THE
MILITARY
BALANCE
2025

published by

for

The International Institute for Strategic Studies
ARUNDEL HOUSE | 6 TEMPLE PLACE | LONDON | WC2R 2PG | UK

THE **MILITARY BALANCE** 2025

The International Institute for Strategic Studies
Arundel House | 6 Temple Place | London | WC2R 2PG | UK

Director-General and Chief Executive **Dr Bastian Giegerich**
Head of Defence and Military Analysis **James Hackett**
Editor **James Hackett**
Assistant Editor **Rupert Schulenburg**

Military Capability and Data **Henry Boyd**
    Land **Michael Tong, Dr Michael Gjerstad, Yurri Clavilier**
    Maritime **Jonathan Bentham, Johannes Fischbach**
    Aerospace **Dzaky Naradichiantama, Giorgio Di Mizio, Fabian Hinz**
Defence Economics **Fenella McGerty, Karl Dewey**
Defence Procurement **Tom Waldwyn, Haena Jo, Matthias Dietrich**
Domain Specialists
    Military Aerospace **Douglas Barrie** MRAeS
    Naval Forces and Maritime Security **Nick Childs**
    Land Warfare **Brigadier (Retd) Benjamin Barry**
Defence Research and Analysis **Jelena Batista, Louis Bearn, Sascha Bruchmann, Joseph Dempsey, Camilla Frank, Zuzanna Gwadera, Jumpei Ishimaru, Jonty Kennon, Yuka Koshino, Meia Nouwens, Albert Vidal Ribe, Ester Sabatino, Rupert Schulenburg, Timothy Wright**
Editorial **Nick Fargher, Jill Lally**
Design, Production, Information Graphics **Alessandra Beluffi, Ravi Gopar, Jade Panganiban, James Parker, Kelly Verity-Cailes**

This publication has been prepared by the Director-General and Chief Executive of the Institute and his Staff, who accept full responsibility for its contents. The views expressed herein do not, and indeed cannot, represent a consensus of views among the worldwide membership of the Institute as a whole.

First published February 2025

© The International Institute for Strategic Studies 2025
All rights reserved. No part of this publication may be reproduced, stored, transmitted, or disseminated, in any form, or by any means, without prior written permission from Taylor & Francis Group, to whom all requests to reproduce copyright material should be directed, in writing.
For Product Safety Concerns and Information please contact our EU representative: GPSR@taylorandfrancis.com, Taylor & Francis Verlag GmbH, Kaufingerstraße 24, 80331 München, Germany

ISBN 978-1-041-04967-8 / eB 978-1-003-63076-0
ISSN 0459-7222

Cover images: Rheinmetall technician working on 155mm ammunition (Axel Heimken/AFP via Getty Images); J-35A aircraft flying during the 15th China International Aviation and Aerospace Exhibition (Chen Jimin/China News Service/VCG via Getty Images); NATO staff member carrying a Swedish flag ahead of Sweden's accession to NATO (Omar Havana/Getty Images); Ansarullah (Houthi) soldiers standing guard on a missile carrier during an official military parade (Mohammed Huwai/AFP via Getty Images); Ukrainian commander of a group of FPV UAVs (Kostya Liberov/Libkos via Getty Images); Ukrainian M142 HIMARS launching a rocket on a Russian position (Serhii Mykhalchuk/Global Images Ukraine via Getty Images); US Army's Mid-Range Capability (or *Typhon*) making its first deployment in the Philippines for *Salaknib* 24 (Captian Ryan DeBooy/US Army); USS *Gravely* launching *Tomahawk* land-attack cruise missiles (Officer Jonathan Word/US Navy) – the appearance of US Department of Defense (DoD) visual information does not imply or constitute DoD endorsement.

Contents

Indexes of Tables, Figures and Maps 4
Editor's Introduction 5

Capabilities, Trends and Economics

Chapter 1   **Defence and military analysis** 6
                 Re-baselining the defence industry 6
                 Global defence spending 10

Chapter 2   **North America** 12
                 Regional trends in 2024 12;   Arms procurement and defence-industrial trends 29;
                 Canada: defence policy 14;   Armed forces data section 31
                 United States: defence policy and economics 15;

Chapter 3   **Europe** 52
                 Regional trends in 2024 52;   Arms procurement and defence-industrial trends 68;
                 Regional defence policy and economics 54;   Armed forces data section 70

Chapter 4   **Russia and Eurasia** 152
                 Regional trends in 2024 152;   Russia: defence policy and economics 157;
                 Regional defence policy and economics 154;   Arms procurement and defence-industrial trends 165;
                 Ukraine: defence policy 155;   Armed forces data section 168

Chapter 5   **Asia** 206
                 Regional trends in 2024 206;   China: defence policy and economics 218;
                 Regional defence policy and economics 208;   Arms procurement and defence-industrial trends 230;
                 Japan: defence policy and economics 215;   Armed forces data section 231

Chapter 6   **Middle East and North Africa** 312
                 Regional trends in 2024 312;   Arms procurement and defence-industrial trends 325;
                 Regional defence policy and economics 314;   Armed forces data section 328

Chapter 7   **Latin America and the Caribbean** 380
                 Regional trends in 2024 380;   Arms procurement and defence-industrial trends 392;
                 Regional defence policy and economics 382;   Armed forces data section 393

Chapter 8   **Sub-Saharan Africa** 440
                 Regional trends in 2024 440;   Regional defence economics 447;
                 West Africa: defence policy 442;   Arms procurement and defence-industrial trends 451;
                 East Africa: defence policy 443;   Armed forces data section 453
                 Central and Southern Africa: defence policy 445;

Reference

Explanatory notes 510
                 Principal land definitions 514; Principal naval definitions 515; Principal aviation definitions 516
List of abbreviations for data sections 518
International comparisons of defence expenditure and military personnel 520
Index of country/territory abbreviations 526
Index of countries and territories 527

Index of TABLES

1. The US DoD budget request by appropriation title, USDbn 26
2. US DoD total budget request by military service, USDbn 27
3. US National Defense Budget Function and other selected budgets, 2000, 2010–25, (USDbn, current year) 28
4. NATO Europe: selected artillery contracts since Feb 2022 69
5. Russia: military expenditure, 2018–25, trillion roubles (current prices) 161
6. China: selected fixed-wing combat-aircraft exports since 2018 ... 223
7. Israel: selected air-force procurements since 2010 315
8. List of abbreviations for data sections 518
9. International comparisons of defence budgets and military personnel 520
10. Index of country/territory abbreviations 526
11. Index of countries and territories 527

Index of FIGURES

North America
1. US: selected current ground-based conventionally armed missile programmes 16
2. US: modernisation of strategic nuclear-weapon delivery platforms 18
3. US Navy: personnel and selected inventory, 1989 and 2024 23
4. US defence budget as % of GDP 25
5. North America: arms procurement and defence-industrial trends, 2024 29
6. US Army: selected air and missile defence (AMD) programmes 30

Europe
7. Europe: selected ongoing submarine procurement programmes ... 56
8. European Union: financial support for the European Defence Technological and Industrial Base (EDTIB) 60
9. Europe: selected countries, fiscal balance, 2019–29 (% of GDP) 62
10. Europe: defence spending by country and sub-region, 2024 64
11. Europe: regional defence spending as % of GDP (average) 65
12. Europe: arms procurement and defence-industrial trends, 2024 .. 68

Russia and Eurasia
13. Ukraine: selected one-way attack (OWA) uninhabited aerial vehicle (UAV) inventory 156
14. Russia: defence expenditure as % of GDP 161
15. Russia and Eurasia: arms procurement and defence-industrial trends, 2024 165
16. Kazakhstan: defence industry 166

Asia
17. Asia: airborne early-warning and control (AEW&C) fleets, 2014–24 210
18. Asia: defence spending by country and sub-region, 2024 211
19. Asia: regional defence spending as % of GDP (average) 212
20. Asia: sub-regional real-terms defence-spending growth, 2023–24 (USDbn, constant 2015) 214
21. Japan: selected missile programmes 217
22. Asia: total active conventional submarines, 2024 222
23. US, Russia and China: submarine fleet evolution, 2014 and 2024 ... 222
24. China: defence budget compared with the rest of Asia (total), 2008–24 (USDbn, constant 2015) 225
25. Thailand: defence industry 228
26. Asia: arms procurement and defence-industrial trends, 2024 230

Middle East and North Africa
27. Ansarullah (Houthis): selected missile forces 318
28. Middle East and North Africa: defence spending by country and sub-region, 2024 322
29. Middle East and North Africa: defence spending as % of GDP (average) 323
30. Middle East and North Africa: arms procurement and defence-industrial trends, 2024 325
31. Saudi Arabia: defence industry 326

Latin America and the Caribbean
32. Latin America and the Caribbean: tactical-aviation fleets, 2014–24 383
33. Brazil's annual core defence budget by function, 2014–24 (BRLbn, current 2015) 386
34. Latin America and the Caribbean: defence spending by country and sub-region, 2024 387
35. Latin America and the Caribbean: regional defence spending as % of GDP (average) 389
36. Brazil: defence industry 390
37. Latin America and the Caribbean: arms procurement and defence-industrial trends, 2024 392

Sub-Saharan Africa
38. Sudan: confirmed aircraft losses in the Sudanese civil war since April 2023 444
39. Sub-Saharan Africa: defence spending by country and sub-region, 2024 447
40. Sub-Saharan Africa: regional defence spending as % of GDP (average) 449
41. Sub-Saharan Africa: total defence spending by sub-region, 2008–24 450
42. Sub-Saharan Africa: arms procurement and defence-industrial trends, 2024 451

Index of MAPS

1. Europe: regional defence spending (USDbn, %ch yoy) 63
2. Russia and Eurasia: regional defence spending (USDbn, %ch yoy) ... 162
3. Asia: regional defence spending (USDbn, %ch yoy) 213
4. Middle East and North Africa: regional defence spending (USDbn, %ch yoy) 321
5. Latin America and the Caribbean: regional defence spending (USDbn, %ch yoy) 388
6. Sub-Saharan Africa: regional defence spending (USDbn, %ch yoy) 448
7. Selected Turkish exports to Sub-Saharan Africa since 2018 452

Editor's Introduction

The complexity of the international security environment was starkly evident in 2024. Countries not only deployed new capabilities but, as they invested more in defence, also considered further equipment priorities. They also paid greater attention to security of supply, defence-industrial capacity, societal resilience and, for many armed forces, personnel strength.

In the Middle East, the collapse of the Assad regime in Syria bookended a year of change. Israel's war against Hamas in Gaza, coupled with its campaign to degrade Hizbullah in Lebanon, shackled Iran's 'Axis of Resistance', though the Houthis in Yemen continued to threaten international shipping in the Red Sea. The year ended with Iran's regional influence weakened, and Israel's military dominance apparent. Israel, however, did require external support to mostly thwart large-scale missile and UAV attacks.

In Europe, there was concern over the kind of threat Russia poses immediately and into the longer term, and recognition that defence challenges extended to disinformation and cyber activities and threats to supply chains, including through sabotage. In NATO's 75th year, its two new Nordic members bolstered the Alliance with additional military capabilities and a security-and-resilience mindset.

The US bolstered its forces in the Middle East, albeit stretching its force posture elsewhere. There was also growing concern about the impact on weapons stockpiles from its actions in the Middle East and support for Ukraine, even as it sought to boost capacity and accelerate innovation. China maintained the pace of its overall force modernisation and reorganisation, while raising the pressure on Taiwan with enhanced exercise activity.

Some of Europe's armed forces are under-strength and struggling with recruitment and retention, not least in high-tech and skilled trades. Militaries have struggled to compete with the rising pay and other attractions of the private sector. Among the responses have been efforts to improve pay and conditions and new career structures, to make military life more appealing. With NATO having agreed significant personnel commitments under its New Force Model, much remains to be done to ensure Western readiness.

Western armed forces examined additional capabilities and began the process of rebuilding stocks depleted after the Cold War. European states' air-launched land-attack cruise missiles, in the form of *Storm Shadow*/SCALP EG at least, were in focus because Ukraine was by year end finally allowed to use them to engage targets, if limited, inside Russia. European states were also exploring options for 1,000+ kilometres ground-launched land-attack systems, a path the US is already treading. More artillery and ground-based air defence is now being procured, and there are investments in large-calibre ammunition production.

There was also growing diversity of defence suppliers. Brazil, Israel, South Korea and Turkiye have all seen their defence sales to Europe grow in recent years. And there are new companies offering uncrewed systems, along with a re-examination of the 'exquisite' approach to system design in favour of affordability and mass, and improvements to defence production processes.

Russia's ambition for its Ukraine invasion seemed undimmed. While it has lost large numbers of personnel and increasing volumes of equipment – our figures indicate that it lost 1,400 main battle tanks in the past year – it bolstered its forces with weapons from Iran and North Korea, as well as troops from the latter. There was also scrutiny over the nature and extent of China's support for Russia, with NATO saying in mid-year that it had become a 'decisive enabler of Russia's war in Ukraine'.

Donald Trump's re-election as US president caused consternation in many European capitals. Last time, he pressured them to spend more on defence. Europe's spending in 2024 is more than 50% higher than in 2014, in nominal terms, though 2022 was really the year when spending accelerated. But at year end, whether NATO's 2%-of-GDP target was enough to rebuild readiness at the pace required was in question. And as states spend more, there is concern that national budgets will be insufficient to support increased production. As a result, there is growing attention on alternative financing methods. Another challenge for Europe, and US partners in the Middle East, is the likely shift in Washington's focus in Trump's second term towards East Asia and China.

Chapter One
Defence and military analysis

Re-baselining the defence industry

Russia's war in Ukraine has harshly exposed the inventory reductions within many NATO members that took place after the end of the Cold War. Traditionally, rectifying this would have been achieved through simply buying far larger volumes of equipment, such as missiles, uninhabited aerial vehicles (UAVs) or munitions, and stockpiling these in case of war. This was because procurement and production cycles, measured in years and not months, were unable to accommodate surges in demand to more quickly meet a deteriorating security environment, or even the outbreak of hostilities. This, however, is changing as novel production techniques and technologies emerge in combination with disruptive new entrants offering to reshape parts of the defence-industrial landscape.

Several factors contribute to what is unfolding. A cadre of defence start-ups are embracing new ways of manufacturing to reduce costs and act with increased agility. There is also recognition among some senior military and political circles that the old models of defence acquisition and production are no longer fully fit for purpose. The existing defence-industrial base is being oriented more toward a war footing, while emerging players are encouraged to offer different and more rapid responses to meet defence-materiel needs.

In 2024, then US Deputy Defense Secretary Kathleen Hicks said that 'America's defence industrial base is at a pivotal moment', with the COVID-19 pandemic revealing the fragility of supply chains, along with Russia's war in Ukraine, Israel's invasion of Gaza and its incursion into Lebanon underscoring the importance of, and sometimes the lack of, production capacity.

Israel's MAFAT, the country's Directorate of Defense Research and Development, hosted an advanced-manufacturing seminar as the country was juggling the competing demands of fighting in Gaza and Lebanon while all along supporting national missile defence. These demands have strained Israel's industrial output, from ammunition to air-defence missiles. At the gathering, MAFAT head Daniel Gold urged industry to embrace mass production and automation and argued further for domestic innovation. The seminar focused on topics including 3D printing, the use of automation and robotics in production, and innovative manufacturing methods.

In the United States, a flag bearer for a disruptive approach to defence manufacturing is defence start-up Anduril Industries. In August 2024, the company unveiled plans for a large defence production facility able to produce thousands of uninhabited vehicles annually. With more than 460,000 square metres of space, the facility would almost approach the size of the Pentagon itself and be one of the world's largest production facilities. The start-up disclosed the ambition soon after completing a USD1.5 billion 'Series F' investment round that valued the seven-year-old business at USD14bn.

Anduril's chief strategy officer, Chris Brose, said that the goal is to use a common set of manufacturing tools and processes to easily scale production. The company has for some time rather grandiosely called for 'rebooting the arsenal of democracy', invoking the United States' ability during the Second World War to surge production on a vast scale, and said the new facility would be called Arsenal-1. The company has suggested it may not be too long before it moves forward with another facility, Arsenal-2, either in the US or abroad. Anduril said it would rely on modularity to build equipment quickly and to avoid dependence on bespoke components. It added that 'Arsenal dismantles the traditional defence production preference for complexity by designing products that are as simple as possible, eliminating requiring unnecessary materials, parts, and specialized processes', adding that around 90% of production at Arsenal-1 will rely on commercially sourced items.

The start-up had previously made other production commitments, including building 200 autonomous underwater vehicles in Rhode Island, in part to meet the requirements of a US Navy contract. Anduril said it made the investment decision to have sufficient capacity to satisfy anticipated demand for its Dive-LD family of underwater systems. Another company goal is to meet orders at pace, signalling how industry recognises that during a time of growing security concerns, military customers are less able to wait for years for equipment. The facility, which is due to open in 2025, should allow Anduril to produce more than 200 hulls per year.

It is not just the new entrants that are innovating to simplify equipment manufacture for military users. Pratt & Whitney is among those that have been working on additive-layer manufacturing, also called 3D printing, to become more efficient. The RTX unit says it has been able to slash the parts count on its TJ-150 small turbojet engine, used on missiles and UAVs, using a process called unitisation, without compromising performance. Rather than using outsourced casting and machining, Pratt & Whitney says it can print the component in-house. The supplier has said that the potential savings on castings and mouldings alone could approach USD1bn. Rolls-Royce is also exploring the use of 3D printing for some of its defence-related activities. The company, for instance, is looking at additive-layer manufacturing as part of its *Orpheus* rapid-development demonstrator-engine effort aimed in part at the United Kingdom's Future Combat Air System Technology Initiative. *Orpheus*, funded jointly by Rolls-Royce and the UK Ministry of Defence, is intended to lead to a family of new small engines to power systems such as cruise missiles and autonomous collaborative platforms, the UK equivalent of the US collaborative combat aircraft. 3D printing of metals as well as plastics is being tested and integrated increasingly by armed services as well as defence industries. For armed forces, using 3D printers holds the promise of shortening supply chains and increasing equipment availability through more flexible spare-parts supply, while also possibly increasing the pace of equipment adaptation and innovation. However, as both industry and the armed forces pursue these technologies, ensuring cyber security will remain a key focus.

The start-up world is thinking even more aggressively. Divergent Technologies, for example, sees a future where some platforms are 3D-made. The company, which is already working with General Atomics, has plans to develop 3D-printed UAV structures and is eyeing the Pentagon's Replicator initiative to produce systems at scale. Divergent supported General Atomics' November 2023 release of an Advanced Air-Launched Effects from the internal weapons bay of an MQ-20 *Avenger*. Ukraine, which has made considerable use of UAVs, has been pursuing 3D-printing technologies rapidly to put systems into the field more quickly and at scale. In late 2023, the country began operating some long-range printed UAVs, demonstrating the utility of such systems.

Interest in greater flexibility and responsiveness is not restricted to the realm of military hardware. Many modern weapons systems are dependent on software for their performance, though this too comes with multiple challenges. Coding, software verification, ensuring new software releases are reliable, and that performance patches do not have an inadvertent effect on existing software, all have to be considered. The Lockheed Martin F-35 *Lightning II*, for example, is a software-intensive platform, and updating the software has been one source of the problems with the aircraft.

The ever-increasing importance of and reliance on software-based systems was apparent in the March 2024 decision by the US Army Contracting Command to award a software-focused contractor, Palantir Technologies, a USD178.4 million major systems integration prime contract. Palantir will develop and deliver the Tactical Intelligence Targeting Access Node (TITAN). TITAN is intended to be the US Army's next-generation intelligence, surveillance and reconnaissance ground station to process data gathered from ground, airborne and space sensors and to employ machine learning. Palantir will oversee the team that also includes more traditional contractors such as Northrop Grumman and L3Harris.

Anduril, a member of Palantir's team, has also stressed that software is key to its approach to defence production. It described its Arsenal platform as 'software-defined' and said that for all Anduril products the software 'serves as a unified system to integrate the design, development, and mass production stages'. Core to its effort is a proprietary manufacturing-execution software system, it said, that spans modelling and simulation, testing, threat-based operational analysis and other functions. Proprietary, however, is not necessarily a positive in the software realm.

More traditional defence companies are also embracing that mindset. In October 2024, Saab chief executive Micael Johansson said 'the way we develop software is incredibly important and that needs to be transformed'. The company, he said, would try to move to more of a 'software factory type of setup' where code can support different programmes. Governments are also adapting to embrace the new approaches to doing business. The US Department of Defense, in October 2024, laid out implementation measures for the Defense Industrial Strategy unveiled in January that year, aimed at strengthening its supply chain and core manufacturing capabilities. The implementation plan then urged the department to adopt 'more flexible pathways to field new capability in a timely fashion'. In some cases, that just requires institutions using newly created acquisition tools to move with greater pace for rapid prototyping and fielding of equipment.

Even though software and additive-layer manufacturing are becoming more critical to equipping armed forces, more traditional concerns have not disappeared. In late September, the Pentagon placed a USD15m Defense Production Act Investment to bolster heavy-forging capacity, with potential use in the manufacture of *Virginia*- and *Columbia*-class submarines, perhaps the clearest sign that industrial-era considerations remain as fundamental to the modern defence-industrial base as new technology concerns.

MISSILE DIALOGUE INITIATIVE

Strengthening international discussion and promoting a high-level exchange of views on missile technologies and related international security dynamics

MISSILE TECHNOLOGY: ACCELERATING CHALLENGES

The IISS Strategic Dossier *Missile Technology: Accelerating Challenges* examines the ballistic- and cruise-missile developments of the world's most prominent users and producers; the impact of development and procurement programmes on regional and strategic stability; the arms-control processes designed to restrain proliferation; and the trajectory of future technological developments, particularly Mach 5+ systems.

FREE DOWNLOAD go.iiss.org/MDISD

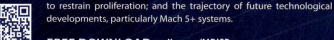

Ballistic-missile Proliferation and the Rise of Middle Eastern Space Programmes

Middle Eastern countries' civilian space ambitions are now largely decoupled from military ballistic-missile programmes, despite lingering mischaracterisations. This report re-examines this nexus and proposes new measures to encourage legitimate space activities, foster regional cooperation in space and maintain robust monitoring mechanisms to detect deviations from this trajectory.

go.iiss.org/49JEEzl

Evaluating Current Arms-control Proposals: Perspectives from the US, Russia and China

Bilateral and multilateral arms control for limiting theatre- and strategic-range missile systems is in a quandary. Even though the US, Russia and China have each put forward proposals for arms-control and risk-reduction measures, conflicting interests and adversarial relations have so far served to stymie any progress. In this report, three experts – one American, one Russian and one Chinese – examine selected arms-control and risk-reduction proposals from their respective countries, and assess their potential contributions to strategic stability.

go.iiss.org/3AnIK47

FREE PAPER DOWNLOAD

www.iiss.org/missile-dialogue-initiative

IISS

Global defence spending

- Global defence spending reached USD2.46 trillion in 2024, up from USD2.24 trillion in 2023. Real-terms growth rose to 7.4% in 2024 compared to 6.5% in 2023 and 3.5% in 2022. All regions, bar Sub-Saharan Africa, grew in real terms in 2024.
- As a proportion of GDP, global spending increased from an average of 1.59% in 2022 to 1.80% in 2023 and 1.94% in 2024.
- Between 2023 and 2024, Russian total military expenditure grew by 41.9% in real terms to USD145.9 billion.
- European defence spending growth surged to 11.7% in real terms in 2024. Significant 23.2% real growth in the German budget, between 2023 and 2024, made it the world's 4th largest defence budget, while Poland became the 15th largest defence spender globally, up from 20th place in 2022.
- Overall, regional spending in Europe was more than 50% higher in nominal terms compared to 2014.
- China's defence budget grew by 7.4% in real terms, outpacing the wider regional average of 3.9% despite significant uplifts in the Japanese and Indonesian budgets. However, stronger uplifts in other regions meant that Asia's share of global spending fell to 21.7% in 2024 from 25.9% in 2021.

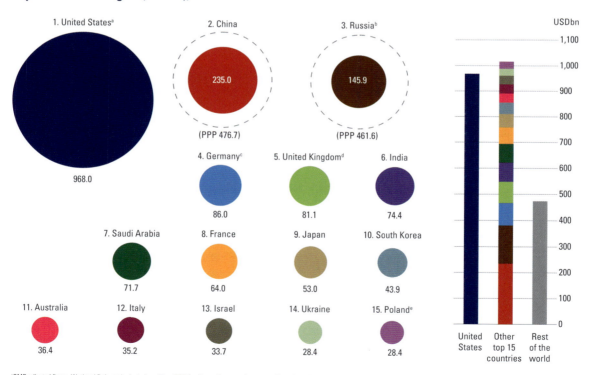

Top 15 defence budgets (USDbn), 2024[†][‡]

1. United States[a] — 968.0
2. China — 235.0 (PPP 476.7)
3. Russia[b] — 145.9 (PPP 461.6)
4. Germany[c] — 86.0
5. United Kingdom[d] — 81.1
6. India — 74.4
7. Saudi Arabia — 71.7
8. France — 64.0
9. Japan — 53.0
10. South Korea — 43.9
11. Australia — 36.4
12. Italy — 35.2
13. Israel — 33.7
14. Ukraine — 28.4
15. Poland[e] — 28.4

[a] OMB adjusted figure. [b] National Defence budget plus military R&D funding, military pensions, paramilitary forces' budgets, and other MoD-related expenses such as housing. [c] Includes 'Sondervermögen' (special fund) allocation, military pensions and military aid to Ukraine. [d] Includes Armed Forces Pension Scheme and military aid to Ukraine. [e] Excludes Armed Forces Support Fund.
[†] At current prices and exchange rates. [‡] Analysis only includes countries for which sufficient comparable data is available. Notable exceptions include Cuba, Eritrea, Libya, North Korea and Syria.
Notes: Unless otherwise indicated, US dollar totals are calculated using average market exchange rates for 2024, derived using IMF data. The relative position of countries will vary not only as a result of actual adjustments in defence spending levels, but also due to exchange-rate fluctuations between domestic currencies and the US dollar. The use of average exchange rates reduces these fluctuations, but the effects of such movements can be significant in a number of cases. US Foreign Military Financing not included in figures. Dashed line reflects an estimate for the value of the Chinese and Russian defence budget in PPP (purchasing power parity) terms to take into account the lower input costs in these countries. These PPP figures are not used in any regional or global totals in this publication and should not be used in comparison with other international data.

©IISS

Real global defence spending changes by region, 2022–24*

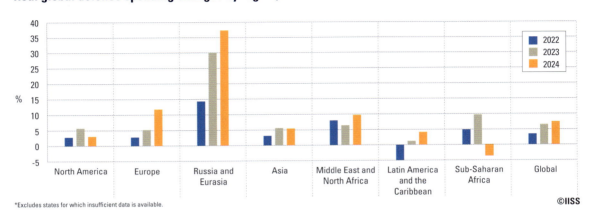

*Excludes states for which insufficient data is available.

©IISS

Top 15 defence budgets as a % of GDP, 2024‡

Ukraine	Algeria	Russia[a]	Saudi Arabia	Israel	Oman	Mali	Armenia	Azerbaijan	Kuwait	Iraq	Burkina Faso	Qatar	Morocco	Myanmar
15.4%	8.2%	6.7%	6.5%	6.4%	6.1%	5.7%	5.4%	5.0%	4.8%	4.8%	4.7%	4.4%	4.2%	4.1%

[a] National Defence budget plus military R&D funding, military pensions, paramilitary forces' budgets, and other MoD-related expenses such as housing. ‡Analysis only includes countries for which sufficient comparable data is available. Notable exceptions include Cuba, Eritrea, Libya, North Korea and Syria.

©IISS

Planned global defence spending by region, 2024†‡

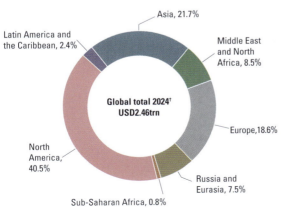

Planned defence spending by country, 2024†‡

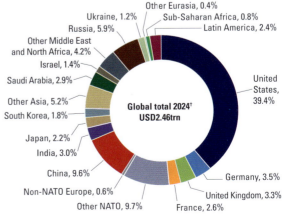

†At current prices and exchange rates. ‡Analysis only includes countries for which sufficient comparable data is available. Notable exceptions include Cuba, Eritrea, Libya, North Korea and Syria.

©IISS

Chapter Two
North America

- The Mid-Range Capability (or *Typhon*) system, capable of launching the *Tomahawk* land-attack cruise missile and the surface-to-air SM-6, made its first deployment in April 2024, during an exercise in the Philippines.
- The US nuclear triad continued to be modernised, with the Pentagon approving the next-generation LGM-35A *Sentinel* intercontinental ballistic missile programme even after major cost overruns.
- The war in Ukraine and adversaries' capability developments are leading the US Army to rebuild short-range air and missile defence capabilities. The army plans to increase the number of M-SHORAD battalions and IFPC battalions, and add dedicated C-UAS capabilities. The US Marine Corps is also expanding its air defence force.
- US military engagements in the Middle East and efforts to support Ukraine's self-defence exposed magazine depth issues. The US Navy is studying reviving the ability to replenish missile stocks at sea, and there has been significant investment in increasing munitions production, such as 155mm for the US Army and Marine Corps.
- In addition to replacing its ageing fleet of CF-18 *Hornet*s with F-35A *Lightning* IIs (the first tranche is to arrive in 2026), the government of Canada announced in 2024 plans to procure 12 conventionally powered submarines to replace its four *Victoria*-class boats.
- Growth in US defence spending remained constrained by the 2023 Fiscal Responsibility Act, leading policymakers to prioritise force readiness and personnel over longer-term modernisation and R&D efforts. Funding reductions are unlikely to be detrimental in the long run, as many programmes have widespread political support, while reduced orders also provide short-term relief for the country's defence industries.

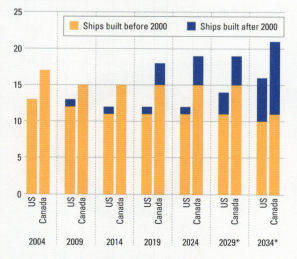

North America: navy and coastguard icebreaker fleets, 2004–34

*Best-case projection based on official schedules.
Notes: Some used on the Great Lakes. US figure includes nine light *Bay*-class icebreakers.

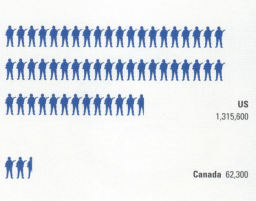

Active military personnel
(25,000 per unit)

US 1,315,600
Canada 62,300

Global total 20,629,000
Regional total 1,378,000
6.7%

Regional defence policy and economics 14 ▶

Arms procurement and defence-industrial trends 29 ▶

Armed forces data section 31 ▶

US Air Force: tanker and tanker/transport aircraft fleets, 2014–24

US Army: selected short-range air defence units, current and planned

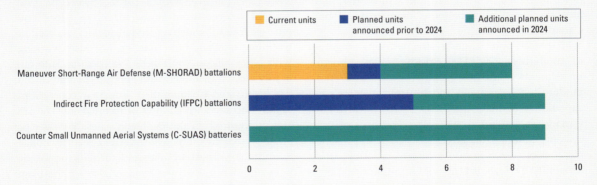

US real-terms defence budget trend, 2014–24

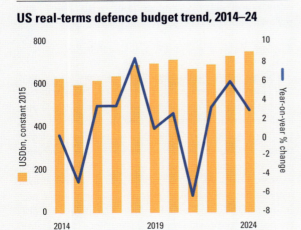

Canada real-terms defence budget trend, 2014–24

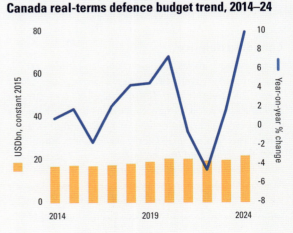

North America

Concerns over China's military modernisation and Russia's continued aggression in Ukraine continued to weigh on defence planners in Canada and the United States. There was also further evidence of defence ties between China and Russia. In July 2024, North American Aerospace Defense Command (NORAD) alerted Canadian and US aircraft to intercept two Russian Tu-95 *Bear* and two Chinese H-6 bombers that had entered Alaska's air defence identification zone (ADIZ). According to the US Department of Defense, this was the first time the two countries' aircraft had been intercepted while operating together and the first time that H-6s had entered the Alaska ADIZ (the aircraft remained in international airspace). This incident followed other Russian and Chinese activity close to North American shores in 2023, when they conducted joint naval activities near Alaska and China flew high-altitude surveillance balloons over parts of both Canada and the US.

The US and Canada are working together to modernise NORAD. Priority areas for new investments include situational awareness, modernised command-and-control systems and capabilities to deter and defeat aerospace threats. Canada is procuring two over-the-horizon radar systems covering the Arctic and polar approaches, the first of which is due to reach initial operating capability by 2028. It is also investing in facilities in its north to prepare for the arrival of its first F-35A combat aircraft in 2026. Meanwhile, the US is looking into options for new space-based missile-warning and observation systems with improved polar coverage. In recent years, NORAD commanders have also expressed concern over the threat posed by cruise missiles, and the US is examining new interceptor capabilities in response, including with Japan as part of the Glide Phase Interceptor project.

Both the US and Canada are also working to reinforce their presence in the Arctic. Canada is constructing the Nanisivik Naval Facility in Nunavat to refuel its offshore patrol ships and improve coastguard refuelling and resupply capacity. The US, meanwhile, is expanding existing port facilities in Nome, Alaska, while the US Coast Guard plans to expand its fleet with the introduction of new heavy Polar Security Cutters, the first of which is estimated to be delivered no earlier than 2029. NORAD Commander General Gregory Guillot told Congress in March 2024 that even with the planned fleet expansion 'we will be severely outnumbered, and that does limit our freedom of maneuver in that region'. As well as working together, both nations are also working with other allies. At NATO's Washington Summit, in July 2024, Canada, Finland and the US announced the Icebreaker Collaboration Effort, a consortium to scale up the shipbuilding of icebreakers. The US also announced, in the Pentagon's new 2024 Arctic Strategy, that it would create an Arctic Security Policy Roundtable with Arctic allies and partners to provide policy guidance, with the strategy also emphasising the need for improved domain awareness and information-sharing, engagement with allies and partners, and exercising in the region.

Canadian defence

Canada maintains its modernisation ambitions. Articulating its security concerns in a new defence paper issued in May 2024, entitled *Our North, Strong and Free*, Ottawa identified the need for new capabilities to guard against global uncertainty and defend its Arctic territories amid waters that will be increasingly navigable in future. 'By 2050', the report said, 'the Arctic Ocean could become the most efficient shipping route between Europe and East Asia'. Some of these new capability plans were known, such as the plan to acquire new long-range missile capabilities and F-35As to replace the ageing fleet of CF-18s. Others were anticipated, such as the announcement that Canada planned to procure 12 conventionally powered submarines. At the same time, Ottawa has made efforts to enhance its contributions to regional security beyond North America. For its forces deployed to the Canada-led NATO enhanced Forward Presence (eFP) battlegroup in Latvia, which Ottawa is working to scale up to an eFP brigade by 2026, it announced plans in February 2024 to procure new air-defence and counter-uninhabited aerial vehicle capabilities. It also continued to provide military assistance to Ukraine.

Between the start of 2022 and September 2024, Ottawa said that it had committed CAD4.5 billion (USD3.3bn) in military assistance to the country. In the Indo-Pacific, Canada deployed three warships to the region in 2024, taking part in multinational exercises and in its forward-presence mission *Operation Horizon*. But as well as investing in new capabilities, reports in 2024 highlighted similar requirements to invest in readiness, including in equipment and personnel availability. But all this is in the context of defence spending that stood at 1.22% of GDP in 2024, lagging well behind NATO's 2% defence-spending target. Prime Minister Justin Trudeau said at the 2024 NATO summit that Canada will only reach the Alliance's spending goal in 2032. Pressure on Canada over its defence-spending levels persisted during the Biden administration, and President Donald Trump, who labelled Canada 'slightly delinquent' on defence spending in 2019, will likely maintain this.

THE UNITED STATES

Donald Trump returned to the White House in January 2025 for a second term as president. In contrast to the initial period after his first election victory, the new administration will likely be able to more rapidly begin implementing the president's national-security agenda. This is likely to include, among others, scrutiny of US alliance partners' defence contributions, and of US commitments to Ukraine's defence. In the wake of Kamala Harris's election defeat, it was noteworthy that the Biden administration subsequently surged defence assistance to Ukraine and loosened long-standing restrictions on the use of some US-supplied equipment, perhaps anticipating a change in the level of US support after 20 January 2025.

New challenges and strategies

The last year of the Biden administration was marked by efforts to support Ukraine's defence against Russia and Israel's military operations against Hamas in Gaza, while it also intervened directly to defend Israel from Iranian attacks as well as striking Ansarullah (Houthi) forces in Yemen and intercepting their attacks on international shipping in the Red Sea. At the same time, the US continued to strengthen its force posture and alliances in the Indo-Pacific. By the end of 2022, the Biden administration had unveiled its major security and defence positions, including the National Security Strategy and the National Defense Strategy. These documents established a focus on China as the 'pacing challenge' and most consequential strategic competitor, with Russia labelled as an 'acute threat' to the US. The Department of Defense's first National Defense Industrial Strategy (NDIS) followed in January 2024 and a new Arctic Strategy in July 2024.

The US-led effort to bolster Ukraine's capabilities, and earlier the COVID-19 pandemic, revealed limitations in the US defence-industrial base. Concerns over stockpile size and production capacity, as well as security of supply, have driven initiatives in several areas. Production-capacity considerations were highlighted by cases including 155mm ammunition production. As of mid-October 2024, the US said that it had committed over three million 155mm rounds to Ukraine's assistance. While US officials stress that there remain adequate supplies for national defence, deficiencies have been highlighted. One press report indicated that 'from summer 2014 to fall 2015, the U.S. added no new [155mm] shells to its stockpile'. A USD4 billion investment, as part of the NDIS, is intended to improve the munitions defence-industrial base. According to Douglas Bush, assistant secretary of the army for acquisition, logistics and technology, speaking at the IISS Prague Defence Summit in November 2024, production is 'now up to 40,000 155-millimetre shells a month. We're going to get to 55,000 a month in December, and we have a path to 100,000 a month in 2025.' Investment is also being made to improve stockpiles, with Bush noting their importance in giving the defence industry time to ramp up production.

An interim assessment of the implementation of the NDIS, released in July 2024, showed that several hundred million dollars, in aggregate, had been allocated to specific production lines and industries to create additional production capacity. Funds of comparable amounts were being distributed to train the future workforce, to improve reliable access to raw materials through 'friendshoring' and 'homeshoring', as well as to increase stockpiles of key ordnance. This included not only 155mm shells but also precision-strike capabilities.

Ukraine and Europe

The Biden administration provided around USD65bn in military assistance to Ukraine following

Figure 1 🇺🇸 US: selected current ground-based conventionally armed missile programmes

After withdrawing in 2019 from the 1987 Intermediate-Range Nuclear Forces (INF) Treaty, citing Russian violations, the US initiated the development of ground-based missile systems with ranges between 500 and 5,500 kilometres – a capability the treaty had prohibited. The development of long-range fires is a key part of the force-modernisation efforts of both the US Army and Marine Corps in order to address the demands of great-power competition, particularly in the Indo-Pacific region. Some of these systems have started to come into inventory. In April 2024, the US Army deployed the Mid-Range Capability system (or *Typhon*) for the first time; this occurred as part of the bilateral exercise *Salaknib 24* in the Philippines. Washington and Berlin announced in July that the US will begin episodic deployments of US ground-based missile systems to Germany from 2026.

ARMY
Long-Range Hypersonic Weapon (LRHW) (*Dark Eagle*)

MISSILE LRHW All Up Round
ROLE Land-attack
RANGE 2,775+ km
LAUNCHER Truck-towed trailer-based transporter erector launcher
CAPACITY Two LRHW All Up Rounds per launch vehicle
STATUS[†] In development

Precision Strike Missile (PrSM)

MISSILE PrSM
ROLES Land-attack (Increments 1, 2, 3 and 4)[††]; anti-ship (Increment 2)
RANGE 499+ km (Increments 1, 2 and 3); 1,000 km (Increment 4)
LAUNCHERS M142 High Mobility Artillery Rocket System (HIMARS) truck-mounted rocket launcher*; M270A2 Multiple Launch Rocket System (MLRS) self-propelled rocket launcher
CAPACITY Two PrSMs per M142 HIMARS launch vehicle; Four PrSMs per M270A2 MLRS launch vehicle
STATUS[†] Operational (Increment 1); in development (Increments 2, 3 and 4)

Mid-Range Capability (*Typhon*)

MISSILES *Tomahawk* / SM-6
ROLES Missile defence and anti-air (SM-6 Block Ia); anti-ship (SM-6 Blocks Ia and Ib, and *Tomahawk* Block Va); land-attack (*Tomahawk* Blocks V, Va and Vb)
RANGE 1,600 km (*Tomahawk*); 240+ km (SM-6)
LAUNCHER Truck-towed trailer-based Mk 70 Payload Delivery System with Mk 41 Vertical Launching System cells
CAPACITY Four SM-6s or four *Tomahawks* per launch canister
STATUS[†] Operational

MARINE CORPS
Long-Range Fires

MISSILE *Tomahawk*
ROLES Anti-ship (Block Va); land-attack (Blocks V, Va and Vb)
RANGE 1,600 km
LAUNCHER ROGUE-Fires uninhabited ground vehicle with a Mk 41 Vertical Launching System cell
CAPACITY One *Tomahawk* per launch vehicle
STATUS[†] First unit forming

*The US Army is testing a modified version of the M142 HIMARS that can be controlled remotely called the Autonomous Multi-Domain Launcher (AML). [†] As of November 2024. [††] PrSM Increment 4 is also known as Long Range Maneuverable Fires.
Sources: US Department of Defense, Kongsberg, Lockheed Martin, Oshkosh Defense and RTX

Russia's full-scale invasion in 2022, though the pace of US assistance was increasingly determined by congressional dynamics. In 2024, the Republican-controlled House of Representatives held up for months a USD95bn foreign-aid bill, which contained around USD61bn in funding relating to Ukraine, before it was signed into law in April 2024. The administration continued to incrementally adjust its policy over end-user restrictions on Ukraine. It was only in the weeks after Trump's victory that the administration acceded to Kyiv's requests and loosened the restriction on use of the 300-kilometre-range Block 1A Army Tactical Missile Systems (ATACMS) short-range ballistic missile. The US also said it would send Ukraine anti-personnel mines, reflective not just of changing risk tolerance in the Biden administration, but also of the gravity of the situation on the battlefield. In Europe, Washington has pushed ahead with new agreements designed to quickly formally integrate the two new Nordic members of NATO. A defence-cooperation agreement with Finland, signed in December 2023, came into force in September 2024. Meanwhile, ahead of Sweden's entry into NATO in March 2024, the US and Sweden signed a defence-cooperation agreement in December 2023. This came into force in August 2024. It established the conditions for US forces to operate in the country and US basing access to 17 military sites in Sweden. Since the start of 2022, the US has increased its overall footprint in Europe, and after an initial surge the total US presence on the continent now numbers around 90,000 troops. In July, the US and Germany announced a planned enhancement to the US force posture on the continent, stating that the US would episodically deploy conventionally armed ground-based missiles with ranges of over 500km to Germany from 2026. This follows the establishment of the 2nd Multi-Domain Task Force (MDTF) in Wiesbaden in September 2021. Each of these MDTFs contains a long-range fires battalion to provide long-range strike capability.

The Middle East

The outbreak of conflict in the Middle East placed another high demand on US resources as it sought to protect Israel and international shipping in the region. Following Hamas's attack on Israel on 7 October 2023, Israel prosecuted efforts to eliminate Hamas in Gaza. At time of writing, US military support to Israel amounted to over 100 separate military transfers. US policy in the region was also focused on preventing a wider regional war following Iran's attacks on Israel. On 13 April 2024, Iran attacked Israel using around 350 uninhabited aerial vehicles (UAVs), cruise missiles and ballistic missiles in response to an attack, by the Israel Defense Forces, on the Iranian consulate in Syria. Tehran attacked Israel again on 1 October, using nearly 200 ballistic missiles, after Israel killed leaders of militias in Lebanon. In both cases US Navy destroyers used air- and missile-defence systems, at the same time as Israel used its own systems, to engage incoming missiles, and after the October attack the US again deployed a battery of THAAD ballistic-missile-defence systems to the country.

In response to Houthi attacks in and around the Red Sea, Washington deployed naval assets including a carrier strike group to support the US-led multinational operations *Prosperity Guardian* and *Poseidon Archer* to protect international shipping. During their nine-month deployment, the ships of the USS *Dwight D. Eisenhower* carrier strike group reportedly launched some 135 *Tomahawk* land-attack cruise missiles, 155 *Standard* surface-to-air missiles and 420 air-to-surface weapons to either intercept Houthi missiles and UAVs or strike Houthi targets in Yemen. The volume of intercepts focused attention on questions of 'magazine depth' and stockpile size. But the high relative costs of the interceptors used, compared to the Houthi missiles and UAVs intercepted, also highlighted the requirement for cost-effective air-defence solutions. The undersecretary of defense for acquisition and sustainment told lawmakers in May 2024 that developing counter-UAV capabilities that have cost-effective exchange ratios is a high priority.

The Indo-Pacific

The US continued efforts to improve its alliances and partnerships against the backdrop of China's rapid military modernisation and growing assertiveness alongside North Korea's advancing nuclear-weapons programme. The US also continued to strengthen its networks in traditional bilateral frameworks but also – as Secretary of Defense Lloyd Austin said at the IISS Shangri-La Dialogue in June 2024 – towards 'a set of overlapping and complementary initiatives and institutions', with the region shifting from the 'hub-and-spokes' model of Indo-Pacific security to this looser 'lattice' of arrangements.

A series of announcements in 2024 indicated further progress as part of the AUKUS partnership, made up of Australia, the United Kingdom and

Figure 2 🇺🇸 US: modernisation of strategic nuclear-weapon delivery platforms

The US is replacing the ageing delivery platforms of its nuclear triad, including its strategic bombers and ballistic missile submarines. It is also introducing new delivery vehicles, such as the AGM-181 Long Range Stand-Off Weapon (LRSO) air-launched cruise missile and modernised B61 gravity bombs, and recently completed a life-extension of the UGM-133A *Trident* II D-5 submarine-launched ballistic missile (SLBM). In January 2024, the US Air Force (USAF) notified Congress that the LGM-35A *Sentinel* intercontinental ballistic missile programme had exceeded its baseline cost projections by well over 25%, a breach of the Nunn–McCurdy statute. After a review,

AIR
Nuclear-capable strategic bomber

CURRENT

B-2A *Spirit*
INTRODUCTION
1997
AIRCRAFT RANGE
11,100 kilometres un-refuelled (18,500 km with one air-to-air refuel)
CAPACITY
Up to 16 nuclear bombs per aircraft
ARMAMENT
Bombs: B61-7 (variable yield from 10 to 340 kilotons), B61-11 (400 kt), B61-12 (variable yield of 0.3 kt, 1.5 kt, 10 kt or 50 kt) and B83-1 (very low yield to 1.2 megatons)
Missile: n.a.
MISSILE RANGE
n.a.

REPLACEMENT*

B-21 *Raider*
INTRODUCTION
Late 2020s (planned)
AIRCRAFT RANGE
n.k.
CAPACITY
n.k.
ARMAMENT
Bombs: B61-12 (variable yield of 0.3 kt, 1.5 kt, 10 kt or 50 kt) and B61-13 (yield similar to the B61-7)
Missile: AGM-181 LRSO air-launched cruise missile with the W80-4 warhead (yield n.k.)
MISSILE RANGE
2,400+ km

LAND
Intercontinental ballistic missile

CURRENT

LGM-30G *Minuteman* III
INTRODUCTION
1970
CAPACITY
Silos: 450 (currently housing only 400 missiles)
Warheads: up to three per missile (currently each missile is only mated with one warhead)
ARMAMENT
Warheads: W87-0 (300 kt) and W78 (335 kt)
MISSILE RANGE
12,000+ km

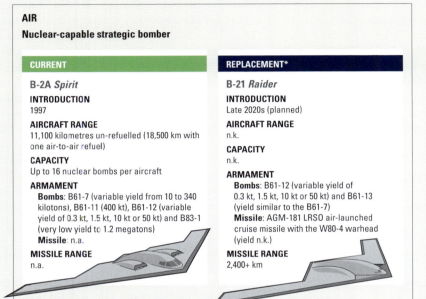

Basing locations of US strategic nuclear-weapon delivery platforms: current and future sites

- **Naval Base Kitsap** — Submarine Squadron 17, Pacific Fleet: 8 *Ohio*-class SSBNs
- **Malmstrom Air Force Base** — 341st Missile Wing, Twentieth Air Force: 150 ICBM silos
- **F. E. Warren Air Force Base** — 90th Missile Wing, Twentieth Air Force: 150 ICBM silos**
- **Dyess Air Force Base** — Planned, B-21 *Raider* bombers

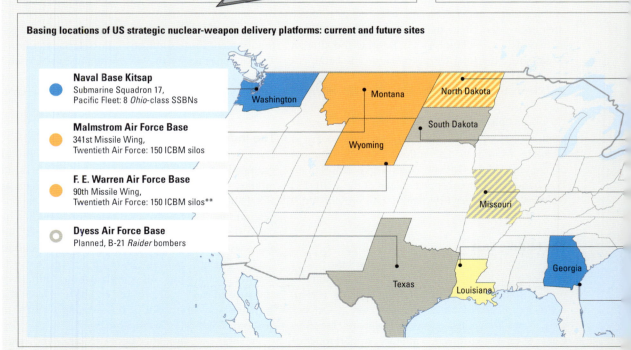

*The B-21 *Raider* will operate alongside the nuclear-capable B-52 *Stratofortress*. **The missile silos assigned to F. E. Warren AFB are deployed in northern Colorado, western Nebraska and eastern Wyoming.

the Pentagon announced in July that the programme will continue, citing its necessity for US national security. Amid China's rapid nuclear expansion and Russia's suspension of its implementation of the New Strategic Arms Reduction Treaty, there is growing concern in Washington that the US may need to re-evaluate its nuclear posture to face two near-peer competitors. In April 2024, Secretary of Defense Lloyd Austin told Congress that the current 'program of record is necessary but may not be sufficient' and Chairman of the Joint Chiefs of Staff General Charles Q. Brown similarly stated, albeit with certainty, that 'our nuclear migration is necessary but not sufficient'.

(ICBM)

REPLACEMENT

LGM-35A *Sentinel*

INTRODUCTION
2030 (planned)

CAPACITY
Silos: 450 (plans to deploy 400 missiles)
Warheads: multiple per missile (each missile will likely be mated with one warhead)

ARMAMENT
Warheads: W87-0 (300 kt) and W87-1 (475 kt)

MISSILE RANGE
Likely 12,000+ km

SEA

Nuclear-powered ballistic missile submarine (SSBN)

CURRENT

Ohio-class

INTRODUCTION
1981

SUBMARINE RANGE
Unlimited (supplies and maintenance permitting)

CAPACITY
Missile tubes: 20 per submarine
Warheads: up to eight per missile

ARMAMENT
Missile: UGM-133A *Trident* II D-5 (life-extended 1) SLBM
Warheads: W76-1 (90 kt), W76-2 (8 kt) and W88 (455 kt)

MISSILE RANGE
12,000+ km

REPLACEMENT

Columbia-class

INTRODUCTION
2028 (planned)

SUBMARINE RANGE
Unlimited (supplies and maintenance permitting)

CAPACITY
Missile tubes: 16 per submarine
Warheads: up to eight per missile

ARMAMENT
Missile: UGM-133A *Trident* II D-5 (LE1 and LE2) SLBM
Warheads: W76-1 (90 kt), W76-2 (8 kt), W88 (455 kt) and W93 (yield n.k.)

MISSILE RANGE
12,000+ km

Minot Air Force Base
91st Missile Wing, Twentieth Air Force: 150 ICBM silos; 5th Bomb Wing, Eighth Air Force: est. 26 B-52H *Stratofortress* bombers

Ellsworth Air Force Base
Planned, B-21 *Raider* bombers

Whiteman Air Force Base
509th Bomb Wing, Eighth Air Force: 20 B-2A *Spirit* bombers; planned, B-21 *Raider* bombers

Barksdale Air Force Base
2nd Bomb Wing, Eighth Air Force: est. 20 B-52H *Stratofortress* bombers

Naval Submarine Base Kings Bay
Submarine Squadron 20, Atlantic Fleet: 6 *Ohio*-class SSBNs

The first sixth-generation aircraft: the B-21 *Raider*
In January 2024, the USAF's next-generation bomber, the Northrop Grumman B-21 *Raider*, entered low-rate initial production. The USAF plans to acquire at least 100 of the low-observable, dual-capable aircraft. The USAF will send the first operational bomber to Ellsworth AFB, one of the three planned main operating bases and the site for the formal training unit. The assistant secretary of the USAF for acquisition, technology and logistics, Andrew P. Hunter, told Congress in May 2024 that the bomber's flight test programme is 'on track' following the B-21's maiden flight in November 2023. He also said that the LRSO, which the service plans to introduce in 2030, is 'tracking well' to meet its timelines.

Current basing
- Nuclear-capable strategic bombers
- Intercontinental ballistic missiles
- Nuclear-powered ballistic missile submarine

Planned additional basing
- Nuclear-capable strategic bombers

©IISS

Note: The capacity and armament categories only cover nuclear weapons.
Sources: IISS analysis, US Department of Defense, US Air Force, US Navy, National Nuclear Security Administration, Government Accountability Office

the US, the main pillar of which is to provide Australia with a nuclear-powered attack-submarine capability. Announcements revealed progress including in building up Australia's industrial and personnel capacities in relation to pillar one, and investments also in pillar two, relating to advanced capabilities. Here there were indications of progress in, among other areas, data sharing, artificial-intelligence-enabled data processing, undersea-warfare capability, and 'offensive and defensive hypersonic technologies'. Meanwhile, the Quad partners, consisting of Australia, India, Japan and the US, agreed in July to geographically expand the Indo-Pacific Partnership for Maritime Domain Awareness, a technology and training initiative to increase transparency in critical waterways, to the Indian Ocean region. Another minilateral, the so-called Squad – composed of Australia, Japan, the Philippines and the US – conducted its first joint maritime patrol within the Philippines' exclusive economic zone in April 2024. The US is also deepening triangular integration of the US–Japan and US–South Korea alliances, including through a multi-year trilateral exercise plan and initiating a mechanism to share early-warning data on North Korean missiles.

On the industrial side, the US worked with its allies and partners to ensure the resilience of economic and military supply chains, endorsing in May 2024 a statement of principles for Indo-Pacific defence-industrial-base collaboration to guide cooperation. Signatories of that joint statement also agreed to establish a Partnership for Indo-Pacific Industrial Resilience, a multinational forum to exchange lessons learned and best practices to work through common acquisition and sustainment issues.

Building on the additional basing access it secured in 2023 from the Philippines and Papua New Guinea, the US continued its efforts to diversify its force posture in the Indo-Pacific. In support of the Agile Combat Employment concept, which aims to improve the resilience of US forces by enabling dispersal across forward operating locations, work began to renovate the runway on Tinian. The US is also building a new radar installation on Palau, between the Philippines and Guam, and is upgrading air bases in Western Australia and in the Northern Territory. The Pentagon announced in August 2024 that more maritime-patrol and reconnaissance aircraft would operate from bases across northern Australia, as well as more frequent rotational bomber deployments. The US also introduced a new capability to the region, deploying the new US Army ground-based intermediate-range missile system known as the Mid-Range Capability (or *Typhon*), capable of launching *Tomahawk*s and SM-6s, as part of the bilateral exercise *Salaknib* 2024. In an effort by Japan and the US to deepen defence coordination, the two countries announced plans in July to upgrade US Forces Japan to a joint force headquarters with expanded missions and operational responsibilities.

While Washington maintained high-level contact with Beijing, including the first official in-person meeting between Secretary of Defense Austin and his Chinese counterpart, Minister for National Defense Admiral Dong Jun, on the margins of the 2024 IISS Shangri-La Dialogue, tensions over Taiwan disrupted communications. In July 2024 Beijing halted talks with Washington over arms control and nuclear proliferation – which had commenced the previous November – in protest at recent US arms sales to Taiwan. The Pentagon has called bolstering Taiwan's defences an 'urgent task' and referred to a Taiwan contingency as the 'pacing scenario'. The April 2024 foreign-aid bill included an additional USD2bn in funding for Foreign Military Financing for US allies and partners in the Indo-Pacific, as well as USD1.9bn in funding for the Pentagon to pay for any defence services that the department provides to Taiwan or to replace equipment that it transfers to Taiwan from its existing materiel supplies. Increased numbers of asymmetric capabilities are being earmarked, and the US Department of State in June approved the potential sale of up to around USD350m-worth of UAVs to Taiwan, including hundreds of *Switchblade* 300 and ALTIUS 600M-V loitering munitions.

Capabilities and personnel

Efforts to modernise each leg of the US nuclear triad continued. Although the Biden administration said it would prioritise reducing the role of nuclear weapons in national-security strategy, some senior administration officials and members of Congress said that the programme of record may not be sufficient to address two near-peer competitors. In July 2024, the Department of Defense approved the continuation of the LGM-35A *Sentinel* next-generation intercontinental ballistic missile programme, even after it exceeded statutory cost thresholds. The modified programme will cost 81% more than the previous 2020 estimate. Moreover, although the administration did not include the submarine-launched cruise missile (SLCM-N) in its budget requests, Congress provided continued funding for the missile and the associated warhead. The US is also pressing forward with its Replicator initiative, intended to deliver multiple thousands of 'all-domain attritable autonomous systems'. Deputy Secretary of Defense Kathleen Hicks announced in May 2024 that the first tranche of Replicator capabilities will include uninhabited surface vehicles, uninhabited aerial systems (UAS) and counter-uninhabited aerial systems (C-UAS) of various sizes and payloads from traditional and non-traditional vendors.

US Army

The ongoing wars in Ukraine and Gaza, as well as sporadic attacks on facilities in the Middle East, have underlined the air- and missile-defence challenges posed to the US Army by both peer opponents and asymmetric actors. Longer-term development plans have had to be balanced against pressing short-term operational requirements, particularly those posed by UAVs.

The army largely mothballed its short-range air defence (SHORAD) capabilities in the aftermath of the Cold War and is now looking at rebuilding capacity in this area, as well as adding dedicated C-UAS capabilities. These efforts combine short-term interim solutions with the ongoing development and fielding of mobile and site-based directed energy (DE) systems.

The US Army is working on a new air- and missile-defence strategy, which is due for completion by the end of October 2025. The army released a white paper in early 2024 that identified increases in air- and missile-defence formation and personnel numbers to be resourced, in part, by reductions to unit numbers and sizes elsewhere in the service. As part of this process the army began inactivating the cavalry squadrons of continental United States-based Infantry and Stryker Brigade Combat Teams in summer 2024.

The army's hard-worked *Patriot* missile-system force is set to be enhanced by the introduction of the RTX Lower Tier Air and Missile Defense Sensor (LTAMDS) and Northrop Grumman's new Integrated Battle Command System (IBCS). The first full IBCS battalion set was delivered in mid-2024, ahead of testing in 2025, while the initial LTAMDS prototypes continued testing in 2024, ahead of the planned fielding of both components in 2027. The army's Lower-Tier Future Interceptor programme, intended to deliver a replacement to the existing *Patriot* missiles, was axed in late 2024.

The army's current mounted SHORAD capability consists of a mix of legacy *Avenger* surface-to-air missile systems and the *Sgt Stout* (formerly M-SHORAD Increment 1) gun-missile system. With both systems dependent on the FIM-92 *Stinger* missile, they represent only a short-term solution pending a replacement missile design. The chosen design is anticipated to commence production in 2028.

In response to the increasing threat of smaller UAVs, the army has deployed SRC's Low, Slow, Small UAS Integrated Defeat System (LIDS) in both fixed-site (FS-LIDS) and mobile (M-LIDS) variants. The current M-LIDS Increment 2 variant, mounted on an Oshkosh M-ATV chassis, requires two separate vehicles operating in tandem, and since 2022, the army has been working on consolidating the system onto a single vehicle variant (SV M-LIDS Increment 2.1) using a *Stryker* chassis.

The US Army is using Dynetics' *Enduring Shield* for the kinetic element of the Indirect Fire Protection Capability (IFPC) Increment 2 programme, and the first battalion set of the latter began testing in 2024. Each of the army's five active-duty MDTF brigades is intended to field one battalion set of *Enduring Shield*.

The fatal UAV attack on US forces based in Jordan in January 2024 led to additional C-UAS systems being deployed to US Central Command (CENTCOM). These included the first platoon of prototype laser-weapon DE M-SHORAD systems, although these reportedly experienced overheating issues in the local climatic conditions. Another DE C-UAS system, Blue Halo's *Locust* Laser Weapon System, has also been operationally deployed in small numbers by the army, likely also with CENTCOM, and is also being tested by the marines. In addition to laser systems, the first prototype battery of Epirus's IFPC High-Power Microwave (IFPC-HPM) was delivered to the army in May 2024, with an aspiration for an initial deployment to CENTCOM in 2025.

Alongside new air-defence equipment, in 2024 the army took delivery of the first production models of the M10 *Booker* light tank. In contrast, the service cancelled two major army development programmes in 2024. Lessons drawn from the role of UAVs in Ukraine contributed to the decision to cut the Future Attack Reconnaissance Aircraft helicopter programme, while development of the Extended Range Cannon Artillery 155mm self-propelled howitzer was also terminated as problems with wear on the gun's 58-calibre barrel proved impossible to surmount. The army is now planning to competitively evaluate future self-propelled 155mm artillery systems in 2025.

US Navy

United States Navy activities were in 2024 dominated by some of the most intensive and sustained naval combat operations seen in decades. These focused on countering the Houthi anti-shipping campaign in and around the Red Sea and helping defend Israel against Iranian missile and UAV attacks.

These engagements saw the first operational use of the SM-3 ballistic-missile interceptor. US Navy warships enjoyed considerable tactical success in engaging multiple air threats in the region, but at the expense of high and potentially unsustainable weapons-expenditure rates. One result has been accelerated navy studies into reviving the ability to replenish missile stocks at sea, including a successful test transfer of an Mk 41 missile canister at sea in October 2024.

While surging assets into the Middle East underscored the navy's unique capacities, it also added to strains on the fleet. This included, for periods, deploying two aircraft carriers simultaneously to the region at the expense of the carrier presence in the Pacific.

In September 2024, the chief of naval operations issued a new Navigation Plan policy paper with a focus on enhanced readiness by the target date of 2027 and accelerating innovation, including integrating more robotic systems. However, despite significant improvements, the previous goal of having a readiness level of 75 warships mission-capable and ready to deploy in 2024 remained a work in progress due to delays in both maintenance and new construction.

Despite efforts to invest in the naval-industrial base, an urgent shipbuilding review directed by the secretary of the navy revealed major shipbuilding delays. This included an up to 16-month delay for the first next-generation nuclear-powered ballistic-missile submarine, USS *District of Columbia*, three years in the case of the *Constellation*-class frigates, and potentially more than two years in delivering the third *Gerald R. Ford*-class aircraft carrier, the future USS *Enterprise*. Concerns continued to be expressed over whether the US shipbuilding industry can deliver the US Navy's own future submarine requirements as well as submarines for Australia under the AUKUS partnership.

After years of falling below recruitment goals, the US Navy and the US Marine Corps announced that they had met or exceeded them in FY24. Nevertheless, a significant shortfall of qualified mariners raised the prospect of Military Sealift Command sidelining up to 17 support ships and auxiliaries.

The navy also announced that it was pressing ahead with plans to award a contract for its new sixth-generation carrier-based fighter, F/A-XX, even as the US Air Force had paused its equivalent plans. In anticipation of introducing the MQ-25 *Stingray* uninhabited airborne refuelling platform, the navy announced that it had installed its first associated control centre aboard the carrier USS *George H. W. Bush*. Boeing delivered the first MQ-25 to the navy in February 2024 for testing. It is due to reach initial operating capability in 2026.

The navy also made steps in augmenting the missile capabilities of its aircraft. During the RIMPAC 2024 exercise, a US F/A-18E *Super Hornet* was seen carrying an AIM-174B – an air-launched version of the SM-6 surface-to-air missile, which could enhance the capability of the service's air assets against high-value targets. Moreover, the navy's carrier-based F-35C in September conducted a flight test to certify its ability to carry the AGM-158C Long-Range Anti-Ship Missile.

As the US Marine Corps (USMC) continues its Force Design 2030 restructuring programme to transform itself into a more agile and flexible force, differences between the navy and the marines appeared to persist over plans for a new medium landing ship design. The navy envisages 18 of the ships, while the corps sees a requirement for 35. The Congressional Budget Office reported that the cost of the new ships could be two to three times that estimated by the navy.

The USMC is in the process of expanding its air-defence force from four to 15 batteries, including reserve units, by 2029 under Force Design 2030. To counter the growing threat posed by small UAV systems, the corps has introduced the Light Marine Air Defense Integrated System (L-MADIS), which is

Figure 3 US Navy: personnel and selected inventory, 1989 and 2024

The mid-to-late 1980s saw a considerable build-up of US Navy strength. This was the era of then-president Ronald Reagan's '600-ship navy' ambition after a period of perceived neglect and decline and in response to a significant Soviet naval build-up. This increase was achieved by a combination of new construction, retaining existing platforms in service, and notably also the attention-grabbing decision to reactivate and modernise four Second World War *Iowa*-class battleships, including the fitting of *Tomahawk* cruise missiles. There were also major capability upgrades, perhaps most significantly the introduction of the *Aegis* combat system.

The fleet never quite reached the 600-ship target. It reached its peak in 1987, and the number fell only slightly until 1989 due to the decommissioning of some of the older surface warships. However, the collapse of the Warsaw Pact and the Soviet Union led to a rapid reduction in the size of the active US fleet in the early 1990s as part of the peace dividend. Other navies also declined dramatically, so the US Navy still remained unrivalled as the most powerful global fleet. But in the absence of any peer threat, its mission focus switched from sea control to power projection.

Today, the US Navy is once again in an era of challenge and a phase of upheaval. Many of the mainstays of the 1980s build-up (*Nimitz*-class aircraft carriers, *Ticonderoga*-class cruisers and *Los Angeles*-class nuclear-powered attack and guided-missile submarines) are now the legacy platforms needing replacement. The same is true for the *Arleigh Burke*-class destroyers that became the workhorses of the post-Cold War navy. However, the service is struggling to procure the new classes (such as *Ford*-class aircraft carriers and *Virginia*-class submarines) in the numbers required, even though they undoubtedly have greater individual capabilities than their predecessors. The new *Columbia*-class submarine programme is also imposing more of a burden on the US Navy than its predecessors did. After abandoning traditional frigates in favour of the experimental Littoral Combat Ship, which has not been considered a success, the US Navy has also returned to frigate construction with the *Constellation*-class, but this is equally facing delays and cost overruns. Consequently, the US Navy is having to look to new approaches and designs, including increased focus on uncrewed platforms, to try to supplement its mainstream warship construction and help rebuild capability.

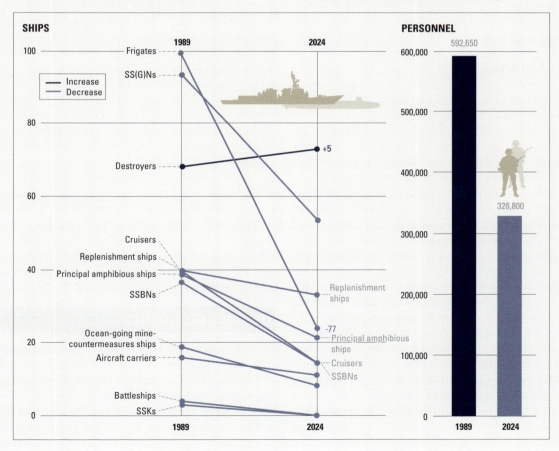

Note: The reporting date for both years is 30 June. Ship-type classifications for 1989 are according to the then-current IISS methodology. The Institute's methodology has changed since 1989, and the categorisations are therefore not completely comparable.
Sources: IISS, *The Military Balance 1990–1991*; Military Balance+, milbalplus.iiss.org

split across two vehicles – one with a sensor package and the other a jammer, with kinetic engagement covered by man-portable missile systems. In 2024, a heavier version of MADIS, incorporating integral gun and missile capabilities on a single Joint Light Tactical Vehicle chassis, began test and evaluation, with the intention of fielding it with the 3rd Marine Littoral Regiment in Hawaii in 2025. The Marine Corps is also planning to incorporate the Israeli *Iron Dome* launcher, with its *Tamir* missiles, into its Mid-Range Intercept Capability system, intended for fielding in 2025.

The US Coast Guard continued to grapple with increased global demand for its presence against a backdrop of personnel shortfalls which have seen the laying up of operational vessels. Like the navy and marine corps, it was anticipating improved recruiting, but this will take time to have effect. Its flagship project for new-generation heavy icebreakers, or Polar Security Cutters, faced further delays with the initial in-service date slipping to 2029 at the earliest.

US Air Force

The United States Air Force (USAF) spent much of 2024 grappling with managing tactical combat aircraft fleets, navigating ongoing difficulties with the Lockheed Martin F-35 *Lighting* II, and, in the latter part of the year, placing a question mark against its strategy for meeting its Next-Generation Air Dominance (NGAD) set of requirements.

The USAF's 'fighter fleet' is now, on average, 26 years old, with the pace of recapitalisation still slower than first planned, and the service will continue to withdraw ageing airframes in FY25. It plans to cut the Boeing F-15C/D *Eagle* fleet by 65 aircraft and pull 26 F-15E *Strike Eagle*s from service. The USAF's ambition to retire the Block 20 version of the Lockheed Martin F-22A *Raptor*, however, continued to be stymied by domestic politics.

Deliveries of the F-35 were halted in mid-2023 due to software and computer-hardware development issues, with the hold lasting around 12 months before the handover of aircraft resumed in mid-2024. Meanwhile, the envisaged high-end complement to the air force's F-35As, the NGAD platform, appeared in limbo when source selection was paused at the end of the second quarter. An engineering manufacturing and development contract had been due to be awarded to either Boeing or Lockheed Martin by the end of 2024.

Instead, the USAF appeared to be reconsidering its approach to the crewed element of the programme, with apparent greater emphasis being placed on the uninhabited elements of NGAD. Air Force Secretary Frank Kendall's suggestion that the crewed element of NGAD would have a unit cost ideally no more than that of the F-35 strained credibility in some quarters. A greater reliance on uninhabited systems could also offset much of the savings from a less capable crewed platform.

The air force's recapitalisation of its bomber fleets has, so far, not hit the turbulence of its fighter fraternity. The first Northrop Grumman B-21 *Raider* bomber, which is set to enter service in the late 2020s, continues in flight test, with five more in various stages of manufacture in the fourth quarter of 2024. The Boeing B-52J *Stratofortress* will form the other leg of the bomber fleet, with the USAF beginning to phase out the Northrop Grumman B-2A *Spirit* and the Rockwell B-1B *Lancer* in the first half of the 2030s. At the core of the B-52J is the commercial-engine replacement programme. The B-52H's Pratt & Whitney TF33 early-generation turbofan engines will be replaced with the modern Rolls-Royce F130. The B-52 radar is also the subject of an upgrade, with the Raytheon APQ-188, a derivative of the APG-79 active electronically scanned array radar, replacing the 1980s-era Raytheon APQ-116.

As the air force attempts to rapidly reconfigure to address peer-competitor threats, it also plans to rebuild its training infrastructure to better prepare for high-end combat, including making greater use of synthetic training in preparing for any confrontation with a peer rival. A key advantage of synthetic training is the ability to use some capabilities that would not be utilised in real-world training for reasons of operational security. The USAF, however, also stresses that such training is a complement to and not a replacement of live training.

DEFENCE ECONOMICS

The Biden administration submitted its FY25 budget request to Congress on 11 March 2024, requesting a total of USD895.2 billion for all discretionary national-defence-related activities. This included base budgets of USD849.8bn for the Department of Defense (DoD), USD34bn for the Department of Energy and a further USD11.5bn for other defence-related activities. In addition to discretionary elements, the inclusion of mandatory requirements brought total US defence spending to USD921bn.

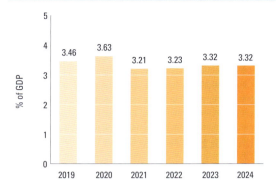

Figure 4 **US defence budget** as % of GDP

Note: Figures refer to the National Defense (050) Budget Function (Budget Authority) as % of GDP.
Source: IISS analysis based on GDP data from IMF World Economic Outlook, October 2024 ©IISS

For discretionary spending, the proposed budget represents a 1% increase on the previous year's request, in line with the 2023 Fiscal Responsibility Act (FRA). Against these funding constraints, in FY25, US policymakers opted to prioritise force readiness and personnel investments over longer-term modernisation and research and development (R&D) efforts. However, in the long run, reductions in funding are unlikely to be detrimental as cuts to popular programmes will increase pressures to ease future spending restraints, while reduced orders also provide breathing space for the country's defence-industrial base, which is struggling to meet demand.

The restrictions also come at a time when support for US allies and partners is driving further spending requirements. To that end, commitments in Europe, the Indo-Pacific and the Middle East suggest that the US will remain reliant on supplemental funding to plug spending shortfalls.

Balancing acts

Budgetary growth remained confined to limits established by the FRA. These were introduced in July 2023, after a political impasse over the national-debt ceiling threatened to shut down all non-essential government activity. As a compromise, lawmakers agreed to increase Washington's debt ceiling but also to place limits on federal spending. This resulted in discretionary spending for defence and the Department of Energy being capped at USD886bn for FY24 and USD895bn for FY25. Despite allowing budgets to increase by USD8.4bn in nominal terms from the FY24 request, in real terms, discretionary defence budgets declined by USD5.5bn, or 0.8% overall.

The cap also limits the flexibility to increase spending against an expanding range of challenges, including the need to continue military support for partners such as Ukraine and Israel. To date, Congress has relied on supplemental funding to make up shortfalls, such as the April 2024 National Security Act, which provided USD60bn in additional funding for Ukraine, over USD14bn for Israel, as well as additional funding for Indo-Pacific allies and partners. Ongoing conflicts mean that calls for US financial support will not dissipate any time soon and that future supplemental budgets should be expected.

That said, another potential route for increasing the DoD's topline budget is through enacting congressional legislation, such as the National Defense Authorization Act (NDAA), which is passed annually to authorise DoD funding levels. In June 2024, the Senate Armed Services Committee used its mark-up process to request that an additional USD28bn be allocated to the DoD via the NDAA. This would increase the DoD's base budget to USD878.4bn. Although the bill underwent other House and Senate mark-ups, it nonetheless indicates a willingness among some in Congress to challenge FRA budget caps.

Readiness over modernisation

Given funding restrictions, US policymakers were forced to make 'difficult but responsible decisions', according to Secretary of Defense Lloyd Austin's budget-release statement. Accordingly, the FY25 budget prioritises readiness and ongoing operations over long-term modernisation plans. This signals Washington's ongoing commitment to allies and partners in Europe, the Indo-Pacific and the Middle East and is reflected by the 2.4% increase in FY25 operations and maintenance (O&M) compared to the initial FY24 budget request. In FY25, O&M spending reached USD337.9bn, forming some 40% of the DoD's defence bill. In contrast, investment budgets declined: procurement spending fell 1.5% to USD167.5bn and spending on research, development, testing and evaluation (RDT&E) dropped by 1.3% to USD143.2bn.

One result of these cuts is a smaller US Navy. The FY25 request only allocated funding for six new ships, down from the seven previously outlined in the five-year budget outlook. In addition to buying one fewer *Virginia*-class nuclear-powered attack submarine, the FY25 budget also earmarked the

Table 1 The US DoD budget request by appropriation title, USDbn

Requests/CR budget by Appropriation Title	FY23	FY24 Request*	FY24 CR**	FY25 Request
Military Personnel	174.210	178.874	173.019	181.881
Operation and Maintenance	339.638	329.749	320.072	337.921
Procurement	176.845	170.049	163.862	167.546
RDT&E	139.820	144.980	139.658	143.157
Revolving and Management Funds	2.178	1.683	1.718	1.721
Offsetting Receipts	-0.025	-0.009	-0.009	
Defense Bill	**832.665**	**825.326**	**798.321**	**832.225**
Military Construction	16.714	14.734	16.673	15.561
Family Housing	2.327	1.941	2.327	1.984
Military Construction Bill	**19.041**	**16.675**	**19.000**	**17.545**
DoD TOTAL	**851.706**	**842.000**	**817.321**	**849.770**

Note: Base budget + FY 2023 Supplemental. Numbers may not add due to rounding.
*FY 2024 excludes supplemental funding request for Ukraine (USD44.4bn), Israel (USD10.6bn), and Submarine Industrial Base (USD3.3bn).
**Reflects Continuing Resolution (CR) (P.L. 118-15), as amended. This was passed in September 2023, as a stopgap measure to prevent a government shutdown.
Source: US Comptroller, Defense Budget Overview, United States Department of Defense Fiscal Year 2025 Budget Request, Revised 4 April 2024

retirement of 19 ships – including ten before the end of their expected service lives – and delayed the next *Ford*-class aircraft carrier by two years. In terms of aircraft procurement, the DoD reduced its total orders of F-35 *Lightning* IIs, decreasing the expected purchase of 83 aircraft in FY24, down to 68 in FY25. The air force also planned to buy six fewer F-15EX *Eagle* IIs, while the navy also deferred funding for several next-generation programmes, including its next-generation fighter (F/A-XX).

Yet the cuts to these high-profile programmes have both strategic and practical implications. Domestically, reductions to favoured modernisation plans are likely to raise questions about the future of American military strength, on both sides of the aisle. As such, the cuts take place against a wider calculus which strategically incentivises Congress to find new ways to protect and increase funding. At the practical level, reduced orders will also ease pressures on the defence-industrial base, which continues to suffer from capacity restraints. Indeed, since 2022, the US submarine shipbuilding industry has only produced an average of between 1.2 and 1.4 *Virginia*-class submarines a year, well below past expectations of two per year. Similarly, the F-35 programme has faced both hardware and software challenges with Technology Refresh-3, leading to delays in delivery and grounding of aircraft. These need to be addressed before the DoD can reasonably expect to hit projected production targets. Thus, cuts provide breathing room for industry, especially as the FY25 budget continues to invest in production infrastructure, such as the national submarine-industrial base.

Smaller, but better paid

In addition to increasing spending on O&M, spending on personnel also increased: the FY25 budget called for a 4.5% pay increase for military personnel and a 2.0% raise for civilians. This came a year after military personnel received a 5.2% pay increase. The FY25 budget also stresses other initiatives to increase the attractiveness of a military career. Indeed, the DoD is amid a 'recruitment crisis', after missing its recruitment targets for the last two years. In 2023, recruitment stood at 10,000 soldiers below target, a 20% shortfall, meaning that there are 41,000 fewer active-duty soldiers than in 2021. DoD called FY23 the 'toughest recruitment year' for the all-volunteer force since its inception, citing a strong economy, a smaller eligible population and the younger generation's distrust of institutions as some of the drivers of the recruitment shortfalls. In line with the 2022 National Defense Strategy, the FY25 budget includes additional support for personnel and their families, including childcare workforce initiatives, investment in suicide prevention and continued efforts to combat sexual assault. That said, the FY25 budget also tacitly acknowledged the ongoing recruitment challenges and reduced the size of the active-duty force by 7,800 people, with large reductions across the navy (5,000), army (2,700) and air-force reserve (2,600). The loss in end strength is mitigated to some degree by an overall increase of 2,100 in the reserve component across services and an increase of 400 space-force personnel, though there is still a net reduction of 5,700 personnel across the services' active-duty and reserve components. Perhaps more concerning, the Pentagon reported that, for the first time, the majority of young people did not even consider military service as an option.

Munitions

The budget includes several other capability priorities, including modernising the nuclear triad and advancing the Replicator initiative – though there remains a lack of guidance on the nature of Replicator funding.

As with FY24, scaling up munitions-manufacturing capability is also singled out as a budget priority, though spending on munitions dropped slightly from USD30.6bn in the FY24 request to USD29.8bn in FY25. Critically, the budget continues the multi-year procurement authorities granted by Congress for seven missiles – the RGM-184A Naval Strike Missile (navy), SM-6 (navy), AIM-120 Advanced Medium-Range Air-to-Air Missile (AMRAAM), AGM-158C Long Range Anti-Ship Missile (LRASM), AGM-158B Joint Air-to-Surface Standoff Missile – Extended Range (JASSM-ER), Guided Multiple Launch Rocket System (GMLRS) rounds (army), and the *Patriot* PAC-3 Missile Segment Enhancement (MSE) (army). These authorities help to ensure a more predictable demand for an industry that has struggled to scale munitions production due to fluctuating DoD requirements.

The military departments
US Army
While top-level service budgets reflect the wider DoD priorities, the allocations within these department budgets give clues to the priority areas for individual services. For example, the army budget request shows a continued focus on prioritising its people by both increasing recruitment and working to retain trained staff by investing in soldier housing and quality-of-life provisions. The budget also seeks to keep most of its modernisation programmes active, as seen by the increase in the service's procurement budget from USD23.4bn to USD24.4bn between the FY24 and FY25 budget requests. The FY25 request focuses on missiles and aircraft, with the budget for aircraft increasing to USD3.2bn from USD3.0bn due to notable increases in CH-47 *Chinook* helicopters, future UAS and small UAS. In contrast, the army RDT&E budget request declined from USD15.8bn in FY24 to USD14.1bn in FY25, with reductions primarily impacting the demonstration and validation phase. Ongoing RDT&E programmes include the Aviation Advanced Development, the Army Integrated Air and Missile Defense, and the Long-Range Hypersonic Weapon programmes.

US Navy
The Department of the Navy's total request of USD257.6bn, split by USD203.9bn for the navy and USD53.7bn for the US Marine Corps, marked a nominal increase of USD1.8bn over the FY24 budget request. Like the army's, the navy's budget prioritises people, readiness and current operations over modernisation. To this end, it reduced funding for high-profile next-generation programmes such as the Large Unmanned Surface Vehicle (LUSV), Extra-Large Uncrewed Underwater Vehicle (XLUUV), Next-Generation Attack Submarine (SSN(X)) and F/A-XX fighter-aircraft programme. Though plans to reduce the total fleet size are likely to provoke congressional disquiet, one area of good news for navy procurement is the update to its long-term shipbuilding plan. This seeks to reach a fleet size of 31 amphibious ships and includes funding for the US Marine Corps' Force Design 2030 transformation effort, including procurement of the Amphibious Combat Vehicle, Marine Air Defense Integrated System (MADIS) and AN/TPS-80 Ground/Air Task Oriented Radar (G/ATOR).

US Air Force and US Space Force
The Department of the Air Force total request is USD262.6bn, though this includes USD45.1bn of 'pass through' funding that does not fund the air force. Key elements of the US Air Force's request include the retirement of 251 aircraft. This includes 56 A-10 *Thunderbolt* IIs, 32 Block 20 F-22A *Raptor*s and a range of older aircraft that are not well suited for conventional deterrent or war-fighting roles. Similar to the navy's budget request, the air force's

Table 2 US DoD total budget request by military service, USDbn

Service	FY24 (requested)	FY25 (requested)	Nominal Change
Department of the Army	185.5	185.9	+0.4
Department of the Navy	255.8	257.6	+1.8
Department of the Air Force	Total: 259.2 / Total (without Pass Through funding): 215.1	Total: 262.6 Total (without Pass Through funding): 217.5	+2.4 absent Pass Through funding
		US Air Force: 188.1 US Space Force: 29.4 Pass Through: 45.1	Air Force: +3.08 Space Force: -0.6

Note: Numbers may not add due to rounding.
Sources: Departments of the Army, Navy and Air Force Budget Reviews

Table 3 US National Defense Budget Function[1] and other selected budgets,[2] 2000, 2010–25, (USDbn, current year)

FY	National Defense Budget Function BA	National Defense Budget Function Outlay	Atomic Energy Defense Activities BA	Other Defense Activities BA	Total National Defense BA	Total National Defense BA**	Total National Defense Outlay	Department of Homeland Security BA	Department of Veterans' Affairs BA	Total Federal Government Outlays	Total Federal Budget Surplus/Deficit
2000	290.3	281.0	12.4	1.3	304.0	300.8	294.4	13.8	45.5	1,789.0	236.2
2010	695.6	666.7	18.2	7.3	721.2	714.1	693.5	45.4	124.3	3,457.1	-1,294.4
2011	691.5	678.1	18.5	7.0	717.0	710.1	705.6	41.6	122.8	3,603.1	-1,299.6
2012	655.4	650.9	18.3	7.7	681.4	669.6	677.9	45.9	124.0	3,526.6	-1,076.6
2013	585.2	607.8	17.5	7.4	610.2	600.4	633.4	61.9	136.0	3,454.9	-679.8
2014	595.7	577.9	18.4	8.2	622.3	606.2	603.5	44.1	165.7	3,506.3	-484.8
2015	570.8	562.5	19.0	8.5	598.4	585.9	589.7	45.3	160.5	3,691.9	-442.0
2016	595.7	565.4	20.1	8.3	624.1	606.8	593.4	46.0	163.3	3,852.6	-584.7
2017	626.2	568.9	21.4	8.7	656.3	634.1	598.7	62.3	178.8	3,981.6	-665.5
2018	694.6	600.8	23.3	9.0	726.9	700.9	631.3	103.0	191.8	4,109.0	-779.1
2019	712.3	653.7	24.0	9.1	745.4	718.8	685.7	61.4	194.2	4,447.0	-983.6
2020	738.7	690.4	26.0	9.7	774.5	756.6	724.6	114.2	233.3	6,553.6	-3,132.5
2021	719.5	717.6	29.4	10.8	759.6	741.7	753.9	123.2	255.4	6,822.5	-2,775.4
2022	795.6	726.5	32.0	11.1	838.6	816.3	765.6	78.0	269.5	6,273.3	-1,375.9
2023	874.4	775.9	33.9	11.5	919.8	894.2	820.3	86.8	303.1	6,134.7	-1,693.7
2024*	920.6	859.5	35.3	12.1	968.0	945.1	907.7	112.3	345.1	6,940.9	-1,859.4
2025*	872.2	878.5	36.9	12.0	921.0	895.2	926.8	88.3	364.3	7,266.0	-1,781.0

Notes

FY = Fiscal Year (1 October–30 September). [1] The National Defense Budget Function subsumes funding for the DoD, the Department of Energy Atomic Energy Defense Activities and some smaller support agencies (including Federal Emergency Management and Selective Service System). It does not include funding for International Security Assistance (under International Affairs), the Veterans Administration, the US Coast Guard (Department of Homeland Security), nor for the National Aeronautics and Space Administration (NASA). Funding for civil projects administered by the DoD is excluded from the figures cited here. [2] Early in each calendar year, the US government presents its defence budget to Congress for the next fiscal year, which begins on 1 October. Until approved by Congress, the budget is called the Budget Request; after approval, it becomes the Budget Authority (BA). *Requests. Note that the FY25 request does not include supplemental funding for Ukraine or Israel. **Discretionary.

procurement budget decreased from USD30.6bn in FY24 to USD29.0bn in FY25. This reflects the trade-offs and tensions associated with the FRA budget caps. Despite the retirement of older aircraft and reduced orders, the air force's FY25 budget nonetheless calls for the procurement of 90 new aircraft. This includes 42 F-35As, 18 F-15EXs and 15 KC-46A *Pegasus* refuelling tankers.

In addition, the B-21 *Raider* received USD323 million in low-rate initial procurement funding. This is accompanied by an additional USD2.7bn for R&D purposes. This will come out of the air force's USD37.7bn RDT&E budget, which increased USD1.5bn above the FY24 request. Other programmes supported by the RDT&E budget include USD2.8bn for the development of the air force's Next-Generation Air Dominance (NGAD) platform and USD680m for the Collaborative Combat Aircraft (CCA) uninhabited system programme. To progress the CCA, the FY25 budget accommodates the prototype building and testing from the five programme contractors.

The decrease in space-force funding was expected and is in part due to a reduction in the number of launches planned in FY25 as part of the National Security Space Launch programme. The programme reduced the number of planned launches from ten in FY24 to seven in FY25, ostensibly as industry did not deliver the payloads on time. As with other services, the space force's FY25 RDT&E budget was also decreased slightly, from USD19.2bn in FY24 to USD18.7bn in FY25. The main impact of this is on the Next-Generation Overhead Persistent Infrared missile warning and tracking constellations, which saw a reduction from USD2.6bn to USD2.1bn across requests.

Figure 5 **North America: arms procurement and defence-industrial trends, 2024**

RAMPING UP AMMUNITION PRODUCTION

US efforts to increase its capacity to produce various munitions have accelerated over the last two years. Greater industrial capacity will support any future need to fight conflicts in different parts of the world simultaneously, but also to supply partners such as Israel and Ukraine. As in Europe, the US has paid much attention to 155mm howitzer-ammunition production, identifying several bottlenecks. The US has invested USD4 billion in ramping up capacity since February 2022 and is now producing over 40,000 rounds a month compared to 14,000 before 2022. This will then increase to 100,000 per month by the end of 2025. Similarly, Raytheon is increasing production of AIM-120 AMRAAM missiles to 1,200 per annum (PA) by the end of 2024, in part to satisfy European and Ukrainian demand for NASAMS air-defence systems. Lockheed Martin has increased *Javelin* anti-tank missile production by 15%, to 2,400 PA in 2024, and is aiming to reach 3,960 by the end of 2026. The company is also ramping up PA production of HIMARS multiple rocket launchers to 96, Guided Multiple Launch Rocket System rounds to 14,000 and *Patriot* PAC-3 MSE surface-to-air missiles to 650 by the end of 2024, 2025 and 2027 respectively. The US is also concerned with the size of its torpedo and long-range missile stocks, on which it would expect to rely in a conflict in the Indo-Pacific. For example, missile strikes against Ansarullah (the Houthis) in Yemen in 2024 placed pressure on the US Navy's *Tomahawk* cruise-missile stocks. However, the service's ambition to double production of that missile by 2027 is hampered by supply-chain weaknesses, particularly in electronics and rocket motors.

VENTURE CAPITAL (VC) FUNDING INTO DEFENCE

Over the last few years in the US, there has been a surge in VC funding (USD130bn from 2021 to mid-2024) for defence and security firms. Several companies have secured major contracts to deliver platforms, software and services to the US Department of Defense (DoD) and the armed forces. Autonomous-systems specialist Anduril Industries has been contracted to act as the US Special Operations Command's counter-UAV systems integrator and shortlisted for the US Air Force's Collaborative Combat Aircraft uninhabited combat air vehicle (UCAV) project. Data-analytics firm Palantir, which went public in 2020, has worked with the US Army since 2008 and has been recently contracted as part of the Pentagon's AI-related Project Maven. Both Anduril and Palantir have been incentivised to invest in defence businesses, due to growing defence spending and the DoD's stated desire to acquire hardware and software more quickly by broadening the number of companies it contracts beyond the largest prime contractors. The 2015 establishment of the Defense Innovation Unit (DIU) in Silicon Valley to speed up the use of commercial technology, and that of the Office of Strategic Capital in 2022 to accelerate private investment into critical component technologies, are examples of this. So too is the Replicator Initiative, launched in 2023 by the DIU, to quickly acquire thousands of 'attritable' uninhabited systems. Despite these efforts, there is concern that the the DoD is neither meeting the pace of its own ambitions nor VC investment in defence start-ups. This is particularly problematic for small start-ups seeking to survive the 'valley of death' between launching a product and securing a contract, which can take several years. On the government side, there is hesitancy to take risks on unproven companies. It remains to be seen how long-term VC interest in the sector will be.

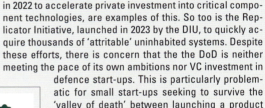

EUROPEAN COMPANIES SEE GROWTH IN THE US

Several European firms, such as BAE Systems and GKN, have long had a substantial presence in the US. Others have begun to establish or grow their presence more recently, encouraged by the steady growth in US defence spending and the success of some European-origin designs in the US market. This has included a Fincantieri frigate, Airbus and Leonardo helicopters, Kongsberg guided weapons, Saab radars and Thales sonars amongst others. In 2021, Germany's Rheinmetall opened a facility in Michigan to manufacture HX3 trucks for the US Army and to compete for that service's *Bradley* armoured-vehicle replacement requirement, the XM30 Mechanized Infantry Combat Vehicle. Having produced its *Protector* series of armoured-vehicle remote weapon stations in the US for two decades, Norway's Kongsberg announced in 2024 that it will build a factory in Virginia for its Naval Strike Missile and Joint Strike Missile. Sweden's Saab has announced it will open a factory in Michigan to produce 'shoulder-fired munitions and precision fire systems', following on from its opening in 2021 of an aerostructures facility in Indiana to support its participation in the T-7A *Red Hawk* training aircraft programme, and has opened an innovation hub in San Diego. Smaller firms have also begun to establish their presence in the US market. Germany's Renk established its US division in 2021 through the acquisition of L3Harris's propulsion-systems business, and Spain's Indra did the same through the 2023 acquisition of Leonardo's US-based air-traffic-control business.

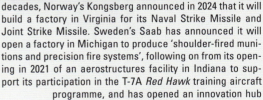

Figure 6 🇺🇸 US Army: selected air and missile defence (AMD) programmes

In 2019, the US Army published its Modernization Strategy which set out six capability priorities, including AMD. This brought together several existing programmes and requirements, some of which the army had already disclosed as far back as 2012 in its Air and Missile Defense Strategy. Of these, M-SHORAD, IFPC, LTAMDS and IBCS are the most significant efforts. To speed up entry into service, the army has used acquisition pathways designed to more quickly prototype and field an initial capability, such as Middle Tier of Acquisition (MTA) and dividing elements of the overall requirement into 'Increments' to be developed separately, a method used for other modernisation priorities. While this has achieved some results, technical challenges have meant that development can take longer than the five years envisaged in the MTA process, as has been the case with LTAMDS. The war in Ukraine and capability developments by adversaries elsewhere have given AMD a greater importance in the army's planning than five years ago. Consequently, the army's 2024 Army Force Structure Transformation outlined plans to double the number of planned M-SHORAD battalions to eight, and to add four new IFPC battalions to its plans, making a total of nine. Challenges remain, however, as the ambition to integrate a wide variety of AMD systems into the IBCS C2 system has run into both hardware and software issues.

Maneuver-Short Range Air Defense (M-SHORAD) Increment 1

TYPE 30mm self-propelled anti-aircraft gun and missile system (SPAAGM)
STATUS Series production since 2020
CONTRACTOR General Dynamics Land Systems
PRODUCTION MILESTONE 2023: first series production delivery
DEVELOPMENT PROCESS Blend of Urgent Capability Acquisition and Middle Tier of Acquisition
REQUIREMENT 8 battalions
REPLACING M1097 *Avenger* point-defence self-propelled surface-to-air missile (SAM)

Indirect Fire Protection Capability (IFPC) Increment 2

TYPE Short-range SAM system
STATUS Rapid prototyping and tests; 'field-able' prototype contract awarded 2021
CONTRACTOR Dynetics
PRODUCTION MILESTONE FY2026: first unit to be fielded
DEVELOPMENT PROCESS Middle Tier of Acquisition
REQUIREMENT 9 battalions
REPLACING *Land Phalanx Weapon System* 20mm towed air defence artillery; *Iron Dome* short-range SAM

Lower Tier Air and Missile Defense Sensor (LTAMDS)

TYPE Active electronically scanned array (AESA) radar
STATUS In test; Low-Rate Initial Production contract awarded 2024
CONTRACTOR Raytheon
PRODUCTION MILESTONE 2024: planned fielding of first system
DEVELOPMENT PROCESS Middle Tier of Acquisition
REQUIREMENT At least 15 battalion sets
REPLACING AN/MPQ-53/65 passive electronically scanned array (PESA) and AN/MPQ-65A AESA radars

Integrated AMD Battle Command System (IBCS)

TYPE AMD command-and-control (C2) system
STATUS Series production since 2021
CONTRACTOR Northrop Grumman
PRODUCTION MILESTONE 2023: Initial Operational Capability achieved
DEVELOPMENT PROCESS Software Acquisition
REQUIREMENT At least 15 battalion sets
REPLACING Multiple AMD C2 systems

©IISS

Sources: IISS analysis, US Department of Defense, US Army, US Government Accountability Office, Congressional Research Service, General Dynamics, Northrop Grumman, RTX, Epirus, Leidos, Lockheed Martin, Dynetics

Canada CAN

Canadian Dollar (CAD)		2023	2024	2025
GDP	CAD	2.89trn	3.02trn	3.16trn
	USD	2.14trn	2.21trn	2.33trn
Real GDP growth	%	1.2	1.3	2.4
Def exp [a]	CAD	37.8bn	41.0bn	
	USD	28.0bn	30.5bn	
Def bdgt [b]	CAD	32.5bn	36.8bn	
	USD	24.1bn	27.0bn	

[a] NATO figure
[b] Department of National Defence and Veterans Affairs

Real-terms defence budget trend (USDbn, constant 2015)

Population		38,794,813				
Age	0–14	15–19	20–24	25–29	30–64	65 plus
Male	8.0%	2.8%	2.7%	3.2%	23.2%	9.7%
Female	7.6%	2.6%	2.6%	3.0%	23.3%	11.4%

Capabilities

Canada's armed forces are focused principally on territorial defence, as well as contributing to international missions, chiefly through NATO. Canada unveiled a new defence vision in April 2024 which focuses on the Arctic, the North and Canada's approaches, and also competition further afield in the Euro-Atlantic and Indo-Pacific. It also emphasises increasing striking power for the armed forces. Canada has faced criticism within NATO over its defence spending, with the government pledging in July 2024 to reach 2% of GDP only by 2032. Nonetheless, in the same month, Ottawa unveiled the ambition to replace its existing four-boat submarine force with twelve new conventionally-powered boats with under-ice capability. It has also pledged to more than double its leadership contribution to a NATO battlegroup in Latvia while also providing military support and training for Ukraine. In November 2022, the government issued a new Indo-Pacific strategy with increased focus and investment there, including naval presence. However, Canadian forces are stretched to maintain commitments in three arenas – the Indo-Pacific, the Arctic and the Euro-Atlantic. Procurement delays continue, while the armed forces have also suffered recruitment and retention problems. Canada maintains a well-developed range of mainly small and medium-sized defence firms. The strongest sector is in combat vehicles and components, though the government is using its latest naval procurements to establish a long-term national shipbuilding strategy.

ACTIVE 62,300 (Army 22,500 Navy 8,400 Air Force 12,100 Other 19,300) **Gendarmerie & Paramilitary 5,800**

RESERVE 29,100 (Army 21,500 Navy 4,100 Air 2,000 Other 1,500)

ORGANISATIONS BY SERVICE

Space
EQUIPMENT BY TYPE
SATELLITES • SPACE SURVEILLANCE 1 *Sapphire*

Army 22,500
FORCES BY ROLE
MANOEUVRE
  Mechanised
  1 (1st) mech bde gp (1 armd regt, 2 mech inf bn, 1 lt inf bn, 1 arty regt, 1 cbt engr regt, 1 log bn)
  2 (2nd & 5th) mech bde gp (1 armd recce regt, 2 mech inf bn, 1 lt inf bn, 1 arty regt, 1 cbt engr regt, 1 log bn)
COMBAT SUPPORT
  1 engr regt
  3 MP pl
AIR DEFENCE
  1 AD regt
EQUIPMENT BY TYPE
ARMOURED FIGHTING VEHICLES
  MBT 74: 34 *Leopard* 2A4 (trg role); 20 *Leopard* 2A4M; 20 *Leopard* 2A6M
  RECCE 61: 5 LAV 6.0 Reconnaissance; 56 LAV-25 *Coyote*
  IFV 550 LAV 6.0 (incl variants)
  APC 295
    APC (T) 140 M113/M577 (CP)
    APC (W) 155 LAV *Bison* (incl EW, amb, repair & recovery variants)
  AUV 507: 7 *Cougar*; 500 TAPV
ENGINEERING & MAINTENANCE VEHICLES
  AEV 23: 5 *Buffalo*; 18 *Wisent* 2
  ARV 11 BPz-3 *Büffel*
ANTI-TANK/ANTI-INFRASTRUCTURE
  MSL • MANPATS TOW-2
  RCL 84mm *Carl Gustaf*
ARTILLERY 178
  TOWED 154 **105mm** 121: 93 C3 (M101); 28 LG1 MkII; **155mm** 33 M777
  MOR 24: **81mm** L16; SP **81mm** 24 LAV *Bison*
UNINHABITED AERIAL VEHICLES
  ISR • Light 5 RQ-21A *Blackjack*

Reserve Organisations 21,500

Canadian Rangers 5,300 Reservists
Provide a limited military presence in Canada's northern, coastal and isolated areas. Sovereignty, public-safety and surveillance roles
FORCES BY ROLE
MANOEUVRE
  Other
  5 (patrol) ranger gp (209 patrols)

Army Reserves 16,200 Reservists

Most units have only coy-sized establishments

FORCES BY ROLE

COMMAND

10 bde gp HQ

MANOEUVRE

Reconnaissance

18 recce regt (sqn)

Light

51 inf regt (coy)

COMBAT SUPPORT

16 fd arty regt (bty)

3 indep fd arty bty

10 cbt engr regt (coy)

1 EW regt (sqn)

4 int coy

10 sigs regt (coy)

COMBAT SERVICE SUPPORT

10 log bn (coy)

3 MP coy

Royal Canadian Navy 8,400

EQUIPMENT BY TYPE

SUBMARINES 4

SSK 4 *Victoria* (ex-UK *Upholder*) (of which 1 in long-term refit) with 6 single 533mm TT with Mk 48 HWT

PRINCIPAL SURFACE COMBATANTS • FRIGATES 12

FFGHM 12 *Halifax* with 2 quad lnchr with RGM-84L *Harpoon* Block II AShM, 2 8-cell Mk 48 mod 0 VLS with RIM-162C ESSM SAM, 2 twin 324mm SVTT Mk 32 mod 9 ASTT with Mk 46 LWT, 1 Mk 15 *Phalanx* Block 1B CIWS, 1 57mm gun (capacity 1 CH-148 *Cyclone* hel)

PATROL AND COASTAL COMBATANTS 4

PSOH 4 *Harry DeWolf* (capacity 1 CH-148 *Cyclone* hel)

MINE WARFARE • MINE COUNTERMEASURES 12

MCO 12 *Kingston* (also used in patrol role)

LOGISTICS AND SUPPORT 10

AORH 1 *Asterix* (*Resolve*) (capacity 2 CH-148 *Cyclone* hel)

AXL 8 *Orca*

AXS 1 *Oriole*

UNINHABITED MARITIME SYSTEMS

UUV • DATA REMUS 100; *Seabotix*

Reserves 4,100 reservists

24 units tasked with crewing 10 of the 12 MCOs, harbour defence & naval control of shipping

Royal Canadian Air Force (RCAF) 12,100

FORCES BY ROLE

FIGHTER/GROUND ATTACK

4 sqn with F/A-18A/B (CF-18AM/BM) *Hornet*

ANTI-SUBMARINE WARFARE

2 sqn with CH-148 *Cyclone*

MARITIME PATROL

2 sqn with P-3 *Orion* (CP-140M *Aurora*)

SEARCH & RESCUE/TRANSPORT

4 sqn with AW101 *Merlin* (CH-149 *Cormorant*); C-130H/H-30 (CC-130) *Hercules*; KC-130H

1 sqn with Bell 412 (CH-146 *Griffon*); C-130J-30 (CC-130) *Hercules*

TANKER/TRANSPORT

1 sqn with A310/A310 MRTT (CC-150/CC-150T); A330 (CC-330)

TRANSPORT

1 sqn with C-17A (CC-177) *Globemaster*

1 sqn with CL-600 (CC-144B/C); CL-650 (CC-144D)

1 sqn with C-130J-30 (CC-130) *Hercules*

1 sqn with DHC-6 (CC-138) *Twin Otter*

TRAINING

1 OCU sqn with F/A-18A/B (CF-18AM/BM) *Hornet*

1 OCU sqn with C295W (CC-295)

1 OCU sqn with C-130H/H-30/J-30 (CC-130) *Hercules*

1 OCU sqn with CH-148 *Cyclone*

1 OCU sqn with Bell 412 (CH-146 *Griffon*)

1 sqn with DHC-8 (CT-142)

1 sqn with P-3 *Orion* (CP-140M *Aurora*)

TRANSPORT HELICOPTER

4 sqn with Bell 412 (CH-146 *Griffon*)

3 (cbt spt) sqn with Bell 412 (CH-146 *Griffon*)

1 sqn with CH-47F (CH-147F) *Chinook*

EQUIPMENT BY TYPE

AIRCRAFT 103 combat capable

FGA 89: 83 F/A-18A/B (CF-18AM/BM) *Hornet*; 6 CF-18AM/BM HEP *Hornet*

ASW 14 P-3 *Orion* (CP-140M *Aurora*)

SAR 8 C295W (CC-295)

TKR/TPT 5: 2 A310 MRTT (CC-150T); 3 KC-130H

TPT 43: **Heavy** 5 C-17A (CC-177) *Globemaster* III; **Medium** 26: 7 C-130H (CC-130) *Hercules*; 2 C-130H-30 (CC-130) *Hercules*; 17 C-130J-30 (CC-130) *Hercules*; **Light** 4 DHC-6 (CC-138) *Twin Otter*; **PAX** 8: 2 A310 (CC-150 *Polaris*); 2 A330 (CC-330) (VIP); 2 CL-600 (CC-144B/C); 2 CL-650 (CC-144D)

TRG 4 DHC-8 (CT-142)

HELICOPTERS

ASW 27 CH-148 *Cyclone*

MRH 75 Bell 412 (CH-146 *Griffon*)

SAR 13 AW101 *Merlin* (CH-149 *Cormorant*)

TPT • Heavy 14 CH-47F (CH-147F) *Chinook*

RADAR 53

AD RADAR • NORTH WARNING SYSTEM 46: 10 AN/FPS-117 (range 200nm); 36 AN/FPS-124 (range 80nm)

STRATEGIC 6: 4 Coastal; 2 Transportable

AIR-LAUNCHED MISSILES

AAM • **IR** AIM-9L *Sidewinder*
ARH AIM-120C AMRAAM
BOMBS
  Laser-guided: GBU-10/-12/-16 *Paveway* II; GBU-24 *Paveway* III
  Laser & INS/GPS-guided GBU-49 *Enhanced Paveway* II
  INS/GPS-guided: GBU-31 JDAM; GBU-38 JDAM

NATO Flight Training in Canada
EQUIPMENT BY TYPE
AIRCRAFT
  TRG 26 T-6A *Texan* II (CT-156 *Harvard* II)

Contracted Flying Services – Southport
EQUIPMENT BY TYPE
AIRCRAFT
  TPT • Light 7 Beech C90B *King Air*
  TRG 13 G-120A
HELICOPTERS
  MRH 9 Bell 412 (CH-146)
  TPT • Light 13 Bell 206 *Jet Ranger* (CH-139)

Canadian Special Operations Forces Command 1,500
FORCES BY ROLE
SPECIAL FORCES
  1 SF regt (Canadian Special Operations Regiment)
  1 SF unit (JTF 2)
COMBAT SERVICE SUPPORT
  1 CBRN unit (Canadian Joint Incident Response Unit – CJIRU)
TRANSPORT
  1 (spec ops) sqn, with Beech 350ER *King Air* (CE-145C *Vigilance*); Bell 412 (CH-146 *Griffon* – from the RCAF)
EQUIPMENT BY TYPE
NBC VEHICLES 4 LAV *Bison* NBC
AIRCRAFT
  ISR 1 Beech 350ER *King Air* (CE-145C *Vigilance*)
HELICOPTERS • MRH 10 Bell 412 (CH-146 *Griffon*)

Canadian Forces Joint Operational Support Group
FORCES BY ROLE
COMBAT SUPPORT
  1 engr spt coy
  1 (close protection) MP coy
  1 (joint) sigs regt
COMBAT SERVICE SUPPORT
  1 (spt) log unit
  1 (movement) log unit

Gendarmerie & Paramiltary 5,800

Canadian Coast Guard 5,800

Incl Department of Fisheries and Oceans; all platforms are designated as non-combatant
EQUIPMENT BY TYPE
PATROL AND COASTAL COMBATANTS 81
  PSOH 1 *Leonard J Cowley*
  PSO 1 *Sir Wilfred Grenfell*
  PCO 13: 2 *Cape Roger*; 1 *Gordon Reid*; 9 *Hero*; 1 *Tanu*
  PBF 1 Response Boat-Medium (RB-M)
  PB 65: 16 *Baie de Plaisance* (SAR); 9 Type-300A (SAR); 36 Type-300B (SAR); 3 *S. Dudka*; 1 *Vakta*
AMPHIBIOUS • LANDING CRAFT 4
  UCAC 4 Type-400
LOGISTICS AND SUPPORT 43
  ABU 4
  AG 8
  AGB 8
  AGBH 11
  AGOR 8
  AGS 2
  ATF 2
HELICOPTERS
  MRH 7 Bell 412EP
  TPT • Light 15 Bell 429

DEPLOYMENT

CYPRUS: UN • UNFICYP (*Operation Snowgoose*) 1
DEMOCRATIC REPUBLIC OF THE CONGO: UN • MONUSCO (*Operation Crocodile*) 7
EGYPT: MFO (*Operation Calumet*) 55; 1 MP team
IRAQ: NATO • NATO Mission Iraq 14
KOSOVO: NATO • KFOR • *Joint Enterprise* (*Operation Kobold*) 5
KUWAIT: *Operation Inherent Resolve* (*Impact*) 200
LATVIA: NATO • Forward Land Forces (*Operation Reassurance*) 1,600; 1 mech inf bde HQ; 1 tk sqn; 1 mech inf BG; 1 fd arty bty
MIDDLE EAST: UN • UNTSO (*Operation Jade*) 4
NORTH SEA: NATO • SNMG 1: 210; 1 FFGHM
POLAND: *Operation Unifier* 40 (UKR trg)
SOUTH SUDAN: UN • UNMISS (*Operation Soprano*) 9
UNITED KINGDOM: Air Task Force Prestwick (ATF-P) 55; 3 C-130J-30 *Hercules* (CC-130J); *Operation Unifier* 170 (UKR trg)

FOREIGN FORCES
United Kingdom BATUS 50
United States 150

United States US

United States Dollar USD		2023	2024	2025
GDP	USD	27.7trn	29.2trn	30.3trn
Real GDP growth	%	2.9	2.8	2.2
Def exp [a]	USD	876bn	968bn	
Def bdgt [b]	USD	920bn	968bn	921bn

[a] NATO figure

[b] National Defense Budget Function (50) Budget Authority. Includes DoD fund ng, as well as funds for nuclear weapons-related activities undertaken by the Department of Energy. Excludes some military retirement and healthcare costs. 2025 figure does not include supplemental funding for Ukraine or Israel.

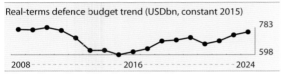

Real-terms defence budget trend (USDbn, constant 2015)

Population	341,963,408				
Age	0–14	15–19	20–24	25–29	30–64	65 plus
Male	9.2%	3.2%	3.3%	3.4%	21.9%	8.3%
Female	8.8%	3.0%	3.1%	3.3%	22.2%	10.2%

Capabilities

The United States remains the world's most capable military power, with a unique ability to project power globally. In January 2025, a second Trump administration succeeded the Biden administration, which had identified China as the 'pacing challenge' and Russia as the 'acute threat' to the US in its main national security documents. In 2024, the Pentagon released a new Arctic Strategy and also issued its first National Defense Industrial Strategy. The US continued to support Ukraine, sending longer-range weapon systems and loosening some end-user restrictions. In Europe, the US has maintained an elevated troop presence to reassure NATO allies and, in 2024, announced plans to deploy new long-range missiles to Germany. In the Indo-Pacific, the US is strengthening its footprint through new basing rights and renovating older facilities across the region. The Pentagon is modernising across domains, including each leg of its nuclear triad, and is aiming to field conventional very-high-speed cruise missiles, hypersonic glide vehicles, and conventionally-armed ground-based long-range missiles. The US maintains an all-volunteer force, including significant reserves, with high levels of training throughout all commands and services. The Pentagon has struggled, though, to meet recruitment targets and is trying to improve readiness. Support for Ukraine and military engagements in the Middle East have placed strains on US munitions stocks, though the US is now making significant investments in rebuilding production capacity and in securing the defence-related supply chain. The US has the world's most capable defence industry, active in all sectors, and with a dominant position in the international defence market.

ACTIVE 1,315,600 (Army 446,950 Navy 330,350 Air Force 316,650 Space Force 9,450 US Marine Corps 171,400 US Coast Guard 40,800)

RESERVE 797,200 (Army 497,000 Navy 92,350 Air Force 168,850 Marine Corps Reserve 32,750 US Coast Guard 6,250)

ORGANISATIONS BY SERVICE

US Strategic Command
HQ at Offutt AFB (NE)

US Navy
EQUIPMENT BY TYPE
SUBMARINES • STRATEGIC • SSBN 14 *Ohio* with up to 20 UGM-133A *Trident* D-5/D-5LE nuclear SLBM, 4 single 533mm TT with Mk 48 ADCAP mod 6/7 HWT

US Air Force • Global Strike Command
FORCES BY ROLE
MISSILE
9 sqn with LGM-30G *Minuteman* III
BOMBER
5 sqn with B-52H *Stratofortress*
2 sqn with B-2A *Spirit* (+1 ANG sqn personnel only)
EQUIPMENT BY TYPE
SURFACE-TO-SURFACE MISSILE LAUNCHERS
ICBM • **Nuclear** 400 LGM-30G *Minuteman* III (1 Mk12A or Mk21 re-entry veh per missile)
AIRCRAFT
BBR 65: 19 B-2A *Spirit*; 46 B-52H *Stratofortress*
AIR-LAUNCHED MISSILES
LACM • **Nuclear** AGM-86B

Strategic Defenses – Early Warning
EQUIPMENT BY TYPE
RADAR
NORTH WARNING SYSTEM 50: 14 AN/FPS-117; 36 AN/FPS-124
SOLID STATE PHASED ARRAY RADAR SYSTEM (SSPARS) 5 AN/FPS-132 Upgraded Early Warning Radar located at Beale AFB (CA), Cape Cod SFS (MA), Clear SFS (AK), Pituffik SB (GL) and RAF Fylingdales (UK)
SPACETRACK SYSTEM 7: 1 AN/FPS-85 Spacetrack Radar at Eglin AFB (FL); 6 contributing radars at Cavalier SFS (ND), Clear SFS (AK), Pituffik SB (GL), RAF Fylingdales (UK), Beale AFB (CA) and Cape Cod SFS (MA); 3 Spacetrack Optical Trackers located at Socorro (NM), Maui (HI), Diego Garcia (BIOT)
PERIMETER ACQUISITION RADAR ATTACK CHARACTERISATION SYSTEM (PARCS) 1 AN/FPQ-16 at Cavalier SFS (ND)
DETECTION AND TRACKING RADARS 5 located at Kwajalein Atoll, Ascension Island, Australia, Kaena Point (HI), MIT Lincoln Laboratory (MA)
GROUND BASED ELECTRO OPTICAL DEEP SPACE SURVEILLANCE SYSTEM (GEODSS) Socorro (NM), Maui (HI), Diego Garcia (BIOT)
STRATEGIC DEFENCES – MISSILE DEFENCES
SEA-BASED: *Aegis* engagement cruisers and destroyers
LAND-BASED: 40 ground-based interceptors at

Fort Greely (AK); 4 ground-based interceptors at Vandenburg SFB (CA)

Space
EQUIPMENT BY TYPE
SATELLITES 263
  COMMUNICATIONS 150: 6 AEHF; 6 DSCS-III; 2 *Milstar*-I; 3 *Milstar*-II; 5 MUOS; 5 SDS-III; 2 SDS-IV; ε84 *Starshield*; 1 *TacSat*-4; 1 *TacSat*-6; 19 Transport Layer Tranche 0; 6 UFO; 10 WGS SV2
  POSITIONING, NAVIGATION & TIMING 30: 12 NAVSTAR Block IIF; 7 NAVSTAR Block IIR; 7 NAVSTAR Block IIRM; 4 NAVSTAR Block III
  METEOROLOGY/OCEANOGRAPHY 5: 4 DMSP-5; 1 WSF-M
  ISR 14: 5 FIA *Radar*; 5 *Evolved Enhanced/Improved Crystal* (visible and infrared imagery); 2 NRO L-71; 2 NRO L-76
  ELINT/SIGINT 33: 8 *Mentor* (advanced *Orion*); 2 *Mercury*; 2 *Nemesis*; 1 *Sharp* (NRO L-67); 3 *Trumpet*; 4 Improved *Trumpet*; 12 Naval Ocean Surveillance System (NOSS); 1 NRO L-85
  SPACE SURVEILLANCE 11: 6 GSSAP; 1 ORS-5; 1 SBSS (Space Based Surveillance System); 3 *Silent Barker* (NRO L-107)
  EARLY WARNING 20: 4 DSP; 2 HTBSS; 6 SBIRS *Geo*; 8 Tracking Layer Tranche 0
REUSABLE SPACECRAFT 1 X-37B OTV
COUNTERSPACE • **EW** Counter Communications System (CCS)

US Army 446,950
FORCES BY ROLE
Sqn are generally bn sized and tp are generally coy sized
COMMAND
  4 (I, III, V & XVIII AB) corps HQ
  1 (2nd) inf div HQ
  1 (56th) arty comd
SPECIAL FORCES
  (see USSOCOM)
MANOEUVRE
  Armoured
  2 (1st Armd & 1st Cav) armd div (3 (1st–3rd ABCT) armd bde (1 armd recce sqn, 2 armd bn, 1 armd inf bn, 1 SP arty bn, 1 cbt engr bn, 1 CSS bn); 1 SP arty bde HQ; 1 log bde; 1 (hy cbt avn) hel bde; 1 SAM bn)
  1 (1st) inf div (2 (1st & 2nd ABCT) armd bde (1 armd recce sqn, 2 armd bn, 1 armd inf bn, 1 SP arty bn, 1 cbt engr bn, 1 CSS bn); 1 SP arty bde HQ; 1 log bde; 1 (cbt avn) hel bde)
  1 (3rd) inf div (2 (1st & 2nd ABCT) armd bde (1 armd recce sqn, 2 armd bn, 1 armd inf bn, 1 SP arty bn, 1 cbt engr bn, 1 CSS bn); 1 lt inf bn; 1 SP arty bde HQ; 1 log bde; 1 (cbt avn) hel bde)
  Mechanised
  1 (4th) inf div (1 (3rd ABCT) armd bde (1 armd recce sqn, 2 armd bn, 1 armd inf bn, 1 SP arty bn, 1 cbt engr bn, 1 CSS bn); 2 (1st & 2nd SBCT) mech bde (3 mech inf bn, 1 arty bn, 1 cbt engr bn, 1 CSS bn); 1 SP arty bde HQ; 1 log bde; 1 (hy cbt avn) hel bde)
  1 (7th) inf div (1 (1st SBCT, 2nd ID) mech bde (1 armd recce sqn, 3 mech inf bn, 1 arty bn, 1 cbt engr bn, 1 CSS bn); 1 (2nd SBCT, 2nd ID) mech bde (3 mech inf bn, 1 arty bn, 1 cbt engr bn, 1 CSS bn))
  2 (2nd & 3rd CR) mech bde (1 armd recce sqn, 3 mech sqn, 1 arty sqn, 1 cbt engr sqn, 1 CSS sqn)
  Light
  1 (10th Mtn) inf div (3 (1st–3rd BCT) lt inf bde (3 inf bn, 1 arty bn, 1 cbt engr bn, 1 CSS bn); 1 log bde; 1 (cbt avn) hel bde)
  1 (25th) inf div (2 (2nd & 3rd BCT) inf bde (1 recce sqn, 2 inf bn, 1 arty bn, 1 cbt engr bn, 1 CSS bn); 1 log bde; 1 (cbt avn) hel bde)
  5 (Sy Force Assist) inf bde(-)
  Air Manoeuvre
  1 (11th) AB div (1 (1st BCT) inf bde (1 recce sqn, 3 inf bn, 1 arty bn, 1 cbt engr bn, 1 CSS bn); 1 (2nd BCT) AB bde (1 recce bn, 2 para bn, 1 arty bn, 1 cbt engr bn, 1 CSS bn))
  1 (82nd) AB div (3 (1st–3rd BCT) AB bde (3 para bn, 1 arty bn, 1 cbt engr bn, 1 CSS bn); 1 (cbt avn) hel bde; 1 log bde)
  1 (101st) air aslt div (1 (1st BCT) air aslt bde (3 air aslt bn, 1 arty bn, 1 cbt engr bn, 1 CSS bn); 1 (2nd BCT) air aslt bde (1 recce coy, 3 air aslt bn, 1 arty bn, 1 cbt engr bn, 1 CSS bn); 1 (3rd BCT) air aslt bde (1 recce sqn, 3 air aslt bn, 1 arty bn, 1 cbt engr bn, 1 CSS bn); 1 (cbt avn) hel bde; 1 log bde)
  1 (173rd BCT) AB bde (1 recce bn, 2 para bn, 1 arty bn, 1 cbt engr bn, 1 CSS bn)
  Other
  1 (11th ACR) trg armd cav regt (OPFOR) (2 armd cav sqn, 1 CSS bn)
COMBAT SUPPORT
  3 MRL bde (2 MRL bn)
  1 MRL bde (1 MRL bn; 1 SSM bn)
  1 MRL bde (5 MRL bn)
  4 engr bde
  2 EOD gp (2 EOD bn)
  10 int bde
  2 int gp
  4 MP bde
  1 NBC bde
  3 (strat) sigs bde
  4 (tac) sigs bde
  1 (1st MDTF) cbt spt bde (1 SSM bn; 1 (MDEB) cbt spt bn)
  2 (2nd & 3rd MDTF) cbt spt bde (1 (MDEB) cbt spt bn)

COMBAT SERVICE SUPPORT
  2 log bde
  3 med bde
  1 tpt bde
ISR
  1 ISR avn bde
HELICOPTER
  2 (cbt avn) hel bde
  1 (cbt avn) hel bde HQ
AIR DEFENCE
  6 SAM bde

Reserve Organisations

Army National Guard 323,450 reservists

Normally dual-funded by DoD and states. Civil-emergency responses can be mobilised by state governors. Federal government can mobilise ARNG for major domestic emergencies and for overseas operations

FORCES BY ROLE
COMMAND
  8 div HQ
SPECIAL FORCES
  (see USSOCOM)
MANOEUVRE
  Reconnaissance
  1 armd recce sqn
  Armoured
  5 (ABCT) armd bde (1 armd recce sqn, 2 armd bn, 1 armd inf bn, 1 SP arty bn, 1 cbt engr bn, 1 CSS bn)
  Mechanised
  2 (SBCT) mech bde (1 armd recce sqn, 3 mech inf bn, 1 arty bn, 1 cbt engr bn, 1 CSS bn)
  Light
  14 (IBCT) inf bde (1 recce sqn, 3 inf bn, 1 arty bn, 1 cbt engr bn, 1 CSS bn)
  6 (IBCT) inf bde (1 recce sqn, 2 inf bn, 1 arty bn, 1 cbt engr bn, 1 CSS bn)
  1 (Sy Force Assist) inf bde(-)
  4 inf bn
  Air Manoeuvre
  1 AB bn
COMBAT SUPPORT
  8 arty bde
  1 SP arty bn
  8 engr bde
  1 EOD regt
  3 int bde
  3 MP bde
  1 NBC bde
  2 (tac) sigs bde
  17 cbt spt bde
COMBAT SERVICE SUPPORT
  10 log bde
  17 (regional) log spt gp

HELICOPTER
  8 (cbt avn) hel bde
  5 (theatre avn) hel bde
AIR DEFENCE
  3 SAM bde

Army Reserve 173,550 reservists

Reserve under full command of US Army. Does not have state-emergency liability of Army National Guard

FORCES BY ROLE
SPECIAL FORCES
  (see USSOCOM)
COMBAT SUPPORT
  4 engr bde
  4 MP bde
  2 NBC bde
  2 sigs bde
  3 cbt spt bde
COMBAT SERVICE SUPPORT
  9 log bde
  11 med bde
HELICOPTER
  2 (exp cbt avn) hel bde

Army Stand-by Reserve 700 reservists

Trained individuals for mobilisation

EQUIPMENT BY TYPE
ARMOURED FIGHTING VEHICLES
  MBT 2,640: ε540 M1A1 SA *Abrams*; ε1,410 M1A2 SEPv2 *Abrams*; ε690 M1A2 SEPv3 *Abrams*; (ε1,500 more M1A1/A2 *Abrams* in store)
  LT TK ε22 M10 *Booker*
  RECCE 1,745: ε1,200 M3A2/A3 *Bradley*; 545 M1127 *Stryker* RV (ε800 more M3 *Bradley* in store)
  IFV 2,800: ε14 LAV-25; ε2,000 M2A2/A3 *Bradley*; ε285 M2A4 *Bradley*; ε300 M7A3/SA BFIST (OP); ε35 M7A4 BFIST (OP); 83 M1296 *Stryker* Dragoon; 83 *Stryker* MCWS (in test); (ε2,000 more M2 *Bradley* in store)
  APC 10,047
    APC (T) 4,590: ε390 M1283 AMPV GP (incl CP and amb variants); ε4,200 M113A2/A3 (ε8,000 more in store)
    APC (W) 2,523: 1,162 M1126 *Stryker* ICV; 240 M1130 *Stryker* CV (CP); 144 M1131 *Stryker* FSV (OP); 173 M1133 *Stryker* MEV (Amb); 44 M1251A1 *Stryker* FSV (OP); 131 M1254A1 *Stryker* MEV (Amb); 108 M1255A1 *Stryker* CV (CP); 521 M1256A1 *Stryker* ICV
    PPV 2,934: 2,633 *MaxxPro* Dash; 301 *MaxxPro* LWB (Amb)
    AUV 22,291: ε15,000 JLTV; 1,175 M1117 ASV; 465 M1200 *Armored Knight* (OP); 5,651 M-ATV
ENGINEERING & MAINTENANCE VEHICLES
  AEV 567: 149 M1150 ABV; 250 M9 ACE; 123 M1132 *Stryker* ESV; 45 M1257A1 *Stryker* ESV
  ARV 1,293+: 360 M88A1; 933 M88A2 (ε1,000 more M88A1 in store); some M578

VLB 410: ε230 M60 AVLB; 120 M1074 Joint Assault Bridge System; 20 REBS; 40 *Wolverine* HAB
MW *Aardvark* JSFU Mk4; some *Husky* 2G; *Hydrema* 910 MCV-2; M58/M59 MICLIC; M139; *Rhino*

NBC VEHICLES 234 M1135 *Stryker* NBCRV

ANTI-TANK/ANTI-INFRASTRUCTURE
  MSL
    SP 1,133: 102 M1134 *Stryker* ATGM; 31 M1253A1 *Stryker* ATGM; ε1,000 M1167 HMMWV TOW
    MANPATS FGM-148 *Javelin*
  RCL 84mm *Carl Gustaf*

ARTILLERY 5,061
  SP 155mm 670: ε370 M109A6; ε300 M109A7 (ε850 more M109A6 in store)
  TOWED 1,212: **105mm** 821 M119A2/3; **155mm** 391 M777A2
  MRL 227mm 622: 368 M142 HIMARS; 184 M270A1; ε70 M270A2 MLRS
  MOR 2,557: **81mm** 990 M252; **120mm** 1,076 M120/M1064A3; **SP 120mm** 491; 322 M1129 *Stryker* MC; 119 M1252A1 *Stryker* MC; ε50 M1287 AMPV MC

SURFACE-TO-SURFACE MISSILE LAUNCHERS
  SSM • Conventional 8 *Typhon*; SM-6 Block IA (launched from *Typhon*)
  SRBM • Conventional MGM-140A/B ATACMS; MGM-168 ATACMS; PrSM (All launched from M270 MLRS or M142 HIMARS MRLs)
  GLCM • Conventional RGM-109E *Tomahawk* Block V (launched from *Typhon*)

AMPHIBIOUS
  PRINCIPAL AMPHIBIOUS SHIPS 8
    LST 8 *Frank Besson* (capacity 24 *Abrams* MBT)
  LANDING CRAFT 26
    LCT 17 LCU 2000 (capacity 5 M1 *Abrams* MBT)
    LCM 9 LCM 8 (capacity either 1 M1 *Abrams* MBT or 200 troops)

AIRCRAFT
  ISR 38: 8 EMARSS-G; 4 EMARSS-V; 7 EMARSS-M; 19 RC-12X *Guardrail* (5 trg)
  SIGINT 3: 2 CL-600 *Artemis* (in test); 1 Global-6500 *Ares* (in test)
  ELINT 9: 4 EMARSS-S; 4 EO-5C ARL-M (COMINT/ELINT); 1 TO-5C (trg)
  TPT 161: **Light** 157: 116 Beech A200 *King Air* (C-12 *Huron*); 30 Cessna 560 *Citation* (UC-35A/B); 11 SA-227 *Metro* (C-26E); **PAX** 4: 1 Gulfstream IV (C-20F); 2 Gulfstream V (C-37A); 1 Gulfstream G550 (C-37B)
  TRG 4 T-6D *Texan* II

HELICOPTERS
  ATK 750: ε160 AH-64D *Apache*; ε590 AH-64E *Apache*
  SAR 365: 19 HH-60L *Black Hawk*; 346 HH-60M *Black Hawk* (medevac)
  TPT 2,846: **Heavy** 465 CH-47F *Chinook*; **Medium** 1,841: ε20 UH-60A *Black Hawk*; ε800 UH-60L *Black Hawk*; 931 UH-60M *Black Hawk*; ε90 UH-60V *Black Hawk*; **Light** 540: 457 UH-72A *Lakota*; 18 UH-72B *Lakota*; 65 UH-1H/V *Iroquois*

UNINHABITED AERIAL VEHICLES 680
  CISR • Heavy ε180 MQ-1C *Gray Eagle*
  ISR • Medium ε500 RQ-7B *Shadow*
  OWA *Switchblade*-600

AIR DEFENCE
  SAM 921+
    Long-range 468 M903 *Patriot* PAC-3 MSE
    Short-range NASAMS
    Point-defence 453+: FIM-92 *Stinger*; 453 M1097 *Avenger*
  SPAAGM 30mm some M-LIDS; ε120 *Sgt Stout*
  GUNS • Towed • 20mm *Phalanx* (LPWS)
  DE 4 DE M-SHORAD (in test)

MISSILE DEFENCE • Long-range 42 THAAD

AIR-LAUNCHED MISSILES
  ASM AGM-114K/L/M/N/R *Hellfire* II; AGM-179A JAGM; AGR-20A APKWS

US Navy 330,350

Comprises 2 Fleet Areas, Atlantic and Pacific. 6 Fleets: 2nd – Atlantic; 3rd – Pacific; 4th – Caribbean, Central and South America; 5th – Arabian Sea, Persian Gulf, Red Sea; 6th – Mediterranean; 7th – Indian Ocean, East Asia, W. Pacific; plus Military Sealift Command (MSC); Naval Reserve Force (NRF). For Naval Special Warfare Command, see US Special Operations Command

EQUIPMENT BY TYPE

SUBMARINES 65
  STRATEGIC • SSBN 14 *Ohio* (opcon US STRATCOM) with up to 20 UGM-133A *Trident* D-5/D-5LE nuclear SLBM, 4 single 533mm TT with Mk 48 ADCAP mod 6/7 HWT
  TACTICAL 51
    SSGN 49:
      4 *Ohio* (mod) with 22 7-cell MAC VLS with UGM-109E *Tomahawk* Block IV/V LACM, 4 single 533mm TT with Mk 48 ADCAP mod 6/7 HWT
      1 *Los Angeles* Flight II with 1 12-cell VLS with UGM-109E *Tomahawk* Block IV/V LACM, 4 single 533mm TT with Mk 48 ADCAP mod 6/7 HWT
      21 *Los Angeles* Flight III with 1 12-cell VLS with UGM-109E *Tomahawk* Block IV/V LACM, 4 single 533mm TT with Mk 48 ADCAP mod 6/7 HWT
      10 *Virginia* Flight I/II with 1 12-cell VLS with UGM-109E *Tomahawk* Block IV/V LACM, 4 single 533mm TT with Mk 48 ADCAP mod 6/7 HWT
      8 *Virginia* Flight III with 2 6-cell VPT VLS with UGM-109E *Tomahawk* Block IV/V LACM, 4 single 533mm TT with Mk 48 ADCAP mod 6/7 HWT
      5 *Virginia* Flight IV with 2 6-cell VPT VLS with UGM-109E *Tomahawk* Block IV/V LACM, 4 single 533mm TT with Mk 48 ADCAP mod 6/7 HWT
    SSN 2 *Seawolf* (one more in long-term repair) with 8

single 660mm TT with UGM-109E *Tomahawk* Block IV LACM/Mk 48 ADCAP mod 6/7 HWT

PRINCIPAL SURFACE COMBATANTS 122

AIRCRAFT CARRIERS • CVN 11:

1 *Gerald R. Ford* with 2 octuple Mk 29 mod 5 GMLS with RIM-162D ESSM SAM, 2 Mk 49 mod 3 GMLS with RIM-116C RAM Block 2 SAM, 3 Mk 15 *Phalanx* Block 1B CIWS (typical capacity 75+ F/A-18E/F *Super Hornet* FGA ac; F-35C *Lightning* II FGA ac; E-2D *Hawkeye* AEW&C ac; EA-18G *Growler* EW ac; MH-60R *Seahawk* ASW hel; MH-60S *Knight Hawk* MRH hel)

10 *Nimitz* with 2 8-cell Mk29 GMLS with RIM-162D ESSM SAM, 2 21-cell Mk 49 GMLS with RIM-116 RAM Block 2 SAM, 3 Mk 15 *Phalanx* Block 1B CIWS (typical capacity 55 F/A-18E/F *Super Hornet* FGA ac; F-35C *Lightning* II FGA ac; 4 EA-18G *Growler* EW ac; 4 E-2C/D *Hawkeye* AEW ac; 6 MH-60R/S *Seahawk/Knight Hawk* hel)

CRUISERS • CGHM 11:

9 *Ticonderoga* with *Aegis* Baseline 5/6/8/9 C2, 2 quad lnchr with RGM-84D *Harpoon* Block 1C AShM, 16 8-cell Mk 41 VLS (of which 2 only 5-cell and fitted with reload crane) with RGM-109E *Tomahawk* Block IV/V LACM/SM-2 Block III/IIIA/IIIB/IV SAM/SM-3 Block IA/B SAM/SM-6 Block I/IA SAM, 2 triple 324mm SVTT Mk 32 ASTT with Mk 54 LWT, 2 Mk 15 *Phalanx* Block 1B CIWS, 2 127mm guns (capacity 2 MH-60R *Seahawk*/MH-60S *Knight Hawk* hels)

1 *Zumwalt* with 20 4-cell Mk 57 VLS with RGM-109E *Tomahawk* Block IV/V LACM/RIM-162 ESSM SAM/SM-2 Block IIIA SAM/ASROC A/S msl, 2 155mm guns (capacity 2 MH-60R *Seahawk* ASW hel or 1 MH-60R *Seahawk* ASW hel and 3 *Fire Scout* UAV)

1 *Zumwalt* with 20 4-cell Mk 57 VLS with RGM-109E *Tomahawk* Block IV/V LACM/RIM-162 ESSM SAM/SM-2 Block IIIA SAM/ASROC A/S msl, 1 155mm gun (capacity 2 MH-60R *Seahawk* ASW hel or 1 MH-60R *Seahawk* ASW hel and 3 *Fire Scout* UAV) (being upgraded to carry CPS msl)

DESTROYERS 74:

DDGHM 45:

5 *Arleigh Burke* Flight IIA with *Aegis* Baseline 5/9 C2, 12 8-cell Mk 41 VLS with RGM-109E *Tomahawk* Block IV/V LACM/RIM-162A ESSM SAM/SM-2 Block III/IIIA/IIIB/IV SAM/SM-3 Block IA/B SAM/SM-6 Block I/IA SAM/ASROC A/S msl, 2 triple 324mm SVTT Mk 32 ASTT with Mk 54 LWT, 2 Mk 15 *Phalanx* Block 1B CIWS, 1 127mm gun (capacity 2 MH-60R *Seahawk*/MH-60S *Knight Hawk* hels)

40 *Arleigh Burke* Flight IIA with *Aegis* Baseline 6/7/9 C2, 12 8-cell Mk 41 VLS with RGM-109E *Tomahawk* Block IV/V LACM/RIM-162A ESSM SAM/SM-2 Block III/IIIA/IIIB/IV SAM/SM-3 Block IA/B SAM/SM-6 Block I/IA SAM/ASROC A/S msl, 2 triple 324mm SVTT Mk 32 ASTT with Mk 54 LWT, 1 Mk 15 *Phalanx* Block 1B CIWS, 1 127mm gun (capacity 2 MH-60R *Seahawk*/MH-60S *Knight Hawk* hels) (of which 3 vessels also with 1 Mk 15 SeaRAM with RIM-116C RAM Block 2 and 8 vessels also with 1 Optical Dazzling Interdictor, Navy (ODIN) LWS)

1 *Arleigh Burke* Flight III with *Aegis* Baseline 10 C2, 12 8-cell Mk 41 VLS with RGM-109E *Tomahawk* Block IV/V LACM/RIM-162A ESSM SAM/SM-2 Block III/IIIA/IIIB/IV SAM/SM-3 Block IA/B SAM/SM-6 Block I/IA SAM/ASROC A/S msl, 2 triple 324mm SVTT Mk 32 ASTT with Mk 54 LWT, 1 Mk 15 *Phalanx* Block 1B CIWS, 1 127mm gun (capacity 2 MH-60R *Seahawk*/MH-60S *Knight Hawk* hels)

DDGM 28 *Arleigh Burke* Flight I/II with *Aegis* Baseline 5/9 C2, 2 quad lnchr with RGM-84D *Harpoon* Block 1C AShM, 12 8-cell Mk 41 VLS (of which 2 only 5-cell and fitted with reload crane) with RGM-109E *Tomahawk* Block IV/V LACM/RIM-162A ESSM SAM/SM-2 Block III/IIIA/IIIB/IV SAM/SM-3 Block IA/B SAM/SM-6 Block I SAM/ASROC A/S msl, 2 triple 324mm SVTT Mk 32 ASTT with Mk 54 LWT, 2 Mk 15 *Phalanx* Block 1B CIWS (of which 5 vessels with 1 Mk 15 SeaRAM with RIM-116C RAM Block 2, 1 Mk 15 *Phalanx* Block 1B instead of 2 *Phalanx*), 1 127mm gun, 1 hel landing platform

FRIGATES 26:

FFGHM 6 *Independence* with 2 quad lnchr with NSM (RGM-184A) AShM, 1 11-cell SeaRAM lnchr with RIM-116C Block 2 SAM, 1 57mm gun (capacity 2 MH-60R/S *Seahawk/Knight Hawk* hel and 3 MQ-8 *Fire Scout* UAV)

FFHM 20:

10 *Freedom* with 1 21-cell Mk 49 lnchr with RIM-116C RAM Block 2 SAM, 1 57mm gun (capacity 2 MH-60R/S *Seahawk/Knight Hawk* hel or 1 MH-60 with 3 MQ-8 *Fire Scout* UAV)

10 *Independence* with 1 11-cell SeaRAM lnchr with RIM-116C Block 2 SAM, 1 57mm gun (capacity 2 MH-60R/S *Seahawk/Knight Hawk* hel and 3 MQ-8 *Fire Scout* UAV)

PATROL AND COASTAL COMBATANTS 107

PBF 107: 32 Combatant Craft Assault; 3 Combatant Craft Heavy; 30 Combatant Craft Medium Mk 1; 42 Defiant 40 (40PB)

MINE WARFARE

MINE COUNTERMEASURES • MCO 8 *Avenger*

COMMAND SHIPS

LCC 2 *Blue Ridge* with 2 Mk 15 *Phalanx* Block 1B CIWS (capacity 3 LCPL; 2 LCVP; 700 troops; 1 med hel) (of which 1 vessel partially crewed by Military Sealift Command personnel)

AMPHIBIOUS

PRINCIPAL AMPHIBIOUS SHIPS 32:

LHA 2 *America* with 2 8-cell Mk 29 GMLS with RIM-162D ESSM SAM, 2 Mk 49 GMLS with RIM-116C RAM Block 2 SAM, 2 Mk 15 *Phalanx* Block 1B CIWS (capacity up to 29 ac/hel incl: 6-13 F-35B *Lightning* II FGA ac (possible 20 as full '*Lightning*' carrier'); 4 AH-1Z *Viper* atk hel; up to 12 MV-22B *Osprey* tpt ac; 2

MH-60S *Knight Hawk* MRH; 4 CH-53E *Sea Stallion* tpt hel; 2 UH-1Y *Iroquois* tpt hel; up to 1,800 troops)
LHD 7 *Wasp* with 2 8-cell Mk 29 GMLS with RIM-7M/P *Sea Sparrow* SAM, 2 Mk 49 GMLS with RIM-116C RAM Block 2 SAM, 2 Mk 15 *Phalanx* Block 1B CIWS (capacity up to 23 ac/hel incl: 6 AV-8B *Harrier* II FGA or F-35B *Lightning* II FGA ac (possible 20 F-35B as full '*Lightning* carrier'); 4 AH-1Z *Viper* atk hel; 4 CH-53E *Sea Stallion* hel; up to 6 MV-22B *Osprey* tpt ac; 3 UH-1Y *Iroquois* tpt hel; 3 LCAC(L); 60 tanks; 1,687 troops)
LPD 13 *San Antonio* with 2 21-cell Mk 49 GMLS with RIM-116C RAM Block 2 SAM (1 vessel also fitted with 1 Solid-State Laser Technology Maturation (SSL-TM) LWS) (capacity 2 CH-53E *Sea Stallion* hel or 2 MV-22 *Osprey*; 2 LCAC(L); 14 AAV; 720 troops)
LSD 10:
    4 *Harpers Ferry* with 2 Mk 49 GMLS with RIM-116C RAM Block 2 SAM, 2 Mk 15 *Phalanx* Block 1B CIWS (capacity 2 CH-53E *Sea Stallion* hel; 2 LCAC(L); 40 tanks; 500 troops)
    6 *Whidbey Island* with 2 Mk 49 GMLS with RIM-116C RAM Block 2 SAM, 2 Mk 15 *Phalanx* Block 1B CIWS (capacity 2 CH-53E *Sea Stallion* hel; 4 LCAC(L); 40 tanks; 500 troops)
LANDING CRAFT 143:
LCU 25 LCU 1610 (capacity either 1 M1 *Abrams* MBT or 350 troops)
LCM 7 LCM 8
LCP 33 Maritime Positioning Force Utility Boat (MPF-UB)
LCAC 78: 68 LCAC(L) (MLU ongoing) (capacity either 1 MBT or 60 troops); 10 *Ship to Shore Connector* (SSC) (capacity 1 MBT or 145 troops)
LOGISTICS AND SUPPORT 13
AGOR 6 (all leased out): 2 *Neil Armstrong*; 3 *Thomas G. Thompson*; 1 *Kilo Moana*
AX 1 *Prevail*
ESB 4 *Lewis B. Puller* (MSC) (capacity 4 MH-53/MH-60 hel)
SSA 2 *Dry Combat Submersible*
UNINHABITED MARITIME PLATFORMS
USV 11
    DATA • **Medium** 1 *Arabian Fox* (MAST-13)
    MW • **Medium** 3 UISS
    UTL 7: **Large** 4: 3 *Ranger*; 1 *Vanguard*; **Medium** 2 *Sea Hunter*; **Small** 1 *Devil Ray* T38
UUV • **UTL** • **Extra-large** 2: 1 *Orca*; 1 *Proteus*
UNINHABITED MARITIME SYSTEMS
USV • **DATA** *Adaro*; *Global Autonomous Response Craft*; *Saildrone Explorer*; *Wave Glider*
UUV
    DATA *Iver*-3; *Kingfish* Mk 18 mod 2; *Knifefish*; LBS-AUV (REMUS 600); LBS-G *Razorback*; *Lionfish* (REMUS 300); *Marlin*; *Riptide Micro*; *Sealion* (*Bluefin*-9); *Submaran*; *Swordfish* Mk 18 mod 1 (REMUS 100); *Viperfish* Mk 18 mod 3 (*Iver*-4 900)
    MW *Archerfish*; EX-116; *Seafox* (AN/SLQ-60); SLQ-48; SRS *Fusion*
    UTL *Bluefin*-12D; CURV 21; *Deep Drone* 8000; HUGIN; *Iver*-4 580; MR2 *Hydros*
MISSILE DEFENCE • **Long-range** 6 8-cell Mk 41 VLS with SM-3 (Poland & Romania)

Naval Reserve Forces 92,350

Selected Reserve 55,350

Individual Ready Reserve 37,000

Naval Inactive Fleet
Notice for reactivation: 60–90 days minimum (still on naval-vessel register)
EQUIPMENT BY TYPE
AMPHIBIOUS 1
    LSD 1 *Whidbey Island*
LOGISTICS AND SUPPORT 2
    ARS 2 *Safeguard*

Military Sealift Command (MSC)

Fleet Oiler (PM1)
EQUIPMENT BY TYPE
LOGISTICS AND SUPPORT 17
    AOR 17: 3 *John Lewis* with 1 hel landing platform; 14 *Henry J. Kaiser* with 1 hel landing platform

Special Mission (PM2)
EQUIPMENT BY TYPE
LOGISTICS AND SUPPORT 22
    AGM 2: 1 *Howard O. Lorenzen*; 1 Sea-based X-band radar
    AGOR 6 *Pathfinder*
    AGOS 5: 1 *Impeccable*; 4 *Victorious*
    AGE 1 *Waters*
    AKRH 1 *Ocean Trader* (long-term chartered, spec ops role)
    ARC 1 *Zeus*
    AS 4 *Arrowhead*
    ATF 2: 1 HOS *Red Dawn*; 1 HOS *Red Rock* (all long-term chartered, surv role)

Prepositioning (PM3)
EQUIPMENT BY TYPE
LOGISTICS AND SUPPORT 23
    AG 2: 1 *V Adm K.R. Wheeler*; 1 *Fast Tempo*
    AK 4: 2 *LTC John U.D. Page* (long-term chartered); 1 *Maj. Bernard F. Fisher* (long-term chartered); 1 *Cpt David I. Lyon* (long-term chartered)
    AKR 11: 2 *Bob Hope*; 1 *Stockham*; 8 *Watson*
    AKRH 4 *2nd Lt John P. Bobo*
    ESD 2 *Montford Point*

Service Support (PM4)
EQUIPMENT BY TYPE
LOGISTICS AND SUPPORT 14

AGE 1 *HOS Resolution* (long-term chartered)
AH 2 *Mercy* with 1 hel landing platform
ARS 2 *Safeguard*
AS 6: 1 *Dominator* (long-term chartered); 2 *Emory S. Land*; 1 *Kellie Chouest* (long-term chartered); 1 *Malama* (long-term chartered); 1 other (long-term chartered)
ATF 3: 1 *Ocean Valor* (long-term chartered, used as AGE); 1 *Powhatan*; 1 other (long-term chartered)

Fleet Ordnance and Dry Cargo (PM6)
EQUIPMENT BY TYPE
LOGISTICS AND SUPPORT 16
AOE 2 *Supply*
AFS 14 *Lewis and Clark*

Expeditionary Fast Transport (PM8)
EQUIPMENT BY TYPE
LOGISTICS AND SUPPORT 16
EPF 16: 2 *Guam*; 14 *Spearhead*

Dry Cargo and Tankers
EQUIPMENT BY TYPE
LOGISTICS AND SUPPORT 12
AK 1 *SLNC Star* (long-term chartered)
AO 11: 1 *Allied Pacific*; 1 *Badlands Trader*; 2 *Empire State*; 1 *Hama Patriot*; 1 *Overseas Mykonos*; 1 *Pohang Pioneer*; 1 *Stena Polaris*; 1 *Yosemite Trader*; 2 other (all long-term chartered)

US Maritime Administration (MARAD)

National Defense Reserve Fleet
EQUIPMENT BY TYPE
LOGISTICS AND SUPPORT 19
AGOS 2 *General Rudder* (trg role)
AGM 2: 1 *Pacific Collector*; 1 *Pacific Tracker*
AK 7: 2 *Cape Ann* (breakbulk); 1 *Cape Chalmers* (breakbulk); 2 *Cape May*; 1 *Del Monte* (breakbulk); 1 *Savannah*
AP 3: 1 *Golden Bear* (trg role); 1 *Kennedy* (trg role); 1 *State of Maine* (trg role)
AX 5: 1 *Freedom Star*; 1 *Invincible*; 1 *Kings Pointer*; 2 *Empire State* (NSMV)

Ready Reserve Force
Ships at readiness up to a maximum of 30 days
EQUIPMENT BY TYPE
LOGISTICS AND SUPPORT 53
AK 4: 2 *Gopher State*; 2 *Keystone State*
AKR 49: 1 *Adm W.M. Callaghan*; 8 *Algol*; 5 *Bob Hope*; 2 *Cape Arundel*; 5 *Cape Ducato*; 1 *Cape Edmont*; 3 *Cape Hudson*; 2 *Cape Knox*; 4 *Cape Island*; 1 *Cape Orlando*; 3 *Cape Race*; 3 *Cape Sable*; 3 *Cape Texas*; 2 *Cape Victory*; 2 *Cape Washington*; 2 *Gordon*; 2 *Wright* (breakbulk)

Naval Aviation 98,600
10 air wg. Each air wing usually comprises 8 sqn: 4 with F/A-18 or F-35; 1 with EA-18G; 1 with E-2D; 1 with MH-60R; 1 with MH-60S

FORCES BY ROLE
FIGHTER/GROUND ATTACK
19 sqn with F/A-18E *Super Hornet*
11 sqn with F/A-18F *Super Hornet*
2 sqn with F-35C *Lightning* II
2 sqn with F-35C *Lightning* II (forming)
ANTI-SUBMARINE WARFARE
12 sqn with P-8A *Poseidon*
1 (special projects) sqn with P-8A *Poseidon*
12 sqn with MH-60R *Seahawk*
3 ASW/ISR sqn with MH-60R *Seahawk*; MQ-8B *Fire Scout*
ELINT
1 sqn with EP-3E *Aries* II
ELINT/ELECTRONIC WARFARE
14 sqn with EA-18G *Growler*
AIRBORNE EARLY WARNING & CONTROL
1 sqn with E-2C *Hawkeye*
8 sqn with E-2D *Hawkeye*
COMMAND & CONTROL
2 sqn with E-6B *Mercury*
MINE COUNTERMEASURES
1 sqn with MH-53E *Sea Dragon*
TRANSPORT
3 sqn with CMV-22B *Osprey*
1 sqn with C-2A *Greyhound*
TRAINING
1 (FRS) sqn with EA-18G *Growler*
1 (FRS) sqn with C-2A *Greyhound*; E-2C/D *Hawkeye*; TE-2C *Hawkeye*
1 sqn with E-6B *Mercury*
2 (FRS) sqn with F/A-18E/F *Super Hornet*
1 (FRS) sqn with F-35C *Lightning* II
1 (FRS) sqn with MH-53 *Sea Dragon*
2 (FRS) sqn with MH-60S *Knight Hawk*; HH-60H *Seahawk*
2 (FRS) sqn with MH-60R *Seahawk*
1 (FRS) sqn with MQ-4C *Triton*; P-8A *Poseidon*
6 sqn with T-6A/B *Texan* II
2 sqn with T-44C *Pegasus*; T-54A
5 sqn with T-45C *Goshawk*
2 hel sqn with TH-57B/C *Sea Ranger*
1 hel sqn with TH-73A
1 (FRS) UAV sqn with MQ-8B/C *Fire Scout*
TRANSPORT HELICOPTER
12 sqn with MH-60S *Knight Hawk*
2 tpt hel/ISR sqn with MH-60S *Knight Hawk*; MQ-8B/C *Fire Scout*
ISR UAV
1 sqn with MQ-4C *Triton*
EQUIPMENT BY TYPE
AIRCRAFT 954 combat capable
FGA 678: 10 F-16A *Fighting Falcon*; 4 F-16B *Fighting Falcon*; 10 F-16C *Fighting Falcon*; 7 F-16D *Fighting Falcon*; 68 F-35C *Lightning* II; 4 F/A-18C *Hornet*; 2 F/A-

18D *Hornet*; 323 F/A-18E *Super Hornet*; 250 F/A-18F *Super Hornet*
ATK 2 AT-6E *Wolverine*
ASW 122: 6 P-3C *Orion*; 116 P-8A *Poseidon*
EW 152 EA-18G *Growler**
ELINT 4 EP-3E *Aries* II
AEW&C 80: 15 E-2C *Hawkeye*; 65 E-2D *Hawkeye*
C2 16 E-6B *Mercury*
TKR/TPT 8: 7 KC-130T *Hercules*; 1 KC-130J *Hercules*
TPT • Light 41: 3 Beech A200 *King Air* (C-12C *Huron*); 6 Beech A200 *King Air* (UC-12F *Huron*); 7 Beech A200 *King Air* (UC-12M *Huron*); 14 C-2A *Greyhound*; 2 DHC-2 *Beaver* (U-6A); 2 Gulfstream G100 (C-38A); 7 SA-227-BC *Metro* III (C-26D)
TRG 410: 43 T-6A *Texan* II; 173 T-6B *Texan* II; 13 T-34C *Turbo Mentor*; 10 T-38C *Talon*; 31 T-44C *Pegasus*; 2 T-54A; 135 T-45C *Goshawk*; 2 TE-2C *Hawkeye*; 1 TE-6B
TILTROTOR • TPT 41 CMV-22B *Osprey*
HELICOPTERS
ASW 221 MH-60R *Seahawk*
MRH 211 MH-60S *Knight Hawk* (Multi Mission Support)
MCM 12 MH-53E *Sea Dragon*
ISR 6 OH-58C *Kiowa*
TPT 16: **Heavy** 1 CH-53E *Sea Stallion*; **Medium** 5 UH-60L *Black Hawk*; **Light** 10: 5 UH-72A *Lakota*; 2 UH-1N *Iroquois*; 3 UH-1Y *Venom*
TRG 136: 26 TH-57B *Sea Ranger*; 52 TH-57C *Sea Ranger*; 58 TH-73A
UNINHABITED AERIAL VEHICLES
CISR 2 MQ-9A *Reaper*
ISR 111: **Heavy** 66: 17 MQ-4C *Triton*; 13 MQ-8B *Fire Scout*; 36 MQ-8C *Fire Scout*; **Medium** 34 RQ-23A *Tigershark*; **Light** 11 RQ-21A *Blackjack*
TKR 1 MQ-25 *Stingray* (in test)
AIR-LAUNCHED MISSILES
AAM • IR AIM-9M *Sidewinder*; **IIR** AIM-9X *Sidewinder* II; **SARH** AIM-7M *Sparrow* (being withdrawn); **ARH** AIM-120C-5/C-7/D AMRAAM
ASM AGM-65F *Maverick*; AGM-114M *Hellfire* II; AGR-20A APKWS
AShM AGM-84D *Harpoon*; AGM-84N *Harpoon* Block II+; AGM-158C LRASM
ARM AGM-88B/C/E HARM/AARGM
LACM • Conventional AGM-84E/H/K SLAM/SLAM-ER
BOMBS
Laser-guided: GBU-10/-12/-16 *Paveway* II; GBU-24 *Paveway* III; GBU-51 LCDB
Laser & INS/GPS-guided: EGBU-12 *Paveway* II; EGBU-24 *Paveway* III; GBU-52 LCDB; GBU-56 Laser JDAM
INS/GPS-guided: GBU-31/-32/-38 JDAM; AGM-154A/C/C-1 JSOW
Multi-mode guided GBU-53/B *Stormbreaker*

Naval Aviation Reserve
FORCES BY ROLE
FIGHTER/GROUND ATTACK
1 sqn with F/A-18E/F *Super Hornet*
ANTI-SUBMARINE WARFARE
2 sqn with P-8A *Poseidon* (forming)
1 sqn with MH-60R *Seahawk*
ELECTRONIC WARFARE
1 sqn with EA-18G *Growler*
TRANSPORT
6 log spt sqn with B-737-700 (C-40A *Clipper*)
1 log spt sqn with Gulfstream V/G550 (C-37A/B)
5 sqn with C-130T/KC-130T *Hercules*
TRAINING
2 (aggressor) sqn with F-5F/N *Tiger* II
1 (aggressor) sqn with F-16C *Fighting Falcon*
EQUIPMENT BY TYPE
AIRCRAFT 73 combat capable
FTR 36: 6 F-5F *Tiger* II; 30 F-5N *Tiger* II
FGA 23: 12 F-16C *Fighting Falcon*; 9 F/A-18E *Super Hornet*; 2 F/A-18F *Super Hornet*
ASW 9 P-8A *Poseidon*
EW 5 EA-18G *Growler**
TKR/TPT 13 KC-130T *Hercules*
TPT 37: **Medium** 16 C-130T *Hercules*; **PAX** 21: 17 B-737-700 (C-40A *Clipper*); 1 Gulfstream V (C-37A); 3 Gulfstream G550 (C-37B)
TRG 152: 76 T-6B *Texan* II; 22 T-44C *Pegasus*; 54 T-45C *Goshawk*
HELICOPTERS
ASW 7 MH-60R *Seahawk*
MCM 7 MH-53E *Sea Dragon*

US Marine Corps 170,800
3 Marine Expeditionary Forces (MEF), 3 Marine Expeditionary Brigades (MEB), 7 Marine Expeditionary Units (MEU) drawn from 3 div. Composition varies with mission requirements
FORCES BY ROLE
SPECIAL FORCES
(see USSOCOM)
MANOEUVRE
Reconnaissance
3 (MEF) recce coy
Amphibious
1 (1st) mne div (2 armd recce bn, 1 recce bn, 3 mne regt (4 mne bn), 1 amph aslt bn, 1 arty regt (3 arty bn, 1 MRL bn, 1 GLCM bty), 1 cbt engr bn, 1 EW bn, 1 int bn, 1 sigs bn)
1 (2nd) mne div (1 armd recce bn, 1 recce bn, 3 mne regt (3 mne bn), 1 amph aslt bn, 1 arty regt (2 arty bn), 1 cbt engr bn, 1 EW bn, 1 int bn, 1 sigs bn)
1 (3rd) mne div (1 recce bn, 1 mne regt (1 mne bn, 1 AD bn, 1 log bn), 1 arty regt HQ, 1 EW bn, 1 int bn, 1 sigs bn)
COMBAT SERVICE SUPPORT
3 log gp

EQUIPMENT BY TYPE
ARMOURED FIGHTING VEHICLES
  IFV 488 LAV-25
  APC • APC (W) 207 LAV variants (66 CP; 127 log; 14 EW)
  AAV 1,524: 1,200 AAV-7A1 (all roles); 324 ACV
  AUV 8,529: 1,725 *Cougar*; ε6,100 JLTV; 704 M-ATV
ENGINEERING & MAINTENANCE VEHICLES
  AEV 42 M1 ABV
  ARV 105: 60 AAVRA1; 45 LAV-R
  MW 38 *Buffalo*; some *Husky* 2G
  VLB ε30 M60 AVLB
ANTI-TANK/ANTI-INFRASTRUCTURE
  MSL
    SP 106 LAV-AT
    MANPATS FGM-148 *Javelin*; FGM-172B SRAW-MPV; TOW
  ARTILLERY 1,459
    TOWED 812: **105mm**: 331 M101A1; **155mm** 481 M777A2
    MRL 227mm 47 M142 HIMARS
    MOR 600: **81mm** 535 M252; **SP 81mm** 65 LAV-M; **120mm** (49 EFSS in store for trg)
UNINHABITED MARITIME PLATFORMS
  USV • Data 5 LRUSV
UNINHABITED AERIAL VEHICLES
  ISR • Light 100 BQM-147 *Exdrone*
  TPT 6 TRV-150C
AIR DEFENCE • SAM • Point-defence FIM-92 *Stinger*

Marine Corps Aviation 34,700
3 active Marine Aircraft Wings (MAW) and 1 MCR MAW
FORCES BY ROLE
FIGHTER/GROUND ATTACK
  2 sqn with AV-8B *Harrier* II
  1 sqn with F/A-18C *Hornet*
  3 sqn with F/A-18C/D *Hornet*
  7 sqn with F-35B *Lightning* II
  1 sqn with F-35B *Lightning* II (forming)
  2 sqn with F-35C *Lightning* II
  1 sqn with F-35C *Lightning* II (forming)
COMBAT SEARCH & RESCUE/TRANSPORT
  1 sqn with Beech A200/B200 *King Air* (UC-12F/M *Huron*); Beech 350 *King Air* (UC-12W *Huron*); Cessna 560 *Citation Ultra/Encore* (UC-35C/D); Gulfstream IV (C-20G)
TANKER
  4 sqn with KC-130J *Hercules*
TRANSPORT
  15 sqn with MV-22B *Osprey*
TRAINING
  2 sqn with F-35B *Lightning* II
  1 sqn with MV-22B *Osprey*
  1 hel sqn with AH-1Z *Viper*; UH-1Y *Venom*
  1 hel sqn with CH-53E *Sea Stallion*
ATTACK HELICOPTER
  6 sqn with AH-1Z *Viper*; UH-1Y *Venom*
TRANSPORT HELICOPTER
  5 sqn with CH-53E *Sea Stallion*
  1 sqn with CH-53K *King Stallion* (forming)
  1 (VIP) sqn with MV-22B *Osprey*; VH-3D *Sea King*; VH-60N *White Hawk*
CISR UAV
  2 sqn with MQ-9A *Reaper*
ISR UAV
  1 sqn with RQ-21A *Blackjack*
AIR DEFENCE
  2 bn with M1097 *Avenger*; FIM-92 *Stinger*
EQUIPMENT BY TYPE
AIRCRAFT 324 combat capable
  FGA 324: 152 F-35B *Lightning* II; 19 F-35C *Lightning* II; 67 F/A-18C *Hornet*; 43 F/A-18D *Hornet*; 38 AV-8B *Harrier* II; 5 TAV-8B *Harrier*
  TKR/TPT 64 KC-130J *Hercules*
  TPT 20: **Light** 18: 2 Beech B200 *King Air* (UC-12F *Huron*); 2 Beech B200 *King Air* (UC-12M *Huron*); 7 Beech 350 *King Air* (C-12W *Huron*); 7 Cessna 560 *Citation Encore* (UC-35D); **PAX** 2 Gulfstream IV (C-20G)
  TRG 26: 3 T-34C *Turbo Mentor*; 23 T-44C *Pegasus*
TILTROTOR • TPT 297 MV-22B *Osprey*
HELICOPTERS
  ATK 117 AH-1Z *Viper*
  TPT 264: **Heavy** 136: 119 CH-53E *Sea Stallion*; 17 CH-53K *King Stallion* (in test); **Medium** 39: 10 VH-3D *Sea King* (VIP); 8 VH-60N *White Hawk* (VIP); 21 VH-92A; **Light** 89 UH-1Y *Venom*
  TRG 52: 8 TH-57B *Sea Ranger*; 14 TH-57C *Sea Ranger*; 30 TH-73A
UNINHABITED AERIAL VEHICLES
  CISR • Heavy 7 MQ-9A *Reaper*
  ISR • Light 40 RQ-21A *Blackjack*
AIR DEFENCE
  SAM • Point-defence FIM-92 *Stinger*; M1097 *Avenger*
AIR-LAUNCHED MISSILES
  AAM • IR AIM-9M *Sidewinder*; IIR AIM-9X *Sidewinder* II; SARH AIM-7M *Sparrow*; ARH AIM-120C/D AMRAAM
  ASM AGM-65E *Maverick*; AGM-114K *Hellfire* II; AGM-176 *Griffin*; AGM-179A JAGM; AGR-20A APKWS
  AShM AGM-84D *Harpoon*; AGM-158C LRASM
  ARM AGM-88E/G AARGM/AARGM-ER
  LACM AGM-84E/H/K SLAM/SLAM-ER
BOMBS
  Laser-guided: GBU-10/-12/-16 *Paveway* II; GBU-51 LCDB
  Laser & INS/GPS-guided: EGBU-12 *Paveway* II; EGBU-24 *Paveway* III; GBU-49 Enhanced *Paveway* II;

GBU-52 LCDB; GBU-54 Laser JDAM; GBU-56 Laser JDAM
INS/GPS guided GBU-31/-32/-38 JDAM; AGM-154A/C/C-1 JSOW
Multi-mode guided GBU-53/B *Stormbreaker*

Reserve Organisations

Marine Corps Reserve 33,200
FORCES BY ROLE
MANOEUVRE
Reconnaissance
  2 MEF recce coy
Amphibious
  1 (4th) mne div (1 armd recce bn, 1 recce bn, 2 mne regt (3 mne bn), 1 amph aslt bn, 1 arty regt (2 arty bn, 1 MRL bn), 1 cbt engr bn, 1 int bn, 1 sigs bn)
COMBAT SERVICE SUPPORT
  1 log gp

Marine Corps Aviation Reserve 12,000 reservists
FORCES BY ROLE
FIGHTER/GROUND ATTACK
  1 sqn with F/A-18C/C+ *Hornet*
TANKER
  1 sqn with KC-130J *Hercules*
TRANSPORT
  2 sqn with MV-22B *Osprey*
TRAINING
  1 sqn with F-5F/N *Tiger* II
ATTACK HELICOPTER
  2 sqn with AH-1Z *Viper*; UH-1Y *Venom*
TRANSPORT HELICOPTER
  1 sqn with CH-53E *Sea Stallion*
EQUIPMENT BY TYPE
AIRCRAFT 24 combat capable
  FTR 15: 3 F-5F *Tiger* II; 12 F-5N *Tiger* II
  FGA 9: 2 F/A-18C *Hornet*; 7 F/A-18C+ *Hornet*
  TKR/TPT 10 KC-130J *Hercules*
  TPT 9: **Light** 7: 2 Beech A200 *King Air* (UC-12F); 2 Beech 350 *King Air* (UC-12W *Huron*); 3 Cessna 560 *Citation Encore* (UC-35D); **PAX** 2 B-737-700 (C-40A *Clipper*)
TILTROTOR • **TPT** 24 MV-22B *Osprey*
HELICOPTERS
  ATK 21 AH-1Z *Viper*
  TPT 28: **Heavy** 8 CH-53E *Sea Stallion*; **Light** 20 UH-1Y *Venom*

Marine Stand-by Reserve 700 reservists
Trained individuals available for mobilisation

US Coast Guard 40,800
9 districts (4 Pacific, 5 Atlantic)
EQUIPMENT BY TYPE
PATROL AND COASTAL COMBATANTS 327

PSOH 24: 1 *Alex Haley*; 13 *Famous* with 1 76mm gun; 10 *Legend* with 1 Mk 15 *Phalanx* Block 1B CIWS, 1 57mm gun (capacity 2 MH-65 hel)
PCO 65: 9 *Reliance* (with 1 hel landing platform) (3 more in reserve); 56 *Sentinel* (Damen 4708)
PCC 7 *Island*
PBF 173 *Response Boat-Medium* (RB-M)
PBI 58 *Marine Protector*
LOGISTICS AND SUPPORT 181
  AAR 117 47-foot *Motor Life Boat*
  ABU 51: 16 *Juniper*; 3 WLI; 14 *Keeper*; 18 WLR
  AGB 12: 9 *Bay*; 1 *Mackinaw*; 1 *Healy*; 1 *Polar* (1 additional *Polar* in reserve)
  AXS 1 *Eagle* (ex-GER *Gorch Fock*)
UNINHABITED MARITIME SYSTEMS
  UUV • **MW** SRS *Fusion*

US Coast Guard Aviation
EQUIPMENT BY TYPE
AIRCRAFT
  SAR 34: 16 HC-130J *Hercules*; 2 HC-144A; 16 HC-144B
  TPT 16: **Medium** 14 C-27J *Spartan*; **PAX** 2: 1 Gulfstream V (C-37A); 1 Gulfstream G550 (C-37B)
HELICOPTERS
  SAR 142: 44 MH-60T *Jayhawk*; 14 AS366G1 (MH-65D) *Dauphin* II; 84 AS366G1 (MH-65E) *Dauphin* II

US Air Force (USAF) 316,650

Global Strike Command (GSC)
2 active air forces (8th & 20th); 8 wg
FORCES BY ROLE
SURFACE-TO-SURFACE MISSILE
  9 ICBM sqn with LGM-30G *Minuteman* III
BOMBER
  4 sqn with B-1B *Lancer*
  2 sqn with B-2A *Spirit*
  5 sqn (incl 1 trg) with B-52H *Stratofortress*
COMMAND & CONTROL
  1 sqn with E-4B
TRANSPORT HELICOPTER
  4 sqn with MH-139A *Grey Wolf*; UH-1N *Iroquois*

Air Combat Command (ACC)
2 active air forces (9th & 12th); 12 wg. ACC numbered air forces provide the air component to CENTCOM, SOUTHCOM and NORTHCOM
FORCES BY ROLE
FIGHTER
  2 sqn with F-22A *Raptor*
FIGHTER/GROUND ATTACK
  4 sqn with F-15E *Strike Eagle*
  3 sqn with F-16C/D *Fighting Falcon* (+4 sqn personnel only)
  4 sqn with F-35A *Lightning* II (+2 sqn personnel only)

GROUND ATTACK
2 sqn with A-10C *Thunderbolt* II (+1 sqn personnel only)
ELECTRONIC WARFARE
1 sqn with EA-18G *Growler* (personnel only – USN aircraft)
2 sqn with EC-130H *Compass Call*
ISR
1 sqn with E-11A
5 sqn with RC-135/WC-135
2 sqn with U-2S
AIRBORNE EARLY WARNING & CONTROL
5 sqn with E-3 *Sentry*
COMBAT SEARCH & RESCUE
2 sqn with HC-130J *Combat King* II
3 sqn with HH-60W *Jolly Green* II
TRAINING
1 (aggressor) sqn with F-16C *Fighting Falcon*
1 (aggressor) sqn with F-35A *Lightning* II
1 sqn with A-10C *Thunderbolt* II
1 sqn with E-3 *Sentry*
2 sqn with F-15E *Strike Eagle*
1 sqn with F-22A *Raptor*
1 sqn with RQ-4A *Global Hawk*; TU-2S
1 UAV sqn with MQ-9A *Reaper*
COMBAT/ISR UAV
8 sqn with MQ-9A *Reaper*
ISR UAV
2 sqn with RQ-4B *Global Hawk*
2 sqn with RQ-170 *Sentinel*
1 sqn with RQ-180

Pacific Air Forces (PACAF)

Provides the air component of INDOPACOM, and commands air units based in Alaska, Hawaii, Japan and South Korea. 3 active air forces (5th, 7th, & 11th); 8 wg
FORCES BY ROLE
FIGHTER
2 sqn with F-15C/D *Eagle*
1 (interceptor) sqn with F-16C/D *Fighting Falcon*
2 sqn with F-22A *Raptor* (+1 sqn personnel only)
FIGHTER/GROUND ATTACK
5 sqn with F-16C/D *Fighting Falcon*
2 sqn with F-35A *Lightning* II
GROUND ATTACK
1 sqn with A-10C *Thunderbolt* II
AIRBORNE EARLY WARNING & CONTROL
2 sqn with E-3 *Sentry*
COMBAT SEARCH & RESCUE
1 sqn with HH-60G *Pave Hawk*; HH-60W *Jolly Green* II
TANKER
1 sqn with KC-135R (+1 sqn personnel only)
TRANSPORT
1 sqn with B-737-200 (C-40B); Gulfstream V (C-37A)

1 sqn with C-17A *Globemaster* (+1 sqn personnel only)
1 sqn with C-130J-30 *Hercules*
1 sqn with Beech 1900C (C-12J); UH-1N *Huey*

United States Air Forces in Europe - Air Forces Africa (USAFE-AFAFRICA)

Provides the air component to both EUCOM and AFRICOM. 1 active air force (3rd); 5 wg
FORCES BY ROLE
FIGHTER/GROUND ATTACK
2 sqn with F-15E *Strike Eagle*
3 sqn with F-16C/D *Fighting Falcon*
2 sqn with F-35A *Lightning* II
COMBAT SEARCH & RESCUE
1 sqn with HH-60G *Pave Hawk*
TANKER
1 sqn with KC-135R *Stratotanker*
TRANSPORT
1 sqn with C-130J-30 *Hercules*
2 sqn with Gulfstream V (C-37A); Learjet 35A (C-21A); B-737-700 (C-40B)

Air Mobility Command (AMC)

Provides strategic and tactical airlift, air-to-air refuelling and aeromedical evacuation. 1 active air force (18th); 12 wg and 1 gp
FORCES BY ROLE
TANKER
4 sqn with KC-46A *Pegasus*
2 sqn with KC-46A *Pegasus* (forming)
6 sqn with KC-135R/T *Stratotanker*
1 sqn with KC-135R/T *Stratotanker* (personnel only)
TRANSPORT
2 sqn with C-5M *Super Galaxy*
8 sqn with C-17A *Globemaster* III
1 sqn with C-17A *Globemaster* III (personnel only)
4 sqn with C-130J-30 *Hercules* (+2 sqn personnel only)
1 sqn with Learjet 35A (C-21A)
1 VIP sqn with B-737-200 (C-40B); B-757-200 (C-32A)
1 VIP sqn with Gulfstream V (C-37A); Gulfstream 550 (C-37B)
1 VIP sqn with VC-25 *Air Force One*

Air Education and Training Command

1 active air force (2nd), 10 active air wg and 1 gp
FORCES BY ROLE
TRAINING
1 sqn with C-17A *Globemaster* III
1 sqn with C-130J-30 *Hercules*
3 sqn with F-16C/D *Fighting Falcon*
6 sqn with F-35A *Lightning* II
1 sqn with F-35A *Lightning* II (forming)
1 sqn with KC-46A *Pegasus*
1 sqn with KC-135R *Stratotanker*
5 (flying trg) sqn with T-1A *Jayhawk*

10 (flying trg) sqn with T-6A *Texan* II
10 (flying trg) sqn with T-38C *Talon*
5 UAV sqn with MQ-9A *Reaper*

EQUIPMENT BY TYPE

SURFACE-TO-SURFACE MISSILE LAUNCHERS
  ICBM • **Nuclear** 400 LGM-30G *Minuteman* III (1 Mk12A or Mk21 re-entry veh per missile)
AIRCRAFT 1,456 combat capable
  BBR 120: 43 B-1B *Lancer*; 19 B-2A *Spirit*; 58 B-52H *Stratofortress* (46 nuclear capable)
  FTR 175: 10 F-15C/D *Eagle*; 165 F-22A *Raptor*
  FGA 1,070: 218 F-15E *Strike Eagle*; 6 F-15EX *Eagle* II; 373 F-16C *Fighting Falcon*; 90 F-16D *Fighting Falcon*; 383 F-35A *Lightning* II
  ATK 91 A-10C *Thunderbolt* II
  CSAR 17 HC-130J *Combat King* II
  EW 7: 3 EA-37B *Compass Call*; 4 EC-130H *Compass Call*
  ISR 42: 2 E-9A; 7 E-11A; 27 U-2S; 3 TU-2S; 3 WC-135R *Constant Phoenix*
  ELINT 22: 8 RC-135V *Rivet Joint*; 9 RC-135W *Rivet Joint*; 3 RC-135S *Cobra Ball*; 2 RC-135U *Combat Sent*
  AEW&C 18: 2 E-3B *Sentry*; 1 E-3C *Sentry*; 15 E-3G *Sentry*
  C2 4 E-4B
  TKR 153: 124 KC-135R *Stratotanker*; 29 KC-135T *Stratotanker*
  TKR/TPT 65 KC-46A *Pegasus*
  TPT 339: **Heavy** 182: 36 C-5M *Super Galaxy*; 146 C-17A *Globemaster* III; **Medium** 105: 10 C-130J *Hercules*; 95 C-130J-30 *Hercules*; **Light** 26: 7 Beech 1900C (C-12J); 19 Learjet 35A (C-21A); **PAX** 26: 4 B-737-700 (C-40B); 4 B-757-200 (C-32A); 9 Gulfstream V (C-37A); 7 Gulfstream 550 (C-37B); 2 VC-25A *Air Force One*
  TRG 1,026: 3 EMB-314 *Super Tucano*; 75 T-1A *Jayhawk*; 444 T-6A *Texan* II; 504 T-38A/C *Talon*
HELICOPTERS
  MRH 8 MH-139A *Grey Wolf*
  CSAR 61: 25 HH-60G *Pave Hawk*; 36 HH-60W *Jolly Green* II
  TPT • **Light** 57 UH-1N *Huey*
UNINHABITED AERIAL VEHICLES 160
  CISR • **Heavy** 134 MQ-9A *Reaper*
  ISR • **Heavy** 26: 9 RQ-4B *Global Hawk*; ε10 RQ-170 *Sentinel*; ε7 RQ-180
AIR DEFENCE
  SAM • **Point-defence** FIM-92 *Stinger*
AIR-LAUNCHED MISSILES
  AAM • **IR** AIM-9M *Sidewinder*; **IIR** AIM-9X *Sidewinder* II; **SARH** AIM-7M *Sparrow*; **ARH** AIM-120C/D AMRAAM
  ASM AGM-65H/K *Maverick*; AGM-114K/M/N/R *Hellfire* II; AGM-130A; AGM-176 *Griffin*; AGR-20A APKWS
  AShM AGM-84D *Harpoon*; AGM-158C LRASM
  LACM
    Nuclear AGM-86B (ALCM)
    Conventional AGM-158A JASSM; AGM-158B JASSM-ER
  ARM AGM-88B/C HARM
  EW MALD/MALD-J
BOMBS
  Laser-guided: GBU-10/-12 *Paveway* II, GBU-24 *Paveway* III; GBU-28
  Laser & INS/GPS-guided: EGBU-24 *Paveway* III; EGBU-28; GBU-49 Enhanced *Paveway* II; GBU-54 Laser JDAM; GBU-56 Laser JDAM
  INS/GPS-guided: AGM-154A/C/C-1 JSOW/JSOW C-1; GBU-15 (with BLU-109 penetrating warhead or Mk84); GBU-31/-32/-38 JDAM; GBU-39B Small Diameter Bomb (250lb); GBU-43B MOAB; GBU-57A/B MOP
  Multi-mode guided: GBU-53/B *Stormbreaker*

Reserve Organisations

Air National Guard 103,150 reservists
FORCES BY ROLE
BOMBER
  1 sqn with B-2A *Spirit* (personnel only)
FIGHTER
  5 sqn with F-15C/D *Eagle*
  1 sqn with F-22A *Raptor* (+1 sqn personnel only)
FIGHTER/GROUND ATTACK
  8 sqn with F-16C/D *Fighting Falcon*
  1 sqn with F-16C/D *Fighting Falcon* (forming)
  3 sqn with F-35A *Lightning* II
GROUND ATTACK
  3 sqn with A-10C *Thunderbolt* II
COMBAT SEARCH & RESCUE
  3 sqn with HC-130J *Combat King* II
  2 sqn with HH-60G *Pave Hawk*
  1 sqn with HH-60W *Jolly Green* II (forming)
TANKER
  1 sqn with KC-46A *Pegasus* (+2 sqn personnel only)
  15 sqn with KC-135R *Stratotanker* (+1 sqn personnel only)
  3 sqn with KC-135T *Stratotanker*
TRANSPORT
  1 sqn with B-737-700 (C-40C)
  6 sqn with C-17A *Globemaster* (+2 sqn personnel only)
  8 sqn with C-130H *Hercules*
  1 sqn with C-130H/LC-130H *Hercules*
  6 sqn with C-130J-30 *Hercules*
TRAINING
  1 sqn with C-130J-30 *Hercules*
  1 sqn with F-15C/D *Eagle*
  4 sqn with F-16C/D *Fighting Falcon*
  1 sqn with MQ-9A *Reaper*
COMBAT/ISR UAV
  10 sqn with MQ-9A *Reaper*
EQUIPMENT BY TYPE
AIRCRAFT 534 combat capable

FTR 125: 95 F-15C *Eagle*; 10 F-15D *Eagle*; 20 F-22A *Raptor*
FGA 346: 2 F-15EX *Eagle* II: 261 F-16C *Fighting Falcon*; 45 F-16D *Fighting Falcon*; 38 F-35A *Lightning* II
ATK 63 A-10C *Thunderbolt* II
CSAR 12 HC-130J *Combat King* II
TKR 159: 136 KC-135R *Stratotanker*; 23 KC-135T *Stratotanker*
TKR/TPT 12 KC-46A *Pegasus*
TPT 183: **Heavy** 50 C-17A *Globemaster* III; **Medium** 130: 78 C-130H *Hercules*; 42 C-130J-30 *Hercules*; 10 LC-130H *Hercules*; **PAX** 3 B-737-700 (C-40C)
HELICOPTERS • CSAR 14: 8 HH-60G *Pave Hawk*; 6 HH-60W *Jolly Green* II
UNINHABITED AERIAL VEHICLES
  CISR • Heavy 24 MQ-9A *Reaper*

Air Force Reserve Command 65,700 reservists
FORCES BY ROLE
BOMBER
  1 sqn with B-52H *Stratofortress* (personnel only)
FIGHTER
  2 sqn with F-22A *Raptor* (personnel only)
FIGHTER/GROUND ATTACK
  1 sqn with F-16C/D *Fighting Falcon* (+1 sqn personnel only)
  1 sqn with F-35A *Lightning* II (+1 personnel only)
GROUND ATTACK
  1 sqn with A-10C *Thunderbolt* II (+2 sqn personnel only)
ISR
  1 (Weather Recce) sqn with WC-130J *Hercules*
AIRBORNE EARLY WARNING & CONTROL
  1 sqn with E-3 *Sentry* (personnel only)
COMBAT SEARCH & RESCUE
  1 sqn with HC-130J *Combat King* II
  2 sqn with HH-60G *Pave Hawk*
TANKER
  1 sqn with KC-46A *Pegasus*
  3 sqn with KC-46A *Pegasus* (personnel only)
  6 sqn with KC-135R *Stratotanker*
  2 sqn with KC-135R *Stratotanker* (personnel only)
TRANSPORT
  2 sqn with C-5M *Super Galaxy* (+2 sqn personnel only)
  3 sqn with C-17A *Globemaster* (+9 sqn personnel only)
  5 sqn with C-130H *Hercules*
  1 sqn with C-130J-30 *Hercules*
  1 VIP sqn with B-737-700 (C-40C)
TRAINING
  1 (aggressor) sqn with A-10C *Thunderbolt* II; F-15C/E *Eagle*; F-16 *Fighting Falcon*; F-22A *Raptor* (personnel only)
  1 sqn with A-10C *Thunderbolt* II
  1 sqn with B-52H *Stratofortress*
  1 sqn with C-5M *Super Galaxy*
  1 sqn with F-16C/D *Fighting Falcon*
  5 (flying training) sqn with T-1A *Jayhawk*; T-6A *Texan* II; T-38C *Talon* (personnel only)
  1 hel trg sqn with MH-139A *Grey Wolf* (forming)
COMBAT/ISR UAV
  2 sqn with MQ-9A *Reaper* (personnel only)
ISR UAV
  1 sqn with RQ-4B *Global Hawk* (personnel only)
EQUIPMENT BY TYPE
AIRCRAFT 128 combat capable
  BBR 18 B-52H *Stratofortress*
  FGA 53: 48 F-16C *Fighting Falcon*; 2 F-16D *Fighting Falcon*; 3 F-35A *Lightning* II
  ATK 57 A-10C *Thunderbolt* II
  CSAR 6 HC-130J *Combat King* II
  ISR 10 WC-130J *Hercules* (Weather Recce)
  TKR 59 KC-135R *Stratotanker*
  TKR/TPT 12 KC-46A *Pegasus*
  TPT 90: **Heavy** 42: 16 C-5M *Super Galaxy*; 26 C-17A *Globemaster* III; **Medium** 44: 34 C-130H *Hercules*; 10 C-130J-30 *Hercules*; **PAX** 4 B-737-700 (C-40C)
HELICOPTERS • CSAR 9 HH-60G *Pave Hawk*

Civil Reserve Air Fleet
Commercial ac numbers fluctuate
  AIRCRAFT • TPT 517 international (391 long-range and 126 short-range); 36 national

Air Force Stand-by Reserve 16,850 reservists
Trained individuals for mobilisation

US Space Force 9,450
Tasked with organising, training and equipping forces to protect US and allied space interests and to provide space capabilities to the joint Combatant Commands
EQUIPMENT BY TYPE
SATELLITES see Space
COUNTERSPACE see Space
RADAR see Strategic Defenses – Early Warning

US Special Operations Command (USSOCOM) 67,500
Commands all active, reserve and National Guard Special Operations Forces (SOF) of all services based in CONUS

Joint Special Operations Command
Reported to comprise elite US SOF, including Special Forces Operations Detachment Delta ('Delta Force'), SEAL Team 6 and integral USAF support

US Army Special Operations Command 36,000
FORCES BY ROLE
SPECIAL FORCES
  5 SF gp (4 SF bn, 1 spt bn)
  1 ranger regt (3 ranger bn; 1 cbt spt bn)

COMBAT SUPPORT
1 civil affairs bde (5 civil affairs bn)
1 psyops gp (3 psyops bn)
1 psyops gp (4 psyops bn)
COMBAT SERVICE SUPPORT
1 (sustainment) log bde (1 sigs bn)
HELICOPTER
1 (160th SOAR) hel regt (4 hel bn)
EQUIPMENT BY TYPE
ARMOURED FIGHTING VEHICLES
APC • **APC (W)** 28: 16 M1126 *Stryker* ICV; 12 *Pandur*
AUV 640 M-ATV
ARTILLERY 20
MOR • **120mm** 20 XM905 AMPS
AIRCRAFT
TPT 12: **Medium** 7 C-27J *Spartan* (parachute training); **Light** 5 C-212 (parachute training)
HELICOPTERS
MRH 51 AH-6M/MH-6M *Little Bird*
TPT 139: **Heavy** 68 MH-47G *Chinook*; **Medium** 71 MH-60M *Black Hawk*
UNINHABITED AERIAL VEHICLES
CISR • **Heavy** 24 MQ-1C *Gray Eagle*
ISR • **Light** 29: 15 XPV-1 *Tern*; 14 XPV-2 *Mako*
TPT • **Heavy** 28 CQ-10 *Snowgoose*
OWA *Roadrunner*-M (AD)
AIR-LAUNCHED MISSILES
AAM • **IR** *Air-to-Air Stinger* (ATAS)
ASM AGM-114R *Hellfire* II

Reserve Organisations

Army National Guard
FORCES BY ROLE
SPECIAL FORCES
2 SF gp (3 SF bn)

Army Reserve
FORCES BY ROLE
COMBAT SUPPORT
2 psyops gp
4 civil affairs comd HQ
8 civil affairs bde HQ
32 civil affairs bn (coy)

US Navy Special Warfare Command 11,000
FORCES BY ROLE
SPECIAL FORCES
8 SEAL team (total: 48 SF pl)
2 SEAL Delivery Vehicle team

Reserve Organisations

Naval Reserve Force
FORCES BY ROLE
SPECIAL FORCES
8 SEAL det
10 Naval Special Warfare det
2 Special Boat sqn
2 Special Boat unit
1 SEAL Delivery Vehicle det

US Marine Special Operations Command (MARSOC) 3,500
FORCES BY ROLE
SPECIAL FORCES
1 SF regt (3 SF bn)
COMBAT SUPPORT
1 int bn
COMBAT SERVICE SUPPORT
1 spt gp

Air Force Special Operations Command (AFSOC) 17,000
FORCES BY ROLE
GROUND ATTACK
4 sqn with AC-130J *Ghostrider*
TRANSPORT
4 sqn with CV-22B *Osprey*
1 sqn with Do-328 (C-146A)
5 sqn with MC-130J *Commando* II
4 sqn with PC-12 (U-28A)
TRAINING
1 sqn with CV-22A/B *Osprey*
1 sqn with HC-130J *Combat King* II; MC-130J *Commando* II
1 sqn with Bell 205 (TH-1H *Iroquois*)
1 sqn with HH-60W *Jolly Green* II; UH-1N *Huey*
COMBAT/ISR UAV
3 sqn with MQ-9 *Reaper*
EQUIPMENT BY TYPE
AIRCRAFT 30 combat capable
ATK 30 AC-130J *Ghostrider*
ISR 21 MC-12 *Javaman*
CSAR 3 HC-130J *Combat King* II
TPT 119: **Medium** 64 MC-130J *Commando* II; **Light** 55: 20 Do-328 (C-146A); 35 PC-12 (U-28A)
TILT-ROTOR 51 CV-22A/B *Osprey*
HELICOPTERS
CSAR 7 HH-60W *Jolly Green* II
TPT • **Light** 34: 28 Bell 205 (TH-1H *Iroquois*); 6 UH-1N *Huey*
UNINHABITED AERIAL VEHICLES • **CISR** • **Heavy** 50 MQ-9 *Reaper*
AIR-LAUNCHED MISSILES
ASM AGM-114R *Hellfire* II; AGM-176 *Griffin*
BOMBS
Laser-guided: GBU-12 *Paveway* II; GBU-69/B *Small Glide Munition*

Reserve Organisations

Air National Guard

FORCES BY ROLE

ELECTRONIC WARFARE
1 sqn with MC-130J *Commando* II

ISR
1 sqn with MC-12W *Liberty*

TRANSPORT
1 flt with B-737-200 (C-32B)

EQUIPMENT BY TYPE

AIRCRAFT
ISR 13 MC-12W *Liberty*
TPT 4: **Medium** 2 MC-130J *Commando* II; **PAX** 2 B-757-200 (C-32B)

Air Force Reserve

FORCES BY ROLE

TRAINING
1 sqn with AC-130J *Ghostrider* (personnel only)

COMBAT/ISR UAV
1 sqn with MQ-9 *Reaper* (personnel only)

DEPLOYMENT

ARABIAN SEA: US Central Command • US Navy • 5th Fleet 7,500: 2 SSGN; 1 CVN, 2 DDGHM, 1 DDGM **Combined Maritime Forces** • TF 53: 3 AKEH; 1 AOR

ARUBA: US Southern Command • 1 Cooperative Security Location at Reina Beatrix Airport

ASCENSION ISLAND: US Strategic Command • 1 detection and tracking radar at Ascension Auxiliary Air Field

AUSTRALIA: US Indo-Pacific Command • 1,700; 1 SEWS at Pine Gap; 1 comms facility at Pine Gap; 1 SIGINT stn at Pine Gap; **US Strategic Command** • 1 detection and tracking radar at Naval Communication Station Harold E. Holt

BAHRAIN: US Central Command • 4,500; 1 HQ (5th Fleet); 4 MCO; 1 ESB; 1 ASW flt with 3 P-8A *Poseidon*; 2 SAM bty with M903 *Patriot* PAC-3 MSE

BELGIUM: US European Command • 1,150

BRITISH INDIAN OCEAN TERRITORY: US Strategic Command • 300; 1 Spacetrack Optical Tracker at Diego Garcia; 1 ground-based electro-optical deep space surveillance system (GEODSS) at Diego Garcia **US Indo-Pacific Command** • 1 MPS sqn (MPS-2 with equipment for one MEB) at Diego Garcia; 1 naval air base at Diego Garcia, 1 support facility at Diego Garcia

BULGARIA: NATO • Forward Land Forces 150; 1 mech inf coy with M1296 *Stryker Dragoon*

CANADA: US Northern Command • 150

CENTRAL AFRICAN REPUBLIC: UN • MINUSCA 10

COLOMBIA: US Southern Command • 70

CUBA: US Southern Command • 550 (JTF-GTMO) at Guantanamo Bay

CURACAO: US Southern Command • 1 Cooperative Security Location at Hato Airport

DEMOCRATIC REPUBLIC OF THE CONGO: UN • MONUSCO 3

DJIBOUTI: US Africa Command • 4,000; 1 tpt sqn with C-130H/J-30 *Hercules*; 1 tpt sqn with 12 MV-22B *Osprey*; 2 KC-130J *Hercules*; 1 spec ops sqn with MC-130J; PC-12 (U-28A); 1 CSAR sqn with HH-60G *Pave Hawk*; 1 CISR UAV sqn with MQ-9A *Reaper*; 1 naval air base

EGYPT: MFO 465; elm 1 ARNG inf bn; 1 ARNG spt bn

EL SALVADOR: US Southern Command • 1 Cooperative Security Location at Comalapa Airport

ESTONIA: US European Command • 700; 1 inf bn

GERMANY: US Africa Command • 1 HQ at Stuttgart **US European Command** • 38,700; 1 Combined Service HQ (EUCOM) at Stuttgart–Vaihingen
US Army 24,400

FORCES BY ROLE

1 HQ (US Army Europe & Africa (USAREUR-AF)) at Wiesbaden; 1 arty comd; 1 spec ops gp; 1 recce bn; 1 mech bde(-); 1 inf bn; 1 fd arty bn; 1 (cbt avn) hel bde; 1 MRL bde (3 MRL bn); 1 (cbt avn) hel bde HQ; 1 int bde; 1 MP bde; 1 sigs bde; 1 (MDTF) cbt spt bde(-); 1 spt bde; 1 SAM bde; 1 (APS) armd bde eqpt set

EQUIPMENT BY TYPE

M1A2 SEPv2/v3 *Abrams*; M2A3/M3A3 *Bradley*; M1296 *Stryker Dragoon*, M109A6; M119A3; M777A2; M270A2; M142 HIMARS; AH-64E *Apache*; CH-47F *Chinook*; UH-60L/M *Black Hawk*; HH-60M *Black Hawk*; M903 *Patriot* PAC-3 MSE; M1097 *Avenger*; Sgt Stout
US Navy 400
USAF 13,250

FORCES BY ROLE

1 HQ (US Air Forces in Europe and Africa) at Ramstein AB; 1 HQ (3rd Air Force) at Ramstein AB; 1 FGA wg at Spangdahlem AB with (1 FGA sqn with 24 F-16C/D *Fighting Falcon*); 1 tpt wg at Ramstein AB with 14 C-130J-30 *Hercules*; 2 Gulfstream V (C-37A); 5 Learjet 35A (C-21A); 1 B-737-700 (C-40B)
US Space Force 150
USMC 500

GREECE: US European Command • 600; 1 hel bn with UH-60M/HH-60M *Black Hawk*; 1 naval base at Makri; 1 naval base at Souda Bay; 1 air base at Iraklion

GREENLAND (DNK): US Strategic Command • 100; 1 AN/FPS-132 Upgraded Early Warning Radar and 1 Spacetrack Radar at Pituffik

GUAM: US Indo-Pacific Command • 9,000; 4 SSGN; 1 MPS sqn (MPS-3 with equipment for one MEB) with 2 AKRH; 4 AKR; 1 ESD; 1 AKEH; 1 tkr sqn with 12 KC-135R *Stratotanker*; 1 tpt hel sqn with MH-60S; 1 ISR UAV unit with 2 MQ-4C *Triton*; 1 SAM bty with THAAD; 1 air base; 1 naval base

HONDURAS: US Southern Command • 400; 1 avn bn with 4 CH-47F *Chinook*; 12 UH-60L/HH-60L *Black Hawk*

HUNGARY: NATO • Forward Land Forces 150; 1 inf coy

ICELAND: US European Command • 50 1 ASW flt with 2 P-8A *Poseidon*

IRAQ: US Central Command • *Operation Inherent Resolve* 2,500; 1 inf bde(-); 2 atk hel bn with AH-64D *Apache*; MQ-1C *Gray Eagle*; 1 spec ops hel bn with MH-47G *Chinook*; MH-60M *Black Hawk*; 1 CISR UAV sqn with MQ-9A *Reaper*; 2 SAM bty with M903 *Patriot* PAC-3 MSE; **NATO** • NATO Mission Iraq 16

ISRAEL: US Strategic Command • 250; 1 SAM bty with THAAD; 1 AN/TPY-2 X-band radar at Mount Keren

ITALY: US European Command • 12,600
US Army 4,100; 1 AB bde(-)
US Navy 3,650; 1 HQ (US Naval Forces Europe-Africa (NAVEUR-NAVAF/6th Fleet) at Naples; 1 LCC; 1 ASW sqn with 5 P-8A *Poseidon* at Sigonella; 1 ISR UAV flt with 2 MQ-4C *Triton* at Sigonella
USAF 4,800; 1 FGA wg with (2 FGA sqn with 21 F-16C/D *Fighting Falcon* at Aviano; 1 CSAR sqn with 8 HH-60G *Pave Hawk* at Aviano); 1 CISR UAV sqn with MQ-9A *Reaper* at Sigonella; 1 ISR UAV flt with RQ-4B *Global Hawk* at Sigonella
USMC 50

JAPAN: US Indo-Pacific Command • 55,750
US Army 2,450; 1 corps HQ (fwd); 1 SF gp; 1 avn bn; 1 SAM bn with M903 *Patriot* PAC-3 MSE
US Navy 22,200; 1 HQ (7th Fleet) at Yokosuka; 1 base at Sasebo; 1 base at Yokosuka

FORCES BY ROLE

2 FGA sqn at Iwakuni with 10 F/A-18E *Super Hornet*; 1 FGA sqn at Iwakuni with 10 F/A-18F *Super Hornet*; 1 FGA sqn with 10 F-35C *Lightning* II; 2 ASW sqn at Misawa/Kadena AB with 5 P-8A *Poseidon*; 2 EW sqn at Iwakuni/Misawa with 5 EA-18G *Growler*; 1 AEW&C sqn at Iwakuni with 5 E-2D *Hawkeye*; 2 ASW hel sqn at Atsugi with 12 MH-60R;1 tpt hel sqn at Atsugi with 12 MH-60S

EQUIPMENT BY TYPE

1 CVN; 1 CGHM; 8 DDGHM; 3 DDGM; 1 LCC; 4 MCO; 1 LHA; 2 LPD; 1 LSD
USAF 13,000

FORCES BY ROLE

1 HQ (5th Air Force) at Kadena AB; 1 ftr wg at Misawa AB with (2 FGA sqn with 22 F-16C/D *Fighting Falcon*); 1 wg at Kadena AB with (2 ftr sqn with 5 F-15C/D *Eagle*; 1 ftr sqn with 12 F-22A *Raptor*; 1 FGA sqn with 12 F-16C/D *Fighting Falcon*; 1 tkr sqn with 15 KC-135R *Stratotanker*; 1 AEW&C sqn with 2 E-3G *Sentry*; 1 CSAR sqn with 10 HH-60G *Pave Hawk*; 1 CISR UAV sqn with 4 MQ-9A *Reaper*); 1 tpt wg at Yokota AB with 10 C-130J-30 *Hercules*; 3 Beech 1900C (C-12J); 1 Spec Ops gp at Kadena AB with (1 sqn with 5 MC-130J *Commando* II; 1 sqn with 5 CV-22B *Osprey*); 1 ISR sqn with RC-135 *Rivet Joint*; 1 ISR UAV flt with 5 RQ-4A *Global Hawk*
US Space Force 100
USMC 20,000

FORCES BY ROLE

1 mne div; 1 mne regt HQ; 1 arty regt HQ; 1 recce bn; 3 mne bn; 1 arty bn; 1 FGA sqn with 12 F/A-18C/D *Hornet*; 2 FGA sqn with 10 F-35B *Lightning* II; 1 tkr sqn with 12 KC-130J *Hercules*; 2 tpt sqn with 12 MV-22B *Osprey*
US Strategic Command • 1 AN/TPY-2 X-band radar at Shariki; 1 AN/TPY-2 X-band radar at Kyogamisaki

JORDAN: US Central Command • *Operation Inherent Resolve* 3,000: 1 FGA sqn with 18 F-15E *Strike Eagle*; 1 CISR UAV sqn with 12 MQ-9A *Reaper*; 2 SAM bty with M903 *Patriot* PAC-3 MSE

KOREA, REPUBLIC OF: US Indo-Pacific Command • 28,500
US Army 19,750

FORCES BY ROLE

1 HQ (8th Army) at Pyeongtaek; 1 div HQ (2nd Inf) located at Pyeongtaek; 1 mech bde; 1 (cbt avn) hel bde; 1 MRL bde; 1 AD bde; 1 SAM bty with THAAD

EQUIPMENT BY TYPE

M1A2 SEPv2 *Abrams*; M2A3/M3A3 *Bradley*; M109A6; M270A1 MLRS; AH-64D/E *Apache*; CH-47F *Chinook*; UH-60L/M *Black Hawk*; M903 *Patriot* PAC-3 MSE; THAAD; FIM-92A *Avenger*; 1 (APS) armd bde eqpt set
US Navy 350
USAF 8,150

FORCES BY ROLE

1 (AF) HQ (7th Air Force) at Osan AB; 1 ftr wg at Osan AB with (1 ftr sqn with 20 F-16C/D *Fighting Falcon*; 1 atk sqn with 24 A-10C *Thunderbolt* II); 1 ftr wg at Kunsan AB with (2 ftr sqn with 20 F-16C/D *Fighting Falcon*); 1 ISR sqn at Osan AB with U-2S
US Space Force 100
USMC 150

KOSOVO: NATO • KFOR • *Joint Enterprise* 598; elm 1 ARNG inf bde HQ; 1 ARNG inf bn HQ; 1 ARNG inf coy; 1 hel flt with UH-60

KUWAIT: US Central Command • 10,000; 1 ARNG armd bn; 1 ARNG inf bn; 1 ARNG MRL bn; 1 (cbt avn) hel bde(-); 1 spt bde; 1 CISR UAV sqn with MQ-9A *Reaper*; 1 (APS) armd bde set; 1 (APS) inf bde set; 2 SAM bty with M903 *Patriot* PAC-3 MSE

LIBYA: UN • UNSMIL 1

LITHUANIA: US European Command • 1,000; 1 armd bn; 1 SP arty bty

MARSHALL ISLANDS: US Strategic Command • 20; 1 detection and tracking radar at Kwajalein Atoll

MEDITERRANEAN SEA: US European Command • 6th Fleet 4,500; 2 SSGN; 1 FFHM; 1 LHD; 1 LPD; 1 LSD

MIDDLE EAST: UN • UNTSO 2

NETHERLANDS: US European Command • 400

NORTH SEA: US European Command • 6th Fleet 7,000; 1 CVN; 1 CGHM; 1 DDGHM; 1 DDGM

NORWAY: US European Command • 1,100; 1 (USMC) MEU eqpt set; 1 (APS) SP 155mm arty bn set

PERSIAN GULF: US Central Command • US Navy • 5th Fleet 200: 6 (Coast Guard) PCC

PHILIPPINES: US Indo-Pacific Command 200

POLAND: NATO • Forward Land Forces 1,000; 1 armd bn with M1A2 SEPv2 *Abrams*; M2A3 *Bradley*; 1 arty bty with M109A6 **US European Command** • 13,000; 1 corps HQ; 1 div HQ; 1 armd bde with M1A2 SEPv2 *Abrams*; M3A3 *Bradley*; M2A3 *Bradley*; M109A6; 1 armd bde(-) with M1A2 SEPv2 *Abrams*; M3A3 *Bradley*; M2A3 *Bradley*; M109A6; 2 SAM bty with M903 *Patriot* PAC-3 MSE; 1 CISR UAV sqn with MQ-9A *Reaper*; 1 *Aegis Ashore* BMD unit with three 8-cell Mk 41 VLS launchers with SM-3; 1 (APS) armd bde eqpt set

PORTUGAL: US European Command • 250; 1 spt facility at Lajes

QATAR: US Central Command • 11,000: 1 bbr flt with 4 B-52H *Stratofortress*; 1 ftr sqn with 12 F-22A Raptor; 1 atk sqn with 12 A-10C Thunderbolt II; 1 ISR sqn with 4 RC-135 *Rivet Joint*; 1 tkr/tpt sqn with 12 KC-46A Pegasus; 2 tkr sqn with 12 KC-135R/T *Stratotanker*; 1 tpt sqn with 4 C-17A *Globemaster*; 2 SAM bty with M903 *Patriot* PAC-3 MSE

RED SEA: US Central Command • 5th Fleet 900; 2 DDGHM; 1 DDGM

ROMANIA: NATO • Forward Land Forces; 150; 1 inf coy **US European Command** • 2,000; 1 inf bde HQ; 1 fd arty bn with M119A3; M777A2; 1 *Aegis Ashore* BMD unit with three 8-cell Mk 41 VLS launchers with SM-3

SAUDI ARABIA: US Central Command • 2,500; 2 FGA sqn with 12 F-16C *Fighting Falcon*; 1 tkr sqn with 12 KC-135R *Stratotanker*; 1 ISR flt with 4 E-11A; 1 AEW&C sqn with 4 E-3B/G *Sentry*; 1 SAM bty with M903 *Patriot* PAC-3 MSE; 1 SAM bty with THAAD **US Strategic Command** • 1 AN/TPY-2 X-band radar

SINGAPORE: US Indo-Pacific Command • 200; 1 log spt sqn; 1 spt facility

SLOVAKIA: NATO • Forward Land Forces 150; 1 inf coy

SOMALIA: US Africa Command • 100

SOUTH SUDAN: UN • UNMISS 7

SPAIN: US European Command • 3,500; 1 DDGHM; 1 DDGM; 1 air base at Morón; 1 naval base at Rota

SYRIA: US Central Command • *Operation Inherent Resolve* 900; 1 armd inf coy; 1 spec ops bn(-); 1 fd arty bty with M777A2; 1 AD bty with M1097 *Avenger*; *Phalanx* (LPWS)

THAILAND: US Indo-Pacific Command • 100

TURKIYE: US European Command • 1,700; 1 air base at Incirlik **US Strategic Command** • 1 AN/TPY-2 X-band radar at Kürecik

UNITED ARAB EMIRATES: US Central Command • 5,000: 1 FGA sqn with 12 F-15E *Strike Eagle*; 1 ISR sqn with 4 U-2S; 1 ISR UAV sqn with RQ-4 *Global Hawk*; 1 ISR UAV flt with 2 MQ-4C *Triton*; 2 SAM bty with M903 *Patriot* PAC-3 MSE

UNITED KINGDOM: US European Command • 10,000
  FORCES BY ROLE
  1 FGA wg at RAF Lakenheath with (2 FGA sqn with 27 F-15E *Strike Eagle*, 1 FGA sqn with 27 F-35A *Lightning* II; 1 FGA sqn with 14 F-35A *Lightning* II); 1 ISR sqn at RAF Mildenhall with RC-135; 1 tkr wg at RAF Mildenhall with 15 KC-135R/T *Stratotanker*; 1 spec ops gp at RAF Mildenhall with (1 sqn with 8 CV-22B *Osprey*; 1 sqn with 8 MC-130J *Commando* II)
US Strategic Command • 1 AN/FPS-132 Upgraded Early Warning Radar and 1 Spacetrack Radar at Fylingdales Moor

WESTERN SAHARA: UN • MINURSO 1

FOREIGN FORCES

Germany Air Force: trg units with 40 T-38 *Talon*; 69 T-6A *Texan* II • Missile trg at Fort Bliss (TX)

Netherlands 1 hel trg sqn with AH-64D *Apache*; CH-47D *Chinook*

Singapore Air Force: trg units with F-16C/D; 12 F-15SG; AH-64D *Apache*; 6+ CH-47D *Chinook* hel

NEW IISS STRATEGIC DOSSIER

Building Defence Capacity in Europe // An Assessment

Launched at the 2024 IISS Prague Defence Summit, the IISS Strategic Dossier *Building Defence Capacity in Europe: An Assessment* examines European NATO countries' efforts to increase their military readiness following Russia's full-scale invasion of Ukraine in February 2022.

It considers the progress they have made – and the significant challenges they still face – as they look to build defence capabilities suitable for potentially fighting a high-intensity war in Europe.

CONTENT INCLUDES:

- Chapters on the transatlantic defence-industrial ecosystem and Europe's defence industries, as well as on European defence spending and important issues around mass and resilience and security of supply.
- A chapter on European defence industries that assesses key defence programmes by sector, accompanied by maps and tables.
- Over 40 bespoke, full-colour graphics, including maps, graphs and charts.
- Seven 'Capability Vignettes' that explore important areas of focus for defence planners, such as artillery and air defence, with tables detailing European equipment holdings.

IISS
THE INTERNATIONAL INSTITUTE
FOR STRATEGIC STUDIES

IISS Prague Defence Summit

AVAILABLE ONLINE:
go.iiss.org/assessment

Chapter Three
Europe

- Six European countries formed the European Long-Range Strike Approach (ELSA), a project aimed at developing a ground-launched cruise missile capability with a range of 1,000–2,000 kilometres by the 2030s.
- The Netherlands became the first of NATO's Dual Capable Aircraft partners to declare its F-35A *Lightning II* operational in the nuclear role, replacing the F-16 *Fighting Falcon*. Meanwhile, 13 years after retiring its main battle tank (MBT) capability, the Netherlands said it intended to buy *Leopard* 2A8s.
- Fighting in Ukraine, and the scale of post-Cold War personnel reductions, have fuelled debates in Europe on the size of armed forces, leading some countries to expand conscription while others are considering measures including military registration.
- Attempts were made to address production capacity and security of supply issues exposed by military support to Ukraine. European countries fell short of their target to send one million 155mm artillery shells to Ukraine by the end of March 2024, but production rates are increasing.
- Europe's defence supplier base is diversifying, with more inventories featuring equipment from non-traditional suppliers, such as Brazil, Israel and South Korea. Regional defence spending grew by 11.7% in real terms in 2024, marking the tenth consecutive year of growth. Defence budgets continue to be supplemented by off-budget funds and increasingly include military aid for Ukraine.
- Uplifts have targeted modernisation and recapitalisation, causing the investment share of defence budgets to increase to 29.9%, up from 14.7% in 2014, with allocations higher among NATO members.
- Policymakers are now shifting their focus to improving readiness, although fiscal constraints may restrict defence budget growth in the medium to long term.

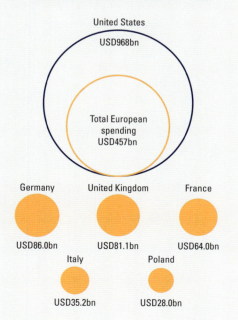

Europe defence spending, 2024 – top 5

United States USD968bn
Total European spending USD457bn
Germany USD86.0bn
United Kingdom USD81.1bn
France USD64.0bn
Italy USD35.2bn
Poland USD28.0bn

Active military personnel – top 10
(15,000 per unit)

Turkiye 355,200
France 202,200
Germany 179,850
Poland 164,100
Italy 161,850
United Kingdom 141,100
Greece 132,000
Spain 122,200
Romania 69,900
Bulgaria 36,950

Global total 20,629,000
Regional total 1,972,000 (9.6%)

Regional defence policy and economics 54 ▶

Arms procurement and defence-industrial trends 68 ▶

Armed forces data section 70 ▶

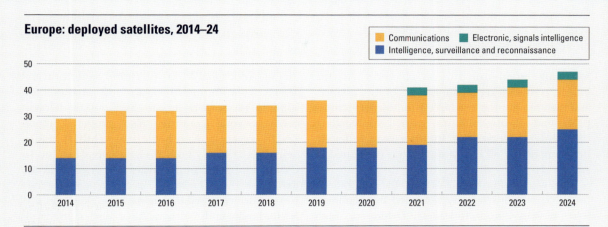

Europe: deployed satellites, 2014–24

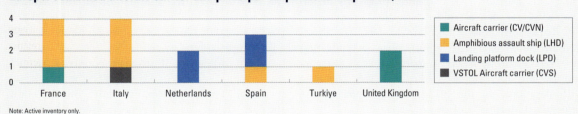

Europe: combined aircraft-carrier and principal-amphibious-ship fleets, 2024

Note: Active inventory only.

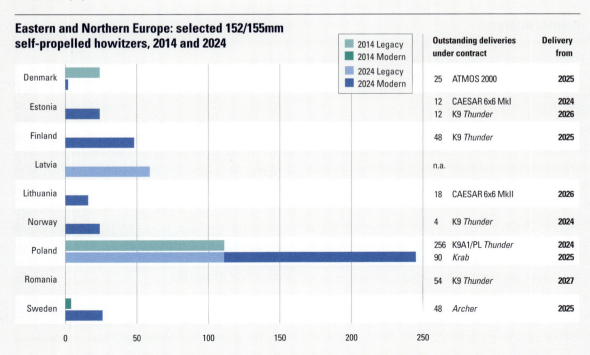

Eastern and Northern Europe: selected 152/155mm self-propelled howitzers, 2014 and 2024

Europe

Confronted throughout 2024 by Russia's ongoing aggression in Ukraine, Europe continued to work on bolstering its collective defence. NATO gained a 32nd member, with Sweden joining in March, following months of Turkish objection. All the Nordic countries are now members of the Alliance, and their integration into NATO military structures proceeded throughout the year. Approaching the third anniversary of Russia's 2022 full-scale invasion, nearly all European nations continued to support Kyiv.

The war in Europe's east and its implications for the continent's security remained the dominant issue among European leaders. Deterrence, both conventional and nuclear, military readiness and sustainability, defence-industrial production capacity, and societal resilience featured prominently in discussions among Europe's leaders. The Royal Netherlands Air Force, in June 2024, was the first of NATO Europe's Dual Capable Aircraft partners to declare its Lockheed Martin F-35A *Lightning II* operational in the nuclear role, replacing the Lockheed Martin F-16 *Fighting Falcon*.

Politics matters

Questions over the continent's capacity to defend itself were given even greater focus by the victory of Donald Trump in the November 2024 US election. In his first term in office (2017–21), he had criticised the level of defence spending in Europe, with similar statements made on the 2024 campaign trail. Election outcomes elsewhere also had an effect, if less dramatic, with the return to power after 14 years of a Labour government in the United Kingdom. The new British government sought to begin to rebuild bridges with its main European defence partners, including harbouring the goal of a UK–European Union defence pact. In October 2024, it signed the Trinity House Agreement with Germany, aimed at deepening military cooperation and defence-industrial ties and promoting inter-operability. The agreement will be followed by a treaty. Discussions on reinforcing the Lancaster House Agreement on defence cooperation with France were also understood to be under way in the latter half of the year.

European defence equipment continued to flow into Ukraine, if not always in the volume Kyiv hoped, nor always with the desired freedom of action to use weaponry against targets inside Russia. Additional MIM-104 *Patriot* batteries were drawn from European stocks and provided to Ukraine to support its air- and missile-defence needs. Several countries also provided more KNDS *Leopard* 2 main battle tanks (MBTs), while deliveries of newly built BAE Systems Hägglunds CV90 infantry fighting vehicles will begin in 2026. Ex-Danish F-16 *Fighting Falcon*s entered active Ukrainian inventory in August 2024. Belgium, the Netherlands and Norway have also committed to provide F-16s withdrawn from service. As of the end of 2024, the number of aircraft handed over remained likely in single figures, though the pledges total 65. The pilot-training pipeline may be a limiting factor.

While numerous European countries signed multi-year security agreements with Kyiv, including France, Germany, Italy, Sweden and the UK, there was also concern over the risk of increasing economic fatigue in supporting Ukraine. In part to alleviate this issue, the EU agreed to transfer the profits from sanctioned Russian assets to Ukraine. This windfall funding will be used to buy military equipment or provide humanitarian aid. An initial EUR1.5 billion (USD1.6bn) was transferred in July 2024 through the EU's off-budget funding mechanism known as the European Peace Facility. In March 2024 the European Council added a further EUR5bn (USD5.4bn) to the facility, with this allocated solely to what it dubbed the Ukraine Assistance Fund. A long-term security-assistance pledge for Ukraine was also part of NATO's July 2024 Washington Summit declaration. This included the provision of EUR40bn (USD43.6bn) through the period to July 2025.

Insecurity of supply

Europe's ongoing efforts to support and supply Kyiv further exposed continuing frailties in production capacity and security of supply. The EU's 2023 Act in Support of Ammunition

Production work programme was aimed at increasing the continent's capacity to produce ammunition and missiles to backfill national inventories and to continue to supply Ukraine. However, the initial target for 155mm ammunition deliveries to Ukraine, to deliver one million shells within a year, was missed at the end of the first quarter of 2024, though production capacity was certainly increasing and the EU estimated that the Act in Support of Ammunition Production (ASAP) would help EU states reach production of 2m shells per year by the end of 2025. The March 2024 European Defence Industrial Strategy marked the latest effort to improve defence readiness and defence-industrial capacity. Kyiv was also working on further shoring up domestic defence-industrial capacity through bilateral and multilateral activity. An EU Defence Innovation Office was opened in Kyiv in September 2024. The core role of the office will be to act as a facilitator in identifying and establishing joint development to meet Kyiv's defence needs. It will also support access to EU funding.

Alongside support for Ukraine, NATO's Washington Summit declaration listed multiple initiatives intended to address the more difficult security environment, with Russia 'the most significant and direct threat to Allies' security'. These included further improvements to integrated air and missile defence (IAMD), the NATO Industrial Capacity Expansion Pledge, and the aim of integrating civilian and defence planning at the national and Alliance levels. Improving private–public cooperation and increasing societal resilience were also identified as goals. The last is also an EU aim, with Brussels in March 2024 commissioning former Finnish president Sauli Niinistö to write a report on how to improve this within Europe. In his November 2024 study, he cautioned that neither the EU nor member states were 'fully prepared' for the most severe scenarios they might face.

Domain developments

With the enduring importance of air and space power only underscored by the war in Ukraine, European countries have sought additional capability. Three of the four *Eurofighter* partner nations, Germany, Italy and Spain, said they would acquire additional aircraft in 2024. Germany and Italy planned a further 20 and 24, respectively, for the Tranche 4 standard of the aircraft to replace earlier and less capable Tranche 1 aircraft. Spain is buying 25 of the Tranche 4 standard of the aircraft, but to replace 20 Boeing F/A-18C/D *Hornet* fighter ground-attack aircraft. The additional aircraft will now keep *Eurofighter* production open at least until 2032. Italy also announced plans to acquire additional F-35s, with 15 more F-35As and ten more F-35Bs to be acquired. This would take Rome's overall order for the type to 115. Greece also signed a Letter of Offer and Acceptance through a US foreign military sale for 20 F-35As in July 2024, with an option for a further 20. In September 2024, the pending sale of 32 F-35As was announced. Delivery of the aircraft will not begin until 2031. The French air force, which has previously had to relinquish both Dassault *Rafale* aircraft from its inventory and delivery slots to support exports, ordered 42 aircraft at the end of 2023.

Europe's two high-profile multinational next-generation combat air system projects also continued, if not without some concern. The change in government in the UK brought with it a Strategic Defence Review and speculation that the Global Combat Air Programme (GCAP), in which the UK is in partnership with Italy and Japan, would be reviewed. In the event, the Labour government continued British support for the programme, with a joint company being formed in December 2024. France, Germany and Spain, meanwhile, continued to work on their equivalent project, the Future Combat Air System. References to cooperation on uninhabited-systems in the Germany–UK Trinity House Agreement, however, raised at the time of the announcement at least a question over Berlin's alignment on this aspect of the Franco-German-Spanish programme.

The NATO goal of integrated air and missile defence came a little closer with the introduction into service of the second *Aegis* Ashore ballistic missile defence (BMD) site. The activation of the Redzikowo site in Poland in July 2024 joined Deveselu in Romania in supporting NATO BMD.

Long-range strike was also given impetus by the multinational European Long-range Strike Approach (ELSA). Launched at the Washington Summit by France, Germany, Italy and Poland, the project was later joined by Sweden and the UK. The aim is to acquire up to a 2,000-kilometre-range land-attack weapon. In the near term, the Biden administration said it would episodically deploy ground-based land-attack systems in Germany from 2026.

Figure 7 Europe: selected ongoing submarine procurement programmes

With the return of a contested maritime environment, European states are refocusing on their submarine capabilities, reflecting the utility of these platforms for anti-surface and anti-submarine warfare, intelligence-gathering and helping to protect critical assets. Many have recognised the need to replace their Cold War-era platforms or expand their fleets. The new boats feature clear qualitative enhancements across the board, not least in the use of air-independent propulsion in almost all designs and the ability to support more capable combat systems and a wider variety of weapons. Additionally, France and the United Kingdom are both rejuvenating their nuclear-powered strategic and attack submarine inventories. However, intergovernmental cooperation remains low, a product of the density of submarine yards in Europe, with many countries producing competing submarine designs, and of the desire to buy domestically. Still, the momentum of recent years underpins Europe's status as a centre of submarine development and construction with global reach.

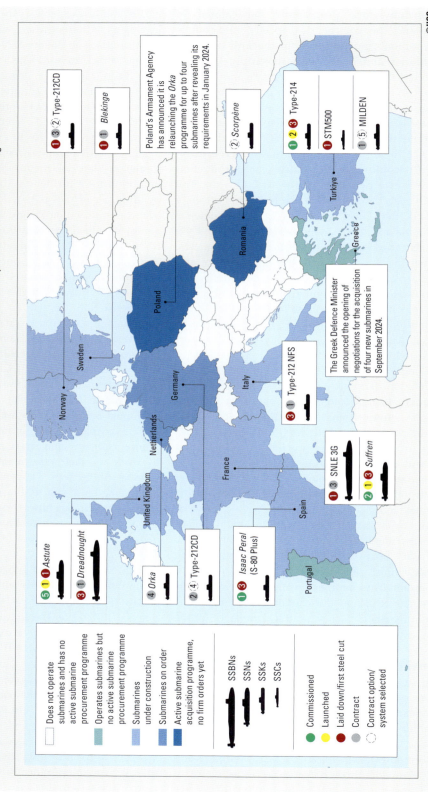

Source: IISS, Military Balance+, milbalplus.iiss.org

Europe considers ground-launched long-range strike

Russia's large-scale use of ballistic- and cruise-missiles in its war against Ukraine has led some European countries to re-evaluate ground-launched conventional long-range strike capabilities. One option is to buy from outside the region, but another is to manufacture either indigenously or in partnership. The latter approach informs the European Long-range Strike Approach (ELSA) project. France, Germany, Italy and Poland launched ELSA in July 2024 with the intention to develop a sovereign capability to improve 'the defence of Europe and to strengthen the European defence industrial and technological base' and to contribute to 'strengthening the European pillar of the Alliance, for better sharing of the burden between Allies'.

ELSA is currently at an early stage and so there are open questions as to which countries may join the project and what type of system may ultimately be developed. In addition to the original four nations, Sweden and the United Kingdom separately announced their participation in October 2024.

The official ELSA announcement refers to developing a new capability for 'long-range strikes' without mentioning the type of weapon being pursued, leaving open the possibility that the parties are considering either a ballistic- or cruise-missile design. The development of a cruise rather than a ballistic missile is more likely because European defence industries are more experienced in developing the former than the latter. Analysts consider that the intention is to develop a ground-launched cruise missile with a range of between 1,000 and 2,000 kilometres to be in service by the 2030s.

If ELSA participants pursue a cruise-missile design, the French division of MBDA has already put itself forward as best placed to meet European needs. Ahead of the ELSA announcement, MBDA France proposed developing a ground-launched version of its sea-launched Missile de Croisière Naval/Naval Cruise Missile (MdCN-NCM) known as the Land Cruise Missile (LCM).

MBDA's proposition to adapt MdCN for ground launch in some ways presents a fait accompli as there are no other European-designed cruise missiles in service or under development that would meet the envisaged 1,000–2,000-km-range requirement. At the same time, procuring non-European systems which meet the project's range requirement, such as the United States' ground-based variant of the *Tomahawk* land-attack cruise missile (LACM) or South Korea's *Hyunmoo*-3 family, will almost certainly fall foul of ELSA's explicit European defence-industrial requirements.

However, there are wider questions about whether adapting existing systems will meet participants' capability requirements for the next several decades. Data from the war in Ukraine has demonstrated the vulnerability of subsonic Russian systems such as the Kh-101 (RS-AS-23A *Kodiak*) to ground-based air defences and missile defences. A supersonic missile or a very low observable system might be seen as a more attractive long-term solution for European needs, but this would increase both development costs and time. As ELSA participants intend to develop a new capability 'within adequate time, cost and volume', a new design may not be feasible due to these constraints.

Involving multiple contributors may lower joint development and production costs, though in this instance, one challenge would be how to effectively manage and harmonise possibly divergent technical and industrial requirements. Similarly, while joint development may lower design and production costs, beyond the six countries that have already signed up, there are few other European NATO members with sufficient defence budgets and industrial bases to support ELSA both financially and technically. Developing an affordable system will be necessary if European countries hope to procure the missile on a large scale while fulfilling their pre-existing orders for stand-off weaponry. Beyond finances, managing the defence-industrial interests of the different stakeholders will be another potential challenge. The number of different guided-weapons development capabilities in the participating countries will make implementing a *juste retour* (a return equal to the level of investment) workshare arrangement challenging without running into the kinds of inefficiencies and duplication that have plagued other multinational European programmes. This assumes, however, that industrial workshare will be more important than expediency.

In the land domain, the Bundestag Budget Committee approved the acquisition of an additional 105 *Leopard* 2A8 MBTs earmarked from 2027 for Germany's brigade that it intends to permanently base in Lithuania. In October, Croatia signed a letter of intent with Berlin to buy up to 50 of the same *Leopard* variant. That month, the Netherlands also said it intended to purchase the *Leopard* 2A8, with delivery of at least 46 tanks to begin in 2027. This will mark the Netherlands' return to nationally fielded heavy armour, since it retired its previous fleet in 2011. A substantial Italian order anticipated in 2024 for the *Leopard* 2A8, however, fell victim to the collapse of talks between KNDS and Leonardo regarding design changes and localisation. Leonardo has now established a joint venture with Rheinmetall and will offer the KF51 *Panther* and KF41 *Lynx* for Italian armoured-vehicle requirements.

In the maritime domain, the German–Norwegian joint project to acquire ThyssenKrupp Marine Systems Type-212CD diesel-electric submarines passed its critical design review in September 2024. Tests of the first boat are due to begin in 2027, with a handover to the Norwegian navy planned for 2029. The design was also on offer to the Netherlands, but in September 2024 the defence ministry contracted France's Naval Group's *Black Sword Barracuda*, with four of the boats planned to replace the navy's ageing *Walrus* class from 2034. Italy meanwhile in June 2024 took the option of contracting for a fourth of the Fincantieri Type-212 Near Future Submarine (NFS) boat to be delivered in 2032. Construction of three of the four boats is already under way with deliveries to take place from 2027 to 2031. The Italian navy is also aiming to acquire at least two additional submarines based on the Type-212 NFS, with the larger development known as the Type-212 NFS EVO. The build programme for these would start in 2030, with both boats delivered in 2036.

Above water, Germany increased its order for the F126 frigate from four to six with contract signature in June 2024. The first of the type is scheduled to be delivered in 2028. A month later, in 2024, Italy contracted for two more FREMM frigates to be built to a new FREMM EVO standard, with the ships to be delivered in 2029 and 2030. In January 2024, Poland awarded a contract to MBDA to fit the *Sea Ceptor* air-defence system for its three PGZ *Miecznik*-class frigates. The first keel of the frigate programme, which is a partnership with the UK, was laid at the end of that month.

Personnel problems and beyond

Europe's lack of depth is not limited to just defence inventories. Recruitment and retention remain an issue for many. In the Baltic region, Latvia's decision to reintroduce male military conscription came into effect in 2024 and all three Baltic republics now have a form of compulsory military service. In Northern Europe, Norway announced plans to increase annual conscription numbers from 9,000 to 13,500 by 2036, while Denmark will introduce female compulsory service from 2026 and changed the regulation over the employment of conscripts. Berlin was also mulling the reintroduction of conscription, suspended in 2011, to help it meet personnel targets, and a draft law requiring military registration was tabled by the Scholz government. This focus on conscription was driven not only by concern over immediate force strength, but also by a desire to generate a deeper reserve, in light of lessons from the war in Ukraine over the need to replenish losses and regenerate in the face of attrition. A further issue for some was the comparatively high average age of military personnel, as well as the challenge of retention. In response, a number of governments were introducing measures including financial incentives and considering the introduction of more flexible career paths. However, increasing personnel numbers comes at a cost – a cost that varies considerably across NATO and EU countries. In terms of the percentage of defence expenditure devoted to personnel, the lowest in NATO is now Sweden at 15.8%, with Italy the highest at 59.4%, according to NATO figures.

In spite of war on Europe's periphery and the focus on rebuilding readiness within the European context, many countries continued with wider military engagements, on top of standing commitments and deployments. Belgium, Denmark, France, Germany, Italy, the Netherlands and the UK sent personnel to take part in the US-led RIMPAC 24. Also notable was Berlin's May-to-December 2024 deployment of two frigates to the region. The ships were used to take part in multinational regional exercises and the EU Coordinated Maritime Presence in the Indian Ocean. France, Germany and Spain took part in *Pacific Skies* 24, while Spain and Italy were first-time participants in the *Pitch Black* 24 air exercise held in Australia. As part of the latter, Italy deployed a total of 21 aircraft to the exercise, while the Italian navy sent the *Cavour* aircraft carrier.

European defence-industrial realignment

Defence cooperation within the EU in 2024 was marked by a focus on continued support for Ukraine, replenishing European inventories and strengthening the capacity of the European Defence Technological and Industrial Base (EDTIB). To help replenish stocks and increase production, ASAP assigned around EUR500m (USD545m) to 31 projects to increase ammunition and missile production in Europe. ASAP is also expected to leverage additional funding from the private sector, up to around EUR1.4bn (USD1.5bn) in total. In the case of Norway, ASAP-allocated fundings are said to have triggered NOK3bn (USD282m) in investments.

Moreover, the European Commission identified five critical and urgent capabilities to be supported with a EUR300m (USD327m) incentive under the European Defence Industrial Reinforcement through common Procurement Act (EDIRPA). Through EDIRPA, the EU is using the EU budget, for the first time, to co-finance joint procurement of EU-origin equipment by EU member states. Allocating EDIRPA co-funding is expected to generate more than EUR11bn-worth (USD12.0bn) of defence products.

Hitherto, a major problem in deepening EU defence and defence-industrial cooperation has been the tendency of member states to eschew cooperation, particularly in times of crisis. ASAP and EDIRPA, both short-term instruments, are intended to overcome this situation.

To provide an overall structure for EU defence-industrial cooperation and enhance industry's capacity and readiness to meet member states' needs, the Commission in 2024 published a European Defence Industrial Strategy (EDIS), together with a proposed European Defence Industrial Programme (EDIP) instrument.

EDIS represents the Commission's first structured effort to transform the European defence-industrial landscape in order to increase the capacity of EU member states to build relevant military capabilities, reduce external dependencies, exploit economies of scale and gain from a more coordinated industrial effort.

It aims to do this by setting ambitious targets for reshaping the EU defence-equipment market. By 2030, at least 40% of procurement in the EU should be carried out jointly and at least 50% of products procured should originate from the EDTIB. By the start of the next decade, 35% of market value should come from intra-community transfers, thus sharpening focus on the elimination of internal barriers to the single market on defence, particularly for small and medium-size enterprises and mid-caps. These entities are widely acknowledged to struggle to integrate into the defence market despite representing the majority of the European defence-industrial base.

The targets are to be realised by implementing multiple new tools and bodies under the EDIP proposal, which at the time of writing had not been endorsed by member states or the European Parliament. The EDIP regulation was originally expected to be adopted by mid-2025 and be operational by autumn that year, though delays might affect this timeline. The activities proposed by EDIS and EDIP aim to improve the EDTIB's output capacity and innovation, improve security of supply, rebuild inventories, enhance access to critical raw materials, stimulate industrial expansion and nurture specialist skills. This would require a significantly increased EU defence budget, along with a coordinated inter-institutional approach. Against this background, to further help improve coordination on common procurement, the European Defence Agency (EDA) will act as demand aggregator as agreed in the 2024 Long Term Review of the agency.

However, EDIP only has an operational budget of EUR1.5bn (USD1.6bn) for 2025–27. This sum is too small to achieve EDIP's ambitious aims of extending ASAP and EDIRPA until 2027, to set up incentives and perform activities related to security of supply, to foster joint armament-development programmes and to expand cooperation with Ukraine. More substantial allocations are expected in the next multiannual financial framework, running from 2028–34. In this context, various innovative financing approaches have been touted, including urging the European Investment Bank to modify its current restrictive lending policy towards the defence sector, and the potential use of cohesion funds to finance defence and dual-use products up until the next multiannual financial framework.

Further avenues being pursued to secure additional funding include the use of Russian windfall profits to continue sustaining Ukraine's defence. Channelled through the European Peace Facility (EPF), EU member states have made EUR1.5bn (USD1.6bn) available to Ukraine, 90% of which is for military acquisition. This funding could have a positive industrial impact on the EDTIB, as the EPF is progressively shifting towards sustaining direct acquisition of equipment from European defence industries with a reimbursement rate of 43%.

Ursula von der Leyen's reappointment as president of the European Commission has reaffirmed the priority of strengthening the EU's defence industry, as evidenced by the creation of the position of defence commissioner. The new commissioner will oversee the implementation of all EU projects affecting the defence industry, including the more than 100 ongoing projects under the European Defence Fund (EDF) and those to be selected for the 2024 call for proposals. A white paper on defence was expected a matter of months after the commissioner takes office.

Figure 8 — European Union: financial support for the European Defence Technological and Industrial Base (EDTIB)

The EU has financially supported the European Defence Technological and Industrial Base (EDTIB) since the late 2010s. The first limited allocations from the EU's budget to sustain joint defence R&D projects occurred through the precursor programmes of the European Defence Fund (EDF), the Preparatory Action on Defence Research (PADR) and the European Defence Industrial Development Programme (EDIDP). But only since the 2021–27 multi-year financial framework has the EU had a 'heading' dedicated to defence. Russia's full-scale invasion of Ukraine since 2022 has driven the launch of the

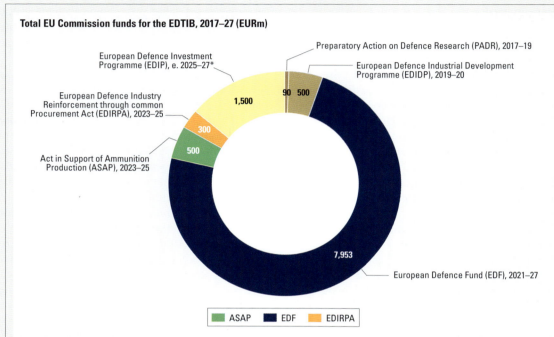

*The EDIP is still under discussion at the EU level. Total expected allocation for the programme is EUR1.5bn for the period 2025–27.
Note: e. = expected.

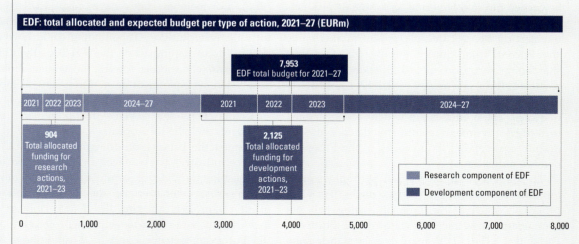

Note: The expected budget for research and development actions of the 2024 allocation is EUR1.1bn.

Source: IISS

Act in Support of Ammunition Production (ASAP) to sustain the later stages of defence production and ramp up the ammunition and missile sectors. The EU also launched the European Defence Industry Reinforcement through common Procurement Act (EDIRPA) to increase cooperation among member states on joint acquisition by providing financial incentives. The temporary character of these initiatives and the necessity to strengthen and systematise the EDTIB triggered the Commission's proposal for a European Defence Industry Programme (EDIP), currently under negotiation at member-state level.

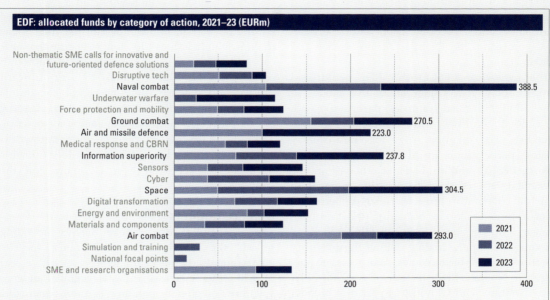

EDF: allocated funds by category of action, 2021–23 (EURm)

Note: Bold text = exceeds 200m; CBRN = chemical, biological, radiological, nuclear; SME = small and medium-sized enterprise.

ASAP: allocated funds by programme, 2023–25 (EURm)

Note: ASAP is a short-term instrument that aims to support a ramp-up in production of ammunition and missiles in Europe. It has funded 31 projects on powder/propellant, explosives, shells, missiles, and testing and reconditioning certification for artillery ammunition. The almost EUR513m allocated for 2023–25 is expected to trigger a total investment of EUR1.5bn for new production capacities across Europe due to the expected co-funding by industry.

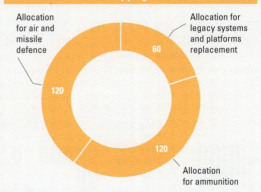

EDIRPA: allocated funds by programme, 2024–25 (EURm)

Note: EDIRPA is a short-term instrument to incentivise common procurement of urgent and critical products among EU member states. Co-funds have been assigned to five projects involving 20 member states and representing critical and urgent capability gaps in the field of ammunition, air and missile defence, and legacy systems and platform replacement.

©IISS

Because of the institutional approach needed to restructure the defence-industrial sector, the first year of the defence commissioner's mandate will come at a significant time, as in 2025 there will be several milestones in addition to the expected operationalisation of the EDIP. By 2025, both the EDF mid-term review and the strategic review of Permanent Structured Cooperation (PESCO) will be completed, opening the way for more coordinated and structured cooperation between the Commission, the External Action Service and member states.

The review of PESCO and EDF could lead EU institutions to consider alternative modes of cooperation with third countries, particularly with like-minded countries with compatible national industries. The onerous rules for third-country entities' participation in EU-sponsored projects, both in PESCO and in EDF, is reflected in the substantial lack of third-country involvement in industrial cooperative projects. This risks becoming a major impediment to bolstering the European defence industry, because of deeply embedded and complex supply chains, unique third-country expertise in some technologies, and access to raw materials. Notably EDIS includes a specific pillar on cooperation with Ukraine, as part of a broader strategy to support the country in countering Russia's invasion.

DEFENCE ECONOMICS

European defence spending surged by 11.7% in real terms in 2024, with most countries bolstering their defence budgets. Uplifts were driven both by national responses to Russia's war in Ukraine – particularly in the Nordic states and former Eastern bloc countries – and by the commitment by NATO members to spend 2% of GDP on defence by 2024. While growth is widespread, it has been uneven, with countries in Southern Europe struggling to implement sustained increases owing to fiscal pressures. Recent spending uplifts have targeted investment and recapitalisation in response to urgent operational requirements. Following these efforts, policymakers are now shifting their focus to improving readiness, looking to ensure that new capabilities can be employed effectively. Although security drivers will continue to exert upward pressure on defence spending, fiscal constraints may dampen growth over the longer term, leading to renewed focus on private financing for defence. The outlook for regional defence-budget growth is moderate to strong but will hinge on developments in major markets, not least Germany and the United Kingdom.

Defence budgets

The 2024 uplift in European defence spending reflects the deterioration of Europe's security environment and marks the tenth consecutive year of real-terms increases in total regional defence spending. Regional spending is more than 50% higher in nominal terms compared to 2014 levels, with real-terms growth averaging 3.6% annually, although some countries posted far stronger increases than others.

Regional growth in 2024 was dominated by the 23.2% real uplift in the German defence budget to reach EUR78.9 billion (USD86.0bn) or 1.83% of GDP. The EUR0.8bn (USD0.9bn) increase in the core defence budget was not the primary driver of

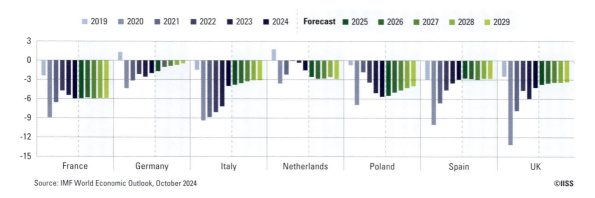

▲ Figure 9 **Europe: selected countries, fiscal balance, 2019–29** (% of GDP)

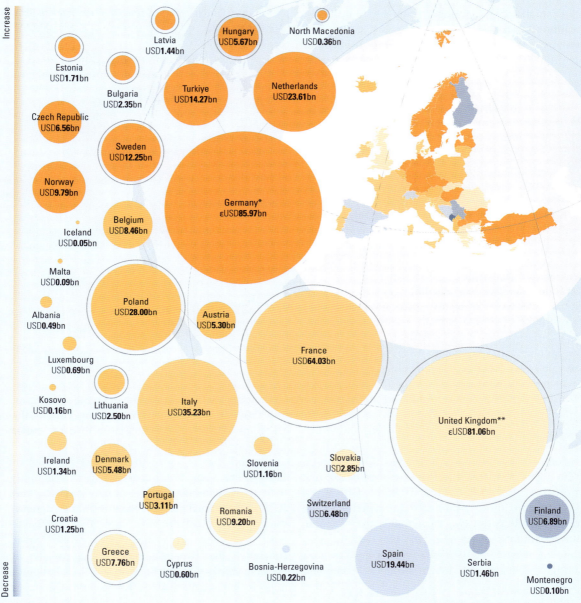

▲ Map 1 **Europe: regional defence spending** (USDbn, %ch yoy)

Sub-regional groupings referred to in defence economics text: Central Europe (Austria, Czech Republic, Germany, Hungary, Poland, Slovakia and Switzerland), Northern Europe (Denmark, Estonia, Finland, Latvia, Lithuania, Norway and Sweden), Southern Europe (Cyprus, Greece, Italy, Malta, Portugal and Spain), Southeastern Europe (Bulgaria, Romania and Turkiye), the Balkans (Albania, Bosnia-Herzegovina, Croatia, Kosovo, Montenegro, North Macedonia, Serbia and Slovenia) and Western Europe (Belgium, France, Iceland, Ireland, Luxembourg, the Netherlands and the United Kingdom).

the overall increase. Rather, it was due to uplifts in funds allocated from the EUR100bn (USD109bn) Sondervermögen or 'special fund' signed in 2022 and in military aid for Ukraine, the first increasing from EUR5.8bn (USD6.3bn) to EUR19.8bn (USD21.6bn), and the latter from EUR5.0bn (USD5.4bn) to EUR7.1bn (USD7.7bn), between 2023 and 2024, respectively. However, defence-budget growth in the short term is projected to be more muted, just 1.9% in real terms, and is subject to a higher degree of uncertainty following the collapse of the ruling 'traffic light' coalition in November 2024. The 'growth initiative', released alongside the 2025 budget, proposed wider fiscal initiatives that, if enacted, may compete with future spending increases for defence. German commitments to reach 2% of GDP on defence by 2029 are also uncertain in light of current political instability and will now depend on the outcome of the 2025 election. This will also shape what will happen when the special fund runs out in 2027. Without substantial and sustainable increases to Germany's core defence budget, or the approval of another extra-budgetary financing instrument, any progress made on strengthening capability may stall and readiness gaps re-emerge.

Inclusion of the special fund and military aid to Ukraine raises the German defence budget to the largest in Europe, surpassing that of the UK, which has been the largest spender in Europe and the second largest in NATO for the last three decades. The British defence budget saw significant real growth in 2021 and 2022 in line with the GBP16.5bn (USD21.2bn) uplift announced for defence in the 2020 Spending Review, though the 2023 increase struggled to contend with the elevated inflation rate, resulting in a 4.86% fall in real terms. The 2024 budget increase was much stronger. Combined with easing inflation, this enabled a 2.93% real uplift to GBP63.5bn (USD81.1bn) or 2.29% of GDP. The Labour government's plan to reach 2.5% of GDP is expected to be outlined in the Strategic Defence Review (SDR), launched in July 2024 and due to be published in the first half of 2025. The October 2024 Autumn Statement clarified that the path to 2.5% would be set at a 'future fiscal event' while also committing to a GBP2.9bn (USD3.7bn) increase for defence in 2025. In the meantime, IISS forecasts in the Military Balance+ database assume that spending will be maintained at a level between 2.2% and 2.3% of GDP given ongoing aid to Ukraine, major programme costs (the strategic deterrent,

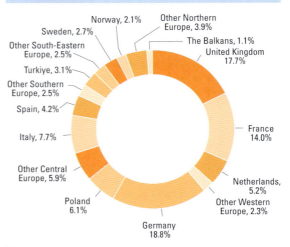

▼ Figure 10 **Europe: defence spending by country and sub-region, 2024**

Note:
Other Western Europe – Belgium, Iceland, Ireland, Luxembourg
Other Central Europe – Austria, Czech Republic, Hungary, Slovakia, Switzerland
Other Northern Europe – Denmark, Estonia, Finland, Latvia, Lithuania
Other Southern Europe – Cyprus, Greece, Malta, Portugal
The Balkans – Albania, Bosnia-Herzegovina, Croatia, Kosovo, Montenegro, North Macedonia, Serbia, Slovenia
Other South-Eastern Europe – Bulgaria, Romania

©IISS

AUKUS and GCAP), recapitalisation requirements and munitions replenishment over the long term. The GBP16.9bn (USD21.5bn) funding gap in the UK's 2023–2033 Equipment Plan will drive either funding uplifts or programme cuts in the SDR.

Beyond the UK, growth is strong in Western Europe. The Netherlands enacted a 35.1% real uplift to defence with the budget reaching EUR21.7bn (USD23.6bn). Such growth means the Dutch defence budget has almost doubled since 2018. Alongside these increases, the Dutch 2024 white paper concluded that 'Russia's unbridled aggression in Ukraine shows that an attack on the NATO alliance is no longer inconceivable'. To this end, the paper committed to major procurements such as new main battle tanks, additional F-35As and additional frigates for anti-submarine warfare. The acquisition of new tanks would restore a capability retired in 2011. In recognition of recruitment challenges, an additional EUR250 million (USD272m) was also allocated towards attracting and retaining personnel. Investment in innovation and the defence industry is also a priority to boost and sustain the production of military equipment.

Meanwhile, France continues to implement increases to defence despite wider fiscal pressures. The 2024 French defence budget grew by 4.5% in real

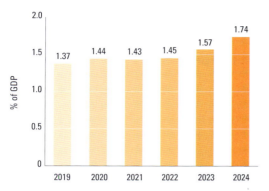

▼ Figure 11 **Europe: regional defence spending** as % of GDP (average)

Source: IISS analysis based on GDP data from IMF World Economic Outlook, October 2024 ©IISS

terms in line with the Military Planning Law (LPM) 2024–30 to reach EUR58.8bn (USD64.0bn). Despite wider public-spending cuts intended to reduce France's fiscal deficit, the 2025 defence budget is also projected to increase to reach EUR62.0bn (USD68.0bn), a 3.5% annual real increase, again in line with the LPM. Defence and security were protected from cuts, along with supporting innovation and reindustrialisation and continuing environmental initiatives. The LPM also highlighted the threat posed by Russia's invasion of Ukraine, which presented a 'strategic shift' in Europe, while instability in the Middle East and the impact of China's strategy and military modernisation on the Indo-Pacific were also used to justify bolstered French commitment to defence.

Beyond Western Europe, growth also continues to strengthen in Eastern and Northern Europe. Prior to Russia's full-scale invasion of Ukraine, Polish defence spending was on a stable upward trajectory with real growth averaging 5.5% in real terms between 2014 and 2022, in line with wider economic growth, with funding fixed as an ever-increasing proportion of GDP by law. The budget has surged since, with real growth of 52.3% implemented in 2023, and 16.9% in 2024. As a result, the defence budget reached PLN118bn (USD28.0bn), making the country the 15th-largest defence budget in the world, compared to 20th in 2022. The 2024 budget reached 3.2% of GDP; however, when including the Armed Forces Support Fund (AFSF), total Polish military expenditure reaches PLN158bn (USD37.5bn) or 4.3% of GDP. The AFSF, established in the 2022 Law on the Defence of the Fatherland, is not part of publicly funded defence. It is financed through the Bank Gospodarstwa Krajowego (BGK), the state development bank, via various means. These include proceeds from treasury securities and BGK bonds, with funding directed towards foreign military acquisitions. The outlook for Polish defence spending is strong in light of ongoing extensive recapitalisation efforts although there are concerns that major purchases have placed extensive pressure on the country's fiscal bandwidth. The 2024 deficit extended to 5.7% of GDP, triggering the European Union's Excessive Deficit Procedure.

Growth has also accelerated considerably in the Nordic states since 2022. The combined budgets of Denmark, Finland, Norway and Sweden grew in real terms by 13.8% and 17.0% in 2023 and 2024. Current official projections for 2025 would result in growth strengthening to 20.5%, largely driven by Norway and Sweden but also by a significant uplift in the Danish budget in line with the Danish Defence Agreement 2024–33. While more recent growth in the Finnish defence budget is not as strong as its neighbours, Helsinki had already made significant uplifts in 2021 and 2023, with funding exceeding the 2% of GDP target level of spending since 2021.

Long-term defence plans are common in the region. In April 2024, Norway launched a Long-Term Plan on Defence that will add NOK600bn (USD56.3bn) to defence spending over the next 12 years (to 2036). As a result, total spending over the period will reach NOK1624bn (USD152.5bn) in a move aimed to strengthen all branches of the armed forces. This includes the purchase of five new frigates with anti-submarine helicopters, at least five submarines and Norway's first long-range air-defence system. Meanwhile the country plans to expand the army from one to three brigades and is increasing the Home Guard to a total of 45,000 soldiers.

Sweden's defence-budget growth, already strong before Russia's full-scale invasion of Ukraine, has surged since 2022, with real growth of 13.5% in 2023 and 29.0% in 2024 to reach SEK129.1bn (USD12.3bn). The budget has effectively doubled over the last four years and reached the NATO target of 2% of GDP in 2024 – up from just 1.1% as recently as 2018. The plans laid out in the Swedish Defence Commission's April 2024 report entitled 'Strengthened Defence Capability, Sweden as an Ally' continue funding increases – albeit at a more measured pace – with the budget reaching SEK185bn (USD17.6bn) by 2030. The Total Defense 2025–30 bill aligned with the recommendations, stating that the budget would reach 2.6% of GDP by 2028 in what would be the most 'powerful strengthening of total defense since the Cold War'. The bill focused on increasing the pace of rearmament, with ambitious procurement plans for all forces and greater investment for innovation, digitalisation and research.

While growth in Central, Eastern, Western and Northern Europe is consistent and has strengthened, growth among countries in Southern Europe has been more muted, particularly as high inflation rates in key markets like Turkiye have eroded real-terms growth. Consequently, combined spending in Southern Europe is the same in real terms as it was in 2008. To overcome soaring inflation rates, Turkiye has enacted significant uplifts to defence since 2023. Despite effectively doubling its spending in lira every year between 2022 and 2024, in real terms this was only sufficient to return spending to 2021 levels owing to respective inflation rates of 72.3%, 53.9% and 60.9% in 2022, 2023 and 2024.

The sub-region's larger spenders, Italy and Spain, have not implemented sustained increases to defence, at odds with the trend across Europe. Prior to 2023, when an 18% real-terms uplift was enacted, the Spanish defence budget had stagnated for well over a decade, with spending in 2022 equivalent to 2008 levels in real terms. Growth stalled again in 2024 as the country failed to pass a budget. This resulted in the 2023 budget being carried over, leading to a decline in real terms. Italy's defence budget also stagnated for over a decade until 2022 with moderate growth also returning spending to 2008 levels, in real terms. The reinstatement of EU fiscal rules to keep deficits below 3% of GDP and debt below 60% of GDP may also curb future growth as both countries are projected to exceed one or both of these rules annually. The exclusion of defence from fiscal-deficit calculations by the EU is currently under debate, particularly for countries like Poland where substantial defence-budget growth since 2022 has caused the deficit to extend to beyond 5% of GDP.

As questions regarding the sustainability of public funding arise, one concern is that national budgets will not be able to sufficiently support increased production and activity in Europe's defence-industrial base, particularly if underlying security threats sharpen and demand also increases further. Attention is increasingly shifting to the role of alternative financing methods. However, adherence to and application of environmental, social and governance (ESG) standards often means that it is hard for industry to secure private financing for research and development (R&D) as well as investment in production capacity.

Spending priorities

The primary focus of increased public funding in Europe has been on modernisation and recapitalisation. The portion of defence budgets allocated to procurement and R&D has increased markedly over the last ten years, with much of the shift evident since 2022. In 2014, the average share of defence budgets spent on procurement and R&D by countries in Europe came to 14.7%. By 2022 this had reached 28.4% and in 2024 it was 29.9%. The share is higher among European NATO members (32.8% in 2024), with countries like Finland, Hungary, the Netherlands, Poland and Sweden allocating over 40% of their defence budgets to investment.

The increasing share of investment is likely to continue in the short term. In the Netherlands, for instance, recent uplifts are evident in the Defensiematerieelbegrotingsfonds or Defense Materiel Budget Fund (DMF), used to fund major acquisitions including frigates, *Patriot* missiles and F-35A aircraft, which increased from EUR6.5bn (USD7.1bn) in 2023 to EUR8.2bn (USD9.0bn) in 2024. Projections for the DMF given in the 2025 budget indicate that increases will continue, with the fund rising to EUR9.8bn (USD10.7bn) and then EUR12.3bn (USD13.5bn) in 2025 and 2026 respectively, remaining around this level to 2029.

However, in some countries, the higher levels of investment may still not be sufficient to counter the impact of Europe's past stagnation and underinvestment in defence. In the UK, for instance, equipment plans have consistently presented affordability gaps since their first publication in 2012. The UK Ministry of Defence estimated in December 2023 that the forecast costs of the UK's current equipment plan to 2033 exceed allocated funding by GBP16.9bn (USD21.0bn). This funding gap could extend to GBP29.8bn (USD37.1bn) if all financial risks materialise. Europe also felt keenly the impact of underinvestment where the surge in demand from 2022 exposed alarming gaps in arms production. Years – if not decades – of 'managed decline' and efficiency savings affected resilience. Rapid increases in production were inhibited by supply-chain challenges and recruitment difficulties.

The increase in spending on investment also impacts other areas of spending. The allocation to military personnel across Europe has fallen from 60% to 40% of the budgets on average since 2014, while the allocation to operations and maintenance (O&M) has not shifted significantly over the decade, increasing mildly from 19% to 23% of defence budgets.

Defence industry

Nonetheless, European defence companies are benefiting from the increase in demand and public funding for acquisitions. The share price of major European defence companies like BAE Systems, Leonardo, Rheinmetall and Saab have all seen significant uplifts since 2022. Companies like BAE Systems are showing increased confidence and conducting recruitment drives. Companies are also expanding capacity through acquisitions, with key examples in 2024 including defence-electronics company Hensoldt's acquisition of system integrator ESG in April 2024 and Fincantieri's purchase of Leonardo's underwater-weapons business in May 2024.

Partnerships are also strengthening in Europe. For example, the Leonardo and Rheinmetall 50:50 joint venture, named Leonardo Rheinmetall Military Vehicles, was formally established in October 2024, and was aimed at forming a 'new European nucleus for the development and production of military combat vehicles in Europe'. Increased investment and public demand are also driving partnerships across the Atlantic, such as the collaboration agreement between Rheinmetall and Lockheed Martin signed in June 2024.

However, the capacity of industry to continue such growth is still in question. Some companies are struggling in the newly competitive and more complex business environment. For example, Airbus announced 2,500 job cuts in October 2024. Underlying issues are not easing in terms of supply chains, longer lead times, a talent shortage and uncertainty over demand at the government level over the long term.

Governments have sought to address concerns around security of demand, as has the EU. The European Commission published its first European Defence Industrial Strategy in 2024, which aimed to incentivise development and joint procurement to address critical EU capability gaps. Initiatives to encourage private-sector investment in defence are also evident at the country level, with Germany releasing an Initiative for Growth in July 2024 which highlighted the role that the German defence and security industry plays in securing peace in Germany and in Europe – thus complying with ESG ideals – while also activating a promotional bank system to finance the industry and considering a top-up to the Future Fund for start-ups which produce military equipment.

Figure 12 Europe: arms procurement and defence-industrial trends, 2024

GREATER INVESTMENTS IN ARMOURED AND MECHANISED FLEETS

During operations in Afghanistan and Iraq, European armed forces deprioritised armoured and mechanised capabilities. However, over the last three years, European states have advanced plans to recapitalise their fleets, with some even announcing ambitions to establish these capabilities from scratch. The Netherlands retired its KNDS *Leopard* 2A6 main battle tanks (MBTs) in 2011 due to budget cuts. However, in late 2024, the country's defence ministry requested approval to acquire up to 52 *Leopard* 2A8s to establish an armoured battalion by 2030. More ambitiously, Lithuania announced that it would also procure a battalion of *Leopard* 2A8s, as well as two battalions of BAE Systems Hägglunds CV90 infantry fighting vehicles (IFVs) and additional ARTEC *Vilkas* wheeled IFVs. Italy is also seeking to expand its armoured fleets. A mid-life upgrade of the CIO *Ariete* is under way, with plans to double the number of MBTs by acquiring a second type. Talks between KNDS and Leonardo to produce an Italian version of the *Leopard* 2A8 collapsed in mid-2024. Since then, Leonardo has established a joint venture (JV) with Rheinmetall to offer the KF51 *Panther* instead. The JV will also offer the KF41 *Lynx* for the Italian army's ambitious programme to acquire over 1,000 vehicles, a significant expansion of its fleet size. Elsewhere. Poland's acquisition of South Korean and US tanks will soon be followed by the production of its indigenous HSW *Borsuk* tracked IFV, with further plans to acquire a heavier platform as well. Efforts across Europe to regenerate capability will not be quick, however, with companies highlighting difficulties in the supply of electronics and armour steel and thus in speeding up delivery of systems to customers.

EUROPE'S MUNITION PRODUCTION RAMP-UP MAKES PROGRESS

European states, defence companies and multinational organisations are racing to increase defence-industrial capacity and production rates as quickly as possible. This is driven by the need to support Ukraine's war effort and to meet European armed forces' own requirements, including deeper ammunition stocks. Particular efforts have been made in artillery-ammunition production, an area where Ukraine has a great need. Rheinmetall, Europe's largest such producer, has increased its global annual production of 155mm artillery rounds by a factor of ten from its pre-2022 capacity to 700,000 rounds, and is planning to reach one million by 2026. The company has achieved this partly through the acquisition of Spanish company EXPAL Systems in 2023 as well as through investing in existing facilities both before and after the signing of long-term production orders. Other producers, such as Franco-German KNDS, are investing in sites in Belgium, France and Italy to achieve an annual rate of 100,000 rounds by 2025, which will be up from 60,000 at the start of 2022. Similarly, Scandinavian company Nammo and the UK's BAE Systems have both received contracts from national governments to increase production. However, a range of factors hamper the speed at which this can take place, including competition for energy and chemicals with the commercial sector and difficulties receiving approval to build new factories. There is also concern over the origin of certain materials, with European states relying heavily on China for the supply of nitrocellulose, for example. In addition to national governments funding production increases, the EU has also provided funds to increase supply, most notably through its 2023 Act in Support of Ammunition Production which allocated funds to sustain the industrial ramp-up and production of the ammunition and missile sector. The EU aims for member states' total annual production capacity to reach two million rounds by the end of 2025.

EUROPEAN STATES DIVERSIFY SUPPLIERS

Since Russia's full-scale invasion of Ukraine began in February 2022, European states have accelerated their modernisation efforts. This has created opportunities for companies outside of Europe, as well as traditional US suppliers, which can either supply equipment more quickly than their European competitors or produce equipment that few or no European companies currently can, such as multiple rocket launchers (MRLs). From February 2022 to the end of October 2024, South Korean companies secured production contracts worth USD18.03 billion from European states. The vast majority of this sum, USD16.88bn, has been contracted by Poland, which is seeking to rapidly modernise and expand the size of its armed forces. This includes the acquisition of large numbers of the Hanwha K9 *Thunder* tracked howitzers now ordered or operated by seven European countries. Israeli firms have also enjoyed success, signing USD6.85bn+ worth of contracts during this time frame. Although the sale of the IAI *Arrow* 3 ballistic-missile-defence system to Germany (USD3.89bn) accounts for most of this, it also includes the sale of Elbit Systems PULS MRLs to Denmark, the Netherlands and Spain. Similarly, since 2019, Brazil's Embraer has signed contracts with five European states for its KC-390 medium airlifter: worth a total of USD4.18bn, of which USD2.96bn has come since February 2022. Some politicians and industrialists in Europe have criticised such acquisitions, arguing that European states should procure from one another or collaborate to develop systems to build up the continent's 'strategic autonomy'. However, other countries, while supporting the overall ambition in the long term, have preferred to acquire non-European systems to achieve capability objectives more quickly.

Table 4 NATO Europe: selected artillery contracts since Feb 2022

The war in Ukraine has reminded planners of the importance of artillery and long-range fires. While European NATO members would expect to fight in a coalition that utilised airpower to a far greater extent than Ukraine is able to, many of these countries have now assessed that their artillery forces are too small and have sought to accelerate procurement. This is particularly the case with rocket artillery, where many countries had either phased out the capability or cut their numbers substantially. Because of this, there are no European systems available to satisfy this requirement outside of those produced in Turkiye. Those countries seeking to rapidly generate this capability have instead acquired Israeli, South Korean and US systems.

Date	Country	Equipment	Type	Quantity	Value	Contractor	Deliveries
May 2022	Belgium	CAESAR 6x6 MkII	155mm self-propelled (SP) artillery	9	USD65.34m	KNDS France	2027
Jul	France	CAESAR 6x6	155mm SP artillery	18	USD89.58m	KNDS France	2023–24
Aug	Poland	K9A1 *Thunder*	155mm SP artillery	212	USD2.67bn	Hanwha Aerospace	2022–26
Sep	Poland	*Krab*	155mm SP artillery	48	USD883.27m	Huta Stalowa Wola (HSW)	2025–27
Nov	Poland	K239 *Chunmoo* (*Homar*-K)	239mm multiple rocket launcher (MRL)	218	USD3.55bn	Hanwha Aerospace	2023–27
	Norway	K9 *Thunder*	155mm SP artillery	4	n.k.	Hanwha Aerospace	2022–24
Dec	Lithuania	CAESAR 6x6 MkII	155mm SP artillery	18	USD137m	KNDS France	By 2027
	Estonia	M142 HIMARS with ATACMS	227mm MRL with short-range ballistic missile	6	USD200m+	Lockheed Martin	From 2024
	Lithuania	M142 HIMARS with ATACMS	227mm MRL with short-range ballistic missile	8	USD495m	Lockheed Martin	From 2025
Jan 2023	Estonia	K9 *Thunder*	155mm SP artillery	12	USD39.18m	Hanwha Aerospace	2026
Mar	Germany	PzH 2000	155mm SP artillery	22	est. USD437.82m	KNDS Deutschland	2025–26
	United Kingdom	*Archer*	155mm SP artillery	14	n.k.	BAE Systems Bofors	2023–24
	Denmark	ATMOS 2000 PULS	155mm SP artillery 306mm MRL	19 8	USD252m	Elbit Systems	2023–26
May	Netherlands	PULS	306mm MRL	20	USD305m	Elbit Systems	2024–27
Sep	Sweden	*Archer*	155mm SP artillery	48	USD471.25m	BAE Systems Bofors	From 2025
Dec	Poland	K9A1 *Thunder* K9PL	155mm SP artillery	6 146	USD2.6bn	Hanwha Aerospace	2025–27
	France	CAESAR 6x6 MkII	155mm SP artillery	109	USD380.91m	KNDS France	2026–31
	Latvia	M142 HIMARS with ATACMS	227mm MRL with short-range ballistic missile	6	USD194.47m	Lockheed Martin	From 2027
	Spain	PULS (SILAM)	306mm MRL	12	USD754.41m	Estribano M&E Rheinmetall Expal Munitions	2024–28
Apr 2024	Poland	K239 *Chunmoo* (*Homar*-K)	239mm MRL	72	USD1.6bn	Hanwha Aerospace	2026–29
Jun	Estonia	CAESAR 6x6 MkII	155mm SP artillery	12	n.k.	KNDS France	2024–25
Jul	Romania	K9 *Thunder*	155mm SP artillery	54	USD1.02bn	Hanwha Aerospace	From 2027

Source: IISS, Military Balance+, milbalplus.iiss.org

Albania ALB

Albanian Lek ALL		2023	2024	2025
GDP	ALL	2.31trn	2.45trn	2.59trn
	USD	22.8bn	26.1bn	28.0bn
Real GDP growth	%	3.5	3.3	3.4
Def exp [a]	ALL	40.3bn	49.8bn	
	USD	397m	510m	
Def bdgt [b]	ALL	40.3bn	45.8bn	51.0bn
	USD	397m	489m	551m

[a] NATO figure
[b] Excludes military pensions

Real-terms defence budget trend (USDm, constant 2015)

Population			3,107,100			
Age	0–14	15–19	20–24	25–29	30–64	65 plus
Male	9.4%	2.8%	3.6%	4.4%	22.1%	6.9%
Female	8.6%	2.5%	3.3%	4.1%	24.1%	8.2%

Capabilities

The 2024 defence directive emphasised the need to improve capabilities and infrastructure and implement the Military Strategy and the Long-Term Development Plan. The latter notes priorities including ground-based air defence and counter-UAV capabilities. Tirana is trying to improve readiness and also recruitment and retention, the latter with improved benefits and pay. Albania contributes to NATO, UN and EU missions but does not possess an independent expeditionary capability. Kuçova Air Base has been modernised, while the naval base Porto Romano is being upgraded. There is developing cooperation with the US, including on cyber defence and air force modernisation, as well as other NATO partners, and Albania will also receive funding under the European Peace Facility. NATO allies Greece and Italy police Albania's airspace. The government plans to regenerate a defence industrial capacity.

ACTIVE 7,500 (Land Force 2,350 Naval Force 700 Air Force 650 Support Command 1,650 Other 2,150)

ORGANISATIONS BY SERVICE

Land Force 2,350
FORCES BY ROLE
SPECIAL FORCES
  1 spec ops regt (1 SF bn, 1 cdo bn)
MANOEUVRE
  Light
  3 lt inf bn
COMBAT SUPPORT
  1 mor bty
  1 NBC coy
EQUIPMENT BY TYPE
ARMOURED FIGHTING VEHICLES
  APC • PPV 40 MaxxPro Plus
ARTILLERY • MOR 32: 82mm 20; 120mm 12

Naval Force 700
EQUIPMENT BY TYPE
All operational patrol vessels under 10t FLD

Coast Guard
EQUIPMENT BY TYPE
PATROL AND COASTAL COMBATANTS 19
  PBF 5 Drini (US Archangel)
  PB 9: 4 Iliria (Damen Stan Patrol 4207); 3 Bora (ex-US Sea Spectre Mk III); 2 Shqypnia
  PBR 5: 2 Type-227; 1 Type-246; 2 Type-2010
LOGISTICS AND SUPPORT • AG 1

Air Force 650
EQUIPMENT BY TYPE
HELICOPTERS
  TPT 18: **Medium** 6: 4 AS532AL Cougar†; 2 UH-60A+ Black Hawk; **Light** 12: 1 AW109; 3 Bell 205 (AB-205); 2 Bell 206C (AB-206C); 4 Bo-105; 2 H145
UNINHABITED AERIAL VEHICLES
  CISR 3 Bayraktar TB2

Military Police
FORCES BY ROLE
COMBAT SUPPORT
  1 MP bn
EQUIPMENT BY TYPE
ARMOURED FIGHTING VEHICLES
  AUV 8 IVECO LMV

Support Command 1,650
FORCES BY ROLE
COMBAT SUPPORT
  1 engr bn
  1 cbt spt bn
COMBAT SERVICE SUPPORT
  1 log bde (1 tpt bn, 1 log bn)
  1 maint unit

DEPLOYMENT

BOSNIA-HERZEGOVINA: EU • EUFOR (Operation Althea) 1
BULGARIA: NATO • Forward Land Forces 30; 1 inf pl
KOSOVO: NATO • KFOR 90
LATVIA: NATO • Forward Land Forces 40; 1 EOD pl
SOUTH SUDAN: UN • UNMISS 3
SUDAN: UN • UNISFA 1

Austria AUT

Euro EUR		2023	2024	2025
GDP	EUR	479bn	492bn	510bn
	USD	518bn	536bn	559bn
Real GDP growth	%	-0.8	-0.6	1.1
Def bdgt [a]	EUR	4.08bn	4.86bn	5.19bn
	USD	4.41bn	5.30bn	5.69bn

[a] Includes military pensions

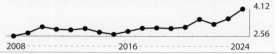
Real-terms defence budget trend (USDbn, constant 2015)

Population	8,967,982				
Age	0–14	15–19	20–24	25–29	30–64	65 plus
Male	7.2%	2.4%	2.6%	3.0%	24.4%	9.4%
Female	6.9%	2.3%	2.5%	3.0%	24.6%	11.8%

Capabilities

Austria is constitutionally non-aligned but is an EU member and actively engaged in the bloc's Common Security and Defence Policy. Vienna bases its defence-policy objectives on the 2013 National Security Strategy, the 2014 Defence Strategy and the 2017 Military Strategy, which direct that military capabilities maintain sovereignty and territorial integrity, enable military assistance to civil authorities and participate in crisis-management missions. Authorities are shifting emphasis from international operations to homeland defence. Austrian assets for international deployments may eventually be embedded in the EUFOR Crisis Response Operation Core. Vienna aims to be able to deploy and sustain a minimum (on average) of 1,100 troops. The military plans to group cyber, CIS and EW capabilities in one directorate. While not a NATO member, Austria joined the Alliance's Partnership for Peace framework in 1995. In early 2023, a defence report highlighted the need to strengthen the armed forces to adapt to a changed security environment, and an investment plan has been drawn up to 2032. Since then, to address shortfalls, Vienna announced plans to upgrade *Leopard* 2 MBTs and *Pandur* wheeled APCs, acquire *Pandur* with an air defence capability, and placed orders for additional IFVs. With the Netherlands, Austria has ordered KC-390 medium transport aircraft and, in 2024, announced it would replace its AB-212 light transport helicopters with twelve UH-60M medium transport helicopters, beginning in 2028. The country's defence-industrial base comprises some 100 companies with niche capabilities and international ties in the areas of weapons and ammunition, communications equipment and vehicles.

ACTIVE 22,800 (Land Forces 11,200 Air 3,100 Support 8,500)

Conscript liability 6 months recruit trg, 30 days reservist refresher trg for volunteers; 120–150 days additional for officers, NCOs and specialists. Authorised maximum wartime strength of 55,000

RESERVE 106,900 (Joint structured 34,200 Joint unstructured 72,700)

Some 8,600 reservists a year undergo refresher trg in tranches

ORGANISATIONS BY SERVICE

Land Forces 11,200

FORCES BY ROLE

MANOEUVRE

Armoured
1 (4th) armd inf bde (1 recce/SP arty bn, 1 tk bn, 2 armd inf bn, 1 spt bn)

Mechanised
1 (3rd) mech inf bde (1 recce/SP arty bn, 3 mech inf bn, 1 cbt engr bn, 1 spt bn)

Light
1 (7th) lt inf bde (1 recce bn, 3 inf bn, 1 cbt engr bn, 1 spt bn)
1 (6th) mtn inf bde (3 mtn inf bn, 1 cbt engr bn, 1 spt bn)

EQUIPMENT BY TYPE

ARMOURED FIGHTING VEHICLES

MBT 56 Leopard 2A4
IFV 112 *Ulan*
APC 163
 APC (T) 32 BvS-10
 APC (W) 131: 71 *Pandur*; 60 *Pandur* EVO
AUV 216: 66 *Dingo* 2; 150 IVECO LMV

ENGINEERING & MAINTENANCE VEHICLES

ARV 65: 27 4KH7FA-SB *Greif* (11 more in store); 28 *Dingo* 2 ARV; 10 M88A1

NBC VEHICLES 12 *Dingo* 2 AC NBC

ANTI-TANK/ANTI-INFRASTRUCTURE

MSL • MANPATS *Bill* 2 (PAL 2000)
RCL 84mm *Carl Gustaf*

ARTILLERY 119

SP 155mm 48 M109A5ÖE
MOR 71+: 81mm L16; 120mm 71 sGrW 86 (22 more in store)

Reserve

FORCES BY ROLE

MANOEUVRE

Light
10 inf bn

Air Force 3,100

The Air Force is part of Joint Forces Comd and consists of 2 bde; Air Support Comd and Airspace Surveillance Comd

FORCES BY ROLE

FIGHTER

2 sqn with Eurofighter *Typhoon*

ISR

1 sqn with PC-6B *Turbo Porter*

TRANSPORT

1 sqn with C-130K *Hercules*

TRAINING

1 trg sqn with PC-7 *Turbo Trainer*

TRANSPORT HELICOPTER
 2 sqn with Bell 212 (AB-212)
 1 sqn with OH-58B *Kiowa*
 1 sqn with S-70A *Black Hawk*
AIR DEFENCE
 2 bn
 1 radar bn
EQUIPMENT BY TYPE
AIRCRAFT 13 combat capable
 FTR 13 Eurofighter *Typhoon* (Tranche 1)
 TPT 11: **Medium** 3 C-130K *Hercules*; **Light** 8 PC-6B *Turbo Porter*
 TRG 16: 4 DA40NG; 12 PC-7 *Turbo Trainer*
HELICOPTERS
 ISR 10 OH-58B *Kiowa*
 TPT 36: **Medium** 9 S-70A-42 *Black Hawk*; **Light** 27: 5 AW169M LUH; 22 Bell 212 (AB-212)
AIR DEFENCE
 SAM • Point-defence *Mistral*
 GUNS 35mm 24 GDF-005 (6 more in store)
AIR-LAUNCHED MISSILES • **AAM** • **IIR** IRIS-T

Special Operations Forces
FORCES BY ROLE
SPECIAL FORCES
 2 SF gp
 1 SF gp (reserve)

Support 8,500
Support forces comprise Joint Services Support Command and several agencies, academies and schools

DEPLOYMENT
BOSNIA-HERZEGOVINA: EU • EUFOR (*Operation Althea*) 134; 1 inf bn HQ; 1 inf coy; 1 hel unit
CYPRUS: UN • UNFICYP 3
KOSOVO: NATO • KFOR 107; 1 recce coy; **UN** • UNMIK 1
LEBANON: UN • UNIFIL 161; 1 log coy
MIDDLE EAST: UN • UNTSO 5
MOZAMBQIUE: EU • EUMAM Mozambique 1
WESTERN SAHARA: UN • MINURSO 5

Belgium BEL

Euro EUR		2023	2024	2025
GDP	EUR	585bn	608bn	628bn
	USD	632bn	662bn	689bn
Real GDP growth	%	1.4	1.1	1.2
Def exp [a]	EUR	7.05bn	7.90bn	
	USD	7.62bn	8.52bn	
Def bdgt [b]	EUR	6.83bn	7.77bn	7.94bn
	USD	7.39bn	8.46bn	8.71bn

[a] NATO figure
[b] Includes military pensions

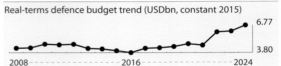
Real-terms defence budget trend (USDbn, constant 2015)

Population		11,977,634				
Age	0–14	15–19	20–24	25–29	30–64	65 plus
Male	8.7%	3.0%	2.9%	3.0%	22.8%	9.0%
Female	8.3%	2.8%	2.8%	2.9%	22.6%	11.3%

Capabilities
Belgium's STAR plan, in June 2022, updated the previous six-year-old strategic defence vision. Soon after, Brussels approved a new military programming law, which heralded increased defence budgets out to 2030. The funds are intended to address three key areas: increasing personnel numbers, strengthening the defence technological and industrial base, and delivering major equipment investments. Recruitment and retention criteria are under scrutiny following retirements and establishment reductions in recent decades. The motorised brigade, medical support and mobility are supposed to secure investments, with over half of the STAR plan's investments slated for the land domain. Belgium is prioritising investments with 'dual capability' to be used in contingencies at home as well as for military operations. NATO, EU and UN membership are central to its defence policy. Belgium often cooperates with neighbours and has committed with Denmark and the Netherlands to form a composite combined special-operations command. In late 2024, Belgium and the Netherlands announced the formation of a Combined-Special Operations Maritime Task Group. A Space Security Centre is intended to be operational by 2029. Brussels is modernising across its forces, including through purchasing fighter aircraft (Belgian F-35A pilots are training in the US), frigates and armoured vehicles, and also modernising its artillery capabilities. Belgium has an advanced, export-focused defence industry, focusing on components and subcontracting, though in FN Herstal, it has one of the world's largest manufacturers of small arms.

ACTIVE 23,500 (Army 9,100 Navy 1,400 Air 4,600 Medical Service 1,450 Joint Service 6,950)

RESERVE 5,900

ORGANISATIONS BY SERVICE

Land Component 9,100

FORCES BY ROLE
SPECIAL FORCES
  1 spec ops regt (1 SF gp, 1 cdo bn, 1 para bn, 1 sigs gp)
MANOEUVRE
  Mechanised
  1 mech bde (1 ISR bn; 3 mech bn; 2 lt inf bn; 1 arty bn; 2 engr bn; 2 sigs gp; 2 log bn)
COMBAT SUPPORT
  1 CIMIC gp
  1 EOD unit
  1 MP coy
COMBAT SERVICE SUPPORT
  1 log bn
EQUIPMENT BY TYPE
ARMOURED FIGHTING VEHICLES
  ASLT 18 *Piranha* III-C DF90
  RECCE 30 *Pandur Recce*
  IFV 17: 7 *Piranha* III-C DF30; 10 *Piranha* III-C DF30S
  APC • APC (W) 78: 64 *Piranha* III-C; 14 *Piranha* III-PC (CP)
  AUV 470: 219 *Dingo* 2 (inc 52 CP); 241 IVECO LMV; 10+ JLTV
ENGINEERING & MAINTENANCE VEHICLES
  AEV 14: 6 Pionierpanzer 2 *Dachs*; 8 *Piranha* III-C
  ARV 13: 4 *Pandur*; 9 *Piranha* III-C
ANTI-TANK/ANTI-INFRASTRUCTURE
  MSL • MANPATS *Spike*-MR
ARTILLERY 60
  TOWED 105mm 14 LG1 MkII
  MOR 46: 81mm 14 Expal; 120mm 32 RT-61
UNINHABITED AERIAL VEHICLES
  ISR • Light RQ-21A *Blackjack*

Naval Component 1,400
EQUIPMENT BY TYPE
PRINCIPAL SURFACE COMBATANTS • FRIGATES 2
  FFGHM 2 *Leopold* I (ex-NLD *Karel Doorman*) with 2 quad lnchr with RGM-84 *Harpoon* AShM, 1 16-cell Mk 48 mod 1 VLS with RIM-7P *Sea Sparrow* SAM, 2 twin 324mm SVTT Mk 32 ASTT with Mk 46 LWT, 1 *Goalkeeper* CIWS, 1 76mm gun (capacity 1 med hel)
PATROL AND COASTAL COMBATANTS 2
  PCC 2 *Castor* (FRA *Kermorvan* mod)
MINE WARFARE • MINE COUNTERMEASURES 5
  MHC 5 *Flower* (*Tripartite*)
LOGISTICS AND SUPPORT 1
  AGOR 1 *Belgica*
UNINHABITED MARITIME PLATFORMS • USV 1
  MW 1 *Inspector* 125
UNINHABITED MARITIME SYSTEMS • UUV
  DATA REMUS 100; *Seascan*
  MW A18-M; *K-Ster* C/I; *Seafox* C/I

Air Component 4,600
FORCES BY ROLE
FIGHTER/GROUND ATTACK/ISR
  4 sqn with F-16AM/BM *Fighting Falcon*
SEARCH & RESCUE
  1 sqn with NH90 NFH
TRANSPORT
  1 sqn with *Falcon* 7X (VIP)
  1 sqn (BEL/LUX) with A400M
TRAINING
  1 OCU sqn with F-16AM/BM *Fighting Falcon*
  1 sqn with SF-260D/M
  1 OCU unit with AW109
TRANSPORT HELICOPTER
  1 sqn with AW109 (ISR)
  1 sqn with NH90 TTH
ISR UAV
  1 sqn with MQ-9B *Sky Guardian* (forming)
EQUIPMENT BY TYPE
AIRCRAFT 50 combat capable
  FTR 50: 42 F-16AM *Fighting Falcon*; 8 F-16BM *Fighting Falcon*
  TPT 9: Heavy 7 A400M; PAX 2 *Falcon* 7X (VIP, leased)
  TRG 12: 4 SF-260D; 8 SF-260M
HELICOPTERS
  ASW 4 NH90 NFH (opcon Navy)
  TPT 14: Medium 4 NH90 TTH; Light 10 AW109 (ISR)
AIR-LAUNCHED MISSILES
  AAM • IR AIM-9M *Sidewinder*; IIR AIM-9X *Sidewinder* II; ARH AIM-120B AMRAAM
BOMBS
  Laser-guided: GBU-10/-12 *Paveway* II; GBU-24 *Paveway* III
  Laser & INS/GPS-guided: GBU-54 Laser JDAM (dual-mode)
  INS/GPS-guided: GBU-31 JDAM; GBU-38 JDAM; GBU-39 Small Diameter Bomb

Medical Service 1,450
FORCES BY ROLE
COMBAT SERVICE SUPPORT
  4 med unit
  1 fd hospital
EQUIPMENT BY TYPE
ARMOURED FIGHTING VEHICLES
  APC • APC (W) 10: 4 *Pandur* (amb); 6 *Piranha* III-C (amb)
  AUV 10 *Dingo* 2 (amb)

DEPLOYMENT

BALTIC SEA: NATO • SNMCMG 1: 50; 1 MHC
BOSNIA-HERZEGOVINA: EU • EUFOR (*Operation Althea*) 5
LITHUANIA: NATO • Forward Land Forces 2
MIDDLE EAST: UN • UNTSO 1

MOZAMBIQUE: EU • EUMAM Mozambique 2

NORTH SEA: NATO • SNMG 1: 150; 1 FFGHM

ROMANIA: NATO • Forward Land Forces 300; 1 mech inf coy with *Piranha* IIIC

FOREIGN FORCES

United States US European Command: 1,150

Bosnia-Herzegovina BIH

Convertible Mark BAM		2023	2024	2025
GDP	BAM	48.9bn	51.4bn	54.2bn
	USD	27.1bn	28.4bn	29.9bn
Real GDP growth	%	1.7	2.5	3.0
Def bdgt	BAM	392m	395m	403m
	USD	217m	218m	222m

Population	3,798,671				
Age	0–14	15–19	20–24	25–29	30–64	65 plus
Male	6.8%	2.3%	2.5%	3.2%	26.3%	7.6%
Female	6.3%	2.1%	2.4%	3.0%	26.4%	10.9%

Capabilities

The primary objectives of Bosnia-Herzegovina's armed forces are to defend territorial integrity and contribute to peacekeeping missions, aiding civil authorities. The armed forces are professional and represent all three ethnic groups. However, low salaries may negatively affect recruitment and retention. In 2023, the country signed agreements with Germany and the US to support the armed forces' infrastructure, and the Ministry of Defence with planning, programming and budgeting. The country is reforming its armed forces and modernising its equipment in accordance with a Defence Review, Development and Modernisation Plan for 2017–27 and its NATO aspirations. Bosnia-Herzegovina joined NATO's Partnership for Peace in 2006 and presented a Membership Action Plan in 2010, though progress has been slow. A new Defence Capacity Building Package for Bosnia-Herzegovina was agreed by NATO defence ministers in 2023. Ethnic tensions persist, with the Serb community threatening to withdraw from national structures, including the armed forces. Bosnia-Herzegovina contributes to EU, NATO and UN missions, but the armed forces have no capacity to deploy independently and self-sustain beyond national borders. The inventory comprises mainly ageing Soviet-era equipment, though some new helicopters have been procured from the US. Bosnia-Herzegovina has little in the way of a domestic defence industry, with only the capability to produce small arms, ammunition and explosives.

ACTIVE 10,650 (Armed Forces 10,650)

RESERVE 6,000 (Armed Forces 6,000)

ORGANISATIONS BY SERVICE

Armed Forces 10,650

1 ops comd; 1 spt comd

FORCES BY ROLE

MANOEUVRE

Light
  3 inf bde (1 recce coy, 3 inf bn, 1 arty bn)

COMBAT SUPPORT

1 cbt spt bde (1 tk bn, 1 engr bn, 1 EOD bn, 1 int bn, 1 MP bn, 1 CBRN coy, 1 sigs bn)

COMBAT SERVICE SUPPORT

1 log comd (5 log bn)

EQUIPMENT BY TYPE

ARMOURED FIGHTING VEHICLES

MBT 45 M60A3

APC • **APC (T)** 20 M113A2

ENGINEERING & MAINTENANCE VEHICLES

VLB MTU

MW *Bozena*

ANTI-TANK/ANTI-INFRASTRUCTURE • **MSL**

SP 60: 8 9P122 *Malyutka*; 9 9P133 *Malyutka*; 32 BOV-1; 11 M-92

MANPATS 9K11 *Malyutka* (RS-AT-3 *Sagger*); 9K111 *Fagot* (RS-AT-4 *Spigot*); 9K115 *Metis* (RS-AT-7 *Saxhorn*); HJ-8; *Milan*

ARTILLERY 224

TOWED 122mm 100 D-30

MRL 122mm 24 APRA-40

MOR 120mm 100 M-75

Air Force and Air Defence Brigade 850

FORCES BY ROLE

HELICOPTER

1 sqn with Bell 205 (UH-1H *Iroquois*); Mi-8MTV *Hip*; Mi-17 *Hip* H

1 sqn with Bell 205 (UH-1H *Huey* II); Mi-8 *Hip*; SA-341H/SA-342L *Gazelle* (HN-42/45M)

AIR DEFENCE

1 AD bn

EQUIPMENT BY TYPE

AIRCRAFT

FGA (7 J-22 *Orao* in store)

ATK (6 J-1 (J-21) *Jastreb*; 3 TJ-1(NJ-21) *Jastreb* all in store)

ISR (2 RJ-1 (IJ-21) *Jastreb** in store)

TRG (1 G-4 *Super Galeb* (N-62)* in store)

HELICOPTERS

MRH 9: 4 Mi-8MTV *Hip*; 1 Mi-17 *Hip* H; 1 SA-341H *Gazelle* (HN-42); ε3 SA-342L *Gazelle* (HN-45M)

TPT 16: **Medium** 8 Mi-8 *Hip* **Light** 8: 5 Bell 205 (UH-1H *Iroquois*) (incl 2 MEDEVAC); 3 Bell 205 (UH-1H *Huey* II) (1 UH-1H *Huey* II in store)

AIR DEFENCE

SAM
Short-range 20 2K12 *Kub* (RS-SA-6 *Gainful*)
Point-defence 9K34 *Strela*-3 (RS-SA-14 *Gremlin*); 9K310 *Igla*-1 (RS-SA-16 *Gimlet*)
GUNS • TOWED 40mm 47: 31 L/60, 16 L/70

DEPLOYMENT

CENTRAL AFRICAN REPUBLIC: EU • EUTM RCA 3

FOREIGN FORCES

Part of EUFOR – *Operation Althea* unless otherwise stated
Albania 1
Austria 134; 1 inf bn HQ; 1 inf coy; 1 hel unit
Belgium 5
Bulgaria 150; 1 inf coy
Chile 6
Czech Republic 2
Denmark 1
France 24
Germany 30
Greece 7
Hungary 250; 1 inf coy
Ireland 4
Italy 180; 1 ISR coy
Macedonia, North 33
Netherlands 10
Poland 49
Romania 470; 2 inf coy
Slovakia 51
Slovenia 20
Spain 2
Switzerland 20
Turkiye 238; 1 inf coy

Bulgaria BLG

Bulgarian Lev BGN		2023	2024	2025
GDP	BGN	184bn	195bn	206bn
	USD	102bn	108bn	116bn
Real GDP growth	%	1.8	2.3	2.5
Def exp [a]	BGN	3.60bn	4.22bn	
	USD	1.99bn	2.33bn	
Def bdgt [b]	BGN	2.41bn	4.22bn	4.35bn
	USD	1.33bn	2.35bn	2.44bn

[a] NATO figure
[b] Excludes military pensions

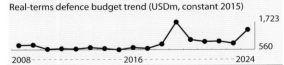
Real-terms defence budget trend (USDm, constant 2015)

Population	6,782,659					
Age	0–14	15–19	20–24	25–29	30–64	65 plus
Male	7.1%	2.8%	2.5%	2.5%	25.4%	8.4%
Female	6.7%	2.6%	2.3%	2.3%	24.8%	12.6%

Capabilities

The main priority of the armed forces is to defend sovereignty and territorial integrity. In 2021, Bulgaria adopted a long-term development plan out to 2032 involving significant re-equipment and modernisation, though because of the cost of the plan's recommendations the country is unlikely to be able to meet all requirements. Bulgaria also updated its 2032 Defence Investment Programme indicating a planned 6,000 increase in personnel. Despite difficulties in retention, the ministry plans to reduce armed forces salaries from January 2025. Bulgaria has several bilateral defence cooperation agreements with regional states and is discussing updating the strategic partnership with France. In July 2024, Bulgaria, Romania and Greece signed a Letter of Intent to create a Military Mobility Corridor, and similar agreements are mooted with other countries. Bulgaria hosts one of NATO's Forward Land Forces multinational battlegroups. Bulgaria decided to acquire the IRIS-T SLM air defence system as part of the European Sky Shield Initiative. Airspace is protected by NATO's Air Policing Mission and Sofia expects to receive new F-16s in 2025, ordering a second batch in 2022. Bulgaria regularly trains and exercises with NATO and regional partners. Units intended for international operations and those with certain readiness levels declared to NATO and the EU receive higher priority in training. The navy is awaiting delivery of two corvettes. Bulgaria's defence industry exports small arms and ammunition but has limited capacity to design and manufacture platforms.

ACTIVE 36,950 (Army 17,000 Navy 4,450 Air 8,500 Central Staff 7,000)

RESERVE 3,000 (Joint 3,000)

ORGANISATIONS BY SERVICE

Army 17,000
FORCES BY ROLE
MANOEUVRE
Reconnaissance
1 recce bn
Armoured
2 tk bn
Mechanised
2 mech bde (4 mech inf bn, 1 SP arty bn, 1 cbt engr bn, 1 log bn, 1 SAM bn)
Light
1 mtn inf regt
COMBAT SUPPORT
1 arty regt (1 fd arty bn, 1 MRL bn)
1 engr regt (1 cbt engr bn, 1 ptn br bn, 1 engr spt bn)
1 NBC bn
COMBAT SERVICE SUPPORT
1 log regt
EQUIPMENT BY TYPE
ARMOURED FIGHTING VEHICLES
MBT 90: 46 T-72M1/M2⁻; 44 T-72M1 (mod)
IFV 160: 90 BMP-1; 70 BMP-23
APC 120
APC (T) 100 MT-LB
APC (W) 20 BTR-60

AUV 89: 45 IAG *Guardian*; 17 M1117 ASV; 27 Plasan *SandCat*

ENGINEERING & MAINTENANCE VEHICLES
 AEV MT-LB
 ARV T-54/T-55; MTP-1; MT-LB
 VLB BLG67; TMM

ANTI-TANK/ANTI-INFRASTRUCTURE
 MSL
  SP 24 9P148 *Konkurs* (RS-AT-5 *Spandrel*)
  MANPATS 9K111 *Fagot* (RS-AT-4 *Spigot*); 9K111-1 *Konkurs* (RS-AT-5 *Spandrel*); (9K11 *Malyutka* (RS-AT-3 *Sagger*) in store)
 GUNS 126: **85mm** (150 D-44 in store); **100mm** 126 MT-12

ARTILLERY 176
 SP 122mm 48 2S1
 TOWED 152mm 24 D-20
 MRL 122mm 24 BM-21
 MOR SP 120mm ε80 *Tundza/Tundza Sani*

SURFACE-TO-SURFACE MISSILE LAUNCHERS
 SRBM • Conventional 9K79 *Tochka* (RS-SS-21 *Scarab*)

AIR DEFENCE
 SAM • Point-defence 9K32 *Strela* (RS-SA-7 *Grail*)‡; 24 9K33 *Osa* (RS-SA-8 *Gecko*)
 GUNS 400
  SP 23mm ZSU-23-4
  TOWED 23mm ZU-23-2; **57mm** S-60

Navy 4,450
EQUIPMENT BY TYPE

PRINCIPAL SURFACE COMBATANTS • FRIGATES 2
 FFM 2 *Drazki* (ex-BEL *Wielingen*) (1 more in reserve) with 1 octuple Mk 29 GMLS with RIM-7P *Sea Sparrow* SAM, 2 single 533mm ASTT with L5 mod 4 HWT, 1 sextuple Bofors ASW Rocket Launcher System 375mm A/S mor, 1 100mm gun (Fitted for but not with 2 twin lnchr with MM38 *Exocet* AShM)

PATROL AND COASTAL COMBATANTS 4
 CORVETTES • FS 1 *Smeli* (ex-FSU *Koni*) with 2 RBU 6000 *Smerch* 2 A/S mor, 2 twin 76mm guns
 PCF 1 *Molnya*† (ex-FSU *Tarantul* II) with 2 AK630M CIWS, 1 76mm gun
 PCT 2 *Reshitelni* (ex-FSU *Pauk* I) with 4 single 406mm TT, 2 RBU 1200 *Uragan* A/S mor, 1 76mm gun

MINE COUNTERMEASURES 10
 MHC 3: 2 *Mesta* (ex-NLD *Alkmaar*); 1 *Tsibar* (ex-BEL *Flower*)
 MSC 3 *Briz* (ex-FSU *Sonya*) (of which 1†)
 MSI 4 *Olya* (ex-FSU)

AMPHIBIOUS • LANDING CRAFT 2
 LCM 2 *Vydra* (capacity either 3 MBT or 200 troops) (of which 1†)

LOGISTICS AND SUPPORT 10
 AG 1 *Dimitar Dobrev*
 AGS 2
 AGOR 1 *Sv Sv Kiril i Metodi*

 AOL 2 *Balchik*
 ARS 1 *Proteo* (ex-ITA *Proteo*)
 ATF 2
 AX 1

UNINHABITED MARITIME SYSTEMS • UUV
 DATA *Gavia*
 MW *Double Eagle* Mk III

Naval Aviation
EQUIPMENT BY TYPE
HELICOPTERS
 ASW 2 AS565MB *Panther*
 MRH 1 AS365N3+ *Dauphin* 2

Air Force 8,500
FORCES BY ROLE

FIGHTER/ISR
 1 sqn with MiG-29/MiG-29UB *Fulcrum*
TRANSPORT
 1 sqn with C-27J *Spartan*; L-410UVP-E; PC-12M
TRAINING
 1 sqn with L-39ZA *Albatros**
 1 sqn with PC-9M
 1 flt with Z-242L
ATTACK HELICOPTER
 1 sqn with Mi-24D/V *Hind* D/E
TRANSPORT HELICOPTER
 1 sqn with AS532AL *Cougar*; Bell 206 *Jet Ranger*; Mi-17 *Hip* H

EQUIPMENT BY TYPE
AIRCRAFT 26 combat capable
 FTR 14: 11 MiG-29 *Fulcrum*; 3 MiG-29UB *Fulcrum*†
 FGA (Some MiG-21bis *Fishbed*/MiG-21UM *Mongol* B in store)
 ATK 6: 5 Su-25K *Frogfoot* K; 1 Su-25UBK *Frogfoot* B
 ISR (1 An-30 *Clank* non-operational)
 TPT 7: **Medium** 3 C-27J *Spartan*; **Light** 4: 1 An-2T *Colt*; 2 L-410UVP-E; 1 PC-12M
 TRG 12: 6 L-39ZA *Albatros**; 6 PC-9M (basic)
HELICOPTERS
 ATK 6 Mi-24V *Hind* E (6 Mi-24D *Hind* D in store)
 MRH 5 Mi-17 *Hip* H
 TPT 18: **Medium** 12 AS532AL *Cougar*; **Light** 6 Bell 206 *Jet Ranger*
AIR DEFENCE
 SAM 20
  Long-range 20: 12 S-200 (RS-SA-5 *Gammon*); 8 S-300PMU (RS-SA-10 *Grumble*)
  Short-range S-125M *Neva*-M (RS-SA-3 *Goa*); 2K12 *Kub* (RS-SA-6 *Gainful*)
AIR-LAUNCHED MISSILES
 AAM • IR R-3 (RS-AA-2 *Atoll*)‡; R-73 (RS-AA-11A *Archer*); **SARH** R-27R (RS-AA-10A *Alamo*)
 ASM Kh-25 (RS-AS-10 *Karen*); Kh-29 (RS-AS-14 *Kedge*)

Special Forces
FORCES BY ROLE
SPECIAL FORCES
1 spec ops bde (1 SF bn, 1 para bn)

DEPLOYMENT
BOSNIA-HERZEGOVINA: EU • EUFOR (*Operation Althea*) 150; 1 inf coy
IRAQ: NATO • NATO Mission Iraq 2
KOSOVO: NATO • KFOR 126; 1 inf coy

FOREIGN FORCES
Albania NATO Forward Land Forces: : 30; 1 inf pl
Greece NATO Forward Land Forces: 30; 1 AT pl
Italy NATO Forward Land Forces: 750; 1 armd inf BG
United States NATO Forward Land Forces: 150; 1 mech inf coy

Croatia CRO

Euro EUR		2023	2024	2025
GDP	EUR	76.5bn	82.3bn	87.5bn
	USD	82.7bn	89.7bn	96.0bn
Real GDP growth	%	3.1	3.4	2.9
Def exp [a]	EUR	1.33bn	1.51bn	
	USD	1.44bn	1.62bn	
Def bdgt [b]	EUR	1.03bn	1.15bn	
	USD	1.12bn	1.25bn	

[a] NATO figure

[b] Includes military pensions

Real-terms defence budget trend (USDm, constant 2015)

Population	4,150,116				
Age	0–14	15–19	20–24	25–29	30–64	65 plus
Male	7.1%	2.6%	2.6%	3.1%	23.3%	9.6%
Female	6.7%	2.4%	2.4%	3.0%	23.7%	13.5%

Capabilities

The principal tasks of the armed forces include defending national sovereignty and territorial integrity, as well as tackling terrorism and contributing to international peacekeeping missions. Croatia reformed and professionalised its armed forces before joining NATO in 2009, but announced it would introduce a two-month conscription system in January 2025. The government has tried to improve conditions of service and to increase the proportion of the budget focused on equipment investment. In 2023, Zagreb deepened defence and security cooperation with the UK and signed a long-term cooperation and support agreement with Ukraine in October 2024. Croatia hosts the NATO Multinational Special Aviation Programme and training centre and participates in EU and NATO missions. The inventory is being upgraded to better align with NATO standards. Air force capabilities have been boosted with the delivery of *Rafale* F3-R aircraft, while there are plans to improve army artillery capabilities. *Bradley* IFVs are being refurbished at a local facility, following delivery from the US in late 2023. Croatia has a limited defence industry, focused on armoured vehicles and naval systems as well as small arms, ammunition, and explosives.

ACTIVE 16,800 (Army 7,800 Navy 1,650 Air 1,600 Joint 5,750)

Conscript liability Two months (planned from Jan 2025)

RESERVE 21,000 (Army 21,000)

ORGANISATIONS BY SERVICE

Army 7,800
FORCES BY ROLE
MANOEUVRE
Armoured
1 armd bde (1 tk bn, 2 armd inf bn, 1 SP arty bn, 1 ADA bn, 1 cbt engr bn)
Mechanised
1 mech bde (3 mech inf bn, 1 lt mech inf bn, 1 fd arty bn, 1 ADA bn, 1 cbt engr bn)
Other
1 inf trg regt
COMBAT SUPPORT
1 arty/MRL regt
1 engr regt
1 MP regt
1 NBC bn
1 sigs bn
COMBAT SERVICE SUPPORT
1 log regt
AIR DEFENCE
1 ADA regt
EQUIPMENT BY TYPE
ARMOURED FIGHTING VEHICLES
MBT 74 M-84
IFV 122: 22 M2A2 *Bradley*; 100 M-80
APC 178
    APC (T) 11: 7 BTR-50; 4 OT M-60
    APC (W) 126 Patria AMV (incl variants)
    PPV 41: 21 *Maxxpro Plus*; 20 RG-33 HAGA (amb)
AUV 63: 10 IVECO LMV; 53 M-ATV
ENGINEERING & MAINTENANCE VEHICLES
ARV 22: 12 JVBT-55A; 2 M-84AI; 1 WZT-2; 2 WZT-3; 5 *Maxxpro Recovery*
VLB 6 MT-55A
MW 4 MV-4
ANTI-TANK/ANTI-INFRASTRUCTURE • MSL
SP 20 BOV-1
MANPATS 9K11 *Malyutka* (RS-AT-3 *Sagger*); 9K111 *Fagot* (RS-AT-4 *Spigot*); 9K111-1 *Konkurs* (RS-AT-5 *Spandrel*); 9K115 *Metis* (RS-AT-7 *Saxhorn*)

ARTILLERY 176
 SP 21: **122mm** 8 2S1 *Gvozdika*; **155mm** 13 PzH 2000
 TOWED 122mm 27 D-30
 MRL 122mm 27: 6 M91 *Vulkan*; 21 BM-21 *Grad*
 MOR 101: **82mm** 55 LMB M96; **120mm** 46 M-75/UBM 52
PATROL AND COASTAL COMBATANTS • PBR 2
UNINHABITED AERIAL VEHICLES
 ISR • Light 6 *Orbiter*-3
AIR DEFENCE
 SAM • Point-defence 9+: 3 9K35 *Strela*-10M3 (RS-SA-13 *Gopher*); 6 9K35 Strela-10CRO; 9K310 Igla-1 (RS-SA-16 *Gimlet*); 9K32M *Strela*-2M (RS-SA-7B *Grail*)‡; Mistral 3
 GUNS SP 20mm 10 BOV-3 SP

Reserve
FORCES BY ROLE
MANOEUVRE
 Light
  6 inf regt
COMBAT SUPPORT
  2 arty regt

Navy 1,650
Navy HQ at Split
EQUIPMENT BY TYPE
PATROL AND COASTAL COMBATANTS 5
 PCFG 1 *Končar* with 2 twin lnchr with RBS15B Mk I AShM, 1 AK630 CIWS, 1 57mm gun
 PCG 4:
  2 *Kralj* with 4 single lnchr with RBS15B Mk I AShM, 1 AK630 CIWS, 1 57mm gun (with minelaying capability)
  2 *Vukovar* (ex-FIN *Helsinki*) with 4 single lnchr with RBS15B Mk I AShM, 1 57mm gun
MINE WARFARE • MINE COUNTERMEASURES 1
 MHI 1 *Korcula*
AMPHIBIOUS • LANDING CRAFT 5:
 LCT 2 *Cetina* (with minelaying capability)
 LCVP 3: 2 Type-21; 1 Type-22
UNINHABITED MARITIME SYSTEMS
 UUV • DATA REMUS 100
COASTAL DEFENCE • AShM 3 RBS15K

Marines
FORCES BY ROLE
MANOEUVRE
 Amphibious
  1 mne coy

Coast Guard 270
FORCES BY ROLE
Two divisions, headquartered in Split (1st div) and Pula (2nd div)
EQUIPMENT BY TYPE
PATROL AND COASTAL COMBATANTS 5

 PB 5: 4 *Mirna*; 1 *Omiš*
LOGISTICS AND SUPPORT 7
 AAR 5: 1 *Faust Vrancic* (YUG *Spasilac*); 4 Other
 AKL 1 PDS 713
 AXL 1 *Andrija Mohorovicic* (POL Project 861)

Air Force and Air Defence 1,600
FORCES BY ROLE
FIGHTER/GROUND ATTACK
 1 sqn with *Rafale* B/C F3-R
TRAINING
 1 sqn with PC-9M; Z-242L
ISR HELICOPTER
 1 hel sqn with Bell 206B *Jet Ranger* II; OH-58D *Kiowa Warrior*
TRANSPORT HELICOPTER
 2 sqn with Mi-171Sh
EQUIPMENT BY TYPE
AIRCRAFT 7 combat capable
 FGA 7: 2 *Rafale* B F3-R; 5 *Rafale* C F3-R
 TRG 21: 17 PC-9M; 4 Z-242L
HELICOPTERS
 MRH 15 OH-58D *Kiowa Warrior*
 TPT 22: **Medium** 14: 10 Mi-171Sh; 4 UH-60M *Black Hawk*; **Light** 8 Bell 206B *Jet Ranger* II
AIR DEFENCE • SAM
 Point-defence 9K31 *Strela*-1 (RS-SA-9 *Gaskin*); 9K34 *Strela*-3 (RS-SA-14 *Gremlin*); 9K310 Igla-1 (RS-SA-16 *Gimlet*)
AIR-LAUNCHED MISSILES
 AAM • IR R-60; R-60MK (RS-AA-8 *Aphid*)
 ASM AGM-114R *Hellfire* II

Special Forces Command
FORCES BY ROLE
SPECIAL FORCES
 5 SF gp

DEPLOYMENT

HUNGARY: NATO • Forward Land Forces 70
INDIA/PAKISTAN: UN • UNMOGIP 8
IRAQ: *Operation Inherent Resolve* 3; **NATO** • NATO Mission Iraq 7
KOSOVO: NATO • KFOR 150; 1 inf coy; 1 hel unit with Mi-171Sh
LEBANON: UN • UNIFIL 1
POLAND: NATO • Forward Land Forces 69; 1 SP arty bty
WESTERN SAHARA: UN • MINURSO 5

Cyprus CYP

Euro EUR		2023	2024	2025
GDP	EUR	29.8bn	31.9bn	34.3bn
	USD	32.2bn	34.8bn	37.7bn
Real GDP growth	%	2.5	3.3	3.1
Def bdgt	EUR	525m	553m	553m
	USD	567m	603m	607m

Real-terms defence budget trend (USDm, constant 2015)

Population		1,320,525				
Age	0–14	15–19	20–24	25–29	30–64	65 plus
Male	8.0%	2.8%	3.3%	4.1%	26.7%	6.3%
Female	7.6%	2.4%	2.7%	3.3%	24.7%	8.1%

Capabilities

The National Guard is focused on protecting territorial integrity and sovereignty, including Cyprus's EEZ. The guard's main objective is to deter any Turkish incursion and to provide enough opposition until military support can be provided by Greece, its primary ally. Greece is a long-time defence partner of Cyprus. Nicosia has pledged to deepen military ties with Israel, while France has renewed and enhanced its defence-cooperation agreement with Cyprus. The US and Cyprus signed a Roadmap for Bilateral Defence Cooperation in 2024. Having reduced conscript liability in 2016, Nicosia began recruiting additional contract-service personnel as part of an effort to modernise and professionalise its forces. Cyprus exercises with several international partners, most notably France, Greece and Israel. External deployments have been limited to some officers joining EU and UN missions. There is little logistics capability to support operations abroad. Equipment comprises a mix of Soviet-era and modern European systems. Cyprus has little in the way of a domestic defence industry, apart from maintenance facilities.

ACTIVE 12,000 (National Guard 12,000)
Gendarmerie & Paramilitary 250

Conscript liability 15 months

RESERVE 50,000 (National Guard 50,000)

Reserve service to age 50 (officers dependent on rank; military doctors to age 60)

ORGANISATIONS BY SERVICE

National Guard 12,000 (incl conscripts)
FORCES BY ROLE
SPECIAL FORCES
1 comd (regt) (1 SF bn)
MANOEUVRE
Armoured
1 armd bde (2 armd bn, 1 armd inf bn)
Mechanised
4 (1st, 2nd, 6th & 7th) mech bde
Light
1 (4th) lt inf bde
2 (2nd & 8th) lt inf regt
COMBAT SUPPORT
1 arty comd (8 arty bn)
COMBAT SERVICE SUPPORT
1 (3rd) spt bde
ISR UAV
1 sqn with *Aerostar*
EQUIPMENT BY TYPE
ARMOURED FIGHTING VEHICLES
MBT 134: 82 T-80U; 52 AMX-30B2
RECCE 72 EE-9 *Cascavel*
IFV 43 BMP-3
APC 295
  APC (T) 168 *Leonidas*
  APC (W) 127 VAB (incl variants)
AUV 8 BOV M16 *Milos*
ENGINEERING & MAINTENANCE VEHICLES
ARV 10: 2 AMX-30D; 8 BREM-80U
ANTI-TANK/ANTI-INFRASTRUCTURE
MSL • SP 37: 15 EE-3 *Jararaca* with Milan; 4 *Enok* with *Spike*-LR; 18 VAB with HOT
GUNS • TOWED 100mm 6 M-1944
ARTILLERY 412
SP 155mm 48: 24 NORA B-52; 12 Mk F3; 12 *Zuzana*
TOWED 60: 105mm 48 M-56; 155mm 12 TR-F-1
MRL 22: 122mm 4 BM-21; 128mm 18 M-63 *Plamen*
MOR 282: 81mm 170 E-44 (70+ M1/M9 in store); 120mm 112 RT61
UNINHABITED AERIAL VEHICLES
ISR • Medium 4 *Aerostar*
AIR DEFENCE
SAM 22+
  Medium-range 4 9K37M1 *Buk* M1-2 (RS-SA-11 *Gadfly*)
  Short-range 18: 12 *Aspide*; 6 9K331 *Tor*-M1 (RS-SA-15 *Gauntlet*)
  Point-defence *Mistral*
GUNS • TOWED 60: 20mm 36 M-55; 35mm 24 GDF-003 (with *Skyguard*)

Maritime Wing
FORCES BY ROLE
COMBAT SUPPORT
1 (coastal defence) AShM bty with MM40 *Exocet* AShM
EQUIPMENT BY TYPE
PATROL AND COASTAL COMBATANTS 7
  PCM 2:
   1 OPV 62 (ISR *Sa'ar* 4.5 derivative) with 1 twin *Simbad* lnchr with *Mistral* SAM
   1 *Alasia* (ex-OMN *Al Mabrukha*) with 1 twin *Simbad* lnchr with *Mistral* SAM, 1 hel landing platform
  PBF 4: 2 Rodman 55; 2 *Vittoria*

PB 1 *Ammachostos* (FIN)

COASTAL DEFENCE • AShM 3 MM40 *Exocet*

Air Wing
EQUIPMENT BY TYPE
HELICOPTERS • MRH 7: 3 AW139 (SAR); 4 SA342L1 *Gazelle* (armed)
AIR-LAUNCHED MISSILES • ASM HOT

Paramilitary 250

Maritime Police 250
EQUIPMENT BY TYPE
PATROL AND COASTAL COMBATANTS 13
   PBF 5: 1 *Odysseus* (ISR *Shaldag* II); 2 *Poseidon*; 2 *Vittoria*
   PB 3 *Kyrenia* (CRO Tehnomont 16m)
   PBI 5 SAB-12

DEPLOYMENT
LEBANON: UN • UNIFIL 2

FOREIGN FORCES
Argentina UNFICYP 333; 2 inf coy; 1 hel flt
Austria UNFICYP 3
Bangladesh UNFICYP 1
Brazil UNFICYP 2
Canada UNFICYP 1
Chile UNFICYP 6
Ghana UNFICYP 1
Greece Army: 950
Hungary UNFICYP 11
India UNFICYP 1
Mongolia UNFICYP 3
Pakistan UNFICYP 4
Russia UNFICYP 4
Serbia UNFICYP 10
Slovakia UNFICYP 240; 2 inf coy; 1 engr pl
United Kingdom 2,260; 2 inf bn; 1 hel sqn with 3 SA330 *Puma* HC2 • Operation Inherent Resolve (*Shader*) 500: 1 FGA sqn with 10 *Typhoon* FGR4; 1 A330 MRTT *Voyager* KC3; 2 A400M *Atlas* • UNFICYP (Operation Tosca) 251: 2 inf coy

NORTHERN CYPRUS

Data here represents the de facto situation on the northern section of the island. This does not imply international recognition as a sovereign state.

Capabilities

ACTIVE 3,000 (Army 3,000) **Gendarmerie & Paramilitary 150**

Conscript liability 15 months

RESERVE 15,000

Reserve liability to age 50

ORGANISATIONS BY SERVICE

Army ε3,000
FORCES BY ROLE
MANOEUVRE
  Light
    5 inf bn
    7 inf bn (reserve)
EQUIPMENT BY TYPE
ANTI-TANK/ANTI-INFRASTRUCTURE
  MSL • MANPATS *Milan*
  RCL • 106mm 36
ARTILLERY • MOR • 120mm 73

Gendarmerie & Paramilitary

Armed Police ε150
FORCES BY ROLE
SPECIAL FORCES
  1 (police) SF unit

Coast Guard
EQUIPMENT BY TYPE
PATROL AND COASTAL COMBATANTS 12
  PBF 8: 3 *Ares* 42; 3 *Ares* 35; 2 *Kaan* 15
  PB 4 Type 80
AMPHIBIOUS • LCM 2 LCM 8 (ex-TUR)

FOREIGN FORCES

TURKIYE

Army ε33,800
FORCES BY ROLE
1 corps HQ; 1 SF regt; 1 armd bde; 2 mech inf div; 1 mech inf regt; 1 arty regt; 1 avn comd
EQUIPMENT BY TYPE
ARMOURED FIGHTING VEHICLES
  MBT 287 M48A5T1
  IFV 145 ACV AIFV
  APC • APC (T) 488: 70 ACV AAPC (incl variants); 418 M113 (incl variants)
ANTI-TANK/ANTI-INFRASTRUCTURE
  MSL
    SP 66 ACV TOW
    MANPATS *Milan*
  RCL 106mm 219 M40A1
ARTILLERY 656
  SP 155mm 178: 30 M44T; 144 M52T1; 4 T-155 *Firtina*
  TOWED 84: **105mm** 36 M101A1; **155mm** 36 M114A2; **203mm** 12 M115
  MRL 122mm 18 T-122
  MOR 376: **81mm** 171; **107mm** 70 M30; **120mm** 135 HY-12

PATROL AND COASTAL COMBATANTS • PB 1
AIRCRAFT • TPT • Light 3 Cessna 185 (U-17)
HELICOPTERS • TPT 3: Medium 2 AS532UL *Cougar*
Light 1 Bell 205 (UH-1H *Iroquois*)
AIR DEFENCE
SAM Point-defence FIM-92 *Stinger*
GUNS • TOWED 150: **20mm** 122: 44 Rh 202; 78 GAI-D01; **35mm** 28 GDF-003

Czech Republic CZE

Czech Koruna CZK		2023	2024	2025
GDP	CZK	7.62trn	7.90trn	8.27trn
	USD	343bn	343bn	360bn
Real GDP growth	%	-0.1	1.1	2.3
Def exp [a]	CZK	101bn	160bn	
	USD	4.54bn	6.83bn	
Def bdgt [b]	CZK	112bn	151bn	154bn
	USD	5.04bn	6.56bn	6.72bn

[a] NATO figure
[b] Includes military pensions

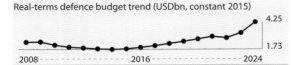
Real-terms defence budget trend (USDbn, constant 2015)

Population	10,837,890					
Age	0–14	15–19	20–24	25–29	30–64	65 plus
Male	8.0%	2.7%	2.4%	2.6%	25.0%	8.5%
Female	7.6%	2.6%	2.3%	2.4%	23.8%	12.0%

Capabilities

The Czech Republic published its latest security strategy in 2023. It identified NATO and EU membership as critical to its security and pointed to Russia and deteriorating international security as key threats to the country. It also raised issues around cyber and information operations. Military modernisation priorities include armoured fighting vehicles, artillery, rotary-wing and transport aviation, short-range air-defence systems and UAVs. Prague, in 2023, said it would buy F-35As to replace its leased *Gripen* fleet. The Czech Republic has signed a letter of intent with Germany to affiliate the 4th Czech Rapid Reaction Brigade with the 10th German Armoured Division under NATO's Framework Nations Concept. There are personnel shortfalls in specialised trades such as engineers and pilots. The armed forces can deploy on international crisis-management operations. The Czech Republic has plans to upgrade military training and simulation facilities. The defence-industrial base includes development and manufacturing capability, in particular small arms, vehicles, and training and light attack aircraft. The holding company Czechoslovak Group brings together several companies across the munitions, vehicles and aerospace sectors. The government has set up an agency to support the defence industry in government-to-government procurement activities.

ACTIVE 26,600 (Army 14,700 Air 5,850 Other 6,050)

ORGANISATIONS BY SERVICE

Army 14,700
FORCES BY ROLE
MANOEUVRE
 Reconnaissance
  1 ISR/EW regt (1 recce bn, 1 EW bn, 1 ISR UAV bn)
 Armoured
  1 (7th) mech bde (1 tk bn, 2 armd inf bn, 1 mot inf bn)
 Mechanised
  1 (4th) rapid reaction bde (2 mech inf bn, 1 mot inf bn)
 Airborne
  1 AB regt
COMBAT SUPPORT
 1 (13th) arty regt (2 arty bn)
 1 engr regt (2 engr bn, 1 EOD bn)
 1 CBRN regt (2 CBRN bn)
COMBAT SERVICE SUPPORT
 1 log regt (2 log bn, 1 maint bn)

Active Reserve
FORCES BY ROLE
COMMAND
 14 (territorial defence) comd
MANOEUVRE
 Armoured
  1 armd coy
 Light
  14 inf coy (1 per territorial comd) (3 inf pl, 1 cbt spt pl, 1 log pl)
EQUIPMENT BY TYPE
ARMOURED FIGHTING VEHICLES
 MBT 44: 14 *Leopard* 2A4; 30 T-72M4CZ
 RECCE 50: 34 BPzV *Svatava*; 8 *Pandur* II (KBV-PZ); 8 *Pandur* II (KBV-PZLOK)
 IFV 227: 120 BMP-2; 107 *Pandur* II (incl 17 CP, 14 comms, 4 amb)
 APC • PPV 62 *Titus*
 AUV 141: 21 *Dingo* 2; 120 IVECO LMV
ENGINEERING & MAINTENANCE VEHICLES
 AEV 4 *Pandur* II (KOT-Z)
 ARV 14+: 1 BPz-3 *Buffel*; 10 VPV-ARV (12 more in store); VT-55A; 3 VT-72M4
 VLB 6 MT-55A (3 more in store)
 MW *Bozena* 5; UOS-155 *Belarty*
NBC VEHICLES BRDM-2RCH
ANTI-TANK/ANTI-INFRASTRUCTURE
 MSL • MANPATS 9K111-1 *Konkurs* (RS-AT-5 *Spandrel*); FGM-148 *Javelin*; *Spike*-LR
 RCL 84mm *Carl Gustaf*
ARTILLERY 96
 SP 152mm 48 M-77 *Dana* (ε25 more in store)
 MOR 48: **81mm** *Expal*; **120mm** 40 M-1982; (45 more in

store); **SP 120mm** 8 SPM-85

UNINHABITED AERIAL VEHICLES
 ISR • **Light** Scan Eagle

Air Force 5,850

Principal task is to secure Czech airspace. This mission is fulfilled within NATO Integrated Extended Air Defence System (NATINADS) and, if necessary, by means of the Czech national reinforced air-defence system.

FORCES BY ROLE
FIGHTER/GROUND ATTACK
 1 sqn with Gripen C/D
 1 sqn with L-159 ALCA; L-159T1*
TRANSPORT
 2 sqn with A319CJ; C295M/MW; L-410FG/UVP-E Turbolet
TRAINING
 1 sqn with L-159 ALCA; L-159T1*; L-159T2*
ATTACK HELICOPTER
 1 sqn with AH-1Z Viper; Mi-35 Hind E
TRANSPORT HELICOPTER
 1 sqn with Mi-17 Hip H; Mi-171Sh; UH-1Y Venom
 1 sqn with Mi-17 Hip H; PZL W-3A Sokol
AIR DEFENCE
 1 (25th) SAM regt (2 AD gp)

EQUIPMENT BY TYPE
AIRCRAFT 38 combat capable
 FGA 14: 12 Gripen C; 2 Gripen D
 ATK 16 L-159 ALCA
 TPT 14: **Light** 12: 4 C295M; 2 C295MW; 2 L-410FG Turbolet; 4 L-410UVP-E Turbolet; **PAX** 2 A319CJ
 TRG 8: 5 L-159T1*; 3 L-159T2*
HELICOPTERS
 ATK 14: 4 AH-1Z Viper; 10 Mi-35 Hind E
 MRH 5 Mi-17 Hip H
 TPT 33: **Medium** 25: 15 Mi-171Sh; 10 PZL W3A Sokol; **Light** 8 UH-1Y Venom
AIR DEFENCE • SAM
 Short-range 8 2K12M2 Kub-M2 (RS-SA-6B Gainful)
 Point-defence 9K35 Strela-10 (RS-SA-13 Gopher); 9K32 Strela-2‡ (RS-SA-7 Grail) (available for trg RBS-70 gunners); RBS-70; RBS-70NG
AIR-LAUNCHED MISSILES
 AAM • IR AIM-9M Sidewinder; **ARH** AIM-120C-5/C-7 AMRAAM
BOMBS
 Laser-guided: GBU-12/-16 Paveway II

Other Forces 6,050

FORCES BY ROLE
SPECIAL FORCES
 1 SF gp
MANOEUVRE

Other
 1 (presidential) gd bde (2 bn)
 1 (honour guard) gd bn (2 coy)
COMBAT SUPPORT
 1 int gp
 1 (central) MP comd
 3 (regional) MP comd
 1 (protection service) MP comd

DEPLOYMENT

BOSNIA-HERZEGOVINA: EU • EUFOR (Operation Althea) 2
CENTRAL AFRICAN REPUBLIC: UN • MINUSCA 3
DEMOCRATIC REPUBLIC OF THE CONGO: UN • MONUSCO 2
EGYPT: MFO 18; 1 C295M
INDIA/PAKISTAN: UN • UNMOGIP 1
IRAQ: Operation Inherent Resolve 3; **NATO** • NATO Mission Iraq 5
KOSOVO: NATO • KFOR 35; **UN** • UNMIK 1
LATVIA: NATO • Forward Land Forces ε70; 1 EW unit; 1 SAM bty
LITHUANIA: NATO • Forward Land Forces 150; 1 SP arty bty
SLOVAKIA: NATO • Forward Land Forces 400; 1 mech inf coy
SYRIA/ISRAEL: UN • UNDOF 4

Denmark DNK

Danish Krone DKK		2023	2024	2025
GDP	DKK	2.80trn	2.84trn	2.96trn
	USD	407bn	412bn	431bn
Real GDP growth	%	2.5	1.9	1.6
Def exp [a]	DKK	56.1bn	68.7bn	
	USD	8.14bn	9.94bn	
Def bdgt [b]	DKK	36.8bn	37.8bn	56.6bn
	USD	5.35bn	5.48bn	8.23bn

[a] NATO figure
[b] Includes military pensions

Real-terms defence budget trend (USDbn, constant 2015)

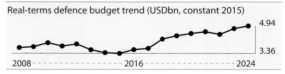

Population	5,973,136				
Age	0–14	15–19	20–24	25–29	30–64	65 plus
Male	8.3%	3.0%	3.1%	3.4%	22.4%	9.6%
Female	7.9%	2.8%	3.0%	3.3%	22.0%	11.2%

Capabilities

Denmark maintains compact but effective armed forces focused on contributing to NATO operations. Ties to NATO, Nordic Defence Cooperation (NORDEFCO) and regional neighbours have increased. In June 2022, the opt-out on Danish participation in EU defence cooperation under the CSDP ended after a referendum. The new defence agreement (2024–33) has been influenced by the changing threat environment. Copenhagen has prioritised the Baltic and the Arctic regions as well as efforts to receive and host allies that deploy to the country as reinforcements. In 2023, Denmark more closely integrated its air force with neighbours Finland, Norway and Sweden. Current defence modernisation priorities include F-35A procurements, new ocean patrol vessels, upgrading the mechanised brigades' armoured vehicles and the acquisition of short- and long-range air defence. Understaffing is among the challenges reportedly limiting operational capability. The armed forces are mostly professional, supplemented by a substantial number of conscripts. By 2033, the number of conscripts will be increased up to 7,500 annually and the national service period will be increased to 11 months. More operational use will be made of conscripts. The Danish armed forces have little ability to deploy independently but have contributed to larger multinational deployments. Denmark maintains a small defence industry focused on exports to Europe and North America. It is strong in defence electronics and the design and manufacture of components and subsystems. The government in 2023 pushed to restart ammunition production, and an ammunition factory is planned to be operational by 2027. Under NATO's DIANA initiative, Denmark hosts a quantum technology centre.

ACTIVE 13,100 (Army 5,700 Navy 2,250 Air 3,000 Joint 2,150)

Conscript liability 4–12 months, most voluntary

RESERVES 44,200 (Army 34,400 Navy 5,300 Air Force 4,500)

ORGANISATIONS BY SERVICE

Army 5,700

Div and a bde HQ transforming into operational formations

FORCES BY ROLE
COMMAND
  1 (MND-N) div HQ
MANOEUVRE
  Mechanised
  1 (1st) mech bde (1 ISR bn, 3 mech inf bn, 1 SP arty bn, 1 cbt engr bn, 1 sigs bn, 1 log bn)
  1 (2nd) mech bde (1 recce bn, 1 tk bn, 1 lt inf bn)
COMBAT SUPPORT
  1 CBRN/construction bn
  1 EOD bn
  1 int bn
  1 MP bn
  2 sigs bn
COMBAT SERVICE SUPPORT
  1 log bn
  1 maint bn
  1 spt bn
EQUIPMENT BY TYPE
ARMOURED FIGHTING VEHICLES
  MBT 44: 44 *Leopard* 2A7V
  IFV 44 CV9035 MkIII
  APC 390
    APC (W) 390: 81 *Piranha* III (incl variants); 309 *Piranha* V
  AUV 143: 84 *Eagle* IV; 59 *Eagle* V
ENGINEERING & MAINTENANCE VEHICLES
  ARV *Wisent*
  VLB 1+: BRP-1 *Biber*; 1 *Leguan*
ANTI-TANK/ANTI-INFRASTRUCTURE
  MSL • MANPATS *Spike*-LR2
  RCL 84mm *Carl Gustaf*
ARTILLERY 25
  SP 155mm 2 ATMOS 2000
  MRL 220mm 8 PULS
  MOR 15: **81mm** M252; **SP 120mm** 15 *Piranha* V with *Cardom*-10; (**120mm** 20 Soltam K6B1 in store)
AIR DEFENCE • SAM • Point-defence FIM-92 *Stinger*

Navy 2,250

Three naval squadrons, headquartered at naval bases in Frederikshavn and Korsør

EQUIPMENT BY TYPE
PRINCIPAL SURFACE COMBATANTS 5
  DESTROYERS • DDGHM 3 *Iver Huitfeldt* with 4 quad lnchr with RGM-84L *Harpoon* Block II AShM, 4 8-cell Mk 41 VLS (to be fitted with SM-2 SAM), 2 12-cell Mk 56 VLS with RIM-162B ESSM SAM, 2 twin 324mm TT with MU90 LWT, 1 *Millennium* CIWS, 2 76mm guns (*Peter Willemoes* 1 76mm gun) (capacity 1 AW101 *Merlin*/MH-60R *Seahawk* hel)
  FRIGATES • FFGHM 2 *Absalon* (flexible support ships) with 4 quad lnchr with RGM-84L *Harpoon* Block II AShM, 3 12-cell Mk 56 VLS with RIM-162B ESSM SAM, 2 twin 324mm TT with MU90 LWT, 2 *Millennium* CIWS, 1 127mm gun (capacity 2 AW101 *Merlin*/MH-60R *Seahawk* hel; 2 LCP, 7 MBT or 40 vehicles; 130 troops)
PATROL AND COASTAL COMBATANTS 12
  PSOH 4 *Thetis* 1 76mm gun (capacity 1 MH-60R *Seahawk*)
  PSO 3 *Knud Rasmussen* with 1 76mm gun, 1 hel landing platform (ice-strengthened hull)
  PCC 5 *Diana* (1 other non-operational)
MINE WARFARE • MINE COUNTERMEASURES 4
  MCI 4 MSF Mk I
LOGISTICS AND SUPPORT 12
  ABU 2 *Gunnar Thorson* (primarily used for marine pollution duties)
  AGS 2 *Holm*
  AKL 3: 1 *Sleipner* 2 *Seatruck*
  AXL 3: 2 *Holm*; 1 *Søløven* (DNK *Flyvefisken*)
  AXS 2 *Svanen*
UNINHABITED MARITIME PLATFORMS
  USV • MW • Medium 2 *Holm*
UNINHABITED MARITIME SYSTEMS
  UUV • MW *Double Eagle* Mk II/SAROV

84   THE MILITARY BALANCE 2025

UNINHABITED AERIAL VEHICLES
ISR • Light S-100 *Camcopter* (owned by European Maritime Safety Agency)

Air Force 3,000

Tactical Air Command
FORCES BY ROLE
FIGHTER/GROUND ATTACK
1 sqn with F-16AM/BM *Fighting Falcon*; F-35A *Lightning* II
1 sqn with F-16AM/BM *Fighting Falcon*
ANTI-SUBMARINE WARFARE
1 sqn with MH-60R *Seahawk*
SEARCH & RESCUE/TRANSPORT HELICOPTER
1 sqn with AW101 *Merlin*
1 sqn with AS550 *Fennec* (ISR)
TRANSPORT
1 sqn with C-130J-30 *Hercules*; CL-604 *Challenger* (MP/VIP)
TRAINING
1 unit with MFI-17 *Supporter* (T-17)
EQUIPMENT BY TYPE
AIRCRAFT 49 combat capable
FTR 39: 30 F-16AM *Fighting Falcon*; 9 F-16BM *Fighting Falcon*; (total of 30 F-16AM/BM operational)
FGA 10 F-35A *Lightning* II
TPT 8: **Medium** 4 C-130J-30 *Hercules*; **PAX** 4 CL-604 *Challenger* (MP/VIP)
TRG 27 MFI-17 *Supporter* (T-17)
HELICOPTERS
ASW 9 MH-60R *Seahawk*
SAR 8 AW101 *Merlin*
MRH 8 AS550 *Fennec* (ISR) (4 more non-operational)
TPT • **Medium** 6 AW101 *Merlin*
AIR-LAUNCHED MISSILES
AAM • IR AIM-9L *Sidewinder*; IIR AIM-9X *Sidewinder* II; ARH AIM-120B/C-7 AMRAAM
BOMBS
Laser-guided GBU-24 *Paveway* III
Laser & INS/GPS-guided EGBU-12 *Paveway* II
INS/GPS guided GBU-31 JDAM

Control and Air Defence Group
1 Control and Reporting Centre, 1 Mobile Control and Reporting Centre. 4 Radar sites

Special Operations Command
FORCES BY ROLE
SPECIAL FORCES
1 SF unit
1 diving unit
EQUIPMENT BY TYPE
ARMOURED FIGHTING VEHICLES
AUV 14 HMT-400

Reserves
Home Guard (Army) 34,400 reservists (to age 50)
2 (local) def region

Home Guard (Navy) 5,300 reservists (to age 50)
EQUIPMENT BY TYPE
PATROL AND COASTAL COMBATANTS 30
PB 30: 18 MHV800; 12 MHV900

Home Guard (Air Force) 4,500 reservists (to age 50)
EQUIPMENT BY TYPE
AIRCRAFT • TPT • **Light** 2 BN-2A *Islander*

DEPLOYMENT
BOSNIA-HERZEGOVINA: EU • EUFOR (*Operation Althea*) 1
IRAQ: NATO • NATO Mission Iraq 15
KOSOVO: NATO • KFOR 35
LATVIA: NATO • Forward Land Forces 800; 1 armd BG
MIDDLE EAST: UN • UNTSO 10
UNITED KINGDOM: *Operation Interflex* 130 (UKR trg)

Estonia EST

Euro EUR		2023	2024	2025
GDP	EUR	38.2bn	39.5bn	41.3bn
	USD	41.3bn	43.0bn	45.3bn
Real GDP growth	%	-3.0	-0.9	1.6
Def exp [a]	EUR	1.14bn	1.33bn	
	USD	1.24bn	1.44bn	
Def bdgt [b]	EUR	1.14bn	1.56bn	1.71bn
	USD	1.24bn	1.71bn	1.88bn
FMA (US)	USD	9.75m	9.75m	9.75m

[a] NATO figure
[b] Includes military pensions

Real-terms defence budget trend (USDm, constant 2015)

Population   1,193,791

Age	0–14	15–19	20–24	25–29	30–64	65 plus
Male	7.8%	2.9%	2.3%	2.2%	23.9%	8.1%
Female	7.4%	2.7%	2.1%	2.0%	24.0%	14.6%

Capabilities

Estonia's principal security concern is Russia. After February 2022, Estonia boosted defence spending and transferred military equipment to Ukraine, including ammunition, anti-armour systems and artillery. The defence ministry publishes medium-term development plans annually covering a four-year period. They are designed to ensure that the goals of a long-term National Defence

Development Plan (NDPP) are achieved within the planned timeframe. The NDPP for 2031, adopted in December 2021, focuses on improving territorial defence and indirect fire and anti-tank capabilities, as well as boosting maritime and surveillance systems. Estonia is procuring HIMARS rocket artillery systems, jointly procuring medium-range air defence systems with Latvia and short-range air defences with Poland. Estonia has joined the German-led European Sky Shield Initiative, to boost air defence capability across the region. Under the Baltic Defence Line Initiative, Estonia plans to build defensive fortifications along its eastern border. Modernisation spending is also intended to improve infrastructure and readiness. NATO in 2022 bolstered its battlegroup based in Estonia, present since mid-2017 as part of the Alliance's Forward Land Forces. The Amari air base hosts a NATO Air Policing detachment. Estonia is a member of the UK-led Joint Expeditionary Force. Tallinn also hosts NATO's Cooperative Cyber Defence Centre of Excellence. The country has limited capability to deploy abroad, though Estonian forces have taken part in EU, NATO and UN missions. There is a small defence industry with niche capabilities, including in robotics, ship repair and digital systems.

ACTIVE 7,100 (Army 3,750 Navy 450 Air 400 Other 2,500)

Conscript liability 8 or 11 months (depending on specialisation; conscripts cannot be deployed)

RESERVE 41,200 (Joint 20,000) Gendarmerie & Paramilitary 21,200

ORGANISATIONS BY SERVICE

Army 1,300; 2,450 conscript (total 3,750)

4 def region. All units except one inf bn are reserve based

FORCES BY ROLE
COMMAND
   1 div HQ
MANOEUVRE
   Mechanised
   1 (1st) mech bde (1 recce coy, 1 armd inf bn; 2 mech inf bn, 1 SP arty bn, 1 AT coy, 1 cbt engr bn, 1 spt bn, 1 AD bn)
   Light
   1 (2nd) inf bde (1 inf bn, 1 spt bn)
EQUIPMENT BY TYPE
ARMOURED FIGHTING VEHICLES
   IFV 44 CV9035EE (incl 2 CP)
   APC • APC (W) 136: 56 XA-180 *Sisu*; 80 XA-188 *Sisu*
ENGINEERING & MAINTENANCE VEHICLES
   AEV 2 Pionierpanzer 2 *Dachs*
   ARV 2 BPz-2
   VLB 2 *Biber*
ANTI-TANK/ANTI-INFRASTRUCTURE
   MSL • MANPATS FGM-148 *Javelin*; *Spike*-SR/-LR
   RCL 84mm *Carl Gustaf*; **90mm** PV-1110
ARTILLERY 180
   SP 155mm 18 K9 *Thunder*
   TOWED 122mm 36 D-30 (H 63)
   MOR 126: **81mm** 60 B455/NM 95/M252; **120mm** 66 2B11/M/41D
AIR DEFENCE
   SAM • Point-defence *Mistral*; *Piorun*
   GUNS • TOWED 23mm ZU-23-2

Reserve

Reserve units subordinate to 2nd inf bde and territorial defence

FORCES BY ROLE
MANOEUVRE
   Reconnaissance
   1 recce coy
   Light
   3 inf bn
   4 (territorial) inf bn
COMBAT SUPPORT
   1 arty bn
   1 AT coy
   1 cbt engr bn
AIR DEFENCE
   1 AD bn

Navy 300; 150 conscript (total 450)

EQUIPMENT BY TYPE
PATROL AND COASTAL COMBATANTS 4
   PCO 1 *Kindral Kurvits* (FIN *Tursas* derivative)
   PB 3: 1 *Pikker*; 1 *Roju* (Baltic 4500WP); 1 *Valve*
MINE WARFARE • MINE COUNTERMEASURES 4:
   MCCS 1 *Tasuja* (ex-DNK *Lindormen*)
   MHC 3 *Admiral Cowan* (ex-UK *Sandown*)
UNINHABITED MARITIME SYSTEMS • UUV
   DATA REMUS 100
   MW A9-M; *Seafox*
COASTAL DEFENCE
   AShM *Blue Spear*

Air Force 400

FORCES BY ROLE
TRANSPORT
   1 sqn with M-28 *Skytruck*
TRANSPORT HELICOPTER
   1 sqn with R-44 *Raven* II
EQUIPMENT BY TYPE
AIRCRAFT
   TPT • Light 2 M-28 *Skytruck*
   TRG 1+ L-39C *Albatros* (leased)
HELICOPTERS • TPT • Light 2 R-44 *Raven* II

Other 1,600; 900 conscript (total 2,500)

Includes Cyber Command, Support Command and Special Operations Forces

FORCES BY ROLE
SPECIAL FORCES
   1 spec ops bn
COMBAT SUPPORT

2 MP coy
1 sigs bn
COMBAT SERVICE SUPPORT
1 log bn

Gendarmerie & Paramilitary

Defence League 21,200 reservists

Subordinate to the Ministry of the Defence. Totals include affiliated Women's Voluntary Defence Organization.

DEPLOYMENT

IRAQ: *Operation Inherent Resolve* 88 • NATO Mission Iraq 1
LEBANON: UN • UNIFIL 1
MIDDLE EAST: UN • UNTSO 1
MOZAMBIQUE: EU • EUMAM Mozambique 1
UNITED KINGDOM: *Operation Interflex* 30 (UKR trg)

FOREIGN FORCES

All NATO Forward Land Forces unless stated
France 350; 1 lt armd pl; 1 inf coy
Spain 150; 1 SAM bty with NASAMS
United Kingdom 1,000; 1 armd BG; 1 SP arty bty; 1 MRL bty; 1 cbt engr coy
United States US European Command: 700; 1 inf bn

Finland FIN

Euro EUR		2023	2024	2025
GDP	EUR	273bn	281bn	292bn
	USD	296bn	306bn	320bn
Real GDP growth	%	-1.2	-0.2	2.0
Def exp [a]	EUR	5.79bn	6.78bn	
	USD	6.27bn	7.31bn	
Def bdgt [b]	EUR	6.49bn	6.32bn	6.81bn
	USD	7.02bn	6.89bn	7.47bn

[a] NATO figure
[b] Includes military pensions

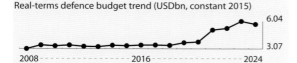
Real-terms defence budget trend (USDbn, constant 2015)

Population		5,626,414				
Age	0–14	15–19	20–24	25–29	30–64	65 plus
Male	8.3%	2.8%	2.8%	3.0%	22.1%	10.4%
Female	7.9%	2.7%	2.6%	2.8%	21.5%	13.1%

Capabilities

Finland's armed forces are primarily focused on defence against Russia. Finland's national security posture has significantly evolved in recent years, spurred by Moscow's full-scale invasion of Ukraine in 2022. Finland's security policy changes culminated in NATO membership in April 2023. Work that same year began on a new defence report to succeed the last version of 2021. The government that took office in Finland in 2023 stated in a policy document that 'Russia's foreign and security policy is irreconcilable with European stability and security'. Finland has been a participant in key multilateral defence relationships, including NORDEFCO, the Northern Group and the Joint Expeditionary Force, and has joined the European Sky Shield Initiative. Integration into NATO structures and exercises is proceeding, and discussions are proceeding on the establishment of a NATO Multi Corps Land Component Command and on the presence of forward land forces in Finland. In 2022, Finland signed a mutual-security agreement with the UK and a Defence Cooperation Agreement with the US entered into force in September 2024. The country contributes to UN peacekeeping missions and to NATO operations. Finland maintains a well-trained military, supported by reserves. The country has emphasised security resilience, including maintaining stockpiles of ammunition. It is modernising equipment, including combat aircraft and air-launched weapons and naval vessels. Finland's defence industry consists largely of privately owned SMEs, concentrating on niche products for international markets, but it also features some internationally competitive larger companies, including Patria which is mostly owned by the Finnish state.

ACTIVE 23,850 (Army 17,400 Navy 3,150 Air 3,300)
Gendarmerie & Paramilitary 2,900

Conscript liability 165, 255 or 347 days (latter for NCOs, officers or those on 'especially demanding' duties)

RESERVE 233,000 (Army 180,000 Navy 24,000 Air 29,000) **Gendarmerie & Paramilitary 12,000**

18,000 reservists a year conduct refresher training: total obligation 80 days (150 for NCOs, 200 for officers) between conscript service and age 50 (NCOs and officers to age 60)

ORGANISATIONS BY SERVICE

Army 4,400; 13,000 conscript (total 17,400)
FORCES BY ROLE

Finland's army maintains a mobilisation strength of about 285,000. In support of this requirement, two conscription cycles, each for about 9,000 conscripts, take place each year. After conscript training, reservist commitment is to the age of 60. Reservists are usually assigned to units within their local geographical area. All service appointments or deployments outside Finnish borders are voluntary for all members of the armed services. All brigades are reserve based

Reserve Organisations 180,000
FORCES BY ROLE
SPECIAL FORCES
  1 SF regt (1 SF bn, 1 tpt hel bn, 1 spt coy)
MANOEUVRE
  Armoured
  2 armd BG (regt)
  Mechanised
  2 (Karelia & Pori Jaeger) mech bde

Light
3 (Jaeger) bde
6 lt inf bde

COMBAT SUPPORT
1 arty bde
1 AD regt
7 engr regt
3 sigs bn

COMBAT SERVICE SUPPORT
3 log regt

EQUIPMENT BY TYPE

ARMOURED FIGHTING VEHICLES
MBT 200: 100 *Leopard* 2A4; 100 *Leopard* 2A6
IFV 212: 110 BMP-2MD; 102 CV9030FIN
APC 1,085
  APC (T) 320 MT-LBu/MT-LBV
  APC (W) 765: 464 XA-180/185 *Sisu*; 101 XA-202 *Sisu* (CP); 48 XA-203 *Sisu*; 90 XA-300; 62 AMV (XA-360)
AUV 44 SISU GTP (incl variants)

ENGINEERING & MAINTENANCE VEHICLES
AEV 5 *Dachs*
ARV 36: 9 BPz-2; 15 MTP-LB; 12 VT-55A
VLB 32: 12 BLG-60M2; 10 *Leopard* 2L AVLB; 10 SISU *Leguan*
MW 3+: *Aardvark* Mk 2; KMT T-55; 3 *Leopard* 2R CEV; RA-140 DS

ANTI-TANK/ANTI-INFRASTRUCTURE
MSL • MANPATS NLAW; *Spike*-MR; *Spike*-LR

ARTILLERY 1,543
SP 122: **122mm** 74 2S1 *Gvozdika* (PsH 74); **155mm** 48 K9 *Thunder*
TOWED 630: **122mm** 474 D-30 (H 63); **152mm** 24 2A36 *Giatsint*-B (K 89); **155mm** 132 K 83/GH-52 (K 98)
MRL 75: **122mm** 34 RM-70; **227mm** 41 M270 MLRS
MOR 716+: **81mm** Krh/71; **120mm** 698 Krh/92; **SP 120mm** 18 XA-361 AMOS

HELICOPTERS
MRH 7: 5 Hughes 500D; 2 Hughes 500E
TPT • Medium 20 NH90 TTH

UNINHABITED AERIAL VEHICLES
ISR • Medium 11 ADS-95 *Ranger*

AIR DEFENCE
SAM 60+
  Short-range 44: 20 *Crotale* NG (ITO 90); 24 NASAMS II FIN (ITO 12)
  Point-defence 16+: 16 ASRAD (ITO 05); FIM-92 *Stinger* (ITO 15); RBS 70 (ITO 05/05M)
GUNS 407+: **23mm** ItK 95/ZU-23-2 (ItK 61); **35mm** GDF-005 (ItK 88); **SP 35mm** 7 *Leopard* 2 ITK *Marksman*

Navy 1,400; 1,750 conscript (total 3,150)

Naval Command HQ located at Turku

EQUIPMENT BY TYPE

PATROL AND COASTAL COMBATANTS 20
PCGM 4 *Hamina* with 2 twin lnchr with *Gabriel* V (PTO2020) AShM, 1 8-cell VLS with *Umkhonto*-IR (ITO2004) SAM; 1 single 400mm ASTT with Torped 45/47 LWT
PBG 4 *Rauma* with 6 single lnchr with RBS15 Mk3 (MTO-85M) AShM
PBF 12 *Jehu* (U-700) (capacity 24 troops)

MINE WARFARE 8
  MINE COUNTERMEASURES 3
    MCC 3 *Katanpää* (ITA *Gaeta* mod)
  MINELAYERS • ML 5:
    2 *Hameenmaa* with 1 8-cell VLS with *Umkhonto*-IR (ITO2004) SAM, 2 RBU 1200 *Uragan* A/S mor, 1 57mm gun (can carry up to 120 mines)
    3 *Pansio* with 50 mines

AMPHIBIOUS • LANDING CRAFT 59
LCVP ε9 *Utö*
LCP 50+

LOGISTICS AND SUPPORT 6
AG 3: 1 *Louhi*; 2 *Hylje*
AXL 3 *Fabian Wrede*

UNINHABITED MARITIME SYSTEMS • UUV
DATA REMUS 100
MW *Double Eagle* Mk II; *Seafox* I
UTL HUGIN 1000

Coastal Defence

FORCES BY ROLE
MANOEUVRE
Amphibious
1 mne bde
COMBAT SUPPORT
1 cbt spt bde (1 AShM bty)

EQUIPMENT BY TYPE
COASTAL DEFENCE
  AShM 4 RBS15K
  ARTY • 130mm 30 K-53tk (static)
ANTI-TANK/ANTI-INFRASTRUCTURE
  MSL • MANPATS *Spike* (used in AShM role)

Air Force 2,000; 1,300 conscript (total 3,300)

3 Air Comds: Satakunta (West), Karelia (East), Lapland (North)

FORCES BY ROLE

FIGHTER/GROUND ATTACK
2 sqn with F/A-18C/D *Hornet*
ISR
1 (survey) sqn with Learjet 35A
TRANSPORT
1 flt with C295M
1 (liaison) flt with PC-12NG
TRAINING
1 sqn with *Hawk* Mk50/51A/66*
1 unit with G-115EA

EQUIPMENT BY TYPE

AIRCRAFT 89 combat capable

FGA 62: 55 F/A-18C *Hornet*; 7 F/A-18D *Hornet*

ELINT 1 C295M

ISR 3 Learjet 35A (survey; ECM trg; tgt-tow)

TPT • Light 8: 2 C295M; 6 PC-12NG

TRG 55: 28 G-115EA; 11 *Hawk* Mk50/51A*; 16 *Hawk* Mk66*

AIR-LAUNCHED MISSILES

AAM • IR AIM-9 *Sidewinder*; **IIR** AIM-9X *Sidewinder*
ARH AIM-120C AMRAAM
LACM • Conventional AGM-158 JASSM

BOMBS

INS/GPS-guided AGM-154C JSOW; GBU-31/-38 JDAM;

Gendarmerie & Paramilitary

Border Guard 2,900

Ministry of Interior. 4 Border Guard Districts and 2 Coast Guard Districts

FORCES BY ROLE

MARITIME PATROL

1 sqn with AS332 *Super Puma*; AW119KE *Koala*; Bell 412EP (AB-412EP) *Twin Huey*; Do-228

EQUIPMENT BY TYPE

PATROL AND COASTAL COMBATANTS 58
  PSO 1 *Turva* with 1 hel landing platform
  PCC 2 *Tursas*
  PB 55

AMPHIBIOUS • LANDING CRAFT 4
  UCAC 4

AIRCRAFT • TPT • Light 2 Do-228

HELICOPTERS
  MRH 2 Bell 412EP (AB-412EP) *Twin Huey*
  TPT 9: **Medium** 5 AS332 *Super Puma*; **Light** 4 AW119KE *Koala*

Reserve 12,000 reservists on mobilisation

DEPLOYMENT

IRAQ: *Operation Inherent Resolve* 70; 1 trg team; **NATO •** NATO Mission Iraq 4

KOSOVO: NATO • KFOR 70

LEBANON: UN • UNIFIL 163; 1 mech inf coy

MIDDLE EAST: UN • UNTSO 16

MOZAMBIQUE: EU • EUMAM Mozambique 5

SOMALIA: EU • EUTM Somalia 12

UNITED KINGDOM: *Operation Interflex* 20 (UKR trg)

France FRA

Euro EUR		2023	2024	2025
GDP	EUR	2.82trn	2.91trn	2.99trn
	USD	3.05trn	3.17trn	3.28trn
Real GDP growth	%	1.1	1.1	1.1
Def exp [a]	EUR	54.9bn	59.6bn	
	USD	59.4bn	64.3bn	
Def bdgt [b]	EUR	55.1bn	58.8bn	62.0bn
	USD	59.6bn	64.0bn	68.0bn

[a] NATO figure
[b] Includes pensions

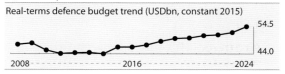

Real-terms defence budget trend (USDbn, constant 2015)

Population	68,374,591				
Age	0–14	15–19	20–24	25–29	30–64	65 plus
Male	8.9%	3.1%	3.1%	2.9%	21.4%	9.7%
Female	8.5%	3.0%	2.9%	2.8%	21.4%	12.3%

Capabilities

France published a National Strategic Review in November 2022, which highlighted the deteriorating security environment, the need to strengthen resilience and the importance of NATO and European strategic autonomy. France plays a leading military role in the EU, NATO and the UN, and maintains globally deployed forces. It is also modernising its nuclear forces and expanding capabilities in non-traditional domains. In 2023, Paris issued a new Military Programming Law (LPM) and increased defence spending. The LPM reflects Russia's 2022 invasion of Ukraine and greater doctrinal emphasis on high-intensity warfare. It increases investment in combat-support capabilities, maintenance, combat training and readiness. The operational reserve should double in size, with higher combat readiness. Incentives are being explored to boost retention, and from 2025 the compulsory 'defence and citizens' day will include a military component. After reorganising armoured and mechanised brigades into two divisions, initially as headquarters formations, France is now filling out these divisional structures. New 'Alpha' commands were created. France aims to be able to deploy a complete division within a NATO framework. As shown by the *Orion* 2023 exercise, France faces challenges in scaling Combat Service Support to the requirements of high-intensity warfare. There is demonstrated capacity to support expeditionary forces, although some strategic and intra-theatre military air-transport requirements have relied on allies and external contractors. Coups and policy decisions led France to reorganise its presence in the Sahel and to reduce its foreign deployments, with mostly training forces or contributions to multinational coalitions. France has a sophisticated multi-domain defence industry, and most procurements are with domestic companies.

ACTIVE 202,200 (Army 113,800 Navy 34,700 Air 38,500, Other Staffs 15,200) Gendarmerie & Paramilitary 95,100

RESERVE 38,500 (Army 22,550 Navy 5,400 Air

5,700 Other Staffs 4,850) Gendarmerie & Paramilitary 31,500

ORGANISATIONS BY SERVICE

Strategic Nuclear Forces

Navy 2,200
EQUIPMENT BY TYPE
SUBMARINES • STRATEGIC 4
  SSBN 4 *Le Triomphant* with 16 M51 SLBM with 6 TN-75 nuclear warheads, 4 single 533mm TT with SM39 *Exocet* AShM/F17 mod 2 HWT
AIRCRAFT • FGA 20 *Rafale* M F3-R with ASMPA msl

Air Force 1,800

Air Strategic Forces Command
FORCES BY ROLE
STRIKE
  2 sqn with *Rafale* B F3-R with ASMPA msl
TANKER
  3 sqn with A330 MRTT; KC-135 *Stratotanker*
EQUIPMENT BY TYPE
AIRCRAFT 20 combat capable
  FGA 20 *Rafale* B F3-R
  TKR/TPT 12 A330 MRTT
  TKR 3 KC-135 *Stratotanker*

Paramilitary

Gendarmerie 40

Space
EQUIPMENT BY TYPE
SATELLITES 14
  COMMUNICATIONS 5: 2 *Syracuse*-3 (designed to integrate with UK *Skynet* & ITA *Sicral*); 2 *Syracuse*-4; 1 *Athena-Fidus* (also used by ITA)
  ISR 6: 1 CSO-1; 1 CSO-2; 1 *Helios* 2A; 1 *Helios* 2B; 2 *Pleiades*
  ELINT/SIGINT 3 CERES

Army 113,800
Regt and BG normally bn size
FORCES BY ROLE
COMMAND
  1 corps HQ (CRR-FR)
MANOEUVRE
  Mechanised
  1 (1st) mech div (1 (7th) armd bde (1 tk regt, 1 armd BG, 3 armd inf regt, 1 SP arty regt, 1 engr regt), 1 (27th) mtn bde (1 armd cav regt, 3 mtn inf regt, 1 arty regt, 1 engr regt), 1 (9th) amph bde (2 armd cav regt, 1 armd inf regt, 2 mech inf regt, 1 SP arty regt, 1 engr regt))
  1 (3rd) mech div (1 (2nd) armd bde (2 tk regt, 1 armd BG(-), 3 armd inf regt, 1 SP arty regt, 1 engr regt), 1 (6th) lt armd bde (2 armd cav regt, 1 armd inf regt, 1 mech inf regt, 1 mech inf regt, 1 SP arty regt, 1 engr regt), 1 (11th) AB bde (1 armd cav regt, 4 para regt, 1 arty regt, 1 engr regt, 1 spt regt))
  1 (FRA/GER) mech bde (1 armd cav regt, 1 mech inf regt)
  1 mech regt HQ (Djibouti)
  Light
  3 inf regt (French Guiana & French West Indies)
  1 inf regt HQ (New Caledonia)
  2 inf bn HQ (Côte d'Ivoire & Gabon)
  Air Manoeuvre
  1 AB regt (La Réunion)
  Other
  4 SMA regt (French Guiana, French West Indies & Indian Ocean)
  3 SMA coy (French Polynesia, Indian Ocean & New Caledonia)
COMBAT SUPPORT
  1 cbt spt div (1 arty bde (1 MRL regt, 1 SAM regt, 1 ISR UAV regt), 1 cyber bde (1 recce regt, 2 EW regt), 1 hel bde (3 hel regt, 1 maint regt))
  1 cyber div (1 cyber bde)
  5 sigs regt
COMBAT SERVICE SUPPORT
  1 spt div (1 engr bde (2 cbt engr regt, 1 EOD bn, 1 geo engr bn, 1 CBRN regt), 1 maint bde (2 maint regt, 4 maint bn), 1 log bde (1 log regt, 5 tpt regt, 1 tpt bn, 1 med regt))

Special Operation Forces 2,200
FORCES BY ROLE
SPECIAL FORCES
  1 SF div (2 SF regt, 1 hel regt)

Reserves 22,550 reservists
Reservists form 79 UIR (Reserve Intervention Units) of about 75 to 152 troops, for 'Proterre' – combined land projection forces bn, and 23 USR (Reserve Specialised Units) of about 160 troops, in specialised regt
EQUIPMENT BY TYPE
ARMOURED FIGHTING VEHICLES
  MBT 200: 166 *Leclerc*; 34 *Leclerc* XLR
  ASLT 192 AMX-10RC
  RECCE 139: 99 EBRC *Jaguar*; 40 ERC-90D *Sagaie*
  IFV 622: 515 VBCI VCI; 107 VBCI VPC (CP)
  APC 2,557
    APC (T) 49 BvS-10
    APC (W) 2,488: 737 VBMR *Griffon*; 11 *Griffon* VOA (OP); ε1,700 VAB: 40 VAB VOA (OP)
    PPV 20 *Aravis*
  AUV 1,677: 1,134 VBL/VB2L; 251 VBL Ultima; 292 VBMR-L *Serval*
ENGINEERING & MAINTENANCE VEHICLES
  AEV 110: 38 AMX-30EBG; 72 VAB GE
  ARV 44: 27 AMX-30D; 17 *Leclerc* DNG; VAB-EHC

VLB 48: 20 EFA; 18 PTA; 10 SPRAT
MW 16+: AMX-30B/B2; 4 *Buffalo*; 12 *Minotaur*
NBC VEHICLES 26 VAB NRBC
ANTI-TANK/ANTI-INFRASTRUCTURE • MSL
  SP 177: 64 VAB *Milan*; 113 VAB with *Akeron*
  MANPATS *Akeron*; *Eryx*; FGM-148 *Javelin*; *Milan*
ARTILLERY 245+
  SP 155mm 92: 32 AU-F-1; 60 CAESAR
  TOWED 155mm 12 TR-F-1
  MRL 227mm 9 M270 MLRS
  MOR 132+: **81mm** LLR 81mm; **120mm** 132 RT-F-1
AIRCRAFT • TPT • Light 13: 5 PC-6B *Turbo Porter*; 5 TBM-700; 3 TBM-700B
HELICOPTERS
  ATK 67: 17 *Tiger* HAP (to be upgraded to HAD); 50 *Tiger* HAD
  MRH 104: 18 AS555UN *Fennec*; 86 SA341F/342M *Gazelle* (all variants)
  TPT 172: **Heavy** 8 H225M *Caracal* (CSAR); **Medium** 129: 24 AS532UL *Cougar*; 2 EC225LP *Super Puma*; 57 NH90 TTH; 46 SA330 *Puma*; **Light** 35 H120 *Colibri* (leased)
AIR DEFENCE • SAM
  Short-range ε6 VL MICA
  Point-defence *Mistral*
AIR-LAUNCHED MISSILES
  ASM AGM-114 *Hellfire* II; HOT

Navy 34,700
EQUIPMENT BY TYPE
SUBMARINES 9
  STRATEGIC • SSBN 4 *Le Triomphant* opcon Strategic Nuclear Forces with 16 M51 SLBM with 6 TN-75 nuclear warheads, 4 single 533mm TT with SM39 *Exocet* AShM/F17 mod 2 HWT
  TACTICAL • SSN 5
    2 *Rubis* with 4 single 533mm TT with SM39 *Exocet* AShM/F17 mod 2 HWT
    1 *Rubis* with 4 single 533mm TT with SM39 *Exocet* AShM/F17 mod 2 HWT/*Artémis* (F-21) HWT
    2 *Suffren* with 4 single 533mm TT with MdCN (SCALP Naval) LACM/SM39 *Exocet* AShM/*Artémis* (F-21) HWT
PRINCIPAL SURFACE COMBATANTS 22
  AIRCRAFT CARRIERS • CVN 1 *Charles de Gaulle* with 4 8-cell *Sylver* A43 VLS with *Aster* 15 SAM, 2 sextuple *Sadral* lnchr with *Mistral* SAM (capacity 30 *Rafale* M FGA ac, 2 E-2C *Hawkeye* AEW&C ac, 8 AS365 *Dauphin*/NH90 NFH hel)
  DESTROYERS • DDGHM 4:
    2 *Aquitaine* (FREMM FREDA) with 2 quad lnchr with MM40 *Exocet* Block 3 AShM, 4 8-cell *Sylver* A50 VLS with *Aster* 15 SAM/*Aster* 30 SAM, 2 twin 324mm B-515 ASTT with MU90 LWT, 1 76mm gun (capacity 1 NH90 NFH hel)
    2 *Forbin* with 2 quad lnchr with MM40 *Exocet* Block 3 AShM, 4 8-cell *Sylver* A50 VLS with *Aster* 30 SAM, 2 8-cell *Sylver* A50 VLS with *Aster* 15 SAM, 2 twin 324mm ASTT with MU90 LWT, 2 76mm gun (capacity 1 NH90 NFH hel)
  FRIGATES 17
    FFGHM 11:
      4 *Aquitaine* (FREMM ASM) with 2 8-cell *Sylver* A70 VLS with MdCN (SCALP Naval) LACM, 2 quad lnchr with MM40 *Exocet* Block 3 AShM, 2 8-cell *Sylver* A43 VLS with *Aster* 15 SAM, 2 twin 324mm B-515 ASTT with MU90 LWT, 1 76mm gun (capacity 1 NH90 NFH hel)
      2 *Aquitaine* (FREMM ASM) with 2 8-cell *Sylver* A70 VLS with MdCN (SCALP Naval) LACM, 2 quad lnchr with MM40 *Exocet* Block 3 AShM, 2 8-cell *Sylver* A50 VLS with *Aster* 15 SAM/*Aster* 30 SAM, 2 twin 324mm B-515 ASTT with MU90 LWT, 1 76mm gun (capacity 1 NH90 NFH hel)
      2 *La Fayette* with 2 quad lnchr with MM40 *Exocet* Block 3 AShM, 2 twin *Simbad* lnchr with *Mistral* SAM, 1 octuple lnchr with *Crotale* SAM, 1 100mm gun (capacity 1 AS565SA *Panther* hel)
      3 *La Fayette* with 2 quad lnchr with MM40 *Exocet* Block 3 AShM, 2 sextuple *Sadral* lnchr with *Mistral* 3 SAM, 1 100mm gun (capacity 1 AS565SA *Panther* hel)
    FFH 6 *Floreal* with 1 100mm gun (fitted for but not with 1 twin *Simbad* lnchr with *Mistral* SAM) (capacity 1 AS565SA *Panther* hel)
PATROL AND COASTAL COMBATANTS 22
  FSM 5 *D'Estienne d'Orves* with 1 twin *Simbad* lnchr with *Mistral* SAM, 1 100mm gun
  PSO 4 *d'Entrecasteaux* (BSAOM) with 1 hel landing platform
  PCO 8: 2 *Auguste Benebig* (POM); 3 *La Confiance*, 1 *Lapérouse*; 1 *Le Malin*; 1 *Fulmar*
  PCC 3 *Flamant*
  PBF 2 *Bir Hakeim* (VFM)
MINE WARFARE • MINE COUNTERMEASURES 16
  MCD 5: 1 *Ophrys* (VSP); 4 *Vulcain*
  MHC 3 *Antarès*
  MHO 8 *Éridan*
AMPHIBIOUS
  PRINCIPAL AMPHIBIOUS SHIPS 3
    LHD 3 *Mistral* with 2 twin *Simbad* lnchr with *Mistral* SAM (capacity up to 16 NH90/SA330 *Puma*/AS532 *Cougar*/*Tiger* hel; 2 LCT or 4 LCM/LCU; 13 MBTs; 50 AFVs; 450 troops)
  LANDING CRAFT 25
    LCU 6 *Arbalète* (EDA-S) (capacity 1 *Leclerc* MBT or 2 *Griffon*/*Jaguar*)
    LCT 4 EDA-R (capacity 2 *Leclerc* MBT or 6 VAB)
    LCM 5 CTM (capacity 2 APC)
    LCVP 10
LOGISTICS AND SUPPORT 35
  ABU 1 *Telenn Mor*
  AG 3: 1 *Alize* (BSP) with 1 hel landing platform;

1 Caouanne (ERF); 1 *Chamois*
AGB 1 *Astrolabe* with 1 hel landing platform
AGE 1 *Thetis* (*Lapérouse* mod) (used as trials ships for mines and divers)
AGI 1 *Dupuy de Lome* with 1 hel landing platform
AGM 1 *Monge* (capacity 2 med hels)
AGOR 2: 1 *Pourquoi pas?* (used 150 days per year by Ministry of Defence; operated by Ministry of Research and Education otherwise); 1 *Beautemps-Beaupre*
AGS 3 *Lapérouse*
AORH 2: 1 *Durance* with 3 twin *Simbad* lnchr with *Mistral* SAM (capacity 1 SA319 *Alouette* III/AS365 *Dauphin*/*Lynx*); 1 *Jacques Chevallier* (BRF) with 2 twin *Simbad* lnchr with *Mistral* SAM (capacity 1 AS365 *Dauphin*/H160)
ARS 4 *Loire* (BSAM)
AXL 12: 2 *Glycine*; 1 *Jules* with 1 hel landing platform; 8 *Léopard*; 1 *Palyvestre* (VSMP mod)
AXS 4: 2 *La Belle Poule*; 1 *La Grand Hermine*; 1 *Mutin*
UNINHABITED MARITIME PLATFORMS
USV • MW • Medium 1 *Artemis*
UNINHABITED MARITIME SYSTEMS • UUV
DATA A18D; *Victor* 6000
MW A9-M; *Double Eagle* Mk II; PAP

Naval Aviation 6,500
FORCES BY ROLE
STRIKE/FIGHTER/GROUND ATTACK
3 sqn with *Rafale* M F3-R
ANTI-SURFACE WARFARE
1 sqn with AS565SA *Panther*
ANTI-SUBMARINE WARFARE
2 sqn with NH90 NFH
MARITIME PATROL
2 sqn with *Atlantique* 2
1 sqn with *Falcon* 20H *Gardian*
1 sqn with *Falcon* 50MI
AIRBORNE EARLY WARNING & CONTROL
1 sqn with E-2C *Hawkeye*
SEARCH & RESCUE
1 sqn with AS365F/N *Dauphin* 2
TRAINING
1 sqn with AS365F/N *Dauphin* 2
1 sqn with EMB 121 *Xingu*
1 unit with *Falcon* 10MER
1 unit with CAP 10M
1 unit with H160B
EQUIPMENT BY TYPE
AIRCRAFT 60 combat capable
FGA 42 *Rafale* M F3-R
ASW 18: 11 *Atlantique*-2 (standard 6); 7 *Atlantique*-2 (being upgraded to standard 6)
AEW&C 3 E-2C *Hawkeye*
SAR 4 *Falcon* 50MS
TPT 25: **Light** 10 EMB-121 *Xingu*; **PAX** 15: 6 *Falcon* 10MER; 5 *Falcon* 20H *Gardian*; 4 *Falcon* 50MI

TRG 5 CAP 10M
HELICOPTERS
ASW 27 NH90 NFH
MRH 33: 3 AS365F *Dauphin* 2; 6 AS365N *Dauphin* 2; 2 AS365N3; 16 AS565SA *Panther*; 6 H160B (leased)
UNINHABITED AERIAL VEHICLES
ISR • Light 4 S-100 *Camcopter*
AIR-LAUNCHED MISSILES
AAM • IIR *Mica* IR; **ARH** *Mica* RF
AShM AM39 *Exocet*
LACM • Nuclear ASMPA
BOMBS
Laser-guided: GBU-12/16 *Paveway* II
INS/GPS-guided AASM *Hammer* 250

Marines 2,400

Commando Units 700
FORCES BY ROLE
MANOEUVRE
Reconnaissance
1 recce gp
Amphibious
2 aslt gp
1 atk swimmer gp
1 raiding gp
COMBAT SUPPORT
1 cbt spt gp
COMBAT SERVICE SUPPORT
1 spt gp

Fusiliers-Marin 1,700
FORCES BY ROLE
MANOEUVRE
Other
2 sy gp
7 sy coy

Reserves 4,900 reservists

Air and Space Force 38,500
FORCES BY ROLE
STRIKE
2 sqn with *Rafale* B F3-R with ASMPA msl
SPACE
1 (satellite obs) sqn
FIGHTER
1 sqn with *Mirage* 2000-5
1 sqn with *Mirage* 2000B
FIGHTER/GROUND ATTACK
3 sqn with *Mirage* 2000D
1 (composite) sqn with *Mirage* 2000-5/D (Djibouti)
3 sqn with *Rafale* B/C F3-R
1 sqn with *Rafale* B/C F3-R (UAE)
ISR
1 sqn with Beech 350ER *King Air*

AIRBORNE EARLY WARNING & CONTROL
1 (Surveillance & Control) sqn with E-3F *Sentry*

SEARCH & RESCUE/TRANSPORT
5 sqn with AS555 *Fennec*; CN235M; SA330 *Puma* (Djibouti, French Guiana, French Polynesia, Indian Ocean & New Caledonia)

TANKER/TRANSPORT
2 sqn with A330; A330 MRTT
1 sqn with KC-135 *Stratotanker*

TRANSPORT
2 sqn with A400M
1 sqn with C-130H/H-30/J-30 *Hercules*; KC-130J *Hercules*
1 sqn (joint FRA-GER) with C-130J-30 *Hercules*; KC-130J *Hercules*
2 sqn with CN235M
1 sqn with *Falcon* 7X (VIP); *Falcon* 900 (VIP); *Falcon* 2000
3 flt with TBM-700A
1 gp with DHC-6-300 *Twin Otter*

TRAINING
1 OCU sqn with AS555 *Fennec*; SA330 *Puma*
1 OCU sqn with *Mirage* 2000D
1 OCU sqn with *Rafale* B/C F3-R
2 (aggressor) sqn with *Alpha Jet**
1 sqn with EMB-121
1 sqn with G 120AF
2 sqn with G 120AF; PC-21

TRANSPORT HELICOPTER
1 sqn with AS332C/L *Super Puma*; H225M; SA330 *Puma*
2 sqn with AS555 *Fennec*

ISR UAV
1 sqn with MQ-9A *Reaper*

AIR DEFENCE
3 sqn with *Crotale* NG; SAMP/T
1 sqn with SAMP/T

EQUIPMENT BY TYPE
SATELLITES *see* Space
AIRCRAFT 238 combat capable
  FTR 34: 27 *Mirage* 2000-5; 7 *Mirage* 2000B
  FGA 159: 60 *Mirage* 2000D (55 being upgraded to *Mirage* 2000D RMV); 56 *Rafale* B F3-R; 43 *Rafale* C F3-R (*Rafale* being upgraded to F4.1 standard)
  ISR 2 Beech 350ER *King Air*
  AEW&C 4 E-3F *Sentry*
  TKR 3 KC-135 *Stratotanker*
  TKR/TPT 14: 12 A330 MRTT; 2 KC-130J *Hercules*
  TPT 114: **Heavy** 21 A400M; **Medium** 16: 5 C-130H *Hercules*; 9 C-130H-30 *Hercules*; 2 C-130J-30 *Hercules*; **Light** 69: 19 CN235M-100; 8 CN235M-300; 5 DHC-6-300 *Twin Otter*; 22 EMB-121 *Xingu*; 15 TBM-700; **PAX** 8: 1 A330 (VIP); 2 *Falcon* 7X; 3 *Falcon* 900 (VIP); 2 *Falcon* 2000
  TRG 124: 45 *Alpha Jet**; 17 D140 Jodel; 3 Extra 300/330; 17 G 120AF (leased); 17 PC-21; 5 *Super Dimona* HK36; 13 SR20 (leased); 7 SR22 (leased)

HELICOPTERS
  MRH 37 AS555 *Fennec*
  TPT 38: **Heavy** 11 H225M *Caracal*; **Medium** 27: 1 AS332C *Super Puma*; 4 AS332L *Super Puma*; 2 H225; 20 SA330B *Puma*

UNINHABITED AERIAL VEHICLES
  CISR • **Heavy** 12 MQ-9A *Reaper*

AIR DEFENCE • **SAM** 60: **Long-range** 40 SAMP/T; **Short-range** 20 *Crotale* NG

AIR-LAUNCHED MISSILES
  AAM • **IR** R-550 *Magic* 2; **IIR** Mica IR; **ARH** Meteor; Mica RF
  ASM *Apache*
  LACM
    Nuclear ASMPA
    Conventional SCALP EG

BOMBS
  Laser-guided: GBU-12/-16 *Paveway* II
  Laser & INS/GPS-guided GBU-49 Enhanced *Paveway* II
  INS/GPS-guided AASM *Hammer* 250

Air Force Special Forces Brigade
FORCES BY ROLE
SPECIAL FORCES
  3 SF gp
MANOEUVRE
  Other
    24 protection units
TRANSPORT
  1 spec ops sqn with C-130H/H-30 *Hercules*
TRANSPORT HELICOPTER
  1 spec ops sqn with H225M; SA330 *Puma*

Reserves 5,700 reservists

Gendarmerie & Paramilitary 95,100

Gendarmerie 95,100; 31,500 reservists
EQUIPMENT BY TYPE
ARMOURED FIGHTING VEHICLES
  APC 112:
    APC (W) 80: 60 VXB-170 (VBRG-170); 20 VAB
    PPV 32 *Centaure*
ARTILLERY • **MOR 81mm** some
PATROL AND COASTAL COMBATANTS 40
  PB 40: 1 *Armoise*; 4 *Géranium*; 3 *Maroni* (VCSM NG); 23 VCSM (1 more non-op); 9 VSMP
HELICOPTERS • **TPT** • **Light** 60: 25 AS350BA *Ecureuil*; 20 H135; 15 H145

DEPLOYMENT

BALTIC SEA: NATO • SNMCMG 1: 50; 1 MHO
BOSNIA-HERZEGOVINA: EU • EUFOR (*Operation Althea*) 24
CENTRAL AFRICAN REPUBLIC: UN • MINUSCA 3

CHAD: 1,000; 1 mech inf BG; 1 FGA det with 3 *Mirage 2000D*; 1 tkr/tpt det with 1 A330 MRTT; 1 C-130H; 2 CN235M

CÔTE D'IVOIRE: 600; 1 inf bn; 1 (army) hel unit with 2 SA330 *Puma*; 2 SA342 *Gazelle*; 1 (air force) hel unit with 1 AS555 *Fennec*

CYPRUS: *Operation Inherent Resolve* 30: 1 *Atlantique*-2

DEMOCRATIC REPUBLIC OF THE CONGO: UN • MONUSCO 2

DJIBOUTI: 1,500; 1 combined arms regt with (2 recce sqn, 2 inf coy, 1 arty bty, 1 engr coy); 1 hel det with 4 SA330 *Puma*; 3 SA342 *Gazelle*; 1 LCM; 1 FGA sqn with 4 *Mirage 2000-5*; 1 SAR/tpt sqn with 1 CN235M; 3 SA330 *Puma*

EGYPT: MFO 1

ESTONIA: NATO • Forward Land Forces(*Operation Lynx*) 350; 1 lt armd pl; 1 inf coy

FRENCH GUIANA: 2,650: 2 inf regt; 1 SMA regt; 2 PCO; 1 tpt sqn with 3 CN235M; 5 SA330 *Puma*; 4 AS555 *Fennec*; 3 gendarmerie coy; 1 AS350BA *Ecureuil*; 1 H145

FRENCH POLYNESIA: 1,000: 1 inf bn; 1 SMA coy; 1 naval HQ at Papeete; 1 FFH; 1 PSO; 1 PCO; 1 AFS; 3 *Falcon 200 Gardian*; 1 SAR/tpt sqn with 2 CN235M; 3 SA330 *Puma*

FRENCH WEST INDIES: 1,100; 1 inf regt; 2 SMA regt; 2 FFH; 1 AS565SA *Panther*; 1 SA319 *Alouette* III; 1 naval base at Fort de France (Martinique); 4 gendarmerie coy; 1 PCO; 1 PB; 2 AS350BA *Ecureuil*

GABON: 350; 1 inf bn

GERMANY: 2,000 (incl elm Eurocorps and FRA/GER bde); 1 (FRA/GER) mech bde (1 armd cav regt, 1 mech inf regt)

GULF OF GUINEA: *Operation Corymbe* 1 LHD

IRAQ: *Operation Inherent Resolve* 6; **NATO** • NATO Mission Iraq 4

JORDAN: *Operation Inherent Resolve* (*Chammal*) 300: 4 *Rafale* F3

KOSOVO: NATO • KFOR 3

LA REUNION/MAYOTTE: 2,100; 1 para regt; 1 inf coy; 1 SMA regt; 1 SMA coy; 2 FFH; 1 PCO; 1 LCM; 1 naval HQ at Port-des-Galets (La Réunion); 1 naval base at Dzaoudzi (Mayotte); 1 *Falcon* 50M; 1 SAR/tpt sqn with 2 CN235M; 5 gendarmerie coy; 1 SA319 *Alouette* III

LEBANON: UN • UNIFIL 578; 1 bn HQ; 1 recce coy, 1 log coy, 1 maint coy, 1 tpt coy, VBCI; VAB; VBL; *Mistral*

MEDITERRANEAN SEA: Navy 500; 1 DDGHM; 1 LHD; **EU** • EUNAVFOR MED • *Operation Irini*: 180; 1 FFGHM

MIDDLE EAST: UN • UNTSO 1

MOZAMBIQUE: EU • EUMAM Mozambique 2

NEW CALEDONIA: 1,500; 1 mech inf regt; 1 SMA coy; 6 ERC-90F1 *Lynx*; 1 FFH; 1 PSO; 1 PCO; 1 base with 2 *Falcon 200 Gardian* at Nouméa; 1 tpt unit with 2 CN235 MPA; 3 SA330 *Puma*; 4 gendarmerie coy; 2 AS350BA *Ecureuil*

NORTH SEA: NATO • SNMG 1: 200; 1 FFGHM; 1 FSM

QATAR: *Operation Inherent Resolve* (*Chammal*) 70; 1 E-3F *Sentry*

ROMANIA: NATO • Forward Land Forces 750; 1 armd BG with *Leclerc*; VBCI; 2 SP arty bty with CAESAR; M270 MLRS; 1 SAM bty with SAMP/T

SAUDI ARABIA: 50 (radar det)

SENEGAL: 350; 1 *Falcon* 50MI

UNITED ARAB EMIRATES: 850: 1 armd BG (1 tk coy, 1 arty bty); *Leclerc*; CAESAR; • *Operation Inherent Resolve* (*Chammal*); 1 FGA sqn with 7 *Rafale* F3

WESTERN SAHARA: UN • MINURSO 2

FOREIGN FORCES

Germany 400 (GER elm Eurocorps)
Singapore 200; 1 trg sqn with 12 M-346 *Master*

Germany GER

Euro EUR		2023	2024	2025
GDP	EUR	4.19trn	4.32trn	4.48trn
	USD	4.53trn	4.71trn	4.92trn
Real GDP growth	%	-0.3	0.0	0.8
Def exp [a]	EUR	67.6bn	90.6bn	
	USD	73.1bn	97.7bn	
Def bdgt [b]	EUR	ε62.0bn	ε78.9bn	ε79.3bn
	USD	ε67.1bn	ε86.0bn	ε87.0bn

[a] NATO figure

[b] Includes 'Sondervermögen' (special fund) allocation, military pensions and military aid to Ukraine

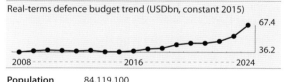

Real-terms defence budget trend (USDbn, constant 2015)
67.4
36.2
2008 — 2016 — 2024

Population		84,119,100				
Age	0–14	15–19	20–24	25–29	30–64	65 plus
Male	7.0%	2.3%	2.5%	2.8%	24.1%	10.6%
Female	6.8%	2.2%	2.4%	2.7%	23.4%	13.1%

Capabilities

Germany released its first National Security Strategy (NSS) in 2023. The NSS was spurred by Russia's 2022 invasion of Ukraine, which prompted Chancellor Olaf Scholz to invoke a turning point, or *Zeitenwende*, in German security policy. Germany pledged to contribute more to security in Europe and the government said it would promote the development and introduction of advanced capabilities. In 2024, it was announced that the US would, from 2026, deploy to Germany conventionally armed surface-to-surface missiles with 500 kilometre-plus ranges. Germany initiated the European Sky Shield Initiative and is improving domestic air and missile defence capability. Berlin is committed to bolstering NATO's eastern flank and has the goal of stationing a brigade in Lithuania by 2027. Defence policy guidelines were updated in November 2023 and changes to organisational structures began with the October 2024 announcement of a new Operational Command and Support Command. The defence ministry has announced its objective to increase authorised active and reserve personnel numbers, but there are recruitment and retention challenges and the armed forces are struggling to improve readiness levels. A draft law on military registration was prepared in late 2024. Germany has indicated that it intends to provide, from 2025, around 35,000 personnel and some 200 vessels and aircraft at 30 days' notice for NATO's New Force Model. Shortages of spare parts and maintenance problems are reported across the services. Germany's defence-industrial base can design and manufacture equipment to meet requirements across all domains, with strengths in land and naval systems. The government is pursuing closer defence-industrial cooperation in Europe.

ACTIVE 179,850 (Army 60,650 Navy 15,350 Air 27,000 Joint Support Service 22,250 Joint Medical Service 20,150 Cyber 13,700 Other 20,750)

Conscript liability Voluntary conscription only. Voluntary conscripts can serve up to 23 months

RESERVE 34,100 (Army 13,500 Navy 2,300 Air 4,800 Joint Support Service 4,850 Joint Medical Service 5,350 Cyber 1,900 Other 1,400)

ORGANISATIONS BY SERVICE

Space
EQUIPMENT BY TYPE
SATELLITES 10
　COMMUNICATIONS 2 COMSATBw (1 & 2)
　ISR 8: 3 SARah; 5 SAR-*Lupe*

Army 60,650
FORCES BY ROLE
COMMAND
　elm 2 (1 GNC & MNC NE) corps HQ
MANOEUVRE
　Armoured
　1 (1st) armd div (1 (9th) armd bde (1 armd recce bn, 2 tk bn, 2 armd inf bn, 1 cbt engr bn, 1 spt bn); 1 (21st) mech inf bde (1 armd recce bn, 3 mech inf bn, 1 cbt engr bn, 1 spt bn); 1 (41st) mech inf bde (1 armd recce bn, 2 armd inf bn, 1 cbt engr bn, 1 sigs coy, 1 spt bn); 1 tk bn (for NLD 43rd Bde); 1 SP arty bn; 1 sigs coy)
　1 (10th) armd div (1 (12th) armd bde (1 armd recce bn, 1 recce bn, 2 tk bn, 2 armd inf bn, 1 cbt engr bn, 1 sigs coy, 1 cbt engr bn, 1 spt bn); 1 (37th) mech inf bde (1 armd recce bn, 1 tk bn, 3 armd inf bn, 1 SP arty bn (forming), 1 engr bn, 1 sigs coy, 1 spt bn); 1 SP arty bn; 1 SP arty trg bn; 2 mech inf bn (GER/FRA bde); 1 arty bn (GER/FRA bde); 1 cbt engr coy (GER/FRA bde); 1 spt bn (GER/FRA bde))
　1 (45th) armd bde (forming)
　Air Manoeuvre
　1 (rapid reaction) AB div (1 SOF bde (3 SOF bn); 1 (23rd) mtn inf bde (1 recce coy, 3 mtn inf bn, 1 engr coy, 1 spt coy); 1 AB bde (2 recce coy, 2 para regt, 2 cbt engr coy); 1 atk hel regt; 2 tpt hel regt; 1 sigs coy)
COMBAT SUPPORT
　1 engr bn(-) (Joint GER-UK unit)
EQUIPMENT BY TYPE

ARMOURED FIGHTING VEHICLES
　MBT 313: 209 *Leopard* 2A5/A6; 104 *Leopard* 2A7V
　RECCE 220 *Fennek* (incl 24 engr recce, 50 fires spt)
　IFV 680: 258 *Marder* 1A3/A4; 72 *Marder* 1A5; 350 *Puma*
　APC 802
　　APC (T) 112: 75 Bv-206S; 37 M113 (inc variants)
　　APC (W) 690: 331 *Boxer* (inc variants); 359 TPz-1 *Fuchs* (inc variants)
　AUV 610: 247 *Dingo* 2; 363 *Eagle* IV/V
　ABCV 73 *Wiesel* 1 Mk20
ENGINEERING & MAINTENANCE VEHICLES
　AEV 50 *Dachs*
　ARV 168: 93 BPz-2 1; 75 BPz-3 *Büffel*
　VLB 42: 5 *Biber*; 7 *Leopard* 2 with *Leguan*; 30 M3
　MW 30: 6 *Fuchs* KAI; 24 *Keiler*
NBC VEHICLES 44 TPz-1 *Fuchs* NBC
ANTI-TANK/ANTI-INFRASTRUCTURE • MSL
　SP 107 *Wiesel* ATGM with TOW or MELLS
　MANPATS *Milan*; *Spike*-LR (MELLS)
ARTILLERY 245
　SP 155mm 109 PzH 2000
　MRL 227mm 38 M270 MLRS
　MOR 98: **120mm** 58 Tampella; **SP 120mm** 40 M113 with Tampella
HELICOPTERS
　ATK 51 *Tiger*
　MRH 1 H145M
　TPT 108: **Medium** 82 NH90 TTH; **Light** 26: 6 Bell 206B3 *Jet Ranger* III (leased); 13 H135; 7 H145 (SAR)
UNINHABITED AERIAL VEHICLES
　ISR 122: **Medium** 35 KZO; **Light** 87 LUNA
AIR-LAUNCHED MISSILES • ASM HOT; PARS 3 LR

Navy 15,350
EQUIPMENT BY TYPE
SUBMARINES 6
　SSK 6 Type-212A (fitted with AIP) with 6 single 533mm TT with DM2A4 HWT
PRINCIPAL SURFACE COMBATANTS 11
　DESTROYERS • DDGHM 3 *Sachsen* (F124) with 2 quad lnchr with RGM-84C *Harpoon* Block 1B AShM, 4 8-cell Mk 41 VLS with SM-2 Block IIIA SAM/RIM-162B ESSM SAM, 2 21-cell Mk 49 GMLS with RIM-116 RAM SAM, 2 triple 324mm SVTT Mk 32 ASTT with MU90 LWT, 1 76mm gun (capacity 2 *Lynx* Mk88A hel)
　FRIGATES • FFGHM 8:
　　4 *Baden-Württemberg* (F125) with 2 quad lnchr with RGM-84C *Harpoon* Block 1B AShM, 2 21-cell Mk 49 GMLS with RIM-116C RAM Block 2 SAM, 1 127mm gun (capacity 2 NH90 hel)
　　4 *Brandenburg* (F123) with 2 quad lnchr with RGM-84C *Harpoon* Block 1B AShM, 2 8-cell Mk 41 VLS with RIM-7P *Sea Sparrow* SAM/RIM-162B ESSM SAM, 2 21-cell Mk 49 GMLS with RIM-116 RAM

SAM, 2 twin 324mm SVTT Mk 32 ASTT with Mk 46 LWT, 1 76mm gun (capacity 2 *Lynx* Mk88A hel)

PATROL AND COASTAL COMBATANTS 5

CORVETTES • FSGM 5 *Braunschweig* (K130) with 2 twin lnchr with RBS15 Mk3 AShM, 2 21-cell Mk 49 GMLS with RIM-116 RAM SAM, 1 76mm gun, 1 hel landing platform

MINE WARFARE • MINE COUNTERMEASURES 12

MHO 10: 7 *Frankenthal* (2 used as diving support); 3 *Frankenthal* (mod. MJ332CL)

MSO 2 *Ensdorf*

LOGISTICS AND SUPPORT 22

AG 4: 2 *Kalkgrund*; 2 *Schwedeneck* (Type-748)

AGI 3 *Oste* (Type-423)

AGOR 1 *Planet* (Type-751)

AOR 8: 2 *Rhön* (Type-704); 6 *Elbe* (Type-404) with 1 hel landing platform (2 specified for PFM support; 1 specified for SSK support; 3 specified for MHO/MSO support)

AORH 3 *Berlin* (Type-702) (fitted for but not with RIM-116 RAM SAM) (capacity 2 NH90 hel)

ATF 2 *Rugen* (Type-722)

AXS 1 *Gorch Fock*

UNINHABITED MARITIME PLATFORMS

USV • MW • Medium 12 *Seehund*

UNINHABITED MARITIME SYSTEMS • UUV

DATA *Deep Trekker Revolution*; REMUS 1000

MW *Seafox*

Naval Aviation 2,100

FORCES BY ROLE

MARITIME PATROL

1 sqn with AP-3C *Orion*; Do-228

ANTI-SUBMARINE WARFARE/SEARCH & RESCUE

1 sqn *Lynx* Mk88A; NH90 NFH (*Sea Lion*)

EQUIPMENT BY TYPE

AIRCRAFT 2 combat capable

ASW 2 AP-3C *Orion*

TPT • Light 2 Do-228 (pollution control)

HELICOPTERS

ASW 22 *Lynx* Mk88A

SAR 18 NH90 NFH (*Sea Lion*)

Naval Special Forces Command

FORCES BY ROLE

SPECIAL FORCES

1 SF coy

Sea Battalion

FORCES BY ROLE

MANOEUVRE

Amphibious

1 mne bn

Air Force 27,000

FORCES BY ROLE

FIGHTER

3 wg (2 sqn with Eurofighter *Typhoon*)

FIGHTER/GROUND ATTACK

1 wg (2 sqn with *Tornado* IDS)

1 wg (2 sqn with Eurofighter *Typhoon*)

ISR

1 wg (1 ISR sqn with *Tornado* ECR/IDS; 1 UAV sqn with *Heron* TP)

TANKER/TRANSPORT

1 (special air mission) wg (3 sqn with A319; A321; A321LR; A350; AS532U2 *Cougar* II; *Global* 5000; *Global* 6000)

1 sqn (joint FRA-GER) with C-130J-30 *Hercules*; KC-130J *Hercules*

TRANSPORT

1 wg (3 sqn with A400M *Atlas*)

TRAINING

1 sqn located at Holloman AFB (US) with *Tornado* IDS

1 unit (ENJJPT) located at Sheppard AFB (US) with T-6A *Texan* II; T-38C *Talon*

1 hel unit located at Fassberg

TRANSPORT HELICOPTER

1 tpt hel wg (3 sqn with CH-53G/GA/GE/GS *Stallion*; 1 sqn with H145M)

AIR DEFENCE

1 wg (3 SAM gp) with M902 *Patriot* PAC-3

1 AD gp with ASRAD *Ozelot*; C-RAM Mantis and trg unit

1 AD trg unit located at Fort Bliss (US) with M902 *Patriot* PAC-3

3 (tac air ctrl) radar gp

Air Force Regiment

FORCES BY ROLE

MANOEUVRE

Other

1 sy regt

EQUIPMENT BY TYPE

AIRCRAFT 226 combat capable

FTR 138 Eurofighter *Typhoon*

ATK 68 *Tornado* IDS (8 in store)

ATK/EW 20 *Tornado* ECR*

ISR 1 A319CJ (Open Skies)

TKR/TPT 3 KC-130J *Hercules*

TPT 65: **Heavy** 47 A400M (several fitted with aerial refuelling kit); **Medium** 3 C-130J-30 *Hercules* **PAX** 15: 1 A321; 2 A321LR; 3 A350 (VIP); 2 A319; 4 *Global* 5000; 3 *Global* 6000

TRG 109: 69 T-6A *Texan* II, 40 T-38C *Talon*

HELICOPTERS

MRH 16 H145M

TPT 63: **Heavy** 60 CH-53G/GA/GS/GE *Stallion*; **Medium** 3 AS532U2 *Cougar* II (VIP)

UNINHABITED AERIAL VEHICLES
ISR • **Heavy** 1 *Heron* TP (leased)
AIR DEFENCE
SAM 93
Long-range ε70 M902 *Patriot* PAC-3
Medium-range 3 IRIS-T SLM
Point-defence 20 ASRAD *Ozelot* (with FIM-92 *Stinger*)
AIR-LAUNCHED MISSILES
AAM • **IR** AIM-9L/Li *Sidewinder*; **IIR** IRIS-T; **ARH** AIM-120B AMRAAM
ARM AGM-88B HARM
LACM Taurus KEPD 350
BOMBS
Laser-guided GBU-24 *Paveway* III; GBU-48 Enhanced *Paveway* II
Laser & INS/GPS-guided GBU-54 Laser JDAM

Joint Support Service 22,250
FORCES BY ROLE
COMBAT SUPPORT
3 MP regt
2 NBC bn
COMBAT SERVICE SUPPORT
1 log regt (4 log bn)
1 log regt (3 log bn)
1 spt regt
EQUIPMENT BY TYPE
ARMOURED FIGHTING VEHICLES
AUV 451: 206 *Dingo* 2; 245 *Eagle* IV/V
ENGINEERING & MAINTENANCE VEHICLES
ARV 35: 23 BPz-2; 12 BPz-3 *Büffel*
NBC VEHICLES 35 TPz-1 *Fuchs* A6/A7/A8 NBC

Joint Medical Services 20,150
FORCES BY ROLE
COMBAT SERVICE SUPPORT
4 med regt
EQUIPMENT BY TYPE
ARMOURED FIGHTING VEHICLES
APC • **APC (W)** 109: 72 *Boxer* (amb); 37 TPz-1 *Fuchs* (amb)
AUV 42 *Eagle* IV/V (amb)

Cyber & Information Command 13,700
FORCES BY ROLE
COMBAT SUPPORT
4 EW bn
6 sigs bn

DEPLOYMENT
BALTIC SEA: NATO • SNMCMG 1: 125; 1 MHO; 1 AOR
BOSNIA-HERZEGOVINA: EU • EUFOR (*Operation Althea*) 30
FRANCE: 400 (incl GER elm Eurocorps)
IRAQ: *Operation Inherent Resolve* 90; **NATO** • NATO Mission Iraq 50
JORDAN: *Operation Inherent Resolve* 150; 1 A400M
LATVIA: NATO • Baltic Air Policing 150; 5 Eurofighter *Typhoon*
KOSOVO: NATO • KFOR 300; 1 inf coy
LEBANON: UN • UNIFIL 78; 1 FSGM
LITHUANIA: NATO • Forward Land Forces 1,000; 1 armd bde HQ; 1 armd inf BG with *Leopard* 2A6; *Fennek*; *Marder* 1A3; *Boxer*
POLAND: 95 (GER elm MNC-NE)
SOUTH SUDAN: UN • UNMISS 11
UNITED STATES: Trg units with 40 T-38 *Talon*; 69 T-6A *Texan* II at Goodyear AFB (AZ)/Sheppard AFB (TX); NAS Pensacola (FL); Fort Rucker (AL); Missile trg at Fort Bliss (TX)
WESTERN SAHARA: UN • MINURSO 4

FOREIGN FORCES
France 2,000; 1 (FRA/GER) mech bde (1 armd cav regt, 1 mech inf regt)
United Kingdom 185
United States
US Africa Command: Army; 1 HQ at Stuttgart
US European Command: 38,700; 1 combined service HQ (EUCOM) at Stuttgart-Vaihingen

Army 24,400; 1 HQ (US Army Europe & Africa (USAREUR-AF) at Wiesbaden; 1 arty comd; 1 SF gp; 1 recce bn; 1 mech bde(-); 1 inf bn; 1 fd arty bn; 1 MRL bde (3 MRL bn); 1 (cbt avn) hel bde; 1 (cbt avn) hel bde HQ; 1 int bde; 1 MP bde; 1 sigs bde; 1 spt bde; 1 (MDTF) cbt spt bde(-); 1 SAM bde; 1 (APS) armd bde eqpt set; M1A2 SEPv2/v3 *Abrams*; M3A3 *Bradley*; M2A3 *Bradley*; M1296 *Stryker Dragoon*; M109A6; M119A3; M777A2; M270A2; M142 HIMARS; AH-64E *Apache*; CH-47F *Chinook*; UH-60L/M *Black Hawk*; HH-60M *Black Hawk*; M903 *Patriot* PAC-3 MSE; M1097 *Avenger*; *Sgt Stout*
Navy 400
USAF 13,250; 1 HQ (US Air Forces Europe & Africa) at Ramstein AB; 1 HQ (3rd Air Force) at Ramstein AB; 1 FGA wg at Spangdahlem AB with (1 FGA sqn with 24 F-16C *Fighting Falcon*); 1 tpt wg at Ramstein AB with 14 C-130J-30 *Hercules*; 2 Gulfstream V (C-37A); 5 Learjet 35A (C-21A); 1 B-737-700 (C-40B)
US Space Force 150
USMC 500

Greece GRC

Euro EUR		2023	2024	2025
GDP	EUR	220bn	232bn	242bn
	USD	238bn	253bn	265bn
Real GDP growth	%	2.0	2.3	2.0
Def exp [a]	EUR	6.22bn	7.13bn	
	USD	6.73bn	7.68bn	
Def bdgt [b]	EUR	6.76bn	7.13bn	6.90bn
	USD	7.31bn	7.76bn	7.58bn

[a] NATO figure

[b] Includes military pensions

Real-terms defence budget trend (USDbn, constant 2015)

Population		10,461,091				
Age	0–14	15–19	20–24	25–29	30–64	65 plus
Male	7.1%	2.9%	3.0%	2.9%	22.6%	10.5%
Female	6.7%	2.6%	2.5%	2.5%	23.7%	13.2%

Capabilities

Greece's National Military Strategy identifies safeguarding sovereignty and territorial integrity as principal defence objectives. The country also expects to employ the armed forces to support Cyprus in the event of a conflict there. In its Force Structure 2020–34 document, Athens established a US-style Special Warfare Command with the ambition to create new units with higher readiness. In early 2024, Athens announced an 'Agenda 2030' modernisation plan, including reorganisation and modernisation initiatives for the armed services. In recent years, Greece signed defence cooperation agreements with Cyprus, Egypt and Israel, and it is developing ties with the UAE and Saudi Arabia. The Mutual Defense Cooperation Agreement is the cornerstone of the close US–Greek defence relationship and provides for a naval-support facility and an airfield at Souda Bay in Crete. More recently, it granted the US access to Greek ports to reinforce NATO's eastern flank. The armed forces contain conscripts, but most personnel are regulars. Troop deployments generally involve limited numbers of personnel and focus on the near abroad, although Greece contributes to EU, NATO and UN missions. Athens is acquiring *Rafale* aircraft and frigates from France as part of a 2021 strategic partnership. Defence spending cuts from 2010–20 cut or postponed numerous modernisation efforts, with the army most affected and now requiring major investment. Greece's defence industry also suffered underinvestment, with this reflected in the Agenda 2030 plan's intent to boost the local defence sector, including by establishing a defence innovation centre, focusing on defence R&D and on dual-use technologies.

ACTIVE 132,000 (Army 93,500 Navy 16,700 Air 21,800) Gendarmerie & Paramilitary 7,400

Conscript liability 9 to 12 months

RESERVE 289,000 (Army 248,900 Navy 6,100 Air 34,000)

ORGANISATIONS BY SERVICE

Army 48,500; 45,000 conscripts (total 93,500)

FORCES BY ROLE
COMMAND
2 corps HQ (incl NRDC-GR)
1 armd div HQ
3 mech inf div HQ
1 inf div HQ
SPECIAL FORCES
1 SF comd
1 cdo/para bde
MANOEUVRE
Reconnaissance
4 recce bn
Armoured
4 armd bde (2 armd bn, 1 mech inf bn, 1 SP arty bn)
Mechanised
10 mech inf bde (1 armd bn, 2 mech bn, 1 SP arty bn)
Light
2 inf regt
Air Manoeuvre
1 air mob bde
1 air aslt bde
Amphibious
1 mne bde
COMBAT SUPPORT
2 MRL bn
3 AD bn (4 with I-*Hawk*, 2 with *Tor* M1)
3 engr regt
2 engr bn
1 EOD bn
1 EW regt
10 sigs bn
COMBAT SERVICE SUPPORT
1 log corps HQ
2 log div
1 log bde
HELICOPTER
1 hel bde (1 hel regt with (2 atk hel bn), 2 tpt hel bn, 4 hel bn)

EQUIPMENT BY TYPE
ARMOURED FIGHTING VEHICLES
MBT 1,385: 170 *Leopard* 2A6HEL; 183 *Leopard* 2A4; 500 *Leopard* 1A4/5; 375 M48A5; 157 M60A3
IFV 169: 129 BMP-1; 40 *Marder* 1A3
APC • APC (T) 2,157: 74 *Leonidas* Mk1/2; 1,862 M113A1/A2; 221 M577 (CP)
AUV 1,217: 975 M1117 *Guardian*; 242 VBL
ENGINEERING & MAINTENANCE VEHICLES
ARV 262: 12 *Büffel*; 43 BPz-2; 94 M88A1; 113 M578
VLB 51: 33 M48/M60 AVLB; 10 *Biber*; 8 *Leopard* 1 with *Leguan*
MW *Giant Viper*

ANTI-TANK/ANTI-INFRASTRUCTURE
MSL
SP 556: 195 HMMWV with 9K135 *Kornet*-E (RS-AT-14 *Spriggan*); 361 M901
MANPATS 9K111 *Fagot* (RS-AT-4 *Spigot*); *Milan*; TOW
RCL 687+: **84mm** *Carl Gustaf*; **90mm** EM-67; **SP 106mm** 687 M40A1

ARTILLERY 3,512
SP 602: **155mm** 444: 420 M109A1B/A2/A3GEA1/A5; 24 PzH 2000; **175mm** 12 M107; **203mm** 146 M110A2
TOWED 439: **105mm** 244: 226 M101; 18 M-56; **155mm** 195 M114
MRL 151: **122mm** 115 RM-70; **227mm** 36 M270 MLRS
MOR 2,320: **81mm** 1,700; **107mm** 620 M30 (incl 231 SP)

SURFACE-TO-SURFACE MISSILE LAUNCHERS
SRBM • Conventional MGM-140A ATACMS (launched from M270 MLRS)

AIRCRAFT • TPT • Light 12: 1 Beech 200 *King Air* (C-12C); 2 Beech 200 *King Air* (C-12R/AP *Huron*); 9 Cessna 185 (U-17A/B) (liaison)

HELICOPTERS
ATK 28: 19 AH-64A *Apache*; 9 AH-64D *Apache*
MRH 60 OH-58D *Kiowa Warrior*
TPT 115: **Heavy** 23: 13 CH-47D *Chinook*; 10 CH-47SD *Chinook*; **Medium** 14 NH90 TTH; **Light** 78: 63 Bell 205 (UH-1H *Iroquois*); 14 Bell 206 (AB-206) *Jet Ranger*; 1 Bell 212 (VIP)
TRG 15 NH-300C

UNINHABITED AERIAL VEHICLES
ISR • Medium 4 *Sperwer*

AIR-LAUNCHED MISSILES
ASM AGM-114K/M *Hellfire* II

AIR DEFENCE
SAM 155+
Medium-range 42 MIM-23B I-*Hawk*
Short-range 21 9K331 *Tor*-M1 (RS-SA-15 *Gauntlet*)
Point-range 92+: 38 9K33 *Osa*-M (RS-SA-8B *Gecko*); 54 ASRAD HMMWV; FIM-92 *Stinger*
GUNS • TOWED 727: **20mm** 204 Rh 202; **23mm** 523 ZU-23-2

National Guard 38,000 reservists
Internal security role
FORCES BY ROLE
MANOEUVRE
  Light
    1 inf div
  Air Manoeuvre
    1 para regt
COMBAT SUPPORT
  8 arty bn
  4 AD bn
HELICOPTER
  1 hel bn

Navy 14,300; 2,400 conscript (total 16,700)
EQUIPMENT BY TYPE
SUBMARINES • SSK 10:
  3 *Poseidon* (GER Type-209/1200) with 8 single 533mm TT with SUT HWT
  1 *Poseidon* (GER Type-209/1200) (fitted with AIP) with 8 single 533mm TT with UGM-84C *Harpoon* Block 1B AShM/SUT HWT
  2 *Glavkos* (GER Type-209/1100) with 8 single 533mm TT with UGM-84C *Harpoon* Block 1B AShM/SUT HWT
  4 *Papanikolis* (GER Type-214) (fitted with AIP) with 8 single 533mm TT with UGM-84C *Harpoon* Block 1B AShM/SUT HWT

PRINCIPAL SURFACE COMBATANTS 13
FRIGATES • FFGHM 13:
  2 *Elli* Batch I (NLD *Kortenaer* mod) with 2 quad lnchr with RGM-84C/G *Harpoon* Block 1B/G AShM, 1 octuple Mk 29 GMLS with RIM-7P *Sea Sparrow* SAM, 2 twin 324mm SVTT Mk 32 mod 9 ASTT with Mk 46 mod 5 LWT, 2 Mk 15 *Phalanx* CIWS, 2 76mm gun (capacity 2 Bell 212 (AB-212) hel or 1 S-70B *Seahawk* hel)
  7 *Elli* Batch II (ex-NLD *Kortenaer*) with 2 quad lnchr with RGM-84C/G *Harpoon* Block 1B/G AShM, 1 octuple Mk 29 GMLS with RIM-7P *Sea Sparrow* SAM, 2 twin 324mm SVTT Mk 32 mod 9 ASTT with Mk 46 mod 5 LWT, 1 Mk 15 *Phalanx* CIWS, 1 76mm gun (capacity 2 Bell 212 (AB-212) hel or 1 S-70B *Seahawk* hel)
  4 *Hydra* (GER MEKO 200) with 2 quad lnchr with RGM-84G *Harpoon* Block 1G AShM, 1 16-cell Mk 48 mod 2 VLS with RIM-162C ESSM SAM, 2 triple 324mm SVTT Mk 32 mod 5 ASTT with Mk 46 mod 5 LWT, 2 Mk 15 *Phalanx* CIWS, 1 127mm gun (capacity 1 S-70B *Seahawk* ASW hel/*Alpha* 900 UAV)

PATROL AND COASTAL COMBATANTS 41
PCGM 7 *Roussen* (UK *Super Vita*) with 2 quad lnchr with MM40 *Exocet* Block 3 AShM (of which 2 still fitted with Block 2), 1 21-cell Mk 49 GMLS with RIM-116 RAM SAM, 1 76mm gun
PCFG 9:
  4 *Kavaloudis* (FRA *La Combattante* IIIB) with 2 twin lnchr with RGM-84C *Harpoon* Block 1B AShM, 2 single 533mm TT with SST-4 HWT, 2 76mm gun
  4 *Laskos* (FRA *La Combattante* III) with 2 twin lnchr with RGM-84C *Harpoon* Block 1B AShM, 2 single 533mm TT with SST-4 HWT, 2 76mm gun
  1 *Votsis* (ex-GER *Tiger*) with 2 twin lnchr with RGM-84C *Harpoon* AShM, 1 76mm gun
PCF 1 *Votsis* (ex-GER *Tiger*) with 1 76mm gun
PCO 8:
  2 *Armatolos* (DNK *Osprey*) with 1 76mm gun
  2 *Kasos* (DNK *Osprey* derivative) with 1 76mm gun
  4 *Machitis* with 1 76mm gun
PCC 2 *Mantouvalos* (ex-US *Island*)
PBF 8: 4 *Aeolos* (ex-US Mk V FPB); 1 *Agenor*; 1 *Okyalos*; 2 ST60
PB 6: 3 *Andromeda* (ex-NOR *Nasty*); 2 *Stamou*; 1 *Tolmi*

MINE WARFARE • MINE COUNTERMEASURES 3
  MHO 3: 1 *Evropi* (ex-UK *Hunt*); 2 *Evniki* (ex-US *Osprey*)
AMPHIBIOUS
  LANDING SHIPS • LST 5 *Chios* (capacity 4 LCVP; 300 troops) with 1 76mm gun, 1 hel landing platform
  LANDING CRAFT 12
    LCU 2 *Folegandros* (ex-GER Type-520)
    LCA 7
    LCAC 3 *Kefallinia* (*Zubr*) with 2 AK630 CIWS (capacity either 3 MBT or 10 APC (T); 230 troops)
LOGISTICS AND SUPPORT 37
  ABU 1 *Thetis*
  AFS 4 *Atlas* I
  AG 4: 2 *Pandora*; 2 *Karavogiannos*
  AGOR 1 *Pytheas*
  AGS 2: 1 *Naftilos*; 1 *Stravon*
  AOL 5: 1 *Ilissos*; 4 *Ouranos*
  AORH 1 *Prometheus* (ITA *Etna*) with 1 Mk 15 *Phalanx* CIWS
  AOR 1 *Axios* (ex-GER *Luneburg*)
  AP 6: 2 Type-520; 4 Other
  AWT 6: 2 *Kerkini*; 1 *Ouranos*; 3 *Prespa*
  AXL 1 *Kyknos*
  AXS 5
UNINHABITED MARITIME SYSTEMS
  UUV • MW *Pluto* Plus

Coastal Defence
EQUIPMENT BY TYPE
COASTAL DEFENCE • AShM 2 MM40 *Exocet*

Naval Aviation
FORCES BY ROLE
ANTI-SUBMARINE WARFARE
  1 div with Bell 212 (AB-212) ASW; MH-60R/S-70B *Seahawk*
EQUIPMENT BY TYPE
AIRCRAFT 1 combat capable
  ASW 1 P-3B *Orion* (4 more undergoing upgrade)
HELICOPTERS
  ASW 18: 4 Bell 212 (AB-212) ASW; 3 MH-60R *Seahawk*; 11 S-70B *Seahawk*
AIR-LAUNCHED MISSILES
  ASM AGM-114 *Hellfire*
  AShM AGM-119 *Penguin*

Air Force 18,800; 3,000 conscripts (total 21,800)

Tactical Air Force
FORCES BY ROLE
FIGHTER/GROUND ATTACK
  1 sqn with F-4E *Phantom* II
  3 sqn with F-16CG/DG Block 30/50 *Fighting Falcon*
  2 sqn with F-16CG/DG Block 52+ *Fighting Falcon*
  2 sqn with F-16C/D Block 52+ ADV *Fighting Falcon*
  1 sqn with F-16V(C/D) Block 72 *Fighting Falcon*
  1 sqn with *Mirage* 2000-5EG/BG Mk2
  1 sqn with *Rafale* B/C F3-R
AIRBORNE EARLY WARNING
  1 sqn with EMB-145H *Erieye*
ISR UAV
  1 sqn with *Heron* 1; *Pegasus* II
EQUIPMENT BY TYPE
AIRCRAFT 230 combat capable
  FGA 230: 32 F-4E *Phantom* II; 70 F-16CG/DG Block 30/50 *Fighting Falcon*; 64 F-16CG/DG Block 52+/Block 52+ ADV *Fighting Falcon*; 20 F-16V(C/D) Block 72 *Fighting Falcon*; 19 *Mirage* 2000-5EG Mk2; 5 *Mirage* 2000-5BG Mk2; 16 *Rafale* C F3-R; 4 *Rafale* B F3-R; (10 *Mirage* 2000EG in store)
  AEW 4 EMB-145AEW (EMB-145H) *Erieye*
UNINHABITED AERIAL VEHICLES
  ISR 4: **Heavy** 2 *Heron* 1 (leased); **Medium** 2 *Pegasus* II (6 more in store)
AIR-LAUNCHED MISSILES
  AAM • IR AIM-9L/P *Sidewinder*; R-550 *Magic* 2; **IIR** IRIS-T; *Mica* IR; **ARH** AIM-120B/C AMRAAM; *Meteor*; *Mica* RF
  ASM AGM-65A/B/G *Maverick*
  AShM AM39 *Exocet*
  ARM AGM-88 HARM
  LACM SCALP EG
BOMBS
  Electro-optical guided: GBU-8B HOBOS
  Laser-guided: GBU-10/-12/-16 *Paveway* II; GBU-24 *Paveway* III; GBU-50 Enhanced *Paveway* II
  INS/GPS-guided AGM-154C JSOW; GBU-31 JDAM

Air Defence
FORCES BY ROLE
AIR DEFENCE
  6 sqn/bty with M901 *Patriot* PAC-2
  2 sqn/bty with S-300PMU1 (RS-SA-20 *Gargoyle*)
  12 bty with *Skyguard*/RIM-7 *Sparrow*/guns; *Crotale* NG/GR; *Tor*-M1 (RS-SA-15 *Gauntlet*)
EQUIPMENT BY TYPE
AIR DEFENCE
  SAM 81
    Long-range 48: 36 M901 *Patriot* PAC-2; 12 S-300PMU1 (RS-SA-20 *Gargoyle*)
    Short-range 33: 9 *Crotale* NG/GR; 4 9K331 *Tor*-M1 (RS-SA-15 *Gauntlet*); 20 RIM-7M *Sparrow* with *Skyguard*
  GUNS 59: **20mm** some Rh-202; **30mm** 35+ Artemis-30; **35mm** 24 GDF-005 with *Skyguard*

Air Support Command
FORCES BY ROLE
SEARCH & RESCUE/TRANSPORT HELICOPTER
  1 sqn with AS332C *Super Puma* (SAR/CSAR)
  1 sqn with AW109; Bell 205A (AB-205A) (SAR); Bell 212 (AB-212) (VIP, tpt)
TRANSPORT
  1 sqn with C-27J *Spartan*

1 sqn with C-130B/H *Hercules*
1 sqn with EMB-135BJ *Legacy*; ERJ-135LR; *Falcon* 7X; Gulfstream V

EQUIPMENT BY TYPE
AIRCRAFT
TPT 27: **Medium** 23: 8 C-27J *Spartan*; 5 C-130B *Hercules*; 10 C-130H *Hercules*; **Light** 2: 1 EMB-135BJ *Legacy*; 1 ERJ-135LR; **PAX** 2: 1 *Falcon* 7X (VIP); 1 Gulfstream V
HELICOPTERS
TPT 31: **Medium** 12 AS332C *Super Puma*; **Light** 19: 3 AW109; 12 Bell 205A (AB-205A) (SAR); 4 Bell 212 (AB-212) (VIP, tpt)

Air Training Command
FORCES BY ROLE
TRAINING
2 sqn with M-346; T-2C/E *Buckeye*
1 sqn with P2002JF
2 sqn with T-6A/B *Texan* II

EQUIPMENT BY TYPE
AIRCRAFT • **TRG** 70: 2 M-346; 12 P2002JF; 28 T-2C/E *Buckeye*; ε13 T-6A *Texan* II; ε15 T-6B *Texan* II

Gendarmerie & Paramilitary

Coast Guard and Customs 7,400
EQUIPMENT BY TYPE
PATROL AND COASTAL COMBATANTS 84
  PCO 1 *Gavdos* (Damen 5509)
  PCC 4: 1 *Arkoi* (UK Vosper *Europatrol* 250); 3 *Fournoi* (ISR *Sa'ar* 4.5 mod)
  PBF 47: 3 CB90; 4 *Marinos Zampatis* (ITA CNV P355); 40 Other
  PB 32: 2 *Faiakas* (CRO POB 24); 30 Other
LOGISTICS AND SUPPORT • **AG** 4
AIRCRAFT • **TPT** • **Light** 7: 2 Cessna 172RG *Cutlass*; 3 F406 *Caravan* II; 2 TB-20 *Trinidad*
HELICOPTERS • **MRH** 6 AS365N3 (SAR)
UNINHABITED AERIAL VEHICLES
  ISR • **Heavy** 1 *Heron* 1 (leased)

DEPLOYMENT

BOSNIA-HERZEGOVINA: EU • EUFOR (*Operation Althea*) 9
BULGARIA: NATO • Forward Land Forces 30; 1 AT pl with M901
CYPRUS: Army 950; 1 mech bde (1 armd bn, 2 mech inf bn, 1 arty bn); 61 M48A5 MOLF MBT; 80 *Leonidas* APC; 12 M114 arty; 6 M110A2 arty
IRAQ: NATO • NATO Mission Iraq 4
KOSOVO: NATO • KFOR 121; 1 inf bn HQ; 2 inf coy
LEBANON: UN • UNIFIL 131; 1 FFGHM
MEDITERRANEAN SEA: EU • EUNAVFOR MED • *Operation Irini*; 180; 1 FFGHM; **NATO** • SNMG 2: 180; 1 FFGHM
MOZAMBIQUE: EU • EUMAM Mozambique 15
RED SEA: EU • EUNAVFOR • *Operation Aspides*; 180; 1 FFGHM;
SAUDI ARABIA: Air Force 100; 1 SAM bty with M901 *Patriot* PAC-2

FOREIGN FORCES

United States US European Command: 600; 1 hel bn with UH-60M/HH-60M *Black Hawk*; 1 naval base at Makri; 1 naval base at Souda Bay; 1 air base at Iraklion

Hungary HUN

Hungarian Forint HUF		2023	2024	2025
GDP	HUF	75.0trn	80.2trn	85.4trn
	USD	212bn	229bn	246bn
Real GDP growth	%	-0.9	1.5	2.9
Def exp [a]	HUF	1.54trn	1.73trn	
	USD	4.36bn	4.89bn	
Def bdgt [b]	HUF	1.56trn	1.99trn	
	USD	4.42bn	5.67bn	

[a] NATO figure
[b] Includes military pensions

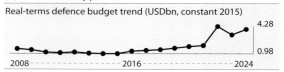
Real-terms defence budget trend (USDbn, constant 2015)

Population	9,855,745					
Age	0–14	15–19	20–24	25–29	30–64	65 plus
Male	7.6%	3.0%	2.8%	2.8%	23.8%	8.8%
Female	6.9%	2.5%	2.5%	2.6%	23.9%	12.7%

Capabilities

Hungary published a National Security Strategy in April 2020 and a National Military Strategy in June 2021. The documents reflect a deteriorating security environment marked by great-power competition. The security strategy also characterises mass migration as a key concern for Hungary. Budapest is implementing the Zrinyi 2026 national-defence and armed-forces modernisation plan. One of NATO's four new post-2022 multinational battlegroups is based in Hungary. Hungary is establishing new territorial defence units. The country, in 2022, set up a Cyber and Information Operations Centre and published a Military Cyberspace Operations Doctrine. Hungary coordinates policy, including on defence, with other member states of the Visegrád Group. The armed forces participate in international crisis-management missions, but have limited organic capacity to deploy forces beyond national borders. In 2023, the government announced its intention to deploy forces to Chad to help the government there deal with security challenges. Hungary's defence forces are modernising, including its armour, artillery, air defence, combat air, communications, and command-and-control capabilities. Hungary's defence-industrial base is limited but developing. In 2023, Rheinmetall and the Hungarian government opened a factory to build *Lynx* IFVs. The defence ministry has set up an inter-ministerial working group to boost domestic capacity in small-arms and ammunition.

ACTIVE 32,150 (Army 10,450 Air 5,750 Joint 15,950)
RESERVE 20,000

ORGANISATIONS BY SERVICE

Hungary's armed forces have reorganised into a joint force

Land Component 10,450 (incl riverine element)

FORCES BY ROLE

SPECIAL FORCES
1 SF bde (4 spec ops bn)

MANOEUVRE
Reconnaissance
1 ISR regt
Armoured
1 (1st) armd inf bde (1 tk bn; 1 armd inf bn, 1 SP arty bn, 1 AT bn, 1 log bn)
Mechanised
1 (11th) mech inf bde (3 mech inf bn, 1 cbt engr coy, 1 sigs coy, 1 log bn)

COMBAT SUPPORT
1 engr regt
1 EOD/rvn regt
1 CBRN bn
1 sigs regt

COMBAT SERVICE SUPPORT
1 log regt

EQUIPMENT BY TYPE

ARMOURED FIGHTING VEHICLES
MBT 80: 12 *Leopard* 2A4HU; 24 *Leopard* 2A7HU; 44 T-72M1
IFV 131+: 120 BTR-80A/AM; 11+ KF41 *Lynx* (in test)
APC 322
  APC (W) 260 BTR-80
  PPV 62: 50 *Ejder Yalcin* 4×4 (*Gidran*); 12 *MaxxPro Plus*

ENGINEERING & MAINTENANCE VEHICLES
AEV 5 BAT-2
ARV 10: 1 BPz-3 *Buffel*; 8 VT-55A; 1 *Wisent* 2
VLB 9+: 8 BLG-60; 1 *Leguan* 2HU, MTU; TMM

NBC VEHICLES 14 BTR-80M-NBC

ANTI-TANK/ANTI-INFRASTRUCTURE
MSL • MANPATS 9K111 *Fagot* (RS-AT-4 *Spigot*); 9K111-1 *Konkurs* (RS-AT-5 *Spandrel*), *Spike* LR

ARTILLERY 73
SP 155mm 23 PzH 2000
MOR 82mm 50 M-37

PATROL AND COASTAL COMBATANTS • PBR 2
MINE COUNTERMEASURES • MSR 3 *Nestin*

Air Component 5,750

FORCES BY ROLE

FIGHTER/GROUND ATTACK
1 sqn with *Gripen* C/D

TRANSPORT
1 sqn with A319; *Falcon* 7X

TRAINING
1 sqn with Z-143LSi; Z-242L; AS350 *Ecureuil*

ATTACK HELICOPTER
1 sqn with Mi-24V/P *Hind* E/F

TRANSPORT HELICOPTER
1 sqn with H145M; H225M

AIR DEFENCE
1 SAM regt (9 bty with *Mistral*; 1 bty with 2K12 *Kub* (RS-SA-6 *Gainful*); 2 bty with NASAMS III)
1 radar regt

EQUIPMENT BY TYPE

AIRCRAFT 14 combat capable
FGA 14: 12 *Gripen* C; 2 *Gripen* D
TPT 5: **Medium** 1 KC-390 *Millenium*; **PAX** 4: 2 A319; 2 *Falcon* 7X
TRG 8: 2 Z-143LSi; 6 Z-242L

HELICOPTERS
ATK 8: 6 Mi-24V *Hind* E; 2 Mi-24P *Hind* F
MRH 20 H145M (incl 2 SAR)
TPT 12: **Heavy** 10 H225M; **Light** 2 AS350 *Ecureuil*

AIR DEFENCE • SAM 24
Medium-range 8 NASAMS III
Short-range 16 2K12 *Kub* (RS-SA-6 *Gainful*)
Point-defence *Mistral*

AIR-LAUNCHED MISSILES
AAM • IR AIM-9 *Sidewinder*; **ARH** AIM-120C AMRAAM
ASM AGM-65 *Maverick*; 3M11 *Falanga* (RS-AT-2 *Swatter*); 9K114 *Shturm*-V (RS-AT-6 *Spiral*)

BOMBS • Laser-guided *Paveway* II

DEPLOYMENT

BOSNIA-HERZEGOVINA: EU • EUFOR (*Operation Althea*) 250; 1 inf coy

CYPRUS: UN • UNFICYP 11

IRAQ: *Operation Inherent Resolve* 20; **NATO** • NATO Mission Iraq 3

KOSOVO: NATO • KFOR 365; 1 inf bn HQ; 2 inf coy; **UN** • UNMIK 1

LEBANON: UN • UNIFIL 15

WESTERN SAHARA: UN • MINURSO 7

FOREIGN FORCES

Croatia NATO Forward Land Forces: 64; 1 MP pl
Italy NATO Forward Land Forces: 260; 1 mech inf coy(+)
United States NATO Forward Land Forces: 150; 1 inf coy

Iceland ISL

Icelandic Krona ISK		2023	2024	2025
GDP	ISK	4.32trn	4.54trn	4.79trn
	USD	31.3bn	32.9bn	35.4bn
Real GDP growth	%	5.0	0.6	2.4
Sy Bdgt [a]	ISK	5.58bn	6.70bn	8.00bn
	USD	40.5m	48.6m	59.1m

[a] Coast Guard budget

Real-terms defence budget trend (USDm, constant 2015)
46.6
27.9
2008 — 2016 — 2024

Population		364,036				
Age	0–14	15–19	20–24	25–29	30–64	65 plus
Male	10.1%	3.3%	3.1%	3.3%	22.2%	8.1%
Female	9.7%	3.2%	3.1%	3.2%	21.8%	9.0%

Capabilities

Iceland is a NATO member but maintains only a coast guard service. In 2016, the country established a National Security Council to implement and monitor security policy. The coast guard controls the NATO Iceland Air Defence System, as well as a NATO Control and Reporting Centre that feeds into NATO air- and missile-defence and air-operations centres. Geographically, Iceland plays an important role in connecting Europe and North America with communication links via subsea cables. In 2022, Iceland published its National Cybersecurity Strategy. Iceland considers its bilateral defence agreement with the US to be an important pillar of its security policy and also participates in NORDEFCO. Iceland joined the UK-led Joint Expeditionary Force in 2021. Iceland hosts NATO and regional partners for exercises, transits and naval task groups, as well as a NATO Icelandic Air Policing mission. Despite there being no standing armed forces, Iceland makes financial contributions and, on occasion, deploys civilian personnel to NATO missions. Iceland hosts US Navy P-8A *Poseidon* maritime-patrol aircraft in a rotational deployment based at Keflavik Air Base.

ACTIVE NIL Gendarmerie & Paramilitary 250

ORGANISATIONS BY SERVICE

Gendarmerie & Paramilitary

Iceland Coast Guard 250

EQUIPMENT BY TYPE
PATROL AND COASTAL COMBATANTS 2
  PSO 2: 1 *Freyja*; 1 *Thor*
LOGISTICS AND SUPPORT • AGS 1 *Baldur*
AIRCRAFT • TPT • Light 1 DHC-8-300 (MP)
HELICOPTERS • TPT • Medium 3 H225 (leased)

FOREIGN FORCES

Icelandic Air Policing: Aircraft and personnel from various NATO members on a rotating basis

United States US European Command: 50; 1 ASW flt with 2 P-8A *Poseidon*

Ireland IRL

Euro EUR		2023	2024	2025
GDP	EUR	510bn	514bn	535bn
	USD	552bn	561bn	587bn
Real GDP growth	%	-5.5	-0.2	2.2
Def bdgt [a]	EUR	1.17bn	1.23bn	1.35bn
	USD	1.27bn	1.34bn	1.48bn

[a] Includes military pensions and capital expenditure

Real-terms defence budget trend (USDbn, constant 2015)
1.24
1.00
2008 — 2016 — 2024

Population		5,233,461				
Age	0–14	15–19	20–24	25–29	30–64	65 plus
Male	9.5%	3.3%	3.0%	3.0%	23.2%	7.5%
Female	9.1%	3.2%	2.8%	3.0%	24.0%	8.4%

Capabilities

The core mission of Ireland's armed forces is to defend the state against armed aggression. Ireland underwent a Defence Policy Review in 2024, issuing a plan to increase the country's defence capabilities and improve its ability to respond to security threats. The government pledged to increase defence spending and boost ranks by around 2,000 personnel. Retention across the armed forces is an issue amongst experienced service personnel due to pay, conditions and opportunities. Dublin plans to create a chief of defence post and elevate the air corps and naval service to branches on par with the army. Ireland is active in EU defence cooperation and contributes to multinational operations, particularly UN deployments. Ireland's Office of Reserve Affairs intends to regenerate the Reserve Defence Force. Ireland is pursuing limited capability upgrades, and the primary radar project, identified in the 2022 Defence Commission Report, received additional funds in the budget. Reports of Russian naval activity over key fibre optic cables near Ireland's southwest coast has increased focus on improving underwater domain awareness capabilities. The country has a small defence industry specialising in areas such as drivetrain technologies for land systems.

ACTIVE 7,400 (Army 5,950 Navy 750 Air 700)
RESERVE 1,500 (Army 1,400 Navy 100)

ORGANISATIONS BY SERVICE

Army 5,950
FORCES BY ROLE
SPECIAL FORCES
  1 ranger coy
MANOEUVRE
  Reconnaissance
  1 armd recce sqn

Mechanised
1 mech inf coy
Light
1 inf bde (1 cav recce sqn, 4 inf bn, 1 arty regt (3 fd arty bty, 1 AD bty), 1 fd engr coy, 1 sigs coy, 1 MP coy, 1 tpt coy)
1 inf bde (1 cav recce sqn, 3 inf bn, 1 arty regt (3 fd arty bty, 1 AD bty), 1 fd engr coy, 1 sigs coy, 1 MP coy, 1 tpt coy)

EQUIPMENT BY TYPE
ARMOURED FIGHTING VEHICLES
RECCE 6 *Piranha* IIIH 30mm
APC 101
    APC (W) 74: 56 *Piranha* III; 18 *Piranha* IIIH
    PPV 27 RG-32M
ANTI-TANK/ANTI-INFRASTURCTURE
MSL • MANPATS FGM-148 *Javelin*
RCL 84mm *Carl Gustaf*
ARTILLERY 131
    TOWED • 105mm 23: 17 L118 Light Gun; 6 L119 Light Gun
    MOR 108: 81mm 84 Brandt; 120mm 24 Ruag M87
AIR DEFENCE
SAM • Point-defence RBS-70

Reserves 1,400 reservists
FORCES BY ROLE
MANOEUVRE
    Reconnaissance
    1 (integrated) armd recce sqn
    2 (integrated) cav sqn
    Mechanised
    1 (integrated) mech inf coy
    Light
    14 (integrated) inf coy
COMBAT SUPPORT
    4 (integrated) arty bty
    2 engr gp
    2 MP coy
    3 sigs coy
COMBAT SERVICE SUPPORT
    2 med det
    2 tpt coy

Naval Service 750
EQUIPMENT BY TYPE
PATROL AND COASTAL COMBATANTS 4
    PSO 2 *Samuel Beckett* (2 more in reserve) with 1 76mm gun; (2 *Roisin* with 1 76mm gun in reserve of which 1 in refit)
    PCC 2 Aoibhinn (ex-NZL *Lake*)
LOGISTICS AND SUPPORT • AXS 2
UNINHABITED MARITIME SYSTEMS
    UUV • DATA REMUS 100

Air Corps 700
2 ops wg; 2 spt wg; 1 trg wg; 1 comms and info sqn

FORCES BY ROLE
MARITIME PATROL
    1 sqn with C295 MPA
TRANSPORT
    1 sqn with Learjet 45; PC-12NG
TRAINING
    1 sqn with PC-9M
HELICOPTER
    1 sqn with AW139; H135
EQUIPMENT BY TYPE
AIRCRAFT
    MP 2 C295 MPA
    TPT • Light 5: 1 Learjet 45 (VIP); 4 PC-12NG
    TRG 8 PC-9M
HELICOPTERS:
    MRH 6 AW139
    TPT • Light 2 H135 (incl trg/medevac)

DEPLOYMENT
BOSNIA-HERZEGOVINA: EU • EUFOR (*Operation Althea*) 4
KOSOVO: NATO • KFOR 13
LEBANON: UN • UNIFIL 355; 1 mech inf bn(-)
MIDDLE EAST: UN • UNTSO 12
SYRIA/ISRAEL: UN • UNDOF 4

Italy ITA

Euro EUR		2023	2024	2025
GDP	EUR	2.13trn	2.18trn	2.24trn
	USD	2.30trn	2.38trn	2.46trn
Real GDP growth	%	0.7	0.7	0.8
Def exp [a]	EUR	31.3bn	32.0bn	
	USD	33.9bn	34.5bn	
Def bdgt [b]	EUR	30.1bn	32.3bn	31.3bn
	USD	32.5bn	35.2bn	34.4bn

[a] NATO figure
[b] Includes military pensions

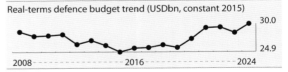
Real-terms defence budget trend (USDbn, constant 2015)

Population	60,964,931				
Age	0–14	15–19	20–24	25–29	30–64	65 plus
Male	6.1%	2.5%	2.5%	2.5%	24.3%	10.4%
Female	5.8%	2.4%	2.5%	2.6%	25.3%	13.2%

Capabilities
Italy's security concerns include challenges in the Euro-Atlantic area and on Europe's southern borders. A defence plan for 2024–26

outlined modernisation goals. The Ministry of Defence is revising its organisational structure, and the roles of the secretariat general of defence and of the national director for armaments have been separated. Italy is looking to reduce the average age of military personnel. Italy is deployed in NATO's air-policing missions, as part of the Alliance's Forward Land Forces in Latvia, is the framework nation for the battlegroup in Bulgaria, and has commanded the EU's *Aspides* mission. The EUNAVFORMED force is headquartered in Rome, while the US Navy's 6th Fleet is based in Naples. The country takes part in and hosts NATO and other multinational exercises and continues to support NATO, EU and UN operations. The parliament modified the authorisation process for military missions to approve them on a case-by-case basis when needed, instead of annually. Rome intends to be able to deploy a limited joint expeditionary force for high-intensity operations for six to eight months. Modernisation plans include C2 and ISR capabilities. Rome is a partner with Japan and the UK on the Global Combat Air Programme to develop a next-generation fighter, and the country takes part in European defence-industrial cooperation activities. Italy has an advanced defence industry capable of producing equipment across all domains, with particular strengths in ship, aircraft and helicopter production. In 2024, a new joint venture was announced between Rheinmetall and Leonardo focused on armoured vehicles.

ACTIVE 161,850 (Army 94,000 Navy 29,300 Air 38,550) Gendarmerie & Paramilitary 178,600

RESERVES 14,500

ORGANISATIONS BY SERVICE

Space
EQUIPMENT BY TYPE
SATELLITES 9
   COMMUNICATIONS 2: 1 *Athena-Fidus* (also used by FRA); 1 *Sicral*
   ISR 7: 4 *Cosmo* (*Skymed*); 2 *Cosmo* SG; 1 OPTSAT-3000

Army 94,000
Regt are bn sized
FORCES BY ROLE
COMMAND
   1 (NRDC-ITA) corps HQ (1 spt bde, 1 sigs regt, 1 spt regt)
   3 div HQ
MANOEUVRE
  Armoured
   1 (*Ariete*) armd bde (1 cav regt, 2 tk regt, 1 armd inf regt, 1 SP arty regt, 1 cbt engr regt, 1 log regt)
   1 (*Garibaldi Bersaglieri*) armd inf bde (1 cav regt, 1 tk regt, 2 armd inf regt, 1 SP arty regt, 1 cbt engr regt, 1 log regt)
  Mechanised
   1 (*Aosta*) mech bde (1 cav regt, 1 armd inf regt, 2 mech inf regt, 1 fd arty regt, 1 cbt engr regt, 1 log regt)
   1 (*Granatieri*) mech bde (1 cav regt, 2 mech inf regt)
   1 (*Pinerolo*) mech bde (1 cav regt, 3 armd inf regt, 1 fd arty regt, 1 cbt engr regt, 1 log regt)
   1 (*Sassari*) lt mech bde (1 armd inf regt, 2 mech inf regt, 1 cbt engr regt, 1 log regt)

  Mountain
   2 mtn bde (1 cav regt, 3 mtn inf regt, 1 arty regt, 1 mtn cbt engr regt, 1 spt bn, 1 log regt)
  Air Manoeuvre
   1 (*Folgore*) AB bde (1 cav regt, 3 para regt, 1 arty regt, 1 cbt engr regt, 1 log regt)
   1 (*Friuli*) air mob bde (1 air mob regt, 2 atk hel regt)
  Amphibious
   1 (*Pozzuolo del Friuli*) amph bde (1 cav regt, 1 amph regt, 1 arty regt, 1 cbt engr regt, 1 log regt);
COMBAT SUPPORT
   1 arty comd (1 arty regt, 1 MRL regt, 1 NBC regt)
   1 AD comd (3 SAM regt)
   1 engr comd (2 engr regt, 1 ptn br regt)
   1 EW/sigs comd (1 EW/ISR bde (1 CIMIC regt, 1 EW regt, 1 int regt, 1 STA regt); 1 sigs bde with (7 sigs regt))
COMBAT SERVICE SUPPORT
   1 log comd (3 log regt, 4 med unit)
HELICOPTER
   1 hel bde (3 hel regt)
EQUIPMENT BY TYPE
ARMOURED FIGHTING VEHICLES
  MBT 150: 147 C1 *Ariete*; 3 C2 *Ariete* AMV (in test)
  ASLT 268: 255 B1 *Centauro*; 13+ *Centauro* II
  IFV 449: 165 VCC-80 *Dardo*; 284 VBM 8×8 *Freccia* (incl 20 CP and 60 with *Spike*-LR)
  APC 370
   APC (T) 138 Bv-206S
   APC (W) 199 *Puma* 6×6
   PPV 33 VTMM *Orso* (incl 16 amb)
  AUV 1,842: 10 *Cougar*; 1,798 IVECO LMV (incl 82 amb); 34 IVECO LMV 2
  AAV 15: 14 AAVP-7; 1 AAVC-7
ENGINEERING & MAINTENANCE VEHICLES
  AEV 25: 25 *Dachs*; M113
  ARV 74: 73 BPz-2; 1 AAVR-7
  VLB 30 *Biber*
  MW 43: 15 *Buffalo*; 3 *Miniflail*; 25 VTMM *Orso*
NBC VEHICLES 14: 5 VBR NBC; 9 VBR NBC Plus
ANTI-TANK/ANTI-INFRASTRUCTURE
  MSL • MANPATS *Spike*
ARTILLERY 708
  SP 155mm 64 PzH 2000
  TOWED 115: **105mm** 25 Oto Melara Mod 56; **155mm** 90 FH-70 (52 more in store)
  MRL 227mm 21 M270 MLRS
  MOR 508: **81mm** 283 Expal; **120mm** 204: 62 Brandt; 142 RT-61 (RT-F1) **SP 120mm** 21 VBM 8×8 *Freccia*
AIRCRAFT • TPT • Light 6: 3 Do-228 (ACTL-1); 3 P.180 *Avanti*
HELICOPTERS
  ATK 33 AW129CBT *Mangusta*
  MRH 13 Bell 412 (AB-412) *Twin Huey*

TPT 148: **Heavy** 16 CH-47F *Chinook*; **Medium** 60 NH90 TTH (UH-90A); **Light** 72: 2 AW169LUH (UH-169B); 29 Bell 205 (AB-205); 28 Bell 206 *Jet Ranger* (AB-206); 13 Bell 212 (AB-212)

AIR DEFENCE • SAM 12+
  Long-range 12 SAMP/T
  Point-defence FIM-92 *Stinger*

AIR-LAUNCHED MISSILES
  ASM *Spike*-ER

Navy 29,300

EQUIPMENT BY TYPE

SUBMARINES • SSK 8:
  4 *Pelosi* (imp *Sauro*, 3rd and 4th series) with 6 single 533mm TT with A184 mod 3 HWT
  4 *Salvatore Todaro* (Type-212A) (fitted with AIP) with 6 single 533mm TT with *Black Shark* HWT

PRINCIPAL SURFACE COMBATANTS 18
  AIRCRAFT CARRIERS • CVS 1
    1 *Cavour* with 4 8-cell *Sylver* A43 VLS with *Aster* 15 SAM, 2 76mm guns (capacity mixed air group of 20 AV-8B *Harrier* II; F-35B *Lightning* II; AW101 *Merlin*; NH90; Bell 212)
  DESTROYERS • DDGHM 3:
    2 *Andrea Doria* with 2 quad lnchr with *Otomat* (*Teseo*) Mk2A AShM, 6 8-cell *Sylver* A50 VLS with *Aster* 15/*Aster* 30 SAM, 2 single 324mm B-515 ASTT with MU90 LWT, 3 76mm guns (capacity 1 AW101 *Merlin*/NH90 hel)
    1 *Luigi Durand de la Penne* (ex-*Animoso*) with 2 quad lnchr with *Otomat* (*Teseo*) Mk2A AShM/*Milas* A/S msl, 1 Mk 13 mod 4 GMLS with SM-1MR Block VI SAM, 1 octuple *Albatros* lnchr with *Aspide* SAM, 2 triple 324mm B-515 ASTT with Mk 46 LWT, 1 127mm gun, 3 76mm guns (capacity 1 NH90 or 2 Bell 212 (AB-212) hel)

  FRIGATES 14
    FFGHM 11:
      4 *Bergamini* (GP) with 2 quad lnchr with *Otomat* (*Teseo*) Mk2A AShM, 2 8-cell *Sylver* A50 VLS with *Aster* 15/*Aster* 30 SAM, 2 triple 324mm B-515 ASTT with MU90 LWT, 1 127mm gun, 1 76mm gun (capacity 2 AW101/NH90 hel)
      4 *Bergamini* (ASW) with 2 twin lnchr with *Otomat* (*Teseo*) Mk2A AShM, 2 twin lnchr with MILAS A/S msl, 2 8-cell *Sylver* A50 VLS with *Aster* 15/*Aster* 30 SAM, 2 triple 324mm B-515 ASTT with MU90 LWT, 2 76mm guns (capacity 2 AW101/NH90 hel)
      2 *Maestrale* with 4 single lnchr with *Otomat* (*Teseo*) Mk2 AShM, 1 octuple *Albatros* lnchr with *Aspide* SAM, 2 triple 324mm SVTT Mk 32 ASTT with Mk 46 LWT, 1 127mm gun (capacity 1 NH90 or 2 Bell 212 (AB-212) hel)
      1 *Paolo Thaon di Revel* (PPA Full) with 2 quad lnchr with *Otomat* (*Teseo*) Mk2A AShM, 2 8-cell *Sylver* A50 VLS with *Aster* 30 SAM, 2 triple 324mm B-515 ASTT with MU90 LWT, 1 127mm gun, 1 76mm gun (capacity 2 NH90 or 1 AW101)
    FFHM 1 *Paolo Thaon di Revel* (PPA Light+) with 2 8-cell *Sylver* A50 VLS with *Aster* 30 SAM, 1 127mm gun, 1 76mm gun (capacity 2 NH90 or 1 AW101)
    FFH 2 *Paolo Thaon di Revel* (PPA Light) with 1 127mm gun, 1 76mm gun (capacity 2 NH90 or 1 AW101)

PATROL AND COASTAL COMBATANTS 16
  PSOH 10:
    4 *Cassiopea* with 1 76mm gun (capacity 1 Bell 212 (AB-212) hel)
    4 *Comandante Cigala Fuligosi* with 1 76mm gun (capacity 1 Bell 212 (AB-212)/NH90 hel)
    2 *Sirio* (capacity 1 Bell 212 (AB-212) or NH90 hel)
  PB 6: 2 *Angelo Cabrini*; 4 *Esploratore*

MINE WARFARE • MINE COUNTERMEASURES 10
  MHO 10: 8 *Gaeta*; 2 *Lerici*

AMPHIBIOUS
  PRINCIPAL AMPHIBIOUS SHIPS • LHD 3:
    2 *San Giorgio* (capacity 3-4 AW101/NH90/Bell 212; 3 LCM; 2 LCVP; 30 trucks; 36 APC (T); 350 troops)
    1 *San Giusto* with 1 76mm gun (capacity 2 AW101 *Merlin*/NH90/Bell 212/S-100; 3 LCM; 2 LCVP; 30 trucks; 36 APC (T); 350 troops)
  LANDING CRAFT 28: 15 **LCVP**; 13 **LCM**

LOGISTICS AND SUPPORT 43
  ABU 5 *Ponza*
  AGE 3: 1 *Leonardo* (coastal); 1 *Raffaele Rosseti*; 1 *Vincenzo Martellota*
  AGI 1 *Elettra*
  AGOR 1 *Alliance*
  AGS 3: 1 *Ammiraglio Magnaghi* with 1 hel landing platform; 2 *Aretusa* (coastal)
  AKL 6 *Gorgona*
  AORH 2: 1 *Etna* with 1 76mm gun (capacity 1 AW101/NH90/Bell 212 hel); 1 *Vulcano* (capacity 2 AW101/NH90/Bell 212)
  AOR 1 *Stromboli* with 1 76mm gun (capacity 1 AW101/NH90 hel)
  AOL 4 *Panarea*
  ARSH 1 *Anteo* (capacity 1 Bell 212 (AB-212) hel)
  ATF 6 *Ciclope*
  AWT 2 *Simeto*
  AXS 8: 1 *Amerigo Vespucci*; 5 *Caroly*; 1 *Italia*; 1 *Palinuro*

UNINHABITED MARITIME SYSTEMS • UUV
  DATA REMUS 1000
  MW *Pluto* Gigas; *Pluto* Plus
  UTL HUGIN 1000

Naval Aviation 2,000

FORCES BY ROLE
FIGHTER/GROUND ATTACK
  1 sqn with AV-8B *Harrier* II; TAV-8B *Harrier* II; F-35B *Lightning* II
ANTI-SUBMARINE WARFARE/TRANSPORT
  5 sqn with AW101 ASW *Merlin*; Bell 212 ASW (AB-212AS); Bell 212 (AB-212); NH90 NFH; S-100 *Camcopter*

MARITIME PATROL
  1 flt with P-180
AIRBORNE EARLY WANRING & CONTROL
  1 flt with AW101 AEW *Merlin*
EQUIPMENT BY TYPE
AIRCRAFT 16 combat capable
  FGA 16: 9 AV-8B *Harrier* II; 1 TAV-8B *Harrier* II; 6 F-35B *Lightning* II
  MP 3 P.180 *Avanti*
HELICOPTERS
  ASW 62: 10 AW101 ASW *Merlin*; 6 Bell 212 ASW; 46 NH90 NFH (SH-90)
  AEW 4 AW101 AEW *Merlin*
  TPT • Medium 20: 10 AW101 *Merlin*; 10 NH90 MITT (MH-90)
UNINHABITED AERHIAL VEHICLES
  ISR • Light 1 S-100 *Camcopter*
AIR-LAUNCHED MISSILES
  AAM • IR AIM-9L *Sidewinder*; ARH AIM-120 AMRAAM
  ASM AGM-65 *Maverick*
  AShM *Marte* Mk 2/S

Marines 3,000
FORCES BY ROLE
MANOEUVRE
  Amphibious
  1 mne regt (1 recce coy, 2 mne bn, 1 log bn)
  1 (boarding) mne regt (2 mne bn)
  1 landing craft gp
  Other
  1 sy regt (3 sy bn)
EQUIPMENT BY TYPE
ARMOURED FIGHTING VEHICLES
  AAV 17: 15 AAVP-7; 2 AAVC-7
  AUV 70 IVECO LMV
ENGINEERING & MAINTENANCE VEHICLES
  ARV 1 AAVR-7
ANTI-TANK/ANTI-INFRASTRUCTURE
  MSL• MANPATS *Spike*
ARTILLERY
  MOR 22: 81mm 16 Expal; 120mm 6 RT-61 (RT-F1)
  AIR DEFENCE • SAM • Point-defence FIM-92 *Stinger*

Air Force 38,550
FORCES BY ROLE
FIGHTER
  5 sqn with Eurofighter *Typhoon*
FIGHTER/GROUND ATTACK
  1 sqn with F-35A *Lightning* II
  1 sqn with F-35A/B *Lightning* II
GROUND ATTACK
  1 sqn with *Tornado* IDS
  1 (SEAD/EW) sqn with *Tornado* ECR
MARITIME PATROL
  1 sqn (opcon Navy) with ATR-72MP (P-72A)
TANKER/TRANSPORT
  1 sqn with KC-767A
COMBAT SEARCH & RESCUE
  1 sqn with AW101 SAR (HH-101A)
SEARCH & RESCUE
  1 wg with AW139 (HH-139A)
TRANSPORT
  1 sqn with C-27J *Spartan*
  2 sqn with C-130J/C-130J-30/KC-130J *Hercules*
  1 (calibration) sqn with P-180 *Avanti*/Gulfstream G550 CAEW
  2 (VIP) sqn with A319CJ; AW139 (VH-139A); *Falcon* 50; *Falcon* 900 *Easy*; *Falcon* 900EX
TRAINING
  1 OCU sqn with Eurofighter *Typhoon*
  1 OCU with F-35A *Lightning* II
  1 sqn with MB-339PAN (aerobatic team)
  1 sqn with MD-500D/E (NH-500D/E)
  1 sqn with MB-339A
  1 sqn with M-346
  1 sqn with SF-260EA; 3 P2006T (T-2006A)
  1 hel sqn with AW101 SAR (HH-101A)
ISR UAV
  1 sqn with MQ-9A *Reaper*
AIR DEFENCE
  2 bty with *Spada*
EQUIPMENT BY TYPE
AIRCRAFT 195 combat capable
  FTR 92 Eurofighter *Typhoon*
  FGA 26: 24 F-35A *Lightning* II; 2 F-35B *Lightning* II
  ATK 34 *Tornado* IDS
  ATK/EW 15 *Tornado* ECR*
  MP 4 ATR-72MP (P-72A)
  SIGINT 1 Beech 350 *King Air*
  AEW&C 3 Gulfstream G550 CAEW
  TKR/TPT 4 KC-767A
  TPT 76: Medium 33: 11 C-130J *Hercules* (5+ KC-130J tanker pods); 10 C-130J-30 *Hercules*; 12 C-27J *Spartan*; Light 35: 17 P-180 *Avanti*; 18 S-208 (liaison); PAX 8: 3 A319CJ; 2 *Falcon* 50 (VIP); 2 *Falcon* 900 *Easy*; 1 *Falcon* 900EX (VIP)
  TRG 114: 21 MB-339A; 28 MB-339CD*; 15 MB-339PAN (aerobatics); 2+ M-345; 22 M-346; 26 SF-260EA
HELICOPTERS
  MRH 54: 13 AW139 (HH-139A/VH-139A); 2 MD-500D (NH-500D); 39 MD-500E (NH-500E)
  CSAR 12 AW101 (HH-101A)
  SAR 17 AW139 (HH-139B)
UNINHABITED AERIAL VEHICLES 6
  CISR • Heavy 6 MQ-9A *Reaper* (unarmed)
AIR DEFENCE • SAM • Short-range SPADA
AIR-LAUNCHED MISSILES
  AAM • IR AIM-9L *Sidewinder*; IIR IRIS-T; ARH AIM-120C AMRAAM; *Meteor*

ARM AGM-88C HARM; AGM-88E AARGM
LACM SCALP EG/*Storm Shadow*
BOMBS
  Laser-guided GBU-16 *Paveway* II; *Lizard* 2
  Laser & INS/GPS-guided GBU-48 Enhanced *Paveway* II; GBU-54 Laser JDAM
  INS/GPS-guided GBU-31/-32/-38 JDAM; GBU-39 Small Diameter Bomb

Joint Special Forces Command (COFS)

Army
FORCES BY ROLE
SPECIAL FORCES
  1 SF regt (9th *Assalto paracadutisti*)
  1 STA regt
  1 ranger regt (4th *Alpini paracadutisti*)
COMBAT SUPPORT
  1 psyops regt
TRANSPORT HELICOPTER
  1 spec ops hel regt

Navy (COMSUBIN)
FORCES BY ROLE
SPECIAL FORCES
  1 SF gp (GOI)
  1 diving gp (GOS)

Air Force
FORCES BY ROLE
SPECIAL FORCES
  1 wg (sqn) (17th *Stormo Incursori*)

Paramilitary

Carabinieri
FORCES BY ROLE
SPECIAL FORCES
  1 spec ops gp (GIS)

Gendarmerie & Paramilitary 178,600

Carabinieri 110,500
The Carabinieri are organisationally under the MoD. They are a separate service in the Italian Armed Forces as well as a police force with judicial competence

Mobile and Specialised Branch
FORCES BY ROLE
MANOEUVRE
  Other
    1 (mobile) paramilitary div (1 bde (1st) with (1 horsed cav regt, 11 mobile bn); 1 bde (2nd) with (1 (1st) AB regt, 2 (7th & 13th) mobile regt))
HELICOPTER
  1 hel gp
EQUIPMENT BY TYPE
ARMOURED FIGHTING VEHICLES
  APC • APC (T) 3 VCC-2
  AUV 30 IVECO LMV
AIRCRAFT • TPT • Light: 2 P.180 *Avanti*
HELICOPTERS
  MRH 15 Bell 412 (AB-412)
  TPT • Light 31: 19 AW109; 2 AW109E; 2 AW139; 8 MD-500D (NH-500D)

Customs 68,100
(Servizio Navale Guardia Di Finanza)
EQUIPMENT BY TYPE
PATROL AND COASTAL COMBATANTS 207
  PCO 3: 1 *Bandiera* (Damen Stan Patrol 5509 mod); 2 *Monti* (Damen Stan Patrol 5509)
  PCF 1 *Antonio Zara*
  PBF 178: 19 *Bigliani*; 3 *Corrubia*; 9 *Mazzei*; 1 *Tenente Petrucci*; 29 V-800; 5 V-1600; 77 V-2000; 8 V-3000; 11 V-5000; 4 V-6000; 12 V-7000
  PB 25: 23 *Buratti*; 2 GL1400
LOGISTICS AND SUPPORT 2
  AX 1 *Giorgio Cini*
  AXS 1 *Grifone*
AIRCRAFT
  MP 8: 4 ATR-42-500MP; 4 ATR-72-600 (P-72B)
  TPT • Light 2 P.180 *Avanti*
HELICOPTERS
  TPT • Light 54: 10 AW109N; 17 AW139; 7 AW169M; 8 Bell 412HP *Twin Huey*; 4 MD-500MC (NH-500MC); 8 MD-500MD (NH-500MD)

DEPLOYMENT

BOSNIA-HERZEGOVINA: EU • EUFOR (*Operation Althea*) 180; 1 ISR coy

BULGARIA: NATO • Forward Land Forces 750; 1 armd inf BG with C1 *Ariete*; B1 *Centauro*; VBM *Freccia* 8×8; IVECO LMV; PzH 2000

DJIBOUTI: 92

EGYPT: MFO 75; 3 PB

GULF OF GUINEA: Navy 190; 1 FFGHM

INDIA/PAKISTAN: UN • UNMOGIP 2

IRAQ: *Operation Inherent Resolve* (*Prima Parthica*) 300; 1 trg unit; 1 hel sqn with 5 NH90; **NATO •** NATO Mission Iraq 75

KOSOVO: NATO • KFOR 855; 1 armd inf BG HQ; 1 inf coy; 1 ISR bn HQ; 1 Carabinieri unit

KUWAIT: *Operation Inherent Resolve* (*Prima Parthica*) 400; 4 Eurofighter *Typhoon*; 2 MQ-9A *Reaper*; 1 C-27J *Spartan*; 1 KC-767A

LATVIA: NATO • Forward Land Forces (*Baltic Guardian*) 300; 1 armd inf coy with C1 *Ariete*; VCC-80 *Dardo*

LEBANON: MIBIL 22; **UN •** UNIFIL 863; 1 bde HQ; 1 inf bn; 1 MP coy; 1 sigs coy; 1 hel sqn

LIBYA: MIASIT 160; 1 inf coy; 1 CRBN unit; 1 trg unit

LITHUANIA: NATO • Baltic Air Policing: 200; 4 Eurofighter *Typhoon*

MEDITERRANEAN SEA: EU • EUNAVFOR MED • *Operation Irini*; 60; 1 PSOH; **NATO** • SNMCMG 2: 40; 1 MHO

MOZAMBIQUE: EU • EUMAM Mozambique 6

NIGER: MISIN 250

RED SEA: EU • EUNAVFOR • *Operation Aspides*; 200; 1 DDGHM

SOMALIA: EU • EUTM Somalia 150

WESTERN SAHARA: UN • MINURSO 2

FOREIGN FORCES

United States US European Command: 12,600
  Army 4,100; 1 AB bde(-)
  Navy 3,650; 1 HQ (US Naval Forces Europe-Africa (NAVEUR-NAVAF)/6th Fleet) at Naples; 1 ASW Sqn with 5 P-8A *Poseidon* at Sigonella; 1 ISR UAV flt with 2 MQ-4C *Triton* at Sigonella
  USAF 4,800; 1 FGA wg with (2 FGA sqn with 21 F-16C/D *Fighting Falcon* at Aviano; 1 CSAR sqn with 8 HH-60G *Pave Hawk*); 1 CISR UAV sqn with MQ-9A *Reaper* at Sigonella; 1 ISR UAV flt with RQ-4B *Global Hawk* at Sigonella
  USMC 50

Kosovo XKX

Euro EUR		2023	2024	2025
GDP	EUR	9.65bn	10.3bn	11.0bn
	USD	10.4bn	11.2bn	11.8bn
Real GDP growth	%	3.3	3.8	4.0
Def bdgt [a]	EUR	123m	152m	155m
	USD	133m	164m	167m

[a] Excludes pensions

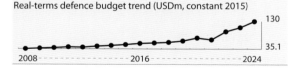

Real-terms defence budget trend (USDm, constant 2015)

Population	1,977,093				
Age	0–14	15–19	20–24	25–29	30–64	65 plus
Male	11.8%	4.3%	4.3%	4.1%	23.3%	3.7%
Female	10.9%	3.9%	4.0%	3.8%	21.2%	4.7%

Capabilities

In February 2008, Kosovo declared itself independent, a move Serbia continues to oppose. While Kosovo has not been admitted to the UN, several states have recognised Kosovo's self-declared status. The Kosovo Security Force (KSF), formed in January 2009, is tasked with defence of the country, support to civil authorities in case of national emergencies and participation in international operations. A series of legislative changes passed by the Kosovo Assembly in 2018 redefined it as a regular military organisation as part of a transformation process intended to be complete by 2028. Plans for a 5,000 strong force have not yet been realised. The EU's EULEX Kosovo and NATO's KFOR missions contribute to security. The KSF's budget has increased in the last years to enable important acquisition programmes, including Bayraktar TB2 UAVs from Turkiye in 2023. A military framework agreement was signed with Turkiye in January 2024. Data here represents the de facto situation in Kosovo. This does not imply international recognition as a sovereign state.

ACTIVE 3,000 (Kosovo Security Force 3,000)

ORGANISATIONS BY SERVICE

Kosovo Security Force 3,000
FORCES BY ROLE
SPECIAL FORCES
  1 spec ops unit
MANOEUVRE
  Light
  1 inf bde (3 inf bn)
COMBAT SUPPORT
  1 spt bde (1 engr bn, 1 EOD bn)
COMBAT/ISR UAV
  1 sqn with *Bayraktar* TB2
EQUIPMENT BY TYPE
ARMOURED FIGHTING VEHICLES
  AUV 71+: 55 M1117 *Guardian*; 16+ *Cobra*
ANTI-TANK/ANTI-INFRASTRUCTURE
  MANPATS OMTAS
ARTILLERY
  MOR 3+: **81mm** some; **120mm** some; **SP 120mm** 3+ *Vuran* with *Alkar*
UNIHABITED AERIAL VEHICLES
  CISR • **Medium** 5 *Bayraktar* TB2

DEPLOYMENT

UNITED KINGDOM: *Operation Interflex* 25 (UKR trg)

FOREIGN FORCES

All under Kosovo Force (KFOR) command unless otherwise specified
Albania 90
Armenia 57
Austria 107; 1 recce coy; • UNMIK 1
Bulgaria 126; 1 inf coy
Canada 5
Croatia 150; 1 inf coy; 1 hel flt with Mi-8
Czech Republic 35 • UNMIK 1
Denmark 35
Finland 70
France 3
Germany 300; 1 inf coy
Greece 121; 1 inf bn HQ; 2 inf coy
Hungary 365; 1 inf bn HQ; 2 inf coy • UNMIK 1
Ireland 13
Italy 855; 1 armd inf regt BG HQ; 1 ISR bn; 1 Carabinieri unit
Latvia 140; 1 inf coy
Lithuania 1

Macedonia, North 68
Moldova 44 • UNMIK 1
Montenegro 2
Poland 247; 1 inf coy • UNMIK 2
Portugal 1
Romania 184; 1 inf coy • UNMIK 1
Slovenia 105; 1 mot inf coy; 1 MP unit; 1 hel unit • UNMIK 1
Sweden 3
Switzerland 211; 1 engr pl; 1 tpt unit; 1 hel flt with AS332
Türkiye 325; 1 inf coy • UNMIK 1
United Kingdom 41
United States 598; elm 1 ARNG inf bde HQ; 1 ARNG inf bn HQ; 1 ARNG inf coy; 1 hel flt with UH-60

Latvia LVA

Euro EUR		2023	2024	2025
GDP	EUR	40.3bn	41.8bn	43.9bn
	USD	43.6bn	45.5bn	48.2bn
Real GDP growth	%	-0.3	1.2	2.3
Def exp [a]	EUR	1.16bn	1.32bn	
	USD	1.25bn	1.42bn	
Def bdgt [b]	EUR	967m	1.32bn	1.45bn
	USD	1.05bn	1.44bn	1.59bn
FMA (US)	USD	9.75m	9.75m	9.75m

[a] NATO figure
[b] Includes military pensions

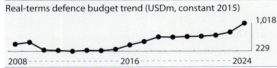
Real-terms defence budget trend (USDm, constant 2015)

Population	1,801,246					
Age	0–14	15–19	20–24	25–29	30–64	65 plus
Male	7.6%	2.8%	2.4%	2.3%	23.8%	7.6%
Female	7.1%	2.6%	2.2%	2.1%	24.9%	14.6%

Capabilities

Latvia's armed forces are focused on maintaining national sovereignty and territorial integrity. The Baltic state relies on NATO membership for security guarantees. Russia is Latvia's overriding security concern. In the wake of the February 2022 invasion of Ukraine, Latvia boosted defence spending and transferred military equipment to Ukraine. The State Defence Service law reintroduced compulsory military service in 2023, with two intakes of conscripts annually. The 2023 National Security Concept emphasised societal resilience and comprehensive defence as well as the importance of border protection. Under the Baltic Defence Line Initiative, Latvia plans to build defensive fortifications along its eastern border. The 2023 National Defence Concept outlined plans to increase the size of the armed forces to 31,000 active personnel and for an additional 30,000 reserves. Latvia hosts a NATO Forward Land Forces multinational battlegroup. Latvia is also a member of the UK-led Joint Expeditionary Force. There is no capacity to independently deploy and sustain forces beyond national boundaries, although the armed forces have taken part in NATO and EU missions. Improvements are being made to logistics and procurement systems. Latvia has recently recapitalised its artillery capability with second-hand howitzers from Austria and is acquiring medium-range air defences jointly with Estonia. Latvia has a niche defence-industrial capability, with strengths in cyber security.

ACTIVE 6,600 (Army 1,500 Navy 500 Air 500 Joint Staff 2,400 National Guard 1,400 Other 300)

Conscript liability 11 months, 18–27 years

RESERVE 16,000 (National Guard 10,000 Other 6,000)

ORGANISATIONS BY SERVICE

Joint 2,400
FORCES BY ROLE
SPECIAL FORCES
   1 SF unit
COMBAT SUPPORT
   1 MP bn

Army 1,500
FORCES BY ROLE
MANOEUVRE
   Mechanised
   1 mech inf bde (2 mech inf bn, 1 SP arty bn, 1 cbt spt bn (1 recce coy, 1 engr coy, 1 AD coy), 1 CSS bn HQ)

National Guard 1,400; 10,000 part-time (11,400 total)
FORCES BY ROLE
MANOEUVRE
   Light
   1 (2nd) inf bde (3 inf bn; 3 spt bn, 1 engr coy, 1 med coy)
   3 (1st, 3rd & 4th) inf bde (3 inf bn; 2 spt bn, 1 engr coy, 1 med coy)
COMBAT SUPPORT
   1 cyber unit
   1 NBC coy
   1 psyops pl
EQUIPMENT BY TYPE
ARMOURED FIGHTING VEHICLES
   RECCE 197 FV107 Scimitar (incl variants)
   APC • APC(W) ε90 XA-300
ANTI-TANK/ANTI-INFRASTRUCTURE
   MANPATS Spike-LR
   RCL 84mm Carl Gustaf; 90mm Pvpj 1110
ARTILLERY 100
   SP 155mm 47 M109A5ÖE
   TOWED 100mm (23 K-53 in store)
   MOR 53: 81mm 28 L16; 120mm 25 M120
   AIR DEFENCE • SAM • Point-defence Piorun

Navy 500 (incl Coast Guard)

Naval Forces Flotilla separated into an MCM squadron

and a patrol-boat squadron. LVA, EST and LTU have set up a joint naval unit, BALTRON, with bases at Liepaja, Riga, Ventspils (LVA), Tallinn (EST), Klaipeda (LTU). Each nation contributes 1–2 MCMVs

EQUIPMENT BY TYPE
PATROL AND COASTAL COMBATANTS 5
  PB 5 *Skrunda* (GER *Swath*)
MINE WARFARE • MINE COUNTERMEASURES 4
  MCCS 1 *Vidar* (ex-NOR)
  MHO 3 *Imanta* (ex-NLD *Alkmaar/Tripartite*)
LOGISTICS AND SUPPORT • AXL 1 *Varonis* (comd and spt ship, ex-NLD)
UNINHABITED MARITIME SYSTEMS
  UUV • MW A18-M

Coast Guard
Under command of the Latvian Naval Forces
EQUIPMENT BY TYPE
PATROL AND COASTAL COMBATANTS 6
  PB 6: 1 *Astra*; 5 KBV 236 (ex-SWE)

Air Force 500
Main tasks are airspace control and defence, maritime and land SAR and air transportation
FORCES BY ROLE
TRANSPORT
  1 (mixed) tpt sqn with An-2 *Colt*; UH-60M *Black Hawk*
AIR DEFENCE
  1 AD bn
  1 radar sqn (radar/air ctrl)
AIRCRAFT
  TPT • Light 4 An-2 *Colt*
  TRG 2 *Tarragon*
HELICOPTERS
  TPT • Medium 4 UH-60M *Black Hawk*
AIR DEFENCE
  SAM • Point-defence RBS-70
  GUNS • TOWED 40mm 24 L/70

Gendarmerie & Paramilitary
State Border Guard
EQUIPMENT BY TYPE
PATROL AND COASTAL COMBATANTS 3
  PB 3: 1 *Valpas* (ex-FIN); 1 *Tiira* (ex-FIN); 1 *Randa*
HELICOPTERS
  TPT • Light 6: 2 AW109E *Power*; 2 AW119Kx; 2 Bell 206B (AB-206B) *Jet Ranger* II

DEPLOYMENT
IRAQ: *Operation Inherent Resolve* 1; **NATO** • NATO Mission Iraq 3
KOSOVO: NATO • KFOR 140; 1 inf coy
MIDDLE EAST: UN • UNTSO 1

FOREIGN FORCES
All NATO Forward Land Forces unless stated
Albania 40; 1 EOD pl
Canada 1,600; 1 mech inf bn HQ; 1 tk sqn; 1 mech inf BG; 1 fd arty bty
Czech Republic 60; 1 EW unit; 1 SAM bty
Denmark 800; 1 armd BG
Germany NATO Baltic Air Policing 150; 5 Eurofighter *Typhoon*
Italy 300; 1 armd inf coy
Macedonia, North 9
Montenegro 11
Poland 200; 1 tk coy
Slovakia 115; 1 arty bty
Slovenia 35
Spain 600; 1 armd inf coy(+); 1 arty bty; 1 cbt engr coy; 1 SAM bty

Lithuania LTU

Euro EUR		2023	2024	2025
GDP	EUR	72.0bn	76.0bn	80.2bn
	USD	77.8bn	82.8bn	88.0bn
Real GDP growth	%	-0.3	2.4	2.6
Def exp [a]	EUR	2.00bn	2.13bn	
	USD	2.17bn	2.30bn	
Def bdgt [b]	EUR	1.87bn	2.29bn	2.52bn
	USD	2.02bn	2.50bn	2.77bn
FMA (US)	USD	9.75m	9.75m	9.75m

[a] NATO figure
[b] Includes military pensions

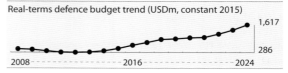
Real-terms defence budget trend (USDm, constant 2015)
2008 – 2016 – 2024; 286 – 1,617

Population	2,628,186					
Age	0–14	15–19	20–24	25–29	30–64	65 plus
Male	7.8%	2.6%	2.5%	2.8%	22.8%	7.7%
Female	7.4%	2.4%	2.4%	2.6%	24.5%	14.5%

Capabilities
Lithuania's armed forces are focused on maintaining sovereignty and territorial integrity, though the country relies on its NATO membership for its security. The country adopted a new National Security Strategy in December 2021, reflecting the worsening regional security environment. An updated National Defence System Development Programme was adopted in March 2024, detailing planned increases in defence spending and capability development. The armed forces are proceeding with plans to establish a divisional formation, built from the existing two regular and one reserve brigades, with support and enabling assets. The annual conscript intake is due to increase from 2025. The number of reservists called to annual exercises is also increasing. Lithuania has a limited medium-airlift capability. It takes part in NATO and EU operations.

Like the other Baltic states, it benefits from NATO's air policing deployment. The country is part of the European Sky Shield initiative and has purchased artillery systems and announced plans to transform a mechanised infantry battalion into a tank battalion. Lithuania hosts a multinatoinal battlegroup as part of NATO's Forward Land Forces. Germany in 2024 started to deploy elements of a permanent brigade to the country, expected to reach full operational capability in 2027. Lithuania is part of the Baltic Defence Line Initiative, designed to improve border defences. The Roadmap for the Development of Lithuania's Defence and Security Industry 2023–27 seeks to help the country's defence industry access new sources of funding, and a defence industry law came into effect in 2024.

ACTIVE 16,100 (Army 10,250 Navy 800 Air 1,850 Other 3,200) Gendarmerie & Paramilitary 18,400

Conscript liability 9 months, 18–23 years

RESERVE 12,950 (Army 7,100 National Defence Voluntary Forces 5,850)

ORGANISATIONS BY SERVICE

Army 10,250
FORCES BY ROLE
MANOEUVRE
  Mechanised
    1 (1st) mech bde (4 mech inf bn, 1 SP arty bn, 1 log bn)
  Light
    1 (2nd) mot inf bde (3 mot inf bn, 1 arty bn)
COMBAT SUPPORT
  1 engr bn
COMBAT SERVICE SUPPORT
  1 trg regt
EQUIPMENT BY TYPE
ARMOURED FIGHTING VEHICLES
  IFV 91 *Boxer* (*Vilkas*) (incl 2 trg)
  APC • APC (T) ε160 M113A1/M577 (CP)
  AUV 350+ JLTV
ENGINEERING & MAINTENANCE VEHICLES
  AEV 8 MT-LB AEV
  ARV 10: 6 BPz-2; 4 M113
ANTI-TANK/ANTI-INFRASTRUCTURE
  MSL
    SP 10 M1025A2 HMMWV with FGM-148 *Javelin*
    MANPATS FGM-148 *Javelin*
  RCL 84mm *Carl Gustaf*
  ARTILLERY 134
  SP 16 PzH 2000
  TOWED 105mm 18 M101
  MOR 100: 120mm 68: 20 2B11; 26 EXPAL 120-MX2-SM; 22 M/41D; SP 120mm 32 M113 with Tampella
AIR DEFENCE • SAM • Point-defence *Grom*

Reserves
National Defence Voluntary Forces 5,850 reservists

FORCES BY ROLE
MANOEUVRE
  Other
    6 (territorial) def unit

Navy 800
LVA, EST and LTU established a joint naval unit, BALTRON, with bases at Liepaja, Riga, Ventpils (LVA), Tallinn (EST), Klaipeda (LTU)
EQUIPMENT BY TYPE
PATROL AND COASTAL COMBATANTS 5:
  PCC 4 *Zemaitis* (ex-DNK *Flyvefisken*) with 1 76mm gun
  PBF 1 *Zaibas*
MINE WARFARE • MINE COUNTERMEASURES 3
  MCCS 1 *Jotvingis* (ex-NOR *Vidar*)
  MHC 2 *Skalvis* (ex-UK *Hunt*)
LOGISTICS AND SUPPORT • AAR 1 *Šakiai*
UNINHABITED MARITIME SYSTEMS
  UUV • MW *K-Ster* C/I; PAP Mk6

Air Force 1,850
FORCES BY ROLE
AIR DEFENCE
  1 AD bn
EQUIPMENT BY TYPE
AIRCRAFT
  TPT 5: Medium 3 C-27J *Spartan*; Light 2 L-410 *Turbolet*
HELICOPTERS
  MRH 3 AS365M3 *Dauphin* (SAR)
  TPT • Medium 3 Mi-8 *Hip* (tpt/SAR)
AIR DEFENCE • SAM 8+
  Medium-range 8 NASAMS III
  Point-defence FIM-92 *Stinger*; RBS-70

Special Operation Force
FORCES BY ROLE
SPECIAL FORCES
  1 SF gp (1 CT unit; 1 Jaeger bn, 1 cbt diver unit)

Other Units 3,200
FORCES BY ROLE
COMBAT SUPPORT
  1 MP bn
COMBAT SERVICE SUPPORT
  1 log bn
  1 trg regt

Gendarmerie & Paramilitary 18.400

Riflemen Union 14,250

State Border Guard Service 4,150
Ministry of Interior

EQUIPMENT BY TYPE

PATROL AND COASTAL COMBATANTS • PB 3:
1 *Gintaras Zagunis*; 1 KBV 041 (ex-SWE); 1 *Barauskas* (Baltic Patrol 2700)

AMPHIBIOUS • LANDING CRAFT • UCAC 2 *Christina* (*Griffon* 2000)

HELICOPTERS • TPT • Light 5: 1 BK-117 (SAR); 2 H120 *Colibri*; 2 H135

DEPLOYMENT

BALTIC SEA: NATO • SNMCMG 1: 40; 1 MHC
CENTRAL AFRICAN REPUBLIC: EU • EUTM RCA 1
IRAQ: NATO • NATO Mission Iraq 30
KOSOVO: NATO • KFOR 1
MOZAMBIQUE: EU • EUMAM Mozambique 2
UNITED KINGDOM: *Operation Interflex* 15 (UKR trg)

FOREIGN FORCES

All NATO Enhanced Forward Presence unless stated
Belgium 2
Czech Republic 150; 1 SP arty bty
Germany 1,000; 1 armd inf bde HQ; 1 armd inf bn(+)
Italy NATO Baltic Air Policing: 200; 4 Eurofighter *Typhoon*
Luxembourg 6
Netherlands 250; 1 armd inf coy
Norway 150; 1 armd inf coy(+)
Portugal 150; 1 mne coy
United States US European Command: 1,000; 1 armd bn; 1 SP arty bty

Luxembourg LUX

Euro EUR		2023	2024	2025
GDP	EUR	79.3bn	83.7bn	88.4bn
	USD	85.8bn	91.2bn	97.0bn
Real GDP growth	%	-1.1	1.3	2.7
Def exp [a]	EUR	594m	728m	
	USD	642m	785m	
Def bdgt	EUR	543m	634m	794m
	USD	587m	691m	871m

[a] NATO figure

Real-terms defence budget trend (USDm, constant 2015)

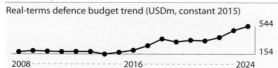

Population		671,254				
Age	0–14	15–19	20–24	25–29	30–64	65 plus
Male	8.6%	2.7%	3.0%	3.5%	25.2%	7.4%
Female	8.1%	2.6%	2.9%	3.4%	23.8%	8.7%

Capabilities

Luxembourg maintains a limited military capability to participate in European collective security and crisis management, primarily focused on providing reconnaissance capability to NATO. The Defence Guidelines for 2035, published in 2023, identify the creation of a joint medium combat reconnaissance battalion with Belgium by 2030 as the centre of this plan. As part of this effort, Luxembourg is making investments in armoured fighting vehicles. Acquisition priorities in the 2028 timeframe include ISR, air transport and surveillance, cyber defence and uninhabited capabilities. There are plans to improve space situational awareness, SATCOM and Earth observation capabilities. Luxembourg has contributed troops to NATO's Enhanced Forward Presence. It is part of the European Multi-Role Tanker Transport Fleet programme, in which it partially funds one A330 MRTT. It has contributed its A400M to an airlift squadron formed jointly with Belgium. The Belgian and Dutch air forces are responsible for policing Luxembourg's airspace. Sustaining the army's personnel strength depends on improving recruiting and retention. The country has a small but advanced space industry, but is largely reliant on imports. The defence guidelines call for the development of a defence industry, innovation and research strategy.

ACTIVE 900 (Army 900) Gendarmerie & Paramilitary 600

ORGANISATIONS BY SERVICE

Space
EQUIPMENT BY TYPE
SATELLITES • COMMUNICATIONS 1 *Govsat-1*

Army 900
FORCES BY ROLE
MANOEUVRE
  Reconnaissance
    2 recce coy (1 to Eurocorps/BEL div, 1 to NATO pool of deployable forces)
EQUIPMENT BY TYPE
ARMOURED FIGHTING VEHICLES
  AUV 50: 48 *Dingo* 2; 2 *Eagle* V
ANTI-TANK/ANTI-INFRASTRUCTURE
  MSL • MANPATS NLAW; TOW
ARTILLERY • MOR 81mm 6+
AIRCRAFT • TPT • Heavy 1 A400M
HELICOPTERS
  MRH 2 H145M (jointly operated with Police)
UNINHABITED AERIAL VEHICLES
  ISR • Light RQ-21A *Blackjack*

Gendarmerie & Paramilitary 600
Gendarmerie 600

DEPLOYMENT

LITHUANIA: NATO • Forward Land Forces 6
ROMANIA: NATO • Forward Land Forces 27; 1 recce pl
MEDITERRANEAN SEA: EU • EUNAVFOR MED 2 *Merlin* IIIC (leased)

Macedonia, North MKD

Macedonian Denar MKD		2023	2024	2025
GDP	MKD	841bn	896bn	959bn
	USD	14.8bn	15.9bn	17.1bn
Real GDP growth	%	1.0	2.2	3.6
Def exp [a]	MKD	15.2bn	20.1bn	
	USD	267m	353m	
Def bdgt	MKD	15.6bn	20.1bn	22.5bn
	USD	274m	356m	402m

[a] NATO figure

Population		2,135,622				
Age	0–14	15–19	20–24	25–29	30–64	65 plus
Male	8.3%	2.7%	3.1%	3.7%	25.2%	6.9%
Female	7.7%	2.6%	2.9%	3.4%	24.8%	8.7%

Capabilities

The primary goals of the armed forces are safeguarding territorial integrity and sovereignty, as well as contributing to operations under the EU, NATO and UN. A 2023–32 Defence Capability Development Plan (DCDP) consolidated long-term goals aimed at implementing reforms and strengthening capabilities. The country donated Mi-8 helicopters to Ukraine, and is replacing these with more modern Western types to support military and civilian tasks. Army investments include *Stryker* armoured vehicles, howitzers, as well as the development of a light infantry unit. Procurements are being supported by allocations from the European Peace Facility. There is now greater cooperation with international partners. In 2023, it has defined a 10-year cooperation roadmap with the US, while in 2024 Skopje signed a framework agreement for military cooperation with Turkiye. There is little in the way of a domestic defence industry, with no ability to design and manufacture modern equipment.

ACTIVE 8,000 (Army 8,000) Gendarmerie & Paramilitary 7,600

RESERVE 4,850

ORGANISATIONS BY SERVICE

Army 8,000
FORCES BY ROLE
SPECIAL FORCES
  1 SF regt (1 SF bn, 1 ranger bn)
MANOEUVRE
  Mechanised
  1 mech inf bde (3 mech inf bn, 1 arty bn, 1 engr bn, 1 int coy, 1 NBC coy, 1 sigs coy)
COMBAT SUPPORT
  1 MP bn
  1 sigs bn
COMBAT SERVICE SUPPORT
  1 log bde (3 log bn)

Reserves
FORCES BY ROLE
  MANOEUVRE Light
  1 inf bde
EQUIPMENT BY TYPE
ARMOURED FIGHTING VEHICLES
  IFV 11: 10 BMP-2; 1 BMP-2K (CP)
  APC 198
    APC (T) 46: 9 *Leonidas*; 27 M113; 10 MT-LB
    APC (W) 152: 56 BTR-70; 12 BTR-80; 84 TM-170 *Hermelin*
  AUV 34: 2 *Cobra*; 32 JLTV
ANTI-TANK/ANTI-INFRASTRUCTURE
  MSL • MANPATS *Milan*
ARTILLERY 131
  TOWED 70: **105mm** 14 M-56; **122mm** 56 M-30 M-1938
  MRL 17: **122mm** 6 BM-21; **128mm** 11
  MOR • **120mm** 44

Marine Wing
EQUIPMENT BY TYPE
PATROL AND COASTAL COMBATANTS 1
  PB 1 *Botica*†

Aviation Brigade
FORCES BY ROLE
TRAINING
  1 flt with Bell 205 (UH-1H *Iroquois*); Bell 206B; Z-242
ATTACK HELICOPTER
  1 sqn with Mi-24V *Hind* E
TRANSPORT HELICOPTER
  1 sqn with Mi-8MTV *Hip*; Mi-17 *Hip* H
AIR DEFENCE
  1 AD bn
EQUIPMENT BY TYPE
AIRCRAFT
  (TPT • **Light** 1 An-2 *Colt* in store)
  TRG 5 Z-242
HELICOPTERS
  ATK 2 Mi-24V *Hind* E (2 Mi-24K *Hind* G2; 6 Mi-24V *Hind* E in store)
  MRH 6: 4 Mi-8MTV *Hip*; 2 Mi-17 *Hip* H
  TPT • **Light** 6: 2 Bell 205 (UH-1H *Iroquois*); 4 Bell 206B *Jet Ranger*
AIR DEFENCE
  SAM • **Point-defence** 8+: 8 9K35 *Strela*-10 (RS-SA-13 *Gopher*); 9K310 *Igla*-1 (RS-SA-16 *Gimlet*)
  GUNS **40mm** 36 L/60

Gendarmerie & Paramilitary 7,600

Police 7,600 (some 5,000 armed)

incl 2 SF units

EQUIPMENT BY TYPE

ARMOURED FIGHTING VEHICLES
  APC • **APC (T)** M113; **APC (W)** BTR-80; TM-170 *Heimlin*
  AUV *Ze'ev*
HELICOPTERS
  MRH 1 Bell 412EP *Twin Huey*
  TPT 3: **Medium** 1 Mi-171; **Light** 2: 1 Bell 206B (AB-206B) *Jet Ranger* II; 1 Bell 212 (AB-212)

DEPLOYMENT

BOSNIA-HERZEGOVINA: EU • EUFOR (*Operation Althea*) 33
IRAQ: NATO • NATO Mission Iraq 4
KOSOVO: NATO • KFOR 68
LATVIA: NATO • Forward Land Forces 9
LEBANON: UN • UNIFIL 5
ROMANIA: NATO • Forward Land Forces 35

Malta MLT

Euro EUR		2023	2024	2025
GDP	EUR	20.7bn	22.4bn	23.9bn
	USD	22.3bn	24.4bn	26.3bn
Real GDP growth	%	7.5	5.0	4.0
Def bdgt [a]	EUR	73.9m	85.7m	
	USD	80.0m	93.4m	

[a] Excludes military pensions

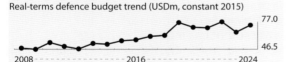

Real-terms defence budget trend (USDm, constant 2015)

Population		469,730				
Age	0–14	15–19	20–24	25–29	30–64	65 plus
Male	7.5%	2.3%	2.5%	3.3%	24.2%	10.7%
Female	7.1%	2.2%	2.3%	2.9%	22.7%	12.4%

Capabilities

The principal roles of the armed forces are external security, including maritime security, and support for civil emergencies and the police. Malta is neutral but has been a member of NATO's Partnership for Peace programme since 1996 and agreed to an Individually Tailored Partnership Programme in February 2024. It also joined the Planning and Review Process in December 2023. A strategy paper for 2016–26 laid out defence-policy objectives, including operational and organisational reforms. The country also participates in bilateral and multilateral exercises. Although deployment capacity is limited, Malta contributes to EU and UN missions. There are personnel retention challenges, with force levels remaining below authorised levels. Italy has assisted Malta in meeting some security requirements, including air surveillance. The European Internal Security Fund is funding some modernisation. Malta has some shipbuilding and ship-repair activity and a small aviation-maintenance industry but no dedicated defence industry.

ACTIVE 1,700 (Armed Forces 1,700)
RESERVE 260 (Volunteer Reserve Force 110 Individual Reserve 150)

ORGANISATIONS BY SERVICE

Armed Forces of Malta 1,700

FORCES BY ROLE

SPECIAL FORCES
  1 SF unit
MANOEUVRE
  Light
  1 (1st) inf regt (3 inf coy, 1 cbt spt coy)
COMBAT SUPPORT
  1 (3rd) cbt spt regt (1 cbt engr sqn, 1 EOD sqn, 1 maint sqn)
COMBAT SERVICE SUPPORT
  1 (4th) CSS regt (1 CIS coy, 1 sy coy)

EQUIPMENT BY TYPE

ARTILLERY • **MOR 81mm** L16
AIR DEFENCE • **GUNS 14.5mm** 1 ZPU-4

Maritime Squadron 500

Organised into 5 divisions: offshore patrol; inshore patrol; rapid deployment and training; marine engineering; and logistics

EQUIPMENT BY TYPE

PATROL AND COASTAL COMBATANTS 9
  PSO 1 P71 (ITA OPV 748) with 1 hel landing platform
  PCO 1 P62 (ex-IRL *Emer*)
  PCC 1 P61 (ITA *Saettia* mod) with 1 hel landing platform
  PB 6: 4 Austal 21m; 2 *Marine Protector*
LOGISTICS AND SUPPORT • **AAR** 2 *Vittoria*

Air Wing

1 base party. 1 flt ops div; 1 maint div; 1 integrated log div; 1 rescue section

EQUIPMENT BY TYPE

AIRCRAFT
  TPT • **Light** 5: 3 Beech 200 *King Air* (MP); 2 BN-2B *Islander*
  TRG 3 *Bulldog* T MK1
  HELICOPTERS MRH 6: 3 AW139 (SAR); 3 SA316B *Alouette* III

DEPLOYMENT

LEBANON: UN • UNIFIL 8

Montenegro MNE

Euro EUR		2023	2024	2025
GDP	EUR	6.85bn	7.44bn	8.06bn
	USD	7.41bn	8.11bn	8.85bn
Real GDP growth	%	6.0	3.7	3.7
Def exp [a]	EUR	106m	150m	
	USD	114m	162m	
Def bdgt [b]	EUR	123m	92.5m	104m
	USD	134m	101m	115m

[a] NATO figure
[b] Includes military pensions

Real-terms defence budget trend (USDm, constant 2015)

Population 599,849

Age	0–14	15–19	20–24	25–29	30–64	65 plus
Male	9.1%	3.1%	3.2%	3.1%	22.6%	7.9%
Female	8.6%	2.9%	3.0%	3.0%	23.4%	10.0%

Capabilities

Montenegro plans to develop an integrated defence system capable of defending and preserving independence, sovereignty and national territory. An action plan to implement its defence strategy was outlined in 2023, focusing on strengthening resilience and cyber structures. Since becoming a NATO member in 2017, Montenegro has accepted Alliance capability targets and has been aligning its defence-planning process, and also procurements including light armoured vehicles for two declared infantry companies. Personnel have deployed to EU, UN and NATO-led operations, although with small contributions. Podgorica intends to replace ageing Soviet-era equipment. In 2024, the government agreed to use reserve funds for defence procurement. As well as light armoured vehicles, procurement priorities include light and medium helicopters, airspace surveillance radars and improved communications capacities. The country has signed defence cooperation agreements with Serbia and Turkiye. Podgorica is acquiring two patrol ships from France and jointly acquiring UAVs with Slovenia. Its defence industry is capable of producing small arms and ammunition.

ACTIVE 2,710 (Army 1,700 Navy 310 Air Force 200 Other 500) Gendarmerie & Paramilitary 4,100

RESERVE 2,800

ORGANISATIONS BY SERVICE

Army 1,700
FORCES BY ROLE
SPECIAL FORCES
  1 SF unit
MANOEUVRE
  Light
    1 mot inf bn
COMBAT SUPPORT
  1 MP coy
  1 sigs coy
  1 cbt spt bn
COMBAT SERVICE SUPPORT
  1 med bn
  1 spt bn
EQUIPMENT BY TYPE
ARMOURED FIGHTING VEHICLES
  APC • **APC (W)** 6 BOV-VP M-86
  AUV 32 JLTV
NBC VEHICLES 1 *Cobra* CBRN
ANTI-TANK/ANTI-INFRASTRUCTURE
  SP 9 BOV-1
  MSL • **MANPATS** 9K111 *Fagot* (RS-AT-4 *Spigot*); 9K111-1 *Konkurs* (RS-AT-5 *Spandrel*)
ARTILLERY 135
  TOWED 122mm 12 D-30
  MRL 128mm 18 M-63/M-94 *Plamen*
  MOR 105: **82mm** 73; **120mm** 32

Reserve
FORCES BY ROLE
MANOEUVRE
  Light
    2 inf bn
COMBAT SUPPORT
  1 arty bn

Navy 310
EQUIPMENT BY TYPE
PATROL AND COASTAL COMBATANTS 5:
  PCC 1 *Rade Končar* with 2 57mm guns (1 more in reserve)
  PBI 4 Coastal Fast Response Boat
LOGISTICS AND SUPPORT • **AXS** 1 *Jadran*

Air Force 200
Golubovci (Podgorica) air base under army command
FORCES BY ROLE
TRAINING
  1 (mixed) sqn with G-4 *Super Galeb*; Utva-75 (none operational)
TRANSPORT HELICOPTER
  1 sqn with SA341/SA342L *Gazelle*
EQUIPMENT BY TYPE
AIRCRAFT • **TRG** (4 G-4 *Super Galeb* non-operational; 4 Utva-75 non-operational)
HELICOPTERS
  MRH 16: 1 Bell 412EP *Twin Huey*; 2 Bell 412EPI *Twin Huey*; 13 SA341/SA342L (HN-45M) *Gazelle*
  TPT • **Light** 2 Bell 505 *Jet Ranger X*

Gendarmerie & Paramilitary ε4,100

Special Police Units ε4,100

DEPLOYMENT

IRAQ: NATO • NATO Mission Iraq 1
KOSOVO: NATO • KFOR 2
LATVIA: NATO • Forward Land Forces 11
WESTERN SAHARA: UN • MINURSO 1

Multinational Organisations
Capabilities

The following represent shared capabilities held by contributors collectively rather than as part of national inventories

ORGANISATIONS BY SERVICE

NATO AEW&C Force

Based at Geilenkirchen (GER). Original participating countries (BEL, CAN, DNK, GER, GRC, ITA, NLD, NOR, PRT, TUR, US) have been subsequently joined by five more (CZE, ESP, HUN, POL, ROM).

FORCES BY ROLE

AIRBORNE EARLY WARNING & CONTROL
1 sqn with B-757 (trg); E-3A *Sentry* (NATO standard)

EQUIPMENT BY TYPE
AIRCRAFT
  AEW&C 14 E-3A *Sentry* (NATO standard)
  TPT • PAX 1 B-757 (trg)

NATO Alliance Ground Surveillance

Based at Sigonella (ITA)
EQUIPMENT BY TYPE
UNINHABITED AERIAL VEHICLES
  ISR • Heavy 5 RQ-4D *Phoenix*

NATO Multinational Multi-Role Tanker Transport Fleet (MMF)

Based at Eindhoven (NLD). Six participating countries (BEL, CZE, GER, NLD, NOR & LUX)
EQUIPMENT BY TYPE
AIRCRAFT • TKR/TPT 8 A330 MRTT

Strategic Airlift Capability

Heavy Airlift Wing based at Papa air base (HUN). 12 participating countries (BLG, EST, FIN, HUN, LTU, NLD, NOR, POL, ROM, SVN, SWE, US)
EQUIPMENT BY TYPE
AIRCRAFT • TPT • Heavy 3 C-17A *Globemaster* III

Strategic Airlift International Solution

Intended to provide strategic-airlift capacity pending the delivery of A400M aircraft by leasing An-124s. 10 participating countries (BEL, CZE, FRA, GER, HUN, NLD, NOR, POL, SVK, SVN)
EQUIPMENT BY TYPE
AIRCRAFT • TPT • Heavy 1 An-124-100 (2 more available on 6–9 days' notice and 2 more subject to availability)

Netherlands NLD

Euro EUR		2023	2024	2025
GDP	EUR	1.07trn	1.12trn	1.16trn
	USD	1.15trn	1.22trn	1.27trn
Real GDP growth	%	0.1	0.6	1.6
Def exp [a]	EUR	15.5bn	19.9bn	
	USD	16.8bn	21.5bn	
Def bdgt [b]	EUR	15.4bn	21.7bn	22.0bn
	USD	16.7bn	23.6bn	24.2bn

[a] NATO figure
[b] Includes military pensions

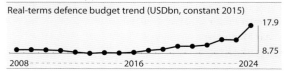
Real-terms defence budget trend (USDbn, constant 2015)

Population 17,772,378

Age	0–14	15–19	20–24	25–29	30–64	65 plus
Male	7.8%	2.8%	3.3%	3.5%	22.6%	9.6%
Female	7.4%	2.7%	3.2%	3.4%	22.5%	11.1%

Capabilities

The armed forces are responsible for territorial defence, supporting national civil authorities and contributing to NATO. Building on defence documents issued in 2022 and 2023, a 2024 white paper announced plans to increase defence spending, including investments in recruitment and retention and equipment purchases. Readiness levels had been criticised in earlier reports. Dutch forces have increasingly integrated with NATO allies, particularly Germany. The Netherlands has air-policing agreements with France, Belgium and Luxembourg, and is a participant in the Joint Expeditionary Force and the European Intervention Initiative. Dutch forces are fully professional and well-trained and can deploy and sustain a medium-scale force for a single operation or a small-scale joint force for an extended period. The Netherlands makes significant contributions to NATO and EU military operations. To support Ukraine, the Netherlands has supplied F-16s to train Ukrainian pilots and delivered main battle tanks. In 2024, the country declared its F-35A aircraft operational in the nuclear role, replacing its F-16s. The country is upgrading all aspects of its forces and has plans to boost defence innovation and research and to expand the Defence Space Security Centre. It also announced plans to buy main battle tanks. The country has an advanced domestic defence industry in areas such as ships and radar systems.

ACTIVE 33,650 (Army 15,350 Navy 7,400 Air 6,400 Other 4,500) **Military Constabulary 6,500**

RESERVE 6,350 (Army 3,900 Navy 1,450 Air 800 Other 200) **Military Constabulary** 300

Reserve liability to age 35 for soldiers/sailors, 40 for NCOs, 45 for officers

ORGANISATIONS BY SERVICE

Army 15,350
FORCES BY ROLE
COMMAND
  elm 1 (1 GNC) corps HQ
SPECIAL FORCES
  4 SF coy
MANOEUVRE
  Reconnaissance
  1 ISR bn (2 armd recce sqn, 1 EW coy, 2 int sqn, 1 UAV bty)
  Mechanised
  1 (13th) mech bde (1 recce sqn, 2 mech inf bn, 1 engr bn, 1 maint coy, 1 med coy)
  1 (43rd) mech bde (1 armd recce sqn, 2 armd inf bn, 1 engr bn, 1 maint coy, 1 med coy)
  Air Manoeuvre
  1 (11th) air mob bde (3 air mob inf bn, 1 engr coy, 1 med coy, 1 supply coy, 1 maint coy)
COMBAT SUPPORT
  1 SP arty bn (3 SP arty bty)
  1 CIMIC bn
  1 engr bn
  2 EOD coy 1 (CIS) sigs bn 1 CBRN coy
COMBAT SERVICE SUPPORT
  1 med bn
  5 fd hospital
  3 maint coy
  2 tpt bn
AIR DEFENCE
  1 SAM comd (1 SAM sqn; 3 SAM bty)

Reserves 3,900 reservists
  National Command
  Cadre bde and corps tps completed by call-up of reservists (incl Territorial Comd)
  FORCES BY ROLE
  MANOEUVRE
    Light
    3 inf bn (could be mobilised for territorial def)
  EQUIPMENT BY TYPE
  ARMOURED FIGHTING VEHICLES
    RECCE 185 *Fennek* (incl 47 OP)
    IFV 117: 113 CV9035NL (being upgraded; 32 more in store); 4 CV9035NL MLU (in test)
    APC • APC (W) 200 *Boxer* (8 driver trg; 52 amb; 36 CP; 92 engr; 12 log)

AUV 332: 92 *Bushmaster* IMV; 140 *Fennek* (incl 4 CP; 10 trg); 100 MTV *Manticore*
ENGINEERING & MAINTENANCE VEHICLES
  AEV 10+: *Dachs*; 10 *Kodiak*
  ARV 25+: BPz-2; 25 BPz-3 *Büffel*
  VLB 28: 16 *Leopard* 1 with *Legaun*; 8 *Leopard* 2 with *Leguan*; 4 MLC70 with *Leguan*
  MW *Bozena*
NBC VEHICLES 6 TPz-1 *Fuchs* NBC
ANTI-TANK/ANTI-INFRASTRUCTURE
  MSL • MANPATS *Spike*-MR, *Spke*-LR
ARTILLERY 124
  SP 155mm 21 PzH 2000 (25 more in store)
  MOR 101: **81mm** 83 L16/M1; **120mm** 18 Brandt
  MRL 306mm 2 PULS
UNINHABITED AERIAL VEHICLES
  ISR • Light RQ-21A *Blackjack*
AIR DEFENCE • SAM 42–
  Long-range 18 M902 *Patriot* PAC-3
  Short-range 6 NASAMS II
  Point-defence 18+: FIM-92 *Stinger*; 18 *Fennek* with FIM-92 *Stinger*

Navy 7,400 (incl Marines)
EQUIPMENT BY TYPE
SUBMARINES 3
  SSK 3 *Walrus* with 4 single 533mm TT with Mk 48 ADCAP mod 7 HWT
PRINCIPAL SURFACE COMBATANTS 5
  DESTROYERS • DDGHM 4:
    3 *De Zeven Provinciën* with 2 quad lnchr with RGM-84C *Harpoon* Block 1B AShM, 5 8-cell Mk 41 VLS with SM-2 Block IIIA/RIM-162B ESSM SAM, 2 twin 324mm SVTT Mk 32 ASTT with Mk 46 LWT, 1 *Goalkeeper* CIWS, 1 127mm gun (capacity 1 NH90 hel)
    1 *De Zeven Provinciën* with 2 quad lnchr with RGM-84C *Harpoon* Block 1B AShM, 5 8-cell Mk 41 VLS with SM-2 Block IIIA/RIM-162B ESSM SAM, 2 twin 324mm SVTT Mk 32 ASTT with Mk 46 LWT, 2 *Goalkeeper* CIWS, 1 127mm gun (capacity 1 NH90 hel)
  FRIGATES • FFGHM 1 *Karel Doorman* (1 more in reserve) with 2 quad lnchr with RGM-84C *Harpoon* Block 1B AShM, 1 16-cell Mk 48 mod 1 VLS with RIM-7P *Sea Sparrow* SAM, 2 twin 324mm SVTT Mk 32 ASTT with Mk 46 LWT, 1 *Goalkeeper* CIWS, 1 76mm gun (capacity 1 NH90 hel)
PATROL AND COASTAL COMBATANTS 4
  PSOH 4 *Holland* with 1 76mm gun (capacity 1 NH90 hel)
MINE WARFARE • MINE COUNTERMEASURES 3
  MHO 3 *Alkmaar* (*Tripartite*)
AMPHIBIOUS
  PRINCIPAL AMPHIBIOUS SHIPS • LPD 2:

1 *Rotterdam* with 2 *Goalkeeper* CIWS (capacity 6 NH90/AS532 *Cougar* hel; either 6 LCVP or 2 LCM and 3 LCVP; either 170 APC or 33 MBT; 538 troops)
1 *Johan de Witt* with 2 *Goalkeeper* CIWS (capacity 6 NH90 hel or 4 AS532 *Cougar* hel; either 6 LCVP or 2 LCM and 3 LCVP; either 170 APC or 33 MBT; 700 troops)

LANDING CRAFT 17
  LCU 5 LCU Mk II
  LCVP 12 Mk5

LOGISTICS AND SUPPORT 10
  AGS 3: 1 *Hydrograaf*; 2 *Snellius*
  AKL 1 *Pelikaan*
  AKR 2: 1 *New Amsterdam* (capacity 200 containers and 300 vehs) (leased); 1 *Southern Rock* (capacity 240 containers and 150 vehs) (leased)
  AORH 1 *Karel Doorman* with 2 *Goalkeeper* CIWS (capacity 6 NH90/AS532 *Cougar* or 2 CH-47F *Chinook* hel; 2 LCVP)
  AS 1 *Mercuur*
  AXL 1 *Van Kingsbergen*
  AXS 1 *Urania*

UNINHABITED MARITIME SYSTEMS
  UUV • **MW** A18-M; *Double Eagle* Mk III; *K-Ster* C/I; *Seafox*; *Seascan*

Marines 2,650

FORCES BY ROLE
SPECIAL FORCES
  1 SF gp (1 SF sqn, 1 CT sqn)
MANOEUVRE
  Amphibious
  2 mne bn
  1 amph aslt gp
COMBAT SERVICE SUPPORT
  1 spt gp (coy)

EQUIPMENT BY TYPE
ARMOURED FIGHTING VEHICLES
  APC • **APC (T)** 64 BvS-10 *Viking* (incl 20 CP)
ENGINEERING & MAINTENANCE VEHICLES
  ARV 8: 4 BvS-10; 4 BPz-2
  MED 4 BvS-10
ANTI-TANK/ANTI-INFRASTRUCTURE
  MSL • **MANPATS** Spike-MR
ARTILLERY • **MOR 81mm** 12 L16/M1
AIR DEFENCE • **SAM** • **Point-defence** FIM-92 *Stinger*

Air Force 6,400

FORCES BY ROLE
FIGHTER/GROUND ATTACK
  3 sqn with F-35A *Lightning* II
ANTI-SUBMARINE WARFARE/SEARCH & RESCUE
  1 sqn with NH90 NFH
TANKER/TRANSPORT
  1 sqn with C-130H/H-30 *Hercules*
  1 sqn with Gulfstream G650ER
TRAINING
  1 OEU sqn with F-35A *Lightning* II
  1 sqn with PC-7 *Turbo Trainer*
  1 hel sqn with AH-64E *Apache*; CH-47F *Chinook* (based at Fort Cavazos, TX)
ATTACK HELICOPTER
  1 sqn with AH-64E *Apache*
TRANSPORT HELICOPTER
  1 sqn with AS532U2 *Cougar* II; NH90 NFH
  1 sqn with CH-47F *Chinook*
ISR UAV
  1 sqn with MQ-9A *Reaper*

EQUIPMENT BY TYPE
AIRCRAFT 40 combat capable
  FGA 40 F-35A *Lightning* II
  TPT 5: **Medium** 4: 2 C-130H *Hercules*; 2 C-130H-30 *Hercules*; **PAX** 1 Gulfstream G650ER
  TRG 13 PC-7 *Turbo Trainer*
HELICOPTERS
  ATK 28: 16 AH-64D *Apache*; 12 AH-64E *Apache*
  ASW 19 NH90 NFH (of which 8 not fitted with sonar)
  TPT 32: **Heavy** 20 CH-47F *Chinook*; **Medium** 12 AS532U2 *Cougar* II
UNINHABITED AERIAL VEHICLES
  CISR • **Heavy** 4 MQ-9 *Reaper* (unarmed)
AIR-LAUNCHED MISSILES
  AAM • **IR** AIM-9L/M *Sidewinder*; **IIR** AIM-9X *Sidewinder* II; **ARH** AIM-120B/C-7 AMRAAM
  ASM AGM-114K *Hellfire* II
BOMBS
  Laser-guided GBU-10/GBU-12 *Paveway* II; GBU-24 *Paveway* III (all supported by LANTIRN)
  INS/GPS guided GBU-39 Small Diameter Bomb

Gendarmerie & Paramilitary 6,500

Royal Military Constabulary 6,500

Subordinate to the Ministry of Defence, but performs most of its work under the authority of other ministries

FORCES BY ROLE
MANOEUVRE
  Other
  1 paramilitary comd (total: 28 paramilitary unit)
EQUIPMENT BY TYPE
ARMOURED FIGHTING VEHICLES
  APC • **APC (W)** 24 YPR-KMar

DEPLOYMENT

BALTIC SEA: NATO • SNMCMG 1: 40; 1 MHO
BOSNIA-HERZEGOVINA: EU • EUFOR (*Operation Althea*) 10
IRAQ: *Operation Inherent Resolve* 7; **NATO** • NATO Mission Iraq 280; 1 inf coy; 1 hel flt with 3 CH-47F *Chinook*
LEBANON: UN • UNIFIL 1

LITHUANIA: NATO • Forward Land Forces 250; 1 armd inf coy

MIDDLE EAST: UN • UNTSO 11

NORTH SEA: NATO • SNMG 1: 150; 1 FFGHM

UNITED KINGDOM: Operation Interflex 90 (UKR trg)

UNITED STATES: 1 hel trg sqn with AH-64E *Apache*; CH-47F *Chinook* based at Fort Cavazos (TX)

FOREIGN FORCES

United States US European Command: 400

Norway NOR

Norwegian Kroner NOK		2023	2024	2025
GDP	NOK	5.13trn	5.37trn	5.45trn
	USD	485bn	504bn	506bn
Real GDP growth	%	0.5	1.5	1.8
Def exp [a]	NOK	93.0bn	112bn	
	USD	8.80bn	10.6bn	
Def bdgt [b]	NOK	75.8bn	104bn	110bn
	USD	7.18bn	9.79bn	10.2bn

[a] NATO figure

[b] Includes military pensions

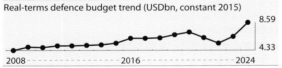
Real-terms defence budget trend (USDbn, constant 2015)

Population		5,509,733				
Age	0–14	15–19	20–24	25–29	30–64	65 plus
Male	8.4%	3.1%	3.1%	3.4%	23.5%	9.0%
Female	8.0%	2.9%	2.9%	3.2%	22.5%	10.1%

Capabilities

Norway sustains small but well-equipped and well-trained armed forces. Territorial defence is at the heart of security policy. The 2020 long-term defence plan argued that the security environment had deteriorated faster than expected and envisaged increased personnel and strengthened readiness and capability in the High North. Following Russia's full-scale invasion of Ukraine in 2022, Norway announced that it would increase funds to strengthen its defence in the North. At any one time, around one-third of troops are conscripts. Senior officers reportedly expressed concerns in 2019 that the force structure was too small. In 2024, a new long-term defence plan detailed objectives including, by 2036, increasing the number of army units, increasing the conscript cohort and fielding three brigades bolstered with more air defence. Norway maintains a small presence in a range of international crisis-management missions. Equipment recapitalisation is ongoing, but large procurements will stretch budgets. In 2023, Norway more closely integrated its air force with neighbours Denmark, Finland and Sweden. The ability to monitor the maritime environment will improve with the introduction of P-8s to replace P-3s. Norway is procuring new submarines as part of a strategic partnership with Germany. Norway has an advanced and diverse defence-industrial base, with a high percentage of SMEs and a mix of private and state-owned companies such as Kongsberg.

ACTIVE 25,400 (Army 8,300 Navy 4,600 Air 4,300 Central Support 7,400 Home Guard 800)

Conscript liability 19 months maximum. Conscripts first serve 12 months from 19–28, and then up to 4–5 refresher training periods until age 35, 44, 55 or 60 depending on rank and function. Conscription was extended to women in 2015

RESERVE 40,000 (Home Guard 40,000)

Readiness varies from a few hours to several days

ORGANISATIONS BY SERVICE

Army 3,900; 4,400 conscript (total 8,300)

The armoured infantry brigade – Brigade North – trains new personnel of all categories and provides units for international operations. At any time around one-third of the brigade will be trained and ready to conduct operations. The brigade includes one high-readiness armoured battalion (Telemark Battalion) with combat-support and combat-service-support units on high readiness

FORCES BY ROLE

MANOEUVRE

Reconnaissance

1 armd recce bn (forming)

1 ISR bn

1 (GSV) bn (1 (border) recce coy, 1 ranger coy, 1 spt coy, 1 trg coy)

Armoured

1 armd inf bde (2 armd bn, 1 lt inf bn, 1 arty bn, 1 engr bn, 1 MP coy, 1 CIS bn, 1 spt bn, 1 med bn)

Light

1 lt inf bn (His Majesty The King's Guards)

EQUIPMENT BY TYPE

ARMOURED FIGHTING VEHICLES

MBT 36 *Leopard* 2A4 (8 more in store)

RECCE 21 CV9030N MkIIIB

IFV 91: 76 CV9030N; 15 CV9030N (CP)

APC 390

  APC (T) 315 M113 (incl variants)

  APC (W) 75 XA-186 *Sisu*/XA-200 *Sisu*/XA-203 (amb)

AUV 165: 20 *Dingo* 2; 25 HMT *Extenda*; 120 IVECO LMV (22 more in store)

ENGINEERING & MAINTENANCE VEHICLES

AEV 34+: 20 CV90 STING; 8 M113 AEV; NM109; 6 *Wisent*-2

ARV 8: 4 BPz-2; 4 *Wisent*-2

VLB 40: 26 *Leguan*; 5 *Leopard* 2 with *Leguan*; 9 *Leopard* 1

MW 9 910 MCV-2

NBC VEHICLES 6 TPz-1 *Fuchs* NBC

ANTI-TANK/ANTI-INFRASTRUCTURE

MANPATS FGM-148 *Javelin*
RCL **84mm** *Carl Gustaf*
ARTILLERY 167
SP 155mm 24 K9 *Thunder*
MOR 143: **81mm** 115 L16; **SP 81mm** 28: 16 CV9030; 12 M125A2
AIR DEFENCE
SAM
Medium-range NASAMS III
Point-defence *Piorun*

Navy 2,350; 2,250 conscripts (total 4,600)

Joint Command – Norwegian National Joint Headquarters. The Royal Norwegian Navy is organised into five elements under the command of the Chief of the Navy: the fleet (*Marinen*), the Coast Guard (*Kystvakten*), the recruit training school (KNM *Harald Haarfagre*), the naval medical branch and the naval bases (*Haakonsvern* and *Ramsund*)

FORCES BY ROLE
MANOEUVRE
  Reconnaissance
  1 ISR coy (Coastal Rangers)
COMBAT SUPPORT
  1 EOD pl
EQUIPMENT BY TYPE
SUBMARINES 6
  SSK 6 *Ula* with 8 single 533mm TT with *SeaHake* (DM2A3) HWT
PRINCIPAL SURFACE COMBATANTS • FRIGATES 4
  FFGHM 4 *Fridtjof Nansen* with *Aegis* C2 (mod), 2 quad lnchr with NSM AShM, 1 8-cell Mk 41 VLS with RIM-162A ESSM SAM, 2 twin 324mm ASTT with *Sting Ray* mod 1 LWT, 1 76mm gun (capacity 1 med hel)
PATROL AND COASTAL COMBATANTS 13
  PSOH 1 *Nordkapp* with 1 57mm gun (capacity 1 med tpt hel)
  PCFG 6 *Skjold* with 8 single lnchr with NSM AShM, 1 76mm gun
  PBF 6 CB90N (capacity 20 troops)
MINE WARFARE • MINE COUNTERMEASURES 4
  MSC 2 *Alta* with 1 twin *Simbad* lnchr with *Mistral* SAM
  MHC 2 *Oksoy* with 1 twin *Simbad* lnchr with *Mistral* SAM
LOGISTICS AND SUPPORT 6
  AGI 1 *Marjata* IV
  AGS 2: 1 *HU Sverdrup* II; 1 *Eger* (*Marjata* III) with 1 hel landing platform
  AORH 1 *Maud* (BMT *Aegir*) (capacity 2 med hel)
  AXL 2 *Reine*
UNINHABITED MARITIME SYSTEMS • UUV
  DATA REMUS 100
  MW *Minesniper* Mk III
  UTL HUGIN 1000

Coast Guard
EQUIPMENT BY TYPE
PATROL AND COASTAL COMBATANTS 13
  PSOH 3 *Jan Mayen* (capacity 2 med hel)
  PSO 5: 3 *Barentshav*; 1 *Harstad*; 1 *Svalbard* with 1 57mm gun, 1 hel landing platform
  PCC 5 *Nornen*

Air Force 2,900; 1,400 conscript (total 4,300)

Joint Command – Norwegian National HQ
FORCES BY ROLE
FIGHTER/GROUND ATTACK
  2 sqn with F-35A *Lightning* II
MARITIME PATROL
  1 sqn with P-8A *Poseidon*
SEARCH & RESCUE
  1 sqn with AW101
TRANSPORT
  1 sqn with C-130J-30 *Hercules*
TRAINING
  1 sqn with MFI-15 *Safari*
TRANSPORT HELICOPTER
  2 sqn with Bell 412SP *Twin Huey*
AIR DEFENCE
  2 bn with NASAMS III
EQUIPMENT BY TYPE
AIRCRAFT 49 combat capable
  FGA 44 F-35A *Lightning* II
  ASW 5 P-8A *Poseidon*
  TPT • Medium 4 C-130J-30 *Hercules*
  TRG 16 MFI-15 *Safari*
HELICOPTERS
  ASW (13 NH90 NFH in store)
  SAR 13 AW101
  MRH 18: 6 Bell 412HP; 12 Bell 412SP
AIR DEFENCE
  SAM • Medium-range 6 NASAMS III
AIR-LAUNCHED MISSILES
  AAM • IR AIM-9L *Sidewinder*; **IIR** AIM-9X *Sidewinder* II; IRIS-T; **ARH** AIM-120B/C-7 AMRAAM
BOMBS
  Laser-guided EGBU-12 *Paveway* II
  INS/GPS guided JDAM

Special Operations Command (NORSOCOM)
FORCES BY ROLE
SPECIAL FORCES
  1 (armed forces) SF comd (2 SF gp)
  1 (navy) SF comd (1 SF gp)
EQUIPMENT BY TYPE
PATROL AND COASTAL COMBATANTS • PBF 2 IC20M

Central Support, Administration and Command 5,850; 1,550 conscripts (total 7,400)

Central Support, Administration and Command includes military personnel in all joint elements and they are responsible for logistics and CIS in support of all forces in Norway and abroad

Home Guard 400; 400 conscripts (40,000 reserves)

The Home Guard is a separate organisation, but closely cooperates with all services. The Home Guard is organised in 11 Districts with mobile Rapid Reaction Forces (3,000 troops in total) as well as reinforcements and follow-on forces (37,000 troops in total)

EQUIPMENT BY TYPE
PATROL AND COASTAL COMBATANTS • PB 11: 4 *Harek*; 2 *Gyda*; 5 *Alusafe* 1290

DEPLOYMENT

EGYPT: MFO 3

IRAQ: *Operation Inherent Resolve* 30; 1 trg unit; **NATO** • NATO Mission Iraq 2

JORDAN: *Operation Inherent Resolve* 20

LITHUANIA: NATO • Forward Land Forces 150; 1 armd inf coy(+); CV9030

MIDDLE EAST: UN • UNTSO 12

NORTH SEA: NATO • SNMG 1: 40; 1 AORH

SOUTH SUDAN: UN • UNMISS 14

UNITED KINGDOM: *Operation Interflex* 150 (UKR trg)

FOREIGN FORCES

United States US European Command: 1,100; 1 (USMC) MEU eqpt set; 1 (APS) 155mm SP Arty bn eqpt set

Poland POL

Polish Zloty PLN		2023	2024	2025
GDP	PLN	3.41trn	3.64trn	3.92trn
	USD	812bn	863bn	915bn
Real GDP growth	%	0.2	3.0	3.5
Def exp [a]	PLN	111bn	151bn	
	USD	26.5bn	35.0bn	
Def bdgt [b]	PLN	97.4bn	118bn	124bn
	USD	23.2bn	28.0bn	29.0bn

[a] NATO figure
[b] Does not include Armed Forces Support Fund

Real-terms defence budget trend (USDbn, constant 2015)

Population		38,746,310				
Age	0–14	15–19	20–24	25–29	30–64	65 plus
Male	7.3%	2.6%	2.5%	2.8%	24.5%	8.0%
Female	6.9%	2.5%	2.4%	2.8%	25.9%	11.9%

Capabilities

Territorial defence and NATO membership are central pillars of Poland's defence policy. The primary focus of the 2017–32 defence concept is to prepare the armed forces to deter Russian aggression. Russia is characterised as a direct threat to Poland and to a stable international order. Protecting the border with Belarus has become an important mission. Poland hosts a multinational battlegroup as part of NATO's Forward Land Forces. Poland has delivered a variety of defence equipment to Ukraine, including armour and anti-armour systems. Warsaw has increased defence outlays to support modernisation projects, including through the 2022 Armed Forces Support Fund for foreign acquisitions. The new coalition government has retained the plan to boost personnel numbers by 2035, as well as establish new divisions. The country released a technical-modernisation plan covering the period 2021–35 in October 2019, which extended the planning horizon from ten to 15 years. Modernisation efforts include acquiring F-35As, with the first in-country deliveries expected by 2026 and new land forces capabilities, including armoured vehicles from South Korea and the US, among other efforts. In 2024, Poland joined the European Sky Shield Initiative as well as the European Long-range Strike Approach, and the Redzikowo *Aegis Ashore* EMD site became operational. Warsaw continues work on strengthening its defence-industrial base, much of which is now consolidated in the state-owned holding company PGZ.

ACTIVE 164,100 (Army 90,600 Navy 6,450 Air Force 18,850 Special Forces 3,400 Territorial 5,300 Joint 39,500) **Gendarmerie & Paramilitary** 14,300

RESERVE 37,500 (Territorial 37,500)

ORGANISATIONS BY SERVICE

Army 90,600

FORCES BY ROLE
COMMAND
  elm 1 (MNC NE) corps HQ
MANOEUVRE
  Reconnaissance
  3 recce regt
  Armoured
  1 (11th) armd cav div (1 armd bde (1 recce coy, 2 tk bn, 1 armd inf bn, 1 SP arty bn, 1 cbt engr coy, 1 log bn, 1 AD bn), 1 armd bde (1 recce coy, 2 tk bn, 1 armd inf bn, 1 SP arty bn, 1 cbt engr coy, 1 log bn), 1 mech bde (1 recce coy, 1 armd inf bn, 2 mech inf bn, 1 SP arty bn, 1 engr bn, 1 log bn, 1 AD bn), 1 arty regt, 1 AD regt)
  1 (1st) mech div (forming)
  1 (16th) mech div (1 recce bn, 1 armd bde (1 recce coy, 2 tk bn, 1 armd inf bn, 1 SP arty bn, 1 cbt engr coy, 1 log bn), 2 armd inf bde (1 recce coy, 1 tk bn, 2 armd inf bn, 1 SP arty bn, 1 cbt engr coy, 1 log bn), 1 arty bde, 1 AT regt, 1 log regt, 1 AD regt)
  1 (18th) mech div (1 recce bn, 1 armd bde (1 recce coy, 2 tk bn, 1 armd inf bn, 1 SP arty bn, 1 cbt engr coy, 1 log bn), 1 armd inf bde (1 tk bn, 2 armd inf bn, 1 SP arty bn, 1 cbt engr coy, 1 log bn), 1 mech bde (1 tk bn, 3 mech inf bn, 1 SP arty bn, 1 cbt engr bn, 1 log bn, 1 AD bn), 1 mech bde (forming), 1 log regt, 1 AD regt)
  Mechanised
  1 (12th) mech div (1 armd inf bde (1 recce coy, 1 tk bn, 2 armd inf bn, 1 SP arty bn, 1 cbt engr coy, 1 log bn), 1 mech bde (1 recce coy, 3 mech inf bn, 1 SP arty bn, 1 cbt engr bn, 1 log bn, 1 AD bn), 1 (coastal) mech bde (1 recce coy, 3 armd inf bn, 1 SP arty bn, 1 cbt engr coy, 1 log bn), 1 arty regt, 1 maint bn, 1 AD regt)
  Air Manoeuvre
  1 (6th) AB bde (3 para bn, 1 log bn)
  1 (25th) air cav bde (2 air cav bn, 2 tpt hel bn, 1 log bn)
COMBAT SUPPORT
  2 engr regt
  2 ptn br regt
  2 chem def regt
COMBAT SERVICE SUPPORT
  1 log bde (3 log bn, 2 maint bn, 1 supply bn, 1 spt bn)
  1 log bde (3 log bn, 1 maint bn, 1 med bn, 1 supply bn, 1 spt bn)
  1 log bde
HELICOPTER
  1 (1st) hel bde (2 atk hel sqn with Mi-24D/V *Hind* D/E, 1 CSAR sqn with Mi-24V *Hind* E; PZL W-3PL *Gluszec*; 2 ISR hel sqn with Mi-2URP; 2 tpt hel sqn with Mi-2)
EQUIPMENT BY TYPE
ARMOURED FIGHTING VEHICLES
  MBT 662: 71 K2; 22 *Leopard* 2A4 (being upgraded to 2PL); 105 *Leopard* 2A5; 64 *Leopard* 2PL; 116 M1A1 *Abrams*; 206 PT-91 *Twardy*; 78 T-72M1/M1R
  RECCE 348: 220 BRDM-2; 38 BWR-1D/S (being upgraded); 90 BRDM-2 R5
  IFV 1,525: 916 BMP-1; 4 *Borsuk* (in test); ε600 *Rosomak* (including variants); 5 *Rosomak* (ZSSW-30)
  APC 100
    PPV 100 *Maxxpro*
  AUV 401: 277 *Cougar*; 124 M-ATV
ENGINEERING & MAINTENANCE VEHICLES
  AEV 97+: IWT; 58 MT-LB AEV; 31 *Rosomak* WRT; 8 MID *Bizon*
  ARV 68: 31 BPz-2; 12 M88A2 *Hercules*; 25 WZT-3M
  VLB 130: 4 *Biber*; 107 BLG67M2; 8 Joint Assault Bridge; 11 MS-20 *Daglezja*
  MW 27: 17 *Bozena* 4; 6 ISM *Kroton*; 4 *Kalina* SUM
ANTI-TANK/ANTI-INFRASTRUCTURE
  MSL • MANPATS 9K11 *Malyutka* (RS-AT-3 *Sagger*); 9K111 *Fagot* (RS-AT-4 *Spigot*); *Spike*-LR
ARTILLERY 793
  SP 451: **122mm** 206 2S1 *Gvozdika*; **152mm** 111: 108 M-77 *Dana*; 3 *Dana*-M; **155mm** 134: 108 K9A1; 26 *Krab*
  MRL 199: **122mm** 131: 27 BM-21; 29 RM-70; 75 WR-40 *Langusta*; **227mm** 18 M142 HIMARS; **239mm** 50 K239 *Chunmoo* (*Homar*-K)
  MOR 143: **120mm** 35 M120; **SP 120mm** 108 SMK120 RAK
HELICOPTERS
  ATK 16 Mi-24D/V *Hind* D/E
  MRH 67: 3 AW149; 7 Mi-8MT *Hip*; 3 Mi-17 *Hip* H; 1 Mi-17AE *Hip* (aeromedical); 5 Mi-17-1V *Hip*; 16 PZL Mi-2URP *Hoplite*; 24 PZL W-3W/WA *Sokol*; 8 PZL W-3PL *Gluszec* (CSAR)
  TPT 41: **Medium** 12: 6 Mi-8T *Hip*; 2 PZL W-3AE *Sokol* (aeromedical); 8 S-70i *Black Hawk*; **Light** 25 PZL Mi-2 *Hoplite*
UNINHABITED AERIAL VEHICLES
  ISR • Light FT-5
AIR DEFENCE
  SAM 162
    Short-range 26: 6 CAMM (*Narew*); 20 2K12 *Kub* (RS-SA-6 *Gainful*)
    Point-defence 136+: 57 9K33M2 *Osa*-AK (RS-SA-8B *Gecko*); GROM; *Piorun*; 79 *Poprad*
  SPAAGM 23mm 56: 36 *Pilica*; 20 ZSU-23-4MP *Biala*
  GUNS 345
    SP 23mm 2+: 2 ZSU-23-4; *Hibneryt*
    TOWED 23mm 343: 268 ZU-23-2; 75 ZUR-23-2KG *Jodek*-G (with GROM msl)
BOMBS • Laser-guided MAM-C/L

Navy 6,450
EQUIPMENT BY TYPE
SUBMARINES • SSK 1 *Orzeł* (ex-FSU *Kilo*) with 6 single 533mm TT with 53-65KE/TEST-71ME HWT
PRINCIPAL SURFACE COMBATANTS • FRIGATES 2
  FFH 2 *Pułaski* (ex-US *Oliver Hazard Perry*) (of which 1 used as training ship) with 2 triple 324mm SVTT Mk 32 ASTT with MU90 LWT, 1 Mk 15 *Phalanx* CIWS, 1 76mm gun (capacity 2 SH-2G *Super Seasprite* ASW hel)

PATROL AND COASTAL COMBATANTS 5
  CORVETTES • FSM 1 *Kaszub* with 2 quad lnchr with 9K32 *Strela*-2 (RS-SA-N-5 *Grail*) SAM, 2 twin 533mm ASTT with SET-53 HWT, 2 RBU 6000 *Smerch* 2 A/S mor, 1 76mm gun
  PSO 1 *Ślązak* (MEKO A-100) with 1 76mm gun, 1 hel landing platform
  PCFGM 3 *Orkan* (ex-GDR *Sassnitz*) with 1 quad lnchr with RBS15 Mk3 AShM, 1 quad lnchr (manual aiming) with 9K32 *Strela*-2M (RS-SA-N-5 *Grail*) SAM, 1 AK630 CIWS, 1 76mm gun
MINE WARFARE • MINE COUNTERMEASURES 21
  MCCS 1 *Kontradmiral Xawery Czernicki*
  MCO 3 *Kormoran II*
  MSI 17: 1 *Gopło*; 12 *Gardno*; 4 *Mamry*
AMPHIBIOUS 8
  LANDING SHIPS • LSM 5 *Lublin* (capacity 9 tanks; 135 troops)
  LANDING CRAFT • LCU 3 *Deba* (capacity 50 troops)
LOGISTICS AND SUPPORT 26
  AGI 2 *Moma*
  AGS 8: 2 *Heweliusz*; 4 *Wildcat 40*; 2 (coastal)
  AOR 1 *Bałtyk*
  AOL 1 *Moskit*
  ARS 4: 2 *Piast*; 2 *Zbyszko*
  ATF 8: 6 *Bolko* (B860); 2 H960
  AXL 1 *Wodnik* with 1 twin AK230 CIWS
  AXS 1 *Iskra*
UNINHABITED MARITIME SYSTEMS • UUV
  DATA *Gavia*
  MW *Double Eagle* Mk III/SAROV
COASTAL DEFENCE • AShM 12 NSM

Naval Aviation 1,300
FORCES BY ROLE
ANTI SUBMARINE WARFARE/SEARCH & RESCUE
  1 sqn with Mi-14PL *Haze* A; Mi-14PL/R *Haze* C
  1 sqn with PZL W-3WA RM *Anakonda*; SH-2G *Super Seasprite*
MARITIME PATROL
  1 sqn with An-28E/RM *Bryza*
TRANSPORT
  1 sqn with An-28TD; M-28B TD *Bryza*
  1 sqn with An-28TD; M-28B; PZL Mi-2 *Hoplite*
EQUIPMENT BY TYPE
AIRCRAFT
  MP 10: 8 An-28RM *Bryza*; 2 An-28E *Bryza*
  TPT • Light 4: 2 An-28TD *Bryza*; 2 M-28B TD *Bryza*
HELICOPTERS
  ASW 8: 4 AW101 ASW Merlin HM2; 3 Mi-14PL *Haze*; 1 SH-2G *Super Seasprite*
  SAR 10: 2 Mi-14PL/R *Haze* C; 8 PZL W-3WA RM *Anakonda*
  TPT • Light 4 PZL Mi-2 *Hoplite*

Air Force 18,850
FORCES BY ROLE
FIGHTER
  1 sqn with MiG-29A/UB *Fulcrum*
FIGHTER/GROUND ATTACK
  3 sqn with F-16C/D Block 52+ *Fighting Falcon*
  1 sqn with FA-50 *Fighting Eagle*
FIGHTER/GROUND ATTACK/ISR
  2 sqn with Su-22M-4 *Fitter*
SEARCH AND RESCUE
  1 sqn with Mi-2; PZL W-3 *Sokol*
TRANSPORT
  1 sqn with C-130H/E; M-28 *Bryza*
  1 sqn with C295M; M-28 *Bryza*
TRAINING
  1 sqn with PZL-130 *Orlik*
  1 sqn with M-346
  1 hel sqn with SW-4 *Puszczyk*
TRANSPORT HELICOPTER
  1 (Spec Ops) sqn with Mi-17 *Hip* H
  1 (VIP) sqn with Mi-8 *Hip*; W-3WA *Sokol*
CISR UAV
  1 sqn with Bayraktar TB2; MQ-9A *Reaper*
AIR DEFENCE
  1 bde with M903 *Patriot* PAC-3 MSE; S-125 *Newa* SC
EQUIPMENT BY TYPE
AIRCRAFT 85 combat capable
  FTR 14: 11 MiG-29A *Fulcrum*; 3 MiG-29UB *Fulcrum*
  FGA 71: 36 F-16C Block 52+ *Fighting Falcon*; 12 F-16D Block 52+ *Fighting Falcon*; 12 FA-50 *Fighting Eagle*; 8 Su-22M4 *Fitter*; 3 Su-22UM3K *Fitter*
  AEW&C 2 Saab 340 *Erieye* (in test)
  TPT 52: **Medium** 8: 3 C-130H *Hercules*; 5 C-130E *Hercules*; **Light** 39: 16 C295M; 10 M-28 *Bryza* TD; 13 M-28 *Bryza* PT; **PAX** 5: 2 Gulfstream G550; 3 B-737-800 (VIP)
  TRG 40: 12 M-346; 28 PZL-130 *Orlik*
HELICOPTERS
  MRH 8 Mi-17 *Hip* H
  TPT 65: **Medium** 29: 9 Mi-8 *Hip*; 10 PZL W-3 *Sokol*; 10 PZL W-3WA *Sokol* (VIP); **Light** 36: 14 PZL Mi-2 *Hoplite*; 22 SW-4 *Puszczyk* (trg)
UNIHABITED AERIAL VEHICLES
  CISR 28: **Heavy** 4 MQ-9A *Reaper* (leased; unarmed); **Medium** 24 Bayraktar TB2
AIR DEFENCE
  SAM 30
    Long-range 16 M903 *Patriot* PAC-3 MSE
    Short-range 14 S-125 *Newa* SC
  SPAAGM 23mm 12 *Pilica* (with *Piorun* msl)
AIR-LAUNCHED MISSILES
  AAM • IR AIM-9 *Sidewinder*; R-60 (RS-A-8 *Aphid*);

R-73 (RS-AA-11A *Archer*); R-27T (RS-AA-10B *Alamo*);
IIR AIM-9X *Sidwinder* II; **ARH** AIM-120C AMRAAM
ASM AGM-65J/G *Maverick*; Kh-25 (RS-AS-10 *Karen*);
Kh-29 (RS-AS-14 *Kedge*)
ALCM • Conventional AGM-158B JASSM-ER
BOMBS
Laser-guided MAM-C/L

Special Forces 3,400
FORCES BY ROLE
SPECIAL FORCES
3 SF units (GROM, FORMOZA & cdo)
COMBAT SUPPORT/
1 cbt spt unit (AGAT)
COMBAT SERVICE SUPPORT
1 spt unit (NIL)
EQUIPMENT BY TYPE
UNINHABITED AERIAL VEHICLES
ISR • Light RQ-21A *Blackjack*; *Scan Eagle*

Territorial Defence Forces 5,300 (plus 37,500 reservists)
FORCES BY ROLE
MANOEUVRE
Other
20 sy bde

Gendarmerie & Paramilitary 14,300
Border Guards 14,300
Ministry of Interior
Maritime Border Guard 2,000
EQUIPMENT BY TYPE
PATROL AND COASTAL COMBATANTS 14
PCO 1 *Jozef Haller* (FRA Socarenam 70m OPV)
PCC 2 *Kaper*
PBF 6: 2 *Strażnik*; 4 IC16M
PB 5: 2 *Wisłoka*; 2 *Baltic* 24; 1 Project MI-6
AMPHIBIOUS
LANDING CRAFT • UCAC 2 *Griffon* 2000TDX

DEPLOYMENT
BOSNIA-HERZEGOVINA: EU • EUFOR (*Operation Althea*) 49
CENTRAL AFRICAN REPUBLIC: EU • EUTM RCA 2
DEMOCRATIC REPUBLIC OF THE CONGO: UN • MONUSCO 1
IRAQ: *Operation Inherent Resolve* 208; **NATO •** NATO Mission Iraq 51
KOSOVO: NATO • KFOR 247; 1 inf coy; **UN •** UNMIK 2
LATVIA: NATO • Forward Land Forces up to 200; 1 tk coy
LEBANON: UN • UNIFIL 195; 1 mech inf coy
MIDDLE EAST: UN • UNTSO 3
ROMANIA: NATO • Forward Land Forces 250; 1 mech inf coy(+)
SOUTH SUDAN: UN • UNMISS 1
WESTERN SAHARA: UN • MINURSO 1

FOREIGN FORCES
All NATO Forward Land Forces unless stated
Canada *Operation Unifier* 40 (UKR trg)
Croatia 69; 1 SP arty bty
Germany MNC-NE corps HQ: 95
Romania 100; 1 sp ADA bty
United Kingdom 140; 1 recce sqn; 1 SAM bty with CAMM (*Land Ceptor*)
United States: 1,000; 1 armd bn with M1A2 SEPv2 *Abarms*; M2A3 *Bradley*; 1 SP arty bty with M109A6 • *Operation Atlantic Resolve* 13,000; 1 corps HQ; 1 div HQ; 1 armd bde with M1A2 SEPv2 *Abrams*; M3A3 *Bradley*; M2A3 *Bradley*; M109A6; 1 armd bde(-) with M1A2 SEPv2 *Abrams*; M3A3 *Bradley*; M2A3 *Bradley*; M109A6; 2 SAM bty with M903 *Patriot* PAC-3 MSE; 1 CISR UAV sqn with MQ-9A *Reaper*; 1 Aegis Ashore BMD unit with three 8-cell Mk 41 VLS launchers with SM-3; 1 (APS) armd bde eqpt set

Portugal PRT

Euro EUR		2023	2024	2025
GDP	EUR	266bn	278bn	292bn
	USD	287bn	303bn	320bn
Real GDP growth	%	2.3	1.9	2.3
Def exp [a]	EUR	3.92bn	4.29bn	
	USD	4.24bn	4.63bn	
Def bdgt	EUR	2.58bn	2.85bn	3.07bn
	USD	2.80bn	3.11bn	3.36bn

[a] NATO figure

Real-terms defence budget trend (USDbn, constant 2015)

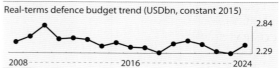

Population	10,207,177

Age	0–14	15–19	20–24	25–29	30–64	65 plus
Male	6.5%	2.6%	2.9%	2.8%	23.6%	8.9%
Female	6.2%	2.5%	2.7%	2.7%	25.1%	13.4%

Capabilities

Principal tasks for Portugal's all-volunteer armed forces are homeland defence, maritime security, multinational operations and responding to humanitarian disasters. Investment plans support Portugal's ambition to field rapid-reaction and maritime surveillance capabilities for territorial defence and multinational operations. The parliament approved a new military programme law for 2019–30, which finances the purchase of five KC-390 aircraft to modernise force projection capacity. Portugal is also upgrading its naval inventory, with plans for tankers and ocean patrol vessels.

The country, in 2022, approved a modest increase in defence spending and suggested further increases were possible. Portugal hosts NATO's cyber-security academy and the country contributes to EU military structures. Portugal has a close relationship with former dependencies and with the US, which operates out of Lajes Air Base. All three services have programmes to modernise and sustain existing equipment. The country has an active defence industry, though principally in relation to shipbuilding, broader maintenance tasks and the manufacture of components, small arms and light weapons, and in 2023, the government adopted a strategy for the development of the defence technological and industrial base 2023–33.

ACTIVE 21,500 (Army 9,250 Navy 6,350 Air 4,350 Other 1,550) Gendarmerie & Paramilitary 22,600

RESERVE 23,500 (Army 10,000 Navy 9,000, Air Force 4,500) Gendarmerie & Paramilitary 220

Reserve obligation to age 35

ORGANISATIONS BY SERVICE

Army 9,250

5 territorial comd (2 mil region, 1 mil district, 2 mil zone)
FORCES BY ROLE
SPECIAL FORCES
  1 SF bn
MANOEUVRE
  Mechanised
  1 mech bde (1 recce sqn, 1 tk regt, 1 mech inf bn, 1 arty bn, 1 AD bty, 1 engr coy, 1 sigs coy, 1 spt bn)
  1 (intervention) mech bde (1 recce regt, 2 mech inf bn, 1 arty bn, 1 AD bty, 1 engr coy, 1 sigs coy, 1 spt bn)
  Air Manoeuvre
  1 (rapid reaction) bde (1 cdo bn, 1 ISR bn, 2 para bn, 1 arty bn, 1 AD bty, 1 engr coy, 1 sigs coy, 1 spt bn)
  Other
  1 (Azores) inf gp (2 inf bn, 1 AD bty)
  1 (Madeira) inf gp (1 inf bn, 1 AD bty)
COMBAT SUPPORT
  1 STA bty
  1 engr bn (1 construction coy; 1 EOD unit; 1 ptn br coy; 1 CBRN coy)
  1 EW coy
  1 MP bn
  1 psyops unit
  1 CIMIC coy (joint)
  1 sigs bn
COMBAT SERVICE SUPPORT
  1 maint coy
  1 log coy
  1 tpt coy
  1 med unit
AIR DEFENCE
  1 AD bn

Reserves 210,000

FORCES BY ROLE
MANOEUVRE
  Light
  3 (territorial) def bde (on mobilisation)
EQUIPMENT BY TYPE
ARMOURED FIGHTING VEHICLES
  MBT 34 Leopard 2A6
  IFV 30 Pandur II MK 30mm
  APC 373
    APC (T) 206: 159 M113A1/M113A2; 47 M577A2 (CP)
    APC (W) 167: 9 V-150 Commando; 12 V-200 Chaimite; 146 Pandur II (incl variants)
  AUV 16 VBL
ENGINEERING & MAINTENANCE VEHICLES
  AEV M728
  ARV 13: 6 M88A1, 7 Pandur II ARV
  VLB M48
ANTI-TANK/ANTI-INFRASTRUCTURE
  MSL
    SP 26: 17 M113 with TOW; 4 M901 with TOW; 5 Pandur II with TOW
    MANPATS Milan
  RCL • **84mm** Carl Gustaf; **106mm** M40A1
ARTILLERY 293
  SP 155mm 18 M109A5; (6 M109A2 in store)
  TOWED 41: **105mm** 17 L119 Light Gun, (21 M101A1 in store); **155mm** 24 M114A1
  MOR 234: **81mm** 143; **SP 81mm** 12: 2 M125A1; 10 M125A2; **107mm** 11 M30; **SP 107mm** 18: 3 M106A1; 15 M106A2; **120mm** 50 Tampella
AIR DEFENCE
  SAM • **Point-defence** FIM-92 Stinger
  GUNS • **TOWED 20mm** 20 Rh 202

Navy 6,350 (incl 950 Marines)
EQUIPMENT BY TYPE
SUBMARINES 2
  SSK 2 Tridente (GER Type-214) (fitted with AIP) with 8 533mm TT with UGM-84L Harpoon Block II AShM/Black Shark HWT
PRINCIPAL SURFACE COMBATANTS • FRIGATES 4
  FFGHM 4:
    2 Bartolomeu Dias (ex-NLD Karel Doorman) with 2 quad lnchr with RGM-84L Harpoon Block II AShM, 1 16-cell Mk 48 mod 1 VLS with RIM-162 ESSM SAM, 2 twin 324mm SVTT Mk 32 ASTT with Mk 46 LWT, 1 Goalkeeper CIWS, 1 76mm gun (capacity 1 Lynx Mk95 (Super Lynx) hel)
    2 Vasco Da Gama (1 other nor. operational) with 2 quad lnchr with RGM-84C Harpoon Block 1B AShM, 1 octuple Mk 29 GMLS with RIM-7M Sea Sparrow SAM, 2 triple 324mm SVTT Mk 32 ASTT with Mk 46 LWT, 1 Mk 15 Phalanx Block 1B CIWS, 1 100mm gun (capacity 2 Lynx Mk95 (Super Lynx) hel)
PATROL AND COASTAL COMBATANTS 21

CORVETTES • FS 2:
  1 *Baptista de Andrade* with 1 100mm gun, 1 hel landing platform
  1 *Joao Coutinho* with 1 twin 76mm gun, 1 hel landing platform
PSO 4 *Viana do Castelo* with 1 hel landing platform
PCC 5: 1 *Cacine*; 4 *Tejo* (ex-DNK *Flyvisken*)
PBR 10: 5 *Argos*; 4 *Centauro*; 1 *Rio Minho*
LOGISTICS AND SUPPORT 20
  AAR 12: 8 *Amelia* (ESP Rodman 46); 4 *Vigilante*
  AGS 4: 2 *D Carlos* I (ex-US *Stalwart*); 2 *Andromeda*
  AXS 4: 1 *Sagres* (ex-GER *Gorch Fock*); 1 *Creoula*; 1 *Polar*; 1 *Zarco*
UNINHABITED MARITIME SYSTEMS
  USV • DATA X-2601
  UUV • DATA *SeaExplorer* • **UTL** *Falcon*; *Navajo*

Marines 950
FORCES BY ROLE
SPECIAL FORCES
  1 SF det
MANOEUVRE
  Light
    1 lt inf bn
COMBAT SUPPORT
  1 mor coy
  1 MP coy
EQUIPMENT BY TYPE
ANTI-TANK/ANTI-INFRASTRUCTURE
  MSL • MANPATS *Milan*; TOW
  RCL • 84mm *Carl Gustaf*
ARTILLERY • MOR 30+: **81mm** some; **120mm** 30

Naval Aviation
EQUIPMENT BY TYPE
HELICOPTERS • ASW 5: 4 *Lynx* Mk95 (*Super Lynx*); 1 *Lynx* Mk95A (*Super Lynx*)

Air Force 4,300
FORCES BY ROLE
FIGHTER/GROUND ATTACK
  2 sqn with F-16AM/BM *Fighting Falcon*
MARITIME PATROL
  1 sqn with P-3C *Orion*
ISR/TRANSPORT
  1 sqn with C295M
COMBAT SEARCH & RESCUE
  2 sqn with with AW101 *Merlin*
TRANSPORT
  1 sqn with C-130H/H-30 *Hercules*
  1 sqn with KC-390 *Millenium*
  1 sqn with *Falcon* 50/900B
TRAINING
  1 sqn with AW119 *Koala*
  1 sqn with TB-30 *Epsilon*
EQUIPMENT BY TYPE
AIRCRAFT 36 combat capable
  FTR 28: 24 F-16AM *Fighting Falcon*; 4 F-16BM *Fighting Falcon*
  ASW 8 P-3C *Orion*
  ISR 5 C295M (maritime surv/photo recce)
  TPT 18: **Medium** 7: 2 C-130H *Hercules*; 3 C-130H-30 *Hercules* (tpt/SAR); 2 KC-390 *Millenium*; **Light** 7 C295M; **PAX** 4: 3 *Falcon* 50 (tpt/VIP); 1 *Falcon* 900B (tpt/VIP)
  TRG 16 TB-30 *Epsilon*
HELICOPTERS
  TPT 21: **Medium** 14: 12 AW101 *Merlin* (6 SAR, 4 CSAR, 2 fishery protection); 2 UH-60A *Black Hawk* (fire fighting); **Light** 7 AW119 *Koala*
AIR-LAUNCHED MISSILES
  AAM • IR AIM-9L/I *Sidewinder*; **ARH** AIM-120C AMRAAM
  ASM AGM-65A *Maverick*
  AShM AGM-84A *Harpoon*
BOMBS
  Laser & INS/GPS-guided GBU-49 Enhanced *Paveway* II
  INS/GPS guided GBU-31 JDAM

Gendarmerie & Paramilitary 22,600
National Republican Guard 22,600
EQUIPMENT BY TYPE
PATROL AND COASTAL COMBATANTS 46
  PBF 15 *Ribamar*
  PBI 30
  PB 1 *Bojador* (Damen FCS 3307)
HELICOPTERS • MRH 7 SA315 *Lama*

DEPLOYMENT
CENTRAL AFRICAN REPUBLIC: EU • EUTM RCA 10; **UN** • MINUSCA 219; 1 AB coy
IRAQ: NATO • NATO Mission Iraq 1
KOSOVO: NATO • KFOR 1
LITHUANIA: NATO • Forward Land Forces 150; 1 mne coy
MOZAMBIQUE: EU • EUMAM Mozambique 50
NORTH SEA: NATO • SNMG 1: 150; 1 FFGHM
ROMANIA: NATO • Forward Land Forces 235; 1 mech inf coy(+)
SLOVAKIA: NATO • Forward Land Forces 25; 1 tk pl
SOMALIA: EU • EUTM Somalia 2

FOREIGN FORCES
United States US European Command: 250; 1 spt facility at Lajes

Romania ROM

Romanian Leu RON		2023	2024	2025
GDP	RON	1.61trn	1.75trn	1.86trn
	USD	351bn	381bn	406bn
Real GDP growth	%	2.1	1.9	3.3
Def exp [a]	RON	25.6bn	40.1bn	
	USD	5.60bn	8.64bn	
Def bdgt [b]	RON	38.8bn	42.2bn	
	USD	8.47bn	9.20bn	

[a] NATO figure

[b] Includes military pensions

Real-terms defence budget trend (USDbn, constant 2015)

Population	18,148,155				
Age	0–14	15–19	20–24	25–29	30–64	65 plus
Male	7.9%	2.8%	2.5%	2.3%	23.3%	9.3%
Female	7.5%	2.7%	2.4%	2.4%	23.6%	13.3%

Capabilities

Romania's armed forces are structured around territorial defence, supporting NATO and EU missions and contributing to regional and global stability and security. According to the National Defence Strategy 2020–24, principal security threats include Russia's increased presence in the Black Sea, hybrid warfare, cyberattacks and terrorism. Romania hosts the *Aegis Ashore* ballistic-missile-defence system at Deveselu. Russia's missile attacks on Ukraine have spurred greater focus on air defence and, after giving one *Patriot* system to Ukraine, Romania is expanding its replacement to also protect critical national infrastructure. SHORAD systems are also being examined. The country contributes to EU and NATO missions. The inventory was comprised of Soviet-era equipment but is undergoing major change, set out in the 2024–33 Romanian Army Equipment Plan. Romanian airspace benefits from NATO's Enhanced Air Policing mission, and Mihail Kogalniceanu airbase will be expanded. The country received approval from the US to buy F-35As, while it is improving its capabilities in other domains such as through the acquisition of mine countermeasures vessels, *Abrams* MBTs, and Turkish UAVs and a planned acquisition of IFVs. The country's defence industry is improving its capacity and competitiveness through a focus on licenced production. Examples include a production facility for *Abrams* ammunition and ongoing discussions with partner countries Turkiye and South Korea.

ACTIVE 69,900 (Army 35,500 Navy 5,200 Air 11,700 Joint 17,500) Gendarmerie & Paramilitary 57,000

RESERVE 55,000 (Joint 55,000)

ORGANISATIONS BY SERVICE

Army 35,500
FORCES BY ROLE
COMMAND
2 div HQ (2nd & 4th)
elm 1 div HQ (MND-SE)
SPECIAL FORCES
1 SF bde (2 SF bn, 1 para bn, 1 log bn)
MANOEUVRE
Reconnaissance
1 recce bde (3 recce bn, 1 AD bn, 1 log bn)
2 recce regt
Mechanised
1 mech bde (2 tk bn, 2 mech inf bn, 1 arty bn, 1 AD bn, 1 log bn)
1 mech bde (1 tk bn, 3 mech inf bn, 1 arty bn, 1 AD bn, 1 log bn)
2 mech bde (1 tk bn, 2 mech inf bn, 1 arty bn, 1 AD bn, 1 log bn)
1 mech bde (4 mech inf bn, 1 arty bn, 1 AD bn, 1 log bn)
1 (MNB-SE) mech inf bde (2 armd inf bn, 1 inf bn, 1 arty bn, 1 AD bn, 1 log br)
Light
2 mtn inf bde (3 mtn inf bn, 1 arty bn, 1 AD bn, 1 log bn)
COMBAT SUPPORT
1 cbt spt bde (1 AB bn, 1 arty bn, 1 CBRN bn, 1 log bn, 1 AD bn)
1 MRL bde (3 MRL bn, 1 STA bn, 1 log bn)
2 arty regt
1 engr bde (1 engr bn, 4 ptn br bn, 1 log bn)
2 engr bn
3 sigs bn
1 CIMIC bn
1 MP bn
2 CBRN bn
COMBAT SERVICE SUPPORT
3 spt bn
AIR DEFENCE
3 AD regt
EQUIPMENT BY TYPE
ARMOURED FIGHTING VEHICLES
    MBT 377: 220 T-55AM; 103 TR-85; 54 TR-85 M1
    IFV 265: 23 MLI-84 (incl CP); 101 MLI-84M *Jderul*; 141 *Piranha* V
    APC 604
        APC (T) 76 MLVM
        APC (W) 468: 69 B33 TAB *Zimbru*; 35 *Piranha* IIIC; 211 TAB-71 (incl variants); 153 TAB-77 (incl variants)
        PPV 60 *Maxxpro*
    AUV 513: 33 JLTV; 480 TABC-79 (incl variants)
ENGINEERING & MAINTENANCE VEHICLES
    ARV 56: 3 MLI-84M TEHEVAC; 1 *Piranha* IIIC; 8 TERA-71L; 44 TERA-77L
    VLB 43 BLG-67
    NBC VEHICLES 110: 1 *Piranha* IIIC CBRN; 109 RCH-84
ANTI-TANK/ANTI-INFRASTRUCTURE
    MSL
        SP 158: 12 9P122 *Malyutka* (RS-AT-3 *Sagger*); 98 9P133

Malyutka (RS-AT-3 *Sagger*); 48 9P148 *Konkurs* (RS-AT-5 *Spandrel*)
  MANPATS Spike-LR
 GUNS
  SP 100mm (23 SU-100 in store)
  TOWED 100mm 218 M-1977
ARTILLERY 1,142
 SP 122mm 40: 6 2S1 *Gvodzika*; 34 Model 89
 TOWED 447: **122mm** 96 (M-30) M-1938 (A-19); **152mm** 351: 247 M-1981; 104 M-1985
 MRL 206: **122mm** 170: 134 APR-40; 36 LAROM; **227mm** 36 M142 HIMARS (ATACMS-capable)
 MOR 449: **SP 82mm** 177: 92 TAB-71AR; 85 TABC-79AR; **120mm** 272: 266 M-1982; 6 Piranha IIIC with *Cardom*
SURFACE-TO-SURFACE MISSILE LAUNCHERS
 SRBM • Conventional MGM-168 ATACMS (Launched from M142 HIMARS MRLS)
AIR DEFENCE
 SAM 96
  Short-range 48: 32 2K12 *Kub* (RS-SA-6 *Gainful*); 16 9K33 *Osa* (RS-SA-8 *Gecko*)
  Point-defence 48 CA-95
 GUNS 65+
  SP 35mm 41 *Gepard*
  TOWED 24+: **14.5mm** ZPU-2; **35mm** 24 GDF-003; **57mm** S-60

Navy 5,200
EQUIPMENT BY TYPE
PRINCIPAL SURFACE COMBATANTS • FRIGATES 3
 FFGH 1 *Marasesti* with 4 twin lnchr with P-22 (RS-SS-N-2C *Styx*) AShM, 2 triple 533mm ASTT with 53–65 HWT, 2 RBU 6000 *Smerch* 2 A/S mor, 4 AK630M CIWS, 2 twin 76mm guns (capacity 2 SA-316 (IAR-316) *Alouette* III hel)
 FFH 2 *Regele Ferdinand* (ex-UK Type-22), with 2 triple STWS Mk.2 324mm TT, 1 76mm gun (capacity 1 SA330 (IAR-330) *Puma*)
PATROL AND COASTAL COMBATANTS 22
 CORVETTES • FS 4:
  2 *Tetal* I with 2 twin 533mm ASTT with SET-53M HWT, 2 RBU 2500 *Smerch* 1 A/S mor, 2 AK230 CIWS, 2 twin 76mm guns
  2 *Tetal* II with 2 twin 533mm ASTT with SET-53M HWT, 2 RBU 6000 *Smerch* 2 A/S mor, 2 AK630 CIWS, 1 76mm gun, 1 hel landing platform
 PCFG 3 *Zborul* (ex-FSU *Tarantul* I (Project 1241RE)) with 2 twin lnchr with P-22 (RS-SS-N-2C *Styx*) AShM, 2 AK630 CIWS, 1 76mm gun
 PCR 8: 5 *Brutar* II with 2 BM-21 122mm MRL, 1 100mm gun; 3 *Kogalniceanu* with 2 BM-21 122mm MRL, 2 100mm guns
 PBR 7: 1 ESM12; 6 VD141 (ex-MSR now used for river patrol)
MINE WARFARE 11
 MINE COUNTERMEASURES 10

  MHC 1 *Ghiculescu* (ex-UK *Sandown*)
  MSO 3 *Musca* with 2 RBU 1200 *Uragan* A/S mor, 2 AK230 CIWS
  MSR 6 VD141
 MINELAYERS • ML 1 *Corsar* with up to 120 mines, 2 RBU 1200 *Uragan* A/S mor, 2 AK230 CIWS
LOGISTICS AND SUPPORT 8
 AE 2 *Constanta* with 2 RBU 1200 *Uragan* A/S mor, 2 AK230 CIWS, 2 twin 57mm guns
 AGOR 1 *Corsar*
 AGS 1 *Catuneanu*
 AOL 2: 1 *Tulcea*; 1 Other
 ATF 1 *Grozavul*
 AXS 1 *Mircea* (GER *Gorch Fock*)

Naval Infantry
FORCES BY ROLE
MANOEUVRE
 Light
  1 naval inf regt
EQUIPMENT BY TYPE
ARMOURED FIGHTING VEHICLES
 AUV 14: 11 ABC-79M; 3 TABC-79M

Air Force 11,700
FORCES BY ROLE
FIGHTER/GROUND ATTACK
 1 sqn with with F-16AM/BM *Fighting Falcon*
 1 sqn with with F-16AM/BM *Fighting Falcon* (forming)
GROUND ATTACK
 1 sqn with IAR-99 *Soim**
TRANSPORT
 1 sqn with An-26 *Curl*; An-30 *Clank*; C-27J *Spartan*
 1 sqn with C-130B/H *Hercules*
TRAINING
 1 sqn with IAR-99 *Soim**
 1 sqn with SA316B *Alouette* III (IAR-316B); Yak-52 (Iak-52)
TRANSPORT HELICOPTER
 2 (multi-role) sqn with IAR-330 SOCAT *Puma*
 3 sqn with SA330L/M *Puma* (IAR-330L/M)
AIR DEFENCE
 1 AD bde
 1 AD regt
COMBAT SERVICE SUPPORT
 1 engr spt regt
EQUIPMENT BY TYPE
AIRCRAFT 53 combat capable
 FTR 29: 24 F-16AM *Fighting Falcon*; 5 F-16BM *Fighting Falcon*
 ISR 2 An-30 *Clank*
 TPT 16: **Medium** 14: 7 C-27J *Spartan*; 4 C-130B *Hercules*; 3 C-130H *Hercules*; **Light** 2 An-26 *Curl*
 TRG 36: 12 IAR-99*; 12 IAR-99C *Soim**; 12 Yak-52 (Iak-52)

HELICOPTERS
  MRH 31: 23 IAR-330 SOCAT *Puma*; 8 SA316B *Alouette III* (IAR-316B)
  TPT • Medium 36: 6 IAR-330L-RM; 14 SA330L *Puma* (IAR-330L); 16 SA330M *Puma* (IAR-330M)
AIR DEFENCE • SAM 16
  Long-range 12 M903 *Patriot* PAC-3 MSE
  Medium-range 4 MIM-23 *Hawk* PIP III
AIR-LAUNCHED MISSILES
  AAM • IR AIM-9M *Sidewinder*; **IIR** AIM-9X *Sidewinder II*; **ARH** AIM-120C AMRAAM
  ASM *Spike*-ER
BOMBS
  Laser-guided GBU-12 *Paveway*
  Laser & INS/GPS-guided GBU-54 Laser JDAM
  INS/GPS guided GBU-38 JDAM

Gendarmerie & Paramilitary ε57,000

  Gendarmerie ε57,000
  Ministry of Interior

DEPLOYMENT

BOSNIA-HERZEGOVINA: EU • EUFOR (*Operation Althea*) 470; 2 inf coy
CENTRAL AFRICAN REPUBLIC: EU • EUTM RCA 60
DEMOCRATIC REPUBLIC OF THE CONGO: UN • MONUSCO 5
INDIA/PAKISTAN: UN • UNMOGIP 2
IRAQ: *Operation Inherent Resolve* 30; **NATO •** NATO Mission Iraq 2
KOSOVO: NATO • KFOR 184; 1 inf coy; **UN •** UNMIK 1
MEDITERRANEAN SEA: NATO • SNMCMG 2: 75; 1 ML
MOZAMBIQUE: EU • EUMAM Mozambique 6
POLAND: NATO • Forward Land Forces ε100; 1 SP ADA bty
SOMALIA: EU • EUTM Somalia 5
SOUTH SUDAN: UN • UNMISS 5
UNITED KINGDOM: *Operation Interflex* 30 (UKR trg)

FOREIGN FORCES

Belgium NATO Forward Land Forces: 300; 1 mech inf coy
France NATO Forward Land Forces: 750; 1 armd BG; 2 arty bty; 1 SAM bty with SAMP/T
Luxembourg NATO Forward Land Forces: 27; 1 recce pl
Macedonia, North NATO Forward Land Forces: 35
Poland NATO Forward Land Forces 250; 1 mech inf coy; *Rosomak*
Portugal NATO Enhanced Vigilance Activities: 235; 1 mech inf coy(+)
Spain NATO Air Policing: 150; 8 F/A-18A *Hornet* MLU (EF-18A MLU)
United States US European Command: 2,000; 1 inf bde HQ; 1 fd arty bn with M119A3; M777A2; 1 *Aegis Ashore* BMD unit with 3 8-cell Mk 41 VLS with SM-3; **NATO**

Forward Land Forces: 150; 1 inf coy; Enhanced Air Policing: 100; 4 F-16C *Fighting Falcon*

Serbia SER

Serbian Dinar RSD		2023	2024	2025
GDP	RSD	8.15trn	8.96trn	9.67trn
	USD	75.2bn	82.6bn	88.6bn
Real GDP growth	%	2.5	3.9	4.1
Def bdgt	RSD	161bn	159bn	
	USD	1.48bn	1.46bn	

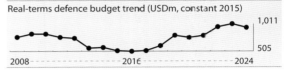
Real-terms defence budget trend (USDm, constant 2015)

Population	6,652,212				
Age	0–14	15–19	20–24	25–29	30–64	65 plus
Male	7.4%	2.7%	2.9%	2.9%	24.5%	8.3%
Female	7.0%	2.5%	2.7%	2.8%	24.5%	11.7%

Capabilities

Serbia's government adopted a Total Defence Concept in 2023, reflected also in a defence white paper. The concept focuses on military neutrality, protection of its sovereignty and citizens, cooperation and partnership, and improvement of national security. Belgrade views separatism, ethnic and religious extremism, climate change and further international recognition of Kosovo as key threats. The Serbian armed forces are modernising to address long-term capability shortfalls and personnel shortages. Priorities include improving combat support, air-defence, cyber and electronic warfare capacities. Serbia is pursuing air force modernisation across most capability types. Belgrade has continued cooperation and dialogue with NATO through the Individual Partnership Action Plan. Serbia maintains a close relationship with Russia, which has provided military equipment. However, the country has also deepened security relations with China, purchasing Chinese military equipment, including air defence systems. Serbia mostly trains with its Balkan neighbours, Russia and NATO countries. It contributes to EU, CSCE and UN peacekeeping missions. Serbia's defence industry focuses on missile and artillery systems, and small arms and ammunition, with a plan to enhance its capabilities. However, the country is reliant on external suppliers for major platforms.

ACTIVE 28,150 (Army 13,250 Air Force and Air Defence 5,100 Training Command 3,000 Guards 1,600 Other MoD 5,200) Gendarmerie & Paramilitary 3,700

Conscript liability 6 months (voluntary)

RESERVE 50,150

ORGANISATIONS BY SERVICE

Army 13,250
FORCES BY ROLE

SPECIAL FORCES
1 spec ops bde (3 spec ops bn, 1 log coy)

MANOEUVRE
Mechanised
1 (1st) bde (1 tk bn, 2 mech inf bn, 1 inf bn, 1 SP arty bn, 1 MRL bn, 1 AD bn, 1 engr bn, 1 log bn)
3 (2nd, 3rd & 4th) bde (1 tk bn, 2 mech inf bn, 2 inf bn, 1 SP arty bn, 1 MRL bn, 1 AD bn, 1 engr bn, 1 log bn)
Air Manoeuvre
1 para bde

COMBAT SUPPORT
1 (mixed) arty bde (4 arty bn, 1 MRL bn, 1 spt bn)
2 ptn bridging bn
1 NBC bn
1 sigs bn
2 MP bn

Reserve Organisations
FORCES BY ROLE
MANOEUVRE
Light
8 (territorial) inf bde

EQUIPMENT BY TYPE
ARMOURED FIGHTING VEHICLES
  MBT 229: 195 M-84; 4+ M-84AS1 (in test); 30 T-72MS
  RECCE 76: 46 BRDM-2; 30 BRDM-2M
  IFV 349+: 26+ BTR-80A; 320 M-80; 3 M-80AB1
  APC 160
    APC(T) 44: 12 BTR-50 (CP); 32 MT-LB (CP)
    APC (W) 106: 20 BOV-KIV (CP); 9 BOV-OT M-21; 39 BOV-VP M-86; 38+ *Lazar*-3 APC
    PPV 10 M-20 MRAP
  AUV 40+ BOV M-16 *Milos*
ENGINEERING & MAINTENANCE VEHICLES
  AEV IWT
  ARV M-84A1; T-54/T-55
  VLB MT-55; TMM
ANTI-TANK/ANTI-INFRASTRUCTURE
  MSL
    SP 48 BOV-1 (M-83) with 9K11 *Malyutka* (RS-AT-3 *Sagger*)
    MANPATS 9K11 *Malyutka* (RS-AT-3 *Sagger*); 9K111 *Fagot* (RS-AT-4 *Spigot*); Kornet-EM
  RCL 90mm M-79
ARTILLERY 461
  SP 85: **122mm** 67 2S1 *Gvozdika*; **155mm** 18 B-52 NORA
  TOWED 132: **122mm** 78 D-30; **130mm** 18 M-46; **152mm** 36 M-84 NORA-A
  MRL 81: **128mm** 78: 18 M-63 *Plamen*; 60 M-77 *Organj*; **262mm** 3 M-87 *Orkan*
  MOR 163: **82mm** 106 M-69; **120mm** 57 M-74/M-75
AIR DEFENCE
  SAM 94+
    Short-range 77 2K12 *Kub* (RS-SA-6 *Gainful*);
    Point-defence 17+: 12 9K31M *Strela*-1M (RS-SA-9 *Gaskin*); 5 9K35M *Strela*-10M; 9K32M *Strela*-2M (RS-SA-7B *Grail*)‡; *Šilo* (RS-SA-16 *Gimlet*); Mistral 3
  GUNS 62+
    SP 40mm 26+ *Pasars*-16
    TOWED 40mm 36 Bofors L/70
UNINHABITED AERIAL VEHICLES
  CISR • Medium 6 CH-92A
AIR-LAUNCHED MISSILES
  ASM FT-8C

River Flotilla
The Serbian–Montenegrin navy was transferred to Montenegro upon independence in 2006, but the Danube flotilla remained in Serbian control. The flotilla is subordinate to the Land Forces

EQUIPMENT BY TYPE
PATROL AND COASTAL COMBATANTS 4
  PBR 4: 3 Type-20; 1 *Jadar*
MINE WARFARE • MINE COUNTERMEASURES 4
  MSI 4 *Nestin* with 1 quad lnchr with 9K32 *Strela*-2M (RS-SA-N-5 *Grail*) SAM
AMPHIBIOUS • LANDING CRAFT 4
  LCVP 4 Type-22 (1 more non-operational)
LOGISTICS AND SUPPORT 3
  AG 1 *Šabac* (degaussing vessel also used for patrol and troop transport) (capacity 80 troops)
  AGF 1 *Kozara*
  AOL 1 RPN-43

Air Force and Air Defence 5,100
FORCES BY ROLE
FIGHTER
1 sqn with MiG-29 *Fulcrum*; MiG-29UB *Fulcrum* B; MiG-29SE *Fulcrum* C
FIGHTER/GROUND ATTACK
1 sqn with J-22/NJ-22 *Orao* 1
TRANSPORT
1 sqn with An-2; An-26; Yak-40 (Jak-40); 1 PA-34 *Seneca* V
TRAINING
1 sqn with G-4 *Super Galeb** (trg/lt atk); *Lasta* 95; SA341/342 *Gazelle*; Utva-75 (basic trg)
ATTACK HELICOPTER
1 sqn with Mi-24 *Hind*; Mi-35M *Hind*; SA341H/342L *Gazelle* (HN-42/45)
TRANSPORT HELICOPTER
2 sqn with H145M; Mi-8 *Hip*; Mi-17 *Hip* H; Mi-17V-5 *Hip*
AIR DEFENCE
1 bde (5 bn with S-125M *Neva*-M (RS-SA-3 *Goa*); 2K12 *Kub* (RS-SA-6 *Gainful*); 9K32 *Strela*-2 (RS-SA-7 *Grail*); 9K310 *Igla*-1 (RS-SA-16 *Gimlet*))
2 radar bn (for early warning and reporting)
COMBAT SUPPORT
1 sigs bn
COMBAT SERVICE SUPPORT
1 maint bn

EQUIPMENT BY TYPE
AIRCRAFT 51 combat capable
FTR 14: 3 MiG-29 *Fulcrum*; 3 MiG-29UB *Fulcrum* B; 8 MiG-29SE *Fulcrum* C
FGA ε18 J-22/NJ-22 *Orao* 1
ISR (10 IJ-22R *Orao* 1* in store)
TPT • Light 9: 1 An-2 *Colt*; 4 An-26 *Curl*; 1 C295W; 2 Yak-40 (Jak-40); 1 PA-34 *Seneca* V
TRG 44: 19 G-4 *Super Galeb**; 11 Utva-75; 14 *Lasta* 95
HELICOPTERS
ATK 12: 2 Mi-24 *Hind*†; 10 Mi-35M *Hind*
MRH 52: 5 H145M; 1 Mi-17 *Hip* H; 5 Mi-17V-5 *Hip*; 2 SA341H *Gazelle* (HI-42); 26 SA341H *Gazelle* (HN-42)/SA342L *Gazelle* (HN-45); 13 SA341H *Gazelle* (HO-42)/SA342L1 *Gazelle* (HO-45)
TPT • Medium 8 Mi-8T *Hip* (HT-40)
AIR DEFENCE
SAM 23+
Long-range 4 FK-3 (HQ-22)
Short-range 19: 4 HQ-17AE (CH-SA-15B); 6 S-125M *Neva-M* (RS-SA-3 *Goa*); 9 2K12 *Kub* (RS-SA-6 *Gainful*)
Point-defence 9K32 *Strela-2* (RS-SA-7 *Grail*)‡; 9K310 *Igla-1* (RS-SA-16 *Gimlet*)
SPAAGM 30mm 6 96K6 *Pantsir-S1* (RS-SA-22 *Greyhound*)
GUNS • TOWED 40mm 24 Bofors L/70
AIR-LAUNCHED MISSILES
AAM • IR R-60 (RS-AA-8 *Aphid*); R-73 (RS-AA-11A *Archer*); **SARH** R-27ER (RS-AA-10C *Alamo*); **ARH** R-77 (RS-AA-12 *Adder*)
ASM A-77 *Thunder*; AGM-65 *Maverick*; Kh-29T (RS-AS-14B *Kedge*)

Guards 1,600
FORCES BY ROLE
MANOEUVRE
Other
1 (ceremonial) gd bde (1 gd bn, 1 MP bn, 1 spt bn)

Gendarmerie & Paramilitary 3,700

Gendarmerie 3,700
EQUIPMENT BY TYPE
ARMOURED FIGHTING VEHICLES
APC • APC (W) 24: 12 *Lazar-3*; 12 BOV-VP M-86
AUV BOV M16 *Milos*

DEPLOYMENT
CENTRAL AFRICAN REPUBLIC: EU • EUTM RCA 7; UN • MINUSCA 72; 1 med coy
CYPRUS: UN • UNFICYP 10
LEBANON: UN • UNIFIL 182; 1 mech inf coy
MIDDLE EAST: UN • UNTSO 1
SOMALIA: EU • EUTM Somalia 6

Slovakia SVK

Euro EUR		2023	2024	2025
GDP	EUR	123bn	131bn	139bn
	USD	133bn	143bn	152bn
Real GDP growth	%	1.6	2.2	1.9
Def exp [a]	EUR	2.26bn	2.63bn	
	USD	2.44bn	2.84bn	
Def bdgt	EUR	2.46bn	2.61bn	2.80bn
	USD	2.66bn	2.85bn	3.07bn

[a] NATO figure

Real-terms defence budget trend (USDbn, constant 2015)

Population	5,563,649					
Age	0–14	15–19	20–24	25–29	30–64	65 plus
Male	8.0%	2.5%	2.4%	2.7%	25.4%	7.3%
Female	7.3%	2.5%	2.4%	2.8%	25.9%	10.8%

Capabilities
Slovakia is looking to modernise its armed forces and replace obsolete equipment while contributing to international crisis management missions. Slovakia cooperates closely with the Visegrád Group. Bratislava has signed an agreement to enable air policing and closer integration of air defence capabilities. The country signed a Defence Cooperation Agreement with the US in 2022 and funds were allocated to Slovakia under the Foreign Military Financing programme to help the country replace part of the military equipment Slovakia sent to Ukraine following Russia's full-scale invasion. In 2022, Germany began delivering *Leopard 2A4* MBTs to Slovakia; Bratislava sent IFVs to Ukraine. The country is modernising its air force and ground forces, with procurements including IFVs and fighter ground-attack aircraft. Slovakia hosts a multinational battlegroup as part of NATO's Forward Land Forces, as well as deploying a company to the battlegroup in Latvia. Part of Slovakia's defence-industrial base is organised within the state-controlled holding company DMD Group, including KONSTRUKTA Defence, which produces land systems. Other companies focus on maintenance, repair and overhaul services.

ACTIVE 12,800 (Army 5,350 Air 4,550 Special Forces 800 Central Staff 2,100)

ORGANISATIONS BY SERVICE

Special Forces 800
FORCES BY ROLE
SPECIAL FORCES
1 (5th) spec ops bn
MANOEUVRE
Air Manoeuvre
1 AB bn
COMBAT SUPPORT
1 psyops unit

Army 5,350
FORCES BY ROLE
MANOEUVRE
Reconnaissance
1 recce bn
Armoured
1 (2nd) armd bde (1 tk bn, 2 armd inf bn, 1 log bn)
Mechanised
1 (1st) mech bde (3 armd inf bn, 1 engr bn, 1 log bn)
COMBAT SUPPORT
1 arty regt (1 mixed SP arty bn, 1 MRL bn)
1 MP bn
1 NBC bn
COMBAT SERVICE SUPPORT
1 spt bde (1 maint bn, 1 spt bn)
EQUIPMENT BY TYPE
ARMOURED FIGHTING VEHICLES
MBT 45: 15 *Leopard* 2A4; 30 T-72M
RECCE 33 BPsVI
IFV 181: 73 BMP-1; 90 BMP-2; 15 BVP-M; 3 Patria AMV (*Vydra*) (including variants)
APC 88+
  APC (T) 66 OT-90
  APC (W) 15: 2 OT-64; 13 *Tatrapan* (6×6)
  PPV 7+ RG-32M
  AUV IVECO LMV
ENGINEERING & MAINTENANCE VEHICLES
ARV MT-55; VT-55A; VT-72B; WPT-TOPAS
VLB AM-50; MT-55A
MW *Bozena*; UOS-155 *Belarty*
ANTI-TANK/ANTI-INFRASTRUCTURE
SP 9S428 with *Malyutka* (RS-AT-3 *Sagger*) on BMP-1; 9P135 *Fagot* (RS-AT-4 *Spigot*) on BMP-2; 9P148 *Konkurs* (RS-AT-5 *Spandrel*) on BRDM-2
MANPATS 9K11 *Malyutka* (RS-AT-3 *Sagger*); 9K111-1 *Konkurs* (RS-AT-5 *Spandrel*)
RCL 84mm *Carl Gustaf*
ARTILLERY 57
SP 29: **152mm** 2 M-77 *Dana*; **155mm** 27: 16 M-2000 *Zuzana*; 11 *Zuzana*-2
MRL 28: **122mm** 4 RM-70; **122/227mm** 24 RM-70/85 MODULAR
AIR DEFENCE
SAM • Point-defence 9K310 *Igla*-1 (RS-SA-16 *Gimlet*)

Air Force 4,550
FORCES BY ROLE
TRANSPORT
1 flt with C-27J *Spartan*
1 flt with L-410FG/T *Turbolet*
TRANSPORT HELICOPTER
1 sqn with Mi-17 *Hip* H
1 sqn with UH-60M *Black Hawk*
TRAINING
1 sqn with L-39CM/ZAM *Albatros**
AIR DEFENCE
1 bde with 2K12 *Kub* (RS-SA-6 *Gainful*)
EQUIPMENT BY TYPE
AIRCRAFT 10 combat capable
FGA 2 F-16C Block 70 *Fighting Falcon*
TPT 5: **Medium** 2 C-27J *Spartan*; **Light** 3: 1 L-410FG *Turbolet*; 2 L-410T *Turbolet*; (4 L-410UVP *Turbolet* in store)
TRG 8: 6 L-39CM *Albatros**; 2 L-39ZAM *Albatros** (1 more in store)
HELICOPTERS
MRH 8 Mi-17 *Hip* H (incl 4 SAR)
TPT • **Medium** 9 UH-60M *Black Hawk*
AIR DEFENCE
SAM • Short-range 2K12 *Kub* (RS-SA-6 *Gainful*)
GUNS • **35mm** 12 C-RAM MANTIS

DEPLOYMENT
BOSNIA-HERZEGOVINA: EU • EUFOR (*Operation Althea*) 51
CYPRUS: UN • UNFICYP 240; 2 inf coy; 1 engr pl
IRAQ: *Operation Inherent Resolve* 1; **NATO** • NATO Mission Iraq 4
LATVIA: NATO • Forward Land Forces 115; 1 arty bty with M-2000 *Zuzana*
MIDDLE EAST: UN • UNTSO 3

FOREIGN FORCES
All under NATO Forward Land Forces
Czech Republic 400; 1 mech inf coy
Portugal 25; 1 tk pl
Slovenia 100; 1 mech inf coy
Spain 800; 1 para BG
United States 150; 1 inf coy

Slovenia SVN

Euro EUR		2023	2024	2025
GDP	EUR	64.0bn	67.2bn	70.5bn
	USD	69.2bn	73.2bn	77.4bn
Real GDP growth	%	2.1	1.5	2.6
Def exp [a]	EUR	845m	880m	
	USD	914m	949m	
Def bdgt [b]	EUR	939m	1.06bn	1.28bn
	USD	1.02bn	1.16bn	1.40bn

[a] NATO figure
[b] Includes military pensions

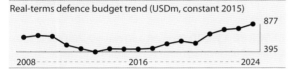

Real-terms defence budget trend (USDm, constant 2015)

Population	2,097,893					
Age	0–14	15–19	20–24	25–29	30–64	65 plus
Male	7.3%	2.5%	2.4%	2.5%	25.2%	10.2%
Female	7.0%	2.4%	2.2%	2.3%	23.1%	13.0%

Capabilities

Since joining NATO and the EU in 2004, territorial defence and the ability to take part in peace-support operations have been central to Slovenia's defence strategy. The government in 2020 published a white paper and in 2022 authorised the Long-Term Development Programme for the Slovenian Armed Forces 2022–35. Subsequently, the government adopted a Medium-Term Development Programme to serve as the guiding document for defence programming and planning. Defence spending is increasing. Short-term plans are focused on developing a medium-weight infantry battalion and an armoured reconnaissance battalion, both to be equipped with new wheeled armoured vehicles. Fixed-wing and rotary-wing transport capabilities are modestly improving with new acquisitions and upgrades. Slovenia acts as the framework nation for the NATO Mountain Warfare Centre of Excellence. Italy and Hungary provide air policing capability under NATO arrangements. The country contributes to EU, NATO and UN operations, including NATO's Forward Land Forces battlegroups in both Latvia and Slovakia. Slovenia's defence industry relies heavily on exports for its revenue and focuses on personal equipment, small arms and ammunition, and CBRN protection and detection.

ACTIVE 6,200 (Army 6,200)

RESERVE 950 (Army 950)

ORGANISATIONS BY SERVICE

Army 6,200
FORCES BY ROLE
Regt are bn sized
SPECIAL FORCES
  1 SF unit (1 spec ops coy, 1 CSS coy)
MANOEUVRE
  Mechanised
  1 (1st) mech inf bde (1 mech inf regt, 1 mtn inf regt, 1 cbt spt bn (1 ISR coy, 1 arty bty, 1 engr coy, 1 MP coy, 1 CBRN coy, 1 sigs coy, 1 SAM bty))
  1 (72nd) mech inf bde (2 mech inf regt, 1 cbt spt bn (1 ISR coy, 1 arty bty, 1 engr coy, 1 MP coy, 1 CBRN coy, 1 sigs coy, 1 SAM bty))
COMBAT SUPPORT
  1 EW coy
COMBAT SERVICE SUPPORT
  1 log bde (1 log regt, 1 maint regt (1 tk coy), 1 med regt)

Reserves
FORCES BY ROLE
MANOEUVRE
  Mountain
  2 inf regt (territorial – 1 allocated to each inf bde)
EQUIPMENT BY TYPE
ARMOURED FIGHTING VEHICLES
  MBT 14 M-84 (trg role) (29 more in store)
  APC 102+:
    APC (W) 95: 65 *Pandur* 6×6 (*Valuk*); 30 *Patria* 8×8 (*Svarun*)
    PPV 7 *Cougar* 6×6 JERRV
  AUV 75 JLTV
ENGINEERING & MAINTENANCE VEHICLES
  ARV VT-55A
  VLB MT-55A
NBC VEHICLES 10 *Cobra* CBRN
ANTI-TANK/ANTI-INFRASTRUCTURE
  MSL • MANPATS *Spike* MR/LR
ARTILLERY 68
  TOWED • **155mm** 18 TN-90
  MOR 50+: **82mm** M-69; **120mm** 50 MN-9/M-74
AIR DEFENCE • **SAM** • **Point-defence** 9K338 *Igla-S* (RS-SA-24 *Grinch*)

Army Maritime Element 130
FORCES BY ROLE
SPECIAL FORCES
  1 SF unit
EQUIPMENT BY TYPE
PATROL AND COASTAL COMBATANTS 2
  PCC 1 *Triglav* III (RUS *Svetlyak*) with 1 AK630 CIWS
  PBF 1 *Super Dvora* MkII
UNINHABITED MARITIME SYSTEMS
  UUV • MW *Comet*-MCM

Air Element 600
FORCES BY ROLE
TRANSPORT
  1 sqn with C-27J *Spartan*; *Falcon* 2000EX; L-410 *Turbolet*; PC-6B *Turbo Porter*
TRAINING
  1 unit with Bell 206 *Jet Ranger* (AB-206); PC-9M*; Z-143L; Z-242L

TRANSPORT HELICOPTER
1 sqn with AS532AL *Cougar*; Bell 412 *Twin Huey*
COMBAT SERVICE SUPPORT
1 maint sqn
EQUIPMENT BY TYPE
AIRCRAFT 9 combat capable
TPT 5: **Medium** 1 C-27J Spartan; **Light** 3: 1 L-410 *Turbolet*; 2 PC-6B *Turbo Porter* **PAX** 1 *Falcon* 2000EX
TRG 19: 9 PC-9M*; 2 Z-143L; 8 Z-242L
HELICOPTERS
MRH 8: 5 Bell 412EP *Twin Huey*; 2 Bell 412HP *Twin Huey*; 1 Bell 412SP *Twin Huey*
TPT 8: **Medium** 4 AS532AL *Cougar*; **Light** 4 Bell 206 *Jet Ranger* (AB-206)

DEPLOYMENT

BOSNIA-HERZEGOVINA: EU • EUFOR (*Operation Althea*) 20
IRAQ: *Operation Inherent Resolve* 3
KOSOVO: NATO • KFOR 105; 1 mot inf coy; 1 MP unit; 1 hel unit; **UN** • UNMIK 1
LATVIA: NATO • Forward Land Forces 35
MIDDLE EAST: UN • UNTSO 2
SLOVAKIA: NATO • Forward Land Forces 100; 1 mech inf coy

Spain ESP

Euro EUR		2023	2024	2025
GDP	EUR	1.50trn	1.59trn	1.67trn
	USD	1.62trn	1.73trn	1.83trn
Real GDP growth	%	2.7	2.9	2.1
Def exp [a]	EUR	17.5bn	19.7bn	
	USD	18.9bn	21.3bn	
Def bdgt [b]	EUR	17.8bn	17.8bn	
	USD	19.3bn	19.4bn	

[a] NATO figure
[b] Includes military pensions. 2024 budget not passed - 2023 budget carried over.

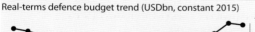
Real-terms defence budget trend (USDbn, constant 2015)

Population	47,280,433				
Age	0–14	15–19	20–24	25–29	30–64	65 plus
Male	6.7%	2.8%	2.6%	2.4%	25.3%	9.0%
Female	6.4%	2.7%	2.5%	2.4%	25.4%	11.9%

Capabilities

The 2021 National Security Strategy emphasised strengthening capacity against hybrid threats. Following Russia's full-scale invasion of Ukraine in February 2022, the government unveiled plans to increase defence spending, though spending levels remain low. The National Defence Directive, issued in June 2020, updated defence policy guidelines and indicated a desire to strengthen the national defence industry. Spain continues to support NATO, EU and UN operations abroad, and hosts one of NATO's two Combined Air Operations Centres. The armed forces are well trained and routinely participate in domestic and multinational exercises. The country's equipment and logistics-support capability appears to be sufficient to meet its national commitments and contribution to NATO operations and exercises. Madrid has significant equipment modernisation plans. Spain participates in the Future Combat Air System project with France and Germany. A space command was initiated in 2023. Spain has broad defence-industrial capabilities, with major firms including state-owned shipbuilder Navantia, Airbus, Indra and General Dynamics European Land Systems – Santa Barbara Sistemas.

ACTIVE 122,200 (Army 70,200 Navy 20,400 Air 20,200 Joint 11,400) **Gendarmerie & Paramilitary 80,500**

RESERVE 13,800 (Army 8,150 Navy 2,700 Air 2,550 Other 400) **Gendarmerie & Paramilitary 6,950**

ORGANISATIONS BY SERVICE

Space
EQUIPMENT BY TYPE
SATELLITES 3
COMMUNICATIONS 2: 1 *Spainsat*; 1 *Xtar-Eur*
ISR 1 *Paz*

Army 70,200

The Land Forces High Readiness HQ Spain provides one NATO Rapid Deployment Corps HQ (NRDC-ESP)
FORCES BY ROLE
COMMAND
1 corps HQ (CGTAD/NRDC-ESP) (1 int regt, 1 MP bn)
2 div HQ
SPECIAL FORCES
1 comd (3 spec ops bn, 1 int coy, 1 sigs coy, 1 log bn)
MANOEUVRE
Reconnaissance
1 armd cav regt (2 armd recce bn)
Mechanised
2 (10th & 11th) mech bde (1 armd regt (1 armd recce bn, 1 tk bn), 1 mech inf regt (1 armd inf bn, 1 mech inf bn), 1 lt inf bn, 1 SP arty bn, 1 AT coy, 1 AD coy, 1 engr bn, 1 int coy, 1 NBC coy, 1 sigs coy, 1 log bn)
1 (12th) mech bde (1 armd regt (1 armd recce bn, 1 tk bn), 1 mech inf regt (1 armd inf bn, 1 mech inf bn), 1 SP arty bn, 1 AT coy, 1 AD coy, 1 engr bn, 1 int coy, 1 NBC coy, 1 sigs coy, 1 log bn)
1 (1st) mech bde (1 armd regt (1 armd recce bn, 1 tk bn), 1 armd inf regt (1 armd inf bn), 1 mot inf bn, 1 SP arty bn, 1 AT coy, 1 AD coy, 1 engr bn, 1 int coy, 1 NBC coy, 1 sigs coy, 1 log bn)
2 (2nd/La Legion & 7th) lt mech bde (1 armd recce bn, 1 mech inf regt (2 mech inf bn), 1 lt inf bn, 1 fd arty bn, 1 AT coy, 1 AD coy, 1 engr bn, 1 int coy, 1 NBC coy, 1 sigs coy, 1 log bn)

Mountain
1 mtn comd (1 mtn inf regt (1 mtn inf bn, 1 mtn inf coy); 1 mtn inf bn)

Air Manoeuvre
1 (6th) bde (1 recce bn, 2 para bn, 1 lt inf bn, 1 fd arty bn, 1 AT coy, 1 AD coy, 1 engr bn, 1 int coy, 1 NBC coy, 1 sigs coy, 1 log bn)

Other
1 (Canary Islands) comd (1 lt inf bde (2 mech inf regt (1 mech inf bn), 1 lt inf regt (1 lt inf bn), 1 fd arty regt,1 AT coy, 1 engr bn, 1 int coy, 1 NBC coy, 1 sigs coy, 1 log bn); 1 EW regt; 1 spt hel bn; 1 AD regt)
1 (Balearic Islands) comd (1 inf regt (1 lt inf bn))
2 (Ceuta and Melilla) comd (1 recce regt, 1 mech inf bn, 1 inf bn, 1 arty regt (1 fd arty bn, 1 ADA bn), 1 engr bn, 1 sigs coy, 1 log bn)

COMBAT SUPPORT
1 arty comd (2 arty regt; 1 coastal arty regt)
1 engr comd (2 engr regt, 1 bridging regt)
1 EW/sigs bde (2 EW regt, 3 sigs regt)
1 NBC regt
1 info ops regt (1 CIMIC bn; 1 Psyops bn)
1 int regt

COMBAT SERVICE SUPPORT
1 log bde (5 log regt; 1 tpt regt; 1 med regt (1 log bn, 2 med bn, 1 fd hospital bn))

HELICOPTER
1 hel comd (1 atk hel bn, 2 spt hel bn, 1 tpt hel bn, 1 sigs bn, 1 log unit (1 spt coy, 1 supply coy))

AIR DEFENCE
1 AD comd (3 SAM regt, 1 sigs unit)

EQUIPMENT BY TYPE
ARMOURED FIGHTING VEHICLES
MBT 274: 55 *Leopard* 2A4 (25 more in store), 219 *Leopard* 2E
ASLT 84 B1 *Centauro*
RECCE 187 VEC-M1
IFV 225: 204 *Pizarro*; 21 *Pizarro* (CP)
APC 915
 APC (T) 484: 61 Bv-206S; 423 M113 (incl variants)
 APC (W) 321: 314 BMR-600/BMR-600M1; 7 VCR 8x8 *Dragon* (in test)
 PPV 110 RG-31
 AUV 258 IVECO LMV

ENGINEERING & MAINTENANCE VEHICLES
AEV 39: 26 CZ-10/25E; 13 *Pizarro* CEV (*Castor*)
ARV 50: 16 *Leopard* REC; 4 BMR REC; 4 *Centauro* REC; 14 *Maxxpro* MRV; 12 M113
VLB 15 M60 AVLB
MW 6 *Husky* 2G

ANTI-TANK/ANTI-INFRASTRUCTURE
MSL • MANPATS *Spike*-LR; TOW

ARTILLERY 1,553
SP 155mm 96 M109A5
TOWED 268: **105mm** 204: 56 L118 Light Gun; 148 Model 56 pack howitzer; **155mm** 64 SBT 155/52 SIAC
MOR 1,189: **81mm** 777; **SP 81mm** 10 VAMTAC with *Cardom* 81mm; **120mm** 402

COASTAL DEFENCE • ARTY 155mm 19 SBT 155/52 APU SBT V07

HELICOPTERS
ATK 18 *Tiger* HAD-E
TPT 86: **Heavy** 17: 13 CH-47D *Chinook* (HT-17D); 4 CH-47F *Chinook*; **Medium** 49: 16 AS332B *Super Puma* (HU-21); 12 AS532UL *Cougar*; 6 AS532AL *Cougar*; 15 NH90 TTH; **Light** 20: 4 Bell 212 (HU.18); 16 H135 (HE.26/HU.26)

UNINHABITED AERIAL VEHICLES
ISR 12: **Medium** 6: 2 *Searcher* MkII-J (PASI); 4 *Searcher* MkIII (PASI); **Light** ε6 Orbiter-3

AIR DEFENCE
SAM 54
 Long-range 18 M901 *Patriot* PAC-2
 Medium-range 28 MIM-23B I-*Hawk* Phase III
 Short-range 8 NASAMS;
 Point-defence *Mistral*
GUNS • TOWED 35mm 67: 19 GDF-005; 48 GDF-007

AIR-LAUNCHED MISSILES • ASM *Spike*-ER

Navy 20,400 (incl Naval Aviation and Marines)
EQUIPMENT BY TYPE
SUBMARINES • SSK 2
1 *Isaac Peral* (S-80 plus) with 6 single 533mm TT with UGM-84L *Harpoon* Block II AShM/DM2A4 HWT
1 *Galerna* with 4 single 533mm TT with F17 mod 2 HWT

PRINCIPAL SURFACE COMBATANTS 11
DESTROYERS • DDGHM 5 *Alvaro de Bazan* with *Aegis* Baseline 5 C2, 2 quad lnchr with RGM-84F *Harpoon* Block 1D AShM, 6 8-cell Mk 41 VLS with SM-2 Block IIIA/RIM-162B ESSM SAM, 2 twin 324mm SVTT Mk 32 mod 9 ASTT with Mk 46 mod 5 LWT, 1 127mm gun (capacity 1 SH-60B *Seahawk* ASW hel)
FRIGATES • FFGH 6 *Santa Maria* with 1 Mk 13 GMLS with RGM-84F *Harpoon* Block 1D AShM, 2 triple 324mm SVTT Mk 32 ASTT with Mk 46 mod 5 LWT, 1 *Sentinel* 25 RFG CIWS, 1 76mm gun (capacity 2 SH-60B *Seahawk* ASW hel)

PATROL AND COASTAL COMBATANTS 22
PSOH 6 *Meteoro* (*Buques de Accion Maritima*) with 1 76mm gun
PSO 3 *Alboran* with 1 hel landing platform
PCO 4 *Serviola* with 1 76mm gun
PCC 3 *Anaga* with 1 76mm gun
PB 4: 1 *Isla Pinto* (Rodman 66); 1 *Isla de Leon* (Rodman 101); 2 *Toralla*
PBR 2: 1 *Cabo Fradera*; 1 P-101

MINE WARFARE • MINE COUNTERMEASURES 6
MHO 6 *Segura*

AMPHIBIOUS
PRINCIPAL AMPHIBIOUS SHIPS 3
 LHD 1 *Juan Carlos* I (capacity 18 hel or 10 AV-8B FGA ac; 4 LCM-1E; 42 APC; 46 MBT; 900 troops)

LPD 2 *Galicia* (capacity 6 Bell 212 hel; 4 LCM or 2 LCM & 8 AAV; 130 APC or 33 MBT; 540 troops)
LANDING CRAFT • LCM 12 LCM 1E
LOGISTICS AND SUPPORT 33
  AGI 1 *Alerta*
  AGOR 2: 1 *Hesperides* with 1 hel landing platform; 1 *Las Palmas*
  AGS 2 *Malaspina*
  AKR 2: 1 *El Camino Espanol*; 1 *Ysabel*
  AORH 2: 1 *Patino* (capacity 3 Bell 212 hel); 1 *Cantabria* (capacity 3 Bell 212 hel)
  AP 1 *Contramaestre Casado* with 1 hel landing platform
  ARS 1 *Carnota*
  ASR 1 *Neptuno*
  ATF 2: 1 *Mar Caribe*; 1 *La Grana*
  AX 1 *Intermares*
  AXL 8: 4 *Maestre de Marineria*; 4 *Guardiamarina*
  AXS 10
UNINHABITED MARITIME SYSTEMS
  USV • DATA *Mariner; Otter*
  UUV
    DATA *Sparus* II
    MW *Pluto* Plus

Naval Aviation 850
FORCES BY ROLE
FIGHTER/GROUND ATTACK
  1 sqn with AV-8B *Harrier* II Plus
ANTI-SUBMARINE WARFARE
  2 sqn with SH-60B/F *Seahawk*
TRANSPORT
  1 (liaison) sqn with Cessna 550 *Citation* II; Cessna 650 *Citation* VII
TRAINING
  1 flt with TAV-8B *Harrier*
  1 hel flt with H135
TRANSPORT HELICOPTER
  1 flt with SH-60F *Seahawk*
  1 sqn with NH90 MSPT (forming)
ISR UAV
  1 sqn with Scan Eagle
EQUIPMENT BY TYPE
AIRCRAFT 11 combat capable
  FGA 11: 10 AV-8B *Harrier* II Plus; 1 TAV-8B *Harrier* (on lease from USMC)
  TPT • Light 3: 2 Cessna 550 *Citation* II; 1 Cessna 650 *Citation* VII
HELICOPTERS
  ASW 18: 12 SH-60B *Seahawk*; 6 SH-60F *Seahawk*
  TPT • Light 4 H135
UNINHABITED AERIAL VEHICLES
  ISR • Light 12+ Scan Eagle
AIR-LAUNCHED MISSILES
  AAM • IR AIM-9L *Sidewinder*; **ARH** AIM-120 AMRAAM
  ASM AGM-65G *Maverick*; AGM-114K/R *Hellfire* II
  AShM AGM-119 *Penguin*

Marines 5,350
FORCES BY ROLE
SPECIAL FORCES
  1 spec ops bn
MANOEUVRE
  Amphibious
    1 mne bde (1 recce unit, 1 mech inf bn, 2 inf bn, 1 arty bn, 1 log bn)
  Other
    1 sy bde (5 mne garrison gp)
EQUIPMENT BY TYPE
ARMOURED FIGHTING VEHICLES
  APC • APC (W) 34: 32 *Piranha* IIIC; 1 *Piranha* IIIC (amb); 1 *Piranha* IIIC EW (EW)
  AAV 18: 16 AAV-7A1/AAVP-7A1; 2 AAVC-7A1 (CP)
ENGINEERING & MAINTENANCE VEHICLES
  AEV 4 *Piranha* IIIC
  ARV 3: 1 AAVR-7A1; 1 M88; 1 *Piranha* IIIC
ARTILLERY 30
  SP 155mm 6 M109A2
  TOWED 105mm 24 Model 56 pack howitzer
ANTI-TANK/ANTI-INFRASTRUCTURE
  MSL • MANPATS *Spike*-LR; TOW-2
AIR DEFENCE • SAM • Point-defence Mistral

Air Force 20,200
The Spanish Air Force is organised in 3 commands – General Air Command, Combat Air Command and Canary Islands Air Command
FORCES BY ROLE
FIGHTER
  2 sqn with Eurofighter *Typhoon*
FIGHTER/GROUND ATTACK
  5 sqn with F/A-18A/B MLU *Hornet* (EF-18A/B MLU)
ISR
  1 sqn with Beech C90 *King Air*
  1 sqn with Cessna 550 *Citation* V
SEARCH & RESCUE
  1 sqn with AS332B/B1 *Super Puma*; CN235 VIGMA
  1 sqn with AS332B *Super Puma*; CN235 VIGMA; H215 (AS332C1) *Super Puma*
  1 sqn with C-212 *Aviocar*; CN235 VIGMA; S-76C
TANKER/TRANSPORT
  1 sqn with A400M
TRANSPORT
  1 VIP sqn with A310; *Falcon* 900
  1 sqn with A400M
  1 sqn with C-212 *Aviocar*
  2 sqn with C295
  1 sqn with CN235
TRAINING
  1 OCU sqn with Eurofighter *Typhoon*

1 OCU sqn with F/A-18A/B (EF-18A/B MLU) *Hornet*
1 sqn with Beech F33C *Bonanza*
1 sqn with C-212 *Aviocar*
1 sqn with PC-21
2 (LIFT) sqn with F-5B *Freedom Fighter*
1 hel sqn with H120 *Colibri*
1 hel sqn with H135

TRANSPORT HELICOPTER
1 sqn with AS332M1 *Super Puma*; AS532UL *Cougar* (VIP)

ISR UAV
1 sqn with MQ-9A *Reaper* (forming)

EQUIPMENT BY TYPE
AIRCRAFT 171 combat capable
 FTR 88: 69 Eurofighter *Typhoon*; 19 F-5B *Freedom Fighter*
 FGA 83: 20 F/A-18A *Hornet* (EF-18A); 51 EF-18A MLU; 12 EF-18B MLU
 MP 8 CN235 VIGMA
 TPT 73: **Heavy** 13 A400M; **Light** 51: 3 Beech C90 *King Air*; 15 Beech F33C *Bonanza*; 10 C-212 *Aviocar* (incl 9 trg); 12 C295; 8 CN235; 3 Cessna 560 *Citation* V (ISR); **PAX** 9: 2 A310; 2 A330 (to be converted to MRTT); 5 *Falcon* 900 (VIP)
 TRG 24 PC-21
HELICOPTERS
 TPT 44: **Medium** 21: 5 AS332B/B1 *Super Puma*; 4 AS332M1 *Super Puma*; 4 H215 (AS332C1) *Super Puma*; 2 AS532UL *Cougar* (VIP); 6 NH90 TTH; **Light** 23: 14 H120 *Colibri*; 1 H135; 8 S-76C
UNINHABITED AERIAL VEHICLES
 CISR • **Heavy** 4 MQ-9A *Reaper* (unarmed)
AIR DEFENCE • **SAM** • **Point-defence** *Mistral*
AIR-LAUNCHED MISSILES
 AAM • **IR** AIM-9L/JULI *Sidewinder*; **IIR** IRIS-T; **SARH** AIM-7P *Sparrow*; **ARH** AIM-120B/C AMRAAM; *Meteor*
 ARM AGM-88B HARM
 ASM AGM-65G *Maverick*
 AShM AGM-84D *Harpoon*
 LACM Taurus KEPD 350
BOMBS
 Laser-guided: BPG-2000; GBU-10/-12/-16 *Paveway* II; GBU-24 *Paveway* III
 Laser & INS/GPS-guided EGBU-16 *Paveway* II

Emergencies Military Unit (UME) 3,500
FORCES BY ROLE
COMMAND
 1 div HQ
MANOEUVRE
 Other
  5 Emergency Intervention bn
  1 Emergency Support and Intervention regt
COMBAT SUPPORT
 1 sigs bn
HELICOPTER
 1 hel bn (opcon Army)

Gendarmerie & Paramilitary 80,500

Guardia Civil 80 500
17 regions, 54 Rural Comds
FORCES BY ROLE
SPECIAL FORCES
 8 (rural) gp
MANOEUVRE
 Other
  15 (traffic) sy gp
  1 (Special) sy bn
EQUIPMENT BY TYPE
PATROL AND COASTAL COMBATANTS 70
 PSO 1 *Rio Segura* with 1 hel landing platform
 PCO 2: 1 *Rio Mino* 1 *Rio Tajo*
 PBF 34: 3 *Aister HS50*; 12 *Alusafe 2100*; 5 *Gondan 21*; 14 *Rodman 55*
 PB 33: 5 *Rio Arlanza* (SAR); 1 *Rio Segre*; 1 Rodman 58; 13 Rodman 66; 1 Rodman 82; 12 Rodman 101
AIRCRAFT • **TPT** • **Light** 3: 2 CN235-300; 1 Beech 350i *King Air*
HELICOPTERS
 MRH 20: 4 AS65N3 *Dauphin*; 16 Bo-105ATH
 TPT • **Light** 21: 8 BK-117; 13 H135

DEPLOYMENT

BOSNIA-HERZEGOVINA: EU • EUFOR (Operation Althea) 2
CENTRAL AFRICAN REPUBLIC: EU • EUTM RCA 8
DJIBOUTI: EU • Operation Atalanta 60; 1 CN235 VIGMA
ESTONIA: NATO • Forward Land Forces 150; 1 SAM bty with NASAMS
GULF OF ADEN & INDIAN OCEAN: EU • Operation Atalanta 220; 1 FFGH
GULF OF GUINEA: Navy 50; 1 PCO
IRAQ: Operation Inherent Resolve 180; 1 trg unit; 1 hel unit with 3 CH-47F *Chinook* **NATO** • NATO Mission Iraq 178; 1 inf coy
LATVIA: NATO • Forward Land Forces 600; 1 armd inf coy(+); 1 arty bty; 1 cbt engr coy; 1 SAM bty with NASAMS
LEBANON: UN • UNIFIL 677; 1 mech bde HQ; 1 mech inf bn(-); 1 engr coy; 1 sigs coy; 1 log coy
MEDITERRANEAN SEA NATO • SNMG 2: 320; 1 DDGHM; 1 AORH; **NATO** • SNMCMG 2 40; 1 MHO
MOZAMBIQUE: EU • EUMAM Mozambique 2
ROMANIA: NATO • Baltic Air Policing: 150; 8 F/A-18A *Hornet* MLU (EF-18A MLU); Forward Land Forces 200; 1 mne coy
SENEGAL: 65; 2 C295M
SLOVAKIA: NATO • Forward Land Forces 800; 1 para BG
SOMALIA: EU • EUTM Somalia 21
TURKIYE: NATO • Operation Active Fence 150; 1 SAM bty with M901 *Patriot* PAC-2

FOREIGN FORCES

United States US European Command: 3,500; 4 DDGHM; 1 DDGM; 1 air base at Morón; 1 naval base at Rota

Sweden SWE

Swedish Krona SEK		2023	2024	2025
GDP	SEK	6.21trn	6.42trn	6.72trn
	USD	585bn	609bn	639bn
Real GDP growth	%	-0.2	0.9	2.4
Def exp [a]	SEK	104bn	140bn	
	USD	9.85bn	13.4bn	
Def bdgt	SEK	97.6bn	129bn	170bn
	USD	9.20bn	12.3bn	16.1bn

[a] NATO figure

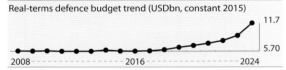

Real-terms defence budget trend (USDbn, constant 2015)

Population	10,589,835					
Age	0–14	15–19	20–24	25–29	30–64	65 plus
Male	8.8%	3.0%	2.9%	3.1%	22.8%	9.7%
Female	8.3%	2.8%	2.6%	2.8%	22.1%	11.0%

Capabilities

Sweden's armed forces remain configured for territorial defence, and there is concern over Russian military activity in the Baltic area. Sweden joined NATO in March 2024 and integration into Alliance military structures is proceeding. In October 2024, Stockholm published a long-term defence bill, with priorities including integration into NATO's integrated air and missile defence, expanding Sweden's air and missile defence capabilities; deployment of a battalion to NATO's Forward Land Forces in Latvia in early 2025; and contributing to NATO's Standing Naval Forces. Defence spending is increasing. Stockholm has also announced measures to enhance societal resilience. Demands for greater interoperability have increased since joining NATO and long-term plans for expanding command and logistics structures have been proposed. The Defence Cooperation Agreement with the US came into force in 2024. In 2023, Sweden more closely integrated its air force with neighbours Denmark, Finland and Norway. Sweden is transforming its two mechanised brigades, while two new additional brigades will be created along with a divisional staff with support elements. These four brigades, including the battlegroup on Gotland, are planned to be operational by 2030. The country is buying additional artillery systems and armoured fighting vehicles and modernising its tank fleet. Readiness challenges in the air force triggered a discussion about extending the service life of the JAS-39C *Gripen* combat aircraft beyond their intended 2026 retirement date. The country's export-oriented defence industry is privately owned and capable of meeting most of the armed forces' equipment needs, including for advanced combat aircraft, conventional submarines and EW equipment.

ACTIVE 14,850 (Army 6,850 Navy 2,350 Air 2,700 Other 2,950) **Voluntary Auxiliary Organisations 21,500**

Conscript liability 4–11 months, depending on branch (selective conscription; 4,000 in total, gender neutral)

RESERVE 21,500 (Home Guard 21,500)

ORGANISATIONS BY SERVICE

Army 6,850

The army has been transformed to provide brigade-sized task forces depending on the operational requirement

FORCES BY ROLE

COMMAND
 1 div HQ
 4 bde HQ

MANOEUVRE
 Reconnaissance
 1 recce bn
 Armoured
 5 armd bn
 1 armd BG
 Mechanised
 1 mech bn
 Light
 1 mot inf bn
 1 lt inf bn
 Air Manoeuvre
 1 AB bn
 Other
 1 sy bn

COMBAT SUPPORT
 2 arty bn
 2 engr bn
 2 MP coy
 1 CBRN coy

COMBAT SERVICE SUPPORT
 1 tpt coy

AIR DEFENCE
 2 AD bn

EQUIPMENT BY TYPE

ARMOURED FIGHTING VEHICLES
 MBT 110 *Leopard* 2A5 (Strv 122)
 IFV 361: 319 CV9040 (Strf 9040; incl CP); 42 Epbv 90 (OP)
 APC 845
  APC (T) 150 BvS-10 MkII
  APC (W) 335+: some *Bastion* APC; 34 XA-180 *Sisu* (Patgb 180); 20 XA-202 *Sisu* (Patgb 202); 148 XA-203 *Sisu* (Patgb 203); 20 XA-300 (Patgb 300); 113 Patria AMV (XA-360/Patgb 360)
 PPV 360 RG-32M
 AUV Sisu GTP

ENGINEERING & MAINTENANCE VEHICLES
 AEV 6 Pionierpanzer-3 *Kodiak* (Ingbv 120)
 ARV 39: 14 Bgbv 120B; 25 Bgbv 90

VLB 6 Brobv 120
MW 33+: *Aardvark* Mk2; 33 Area Clearing System
ANTI-TANK/ANTI-INFRASTRUCTURE
  MSL • MANPATS NLAW; RBS-55
  RCL 84mm *Carl Gustaf*
ARTILLERY 254
  SP 155mm 26 *Archer*
  MOR 228: **81mm** 108 M/86; **120mm** 80 M/41D **SP 120mm** 40 CV90 *Mjolner* (Gkpbv 90)
AIR DEFENCE
  SAM 20+
    Long-range 12 M903 *Patriot* PAC-3 MSE
    Medium-range MIM-23B *Hawk* (RBS-97)
    Short-range 8+: 8 IRIS-T SLS (RBS-98); RBS-23 BAMSE
    Point-defence RBS-70
  GUNS • SP 40mm 30 Lvkv 90

Navy 1,250; 1,100 Amphibious (total 2,350)
EQUIPMENT BY TYPE
SUBMARINE • SSK 4:
  1 *Gotland* (fitted with AIP) with 2 single 400mm TT with Torped 431 LWT/Torped 451 LWT, 4 single 533mm TT with Torped 613 HWT/Torped 62 HWT
  2 *Gotland* mod (fitted with AIP) with 2 single 400mm TT with Torped 431 LWT/Torped 451 LWT, 4 single 533mm TT with Torped 613 HWT/Torped 62 HWT
  1 *Södermanland* (fitted with AIP) with 3 single 400mm TT with Torped 431 LWT/Torped 451 LWT, 6 single 533mm TT with Torped 613 HWT/Torped 62 HWT
PATROL AND COASTAL COMBATANTS 154
  CORVETTES • FSG 5 *Visby* with 2 quad lnchr with RBS15 Mk2 AShM, 4 single 400mm ASTT with Torped 45 LWT, 1 57mm gun, 1 hel landing platform
  PCGT 4:
    2 *Göteborg* with 4 twin lnchr with RBS15 Mk2 AShM, 4 single 400mm ASTT with Torped 431 LWT, 1 57mm gun
    2 *Stockholm* with 4 twin lnchr with RBS15 Mk2 AShM, 4 single 400mm ASTT with Torped 431 LWT, 1 57mm gun
  PBF 145: 100+ Combat Boat 90H (capacity 18 troops); 27 Combat Boat HS (capacity 18 troops); ε18 Combat Boat 90HSM (capacity 18 troops)
  PB 8: 3 *Tapper* (Type 80); 5 *Tapper* mod (Type 88)
MINE WARFARE • MINE COUNTERMEASURES 7
  MCC 5 *Koster* (SWE *Landsort* mod)
  MCD 2 *Spårö* (*Styrsö* mod)
AMPHIBIOUS • LANDING CRAFT 6
  LCVP 3 *Trossbat*
  LCAC 3 *Griffon* 8100TD
LOGISTICS AND SUPPORT 15
  AG 2: 1 *Carlskrona* with 1 hel landing platform (former ML); 1 *Trosso* (spt ship for corvettes and patrol vessels but can also be used as HQ ship)
  AGF 2 *Ledningsbåt* 2000

AGI 1 *Artemis*
AKL 1 *Loke*
ARS 2: 1 *Belos* III; 1 *Furusund* (former ML)
AXL 5 *Altair*
AXS 2: 1 *Falken*; 1 *Gladan*
UNINHABITED MARITIME SYSTEMS • UUV
  MW AUV62-MR; *Double Eagle* Mk II,III; *Seafox*
  UTL AUV62-AT

Amphibious 1,100
FORCES BY ROLE
MANOEUVRE
  Amphibious
  2 amph bn
EQUIPMENT BY TYPE
ARTILLERY • MOR 81mm 12 M/86
COASTAL DEFENCE • AShM 8 RBS-17 *Hellfire*

Coastal Defence
FORCES BY ROLE
COASTAL DEFENCE
  1 AShM bty with RBS-15
EQUIPMENT BY TYPE
COASTAL DEFENCE • AShM RBS-15

Air Force 2,700
FORCES BY ROLE
FIGHTER/GROUND ATTACK/ISR
  6 sqn with JAS 39C/D *Gripen*
TRANSPORT/ISR/AEW&C
  1 sqn with C-130H *Hercules* (Tp-84); KC-130H *Hercules* (Tp-84); Gulfstream IV SRA-4 (S-102B); S-100B/D *Argus*
TRAINING
  1 unit with G 120TP (Sk-40)
AIR DEFENCE
  1 (fighter control and air surv) bn
EQUIPMENT BY TYPE
AIRCRAFT 99 combat capable
  FGA 99: 96 JAS 39C/D *Gripen*; 3 JAS 39E *Gripen* (in test)
  ELINT 2 Gulfstream IV SRA-4 (S-102E)
  AEW&C 3: 1 S-100B *Argus*; 2 S-100D *Argus*
  TKR/TPT 1 KC-130H *Hercules* (Tp-84)
  TPT 8: **Medium** 5 C-130H *Hercules* (Tp-84); **Light** 2 Saab 340 (OS-100A/Tp-100C); **PAX** 1 Gulfstream 550 (Tp-102D)
  TRG 10 G 120TP (Sk-40)
UNINHABITED AERIAL VEHICLES
  ISR • Medium 8 RQ-7 *Shadow* (AUV 3 *Örnen*)
AIR-LAUNCHED MISSILES
  AAM • IR AIM-9L *Sidewinder* (RB-74); **IIR** IRIS-T (RB-98); **ARH** AIM-120B AMRAAM (RB-99); *Meteor*
  ASM AGM-65 *Maverick* (RB-75)
  AShM RB-15F

BOMBS

Laser-Guided GBU-12 *Paveway* II
INS/GPS guided GBU-39 Small Diameter Bomb

Armed Forces Hel Wing
FORCES BY ROLE
TRANSPORT HELICOPTER
  3 sqn with AW109 (Hkp 15A); AW109M (Hkp-15B); NH90 TTH (Hkp-14) (SAR/ASW); UH-60M *Black Hawk* (Hkp-16)
EQUIPMENT BY TYPE
HELICOPTERS
  TPT 53: **Medium** 33: 15 UH-60M *Black Hawk* (Hkp-16); 18 NH90 TTH (Hkp-14) (incl 9 ASW); **Light** 20: 12 AW109 (Hkp-15A); 8 AW109M (Hkp-15B)

Special Forces
FORCES BY ROLE
SPECIAL FORCES
  1 spec ops gp
COMBAT SUPPORT
  1 cbt spt gp

Other 2,950
Includes staff, logistics and intelligence personnel
FORCES BY ROLE
COMBAT SUPPORT
  1 EW bn
  1 psyops unit
COMBAT SERVICE SUPPORT
  2 log bn
  1 maint bn
  4 med coy
  1 tpt coy

Home Guard 21,500
FORCES BY ROLE
MANOEUVRE
  Other
    40 Home Guard bn

DEPLOYMENT
INDIA/PAKISTAN: UN • UNMOGIP 2
IRAQ: *Operation Inherent Resolve* 1; **NATO** • NATO Mission Iraq 1
KOREA, REPUBLIC OF: NNSC • 5
KOSOVO: NATO • KFOR 3
MIDDLE EAST: UN • UNTSO 5
SOMALIA: EU • EUTM Somalia 9
UNITED KINGDOM: *Operation Interflex* 50 (UKR trg)

Switzerland CHE

Swiss Franc CHF		2023	2024	2025
GDP	CHF	804bn	825bn	845bn
	USD	895bn	942bn	1.00trn
Real GDP growth	%	0.7	1.3	1.3
Def bdgt [a]	CHF	5.61bn	5.68bn	5.93bn
	USD	6.24bn	6.48bn	7.02bn

[a] Includes military pensions

Real-terms defence budget trend (USDbn, constant 2015)

Population	8,860,574				
Age	0–14	15–19	20–24	25–29	30–64	65 plus
Male	7.7%	2.4%	2.5%	2.9%	24.7%	9.4%
Female	7.3%	2.3%	2.4%	2.9%	24.4%	11.0%

Capabilities

The conscript-based armed forces are postured for territorial defence and limited participation in international peace-support operations. The government has begun to reduce its armed forces, reflecting an assessment that in the militia-based system, not all personnel would realistically be available for active service. Permanent neutrality a core feature of foreign and security policy, though Switzerland joined NATO's Partnership for Peace programme in 1996 and on occasion contributes to NATO- and EU-led operations alongside its engagement in UN or OSCE missions. Following Russia's invasion of Ukraine in 2022, Switzerland is adjusting and reworking its foreign and defence strategies. In 2023, Switzerland created a state secretariat for security, reflecting the deteriorating security environment, with the mission to coordinate national security policy starting in 2024. The Swiss government intends to increase ways to contribute to European security while remaining neutral. In 2024, the country joined the European Sky Shield Initiative. Under the Armaments Program 2024, Switzerland will invest in C2, reconnaissance and sensor systems, artillery, ATGMs, and short- and long-range air defence systems. The country is also procuring F-35As. Switzerland's defence industry has capabilities in the armoured vehicles, air defence and training aircraft sectors.

ACTIVE 21,300 (Armed Forces 21,300)

Conscript liability 260–600 compulsory service days depending on rank. 18 or 23 weeks' training (depending on branch) generally at age 20, followed by 6 refresher trg courses (3 weeks each). Alternative service available

RESERVE 123,450

Civil Defence 73,000 (51,000 Reserve)

ORGANISATIONS BY SERVICE

Armed Forces 3,100 active; 18,200 conscript (21,300 total)

Operations Command 72,600 on mobilisation
4 Territorial Regions. With the exception of military police all units are non-active

FORCES BY ROLE
COMMAND
4 regional comd
SPECIAL FORCES
2 SF bn
MANOEUVRE
  Armoured
  2 (1st & 11th) bde (1 recce bn, 1 tk bn, 2 armd inf bn, 1 SP arty bn, 1 engr bn, 1 sigs bn)
  Mechanised
  1 (4th) bde (2 recce bn, 2 SP arty bn, 1 ptn br bn)
  Light
  10 inf bn
  7 mtn inf bn
  1 mtn inf unit
COMBAT SUPPORT
4 engr bn
4 MP bn
1 NBC bn
1 int unit
COMBAT SUPPORT
4 engr rescue bn

EQUIPMENT BY TYPE
ARMOURED FIGHTING VEHICLES
  MBT 134 *Leopard* 2 (Pz-87 *Leo*)
  IFV 186: 154 CV9030CH; 32 CV9030 (CP)
  APC 1,113
    APC (T) 309 M113A2 (incl variants)
    APC (W) 804 *Piranha* I/II/IIIC
  AUV 292: 173 *Eagle* II; 119 *Eagle* III (CP)
ENGINEERING & MAINTENANCE VEHICLES
  AEV 12 *Kodiak*
  ARV 25 *Büffel*
  VLB 9 *Leopard* 2 with *Leguan*
  MW 46: 26 Area Clearing System; 20 M113A2
NBC VEHICLES 12 *Piranha* IIIC CBRN
ANTI-TANK/ANTI-INFRASTRUCTURE
  MSL • MANPATS NLAW
ARTILLERY 349
  SP 155mm 133 M109 KAWEST
  MOR • 81mm 216 Mw-72
PATROL AND COASTAL COMBATANTS 14
  PB 14 *Watercat* 1250
AIR DEFENCE • SAM • Point-defence FIM-92 *Stinger*

Air Force 18,900 on mobilisation
FORCES BY ROLE
FIGHTER
  2 sqn with F-5E/F *Tiger* II
  3 sqn with F/A-18C/D *Hornet*
TRANSPORT
  1 sqn with Beech 350 *King Air*; DHC-6 *Twin Otter*; PC-6 *Turbo Porter*; PC-12
  1 VIP Flt with Cessna 560XL *Citation*; CL-604 *Challenger*; *Falcon* 900EX
TRAINING
  1 sqn with PC-7CH *Turbo Trainer*; PC-21
  1 OCU Sqn with F-5E/F *Tiger* II
TRANSPORT HELICOPTER
  6 sqn with AS332M *Super Puma*; AS532UL *Cougar*; H135M
ISR UAV
  1 sqn with *Hermes* 900

EQUIPMENT BY TYPE
AIRCRAFT 48 combat capable
  FTR 18: 14 F-5E *Tiger* I; 4 F-5F *Tiger* II
  FGA 30: 25 F/A-18C *Hornet*; 5 F/A-18D *Hornet*
  TPT 20: **Light** 17: 1 Beech 350 *King Air*; 1 Cessna 560XL *Citation*; 1 DHC-6 *Twin Otter*; 14 PC-6 *Turbo Porter*; **PAX** 3: 2 CL-604 *Challenger*; 1 *Falcon* 900EX
  TRG 34: 27 PC-7CH *Turbo Trainer*; 7 PC-21
HELICOPTERS
  MRH 20 H135M
  TPT • Medium 24: 15 AS332M *Super Puma*; 9 AS532UL *Cougar*
UNINHABITED AERIAL VEHICLES
  ISR • Medium 2 *Hermes* 900
AIR-LAUNCHED MISSILES • AAM • IIR AIM-9X *Sidewinder* II; **ARH** AIM-120B/C-7 AMRAAM

Ground Based Air Defence (GBAD)
GBAD assets can be used to form AD clusters to be deployed independently as task forces within Swiss territory

EQUIPMENT BY TYPE
AIR DEFENCE
  SAM • Point-defence 56+: 56 *Rapier*; FIM-92 *Stinger*
  GUNS 35mm 27 GDF-003/-005 with *Skyguard*

Armed Forces Logistic Organisation 14,500 on mobilisation
FORCES BY ROLE
COMBAT SERVICE SUPPORT
1 log bde (6 log bn; 1 tpt bn; 6 med bn)

Command Support Organisation 15,300 on mobilisation
FORCES BY ROLE
COMBAT SERVICE SUPPORT
1 spt bde

Training Command 25,100 on mobilisation
COMBAT SERVICE SUPPORT
5 trg unit

Civil Defence 73,000 (51,000 Reserve)
(not part of armed forces)

DEPLOYMENT
BOSNIA-HERZEGOVINA: EU • EUFOR (*Operation Althea*) 20

DEMOCRATIC REPUBLIC OF THE CONGO: UN • MONUSCO 1

INDIA/PAKISTAN: UN • UNMOGIP 3

KOREA, REPUBLIC OF: NNSC • 5

KOSOVO: NATO • KFOR 211 (military volunteers); 1 engr pl; 1 tpt unit; 1 hel flt with AS332M *Super Puma*

MIDDLE EAST: UN • UNTSO 12

SOUTH SUDAN: UN • UNMISS 1

WESTERN SAHARA: UN • MINURSO 2

Turkiye TUR

New Turkish Lira TRY		2023	2024	2025
GDP	TRY	26.5trn	43.8trn	59.0trn
	USD	1.13trn	1.34trn	1.46trn
Real GDP growth	%	5.1	3.0	2.7
Def exp [a]	TRY	394bn	848bn	
	USD	16.6bn	22.8bn	
Def bdgt [b]	TRY	206bn	464bn	648bn
	USD	8.78bn	14.3bn	16.0bn

[a] NATO figure

[b] Includes funding for Undersecretariat of Defence Industries; Defence Industry Support Fund; TUBITAK Defense Industries R&D Institute (SAGE); and military pensions.

Population	84,119,531					
Age	0–14	15–19	20–24	25–29	30–64	65 plus
Male	11.1%	3.9%	3.8%	3.7%	23.2%	4.4%
Female	10.6%	3.7%	3.7%	3.6%	22.9%	5.3%

Capabilities

Turkiye has large, generally well-equipped armed forces, that are primarily structured for national defence, with a six-month-minimum compulsory military service for men. The Turkish Armed Forces (TSK) have conducted ground operations in Syria since 2016 and resumed missions in Iraq in 2019. Turkiye has also deployed forces to assist the UN-recognised government in Libya since 2020. The conflict with various Kurdish armed groups, both in and outside of Turkiye, continues, with Ankara treating the different groups as parts of a whole. Ankara spends increasing amounts of the budget locally. Turkiye maintains close relationships with Azerbaijan, Libya and Qatar, which has included training, deployments, arms sales and, in the case of Libya, direct military support. Turkiye has bases in Qatar and Somalia. Following the attempted coup in July 2016, Ankara made several organisational changes in the MoD and armed forces. The TSK trains regularly, including with NATO allies, but also increasingly with countries such as Azerbaijan and Pakistan. Turkiye is investing substantially in its naval capability. Ankara controversially agreed to buy Russia's S-400 air-defence system, with deliveries starting in 2019. In response, the US government terminated Turkiye's participation in the F-35 programme. Many of Turkiye's largest defence companies (such as ASELSAN, Roketsan and TAI) are either entirely or majority-owned by the Turkish Armed Forces Foundation. The country also has important privately-owned enterprises in land systems, shipbuilding and UAV production. Turkish defence exports have grown substantially.

ACTIVE 355,200 (Army 260,200 Navy 45,000 Air 50,000) **Gendarmerie & Paramilitary 160,800**

Conscript liability 12 months (5.5 months for university graduates; 21 days for graduates with exemption) (reducing to 6 months)

RESERVE 378,700 (Army 258,700 Navy 55,000 Air 65,000)

Reserve service to age 41 for all services

ORGANISATIONS BY SERVICE

Space
EQUIPMENT BY TYPE
SATELLITES 3
  COMMUNICATIONS 1 Turksat-6A
  ISR 2 *Gokturk*

Army ε260,200 (incl conscripts)
FORCES BY ROLE
COMMAND
  4 army HQ
  9 corps HQ
SPECIAL FORCES
  15 cdo bde
  1 cdo regt
MANOEUVRE
  Armoured
  8 armd bde
  Mechanised
  2 (28th & 29th) mech div
  14 mech inf bde
  Light
  1 (52nd) mot inf div (2 cdo bde)
  1 (3rd) inf div (1 mtn cdo bde, 1 mot inf bde, 1 sy bde, 1 arty regt)
  1 (23rd) inf div (1 cdo bde, 1 armd bde, 1 sy bde)
  1 mot inf bde
  Other
  2 (border) sy bde
COMBAT SUPPORT
  2 arty bde
  1 trg arty bde
  6 arty regt
  2 engr regt
HELICOPTER
  4 hel regt
  4 hel bn
COMBAT/ISR UAV
  3 bn with *Akinci*; *Bayraktar* TB2

EQUIPMENT BY TYPE
ARMOURED FIGHTING VEHICLES
 MBT 2,378: 316 *Leopard 2A4* (being upgraded); 170 *Leopard 1A4*; 227 *Leopard 1A3*; 100 *M60A1*; 650 *M60A3 TTS*; 165 *M60TM Firat*; 750 *M48A5 T2 Patton*
 IFV 645 *ACV AIFV*
 APC 6,403
  APC (T) 3,636: 823 *ACV AAPC*; 2,813 *M113/M113A1/M113A2*
  APC (W) 57 *Pars 6×6* (incl variants)
  PPV 2,710: 360 *Edjer Yalcin 4×4*; ε2,000 *Kirpi/Kirpi-II*; ε350 *Vuran*
  AUV 1,450: ε250 *Akrep*; 800+ *Cobra*; ε400 *Cobra II*
ENGINEERING & MAINTENANCE VEHICLES
 AEV 12+: *AZMIM*; 12 *M48 AEV*; *M113A2T2*
 ARV 150: 12 *BPz-2*; 105 *M48T5*; 33 *M88A1*
 VLB 88: 36 *Leguan*; 52 Mobile Floating Assault Bridge
 MW 14+: 4 *Husky 2G*; 10 *Meti*; *Tamkar*; *Bozena*
ANTI-TANK/ANTI-INFRASTRUCTURE
 MSL
  SP 709: 365 *ACV TOW*; 208 *Kaplan STA*; *Kaplan ZTA-UC/P*; 136 *Pars STA 4×4*
  MANPATS 9K135 *Kornet-E* (RS-AT-14 *Spriggan*); *Eryx*; FGM-148 *Javelin*; *Milan*; *OMTAS*; *Sungur*
 RCL 106mm M40A1
ARTILLERY 2,762
 SP 1,061: **155mm** 806: ε150 *M44T1*; 365 *M52T* (mod); ε280 *T-155 Firtina*; 11 *T-155 Firtina II*; **175mm** 36 *M107*; **203mm** 219 *M110A2*
 TOWED 675+: **105mm** 82: 7 *Boran* (in test); 75+ *M101A1*; **155mm** 557: 517 *M114A1/M114A2*; 40 *Panter*; **203mm** 36+ *M115*
 MRL 98+: **122mm** ε36 *T-122*; **227mm** 12 *M270 MLRS*; **302mm** 50+ *TR-300 Kasirga* (WS-1)
 MOR 928+
  SP 350+: **81mm** some; **107mm** ε150 *M106*; **120mm** ε200
  TOWED 578+: **81mm** some; **120mm** 578 HY12
SURFACE-TO-SURFACE MISSILE LAUNCHERS
 SRBM • Conventional *Bora*; MGM-140A ATACMS (launched from M270 MLRS); J-600T *Yildrim* (B-611/CH-SS-9 mod 1)
AIRCRAFT
 ISR 5 *Beech 350 King Air*
 TPT • Light 8: 5 *Beech 200 King Air*; 3 *Cessna 421*
 TRG 49: 45 *Cessna T182*; 4 *T-42A Cochise*
HELICOPTERS
 ATK 91: 18 *AH-1P Cobra*; 12 *AH-1S Cobra*; 4 *TAH-1P Cobra*; 9 *T129A*; 48 *T129B*
 MRH 28 *Hughes 300C*
 TPT 216: **Heavy** 6 *CH-47F Chinook*; **Medium** 71: 28 *AS532UL Cougar*; 40 *S-70A Black Hawk*; 3 *T-70 Black Hawk* **Light** 139: 12 *Bell 204B (AB-204B)*; ε43 *Bell 205 (UH-1H Iroquois)*; 64 *Bell 205A (AB-205A)*; 20 *Bell 206 Jet Ranger*

UNINHABITED AERIAL VEHICLES
 CISR 73: **Heavy** 3 *Bayraktar Akinci*; **Medium** ε70 *Bayraktar TB2*
 ISR • Heavy *Falcon 600/Firebee*; **Medium** *CL-89*; *Gnat*
 OWA *Harpy*
AIR-LAUNCHED MISSILES • ASM *Mizrak-U (UMTAS)*
BOMBS • Laser-guided MAM-C/L
AIR DEFENCE
 SAM
  Short-range *Hisar-A/A+*; *Hisar-O*
  Point-defence 148+: 70 *Atilgan* PMADS octuple *Stinger* lnchr, 78 *Zipkin* PMADS quad *Stinger* lnchr; FIM-92 *Stinger*, *Sungur*
 GUNS 1,404
  SP 35mm 42 *Korkut*
  TOWED 1,362: **20mm** ε39 GAI-D01/Rh-202; **35mm** 120 GDF-001/-003; **40mm** 803 L/60/L/70

Navy ε45,000 (incl conscripts)
EQUIPMENT BY TYPE
SUBMARINES • SSK 13
 4 *Atilay* (GER Type-209/1200) with 8 single 533mm TT with SST-4 HWT
 4 *Gur* (GER Type-209/1400) with 8 single 533mm TT with UGM-84 *Harpoon* AShM/*Akya* HWT/Mk 24 *Tigerfish* mod 2 HWT/*SeaHake* mod 4 (DM2A4) HWT
 4 *Preveze* (GER Type-209/1400) (MLU ongoing) with 8 single 533mm TT with UGM-84 *Harpoon* AShM/*Akya* HWT/Mk 24 *Tigerfish* mod 2 HWT/*SeaHake* mod 4 (DM2A4) HWT
 1 *Reis* (GER Type-214) (fitted with AIP) with 8 single 533mm TT with *Akya* HWT/*SeaHake* mod 4 (DM2A4) HWT/Mk 48 HWT
PRINCIPAL SURFACE COMBATANTS • FRIGATES 17
 FFGHM 17:
 3 *Barbaros* (GER MEKO 200 mod) with 2 quad lnchr with RGM-84C *Harpoon* Block 1B AShM, 2 8-cell Mk 41 VLS with RIM-162B ESSM SAM, 2 triple 324mm SVTT Mk 32 ASTT with Mk 46 LWT, 3 *Sea Zenith* CIWS, 1 127mm gun (capacity 1 Bell 212 (AB-212) hel)
 1 *Barbaros* (GER MEKO 200 mod) with 4 quad lnchr with *Atmaca* AShM, 2 8-cell Mk 41 VLS with RIM-162B ESSM SAM, 2 triple 324mm SVTT Mk 32 ASTT with Mk 46 LWT, 1 Mk 15 *Phalanx* CIWS, 1 *Gokdeniz* CIWS, 1 127mm gun (capacity 1 Bell 212 (AB-212) hel)
 4 *Gabya* (ex-US *Oliver Hazard Perry*) with 1 Mk 13 GMLS with RGM-84C *Harpoon* Block 1B AShM/SM-1MR Block VI SAM, 1 8-cell Mk 41 VLS with RIM-162B ESSM SAM, 2 triple 324mm SVTT Mk 32 ASTT with Mk 46 LWT, 1 Mk 15 *Phalanx* Block 1B CIWS, 1 76mm gun (capacity 1 S-70B *Seahawk*/AB-212 ASW hel)
 4 *Gabya* (ex-US *Oliver Hazard Perry*) with 1 Mk 13 GMLS with RGM-84C *Harpoon* Block 1B AShM/SM-1MR Block VI SAM, 2 triple 324mm SVTT Mk 32 ASTT with Mk 46 LWT, 1 Mk 15 *Phalanx* Block

1B CIWS, 1 76mm gun (capacity 1 S-70B *Seahawk*/ AB-212 ASW hel)

1 *Istif* (MILGEM) with 4 quad lnchr with *Atmaca* AShM, 1 16-cell MIDLAS VLS with *Hisar*-D SAM, 2 triple 324mm ASTT with Mk 46 LWT/*Orka* LWT, 1 *Gokdeniz* CIWS, 1 76mm gun (capacity 1 S-70B *Seahawk* hel)

4 *Yavuz* (GER MEKO 200TN) with 2 quad lnchr with RGM-84C *Harpoon* Block 1B AShM, 1 octuple Mk 29 GMLS with RIM-7M *Sea Sparrow* SAM, 2 triple 324mm SVTT Mk 32 ASTT with Mk 46 LWT, 3 *Sea Zenith* CIWS, 1 127mm gun (capacity 1 Bell 212 (AB-212) hel)

PATROL AND COASTAL COMBATANTS 50

CORVETTES 9:

FSGHM 4 *Ada* with 2 quad lnchr with ATMACA AShM/RGM-84C *Harpoon* Block 1B AShM, 1 Mk 49 21-cell lnchr with RIM-116 SAM, 2 twin 324mm SVTT Mk 32 ASTT with Mk 46 LWT, 1 76mm gun (capacity 1 S-70B *Seahawk* hel)

FSG 5 *Burak* (ex-FRA *d'Estienne d'Orves*) with 2 single lnchr with MM38 *Exocet* AShM, 4 single 324mm ASTT with Mk 46 LWT, 1 Creusot-Loire Mk 54 A/S mor, 1 100mm gun (1 vessel with 1 76mm gun instead)

PCFG 18:

3 *Dogan* (GER Lurssen-57) with 2 quad lnchr with RGM-84C *Harpoon* Block 1B AShM, 1 76mm gun

9 *Kilic* (GER Lurssen-62) with 2 quad lnchr with RGM-84C *Harpoon* Block 1B AShM, 1 76mm gun

4 *Rüzgar* (GER Lurssen-57) with 2 quad lnchr with RGM-84C *Harpoon* Block 1B AShM, 1 76mm gun

2 *Yildiz* with 2 quad lnchr with RGM-84C *Harpoon* Block 1B AShM, 1 76mm gun

PCC 16 *Tuzla*

PBF 7: 2 *Kaan* 20 (MRTP 20); 3 MRTP 22; 2 MRTP 24/U

MINE WARFARE • MINE COUNTERMEASURES 11

MHO 11: 5 *Engin* (ex-FRA *Circe*); 6 *Aydin*

AMPHIBIOUS

PRINCIPAL AMPHIBIOUS SHIPS • LHD 1 *Anadolu* (ESP *Juan Carlos* I mod) with 2 Mk 15 *Phalanx* CIWS (capacity 21 hel; 4 LCM or 2 LCAC; up to 80 vehicles; 900 troops)

LANDING SHIPS • LST 5:

2 *Bayraktar* with 2 Mk 15 *Phalanx* Block 1B CIWS, 1 hel landing platform (capacity 20 MBT; 250 troops)

1 *Osmangazi* with 1 Mk 15 *Phalanx* CIWS (capacity 4 LCVP; 17 tanks; 980 troops; 1 hel landing platform)

2 *Sarucabey* with 1 Mk 15 *Phalanx* CIWS (capacity 11 tanks; 600 troops; 1 hel landing platform)

LANDING CRAFT 39

LCT 21: 2 C-120/130; 11 C-140; 8 C-151

LCM 10: 4 LCM-1E; 6 LCM 8

LCVP 8 Anadolu 16m

LOGISTICS AND SUPPORT 37

ABU 2: 1 AG5; 1 AG6 with 1 76mm gun

AG 2 *Dalgic*

AGI 1 *Ufuk* (MILGEM) (capacity 1 S-70B *Seahawk* hel)

AGS 2: 1 *Cesme* (ex-US *Silas Bent*); 1 *Cubuklu*

AO 4: 2 *Burak*; 2 *Yuzbasi Gungor Durmus* with 1 hel landing platform

AOR 2 *Akar* with 1 Mk 15 *Phalanx* CIWS, 1 hel landing platform

AORH 1 *Derya* (DIMDEG) with 2 *Gokdeniz* CIWS (capacity 2 med hels)

AP 4: 1 *Iskenderun*; 3 *Mugla*

ASR 3: 1 *Alemdar* with 1 hel landing platform; 2 *Isin* II

ATF 5: 1 *Akbas*; 1 *Darica*; 1 *Inebolu*; 2 *Kizilirmak*

AWT 3 *Sogut*

AXL 8

UNINHABITED MARITIME PLATFORMS

USV • MARSEC 14: **Medium** 6: 1 *Marlin*; 2 *Mir*; 1 *Salvo*; 1 *Sancar*; 1 ULAQ; **Small** 8 *Albatros* S

UNINHABITED MARITIME SYSTEMS

UUV • MW PAP

Marines 3,000

FORCES BY ROLE

MANOEUVRE

Amphibious

1 mne bde (3 mne bn; 1 arty bn)

ARMOURED FIGHTING VEHICLES

AAV 25 MAV ZAHA

ENGINEERING & MAINTENANCE VEHICLES

ARV 2 ZAHA ARV

Naval Aviation

FORCES BY ROLE

ANTI-SUBMARINE WARFARE

2 sqn with Bell 212 ASW (AB-212 ASW); S-70B *Seahawk*

1 sqn with ATR-72-600; CN235M-100; TB-20 *Trinidad*

ATTACK HELICOPTER

1 sqn with AH-1W *Cobra*

CISR UAV

1 sqn with *Aksungur*; Anka-S; Bayraktar TB2

EQUIPMENT BY TYPE

AIRCRAFT 6 combat capable

ASW 6 ATR-72-600 (P-72)

MP 6 CN235M-100

TPT • Light 7: 3 ATR-72-600; 4 TB-20 *Trinidad*

HELICOPTERS

ATK 10 AH-1W *Cobra*

ASW 33: 9 Bell 212 ASW (AB-212 ASW); 24 S-70B *Seahawk*

UNINHABITED AERIAL VEHICLES 20

CISR 22: **Heavy** 13: 5 *Aksungur*; 8 Anka-S; **Medium** 9 Bayraktar TB2

AIR-LAUNCHED MISSILES

ASM AGM-114M *Hellfire* II

BOMBS • Laser-guided MAM-C/L

Air Force ε50,000

2 tac air forces (divided between east and west)

FORCES BY ROLE
FIGHTER/GROUND ATTACK
  1 sqn with F-4E *Phantom* 2020
  8 sqn with F-16C/D *Fighting Falcon*
ISR
  1 sqn with F-16C/D *Fighting Falcon*
  1 unit with *King Air* 350
AIRBORNE EARLY WARNING & CONTROL
  1 sqn (forming) with B-737 AEW&C
EW
  1 unit with CN235M EW
SEARCH & RESCUE
  1 sqn with AS532AL/UL *Cougar*; T-70 *Black Hawk*
TANKER
  1 sqn with KC-135R *Stratotanker*
TRANSPORT
  1 sqn with A400M
  1 sqn with C-130B/E *Hercules*
  3 sqn with CN235M
  1 (VIP) sqn with Cessna 550 *Citation* II (UC-35); Cessna 650 *Citation* VII; CN235M; Gulfstream 550
  10 (liaison) flt with Bell 205 (UH-1H *Iroquois*); CN235M
TRAINING
  1 sqn with F-16C/D *Fighting Falcon*
  1 sqn (display team) with NF-5A-2000/NF-5B-2000 *Freedom Fighter*
  1 sqn with MFI-395 *Super Mushshak*; SF-260D
  1 sqn with *Hurkus*-B; KT-IT
  1 sqn with T-38A/M *Talon*
  1 sqn with T-41D *Mescalero*
COMBAT/ISR UAV
  1 sqn with *Bayraktar Akinci*
AIR DEFENCE
  4 bn with S-400 (RS-SA-21 *Growler*)
  4 sqn with MIM-14 *Nike Hercules*
  2 sqn with *Rapier*
  8 (firing) unit with MIM-23 *Hawk*
MANOEUVRE
  Air Manoeuvre
  1 AB bde
EQUIPMENT BY TYPE
AIRCRAFT 293 combat capable
  FTR 14: 8 NF-5A-2000 *Freedom Fighter* (display team); 6 NF-5B-2000 *Freedom Fighter* (display team)
  FGA 279: 19 F-4E *Phantom* 2020; 27 F-16C *Fighting Falcon* Block 30; 162 F-16C *Fighting Falcon* Block 50; 14 F-16C *Fighting Falcon* Block 50+; 8 F-16D Block 30 *Fighting Falcon*; 33 F-16D *Fighting Falcon* Block 50; 16 F-16D *Fighting Falcon* Block 50+
  ISR 7: 5 Beech 350 *King Air*; 1 C-160D *Transall*; 1 CN235M (Open Skies)
  EW 1 C-160D *Transall*
  SIGINT 3 CN235M
  AEW&C 4 B-737 AEW&C
  TKR 7 KC-135R *Stratotanker*
  TPT 79: **Heavy** 10 A400M; **Medium** 19: 6 C-130B *Hercules*; 13 C-130E *Hercules*; **Light** 49: 2 Cessna 550 *Citation* II (UC-35 - VIP); 2 Cessna 650 *Citation* VII; 45 CN235M; **PAX** 1 Gulfstream 550
  TRG 173: 4 *Hurkus*-B; 39 KT-IT; 3 MFI-395 *Super Mushshak*; 32 SF-260D; 70 T-38A/M *Talon*; 25 T-41D *Mescalero*
HELICOPTERS
  TPT 37: **Medium** 23: 6 AS532AL *Cougar* (CSAR); 14 AS532UL *Cougar* (SAR); 3 T-70 *Black Hawk*; **Light** 14 Bell 205 (UH-1H *Iroquois*)
UNINHABITED AERIAL VEHICLES
  CISR • Heavy 31: 19 *Anka*-S; 12 *Bayraktar Akinci*
  ISR 27: **Heavy** 9 *Heron*; **Medium** 18 *Gnat* 750
AIR DEFENCE • SAM 58+
  Long-range 34+: MIM-14 *Nike Hercules*; 32 S-400 (RS-SA-21 *Growler*); 2+ *Siper* Block-1
  Medium-range ε24 MIM-23 *Hawk*
  Point-defence *Rapier*
AIR-LAUNCHED MISSILES
  AAM • IR AIM-9S *Sidewinder*; *Shafrir* 2‡; **IIR** AIM-9X *Sidewinder* II; **SARH** AIM-7E *Sparrow*; **ARH** AIM-120A/B AMRAAM
  ARM AGM-88A HARM
  ASM AGM-65A/G *Maverick*; *Popeye* I
  LACM • Conventional AGM-84K SLAM-ER
BOMBS
  Electro-optical guided GBU-8B HOBOS (GBU-15)
  Laser-guided MAM-C/-L; *Paveway* I/II
  INS/GPS guided AGM-154A JSOW; AGM-154C JSOW

Special Forces Command
FORCES BY ROLE
SPECIAL FORCES
  4 spec ops bde
  1 spec ops regt
EQUIPMENT BY TYPE
ARMOURED FIGHTING VEHICLES
APC • APC(W) 12 Pars IV 6×6
HELICOPTERS
  TPT 14: **Heavy** 5 CH-47F *Chinook*; **Medium** 9: 8 S-70A *Black Hawk*; 1 T-70 *Black Hawk*

Gendarmerie & Paramilitary 160,800

Gendarmerie 152,100
Ministry of Interior; Ministry of Defence in war
FORCES BY ROLE
SPECIAL FORCES
  1 cdo bde
MANOEUVRE
  Other

1 (border) paramilitary div
2 paramilitary bde

EQUIPMENT BY TYPE
ARMOURED FIGHTING VEHICLES
  RECCE 57+: *Akrep*; 57 *Ates*
  APC 760+
    APC (W) 560: 535 BTR-60/BTR-80; 25 *Condor*
    PPV 200+: *Edjer Yaclin* 4×4; *Kirpi*; 200 *Kirpi* II; *Vuran*
  AUV *Cobra*; *Cobra* II; Otokar *Ural*
ARTILLERY • MOR • SP 120mm *Vuran* with *Alkar*
AIRCRAFT
  ISR Some O-1E *Bird Dog*
  TPT • **Light** 2 Do-28D
HELICOPTERS
  ATK 13 T129B
  MRH 19 Mi-17 *Hip* H
  TPT 36: **Medium** 12 S-70A *Black Hawk*; **Light** 24: 8 Bell 204B (AB-204B); 6 Bell 205A (AB-205A); 8 Bell 206A (AB-206A) *Jet Ranger*; 1 Bell 212 (AB-212); 1 T625 *Gokbey*
UNINHABITED AERIAL VEHICLES
  CISR 42: **Heavy** 6 *Anka*-S; **Medium** ε36 *Bayraktar* TB2
BOMBS • Laser-guided MAM-C/-L

Coast Guard 8,700
EQUIPMENT BY TYPE
PATROL AND COASTAL COMBATANTS 197
  PSOH 4 *Dost*
  PBF 151: 84 *Ares* 35; 10 *Ares* 42; 18 *Kaan* 15; 17 *Kaan* 19; 9 *Kaan* 29; 13 *Kaan* 33
  PB 42: 15 Damen SAR 1906; 5 *Saar* 33; 4 *Saar* 35; 18 Type-80
AIRCRAFT • MP 3 CN235 MPA
HELICOPTERS • MRH 14 Bell 412EP (AB-412EP) (SAR)
UNINHABITED AERIAL VEHICLES 6
  CISR • **Medium** 6 *Bayraktar* TB2

DEPLOYMENT
AZERBAIJAN: Army 170; 1 EOD unit
BOSNIA-HERZEGOVINA: EU • EUFOR • *Operation Althea* 238; 1 inf coy
CYPRUS (NORTHERN): ε33,800; 1 army corps HQ; 1 SF regt; 1 armd bde; 2 mech inf div; 1 mech inf regt; 1 arty regt; 1 avn comd; 287 M48A5T2; 145 ACV AIFV; 70 ACV AAPC (incl variants); 418 M113 (incl variants); 36 M101A1; 36 M114A2; 12 M115; 30 M44T; 144 M52T1; 4 T-155; 18 T-122; 171 81mm mor; 70 M30; 135 HY-12; *Milan*; 66 ACV TOW; 219 M40A1; FIM-92 *Stinger*; 44 Rh 202; 78 GAI-D01; 16 GDF-003; 3 Cessna 185 (U-17); 2 AS532UL *Cougar*; 1 Bell 205 (UH-1H *Iroquois*); 1 PB
IRAQ: Army: 4,000; **NATO** • NATO Mission Iraq 86
KOSOVO: NATO • KFOR 325; 1 inf coy; UN • UNMIK 1
LEBANON: UN • UNIFIL 92; 1 FSG

LIBYA: ε500; ACV-AAPC; *Kirpi*; 1 arty unit with T-155 *Firtina*; 1 AD unit with *Hisar*-O; *Korkut*; GDF-003; 1 CISR UAV unit with *Bayraktar* TB2
MEDITERRAEAN SEA: NATO • SNMG 2: 200; 1 FFGHM; SNMCMG 2: 50; 1 MHO
QATAR: Army: 300 (trg team); 1 mech inf coy; 1 arty unit; 12+ ACV AIFV/AAPC; 2 T-155 *Firtina*
SOMALIA: 200 (trg team); UN • UNSOM 1
SYRIA: ε3,000; some cdo units; 3 armd BG; 1 SAM unit; 1 gendarmerie unit

FOREIGN FORCES
Spain *Active Fence*: 150; 1 SAM bty with M901 *Patriot* PAC-2
United States US European Command: 1,700; 1 spt facility at Izmir; 1 spt facility at Ankara; 1 air base at Incirlik • **US Strategic Command**: 1 AN/TPY-2 X-band radar at Kürecik

United Kingdom UK

British Pound GBP		2023	2024	2025
GDP	GBP	2.72trn	2.81trn	2.90trn
	USD	3.38trn	3.59trn	3.73trn
Real GDP growth	%	0.3	1.1	1.5
Def exp [a]	GBP	61.9bn	64.6bn	
	USD	76.9bn	82.1bn	
Def bdgt [b]	GBP	ε60.4bn	ε63.5bn	ε66.5bn
	USD	ε75.0bn	ε81.1bn	ε85.5bn

[a] NATO figure
[b] Includes total departmental expenditure limits; costs of military operations; Armed Forces Pension Service; military aid to Ukraine; and external income earned by the MoD.

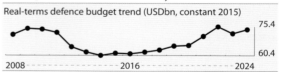
Real-terms defence budget trend (USDbn, constant 2015)

Population	68,459,055					
Age	0–14	15–19	20–24	25–29	30–64	65 plus
Male	8.6%	3.0%	2.9%	3.3%	23.0%	8.9%
Female	8.2%	2.9%	3.0%	3.3%	22.5%	10.5%

Capabilities

UK armed forces provide nuclear and conventional deterrence, with a broad range of deployable forces. Most conventional forces are assigned to NATO, 'optimised' to fight in the Euro-Atlantic area. The UK maintains forces in Poland and Estonia as part of NATO's Forward Land Forces battlegroups. Naval and air forces have seen combat in the Red Sea and in defending Israel. A modest military 'tilt' to the Indo-Pacific is being sustained. The UK continues to support Ukraine, donating materiel, which exposed weaknesses in logistic stockpiles, resulting in significant new investment in munitions production. The UK is partnering with Italy and Japan in the Global Combat Air Programme for a next-generation fighter and with Australia and the US in the AUKUS partnership to collaboratively develop nuclear submarines and advanced military technology. Nuclear programmes absorb an increasingly significant proportion of defence funding. Parliamentary committees and the defence secretary have questioned readiness, force levels and stockpiles, among others. The UK's defence industry is globally competitive in some areas, particularly aerospace, but does not meet the full range of capability requirements, particularly for land equipment. There is currently an effort to reform defence acquisition. The new government has begun a strategic defence review, which will report by mid-2025, and has committed to increase defence spending to 2.5% of GDP 'when circumstances allow'.

ACTIVE 141,100 (Army 78,800 Navy 31,800 Air 30,500)

RESERVE 70,450 (Regular Reserve 36,500 (Army 22,850, Navy 6,800, Air 6,850); Volunteer Reserve 32,050 (Army 25,800, Navy 3,250, Air 3,000); Sponsored Reserve 1,900)

Includes both trained and those currently under training within the Regular Forces, excluding university cadet units

ORGANISATIONS BY SERVICE

Strategic Forces 1,000

Royal Navy
EQUIPMENT BY TYPE
SUBMARINES • STRATEGIC
SSBN 4 *Vanguard* with 16 UGM-133A *Trident* II D-5/D-5LE nuclear SLBM, 4 533mm TT with *Spearfish* HWT (recent deployment practice of no more than 8 missiles/40 warheads per boat; each missile could carry up to 12 MIRV; some *Trident* D-5 capable of being configured for sub-strategic role)
MSL • SLBM • Nuclear 48 UGM-133A *Trident* II D-5

Royal Air Force
EQUIPMENT BY TYPE
RADAR • STRATEGIC 1 Ballistic Missile Early Warning System (BMEWS) at Fylingdales Moor

Space
EQUIPMENT BY TYPE
SATELLITES 7
COMMUNICATIONS 6: 2 *Skynet*-4; 4 *Skynet*-5
ISR 1 *Tyche*

Army 74,600; 4,200 Gurkhas (total 78,800)
Regt normally bn size. Many cbt spt and CSS regt and bn have reservist sub-units
FORCES BY ROLE
COMMAND
  1 (ARRC) corps HQ
MANOEUVRE
  Armoured
  1 (3rd) armd inf div (1 armd recce/arty bde (2 armd recce regt, 1 recce regt, 2 SP arty regt, 2 MRL regt, 1 STA regt, 1 maint bn); 1 (12th) armd inf bde (2 tk regt, 2 armd inf bn, 1 log regt, 1 maint regt, 1 med regt); 1 (20th) armd inf bde (1 armd recce regt, 1 tk regt, 2 armd inf bn, 1 log regt, 1 maint regt, 1 med regt); 1 cbt engr gp (3 cbt engr regt); 1 int bn; 1 sigs gp (3 sigs regt); 1 log bde (2 log regt); 1 AD gp (2 SAM regt))
  Light
  1 (1st) inf div (1 (4th) inf bde (1 recce regt, 6 inf bn); 1 (7th) lt mech inf bde (1 recce regt, 4 lt mech inf bn, 2 inf bn; 1 fd arty regt; 1 cbt engr regt, 1 log regt, 1 maint bn, 1 med regt); 1 (11th) inf bde (4 inf bn, 1 info ops gp); 1 engr bde (1 CBRN regt, 3 EOD regt, 1 (MWD) EOD search regt, 1 engr regt, 1 (air spt) engr regt); 1 int bn; 1 sigs regt; 1 log bde (1 log regt; 1 maint bn))
  1 inf bn
  Air Manoeuvre
  1 (16th) air aslt bde (1 recce pl, 2 para bn, 1 air aslt bn, 1 inf bn, 1 fd arty regt, 1 cbt engr regt, 1 log regt, 1 med regt)
  Other
  1 inf bn (trials gp)
COMBAT SUPPORT
  1 (6th) cbt spt div (1 ranger bde (4 ranger bn); 1 (77th) info ops bde (2 info ops gp, 1 spt gp, 1 engr spt/log gp); 1 int bn)
  1 (geographic) engr regt
  1 cyber/EW gp (1 cyber regt, 2 EW regt)
  1 ISR gp (1 int bn, 2 ISR UAV regt)
  1 MP bde (2 MP regt)
  1 sigs bde (4 sigs regt)
COMBAT SERVICE SUPPORT
  1 log bde (3 log regt; 2 maint regt)
  1 maint bn
  1 med bde (2 fd hospital)
  1 (ARRC) spt bn

Reserves

Army Reserve 25,900 reservists
The Army Reserve (AR) generates individuals, sub-units and some full units. The majority of units are subordinate to regular-formation headquarters and paired with one or more regular units
FORCES BY ROLE
MANOEUVRE
  Reconnaissance
  1 recce regt
  Armoured
  1 armd regt
  Light
  1 inf bde (2 recce regt, 8 inf bn)
  7 inf bn
  Air Manoeuvre
  1 para bn
COMBAT SUPPORT
  3 arty regt

1 STA regt
1 MRL regt
3 engr regt
1 EOD regt
3 int bn
4 sigs regt

COMBAT SERVICE SUPPORT
11 log regt
3 maint regt
5 med regt
9 fd hospital

AIR DEFENCE
1 AD regt

EQUIPMENT BY TYPE

ARMOURED FIGHTING VEHICLES
MBT 213 *Challenger* 2
RECCE 59 *Ajax* (in test)
IFV 388+: 388 FV510 *Warrior*; FV511 *Warrior* (CP); FV514 *Warrior* (OP); FV515 *Warrior* (CP)
APC 875
  APC (T) 615: 41 *Ares* (in test); 26 *Athena* (in test); 97 FV103 *Spartan*; 21 FV105 *Sultan* (CP); 409 FV430 *Bulldog* (incl variants); 17 *Spartan* Mk2; 4 *Sultan* Mk2
  APC (W) 4 *Boxer* (in test)
  PPV 256 *Mastiff* (6×6)
AUV 1,355: 398 *Foxhound*; (CP); 197 *Jackal*; 110 *Jackal* 2; 130 *Jackal* 2A; 380 *Panther* CLV; 140 *Ridgback*

ENGINEERING & MAINTENANCE VEHICLES
AEV 104: 16 *Argus* (in test); 56 *Terrier*; 32 *Trojan*
ARV 283: 21 *Apollo* (in test); 19 *Atlas* (in test); 80 *Challenger* ARRV; 12 FV106 *Samson*; 5 *Samson* Mk2; 105 FV512 *Warrior*; 41 FV513 *Warrior*
MW 64 *Aardvark*
VLB 60: 27 M3; 33 *Titan*

NBC VEHICLES 8 TPz-1 *Fuchs* NBC

ANTI-TANK/ANTI-INFRASTRUCTURE • MSL
SP *Exactor*-2 (*Spike* NLOS)
MANPATS FGM-148 *Javelin*; NLAW

ARTILLERY 553
SP 155mm 53: 14 *Archer*; 39 AS90
TOWED 105mm 114 L118 Light Gun
MRL 227mm 26 M270B1 MLRS
MOR 81mm 360 L16A1

AMPHIBIOUS • LCM 3 Ramped Craft Logistic

AIR DEFENCE • SAM 50+
Short-range ε12 CAMM (*Land Ceptor*)
Point-defence 38 FV4333 *Stormer* with *Starstreak*; *Starstreak* (LML)

UNINHABITED AERIAL VEHICLES • ISR • Medium
12 *Watchkeeper* (33 more in store)

Joint Helicopter Command

Tri-service joint organisation including Royal Navy, Army and RAF units

Army
FORCES BY ROLE
ATTACK HELICOPTER
1 bde (1 atk hel regt (3 sqn (incl 1 trg) with AH-64E *Apache*); 1 atk hel regt (2 sqn with AH-64E *Apache*); 1 regt (3 sqn (incl 1 trg) with AW159 *Wildcat* AH1); 1 (spec ops) sqn with AS365N3; 1 maint regt)
TRAINING
1 hel trg regt (1 sqn with AH-64E *Apache*; 1 sqn with AS350B *Ecureuil*)

Army Reserve
FORCES BY ROLE
HELICOPTER
1 hel regt (4 sqn personnel only)

Royal Navy
FORCES BY ROLE
ATTACK HELICOPTER
1 lt sqn with AW159 *Wildcat* AH1
TRANSPORT HELICOPTER
2 sqn with AW101 *Merlin* HC4/4A

Royal Air Force
FORCES BY ROLE
TRANSPORT HELICOPTER
3 sqn with CH-47D/F/SD *Chinook* HC6A/6/5
2 sqn with SA330 *Puma* HC2
TRAINING
1 OCU sqn with CH-47D/SD/F *Chinook* HC3/4/4A/6; SA330 *Puma* HC2

EQUIPMENT BY TYPE
HELICOPTERS
ATK 44 AH-64E *Apache*
MRH 39: 5 AS365N3; 34 AW159 *Wildcat* AH1
TPT 103: **Heavy** 57: 35 CH-47D *Chinook* HC6A; 14 CH-47F *Chinook* HC6; 8 CH-47SD *Chinook* HC5; **Medium** 37: 24 AW101 *Merlin* HC4/4A; 13 SA330 *Puma* HC2; (7 SA330 *Puma* HC2 in store); **Light** 9 AS350B *Ecureuil*

Royal Navy 31,800

EQUIPMENT BY TYPE
SUBMARINES 10
STRATEGIC • SSBN 4 *Vanguard*, opcon Strategic Forces with 16 UGM-133A *Trident* II D-5/D-5LE nuclear SLBM, 4 single 533mm TT with *Spearfish* HWT (recent deployment practice of no more than 8 missiles/40 warheads per boat; each missile could carry up to 12 MIRV; some *Trident* D-5 capable of being configured for sub-strategic role)
TACTICAL • SSN 6
1 *Trafalgar* with 5 single 533mm TT with UGM-109E *Tomahawk* Block IV/V LACM/*Spearfish* HWT
5 *Astute* with 6 single 533mm TT with UGM-109E *Tomahawk* Block IV/V LACM/*Spearfish* HWT

PRINCIPAL SURFACE COMBATANTS 16
AIRCRAFT CARRIERS 2:

CV 2 *Queen Elizabeth* with up to 3 Mk 15 *Phalanx* Block 1B CIWS (capacity 40 ac/hel, incl 24+ F-35B *Lightning* II, 14+ *Merlin* HM2/*Wildcat* HMA2/CH-47 *Chinook* hel)

DESTROYERS 6:
DDGHM 3 *Daring* (Type-45) with 2 quad lnchr with RGM-84D *Harpoon* Block 1C AShM, 6 8-cell *Sylver* A50 VLS with *Aster* 15/30 (*Sea Viper*) SAM, 2 Mk 15 *Phalanx* Block 1B CIWS, 1 114mm gun (capacity 1 AW159 *Wildcat*/AW101 *Merlin* hel)
DDHM 3 *Daring* (Type-45) with 6 8-cell *Sylver* A50 VLS with *Aster* 15/30 (*Sea Viper*) SAM, 2 Mk 15 *Phalanx* Block 1B CIWS, 1 114mm gun (capacity 1 AW159 *Wildcat*/AW101 *Merlin* hel)

FRIGATES • FFGHM 8:
7 *Duke* (Type-23) with 2 quad lnchr with RGM-84D *Harpoon* Block 1C AShM, 1 32-cell VLS with *Sea Ceptor* SAM, 2 twin 324mm ASTT with *Sting Ray* LWT, 1 114mm gun (capacity either 2 AW159 *Wildcat* or 1 AW101 *Merlin* hel)
1 *Duke* (Type-23) with 2 quad lnchr with NSM AShM, 1 32-cell VLS with *Sea Ceptor* SAM, 2 twin 324mm ASTT with *Sting Ray* LWT, 1 114mm gun (capacity either 2 AW159 *Wildcat* or 1 AW101 *Merlin* hel)

PATROL AND COASTAL COMBATANTS 26
PSO 8: 3 *River* Batch 1; 5 *River* Batch 2 with 1 hel landing platform
PBF 2 *Cutlass*
PBI 16 *Archer* (14 in trg role, 2 deployed to Gibraltar sqn)

MINE WARFARE • MINE COUNTERMEASURES 7
MCO 6 *Hunt* (incl 4 mod *Hunt*)
MHC 1 *Sandown*

LOGISTICS AND SUPPORT 4
AGB 1 *Protector* with 1 hel landing platform
AGE 1 XV *Patrick Blackett* (Damen Fast Crew Supplier 4008)
AGS 2: 1 *Scott* with 1 hel landing platform; 1 *Magpie*

UNINHABITED MARITIME PLATFORMS
USV • MW 8: **Medium** 1 *Hebe* (*Hussar* mod); **Small** 7: 2 *Apollo*; 5 *Hussar*

UNINHABITED MARITIME SYSTEMS • UUV
DATA *Gavia*; *Iver-4 580*; REMUS 100/600; *Slocum* G3 *Glider*
MW *Seafox* C/I
UTL AUV62-AT

Royal Fleet Auxiliary

Support and miscellaneous vessels are mostly crewed and maintained by the Royal Fleet Auxiliary (RFA), a civilian fleet owned by the UK MoD, which has approximately 1,900 personnel with type comd under Fleet Commander

MINE WARFARE • MINE COUNTERMEASURES 1
MCCS 1 *Stirling Castle*

AMPHIBIOUS • PRINCIPAL AMPHIBIOUS SHIPS 3:
LSD 3 *Bay* (capacity 4 LCU; 2 LCVP; 24 *Challenger* 2 MBT; 350 troops)

LOGISTICS AND SUPPORT 10
AORH 4 *Tide* (capacity 1 AW159 *Wildcat*/AW101 *Merlin* hel); (1 *Fort Victoria* with 2 Mk 15 *Phalanx* Block 1B CIWS in reserve)
AGE 1 *Proteus*
AG 1 *Argus* with 1 Mk 15 *Phalanx* Block 1B CIWS (primary casualty-receiving ship with secondary aviation trg ship role)
AKR 4 *Point* (not RFA manned)

Naval Aviation (Fleet Air Arm) 4,900
FORCES BY ROLE
FIGHTER/GROUND ATTACK
1 sqn with F-35B *Lightning* II (form rg)
ANTI-SUBMARINE WARFARE
3 sqn with AW101 ASW *Merlin* HM2
2 sqn with AW159 *Wildcat* HMA2
TRAINING
1 sqn with Beech 350ER *King Air*
1 sqn with G-115

EQUIPMENT BY TYPE
AIRCRAFT
TPT • Light 4 Beech 350ER *King Air* (*Avenger*)
TRG 5 G-115
HELICOPTERS
ASW 58: 28 AW159 *Wildcat* HMA2; 30 AW101 ASW *Merlin* HM2
AIR-LAUNCHED MISSILES • ASM *Martlet*

Royal Marines 6,600
FORCES BY ROLE
MANOEUVRE
Amphibious
1 (3rd Cdo) mne bde (2 mne bn; 2 sp In; 1 amph gp; 1 amph aslt sqn; 1 (army) arty regt; 1 (army) engr regt; 1 ISR gp (1 EW sqn; 1 cbt spt sqn; 1 sigs sqn; 1 log sqn), 1 log regt)
2 amph sqn

EQUIPMENT BY TYPE
ARMOURED FIGHTING VEHICLES
APC (T) 99 BvS-10 Mk2 *Viking* (incl 15 cabs with 81mm mor)
ANTI-TANK/ANTI-INFRASTRUCTURE
MSL • MANPATS FGM-148 *Javelin*
ARTILLERY 39
TOWED 105mm 12 L118 Light Gun
MOR 81mm 27 L16A1
PATROL AND COASTAL COMBATANTS • PB 2 *Island*
AMPHIBIOUS • LANDING CRAFT 26
LCU 10 LCU Mk10 (capacity 4 *Viking* APC or 120 troops)
LCVP 16 LCVP Mk5B (capacity 35 troops)
AIR DEFENCE • SAM • Point-defence *Starstreak*

Royal Air Force 30,500
FORCES BY ROLE
FIGHTER
 2 sqn with *Typhoon* FGR4/T3
FIGHTER/GROUND ATTACK
 1 sqn with F-35B *Lightning* II
 4 sqn with *Typhoon* FGR4/T3 (incl one joint QTR-UK sqn)
 1 sqn with *Typhoon* FGR4/T3 (aggressor)
ANTI-SUBMARINE WARFARE
 2 sqn with P-8A *Poseidon* (MRA Mk1)
ISR
 1 sqn with *Shadow* R1
ELINT
 1 sqn with RC-135W *Rivet Joint*
SEARCH & RESCUE
 1 sqn with SA330 *Puma* HC2
TANKER/TRANSPORT
 2 sqn with A330 MRTT *Voyager* KC2/3
TRANSPORT
 2 sqn with A400M *Atlas*
 1 sqn with C-17A *Globemaster*
 1 (VIP) sqn with *Falcon* 900LX (*Envoy* IV CC Mk1)
TRAINING
 1 OCU sqn with A400M *Atlas*; C-17A *Globemaster*
 1 OCU sqn with F-35B *Lightning* II
 1 OCU sqn with *Typhoon* FGR4/T3
 1 OCU sqn with RC-135W *Rivet Joint*
 1 sqn with EMB-500 *Phenom* 100
 2 sqn with *Hawk* T2
 1 sqn with T-6C *Texan* II
 2 sqn with G-115E *Tutor*
COMBAT/ISR UAV
 1 sqn with MQ-9A *Reaper*
EQUIPMENT BY TYPE
AIRCRAFT 210 combat capable
 FGA 159: 32 F-35B *Lightning* II; 121 *Typhoon* FGR4; 6 *Typhoon* T3; (10 *Typhoon* FGR4 in store)
 ASW 9 P-8A *Poseidon* (MRA Mk1)
 ISR 8 *Shadow* R1
 ELINT 3 RC-135W *Rivet Joint*
 AEW&C 3 E-3D *Sentry*
 TKR/TPT 10: 3 A330 MRTT *Voyager* KC2 (incl 1 VIP); 7 A330 MRTT *Voyager* KC3
 TPT 32: **Heavy** 30: 22 A400M *Atlas*; 8 C-17A *Globemaster*; **PAX** 2 *Falcon* 900LX (*Envoy* IV CC Mk1)
 TRG 147: 5 EMB-500 *Phenom* 100; 86 G-115E *Tutor*; 28 *Hawk* T2*; 14 *Hawk* T1* (Red Arrows) (ε53 more in store); 14 T-6C *Texan* II
HELICOPTERS
 TPT • Medium 3 SA330 *Puma* HC2
UNINHABITED AERIAL VEHICLES
 CISR • Heavy 11: 10 MQ-9A *Reaper*; 1 MQ-9B *Sky Guardian* (*Protector* RG Mk1)
AIR-LAUNCHED MISSILES
 AAM • IR AIM-9L/L(I) *Sidewinder*; **IIR** ASRAAM; **ARH** AIM-120C-5 AMRAAM; *Meteor*
 ASM AGM-114 *Hellfire*; *Brimstone*; *Brimstone* II; Dual-Mode *Brimstone*
 LACM *Storm Shadow*
BOMBS
 Laser-guided GBU-10 *Paveway* II; GBU-24 *Paveway* III
 Laser & INS/GPS-guided Enhanced *Paveway* II/III; *Paveway* IV

Royal Air Force Regiment
FORCES BY ROLE
MANOEUVRE
 Other
 6 sy sqn

No. 1 Flying Training School (Tri-Service Helicopter Training)
FORCES BY ROLE
TRAINING
 1 hel sqn with H135 (*Juno* HT1); H145 (*Jupiter*)
 3 hel sqn with H135 (*Juno* HT1)
EQUIPMENT BY TYPE
HELICOPTERS
 MRH 7 H145 (*Jupiter*)
 TPT • Light 31: 2 AW109E; 29 H135 (*Juno* HT1)

Volunteer Reserve Air Forces
(Royal Auxiliary Air Force/RAF Reserve)
MANOEUVRE
 Other
 5 sy sqn
COMBAT SUPPORT
 2 int sqn
COMBAT SERVICE SUPPORT
 1 med sqn
 1 (air movements) sqn
 1 (HQ augmentation) sqn
 1 (C-130 Reserve Aircrew) flt

UK Special Forces
Includes Royal Navy, Army and RAF units
FORCES BY ROLE
SPECIAL FORCES
 1 (SAS) SF regt
 1 (SBS) SF regt
 1 (Special Reconnaissance) SF regt
 1 SF BG (based on 1 para bn)
AVIATION
 1 wg (includes assets drawn from 3 Army hel sqn, 1 RAF tpt sqn and 1 RAF hel sqn)
COMBAT SUPPORT
 1 sigs regt

Reserve
FORCES BY ROLE
SPECIAL FORCES
  2 (SAS) SF regt
EQUIPMENT BY TYPE
ARMOURED FIGHTING VEHICLES
  AUV 24 *Bushmaster* IMV
ANTI-TANK/ANTI-INFRASTRUCTURE • MSL
  MANPATS FGM-148 *Javelin*; NLAW

DEPLOYMENT

ASCENSION ISLAND: 20
ATLANTIC (NORTH)/CARIBBEAN: 140; 1 PSO; 1 AOEH
ATLANTIC (SOUTH): 40; 1 PSO
BAHRAIN: *Operation Kipion* 1,000; 1 FFGHM; 2 MCO; 2 MHC; 1 LSD; 1 naval facility
BELIZE: BATSUB 12
BRITISH INDIAN OCEAN TERRITORY: 40; 1 navy/marine det
BRUNEI: 1,200; 1 (Gurkha) lt inf bn; 1 jungle trg centre; 1 hel sqn with 3 SA330 *Puma* HC2
CANADA: BATUS 50
CYPRUS: 2,260; 2 inf bn; 1 SAR sqn with 3 SA330 *Puma* HC2; 1 radar (on det); *Operation Shader* 450: 1 FGA sqn with 10 *Typhoon* FGR4; 1 A330 MRTT *Voyager*; 2 A400M *Atlas*; **UN** • UNFICYP (*Operation Tosca*) 251; 2 inf coy
DEMOCRATIC REPUBLIC OF THE CONGO: UN • MONUSCO 3
EGYPT: MFO 2
ESTONIA: NATO • Forward Land Forces (*Operation Cabrit*) 1,000; 1 armd BG; 1 SP arty bty; 1 MRL bty; 1 cbt engr coy
FALKLAND ISLANDS: 1,200: 1 inf coy(+); 1 sigs unit; 1 AD det with CAMM (*Land Ceptor*); 1 PSO; 1 ftr flt with 4 *Typhoon* FGR4; 1 tkr/tpt flt with 1 A330 MRTT *Voyager*; 1 A400M; 1 hel flt with 2 *Chinook*
GERMANY: 185
GIBRALTAR: 480: 1 inf bn(-) (Royal Gibraltar Regt); 1 PSO; 2 PBI
IRAQ: *Operation Shader* 70; 1 inf coy; **NATO •** NATO Mission Iraq 27
KENYA: BATUK 350; 1 trg unit
KOSOVO: NATO • KFOR 41
KUWAIT: *Operation Shader* 50; 1 CISR UAV sqn with 8 MQ-9A *Reaper*
LEBANON: UN • UNIFIL 1
MEDITERRANEAN SEA: 200; 1 DDGHM
NEPAL: 60 (Gurkha trg org)
NIGERIA: 80 (trg team)
OMAN: 90
PACIFIC OCEAN: 60; 2 PSO
POLAND: Army; 1 SAM bty with CAMM (*Land Ceptor*); **NATO •** Forward Land Forces 140; 1 recce sqn
SAUDI ARABIA: *Operation Crossways* 100; 1 SAM bty with FV4333 *Stormer* with *Starstreak*
SOMALIA: 65 (trg team); **UN • UNSOM (***Operation Praiser***) 2; UN •** UNSOS (*Operation Catan*) 7
SOUTH SUDAN: UN • UNMISS (*Operation Vogul*) 4
UNITED ARAB EMIRATES: 100

FOREIGN FORCES

Australia *Operation Kudu* (*Interflex*) 70 (UKR trg)
Canada Air Task Force Prestwick (ATF-P) 55; 3 C-130J-30 *Hercules* (CC-130J); *Operation Unifier* 170 (UKR trg)
Denmark *Operation Interflex* 120 (UKR trg)
Estonia *Operation Interflex* 30 (UKR trg)
Finland *Operation Interflex* 20 (UKR trg)
Kosovo *Operation Interflex* 25 (UKR trg)
Lithuania *Operation Interflex* 15 (UKR trg)
Netherlands *Operation Interflex* 90 (UKR trg)
New Zealand *Operation Tieke* (*Interflex*) 71 (UKR trg)
Norway *Operation Interflex* 150 (UKR trg)
Romania *Operation Interflex* 30 (UKR trg)
Sweden *Operation Interflex* 50 (UKR trg)
United States US European Command: 10,000; 1 FGA wg at RAF Lakenheath (2 FGA sqn with 27 F-15E *Strike Eagle*, 1 FGA sqn with 27 F-35A *Lightning* II; 1 FGA sqn with 14 F-35 *Lightning* II); 1 ISR sqn at RAF Mildenhall with RC-135; 1 tkr wg at RAF Mildenhall with 15 KC-135R/T *Stratotanker*; 1 spec ops gp at RAF Mildenhall (1 sqn with 8 CV-22B *Osprey*; 1 sqn with 8 MC-130J *Commando* II) • **US Strategic Command:** 1 AN/FPS-132 Upgraded Early Warning Radar and 1 *Spacetrack* radar at Fylingdales Moor

Chapter Four
Russia and Eurasia

- Russia has suffered continued attrition to equipment, losing over 4,100 main battle tanks since February 2022. However, stockpiles of Cold-War era armour and artillery have allowed Russia to keep pace with heavy attrition.
- Russian forces continue to suffer high personnel attrition, with Ukrainian figures indicating over 45,000 casualties in November 2024 alone. Recruitment in 2024 was lower than the year before. In late 2024, Russia augmented its forces with troops from North Korea and deployed them to Russia's Kursk region.
- Ukraine has received more advanced Western equipment and started to use its F-16s in combat in 2024. Western restrictions were relaxed, enabling it to use precision-strike capabilities inside Russia.
- Pressures from the war on Russia's defence industry have resulted in closer cooperation with Iran and North Korea. In 2024, Tehran provided *Fateh*-360 short-range ballistic missiles to Russia, while North Korea transferred thousands of containers of supplies and *Hwasong*-11A (KN-23) short-range ballistic missiles.
- States in Central Asia deepened defence ties among themselves and with extra-regional actors. Kazakhstan retains ambitions to expand its defence industry, and there are longstanding political, economic and defence industrial ties with Turkiye and other European countries, South Africa, and Russia.
- Russia's total military expenditure in 2024 reached an estimated RUB13.1 trillion (USD145.9 billion), equivalent to 6.7% of GDP – more than double the average of 2.8% seen in the years immediately prior to large-scale fighting. In purchasing-power-parity terms, total military expenditure in 2024 would come to I$461.6bn (international dollars), which is close to total European defence spending.

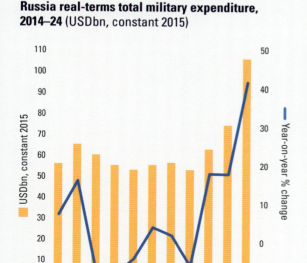

Russia real-terms total military expenditure, 2014–24 (USDbn, constant 2015)

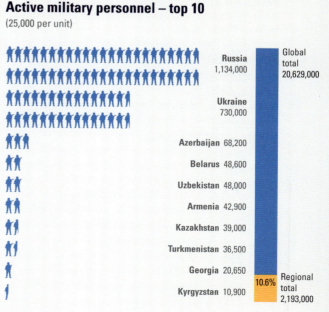

Active military personnel – top 10
(25,000 per unit)

Regional defence policy and economics 154
Arms procurement and defence-industrial trends 165
Armed forces data section 168

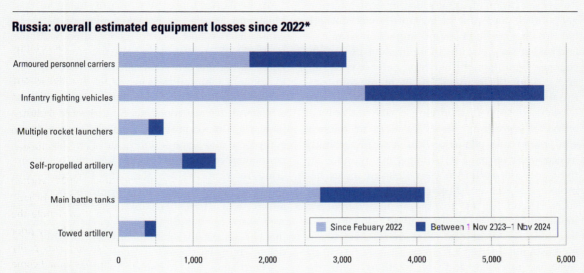

Russia: overall estimated equipment losses since 2022*

*Data as of 1 November 2024
Note: IISS equipment losses are estimated beyond what is reportedly observed. Losses counted here are only non-recoverable losses, excluding damaged and abandoned equipment which is possibly recoverable.

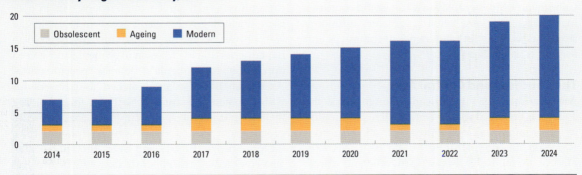

Russia's navy: frigate inventory, 2014–24

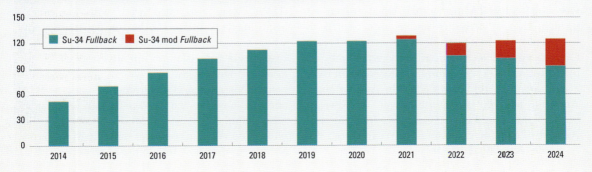

Russia: Su-34 *Fullback* and Su-34 mod *Fullback* inventory, 2014–24

Russia and Eurasia

Russia's invasion of Ukraine continues to affect the geopolitical landscape of the post-Soviet states. It has not only had a profound impact on Ukraine – and on Russia – but it is more broadly prompting changes to military partnerships, defence spending and diplomatic relationships in many countries. Russia remains committed to its effort to subdue Ukraine, despite this proving costly not only in terms of significant losses of Russian military equipment and personnel but also increasingly in economic terms. For Ukraine, maintaining the fight and attempting to eject Russian forces has mobilised significant Western political and military support, and has led to military adaptation and innovation that is being studied globally, but has come at great cost. Elsewhere, Armenia is increasingly estranged from Russia; Georgia remains unsettled and its relations with the European Union are cooling; while further west, Moldova's alignment with Ukraine underscores its commitment to European integration. Russia has allegedly pursued information operations in both Georgia and Moldova. Meanwhile, some countries in Central Asia are seeking greater autonomy from Russia, pursuing independent initiatives and forging relationships.

The Caucasus and Central Asia

Armenia has seen significant change since the 2020 Nagorno-Karabakh war, which culminated in Azerbaijan taking control of all Nagorno-Karabakh in 2023. Despite Russia being a treaty ally of Armenia, Moscow provided no direct political or military support, demonstrating to Yerevan that Russia's security guarantees were ineffective. Armenia has since frozen its participation in activities and events related to the Russia-dominated Collective Security Treaty Organization (CSTO) and, after the 2022 flare-up, opted for an EU civilian monitoring mission over a similar offer from the CSTO. In August 2024, Armenia secured the withdrawal of Russian border guards from Zvartnots International Airport (the country's main airport) and from the Armenia–Azerbaijan border.

Armenia has forged new security relationships. India and France are now key defence partners, while defence and security cooperation with the United States and the EU has also increased. Indeed, India has become a more significant defence supplier to Armenia, with contracts for air defence and rocket artillery agreed in 2020 and the two sides signing a bilateral defence cooperation agreement in 2024. Similarly, France provides Armenia with military equipment and some training, and Paris has sent a permanent military adviser to Yerevan to support army reforms. In July 2024, the EU, under the European Peace Facility (EPF), approved non-lethal aid worth EUR10 million (USD10.9m). For its part, as well as another iteration of the *Eagle Partner* exercise, the US agreed to send an adviser to Armenia's defence ministry to assist with defence reforms.

Azerbaijan has maintained its relations with Russia. In August 2024, President Vladimir Putin made a state visit to Baku, his first trip to Azerbaijan in six years. Azerbaijan continues to pressure Armenia militarily during peace negotiations, which have yet to result in a final agreement; tensions remain over issues including Azerbaijan's access to its exclave of Nakhchivan. Alongside Russian officials, Azerbaijan has criticised the EU Mission in Armenia and voiced opposition to Armenia's defence procurements. Azerbaijan has also strengthened its partnerships with Pakistan and Turkiye, with the three holding their first trilateral summit in July 2024. Defence procurement has focused on equipment from Eastern Europe, Turkiye and Israel, though Pakistan also emerged as a supplier in 2024 with Azerbaijan agreeing to acquire JF-17 *Thunder* combat aircraft. Additional Turkish uninhabited aerial vehicles (UAVs) were also introduced, with the country acquiring Baykar *Akinci* UAVs to add to its inventory, which includes *Bayraktar* TB2s.

Georgia's legislative initiatives, such as the 'foreign agents law' – which imposes severe restrictions on non-governmental organisations and media outlets that receive foreign funding and echoes similar Russian legislation – strained relations with those Western countries that regard this law as a threat to domestic freedoms. In response, the EU froze its EUR30m (USD32.7m) military aid under the EPF framework to Georgia. The economy has grown due to the relocation of Western companies and employees from Russia, which has enabled an increased defence budget. In 2024, Georgia procured air-defence systems from Poland and received armoured vehicles from Turkiye. The parliamentary election in October 2024, which saw the Georgian Dream party remain in power, will likely lead to further friction in relations with Western states. In late November 2024, Georgia announced it was suspending talks towards EU candidacy that began in December 2023. Meanwhile, it was reported that construction continues at Ochamchira, in the breakaway region of Abkhazia, where Russia is building-out the existing naval and shore facilities.

Further west, **Moldova** has maintained its pro-Ukrainian stance and has received a significant number of Ukrainian refugees. The EU opened accession negotiations with Moldova in December 2023 and, in May 2024, Moldova signed a security and defence partnership with the EU, focused on countering hybrid threats, cyber security and training, and capacity-building. Through the EPF, in June 2024, the EU provided Moldova with a EUR50m (USD54.5m) aid package to help modernise military mobility, air surveillance, electronic warfare and logistics. Separately, Moldova signed a defence cooperation agreement with France in March 2024 that included an intent to bolster resilience through training support and intelligence-sharing.

Russia's war in Ukraine continues to shape **Central Asia's** security and economic environment. Some economies have benefitted from Russia's military-spending-fuelled growth and from Russian efforts to use these countries as transit routes for sanctions evasion. This carries risks, however, as Western states seek to escalate their use of anti-evasion measures. There is quiet concern in the region about Russia's longer-term ambitions, as well as more immediate concerns about Moscow's policies regarding labour migrants, which could impact income from remittances.

Intra-regional tensions subsided as Kyrgyzstan and Tajikistan, locked in a border dispute, progressed in the delimitation of their mutual border. Azerbaijan became a new security actor in Central Asia, promoting military and defence cooperation bilaterally and through the Organization of Turkic States. Kazakhstan hosted the *Birlestik*-2024 military exercise in July, which included Azerbaijan and four Central Asian states but no participation by Russia or China. Kazakhstan is an increasingly important partner for the EU: the two sides reached a memorandum of understanding on strategic materials cooperation in 2022, amid growing European concerns about supply-chain security. Astana retains ambitions to expand its defence industry, and there are long-standing political, economic and defence-industrial ties with Turkiye, as well as with South Africa, European states (Kazakhstan has acquired C295s and has contracted for A400M) and, of course, Russia. Russian bilateral security cooperation continues with most Central Asian states, with Russian and Soviet-era military equipment still predominant in regional inventories. In 2024, Moscow reportedly discussed a rearmament programme with Uzbekistan relating to airpower, air defence and land forces while, notwithstanding its defence ties further afield, Kazakhstan continued to receive Russian-origin equipment, reportedly including additional Su-30SM *Flanker* H fighter ground-attack aircraft.

UKRAINE

Throughout 2024, Ukraine's Western partners continued to deliver military support, including for the first time advanced combat aircraft, and lifted some important end-user restrictions. However, the pledged Western military supplies appear insufficient to enable a sustained Ukrainian counter-offensive. The temporary suspension of US arms deliveries gave Russia additional advantages on the battlefield, such as an increased overmatch in artillery. While Ukraine has proved its ability to resist Russia's invasion in the air, land and maritime domains, it has found it difficult to mobilise sufficient troops to keep pace with its casualties.

Ukraine's air force, even with a far smaller number of combat aircraft than Russia's, continued to remain operational. Sukhoi Su-27 *Flanker* B and MiG-29 *Fulcrum* aircraft provided air defence and air-to-surface attack, using glide bombs to achieve greater survivability against surface-to-air missiles by enabling stand-off launches. Both types have also been equipped with the Raytheon AGM-88 High-speed Anti-Radiation Missile for suppression of air defences.

The air force began operations with the Lockheed Martin F-16AM *Fighting Falcon* in the third quarter of 2024, using the type to counter Russia's

Figure 13 Ukraine: selected one-way attack (OWA) uninhabited aerial vehicle (UAV) inventory

At the start of Russia's full-scale invasion of Ukraine, many UAVs in Ukrainian service were Western donations and local production lagged behind demand. However, since 2023, Ukraine's UAV capabilities have markedly grown. Ukraine's inferiority vis-à-vis the Russian Aerospace Forces, its lack of longer-range precision-strike systems, and restrictions on the use of Western-supplied cruise missiles led to a surge in OWA UAV strikes deep into Russian territory. The first strikes relied on converted fixed-wing UAVs sourced from the civilian market. Ukraine continues to use systems converted to OWA UAVs, such as an OWA version of a jet-powered Banshee target drone and an OWA UAV conversion of the A-22 light aircraft. It has employed the latter in some of its longest-range strikes, including on the Alabuga Special Economic Zone where Iranian Shahed 136 OWA UAVs are assembled and produced. Most of its OWA UAV operations now rely on purpose-built systems. These include foreign designs such as the Lord, optimised for low costs and ease of production, and indigenous ones like the AQ 400 Scythe and An-196 Lyutyy, used against petrochemical facilities, industrial plants, arms depots and air bases. Ukraine improves longer-range OWA UAV survivability through jamming-resistant GNSS antennas, careful mission planning to exploit air-defence gaps, and decoy UAVs like the Rubaka.

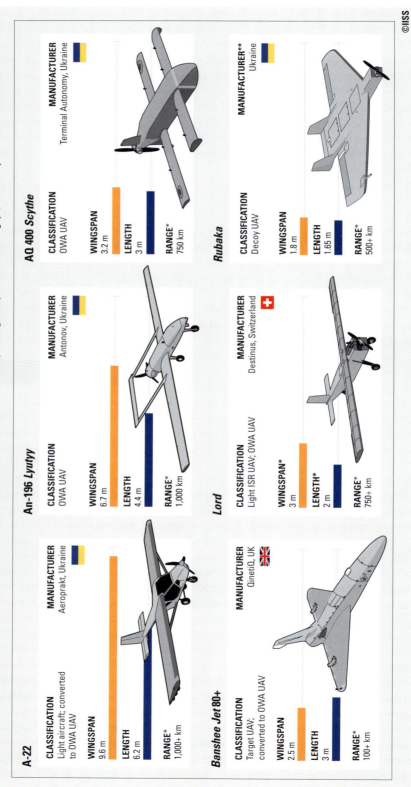

A-22
- CLASSIFICATION: Light aircraft; converted to OWA UAV
- MANUFACTURER: Aeroprakt, Ukraine
- WINGSPAN: 9.6 m
- LENGTH: 6.2 m
- RANGE*: 1,000+ km

An-196 Lyutyy
- CLASSIFICATION: OWA UAV
- MANUFACTURER: Antonov, Ukraine
- WINGSPAN: 6.7 m
- LENGTH: 4.4 m
- RANGE*: 1,000 km

AQ 400 Scythe
- CLASSIFICATION: OWA UAV
- MANUFACTURER: Terminal Autonomy, Ukraine
- WINGSPAN: 3.2 m
- LENGTH: 3 m
- RANGE*: 750 km

Banshee Jet 80+
- CLASSIFICATION: Target UAV; converted to OWA UAV
- MANUFACTURER: QinetiQ, UK
- WINGSPAN: 2.5 m
- LENGTH: 3 m
- RANGE*: 100+ km

Lord
- CLASSIFICATION: Light ISR UAV, OWA UAV
- MANUFACTURER: Destinus, Switzerland
- WINGSPAN*: 3 m
- LENGTH*: 2 m
- RANGE*: 750+ km

Rubaka
- CLASSIFICATION: Decoy UAV
- MANUFACTURER**: Ukraine
- WINGSPAN: 1.8 m
- LENGTH: 1.65 m
- RANGE*: 500+ km

*Estimated. **Exact manufacturer not confirmed.
Source: IISS, Military Balance+, milbalplus.iiss.org

employment of UAVs and land-attack missiles. The US also approved the provision of the Raytheon AGM-154 Joint Standoff Weapon for Ukraine in September 2024, which will form part of the F-16AM weapons inventory. Ukraine continued to use its small number of Sukhoi Su-24M *Fencer* D ground-attack aircraft in combination with the Franco-British MBDA SCALP EG/*Storm Shadow* land-attack cruise missile, including for the first time against targets inside Russia in November 2024.

Ukraine continued to inflict heavy losses on Russian ground forces. Western officials claimed in October 2024 that the number of Russian troops killed and wounded sometimes exceeded 1,200 a day, with a total of 700,000 casualties since the start of the war. While Russia appears to be able to sustain the manning of its forces, evidence suggests that Ukraine, which generally kept its casualty figures secret, has suffered a serious drain on its personnel – with many ground units under-strength. In a rare announcement in December, President Volodymyr Zelenskyy said that 43,000 Ukrainian soldiers had been killed since February 2022. Changes to Kyiv's military-service laws, such as lowering the conscription age from 27 to 25, have not yet seemed to have had significant effect, and Kyiv has resisted suggestions that it lower the age further.

Ukraine, in its August surprise attack into Russia's Kursk oblast, seized a relatively small salient of territory which, as of late November 2024, Russia had not fully retaken. Kyiv's move, while seizing the initiative and setting out a 'buffer zone' (as described by President Zelenskyy), carried considerable risk, and there remained the possibility of overstretching Ukrainian ground forces. Ukraine's extensive belts of fortifications, minefields, ditches and other obstacles continued to prove effective in countering Russian attempts to gain further large swathes of territory.

The situation in the Black Sea during 2024 fuelled a debate over whether Ukraine, through its innovative combination of attacks using uninhabited surface vessels, missiles and special forces, had inflicted a notable defeat upon Russia's Black Sea Fleet. There was little indication that the Russian fleet was able to regain the naval initiative, instead suffering incremental losses including at least one patrol ship and a further amphibious vessel. Ukraine appears to have deterred the fleet from operating in the western Black Sea, undercutting its ability to mount an effective blockade of Ukraine and negating the advantage it might have enjoyed from its occupation of Crimea. Indeed, Russia continued to re-base its units away from Crimea, further east, and even into the Caspian Sea.

Moscow targeted port infrastructure in and around Odesa and, reportedly, carried out sporadic attacks on a handful of merchant ships trading with Ukraine. Nevertheless, while Russia still carried out threats of a more general campaign against shipping, it appeared somewhat constrained, enabling Ukraine to establish a de facto maritime corridor utilising the territorial waters of Romania, Bulgaria and Turkiye for grain and other shipments. While these have not rebounded to pre-war levels, they have had a significant impact in helping to sustain Ukraine's war economy.

RUSSIA

Russia's war against Ukraine has become its costliest, in blood and treasure, since 1945. It has become the overriding purpose of President Putin's government, which is mobilising every aspect of Russia's society, economy and polity around the war. The Kremlin is calibrating its war effort with domestic and external constraints in mind. It seeks to ensure that the pace and scale of mobilisation neither impose severe strains on domestic stability – and thus call the administration's future into question – nor harden the West's commitment to Ukraine – and thus reverse the gradual loss of resolve that Putin expects.

Yet the Kremlin appears concerned about how deep popular support for the war runs, and understands that most Russians want to remain untouched by the conflict. Throughout 2024 the Kremlin remained determined to avoid a second 'partial mobilisation' (after the first one in September 2022) that would compel some citizens to fight, and has dramatically raised military pay to attract more recruits. It downplayed Ukraine's August 2024 incursion into Russian territory, rather than using this to rally the population around the flag. Nonetheless, Russia has so far been able to replenish its troop supply. In September 2024, Putin announced plans to increase the armed forces' establishment strength to 1.5m active service members. Western sanctions compound these problems. In December 2023, the US Department of the Treasury began imposing secondary sanctions on Russia, targeting any financial institution in the world, not only US ones, that conduct business with certain Russian entities. These restrictions grew more severe in June 2024. But the difficulties that a major war and severe sanctions impose are currently chronic and cumulative, not acute and crisis-inducing. Russia can still bear the overall costs of war, but what is less clear is whether the economy will face bottlenecks that lead to critical shortages of militarily important outputs.

The war has also driven shifts in elite politics. In May, Andrei Belousov replaced Sergei Shoigu as defence minister. Analysts saw Belousov's appointment as reflecting growing concern about the economic efficiency of the war effort. Shoigu, who had been minister since 2012, became secretary of the Security Council, replacing Putin's close ally, the hardline Nikolai Patrushev. A purge of Shoigu's old team at the Ministry of Defence (MoD) followed, with a dozen senior officials arrested on corruption charges between April and August 2024. Chief of the General Staff Valery Gerasimov, who, like Shoigu, is closely linked to Russia's battlefield performance, remains in place.

Concerns about military performance may also help explain why the Federal Security Service (FSB), and not the army, was assigned the lead role in the 'counter-terrorist operation' mounted in response to Ukraine's incursion into Russia. Meanwhile, Russia's focus on the war has diverted attention from domestic security threats. On 22 March 2024, Islamic State Khorasan Province (ISIS–K) conducted a terrorist attack in central Moscow that killed 145 people – the worst such attack in Russia since 2002. Three months later, further attacks in the southern region of Dagestan killed 22 people.

President Putin's objective seems to be not only to wear down Ukraine militarily but also to outlast the West politically, and to avoid impelling the West to escalate its involvement to a scale that jeopardises Russia's aims. He has relied heavily on threats of nuclear weapons use in Ukraine to do so, mostly to no avail. But in September 2024, he stepped up these warnings in an effort to deter the West from authorising Ukraine's use of its precision-strike missiles against targets in Russia. On 25 September, he announced that Russia's nuclear doctrine had been updated. Russia would now consider an attack by a non-nuclear state that was backed by a nuclear one to be a 'joint attack'. Russia would also consider using nuclear weapons in response to 'a massive launch of air and space attack weapons', a category he said included UAVs and cruise missiles. When, in November, some Western states relaxed end-user restrictions on high-precision systems supplied to Ukraine, enabling Ukrainian strikes inside Russia, Russia attacked the Ukrainian city of Dnipro using what appeared to be an intermediate-range ballistic missile, employing multiple warheads – possibly without charges. Putin said this was a new system called *Oreshnik*, though Western analysts indicated it was likely a modified version of the developmental *Rubezh* (RS-SS-X-28) system.

Ground forces

Since February 2022, Russia's ground forces have been expanding the number of manoeuvre and support units, and in 2024, the Kremlin recreated the Moscow and Leningrad Military Districts, indicating that it still considers mass a priority.

Although Ukraine has been innovative in its battlefield adaptations, especially with fielding first-person-view UAVs, Russia has also adapted. Russia now has improved intelligence, surveillance and reconnaissance (ISR) capabilities for artillery spotting and targeting Ukraine's rear. Its ground forces also retain the ability to concentrate enough forces in Ukraine's weakest areas and have been able to achieve tactical gains, albeit with high losses.

Stockpiles of Cold War-era armour and artillery have allowed Russia to keep pace with heavy attrition throughout its invasion. The remaining equipment in store could allow Russia to sustain the current rate of loss in the short term, but a significant number of these platforms would require deep and costly refurbishment. In that case, Russia's defence-industrial sector may struggle to deliver as much refurbished equipment as it did in 2023–24 as it clashes with Moscow's plans to create additional units. Such a shortfall would almost certainly result in many units being below established strength.

Nonetheless, even if Russia effectively exhausts its stockpile of useful platforms, it would likely still be able to reconstitute through a rearmament plan over the medium to long term, though rearmament would rely on imports or a significant expansion of domestic industrial capacity in order to increase the output of newly built platforms. Production of new-build platforms has increased, but Russia still depends on its equipment stocks and support from foreign partners.

Due to a relative scarcity of armoured fighting vehicles, it is likely that personnel losses will continue to rise if Russia maintains in 2025 the same offensive posture as in 2024. Moscow has utilised existing equipment to augment its forces in an improvised and supplementary fashion, such as ad hoc additional armour and screening adaptations to improve protection against Ukrainian UAVs, although this comes at the expense of speed and situational awareness. Armour shortages may force Russia to become even more reliant on infantry-based assaults and other stopgap capabilities.

Russia was able to recruit enough to offset its heavy losses and expand its forces in 2023. Recruitment numbers for 2024 were lower, ranging from 25,000 to 30,000 per month from January to June, than the year before. Enlistment bonuses have, so far, enabled Moscow to find enough replacement personnel. Ensuring that there are enough personnel for Russia's ambitious force-expansion plans, without significant and costly changes to recruitment and retention, will be a challenge. The average age of most personnel now in the Russian Ground Forces, Naval Infantry and Airborne Forces is reported to be above 37. It is uncertain if current recruitment targets can be achieved without further expensive payouts, taking into consideration also the general labour market. The training period for most recruits lies somewhere between one to six months, which does not substantially increase the survivability of the individual soldier, taking into consideration also how recruits have been deployed in battle. But for all this, Moscow still needed more, a need which was met also by October with the deployment to Russia's Kursk region of up to 10,000 North Korean troops, with much speculation over what Russia may be offering North Korea in return, perhaps in the form of technical military assistance.

Russian navy
Russia's Black Sea Fleet continued to suffer significant setbacks at the hands of Ukraine, which employed a combination of innovative and audacious tactics and large-scale use of uncrewed vessels and Western-supplied cruise missiles. Ukraine forced the fleet to be increasingly on the defensive and made it withdraw further to the east, reducing its room for manoeuvre, restricting its ability to blockade Ukraine, and even inhibiting its ability to mount stand-off land-attack cruise-missile strikes. Among the Black Sea Fleet's most significant losses have been those to its amphibious shipping, in part perhaps because of Ukrainian targeting as well as the fact that these vessels have been relatively easy prey. The losses have made Russian amphibious operations even more challenging and have also hit Moscow's ability to support its own land operations from the sea. The extent to which the leadership, training and equipment shortfalls of the Black Sea Fleet are mirrored in the rest of the navy remains uncertain.

Part of the fallout from the Black Sea Fleet's losses was that they drove a shake-up in March 2024 of the Russian navy leadership, including the replacement of both the chief of the navy and the Black Sea Fleet commander. Restoring both the reputation and perceived effectiveness of the navy will likely be one of their priorities, including as a symbol of Russia's continuing great-power status. This might explain the high-profile deployment in June 2024 of the *Yasen*-M submarine *Kazan* and the Project 22350 frigate *Admiral Gorshkov* to Cuba, followed a month later by another flotilla from the Russian Baltic Fleet. It may also account for the large-scale *Okean 2024* exercise in the Pacific and Arctic oceans and the Mediterranean, Baltic and Caspian seas, which also involved Chinese navy units (and harked back to the Soviet navy's pan-oceanic *Okean* exercises in the latter period of the Cold War). However, the late-2024 fall of Russia's Syrian partner Bashar al-Assad, and the resulting uncertainty over the future of Russia's Mediterranean Sea naval base at Tartus, will have dented these hopes.

The navy has made efforts to be seen still out on the world's oceans and to exercise with partners like China and Iran. As part of these activities, a Russian Pacific Fleet flotilla consisting of a cruiser and destroyer undertook a seven-month deployment to the Indian Ocean, the Middle East and the Mediterranean Sea. These moves will be key to maintaining the value of the navy to the Kremlin as a tool of both deterrence and strategic signalling and as a symbol of its major-power status. Whether it will be able to maintain its pipeline of new additions to the fleet in the long term will depend on the pressures on the Russian defence-industrial base as it seeks to recapitalise its land forces. That said, the navy did receive capability enhancements in 2024, including a fourth *Borey*-A (Project 955A) nuclear-powered ballistic-missile submarine, a third *Yasen*-M (Project 08851) nuclear-powered guided-missile submarine, and a third Project 22350 (*Gorshkov*) guided-missile frigate.

Aerospace forces

Symptomatic of the Russian air force's lacklustre performance in Ukraine was the deliberate friendly shoot-down in October 2024 of a Sukhoi S-70 uninhabited combat aerial vehicle (UCAV) prototype. The fourth S-70 was apparently being tested in a combat environment when the air force was forced to use a crewed combat aircraft to destroy the UCAV, presumably due to a technical problem with it.

The war in Ukraine continues to expose shortcomings in the air force at the equipment and operational levels, failings perhaps overlooked or not exposed during Moscow's intervention in Syria. The air force has also suffered aircrew and aircraft losses, with fixed-wing combat fleets suffering up to 20% attrition so far throughout the campaign in Ukraine. As of November 2024, the air force had lost at least 31 Sukhoi Su-34 *Fullback* fighter ground-attack aircraft out of a pre-war strength of 124 aircraft. Most of these, but not all, have been made up through the delivery of an estimated 27 Su-34 NVO aircraft.

During 2023, the air force made increasing use of low-cost glide bombs with comparatively crude kits for the FAB family of bombs as well as the UMPB D-30SN glide munition. Open-source imagery suggests that the Su-34 is the primary delivery platform for this class of weapon. The stand-off range also allows the Su-34 to be flown outside the range of short-to-medium-range ground-based air defences.

Air-launched cruise-missile attacks continued but only sporadically, suggesting that the air force has to rebuild stocks of the Raduga Kh-101 (RS-AS-23A *Kodiak*) between attacks. Whether the service has been forced to draw on any 'reserve' holding of these missiles in case of a full-scale war with NATO is unknown. Cruise-missile attacks were supported by a far greater number of *Geran*-2 (*Shahed* 136) one-way-attack UAVs. The air force also employed some of the Raduga Kh-69, a smaller air-launched cruise missile.

Underlying the air force's poor performance is a lack of both doctrinal support for, and operational experience of, integrated offensive combat air operations. The service appeared either unable to, or not expecting to, need to plan and sustain an integrated offensive operation against Ukraine's air force and ground forces. While there has long been recognition at the requirements-level of the absence of the capabilities needed to prosecute such a campaign, development programmes and procurements have been unable to adequately address this. Multiple levels of air-force ISR, for example, have been found wanting. Available platforms are generally ageing with inadequate numbers, while intended replacement programmes have been delayed and often reduced in scope.

Two decades after the air force set a requirement for a new multi-role fighter, Sukhoi's Su-57 *Felon* began to enter initial service in 2023. Efforts are being made to increase the currently-single-figure rate of production. Other air-force projects could fare less well: bomber and medium and heavy transport aircraft programmes lag considerably behind their ambitious schedules.

DEFENCE ECONOMICS

Russia's defence spending continued to rise in 2024, with increases set to continue in 2025, albeit at a slower rate. But even with this slowdown in growth, spending increases will further raise an already elevated top line which, in real terms, has doubled from 2014 when Russia initially invaded Crimea.

The true extent of the national defence burden, however, is becoming increasingly difficult to quantify as the costs of war are increasingly placed on regions, corporations and families across Russia. For example, sign-up inducements – classed as 'social payments' – are funded from outside the defence budget, as are compensation payments to the families of those killed or seriously wounded in action. Additionally, Russia's regional governments and private enterprises are also increasingly required to sponsor those travelling to and from the battlefield, while families are also expected to help supply basic equipment and other provisions to those drafted. Such dynamics will only increase as a September 2024 decree set a higher establishment-strength target for Russia's military, up to nearly 2.4m personnel.

Russia's expanding defence spending is also having macroeconomic effects by driving inflation through overstimulating demand, and squeezing social provisions such as education and healthcare. Nonetheless, Russia's economy remains resilient, as non-energy revenues make it possible to increase spending while maintaining a modest budget deficit and the central bank actively manages wider economic risks, allowing elevated levels of defence spending to continue. To further support the war effort, Putin has introduced additional reforms to the national defence industry, mainly focusing on priority areas such as munitions production and expanding the country's defence-industrial base across the wider economy.

Defence spending

Accurately estimating Russian defence spending became increasingly difficult after February 2022, when Russian authorities began restricting all information related to defence issues. Detailed budget information is now unavailable, although comparing available information with Russia's historical spending patterns still enables analysis of broad trends. Russia's 2024 budget allocated RUB10.4 trillion (USD115.6 billion) to 'national defence', the budget chapter that supports the MoD, equal to 5.29% of GDP. The final core budget figure for the year was forecast to be RUB10.8trn (USD120.3bn) or 5.51% of GDP. This is almost double the average of 2.8% seen in the years immediately prior to large-scale fighting. In terms of total military expenditure, spending in 2024 will likely reach RUB13.1trn (USD145.9bn), equivalent to 6.68% of GDP. In purchasing-power-parity terms, total military expenditure in 2024 would come to I$461.6bn (international dollars) which is close to total European defence spending.

Despite the already elevated levels of spending, further increases are expected in 2025. According to the 2025 draft budget, 'national defence' will receive RUB13.2trn (USD139.3bn), pushing the defence burden up to 6.34% of GDP. As a result, total military expenditure will likely rise to

Table 5 **Russia: military expenditure, 2018–25**, trillion roubles (current prices)

Year	'National Defence' RUB (trn)	'National Defence' % of GDP	Total military expenditure[1] RUB (trn)	Total military expenditure[1] % of GDP	% change real terms
2025[DB]	13.200	6.34	ε15.600	7.50	+13.73
2024[F]	ε10.800	5.51	ε13.100	6.68	+41.89
2024[B]	10.378	5.29	ε12.368	6.31	+33.96
2023[B]	6.407	3.72	ε8.400	4.88	+18.06
2022	5.110	3.29	6.648	4.28	+18.21
2021	3.573	2.63	4.859	3.58	-5.91
2020	3.169	2.94	4.335	4.03	+2.07
2019	2.997	2.73	4.209	3.84	+4.23
2018	2.827	2.72	3.911	3.77	-4.01

DB = Draft Budget. B = Budget. F = Forecast.
[1]According to NATO definition.
Source: IISS analysis based on GDP and deflator data from IMF World Economic Outlook, October 2024

RUB15.6trn (USD164.6bn) or 7.50% of GDP and 39% of total federal budget spending. Despite the continued increases, this nonetheless suggests that, in real terms, the rate of growth is moderating as the war continues.

Spreading the load

As the war continues, it is increasingly apparent that the federal budget's 'national defence' chapter is no longer an adequate basis for capturing all military-related activities. The chapter covers the basic pay of service people and civilians employed by the MoD, alongside other provisions such as equipment and operational spending. However, the one-off payments to newly mobilised and contracted troops – which are both rapidly growing in number and becoming increasingly large – are classed as 'social payments' and are thus covered by the 'social policy' budget chapter. So too are compensation payments to the families of those killed or seriously wounded in the war. In addition, the regions, republics and other 'subjects of the federation' all make their own payments to those embarking on military service or provide compensation to families of those killed or wounded. They also offer bonuses for combat-related achievements, such as disabling or capturing enemy tanks or being deployed to the front for extended periods. Large companies contribute as well to the cost of personal equipment and other support for troops, while the emergence of a new 'popular' defence industry further disperses

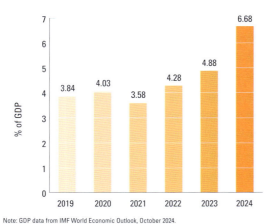

▲ Figure 14 **Russia: defence expenditure** as % of GDP

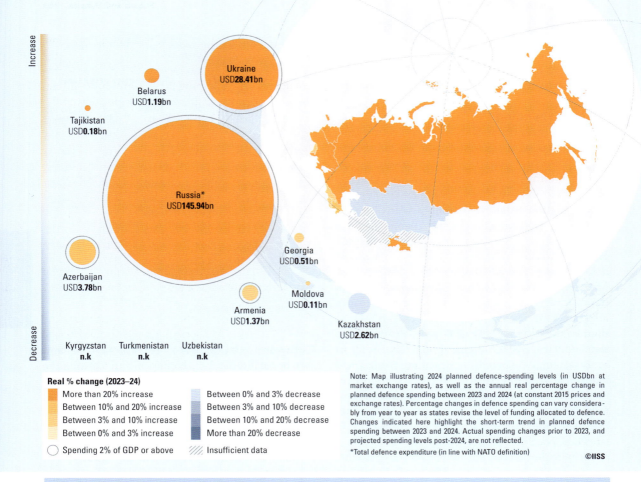

▲ Map 2 **Russia and Eurasia: regional defence spending** (USDbn, %ch yoy)

the national defence burden. Lastly, the families of newly mobilised troops are expected to make up shortfalls in kit and provisions, with countless reports emerging of new conscripts receiving poor-quality training and provisions. Although some elements of these costs – for example, the rates of payment offered by different regional governments – can be reliably established, the total amount of money paid out from outside the central budget structure is impossible to ascertain. However, these hidden sums must be large and can be expected to grow alongside increasing mobilisation and growing numbers of casualties.

Despite the silently increasing burden, the Russian economy remains resilient, growing throughout 2023 and 2024. However, there are signs that the economy is overheating: inflation averaged 7.86% over the course of 2024, while the unemployment rate fell from 3.2% in 2023 to nearly 2.6% in 2024. This has led to acute labour shortages, which in turn has prompted rapidly growing wages and other incomes. As a result, the central bank has repeatedly increased the key interest rate, which reached 21.0% at the end of October, in addition to maintaining currency controls and other measures. Moreover, although sanctions reduced earnings from oil and gas exports, the growing economy allowed Moscow to increase non-energy budget revenues, thus permitting the central government to increase spending while maintaining a modest budget deficit into 2024.

Work has been under way for quite a long time on a new state armament programme for the years 2025 to 2034, the existence of which Putin first announced in September 2023. This has been difficult at a time of uncertain economic prospects and lessons to be learnt on military technology priorities from the experience of using weapons in the war. It is not clear when the new programme will be approved. Meanwhile, the annual state defence order continues to guide weapons procurement, though it is clearly frequently amended and updated and its scale and priorities are strictly classified.

Defence industry

Since Russia launched its full-scale invasion of Ukraine, Russia's defence industry has undergone several reforms as the protracted conflict led to unexpected levels of equipment shortages. Major reforms include the creation of the Coordination Council to monitor orders and logistics, the consolidation of state enterprises and the formation of the Tecmash holding company – a specialised holding company of the Rostec state corporation. Subsequent reforms have sought to work within, and refine, these changes. For example, administrative reshuffles are likely aimed at furthering long-standing ambitions of increasing productivity, while also reducing costs and corruption. That said, in 2024, established elements of the country's defence-industrial base also underwent further consolidation to boost priority areas such as ammunition production, while ownership changes were required in loss-making areas such as shipbuilding and space launches. The industrial base itself also expanded as many more industries involved themselves in the war effort, including growing elements from civil society. Arms exports, however, continue to suffer as the war diverts equipment to the Ukrainian front, with many key orders delayed or lost as customers find alternative suppliers.

Administrative reshuffle

Following Vladimir Putin beginning his fifth term as president in March 2024, the government enacted several significant personnel changes. The economist Andrei Belousov replaced Sergei Shoigu as defence minister, with Shoigu becoming the chair of the Security Council. Denis Manturov, previously industry minister, was elevated to first deputy prime minister. As industry minister, Manturov was responsible for overseeing the defence industry and appears to have retained overall responsibility for military production in his new role. Manturov was succeeded as industry minister by Anton Alikhanov, former governor of Kaliningrad oblast. A new department for the military-industrial complex was also formed within the presidential administration. This is led by Aleksey Dyumin, the former governor of the Tula region and one-time deputy defence minister; while Patrushev, former chair of the Security Council, took up an advisory role in matters concerning the sea and shipbuilding. There were also changes in the composition of the Military-Industrial Commission, with Dyumin being appointed as its deputy chair. These changes appear to have been aimed at increasing the effectiveness of the defence sector in producing weaponry, while also reducing costs and corruption. In parallel, the Coordination Council, formed in late 2022 and chaired by Prime Minister Mikhail Mishustin, continued to meet on a regular basis

Further industrial consolidation

The need to develop and produce artillery systems and munitions remains a top priority for the Russian MoD and, throughout 2023 and 2024, the country significantly increased its volume of munitions for artillery and other weapons used by the ground forces. This was possible because of several organisational changes, including the grouping of many, previously independent, organisations into the Tecmash holding company. The move was designed to better link munitions and artillery production. In addition to improved efficiencies, many Tecmash enterprises were enlarged and re-equipped, and switched to multi-shift work patterns. In parallel, import substitution has reduced import dependencies, in particular with the replacement of cotton-based nitrocellulose by timber-based equivalents; Russia has no shortage of forests.

Other organisational changes focused on loss-making enterprises. For example, management of the United Shipbuilding Corporation (USC) was temporarily transferred for a five-year period to VTB Bank, a Russian majority state-owned bank. This was ostensibly to improve USC's work and financial position after an audit of its enterprises revealed debts of more than RUB1trn (USD11.4bn). This is perhaps unsurprising as long lead times mean that contract prices established with the MoD at the start of a programme are often substantially under the final cost, with the ministry rarely agreeing to price increases. Roscosmos, responsible for the space industry and the production of strategic and other missiles, is also in financial difficulties after losing almost all its foreign customers for space launches and other joint activities. In 2024 it was reported that it had lost income of USD180m since 2022.

Industrial expansion

Russia's civilian enterprises are also involved in the production of components for weapons and munitions, leading to a significant increase in defence-industry employment. According to First Deputy Prime Minister Manturov, interviewed in September 2024, defence-industry employment had reached 3.8m. This includes an additional 500,000 people who joined the industry in 2023, and 100,000 more who joined in the first half of 2024. The shortage of new workers has intensified, leading to efforts to increase efficiencies, with labour productivity reported to have risen by 18% in 2023. Rates of pay have increased significantly, with some companies attracting new skilled workers and engineers by offering cheap housing, education and training and, when possible, exemption from military service.

A further development has been the emergence of a new 'popular' defence industry, with the development and production of new weapons initiated at a local level by technology enthusiasts and grassroots organisations committed to improving the equipment of those engaged in fighting. These activities have focused on UAVs, protective equipment for individual soldiers, and weapons. The MoD has increasingly shown interest in the work of this new, non-state, defence sector, monitoring activities through its Main Directorate for Innovative Development. In 2023, the Directorate analysed almost 130 new UAV developments, many from this sector, and purchased five types for use in Ukraine.

Arms exports

Since the start of the war and the imposition of Western sanctions, Russian arms exports have contracted to a quite significant extent, though no information on their volume is made public. Rosoboronexport has reduced its participation in international export events but claims that it still has a large volume of orders. In August 2023, its director general Aleksandr Mikheev claimed that it had a USD50bn backlog of export orders, 75% of which represented deals for aircraft and air-defence equipment, and a year later he gave a similar (though higher) total of USD60bn.

However, it is not at all clear when the arms will be delivered, as customers are being told that meeting the needs of the Russian armed forces is the priority. Despite being a major customer, India has been informed that it is unlikely to receive the last two squadrons of S-400 (RS-SA-21 *Growler*) air-defence systems until late 2026 because of the pressure of current domestic demand. The prioritisation of Russian domestic needs, plus unwillingness to face possible US sanctions, has led some countries to cancel orders. Peru, for example, cancelled in July 2024 its order for Yak-130 *Mitten* trainers. In pursuing new export orders, Russia has sought to make inroads in Africa, but it is unlikely that any very large new deals will be concluded, much less implemented, until the war is over.

Russia also continues to import arms and munitions, above all from Iran and North Korea. Iranian SAIRC *Shahed* 136 one-way-attack UAVs are being manufactured in Russia's Tatarstan region as the *Geran*-2, and North Korea has supplied munitions in breach of United Nations resolutions. China has supplied dual-use items such as electronic components and machine tools. Belarus also supplies dual-use items and military vehicles. However, Russia has not been able to persuade other countries to offer direct military support.

Figure 15 **Russia and Eurasia: arms procurement and defence-industrial trends, 2024**

RUSSIA TRADES QUALITY FOR QUANTITY

Russia is increasingly trading quality for quantity to support its war effort. While Russia appears to have increased production of some of its more advanced systems, such as the T-90M tank, the scale of its equipment losses fighting against Ukraine has meant that, to keep units equipped, it has had to draw down from its stocks of Soviet-era armour. This includes 1950s-vintage BTR-50 armoured personnel carriers in small numbers and 1960s-vintage T-62 tanks, with a resulting drop in frontline-unit quality. In contrast, the much slower rates of supply from Western partners to Ukraine are increasingly comprised of more modern systems. In January 2024, Ukrainian intelligence assessed that Russia had produced approximately two million 152mm and 122mm artillery rounds in 2023. As these munitions are typically less accurate than those being supplied to Ukraine, Russia must fire more rounds to achieve a similar effect. Because of this, Moscow has acquired ammunition stocks from partners such as Belarus, Iran and North Korea. Both the quality of manufacturing conducted in those countries and the conditions in which munitions are stored are unclear, but they are likely to vary. In the air domain, Russian production of modern combat aircraft continues and can seemingly keep pace with losses, which have decreased compared to 2022. However, production of the advanced Su-57 *Felon* multirole fighter aircraft appears to be significantly behind schedule, having produced an estimated 18 aircraft by late 2024 despite originally envisaging 60 by 2020. Furthermore, Russia's production of precision-guided munitions, including 9K720 *Iskander*-M (RS-SS-26 *Stone*) ballistic and Kh-101 (RS-AS-23A *Kodiak*) cruise missiles, has not kept pace with the extent of Russia's use as it has sought to overwhelm Ukrainian air defences. Russia must now stockpile these weapons before carrying out such attacks. Instead, since 2023, Russia has made greater use of bombs fitted with glide kits, which allow its aircraft to remain out of range of Ukrainian air defences.

RUSSIAN ACQUISITION OF COMPONENTS THROUGH THIRD COUNTRIES

Western states were quick to impose sanctions limiting or halting the supply of components to Russia following its full-scale invasion of Ukraine. Russia was equally quick to adapt. Since 2008, Russia's defence industry has relied on machine tools and electronics imported from US and European firms to support the country's modernisation efforts. The attempts to halt this trade since 2022, therefore, have posed serious problems for Russia's war effort. As well as raiding civilian industry for parts, Russian industry and intelligence services have made a significant effort to acquire Western materials through third countries in the Caucasus and Asia, often through 'cut-out' and 'front' companies created specifically for the purpose. Russian ingenuity in this area descends from Soviet practices. However, Western states, the US in particular, have responded to this by placing pressure – through threatening sanctions – on those countries enabling this practice. As a result, some data suggests that there has been a steep reduction in the supply of critical items from certain countries. However, China remains by far the most significant external supplier of high-priority materials for the Russian defence industry. As Chinese companies produce these items themselves rather than selling on Western-origin goods, the US and others will find this far harder to constrain. Nonetheless, Washington is considering 'secondary sanctions' on Chinese banks that help facilitate this trade

EUROPEAN COMPANIES SETTING UP SHOP IN UKRAINE

A growing number of European defence companies have begun establishing either their own subsidiaries in Ukraine or joint ventures (JVs) with the state-owned Ukrainian Defense Industry (UDI) conglomerate, formerly UkrOboronProm. Among the first to do so was BAE Systems, which established a Ukrainian legal entity in 2023 to explore production of and support for its 105mm L119 Light Gun in Ukraine, and was awarded a contract by the UK government to do the latter in 2024. Germany's Rheinmetall has gone further. Having established a JV with UDI in 2023, the company has opened a maintenance, repair and overhaul (MRO) facility for its equipment in Ukraine, such as the *Marder* infantry fighting vehicle (IFV). Rheinmetall has also been contracted to open an ammunition factory in Ukraine and will begin producing its *Lynx* IFV locally before the end of 2024. Similarly, Thales has signalled its intent to establish a JV in Ukraine to work on electronics, and KNDS has established a Ukrainian subsidiary. A rare example in the aerospace domain includes German uninhabited aerial vehicle (UAV) company Quantum-Systems opening a factory in the country in 2024. A number of factors are driving all this activity. The donation of large amounts of equipment to Ukraine has created a corresponding MRO requirement that is more effectively served closer to the front. European companies also expect Ukrainian defence spending to remain high beyond the current phase of the war, and for their home governments to be willing to fund the acquisition of equipment produced in Ukraine for that country. Furthermore, Ukraine's broader reconstruction ambitions envisage a strong defence industry supported by exports, and Ukrainian companies have growing prowess in uninhabited systems. However, the obvious security concerns and duty of care to staff will make European companies' ambitions to deepen their presences in Ukraine challenging to realise.

Figure 16 — Kazakhstan: defence industry

Following the collapse of the Soviet Union, Kazakhstan's highly integrated defence industry suffered from Russia's and Kazakhstan's low defence spending during the 1990s. As part of the Soviet Union, Kazakh defence companies had strong competencies in rocketry, including the manufacture of rocket casings and propellants for 9K79/-1 *Tochka*/-U (RS-SS-21/B *Scarab*) short-range ballistic missiles (SRBMs) and through the Baikonur Cosmodrome space launch facility. Today, local production of the former has ceased and the latter is leased to Russia until 2050. To address these issues and generate capability, the government established the Kazakhstan Engineering (KE) conglomerate in 2003 to consolidate state-owned industry under one organisation and adapt to market conditions. While this ensured that many companies survived the lean years, most did so by diversifying more or entirely into the commercial sector. Another approach has been establishing joint ventures (JVs) with foreign companies in the late 2000s and early 2010s, which has allowed for the production and assembly of new equipment to complement the maintenance, repair and overhaul (MRO) of Soviet-era equipment still in Kazakhstan's inventory. JVs include those with Airbus (2010) for helicopters and satellites, Turkiye's ASELSAN (2011) for defence electronics and South Africa's Paramount Group (2014) for armoured vehicles. More recently, as part of the 2050 national strategy, Kazakhstan has embarked on a wide-ranging privatisation of state-owned assets to modernise the economy and attract private capital. This has recently extended to the defence sector, with foreign investors sought from Europe (including Turkiye), Israel and the United States. In the uninhabited-systems sector, Kazakhstan Aviation Industry (KAI) has recently concluded agreements with Chinese, Israeli and Turkish companies to manufacture their uninhabited aerial vehicles (UAVs) locally and R&D Center Kazakhstan Engineering has performed flight tests on its *Leyla* and *Shagala* designs.

M = Multinational. *Companies that are part of the KE conglomerate.
Source: IISS, Military Balance+, milbalplus.iiss.org

Selected Kazakhstani defence companies

	Aircraft Repair Plant No. 405	MRO of Soviet/Russian-design helicopters such as Mi-8/17 *Hip* transport helicopters. Formerly KE-owned but privatised in 2016. Assembly of Mi-171E helicopter kits from Russia since 2016.
	Eurocopter Kazakhstan Engineering	Following a 2010 agreement to locally assemble 45 H145 light transport helicopters for Kazakhstan's air force and government agencies, including the Ministry for Emergency Situations, a fifty–fifty joint venture was formed in 2011 by KE and Eurocopter (now Airbus Helicopters).
	Kazakhstan ASELSAN Engineering (KAE)	JV founded in 2011 between KE and ASELSAN. KAE is involved in Kazakhstan's army vehicle upgrades including T-72 main battle tank (MBT) modernisation by Semey Engineering, and produces soldier night-vision and thermal sights.
	Kazakhstan Aviation Industry (KAI)	KAI conducts MRO for a variety of Kazakh aircraft, including Su-27/30 *Flanker* fighter aircraft, Su-25 *Frogfoot* attack aircraft and An-72/74 *Coaler* light transport aircraft. Agreement in 2019 to assemble Elbit Systems *Skylark* I-LEX man-portable UAVs.
	Kazakhstan Gharysh Sapary (KGS)	Established in 2005, KGS has collaborated with Airbus since the late 2000s. This has included the establishment of the Ghalam joint venture in 2010 and the launching of the KazEOSat-1 and KazEOSat-2 observation and monitoring satellites in 2014. While provided by Airbus, the satellites are operated by KGS.
	Kazakhstan Paramount Engineering (KPE)	Joint venture formed in 2014 by KE and Paramount Group to develop and manufacture armoured vehicles. The *Barys* series of wheeled armoured personnel carriers (APCs), based on Paramount's *Mbombe* series, was unveiled in 2016 at KADEX. Despite trials, the vehicle has yet to enter service. Kazakhstan signed an MoU with KPE in 2017 for the supply of up to 274 *Arlan* protected patrol vehicles based on Paramount's *Marauder* design. 170 delivered as of mid-2023 to Kazakhstan's army and other services. A 2015 agreement with Jordan's King Abdullah Design and Development Bureau (KADDB; now the Jordan Design and Development Bureau, or JODDB) for 50 *Arlans* does not seem to have progressed further. Indigenously designed *Alan*-2, unveiled in 2022, is currently in trials with the Ministry for Emergency Situations and the Ministry of Defence.
	Petropavlovsk Plant of Heavy Machine Building (PZTM)	Having produced SRBMs during the Cold War, PZTM now focuses on the oil and gas and railway sectors. In the late 2000s, PZTM built *Naiza* multiple rocket launchers in cooperation with Israeli companies although the effort was reportedly unsuccessful. A modernised version of the system was displayed in 2016, but the design does not appear to have progressed further. PZTM has worked on BM-21 *Grad* modernisation, in cooperation with Russia's Motovilikha Plants, since 2016. PZTM displayed locally assembled Chinese UAVs in 2023.
	Semey Engineering	MRO and upgrade of Kazakh army Soviet-era vehicles, such as T-72 MBTs. EMP-2 infantry fighting vehicles and BTR-70/80 APCs, in cooperation with Russian and Turkish industry.
	Special Design Bureau (SKTB) Granit	Modernisation of S-125 *Pechora* (RS-SA-3 *Goa*) surface-to-air missile (SAM) system in 2021, in collaboration with Belarusian company Tetraedr, as well as MRO of S-300PS (RS-SA-10B *Grumble*) SAM system. Fifty–fifty joint venture with Thales established in 2009, plus 2014 MoU to produce Ground Master 400 radars (called *Nur* locally). However, company is now in the process of being liquidated.
	Steel Manufacturing	Established in 2016 to manufacture small-arms ammunition including 5.45mm and 7.62mm calibres.
	Tynys	Privatised by KE in 2023. Manufactures protective equipment, and parts for aircraft.
	Uralsk Plant Zenit	A variety of patrol craft based on Russian designs built for navy and coastguard since 1990s, including the *Kazakhstan*-class (Project 0250) missile boats in the 2010s. Zenit is currently constructing a multipurpose auxiliary vessel, but the effort is delayed due to supply-chain disruptions caused by sanctions imposed on Russia.

©IISS

Armenia ARM

Armenian Dram AMD		2023	2024	2025
GDP	AMD	9.45trn	10.2trn	11.0trn
	USD	24.1bn	25.3bn	26.6bn
Real GDP Real GDP growth	%	8.3	6.0	4.9
Def bdgt [a]	AMD	501bn	550bn	665bn
	USD	1.28bn	1.37bn	1.60bn

[a] Excludes military pensions

Real-terms defence budget trend (USDm, constant 2015)

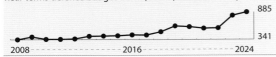

Population	2,976,765					
Age	0–14	15–19	20–24	25–29	30–64	65 plus
Male	9.3%	2.9%	2.8%	3.2%	24.3%	6.4%
Female	8.4%	2.7%	2.6%	3.0%	25.4%	8.9%

Capabilities

The focus of the armed forces is on maintaining territorial integrity. Armenia lost control of the disputed Nagorno-Karabakh territory to Azerbaijan in September 2023, and for much of 2024 the two sides have been attempting to agree a peace treaty covering state borders. The goal of moving the armed forces from a conscript to a contract-based force remains an ambition, though with no clear timetable. The Defence Ministry introduced in 2022 the Motherland Defender initiative with a financial incentive to encourage enlistment on a contract basis. The 2020 National Security Strategy identified Azerbaijan as Armenia's primary security concern, while also highlighting the role it claims Turkiye plays in supporting Azerbaijan's policy aims. Relations with Russia have been strained by the loss of Nagorno-Karabakh, Moscow's lack of intervention and steps Yerevan has taken to improve relations with the West. Armenia remains a member of the CSTO but did not participate in the October 2024 *Rubezh-2024* exercise. Armenia held a joint peacekeeping exercise with the US, dubbed *Eagle Partner*, in July 2024, to the displeasure of Moscow. Armenia is engaged in a NATO Individual Partnership Action Plan. Yerevan has also distanced itself from Russia's war on Ukraine.

ACTIVE 42,900 (Army 40,000 Air/AD Aviation Forces (Joint) 1,100 other Air Defence Forces 1,800) Paramilitary 4,300

Conscript liability 24 months

RESERVE

Some mobilisation reported, possibly 210,000 with military service within 15 years

ORGANISATIONS BY SERVICE

Army ε40,000
FORCES BY ROLE
SPECIAL FORCES
1 SF bde

MANOEUVRE
Mechanised
1 (Special) corps (1 recce bn, 1 tk bn(-), 5 MR regt, 1 sigs bn, 1 maint bn)
1 (2nd) corps (1 recce bn, 1 tk bn, 2 MR regt, 1 lt inf regt, 1 arty bn)
1 (3rd) corps (1 recce bn, 1 tk bn, 5 MR regt, 1 arty bn, 1 MRL bn, 1 sigs bn, 1 maint bn)
1 (5th) corps (2 MR regt)
Other
1 indep MR trg bde

COMBAT SUPPORT
1 arty bde
1 MRL bde
1 AT regt
1 AD bde
2 AD regt
2 (radiotech) AD regt
1 engr regt

SURFACE-TO-SURFACE MISSILE
1 SRBM regt

EQUIPMENT BY TYPE
Available estimates should be treated with caution following losses suffered in the fighting since late 2020 in Nagorno-Karabakh

ARMOURED FIGHTING VEHICLES
MBT 109: 3 T-54; 5 T-55; ε100 T-72A/B; 1 T-90A
RECCE 12 BRM-1K (CP)
IFV 140: 100 BMP-1; 25 BMP-1K (CP); 15 BMP-2
APC 171
  APC (T) 20 MT-LB
  APC (W) 151: 21+ *Bastion* APC; 108 BTR-60 (incl variants); 18 BTR-70; 4 BTR-80
AUV *Tigr*

ENGINEERING & MAINTENANCE VEHICLES
AEV MT-LB
ARV BREhM-D; BREM-1

ANTI-TANK/ANTI-INFRASTRUCTURE
MSL • SP 22+: 9 9P148 *Konkurs* (RS-AT-5 *Spandrel*); 13 9P149 *Shturm* (RS-AT-6 *Spiral*); 9K129 *Kornet*-E (RS-AT-14 *Spriggan*)

ARTILLERY 231
SP 37: **122mm** 9 2S1 *Gvozdika*; **152mm** 28 2S3 *Akatsiya*
TOWED 128: **122mm** 60 D-30; **152mm** 62: 26 2A36 *Giatsint*-B; 2 D-1; 34 D-20; **155mm** 6 ATAGS (reported)
MRL 54: **122mm** up to 50 BM-21 *Grad*; **214mm** some *Pinaka* (reported); **273mm** 2 WM-80; **300mm** 2 9A52 *Smerch*
MOR 120mm 12 M120

SURFACE-TO-SURFACE MISSILE LAUNCHERS
SRBM • Conventional 14: 7+ 9K72 *Elbrus* (RS-SS-1C *Scud* B); 3+ 9K79 *Tochka* (RS-SS-21 *Scarab*); 4 9K720 *Iskander*-E

UNINHABITED AERIAL VEHICLES
ISR • Light *Krunk*

AIR DEFENCE
SAM
Medium-range 2K11 *Krug* (RS-SA-4 *Ganef*); S-75 *Dvina* (RS-SA-2 *Guideline*); 9K37M *Buk*-M1 (RS-SA-11 *Gadfly*); *Akash*

Short-range 2K12 *Kub* (RS-SA-6 *Gainful*); S-125 *Pechora* (RS-SA-3 *Goa*); 9K331MKM *Tor*-M2KM

Point-defence 9K33M2 *Osa*-AK (RS-SA-8B *Gecko*); 9K35M *Strela*-10 (RS-SA-13 *Gopher*); 9K310 *Igla*-1 (RS-SA-16 *Gimlet*); 9K38 *Igla* (RS-SA-18 *Grouse*); 9K333 *Verba* (RS-SA-29 *Gizmo*); 9K338 *Igla*-S (RS-SA-24 *Grinch*)

GUNS
SP 23mm ZSU-23-4 *Shilka*
TOWED 23mm ZU-23-2

Air and Air Defence Aviation Forces 1,100
1 Air & AD Joint Command
FORCES BY ROLE
GROUND ATTACK
1 sqn with Su-25/Su-25UBK *Frogfoot*
EQUIPMENT BY TYPE
AIRCRAFT 17 combat capable
FGA 4 Su-30SM *Flanker* H
ATK 13: up to 12 Su-25 *Frogfoot*; 1 Su-25UBK *Frogfoot*
TPT 4: **Heavy** 3 Il-76 *Candid*; **PAX** 1 A319CJ
TRG 13: 4 L-39 *Albatros*; up to 9 Yak-52
HELICOPTERS
ATK 7 Mi-24P *Hind*
ISR 4: 2 Mi-24K *Hind*; 2 Mi-24R *Hind* (cbt spt)
MRH 14: 10 Mi-8MT (cbt spt); 4 Mi-8MTV-5 *Hip*
C2 2 Mi-9 *Hip* G (cbt spt)
TPT • **Light** 7 PZL Mi-2 *Hoplite*
AIR DEFENCE • **SAM** • **Long-range** S-300PT (RS-SA-10 *Grumble*); S-300PS (RS-SA-10B *Grumble*)
AIR-LAUNCHED MISSILES
AAM • **IR** R-73 (RS-AA-11A *Archer*); **SARH** R-27R (RS-AA-10A *Alamo*)

Gendarmerie & Paramilitary 4,300
Police
FORCES BY ROLE
MANOEUVRE
Other
4 paramilitary bn
EQUIPMENT BY TYPE
ARMOURED FIGHTING VEHICLES
RECCE 5 BRM-1K (CP)
IFV 45: 44 BMP-1; 1 BMP-1K (CP)
APC • APC (W) 24 BTR-60/BTR-70/BTR-152
ABCV 5 BMD-1

Border Troops
Ministry of National Security

EQUIPMENT BY TYPE
ARMOURED FIGHTING VEHICLES
RECCE 3 BRM-1K (CP)
IFV 35 BMP-1
APC • APC (W) 23: 5 BTR-60; 18 BTR-70
ABCV 5 BMD-1

DEPLOYMENT
KOSOVO: NATO • KFOR 57
LEBANON: UN • UNIFIL 1

FOREIGN FORCES
Russia 3,000: 1 mil base with (1 MR bde; 74 T-72; 80 BMP-1; 80 BMP-2; 12 2S1; 12 BM-21); 1 ftr sqn with 10 MiG-29 *Fulcrum*; 1 hel sqn with 8 Mi-24P *Hind*; 4 Mi-8AMTSh *Hip*; 4 Mi-8MT *Hip*; 2 SAM bty with S-300V (RS-SA-12 *Gladiator/Giant*); 1 SAM bty with *Buk*-M1-2 (RS-SA-11 *Gadfly*)

Azerbaijan AZE

Azerbaijani New Manat AZN		2023	2024	2025
GDP	AZN	123bn	129bn	131bn
	USD	72.4bn	75.6bn	77.0bn
Real GDP growth	%	1.1	3.2	2.5
Def bdgt	AZN	5.32bn	6.42bn	
	USD	3.13bn	3.78bn	

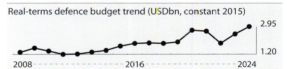
Real-terms defence budget trend (USDbn, constant 2015)

Population	10,650,239					
Age	0–14	15–19	20–24	25–29	30–64	65 plus
Male	11.9%	3.9%	3.2%	3.6%	23.7%	3.8%
Female	10.4%	3.4%	2.7%	3.3%	25.0%	5.2%

Capabilities

The armed forces' main focus is territorial defence. In September 2023, Azerbaijan seized the territory of Nagorno-Karabakh from Armenia. It has since been in discussion with Armenia over a draft peace treaty. While Russia has been the traditional defence partner for Azerbaijan, more recently, it has bought weapons from Israel and forged a strategic relationship with Turkiye. In June 2021, Baku and Ankara signed the Shusha Declaration, which included cooperation if either nation is threatened by a third state. Pakistan has emerged as a defence-industrial partner and a deal to purchase JF-17 combat aircraft was reportedly agreed in late 2024. Azerbaijan maintains a defence relationship with NATO. Readiness varies between units. Azerbaijan has taken part in multilateral exercises and its forces have also trained bilaterally and multilaterally with Georgia and Turkiye, and began joint exercises with Iran in 2024. The armed forces have little expeditionary capability. Defence modernisation and procurement have been intended to replace the ageing inventory of mainly Soviet-era equipment. Recent orders include air-defence and artillery systems and wheeled and tracked armoured vehicles, predominantly of Russian origin. In 2023, Azerbaijan agreed bilateral defence cooperation deals with Uzbekistan and Kazakhstan. The Ministry of Defence Industry, manages and oversees the production of small arms and light weapons. While the country is reliant on external suppliers for major defence equipment, some local defence companies have started to export.

ACTIVE 68,200 (Army 57,800 Navy 1,750 Air 8,650)
Gendarmerie & Paramilitary 15,000

Conscript liability 18 months (12 for graduates)

RESERVE 300,000

Some mobilisation reported; 300,000 with military service within 15 years

ORGANISATIONS BY SERVICE

Army 57,800
FORCES BY ROLE
COMMAND
  5 corps HQ
SPECIAL FORCES
  9 cdo bde
MANOEUVRE
  Mechanised
  4 MR bde
  Light
  13 MR bde
COMBAT SUPPORT
  2 arty bde
  1 MRL bde
  1 engr bde
  1 sigs bde
COMBAT SERVICE SUPPORT
  1 log bde
SURFACE TO SURFACE MISSILE
  1 SRBM bde
EQUIPMENT BY TYPE
ARMOURED FIGHTING VEHICLES
MBT 506: 8 T-55; 405 T-72A/AV/B/SIM2; 93 T-90S
  RECCE 7 BRM-1K
  IFV 311: 60 BMP-1; 91 BMP-2; 46 BMP-3; 7 BTR-80A; 107 BTR-82A
  APC 506
    APC (T) 336 MT-LB
    APC (W) 142: 10 BTR-60; 132 BTR-70
    PPV 28: 14 *Marauder*; 14 *Matador*
  AUV 141: 35 *Cobra*; 106 *SandCat*
  ABCV 20 BMD-1
ENGINEERING & MAINTENANCE VEHICLES
  AEV 10+: 1 IMR-2; 9 IMR-3M; MT-LB
  ARV BREM-L *Brelianka*
  MW 4+: *Bozena*; GW-3 (minelayer); 3 UR-67; 1 UR-77
  VLB 17: 1 MTU-20; 16 MTU-90M

ANTI-TANK/ANTI-INFRASTRUCTURE
  MSL
    SP 53+: 18 9P157-2 *Khrizantema-S* (RS-AT-15 *Springer*); *Cobra* with *Skif*; 26 SandCat with *Spike*-ER; 9 *SandCat* with *Spike*-LR
    MANPATS 9K11 *Malyutka* (RS-AT-3 *Sagger*); 9K111 *Fagot* (RS-AT-4 *Spigot*); 9K111-1 *Konkurs* (RS-AT-5 *Spandrel*); 9K115 *Metis* (RS-AT-7 *Saxhorn*); 9K135 *Kornet* (RS-AT-14 *Spriggan*) (reported); *Spike*-LR
  GUNS • TOWED 85mm some D-44
ARTILLERY 1,240
  SP 159: **122mm** 74 2S1 *Gvozdika*; **152mm** 68: 14 2S3 *Akatsiya*; 18 2S19 *Msta-S*; 36 *Dana*-M1M; **155mm** 5 ATMOS 2000; *Dita*; **203mm** 12 2S7 *Pion*
  TOWED 583: **122mm** 462 D-30; **130mm** 30 M-46; **152mm** 91: 49 2A36 *Giatsint*-B; 42 D-20
  GUN/MOR 120mm 17 2S31 *Vena*
  MRL 273: **107mm** 68 T-107; **122mm** 108: 50 BM-21 *Grad*; 22 BM-21V; 18 RM-70 *Vampir*; 18 T-122; **128mm** 10 RAK-12; **220mm** 17 TOS-1A; **300mm** 36: 30 9A52 *Smerch*; 6 *Polonez*; **302mm** 18 T-300 *Kasirga*; **306mm** 16 IMI *Lynx*
  MOR 208: **120mm** 191: 5 *Cardom*; 14 M-1938 (PM-38); 172 2S12; **SP 120mm** 17 *SandCat* with *Spear*
SURFACE-TO-SURFACE MISSILE LAUNCHERS
  SRBM • Conventional 7: 4 IAI LORA; 3 9K79-1 *Tochka-U* (RS-SS-21B *Scarab*)
UNINHABITED AERIAL VEHICLES
  ISR • Light *Orbiter*-3
AIR DEFENCE
  SAM
    Short-range 9K33-1T *Osa*-1T (RS-SA-8 *Gecko*)
    Point-defence 9K35 *Strela*-10 (RS-SA-13 *Gopher*); 9K32 *Strela* (RS-SA-7 *Grail*)‡; 9K34 *Strela*-3 (RS-SA-14 *Gremlin*); 9K310 *Igla*-1 (RS-SA-16 *Gimlet*); 9K338 *Igla*-S (RS-SA-24 *Grinch*)
  GUNS
    SP 23mm ZSU-23-4
    TOWED 23mm ZU-23-2

Navy 1,750
EQUIPMENT BY TYPE
PATROL AND COASTAL COMBATANTS 13
  CORVETTES • FS 1 *Kusar* (ex-FSU *Petya* II) with 2 RBU 6000 *Smerch* 2 A/S mor, 2 twin 76mm gun
  PSO 1 *Luga* (*Wodnik* 2) (FSU Project 888; additional trg role)
  PCC 4: 3 *Petrushka* (FSU UK-3; additional trg role); 1 *Shelon* (ex-FSU Project 1388M)
  PB 3: 1 *Araz* (ex-TUR AB 25); 1 *Bryza* (ex-FSU Project 722); 1 *Poluchat* (ex-FSU Project 368)
  PBF 4 *Stenka*
MINE WARFARE • MINE COUNTERMEASURES 4
  MHC 4: 2 *Korund* (Project 1258 (*Yevgenya*)); 2 *Yakhont* (FSU *Sonya*)
AMPHIBIOUS 5

LSM 2: 1 Project 770 (FSU *Polnochny* A) (capacity 6 MBT; 180 troops); 1 Project 771 (*Polnochny* B) (capacity 6 MBT; 180 troops)
LCM 3: 2 T-4 (FSU); 1 *Vydra*† (FSU) (capacity either 3 MBT or 200 troops)
LOGISTICS AND SUPPORT • **ATF** 2 *Neftegaz* (Project B-92) (ex-Coast Guard)

Marines
FORCES BY ROLE
MANOEUVRE
  Amphibious
    1 mne bn

Air Force and Air Defence 8,650
FORCES BY ROLE
FIGHTER
1 sqn with MiG-29 *Fulcrum* A; MiG-29UB *Fulcrum* B
GROUND ATTACK
1 regt with Su-25 *Frogfoot*; Su-25UB *Frogfoot* B
TRANSPORT
1 sqn with C-27J Spartan; Il-76TD *Candid*
TRAINING
1 sqn with L-39 *Albatros*
ATTACK/TRANSPORT HELICOPTER
1 regt with Bell 407; Bell 412; Ka-32 *Helix* C; MD-530; Mi-8 *Hip*; Mi-17-1V *Hip*; Mi-24 *Hind*; Mi-35M *Hind*
EQUIPMENT BY TYPE
AIRCRAFT 52 combat capable
  FTR 14: 11 MiG-29 *Fulcrum* A; 3 MiG-29UB *Fulcrum* B
  ATK 38: 33 Su-25 *Frogfoot*; 5 Su-25UB *Frogfoot* B
  TPT 3: **Heavy** 2 Il-76TD *Candid*; **Medium** 1 C-27J *Spartan*
  TRG 34: 24 L-39 *Albatros*; 10 *Super Mushshak*
HELICOPTERS
  ATK 47: 23 Mi-24 *Hind*; 24 Mi-35M *Hind*
  MRH 38: 1 Bell 407; 3 Bell 412; 1 MD-530; 33 Mi-17-1V *Hip*
  TPT • **Medium** 11: 3 Ka-32 *Helix* C; 8 Mi-8 *Hip*
UNINHABITED AERIAL VEHICLES
  CISR 7+: **Heavy** 1+ *Bayraktar Akinci*; **Medium** 6+ *Bayraktar TB2*
  ISR 7+: **Heavy** 3+ *Heron*; **Medium** 4+ *Aerostar*
AIR DEFENCE • **SAM**
  Long-range S-200 *Vega* (RS-SA-5 *Gammon*); S-300PMU2 (RS-SA-20 *Gargoyle*)
  Medium-range 24+: *Barak*-LRAD; *Barak*-MRAD; *Buk*-MB; S-75 *Dvina* (RS-SA-2 *Guideline*); ε24 S-125-2TM *Pechora*-2TM; 9K37M *Buk*-M1 (RS-SA-11 *Gadfly*)
AIR-LAUNCHED MISSILES
  AAM • **IR** R-27T (RS-AA-10B *Alamo*); R-60 (RS-AA-8 *Aphid*); R-73 (RS-AA-11A *Archer*); **SARH** R-27R (RS-AA-10A *Alamo*)
  ASM *Barrier*-V
BOMBS
  Laser-guided MAM-L
  INS/GPS-guided KGK-82; KGK-83

Gendarmerie & Paramilitary ε 5,000
State Border Service ε5,000
Ministry of Internal Affairs
EQUIPMENT BY TYPE
ARMOURED FIGHTING VEHICLES
  IFV 168 BMP-1/BMP-2
  APC • **APC (W)** 19 BTR-60/70/80
  PPV *Titan-S*
ANTI-TANK/ANTI-INFRASTRUCTURE
  RCL 73mm SPG-9
ARTILLERY
  MOR 120mm 2B11
AIR DEFENCE
  GUNS • **TOWED** 23mm ZU-23-2
AIRCRAFT • **TPT** • **Light** 40 An-2 *Colt* (modified for use as decoys)
UNINHABITED AERIAL VEHICLES
  ISR • **Medium** 7+: 4+ *Hermes* 450; 3+ *Hermes* 900
  OWA *Harop*; *Skystriker* (two variants)

Coast Guard
The Coast Guard was established in 2005 as part of the State Border Service
EQUIPMENT BY TYPE
PATROL AND COASTAL COMBATANTS 20
  PCG 6 *Sa'ar* 62 with 1 8-cell *Typhoon* MLS-NLOS lnchr with *Spike* NLOS SSM, 1 hel landing platform
  PBF 9: 1 Project 205 (FSU *Osa* II); 6 *Shaldag* V; 2 Silver Ships 48ft
  PB 5: 3 Baltic 150; 1 *Point* (US); 1 *Grif* (FSU *Zhuk*)
LOGISTICS AND SUPPORT 3
  ATF 3 *Neftegaz* (Project B-92) (also used for patrol duties)

Internal Troops 10,000+
Ministry of Internal Affairs
EQUIPMENT BY TYPE
ARMOURED FIGHTING VEHICLES
  APC • **APC (W)** 7 BTR-60/BTR-70/BTR-80

DEPLOYMENT
SOUTH SUDAN: UN • UNMISS 2

FOREIGN FORCES
Turkiye 170; 1 EOD unit

Belarus BLR

Belarusian Ruble BYN		2023	2024	2025
GDP	BYN	216bn	235bn	256bn
	USD	71.8bn	73.1bn	76.9bn
Real GDP growth	%	3.9	3.6	2.3
Def bdgt	BYN	3.00bn	3.82bn	
	USD	996m	1.19bn	

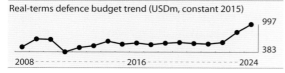
Real-terms defence budget trend (USDm, constant 2015)

Population	9,501,451					
Age	0–14	15–19	20–24	25–29	30–64	65 plus
Male	8.3%	2.7%	2.4%	2.6%	24.6%	6.0%
Female	7.8%	2.5%	2.3%	2.5%	26.4%	11.8%

Capabilities

The armed forces' main task is maintaining territorial integrity, though the army has also been used for internal security tasks. In April 2024, a revised national security concept was approved by parliament, and an updated military doctrine succeeded its 2016 predecessor. The military doctrine was updated to take account of the use of nuclear weapons. Moscow and Minsk have previously discussed locating Russian nuclear warheads in Belarus, with work apparently undertaken on possible storage sites. Moscow said in April 2023 that Belarusian troops were being trained in the use of the 9M723 (RS-SS-26 *Stone*) SRBM, including the use of 'special warheads', in this context referring to tactical nuclear payloads. Warheads located in Belarus would almost certainly remain under Russian control. Belarus is a member of the CSTO and became an SCO member in 2024. Russia remains the country's principal defence partner and has used Belarussian territory to launch attacks on Ukraine. Joint training continued with Russian forces during 2024, including a tactical nuclear weapons exercise. Russian forces also continue to train in Belarus prior to deployment in Ukraine. Minsk's forces remain conscript-based and train regularly with other CSTO partners. The country has no requirement to independently deploy and sustain the armed forces. Russia is Minsk's main defence-equipment supplier. The local defence industry manufactures vehicles, guided weapons and electronic warfare systems, among other equipment.

ACTIVE 48,600 (Army 13,100 Air 10,700 Special Operations Forces 6,300 Joint 18,500) **Gendarmerie & Paramilitary 110,000**

Conscript liability 18 months; 12 months for graduates (alternative service option)

RESERVE 289,500

(Joint 289,500 with mil service within last 5 years)

ORGANISATIONS BY SERVICE

Army 13,100
FORCES BY ROLE

COMMAND
  2 comd HQ (West & North West)

MANOEUVRE
  Mechanised
  4 mech bde

COMBAT SUPPORT
  2 arty bde
  1 engr bde
  1 engr regt
  2 EW bn
  2 sigs regt

COMBAT SERVICE SUPPORT
  2 log regt
  1 tpt bde

EQUIPMENT BY TYPE

ARMOURED FIGHTING VEHICLES
  MBT 497: 477 T-72B; 20 T-72B3 mod
  RECCE 132 BRM-1
  IFV 976: 906 BMP-2; 70 BTR-82A
  APC • APC (T) 58 MT-LB
  AUV *Tigr*; *Volat* V1

ENGINEERING & MAINTENANCE VEHICLES
  AEV BAT-2; IMR-2; MT-LB
  ARV 2+: 2 BREM-K; BREM-1
  VLB 24: 20 MTU-20; 4 MT-55A
  MW UR-77

NBC VEHICLES BRDM-2RKhB; *Cayman* NRBC *Chimera*; RKhM-4; RKhM-K

ANTI-TANK/ANTI-INFRASTRUCTURE • MSL
  SP 160: 75 9P148 *Konkurs* (RS-AT-5 *Spandrel*); 85 9P149 *Shturm* (RS-AT-6 *Spiral*)
  MANPATS 9K111 *Fagot* (RS-AT-4 *Spigot*); 9K111-1 *Konkurs* (RS-AT-5 *Spandrel*); 9K115 *Metis* (RS-AT-7 *Saxhorn*)

ARTILLERY 571
  SP 321: **122mm** 125 2S1 *Gvozdika*; **152mm** 196: 125 2S3 *Akatsiya*; 71 2S5 *Giatsint*-S
  TOWED 152mm 72 2A65 *Msta-B*
  MRL 164: **122mm** 128 BM-21 *Grad*; **220mm** 36 9P140 *Uragan*
  MOR 120mm 14 2S12

AIR DEFENCE
  SAM Point-defence 2K22 *Tunguska* (RS-SA-19 *Grison*)
  GUNS • SP 23mm ZU-23-2 (tch)

Air Force and Air Defence Forces 10,700
FORCES BY ROLE

FIGHTER
  2 sqn with MiG-29/S/UB *Fulcrum* A/C/B
  1 sqn with Su-30SM *Flanker* H

GROUND ATTACK
  2 sqn with L-39 *Albatros**; Su-25K/UBK *Frogfoot* A/B; Yak-130 *Mitten**

TRANSPORT
1 base with An-26 *Curl*; Il-76 *Candid*; Tu-134 *Crusty*

TRAINING
Some sqn with L-39 *Albatros*

ATTACK HELICOPTER
Some sqn with Mi-24 *Hind*; Mi-24K *Hind*; Mi-35M *Hind*

TRANSPORT HELICOPTER
Some (cbt spt) sqn with Mi-8 *Hip*; Mi-8MTV-5 *Hip*

EQUIPMENT BY TYPE
AIRCRAFT 63 combat capable
FTR 18 MiG-29/UB/S *Fulcrum* A/B/C (16 more in store); (21 Su-27/Su-27UB *Flanker* B/C in store)
FGA 4 Su-30SM *Flanker* H
ATK 21 Su-25K/UBK *Frogfoot* A/B
TPT 5: **Heavy** 2 Il-76 *Candid* (+9 civ Il-76 available for mil use); **Light** 3: 2 An-26 *Curl*; 1 Tu-134 *Crusty*
TRG 20: 9 L-39 *Albatros**; 11 Yak-130 *Mitten**

HELICOPTERS
ATK 15: 7 Mi-24 *Hind*; 8 Mi-35M *Hind*
ISR 5 Mi-24K *Hind*
TPT • **Medium** 20: 8 Mi-8 *Hip*; 12 Mi-8MTV-5 *Hip*

UNINHABITED AERIAL VEHICLES
OWA *Geran*-2 (Shahed 136)

AIR-LAUNCHED MISSILES
AAM • **IR** R-60 (RS-AA-8 *Aphid*); R-73 (RS-AA-11A *Archer*) **SARH** R-27R (RS-AA-10 *Alamo* A); R-27ER (RS-AA-10C *Alamo*)
ASM Kh-25 (RS-AS-10 *Karen*); Kh-29 (RS-AS-14 *Kedge*)
ARM Kh-58 (RS-AS-11 *Kilter*) (likely WFU)
BOMBS • **TV-guided** KAB-500KR

Air Defence

AD data from Uzal Baranovichi EW radar
FORCES BY ROLE
AIR DEFENCE
1 bde with S-300PT (RS-SA-10A *Grumble*); S-400 (RS-SA-21 *Growler*); 9K331MK *Tor*-M2K
4 regt with S-300PS (RS-SA-10B *Grumble*)
1 bde with 9K37 *Buk* (RS-SA-11 *Gadfly*); 9K331ME *Tor*-M2E (RS-SA-15 *Gauntlet*)
1 regt with 9K331ME *Tor*-M2E (RS-SA-15 *Gauntlet*)
2 regt with 9K33 *Osa* (RS-SA-8 *Gecko*)

EQUIPMENT BY TYPE
AIR DEFENCE • SAM
Long-range 124: 60 S-300PT (RS-SA-10 *Grumble*); 48 S-300PS (RS-SA-10B *Grumble*); 16 S-400 (RS-SA-21 *Growler*)
Medium-range 9K37 *Buk* (RS-SA-11 *Gadfly*)
Short-range 25: 21 9K331ME *Tor*-M2E (RS-SA-15 *Gauntlet*); 4 9K331MK *Tor*-M2K
Point-defence 9K33 *Osa* (RS-SA-8 *Gecko*); 9K35 *Strela*-10 (RS-SA-13 *Gopher*)

Special Operations Command 6,300

FORCES BY ROLE
SPECIAL FORCES
1 SF bde
MANOEUVRE
Mechanised
2 mech bde

EQUIPMENT BY TYPE
ARMOURED FIGHTING VEHICLES
RECCE 13+ *Cayman* BRDM
IFV 30+ BTR-82A
APC • **APC (W)** 217: 64 BTR-70M1; 153 BTR-80
AUV 12 CS/VN3B mod
ARTILLERY 114
TOWED **122mm** 24 D-30
GUN/MOR • **TOWED 120mm** 18 2B23 NONA-M1
ANTI-TANK/ANTI-INFRASTRUCTURE • MSL
MANPATS 9K111 *Fagot* (RS-AT-4 *Spigot*); 9K111-1 *Konkurs* (RS-AT-5 *Spandrel*); 9K115 *Metis* (RS-AT-7 *Saxhorn*)

Joint 18,500 (Centrally controlled units and MoD staff)

FORCES BY ROLE
SURFACE-TO-SURFACE MISSILE
1 SRBM bde with 9K720 *Iskander*-M (RS-SS-26 *Stone*)
COMBAT SUPPORT
1 arty bde
1 MRL bde
2 engr bde
1 EW regt
1 NBC bde
3 sigs bde
COMBAT SUPPORT
2 tpt bde

EQUIPMENT BY TYPE
ARMOURED FIGHTING VEHICLES
APC • **APC (T)** 20 MT-LB
AUV *Volat* V1
NBC VEHICLES BRDM-2RKhB, RKhM-4; RKhM-K
ARTILLERY 118
SP **152mm** 36 2S5 *Giatsint*-S
TOWED **152mm** 36 2A65 *Msta*-B
MRL **300mm** 46: 36 9A52 *Smerch*; 6 *Polonez*; 4 *Polonez*-M
SURFACE-TO-SURFACE MISSILE LAUNCHERS
SRBM • **Dual-capable** 8 9K720 *Iskander*-M (RS-SS-26 *Stone*)

Gendarmerie & Paramilitary 110,000

State Border Troops 12,000
Ministry of Interior

Militia 87,000
Ministry of Interior

Internal Troops 11,000

FOREIGN FORCES

Russia 2,000; 2 SAM bn with S-400; 1 radar station at Baranovichi (*Volga* system; leased); 1 naval comms site

Georgia GEO

Georgian Lari GEL		2023	2024	2025
GDP	GEL	80.2bn	89.8bn	98.6bn
	USD	30.5bn	33.2bn	35.9bn
Real GDP growth	%	7.5	7.6	6.0
Def bdgt	GEL	1.26bn	1.37bn	
	USD	479m	506m	
FMA (US)	USD	35m	25m	25m

Real-terms defence budget trend (USDm, constant 2015)

Population	4,900,961				
Age	0–14	15–19	20–24	25–29	30–64	65 plus
Male	10.6%	2.9%	2.7%	3.1%	21.9%	6.6%
Female	10.0%	2.7%	2.4%	2.8%	24.2%	10.1%

Capabilities

Georgia's security concerns principally focus on Russian military deployments and the breakaway regions of Abkhazia and South Ossetia, which were heightened by Moscow's 2022 invasion of Ukraine. Domestic political developments in late 2024 created uncertainty over previous ambitions to join NATO; there has been no real progress beyond a package of 'tailored support measures' agreed at the alliance's 2022 Madrid Summit. The US put on hold planned military exercises with the country in July 2024 due to concerns over Georgian domestic politics. EU relations with Georgia have also cooled, with defence funding support blocked in July 2024. Georgia's armed forces have taken part in several NATO multinational exercises but have limited expeditionary logistic capability. A revised Defense Code will come into force in 2025 aimed at closing loopholes in conscription. Revised defence procurement laws were also due to take effect in 2025. The backbone of the armed forces' military equipment remains legacy Soviet-era systems. The Major Systems Acquisitions Strategy 2019–25 outlines efforts to procure new equipment, though funding availability will be key to meeting aspirations including to boost special forces capacity, anti-armour and air-defence capability. The country has begun to develop a defence-industrial base. The State Military Scientific-Technical Center has demonstrated some maintenance, repair, overhaul and design capabilities to produce light armoured vehicles.

ACTIVE 20,650 (Army 17,050 Special Forces 2,000 National Guard 1,600) Gendarmerie & Paramilitary 5,400

Conscript liability 12 months

ORGANISATIONS BY SERVICE

Army 13,000; 4,050 conscript (total 17,050)
FORCES BY ROLE
MANOEUVRE
  Mechanised
  1 (4th) mech inf bde (1 armd bn, 2 mech inf bn, 1 SP arty bn)
  Light
  1 (1st) inf bde (1 mech inf bn, 3 inf bn)
  1 (2nd) inf bde (3 inf bn, 1 fd arty bn)
  1 (3rd) inf bde (3 inf bn, 1 SP arty bn)
  Amphibious
  2 mne bn (1 cadre)
COMBAT SUPPORT
  1 (5th) arty bde (1 fd arty bn; 1 MRL bn)
  1 (6th) arty bde (1 SP arty bn; 1 MRL bn)
  1 engr bde
  1 engr bn
  1 sigs bn
  1 SIGINT bn
  1 MP bn
COMBAT SERVICE SUPPORT
  1 med bn
EQUIPMENT BY TYPE
ARMOURED FIGHTING VEHICLES
  MBT 123: 23 T-55AM2; 100 T-72B/SIM1
  RECCE 41: 1 BRM-1K; 40+ *Didgori*-2
  IFV 71: 25 BMP-1; 46 BMP-2
  APC 267
    APC (T) 69+: 3+ *Lazika*; 66 MT-LB
    APC (W) 152+: 25 BTR-70; 19 BTR-80; 40+ *Didgori*-1; 3+ *Didgori*-3; 65 *Ejder*
    PPV 46: 46 BMC *Vuran*
  AUV 10+: ATF *Dingo*; *Cobra*; 10 *Cougar*
ENGINEERING & MAINTENANCE VEHICLES
  ARV IMR-2
ANTI-TANK/ANTI-INFRASTRUCTURE
  MSL • MANPATS 9K111 *Fagot* (RS-AT-4 *Spigot*); 9K111-1 *Konkurs* (RS-AT-5 *Spandrel*); FGM-148 *Javelin*
  GUNS • TOWED ε40: 85mm D-44; 100mm T-12
ARTILLERY 240
  SP 67: 122mm 20 2S1 *Gvozdika*; 152mm 46: 32 M-77 *Dana*; 13 2S3 *Akatsiya*; 1 2S19 *Msta-S*; 203mm 1 2S7 *Pion*
  TOWED 71: 122mm 58 D-30; 152mm 13: 3 2A36 *Giatsint-B*; 10 2A65 *Msta-B*
  MRL 122mm 37: 13 BM-21 *Grad*; 6 GradLAR; 18 RM-70
  MOR 120mm 65: 14 2S12 *Sani*; 33 M-75; 18 M120
AIR DEFENCE • SAM
  Short-range *Spyder*-SR
  Point-defence *Grom*; *Mistral*-2; 9K32 *Strela*-2 (RS-SA-7 *Grail*)‡; 9K35 *Strela*-10 (RS-SA-13 *Gopher*); 9K36 *Strela*-3 (RS-SA-14 *Gremlin*); 9K310 *Igla*-1 (RS-SA-16 *Gimlet*)

Aviation and Air Defence Command 1,300 (incl 300 conscript)

1 avn base, 1 hel air base

FORCES BY ROLE

AIR DEFENCE

1 AD bde

EQUIPMENT BY TYPE

AIRCRAFT 4 combat capable

ATK 4: 2 Su-25KM *Frogfoot*; 2 Su-25UB *Frogfoot* B (2 Su-25 *Frogfoot* in store)

TPT • **Light** 8: 6 An-2 *Colt*; 2 Yak-40 *Codling*

HELICOPTERS

ATK 6 Mi-24 *Hind*

TPT 18: **Medium** 17 Mi-8T *Hip*; **Light** 1+ Bell 205 (UH-1H *Iroquois*) (up to 8 more in store)

UNINHABITED AERIAL VEHICLES

ISR • **Medium** 1+ *Hermes* 450

AIR DEFENCE • SAM

Medium-range 9K37 *Buk*-M1 (RS-SA-11 *Gadfly*) (1–2 bn)

Point-defence 8 9K33M2 *Osa*-AK (RS-SA-8B *Gecko*) (two bty); 6-10 9K33M3 *Osa*-AKM (RS-SA-8B *Gecko*)

Special Operations Forces Command ε2,000

FORCES BY ROLE

SPECIAL FORCES

2 SF bn

1 ranger bn

National Guard 1,600 active reservists opcon Army

FORCES BY ROLE

MANOEUVRE

Light

1 (10th) inf bde (4 inf bn)

1 (20th) inf bde (4 inf bn)

Gendarmerie & Paramilitary 5,400

Border Police 5,400

EQUIPMENT BY TYPE

HELICOPTERS

TPT • **Medium** 3 Mi-8MTV-1 *Hip*

Coast Guard

HQ at Poti. The Navy was merged with the Coast Guard in 2009 under the auspices of the Georgian Border Police, within the Ministry of the Interior

EQUIPMENT BY TYPE

PATROL AND COASTAL COMBATANTS 11+

PCC 2 *Ochamchira* (ex-US *Island*)

PBF 2+: some Ares 43m; 1 *Kaan* 33; 1 *Kaan* 20

PB 7+: 2 *Dauntless*; 2 *Dilos* (ex-GRC); 1 *Kutaisi* (ex-TUR AB 25); 2 *Point*; some *Zhuk* (3 ex-UKR)

TERRITORY WHERE THE GOVERNMENT DOES NOT EXERCISE EFFECTIVE CONTROL

Following the August 2008 war between Russia and Georgia, the areas of Abkhazia and South Ossetia declared themselves independent. Data presented here represents the de facto situation and does not imply international recognition as sovereign states.

FOREIGN FORCES

Russia ε4,000; 1 mil base at Gudauta (Abkhazia) with 1 MR bde(-); 1 SAM regt with S-300PS; 1 mil base at Djava/Tskhinvali (S. Ossetia) with 1 MR bde(-)

Kazakhstan KAZ

Kazakhstani Tenge KZT		2023	2024	2025
GDP	KZT	121trn	133trn	146trn
	USD	263bn	293bn	307bn
Real GDP growth	%	5.1	3.5	4.6
Def bdgt	KZT	1.15trn	1.19trn	1.22trn
	USD	2.51bn	2.62bn	2.55bn

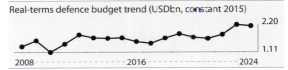

Real-terms defence budget trend (USDbn, constant 2015)

Population	20,260,006					
Age	0–14	15–19	20–24	25–29	30–64	65 plus
Male	14.2%	3.9%	3.0%	3.2%	20.8%	3.5%
Female	13.4%	3.7%	2.8%	3.0%	22.5%	6.1%

Capabilities

Kazakhstan's 2022 military doctrine updated its 2017 predecessor by consolidating the authority of the president's office, enhancing the capabilities of the national guard to respond to domestic disorder, strengthening cyber and information capabilities across all security agencies, and creating a new military territorial directorate. Kazakhstan has a military agreement with Uzbekistan to cooperate on training and education, countering violent extremism and reducing militant movements in their region. In February 2024, parliament ratified a Treaty on Allied Relations, signed with Uzbekistan in 2022. Relations with Turkiye are growing. Russia remains a traditional defence partner. The relationship with Moscow is reinforced by CSTO and SCO membership, though Kazakhstan in late 2024 reportedly declined to join the BRICS grouping. Moscow operates a radar station at Balkash. Kazakhstan takes part in regional and CSTO exercises, including anti-terror drills. The armed forces are reportedly integrating lessons from the war in Ukraine, including a desire to improve artillery, reconnaissance and UAV capabilities. Salary increases were announced in 2023, particularly for specialist trades, including pilots. Joint ventures with foreign firms, such as Airbus, ASELSAN and Paramount Group, make up the most advanced elements of Kazakhstan's defence industry. As part of the 2050 strategy, Kazakhstan is privatising businesses including in the defence sector.

ACTIVE 39,000 (Army 20,000 Navy 3,000 Air 12,000

MoD 4,000) **Gendarmerie & Paramilitary** 31,500

Conscript liability 12 months (due to be abolished)

ORGANISATIONS BY SERVICE

Army 20,000

4 regional comd: Astana, East, West and Southern

FORCES BY ROLE

MANOEUVRE

 Armoured

  2 tk bde

  2 mech bde

  1 aslt bde

 Mechanised

  1 naval inf bde

  1 (peacekeeping) inf regt

 Air Manoeuvre

  4 air aslt bde

COMBAT SUPPORT

 3 arty bde

 1 SRBM unit

 3 cbt engr regt

EQUIPMENT BY TYPE

ARMOURED FIGHTING VEHICLES

 MBT 350 T-72BA; (ε950 T-72A in store)

 TSV 3 BMPT

 RECCE 100: 40 BRDM-2; 60 BRM-1

 IFV 413: 280 BMP-2; 70 BTR-80A; 63 BTR-82A; (ε800 BMP-1/2 in store)

 APC 372

  APC (T) 50 MT-LB; (ε200 MT-LB in store)

  APC (W) 152: 2 BTR-3E; 150 BTR-80; (ε300 BTR-60/70 in store)

  PPV up to 170 *Arlan*

  AUV 17+: 17 *Cobra*; Roshel *Senator*; *SandCat*

ENGINEERING & MAINTENANCE VEHICLES

 AEV MT-LB

ANTI-TANK/ANTI-INFRASTRUCTURE

 MSL

  SP 6+: HMMWV with 9K111-1 *Konkurs* (RS-AT-5 *Spandrel*); 6 9P149 *Shturm* (MT-LB with RS-AT-6 *Spiral*)

  MANPATS 9K111 *Fagot* (RS-AT-4 *Spigot*); 9K111-1 *Konkurs* (RS-AT-5 *Spandrel*); 9K115 *Metis* (RS-AT-7 *Saxhorn*)

 GUNS 100mm 20 MT-12; (ε26 MT-12 in store)

ARTILLERY 490

 SP 126: **122mm** 66: 60 2S1 *Gvozdika*; 6 *Semser*; **152mm** 60 2S3M *Akatsiya*

 TOWED 194: **122mm** 100 D-30; (ε250 D-30 in store); **152mm** 94: 70 2A65 *Msta-B*; 24 D-20; (ε500 D-20 in store); (ε300 2A36 *Giatsint-B* in store)

 GUN/MOR 120mm (ε35 2S9 *Nona* in store)

 MRL 107: 122mm 80 BM-21 *Grad*; **220mm** 3 TOS-1A; (ε100 9P140 *Uragan* in store); **300mm** 24: 6 BM-30 *Smerch*; 18 IMI *Lynx* (with 50 msl)

 MOR 63+: **82mm** some; **SP 120mm** 18 *Cardom*; **120mm** 45 2B11 *Sani*/M120; **SP 240mm** (ε7 2S4 *Tyulpan* in store)

SURFACE-TO-SURFACE MISSILE LAUNCHERS

 SRBM • Conventional 12 9K79 *Tochka* (RS-SS-21 *Scarab*)

Navy 3,000

EQUIPMENT BY TYPE

PATROL AND COASTAL COMBATANTS 14

 PCGM 3 *Kazakhstan* with 1 4-cell lnchr with 4 *Barrier-VK* SSM, 1 *Arbalet-K* lnchr with 4 9K38 *Igla* (RS-SA-18 *Grouse*), 1 AK630 CIWS

 PCC 1 *Kazakhstan* with 1 122mm MRL

 PBF 3 *Sea Dolphin*

 PB 7: 3 *Archangel*; 1 *Dauntless*; 1 *Lashyn*; 1 *Turk* (AB 25); 1 Other

MINE WARFARE • MINE COUNTERMEASURES 1

 MCC 1 *Alatau* (Project 10750E)

LOGISTICS AND SUPPORT • AGS 1 *Zhaik*

UNINHABITED MARITIME SYSTEMS • UUV

 DATA *Alister* 9 (A9-E)

 MW K-Ster I/C

Air Force 12,000 (incl Air Defence)

FORCES BY ROLE

FIGHTER/GROUND ATTACK

 1 sqn with Su-27/Su-27UB *Flanker* B/C

 1 sqn with Su-27/Su-30SM *Flanker* B/H

GROUND ATTACK

 1 sqn with Su-25 *Frogfoot*

TRANSPORT

 1 unit with Tu-134 *Crusty*; Tu-154 *Careless*

 1 sqn with An-12 *Cub*, An-26 *Curl*, An-30 *Clank*, An-72 *Coaler*, C295M

TRAINING

 1 sqn with L-39 *Albatros*

ATTACK HELICOPTER

 5 sqn with Mi-24V *Hind*

TRANSPORT HELICOPTER

 Some sqn with Bell 205 (UH-1H *Iroquois*); H145; Mi-8 *Hip*; Mi-17V-5 *Hip*; Mi-171Sh *Hip*; Mi-26 *Halo*

COMBAT/ISR UAV

 1 sqn with *Anka-S* (forming)

AIR DEFENCE

 1 bty with 9K317M2 *Buk-M2E* (RS-SA-17 *Grizzly*)

 2 bty with S-75M *Volkhov* (RS-SA-2 *Guideline*)

 1 bty with S-125-1T

 1 bty with S-200 *Angara* (RS-SA-5 *Gammon*)

 10 bty with S-300PS (RS-SA-10 *Grumble*)

 Some regt with 2K12 *Kub* (RS-SA-6 *Gainful*)

EQUIPMENT BY TYPE

AIRCRAFT 67 combat capable

FGA 53: 20 Su-27 *Flanker*; 4 Su-27UB *Flanker*; 29 Su-30SM *Flanker* H
ATK 14: 12 Su-25 *Frogfoot*; 2 Su-25UB *Frogfoot*
ISR 1 An-30 *Clank*
TPT 20: **Medium** 2 An-12 *Cub*; **Light** 17: 6 An-26 *Curl*; 2 An-72 *Coaler*; 8 C295; 1 C295W; **PAX** 1 Tu-154 *Careless*
TRG 19: 17 L-39 *Albatros*; 2 Z-242L

HELICOPTERS
ATK 32: 20 Mi-24V *Hind* (some upgraded); 12 Mi-35M *Hind*
MRH 26: 20 Mi-17V-5 *Hip*; 6 Mi-171Sh *Hip*
TPT 26: **Heavy** 4 Mi-26 *Halo*; **Medium** 10 Mi-8T *Hip*; **Light** 12: 4 Bell 205 (UH-1H *Iroquois*); 8 H145

UNINHABITED AERIAL VEHICLES
CISR • **Heavy** 5: 3 *Anka-S* (in test); 2 *Wing Loong* (GJ-1)

AIR DEFENCE • **SAM**
Long-range 43+: 3 S-200 *Angara* (RS-SA-5 *Gammon*); 40+ S-300PS (RS-SA-10B *Grumble*)
Medium-range 15: 3 9K317M2 *Buk-M2E* (RS-SA-17 *Grizzly*); 12 S-75M *Volkhov* (RS-SA-2 *Guideline*)
Short-range 3+: some 2K12 *Kub* (RS-SA-6 *Gainful*); 3 S-125-1T
Point-defence 9K35 *Strela*-10 (RS-SA-13 *Gopher*)

AIR-LAUNCHED MISSILES
AAM • **IR** R-27T (RS-AA-10B *Alamo*); R-60 (RS-AA-8 *Aphid*); R-73 (RS-AA-11A *Archer*); **SARH** R-27ER (RS-AA-10C *Alamo*); R-27R (RS-AA-10A *Alamo*); **ARH** R-77 (RS-AA-12A *Adder*)
ASM Kh-25 (RS-AS-10 *Karen*); Kh-29 (RS-AS-14 *Kedge*)
ARM Kh-27 (RS-AS-12 *Kegler*); Kh-58 (RS-AS-11 *Kilter*)

Gendarmerie & Paramilitary 31,500

National Guard ε20,000
Ministry of Interior
EQUIPMENT BY TYPE
ARMOURED FIGHTING VEHICLE
  APC
    APC (W) Kamaz-43629 *Vystrel*
    PPV Ural-VV
  AUV 4+: 4+ *Cobra II*; *Alan* 2
AIRCRAFT
  TPT • **Medium** 2 Y-8F-200WA

State Security Service 2,500

Border Service ε9,000
Ministry of Interior
EQUIPMENT BY TYPE
AIRCRAFT
  TPT 7: **Light** 6: 3 An-26 *Curl*; 1 An-74T; 1 An-74TK; 1 C295W; **PAX** 1 SSJ-100
HELICOPTERS • **TPT** • **Medium** 15: 1 Mi-171; 14 Mi-171Sh

Coast Guard
EQUIPMENT BY TYPE
PATROL AND COASTAL COMBATANTS 25
  PBF 12: 2 *Aibar* (Project 0210); 8 FC-19; 2 *Saygak*
  PB 13: 7 *Almaty*; 6 *Sardar*

DEPLOYMENT
CENTRAL AFRICAN REPUBLIC: UN • MINUSCA 1
DEMOCRATIC REPUBLIC OF THE CONGO: UN • MONUSCO 2
LEBANON: UN • UNIFIL 9
SYRIA/ISRAEL: UN • UNDOF 140; 1 recce coy
WESTERN SAHARA: UN • MINURSO 6

Kyrgyzstan KGZ

Kyrgyzstani Som KGS		2023	2024	2025
GDP	KGS	1.23trn	1.39trn	1.53trn
	USD	14.0bn	15.8bn	17.4bn
Real GDP growth	%	6.2	6.5	5.0
Def bdgt	KGS	n.k.	n.k.	n.k.
	USD	n.k.	n.k.	n.k.
Population	6,172,101			

Age	0–14	15–19	20–24	25–29	30–64	65 plus
Male	14.9%	4.5%	3.6%	3.8%	19.4%	2.7%
Female	14.1%	4.3%	3.5%	3.7%	21.1%	4.3%

Capabilities

Kyrgyzstan is expanding ties with its neighbours on issues such as defence-industrial cooperation, though it remains generally dependent on Russian assistance for its defence requirements. Moscow has a military presence in the country, including a squadron of ground-attack aircraft at Kant air base, which it has leased since 2003. Talks are ongoing over a possible second Russian base. In 2023, Russia said it would 'develop' its facilities in Kyrgyzstan, following a meeting between the countries' leaders. Russia's government has approved plans to set up a common air defence system, which Kyrgyzstan's parliament endorsed in 2023. Kyrgyzstan is a member of the CSTO and SCO. The country hosted the CSTO command staff drill *Interaction-2024*. There is joint training with regional countries, including anti-terror drills, but combat readiness remains a challenge. Kyrgyzstan has a limited capability to deploy externally, though personnel have been deployed to OSCE and UN missions. The armed forces possess ageing land equipment and limited air capabilities, relying instead on Russian support, training and deployments. The country acquired additional air-defence equipment from Belarus that arrived in 2023, alongside upgraded helicopters. UAV capabilities have improved with the addition of Turkish-origin equipment. There is little local defence industry. Kyrgyzstan has increased defence ties with India and formed a joint working group on defence cooperation.

ACTIVE 10,900 (Army 8,500 Air 2,400) **Gendarmerie & Paramilitary 9,500**

Conscript liability 18 months

ORGANISATIONS BY SERVICE

Army 8,500
FORCES BY ROLE
SPECIAL FORCES
  1 SF bde
MANOEUVRE
  Mechanised
  2 MR bde
  1 (mtn) MR bde
COMBAT SUPPORT
  1 arty bde
  1 AD bde
EQUIPMENT BY TYPE
ARMOURED FIGHTING VEHICLES
  MBT 150 T-72
  RECCE 39: 30 BRDM-2; 9 BRDM-2M
  IFV 320: 230 BMP-1; 90 BMP-2
  APC • APC (W) 55: 25 BTR-70; 20 BTR-70M; 10 BTR-80
ANTI-TANK/ANTI-INFRASTRUCTURE
  MSL • MANPATS 9K11 *Malyutka* (RS-AT-3 *Sagger*); 9K111 *Fagot* (RS-AT-4 *Spigot*); 9K111-1 *Konkurs* (RS-AT-5 *Spandrel*)
  RCL 73mm SPG-9
  GUNS 100mm 36: 18 MT-12/T-12; 18 M-1944
ARTILLERY 228
  SP 122mm 18 2S1 *Gvozdika*
  TOWED 123: **122mm** 107: 72 D-30; 35 M-30 (M-1938); **152mm** 16 D-1
  GUN/MOR 120mm 12 2S9 NONA-S
  MRL 21: 122mm 15 BM-21; **220mm** 6 9P140 *Uragan*
  MOR 120mm 54: 6 2S12; 48 M-120
AIR DEFENCE
  SAM • Point-defence 9K32 *Strela*-2 (RS-SA-7 *Grail*)‡; 9K35 *Strela*-10 (RS-SA-13 *Gopher*)
  GUNS 48
    SP 23mm 24 ZSU-23-4
    TOWED 57mm 24 S-60

Air Force 2,400
FORCES BY ROLE
FIGHTER
  1 regt with L-39 *Albatros**
TRANSPORT
  1 regt with An-2 *Colt*; An-26 *Curl*
ATTACK/TRANSPORT HELICOPTER
  1 regt with Mi-24 *Hind*; Mi-8/-8MT/-17V-5 *Hip*
AIR DEFENCE
  2 bty with S-125 *Neva*-M1 (RS-SA-3 *Goa*)
  1 bty with S-75M3 *Dvina* (RS-SA-2 *Guideline*)
EQUIPMENT BY TYPE
AIRCRAFT 4 combat capable
  TPT • Light 6: 4 An-2 *Colt*; 2 An-26 *Curl*
  TRG 4 L-39 *Albatros**
HELICOPTERS
  ATK 2 Mi-24 *Hind*
  MRH 5: 2 Mi-17V-5 *Hip* H; 3 Mi-8MT *Hip*
  TPT • Medium 8 Mi-8 *Hip*
AIR DEFENCE • SAM
  Medium-range 6 S-75M3 *Dvina* (RS-SA-2 *Guideline*)
  Short-range 8 S-125M1 *Neva*-M1 (RS-SA-3 *Goa*)

Gendarmerie & Paramilitary 9,500

Border Guards 5,000 (KGZ conscript, RUS officers)
FORCES BY ROLE
CISR UAV
  1 sqn with *Aksungur*; *Bayraktar Akinci*; *Bayraktar* TB2
EQUIPMENT BY TYPE
ARMOURED FIGHTING VEHICLES
  AUV 54 *Tigr*
UNINHABITED AERIAL VEHICLES
  CISR 6: **Heavy** 3: 1 *Aksungur*; 2 *Bayraktar Akinci*; **Medium** 3 *Bayraktar* TB2
  BOMBS • Laser-guided MAM-L/T

Internal Troops 3,500

National Guard 1,000

DEPLOYMENT
SOUTH SUDAN: UN • UNMISS 2
SUDAN: UN • UNISFA 2
WESTERN SAHARA: UN • MINURSO 1

FOREIGN FORCES
Russia ε500 Military Air Forces: 13 Su-25SM *Frogfoot*; 2 Mi-8 *Hip*

Moldova MDA

Moldovan Leu MDL		2023	2024	2025
GDP	MDL	300bn	329bn	360bn
	USD	16.6bn	18.1bn	19.6bn
Real GDP growth	%	0.7	2.6	3.7
Def bdgt	MDL	1.70bn	1.97bn	1.84bn
	USD	93.7m	108m	100m

Real-terms defence budget trend (USDm, constant 2015)

Population	3,599,528					
Age	0–14	15–19	20–24	25–29	30–64	65 plus
Male	7.4%	2.9%	2.7%	3.0%	25.4%	5.7%
Female	7.4%	2.9%	2.7%	3.1%	27.4%	9.3%

Capabilities

The primary role of Moldova's armed forces is to maintain territorial integrity. The country is constitutionally neutral. Tensions with Russia over the breakaway region of Transnistria, which Moscow supports, worsened following Russia's 2022 invasion of Ukraine. Russian 'peacekeeping' forces in Transnistria remain a source of concern for Moldova. The Moldovan government during 2024 continued to warn of Russian attempts to destabilise the country. A state of emergency was declared after Russia's 2022 invasion of Ukraine, which only ended in December 2023. Moldova is building relations with European states and NATO. NATO defence ministers approved an Enhanced Defence Capacity Building package in February 2023. A Long-Term Military Capabilities Development Plan was approved in March 2020, covering the period to 2030. The country retains the goal of fielding a fully professional military. There are plans to improve land forces mobility, develop more capable ground-based air defences and replace Soviet-era equipment. The services exercise regularly with NATO members. Moldova has no requirement or capability to independently deploy and support its forces overseas, though personnel were again deployed to the NATO-led KFOR mission in 2023. Moldova has no defence-industrial capabilities beyond the basic maintenance of front-line equipment.

ACTIVE 5,150 (Army 3,250 Air 600 Logistic Support 1,300) **Gendarmerie & Paramilitary 900**

Conscript liability 12 months (3 months for university graduates)

RESERVE 58,000 (Joint 58,000)

ORGANISATIONS BY SERVICE

Army 1,300; 1,950 conscript (total 3,250)
FORCES BY ROLE
SPECIAL FORCES
  1 SF bn
MANOEUVRE
  Light
    3 mot inf bde
    1 lt inf bn
  Other
    1 gd bn
COMBAT SUPPORT
  1 arty bn
  1 engr bn
  1 NBC coy
  1 sigs bn
EQUIPMENT BY TYPE
ARMOURED FIGHTING VEHICLES
  APC 172
    APC (T) 61: 9 BTR-D; 52 MT-LB (variants)
    APC (W) 111: 12 BTR-80; 19 *Piranha*-IIIH; 80 TAB-71
  ABCV 44 BMD-1
ANTI-TANK/ANTI-INFRASTRUCTURE
  MSL • MANPATS 9K111 *Fagot* (RS-AT-4 *Spigot*); 9K111-1 *Konkurs* (RS-AT-5 *Spandrel*)
  RCL 73mm SPG-9
  GUNS 100mm 31 MT-12
ARTILLERY 219
  TOWED 67: **122mm** 16 M-30 (M-1938); **152mm** 51: 20 2A36 *Giatsint*-B; 31 D-20
  GUN/MOR • SP 120mm 9 2S9 NONA-S
  MRL 220mm 11 9P140 *Uragan*
  MOR 132: **82mm** 75 BM-37; **120mm** 57: 50 M-1989; 7 PM-38
AIR DEFENCE • GUNS • TOWED 39: **23mm** 28 ZU-23; **57mm** 11 S-60

Air Force 600 (incl 250 conscripts)
FORCES BY ROLE
TRANSPORT
  1 sqn with An-2 *Colt*; Mi-8MTV-1/PS *Hip*; Yak-18
AIR DEFENCE
  1 regt with S-125M1 *Neva*-M1 (RS-SA-3 *Goa*)
EQUIPMENT BY TYPE
AIRCRAFT
  TPT • Light 3: 2 An-2 *Colt*; 1 Yak-18 *Max*
HELICOPTERS
  TPT • Medium 6: 2 Mi-8PS *Hip*; 4 Mi-8MTV-1 *Hip*
AIR DEFENCE • SAM • Short-range 3 S-125M1 *Neva*-M1 (RS-SA-3 *Goa*)

Gendarmerie & Paramilitary 900
Special Police Brigade 900
Ministry of Interior

DEPLOYMENT

CENTRAL AFRICAN REPUBLIC: UN • MINUSCA 4
KOSOVO: NATO • KFOR 44; **UN • UNMIK** 1
LEBANON: UN • UNIFIL 32
SOUTH SUDAN: UN • UNMISS 4

TRANSNISTRIA

Data presented here represents the de facto situation in the territory of Transnistria and does not imply international recognition.

FOREIGN FORCES

Russia ε1,500 (including 400 peacekeepers); 7 Mi-24 *Hind*/Mi-8 *Hip*

Russia RUS

Russian Rouble RUB		2023	2024	2025
GDP	RUB	172trn	196trn	208trn
	USD	2.01trn	2.18trn	2.20trn
Real GDP growth	%	3.6	3.6	1.3
Def exp [a]	RUB	8.40trn	13.1trn	15.6trn
	USD	98.1bn	146bn	164bn
Def bdgt	RUB	6.41trn	10.8trn	13.2trn
	USD	74.8bn	120bn	139bn

[a] Calculated to be comparable with NATO definition of defence expenditure

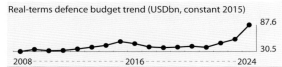

Real-terms defence budget trend (USDbn, constant 2015)

Population	140,820,810					
Age	0–14	15–19	20–24	25–29	30–64	65 plus
Male	8.5%	2.9%	2.5%	2.4%	24.2%	6.1%
Female	8.0%	2.7%	2.4%	2.3%	26.3%	11.7%

Capabilities

Russia fields large conventional military forces and retains the world's second-largest nuclear arsenal. However, its ground forces have suffered extensive losses in personnel and equipment since the country's 2022 full-scale invasion of Ukraine. Moscow, in September 2024, revised its nuclear doctrine in response to Western support for Ukraine, reducing the threshold for nuclear weapons use. Its 2022 attack exposed weaknesses in leadership, planning, personnel and equipment, particularly within the ground and airborne forces. A lack of airborne intelligence, surveillance and reconnaissance systems was evident in Moscow's initial poor performance. The economy has been put on a war footing. Western estimates of Russian personnel losses vary, but these may have reached over 500,000 killed or wounded. Losses have at times rendered ground combat units ineffective. The ground forces have lost large numbers of its most modern MBTs and AFVs. The air force and navy have also suffered losses, with Ukraine destroying or damaging several Black Sea Fleet vessels. The 2027 State Armament Programme (SAP) and the follow-on SAP 2033 are being modified. Substantial recapitalisation of ground forces equipment will be required. Russia is the leading member of both the CSTO and the SCO. Before its 2022 invasion of Ukraine, volunteers outweighed conscripts, following post-2008 reforms that emphasised the shift from a conscript-based mass-mobilisation army to smaller, more professional ground forces. However, Ukraine has revealed the limits of this process. Setbacks and losses led President Putin to introduce a partial mobilisation in September 2022. After the Wagner Group's June 2023 rebellion, Wagner units came under the control of the Russian National Guard, with units reportedly fighting in Ukraine in early 2024. Similar groups deploy personnel to some African states. North Korean ground forces have from October 2024 deployed in the Kursk region in support of Russia. Before the invasion, Russia's armed forces could independently deploy and sustain forces on a global scale, although only in modest size at extended distances. Ground force losses in Ukraine, however, further limit the size and the competency of the units Moscow can deploy. Russia continues to modernise its nuclear and conventional weapons. Russia can design, develop, and manufacture advanced nuclear and conventional weaponry. However, Western sanctions aimed at curtailing access to key components are forcing import substitution and has slowed the production of some weapons.

ACTIVE 1,134,000 (Army 550,000 Navy 119,000 Air 170,000 Strategic Rocket Force 50,000 Airborne 35,000 Special Operations Forces 1,000 Railway Forces 29,000 Command and Support 180,000) **Gendarmerie & Paramilitary 569,000**

Conscript liability 12 months (conscripts now can opt for contract service immediately, which entails a 24-month contract)

RESERVE 1,500,000 (all arms)

Some 1,500,000 with service within last 5 years; reserve obligation to age 50

ORGANISATIONS BY SERVICE

Strategic Deterrent Forces ε80,000 (incl personnel assigned from the Navy and Aerospace Forces)

Navy
EQUIPMENT BY TYPE
SUBMARINES • STRATEGIC • SSBN 12:
  6 *Delfin* (Project 667BDRM (*Delta* IV)) with 16 R-29RMU2 *Sineva*/R-29RMU2.1 *Layner* (RS-SS-N-23 *Skiff*) nuclear SLBM, 4 single 533mm TT with 53-65K HWT/SET-65K HWT/USET-80K *Keramika* HWT
  3 *Borey* (Project 955 (*Dolgorukiy*)) with 16 *Bulava* (RS-SS-N-32) nuclear SLBM, 6 single 533mm TT with USET-80K *Keramika* HWT/UGST *Fizik* HWT
  3 *Borey*-A (Project 955A) with 16 *Bulava* (RS-SS-N-32) nuclear SLBM, 6 single 533mm TT with USET-80K *Keramika* HWT/UGST *Fizik* HWT
UNINHABITED MARITIME PLATFORMS • UUV
  ATK • Nuclear • Extra-Large *Poseidon* (*Status*-6) (nuclear powered) (in test)

Strategic Rocket Forces 50,000

3 Rocket Armies operating silo and mobile launchers organised in 12 divs. Regt normally with 6 to 10 silos or 9 mobile launchers, and one control centre
FORCES BY ROLE
SURFACE-TO-SURFACE MISSILE

8 ICBM regt with RS-12M2 *Topol*-M (RS-SS-27 mod 1)
2 ICBM regt with RS-18 with Avangard HGV (RS-SS-19 mod 4 *Stiletto*)
6 ICBM regt with RS-20 (RS-SS-18 *Satan*)
14 ICBM regt with RS-24 *Yars* (RS-SS-27 mod 2)
8 ICBM regt with *Yars*-S

EQUIPMENT BY TYPE
SURFACE-TO-SURFACE MISSILE LAUNCHERS
ICBM • **Nuclear** 324: 60 RS-12M2 *Topol*-M (RS-SS-27 mod 1) silo-based (single warhead); 18 RS-12M2 *Topol*-M (RS-SS-27 mod 1) road mobile (single warhead); ε10 RS-18 with *Avangard* HGV (RS-SS-19 mod 4 *Stiletto*); ε40 RS-20 (RS-SS-18 *Satan*) (mostly mod 5, 10 MIRV per msl); ε99 RS-24 *Yars* (RS-SS-27 mod 2; ε3 MIRV per msl) road mobile; ε25 RS-24 *Yars* (RS-SS-27 mod 2; ε3 MIRV per msl) silo-based; ε72 *Yars*-S (ε3 MIRV per msl) road mobile
IRBM • **Dual-capable** some *Oreshnik* (RS-SS-28 mod)
COUNTERSPACE • DE • **Laser** *Peresvet*

Long-Range Aviation Command
FORCES BY ROLE
BOMBER
1 sqn with Tu-160/Tu-160 mod *Blackjack*
3 sqn with Tu-95MS/MS mod *Bear*

EQUIPMENT BY TYPE
AIRCRAFT
BBR 71: 6 Tu-160 *Blackjack* with Kh-55SM (RS-AS-15B *Kent*) nuclear LACM; 7 Tu-160 mod *Blackjack* with Kh-55SM (RS-AS-15B *Kent*)/Kh-102 (RS-AS-23B *Kodiak*) nuclear LACM; 31 Tu-95MS *Bear* H with Kh-55SM (RS-AS-15B *Kent*) nuclear LACM; 27 Tu-95MS mod *Bear* H with Kh-55SM (RS-AS-15B *Kent*)/Kh-102 (RS-AS-23B *Kodiak*) nuclear LACM; (3 Tu-160M in test)

Space Command
EQUIPMENT BY TYPE
SATELLITES 101
COMMUNICATIONS 32: 4 *Blagovest*; 1 *Garpun*; 3 *Globus*-M (*Raduga*-1M); 6 *Meridian*; 3 *Meridian*-M; 15 *Rodnik*-S (*Strela*-3M)
POSITIONING, NAVIGATION & TIMING 26: 4 GLONASS-K1; 1 GLONASS-K2; 21 GLONASS-M
ISR 18: 6 *Bars*-M; 1 EMKA; 2 GEO-IK-2; 2 *Kosmos*-2574; 2 *Kosmos*-2577; 1 *Kondor*-FKA; 1 *Neitron*; 2 *Persona*; 1 *Resurs*-P
ELINT/SIGINT 10: 8 *Lotos*-S; 1 *Pion*-NKS; 1 *Tselina*-2
EARLY WARNING 6 *Tundra* (EKS)
RENDEZVOUS & PROXIMITY OPERATIONS 9: 7 *Nivelir*; 2 *Olymp*-K (*Luch*)
MISSILE DEFENCE some S-500 (entering service)
RADAR 12; Russia leases ground-based radar stations in Baranovichi (Belarus) and Balkhash (Kazakhstan). It also has radars on its own territory at Lekhtusi (St Petersburg); Armavir (Krasnodar); Olenegorsk (Murmansk); Mishelevka (Irkutsk); Kaliningrad; Pechora (Komi); Yeniseysk (Krasnoyarsk); Barnaul (Altayskiy); Orsk (Orenburg); and Gorodets/Kovylkino (OTH)

Aerospace Defence Command
FORCES BY ROLE
AIR DEFENCE
2 AD div HQ
4 SAM regt with S-300PM1/PM2 (RS-SA-20 *Gargoyle*)
5 SAM regt with S-400 (RS-SA-21 *Growler*), 96K6 *Pantsir*-S1 (RS-SA-22 *Greyhound*)

EQUIPMENT BY TYPE
AIR DEFENCE
SAM • **Long-range** 186: 90 S-300PM1/PM2 (RS-SA-20 *Gargoyle*); 96 S-400 (RS-SA-21 *Growler*)
SPAAGM 30mm 36 96K6 *Pantsir*-S1 (RS-SA-22 *Greyhound*)
MISSILE DEFENCE 68 53T6 (RS-AB-4A *Gazelle*)
RADAR 1 BMD engagement system located at Sofrino (Moscow)

Army ε550,000 (incl ε100,000 conscripts)
FORCES BY ROLE
As a result of sustained heavy losses suffered during the invasion of Ukraine, almost all of the manoeuvre formations listed are currently understrength.

COMMAND
16 army HQ
7 corps HQ

SPECIAL FORCES
8 (Spetsnaz) SF bde
1 (Spetsnaz) SF regt

MANOEUVRE
Reconnaissance
3 recce bde

Armoured
1 (4th) tk div (2 tk regt, 1 MR regt, 1 arty regt, 1 AD regt)
1 (47th) tk div (1 tk regt, 2 MR regt)
1 (90th) tk div (2 tk regt, 1 MR regt, 1 arty regt)
2 tk bde
2 tk regt (mobilised)

Mechanised
1 (150th) MR div (2 tk regt, 2 MR regt, 1 arty regt, 1 AD regt)
1 (127th & 144th) MR div (1 tk regt, 3 MR regt, 1 arty regt, 1 AD regt)
1 (2nd) MR div (1 tk regt, 2 MR regt, 1 arty regt, 1 AD regt)
1 (6th) MR div (1 tk regt, 3 MR regt, 1 arty regt)
3 (3rd & 70th) MR div (1 tk regt, 2 MR regt, 1 arty regt)
1 (18th) MR div (1 tk regt, 2 MR regt, 1 AD regt)
1 (67th) MR div (1 tk regt, 3 MR regt)
1 (42nd) MR div (4 MR Regt, 1 arty regt)
1 (20th) MR div (3 MR regt, 1 arty regt)
1 (27th) MR div (3 MR regt)
1 (19th) MR div (2 MR regt, 1 arty regt)
1 (72nd) MR div (2 MR regt) (forming)
2 (47th & 69th) MR div (1 MR regt) (forming)
39 MR bde
17 MR regt

1 (18th) MGA div (1 tk bn, 2 MGA regt, 1 arty regt, 2 AD bn)
Light
ε78 MR regt (mobilised)

SURFACE-TO-SURFACE MISSILE
13 SRBM/GLCM bde with 9K720 *Iskander*-M (RS-SS-26 *Stone*/RS-SSC-7 *Southpaw*) (3+ brigades also with 9M729 (RS-SSC-8 *Screwdriver*))

COMBAT SUPPORT
15 arty bde
2 hy arty bde
1 arty regt
1 arty regt (mobilised)
1 arty bn (mobilised)
4 MRL bde
4 engr bde
7 engr regt
1 ptn br bde
5 EW bde
5 NBC bde
10 NBC regt

COMBAT SERVICE SUPPORT
11 log bde

AIR DEFENCE
16 SAM bde
1 SAM regt

EQUIPMENT BY TYPE (ε)
Surface-to-surface missile systems may have very limited numbers of available missiles remaining.

ARMOURED FIGHTING VEHICLES
  MBT 2,730: 70 T-55A; 600 T-62M/MV; 50 T-64A/BV; 700 T-72A/AV/B/BA; 470 T-72B3/B3M; 200 T-80BV/U; 270 T-80BVM; some T-90A/S; 370 T-90M; (2,900+ T-55A/T-62M/T-62MV/T-64/T-72/T-72A/T-72B/T-80B/T-80BV/T-80U in store)
  TSV 8+ BMPT
  RECCE 200+: some BRDM-2/-2A; 200 BRM-1K (CP); (100 BRDM-2/-2A in store; 500 BRDM-2 (variants) in store)
  IFV 3,280: 750 BMP-1/-1AM; 550 BMP-2/-2M; 650 BMP-3/-3M; 100 BTR-80A; 1,230 BTR-82A/AM; (3,000 BMP-1/-2 (incl variants) in store)
  APC 4,500+
    APC (T) 2,950+: some BMO-T; 50 BTR-50; 2,900 MT-LB/MT-LB VM1K (incl variants; (1,200 MT-LB (incl variants) in store)
    APC (W) 1,550: 600 BTR-60/-70 (incl variants); 950 BTR-80; (1,500 BTR-60/-70/-80 (incl variants) in store)
    PPV *Typhoon*-K 4×4; *Typhoon*-K 6×6
    AUV IVECO LMV; *Linza*; *Tigr*; *Tigr*-M; *Tigr*-M SpN; *Vystrel*

ENGINEERING & MAINTENANCE VEHICLES
  AEV BAT-2; IMR; IMR-2; IMR-3; IRM; MT-LB
  ARV BMP-1; BREM-1/64/K/L; BTR-50PK(B); M1977; MTP-LB; RM-G; T-54/55; VT-72A
  VLB KMM; MT-55A; MTU; MTU-20; MTU-72; PMM-2

  MW BMR-3M; GMX-3; MCV-2 (reported); MTK; MTK-2; UR-77

ANTI-TANK/ANTI-INFRASTRUCTURE
  MSL
    SP 9P149 with 9K114 *Shturm* (RS-AT-6 *Spiral*); 9P149M with 9K132 *Shturm*-SM (RS-AT-9 *Spiral*-2); 9P157-2 with 9K123 *Khrizantema* (RS-AT-15 *Springer*); 9P163-3 with 9M133 *Kornet* (RS-AT-14 *Spriggan*); 9K128-1 *Kornet*-T (RS-AT-14 *Spriggan*); M-2010 ATGW
    MANPATS 9K111M *Fagot* (RS-AT-4 *Spigot*); 9K111-1 *Konkurs* (RS-AT-5 *Spandrel*); 9K115 *Metis* (RS-AT-7 *Saxhorn*); 9K115-1 *Metis*-M (RS-AT-13); 9K115-2 *Metis*-M1 (RS-AT-13); 9K135 *Kornet* (RS-AT-14 *Spriggan*)
  RCL 73mm SPG-9
  GUNS • TOWED 100mm 500 MT-12 (**100mm** 800 T-12/MT-12 in store)
  ARTILLERY 5,157
    SP 1,703: **122mm** 400 2S1 *Gvozdika*; **152mm** 1,178: 600 2S3/2S3M *Akatsiya*; 100 2S5 *Giatsint*-S; 150 2S19/2S19M1 *Msta*-S; 300 2S19M2/2S33 *Msta*-SM; 8 2S35 *Koalitsiya*-SV (in test); 20 2S43 *Malva*; **203mm** 125: 50 2S7M *Malka*; 75 2S7 *Pion*; (1,900 in store: **122mm** 1,000 2S1 *Gvozdika*; **152mm** 850: 500+ 2S3 *Akatsiya*; 300 2S5 *Giatsint*-S; 50 2S19 *Msta*-S; **203mm** 50+ 2S7 *Pion*)
    TOWED 670: **122mm** 250: 200 D-30; 50 M-30 (M-1938); **130mm** 50 M-46; **152mm** 370: 150 2A36 *Giatsint*-B; 150 2A65 *Msta*-B; 20+ D-1 (M-1943); 50 D-20; (4,050 in store: **122mm** 2,000: 1,000+ D-30; 1,000+ M-30 (M-1938); **130mm** 300 M-46; **152mm** 1,750: 350 2A36 *Giatsint*-B; 100 2A65 *Msta*-B; 500 D-1 (M-1943); 700 D-20; 100 M-1937 (ML-20))
    GUN/MOR 139
      SP 120mm 64+: 24 2S23 NONA-SVK; 40 2S34; some 2S40 *Phlox*
      TOWED 120mm 75 2B16 NONA-K
    MRL 1,131: **122mm** 850: 650 BM-21 *Grad*; 200 9K51M *Tornado*-G; **220mm** 211+: 175 9P140 *Uragan*/9K512 *Uragan*-1M; 36 TOS-1A; some TOS-2; some TOS-3 (in test); **300mm** 70: 50 9A52 *Smerch*; 20 9K515 *Tornado*-S; (1,350 in store: **122mm** 700: 500 BM-21 *Grad*; 200 9P138; **132mm** 100 BM-13; **220mm** 550 9P140 *Uragan*)
    MOR 1,514: **82mm** 800+ 2B14; **120mm** 675 2S12 *Sani*; **240mm** 39 2S4 *Tulpan* (1,260 in store: **120mm** 950: 500 2S12 *Sani*; 450 M-1938 (PM-38); **160mm** 150 M-160; **SP 240mm** 160 2S4 *Tulpan*)

SURFACE-TO-SURFACE MISSILE LAUNCHERS
  SRBM
    Conventional *Fateh*-360; *Hwasong*-11A (KN-23)
    Dual-capable 212: 50 9K79-1 *Tochka*-U (RS-SS-21B *Scarab*); 162 9K720 *Iskander*-M (RS-SS-26 *Stone*)
  GLCM • Dual-capable Some 9M728 (RS-SSC-7 *Southpaw*); some 9M729 (RS-SSC-8 *Screwdriver*)

UNINHABITED AERIAL VEHICLES
  ISR • Light BLA-07; *Eleron* T-16; *Granat*-4; *Merlin*-VR; *Orlan*-30; *Takhion*

OWA *Geran* 1 (*Shahed* 131); *Geran* 2 (*Shahed* 136); KUB-BLA; (multiple systems below 20kg in weight)

AIR DEFENCE

SAM 839+

Long-range S-300V (RS-SA-12A/B *Gladiator/Giant*); S-300V4 (RS-SA-23)

Medium-range 310: ε150 9K37M1-2 *Buk*-M1-2 (RS-SA-11 *Gadfly*); ε90 9K317 *Buk*-M2 (RS-SA-17 *Grizzly*); 70+ 9K317M *Buk*-M3 (RS-SA-27); (100 9K37 *Buk* (RS-SA-11 *Gadfly*) in store)

Short-range 129: 120+ 9K331/9K331M/9K331MU *Tor*-M1/M2/M2U (RS-SA-15 *Gauntlet*) (9M338 msl entering service); 9 *Tor*-M2DT

Point-defence 400+: 100 9K33M3 *Osa*-AKM (RS-SA-8B *Gecko*); 300 9K35M3 *Strela*-10 (RS-SA-13 *Gopher*); 9K310 *Igla*-1 (RS-SA-16 *Gimlet*); 9K34 *Strela*-3 (RS-SA-14 *Gremlin*); 9K38 *Igla* (RS-SA-18 *Grouse*); 9K333 *Verba* (RS-SA-29 *Gizmo*); 9K338 *Igla*-S (RS-SA-24 *Grinch*); (150 9K33M3 *Osa*-AKM (RS-SA-8B *Gecko*) in store)

SPAAGM 30mm 190 2K22M *Tunguska* (RS-SA-19 *Grison*); (50 more in store)

GUNS

SP 23mm (100 ZSU-23-4 in store)

TOWED 23mm ZU-23-2; **57mm** S-60

Navy ε119,000 (incl conscripts)

4 major fleet organisations (Northern Fleet, Pacific Fleet, Baltic Fleet, Black Sea Fleet) and Caspian Sea Flotilla

EQUIPMENT BY TYPE

SUBMARINES 51

STRATEGIC • SSBN 12:

5 *Delfin* (Project 667BDRM (*Delta* IV)) with 16 R-29RMU2 *Sineva*/R-29RMU2.1 *Layner* (RS-SS-N-23 *Skiff*) nuclear SLBM, 4 single 533mm TT with 53-65K HWT/SET-65K HWT/USET-80K *Keramika* HWT (1 more non-op)

3 *Borey* (Project 955 (*Dolgorukiy*)) with 16 *Bulava* (RS-SS-N-32) nuclear SLBM, 6 single 533mm TT with USET-80K *Keramika* HWT/UGST *Fizik* HWT

4 *Borey*-A (Project 955A) with 16 *Bulava* (RS-SS-N-32) nuclear SLBM, 6 single 533mm TT with USET-80K *Keramika* HWT/UGST *Fizik* HWT

TACTICAL 39

SSGN 10:

6 *Antey* (Project 949A (*Oscar* II)) (1 more non-operational, in long-term refit) with 24 single SM-225A lnchr with 3M45 *Granit* (RS-SS-N-19 *Shipwreck*) dual-capable AShM, 2 single 650mm TT each with T-65 HWT/RPK-7 (RS-SS-N-16 *Stallion*) ASW msl, 4 single 553mm TT with 53-65K HWT/SET-65K HWT/USET-80K *Keramika* HWT

1 *Yasen* (Project 885 (*Severodvinsk* I)) with 8 4-cell SM-346 VLS with 3M14K (RS-SS-N-30A *Sagaris*) dual-capable LACM/3M54K1 (RS-SS-N-27) AShM/3M54K (RS-SS-N-27B *Sizzler*) AShM/3M55 *Oniks* (RS-SS-N-26 *Strobile*) AShM (3M54K/K1 operational status unclear); 10 single 533mm TT with USET-80K *Keramika* HWT/UGST *Fizik* HWT

3 *Yasen*-M (Project 08851 (*Severodvinsk* II)) with 8 4-cell SM-346 VLS with 3M14K (RS-SS-N-30A *Sagaris*) dual-capable LACM/3M54K1 (RS-SS-N-27) AShM/3M54K (RS-SS-N-27B *Sizzler*) AShM/3M55 *Oniks* (RS-SS-N-26 *Strobile*) AShM (3M54K/K1 operational status unclear); up to 10 single 533mm TT with UGST *Fizik* HWT

SSN 10:

1 *Kalmar* (Project 667BDR (*Delta* III)) with 2 single 400mm TT with SET-72 LWT, 4 single 533mm TT with 53-65K HWT/SET-65K HWT/USET-80K *Keramika* HWT (re-roled SSBN)

2 *Kondor* (Project 945A (*Sierra* II)) with 4 single 533mm TT with TEST-71M HWT/USET-80K *Keramika* HWT (unclear if dual-capable 3M14 (RS-SS-N-30A *Sagaris*) has replaced 3M10 *Granat* (RS-SS-N-21 *Sampson*) nuclear LACM which is possibly withdrawn; AShM capability unconfirmed), 4 single 650mm TT with 65-73 HWT

2 *Schuka* (Project 671RTMK (*Victor* III)) with 4 single 533mm TT with 53-65K HWT/SET-65K HWT/USET-80K *Keramika* HWT (unclear if dual-capable 3M14 (RS-SS-N-30A *Sagaris*) has replaced 3M10 *Granat* (RS-SS-N-21 *Sampson*) nuclear LACM which is possibly withdrawn; AShM capability unconfirmed), 2 single 650mm TT with 65-73 HWT

3 *Schuka*-B (Project 971 (*Akula* I)) (5 more non-operational, return to service significantly delayed) with 4 single 533mm TT with 53-65K HWT/TEST-71M HWT/USET-80K *Keramika* HWT (unclear if dual-capable 3M14 (RS-SS-N-30A *Sagaris*) has replaced 3M10 *Granat* (RS-SS-N-21 *Sampson*) nuclear LACM which is possibly withdrawn; AShM capability unconfirmed), 4 single 650mm TT with 65-73 HWT/RPK-7 (RS-SS-N-16 *Stallion*) ASW msl

2 *Schuka*-B (Project 971/09711 (*Akula* II)) with 4 single 533mm TT with 53-65K HWT/TEST-71M HWT/USET-80K *Keramika* HWT (unclear if dual-capable 3M14 (RS-SS-N-30A *Sagaris*) has replaced 3M10 *Granat* (RS-SS-N-21 *Sampson*) nuclear LACM which is possibly withdrawn; AShM capability unconfirmed), 4 single 650mm TT with 65-73 HWT/RPK-7 (RS-SS-N-16 *Stallion*) ASW msl

SSK 19:

9 *Paltus* (Project 877 (*Kilo*)) (1 more non-operational, in long-term refit) with 6 single 533mm TT with 53-65K HWT/TEST-71M HWT/USET-80K *Keramika* HWT

10 *Varshavyanka* (Project 06363 (*Improved Kilo*)) (1 more non-operational) with 6 single 533mm TT with 3M14K *Kalibr*-PL (RS-SS-N-30A *Sagaris*) dual-capable LACM/3M54K (RS-SS-N-27B *Sizzler*) AShM/3M54K1 (RS-SS-N-27) AShM/53-65K HWT/TEST-71M HWT/USET-80K *Keramika* HWT (3M54K/K1 operational status unclear)

(1 *Lada* (Project 677 (*Petersburg*)) with 6 single 533mm TT with 3M14K *Kalibr*-PL (RS-SS-N-30A

Sagaris) dual-capable LACM/3M54K (RS-SS-N-27B *Sizzler*) AShM/3M54K1 (RS-SS-N-27) AShM/USET-80K *Keramika* HWT (3M54K/K1 operational status unclear) non-operational)

PRINCIPAL SURFACE COMBATANTS 34

AIRCRAFT CARRIERS • CV 1 *Admiral Kuznetsov* (in extended refit) with 12 single SM-233A lnchr with 3M45 *Granit* (RS-SS-N-19 *Shipwreck*) AShM, 24 8-cell 3S95 VLS with 3K95 *Kinzhal* (RS-SA-N-9 *Gauntlet*) SAM, 2 RBU 12000 *Udav* 1 A/S mor, 8 3M87 *Kortik* CIWS with 9M311 SAM (RS-CADS-N-1), 6 AK630M CIWS (capacity 18–24 Su-33 *Flanker* D/MiG-29KR/KUBR Ftr/FGA ac; 15 Ka-27 *Helix* ASW hel, 2 Ka-31R *Helix* AEW hel)

CRUISERS 3:

CGHMN 1 *Orlan* (Project 11442 (*Kirov* I)) (1 other non-operational; undergoing extensive refit and planned to return to service in 2024) with 20 single SM-233 lnchr with 3M45 *Granit* (RS-SS-N-19 *Shipwreck*) AShM, 6 8-cell B-203A VLS with S-300F *Fort* (RS-SA-N-6 *Grumble*) SAM, 6 8-cell B-203A VLS with S-300FM *Fort*-M (RS-SA-N-20 *Gargoyle*) SAM, 16 8-cell 3S95 VLS with 3K95 *Kinzhal* (RS-SA-N-9 *Gauntlet*) SAM, 2 quintuple 533mm TT with RPK-6M *Vodopad*-NK (RS-SS-N-16 *Stallion*) A/S msl, 1 RBU 6000 *Smerch* 2 A/S mor, 2 RBU 1000 *Smerch* 3 A/S mor, 6 3M87 *Kortik* CIWS with 9M311 SAM (RS-CADS-N-1), 1 twin 130mm gun (capacity 3 Ka-27 *Helix* ASW hel)

CGHM 2 *Atlant* (Project 1164 (*Slava*)) with 8 twin SM-248 lnchr with 3M70 *Vulkan* (RS-SS-N-12 mod 2 *Sandbox*) AShM, 8 octuple VLS with S-300F *Fort* (RS-SA-N-6 *Grumble*) SAM/S-300FM *Fort* M (RS-SA-N-20 *Gargoyle*) SAM, 2 twin ZIF-122 lnchr with 4K33 *Osa*-M (RS-SA-N-4 *Gecko*) SAM, 2 quintuple 533mm PTA-53-1164 ASTT with SET-65K HWT, 2 RBU 6000 *Smerch* 2 A/S mor, 6 AK630 CIWS, 1 twin 130mm gun (capacity 1 Ka-27 *Helix* ASW hel)

DESTROYERS • DDGHM 11:

3 *Sarych* (Project 956 (*Sovremenny* I)) with 2 quad lnchr with 3M80 *Moskit* (RS-SS-N-22 *Sunburn*) AShM, 2 twin 3S90 lnchr with 9M317 *Yezh* (RS-SA-N-7B) SAM, 2 twin DTA-53-956 533mm TT with 53-65K HWT/SET-65K HWT, 2 RBU 1000 *Smerch* 3 A/S mor, 4 AK630 CIWS, 2 twin 130mm guns (capacity 1 Ka-27 *Helix* ASW hel)

6 *Fregat* (Project 1155 (*Udaloy* I)) with 2 quad lnchr with URK-5 *Rastrub*-B (RS-SS-N-14 *Silex*) AShM/ASW, 8 8-cell 3S95 VLS with 3K95 *Kinzhal* (RS-SA-N-9 *Gauntlet*) SAM, 2 quad 533mm ChTA-53-1155 ASTT with 53-65K HWT/SET-65K HWT, 2 RBU 6000 *Smerch* 2 A/S mor, 4 AK630 CIWS, 2 100mm guns (capacity 2 Ka-27 *Helix* ASW hel)

1 *Fregat* (Project 1155 (*Udaloy* I)) with 2 8-cell 3S14 UKSK VLS with with 3M14T *Kalibr*-NK (RS-SS-N-30A *Sagaris*) dual-capable LACM/3M54T (RS-SS-N-27B *Sizzler*) AShM/3M54T1 (RS-SS-N-27) AShM/3M55 *Oniks* (RS-SS-N-26 *Strobile*) AShM (3M54T/T1 operational status unclear), 2 quad lnchr with 3M24 *Uran* (RS-SS-N-25 *Switchblade*) AShM, 2 quad 533mm ChTA-53-1155 ASTT with 53-65K HWT/SET-65K HWT, 2 RBU 6000 *Smerch* 2 A/S mor, 4 AK630 CIWS, 1 100mm gun (capacity 2 Ka-27 *Helix* ASW hel)

1 *Fregat* (Project 11551 (*Udaloy* II)) (in refit) with 2 quad lnchr with 3M80 *Moskit* (RS-SS-N-22 *Sunburn*) AShM, 8 8-cell 3S95 VLS with 3K95 *Kinzhal* (RS-SA-N-9 *Gauntlet*) SAM, 2 3M87 *Kortik* CIWS with 9M311 SAM (RS-CADS-N-1), 2 RBU 6000 *Smerch* 2 A/S mor, 1 twin 130mm gun (capacity 2 Ka-27 *Helix* ASW hel)

FRIGATES 20

FFGHM 18:

3 Project 11356 (*Grigorovich*) with 1 8-cell 3S14 UKSK VLS with 3M14T *Kalibr*-NK (RS-SS-N-30A *Sagaris*) dual-capable LACM/3M54T (RS-SS-N-27B *Sizzler*) AShM/3M54T1 (RS-SS-N-27) AShM/3M55 *Oniks* (RS-SS-N-26 *Strobile*) AShM/91RT2 A/S msl (3M54T/T1 operational status unclear), 2 12-cell 3S90.1 VLS with 9M317 *Yezh* (RS-SA-N-7B) SAM/9M317M *Yezh* (RS-SA-N-7C) SAM, 2 twin DTA-53-11356 533mm TT with 53-65K HWT/SET-65K HWT, 1 RBU 6000 A/S mor, 2 AK630 CIWS, 1 100mm gun (capacity 1 Ka-27 *Helix* ASW hel)

2 *Jastreb* (Project 11540 (*Neustrashimyy*)) with 2 quad lnchr with 3M24 *Uran* (RS-SS-N-25 *Switchblade*) AShM, 4 8-cell 3S95 VLS with 3K95 *Kinzhal* (RS-SA-N-9 *Gauntlet*), 6 single 533mm ASTT with RPK-6M *Vodopad*-NK (RS-SS-N-16 *Stallion*) A/S msl, 1 RBU 6000 *Smerch* 2 A/S mor, 2 3M87 *Kortik* CIWS with 9M311 SAM (RS-CADS-N-1), 1 100mm gun (capacity 1 Ka-27 *Helix* ASW hel)

1 Project 20380 (*Steregushchiy* I) with 2 quad lnchr with 3M24 *Uran* (RS-SS-N-25 *Switchblade*) AShM, 2 quad 324mm SM-588 ASTT with MTT LWT, 1 3M87 *Kortik*-M CIWS with 9M311 SAM (RS-CADS-N-1), 2 AK630 CIWS, 1 100mm gun (capacity 1 Ka-27 *Helix* ASW hel)

8 Project 20380 (*Steregushchiy* II) with 2 quad lnchr with 3M24 *Uran* (RS-SS-N-25 *Switchblade*) AShM, 3 4-cell 3S97 VLS with 3K96-3 *Redut* (RS-SA-N-28) SAM, 2 quad 324mm SM-588 ASTT with MTT LWT, 2 AK630 CIWS, 1 100mm gun (capacity 1 Ka-27 *Helix* ASW hel)

1 Project 20385 (*Gremyashchiy*) with 1 8-cell 3S14 UKSK VLS with 3M14T *Kalibr*-NK (RS-SS-N-30A *Sagaris*) dual-capable LACM/3M54T (RS-SS-N-27B *Sizzler*) AShM/3M54T1 (RS-SS-N-27) AShM/3M55 *Oniks* (RS-SS-N-26 *Strobile*) AShM (3M54T/T1 operational status unclear), 4 4-cell 3S97 VLS with 3K96-2 *Poliment-Redut* (RS-SA-N-28) SAM, 2 quad 324mm TT with MTT LWT, 2 AK630 CIWS, 1 100mm gun (capacity 1 Ka-27 *Helix* ASW hel)

3 Project 22350 (*Gorshkov*) with 2 8-cell 3S14 UKSK VLS with 3M14T *Kalibr*-NK (RS-SS-N-30A *Sagaris*) dual-capable LACM/3M54T (RS-SS-N-27B *Sizzler*) AShM/3M54T1 (RS-SS-N-27) AShM/3M55 *Oniks* (RS-SS-N-26 *Strobile*) AShM (3M54T/T1

operational status unclear), 4 8-cell 3S97 VLS with 3K96-2 *Poliment-Redut* (RS-SA-N-28) SAM, 2 quad 324mm TT with MTT LWT, 2 3M89 *Palash* CIWS (RS-CADS-N-2), 1 130mm gun (capacity 1 Ka-27 *Helix* ASW hel)

FFGM 2:
- 1 *Burevestnik* (Project 1135 (*Krivak* I))† with 1 quad lnchr with URK-5 *Rastrub-B* (RS-SS-N-14 *Silex*) AShM/ASW, 1 twin ZIF-122 lnchr with *Osa-M* (RS-SA-N-4 *Gecko*) SAM, 2 quad 533mm ChTA-53-1135 ASTT with 53-65K HWT/SET-65K HWT, 2 RBU 6000 *Smerch* 2 A/S mor, 2 twin 76mm guns
- 1 *Burevestnik* M (Project 1135M (*Krivak* II)) with 1 quad lnchr with URK-5 *Rastrub-B* (RS-SS-N-14 *Silex*) AShM/ASW, 2 twin ZIF-122 lnchr with 4K33 *Osa-M* (RS-SA-N-4 *Gecko* SAM), 2 quad 533mm ChTA-53-1135 ASTT with 53-65K HWT/ SET-65K HWT, 2 RBU 6000 *Smerch* 2 A/S mor, 2 100mm guns

PATROL AND COASTAL COMBATANTS 124

CORVETTES 45

FSGM 17
- 11 *Buyan*-M (Project 21631 (*Sviyazhsk*)) with 1 8-cell 3S14 UKSK VLS with 3M14T *Kalibr-NK* (RS-SS-N-30A *Sagaris*) dual-capable LACM/3M54T (RS-SS-N-27B *Sizzler*) AShM/3M54T1 (RS-SS-N-27) AShM/3M55 *Oniks* (RS-SS-N-26 *Strobile*) AShM (3M54T/T1 operational status unclear), 2 sextuple 3M47 *Gibka* lnchr with *Igla*-1M (RS-SA-N-10 *Grouse*) SAM, 1 AK630M-2 CIWS, 1 100mm gun
- 2 *Karakurt* (Project 22800 (*Uragan*)) with 1 8-cell 3S14 UKSK VLS with 3M14T *Kalibr-NK* (RS-SS-N-30A *Sagaris*) dual-capable LACM/3M54T (RS-SS-N-27B *Sizzler*) AShM/3M54T1 (RS-SS-N-27) AShM/3M55 *Oniks* (RS-SS-N-26 *Strobile*) AShM (3M54T/T1 operational status unclear), 2 *Pantsir*-M with 57E6 SAM, 1 76mm gun
- 1 Project 11661K (*Gepard* I) with 2 quad lnchr with 3M24 *Uran* (RS-SS-N-25 *Switchblade*) AShM, 1 twin ZIF-122 lnchr with 4K33 *Osa-M* (RS-SA-N-4 *Gecko*) SAM, 2 AK630 CIWS, 1 76mm gun
- 1 Project 11661K (*Gepard* II) with 1 8-cell VLS with 3M14T *Kalibr-NK* (RS-SS-N-30A *Sagaris*) dual-capable LACM/3M54T (RS-SS-N-27B *Sizzler*) AShM/3M54T1 (RS-SS-N-27) AShM/3M55 *Oniks* (RS-SS-N-26 *Strobile*) AShM (3M54T/T1 operational status unclear), 1 3M89 *Palash* CIWS with 9M337 *Sosna-R* SAM (RS-CADS-N-2), 1 76mm gun
- 2 *Sivuch* (Project 1239 (*Dergach*)) with 2 quad lnchr with 3M80 *Moskit* (RS-SS-N-22 *Sunburn*) AShM, 1 twin ZIF-122 lnchr with 4K33AM *Osa-MA2* (RS-SA-N-4 *Gecko*) SAM, 2 AK630M CIWS, 1 76mm gun

FSG 2 *Karakurt* (Project 22800 (*Uragan*)) with 1 8-cell 3S14 VLS with 3M14T *Kalibr-NK* (RS-SS-N-30A *Sagaris*) dual-capable LACM/3M54T (RS-SS-N-27B *Sizzler*) AShM/3M54T1 (RS-SS-N-27) AShM/3M55 *Oniks* (RS-SS-N-26 *Strobile*) AShM (3M54T/T1 operational status unclear), 2 AK630M CIWS, 1 76mm gun

FSM 26:
- 2 *Albatros* (Project 1124 (*Grisha* III)) with 1 twin ZIF-122 lnchr with 4K33 *Osa-M* (RS-SA-N-4 *Gecko*) SAM, 2 twin 533mm DTA-53-1124 ASTT, 2 RBU 6000 *Smerch* 2 A/S mor, 1 twin 57mm gun
- 18 *Albatros* (Project 1124M (*Grisha* V)) with 1 twin ZIF-122 lnchr with 4K33 *Osa-M* (RS-SA-N-4 *Gecko*) SAM, 2 twin 533mm DTA-53-1124 ASTT, 1 RBU 6000 *Smerch* 2 A/S mor, 1 AK630 CIWS, 1 76mm gun
- 6 Project 1331M (*Parchim* II) with 2 quad lnchr with 9K32 *Strela*-2 (RS-SA-N-5 *Grail*) SAM, 2 twin 533mm ASTT, 2 RBU 6000 *Smerch* 2 A/S mor, 1 AK630 CIWS, 1 76mm gun

PSOH 4 Project 22160 (*Bykov*) (of which 1†) with 1 76mm gun (capacity 1 Ka-27 *Helix* ASW hel)

PCGM 7:
- 6 *Ovod*-1 (Project 1234.1 (*Nanuchka* III)) (1 more in reserve) with 2 triple lnchr with P-120 *Malakhit* (RS-SS-N-9 *Siren*) AShM, 1 twin ZIF-122 lnchr with 4K33 *Osa-M* (RS-SA-N-4 *Gecko*) SAM, 1 AK630 CIWS, 1 76mm gun
- 1 *Ovod*-1 (Project 1234.1 (*Nanuchka* III)) with 4 quad lnchr with 3M24 *Uran* (RS-SS-N-25 *Switchblade*) AShM, 1 twin lnchr with 4K33 *Osa-M* (RS-SA-N-4 *Gecko*) SAM, 1 AK630 CIWS, 1 76mm gun

PCFG 20:
- 4 *Molnya* (*Tarantul* II) with 2 twin lnchr with P-22 *Termit-R* (RS-SS-N-2D *Styx*) AShM, 2 AK630M CIWS, 1 76mm gun
- 15 *Molnya* (*Tarantul* III) with 2 twin lnchr with 3M80 *Moskit* (RS-SS-N-22 *Sunburn*) AShM, 2 AK630M CIWS, 1 76mm gun
- 1 *Molnya* (*Tarantul* III) with 2 twin lnchr with 3M80 *Moskit* (RS-SS-N-22 *Sunburn*) AShM, 1 3K89 *Palash* (RS-CADS-N-2) CIWS, 1 76mm gun

PCM 3 *Buyan* (Project 21630 (*Astrakhan*)) with 1 sextuple lnchr with 3M47 *Gibka* lnchr with *Igla*-1M (RS-SA-N-10 *Grouse*) SAM, 1 A-215 *Grad-M* 122mm MRL, 1 100mm gun

PBF 14: 12+ *Raptor* (capacity 20 troops); 2 *Mangust*

PBR 4 *Shmel* with 1 17-cell BM-14 MRL, 1 76mm gun

PB 27 *Grachonok*

MINE WARFARE • MINE COUNTERMEASURES 44

MCC 8 *Alexandrit* (Project 12700)

MHI 7 *Sapfir* (Project 10750 (*Lida*)) with 1 AK630 CIWS

MHO 2 *Rubin* (Project 12660 (*Gorya*)) with 2 quad lnchr with 9K32 *Strela-2* (RS-SA-N-5 *Grail*) SAM, 1 AK630 CIWS, 1 76mm gun

MSC 20: 19 *Yakhont* (Project 1265 (*Sonya*)) with 4 AK630 CIWS (some with 2 quad lnchr with 9K32 *Strela-2* (RS-SA-N-5 *Grail*) SAM); 1 *Korund-E* (Project 1258E (*Yevgenya*))

MSO 7: 6 *Akvamaren-M* (Project 266M (*Natya*)); 1 *Agat* (Project 02668 (*Natya* II)) (all with 2 quad lnchr (manual aiming) with 9K32 *Strela-2* (RS-SA-N-5 *Grail*) SAM, 2 RBU 1200 *Uragan* A/S mor, 2 twin AK230 CIWS

AMPHIBIOUS

LANDING SHIPS • LST 17

9 Project 775 (*Ropucha* I/II) (2 more non-operational) with 2 twin 57mm guns (capacity either 10 MBT and 190 troops or 24 APC (T) and 170 troops)

3 Project 775M (*Ropucha* III) with 2 AK630 CIWS, 1 76mm gun (capacity either 10 MBT and 190 troops or 24 APC (T) and 170 troops)

3 *Tapir* (Project 1171 (*Alligator*)) with at least 2 twin lnchr with 9K32 *Strela*-2 (RS-SA-N-5 *Grail*) SAM, 2 twin 57mm guns (capacity 20 tanks; 300 troops)

2 Project 11711 (*Gren*) with 1 AK630M-2 CIWS, 2 AK630M CIWS (capacity 1 Ka-29 *Helix* B hel; 13 MBT/36 AFV; 300 troops)

LANDING CRAFT 26

LCM 24: 8 *Akula* (Project 1176 (*Ondatra*)) (capacity 1 MBT); 5 *Dyugon* (Project 21820) (capacity 5 APC or 100 troops); 11 *Serna* (Project 11770) (capacity 2 APC or 100 troops)

LCAC 2 *Zubr* (Project 12322 (*Pomornik*)) with 2 22-cell 140mm MS-227 *Ogon* MRL, 2 AK630 CIWS (capacity 230 troops; either 3 MBT or 10 APC(T))

LOGISTICS AND SUPPORT 284

SSAN 9:
1 *Belgorod* (Project 22870 (*Oscar* II mod))
2 *Halibut* (Project 18511 (*Paltus*))
3 *Kashalot* (Project 1910 (*Uniform*))
1 *Nelma* (Project 1851 (*X-Ray*))
1 *Orenburg* (*Delta* III Stretch)
1 *Podmoskovye* (Project 09787)
(1 non-operational *Losharik* (Project 10831 (*Norsub*-5)) reportedly damaged by fire in 2019)

SSA 1 *Sarov* (Project 20120)

ABU 12: 8 *Kashtan*; 4 Project 419 (*Sura*)

AE 9: 6 *Muna*; 1 *Dubnyak*; 2 *Akademik Kovalev* (Project 20181) with 1 hel landing platform

AEM 2: 1 *Kalma*-3 (Project 1791R); 1 *Lama*

AFS 2 *Longvinik* (Project 23120)

AGB 6: 1 *Dobrynya Mikitich*; 1 *Ilya Muromets*; 1 *Ilya Muromets* (Project 21180); 2 *Ivan Susanin*; 1 *Vladimir Kavraisky*

AGE 2: 1 *Potok*; 1 *Tchusovoy*

AGI 14: 2 *Alpinist*; 2 *Dubridium* (Project 1826); 1 *Moma*; 7 *Vishnya*; 2 *Yuri Ivanov*

AGM 1 *Marshal Nedelin*

AGOR 6: 1 *Akademik Alexandrov* (Project 20183); 1 *Akademik Krylov*; 2 *Seliger*; 2 *Vinograd*

AGOS 1 *Yantar*

AGS 77: 7 *Baklan* (Project 19920); 5 *Baklan* (Project 19920B); 8 *Biya*; 16+ *Finik*; 7 *Kamenka*; 5 *Moma*; 8+ *Onega*; 4 Project 19910; 6 Project 23040G; 2 *Sibiriyakov*; 9+ *Yug*

AGSH 1 *Samara*

AH 3 *Ob*†

AK 1 *Pevek*

AKL 2 *Irgiz*

AO 9: 3+ *Altay* (mod); 2+ *Dubna*; 3 *Uda*; 1 *Platforma-Arktika* (Project 03182) with 1 hel landing plaftorm

AOL 1 *Luza*

AOR 6: 1 *Akademik Pashin* (Project 23130); 3 *Boris Chilikin*; 1+ *Kaliningradneft*; 1 *Olekma*

AR ε7 *Amur*

ARC 5: 4 *Emba*; 1 Improved *Klasma*

ARS 38: 1 *Kommuna*; 5 *Goryn*; 4 *Mikhail Rudnitsky*; 5 Project 22870; 22 Project 23040; 1 *Zvezdochka* (Project 20180)

AS 3 Project 2020 (*Malina*)

ASR 2: 1 *Elbrus*; 1 *Igor Belousov*

ATF 54: 1 *Okhotsk*; 1 *Baklan*; ε3 *Katun*; 3 *Ingul*; 1 *Neftegaz*; 10 *Okhtensky*; 13 *Prometey*; 3 Project 23470 with 1 hel landing platform; 1 *Prut*; 4 *Sliva*; 14 *Sorum*

AWT 1 *Manych*

AX 2 *Smolny* with 2 RBU 2500 *Smerch* 1 A/S mor, 2 twin 76mm guns

AXL 7 *Petrushka*

UNINHABITED MARITIME PLATFORMS

USV • MW • Small 3 *Inspektor* Mk2

UUV
ATK • Nuclear • Extra-Large *Poseidon* (*Status*-6) (nuclear powered) (in test)
DATA • Extra-Large *Klavesin*-1R (*Harpsichord*); *Klavesin*-2R-PM (*Harpsichord*); *Vityaz*-D
UTL • Extra-Large *Sarma*; *Sarma*-D (*Sarma* mod)

UNINHABITED MARITIME SYSTEMS • USV
DATA *Alister* 9 (A9-E); *Galtel*
MW K-Ster C/I; SEASCAN

Naval Aviation ε25,000

FORCES BY ROLE

FIGHTER
1 regt with MiG-31B/BS/BM *Foxhound*
1 regt with Su-33 *Flanker* D; Su-25UTG *Frogfoot*

FIGHTER/GROUND ATTACK
1 regt with MiG-29KR/KUBR *Fulcrum*

ANTI-SURFACE WARFARE/ISR
2 regt with Su-24M/MR *Fencer*; Su-30SM

ANTI-SUBMARINE WARFARE
1 regt with Il-38/Il-38N *May**; Il-18D; Il-20RT *Coot* A; Il-22 *Coot* B
2 sqn with Il-38/Il-38N *May**; Il-18D; Il-20RT *Coot* A; Il-22 *Coot* B
1 regt with Ka-27/Ka-29 *Helix*
1 sqn with Ka-27/Ka-29 *Helix*
2 sqn with Tu-142MK/MZ/MR *Bear* F/J*
1 unit with Ka-31R *Helix*

MARITIME PATROL/TRANSPORT
1 regt with An-26 *Curl*; Be-12 *Mail**; Ka-27 *Helix*; Mi-8 *Hip*

SEARCH & RESCUE/TRANSPORT
1 sqn with An-12PS *Cub*; An-26 *Curl*; Tu-134

TRANSPORT
1 sqn with An-12BK *Cub*; An-24RV *Coke*; An-26 *Curl*; An-72 *Coaler*; An-140
2 sqn with An-26 *Curl*; Tu-134

TRAINING
1 sqn with L-39 *Albatros*; Su-25UTG *Frogfoot*

1 sqn with An-140; Tu-134; Tu-154, Il-38 *May*
ATTACK/TRANSPORT HELICOPTER
1 sqn with Mi-24P *Hind*; Mi-8 *Hip*
TRANSPORT HELICOPTER
1 sqn with Mi-8 *Hip*
COMBAT/ISR UAV
1 regt with *Forpost* (*Searcher* II); *Inokhodets*
AIR DEFENCE
2 AD div HQ
3 SAM regt with S-400 (RS-SA-21 *Growler*); 96K6 *Pantsir-S1* (RS-SA-22 *Greyhound*)
EQUIPMENT BY TYPE
AIRCRAFT 163 combat capable
 FTR 35: 9 MiG-31B/BS *Foxhound*; 9 MiG-31BM *Foxhound* C; 17 Su-33 *Flanker* D
 FGA 47: 19 MiG-29KR *Fulcrum*; 3 MiG-29KUBR *Fulcrum*; ε17 Su-30SM *Flanker* H; 8+ Su-30SM2 *Flanker* H
 ATK 25: 20 Su-24M *Fencer*; 5 Su-25UTG *Frogfoot* (trg)
 ASW 44: 12 Tu-142MK/MZ *Bear* F; 10 Tu-142MR *Bear* J (comms); 15 Il-38 *May*; 7 Il-38N *May*
 MP 7: 6 Be-12PS *Mail**; 1 Il-18D
 ISR 6 Su-24MR *Fencer* E*
 SAR 4: 3 An-12PS *Cub*; 1 Be-200ES
 ELINT 4: 2 Il-20RT *Coot* A; 2 Il-22 *Coot* B
 TPT 49: **Medium** 2 An-12BK *Cub*; **Light** 45: 1 An-24RV *Coke*; 24 An-26 *Curl*; 6 An-72 *Coaler*; 4 An-140; 9 Tu-134; 1 Tu-134UBL; **PAX** 2 Tu-154M *Careless*
 TRG 4 L-39 *Albatros*
HELICOPTERS
 ATK 7 Mi-24P *Hind*
 ASW 67: ε45 Ka-27PL *Helix*; 22 Ka-27M *Helix*
 EW 8 Mi-8 *Hip* J
 AEW 2 Ka-31R *Helix*
 SAR 16 Ka-27PS *Helix* D
 TPT 40: **Medium** 34: 26 Ka-29 *Helix*; 4 Mi-8T *Hip*; 4 Mi-8MT *Hip*; **Light** 6 Ka-226T
AIR DEFENCE
 SAM • Long-range 64 S-400 (RS-SA-21 *Growler*)
 SPAAGM 30mm 30 96K6 *Pantsir-S1* (RS-SA-22 *Greyhound*)
UNINHABITED AERIAL VEHICLES
 CISR • Heavy *Inokhodets*
 ISR • Medium *Forpost* (*Searcher* II)
AIR-LAUNCHED MISSILES
 AAM • IR R-27T/ET (RS-AA-10B/D *Alamo*); R-60 (RS-AA-8 *Aphid*); R-73 (RS-AA-11A *Archer*); R-74M (RS-AA-11B *Archer*); **ARH** R-37M (RS-AA-13A *Axehead*); R-77-1 (RS-AA-12B *Adder*); **SARH** R-27R/ER (RS-AA-10A/C *Alamo*); R-33 (RS-AA-9A *Amos*)
 ARM Kh-25MP (RS-AS-12A *Kegler*); Kh-31P (RS-AS-17A *Krypton*); Kh-58 (RS-AS-11 *Kilter*)
 ASM Kh-59 (RS-AS-13 *Kingbolt*); Kh-59M (RS-AS-18 *Kazoo*); Kh-29T (RS-AS-14 *Kedge*)
 AShM Kh-31A/AM (RS-AS-17B/D *Krypton*)

Naval Infantry (Marines) ε10,000
FORCES BY ROLE
As a result of sustained heavy losses suffered during the invasion of Ukraine, almost all of the manoeuvre formations listed are currently understrength.
SPECIAL FORCES
 4 (OMRP) SF unit
 11 (PDSS) cbt diver unit
MANOEUVRE
 Mechanised
 6 naval inf bde
 1 naval inf regt
COMBAT SUPPORT
 3 engr regt
 1 engr bn
EQUIPMENT BY TYPE (ε)
ARMOURED FIGHTING VEHICLES
 MBT 90: 30 T-55A; 30 T-72B/B3/3M; 30 T-80BV/BVM
 IFV 340: 100 BMP-2; 40 BMP-3F; 200 BTR-82A
 APC 350
  APC (T) 250 MT-LB
  APC (W) 100 BTR-80
 AUV *Vystrel*
ANTI-TANK/ANTI-INFRASTRUCTURE
 MSL
  SP 30+: 9P148 with 9K111-1 *Konkurs* (RS-AT-5 *Spandrel*); 30 9P149 with 9K114 *Shturm* (RS-AT-6 *Spiral*); 9P157-2 with 9K123 *Khrisantema* (RS-AT-15 *Springer*)
  MANPATS 9K111-1 *Konkurs* (RS-AT-5 *Spandrel*); 9K135 *Kornet* (RS-AT-14 *Spriggan*)
 GUNS 100mm T-12
ARTILLERY 300
 SP 68: **122mm** 16 2S1 *Gvozdika*; **152mm** 52: 16 2S3 *Akatsiya*; 36 2S19M1 *Msta-S*
 TOWED 130: **122mm** 30 D-30; **152mm** 100: 50 2A36 *Giatsint-B*; 50 2A65 *Msta-B*
 GUN/MOR 66
  SP 120mm 42: 12 2S23 NONA-SVK; 30 2S9 NONA-S
  TOWED 120mm 24 2B16 NONA-K
 MRL • 122mm 36 BM-21 *Grad/Tornado-G*
AIR DEFENCE
 SAM
  Point-defence 70+: 20 9K33 *Osa* (RS-SA-8 *Gecko*); 40 9K31 *Strela-1*/9K35 *Strela-10* (RS-SA-9 *Gaskin*/RS-SA-13 *Gopher*); 9K338 *Igla-S* (RS-SA-24 *Grinch*)
 GUNS • SP 23mm 60 ZSU-23-4

Coastal Missile and Artillery Forces 2,000
FORCES BY ROLE
COASTAL DEFENCE
 5 AShM bde
 1 AShM regt
EQUIPMENT BY TYPE

COASTAL DEFENCE
ARTY • SP 130mm 36 A-222 *Bereg*
AShM 96+: 40 3K60 *Bal* (RS-SSC-6 *Sennight*); 56 3K55 *Bastion* (RS-SSC-5 *Stooge*); some 4K44 *Redut* (RS-SSC-1 *Sepal*); some 4K51 *Rubezh* (RS-SSC-3 *Styx*)
UNINHABITED AERIAL VEHICLES
ISR • Light *Granat-4*

Aerospace Forces ε170,000 (incl conscripts)

A joint CIS Unified Air Defence System covers RUS, ARM, BLR, KAZ, KGZ, TJK, TKM and UZB

FORCES BY ROLE
BOMBER
3 regt with Tu-22M3 *Backfire* C
3 sqn with Tu-95MS/MS mod *Bear*
1 sqn with Tu-160/Tu-160 mod *Blackjack*
FIGHTER
1 sqn with MiG-29/MiG-29UB *Fulcrum* (Armenia)
2 regt with MiG-31BM *Foxhound* C
1 regt with MiG-31BM *Foxhound* C; Su-35S *Flanker* M
1 regt with Su-27/Su-27UB *Flanker*
1 regt with Su-27/Su-27SM/Su-27UB *Flanker* B/J/C; Su-30M2 *Flanker* G
2 regt with Su-30SM *Flanker* H
FIGHTER/GROUND ATTACK
1 regt with MiG-31BM *Foxhound*; Su-24M/M2/MR *Fencer*
1 regt with MiG-31BM *Foxhound* C; Su-27SM *Flanker* J; Su-30M2 *Flanker* G; Su-30SM *Flanker* H; Su-35S *Flanker* M
1 regt with Su-27SM *Flanker* J; Su-35S *Flanker* M
1 regt with Su-35S *Flanker* M; Su-30SM *Flanker* H
1 regt with Su-27SM3 *Flanker*; Su-30M2 *Flanker* G
1 regt with Su-25 *Frogfoot*; Su-30SM *Flanker* H
GROUND ATTACK
1 regt with MiG-31K
1 regt with Su-24M/M2 *Fencer*; Su-34 *Fullback*
1 regt with Su-24M *Fencer*; Su-25SM *Frogfoot*
3 regt with Su-25SM/SM3 *Frogfoot*
1 sqn with Su-25SM *Frogfoot* (Kyrgyzstan)
3 regt with Su-34 *Fullback*
GROUND ATTACK/ISR
1 regt with Su-24M/MR *Fencer*
ISR
3 sqn with Su-24MR *Fencer*
1 flt with An-30 *Clank*
AIRBORNE EARLY WARNING & CONTROL
1 sqn with A-50U *Mainstay*
TANKER
1 sqn with Il-78/Il-78M *Midas*
TRANSPORT
6 regt/sqn with An-12BK *Cub*; An-148-100E; An-26 *Curl*; Tu-134 *Crusty*; Tu-154 *Careless*; Mi-8 *Hip*
1 regt with An-124 *Condor*; Il-76MD *Candid*
1 regt with An-124 *Condor*; Il-76MD/MD-90A *Candid*
1 regt with An-12BK *Cub*; Il-76MD *Candid*
3 regt with Il-76MD *Candid*
1 sqn with An-22 *Cock*
ATTACK/TRANSPORT HELICOPTER
1 bde with Ka-52A *Hokum* B; Mi-28N *Havoc* B; Mi-35 *Hind*; Mi-26 *Halo*; Mi-8MTV-5 *Hip*
1 bde with Ka-52A *Hokum* B; Mi-26 *Halo*; Mi-8 *Hip*
1 bde with Mi-28N *Havoc* B; Mi-35 *Hind*; Mi-26 *Halo*; Mi-8 *Hip*
2 regt with Ka-52A *Hokum* B; Mi-28N *Havoc* B; Mi-35 *Hind*; Mi-8 *Hip*
1 regt with Ka-52A *Hokum* B; Mi-24P *Hind*; Mi-8MTPR-1 *Hip*; Mi-8 *Hip*
1 regt with Ka-52A *Hokum* B; Mi-8 *Hip*
1 regt with Mi-28N *Havoc* B; Mi-35 *Hind*; Mi-8 *Hip*
1 regt with Mi-28N *Havoc* B; Mi-24P *Hind*; Mi-35 *Hind*; Mi-8 *Hip*
2 regt with Mi-24P *Hind*; Mi-8 *Hip*
2 sqn with Mi-24P *Hind*; Mi-8 *Hip*
AIR DEFENCE
11 AD div HQ
4 regt with 9K37M1-2 *Buk-M1-2* (RS-SA-11 *Gadfly*); 9K317 *Buk-M2* (RS-SA-17 *Grizzly*); S-300V (RS-SA-12 *Gladiator/Giant*)
1 bde with S-300PS (RS-SA-10B *Grumble*)
3 regt with S-300PS (RS-SA-10B *Grumble*)
6 regt with S-300PM1/PM2 (RS-SA-20 *Gargoyle*)
1 SAM regt with S-300PM1 (RS-SA-20 *Gargoyle*); S-300PS (RS-SA-10B *Grumble*)
1 SAM regt with S-300PM1 (RS-SA-20 *Gargoyle*); S-400 (RS-SA-21 *Growler*); 96K6 *Pantsir-S1* (RS-SA-22 *Greyhound*)
1 SAM regt with S-300PS (RS-SA-10B *Grumble*); S-400 (RS-SA-21 *Growler*); 96K6 *Pantsir-S1* (RS-SA-22 *Greyhound*)
13 regt with S-400 (RS-SA-21 *Growler*); 96K6 *Pantsir-S1* (RS-SA-22 *Greyhound*)
EQUIPMENT BY TYPE
AIRCRAFT 1,224 combat capable
BBR 127: 55 Tu-22M3 *Backfire* C; 1 Tu-22MR *Backfire*† (in overhaul); 31 Tu-95MS *Bear*; 27 Tu-95MS mod *Bear*; 6 Tu-160 *Blackjack*; 7 Tu-160 mod *Blackjack*; (3 Tu-160M *Blackjack* in test)
FTR 220: 70 MiG-29/MiG-29UB *Fulcrum*; 102 MiG-31BM *Foxhound* C; 24 Su-27 *Flanker* B; 24 Su-27UB *Flanker* C
FGA 449: 14 MiG-29SMT *Fulcrum*; 2 MiG-29UBT *Fulcrum*; 46 Su-27SM *Flanker* J; 24 Su-27SM3 *Flanker* J; 19 Su-30M2 *Flanker* G; ε80 Su-30SM *Flanker* H; 4+ Su-30SM2 *Flanker* H; ε93 Su-34 *Fullback*; ε31 Su-34 mod *Fullback*; ε117 Su-35S *Flanker* M; ε19 Su-57 *Felon*; (4 MiG-35S *Fulcrum*; 2 MiG-35UB *Fulcrum* in test)
ATK 262: ε24 MiG-31K; 77 Su-24M/M2 *Fencer*; ε37 Su-25 *Frogfoot*; ε109 Su-25SM/SM3 *Frogfoot*; 15 Su-25UB *Frogfoot*
ISR 62: 4 An-30 *Clank*; up to 54 Su-24MR *Fencer**; 2 Tu-214ON; 2 Tu-214R
EW 3 Il-22PP *Mute*
ELINT 14 Il-20M *Coot* A
AEW&C 7 A-50U *Mainstay*

C2 24: 5 Il-22 *Coot* B; 11 Il-22M *Coot* B; 2 Il-80 *Maxdome*; 1 Il-82; 4 Tu-214SR; 1 Tu-214PU-SBUS

TKR 15: 5 Il-78 *Midas*; 10 Il-78M *Midas*

TPT 423: **Heavy** 124: 10 An-124 *Condor*; 4 An-22 *Cock*; 92 Il-76MD *Candid*; 3 Il-76MD-M *Candid*; 15 Il-76MD-90A *Candid*; **Medium** 45 An-12BK *Cub*; **Light** 224: ε113 An-26 *Curl*; 25 An-72 *Coaler*; 5 An-140; 27 L-410; 54 Tu-134 *Crusty*; **PAX** 32: 15 An-148-100E; 17 Tu-154 *Careless*

TRG 234: 35 DA42T; 87 L-39 *Albatros*; 112 Yak-130 *Mitten**

HELICOPTERS

ATK 334: ε62 Ka-52A *Hokum* B; ε20 Ka-52M *Hokum*; ε96 Mi-24D/V/P *Hind*; ε67 Mi-28N *Havoc* B; ε9 Mi-28NM *Havoc*; 24 Mi-28UB *Havoc*; ε56 Mi-35 *Hind*

EW ε16 Mi-8MTPR-1 *Hip*

TPT 304: **Heavy** 33 Mi-26/Mi-26T *Halo*; **Medium** 271 Mi-8/AMTSh/AMTSh-VA/MT/MTV-5/MTV-5-1 *Hip*

TRG 36: 19 Ka-226U; 17 Ansat-U

UNINHABITED AERIAL VEHICLES

CISR • **Heavy** some *Inokhodets*; **Medium** *Forpost* R; *Mohajer* 6

ISR • **Medium** *Forpost (Searcher)* II); *Korsar*

AIR DEFENCE

SAM 796:

Long-range 716: 200 S-300PS (RS-SA-10B *Grumble*); 206 S-300PM1/PM2 (RS-SA-20 *Gargoyle*); 20 S-300V (RS-SA-12 *Gladiator/Giant*); 6 S-350 *Vityaz* (RS-SA-28); 284 S-400 (RS-SA-21 *Growler*)

Medium-range 80 9K37M1-2 *Buk*-M1-2/9K317 *Buk*-M2 (RS-SA-11 *Gadfly*/RS-SA-17 *Grizzly*)

SPAAGM 30mm 50 96K6 *Pantsir*-S1/S2 (RS-SA-22 *Greyhound*)

AIR-LAUNCHED MISSILES

AAM • **IR** *Igla*-V; R-27T/ET (RS-AA-10B/D *Alamo*); R-73 (RS-AA-11A *Archer*); R-74M (RS-AA-11B *Archer*); R-60T (RS-AA-8 *Aphid*); **SARH** R-27R/ER (RS-AA-10A/C *Alamo*); R-33 (RS-AA-9A *Amos*); **ARH** R-77-1 (RS-AA-12B *Adder*); R-37M (RS-AA-13A *Axehead*); **PRH** R-27P/EP (RS-AA-10E/F *Alamo*)

ARM Kh-25MP (RS-AS-12A *Kegler*); Kh-31P/PM (RS-AS-17A/C *Krypton*); Kh-58 (RS-AS-11 *Kilter*)

ASM 9M133; *Grom*-1; Item 305/LMUR; Kh-25ML (RS-AS-12B *Kegler*); Kh-29 (RS-AS-14 *Kedge*); Kh-38ML; Kh-59 (RS-AS-13 *Kingbolt*) Kh-59M (RS-AS-18 *Kazoo*); 9M114 *Kokon* (RS-AT-6 *Spiral*); 9M120 *Ataka* (RS-AT-9 *Spiral* 2); 9M120-1 *Vikhr* (RS-AT-16 *Scallion*)

AShM Kh-22 (RS-AS-4 *Kitchen*); Kh-31A/AM (RS-AS-17B/D *Krypton*); Kh-32 (RS-AS-4A mod); Kh-35U (RS-AS-20 *Kayak*)

ALBM *Kinzhal* (RS-AS-24 *Killjoy*)

LACM

Nuclear Kh-55SM (RS-AS-15B *Kent*); Kh-102 (RS-AS-23B *Kodiak*)

Conventional Kh-69; Kh-101 (RS-AS-23A *Kodiak*); Kh-555 (RS-AS-22 *Kluge*)

BOMBS

INS/SAT-guided FAB-250 UMPK; FAB-500 UMPK; FAB-1500 UMPK; FAB-3000 UMPK; *Grom*-2; KAB-20S (reported); KAB-500S; ODAB-500 UMPK; ODAB-1500 UMPK; OFAB-250-270 UMPK; UMPB D-30SN; UPAB-1500B

Laser-guided KAB-20L (reported); KAB-250LG-E; KAB-500L; KAB-1500L/LG

TV-guided *Ghaem*-5; KAB-500KR; KAB-1500KR; KAB-500OD; UPAB 1500

Airborne Forces ε35,000

FORCES BY ROLE

As a result of sustained heavy losses suffered during the invasion of Ukraine, almost all of the manoeuvre formations listed are currently understrength.

SPECIAL FORCES

1 (AB Recce) SF bde

MANOEUVRE

Air Manoeuvre

1 (7th) AB div (1 tk bn, 3 air aslt regt, 1 arty regt, 1 NBC unit, 1 AD regt)

1 (76th) AB div (1 tk bn, 3 air aslt regt, 1 arty regt, 1 AD regt)

1 (106th) AB div (1 tk bn, 2 para regt, 1 inf regt, 1 arty regt, 1 AD regt)

1 (98th) AB div (2 para regt, 1 inf regt, 1 arty regt, 1 AD regt)

1 (104th) AB div (2 para regt)

1 (44th) AB div (forming)

2 air aslt bde

COMBAT SUPPORT

1 arty bde

EQUIPMENT BY TYPE

ARMOURED FIGHTING VEHICLES(a)

MBT 80: 50 T-72B3/B3M; 30 T-90M

IFV 170: 50 BMP-2; 120 BTR-82AM

APC 300+

APC (T) 300: 150 BTR-D; 150 BTR-MDM

PPV *Typhoon*-VDV

ABCV 850: 650 BMD-2; 200 BMD-4M; (150 BMD-1 in store)

AUV GAZ *Tigr*; UAMZ *Toros*

ENGINEERING & MAINTENANCE VEHICLES

ARV BREM-D; BREhM-D

ANTI-TANK/ANTI-INFRASTRUCTURE

MSL

SP 100 BTR-RD

MANPATS 9K111 *Fagot* (RS-AT-4 *Spigot*); 9K113 *Konkurs* (RS-AT-5 *Spandrel*); 9K115 *Metis* (RS-AT-7 *Saxhorn*); 9K115-1 *Metis*-M (RS-AT-13); 9K135 *Kornet* (RS-AT-14 *Spriggan*)

RCL 73mm SPG-9

GUNS • **SP 125mm** 36+ 2S25 *Sprut*-SD

ARTILLERY 633+

SP 34: **122mm** 16 2S1 *Gvozdika*; **152mm** 18 2S5 *Giatsint*-S

TOWED 100+: **122mm** 100 D-30; **152mm** 2A36 *Giatsint*-B

GUN/MOR • **SP 120mm** 260+: 230 2S9 NONA-S; 30 2S9 NONA-SM; some 2S31 *Vena*; (250 2S9 NONA-S in store)

MRL 39: **122mm** 36 BM-21 *Grad*; **220mm** 3+: some 9P140 *Uragan*; 3 TOS-1A
MOR • TOWED 200+ **82mm** 150 2B14; **120mm** 50+ 2B23 NONA-M1

AIR DEFENCE
SAM • Point-defence 30+: 30 *Strela*-10MN (RS-SA-13 *Gopher*); 9K310 *Igla*-1 (RS-SA-16 *Gimlet*); 9K38 *Igla* (RS-SA-18 *Grouse*); 9K333 *Verba* (RS-SA-29 *Gizmo*); 9K338 *Igla*-S (RS-SA-24 *Grinch*); 9K34 *Strela*-3 (RS-SA-14 *Gremlin*)
GUNS • SP **23mm** 150 BTR-ZD

UNINHABITED AERIAL VEHICLES
ISR • Light *Granat*-4

Special Operations Forces ε1,000
FORCES BY ROLE
SPECIAL FORCES
3 SF unit

Railway Forces ε29,000
4 regional commands
FORCES BY ROLE
COMBAT SERVICE SUPPORT
10 (railway) tpt bde

Russian Military Districts
5 military districts each with a unified Joint Strategic Command. Organisational data presented here represents peacetime assignments rather than operational deployments resulting from Russia's full-scale invasion of Ukraine and does not include mobilised units whose peacetime assignment is unclear.

Moscow Military District
HQ at Moscow

Army
FORCES BY ROLE
COMMAND
2 army HQ
SPECIAL FORCES
1 (Spetsnaz) SF bde
MANOEUVRE
Reconnaissance
1 recce bde
Armoured
2 tk div
Mechanised
3 MR div
1 MR bde
SURFACE-TO-SURFACE MISSILE
2 SRBM/GLCM bde with *Iskander*-M
COMBAT SUPPORT
2 arty bde
1 (hy) arty bde
1 MRL bde
1 engr bde
2 engr regt
1 ptn br bde
1 EW bde
1 NBC bde
1 NBC regt
COMBAT SERVICE SUPPORT
2 log bde
AIR DEFENCE
3 AD bde

Military Air Force

6th Air Force & Air Defence Army
FORCES BY ROLE
FIGHTER
1 regt with Su-30SM *Flanker* H
1 regt with MiG-31BM *Foxhound* C; Su-35S *Flanker* M
GROUND ATTACK
1 regt with Su-34 *Fullback*
ISR
1 sqn with Su-24MR *Fencer* E
TRANSPORT
1 regt with An-12 *Cub*; An-26 *Curl*; Tu-134 *Crusty*
ATTACK HELICOPTER
1 regt with Mi-24P *Hind*; Ka-52A *Hokum* B; Mi-8 *Hip*; Mi-8MTPR-1 *Hip*
AIR DEFENCE
2 SAM regt with S-300PM1/PM2 (RS-SA-20 *Gargoyle*)

Airborne Forces
FORCES BY ROLE
SPECIAL FORCES
1 (AB Recce) SF bde
MANOEUVRE
Air Manoeuvre
3 AB div
1 AB div (forming)

Leningrad Military District
HQ at St Petersburg

Army
FORCES BY ROLE
COMMAND
1 army HQ
3 corps HQ
SPECIAL FORCES
1 (Spetsnaz) SF bde
MANOEUVRE
Mechanised
1 MR div
2 MR div (forming)

3 MR bde
1 MR regt
SURFACE-TO-SURFACE MISSILE
2 SRBM/GLCM bde with *Iskander*-M
COMBAT SUPPORT
2 arty bde
1 engr regt
1 NBC regt
COMBAT SERVICE SUPPORT
1 log bde
AIR DEFENCE
1 AD bde
1 AD regt

Baltic Fleet
EQUIPMENT BY TYPE
SUBMARINES • TACTICAL • SSK 1
PRINCIPAL SURFACE COMBATANTS 7: 1 **DDGHM**; 6 **FFGHM**
PATROL AND COASTAL COMBATANTS 36: 5 **FSGM**; 2 **FSG**; 6 **FSM**; 4 **PCGM**; 6 **PCFG**; 9 **PBF**; 1 **PB**
MINE WARFARE • MINE COUNTERMEASURES 12: 2 **MCC**; 4 **MSC**; 6 **MHI**
AMPHIBIOUS 13: 4 **LST**; 7 **LCM**; 2 **LCAC**

Naval Aviation
FORCES BY ROLE
ANTI-SURFACE WARFARE/ISR
1 regt with Su-24M/MR *Fencer*; Su-30SM *Flanker* H
TRANSPORT
1 sqn with An-26 *Curl*; Tu-134 *Crusty*
ATTACK/TRANSPORT HELICOPTER
1 regt with Ka-27/Ka-29 *Helix*; Mi-24P *Hind*; Mi-8 *Hip*
AIR DEFENCE
2 SAM regt with S-400 (RS-SA-21 *Growler*); 96K6 *Pantsir*-S1 (RS-SA-22 *Greyhound*)

Naval Infantry
FORCES BY ROLE
MANOEUVRE
Mechanised
1 naval inf bde

Coastal Artillery and Missile Forces
FORCES BY ROLE
COASTAL DEFENCE
1 AShM regt

Northern Fleet
EQUIPMENT BY TYPE
SUBMARINES 22
STRATEGIC 6 **SSBN** (of which 2 in refit)
TACTICAL 16: 4 **SSGN**; 8 **SSN**; 4 **SSK**
PRINCIPAL SURFACE COMBATANTS 11: 1 **CV** (in refit); 1 **CGHMN**; 1 **CGHM**; 5 **DDGHM** (1 more in reserve); 3 **FFGHM**
PATROL AND COASTAL COMBATANTS 15: 6 **FSM**; 1 **PCGM**; 8 **PB**
MINE WARFARE • MINE COUNTERMEASURES 7: 1 **MHO**; 6 **MSC**
AMPHIBIOUS 8: 6 **LST**; 2 **LCM**

Naval Aviation
FORCES BY ROLE
FIGHTER
1 regt with Su-33 *Flanker* D; Su-25UTG *Frogfoot*
FIGHTER/GROUND ATTACK
1 regt with MiG-29KR/KUBR *Fulcrum*
ANTI-SUBMARINE WARFARE
1 regt with Il-38/Il-38N *May*; Il-20RT *Coot A*; Tu-134
1 regt with Ka-27/Ka-29 *Helix*
1 sqn with Tu-142MK/MZ/MR *Bear* F/J

Naval Infantry
FORCES BY ROLE
MANOEUVRE
Mechanised
2 naval inf bde
COMBAT SUPPORT
1 engr regt

Coastal Artillery and Missile Forces
FORCES BY ROLE
COASTAL DEFENCE
1 AShM bde

Military Air Force

45th Air Force & Air Defence Army
FORCES BY ROLE
FIGHTER
1 regt with Su-27 *Flanker* B
1 regt with Su-27SM *Flanker* J; Su-35S *Flanker* M
FIGHTER/GROUND ATTACK/ISR
1 regt with MiG-31BM *Foxhound* C; Su-24M/M2/MR *Fencer*
ATTACK HELICOPTER
1 bde with Ka-52A *Hokum* B; Mi-28N *Havoc* B; Mi-35 *Hind*; Mi-26 *Halo*; Mi-8MTV-5 *Hip*
1 regt with Mi-24P/Mi-35 *Hind*; Mi-28N *Havoc* B; Mi-8 *Hip*
AIR DEFENCE
4 SAM regt with S-300PS (RS-SA-10B *Grumble*); S-300PM1 (RS-SA-20 *Gargoyle*); S-400 (RS-SA-21 *Growler*); 96K6 *Pantsir*-S1 (RS-SA-22 *Greyhound*)
1 SAM regt with S-300PM1/PM2 (RS-SA-20 *Gargoyle*)
5 SAM regt with S-400 (RS-SA-21 *Growler*); 96K6 *Pantsir*-S1 (RS-SA-22 *Greyhound*)

Airborne Forces
FORCES BY ROLE

MANOEUVRE
Air Manoeuvre
1 AB div

Central Military District
HQ at Yekaterinburg

Army
FORCES BY ROLE
COMMAND
3 army HQ
1 corps HQ
SPECIAL FORCES
2 (Spetsnaz) SF bde
MANOEUVRE
Armoured
1 tk div
1 tk bde
Mechanised
3 MR div
6 MR bde
SURFACE-TO-SURFACE MISSILE
2 SRBM/GLCM bde with *Iskander*-M
COMBAT SUPPORT
3 arty bde
1 hy arty bde
1 MRL bde
1 engr bde
3 engr regt
1 EW bde
2 NBC bde
2 NBC regt
COMBAT SERVICE SUPPORT
2 log bde
AIR DEFENCE
3 AD bde

Military Air Force

14th Air Force & Air Defence Army
FORCES BY ROLE
FIGHTER
2 regt with MiG-31BM *Foxhound* C
GROUND ATTACK
1 regt with Su-34 *Fullback*
1 sqn with Su-25SM *Frogfoot* (Kyrgyzstan)
ISR
1 sqn with Su-24MR *Fencer* E
TRANSPORT
1 regt with An-12 *Cub*; An-26 *Curl*; Tu-134 *Crusty*; Tu-154; Mi-8 *Hip*
ATTACK/TRANSPORT HELICOPTER
1 bde with Mi-24P *Hind*; Mi-8 *Hip*
1 regt with Mi-24P *Hind*; Mi-8 *Hip*
1 sqn with Mi-24P *Hind*; Mi-8 *Hip* (Tajikistan)

AIR DEFENCE
1 regt with S-300PS (RS-SA-10B *Grumble*)
1 bde with S-300PS (RS-SA-10B *Grumble*)
1 regt with S-300PM2 (RS-SA-20 *Gargoyle*)
4 regt with S-400 (RS-SA-21 *Growler*); 96K6 *Pantsir*-S1 (RS-SA-22 *Greyhound*)

Airborne Troops
FORCES BY ROLE
MANOEUVRE
Air Manoeuvre
1 AB div

Southern Military District
HQ at Rostov-on-Don

Army
FORCES BY ROLE
COMMAND
6 army HQ
2 corps HQ
SPECIAL FORCES
3 (Spetsnaz) SF bde
1 (Spetsnaz) SF regt
MANOEUVRE
Reconnaissance
1 recce bde
Mechanised
5 MR div
1 MR div (forming)
15 MR bde
1 MR regt
1 MR bde (Armenia)
1 MR bde (South Ossetia)
1 MR bde (Abkhazia)
SURFACE-TO-SURFACE MISSILE
3 SRBM/GLCM bde with *Iskander*-M
COMBAT SUPPORT
3 arty bde
1 arty regt
1 MRL bde
1 engr bde
1 EW bde
1 NBC bde
2 NBC regt
COMBAT SERVICE SUPPORT
2 log bde
AIR DEFENCE
3 AD bde
1 AD regt

Black Sea Fleet
The Black Sea Fleet is primarily based in Crimea, at Sevastopol, Karantinnaya Bay and Streletskaya Bay
EQUIPMENT BY TYPE

SUBMARINES • TACTICAL 5 SSK
PRINCIPAL SURFACE COMBATANTS 6: 4 FFGHM; 2 FFGM
PATROL AND COASTAL COMBATANTS 30: 6 FSGM; 6 FSM; 4 PSOH; 4 PCFG; 4 PBF; 6 PB
MINE WARFARE • MINE COUNTERMEASURES 10: 3 MCC; 1 MHO; 5 MSO; 1 MSC
AMPHIBIOUS 4: 3 LST; 1 LCM

Naval Aviation
FORCES BY ROLE
FIGHTER
ANTI-SURFACE WARFARE/ISR
  1 regt with Su-24M/MR *Fencer*; Su-30SM *Flanker H*
  MARITIME PATROL/TRANSPORT
  1 regt with Ka-27 *Helix*; An-26 *Curl*; Be-12PS *Mail*; Mi-8 *Hip*
    TPT • Medium Mi-8 *Hip*

Naval Infantry
FORCES BY ROLE
COMMAND
  1 corps HQ
MANOEUVRE
  Mechanised
  2 naval inf bde
COMBAT SUPPORT
  1 arty regt
  1 engr regt
AIR DEFENCE
  1 SAM regt

Coastal Artillery and Missile Forces
FORCES BY ROLE
COASTAL DEFENCE
  2 AShM bde

Caspian Sea Flotilla
EQUIPMENT BY TYPE
PATROL AND COASTAL COMBATANTS 18: 6 FSGM; 1 PCFG; 3 PCM; 3 PB; 1 PBF; 4 PBR
MINE WARFARE 3: 2 MSC; 1 MHI
AMPHIBIOUS 9 LCM

Naval Infantry
FORCES BY ROLE
MANOEUVRE
  Mechanised
  1 naval inf regt

Military Air Force

4th Air Force & Air Defence Army
FORCES BY ROLE
FIGHTER
  1 regt with Su-30SM *Flanker H*
  1 sqn with MiG-29 *Fulcrum*; Su-30SM *Flanker H* (Armenia)
FIGHTER/GROUND ATTACK
  1 regt with Su-27/Su-27SM *Flanker B/J*; Su-30M2 *Flanker G*
  1 regt with Su-27SM3 *Flanker*; Su-30M2 *Flanker G*
GROUND ATTACK
  1 regt with Su-24M *Fencer*; Su-25SM *Frogfoot*
  2 regt with Su-25SM/SM3 *Frogfoot*
  1 regt with Su-34 *Fullback*
GROUND ATTACK/ISR
  1 regt with Su-24M*/MR *Fencer D/E*
TRANSPORT
  1 regt with An-12 *Cub*/Mi-8 *Hip*
ATTACK/TRANSPORT HELICOPTER
  1 bde with Mi-28N *Havoc B*; Mi-35 *Hind*; Mi-8 *Hip*; Mi-26 *Halo*
  1 regt with Mi-28N *Havoc B*; Mi-35 *Hind*; Mi-8 *Hip*
  2 regt with Ka-52A *Hokum B*; Mi-28N *Havoc B*; Mi-35 *Hind*; Mi-8AMTSh *Hip*
  1 sqn with Mi-24P *Hind*; Mi-8 *Hip* (Armenia)
AIR DEFENCE
  1 SAM regt with 9K317 *Buk-M2* (RS-SA-17 *Grizzly*)
  1 SAM regt with S-300PM1 (RS-SA-20 *Gargoyle*)
  3 SAM regt with S-400 (RS-SA-21 *Growler*); 96K6 *Pantsir*-S1 (RS-SA-22 *Greyhound*)

Airborne Forces
FORCES BY ROLE
MANOEUVRE
  Air Manoeuvre
  1 AB div

Eastern Military District
HQ at Khabarovsk

Army
FORCES BY ROLE
COMMAND
  4 army HQ
SPECIAL FORCES
  1 (Spetsnaz) SF bde
MANOEUVRE
  Armoured
  1 tk bde
  Mechanised
  1 MR div
  8 MR bde
  1 MGA div
SURFACE-TO-SURFACE MISSILE
  4 SRBM/GLCM bde with *Iskander-M*
COMBAT SUPPORT
  4 arty bde
  1 MRL bde

1 engr bde
1 EW bde
1 NBC bde
4 NBC regt
COMBAT SERVICE SUPPORT
4 log bde
AIR DEFENCE
5 AD bde

Pacific Fleet
EQUIPMENT BY TYPE
SUBMARINES 23
  STRATEGIC 6 **SSBN**
  TACTICAL 17: 6 **SSGN** (2 more non-operational in long-term refit); 2 **SSN** (3 more non-operational in long-term refit; 9 **SSK**
PRINCIPAL SURFACE COMBATANTS 11: 1 **CGHM**; 5 **DDGHM**; 5 **FFGHM**
PATROL AND COASTAL COMBATANTS 25: 8 **FSM**; 2 **PCGM**; 9 **PCFG**; 6 **PB**
MINE WARFARE 12: 3 **MCC**; 2 **MSO**; 7 **MSC**
AMPHIBIOUS 9: 4 **LST**; 5 **LCM**

Naval Aviation
FORCES BY ROLE
FIGHTER
  1 sqn with MiG-31BS/BM *Foxhound* A/C
ANTI-SUBMARINE WARFARE
  1 sqn with Ka-27/Ka-29 *Helix*
  2 sqn with Il-38/Il-38N *May*; Il-18D; Il-22 *Coot* B
  1 sqn with Tu-142MK/MZ/MR *Bear* F/J
TRANSPORT
  1 sqn with An-12BK *Cub*; An-26 *Curl*; Tu-134
AIR DEFENCE
  1 SAM regt with S-400 (RS-SA-21 *Growler*); 96K6 *Pantsir*-S1 (RS-SA-22 *Greyhound*)

Naval Infantry
FORCES BY ROLE
MANOEUVRE
  Mechanised
  2 naval inf bde

Coastal Artillery and Missile Forces
FORCES BY ROLE
COASTAL DEFENCE
  2 AShM bde

Military Air Force

11th Air Force & Air Defence Army
FORCES BY ROLE
FIGHTER/GROUND ATTACK
  1 regt with MiG-31BM *Foxhound* C; Su-27SM *Flanker* J; Su-30M2 *Flanker* G; Su-30SM *Flanker* H; Su-35S *Flanker* M

  1 regt with Su-35S *Flanker* M; Su-30SM *Flanker* H
  1 regt with Su-25 *Frogfoot*; Su-30SM *Flanker* H
GROUND ATTACK
  1 regt with Su-24M/M2 *Fencer* D/D mod; Su-34 *Fullback*
  1 regt with Su-25SM *Frogfoot*
ISR
  1 sqn with Su-24MR *Fencer* E
TRANSPORT
  1 regt with An-12 *Cub*; An-26 *Curl*; Tu-134 *Crusty/*Tu-154 *Careless*
ATTACK/TRANSPORT HELICOPTER
  1 bde with Ka-52A *Hokum* B; Mi-8 *Hip*; Mi-26 *Halo*
  1 regt with Ka-52A *Hokum* B; Mi-8 *Hip*; Mi-26 *Halo*
  1 regt with Mi-24P *Hind*; Mi-8 *Hip*
AIR DEFENCE
  1 regt with 9K37M *Buk*-M1-2 (RS-SA-11 *Gadfly*);
  1 regt with S-300V (RS-SA-12 *Gladiator/Giant*); S-400 (RS-SA-21 *Growler*)
  4 regt with S-300PS (RS-SA-10B *Grumble*); S-400 (RS-SA-21 *Growler*); 96K6 *Pantsir*-S1 (RS-SA-22 *Greyhound*)

Airborne Forces
FORCES BY ROLE
MANOEUVRE
  Air Manoeuvre
  2 air aslt bde

Gendarmerie & Paramilitary 569,000

Border Guard Service ε160,000
Subordinate to Federal Security Service
FORCES BY ROLE
10 regional directorates
MANOEUVRE
  Other
  7 frontier gp
EQUIPMENT BY TYPE
ARMOURED FIGHTING VEHICLES
  IFV/APC (W) 1,000 BMP/BTR
  AUV BPM-97
ARTILLERY 90
  SP 122mm 2S1 *Gvozdika*
  GUN/MOR • SP 120mm 2S9 NONA-S
  MOR 120mm 2S12 *Sani*
PATROL AND COASTAL COMBATANTS 205
  PSO 7: 4 *Komandor*; 3 *Okean* (Project 22100) with 1 76mm gun, 1 hel landing platform
  PCM 1 *Okhotnik* (Project 22460) with 1 sextuple GMLS with *Igla*-1M (RS-SA-N-10 *Grouse*) SAM, 1 AK630 CIWS
  PCO 31: 8 *Alpinist* (Project 503); 1 *Sprut*; 13 *Okhotnik* (Project 22460) with 1 AK630M CIWS, 1 hel landing platform; 9 *Purga* with 1 hel landing platform

PCC 33: 4 *Molnya* II (*Pauk* II); 6 *Svetlyak* (Project 10410); 13 *Svetlyak* (Project 10410) with 1 AK630M CIWS, 1 76mm gun; 8 *Svetlyak* (Project 10410) with 2 AK630M CIWS; 1 *Svetlyak* (Project 10410) with 1 AK630M CIWS; 1 *Yakhont*

PCR 1 *Slepen* (*Yaz*) with 1 AK630 CIWS, 2 100mm guns

PBF 87: 57 *Mangust*; 3 *Mirazh* (Project 14310); 4 *Mustang*-2 (Project 18623); 21 *Sobol*; 2 *Sokzhoi*

PBR 27: 4 *Ogonek*; 8 *Piyavka* with 1 AK630 CIWS; 15 *Moskit* (*Vosh*) with 1 AK630 CIWS, 1 100mm gun

PB 18: 6 *Gyuys* (Project 03050); 2 *Morzh* (Project 1496M); 10 *Lamantin* (Project 1496M1)

LOGISTICS AND SUPPORT 30

AE 1 *Muna*

AGB 2 *Ivan Susanin* (primarily used as patrol ships) with 2 AK630 CIWS, 1 76mm gun, 1 hel landing platform

AK 4 *Pevek*

AKL 5 *Kanin*

AO 3: 1 *Ishim* (Project 15010); 2 *Evoron*

ATF 15: 14 *Sorum* (primarily used as patrol ships) with 2 AK230M CIWS; 1 *Sorum* (primarily used as patrol ship)

AIRCRAFT • TPT ε86: 70 An-24 *Coke*/An-26 *Curl*/An-72 *Coaler*/Il-76 *Candid*/Tu-134 *Crusty*/Yak-40 *Codling*; 16 SM-92

HELICOPTERS: ε200 Ka-27PS *Helix*/Mi-24 *Hind*/Mi-26 *Halo*/Mi-8 *Hip*

Federal Guard Service ε40,000–50,000

Org include elm of ground forces (mech inf bde and AB regt)

FORCES BY ROLE
MANOEUVRE
 Mechanised
  1 mech inf regt
 Air Manoeuvre
  1 AB regt
 Other
  1 (Presidential) gd regt

Federal Security Service Special Purpose Centre ε4,000

FORCES BY ROLE
SPECIAL FORCES
 2 SF unit (Alfa and Vympel units)

National Guard ε335,000

FORCES BY ROLE
MANOEUVRE
 Other
  10 paramilitary div (2–5 paramilitary regt)
  17 paramilitary bde (3 mech bn, 1 mor bn)
  36 indep paramilitary rgt
  90 paramilitary bn (incl special motorised units)

COMBAT SUPPORT
 1 arty regt

TRANSPORT
 8 sqn

EQUIPMENT BY TYPE
ARMOURED FIGHTING VEHICLES
 MBT T-80BV
 RECCE some BRDM-2A
 IFV/APC (W) 1,600 BMP-1/BMP-2/BTR-70M/BTR-80/BTR-82A/BTR-82AM
 PPV *Arlan*; SPM-3 *Medved*; *Ural-VV*; Z-STS *Akhmat*
 AUV *Patrol-A*; *Tiger* 4×4; *Tigr*
ARTILLERY 35
 TOWED 122mm 20 D-30
 MOR 120mm 15 M-1938 (PM-38), 2S12 *Sani*
PATROL AND COASTAL COMBATANTS 5
 PBF 3 BK-16 (Project 02510)
 PB 2+ *Grachonok*
AIRCRAFT
 TPT 29: **Heavy** 9 Il-76 *Candid*; **Medium** 2 An-12 *Cub*; **Light** 18: 12 An-26 *Curl*; 6 An-72 *Coaler*
HELICOPTERS
 TPT 71: **Heavy** 10 Mi-26 *Halo*; **Medium** 60+: 60 Mi-8 *Hip*; some Mi-8AMTSh *Hip*; **Light** 1 Ka-226T

Private Military Companies (PMC) ε20,000

Elements of Russian private military companies integrated into the Russian command structure within Ukraine or deployed to Africa and the Middle East.

DEPLOYMENT

ARMENIA: 3,000: 1 mil base with (1 MR bde; 74 T-72; 80 BMP-1; 80 BMP-2; 12 2S1; 12 BM-21); 1 ftr sqn with 10 MiG-29 *Fulcrum*; 1 hel sqn with 8 Mi-24P *Hind*; 4 Mi-8AMTSh *Hip*; 4 Mi-8MT *Hip*; 2 AD bty with S-300V; 1 AD bty with *Buk*-M1-2)

BELARUS: 2,000; 2 SAM bn with S-400, 1 radar station at Baranovichi (*Volga* system; leased); 1 naval comms site

BURKINA FASO: ε200 (PMC)

CENTRAL AFRICAN REPUBLIC: ε1,500 (PMC); UN • MINUSCA 13

CYPRUS: UN • UNFICYP 4

DEMOCRATIC REPUBLIC OF THE CONGO: UN • MONUSCO 6

EQUATORIAL GUINEA: ε200 (PMC)

GEORGIA: ε4,000; Abkhazia: 1 mil base with 1 MR bde(-); 1 SAM regt with S-300PS; South Ossetia: 1 mil base with 1 MR bde(-)

KAZAKHSTAN: 1 radar station at Balkash (*Dnepr* system; leased)

KYRGYZSTAN: ε500; 13 Su-25SM *Frogfoot*; 2 Mi-8 *Hip*

LIBYA: ε3,500 (PMC)

MALI: ε1,500 (PMC)

MEDITERRANEAN SEA: 2 SSK; 1 FFGHM; 1 FFGM; 1 AGI

MIDDLE EAST: UN • UNTSO 4

MOLDOVA: Transnistria ε1,500 (including 400 peacekeepers): 2 MR bn; 7 Mi-24 *Hind*; some Mi-8 *Hip*

NIGER: ε200 (PMC)

SOUTH SUDAN: UN • UNMISS 4

SYRIA: 4,000: 1 inf BG; 3 MP bn; 1 engr unit; ε10 T-72B3; ε20 BTR-82A; BPM-97; *Typhoon*-K; *Tigr*; 6 D-30; 12 2A65; 4 9A52 *Smerch*; 10 Su-24M *Fencer* D; 6 Su-34; 6 Su-35S *Flanker* M; 1 Il-20M; 12 Mi-24P/Mi-35M *Hind*; 4 Mi-8AMTSh *Hip*; 1 UAV unit with *Forpost*-R; 1 AShM bty with 3K55 *Bastion*; 1 SAM bty with S-400; 1 SAM bty with *Pantsir*-S1/S2; air base at Latakia; naval facility at Tartus

TAJIKISTAN: ε3,000; 1 (201st) mil base with 1 MR bde(-); 1 hel sqn with 4 Mi-24P *Hind*; 4 Mi-8MTV *Hip*; 2 Mi-8MTV-5-1 *Hip*; 1 SAM bn with 8 S-300PS

UKRAINE: ε450,000; 16 army; 7 corps

WESTERN SAHARA: UN • MINURSO 12

FOREIGN FORCES

Korea, Democratic Peoples' Republic of 11,000; 4 inf bde
Ukraine ε20,000

Tajikistan TJK

Tajikistani Somoni TJS		2023	2024	2025
GDP	TJS	129bn	144bn	160bn
	USD	11.9bn	13.0bn	14.2bn
Real GDP growth	%	8.3	6.8	4.5
Def bdgt [a]	TJS	ε1.53bn	ε1.95bn	
	USD	ε141m	ε176m	

[a] Excl. budget for law enforcement

Population	10,394,063				
Age	0–14	15–19	20–24	25–29	30–64	65 plus
Male	18.8%	4.5%	3.9%	3.6%	17.8%	1.7%
Female	18.1%	4.3%	3.8%	3.5%	18.0%	2.1%

Capabilities

Tajikistan's armed forces are largely focused on addressing regional security and terrorism concerns, especially given the border with Afghanistan. The country has recently increased border deployments in response to security concerns. The forces have little capacity to deploy other than in token numbers. Most equipment is of Soviet-era origin. In late 2022, the president indicated that a national defence concept was under development. Tajikistan has been building its military capability by hosting CSTO counterterrorism exercises and participating in exercises organised by US Central Command. Tajikistan is a member of the CSTO and the SCO, and the armed forces also conduct exercises with Russian troops based at Russia's 201st military base. Reports began to emerge in 2019 suggesting the development of a Chinese military facility, more recently identified in Tajikistan's eastern highlands. Neither Beijing nor Dushanbe have confirmed this. A military cooperation agreement with Turkiye was reportedly ratified in early 2024 by the Tajik Parliament. This will provide access to Turkish funding for defence equipment purchases from Ankara. Moscow is the historic arms provider to the country, though the US has made some equipment donations. Tajikistan has only minimal defence-industrial capacity, though, in 2022, a facility to produce Iranian UAVs was opened in the country. A military vehicle assembly facility was opened in 2023 by Tajikistan's Shield Group, with parts reportedly produced by the UAE's Streit Group.

ACTIVE 8,800 (Army 7,300 Air Force/Air Defence 1,500) Gendarmerie & Paramilitary 7,500

Conscript liability 24 months

RESERVE 20,000 (Army 20,000)

ORGANISATIONS BY SERVICE

Army 7,300

FORCES BY ROLE

MANOEUVRE
  Mechanised
    3 MR bde
  Air Manoeuvre
    1 air aslt bde

COMBAT SUPPORT
  1 arty bde

AIR DEFENCE
  1 SAM regt

EQUIPMENT BY TYPE

ARMOURED FIGHTING VEHICLES
  MBT 38: 28 T-72 Ural/T-72A/T-72AV/T-72B; 3 T-72B1; 7 T-62/T-62AV/T-62AM
  RECCE 31: 9 BRDM-2; 22 BRDM-2M
  IFV 23: 8 BMP-1; 15 BMP-2
  APC 36
    APC (W) 23 BTR-60/BTR-70/BTR-80
    PPV 13 VP11
  AUV 24 CS/VN3B mod; *Tigr*

ARTILLERY 40
  SP 122mm 3 2S1 *Gvozdika*
  TOWED 122mm 13 D-30
  MRL 14+: **122mm** 14 BM-21 *Grad*; **220mm** some TOS-1A
  MOR 10+: **SP 82mm** CS/SS4; **120mm** 10

AIR DEFENCE
  SAM
    Medium-range 3 S-125 *Pechora*-2M (RS-SA-26)
    Short-range 5 S-125M1 *Neva*-M1 (RS-SA-3 *Goa*)
    Point-defence 9K32 *Strela*-2 (RS-SA-7 *Grail*)‡
  GUNS
    SP 23mm 8 BTR-ZD
    TOWED 23mm ZU-23M1

Air Force/Air Defence 1,500
FORCES BY ROLE
TRANSPORT
  1 sqn with Tu-134A *Crusty*
ATTACK/TRANSPORT HELICOPTER
  1 sqn with Mi-24 *Hind*; Mi-8 *Hip*; Mi-17TM *Hip* H
EQUIPMENT BY TYPE
AIRCRAFT
  TPT • **Light** 1 Tu-134A *Crusty*
  TRG 4+: 4 L-39 *Albatros*; some Yak-52
HELICOPTERS
  ATK 4 Mi-24 *Hind*
  TPT • **Medium** 11 Mi-8 *Hip*/Mi-17TM *Hip* H

Gendarmerie & Paramilitary 7,500

Internal Troops 3,800
National Guard 1,200
Emergencies Ministry 2,500
Border Guards

FOREIGN FORCES
China ε300 (trg)
Russia ε3,000; 1 (201st) mil base with 1 MR bde(-); 1 hel sqn with 4 Mi-24P *Hind*; 4 Mi-8MTV *Hip*; 2 Mi-8MTV-5-1 *Hip*; 1 SAM bn with 8 S-300PS

Turkmenistan TKM

Turkmen New Manat TMT		2023	2024	2025
GDP	TMT	272bn	294bn	319bn
	USD	77.7bn	83.9bn	91.2bn
Real GDP growth	%	2.0	2.3	2.3
Def bdgt	TMT	n.k.	n.k.	n.k.
	USD	n.k.	n.k.	n.k.
Population	5,744,151			

Age	0–14	15–19	20–24	25–29	30–64	65 plus
Male	12.4%	3.8%	3.8%	4.2%	22.3%	3.0%
Female	12.1%	3.7%	3.7%	4.2%	22.9%	3.9%

Capabilities

Turkmenistan has concerns over potential spillover from security challenges in Afghanistan, but its armed forces lack significant capabilities and equipment. Ashgabat has maintained a policy of neutrality since 1995. Turkmenistan is not a member of the CSTO or the SCO. In 2022, Turkmenistan participated in the Organization of Turkic States as an observer, and as of 2024, remains so. While the ground forces are shifting from a Soviet-era divisional structure to a brigade system, progress is slow. The armed forces are largely conscript-based and reliant on Soviet-era equipment and doctrine. The government wants to improve service conditions. Turkmenistan has participated in multinational exercises and is reported to have restarted joint exercises with Russia and Uzbekistan. There is limited capacity to deploy forces abroad. The country has plans to strengthen the border guard with new equipment and facilities and has purchased UAVs, including from China and Turkiye. Apart from maintenance facilities, Turkmenistan has little domestic defence industry, although it is building, under licence, patrol vessels of Turkish design.

ACTIVE 36,500 (Army 33,000 Navy 500 Air 3,000)
Gendarmerie & Paramilitary 20,000

Conscript liability 24 months

ORGANISATIONS BY SERVICE

Army 33,000
5 Mil Districts
FORCES BY ROLE
SPECIAL FORCES
  1 spec ops regt
MANOEUVRE
  Armoured
  1 tk bde
  Mechanised
  1 (3rd) MR div (1 tk regt; 3 MR regt, 1 arty regt)
  1 (22nd) MR div (1 tk regt; 1 MR regt, 1 arty regt)
  4 MR bde
  1 naval inf bde
  Other
  1 MR trg div
SURFACE-TO-SURFACE MISSILE
  1 SRBM bde with 9K72 *Elbrus* (RS-SS-1C *Scud* B)
COMBAT SUPPORT
  1 arty bde
  1 (mixed) arty/AT regt
  1 MRL bde
  1 AT regt
  1 engr regt
AIR DEFENCE
  2 SAM bde
EQUIPMENT BY TYPE†
ARMOURED FIGHTING VEHICLES
  MBT 654: 4 T-90S; 650 T-72/T-72UMG
  RECCE 260+: 200 BRDM-2; 60 BRM-1; Nimr *Ajban*
  IFV 1,050: 600 BMP-1/BMP-1M; 4 BMP-1UM; 430 BMP-2; 4 BMP-2D; 4 BMP-3; 4 BTR-80A; 4 BTR-80 *Crom*
  APC 907+
    APC (W) 870+: 120 BTR-60 (all variants); 300 BTR-70; 450 BTR-80
    PPV 37+: 28+ *Kirpi*; 9+ Titan-DS; some *Typhoon*-K
  AUV 12+: 8 Nimr *Ajban* 440A; 4+ *Cobra*
  ABCV 8 BMD-1
ANTI-TANK/ANTI-INFRASTRUCTURE
  MSL
    SP 58+: 8 9P122 *Malyutka*-M (RS-AT-3 *Sagger* on

BRDM-2); 8 9P133 *Malyutka*-P (RS-AT-3 *Sagger* on BRDM-2); 2 9P148 *Konkurs* (RS-AT-5 *Spandrel* on BRDM-2); 36 9P149 *Shturm* (RS-AT-6 *Spiral* on MT-LB); 4+ *Baryer* (on *Karakal*)

MANPATS 9K11 *Malyutka* (RS-AT-3 *Sagger*); 9K111 *Fagot* (RS-AT-4 *Spigot*); 9K111-1 *Konkurs* (RS-AT-5 *Spandrel*); 9K115 *Metis* (RS-AT-7 *Saxhorn*)

GUNS 100mm 60 MT-12/T-12

ARTILLERY 769

SP 122mm 40 2S1

TOWED 457: **122mm** 350 D-30; **130mm** 6 M-46; **152mm** 101: 17 D-1; 72 D-20; 6 2A36 *Giatsint*-B; 6 2A65 *Msta*-B

GUN/MOR 120mm 17 2S9 NONA-S

MRL 158: **122mm** 92: 18 9P138; 70 BM-21 *Grad*; 4 BM-21A; RM-70; **220mm** 60 9P140 *Uragan*; **300mm** 6 9A52 *Smerch*

MOR 97: **82mm** 31; **120mm** 66 M-1938 (PM-38)

SURFACE-TO-SURFACE MISSILE LAUNCHERS

SRBM • **Conventional** 16 9K72 *Elbrus* (RS-SS-1C *Scud* B)

AIR DEFENCE

SAM

Short-range: FM-90 (CH-SA-4); 2K12 *Kub* (RS-SA-6 *Gainful*)

Point-defence 53+: 40 9K33 *Osa* (RS-SA-8 *Gecko*); 13 9K35 *Strela*-10 mod (RS-SA-13 *Gopher*); 9K38 *Igla* (RS-SA-18 *Grouse*); 9K32M *Strela*-2M (RS-SA-7 *Grail*)‡; 9K34 *Strela*-3 (RS-SA-14 *Gremlin*); *Mistral* (reported); QW-2 (CH-SA-8)

GUNS 70

SP 23mm 48 ZSU-23-4

TOWED 22+: **23mm** ZU-23-2; **57mm** 22 S-60

AIR-LAUNCHED MISSILES

ASM CM-502KG; AR-1

Navy 500

EQUIPMENT BY TYPE

PATROL AND COASTAL COMBATANTS 5

CORVETTES • **FSGM** 1 *Deñiz Han* with 4 twin lnchr with *Otomat* AShM, 1 16-cell CLA VLS with VL MICA, 1 Roketsan ASW Rocket Launcher System A/S mor, 1 *Gokdeniz* CIWS, 1 76mm gun, 1 hel landing platform

PCFG 2 *Edermen* (RUS *Molnya*) with 4 quad lnchr with 3M24E *Uran*-E (RS-SS-N-25 *Switchblade*) AShM, 2 AK630 CIWS, 1 76mm gun

PCGM 2 *Arkadag* (TUR *Tuzla*) with 2 twin lnchr with *Otomat* AShM, 2 twin *Simbad*-RC lnchr with *Mistral* SAM, 1 Roketsan ASW Rocket Launcher System A/S mor

AMPHIBIOUS • **LANDING CRAFT** • **UCAC** 1 *Berdaşly*

LOGISTICS AND SUPPORT • **AGS** 1 (Dearsan 41m)

Air Force 3,000

FORCES BY ROLE

FIGHTER

2 sqn with MiG-29A/S/UB *Fulcrum*

GROUND ATTACK

1 sqn with Su-25 *Frogfoot*

1 sqn with Su-25MK *Frogfoot*

1 sqn with M-346FA*

TRANSPORT

1 sqn with An-26 *Curl*; Mi-8 *Hip*; Mi-24 *Hind*

TRAINING

1 unit with EMB-314 *Super Tucano**

1 unit with L-39 *Albatros*

AIR DEFENCE

1 bty with FD-2000 (CH-SA-9)

1 bty with KS-1C (CH-SA-12)

3 bty with S-125 *Neva*-M1 (RS-SA-3 *Goa*)

1 bty with S-125 *Pechora*-2M (RS-SA-26)

2 bty with S-200 *Angara* (RS-SA-5 *Gammon*)

EQUIPMENT BY TYPE

AIRCRAFT 65 combat capable

FTR 24: 22 MiG-29A/S *Fulcrum*; 2 MiG-29UB *Fulcrum*

ATK 31: 19 Su-25 *Frogfoot*; 12 Su-25MK *Frogfoot*

TPT 5: **Medium** 2 C-27J *Spartan*; **Light** 3: 1 An-26 *Curl*; 2 An-74TK *Coaler*

TRG 12: 5 EMB-314 *Super Tucano**; 5 M-346FA*; 2 L-39 *Albatros*

HELICOPTERS

ATK 10 Mi-24P *Hind* F

MRH 2+ AW139

TPT 11+: **Medium** 8: 6 Mi-8 *Hip*; 2 Mi-17V-V *Hip*; **Light** 3+ AW109

UNINHABITED AERIAL VEHICLES

CISR 3+: **Heavy** CH-3A; WJ-600; **Medium** 3+ *Bayraktar* TB2

ISR 3+: **Medium** 3+ *Falco* **Light** *Orbiter*-3

OWA *Skystriker*

AIR DEFENCE • **SAM**

Long-range 18: 2 2K11 *Krug* (RS-SA-4 *Ganef*); 4 FD-2000 (CH-SA-9); 12 S-200 *Angara* (RS-SA-5 *Gammon*);

Medium-range 8: 4 S-125 *Pechora*-2M (RS-SA-26); 4 KS-1A (CH-SA-12)

Short-range 12: 12 S-125M1 *Neva*-M1 (RS-SA-3 *Goa*); some S-125-2BM *Pechora*

AIR-LAUNCHED MISSILES

AAM • **IR** R-60 (RS-AA-8 *Aphid*); R-73 (RS-AA-11A *Archer*)

BOMBS • **Laser-guided** MAM-C/-L

Gendarmerie & Paramilitary 20,000

Internal Troops ε15,000

EQUIPMENT BY TYPE

ARMOURED FIGHTING VEHICLES

IFV 2+ *Lazar*-3

APC • **PPV** 9: 4+ *Survivor* II; 5 *Titan*-DS

AUV 4+ Plasan *Stormrider*

Federal Border Guard Service ε5,000
EQUIPMENT BY TYPE
ARMOURED FIGHTING VEHICLES
APC • **PPV** 8: 4+ *Kirpi*; 4+ *Survivor* II
AUV 6+ *Cobra*
ARTILLERY • **MRL 122mm** 4 BM-21A
AIR DEFENCE
GUNS • **TOWED** • **23mm** ZU-23-2
PATROL AND COASTAL COMBATANTS 33
PCGM 8 *Arkadag* (TUR *Tuzla*) with 2 twin lnchr with *Otomat* AShM, 2 twin *Simbad*-RC lnchr with *Mistral* SAM, 1 Roketsan ASW Rocket Launcher System A/S mor
PBFG 6 *Nayza* (Dearsan 33) with 2 single lnchr with *Marte* Mk2/N AShM
PBF 18: 10 *Bars*-12; 5 *Grif*-T; 3 *Sobol*
PB 1 *Point*
AMPHIBIOUS • **LCM** 1 Dearsan LCM-1
HELICOPTERS
MRH 2 AW139
TPT 3+: **Medium** some Mi-8 *Hip*; **Light** 3 AW109

Ukraine UKR

Ukrainian Hryvnia UAH		2023	2024	2025
GDP	UAH	6.54trn	7.54trn	8.54trn
	USD	178bn	184bn	190bn
Real GDP growth	%	5.3	3.0	2.5
Def bdgt	UAH	858bn	1.16trn	1.57trn
	USD	23.4bn	28.4bn	34.8bn
FMA (US)	USD	77.8m	165m	94.6m

Real-terms defence budget trend (USDbn, constant 2015)

Population		35,661,826			
Age	0–14	15–19	20–24	25–29	30–64	65 plus
Male	6.4%	2.6%	2.4%	3.0%	27.9%	6.9%
Female	6.0%	2.3%	1.9%	2.3%	25.5%	13.0%

Capabilities

After absorbing the initial assault of Russia's February 2022 invasion, Ukrainian forces halted Russia's attempt to seize Kyiv. Ukrainian counter-offensives in 2022 recovered much of the territory initially lost. Counter-offensives in 2023, however, regained far less territory and suffered considerable personnel and equipment costs. A slow Russian offensive through 2024 again put Ukrainian forces under pressure, with Russia slowly gaining territory in Ukraine's East. In August, Ukraine launched a surprise incursion into Russia's Kursk region, reportedly redeploying capable units for this, with initial gains reducing by late-year after Russian offensives. Western states have continued to support Ukraine, sending military materiel. The trajectory of US support was unclear following Donald Trump's 2024 election victory. Ukraine received air-launched cruise missiles and short-range ballistic missiles in 2023, and in late 2024 some states loosened restrictions on end-use. Kyiv remains intent on securing membership of the European Union and NATO. President Volodymyr Zelenskyy announced Ukraine's application to join NATO in response to Russia's September 2022 annexation of several regions. Zelenskyy signed a decree on general mobilisation in February 2022, but as of late 2024, had resisted drafting under-25s. The minimum draft age was lowered earlier in 2024 from 27 to 25.) At the outset of the war, Ukraine's equipment inventory consisted predominantly of Soviet-era weaponry, though more modern ground equipment from Western sources has increasingly supplemented and replaced Russian systems. A number of Western states provide training assistance in their own nations to Ukrainian troops, ranging from basic training to instruction on new equipment, including F-16 aircraft. Foreign partners also provide maintenance support. The war is accelerating Kyiv's ambition to replace its Soviet-era equipment, though the country will need considerable financial support to meet this goal and to fund reconstruction efforts. Ukraine has a broad defence-industrial base, operating in all sectors, though its capability remains shaped and limited by its Soviet heritage. The condition of its defence-industrial facilities, many of which have been attacked by Russia, is unclear. Western companies have pledged to help rebuild key industrial capacities. Ongoing combat and Ukraine's mobilisation mean accurate equipment, forces and personnel assessments are problematic.

ACTIVE ε730,000 (Army ε500,000 Navy ε40,000 Air Force ε35,000 Airborne ε45,000 Special Operations Forces ε5,000 Territorial Defence ε100,000 Unmanned Systems Force ε5,000) **Gendarmerie & Paramilitary ε260,000**

Conscript liability Army, Air Force 18 months, Navy 2 years. Minimum age for conscription reduced from 27 to 25 in 2024.

ORGANISATIONS BY SERVICE

Army ε500,000

4 regional HQ
FORCES BY ROLE
COMMAND
3 corps HQ
MANOEUVRE
Reconnaissance
1 recce regt
5 recce bn
Armoured
4 tk bde
2 armd bde
Mechanised
3 (aslt) mech inf bde
40 mech inf bde
7 mech inf bde (forming)
1 (aslt) mech inf regt
1 (volunteer) mech inf regt
2 (aslt) mech inf bn
2 mtn bde
Light

4 mot inf bde
4 inf bde
2 (volunteer) inf bn
3 (territorial def) inf bde
Other
2 sy bde
SURFACE-TO-SURFACE MISSILES
1 SRBM bde
COMBAT SUPPORT
9 arty bde
2 MRL bde
1 STA regt
4 cbt engr bde
1 engr bde
1 engr regt
2 ptn br bde
1 EOD bde
3 construction bde
1 EW regt
1 EW bn
2 EW coy
1 CBRN regt
4 sigs regt
COMBAT SERVICE SUPPORT
1 engr spt bde
3 maint regt
1 maint coy
2 tpt bde
HELICOPTERS
4 avn bde
AIR DEFENCE
4 AD regt
EQUIPMENT BY TYPE (ε)
ARMOURED FIGHTING VEHICLES
MBT 1,146: ε85 Leopard 1A5/1A5BE; ε35 Leopard 2A4; ε6 Leopard 2A5 (Strv 122); ε11 Leopard 2A6; 26 M-55S; ε18 PT-91 Twardy; ε40 T-62M/MV; 250+ T-64BM/BV/BV mod 2017; 550+ T-72AMT/AV/AV mod 2021/B1/B3/EA/M1/M1R; ε100 T-80BV/BVM/U; some T-90A/M; 5 T-84 Oplot; ε20 M1A1 SA Abrams
ASLT 18 AMX-10RC
RECCE 193: 120 BRDM-2/-2L1/-2T; 50 BRM-1K (CP); 23 FV107 Scimitar, Fennek
IFV 1,813: ε800 BMP-1/-1AK/-2; 60 BMP-3; some BTR-3DA/-3E1/-4E/-4MV1; ε100 BTR-82A; 29 BVP M-80A; ε220 M2A2 Bradley/M7SA BFIST; 45 CV9040; 94 Rosomak IFV (including variants); 45 PbV-501; 160 YPR-765; ε110 Marder 1A3; ε150 Pbv-302
APC 2,187
APC (T) 1037+: ε800 M113A1/AS4/G3DK/G4DK/M577 (CP); 125 MT-LB; 10 ATTC Bronco (CP); Bv-206; 30 FV103 Spartan; 50+ FV430; 22 FV105 Sultan
APC (W) 571: 43 ACSV; ε350 BTR-60/-70/-80; 20 Pandur 6×6 (Valuk); 10 XA-180 Sisu; Puma 6×6; 20 BOV-VP (M-86); 128 VAB
PPV 579+: Kozak-2/-2M/-5/-7; 440 Maxxpro; Varta; 139 BATT UMG
AUV: Dingo 2; IVECO LMV; Novator; Panthera T6; Roshel Senator; M1117 ASV; Eagle I; Cobra II; Gurkha LAPV
ENGINEERING & MAINTENANCE VEHICLES
AEV 108+: 40 BAT-2; M1150 ABV; MT-LB; 12 Pionierpanzer 2 Dachs; 56 Wisent; FV180 Combat Engineer Tractor
ARV 44+: 19+ BPz-2; BPz-3 Buffel; BREM-1; BREM-M; BREM-2; BREM-64; BTS-4; IMR-2; VT-72M4CZ; 5 ATTC Bronco; 15 M88A2; 5 FV106 Samson
MW 2+: 2 Bozena; Hydrema 910 MCV-2
VLB 27+: ε27 Biber; MTU-20; M60 AVLB
ANTI-TANK/ANTI-INFRASTRUCTURE
MSL
SP 9P148 Konkurs (RS-AT-5 Spandrel); 9P148 with Stugna-P; 9P149 with 9K114 Shturm (RS-AT-6 Spiral); M1064A1 HMMWV with TOW; Brimstone; Brimstone II
MANPATS 9K111 Fagot (RS-AT-4 Spigot); 9K113 Konkurs (RS-AT-5 Spandrel); Corsar; FGM-148 Javelin; Milan; NLAW; Stugna-P
GUNS 100mm ε200 MT-12/T-12
ARTILLERY 1,857
SP 714: **105mm** 1 Hawkeye; **122mm** 125 2S1 Gvozdika; **152mm** 177+: 120 2S3 Akatsiya; some 2S5 Giatsint-S; ε45 2S19 Msta-S; some Dana-M2; 12 M-77 Dana; **155mm** 391: 8 Archer; ε50 AS90; ε80 2S22 Bohdana; 50+ CAESAR 6×6; 17 CAESAR 8×8; ε40 Krab; ε100 M109A3GN/A4/A5Oe/A6/L; 38 PzH 2000; 8 Zuzana-2; **203mm** 20 2S7 Pion
TOWED 543: **105mm** 103: 100 L119 Light Gun/M119A3; 3+ M101; **122mm** 60 D-30; **130mm** 15 M-46; **152mm** 195: 75 2A36 Giatsint-B; 70 2A65 Msta-B; 50 D-20; **155mm** 170: 20 FH 70; 130 M777A2; 20 TR-F1
GUN/MOR • 120mm • TOWED 2B16 NONA-K
MRL 258: **122mm** 112: 100 9K51M Tornado-G/BM-21 Grad; 4 APR-40; 8 RM-70 Vampir; **220mm** 45: up to 10 Bureivy; 35 9P140 Uragan; **227mm** 61: 38 M142 HIMARS; 23 M270A1/B1 MLRS; **300mm** 40+: some Vilkha/Vilkha-M; 40 9A52 Smerch†; MCL
MOR 342+: **82mm** HM-19; M-69A **SP 107mm** M106; **120mm** 310: 100 2S12 Sani; 140 EM-120; some Krh/92; 60 M120-15; HM-15; HM-16; 10+ MO-120 **SP 120mm** 32: BTR-3M2; 10 M113 with Tampella; 22 SMK120 RAK
SURFACE-TO-SURFACE MISSILE LAUNCHERS
SRBM • Conventional 9K79 Tochka-U (RS-SS-21 Scarab)†; MGM-140A/B ATACMS (launched from M142 HIMARS MRL and M270 MRL)
COASTAL • DEFENCE AShM RBS-17 Hellfire
HELICOPTERS
ATK ε46 Mi-24/Mi-35 Hind
MRH 17 Mi-17V-5 Hip
TPT • Medium ε12 Mi-8 Hip
UNINHABITED AERIAL VEHICLES

CISR (Multiple systems below 20kg in weight)
ISR • Medium *Primoco* UAV *One* 150; **Light** AR3; *Luna* NG; MQ-35A V-*Bat*; *Penguin* C; *Poseidon* H10; *Scan Eagle*
OWA FP-1; *Phoenix Ghost*; *Switchblade* 600; (Multiple other systems below 20kg in weight)

AIR DEFENCE
SAM 91+
  Long-range Some S-300V (RS-SA-12A *Gladiator*)
  Short-range 10: 4 *Crotale* NG; up to 6 9K330 *Tor*-M (RS-SA-15 *Gauntlet*)
  Point-defence ε65 9K33 *Osa*-AKM (RS-SA-8 *Gecko*); 9K35 *Strela*-10 (RS-SA-13 *Gopher*); 9K38 *Igla* (RS-SA-18 *Grouse*); ε10 FV4333 *Stormer* with *Starstreak*; 6 M1097 *Avenger*; *Martlet*; *Mistral*; *Piorun*; *Starstreak*
SPAAGM 30mm 75 2K22 *Tunguska* (RS-SA-19 *Grison*)
GUNS
  SP 20mm 6 BOV-3 **23mm** ZSU-23-4 *Shilka*; Hybneryt **35mm** 55 *Gepard*; **100mm** 2 KS-19
  TOWED 23mm ZU-23-2; **40mm** 36 L/70; **57mm** S-60
AIR-LAUNCHED MISSILES • ASM *Barrier*-V

Navy ε40,000

After Russia's annexation of Crimea, HQ shifted to Odessa. Several additional vessels remain in Russian possession in Crimea.

EQUIPMENT BY TYPE
PATROL AND COASTAL COMBATANTS 15
  PCC 3 *Slavyansk* (ex-US *Island*)
  PBG 3 *Gyurza*-M (Project 51855) with 2 *Katran*-M RWS with *Barrier* SSM
  PBF 7: 6 *Defiant* 40; 1 *Kentavr*-LK†
  PB 2 *Irpin* (ex-EST *Roland*)
MINE WARFARE • MINE COUNTERMEASURES 2
  MHC 2 *Chernihiv* (ex-UK *Sandown*)
LOGISTICS AND SUPPORT 8
  ABU 1 Project 419 (*Sura*)
  AG 1 *Bereza*
  AGI 1 *Muna*
  AKL 1
  AWT 1 *Sudak*
  AXL 3 *Petrushka*
UNINHABITED MARITIME PLATFORMS • USV
  ATK *Kherson*; *Magura* V5
UNINHABITED MARITIME SYSTEMS • UUV
  ATK *Toloka*

Naval Aviation ε1,000
EQUIPMENT BY TYPE
FIXED-WING AIRCRAFT
  ASW (2 Be-12 *Mail* non-operational)
  TPT • Light (2 An-26 *Curl* in store)
HELICOPTERS
  ASW 2+: some Ka-27 *Helix* A; 1 Mi-14PS *Haze* A; 1 Mi-14PL *Haze* C
  TPT • Medium 3 *Sea King* HU5
  TRG 1 Ka-226
UNINHABITED AERIAL VEHICLES
  CISR • Medium *Bayraktar* TB2
BOMBS • Laser-guided MAM-C/-L

Marine Corps ε30,000
FORCES BY ROLE
COMMAND
  1 corps HQ
MANOEUVRE
  Reconnaissance
  1 recce bn
  Mechanised
  4 mne bde
  Light
  2 (territorial def) inf bde
COMBAT SUPPORT
  2 arty bde
COMBAT SERVICE SUPPORT
  1 spt regt
  1 log bn
COMBAT/ISR UAV
  1 CISR UAV regt
  1 CISR UAV bn
AIR DEFENCE
  1 SAM bn
EQUIPMENT BY TYPE
ARMOURED FIGHTING VEHICLES
  MBT T-64BV
  ASLT 35 AMX-10RC
  IFV BMP-1; BMP-3; *Marder* 1A3
  APC
    APC (T) MT-LB
    APC (W) 26+: BTR-60; BTR-80; 26 XA-185 *Sisu*; ACSV
    PPV 17+: *Kirpi*; 17 *Mastiff*; *Varta*
  AUV M-ATV
ANTI-TANK/ANTI-INFRASTRUCTURE
  GUNS 100mm MT-12
ARTILLERY
  SP 122mm 2S1 *Gvozdika*; **155mm** 2S22 *Bohdana*
  TOWED 152mm 2A36 *Giatsint*-B; D-20
  MRL 220mm 9P140 *Uragan*
AIR DEFENCE
  GUNS • SP 23mm ZSU-23-4

Coastal Defence ε1,500
FORCES BY ROLE
COASTAL DEFENCE
  1 AshM bde
EQUIPMENT BY TYPE
COASTAL DEFENCE
  AShM *Maritime Brimstone*; RGM-84 *Harpoon*; RK-360MC *Neptun*

Air Forces ε35,000

4 Regional HQ

FORCES BY ROLE

MANOEUVRE

Light
1 inf bde

FIGHTER
4 bde with MiG-29 *Fulcrum*; Su-27 *Flanker* B; L-39 *Albatros*

FIGHTER/GROUND ATTACK
2 bde with Su-24M *Fencer*; Su-25 *Frogfoot*

GROUND ATTACK/ISR
1 sqn with Su-24MR *Fencer* E*

TRANSPORT
3 bde with An-24 *Curl*; An-26 *Coke*; An-30 *Clank*; Il-76 *Candid*; Tu-134 *Crusty*

TRAINING
Some sqn with L-39 *Albatros*

TRANSPORT HELICOPTER
Some sqn with Mi-8 *Hip*; Mi-9 *Hip*; PZL Mi-2 *Hoplite*

AIR DEFENCE
6 SAM bde
9 SAM regt

EQUIPMENT BY TYPE

AIRCRAFT 66 combat capable
FTR 43: ε7 F-16AM *Fighting Falcon*; ε15 MiG-29 *Fulcrum*; ε21 Su-27 *Flanker* B
ATK 15: ε5 Su-24M *Fencer* D; ε10 Su-25 *Frogfoot*
ISR 11: 3 An-30 *Clank*; ε8 Su-24MR *Fencer* E*
TPT 22: **Heavy** (7 Il-76 *Candid* non-operational); **Medium** 1 An-70; **Light** ε21: 3 An-24 *Coke*; ε17 An-26 *Curl*; 1 Tu-134 *Crusty*
TRG ε27 L-39 *Albatros*

HELICOPTERS
C2 2+ Mi-9 *Hip*
MRH 17: 10 Mi-8MTV *Hip* H; ε7 Mi-17 *Hip*
TPT 24: **Medium** ε18 Mi-8 *Hip*; **Light** 6: ε5 PZL Mi-2 *Hoplite*; 1 Mi-2MSB

AIR DEFENCE
SAM 321:
  Long-range 223: ε170 S-300PS/PT (RS-SA-10 *Grumble*); 8 S-300PMU (RS-SA-10 *Grumble*); ε37 M902 *Patriot* PAC-3; 8 SAMP/T
  Medium-range 68+: ε50 9K37M *Buk-M1* (RS-SA-11 *Gadfly*) (some systems converted to AIM-7); 14 IRIS-T SLM; 4+ MIM-23B *I-Hawk*
  Short-range 30+, ε14 NASAMS; 4+ *Skyguard/Aspide*; 12 IRIS-T SLS

GUNS
SP 35mm: 8: ε8 *Skynex*
TOWED 23mm some ZU-23-2

AIR-LAUNCHED MISSILES
AAM • IR AIM-9L *Sidewinder*; R-27ET (RS-AA-10D *Alamo*); R-60 (RS-AA-8 *Aphid*); R-73 (RS-AA-11A *Archer*); **SARH** R-27R (RS-AA-10A *Alamo*); R-27ER (RS-AA-10C *Alamo*); **ARH** AIM-120B AMRAAM
ASM Kh-25 (RS-AS-10 *Karen*); Kh-29 (RS-AS-14 *Kedge*)
ARM AGM-88 HARM; Kh-25MP (RS-AS-12A *Kegler*); Kh-58 (RS-AS-11 *Kilter*)
EW MALD
LACM SCALP EG; *Storm Shadow*

BOMBS
INS/GPS-guided AASM *Hammer* 250; JDAM-ER
Laser-guided MAM-C/-L

Airborne Assault Troops ε45,000

FORCES BY ROLE

COMMAND
1 corps HQ

MANOEUVRE

Reconnaissance
1 recce bn

Mechanised
4 air aslt bde
1 air aslt regt
4 air mob bde

Air Manoeuvre
1 AB bde

COMBAT SUPPORT
1 SP arty bde

COMBAT SERVICE SUPPORT
1 log regt

COMBAT/ISR UAV
1 CISR UAV bn

EQUIPMENT BY TYPE

ARMOURED FIGHTING VEHICLES
MBT 12+ 12 *Challenger* 2; T-80BV mod
IFV BTR-3E1; BTR-4 *Bucephalus*; M2A2 *Bradley*; *Marder* 1A3
APC 643
  APC (T) 30 BTR-D
  APC (W) 443+: BTR-80; *Dozor-B*; 180 M1126 *Stryker* ICV; *Oncilla*; 263+ VAB
  PPV 170 *Kirpi*
ABCV BMD-2
AUV *Bushmaster*; IVECO LMV; KrAZ *Spartan*; MLS *Shield*; *Novator*

ANTI-TANK/ANTI-INFRASTRUCTURE
MSL • MANPATS 9K111 *Fagot* (RS-AT-4 *Spigot*); 9K111-1 *Konkurs* (RS-AT-5 *Spandrel*); NLAW

ARTILLERY
SP 122mm 2S1 *Gvozdika*; **152mm** 2S3 *Akatsiya*
TOWED 105mm M119A3; **122mm** D-30; **155mm** M777A2
MRL 122mm BM-21 *Grad*
GUN/MOR • SP • 120mm 20 2S9 NONA-S; 2S17-2 NONA-SV; 2S23 NONA-SVK
MOR 120mm 2S12 *Sani*

AIR DEFENCE
  SAM • **Point-defence** 9K35M *Strela*-10M; LMM; *Piorun*
  GUNS • **SP 23mm** some ZU-23-2 (truck mounted)

Special Operations Forces ε5,000
FORCES BY ROLE
SPECIAL FORCES
  1 SF regt
  1 SF bn
  3 spec ops regt
  1 (volunteer) spec ops regt
  2 spec ops bn
  2 ranger regt
  2 ranger regt (forming)
COMBAT SUPPORT
  4 psyops bn
EQUIPMENT BY TYPE
UNINHABITED AERIAL VEHICLES
  OWA An-196 *Lyutyy*; AQ 400 *Scythe*; *Banshee* mod; *Morok*; Tu-141 *Strizh* mod; Tu-143 *Reys* mod; UJ-26 *Bober*
  ISR • **Light** *Lord* (OWA role); UJ-22 (OWA role)

Territorial Defence Force ε100,000
FORCES BY ROLE
MANOEUVRE
  Light
    26 (territorial def) inf bde

Unmanned Systems Force ε5,000
FORCES BY ROLE
COMBAT/ISR UAV
  1 CISR UAV regt
  6 CISR UAV bn
  1 CISR UAV bn (forming)
UNINHABITED AERIAL VEHICLES
  CISR • **Medium** *Bayraktar* TB2; (Multiple other systems below 20kg in weight)
  OWA (Multiple systems below 20kg in weight)

Gendarmerie & Paramilitary ε260,000

National Guard ε100,000
Ministry of Internal Affairs; 5 territorial comd
FORCES BY ROLE
SPECIAL FORCES
  1 spec ops regt
MANOEUVRE
  Mechanised
    7 (aslt) mech inf bde
    1 mech inf regt
  Other
    5 sy bde
    1 sy regt
COMBAT SUPPORT
  1 SP arty bde
EQUIPMENT BY TYPE
ARMOURED FIGHTING VEHICLES
  MBT T-64; T-64BV; T-64BM; T-72;
  IFV BMP-2; BTR-3; BTR-3E1; BTR-4 *Bucephalus*; BTR-4E; YPR-765
  APC
    APC (W) BTR-70; BTR-80
    PPV Streit *Cougar*; Streit *Spartan*; *Kozak*-2; *Varta*
  AUV *Novator*; *Novator* 2
ANTI-TANK/ANTI-INFRASTRUCTURE
  MSL • **MANPATS** NLAW
  RCL **73mm** SPG-9
ARTILLERY
  SP **155mm** 2S22 *Bohdana*; *Dita*
  TOWED **122mm** D-30
  MOR **120mm** some
AIRCRAFT
  TPT • **Light** 24: 20 An-26 *Curl*; 2 An-72 *Coaler*; 2 Tu-134 *Crusty*
  HELICOPTERS • **TPT** 14: **Medium** 13: 4 H225; 7 Mi-8 *Hip*; **Light** 3: 2 H125; 1 Mi-2MSB
AIR DEFENCE
  SAM • **Point-defence** 9K38 *Igla* (RS-SA-18 *Grouse*); *Piorun*
  GUNS • **SP 23mm** some ZU-23-2 (tch)

Border Guard ε60,000
FORCES BY ROLE
MANOEUVRE
  Mechanised
    3 (aslt) lt mech bde
  Light
    1 (mobile) inf regt
  Other
    17 sy bn
EQUIPMENT BY TYPE
ARMOURED FIGHTING VEHICLES
  APC • **PPV** *Kozak*-2; *Mamba* (Alvis 4)
  AUV *Triton*-01
AIR DEFENCE
  GUNS • **TOWED 100mm** 3 KS-19

Maritime Border Guard
The Maritime Border Guard is an independent subdivision of the State Commission for Border Guards and is not part of the navy
EQUIPMENT BY TYPE
PATROL AND COASTAL COMBATANTS 21
  PCT 1 *Molnya* (*Pauk* I) with 4 single 406mm TT, 2 RBU 1200 *Uragan* A/S mor, 1 76mm gun
  PCC 4 *Tarantul* (*Stenka*)
  PB 12: 11 *Zhuk*; 1 *Orlan*
  PBR 4 *Shmel* with 1 76mm gun

LOGISTICS AND SUPPORT • AGF 1
AIRCRAFT • TPT Medium An-8 *Camp*; Light An-24 *Coke*; An-26 *Curl*; An-72 *Coaler*
HELICOPTERS • ASW: Ka-27 *Helix* A

National Police ε100,000

Ministry of Internal Affairs

FORCES BY ROLE
MANOEUVRE
Mechanised
1 mech bde
2 lt mech bde
1 lt mech regt
Light
1 lt inf bn
23 lt inf bn (forming)

DEPLOYMENT

RUSSIA: 20,000

SOUTHERN AND EASTERN UKRAINE

Russia annexed the Ukrainian region of Crimea in March 2014, having occupied the territory the previous month. Following Russia's full-scale invasion of Ukraine in February 2022, Moscow declared that it had also annexed undefined areas in Donetsk, Kherson, Luhansk and Zaporizhzhia oblasts. Data presented here represents the de facto situation and does not imply international recognition.

FOREIGN FORCES

Russia 450,000; 16 army; 7 corps

Uzbekistan UZB

Uzbekistani Som UZS		2023	2024	2025
GDP	UZS	1.19qrn	1.42qrn	1.68qrn
	USD	102bn	113bn	127bn
Real GDP growth	%	6.3	5.6	5.7
Def exp	UZS	n.k.	n.k.	n.k.
	USD	n.k.	n.k.	n.k.
Population		36,520,593		

Age	0–14	15–19	20–24	25–29	30–64	65 plus
Male	15.3%	3.9%	3.5%	3.9%	20.6%	3.0%
Female	14.3%	3.7%	3.3%	3.9%	21.0%	3.7%

Capabilities

Uzbekistan's most recent military doctrine emphasises border security and hybrid-warfare concerns while spelling out a requirement for military modernisation and defence industrial improvements. Uzbekistan is a member of the SCO but suspended its CSTO membership in 2012. The country is a member of the Organization of Turkic States. It maintains bilateral defence ties with Moscow. Uzbek forces exercise regularly with other countries in the region, including Azerbaijan and Kazakhstan. The armed forces are army-dominated and conscript-based. Uzbekistan has no foreign deployments and limited capacity for such operations. It inherited a sizeable air fleet from the Soviet Union, but the active inventory has shrunk in the absence of recapitalisation. It may benefit from inheriting some US light fixed-wing aircraft once operated by the previous government in Afghanistan. It is purchasing armed UAVs from China and Turkiye. Logistical and maintenance shortcomings hinder aircraft availability. Uzbekistan relies on foreign suppliers for advanced military equipment. It held meetings with India in 2020 to advance defence cooperation, and, in 2021, signed a defence cooperation pact with Pakistan. A State Committee for the Defence Industry was established in late 2017 to organise domestic industry and defence orders. In recent years, Uzbekistan's defence industry has showcased domestically produced light armoured vehicles and armoured personnel carriers.

ACTIVE 48,000 (Army 24,500 Air 7,500 Joint 16,000)
Gendarmerie & Paramilitary 20,000

Conscript liability 12 months

ORGANISATIONS BY SERVICE

Army 24,500

4 Mil Districts; 2 op comd; 1 Tashkent Comd

FORCES BY ROLE
SPECIAL FORCES
1 SF bde
MANOEUVRE
Armoured
1 tk bde
Mechanised
11 MR bde
Air Manoeuvre
1 air aslt bde
1 AB bde
Mountain
1 lt mtn inf bde
COMBAT SUPPORT
3 arty bde
1 MRL bde

EQUIPMENT BY TYPE
ARMOURED FIGHTING VEHICLES
MBT 340: 70 T-72; 100 T-64B/MV; 170 T-62
RECCE 19: 13 BRDM-2; 6 BRM-1
IFV 370: 270 BMP-2; ε100 BTR-82A
APC 388
  APC (T) 50 BTR-D
  APC (W) 259: 24 BTR-60; 25 BTR-70; 210 BTR-80
  PPV 79: 24 *Ejder Yalcin*; 50 *Maxxpro+*; 5 *Typhoon*-K 4×4
ABCV 129: 120 BMD-1; 9 BMD-2
AUV 11+: 7 *Cougar*; 4+ M-ATV; some *Tigr*-M
ENGINEERING & MAINTENANCE VEHICLES
ARV 20 *Maxxpro* ARV
ANTI-TANK/ANTI-INFRASTRUCTURE

MSL • MANPATS 9K11 *Malyutka* (RS-AT-3 *Sagger*); 9K111 *Fagot* (RS-AT-4 *Spigot*)
GUNS 100mm 36 MT-12/T-12

ARTILLERY 487+
SP 83+: **122mm** 18 2S1 *Gvozdika*; **152mm** 17+: 17 2S3 *Akatsiya*; 2S5 *Giatsint*-S (reported); **203mm** 48 2S7 *Pion*
TOWED 200: **122mm** 60 D-30; **152mm** 140 2A36 *Giatsint*-B
GUN/MOR 120mm 54 2S9 NONA-S
MRL 108: **122mm** 60: 36 BM-21 *Grad*; 24 9P138; **220mm** 48 9P140 *Uragan*
MOR 120mm 42: 5 2B11 *Sani*; 19 2S12 *Sani*; 18 M-120

AIR DEFENCE • SAM
Point-defence QW-18 (CH-SA-11)

Air Force 7,500
FORCES BY ROLE
FIGHTER
1 sqn with MiG-29/MiG-29UB *Fulcrum* A/B
GROUND ATTACK
1 sqn with Su-25/Su-25BM *Frogfoot*
TRANSPORT
1 regt with An-12 *Cub*; An-26 *Curl*; C295W; Il-76 *Candid*; Tu-134 *Crusty*
TRAINING
1 sqn with L-39 *Albatros*
ATTACK/TRANSPORT HELICOPTER
1 regt with Mi-8 *Hip*; Mi-24 *Hind*; Mi-26 *Halo*; Mi-35M *Hind*
AIR DEFENCE
1 bty with FD-2000 (CH-SA-9)
1 bty with S-125-2M *Pechora*-2M (RS-SA-26)
2 bty with S-125M1 *Neva*-M1 (RA-SA-3 *Goa*)

EQUIPMENT BY TYPE
AIRCRAFT 24 combat capable
FTR 12 MiG-29/MiG-29UB *Fulcrum* A/B; (18 more in store); (26 Su-27/Su-27UB *Flanker* B/C in store)
ATK 12 Su-25/Su-25BM *Frogfoot*; (15 Su-24 *Fencer* in store)
TPT 11: **Heavy** 2 Il-76 *Candid*; **Medium** 2 An-12 *Cub*; **Light** 7: 2 An-26 *Curl*; 4 C295W; 1 Tu-134 *Crusty*
TRG 6 L-39 *Albatros*

HELICOPTERS
ATK 41: 29 Mi-24 *Hind*; 12 Mi-35M *Hind*
TPT 32: **Heavy** 9: 8 H225M *Caracal*; 1 Mi-26 *Halo*; **Medium** ε15 Mi-8 *Hip*; **Light** 8 AS350 *Ecureuil*

UNINHABITED AERIAL VEHICLES
CISR 4+: **Heavy** *Wing Loong*; **Medium** 4+ *Bayraktar* TB2

AIR DEFENCE • SAM 18
Long-range 4 FD-2000 (CH-SA-9)
Medium-range 4 S-125-2M *Pechora*-2M (RS-SA-26)
Short-range 10 S-125M1 *Neva*-M1 (RS-SA-3 *Goa*)

AIR-LAUNCHED MISSILES
AAM • IR R-60 (RS-AA-8 *Aphid*); R-73 (RS-AA-11 *Archer*); IR/SARH R-27 (RS-AA-10 *Alamo*)
ASM Kh-25 (RS-AS-10 *Karen*)
ARM Kh-25MP (RS-AS-12A *Kegler*); Kh-28 (RS-AS-9 *Kyle*); Kh-58 (RS-AS-11 *Kilter*)

BOMBS • Laser-guided MAM-L

Gendarmerie & Paramilitary up to 20,000

Internal Security Troops up to 19,000
Ministry of Interior

National Guard 1,000
Ministry of Defence

Chapter Five
Asia

- In April, China's Central Military Commission announced that the Strategic Support Force, a service branch, would be disbanded and split into three new arms: a new Information Support Force, and a re-designated Aerospace Force and Cyberspace Force.
- Japan is progressing in its planned acquisition of various types of stand-off missile capabilities, with deliveries of the American *Tomahawk* land-attack cruise missile and an improved version of the indigenous ground-based Type-12 anti-ship missile set to begin in 2025.
- China's military exercises around Taiwan continued, including the large-scale *Joint Sword*-2024A and *Joint Sword*-2024B exercises around the island reportedly including the People's Liberation Army's four services: the Ground Force (Army), Navy, Air Force and Rocket Force.
- Southeast Asian states have been at the forefront of new defence cooperative arrangements in the Indo-Pacific.
- The Philippines and Japan signed a Reciprocal Access Agreement on 8 July 2024. This marked the Philippines' third such agreement, its others being with Australia and the US. It will likely boost the 'latticework' structure of American partnerships and alliances in the region.
- The UK and Australia moved ahead with the design phase for the new submarine that will equip the Royal Navy from the late 2030s and the Royal Australian Navy from the early 2040s. Defence industrial investments are underway, though doubts remain about the project's overall viability.
- Robust and steady growth in Asian defence budgets continued in 2024. This continuity comes as strategic drivers – such as China's increasing assertiveness and North Korean belligerence – galvanise threat perceptions and well-funded investment programmes, with significant spending increases coming from the region's larger, more mature economies.

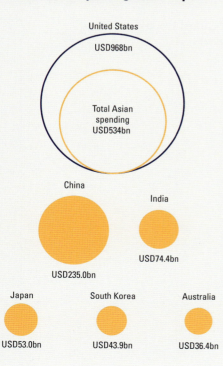

Asia defence spending, 2024 – top 5

United States USD968bn
Total Asian spending USD534bn
China USD235.0bn
India USD74.4bn
Japan USD53.0bn
South Korea USD43.9bn
Australia USD36.4bn

Active military personnel – top 10
(25,000 per unit)

China 2,035,000
India 1,475,750
North Korea 1,280,000
Pakistan 660,000
South Korea 500,000
Vietnam 450,000
Indonesia 404,500
Thailand 360,850
Sri Lanka 262,500
Japan 247,150

Global total 20,629,000
Regional total 8,983,000 (43.5%)

Regional defence policy and economics 208 ▶
Arms procurement and defence-industrial trends 230 ▶
Armed forces data section 231 ▶

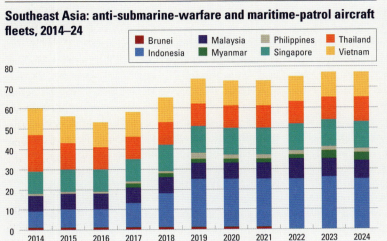

Southeast Asia: anti-submarine-warfare and maritime-patrol aircraft fleets, 2014–24

Note: Fleets include fixed-wing and rotary-wing aircraft.

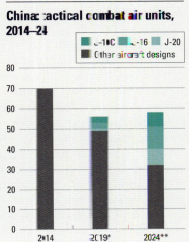

China: tactical combat air units, 2014–24

*Includes 3 J-10C brigades, 3 J-16 brigades and 1 J-20 brigade.
**Includes 7 J-10C brigades, 11 J-16 brigades and 8 J-20 brigades.

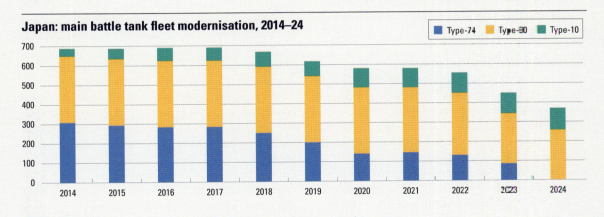

Japan: main battle tank fleet modernisation, 2014–24

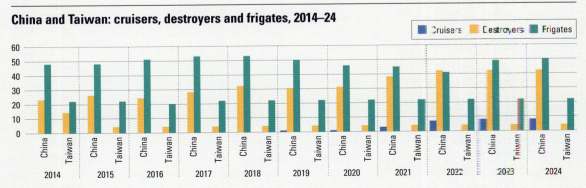

China and Taiwan: cruisers, destroyers and frigates, 2014–24

Note: Active inventory only.

Asia

Defence investments and modernisation plans continued across the region in 2024. Defence budgets are still rising, international partnerships are expanding, and new capabilities continue to be introduced. The United States continued to work to enhance its defence relations and presence in the region, renovating old facilities and securing new access, and at the same time looking to deepen its network of alliances and partnerships. Military modernisation continued in China, though the People's Liberation Army (PLA) was tarred by corruption scandals at senior levels, in a year when it conducted another service reorganisation to help achieve greater 'informatisation'. Beijing undertook yet more major military exercises around Taiwan, and Chinese assets engaged in confrontations with other regional states at more locations in the South China Sea. North Korea, meanwhile, continued to make advances in its nuclear weapons programme, testing a second solid-propellant intercontinental ballistic-missile design.

Northeast and Southeast Asia

Defence establishments across Northeast and Southeast Asia continued to seek qualitative improvements in their operational readiness and war-fighting proficiency. The growing complexity and scope of combined-military exercises, including the introduction of new capabilities, the upgrading of defence partnership agreements and the organisational restructuring of command-and-control (C2) systems, were noteworthy. Alliances and defence partnerships, from agreements to exercises, are increasingly critical components in capability development plans across the region.

Important changes to the regional C2 architecture within the US alliance system in Asia took place in 2024. In July, the US announced that it would upgrade US Forces Japan (USFJ) to a joint force headquarters with expanded missions and operational responsibilities. The new USFJ joint force headquarters will work closely with the Japan Self-Defense Forces (JSDF) Joint Operations Command (J-JOC), a new permanent joint headquarters announced in September 2023, and which could be operational before March 2025. The reconfigured USFJ will assume command responsibilities for the roughly 55,000 personnel stationed in Japan from the US Indo-Pacific Command (INDOPACOM) and is intended to ensure quicker joint decision-making and coordination during contingencies. It will also allow INDOPACOM officers to interact more frequently with their Japanese counterparts across a wide range of joint activities, and operational planning and intelligence-sharing. Japan's planned acquisition of various domestic- and foreign-sourced stand-off capabilities places a premium on improved coordination with the US on the use of force.

South Korea launched a new Strategic Command in early October 2024 to coordinate combined operations involving US nuclear forces and conventional South Korean weapons systems. The new structure seeks to integrate South Korea's major conventional assets with the US extended deterrence architecture. The challenges posed by North Korea's continued missile and nuclear weapons activities and its deepening collaboration with Russia, along with China's increasingly aggressive posture over Taiwan and the South China Sea, have given new impetus for Japan and South Korea to revamp alliance architectures with the US. These threats have also given momentum to the trilateral cooperation between Japan, South Korea and the US: as demonstrated by the Camp David Summit in August 2023, and a joint statement in 2024 that also noted long-standing plans such as to improve trilateral cooperation over missile defence.

The three countries held the inaugural trilateral multi-domain exercise *Freedom Edge* in late June 2024, including serials in cooperative ballistic-missile defence, air defence, anti-submarine warfare and defensive cyber tasks. These activities took place across multiple domains and represented an important step in improving cross-domain inter-operability between the three armed forces. Following the conclusion of the exercise, the three countries' defence ministers signed the Memorandum of Cooperation on the Trilateral Security Cooperation Framework (TSCF) in July.

The TSCF seeks to institutionalise a range of security cooperation initiatives including senior-level policy consultations, information-sharing, exercises and defence exchanges.

The region also witnessed several military exercise 'firsts'. In May 2024, the tenth iteration of *Valiant Shield* – a biennial large-scale military exercise the US initiated in 2006 – saw US allies Canada, France and Japan join for the first time. The Philippines, meanwhile, took part in the 'most expansive' combined-exercise *Balikatan* in April 2024, which included personnel from Australia and France as well as the US. There were observers from over a dozen countries, including Canada, Germany, India, Japan and South Korea, and others from Southeast Asia. For the first time, the US and the Philippines conducted parts of the exercise outside of the Philippines' territorial waters, including in its exclusive economic zone. During the exercise, the Philippine Navy's guided-missile frigate *Jose Rizal* fired a C-Star (*Haesong*) anti-ship cruise missile for the first time. During the US–Philippine exercise *Salaknib* in April, the US conducted its first deployment of its Mid-Range Capability (or *Typhon*) system – its new ground-based missile launcher, capable of employing the *Tomahawk* land-attack cruise missile and the surface-to-air SM-6.

New capabilities were introduced across other major combined-military exercises over the past year. The US–Thailand-anchored multinational *Cobra Gold* exercise from February to March 2024 saw space capabilities integrated into humanitarian and crisis-response serials, under a Combined Space Force Coordination Center that included personnel from Australia, Indonesia, Japan, Malaysia, Singapore, South Korea, Thailand and the US. The US–Indonesia-anchored *Super Garuda Shield* exercise in August and September 2024 included a major cyber exercise for the first time. China also claimed to have introduced new elements in its *Falcon Strike* exercise with Thailand in August 2024. The PLA Air Force reportedly deployed multiple military aircraft, including the Y-20 transport aircraft and the J-10 combat aircraft. And in October 2024, the Five Power Defence Arrangements exercise *Bersama Lima* saw the inaugural participation of F-35As from Australia and a P-8A maritime-patrol aircraft from New Zealand.

Southeast Asian states have been at the forefront of new defence cooperative arrangements in the Indo-Pacific. The Philippines and Japan signed a Reciprocal Access Agreement (RAA) on 8 July 2024. This marked the Philippines' third such agreement, its others being with Australia and the US. Formal negotiations for the agreement coincided with Japan's provision of a coastal-surveillance radar system in November 2023. The agreement is a key mechanism to streamline the burdensome bureaucratic procedures currently required for both forces to train, exercise or conduct exchanges in each other's territory. The RAA, however, explicitly forbids efforts to establish any permanent military facilities in the territory of each country. The legal framework will likely boost the latticework structure of US partnerships and alliances in the region.

In a similar vein, Australia and Indonesia signed a 'treaty-level' Defence Cooperation Agreement (DCA) in late August 2024. While the DCA also facilitates improved bureaucratic procedures for both countries' armed forces to conduct more complex joint activities and exercises and operate in each other's territory, it also seeks to boost other areas of cooperation such as maritime security, counter-terrorism and humanitarian and disaster relief, as well as defence-industrial collaboration. The DCA complements existing bilateral frameworks, including the 2006 Lombok Treaty and 2018 Comprehensive Strategic Partnership.

Other Southeast Asian states are also enhancing their defence cooperative arrangements. In mid-August 2024, Laos and Russia signed an updated bilateral agreement boosting military-to-military cooperation. The agreement was then followed by a combined military exercise, *Laros 2024*. Meanwhile, in late August 2024, the Philippines and Vietnam announced plans to sign a Memorandum of Understanding (MoU) on defence cooperation. This followed a defence-cooperation MoU signed by the Philippines and Singapore the previous month, which will likely serve as a framework to promote cooperation in areas of mutual interest such as military education and counter-terrorism. The Philippines is looking to form more partnerships, having signed, or announced its intention to sign, similar defence MoUs with Canada, France, Germany and South Korea.

While less formal than an RAA or DCA, the European Union and Japan signed a Security and Defence Partnership agreement in November 2024. This upgrades the existing informal, regular

Figure 17 Asia: airborne early-warning and control (AEW&C) fleets, 2014–24

Amid regional tensions, Asian militaries continue to acquire AEW&C aircraft, recognising their importance as key command-and-control nodes and surveillance assets. China continues production of the KJ-500. Introduced in 2015, and now the most numerous AEW&C aircraft in service in China, the KJ-500 are primarily stationed on China's east coast. Concurrently, the Y-20-based KJ-3000 and the carrier-based KJ-600 are reportedly in development. Taiwan, meanwhile, has only recently renewed interest in acquiring more AEW&C aircraft. Japan continues procurement of the E-2D *Hawkeye* to replace some of its older E-2C variants. In 2020, South Korea outlined a requirement for four additional AEW&C aircraft to operate alongside its B-737 AEWs. South Korea will likely use these to detect North Korean missile launches and coordinate air defences and counter-strikes. Elsewhere, Pakistan introduced its eighth Saab 2000 *Erieye* in 2024, possibly with the improved *Erieye* Extended Range radar. The status of its Chinese-manufactured ZDK-03, often operating alongside the navy, remained unclear as of October 2024. India, meanwhile, is pursuing domestic development to supplement imported aircraft types. Two *Netra* AEW aircraft are stationed in the north, alongside three Il-76TD *Phalcon*. More *Netra* are planned, as are Airbus A321-based AEW&C aircraft.

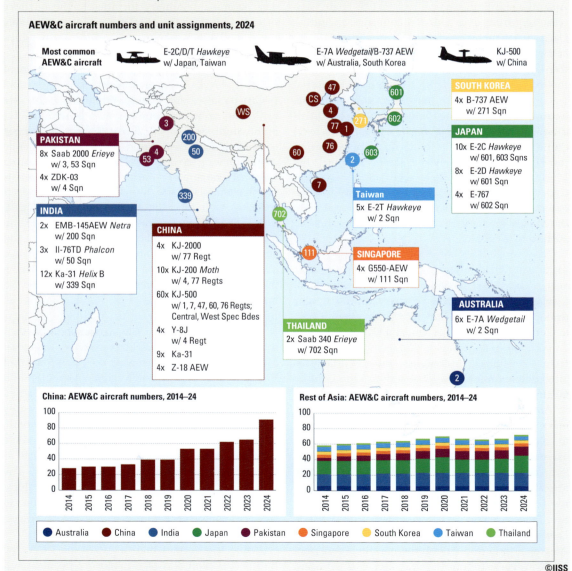

Note: all data and information as of October 2024.
Source: IISS, Military Balance+, milbalplus.iiss.org

consultations between security officials to an annual Security and Defence Dialogue at director-general/managing director level. The agreement covers a wide range of security issues, from naval cooperation, space and cyber security to nuclear non-proliferation. The EU also announced a similar agreement with South Korea in the same week, during the inaugural EU–South Korea Strategic Dialogue.

South Asia

India's military modernisation has been spurred by China's posture and actions on India's northern land border, and by the expansion of China's presence in the Indian Ocean. This effort is taking place alongside India's traditional threat posed by Pakistan on its western border, increasingly being seen in conjunction with China, as well as the sudden change of government in Bangladesh.

Following a clash between Indian and Chinese troops in June 2020 in the Galwan Valley, and after a two-year-long stall in border talks, India and China reached on 21 October 2024 an agreement to completely disengage those troops across the Line of Actual Control, dividing each side's controlled territory in the Himalayan region. Despite India's successes in building dual-use infrastructure such as tunnels and all-weather border roads, China continues to outpace and outspend India's efforts. India's three armed services made progress in 2024 towards forming theatre commands, which are planned to boost interservice cooperation and integrate capabilities to optimise their resources during operations. There were plans to unveil structures to develop joint training, administration and logistics by the end of 2024. India plans to launch unified theatre commands by June 2025, over a decade after China formed its theatre commands.

Amid economic difficulties, Pakistan's focus remains on preventing domestic and Afghanistan-linked terrorist and insurgent attacks and maintaining a form of conventional- and strategic-forces equilibrium with India. Toward the latter, with Chinese assistance, Pakistan is producing new tanks and conventionally powered advanced submarines, as well as importing J-10 combat aircraft. Pakistan's defence trade and industrial partnership with Turkiye is growing. This includes a 2024 agreement between Turkish company Repkon and Pakistani firm Wah Industries to establish 155mm artillery-shell production.

DEFENCE ECONOMICS

Asian defence budgets continued to grow in 2024, with combined spending reaching USD524 billion. Growth was robust in real terms at 5.4%, which was largely in line with the 2023 growth rate. Excluding China, real growth in the Asia-Pacific still reached 3.9%. This continuity comes as strategic drivers – such as China's increasing assertiveness and North Korean belligerence – galvanise threat perceptions and investment programmes, with significant spending increases coming from the region's larger, more mature economies.

In addition to driving the regional top line, spending trends among key US allies have diverged from those seen in developing Asia-Pacific economies, with defence budgets in Western-aligned states now growing at faster rates on average. This dynamic represents a reversal of the previous prevailing trend, whereby higher-growth emerging economies were the primary driving force behind year-on-year real-terms increases.

There is a longer-term question about the sustainability of these rapid spending increases by relatively low-growth economies. Conscious decisions to raise spending as a percentage of GDP in response to the perceived deterioration of the regional security environment have driven recent growth. Whether spending can be maintained at these new elevated levels remains to be seen.

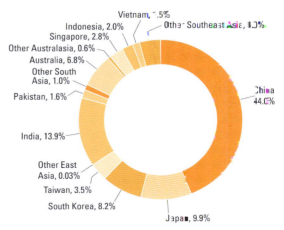

▲ Figure 18 **Asia: defence spending by country and sub-region, 2024**

Defence spending

In April 2024, **Australia** released a new National Defence Strategy (NDS) and a revised Integrated Investment Program (IIP) which outlined plans for significant increases to defence spending. According to this budgetary outlook, Australia's defence budget (including allocations for the Australian Signals Directorate and a newly established Australian Submarine Agency) will rise nominally by over 80% over the next decade. The core budget (excluding special appropriations for pensions) will rise from AUD55.5bn (USD36.7bn) in FY2024–25 to AUD100.4bn (USD66.4bn) by FY2033–34. To achieve this, budgets will grow at an average rate of 7.0% a year in nominal terms, or just less than 5.0% annually in real terms. Compared to previous plans, this raises the defence budget by an additional AUD5.7bn (USD3.8bn) over the next four years, and an additional AUD50.3bn (USD33.3bn) over the decade.

The new funding will enable the Australian government to spend at least AUD330bn (USD218.4bn) over the next ten years acquiring the capabilities outlined in the IIP. Of this, the NDS prioritises Australia's maritime domain, which receives 38.0% of the total investment plan. Undersea-warfare capabilities – predominantly Australia's commitment to acquire a fleet of nuclear-powered submarines through the Australia–United Kingdom–United States (AUKUS) partnership – will account for the biggest portion and are projected to cost AUD53–63bn (USD35.1–41.7bn) over the decade. A further 16.0% of the investment budget will go towards bolstering surface-warfare capabilities, including AUD22–32bn (USD14.6–21.2bn) for six new *Hunter*-class frigates, AUD7–10bn (USD4.6–6.6bn) for 11 new 'general purpose frigates' to replace the *Anzac*-class (MEKO 200) frigates, and AUD6.5–8.5bn (USD4.3–5.6bn) to upgrade the navy's fleet of three *Hobart*-class destroyers fitted with the *Aegis* combat-management system.

Japan's Defense Build-Up Program (DBP) saw the 2024 defence budget boosted by a nominal 16.5% from the previous year, which itself had increased by 10.5% from 2022 levels. Growth is set to continue, with the Ministry of Defense's (MoD's) request of JPY8.5 trillion (USD59.5bn) for 2025 representing a further 7.4% rise. Should the latest request be granted, the MoD's budget will have grown by 38.3% in nominal terms in just three years as the government looks to move military spending towards 2% of GDP. Following this, with

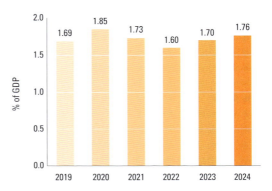

▼ Figure 19 **Asia: regional defence spending** as % of GDP (average)

Note: Analysis excludes Afghanistan, North Korea and Laos.
Source: IISS analysis based on GDP data from IMF World Economic Outlook, October 2024 ©IISS

plans to raise spending to JPY8.9trn (USD62bn) by 2027, growth looks set to slow from 2026 onwards, assuming the MoD's 2025 budget request is granted.

Priorities within the 2024 budget include enhancing air-defence capabilities, expanding munitions stocks, continuing to develop stand-off capabilities (including new anti-ship and hypersonic missiles), and improving military readiness. These activities will be pursued alongside other modernisation plans including the construction of a further two *Mogami*-class frigates, funding three new Kawasaki P-1 anti-submarine-warfare aircraft, and a further 15 F-35 *Lightning* II fighter ground-attack aircraft. The budget also allocated JPY63.7bn (USD444 million) for the ongoing preliminary design phase of the Global Combat Air Programme (GCAP) being pursued in conjunction with the UK and Italy.

In **Singapore** the defence-ministry budget increased by 12.6% compared to the initial 2023 budget, rising to SGD20.2bn (USD15.2bn). Strong growth, over four consecutive years, has reversed a recent relative decline in defence spending as a proportion of GDP. Indeed, despite rising in real terms, defence budgets in relation to GDP consistently fell in 2010–22. Spending has since risen from the 2022 low point of 2.5% of GDP, up to 2.9% for 2024, although this remains below the 3.5% average seen in the late 2000s. According to the Ministry of Finance, a key reason for the uplifts were 'heightened inflationary pressures', though the scale of recent increases far exceeds inflationary pressures, with the 2024 defence budget representing a 20.9% real-terms increase compared to 2022.

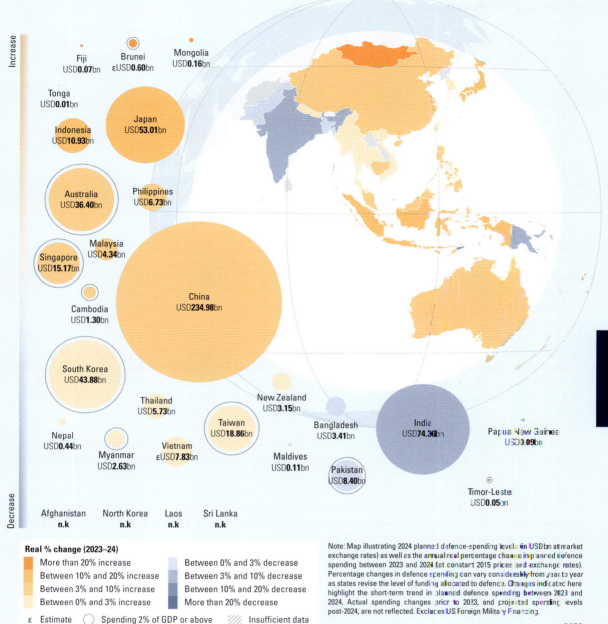

▲ Map 3 **Asia: regional defence spending** (USDbn, %ch yoy)

Defence budgets also continued to rise in **Taiwan**, although this looks set to peak in 2025 as extra-budgetary support for military modernisation priorities gradually draws down. Allocations from two special budgets – one for the acquisition of 66 F-16 Block 70 *Fighting Falcon* fighter aircraft, and one for the wider Naval and Air Force Enhancement Program – are projected to decline. These will decrease from TWD94.5bn (USD2.9bn) in 2024 to TWD90.4bn (USD2.8bn) in 2025, and then more steeply to TWD69.2bn (USD2.2bn) in 2026. By 2027, both funds will be exhausted with no publicly announced plans to approve additional new special budgets.

Similarly, there are signs of a slowdown in **South Korea**. Between 2018 and 2021, Seoul's defence budgets achieved average real-terms annual growth of 5.7%, compared to 1.7% between 2022 and 2024. The proposed budget for 2025 continues this trend with a 1.8% uplift for defence in real terms. Nevertheless, the defence budget will remain a third higher in real terms in 2025 than in 2017, with spending standing at 2.3% of GDP. In terms of priorities, the Defense Acquisition Program Administration's (DAPA) plan for 2024 remained focused on enhancing military capabilities (principally through further implementing the 'three axis' system), investment in indigenous research and development (R&D), and the continued expansion of South Korean defence exports.

Elsewhere in Asia, economic and fiscal conditions still primarily drove the pace of defence spending growth. In 2024, GDP growth slowed across the region as the post-COVID-19 economic recovery waned and economic performance remained subdued relative to pre-pandemic levels. Against this lacklustre backdrop, and mindful of the vast government spending prompted by the pandemic, the IMF urged governments to reduce budget deficits, rebuild buffers against future shocks and address rising levels of debt in the region.

In contrast to this guidance, reports emerged in June 2024 that then **Indonesian** president-elect Prabowo Subianto was exploring ways to adjust the legally mandated 3.0%-of-GDP ceiling on his country's fiscal deficit and raise the 60%-of-GDP limit on sovereign debt. The move is ostensibly aimed at accelerating economic growth, although there are signs that any increases would also benefit the defence ministry. Indonesia's draft budget for 2025 included a IDR165.2trn (USD10.2bn) allocation for defence, an increase of 21.9% compared to the 2024 draft budget. However, the 2024 budget itself was also revised upwards significantly, rising from an initial IDR135.4trn (USD8.5bn) to a projected level of IDR171.5trn (USD10.9bn), which is higher than the 2025 draft figure. This new funding primarily aims at military modernisation plans. According to the new draft budget, 45.4% of total spending – approximately IDR79.5trn (USD5bn) – will contribute towards modernisation in 2024, with a further 41.8% – IDR69trn (USD4.3bn) – allocation in 2025. Although Indonesia had previously planned to achieve its 'Minimum Essential Force' military modernisation concept by 2024, the budget provides continued funding to realise these goals into 2025.

India has sought to redefine its spending limits, announcing plans to tie fiscal policy to debt levels that are expressed in relation to GDP rather than to the deficit. Reflecting these wider difficulties, Indian military spending has reduced in relation to both overall government spending and GDP – a trend which continued this year. Under the 2024–25 budget, total spending on defence came to INR6.21trn (USD74.4bn). This was a 4.7% nominal increase over the initial 2023–24 budget, though the budget was revised during the year as part of the standard budget cycle. Compared to the 2023–24 revised budget of INR6.24tr (USD75.4bn), the 2024–25 budget in fact fell nominally by 0.4%. In real terms, the 2024–25 budget equated to a reduction of around 6.0% from the previous year, causing it to drop to its lowest level against GDP since the 1960s. A side effect of these funding constraints has

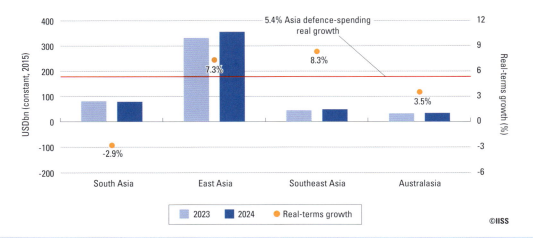

▲ Figure 20 **Asia: sub-regional real-terms defence-spending growth, 2023–24** (USDbn, constant 2015)

been the prioritisation of local programmes in line with the country's flagship 'Make in India' policy. According to the Standing Committee on Defence, just over 65.0% of the 2021–22 capital budget was spent with local companies, with subsequent budgets seeking to raise this to 68.0% in 2022–23 and 75.0% in 2023–24.

Defence industry

Alongside spending increases, regional states continued to prioritise bolstering indigenous defence-industrial capabilities, both as a means of economic development and increasingly to build resilience in the face of potential conflict. Australia's NDS, for example, highlighted the importance of increasing the defence sector's 'capacity to support the [Australian Defence Force] during crisis or conflict'. Indeed, a central theme of the Defence Industry Development Strategy, released ahead of the NDS and IIP, is the fulfilment of seven Sovereign Defence Industrial Priorities including military aircraft maintenance, shipbuilding, guided-weapons production, and the development of autonomous systems.

As with Australia, Japan's most recent defence white paper also emphasised the importance of reinforcing the defence-industrial base as part of wider efforts to enhance military capabilities and preparedness. Tokyo's position is arguably even more ambitious, aimed at ensuring that local industry is capable of development, manufacture and through-life support of the equipment operated by the military, and at ensuring technological superiority over potential adversaries. Such ambitions are mirrored by the South Korean government, which is also bolstering the position of its local defence sector. To enable this, DAPA has plans to invest KRW2.4trn (USD1.8bn) in defence technology R&D including funding for ten strategic areas: artificial intelligence (AI), quantum technologies, space, energy, advanced materials, cyber, uncrewed systems, sensor and electromagnetic warfare, propulsion systems, and weapons-of-mass-destruction response.

DAPA intends to pursue these goals in cooperation with international partners including Australia, the UK and the US. Indeed, the drive to enhance self-reliance in the Asia-Pacific is intrinsically linked to closer cooperation with key partners both in the region and further afield. The AUKUS and Global Combat Air Programme (GCAP) partnerships represent perhaps the highest-profile examples of closer industrial cooperation between regional states and their allies and partners in Europe and North America, ultimately aimed at sustaining and enhancing the local defence sector.

Both sides are driving this renewed spirit of cooperation, with Western states also looking to improve security within their key defence supply chains. This reassessment of overseas industrial partnerships has emphasised the need to improve the security and reliability of global supply chains, with the US in particular deepening relationships with key regional allies and partners. To support this, Singapore signed an MoU with the US in May to enhance cooperation on defence innovation, focusing on areas such as AI, autonomy, and technologies to improve maritime security. This was followed in September by reports that Singapore intended to join the Partnership for Indo-Pacific Industrial Resilience, a US initiative that aims to explore opportunities for joint production and sustainment of defence equipment and weapons.

JAPAN

Amid a deteriorating security environment, Japan has committed to 'fundamentally reinforce' the Japan Self-Defense Forces' (JSDF's) defence capabilities to prepare for a potential major contingency in the region. Based on the three strategic documents laid out in December 2022 – the revised National Security Strategy, National Defense Strategy and the Defense Buildup Program for FY23–27 – Japan is doubling its defence-related spending by FY27 to upgrade its capabilities. Priority areas include acquiring stand-off capabilities, enhancing cross-domain operations and strengthening the defence of the country's southwest.

In 2024, the JSDF continued discussing the planned organisational change of establishing the JSDF Joint Operations Command, a permanent joint headquarters to unify the command of all branches to enhance cross-domain operational capabilities and improve operational coordination with INDOPACOM. To improve military readiness, the JSDF has been expanding its ammunition and equipment availability. Personnel shortages and the heavy use of uninhabited aerial vehicles (UAVs) in recent and ongoing conflicts are driving the JSDF to develop new doctrines, units and R&D programmes to utilise uninhabited assets.

Japan's air force (JASDF) is going through major organisational change as it takes on expanding roles and missions including space domain awareness, missile early-warning and counterstrike operations under the 2023 Space Security Initiative. In FY25, it plans to expand its Space Operations Group into a command and increase its personnel. Its space situational-awareness system became fully operational in 2023 and began sharing information with the US Space Force that same year. The deployment of its Space Domain Awareness satellite is scheduled for FY26. The JASDF also plans in FY25 to start procuring a satellite constellation system to provide detection and targeting capabilities necessary for stand-off missiles to become operational by the end of FY27.

Intensified activities by China's and Russia's air forces continue to absorb the JASDF's attention. In August 2024, a Chinese electronic-intelligence aircraft made an unprecedented two-minute violation of Japanese airspace near Nagasaki Prefecture. Since 2022, Chinese heavy intelligence, surveillance and reconnaissance (ISR) UAVs have flown multiple times between some of Japan's southwest islands. The JSDF is exploring the possibility of using UAVs in the future to conduct surveillance and warning missions that crewed aircraft currently conduct.

The GCAP, a next-generation combat aircraft development project with the UK and Italy, is intended to replace Japan's F-2s from 2035. The GCAP hit several milestones, including the treaty to set up the GCAP International Government Organisation, in 2024. Japan's Ministry of Defense (JMOD) also signed an MoU with the US Department of Defense to jointly research collaborative autonomous technologies to be applied for UAVs operating alongside Japan's future fighters.

Japan's navy (JMSDF) also unveiled a major reorganisation. The Fleet Escort Force under the JMSDF Fleet Command will be revamped into the Surface Force, the Amphibious Mine Warfare Group, and the Patrol Defense Group. The changes reflect major capability upgrades and expanded roles for escort flotillas, such as converting the *Izumo*-class helicopter carriers to carry F-35Bs and stand-off missiles. The JSDF plans to establish new Maritime Transport Units among the three service branches to improve mobile and rapid response capabilities. The JMSDF is also set to consolidate its units on intelligence, cyber and communications, as well as meteorology and oceanography, to establish a new command for information warfare. Further, since 2023, the JMSDF has conducted exercises with the Japan Coast Guard to prepare for contingencies that would bring the agency under the defence minister's control.

Pursuing integrated air and missile defence continues to be a JMSDF priority. In 2024, it signed construction contracts for two *Aegis*-equipped vessels dedicated exclusively to ballistic-missile defence that are expected to be commissioned in FY27 and FY28 respectively. JMOD also signed the Glide Phase Interceptor Cooperative Development Project Arrangement with the Pentagon in May 2024, and seeks to develop ship-launched interceptors in the 2030s. Driven by Japan–South Korea rapprochement, the US, Japan and South Korea initiated a real-time North Korean missile-warning data-sharing mechanism in December 2023.

Japan's ground force (JGSDF) is accelerating the fielding of stand-off missiles, having moved up the schedule to deploy ground-launched upgraded Type-12 surface-to-ship missiles in 2025. In Okinawa Prefecture, it established a new camp on Ishigaki Island in March 2023 where it stationed its Yaeyama Area Security Force, anti-ship missile and surface-to-air missile units. In March 2024, it also established the 7th Surface-to-Ship Missile Regiment at Vice-Camp Katsuren on Okinawa Island. In April 2024, it upgraded the Western Field Artillery Unit at Camp Yufuin in Oita Prefecture to the 2nd Artillery Brigade, to oversee missile units and regiments across Kyushu island and Okinawa Prefecture. The JGSDF plans to establish the 8th Surface-to-Ship Missile Regiment at Yufuin in FY25.

The JGSDF also established the 3rd Amphibious Rapid Deployment Regiment at Camp Takematsu in Nagasaki Prefecture, in March 2024, and plans to reorganise the 15th Brigade at Okinawa Prefecture's Camp Naha into a division. When combined with the US Marine Corps's establishment of the US Marine Littoral Regiment, the JGSDF's expanded footprint is also looking to improve interoperability between the two forces through joint exercises. However, increasing activities continue to face local opposition and protests because of factors including sexual-assault cases involving US military personnel and safety concerns following US V-22 *Osprey* tiltrotor aircraft crashes.

Figure 21 • Japan: selected missile programmes

As part of a major national security policy transformation, the Japan Self-Defense Forces (JSDF) are in the process of acquiring a suite of new stand-off missile capabilities through domestic developments and imports. Tokyo's perception of a deteriorating security environment – shaped by North Korea's military developments and nuclear programme and also China's capability advances and increasingly assertive behaviour – is driving these investments. The Japanese Ministry of Defense's 2024 white paper states that acquiring these long-range missile systems for the air, ground and maritime services of the JSDF will have a deterrent effect on potential adversaries. Japan could use these capabilities to strike an enemy's missile launchers, command-and-control systems and ships, degrading their ability to mount attacks against Japan and its forces. In 2025, Tokyo plans to start taking deliveries of the 900+ kilometre-range Upgraded Type-12 anti-ship missile (ground-based version) and the 1,600 km-range *Tomahawk* Block IV land-attack cruise missile.

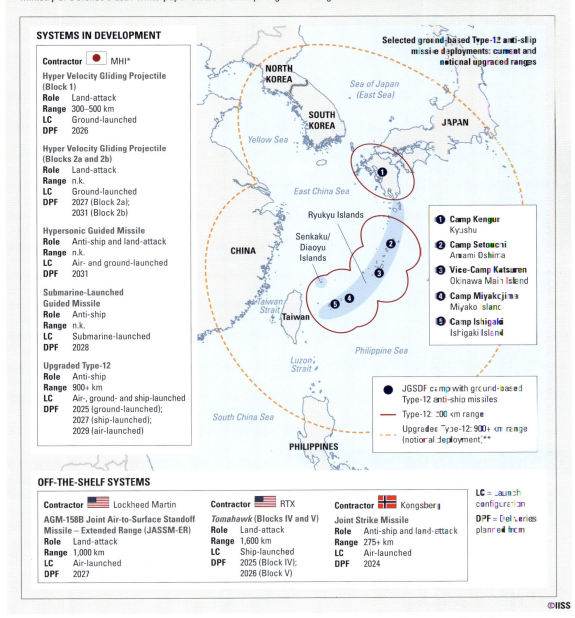

*Mitsubishi Heavy Industries. **Japan has not yet announced where it will deploy ground-based Upgraded Type-12 anti-ship missiles.
Sources: IISS analysis, US Department of Defense, Japan Ministry of Defense, MHI, Kongsberg, RTX, Lockheed Martin

AUKUS partnership developments

In the past year, the three AUKUS partners have made significant progress in their core objectives: to create a nuclear-powered attack submarine (SSN) capability for the Royal Australian Navy (RAN) under Pillar 1 of the arrangement, and to cooperate on other advanced defence capabilities under Pillar 2. Nevertheless, the project remains controversial and challenging given the scale of commitments involved and the sustained effort and political support required. While the new UK government pledged strong support for AUKUS, a cloud of uncertainty hangs over the second Trump administration's attachment to the partnership.

Regarding the planned SSN-AUKUS, the UK and Australia moved ahead with the design phase for the new boat that will equip the Royal Navy (RN) from the late 2030s and the RAN from the early 2040s. In March 2024, it was announced that BAE Systems and the Australian shipbuilder ASC would partner to produce the SSN-AUKUS. All the nuclear reactor sections for the submarines will be built by Rolls-Royce in the UK. In August 2024, the three governments concluded a nuclear-propulsion cooperation agreement that will enable the transfer of nuclear reactor technology and nuclear material between them. In October 2024, the Australian and UK governments announced that they would start negotiations on a bilateral treaty to cover the development and delivery of the SSN-AUKUS submarines. As for the planned sale of US boats to Australia, the US Congress passed a National Defense Authorization Act at the end of 2023 which included provisions clearing the way for the sale of at least three US *Virginia*-class submarines to Australia from 2032. This is envisaged as an initial phase to get an RAN nuclear-powered-submarine force under way before the SSN-AUKUS boats start arriving.

Despite these multiple incremental steps, there remain doubts over whether Australia and the UK will have the capacity to deliver the SSN-AUKUS programme as planned, and whether the US industrial base will be able to satisfy the requirements of both the US Navy (USN) and the RAN for *Virginia*-class submarines in the 2030s. This concern continues despite the significant investments each is making in their industries and with Australia contributing to the UK and US industrial bases as well.

Considerable efforts are also under way to train Australians to build, operate and maintain SSNs. Scores of RAN personnel are either in the US submarine training pipeline or are due to join during 2025. Small numbers of personnel are already trained and gaining operational experience aboard US submarines. A small number of RAN officers have also passed the UK nuclear reactor training course and are serving in RN submarines. RAN personnel have also been training to maintain nuclear-powered submarines and, jointly with US personnel, carried out a first maintenance period for a visiting US nuclear-powered submarine in Perth in September 2024. As well as helping to build Australian expertise, this will support the planned rotational deployment of US submarines to Australia from 2027, as well as eventually an RN boat.

On the Pillar 2 advanced-technologies front, the partners overcame a major hurdle to cooperation in August 2024 with the US determination that Australian and UK export-control regimes now comply sufficiently to allow exemptions under US export-control regulations. How smoothly these arrangements can be implemented, and in what key technology areas, however, is unclear. The partners announced progress in several areas, including exercises to test their ability to operate crewed and uncrewed platforms under the Maritime Big Play concept. The three partners also announced that they would introduce an AI-based data processing algorithm for their P-8A *Poseidon* maritime-patrol aircraft fleets. Further, the partners claimed advances in various undersea capabilities, a key focus of Pillar 2. This included beginning to scale up the ability to launch and recover uninhabited underwater systems from torpedo tubes on current classes of RN and USN submarines.

CHINA

In 2024, China celebrated the 97th anniversary of the founding of the People's Liberation Army (PLA), though the three main themes that characterised China's defence policy and modernisation were corruption, reorganisation and reform.

Since 2023, President Xi Jinping has conducted a second purge of Chinese Communist Party (CCP) officials across different sectors of the party-state system. The government has also implicated figures working in defence, with reports of procurement corruption in the PLA Rocket Force (PLARF). As a result, officials and officers have faced prosecution and dismissal from the PLARF, the Equipment Development Department, the Strategic Support Force (SSF), state-owned defence-industrial enterprises and defence-related universities. Public notices indicated that they had been found guilty of violating party discipline and law (i.e. financial corruption). The two highest-profile dismissals were former ministers of national defence, Li Shangfu and Wei Fenghe, who were expelled from the CCP in July 2024 before being prosecuted. Former PLARF Commander Li Yuchao,

Deputy Commander Liu Guangbin, former Deputy Commander Zhang Zhenzhong, Political Commissar Xu Zhongbo, and former PLARF Chief of Staff Sun Jinming were also removed from their positions and placed under investigation, with Li and Sun eventually expelled from the party. In August 2024, the PLARF's Logistics Department Procurement Supply Bureau issued a notice banning three engineering universities with close ties to the PLA (Xi'an Technological University, Xi'an Jiaotong University and Southwest Jiaotong University) from procurement activities for three years for their part in bid-rigging. Following the corruption scandal, the CCP appointed Admiral Dong Jun as the new defence minister in December 2023. However, unlike his predecessors, Dong does not yet have a seat on the Central Military Commission (CMC), nor a state councillor position. This could be a permanent new feature of Chinese domestic politics, or it could be a sign that President Xi seeks to take greater caution in his appointments following a year of corruption scandals.

The government's removal of senior PLARF personnel has also meant that the service's current leadership comprises the former deputy commander of the PLA Navy – Admiral Wang Houbin, now the PLARF commander – as well as the former deputy political commissar of the Southern Theatre Command, PLA Air Force General Xu Xisheng, who is currently serving as the PLARF's political commissar. While it is unusual for a service to be commanded by officers from different branches, it is not unprecedented. However, the reported return of Wang Liyan from the Joint Logistics Support Force to the PLARF as deputy commander might suggest a return to a situation whereby the PLARF is led by career PLARF officers. A wider rehabilitation effort of the PLARF following the purges could be under way, signalled by Xi's visit to 611 Brigade and the DF-31AG test on 25 September 2024.

At the end of November 2024, Miao Hua, the director of the CMC's Political Work Department, was suspended and placed under investigation for 'serious violations of discipline'. This could signal that a wider corruption investigation is taking place across the PLA.

Reorganisation

The year was also marked by the PLA's announcement that it was restructuring its information-support forces, which has resulted in the PLA now comprising four services and four arms. In April, the CMC announced that the SSF, a service branch, would be disbanded and split into three new arms: a new Information Support Force (ISF), and a re-designated Aerospace Force (ASF) and Cyberspace Force (CSF), previously the SSF Aerospace Systems and Network Systems departments, respectively. All three new arms now report to the CMC but hold a deputy-theatre-command leader grade, positioning them in the PLA's organisational hierarchy just below services and theatre commands.

The resulting ASF, CSF and ISF differ in their capabilities and roles. While the CSF and ASF control capabilities in their respective domains and therefore play distinct roles within the wider PLA, the ISF likely remains a support function for the military. The ASF will continue to command the PLA's space forces, while the CSF will continue to conduct defensive and offensive information operations. The ISF will be responsible for the construction and implementation of joint information support to 'build a network information system that fulfils the requirement of modern warfare'. In establishing the ISF, President Xi likely considered that the provision of information support required greater prominence generally and specifically at the interservice and inter-theatre levels.

The CMC has not officially stated the reasons for dissolving the SSF into three separate arms. However, it is likely that both political and operational considerations drove the decision. By removing layers of bureaucracy between the CMC and the three arms, President Xi has greater oversight over the arms' activities, which cross over into politically sensitive areas of Chinese foreign affairs. The establishment of the ISF as its own arm suggests that Xi may have been dissatisfied with the level of support and operations by the SSF. More importantly, the reorganisation offers a window into the PLA's modernisation progress. The establishment of the three separate arms and their contribution toward achieving greater 'informatisation' could serve as an important indicator of the PLA's progress towards their concurrent ambition of building an 'intelligentised' military.

Reform

The CCP proposed new military reforms in July 2024 intended to contribute to improving military governance and modernisation progress towards the PLA's centennial 2027 goal. Firstly, the CCP proposed deepening military–civil fusion (MCF) through improving both procurement processes between military and civilian stakeholders across industry, and R&D across domains. This would be achieved by reforming how stakeholders report on defence-related military needs, and by coordinating standards between military and civilian sectors. Secondly, the reforms aim to address professionalism and loyalty within the PLA by refining consultation and evaluation processes for major decision-making, developing new approaches to strategic management, and reforming military academies and PLA-affiliated enterprises. Lastly, the reforms seek to enhance the PLA's joint-operations capabilities by 'establishing new domain forces with new combat capabilities' and improving the composition of command centres for joint theatre operations and joint task-force operations. In 2024, the National People's Congress Standing Committee revised the National Defence Education Law with the aim of 'modernising China's system and capacity for national security'. The law calls for whole-of-nation defence education, while the government that same year stressed the need to raise public awareness of national defence. The amendment to the law signals the government's efforts to promote patriotism and consolidate unity between the military, government and citizens.

Cross-Strait relations

2024 also saw changes to China's cross-Strait policy related to the 2005 Anti-Secession Law, and an uptick in large-scale military exercises around Taiwan. The PLA conducted two such exercises in 2024 under the banner of *Joint Sword*-2024A and *Joint Sword*-2024B. *Joint Sword* exercises are not new, however: the PLA conducted an earlier edition in April 2023, timed to coincide with then-president Tsai Ing-wen's transit through the US and in-person meeting with then-speaker of the US House of Representatives Kevin McCarthy. The two iterations of *Joint Sword* in 2024 were also timed with politically significant events. *Joint Sword*-2024A took place following the swearing-in of Taiwan's newly elected president Lai Ching-te, while *Joint Sword*-2024B took place following President Lai's National Day speech. The PLA's Eastern Theatre Command said that all three *Joint Sword* exercises would serve as warnings against 'Taiwan independence' and 'separatist forces' collusion with external forces.

However, the exercises – planned in advance – were likely deployed when needed to serve as political signals to Taiwan and its partners. They present important opportunities for the PLA to exercise varying capabilities useful for any potential cross-Strait contingency. All three exercises reportedly included joint operations of the PLA Army, Navy, Air Force and Rocket Force. Some exercises included live-fire drills, but not all. *Joint Sword*-2024B included a significant role for the China Coast Guard (CCG). The different iterations of the exercise series likely sought to practice different elements of a blockade or economic quarantine of Taiwan, with *Joint Sword*-2024A focused on scenarios related to Taiwan's main ports and naval bases, and 2024B focusing on scenarios related to its main air bases and airports.

In June, China announced a new interpretation of the 2005 Anti-Secession Law. Known as the '22 Articles', the interpretation imposed criminal punishment on advocates of 'Taiwan independence'. The articles outlined the precise crimes of secession that China would punish, and are extraterritorial in application. In addition to the increasing number of Taiwanese citizens detained in China, grey-zone activities in the Taiwan Strait also intensified, including over 44 incursions by CCG vessels into the protected waters around Kinmen Island. In sum, these developments should be regarded as part of the PLA's 'Three Warfares' against Taiwan, including psychological warfare, public-opinion warfare and legal warfare (or lawfare), which attempt to make progress towards China's ambition of peaceful reunification if possible, or to shape the future battlefield across the Taiwan Strait if needed.

Ground Force (Army)

Units equipped with the modular PCH-191 multiple-rocket launcher (MRL) provided the PLA Army's most prominent contributions to the Taiwan-focused *Joint Sword*-2024A and -2024B exercises. This indicates the increased prominence that organic long-range precision-fire support capabilities have played in PLA Army capability development since the PCH-191 was first displayed in public at the 2019 National Day parade.

Following decades of incremental adjustments to PLA force structure, in 2017, President Xi's Deepening Reform of National Defense and the Armed Forces policy began a comprehensive restructuring of the PLA Army. This left its 13 remaining group armies with a common order of battle, each controlling six combined-arms manoeuvre brigades and six supporting brigades. Since 2017, however, this new structure has undergone several incremental adjustments, slowly diverging from the initial template as existing brigades have been disbanded and new brigades formed. This renewed structural change likely indicates that the PLA Army seeks to continue to learn and adapt based on lessons drawn from its own experiences, as well as the observed experiences of other armed forces. Among the most notable additions to the PLA Army's order of battle, as part of this process, are at least two new long-range fire support brigades. One brigade had formed at Fuqing in the Eastern Theatre Command by early 2023 and is believed to report to the 72nd Group Army. By mid-2024, another brigade had likely formed at Linze in the Western Theatre Command and been assigned to the 76th Group Army.

These new brigades are based around the capabilities of the PCH-191 MRL. The launcher's modular configuration allows it to use a variety of ammunition, including precision-guided 300mm and 370mm artillery rockets and a 750mm short-range ballistic missile (SRBM) design that is likely a domestic analogue to the export model *Fire Dragon* 480 SRBM. As such, the PCH-191 MRL has sufficient range and accuracy to target positions in Taiwan from the Chinese mainland. Battalion sets also serve in the artillery brigades of all three Eastern Theatre Command group armies, as well as the amphibious 74th Group Army of the Southern Theatre Command. In addition, the PCH-191 has been issued to units in the PLA's Western and Northern Theatre Commands, likely reflecting that the PLA Army considers organic long-range fire support has strong utility for the service more broadly and not just in relation to a Taiwan contingency.

The PLA Army continues to experiment with a wide range of uninhabited ground vehicle (UGV) designs in its exercises, both domestically and with bilateral partners, including Cambodia and Laos. Unlike in the aerial domain, however, these UGV designs do not appear to have entered serial production.

China North Industries Corporation (NORINCO) completed an initial production batch of a new wheeled infantry fighting vehicle design (possibly designated as ZBL-19) at the end of 2023, likely for PLA Army service. This features a new, unmanned turret design and appears to be a successor to the existing ZBL-08 family of vehicles, suggesting that they are intended to replace the latter in service with the army's medium-weight forces. The army also appears to be fitting its existing ZTZ-99A main battle tanks with a version of NORINCO's GL5 hard-kill active protection system, previously seen on export VT-4 and VT-5 tank designs.

Navy and Coast Guard

In May 2024, the People's Liberation Army Navy's (PLAN's) newest aircraft carrier, the *Fujian*, embarked on its first sea trials. Further trials followed during the year of what is the PLAN's largest and most capable carrier so far, equipped with electromagnetic catapults and arrester gear. When the *Fujian* enters operational service, which may not be until late 2025 or 2026, it will mark another step up in capability for the PLAN fleet. In the meantime, the navy's first carrier – the *Liaoning*, which emerged from a year-long refit in March – and the second vessel, the *Shandong*, continued to mature the PLAN's carrier-operating experience. Between them, they undertook a number of carrier group deployments in the South China Sea, off Taiwan, and in the Philippine Sea, which included more evidence of the ability of the air groups to undertake sustained sorties.

A fourth and even larger carrier is believed to be under construction. The PLAN also appears to be following the rapid introduction of its Type-075 large-deck amphibious assault ships (LHDs) with an even bigger version, dubbed Type-076. Satellite imagery of the first such vessel under construction suggests it could eclipse even the US Navy's LHDs in size, and uniquely could also be equipped with an electromagnetic catapult, adding to speculation about the breadth of its intended roles. Overall, the PLAN continued to develop and expand its capabilities. Its carriers have also been operating with increasingly varied escort groups, now regularly including Type-055 cruisers and Type-052D destroyers.

There is continuing expectation of the arrival of the Type-096 and Type-095 new-generation nuclear-powered ballistic-missile and attack submarines. However, the precise trajectory of the PLAN's submarine force remains uncertain, with reports of new variants of existing nuclear- and conventionally powered attack submarines emerging, including vessels possibly equipped for the first time with vertical launch systems. There is uncertainty also surrounding US-based reporting of a suspected incident in mid-2024 in which a new-design vessel may have accidentally sunk at a berth while under construction at a submarine building yard in Wuhan. It was speculated that the vessel may have been a new design of a relatively small nuclear-powered or nuclear/conventional hybrid. Beijing remained silent on the matter.

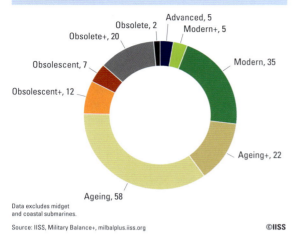

▼ Figure 22 **Asia: total active conventional submarines, 2024**

Data excludes midget and coastal submarines.
Source: IISS, Military Balance+, milbalplus.iiss.org ©IISS

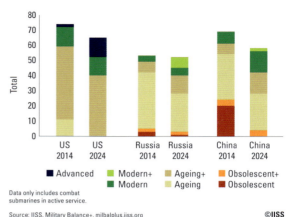

▼ Figure 23 **US, Russia and China: submarine fleet evolution, 2014 and 2024**

Data only includes combat submarines in active service.
Source: IISS, Military Balance+, milbalplus.iiss.org ©IISS

China's Coast Guard and other supporting vessels maintained an aggressive posture in tensions with the Philippines over disputed waters and features, including a number of rammings and violent clashes. Amid growing concerns about escalation, in mid-July, Beijing and Manila announced a 'provisional agreement' to reduce tensions. However, the impact of this deal remained uncertain at best.

Meanwhile, the PLAN continued to sustain the counter-piracy naval-task-group presence which it first established in 2008 in and around the Gulf of Aden. However, it exercised a minimal role in countering the Ansarullah (Houthi) campaign against shipping in the Gulf of Aden and the southern Red Sea. In contrast, ships from the group conducted presence missions and visits to South Africa, to the Baltic for Russia's Navy Day review in St Petersburg, and to take part in the latest in a series of joint Chinese–Iranian–Russian exercises which began in 2018.

China continued to increase the tempo of its joint naval manoeuvres with Russia, especially in the Pacific, although they remained relatively modest in terms of operational integration. China's first deployment to the Arctic of three icebreaking vessels operated by different research organisations also underscored Beijing's growing interests in that region.

Air Force

2024 marked the first time Chinese bomber aircraft operated within the Alaska Air Defense Identification Zone (ADIZ). Two PLAAF Xi'an H-6K medium bombers flew along with two Russian air force Tupolev Tu-95MS *Bear* H heavy bombers within the ADIZ; the formation was tracked and intercepted by the North American Aerospace Defense Command. While notable mainly for its symbolism, the exercise also indicated the increasing confidence of the PLAAF and the growing military ties between Beijing and Moscow.

Despite its age, the Xi'an H-6 remains in production and has been the subject of multiple upgrades. It will likely be the primary delivery vehicle for the PLAAF's nascent nuclear role until the H-20 bomber, now in development, enters service. Within the PLAAF tactical air fleets, however, legacy designs have increasingly been replaced.

Delivery of the Chengdu J-20 heavy multi-role fighter continues, with likely at least a brigade's worth of the aircraft introduced in 2024. At least eight front-line units, three more than the year prior, are now assessed to be operating the type. Two of the twin-seat variant remain in flight test, while a single-seat aircraft was fitted with the Shenyang WS-15 turbofan engine with afterburner. The WS-15 is intended to succeed the Shenyang WS-10 now fitted to J-20A production aircraft.

Alongside the J-20, the Shenyang J-16 *Flanker* N and the Shenyang J-10C *Firebird* continue in production for the PLAAF. Annual production rates are higher for the J-20 and the J-16, likely around double that of the J-10C. It is possible that the J-10C will increasingly be focused on the export

Table 6 China: selected fixed-wing combat-aircraft exports since 2018

China's combat-aircraft exports have seen varying degrees of success over the past two decades. The JF-17 multi-role fighter, jointly developed by Chengdu Aircraft Industrial Group (CAC) and Pakistan Aeronautical Complex (PAC), is among China's biggest export successes. As of September 2024, Pakistan has 158 aircraft across three Blocks. Myanmar and Nigeria also operate Block IIs. In September 2024, Azerbaijan confirmed the purchase of Block IIIs. However, reports from Myanmar, for example, suggest reliability issues. Moreover, despite being equipped with active electronically scanned array radars and the CAMA PL-15 air-to-air missile, it failed to secure orders from Argentina and Malaysia. Meanwhile, only Pakistan operates Chengdu J-10CEs, while Myanmar and Sudan operate Guizhou FTC-2000Gs. Jet trainers have historically fared better with countries looking to expand their training and combat fleets at relatively lower costs. The Hongdu K-8W remains among China's most popular exports.

Competitive prices, co-production deals, and few end-user restrictions all contributed to the export success of armed Chinese uninhabited aerial vehicles (UAVs) over the last decade. However, reports of reliability issues, with both Jordan and Iraq experiencing poor availability on their CH-4B fleets, have likely negatively impacted export chances more recently. Furthermore, since 2018, Chinese firms have faced strong competition from Turkish companies. Since 2018, countries still procuring Chinese combat aircraft are typically those which maintain close political–economic ties with China, as is the case with Algeria, Myanmar, Nigeria and Pakistan. Saudi Arabia and the United Arab Emirates may also be seeking closer political–economic ties. Both countries have also sought to diversify their supplier base, after being denied armed UAVs by the United States, and to generate a defence-industrial capability in this area. Saudi Arabia, for example, plans to open production lines for the CH-4B, TB-001 and *Wing Loong* I.

Date	Recipient	Equipment	Type	Quantity	Contractor	Deliveries
2018	Angola	K-8W *Karakorum*	Training aircraft	12	Hongdu Aviation Industry Group (HAIG)	2020
	Pakistan	JF-17B *Thunder* Block II JF-17 *Thunder* Block III	FGA aircraft	26+ 23+	PAC; CAC	2019–ongoing
	Nigeria	JF-17 *Thunder* Block II	FGA aircraft	3+	PAC	2021–ongoing
Jun	Bangladesh	K-8W *Karakorum*	Training aircraft	7	HAIG	2020
2019	Indonesia	CH-4B	Heavy CISR UAV	6	Aerospace CH UAV	2019–20
2020	Pakistan	*Wing Loong* II	Heavy CISR UAV	n.k.	CAC	c. 2021
	Myanmar	FTC-2000G	FGA aircraft	6+	Guizhou Aircraft Industry Corporation (GAIC)	2022
	Nigeria	CH-4B	Heavy CISR UAV	4	Aerospace CH UAV	2022
	Nigeria	*Wing Loong* II	Heavy CISR UAV	5	CAC	2021–23
	Pakistan	CH-4	Heavy CISR UAV	4+	Aerospace CH UAV	2021
2021	Algeria	*Wing Loong* II	Heavy CISR UAV	24	CAC	c. 2023
Feb	Saudi Arabia	TB-001	Heavy CISR UAV	n.k.	Sichuan Tengden Technology Company	n.k.
Jun	Pakistan	J-10CE *Firebird*	FGA aircraft	20+	CAC	2022–ongoing
Dec	Algeria	WJ-700	Heavy CISR UAV	4	China Aerospace Science and Industry Corporation (CASIC)	Pending
2022	Algeria	CH-5	Heavy CISR UAV	6	Aerospace CH UAV	Pending
	Morocco	*Wing Loong* II	Heavy CISR UAV	n.k.	CAC	2023
2023	Iraq	CH-5	Heavy CISR UAV	n.k.	Aerospace CH UAV	2024
	Laos	K-8W *Karakorum*	Training aircraft	4	HAIG	2024
	Saudi Arabia	*Wing Loong*-10B	Heavy CISR UAV	n.k.	CAC	Pending
Feb	UAE	L-15	Training aircraft	12	HAIG	2023–ongoing
2024	Azerbaijan	JF-17 *Thunder* Block III	FGA aircraft	n.k.	PAC	n.k

CISR = combat intelligence, surveillance and reconnaissance; FGA = fighter ground-attack
Source: IISS, Military Balance+, milbalplus.iiss.org

market rather than the PLAAF. The J-16 airframe, meanwhile, has also been used as the basis for an electronic-warfare aircraft, the J-16D, with a small number of the type now in service. The Shenyang J-35 programme also continued, with a J-35A shown in PLAAF colours during the November 2024 Airshow China held in Zhuhai. The programme has previously been associated mainly with the PLAN.

The PLAAF continued to develop and introduce a broad range of UAVs during 2024. A few additional GAIC WZ-7 turbofan-powered ISR large UAVs were likely provided to the air force over the course of the year. The WZ-7 has been used for missions within Taiwan's ADIZ since 2022, while more recently, it has also been operated over the Sea of Japan. A Chengdu WZ-10 ISR UAV was also intercepted over the East China Sea by the Japan Air Self-Defense Force for the first time in May 2024.

Air activity in Taiwan's ADIZ also included PLAAF participation in *Joint Sword*-2024A, where J-16 and J-20 equipped units took part in the three-day exercise.

The J-20 is not the only PLAAF aircraft that is the focus of an engine upgrade. The Xi'an Y-20 heavy transport is now being fitted with the WS-20 high-bypass turbofan. The Y-20 airframe is also being used in the tanker/transport role, with the YY-20A already in service in limited numbers. A variant re-engined with the WS-20, the YY-20B, was in flight test during 2024.

DEFENCE ECONOMICS

China's military modernisation programme continued to drive increases in national defence spending, with Beijing allocating an estimated CNY1.7trn (USD235bn) to defence in 2024 including estimated funding for local militia. The nominal uplift of 7% continued the long-term trend of increasing budgets, though the country's wider economic slowdown will likely moderate future growth.

To support national goals of having a 'modernised' military by 2035 and a 'world class' military by 2050, China's defence industry continues to strengthen, with President Xi's new development philosophy of 'integrated national strategic systems and capabilities' being complemented by a renewed emphasis on high-end technology and calls for 'new quality productive forces'. As a continuation of the wider MCF paradigm, Xi's reforms have encouraged the greater centralisation of China's national defence industry, with governance structures being reformed to facilitate more efficient resource allocation. In parallel, the country continued its steady progress towards technological self-sufficiency in the production and development of defence materiel.

Defence spending

In terms of core defence spending, in March 2024, Chinese officials proposed an FY24 defence budget of CNY1.67trn (USD231.5bn). This represented a nominal increase of 7.2% on the previous year, and another consecutive year of growth. Such growth matches that seen in 2023 and is comparable to the ten-year average of 7.5%. Indeed, 2024 was the 30th consecutive year that the budget has increased.

As a proportion of GDP, China's core defence budget comes to 1.3%, well below the global average of 1.8% and the 2% target for NATO countries. Even with the addition of funding for local militia, which the IISS estimates amounted to CNY25.3bn (USD3.5bn) in 2024, core defence funding still reaches just 1.3% of GDP. However, total Chinese military expenditure – including government-funded R&D and central funding for the People's Armed Police – is estimated to be closer to CNY2.2trn (USD305.4bn) in 2024. Furthermore, converting the Chinese yuan using the purchasing-power parity (PPP) rate suggests that the core 2024 defence budget comes to USD469.6bn, while total military expenditure reaches USD619.5bn.

Regardless of the measures used, ongoing modernisation plans mean that defence spending will continue to increase, though the extent of growth will depend on China's wider economic performance – particularly as China's leaders remain alert to the importance of domestic needs. In his March address to the National People's Congress, Premier Li Qiang pointed to an 'unusually complex international environment', in likely reference to the heightened prospects of cross-domain conflict in disputes with India and Taiwan and in the South China Sea. However, Li also pointed to 'the challenging tasks of advancing reform and development and ensuring stability at home' and vowed that the government would 'make every effort to deliver, and do its utmost to live up to the expectations and trust of the people'. In part, these internal challenges are being driven by a slowdown in the Chinese economy, which is facing strong deflationary pressures caused by a weak property market, a fluctuating export environment and sluggish domestic demand.

In response, China's central bank has introduced a range of policies, while in September 2024, the Politburo also convened to study the problem. Though the meeting reiterated central bank policies – which had been announced just days before – its timing broke with the usual convening schedule, highlighting the continuing importance placed on fixing the lagging economy. It also highlighted the importance placed on fixing China's venture capital system, which has been part of the CCP's recent financial reforms as it realises the growing need for venture capital to fund China's strategic industries. Following these measures, in November, Chinese officials unveiled a CNY10.0trn (USD1.4trn) financial package. Designed to fix the country's liquidity crisis, the package is scheduled to run for five years, with measures designed to reduce the levels of 'hidden debt' held by local government. According to government officials, the package will help reduce local government debt from CNY14.3trn (USD2trn) to CNY2.3trn (USD319.6bn). However, this will likely not resolve the full problem, with the IMF calculating that local-government financial vehicles have current total debts of CNY60trn (USD8.3trn).

Against these wider constraints, authorities face increasingly sharp questions about which areas to prioritise. According to Chinese officials, central defence spending will be allocated across four priorities. These include the continuing emphasis on improving core capabilities through the delivery of major projects and key programmes, as well as strengthening military training and combat preparedness. In addition, funds will go towards accelerating innovation in defence-related science and technology (S&T), specifically for weapons systems and logistics construction. Funds will also go towards deepening defence and military reforms – including the improvement of military governance systems – while the budget makes provisions to improve training and living conditions too. Within this, most defence spending will be allocated to procurement, personnel and training as the PLA seeks to improve its combat readiness.

Defence industry

China's modernisation drive has impelled significant qualitative leaps in its national defence-industrial capacity. Industry continues to benefit from the wider MCF paradigm, which encourages increased links between the country's civilian and commercial sectors and the armed forces, law enforcement and defence industry. In addition, other key policy lines, including Xi's programme of 'integrated national strategic systems and capabilities', and the recent emphasis on the development of 'new quality productive forces,' represent further evolution and development of the MCF model.

MCF remains controversial, with the US State Department highlighting the often 'clandestine and non-transparent manner' in which China acquires intellectual property and research. However, China also spends considerable amounts on domestic R&D. For example, in March 2024, China's Ministry of Science and Technology (MoST) reported that it

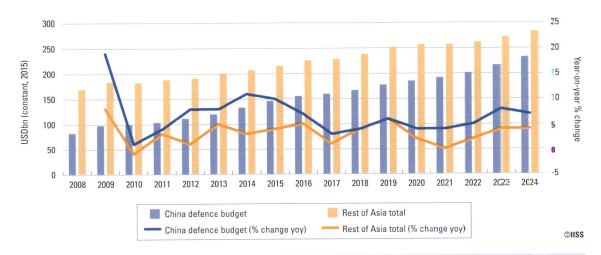

▲ Figure 24 **China: defence budget compared with the rest of Asia (total), 2008–24 (USDbn, constant 2015)**

had spent over CNY3.3trn (USD458.6bn) on R&D in 2023, 8.1% more than the previous year. Of this, CNY221.2bn (USD30.7bn) was spent on 'basic research', which itself was an annual increase of 9.3%. State institutions also continue to play a central role in fostering the innovation landscape: in August 2024, MoST launched a national trial for an 'innovation points system', with the aim of easing financing for innovative firms. This is in addition to the investment instruments – already available at every level of government – to funnel capital into China's S&T sector, especially towards industries and technological capabilities prioritised by the state.

As a result of these policies, innovation indices such as patent filings indicate that China is moving from an imitator to an innovator. For example, statistics from the World Intellectual Property Organization (WIPO) show that China held the largest number of Patent Cooperation Treaty (PCT) applications in 2023. The majority of these came from Chinese telecoms giant Huawei Technologies, with its 6,494 published PCT applications – almost double South Korean Samsung Electronics' 3,924 applications and US firm Qualcomm's 3,410. In terms of patents in force, China accounted for the highest number, comprising approximately a quarter of the world's total in 2022, according to the WIPO. Similarly, according to April 2024's China Patent Survey Report – published by the China National Intellectual Property Administration – the rate of Chinese invention patents has grown steadily, with the 'industrialisation rate' of patents reaching 39.6% in 2023, up 2.9% over the previous year. According to the survey, industry–academia–research collaboration also enhanced patent conversion, with such collaboration resulting in 24.5% higher revenues compared to other enterprise-derived patents.

This focus on industry–academia–research collaboration is a key aspect of President Xi's vision for 'integrated national strategic systems and capabilities', which coalesces strategic planning, resources and strengths across sectors to 'systematically upgrade the country's overall ability to cope with strategic risks, safeguard strategic interests and realise strategic objectives'. These efforts, and the larger MCF paradigm, are being further refined through new policy constructs. For example, in September 2023, Chinese officials introduced the idea of 'new quality productive forces'. Following its introduction, the concept was also emphasised during the 11th study group of the Politburo Central Committee, which was held at the beginning of 2024. Here, the committee emphasised the role of 'new productive forces' in both ensuring the development of high-quality goods and services and contributing to high levels of economic security more generally. The term was also highlighted in other government forums, including March 2024's National People's Congress and the Third Plenum of the Communist Party's Central Committee, which was held in July. According to Chinese media, 'new forces' refer to advanced forms of production, with innovation characterised by high technology, high efficiency and high quality. However, achieving this also requires institutional reform. According to Chinese scholars, the key to successful reform lies in the coordinated formulation of strategy and allocation of resources so that high-quality factors – such as capital, data and talent – flow smoothly and maximise efficiency. In this sense, the reorganisation and centralisation of scientific and technological institutions that 'new productive forces' require also complements Xi's policy of 'integrated national strategic system and capabilities', which in turn strengthens the wider MCF ecosystem.

As China has progressed in developing indigenous technological capabilities, the US has used export controls to limit China's ability to access and develop advanced computing and semiconductor manufacturing items. In place since 2022, these may have the potential to derail China's expansion efforts, with industry leaders reportedly expressing concerns that developments in China's semiconductor industry may have plateaued because of the inability to access lithography equipment.

In addition to qualitative improvements, China has made considerable strides in meeting domestic demand for new equipment. As a sign of its increasing capabilities, imports of defence equipment have also contracted in recent years, with available data suggesting that imports are limited to just four categories: air-defence systems, naval guns, engines and transport helicopters. Yet much of this growing capability has been driven by the rapid expansion of China's defence-industrial base which, in the face of increasingly saturated demand, will likely see calls for further reform and consolidation. Such processes are already under way. For example, in September 2024, Chinese authorities announced the merger of China State Shipbuilding Corporation (CSSC) and China Shipbuilding Industry Corporation (CSIC)

– two of China's largest shipbuilders – through a share swap with CSIC being absorbed into CSSC Holdings. The reorganisation, first foreshadowed in 2019, was designed to resolve the issue of unnecessary competition in the shipbuilding sector. Consolidation will also streamline operations and accelerate development, particularly because both CSSC and CSIC foster a large number of research institutions with overlapping research scopes.

Overcapacity in relation to domestic demand may help drive a push for greater exports as a means of increasing revenues. However, although three Chinese defence companies rank highly in lists of successful defence firms, they face stiffer competition in the global market. In 2023, Aviation Industry Corporation of China's (AVIC's) defence production-related revenue increased by 52.6%, and CSSC's grew by 25.7% year-on-year. However, NORINCO saw its revenue dip by 2.6%. Consolidating capabilities, along with steadily absorbing innovation through MCF, will likely also aid the growth of Chinese defence exports.

Figure 25 🇹🇭 **Thailand: defence industry**

Over the last 15 years, Thailand has sought to diversify its arms suppliers away from heavy reliance on the United States. In acquiring platforms from foreign contractors, Thailand prefers to do so off-the-shelf via a government-to-government agreement accompanied by offset deals focusing on technology transfer. In recent years, Thailand has prioritised the acquisition of ground-based radars, multi-role fighter aircraft and a submarine. The last of these has been particularly difficult, with an earlier attempt in 2011 to acquire a second-hand Type-206A coastal submarine from Germany for THB7.7 billion (USD252.57 million) falling through before Thailand concluded a contract for a Chinese S26T, based on the Type-039A/B (*Yuan*-class), in 2017 for THB13.5bn (USD397.74m) which also failed to proceed due to difficulties in acquiring a German engine. Partnership agreements with Chinese, Israeli, Italian, Russian, South Korean and Swedish companies have led to the creation of local assembly/production lines and maintenance, repair and overhaul centres in Thailand. Thai industry consists of 40 state-owned defence factories, research and development (R&D) centres and maintenance sites with privately owned local companies playing a supporting role to them. The creation of the Defence Technology Institute (DTI) in 2009, a state-owned R&D agency, is a major element of Thailand's efforts to strengthen its defence-industrial base. Following Chinese technology transfer, the DTI developed the DTI-1 multiple rocket launcher (MRL) and its Nakhon Sawan centre will produce rockets for the SR-4 MRLs in partnership with China North Industries Corporation (NORINCO). The facility will also produce Israeli Rafael *Spike* anti-tank missiles. The Weapon Production Centre (WPC), another state-owned facility in Lopburi, has been licence-producing Israel's Elbit Systems ATMOS 2000 155mm wheeled howitzer for the army and marines and the Elbit Systems *Spear* 120mm self-propelled mortar for the army. Chaiseri Metal and Rubber, a local privately-owned company based in Pathum Thani, has developed and exported *First Win*, a 4×4 multi-purpose armoured vehicle, to Bhutan and Malaysia.

Source: IISS, Military Balance+, milbalplus.iiss.org

Thailand: selected non-US equipment procurement programmes involving local industry since 2010

Company	Equipment	Type	Quantity	Value (USDm)	Service
[M] Airbus	H225M	Combat search-and-rescue helicopter	12	approx. 390.39	Air force
	A320CJ	Passenger transport aircraft (PAX)	2	est. 213.43	Air force
	C295W	Light transport aircraft	3	125.32	Army
	H145M	Light transport helicopter	11	105.89	Army; navy
	H125M (AS550) *Fennec*	Multi-role helicopter (MRH)	8	49.20	Army
	H135 T3H	Light transport helicopter	6	42.43	Army
Saab	*Gripen* E/F**	FGA aircraft	4	548.76	Air force
	Gripen C*	Fighter ground-attack (FGA) aircraft	6	305.24	Air force
Korea Aerospace Industries (KAI)	T-50TH *Golden Eagle****	Training aircraft	14	530.36	Air force
NORINCO	VT-4 (MBT-3000)	Main battle tank	62	330.33	Army
	VN-1	Infantry fighting vehicle	52	140.28	Army
	VS-27	Armoured recovery vehicle	11		
	PLL-05	120mm self-propelled (SP) gun/mortar	12		
	SR-4	122mm MRL	4	20.88	Army
	VN-16	Light tank	3	12.72	Marines
Daewoo Shipbuilding & Marine Engineering (DSME, now Hanwha Ocean)	*Bhumibol Adulyadej* (DW3000F)	Frigate	1	474.07	Navy
Elbit Systems	ATMOS 2000	155mm SP artillery	60–	n.k.	Army; marines
	Hermes 900	Medium intelligence, surveillance and reconnaissance (ISR) uninhabited aerial vehicle (UAV)	7	120	Navy
	Spear	120mm SP mortar	34	est. 55	Army
	Hermes 450	Medium ISR UAV	4	25.51	Army
Rostec	Mi-17V-5 *Hip* H	MRH	7	168.66	Army
	SSJ-100-95LR	PAX	3	est. 146.46	Air force
Leonardo	AW139	MRH	10	38.81	Army
	AW149	MRH	5	38.53	Army
	Kronos	Radar	2	34.79	Air force; navy
	RAT 31DL	Radar	2	n.k.	Air force

[M] = Multinational.
*A follow-up order to the 2008 contract for 2x *Gripen* C, 4x *Gripen* D, 1x Saab 340 AEW&C and 1x Saab 340 aircraft worth SEK2bn (USD303.44m) in total; additional Saab 340 orders from 2011 onwards not included in the table due to being second-hand. **Not yet signed selection announced in Aug 2024; delivery planned from 2025. ***Capable of combat use.

Figure 26 Asia: arms procurement and defence-industrial trends, 2024

AUSTRALIA'S MARITIME PROCUREMENT INVESTMENTS TO GROW WITH CHANGES TO PLANS

In April 2024, Australia announced that investments in acquiring new capabilities would rise gradually from AUD17.6 billion (USD11.64bn) in FY2024, with expectations of reaching AUD42.1bn (USD27.85bn) by FY2034. Of this, 38% is to be earmarked for the maritime domain, largely due to the acquisition of nuclear-powered submarines through Pillar 1 of the AUKUS partnership. The financial commitment required for this, however, has meant that Australia needed to adjust other major programmes. This includes a reduction in the planned purchase of *Hunter*-class frigates, based on the United Kingdom's Type-26 design, from nine to six after the total expected programme cost grew in 2023 to AUD45.6bn (USD30.32bn). This increase was due to delays caused by the COVID-19 pandemic and changes to the base design to meet Australian requirements. With Australia aiming to spend AUD22–32bn (USD14.6–21.2bn) from 2024–34 for the amended programme, the construction contract for the first three vessels was signed in June 2024 with the aim of beginning deliveries from 2034. Similarly, Australia has also halved the number of *Arafura*-class offshore-patrol vessels to six. This cut frees up funding for up to 11 'general purpose frigates' worth around AUD7–10bn (USD4.6–6.6bn) in 2024–34. Whilst Australia is making significant investments in its naval capabilities, it has repeatedly revised its plans over the last few years, most significantly with the cancellation of the *Attack*-class diesel-electric attack submarine programme with France's Naval Group to pursue nuclear-powered submarines through AUKUS. Following the latest fleet review, industry will be hoping that Australia's naval plans remain more stable to allow them to make the required investments with greater confidence. Similarly, changes to fleet plans delay modernisation objectives, affecting Australia's short-term defence posture.

JAPAN'S PREPAREDNESS TO GO INTERNATIONAL IN QUESTION

In the two years since the launch of the Italy–Japan–UK Global Combat Air Programme (GCAP), the structure of the project's management has begun to take shape for the highly ambitious 2035 in-service date. This included the establishment of the GCAP International Government Organisation (GIGO) in December 2023, after having reflected on the experiences of other joint development programmes which often lacked clear leadership and struggled to divide the workshare between participating nations. The UK ratified the GIGO as an international treaty in October, while Italy and Japan aim to do so before the end of 2024 (as of November 2024). The GIGO will not come into force until all three countries complete their respective ratification processes. Additionally, in March 2024, Japan relaxed further its defence export policy to allow the sales of GCAP aircraft to other countries from the mid-2030s onwards. However, Japanese industry has struggled to grow defence exports due to self-imposed restrictions since 1967. Currently, Japan can export defence equipment and technology only to 15 countries. While the share of Japanese-designed systems is growing, Japan still acquires much of its defence equipment from abroad, particularly the United States. Although some of this is assembled locally, it is often in small quantities, resulting in high unit costs. Because of this, the number of Japanese companies working in the defence sector has reportedly dropped by approximately 100 from 1,500 over the last decade. Whether continued revisions to its defence export rules will have a significant effect on this in the period leading up to the late 2030s remains to be seen.

SOUTH KOREAN ARMS EXPORTS GROWTH NOT WITHOUT CHALLENGES

A strategy of promoting government-to-government arrangements, combined with a top-down approach when securing exports, has led to significant increases in South Korea's defence exports. The country's firms have also learnt lessons from Western competitors and adjusted their strategies to seek repeat sales, rather than intermittent ones, to achieve greater export success. This government-led approach has other benefits for firms, including sharing responsibilities for export customers' offset requirements and generous financing options through the Export–Import Bank of Korea (KEXIM). The amended KEXIM Act, passed in February 2024, increased South Korea's capital lending limit for defence exports from USD11.4bn to USD19bn. All of this is designed to help the country achieve its objective, stated in 2023, of becoming the world's fourth-largest defence exporter, behind the US, Russia and France, by 2027. However, despite these advantages, export growth has faced some challenges. While South Korean industry now offers an increasing number of indigenously designed platforms, many are fitted with key components and subsystems from abroad, which has sometimes meant difficulties in securing and delivering exports. For example, for the T-50 *Golden Eagle* training aircraft, Korea Aerospace Industries had to replace the Israeli EL/M-2032 AESA radar with radars from Lockheed Martin and Raytheon in export deals with Iraq and Malaysia respectively, due to those countries' objections to acquiring Israeli systems. Similarly, the German diesel engines for Hanwha's sale of K9 *Thunder* 155mm self-propelled howitzers to Egypt stalled the programme for two years until a test vehicle was shipped in mid-2024 with an engine supplied by South Korea's STX Engine instead.

Afghanistan AFG

Definitive macro- and defence-economic data not available

Population		40,121,552				
Age	0–14	15–19	20–24	25–29	30–64	65 plus
Male	20.1%	5.3%	4.9%	4.7%	14.4%	1.3%
Female	19.5%	5.1%	4.7%	4.5%	14.0%	1.6%

Capabilities

The strength and capability of the Afghan Taliban's armed forces remains difficult to assess. Their ability to use the foreign-supplied equipment, seized from the former Afghan National Security and Defence Forces (ANSDF) following the 2021 government collapse, is declining, along with the country's military capability. US authorities indicated that the Taliban is reorganising its defence ministry, and has retained some formation structures used by the ANSDF. Modernisation of the security forces has been hindered by the Taliban's lack of international recognition. The Taliban have utilised armoured vehicles, and a small number of Soviet-era helicopters for troop movements, including equipment the West provided the ANSDF. Taliban efforts to recruit former ANSDF personnel, including pilots and maintainers, have been hampered by attacks on some of those personnel. The Taliban government's priority is internal and border security. It has prioritised operations against Islamic State-Khorasan Province (ISKP), and the National Resistance Front in the mountainous east of the country. The former General Directorate of Intelligence, now the Islamic Emirate of Afghanistan's intelligence agency, has an outward-facing mandate.

ACTIVE 172,000 (Taliban 172,000)

ORGANISATIONS BY SERVICE

Taliban ε172,000
The Taliban has announced plans to expand their regular armed forces to 200,000 personnel

FORCES BY ROLE
SPECIAL FORCES
　3 spec ops bn
MANOEUVRE
　Light
　　8 inf corps
EQUIPMENT BY TYPE
ARMOURED FIGHTING VEHICLES
　MBT T-62M†
　APC • PPV *Maxxpro*
　AUV MSFV
ARTILLERY
　TOWED 122mm D-30
　MRL 122mm BM-21
　MOR 82mm 2B14
AIRCRAFT • TPT • Light 6: ε3 An-26 *Curl*; 1 An-32 *Cline*; ε2 Cessna 208B *Grand Caravan*
HELICOPTERS
　ATK 5: 1 Mi-25 *Hind*; 4 Mi-35 *Hind*
MRH 14: 8 MD-530F; 6 Mi-17 *Hip* H
TPT • Medium 4 UH-60A *Black Hawk*

Australia AUS

Australian Dollar AUD		2023	2024	2025
GDP	AUD	2.62trn	2.72trn	2.84trn
	USD	1.74trn	1.80trn	1.88trn
Real GDP growth	%	2.0	1.2	2.1
Def bdgt [a]	AUD	51.7bn	55.0bn	58.1bn
	USD	34.4bn	36.4bn	38.5bn

[a] Includes pensions

Real-terms defence budget trend (USDbn, constant 2015)

Population		26,768,598				
Age	0–14	15–19	20–24	25–29	30–64	65 plus
Male	9.4%	3.2%	3.4%	3.8%	22.1%	7.8%
Female	8.9%	3.0%	3.1%	3.5%	22.7%	9.2%

Capabilities

The Australian Defence Force (ADF) is well-trained and well-equipped. It has considerable recent operational experience, with capabilities across domains and an ability to support deployments abroad. Canberra released its inaugural National Defence Strategy in April 2024, along with an Integrated Investment Program, which noted the government's plan to transform the ADF away from a balanced force to an integrated, focused force with a strategy of denial as the cornerstone of its defence planning. This framing appeared in the 2023 Defence Strategic Review, which called for strengthening the armed forces to address 'the significant military challenge posed by China' and committed Australia to close security ties with the US. Australia plans to improve the ADF's force projection and positioning, notably in the country's north, as well as its air-defence and long-range strike capabilities. In addition to its alliance with the US, Australia is forging closer defence ties with India, Japan, South Korea and the UK, while remaining committed to the Five Power Defence Arrangements and its alliance with New Zealand. Cooperation continues with London and Washington in implementing the AUKUS partnership, intended to provide Australia with nuclear-powered submarines, first by acquiring US *Virginia*-class boats, followed by the development and production of the new SSN-AUKUS. A second pillar of the partnership centres on jointly developing advanced capabilities. Before the arrival of the new submarines, the UK and US have pledged to increase submarine visits to Australia, while Canberra will update other elements of its force, including by acquiring *Tomahawk* land-attack cruise missiles. Australia imports most of its defence equipment but is looking to develop domestic defence industrial capability.

ACTIVE 58,200 (Army 28,400 Navy 15,000 Air 14,800)

RESERVE 21,500 (Army 15,600 Navy 1,950 Air 3,950)

Integrated units are formed from a mix of reserve and regular personnel.

ORGANISATIONS BY SERVICE

Space
EQUIPMENT BY TYPE
SATELLITES • COMMUNICATIONS 1 *Optus* C1 (dual use for civil/mil comms)

Army 28,400
FORCES BY ROLE
COMMAND
1 (1st) div HQ (1 sigs regt)
MANOEUVRE
Mechanised
2 (3rd & 7th) mech inf bde (1 armd cav regt, 1 mech inf bn, 1 lt mech inf bn, 1 arty regt, 1 cbt engr regt, 1 sigs regt, 1 spt bn)
1 (1st) mech inf bde (1 lt mech inf bn, 1 arty regt, 1 cbt engr regt, 1 sigs regt, 1 spt bn)
1 (9th) mech inf bde (integrated) (1 armd cav regt, 1 mech inf bn)
Amphibious
1 (2nd RAR) amph bn
Aviation
1 (16th) avn bde (1 regt (2 ISR hel sqn), 1 regt (3 tpt hel sqn), 1 regt (2 spec ops hel sqn, 1 avn sqn))
COMBAT SUPPORT
1 (6th) cbt spt bde (1 STA regt (1 STA bty, 2 UAV bty, 1 spt bty), 1 AD/FAC regt (integrated), 1 engr regt (2 construction sqn, 1 EOD sqn), 1 EW regt, 1 int bn, 1 MP bn)
COMBAT SERVICE SUPPORT
1 (17th) log bde (3 log bn, 1 sigs coy)
1 (2nd) med bde (4 med bn)

Special Operations Command
FORCES BY ROLE
SPECIAL FORCES
1 (SAS) SF regt
1 (SF Engr) SF regt
2 cdo regt
COMBAT SUPPORT
3 sigs sqn (incl 1 reserve sqn)
COMBAT SERVICE SUPPORT
1 CSS sqn
EQUIPMENT BY TYPE
ARMOURED FIGHTING VEHICLES
AUV 119 Supacat HMT

Reserve Organisations 15,600 reservists
FORCES BY ROLE
COMMAND
1 (2nd) div HQ
MANOEUVRE
Reconnaissance
1 recce sqn (assigned to 9th Bde)
3 (regional force) surv unit (integrated)
Light
1 (4th) inf bde (1 recce regt, 3 inf bn, 1 engr regt, 1 spt bn)
1 (5th) inf bde (1 recce regt, 4 inf bn, 1 engr regt, 2 spt bn)
1 (11th) inf bde (1 recce regt, 3 inf bn, 1 engr regt, 1 spt bn)
1 (13th) inf bde (1 recce sqn, 2 inf bn, 1 spt bn)
1 inf bn (assigned to 9th Bde)
COMBAT SUPPORT
1 arty regt
1 sigs regt
COMBAT SERVICE SUPPORT
1 trg bde

EQUIPMENT BY TYPE
ARMOURED FIGHTING VEHICLES
MBT 27 M1A2 SEPv3 *Abrams*
RECCE 25 *Boxer* CRV (incl variants)
IFV 221 ASLAV-25 (incl variants)
APC • APC (T) 416 M113AS4
AUV 1,875: ε875 *Bushmaster* IMV; 1,000 *Hawkei*
ENGINEERING & MAINTENANCE VEHICLES
ARV 45: 15 ASLAV-F; 17 ASLAV-R; 13 M88A2
VLB 5 *Biber*
MW 20: 12 *Husky*; 8 MV-10
ANTI-TANK/ANTI-INFRASTRUCTURE
MSL • MANPATS FGM-148 *Javelin*
RCL • 84mm *Carl Gustaf*
ARTILLERY 264
TOWED 155mm 48 M777A2
MOR 81mm 216: 40 L16; 176 M252A1
AIR DEFENCE
SAM 9+
Point-defence RBS-70
Medium-range 9 NASAMS III
AMPHIBIOUS 15 LCM 8 (capacity either 1 MBT or 200 troops)
HELICOPTERS
ATK 22 *Tiger*
MRH 2 AW139 (leased)
TPT 17: **Heavy** 14 CH-47F *Chinook*; **Medium** 3 UH-60M *Black Hawk*
UNINHABITED AERIAL VEHICLES
ISR • Medium 15 RQ-7B *Shadow* 200
AIR-LAUNCHED MISSILES
ASM AGM-114M *Hellfire* II

Navy 15,000
EQUIPMENT BY TYPE
SUBMARINES 6
SSK 6 *Collins* with 6 single 533mm TT with UGM-84C *Harpoon* Block 1B AShM/Mk 48 ADCAP mod 7 HWT
PRINCIPAL SURFACE COMBATANTS 10
DESTROYERS • DDGHM 3

2 *Hobart* with *Aegis* Baseline 8.1 C2, 2 quad lnchr with RGM-84L *Harpoon* Block II AShM, 6 8-cell Mk 41 VLS with SM-2 Block IIIB SAM/RIM-162A ESSM SAM, 2 twin 324mm SVTT Mk 32 mod 9 ASTT with MU90 LWT/Mk 54 LWT, 1 MK 15 *Phalanx* Block 1B CIWS, 1 127mm gun (capacity 1 MH-60R *Seahawk*)

1 *Hobart* with *Aegis* Baseline 8.1 C2, 2 quad lnchr with NSM AShM, 6 8-cell Mk 41 VLS with SM-2 Block IIIB SAM/SM-6 Block IA SAM/RIM-162A ESSM SAM, 2 twin 324mm SVTT Mk 32 mod 9 ASTT with MU90 LWT/Mk 54 LWT, 1 MK 15 *Phalanx* Block 1B CIWS, 1 127mm gun (capacity 1 MH-60R *Seahawk*)

FRIGATES • FFGHM 7 *Anzac* (GER MEKO 200) with 2 quad lnchr with RGM-84L *Harpoon* Block II AShM, 1 8-cell Mk 41 VLS with RIM-162B ESSM SAM, 2 triple 324mm SVTT Mk 32 mod 5 ASTT with MU90 LWT, 1 127mm gun (capacity 1 MH-60R *Seahawk* hel)

PATROL AND COASTAL COMBATANTS 13

PCO 13: 3 *Armidale* (*Bay* mod); 10 *Cape* (of which 2 leased)

MINE WARFARE • MINE COUNTERMEASURES 3

MHC 3 *Huon*

AMPHIBIOUS

PRINCIPAL AMPHIBIOUS SHIPS 3

LHD 2 *Canberra* (capacity 18 hel; 4 LCM-1E; 110 veh; 12 M1 *Abrams* MBT; 1,000 troops)

LSD 1 *Choules* (ex-UK *Bay*) (capacity 2 med hel; 32 MBT; 350 troops)

LANDING CRAFT • LCM 12 LCM-1E

LOGISTICS AND SUPPORT 11

AGE 1 *Guidance* with 1 hel landing platform

AGS 1 *Leeuwin* with 1 hel landing platform

AORH 2 *Supply* (ESP *Cantabria*) (capacity 1 MH-60R *Seahawk* hel)

AXS 1 *Young Endeavour*

The following vessels are operated by a private company:

AFS 2: 1 *Ocean Protector* with 1 hel landing platform; 1 *Reliant* with 1 hel landing platform

ASR 2: 1 *Besant*; 1 *Stoker*

AX 1 *Sycamore* (capacity 1 med hel)

AXL 1 *Mercator* (*Pacific* mod)

UNINHABITED MARITIME PLATFORMS • USV 10

DATA • Small 6 *Bluebottle*

MW • Small 3 SEA 1778

UTL • Small 1 *Devil Ray* T38

UNINHABITED MARITIME SYSTEMS • UUV

DATA *Bluefin*-9/12

MW *Double Eagle* Mk II; *SeaFox*

Naval Aviation 1,450

FORCES BY ROLE

ANTI SUBMARINE WARFARE

2 sqn with MH-60R *Seahawk*

TRAINING

1 OCU sqn with MH-60R *Seahawk*

1 sqn with H135

EQUIPMENT BY TYPE

HELICOPTERS

ASW 23 MH-60R *Seahawk*

TPT • **Light** 20 H135 (5 leased)

UNINHABITED AERIAL VEHICLES

ISR • **Light** ε6 S-100 *Camcopter*

AIR-LAUNCHED MISSILES

ASM AGM-114N *Hellfire* II; AGR-20A APKWS

Clearance Diving Branch

FORCES BY ROLE

SPECIAL FORCES

2 diving unit

Air Force 14,800

FORCES BY ROLE

FIGHTER/GROUND ATTACK

1 sqn with F/A-18F *Super Hornet*

3 sqn with F-35A *Lightning* II

ANTI SUBMARINE WARFARE

1 sqn with P-8A *Poseidon*

ELECTRONIC WARFARE

1 sqn with EA-18G *Growler*

ISR

1 (FAC) sqn with PC-21

AIRBORNE EARLY WARNING & CONTROL

1 sqn with E-7A *Wedgetail*

TANKER/TRANSPORT

1 sqn with A330 MRTT (KC-30A)

TRANSPORT

1 sqn with C-17A *Globemaster* III

1 sqn with C-27J *Spartan*

1 sqn with C-130J-30 *Hercules*

1 VIP sqn with B-737BBJ; *Falcon* 7X

TRAINING

1 OCU sqn with F-35A *Lightning* II

1 sqn with Beech 350 *King Air*

2 sqn with PC-21

2 (LIFT) sqn with *Hawk* MK127*

ISR UAV

1 sqn with MQ-4C *Triton* (forming)

EQUIPMENT BY TYPE

AIRCRAFT 144 combat capable

FGA 87: 24 F/A-18F *Super Hornet*; 63 F-35A *Lightning* II

ASW 12 P-8A *Poseidon*

EW 12 EA-18G *Growler**

AEW&C 6 E-7A *Wedgetail*

TKR/TPT 7 A330 MRTT (KC-30A)

TPT 47: **Heavy** 8 C-17A *Globemaster* III; **Medium** 22: 10 C-27J *Spartan*; 12 C-130J-30 *Hercules*; **Light** 12 Beech 350 *King Air*; **PAX** 5: 2 B-737BBJ (VIP); 3 *Falcon* 7X (VIP)

TRG 82: 33 *Hawk* Mk127*; 49 PC-21

UNINHABITED AERIAL VEHICLES

ISR • **Heavy** 1 MQ-4C *Triton*

AIR-LAUNCHED MISSILES

AAM • IIR AIM-9X *Sidewinder* II; ASRAAM; **ARH** AIM-120B/C-5/C-7 AMRAAM

ARM AGM-88B HARM; AGM-88E AARGM

AShM AGM-84A *Harpoon*

LACM • Conventional AGM-158A JASSM

BOMBS

Laser-guided GBU-12 *Paveway* II

Laser & INS/GPS-guided GBU-54 Laser JDAM; *Paveway* IV

INS/GPS-guided AGM-154C JSOW; GBU-31 JDAM; GBU-39 Small Diameter Bomb

DEPLOYMENT

EGYPT: MFO (*Operation Mazurka*) 27

IRAQ: *Operation Inherent Resolve* (*Okra*) 110; 1 SF gp; **NATO** • NATO Mission Iraq 2

MALAYSIA: 120; 1 inf coy (on 3-month rotational tours); 1 P-8A *Poseidon* (on rotation)

MIDDLE EAST: UN • UNTSO (*Operation Paladin*) 12

PHILIPPINES: *Operation Augury* 100 (trg team)

SOUTH SUDAN: UN • UNMISS (*Operation Aslan*) 14

SYRIA/ISRAEL: UN • UNDOF 2

UNITED ARAB EMIRATES: *Operation Accordion* 400: 1 tpt det with 2 C-130J-30 *Hercules*

UNITED KINGDOM: *Operation Interflex* (*Kudu*) 70 (UKR trg)

FOREIGN FORCES

Singapore 230: 1 trg sqn at Pearce with PC-21 trg ac; 1 trg sqn at Oakey with 12 AS332 *Super Puma*; AS532 *Cougar*

United States US Indo-Pacific Command: 1,700; 1 SEWS at Pine Gap; 1 comms facility at NW Cape; 1 SIGINT stn at Pine Gap • US Strategic Command: 1 detection and tracking radar at Naval Communication Station Harold E. Holt

Bangladesh BGD

Bangladeshi Taka BDT		2023	2024	2025
GDP	BDT	44.9trn	50.1trn	57.7trn
	USD	452bn	451bn	482bn
Real GDP growth	%	5.8	5.4	4.5
Def bdgt	BDT	363bn	378bn	420bn
	USD	3.65bn	3.41bn	3.51bn

Real-terms defence budget trend (USDbn, constant 2015)

Population		168,697,184				
Age	0–14	15–19	20–24	25–29	30–64	65 plus
Male	12.8%	4.2%	4.3%	4.3%	19.9%	3.6%
Female	12.3%	4.1%	4.3%	4.5%	21.7%	4.2%

Capabilities

Bangladesh's limited military capability is focused on border and domestic security, including disaster relief, and has an operational legacy of UN peacekeeping deployments, predominantly to Africa. The country embarked on a defence modernisation plan called Forces Goal 2030, which it revised in 2017. Funding for the programme and its procurement objectives is additional to the defence budget. Dhaka is pursuing naval-recapitalisation and expansion, including through local manufacture of patrol boats, to better protect the country's large EEZ. It procured several former Chinese naval vessels. In April 2024, it announced its first joint military exercises with China, based on UN peacekeeping and counter-terrorism operations. In March 2023, Bangladesh established its first submarine base, which will host Chinese-designed submarines. The country has close defence ties with India, its longest standing defence partner, and also with France. There are plans to recapitalise the combat air fleet and Dhaka has invested in its fixed-wing training inventory. Bangladesh has relied on Chinese and Russian aid, and credit, to augment organic funding for procurement. The armed forces reportedly retain extensive commercial interests. Recent border tensions with Myanmar have increased, which could lead to a greater focus on border security in the future.

ACTIVE 173,650 (Army 132,150 Navy 27,500 Air 14,000) **Gendarmerie & Paramilitary 63,900**

ORGANISATIONS BY SERVICE

Army 132,150

FORCES BY ROLE

COMMAND

10 inf div HQ

SPECIAL FORCES

1 cdo bde (2 cdo bn)

MANOEUVRE

Armoured

1 armd bde

2 armd regt
1 lt armd regt
Light
25 inf bde
2 (composite) bde
COMBAT SUPPORT
10 arty bde
1 engr bde
1 sigs bde
AVIATION
1 avn regt (1 avn sqn; 1 hel sqn)
AIR DEFENCE
1 AD bde
EQUIPMENT BY TYPE
ARMOURED FIGHTING VEHICLES
MBT 276: 174 Type-59/-59G(BD); 58 Type-69/-69G; 44 Type-90-II (MBT-2000)
LT TK 52: 8 Type-62; 44 VT-5
RECCE 8+ BOV M11
APC 545
  APC (T) 134 MT-LB
  APC (W) 330 BTR-80
  PPV 81+ *Maxxpro*
  AUV 188: 36 *Cobra*; 152 *Cobra* II
ENGINEERING & MAINTENANCE VEHICLES
AEV MT-LB
ARV 3+: T-54/T-55; Type-84; 3 Type-654
VLB MTU
ANTI-TANK/ANTI-INFRASTRUCTURE
MSL • MANPATS 9K115-2 *Metis* M1 (RS-AT-13)
RCL 106mm 238 M40A1
ARTILLERY 907+
SP 155mm 18 NORA B-52
TOWED 363+: **105mm** 170 Model 56 pack howitzer; **122mm** 131: 57 Type-54/54-1 (M-30); 20 Type-83; 54 Type-96 (D-30), **130mm** 62 Type-59-1 (M-46)
MRL 54: **122mm** 36+ WS-22; **302mm** 18 T-300
MOR 472: **81mm** 11 M29A1; **82mm** 366 Type-53/type-87/M-31 (M-1937); **120mm** 95 AM-50/UBM 52
AIR DEFENCE • GUNS 35mm PG99
AMPHIBIOUS • LANDING CRAFT 3: 1 **LCT**; 2 **LCVP**
AIRCRAFT • TPT • Light 5: 4 Cessna 152;
1 Cessna 208B
HELICOPTERS
MRH 2 AS365N3 *Dauphin*
TPT 9: **Medium** 6 Mi-171Sh **Light** 3: 1 Bell 206L-4 *Long Ranger* IV; 2 Bell 407GXi
UNINHABITED AERIAL VEHICLES
CISR • Medium 6 *Bayraktar* TB2
BOMBS • Laser-guided MAM-L
AIR DEFENCE
SAM
  Short-range FM-90 (CH-SA-4)
  Point-defence FN-16 (CH-SA-14); QW-2 (CH-SA-8)
GUNS • TOWED 174: **35mm** 8 GDF-009 (with *Skyguard*-3); **37mm** 132 Type-65/74; **57mm** 34 Type-59 (S-60)

Navy 27,500
EQUIPMENT BY TYPE
SUBMARINES 2
  SSK 2 *Nabajatra* (ex-PRC Type-035G (*Ming*)) with 8 single 533mm TT with Yu-3/Yu-4 HWT
PRINCIPAL SURFACE COMBATANTS • FRIGATES 5
  FFGHM 3:
    1 *Bangabandhu* (ROK modified *Ulsan*) with 2 twin lnchr with *Otomat* Mk2 AShM, 1 octuple FM-90N (CH-SA-N-4) SAM, 2 triple ILAS-3 (B-515) 324mm TT with A244/S LWT, 1 76mm gun (capacity 1 AW109E hel)
    2 *Umar Farooq* (ex-PRC Type-053H3 (*Jiangwei* II)) with 2 quad lnchr with C-802A AShM, 1 octuple CMLS with HHQ-7 (CH-SA-N-4) SAM, 2 FQF 3200 A/S mor, 1 twin 100mm gun (capacity 1 hel)
  FFG 2 *Abu Bakr* (ex-PRC Type-053H2 (*Jianghu* III)) with 2 quad lnchr with C-802A AShM, 2 RBU 1200 *Uragan* A/S mor, 2 twin 100mm gun
PATROL AND COASTAL COMBATANTS 48
  CORVETTES 6
    FSGM 4 *Shadhinota* (PRC C13B) with 2 twin lnchr with C-802 (CH-SS-N-6) AShM, 1 octuple lnchr with FL-3000N (HHQ-10) (CH-SA-N-17) SAM, 1 76mm gun, 1 hel landing platform
    FSG 2 *Bijoy* (ex-UK *Castle*) with 2 twin lnchr with C-704 AShM, 1 76mm gun, 1 hel landing platform
  PSOH 2 *Somudra Joy* (ex-US *Hero*) with 1 76mm gun, hel landing platform (1 used for trg)
  PCFG 4 *Durdarsha* (ex-PRC *Huangfeng*) with 4 single lnchr with C-704 AShM
  PCG 2 *Durjoy* with 2 twin lnchr with C-704 AShM, 1 76mm gun
  PCO 8: 1 *Madhumati* (ROK *Sea Dragon*) with 1 57mm gun; 5 *Kapatakhaya* (ex-UK *Island*); 2 *Durjoy* with 2 triple 324mm ASTT, 1 76mm gun
  PCC 11: 2 *Meghna* with 1 57mm gun (fishery protection); 9 *Padma*
  PBF 12: 8 X12 *Combat Craft*; 4 *Titas* (RCK *Sea Dolphin*) (1 used for trg)
  PB 3: 1 *Barkat* (ex-PRC *Shanghai* III); 1 *Salam* (ex-PRC *Huangfen*); 1 other
MINE WARFARE • MINE COUNTERMEASURES 5
  MSO 5: 1 *Sagar*; 4 *Shapla* (ex-UK *River*)
AMPHIBIOUS
  LANDING SHIPS • LSL 1
  LANDING CRAFT 20
    LCU 12: 4 *Dolphin*; 8 Other (of which 2-)
    LCT 2
    LCM 3 *Darshak* (ex-PRC Type-069 (*Yuchin*))

LCVP 3†
LOGISTICS AND SUPPORT 9
 AGS 5: 1 *Anushandhan* (ex-UK *Roebuck*); 2 *Darshak*; 2 *Jarip*
 AG 1
 AOR 1 *Khan Jahan Ali*
 AR 1†
 ATF 1 *Khadem* (ex-PRC *Hujiu*)†

Naval Aviation
EQUIPMENT BY TYPE
AIRCRAFT • MP 4 Do-228NG
HELICOPTERS • TPT • Light 2 AW109E *Power*

Special Warfare and Diving Command 300

Air Force 14,000
FORCES BY ROLE
FIGHTER
 1 sqn with MiG-29/MiG-29UB *Fulcrum*
FIGHTER/GROUND ATTACK
 1 sqn with F-7MB/FT-7B *Airguard*
 1 sqn with F-7BG/FT-7BG *Airguard*
 1 sqn with F-7BGI/FT-7BGI *Airguard*
GROUND ATTACK
 1 sqn with Yak-130 *Mitten**
TRANSPORT
 1 sqn with An-32 *Cline*
 1 sqn with C-130B/J *Hercules*
 1 sqn with L-410UVP
TRAINING
 1 sqn with G 120TP
 1 sqn with K-8W *Karakorum**; L-39ZA *Albatros**
 1 sqn with PT-6
 1 hel sqn with AW119 *Koala*; Bell 206L *Long Ranger*
TRANSPORT HELICOPTER
 1 sqn with AW139; Mi-17 *Hip* H; Mi-17-1V *Hip* H; Mi-171Sh
 1 sqn with Mi-17 *Hip* H; Mi-17-1V *Hip* H; Mi-171Sh
 1 sqn with Bell 212
EQUIPMENT BY TYPE
AIRCRAFT 87 combat capable
 FTR 53: 9 F-7MB *Airguard*; 11 F-7BG *Airguard*; 12 F-7BGI *Airguard*; 5 FT-7B *Airguard*; 4 FT-7BG *Airguard*; 4 FT-7BGI *Airguard*; 6 MiG-29 *Fulcrum*; 2 MiG-29UB *Fulcrum* B
 TPT 17: **Medium** 9: 4 C-130B *Hercules*; 5 C-130J *Hercules*; **Light** 8: 3 An-32 *Cline*†; 2 C295W; 3 L-410UVP
 TRG 86: 4 DA40NG; 24 G 120TP; 15 K-8W *Karakorum**; 7 L-39ZA *Albatros**; ε24 PT-6; 12 Yak-130 *Mitten**
HELICOPTERS
 MRH 18: 4 AW139 (SAR); 12 Mi-17 *Hip* H; 2 Mi-17-1V *Hip* H (VIP)
 TPT 27: **Medium** 11 Mi-171Sh; **Light** 16: 2 AW119 *Koala*; 4 Bell 206L *Long Ranger*; 10+ Bell 212

UNINHABITED AERIAL VEHICLES
 ISR • **Medium** 1 *Falco Astore*
AIR-LAUNCHED MISSILES
 AAM • IR R-73 (RS-AA-11A *Archer*); PL-5; PL-7; PL-9C;
 SARH R-27R (RS-AA-10A *Alamo*)
 ASM Cirit

Gendarmerie & Paramilitary 63,900

Ansars 20,000+
Security Guards

Rapid Action Battalions 5,000
Ministry of Home Affairs
FORCES BY ROLE
MANOEUVRE
 Other
 14 paramilitary bn

Border Guard Bangladesh 38,000
FORCES BY ROLE
MANOEUVRE
 Amphibious
 1 rvn coy
 Other
 54 paramilitary bn

Coast Guard 900
EQUIPMENT BY TYPE
PATROL AND COASTAL COMBATANTS 54
 PSO 4 *Syed Nazrul* (ex-ITA *Minerva*) with 1 hel landing platform
 PCC 7 *Sobuj Bangla* (*Padma* mod)
 PBF 13: 3 *Hurricane*; 10 X12 *Combat Craft*
 PB 25: 1 *Ruposhi Bangla*; 2 *Shetgang*; 2 *Sonadia*; 4 *Tawfiq* (ex-PRC Type-062 (*Shanghai* II)); 16 Other
 PBR 5 *Pabna*
LOGISTICS AND SUPPORT • AAR 5

DEPLOYMENT

CENTRAL AFRICAN REPUBLIC: UN • MINUSCA 1,421; 1 cdo coy; 1 inf bn; 2 med coy; 1 hel coy
CYPRUS: UN • UNFICYP 1
DEMOCRATIC REPUBLIC OF THE CONGO: UN • MONUSCO 1,774; 1 inf bn; 1 engr coy; 1 MP coy; 1 tpt flt with 1 C-130B *Hercules*; 1 hel coy with 6 Mi-17/Mi-171Sh
LEBANON: UN • UNIFIL 120; 1 FSGM
LIBYA: UN • UNSMIL 1
SOUTH SUDAN: UN • UNMISS 1,631; 1 inf bn; 2 rvn coy; 2 engr coy
SUDAN: UN • UNISFA 711; 1 inf bn(-)
WESTERN SAHARA: UN • MINURSO 30; 1 fd hospital

Brunei BRN

Brunei Dollar BND		2023	2024	2025
GDP	BND	20.3bn	21.0bn	22.0bn
	USD	15.1bn	15.7bn	16.7bn
Real GDP growth	%	1.4	2.4	2.5
Def bdgt	BND	ε620m	796m	
	USD	ε462m	597m	

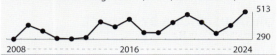

Population		491,900				
Age	0–14	15–19	20–24	25–29	30–64	65 plus
Male	11.2%	3.4%	4.0%	4.5%	21.9%	3.6%
Female	10.5%	3.3%	4.1%	4.7%	24.9%	3.9%

Capabilities

Brunei's core defence missions include ensuring territorial integrity, counter-terrorism and counter-insurgency operations, and assisting civil authorities. In May 2021, the government published Brunei's fourth defence white paper, its first in 17 years. Brunei is looking to improve its C4ISR capabilities – especially aerial, maritime, and underwater surveillance capabilities – to offset the relatively small size of the forces. In 2022, Brunei began operating its first uninhabited aerial platforms and, in 2023, received two ex-Singapore patrol vessels. C4ISR, medium airlift, rotary wing CAS and ISR capabilities were boosted in 2024. Under a long-standing bilateral arrangement, which currently extends to 2025, Brunei hosts a British military presence including a Gurkha infantry battalion, a helicopter-flight and a jungle-warfare school. Brunei has a close defence relationship with Singapore and hosts a permanent Singapore Armed Forces training facility. It participates in regular bilateral exercises with Singapore and other Southeast Asian countries. The armed forces also participate in multinational exercises organised by ASEAN and the ADMM–Plus. Brunei has limited capacity to deploy forces abroad without assistance but has nevertheless maintained a small deployment to UNIFIL in Lebanon since 2008. Brunei has no domestic defence industry.

ACTIVE 7,200 (Army 4,400 Navy 1,200 Air 1,100 Special Forces 500) Gendarmerie & Paramilitary 400–500

RESERVE 700 (Army 700)

ORGANISATIONS BY SERVICE

Army 4,400
FORCES BY ROLE
MANOEUVRE
Light
  3 inf bn
COMBAT SUPPORT
  1 cbt spt bn (1 armd recce sqn, 1 engr sqn)

Reserves 700
FORCES BY ROLE
MANOEUVRE
Light
  1 inf bn
EQUIPMENT BY TYPE
ARMOURED FIGHTING VEHICLES
  LT TK 20 FV101 *Scorpion* (incl FV105 *Sultan* CP)
  APC • APC (W) 45 VAB
ENGINEERING & MAINTENANCE VEHICLES
  ARV 2 *Samson*
ARTILLERY • MOR 81mm 24

Navy 1,200
FORCES BY ROLE
SPECIAL FORCES
  1 SF sqn
EQUIPMENT BY TYPE
PATROL AND COASTAL COMBATANTS 11
  CORVETTES • **FSG** 4 *Darussalam* with 2 twin lnchr with MM40 *Exocet* Block 2 AShM, 1 57mm gun, 1 hel landing platform
  PCO 2 *As-Siddiq* (ex-SGP *Fearless*)
  PCC 4 *Ijtihad*
  PBF 1 *Mustaed*
AMPHIBIOUS • **LANDING CRAFT** • **LCM 4**: 2 *Damuan* (*Cheverton Loadmaster*); 2 *Teraban*

Air Force 1,100
FORCES BY ROLE
MARITIME PATROL
  1 flt with CN235M
TRAINING
  1 sqn with Bell 206B *Jet Ranger* II
TRANSPORT HELICOPTER
  1 sqn with Bell 214 (SAR)
  1 sqn with S-70i *Black Hawk*
AIR DEFENCE
  1 sqn with *Mistral*
  1 sqn with *Rapier*
EQUIPMENT BY TYPE
AIRCRAFT
  TPT • Light 3: 2 C295W; 1 CN235M
  TRG 4 PC-7
HELICOPTERS
  TPT 15: **Medium** 13: 1 Bell 214 (SAR); 12 S-70i *Black Hawk*; **Light** 2 Bell 206B *Jet Ranger* II
UNINHABITED AERIAL VEHICLES
  ISR • Light 1 *Integrator*
AIR DEFENCE • **SAM** • **Point-defence** *Mistral*, *Rapier*

Special Forces Regiment ε500

FORCES BY ROLE
SPECIAL FORCES
1 SF regt

Gendarmerie & Paramilitary 400–500

Gurkha Reserve Unit 400–500
FORCES BY ROLE
MANOEUVRE
Light
2 inf bn(-)

DEPLOYMENT
LEBANON: UN • UNIFIL 29

FOREIGN FORCES
Singapore 1 trg camp with infantry units on rotation; 1 trg school; 1 hel det with AS332 *Super Puma*
United Kingdom 1,200; 1 (Gurkha) inf bn; 1 jungle trg centre; 1 hel sqn with 3 SA330 *Puma* HC2

Cambodia CAM

Cambodian Riel KHR		2023	2024	2025
GDP	KHR	178trn	193trn	210trn
	USD	43.3bn	47.1bn	51.2bn
Real GDP growth	%	5.0	5.5	5.8
Def bdgt [a]	KHR	5.02trn	5.32trn	
	USD	1.22bn	1.30bn	

[a] Defence and security budget

Real-terms defence budget trend (USDm, constant 2015)

Population	17,063,669				
Age	0–14	15–19	20–24	25–29	30–64	65 plus
Male	14.6%	4.5%	3.8%	3.7%	20.0%	1.9%
Female	14.3%	4.5%	4.0%	4.0%	21.4%	3.4%

Capabilities

The Royal Cambodian Armed Forces (RCAF) were established in 1993 after the merger of the Communist government's Cambodian People's Armed Forces and two non-communist resistance armies. The country does not face any direct external military threats, although Cambodia continues to emphasise its border security with Laos, Thailand and Vietnam. Internal security concerns include civil unrest and transnational threats, such as drug trafficking. Cambodia's most important international defence links are with China and Vietnam. Despite a traditional reliance on Russia for defence equipment, China has emerged as a key supplier. Beijing is funding upgrades at the Ream naval base located on the Gulf of Thailand. Cambodia and China also take part in military exercises. The US imposed a largely symbolic arms embargo on Cambodia in December 2021 over the country's military links to China. Phnom Penh's equipment funding is limited, although the 2022 National Defence white paper stated that military modernisation is the top priority. The document also encouraged the development of a domestic defence industry; Cambodia currently lacks the ability to design and manufacture modern equipment for its armed forces.

ACTIVE 124,300 (Army 75,000 Navy 2,800 Air 1,500 Provincial Forces 45,000) Gendarmerie & Paramilitary 67,000

Conscript liability 18 months service authorised but not implemented since 1993

ORGANISATIONS BY SERVICE

Army ε75,000

6 Military Regions (incl 1 special zone for capital)

FORCES BY ROLE
SPECIAL FORCES
1 (Spec Ops Comd) AB/SF Bde
MANOEUVRE
Light
2 (2nd & 3rd Intervention) inf div (3 inf bde)
5 (Intervention) indep inf bde
8 indep inf bde
Other
1 (70th) sy bde (4 sy bn)
17 (border) sy bn
COMBAT SUPPORT
2 arty bn
4 fd engr regt
COMBAT SERVICE SUPPORT
1 (construction) engr regt
2 tpt bde
AIR DEFENCE
1 AD bn

EQUIPMENT BY TYPE
ARMOURED FIGHTING VEHICLES
MBT 200+: 50 Type-59; 150+ T-54/T-55
LT TK 20+: Type-62; 20 Type-63
RECCE 20+ BRDM-2
IFV 70 BMP-1
APC 230+
   APC (T) M113
   APC (W) 230: 200 BTR-60/BTR-152; 30 OT-64
AUV 27: 12 Dongfeng *Mengshi*; 15 *Tiger* 4×4
ENGINEERING & MAINTENANCE VEHICLES
ARV T-54/T-55
MW *Bozena*; RA-140 DS
ANTI-TANK/ANTI-INFRASTRUCTURE
RCL 82mm B-10; **107mm** B-11
ARTILLERY 486+
   SP 155mm 12 SH-1
   TOWED 400+: **76mm** ZIS-3 (M-1942)/**122mm** D-30/**122mm** M-30 (M-1938)/**130mm** Type-59-I

MRL 74+: **107mm** Type-63; **122mm** 48+: 8 BM-21; ε20 PHL-81; some PHL-90B; 20 RM-70; **132mm** BM-13-16 (BM-13); **140mm** 20 BM-14-16 (BM-14); **300mm** 6 PHL-03
MOR 82mm M-37; **120mm** M-43; **160mm** M-160

AIR DEFENCE
SAM
Point-defence FN-6 (CH-SA-10); FN-16 (CH-SA-14) (reported)
Medium-range KS-1C (CH-SA-12)
GUNS • TOWED 14.5mm ZPU-1/ZPU-2/ZPU-4; **37mm** M-1939; **57mm** S-60

Navy ε2,800 (incl 1,500 Naval Infantry)
EQUIPMENT BY TYPE
PATROL AND COASTAL COMBATANTS 13
  PBF 4 Project 205P (ex-FSU *Stenka*)
  PB 7: 3 (PRC 20m); 4 (PRC 46m)
  PBR 2 *Kaoh Chhlam*
AMPHIBIOUS • LANDING CRAFT 1
  LCU 1 Type-067 (*Yunnan*)

Naval Infantry 1,500
FORCES BY ROLE
MANOEUVRE
  Light
    1 (31st) nav inf bde
COMBAT SUPPORT
  1 arty bn

Air Force 1,500
FORCES BY ROLE
ISR/TRAINING
  1 flt with P-92 *Echo*
TRANSPORT
  1 VIP sqn (reporting to Council of Ministers) with A320; AS350 *Ecureuil*; AS355F2 *Ecureuil* II
  1 flt with MA60; Y-12 (II)
TRANSPORT HELICOPTER
  1 sqn with Mi-17 *Hip* H; Mi-8 *Hip*; Z-9
EQUIPMENT BY TYPE
AIRCRAFT
  TPT 10: **Light** 9: 2 MA60; 5 P-92 *Echo* (pilot trg/recce); 2 Y-12 (II) (2 An-24RV *Coke*; 1 BN-2 *Islander* in store); **PAX** 1 A320 (VIP)
  TRG (5 L-39C *Albatros** in store)
HELICOPTERS
  MRH 16: 6 Mi-17 *Hip* H; 10 Z-9
  TPT 10: **Heavy** (2 Mi-26 *Halo* in store); **Medium** ε4 Mi-8 *Hip* (2 more in store); **Light** 6: 2 AW109 (reported); 2 AS350 *Ecureuil*; 2 AS355F2 *Ecureuil* II

Provincial Forces 45,000+
Reports of at least 1 inf regt per province, with varying numbers of inf bn (with lt wpn)

Gendarmerie & Paramilitary 67,000
Police 67,000 (including gendarmerie)

DEPLOYMENT
CENTRAL AFRICAN REPUBLIC: UN • MINUSCA 345; 1 engr coy
DEMOCRATIC REPUBLIC OF THE CONGO: UN • MONUSCO 1
LEBANON: UN • UNIFIL 181; 1 EOD coy
SOUTH SUDAN: UN • UNMISS 85; 1 MP coy
SUDAN: UN • UNISFA 1

FOREIGN FORCES
China 120; 2 FSGM

China, People's Republic of PRC

Chinese Yuan Renminbi CNY		2023	2024	2025
GDP	CNY	126tr	131trn	140trn
	USD	17.8tn	18.3trn	19.5trn
Real GDP growth	%	5.3	4.8	4.5
Def exp [a]	CNY	ε2.08trn	ε2.20trn	
	USD	ε294bn	ε305bn	
Def bdgt [b]	CNY	1.58trn	ε1.59trn	
	USD	223bn	ε235bn	

[a] Includes central and local defence budget; foreign weapons purchases; R&D spending; and central People's Armed Police budget.

[b] Central Expenditure budget including local militia funding

Real-terms defence budget trend (USDbn, constant 2015)

Population	1,423,985,517					
Age	0–14	15–19	20–24	25–29	30–64	65 plus
Male	8.7%	2.9%	2.9%	3.4%	26.4%	6.7%
Female	7.6%	2.5%	2.5%	3.0%	25.7%	7.7%

Capabilities

The People's Liberation Army (PLA) is the world's largest armed force, with an increasingly advanced equipment inventory. Its operational effectiveness, however, remains hampered by training and doctrine issues. In 2021, amendments to the National Defense Law handed full responsibility for defence mobilisation to the Central Military Commission and removed the role of the State Council. In 2024, the PLA saw continued anti-corruption investigations. In 2024, the CMC disbanded the Strategic Support Force and reorganised its constituent parts as three independent PLA arms focused individually on cyber, space and information support operations. China has several defence relationships with regional states and through its membership of the SCO. It has also worked to develop defence ties with African and Middle Eastern states. In

February 2022, China and Russia announced a friendship with 'no limits', and Western states have said that Beijing has assisted Moscow's war on Ukraine through the supply of components, and in return is receiving Russian technical assistance. The PLA lacks any significant recent combat experience, and its training has suffered from over-scripted and unrealistic exercises. It is unclear how effective the newly established structures will be at generating and controlling high-intensity combined-arms capabilities. The PLA conscripts twice a year with the aim of improving readiness. Recruitment focuses on college graduates and those skilled in science and engineering, particularly with specialisms in cyber and space. In 2023, China adopted the Reserve Personnel Law, which instituted a system for military personnel replenishment. A requirement for out-of-area operations is relatively new for the PLA; the navy is the only service to have experience in extended deployments, assisted by its support base in Djibouti. Major platform inventories in all the services comprise a mix of modern, older and obsolescent designs as modernisation efforts continue. China has an extensive defence-industrial base, capable of producing advanced equipment across all domains, although questions persist over quality and reliability.

ACTIVE 2,035,000 (Ground Forces 960,000 Navy 252,000 Air Force 403,000 Strategic Missile Forces 125,000 Other 295,000) Gendarmerie & Paramilitary 500,000

Conscript liability Selective conscription; all services 24 months

RESERVE ε510,000

ORGANISATIONS BY SERVICE

Strategic Missile Forces 125,000+

People's Liberation Army Rocket Force

Controls nuclear and conventional missile units Organised as launch brigades subordinate to 6 army-level missile bases.

FORCES BY ROLE
SURFACE-TO-SURFACE MISSILE
  5 ICBM bde with DF-5A/B/C
  2 ICBM bde with DF-31A
  5 ICBM bde with DF-31A(G)
  3 ICBM bde with DF-31 (silo) (forming)
  5 ICBM bde with DF-41
  8 IRBM bde with DF-26
  4 MRBM bde with DF-17 with HGV
  1 MRBM bde with DF-21A/E
  2 MRBM bde with DF-21C/D
  2 SRBM bde with DF-11A/DF-15B
  2 SRBM bde with DF-16
  3 GLCM bde with CJ-10/CJ-10A/CJ-100
  4 SSM bde (forming)

EQUIPMENT BY TYPE
SURFACE-TO-SURFACE MISSILE LAUNCHERS
  ICBM • Nuclear 148: 18+ DF-5A/B/C (CH-SS-4 Mod 2/3/4); ε6 DF-31 (silo); ε24 DF-31A (CH-SS-10 Mod 2); ε56 DF-31A(G); ε44 DF-41 (CH-SS-20)

  IRBM • Dual-capable 250: ε250 DF-26 (CH-SS-18); DF-27 with HGV (CH-SS-X-24) (entering service)
  MRBM 102: **Nuclear** ε24 DF-21A/E (CH-SS-5 Mod 2/6); **Conventional** 78: ε48 DF-17 with HGV (CH-SS-22); ε30 DF-21C/D (CH-SS-5 Mod 4/5)
  SRBM • Conventional 225: ε108 DF-11A (CH-SS-7 Mod 2); ε81 DF-15B (CH-SS-6 Mod 3); ε36 DF-16 (CH-SS-11 Mod 1/2)
  GLCM • Conventional 126: ε72 CJ-10/CJ-10A (CH-SSC-9 Mod 1/2); ε54 CJ-100 (CH-SSC-13 *Splinter*)
UNINHABITED AERIAL VEHICLES
  ISR • Heavy TB-001

Navy
EQUIPMENT BY TYPE
SUBMARINES • STRATEGIC 6
  SSBN 6 Type-094 (*Jin*) with up to 12 JL-2 (CH-SS-N-14)/JL-3 (CH-SS-N-20) nuclear SLBMs, 6 single 533mm TT with Yu-6 HWT

Defensive
EQUIPMENT BY TYPE
RADAR • STRATEGIC: 4+ large phased array radars; some detection and tracking radars

Space
EQUIPMENT BY TYPE
SATELLITES 267
  COMMUNICATIONS 12: 2 *Shen Tong*-1; 4 *Shen Tong*-2; 2 *Feng Huo*-1; 3 *Feng Huo*-2; 1 *Feng Huo*-3
  POSITIONING, NAVIGATION & TIMING 45: 3 *Beidou*-2(M); 5 *Beidou*-2(G); 7 *Beidou*-2(IGSO); 24 *Beidou*-3(M); 3 *Beidou*-3(G); 3 *Beidou*-3(ISGO)
  METEOROLOGY/OCEANOGRAPHY 8: 2 *Yunhai*-1; 6 *Yunhai*-2
  ISR 115: 2 *Jianbing*-5; 4 *Jianbing*-6; 4 *Jianbing*-7; 5 *Jianbing*-9; 3 *Jianbing*-10; 3 *Jianbing*-11/-12; 3 *Jianbing*-16; 4 LKW; 12 *Tianhui*; 5 *Yaogan*-29; 4 *Yaogan*-34; 15 *Yaogan*-35; 15 *Yaogan*-36; 15 *Yaogan*-39; 3 *Yaogan*-40; 18 *Yaogan*-43
  ELINT/SIGINT 81: 30 *Chuangxin*-5 (*Yaogan*-30); 15 *Jianbing*-8; 3 *Qianshao*-3; 10 *Shijian*-6 (5 pairs – reported ELINT/SIGINT role); 7 *Shijian*-11 (reported ELINT/SIGINT role); 12 *Yaogan*-31; 4 *Yaogan*-32
  EARLY WARNING 3 *Huoyan*-1
  RENDEZVOUS & PROXIMITY OPERATIONS 3: 1 *Shijian*-17; 1 *Shijian*-21; 1 *Shijian*-23
REUSABLE SPACECRAFT 1 CSSHQ
COUNTERSPACE • MSL SC-19 (reported)

Army ε960,000
FORCES BY ROLE
COMMAND
  13 (Group) army HQ
SPECIAL FORCES
  15 spec ops bde

MANOEUVRE
  Armoured
  32 (cbd arms) armd bde
  Mechanised
  1 (high alt) mech inf div (1 (cbd arms) armd regt, 2 (cbd arms) mech regt, 1 arty /AD regt)
  18 (cbd arms) mech inf bde
  2 indep mech inf regt
  Light
  3 (high alt) inf div (1 (cbd arms) armd regt, 2 (cbd arms) inf regt, 1 arty/AD regt)
  24 (cbd arms) inf bde
  Air Manoeuvre
  2 air aslt bde
  Amphibious
  6 amph aslt bde
  Other
  1 (OPFOR) armd bde
  1 mech gd div (1 armd regt, 2 mech inf regt, 1 arty regt, 1 AD regt)
  1 sy gd div (4 sy regt)
  16 (border) sy bde
  15 (border) sy regt
  1 (border) sy gp
COMBAT SUPPORT
  15 arty bde
  2 MRL bde
  10 engr/NBC bde
  5 engr bde
  5 NBC bde
COMBAT SERVICE SUPPORT
  13 spt bde
COASTAL DEFENCE
  19 coastal arty/AShM bde
AVIATION
  1 mixed avn bde
HELICOPTER
  12 hel bde
CISR UAV
  1 bde with CH-4B
TRAINING
  4 hel trg bde
AIR DEFENCE
  14 AD bde

Reserves

The People's Liberation Army Reserve Force is being restructured, and the army component reduced. As a result some of the units below may have been re-roled or disbanded

FORCES BY ROLE
MANOEUVRE
  Armoured
    2 armd regt
  Light
    18 inf div
    4 inf bde
    3 indep inf regt
COMBAT SUPPORT
  3 arty div
  7 arty bde
  15 engr regt
  1 ptn br bde
  3 ptn br regt
  10 chem regt
  10 sigs regt
COMBAT SERVICE SUPPORT
  9 log bde
  1 log regt
AIR DEFENCE
  17 AD div
  8 AD bde
  8 AD regt

EQUIPMENT BY TYPE
ARMOURED FIGHTING VEHICLES
  MBT 4,700: 400 ZTZ-59/-59-II/-59D; 200 ZTZ-79; 300 ZTZ-88A/B; 1,000 ZTZ-96; 1,500 ZTZ-96A; 600 ZTZ-99; 700 ZTZ-99A
  LT TK 1,250: 750 ZTD-05; 500 ZTQ-15
  ASLT 1,200 ZTL-11
  IFV 8,060: 400 ZBD-04; 2,000 ZBD-04A; 3,250 ZBL-08; 10+ ZBL-19 (reported); 600 ZBD-86; 650 ZBD-86A; 550 ZSL-92; 600 ZSL-92B
  APC 3,600
    APC (T) 1,950: 200 ZSD-63; 1,750 ZSD-89/-89A
    APC (W) 1,650: 700 ZSL-92A; 900 ZSL-10; 50 ZSL-93
  AAV 750 ZBD-05
  AUV Dongfeng Mengshi; *Tiger* 4×4
ENGINEERING & MAINTENANCE VEHICLES
  ARV Type-73; Type-84; Type-85; Type-97; Type-654
  VLB MTU; TMM; GQL-110A (Type-84A); GQL-111 (HZQL75); GQL-321 (HZQL22); GQL-410; High Altitude VLB; HZQL-18; ZGQ-84
  MW Type-74; Type-79; Type-81-II; Type-84
ANTI-TANK/ANTI-INFRASTRUCTURE
  MSL
    SP 1,125: 450 HJ-8 (veh mounted); 200 HJ-10; 25 HJ-10A; 450 ZSL-02B
    MANPATS HJ-73D; HJ-8A/C/E, HJ-11; HJ-12
  RCL 3,966: **75mm** PF-56; **82mm** PF-65 (B-10); PF-78; **105mm** PF-75; **120mm** PF-98
  GUNS 1,788
    SP 480: **100mm** 250 PTL-02; **120mm** 230 PTZ-89
    TOWED • **100mm** 1,308 PT-73 (T-12)/PT-86
ARTILLERY 9,580
  SP 3,240: **122mm** 2,170: 300 PLZ-89; 550 PLZ-07A; 150

PLZ-07B; 300 PCL-09; 600 PLL-09; 120 PCL-161; 120 PCL-171; 30 PCL-181 **152mm** 150 PLZ-83A/B; **155mm** 920: 320 PLZ-05; 600 PCL-181; (600 in store: **122mm** 400 PLZ-89; **152mm** 200 PLZ-83A)

TOWED 900: **122mm** 300 PL-96 (D-30); **130mm** 100 PL-59 (M-46)/PL-59-I; **152mm** 500 PL-66 (D-20); (4,700 in store: **122mm** 3,000 PL-54-1 (M-1938)/PL-83/PL-60 (D-74)/PL-96 (D-30); **152mm** 1,700 PL-54 (D-1)/PL-66 (D-20))

GUN/MOR 120mm 1,250: 450 PLL-05; 800 PPZ-10

MRL 1,390+ **107mm** PH-63; **122mm** 1,095: 200 PHL-81/PHL-90; 350 PHL-11; 375 PHZ-89; 120 PHZ-11; 30 PHL-20; 10+ PHL-21; 10 PHL-161; **300mm** 175 PHL-03; **370mm** 120+ PCH-191; (1,000 in store: **122mm** 1,000 PHL-81)

MOR 2,800: **82mm** PP-53 (M-37)/PP-67/PP-82/PP-87; **SP 82mm** PCP-001; **100mm** PP-89

SURFACE-TO-SURFACE MISSILE LAUNCHERS

SRBM • Conventional *Fire Dragon*-480 mod (launched from PCH-191 MRL)

COASTAL DEFENCE

AShM HY-1 (CH-SSC-2 *Silkworm*); HY-2 (CH-SSC-3 *Seersucker*); HY-4 (CH-SSC-7 *Sadsack*); YJ-62

PATROL AND COASTAL COMBATANTS 26

PB 26: 10 *Huzong*; 16 *Shenyang*

AMPHIBIOUS

LANDING SHIPS • LSM 2+ *Yujiu*

LANDING CRAFT • LCM 234: 3+ *Yugong*; 40+ *Yunnan* II; 100+ *Yupen*; 16+ *Yutu*; 75+ *Yuwei*

LOGISTICS AND SUPPORT 23

AK 6+ *Leizhuang*

AKR 2 *Yunsong* (capacity 1 MBT; 1 med hel)

ARC 1

AO 11: 1 *Fuzhong*; 8 *Fubing*; 2 *Fulei*

ATF 2 *Huntao*

AX 1 *Haixun* III

AIRCRAFT • TPT 6: **Medium** 4: 2 Y-8; 2 Y-9; **Light** 2 Y-7

HELICOPTERS

ATK 320+: 200 WZ-10; 120+ WZ-19

MRH 208: 22 Mi-17 *Hip* H; 3 Mi-17-1V *Hip* H; 38 Mi-17V-5 *Hip* H; 25 Mi-17V-7 *Hip* H; ε120 Z-9WZ

TPT 512: **Heavy** 135: 9 Z-8A; 96 Z-8B; ε30 Z-8L; **Medium** 309: 140 Mi-171; 19 S-70C2 (S-70C) *Black Hawk*; ε150 Z-20; **Light** 68: 15 H120 *Colibri*; 53 Z-11

UNINHABITED AERIAL VEHICLES

CISR • Heavy 5+ CH-4B

ISR • Heavy BZK-005; BZK-009 (reported); **Medium** BZK-006 (incl variants); BZK-007; BZK-008

OWA *Harpy*

AIR DEFENCE

SAM 754+

Medium-range 250 HQ-16A/B (CH-SA-16)

Short-range 504: 24 9K331 *Tor*-M1 (RS-SA-15 *Gauntlet*); 30 HQ-6D (CH-SA-6); 200 HQ-7A/B (CH-SA-4); 200 HQ-17 (CH-SA-15A); 50 HQ-17A (CH-SA-15B)

Point-defence HN-5A/B (CH-SA-3); FN-6 (CH-SA-10); QW-1 (CH-SA-7); QW-2 (CH-SA-8)

SPAAGM 25mm 270 PGZ-04A

GUNS 7,126+

SP 126: **30mm** some PGL-19; **35mm** 120 PGZ-07; **37mm** 6 PGZ-88

TOWED 7,000+: **25mm** PG-87; **35mm** PG-99 (GDF-002); **37mm** PG-55 (M-1939)/PG-65/PG-74; **57mm** PG-59 (S-60); **100mm** PG-59 (KS-19)

AIR-LAUNCHED MISSILES

AAM • IR AKK-90

ASM AKD-8; AKD-9; AKD-10; CM-501GA; CM-502KG; LJ-21

Navy ε252,000

The PLA Navy is organised into five service arms: submarine, surface, naval aviation, coastal defence and marine corps, as well as other specialised units. There are three fleets, one each in the Eastern, Southern and Northern theatre commands

EQUIPMENT BY TYPE

SUBMARINES 59

STRATEGIC • SSBN 6 Type-094 (*Jin*) with up to 12 JL-2 (CH-SS-N-14)/JL-3 (CH-SS-N-20) nuclear SLBMs, 6 single 533mm TT with Yu-6 HWT

TACTICAL 53

SSN 6:

2 Type-093 (*Shang* I) with 6 single 533mm TT with YJ-82 (CH-SS-N-7) AShM or YJ-18 (CH-SS-N-13) AShM/Yu-3 HWT/Yu-6 HWT

4 Type-093A (*Shang* II) with 6 single 533mm TT with YJ-82 (CH-SS-N-7) AShM or YJ-18 (CH-SS-N-13) AShM/Yu-3 HWT/Yu-6 HWT

(3 Type-091 (*Han*) in reserve with 6 single 533mm TT with YJ-82 (CH-SS-N-7) AShM/Yu-3 HWT)

SSK 46:

2 Project 636 (Improved *Kilo*) with 6 single 533mm TT with TEST-71ME HWT/53-65KE HWT

8 Project 636M (Improved *Kilo*) with 6 single 533mm TT with TEST-71ME HWT/53-65KE HWT/3M54E *Klub*-S (RS-SS-N-27B *Sizzler*) AShM

4 Type-035B (*Ming*) with 8 single 533mm TT with Yu-3 HWT/Yu-4 HWT

12 Type-039(G) (*Song*) with 6 single 533mm TT with YJ-82 (CH-SS-N-7) AShM or YJ-18 (CH-SS-N-13) AShM/Yu-3 HWT/Yu-6 HWT

4 Type-039A (*Yuan*) (fitted with AIP) with 6 533mm TT with YJ-82 (CH-SS-N-7) AShM or YJ-18 (CH-SS-N-13) AShM/Yu-3 HWT/Yu-6 HWT

14 Type-039B (*Yuan*) (fitted with AIP) with 6 533mm TT with YJ-82 (CH-SS-N-7) AShM or YJ-18 (CH-SS-N-13) AShM/Yu-3 HWT/Yu-6 HWT

2 Type-039B mod (*Yuan*) (fitted with AIP) with 6 533mm TT with YJ-82 (CH-SS-N-7) AShM or YJ-18 (CH-SS-N-13) AShM/Yu-3 HWT/Yu-6 HWT

(up to 10 Type-035(G) (*Ming*) in reserve with 8 single 533mm TT with Yu-3 HWT/Yu-4 HWT)

SSB 1 Type-032 (*Qing*) (SLBM trials)

PRINCIPAL SURFACE COMBATANTS 102
AIRCRAFT CARRIERS • CV 2:
1 Type-001 (*Kuznetsov*) with 3 18-cell GMLS with HHQ-10 (CH-SA-N-17) SAM, 2 RBU 6000 *Smerch* 2 A/S mor, 3 H/PJ-11 CIWS (capacity 18–24 J-15 ac; 17 Ka-28/Ka-31/Z-8S/Z-8JH/Z-8AEW hel)
1 Type-002 (*Kuznetsov* mod) with 3 18-cell GMLS with HHQ-10 (CH-SA-N-17) SAM, 2 RBU 6000 *Smerch* 2 A/S mor, 3 H/PJ-11 CIWS (capacity 32 J-15 ac; 12 Ka-28/Ka-31/Z-8S/Z-8JH/Z-8AEW hel)
CRUISERS • CGHM 8 Type-055 (*Renhai*) with 14 8-cell VLS (8 fore, 6 aft) with YJ-18A (CH-SS-N-13) AShM/HHQ-9B (CH-SA-N-21) SAM/Yu-8 A/S msl, 1 24-cell GMLS with HHQ-10 (CH-SA-N-17) SAM, 2 triple 324mm ASTT with Yu-7 LWT, 1 H/PJ-11 CIWS, 1 130mm gun (capacity 2 med hel)
DESTROYERS 42
DDGHM 40:
2 *Hangzhou* (RUS Project 956EM (*Sovremenny* II)) with 2 quad lnchr with 3M80MVE *Moskit*-E (RS-SS-N-22B *Sunburn*) AShM, 2 single 3S90E lnchr with 9M38E M-22E *Shtil* (RS-SA-N-7 *Gadfly*) SAM, 2 twin 533mm DTA-53-956 ASTT with SET-65KE HWT/53-65KE HWT, 2 RBU 1000 *Smerch* 3 A/S mor, 2 *Kashtan* (RS-CADS-N-1) CIWS, 1 twin 130mm gun (capacity 1 Z-9C/Ka-28 *Helix* A hel)
2 *Hangzhou* (RUS Project 956E (*Sovremenny* III)) with 2 quad lnchr with YJ-12A AShM, 4 8-cell H/AJK-16 VLS with HHQ-16 (CH-SA-N-16) SAM/Yu-8 A/S msl, 2 triple 324mm ASTT with Yu-7 LWT, 4 AK630M CIWS, 2 twin 130mm gun (capacity 1 Z-9C/Ka-28 *Helix* A hel)
1 Type-051B (*Luhai*) with 4 quad lnchr with YJ-12A AShM, 4 8-cell H/AJK-16 VLS with HHQ-16 (CH-SA-N-16) SAM/Yu-8 A/S msl, 2 triple 324mm ASTT with Yu-7 LWT, 2 H/PJ-11 CIWS, 1 twin 100mm gun (capacity 2 Z-9C/Ka-28 *Helix* A hel)
2 Type-052 (*Luhu*) with 4 quad lnchr with YJ-83 AShM, 1 octuple lnchr with HHQ-7 (CH-SA-N-4) SAM, 2 triple 324mm ASTT with Yu-7 LWT, 2 FQF 2500 A/S mor, 2 H/PJ-12 CIWS, 1 twin 100mm gun (capacity 2 Z-9C hel)
2 Type-052B (*Luyang* I) (in refit) with 4 quad lnchr with YJ-83 AShM, 2 single 3S90E lnchr with 9M317E *Shtil*-1 (RS-SA-N-7B) SAM, 2 triple 324mm ASTT with Yu-7 LWT, 2 H/PJ-12 CIWS, 1 100mm gun (capacity 1 Ka-28 *Helix* A hel)
6 Type-052C (*Luyang* II) (of which 1 in refit) with 2 quad lnchr with YJ-62 AShM, 8 8-cell VLS with HHQ-9 (CH-SA-N-9) SAM (CH-SA-N-9), 2 triple 324mm ASTT with Yu-7 LWT, 2 H/PJ-12 CIWS, 1 100mm gun (capacity 2 Ka-28 *Helix* A hel)
10 Type-052D (*Luyang* III) with 8 8-cell VLS with YJ-18A (CH-SS-N-13) AShM/HHQ-9B (CH-SA-N-21) SAM/Yu-8 A/S msl, 1 24-cell GMLS with HHQ-10 (CH-SA-N-17) SAM, 2 triple 324mm ASTT with Yu-7 LWT, 1 H/PJ-12 CIWS, 1 130mm gun (capacity 2 Ka-28 *Helix* A hel)
3 Type-052D (*Luyang* III) with 8 8-cell VLS with YJ-18A (CH-SS-N-13) AShM/HHQ-9B (CH-SA-N-21) SAM/Yu-8 A/S msl, 1 24-cell GMLS with HHQ-10 (CH-SA-N-17) SAM, 2 triple 324mm ASTT with Yu-7 LWT, 1 H/PJ-11 CIWS, 1 130mm gun (capacity 2 Ka-28 *Helix* A hel)
12 Type-052D mod (*Luyang* III mod) with 8 8-cell VLS with YJ-18A (CH-SS-N-13) AShM/HHQ-9B (CH-SA-N-21) SAM/Yu-8 A/S msl, 1 24-cell GMLS with HHQ-10 (CH-SA-N-17) SAM, 2 triple 324mm ASTT with Yu-7 LWT, 1 H/PJ-11 CIWS, 1 130mm gun (capacity 2 Z-9/Z-20 hel)
DDGM 2 Type-051C (*Luzhou*) with 2 quad lnchr with YJ-83 AShM; 6 6-cell B-204 VLS with S-300FM *Rif*-M (RS-SA-N-20 *Gargoyle*) SAM, 2 H/PJ-12 CIWS, 1 100mm gun, 1 hel landing platform
FRIGATES • FFGHM 50
2 Type-053H3 (*Jiangwei* II) with 2 quad lnchr with YJ-83 AShM, 1 octuple lnchr with HHQ-7 (CH-SA-N-4) SAM, 2 RBU 1200 A/S mor, 1 twin 100mm gun (capacity 1 Z-9C hel)
6 Type-053H3 (*Jiangwei* II Upgrade) with 2 quad lnchr with YJ-83 AShM, 1 8-cell GMLS with HHQ-10 (CH-SA-N-17) SAM, 2 RBU 1200 A/S mor, 1 twin 100mm gun (capacity 1 Z-9C hel)
2 Type-054 (*Jiangkai*) with 2 quad lnchr with YJ-83 AShM, 1 24-cell GMLS with HHQ-10 (CH-SA-N-17) SAM, 2 triple 324mm ASTT with Yu-7 LWT, 2 RBU 1200 A/S mor, 4 AK630 CIWS, 1 100mm gun (capacity 1 Ka-28 *Helix* A/Z-9C hel)
40 Type-054A (*Jiangkai* II) with 2 quad lnchr with YJ-83 AShM, 4 8-cell VLS with Yu-8 A/S msl/HHQ-16 (CH-SA-N-16) SAM, 2 triple 324mm ASTT with Yu-7 LWT, 2 FQF 3200 A/S mor, 2 H/PJ-11/12 CIWS, 1 76mm gun (capacity 1 Ka-28 *Helix* A/Z-9C hel)
PATROL AND COASTAL COMBATANTS 142+
CORVETTES • FSGM 50 Type-056A (*Jiangdao*) with 2 twin lnchr with YJ-83 AShM, 1 8-cell GMLS with HHQ-10 (CH-SA-N-17) SAM, 2 triple 324mm ASTT with Yu-7 LWT, 1 76mm gun, 1 hel landing platform
PCFG ε60 Type-022 (*Houbei*) with 2 quad lnchr with YJ-83 AShM, 1 H/PJ-13 CIWS
PCG ε22: (some Type-037-II (*Houjian*) with 2 triple lnchr with YJ-8 (CH-SS-N-4) AShM; some Type-037-IG (*Houxin*) with 2 twin lnchr with YJ-8 (CH-SS-N-4) AShM)
PCC some Type-037-IS (*Haiqing*) with 2 FQF-3200 A/S mor
PB up to 10 Type-062-1 (*Shanghai* III)
MINE WARFARE • MINE COUNTERMEASURES 40:
MCO 24: 4 Type-081 (*Wochi*); 10+ Type-081A (*Wochi* mod); 10+ Type-082-II (*Wozang*)
MSC 16: 4 Type-082 (*Wosao*); 12 Type-082-I (*Wosao* II)
AMPHIBIOUS
PRINCIPAL AMPHIBIOUS SHIPS 11:
LHD 3 Type-075 (*Yushen*) with 2 24-cell GMLS with HHQ-10 (CH-SA-N-17) SAM, 2 H/PJ-11 CIWS (capacity 3 Type-726 (*Yuyi*) LCAC; 800 troops; 60+ AFV; 28 hel)
LPD 8 Type-071 (*Yuzhao*) with 4 AK630 CIWS, 1

76mm gun (capacity 4 Type-726 (*Yuyi*) LCAC plus supporting vehicles; 800 troops; 60 AFV; 4 hel)

LANDING SHIPS 39
  LST 25:
    1 Type-072-IIG (*Yukan*) (capacity 2 LCVP; 10 tk; 200 troops)
    9 Type-072-II/III (*Yuting* I) (capacity 10 tk; 250 troops; 2 hel)
    9 Type-072A (*Yuting* II) (capacity 4 LCVP; 10 tk; 250 troops)
    6 Type-072B (*Yuting* II) (capacity 4 LCVP; 10 tk; 250 troops)
  LSM 14:
    1 Type-073-II (*Yudeng*) with 1 twin 57mm gun (capacity 5 tk or 500 troops)
    10 Type-073A (*Yunshu*) (capacity 6 tk)
    3 Type-074 mod (*Yuhai* mod) (capacity 2 tk, 250 troops)

LANDING CRAFT 82
  LCU 11 Type-074A (*Yubei*) (capacity 10 tanks or 150 troops)
  LCM ε25: 10+ *Yubu*; (some Type-067A (*Yunnan*))
  LCAC 46: 40+ Type-726 (*Yuyi*); 6 *Zubr*

LOGISTICS AND SUPPORT 173
  ABU 1 Type-744A (*Yannan*)
  AFS 1 Type-904A (*Danyao* I)
  AFSH 2 Type-904B (*Danyao* II)
  AG 7: 1 *Kanwu*; 6 Type-639 (*Kanhai*)
  AGB 2 Type-272 (*Yanrao*) with 1 hel landing platform
  AGE 11: 2 Type-909 (*Dahua*) with 1 hel landing platform (weapons test platform); 3+ *Dubei*; 1 *Kantan*; 4 Type-636 (*Shupang*); 1 *Yuting* I (naval rail gun test ship)
  AGI 17: 1 Type-815 (*Dongdiao*) with 1 hel landing platform; 8 Type-815A (*Dongdiao*) with 1 hel landing platform; 8 FT-14
  AGOR 2 *Dahua*
  AGOS 6 Type-927 (*Dongjian*)
  AGS 9 Type-636A (*Shupang*) with 1 hel landing platform
  AH 9: 5 *Ankang*; 2 Type-919 (*Anshen*); 2 Type-920 (*Anwei*)
  AOEH 2 Type-901 (*Fuyu*) with 2 H/PJ-13 CIWS
  AORH 10: 2 Type-903 (*Fuchi*); 7 Type-903A (*Fuchi* II); 1 Type-908 (*Fusu*)
  AO 22: 4 *Fubai*; 16 Type-632 (*Fujian*); 2 Type-637 (*Fuxiao*)
  AOL 6 Type-631 (*Fuchang*)
  AP 4: 2 *Daguan*; 2 *Darong*
  ARC 3 *Youlan*
  ARS 24: 7 *Datuo*; 6 *Hai Jiu* 101 with 1 hel landing platform; 1 Type-648 (*Dadao*); 3 Type-917 (*Dasan*); 1 Type-922-III (*Dalang* II); 3 Type-922-IIIA (*Dalang* III); 2 Type-946 (*Dazhou*); 1 Type-946A (*Dadong*)
  ASR 7: 1 *Dalao* mod; 3 Type-926 (*Dalao*); 3 Type-925 (*Dajiang*) (capacity 2 Z-8)
  ATF 14: 3 *Tuqiang*; ε11 Type-837 (*Hujing*)
  AWT 9+: 3 *Fushi*; 2 *Fuzi*; (some *Fuzi* mod); 4 Type-632 (*Fujian*)
  AX 3:
    1 Type-679 (*Daxin*) with 2 FQF 1200 A/S mor, 1 57mm gun, 1 hel landing platform
    1 Type-680 (*Dadu*) with 1 76mm gun, 1 hel landing platform
    1 Type-891A (*Dashi*) with 2 hel landing platforms
  AXS 1 *Polang*
  ESD 1 *Donghaidao*

UNINHABITED MARITIME PLATFORMS
  USV 32+
    MARSEC 2+: 1 JARI; 1 JARI mod; Others
    MW 30+ Type-529 (*Wonang*) (operated by *Wozang* MCO)
  UUV • UTL • Extra-Large 2 HSU001

UNINHABITED MARITIME SYSTEMS
  UUV • DATA *Haiyi* 300; *Haiyi* 1000-I/II

COASTAL DEFENCE • AShM 72 YJ-12/YJ-62 (3 regt)

Naval Aviation 18,000
FORCES BY ROLE
FIGHTER/GROUND ATTACK
  1 bde with J-11B/BS *Flanker* L
  3 bde with J-15/J-15T *Flanker* K
ANTI-SUBMARINE WARFARE
  2 regt with Y-9 ASW
  2 hel regt with Z-9C; Z-9D; Z-18F
ELINT/ISR/ASW
  1 regt with Y-8JB/X; Y-9JZ; Y-9 ASW
AIRBORNE EARLY WARNING & CONTROL
  3 regt with Y-8J; KJ-200; KJ-500
TRANSPORT
  1 regt with Y-7H; Y-8C; CRJ-200/700
TRAINING
  1 regt with CJ-6A
  1 regt with HY-7
  2 regt with JL-8
  1 regt with JL-9G
  1 regt with JL-9
  1 regt with JL-10
  1 hel regt with Z-9C
HELICOPTER
  1 regt with Ka-27PS; Ka-28; Ka-31
  1 regt with AS365N; Z-9C/D; Z-8J/JH
  1 regt with Y-7G; Z-8; Z-8J; Z-8S; Z-9C/D
ISR UAV
  1 regt with BZK-005

EQUIPMENT BY TYPE
AIRCRAFT 219 combat capable
  FGA 120: ε50 J-11B/BS *Flanker* L; ε60 J-15 *Flanker* K; 10+ J-15T *Flanker* K
  ASW 25+ Y-9 ASW
  EW ε6 J-15D *Flanker**
  ELINT 17: 4 Y-8JB *High New* 2; 3 Y-8X; 10 Y-9JZ

AEW&C 30: 6 KJ-200 *Moth*; 20+ KJ-500; 4 Y-8J *Mask*
TPT 38: **Medium** 6 Y-8C; **Light** 28: 20 Y-5; 2 Y-7G; 6 Y-7H; **PAX** 4: 2 CRJ-200; 2 CRJ-700
TRG 118: 38 CJ-6; 12 HY-7; 16 JL-8*; 28 JL-9*; 12 JL-9G*; 12 JL-10*

HELICOPTERS
ASW 38: 14 Ka-28 *Helix* A; 14 Z-9C; 10 Z-18F
AEW 13: 9 Ka-31; 4+ Z-18 AEW
MRH 18: 7 AS365N; 11 Z-9D
SAR 11: 3 Ka-27PS; 4 Z-8JH; 2 Z-8S; 2 Z-9S
TPT 42: **Heavy** 34: 8 SA321 *Super Frelon*; 9 Z-8; 13 Z-8J; 4 Z-18; **Medium** 8 Mi-8 *Hip*

UNINHABITED AERIAL VEHICLES
ISR • **Heavy** BZK-005; WZ-7; **Medium** BZK-007

AIR-LAUNCHED MISSILES
AAM • **IR** PL-8; PL-9; **IR/SARH** R-27 (RS-AA-10 *Alamo*); **SARH** PL-11; **ARH** PL-12 (CH-AA-7A *Adze*; PL-12A (CH-AA-7B *Adze*); R-77 (RS-AA-12A *Adder*); R-77-1 (RS-AA-12B *Adder*)
ASM KD-88
AShM YJ-8K; YJ-83K; YJ-9; YJ-12
ARM YJ-91

BOMBS
Laser-guided: LS-500J; LT-2

Marines ε35,000
FORCES BY ROLE
SPECIAL FORCES
1 spec ops bde
MANOEUVRE
Amphibious
6 mne bde
HELICOPTER
1 bde with Z-8C
EQUIPMENT BY TYPE
ARMOURED FIGHTING VEHICLES
LT TK 80+: ε80 ZTD-05; some ZTQ-15
ASLT ε50 ZTL-11
IFV ε150 ZBL-08
AAV ε240 ZBD-05
ANTI-TANK/ANTI-INFRASTRUCTURE
MSL • **MANPATS** HJ-73; HJ-8
RCL 120mm Type-98
ARTILLERY 40+
SP 122mm 40+: 20+ PLZ-07; 20+ PLZ-89
MRL 107mm PH-63
MOR 82mm PP-87
HELICOPTERS
TPT • **Heavy** 28 Z-8C
AIR DEFENCE • **SAM** • **Point-defence** HN-5 (CH-SA-3); FN-6 (CH-SA-10); QW-2 (CH-SA-8)

Air Force 403,000
FORCES BY ROLE

BOMBER
2 regt with H-6DU/G/J
1 regt with H-6H
5 regt with H-6K
1 regt with H-6M; WZ-8
1 bde with H-6N (forming)

FIGHTER
1 bde with J-7 *Fishcan*
5 bde with J-7E/G *Fishcan*
1 bde with J-11A/Su-27UBK *Flanker*
3 bde with J-11A/J-11B/Su-27UBK *Flanker*
2 bde with J-11B/BG/BS *Flanker* L

FIGHTER/GROUND ATTACK
1 bde with J-8F *Finback*; JH-7A *Flounder*
5 bde with J-10A/S *Firebird*
1 bde with J-10A/S *Firebird*; Su-30MK2/MKK *Flanker* G
1 bde with J-10B/S *Firebird*
7 bde with J-10C/S *Firebird*
1 bde with J-11B/BG/BS *Flanker* L; JH-7A *Flounder*
11 bde with J-16 *Flanker* N
1 bde with J-16 *Flanker* N; Su-30MKK *Flanker* G; Su-35 *Flanker* M
8 bde with J-20A
1 bde with Su-30MKK *Flanker* G

GROUND ATTACK
5 bde with JH-7A *Flounder*

ELECTRONIC WARFARE
4 regt with KJ-500; Y-8CB/DZ/G/XZ; Y-9G/XZ

ISR
1 regt with JZ-8F *Finback**
1 bde with JZ-8F *Finback**

AIRBORNE EARLY WARNING & CONTROL
2 bde with KJ-500; Y-9LG; Y-9Z
1 regt with KJ-500; Y-9Z
1 regt with KJ-200 *Moth*; KJ-2000; Y-8T

SEARCH & RESCUE
4 bde with Mi-171E; Y-5; Y-7; Y-8; Z-8; Z-9; Z-20S
1 regt with Mi-171E; Y-7; Y-9; Z-8

TANKER
1 bde with H-6U

TRANSPORT
1 regt with Il-76MD/TD *Candid*; Il-78 *Midas*
1 regt with Y-7
2 regt with Y-9 *Claw*
3 regt with Y-20A; YY-20A
1 (VIP) regt with A319; B-737; CRJ-200/-700

TRAINING
5 bde with CJ-6/6A/6B; Y-5
3 bde with J-7; JJ-7A
14 bde with JJ-7A; JL-8; JL-9; JL-10; J-10AS
1 bde with Y-7; Y-8C

TRANSPORT HELICOPTER
  1 (VIP) regt with AS332 *Super Puma*; H225
ISR UAV
  2 bde with GJ-1; GJ-2
  1 regt with WZ-7; WZ-10
AIR DEFENCE
  1 SAM div (3 SAM regt)
  26 SAM bde
EQUIPMENT BY TYPE
  AIRCRAFT 2,989 combat capable
    BBR 219: ε12 H-6A (trg role); 27 H-6G/G mod; 18 H-6J ε40 H-6H/M; ε110 H-6K; 12+ H-6N
    FTR 456: 50 J-7 *Fishcan*; 119 J-7E *Fishcan*; 120 J-7G *Fishcan*; 40 J-8F/H *Finback*; 95 J-11; 32 Su-27UBK *Flanker*
    FGA 1,409: 236 J-10A *Firebird* A; 55 J-10B *Firebird*; 240 J-10C *Firebird* C; 77 J-10S *Firebird*; 110 J-11B/BS *Flanker* L; 40 J-11BG *Flanker*; 300 J-16 *Flanker* N; 230+ J-20A; 24 Su-30MK2 *Flanker* G; 73 Su-30MKK *Flanker* G; 24 Su-35 *Flanker* M
    ATK 200 JH-7A *Flounder*
    EW 34: ε12 J-16D *Flanker**; 4 Y-8CB *High New* 1; 2 Y-8DZ; 9 Y-8G *High New* 3; 2 Y-8XZ *High New* 7; 3 Y-9G; 2 Y-9XZ
    ELINT 10: 4 Tu-154M/D *Careless*; 2 Y-9LG; 4 Y-9Z
    ISR 48: 24 JZ-8 *Finback**; 24 JZ-8F *Finback**
    AEW&C 48: 4 KJ-200 *Moth*; 40 KJ-500; 4 KJ-2000
    C2 8: 2 B-737; 6 Y-8T *High New* 4
    TKR 18: 10 H-6U; 5 H-6DU; 3 Il-78 *Midas*
    TKR/TPT 17 YY-20A
    TPT 280: **Heavy** 75: 20 Il-76MD/TD *Candid*; 55 Y-20; **Medium** 60: 30 Y-8C; 30 Y-9 *Claw*; **Light** 114: 3 Learjet 35A; 70 Y-5; 41 Y-7/Y-7H; **PAX** 31: 3 A319; 10 B-737 (VIP); 5 CRJ-200; 5 CRJ-700; 8 Tu-154M *Careless*
    TRG 1,057+: 400 CJ-6/-6A/-6B; 12+ HY-7; 50 JJ-7*; 150 JJ-7A*; 350 JL-8*; 45 JL-9*; 50+ JL-10*
  HELICOPTERS
    SAR 20+ Z-20S
    MRH 22: 20 Z-9; 2 Mi-17V-5 *Hip* H
    TPT 31+: **Heavy** 18+ Z-8; **Medium** 13+: 6+ AS332 *Super Puma* (VIP); 3 H225 (VIP); 4+ Mi-171
  UNINHABITED AERIAL VEHICLES
    CISR • Heavy 12+: 12+ GJ-1; some GJ-2; GJ-11 (in test)
    ISR • Heavy 14+: 12+ WZ-7; 2+ WZ-8; some WZ-10 (ELINT/ISR)
  AIR DEFENCE
    SAM 898+
      Long-range 670+: 196 HQ-9 (CH-SA-9); 96 HQ-9B (CH-SA-21); 130+ HQ-22 (CH-SA-20); 32 S-300PMU (RS-SA-10 *Grumble*); 64 S-300PMU1 (RS-SA-20 *Gargoyle*); 120 S-300PMU2 (RS-SA-20 *Gargoyle*); 32 S-400 (RS-SA-21B *Growler*)
      Medium-range 150 HQ-12 (CH-SA-12)
      Short-range 78+: 50+ HQ-6A (CH-SA-6); 24 HQ-6D (CH-SA-6); 4+ HQ-11

  GUNS • TOWED • 57mm PG-59 (S-60)
AIR-LAUNCHED MISSILES
  AAM • IR PL-5B/C; PL-8; PL-9; R-73 (RS-AA-11A *Archer*); **IIR** PL-10 (CH-AA-9); **IR/SARH** R-27 (RS-AA-10 *Alamo*); **SARH** PL-11; **ARH** PL-12 (CH-AA-7A *Adze*); PL-12A (CH-AA-7B *Adze*); PL-15 (CH-AA-10 *Abaddon*); PL-17 (CH-AA-X-12) (entering service); R-77 (RS-AA-12A *Adder*); R-77-1 (RVV-SD) (RS-AA-12B *Adder*)
  ASM AKD-9; AKD-10; AR-1/2; CM-502KG; KD-88; Kh-29 (RS-AS-14 *Kedge*); Kh-59M (RS-AS-18 *Kazoo*)
  AShM Kh-31A (RS-AS-17B *Krypton*); YJ-12; YJ-8K; YJ-83K; YJ-83KH
  ARM Kh-31P (RS-AS-17A *Krypton*); YJ-91 (domestically produced Kh-31P variant)
  LACM • Conventional CJ-20; YJ(KD)-63
BOMBS
  Laser-guided: FT-7A; LS-500J; LT-2
  INS/GPS-guided: FT-7; FT-9
  EO-guided: KAB-500KR; KAB-1500KR

Airborne Corps
FORCES BY ROLE
SPECIAL FORCES
  1 spec ops bde
MANOEUVRE
  Air Manoeuvre
  5 AB bde
  1 air aslt bde
COMBAT SERVICE SUPPORT
  1 spt bde
TRANSPORT
  1 bde with Y-5; Y-7; Y-8; Y-12
HELICOPTER
  1 regt with WZ-10K; Z-8KA; Z-9WZ; Z-20K
EQUIPMENT BY TYPE
  ARMOURED FIGHTING VEHICLES
    ABCV 180 ZBD-03
    APC • APC (T) 4 ZZZ-03 (CP)
    AUV CS/VN3 mod
  ANTI-TANK/ANTI-INFRASTRUCTURE
    SP some HJ-9
  ARTILLERY 162+
    TOWED 122mm ε54 PL-96 (D-30)
    MRL 107mm ε54 PH-63
    MOR 54+: **82mm** some; **100mm** 54
  AIRCRAFT • TPT 40: **Medium** 6 Y-8; **Light** 34: 20 Y-5; 2 Y-7; 12 Y-12D
  HELICOPTERS
    ATK 8 WZ-10K
    CSAR 8 Z-8KA
    MRH 12 Z-9WZ
    TPT • Medium 6 Z-20K
  AIR DEFENCE

SAM • **Point-defence** QW-1 (CH-SA-7)
GUNS • **TOWED 25mm** 54 PG-87
AIR-LAUNCHED MISSILES
AAM • **IR** AKK-90
ASM AKD-8; AKD-9; AKD-10; LJ-21

Aerospace Force

The Aerospace Force was created from the former Aerospace Systems Department of the Strategic Support Force in 2024 and is responsible for the PLA's space capabilities

EQUIPMENT BY TYPE

SATELLITES see Space

REUSABLE SPACECRAFT see Space

COUNTERSPACE see Space

LOGISTICS AND SUPPORT • **AGM** 4 Type-718 (*Yuan Wang*) (space and missile tracking)

Cyberspace Force

The Cyberspace Force was created from the former Network Systems Department of the Strategic Support Force in 2024 and is responsible for the PLA's cyber capabilities

Information Support Force

The Information Support Force was formed in 2024 from elements of the former Strategic Support Force

Joint Logistics Support Force

The Joint Logistics Support Force was established in 2016 to oversee the operational aspects of the PLA's logistics requirements

Theatre Commands

Eastern Theatre Command

Eastern Theatre Ground Forces

71st Group Army
(1 spec ops bde, 4 armd bde, 1 mech inf bde, 1 inf bde, 1 arty bde, 1 engr/NBC bde bde, 1 spt bde, 1 hel bde, 1 AD bde)

72nd Group Army
(1 spec ops bde, 1 armd bde, 2 mech inf bde, 1 inf bde, 2 amph bde, 1 arty bde, 1 MRL bde, 1 engr bde, 1 NBC bde, 1 spt bde, 1 hel bde)

73rd Group Army
(1 spec ops bde, 1 armd bde, 1 mech inf bde, 2 inf bde, 2 amph bde, 1 arty bde, 1 engr/NBC bde, 1 spt bde, 1 hel bde, 1 AD bde)

Other Forces
(1 CISR UAV bde)

Eastern Theatre Navy

Coastal defence from south of Lianyungang to Dongshan (approx. 35°10′N to 23°30′N), and to seaward; HQ at Ningbo; support bases at Fujian, Zhoushan, Ningbo
18 **SSK**; 16 **DDGHM**; 25 **FFGHM**; 2 **FSGM**; ε24 **PCFG/PCG**; 14 **MCMV**; 2 **LHD**; 3 **LPD**; ε16 **LSM/LST**

Eastern Theatre Navy Aviation

1st Naval Aviation Division
(1 AEW&C regt with KJ-500; 1 ASW regt with Y-9 ASW)

Other Forces
(1 hel regt with Ka-27PS; Ka-28; Ka-31; 1 UAV regt with BZK-005)

Eastern Theatre Air Force

10th Bomber Division
(2 bbr regt with H-6K; 1 bbr regt with H-6M/WZ-8)

26th Special Mission Division
(1 AEW&C regt with KJ-500; 1 AEW&C regt with KJ-200/KJ-2000/Y-8T)

Fuzhou Base
(1 FGA bde with J-10C; 1 FGA bde with J-16; 1 FGA bde with J-20A; 1 FGA bde with Su-30MKK; 3 SAM bde)

Shanghai Base
(1 ftr bde with J-11B; 1 FGA bde with J-10A; Su-30MK2; 2 FGA bde with J-16; 2 FGA bde with J-20A; 2 atk bde with JH-7A; 1 trg bde with J-10/JL-10; Su-27UBK; 2 SAM bde)

Other Forces
(1 bbr regt with H-6DU/G/J; 1 ISR bde with JZ-8F; 1 SAR bde; 1 Flight Instructor Training Base with CJ-6/JL-8/JL-9/JL-10)

Other Forces

Marines
(2 mne bde)

Southern Theatre Command

Southern Theatre Ground Forces

74th Group Army
(1 spec ops bde, 1 armd bde, 1 mech inf bde, 2 inf bde, 2 amph bde, 1 arty bde, 1 engr bde, 1 NBC bde, 1 spt bde, 1 hel bde, 1 AD bde)

75th Group Army
(1 spec ops bde, 2 armd bde, 1 mech inf bde, 3 inf bde, 1 air aslt bde, 1 arty bde, 1 engr/NBC bde, 1 spt bde, 1 AD bde)

Other Forces
(1 (composite) inf bde (Hong Kong); 1 hel sqn (Hong Kong), 1 AD bn (Hong Kong))

Southern Theatre Navy

Coastal defence from Dongshan (approx. 23°30′N) to VNM border, and to seaward (including Paracel and Spratly islands); HQ at Zhanjiang; support bases at Yulin, Guangzhou

6 **SSBN**; 2 **SSN**; 16 **SSK**; 1 **CV**; 4 **CGHM**; 14 **DDGHM**; 14 **FFGHM**; 20 **FSGM**; ε30 **PCFG/PCG**; 13 **MCMV**; 1 **LHD**; 5 **LPD**; ε20 **LSM/LST**

Southern Theatre Navy Aviation

3rd Naval Aviation Division
(1 ASW regt with Y-9 ASW; 1 AEW&C regt with KJ-500)
Other Forces
(1 FGA bde with J-11B; 1 FGA bde with J-15; 1 tpt/hel regt with Y-7G; Z-8; Z-8J; Z-8S; Z-9C/D)

Southern Theatre Air Force

8th Bomber Division
(2 bbr regt with H-6K)
20th Special Mission Division
(3 EW regt with KJ-500; Y-8CB/DZ/G/XZ; Y-9G/LG/XZ)
Kunming Base
(1 FGA bde with J-10A; 1 FGA bde with J-10C; 1 trg bde with JJ-7A; 1 SAM bde)
Nanning Base
(1 ftr bde with J-11A; 1 FGA bde with J-11B; JH-7A; 1 FGA bde with J-10A; 3 FGA bde with J-16; 1 FGA bde with J-16; Su-30MKK; Su-35; 1 FGA bde with J-20A; 1 atk bde with JH-7A; 3 SAM bde)
Other Forces
(1 bbr regt with H-6DU/G/J; 1 tkr bde with H-6U; 1 SAR bde; 1 UAV bde)

Other Forces

Marines
(1 spec ops bde; 2 mne bde)

Western Theatre Command

Western Theatre Ground Forces

76th Group Army
(1 spec ops bde, 3 armd bde, 2 inf bde, 1 arty bde, 1 MRL bde, 1 engr/NBC bde, 1 spt bde, 1 hel bde, 1 AD bde)
77th Group Army
(1 spec ops bde, 2 armd bde, 1 mech inf bde; 3 inf bde, 1 arty bde, 1 engr bde, 1 NBC bde, 1 spt bde, 1 hel bde, 1 AD bde)
Xinjiang Military District
(1 spec ops bde, 1 (high alt) mech div, 3 (high alt) inf div, 2 mech inf regt, 1 arty bde, 1 AD bde, 1 engr/NBC bde, 1 hel bde)
Xizang Military District
(1 spec ops bde; 2 armd bde; 2 inf bde; 1 arty bde, 1 AD bde, 1 engr/NBC bde, 1 hel bde)

Western Theatre Air Force

4th Transport Division
(2 tpt regt with Y-9; 1 tpt regt with Y-20A)
Lanzhou Base
(1 ftr bde with J-11A/B; 1 FGA bde with J-10C; 1 FGA bde with J-16; 1 FGA bde with J-20A; 1 SAM bde)

Urumqi Base
(1 ftr bde with J-11A/B; 1 FGA bde with J-16; 1 FGA bde with J-20A; 1 atk bde with JH-7A; 2 SAM bde)
Lhasa Base
(1 SAM bde)
Xi'an Flying Academy
(1 trg bde with JJ-7A; 1 trg bde with JL-9A; 2 trg bde with JL-8; 1 trg bde with Y-7; Y-8)
Other Forces
(1 AEW&C bde with KJ-500; 1 SAR regt)

Northern Theatre Command

Northern Theatre Ground Forces

78th Group Army
(1 spec ops bde, 4 armd bde, 1 mech inf bde, 1 inf bde, 1 arty bde, 1 engr/NBC bde, 1 spt bde, 1 hel bde, 1 AD bde)
79th Group Army
(1 spec ops bde, 4 armd bde, 1 mech inf bde, 1 inf bde, 1 arty bde, 1 engr bde, 1 NBC bde, 1 spt bde, 1 hel bde, 1 AD bde)
80th Group Army
(1 spec ops bde, 1 armd bde; 2 mech inf bde, 3 inf bde, 1 arty bde, 1 engr/NBC bde, 1 spt bde, 1 hel bde, 1 AD bde)

Northern Theatre Navy

Coastal defence from the DPRK border (Yalu River) to south of Lianyungang (approx 35°10′N), and to seaward; HQ at Qingdao; support bases at Lushun, Qingdao.
4 **SSN**; 12 **SSK**; 1 **CV**; 4 **CGHM**; 10 **DDGHM**; 2 **DDGM**; 11 **FFGHM**; 10 **FSGM**; ε18 **PCFG/PCG**; 9 **MCMV**; ε2 **LST**

Northern Theatre Navy Aviation

2nd Naval Air Division
(1 EW/ISR/ASW regt with Y-8JB/X; Y-9JZ; Y-9 ASW; 1 AEW&C regt with Y-8J; KJ-200; KJ-500)
Other Forces
(1 FGA bde with J-15; 1 hel regt with AS365N; Z-8J/JH; Z-9C/D; 1 tpt regt with Y-7H/Y-8C/CRJ-200/CRJ-700; 1 trg regt with CJ-6A; 2 trg regt with JL-8; 1 trg regt with HY-7; 1 trg regt with JL-9G; 1 trg regt with JL-9; 1 trg regt with JL-10)

Northern Theatre Air Force

16th Special Mission Division
(1 EW regt with Y-8CB/G/Y-9LG; 1 ISR regt with JZ-8F; 1 UAV regt with WZ-7/WZ-10)
Dalian Base
(1 ftr bde with J-7; 1 ftr bde with J-7E; 1 FGA bde with J-10B; 1 FGA bde with J-10C; 2 FGA bde with J-16; 1 FGA bde with J-20A; 1 atk bde with JH-7A; 4 SAM bde)
Jinan Base
(1 FGA bde with J-8F; JH-7A; 1 FGA bde with J-10C; 1 FGA bde with J-16; 2 SAM bde)
Harbin Flying Academy

(1 trg bde with CJ-6/J-11B/JL-9; Y-5; 1 trg bde with H-6; HY-7; 2 trg bde with JL-8; 1 trg bde with JL-9)
Other Forces
(1 SAR bde)

Other Forces
Marines
(2 mne bde; 1 hel bde)

Central Theatre Command
Central Theatre Ground Forces
81st Group Army
(1 spec ops bde, 2 armd bde, 1 (OPFOR) armd bde, 2 mech inf bde, 1 inf bde, 1 arty bde, 1 engr/NBC bde, 1 spt bde, 1 avn bde, 1 AD bde)
82nd Group Army
(1 spec ops bde, 4 armd bde, 1 mech bde, 2 inf bde, 1 arty bde, 1 engr bde, 1 NBC bde, 1 spt bde, 1 hel bde, 1 AD bde)
83rd Group Army
(1 spec ops bde, 2 armd bde, 4 mech inf bde, 1 air aslt bde, 1 arty bde, 1 engr/NBC bde, 1 spt bde, 1 AD bde)
Other Forces
(2 (Beijing) gd div)

Central Theatre Air Force
13th Transport Division
(2 tpt regt with Y-20A; YY-20A; 1 tpt regt with Il-76MD; Il-78)
34th VIP Transport Division
(1 tpt regt with A319; B-737; CRJ200/700; 1 tpt regt with Y-7)
36th Bomber Division
(2 bbr regt with H-6K)
Datong Base
(1 ftr bde with J-7E/G; 1 ftr bde with J-11A/B; 2 FGA bde with J-10A; 2 FGA bde with J-10C; 1 SAM div; 5 SAM bde)
Wuhan Base
(2 ftr bde with J-7E/G; 1 ftr bde with J-11A/B; Su-27UBK; 1 FGA bde with J-20A; 1 trg bde with J-7/JJ-7A; 2 SAM bde)
Shijiazhuang Flying Academy
(3 trg bde with JL-8; 1 trg bde with JL-8; JL-10)
Airborne Corps
(5 AB bde; 1 air aslt bde; 1 tpt bde; 1 hel regt)
Other Forces
(1 bbr bde with H-6N; 1 AEW&C bde with KJ-500; 1 SAR bde)

Gendarmerie & Paramilitary 500,000+ active

People's Armed Police ε500,000
In 2018 the People's Armed Police (PAP) divested its border-defence, firefighting, gold, forest, hydropower and security-guard units. In addition to the forces listed below, PAP also has 32 regional commands each with one or more mobile units

FORCES BY ROLE
MANOEUVRE
  Other
  1 (1st Mobile) paramilitary corps (3 SF regt; 9 (mobile) paramilitary units; 1 engr/CBRN unit; 1 hel unit)
  1 (2nd Mobile) paramilitary corps (2 SF unit; 9 (mobile) paramilitary units; 1 engr/CBRN unit; 1 hel unit)

China Coast Guard (CCG)
In 2018 the CCG was moved from the authority of the State Oceanic Administration to that of the People's Armed Police. The CCG is currently reorganising its pennant-number system, making it problematic to assess the number of vessels that entered service since 2019.

EQUIPMENT BY TYPE
PATROL AND COASTAL COMBATANTS 546
  PSOH 39:
    2 *Zhaotou* with 1 76mm gun (capacity 2 med hel)
    3 Type-053H2G (*Jiangwei* I) (capacity 1 med hel) (ex-PLAN)
    6 Type-054 mod (*Zhaoduan*) with 1 76mm gun (capacity 1 med hel)
    4 *Shuoshi* II (capacity 1 med hel)
    10 *Shucha* II (capacity 1 med hel)
    12 *Zhaoyu* (capacity 1 med hel)
    1 *Zhaochang* (capacity 1 med hel)
    1 *Zhongyang* (capacity 1 med hel)
  PSO 51:
    9 Type-718B (*Zhaojun*) with 1 76mm gun, 1 hel landing platform
    1 Type-922 (*Dalang* I) (ex-PLAN)
    1 Type-625C (*Hai Yang*) (ex-PLAN)
    1 *Haixun*
    1 Type-053H (*Jianghu* I) (ex-PLAN)
    1 Type-636A (*Kanjie*) with 1 hel landing platform (ex-PLAN)
    6 *Shusheng* with 1 hel landing platform
    3 *Shuwu*
    3 *Tuzhong* (ex-PLAN)
    1 Type-918 (*Wolei*) (ex-PLAN)
    1 *Xiang Yang Hong 9* (ex-PLAN)
    3 *Zhaogao* with 1 hel landing platform
    4 *Zhaolai* with 1 hel landing platform
    2 *Zhaolai* II with 1 hel landing platform
    13 *Zhaotim*
    1 *Zhongpa*
  PCOH 22 Type-056 (*Jiangdao*) (ex-PLAN) with 1 76mm gun
  PCO 30: 1 *Shuke* I; 4 *Shuke* II; 15 *Shuke* III; 3 *Shuyou*; 4 *Zhaodai*; 3 *Zhaoming*
  PCC 104: 25+ Type-618B-II; 45 *Hailin* I/II; 1 *Shuzao* II;

14 *Shuzao* III; 10 *Zhongeng*; 2 *Zhongmel*; 7 *Zhongsui*
PB/PBF 300+
AMPHIBIOUS • LANDING SHIPS 2
  LST 2 Type-072-II (*Yuting* I) (ex-PLAN; used as hospital vessels and island supply)
LOGISTICS AND SUPPORT 28
  AG 7: 6+ *Kaobo*; 1 *Shutu*
  AGB 1 Type-210 (*Yanbing*) (ex-PLAN)
  AGOR 8: 3 *Haijian*; 3 *Shuguang* 04 (ex-PLAN); 2 *Xiang Yang Hong* 9
  AKR 1 *Yunsong*
  ATF 11
AIRCRAFT
  MP 2+ MA60H
  TPT • Light ε7 Y-12 (MP role)
HELICOPTERS
  MRH 36: 26 H425; 10+ Z-9
  TPT • Heavy ε5 Z-18

Maritime Militia

Composed of full- and part-time personnel. Reports to PLA command and trains to assist PLAN and CCG in a variety of military roles. These include ISR, maritime law enforcement, island supply, troop transport and supporting sovereignty claims. The Maritime Militia operates a variety of civilian vessels including fishing boats and oil tankers.

DEPLOYMENT

CAMBODIA: 120; 2 FSGM
DEMOCRATIC REPUBLIC OF THE CONGO: UN • MONUSCO 14
DJIBOUTI: 400; 1 spec ops coy; 1 mne coy; 1 med unit; 2 ZTL-11; 8 ZBL-08
GULF OF ADEN: 1 DDGHM; 1 FFGHM; 1 AORH
LEBANON: UN • UNIFIL 418; 2 engr coy; 1 med coy
MIDDLE EAST: UN • UNTSO 5
SOUTH SUDAN: UN • UNMISS 1,051; 1 inf bn; 1 engr coy; 1 fd hospital
SUDAN: UN • UNISFA 284; 1 inf coy; 1 hel flt with 2 Mi-171
TAJIKISTAN: ε300 (trg)
WESTERN SAHARA: UN • MINURSO 6

Fiji FJI

Fijian Dollar FJD		2023	2024	2025
GDP	FJD	12.2bn	13.3bn	14.2bn
	USD	5.44bn	5.77bn	6.08bn
Real GDP growth	%	7.5	3.0	3.4
Def bdgt	FJD	109m	159m	170m
	USD	48.4m	69.0m	72.8m

Real-terms defence budget trend (USDm, constant 2015)

Population	951,611				
Age	0–14	15–19	20–24	25–29	30–64	65 plus
Male	12.6%	4.3%	3.6%	3.8%	22.3%	4.1%
Female	12.1%	4.1%	3.5%	3.6%	21.2%	4.8%

Capabilities

The Republic of Fiji Military Forces (RFMF) has intervened in Fiji's domestic politics, and after a third coup in 2006, democracy was effectively suspended until 2014. Guidelines issued in 2018 emphasised the need to confront non-traditional threats such as climate change, terrorism and transnational crime. The government embarked on a defence review in 2023 and, in September 2024, published its first foreign policy white paper, which called the prospect of an unstable Indo-Pacific the most significant threat to its security. The RFMF is developing a deployable-force headquarters, funded by Australia, which will also administer and train personnel for peacekeeping and HADR roles. It issued a Security Framework in 2023, addressing information-security concerns. International peacekeeping operations are an important source of revenue for the government. Fiji's principal defence relationships are with Australia and New Zealand. A status of forces agreement was signed with Australia in 2022, and with New Zealand and France in 2023. Defence relations with China, South Korea and the US are growing, with all three countries providing training or donating equipment. The RFMF is attempting to improve the quality of senior NCOs and to raise standards across the rest of the force. Fiji has little defence-industrial capability and is only able to carry out basic equipment maintenance domestically. Significant upgrade and maintenance work is usually conducted in Australia.

ACTIVE 4,040 (Army 3,700 Navy 340)
RESERVE ε6,000
(to age 45)

ORGANISATIONS BY SERVICE

Army 3,700 (incl 300 recalled reserves)
FORCES BY ROLE
SPECIAL FORCES
  1 spec ops coy
MANOEUVRE
  Light
    3 inf bn

COMBAT SUPPORT
  1 arty bty
  1 engr bn
COMBAT SUPPORT
  1 log bn

Reserves 6,000
  FORCES BY ROLE
  MANOEUVRE
    Light
    5 inf bn
  EQUIPMENT BY TYPE
  ARMOURED FIGHTING VEHICLES
    AUV 10 *Bushmaster* IMV
  ARTILLERY • MOR 81mm 24 L16

Navy 340
EQUIPMENT BY TYPE
PATROL AND COASTAL COMBATANTS 3
  PCO 3 *Guardian* (AUS *Bay* mod)
LOGISTICS AND SUPPORT 2
  AGS 2: 1 *Kacau*; 1 *Volasiga*

DEPLOYMENT
EGYPT: MFO 170; elm 1 inf bn
IRAQ: UN • UNAMI 157; 2 sy unit
LEBANON: UN • UNIFIL 1
MIDDLE EAST: UN • UNTSO 2
SOUTH SUDAN: UN • UNMISS 2
SYRIA/ISRAEL: UN • UNDOF 149; 1 inf coy

India IND

Indian Rupee INR		2023	2024	2025
GDP	INR	295trn	325trn	359trn
	USD	3.57trn	3.89trn	4.27trn
Real GDP growth	%	8.2	7.0	6.5
Def bdgt [a]	INR	6.24trn	6.22trn	
	USD	75.4bn	74.4bn	

[a] Includes defence civil estimates, which include military pensions

Real-terms defence budget trend (USDbn, constant 2015)

Population	1,409,128,296				
Age	0–14	15–19	20–24	25–29	30–64	65 plus
Male	12.9%	4.5%	4.6%	4.6%	21.8%	3.1%
Female	11.6%	4.1%	4.1%	4.1%	20.9%	3.7%

Capabilities

India's armed forces are orientated towards territorial disputes with Pakistan. India is improving its military infrastructure on its northern border. Mutual reaffirmation of the 2003 ceasefire agreement between India and Pakistan reduced conflict across the Line of Control in the disputed region of Kashmir. A large number of paramilitary forces are also employed for internal security. India is now pivoting towards security concerns posed by China. The government is increasingly focused on Indian Ocean security. Indian forces participate in multilateral exercises and the country is one of the main troop contributors to UN peacekeeping operations. In 2023, India joined the Combined Maritime Forces multi-national maritime partnership. In 2022, India began setting up integrated battlegroups in the border area with China and Pakistan. In May 2024, the Inter-Services Organisations (Command, Control & Discipline) Act was unveiled, amid a move to establish theatre commands, designed to improve integration. India continues to develop its nuclear capabilities. In 2024, India tested its *Agni*-V ICBM, employing MIRVs. India operates significant quantities of Soviet- and Russian-origin equipment, and the two countries cooperate on missile developments. Recent Indian imports of foreign equipment have primarily been from the US and France. India and the US signed a defence and technology cooperation agreement in 2023, as part of wider efforts to strengthen security ties. Recruitment of term-limited personnel continues under the Agnipath scheme. The overall capability of India's large conventional forces is limited by inadequate logistics, shortages of ammunition, spare parts and maintenance personnel. Modernisation projects have seen delays and cost overruns. The government's Make in India policy aims to strengthen the defence-industrial base, but progress is slow with limited foreign direct investment in defence. India seeks to establish itself as a reliable partner for global defence supply chains.

ACTIVE 1,475,750 (Army 1,237,000 Navy 75,500 Air 149,900 Coast Guard 13,350) Gendarmerie & Paramilitary 1,616,050

RESERVE 1,155,000 (Army 960,000 Navy 55,000 Air 140,000) Gendarmerie & Paramilitary 941,000

Army first-line reserves (300,000) within 5 years of full-time service, further 500,000 have commitment to age 50

ORGANISATIONS BY SERVICE

Strategic Forces Command

Strategic Forces Command (SFC) is a tri-service command established in 2003. The commander-in-chief of SFC, a senior three-star military officer, manages and administers all strategic forces through army, navy and air-force chains of command

FORCES BY ROLE
SURFACE-TO-SURFACE MISSILE
  1 SRBM bde with *Agni* I
  1 IRBM bde with *Agni* II/III
  2 SRBM bde with SS-250 *Prithvi* II
EQUIPMENT BY TYPE
SURFACE-TO-SURFACE MISSILE LAUNCHERS 66
  ICBM • **Nuclear** *Agni* V (in test)
  IRBM • **Nuclear** 4+: ε4 *Agni* III; *Agni* IV (entering service

MRBM • Nuclear ε8 *Agni* II
SRBM • Nuclear 54: ε12 *Agni* I; ε42 SS-250 *Prithvi* II; some SS-350 *Dhanush* (naval testbed)
SUBMARINES • STRATEGIC • SSBN 2 *Arihant* with 4 1-cell VLS with K-15 *Sagarika* SLBM, 6 533mm TT
AIR-LAUNCHED MISSILES • ALCM • Nuclear *Nirbhay* (likely nuclear capable; in development)
Some Indian Air Force assets (such as *Mirage* 2000H, *Rafale* or Su-30MKI) may be tasked with a strategic role

Space
EQUIPMENT BY TYPE
SATELLITES 26
  NAVIGATION, POSITIONING, TIMING: 8 IRNSS
  COMMUNICATIONS: 2 GSAT-7/-7A
  ISR 15: 9 *Cartosat*; 6 RISAT
  ELINT/SIGINT 1 EMISAT

Army 1,237,000
6 Regional Comd HQ (Northern, Western, Central, Southern, Eastern, Southwestern), 1 Training Comd (ARTRAC)
FORCES BY ROLE
COMMAND
  4 (strike) corps HQ
  10 (holding) corps HQ
SPECIAL FORCES
  8 SF bn
MANOEUVRE
  Armoured
  2 armd div (3 armd bde, 1 arty bde (2 arty regt))
  1 armd div (3 armd bde, 1 SP arty bde (2 SP arty regt))
  8 indep armd bde
  Mechanised
  6 (RAPID) mech inf div (1 armd bde, 2 mech inf bde, 1 arty bde)
  2 indep mech bde
  Light
  15 inf div (2–5 inf bde, 1 arty bde)
  1 inf div (forming)
  7 indep inf bde
  12 mtn div (3-4 mtn inf bde, 1 arty bde)
  2 indep mtn bde
  Air Manoeuvre
  1 para bde
SURFACE-TO-SURFACE MISSILE
  1 IRBM bde with *Agni* II/III
  1 SRBM bde with *Agni* I
  2 SRBM bde with SS-250 *Prithvi* II
  3 GLCM regt with PJ-10 *Brahmos*
COMBAT SUPPORT
  3 arty div (2 arty bde, 1 MRL bde)
  2 indep arty bde
  4 engr bde
ATTACK HELICOPTER
  2 atk hel sqn (1 forming)
TRANSPORT HELICOPTER
  1 spec ops sqn
HELICOPTER
  23 hel sqn
AIR DEFENCE
  8 AD bde

Reserve Organisations
Reserves 300,000 reservists (first-line reserve within 5 years full-time service); 500,000 reservists (commitment until age 50) (total 800,000)

Territorial Army 160,000 reservists (only 40,000 regular establishment)
FORCES BY ROLE
MANOEUVRE
  Light
  42 inf bn
COMBAT SUPPORT
  6 (Railway) engr regt
  2 engr regt
  1 sigs regt
COMBAT SERVICE SUPPORT
  6 ecological bn
EQUIPMENT BY TYPE
ARMOURED FIGHTING VEHICLES
  MBT 3,750: 122 *Arjun*; 2,418 T-72M1; 10 T-90 MkIII; ε1,200 T-90S (ε1,100 various models in store)
  RECCE *Ferret* (used for internal-security duties along with some indigenously built armd cars)
  IFV 3,100: 700 BMP-1; 2,400 BMP-2 *Sarath* (incl some BMP-2K CP)
  APC 212+
    APC (W) 6 TASL IPMV
    PPV 206+: 165 *Casspir*; 27 *Kalyani* M4; some TASL QRFV; 14+ *Yukthirath* MPV
ENGINEERING & MAINTENANCE VEHICLES
  AEV BMP-2; FV180
  ARV 730+: T-54/T-55; 156 VT-72B; 222 WZT-2; 352 WZT-3
  VLB AM-50; BLG-60; BLG T-72; *Kartik*; MTU-20; MT-55; *Sarvatra*
  MW 24 910 MCV-2
ANTI-TANK/ANTI-INFRASTRUCTURE
  MSL
    SP 110 9P148 *Konkurs* (RS-AT-5 *Spandrel*)
    MANPATS 9K113 *Konkurs* (RS-AT-5 *Spandrel*); *Milan* 2
  RCL 3,000+: **84mm** *Carl Gustaf*; **106mm** 3,000+ M40A1 (10 per inf bn)
ARTILLERY 10,001+
  SP 155mm 100 K9 *Vajra*-T

TOWED 3,095+: **105mm** 1,350+: 600+ IFG Mk1/Mk2/Mk3; up to 700 LFG; 50 M-56; **122mm** 520 D-30; **130mm** ε600 M-46 (500 in store) **155mm** 625: ε300 FH-77B; ε200 M-46 (mod); 125 M777A2

MRL 306: **122mm** ε150 BM-21/LRAR; **214mm** 114 *Pinaka*; **300mm** 42 9A52 *Smerch*

MOR 6,500+: **81mm** 5,000+ E1; **120mm** ε1,500 AM-50/E1; **SP 120mm** E1

SURFACE-TO-SURFACE MISSILE LAUNCHERS
IRBM • Nuclear 4+: ε4 *Agni* III; *Agni* IV (entering service)

MRBM • Nuclear ε8 *Agni*-II

SRBM • Nuclear 54: ε12 *Agni*-I; ε42 250 *Prithvi* II

GLCM • Conventional 15 PJ-10 *Brahmos*

HELICOPTERS
ATK 5 LCH *Prachand*

MRH 339: 78 *Dhruv*; 12 *Lancer*; 74 *Rudra*; 115 SA315B *Lama* (*Cheetah*); 60 SA316B *Alouette* III (*Chetak*)

UNINHABITED AERIAL VEHICLES
ISR • Heavy 4 *Heron* (leased); **Medium** 25: 13 *Nishant*; 12 *Searcher* Mk I/II

AIR DEFENCE
SAM 748+

Medium-range ε48 *Akash*

Short-range 180 2K12 *Kub* (RS-SA-6 *Gainful*)

Point-defence 500+: 50+ 9K33AKM *Osa*-AKM (RS-SA-8 *Gecko*); 200 9K31 *Strela*-1 (RS-SA-9 *Gaskin*); 250 9K35 *Strela*-10 (RS-SA-13 *Gopher*); 9K310 *Igla*-1 (RS-SA-16 *Gimlet*); 9K38 *Igla* (RS-SA-18 *Grouse*)

SPAAGM 30mm up to 80 2K22 *Tunguska* (RS-SA-19 *Grison*)

GUNS 2,315+

SP 23mm 75 ZSU-23-4; ZU-23-2 (truck-mounted); **TOWED** 2,240+: **20mm** Oerlikon (reported); **23mm** 320 ZU-23-2; **40mm** 1,920 L40/70

Navy 75,500 (incl 7,000 Naval Avn and 1,200 Marines)

Fleet HQ New Delhi. Commands located at Mumbai, Vishakhapatnam, Kochi and Port Blair

EQUIPMENT BY TYPE
SUBMARINES 18
STRATEGIC • SSBN 2 *Arihant* with 4 1-cell VLS with K-15 *Sagarika* SLBM, 6 533mm TT

TACTICAL 16

SSK 16:

5 *Kalvari* (FRA *Scorpene*) with 6 533mm TT with SM39 *Exocet* Block 2 AShM/SUT HWT

3 *Shishumar* (GER Type-209/1500) with 8 single 533mm TT with SUT mod 1 HWT

1 *Shishumar* (GER Type-209/1500) with 8 single 533mm TT with UGM-84L *Harpoon* II AShM/SUT mod 1 HWT

7 *Sindhughosh* (FSU Project 877EKM (*Kilo*) with 6 single 533mm TT with 3M54E1/E *Klub*-S (RS-SS-N-27A/B) (*Klub*-S AShM variant unclear) AShM/53-65KE HWT/TEST-71ME HWT/SET-65E HWT

PRINCIPAL SURFACE COMBATANTS 29
AIRCRAFT CARRIERS • CV 2
1 *Vikramaditya* (ex-FSU *Kiev* mod) with 8-cell VLS with *Barak*-1 SAM, 4 AK630M CIWS (capacity 12 MiG-29K/KUB *Fulcrum* FGA ac; 6 Ka-28 *Helix* A ASW hel/Ka-31 *Helix* B AEW hel)

1 *Vikrant* with 3 AK630M CIWS (to be fitted with *Barak* 8 SAM) (capacity 30 aircraft including MiG-29K/KUB *Fulcrum*, Ka-31 *Helix* B, MH-60R *Seahawk*, *Dhruv*)

DESTROYERS 12
DDGHM 9:

3 *Delhi* (Project 15) with 2 quad lnchr with *Brahmos* AShM, 2 single 3S90E lnchr with 9M-38E M-22E *Shtil* (RS-SA-N-7 *Gadfly*) SAM, 4 8-cell VLS with *Barak*-1 SAM, 5 single 533mm ASTT with SET-65E HWT/*Varunastra* HWT, 2 RBU 6000 *Smerch* 2 A/S mor; 2 AK630 CIWS, 1 76mm gun (capacity either 2 *Dhruv* hel/*Sea King* Mk42A ASW hel)

3 *Kolkata* (Project 15A) with 2 8-cell UVLM VLS with *Brahmos* AShM, 4 8-cell VLS with *Barak*-8 SAM; 2 twin 533mm TT with SET-65E HWT *Varunastra* HWT, 2 RBU 6000 *Smerch* 2 A/S mor, 4 AK630M CIWS, 1 76mm gun (capacity 2 *Dhruv*/*Sea King* Mk42B hel)

3 *Visakhapatnam* (Project 15B) with 2 8-cell UVLM VLS with *Brahmos* AShM, 4 8-cell VLS with *Barak*-8 SAM; 2 twin 533mm TT with *Varunastra* HWT, 2 RBU 6000 *Smerch* 2 A/S mor, 4 AK630M CIWS, 1 76mm gun (capacity 2 *Dhruv*/*Sea King* Mk42B hel)

DDGM 3:

1 *Rajput* (FSU Project 61 (*Kashin*)) with 2 twin lnchr with P-27 *Termit*-R (RS-SS-N-2D *Styx*) AShM, 2 8-cell VLS with VL-SRSAM SAM, 1 twin ZIF-101 lnchr with 4K91 M-1 *Volnya* (RS-SA-N-1 *Goa*) SAM, 1 quintuple 533mm PTA-51-6 ME ASTT with SET-65E HWT/*Varunastra* HWT, 2 RBU 6000 *Smerch* 2 A/S mor, 4 AK630M CIWS, 1 76mm gun (capacity Ka-28 *Helix* A hel)

2 *Rajput* (FSU Project 61 (*Kashin*)) with 1 8-cell UVLM VLS with *Brahmos* AShM, 2 twin lnchr with P-27 *Termit*-R (RS-SS-N-2D *Styx* AShM, 2 8-cell VLS with *Barak*-1 SAM, 1 twin ZIF-102 lnchr with 4K91 M-1 *Volnya* (RS-SA-N-1 *Goa*) SAM, 1 quintuple 533mm ASTT with SET-65E HWT/ *Varunastra* HWT, 2 RBU 6000 *Smerch* 2 A/S mor, 2 AK630M CIWS, 1 76mm gun (capacity 1 Ka-28 *Helix* A hel)

FRIGATES 15
FFGHM 11:

2 *Brahmaputra* (Project 16A) with 4 quad lnchr with 3M24E *Uran*-E (RS-SS-N-25 *Switchblade*) AShM, 3 8-cell VLS with *Barak*-1 SAM, 2 triple ILAS-3 (B-515) 324mm ASTT with A244 LWT, 4 AK630M CIWS, 1 76mm gun (capacity 2 SA319 *Alouette* III (*Chetak*)/*Sea King* Mk42 ASW hel) 1 more non-operational)

3 *Shivalik* (Project 17) with 1 8-cell 3S14E VLS with 3M54TE *Klub*-N (RS-SS-N-27B *Sizzler*) AShM/*Brahmos* AShM, 4 8-cell VLS with *Barak*-1 SAM, 1 single 3S90E lnchr with 9M317E *Shtil*-1 (RS-SA-N-7B) SAM, 2 triple 324mm ILAS-3 (B-515) ASTT, 2 RBU 6000 *Smerch* 2 A/S mor, 2 AK630M CIWS, 1 76mm gun (capacity 1 *Sea King* Mk42B ASW hel)

3 *Talwar* I (RUS Project 11356 (*Krivak* IV)) with 1 8-cell 3S14E VLS with 3M54TE *Klub*-N (RS-SS-N-27B *Sizzler*) AShM, 1 single 3S90E lnchr with 9M317E *Shtil*-1 (RS-SA-N-7B) SAM, 2 twin 533mm DTA-53-11356 ASTT with SET-65E HWT/*Varunastra* HWT, 2 RBU 6000 *Smerch* 2 A/S mor, 2 *Kashtan* (RS-CADS-N-1) CIWS, 1 100mm gun (capacity 1 *Dhruv*/Ka-28 *Helix* A ASW hel)

3 *Talwar* II (RUS Project 11356 (*Krivak* IV)) with 1 8-cell UVLM VLS with *Brahmos* AShM, 1 single 3S90E lnchr with 9M317E *Shtil*-1 (RS-SA-N-7B) SAM, 2 twin 533mm DTA-53-11356 ASTT with SET-65E HWT/*Varunastra* HWT, 2 RBU 6000 *Smerch* 2 A/S mor, 2 AK630M CIWS, 1 100mm gun (capacity 1 *Dhruv*/Ka-28 *Helix* A ASW hel)

FFH 4 *Kamorta* (Project 28) with 2 twin 533mm ITTL ASTT with *Varunastra* HWT, 2 RBU 6000 *Smerch* 2 A/S mor, 2 AK630 CIWS, 1 76mm gun (capacity 1 *Dhruv*/Ka-28 *Helix* A ASW hel)

PATROL AND COASTAL COMBATANTS 159
CORVETTES • FSGM 6:

2 *Khukri* (Project 25) with 2 twin lnchr with P-27 *Termit*-R (RS-SS-N-2D *Styx*) AShM, 2 twin lnchr (manual aiming) with 9K32M *Strela*-2M (RS-SA-N-5 *Grail*) SAM, 2 AK630M CIWS, 1 76mm gun, 1 hel landing platform (for *Dhruv*/SA316 *Alouette* III (*Chetak*))

4 *Kora* (Project 25A) with 4 quad lnchr with 3M24E *Uran*-E (RS-SS-N-25 *Switchblade*) AShM, 1 quad lnchr (manual aiming) with 9K32M *Strela*-2M (RS-SA-N-5 *Grail*) SAM, 2 AK630M CIWS, 1 76mm gun, 1 hel landing platform (for *Dhruv*/SA316 *Alouette* III (*Chetak*))

PSOH 10: 4 *Saryu* with 2 AK630M CIWS, 1 76mm gun (capacity 1 *Dhruv*); 6 *Sukanya* with 4 RBU 2500 A/S mor (capacity 1 SA316 *Alouette* III (*Chetak*))

PCFGM 7:

5 *Veer* (FSU *Tarantul*) with 4 single lnchr with P-27 *Termit*-R (RS-SS-N-2D *Styx*) AShM, 2 quad lnchr (manual aiming) with 9K32M *Strela*-2M (RS-SA-N-5 *Grail*), 2 AK630M CIWS, 1 76mm gun

2 *Prabal* (mod *Veer*) with 4 quad lnchr with 3M24E *Uran*-E (RS-SS-N-25 *Switchblade*) AShM, 1 quad lnchr (manual aiming) with 9K32M *Strela*-2M (RS-SA-N-5 *Grail*) SAM, 2 AK630M CIWS, 1 76mm gun

PCMT 1 *Abhay* (FSU *Pauk* II) with 1 quad lnchr (manual aiming) with 9K32M *Strela*-2M (RS-SA-N-5 *Grail*) SAM, 2 twin 533mm DTA-53 ASTT with SET-65E, 2 RBU 1200 *Uragan* A/S mor, 1 AK630M CIWS, 1 76mm gun

PCC 16: 10 *Car Nicobar*; 6 *Trinkat* (*Bangaram* SDB Mk5)

PCF 3 *Tarmugli* (*Car Nicobar* mod)

PBF 116: 9 Immediate Support Vessel (Rodman 78); 14 Immediate Support Vessel (Craftway); 15 Plascoa 1300 (SPB); 3 *Super Dvora*; 75 Solas Marine Interceptor

AMPHIBIOUS
PRINCIPAL AMPHIBIOUS VESSELS 1

LPD 1 *Jalashwa* (ex-US Austin) with 1 Mk 15 *Phalanx* CIWS (capacity up to 6 med spt hel; either 9 LCM or 4 LCM and 2 LCAC; 4 LCVP; 930 troops)

LANDING SHIPS 4

LST 4: 1 *Magar* with 2 MS-227 *Ogon*' MRL with 1 hel landing platform (capacity 15 MBT or 8 APC or 10 trucks; 500 troops); 3 *Shardul* (*Magar* mod) with 2 MS-227 *Ogon*' MRL with 1 hel landing platform (capacity 11 MBT or 8 APC or 10 trucks; 500 troops)

LANDING CRAFT 12

LCT 8 LCU Mk-IV (capacity 1 *Arjun* MBT/2 T-90 MBT/4 IFV/160 troops)

LCM 4 LCM 8 (for use in *Jalashwa*)

LOGISTICS AND SUPPORT 41

AGOR 1 *Sagardhwani* with 1 hel landing platform

AGSH 2 *Sandhayak* II (capacity 1 med hel)

AGS 6: 1 *Makar*; 5 *Sandhayak* with 1 hel landing platform

AGM 2: 1 *Anvesh*; 1 *Dhruv*

AOL 14: 1 *Ambika*; 4 GSL 1,000T Fuel Barge; 2 *Poshak*; 7 *Purak*

AOR 1 *Jyoti* with 1 hel landing platform

AORH 3: 1 *Aditya* (capacity 1 med hel); 2 *Deepak* with 4 AK630 CIWS (capacity 1 *Sea King* Mk42B)

AP 2 *Nicobar* with 1 hel landing platform

ASR 1

ATF 1 *Gaj*

AWT 3 *Ambuda*

AX 1 *Tir* with 1 hel landing platform

AXS 4: 2 *Mhadei*; 2 *Tarangini*

UNINHABITED MARITIME PLATFORMS • USV 3
DATA • Small 3 SSO

UNINHABITED MARITIME SYSTEMS • UUV

UTL *Atom* Mk 1; Hugin

Naval Aviation 7,000

FORCES BY ROLE
FIGHTER/GROUND ATTACK

2 sqn with MiG-29K/KUB *Fulcrum*

ANTI-SUBMARINE WARFARE

1 sqn with MH-60R *Seahawk*

1 sqn with Ka-28 *Helix* A

1 sqn with *Sea King* Mk42B

MARITIME PATROL

5 sqn with Do-228; Do-228-101

3 sqn with P-8I *Neptune*

AIRBORNE EARLY WARNING & CONTROL

1 sqn with Ka-31 *Helix* B

SEARCH & RESCUE

1 sqn with SA316B *Alouette* III (*Chetak*); *Sea King* Mk42C

4 sqn with *Dhruv* MkI/MkIII
TRANSPORT
1 sqn with Do-228
TRAINING
1 sqn with Do-228; Do-228-101; *Virus* SW-80
1 sqn with *Hawk* Mk132*; HJT-16 *Kiran* MkI/II
1 hel sqn with *Sea King* Mk42B
TRANSPORT HELICOPTER
1 spec ops sqn with *Sea King* Mk42C
ISR UAV
3 sqn with *Heron*; *Searcher* MkII
EQUIPMENT BY TYPE
AIRCRAFT 69 combat capable
  FTR 40: 33 MiG-29K *Fulcrum*; 7 MiG-29KUB *Fulcrum*
  ASW 12 P-8I *Neptune*
  MP 12+ Do-228-101
  TPT • Light 10 Do-228; (17 BN-2 *Islander* in store)
  TRG 41: 17 *Hawk* Mk132*; 7 HJT-16 *Kiran* MkI; 5 HJT-16 *Kiran* MkII; 12 *Virus* SW-80
HELICOPTERS
  ASW 36: 12 Ka-28 *Helix* A; 6 MH-60R *Seahawk*; 18 *Sea King* Mk42B
  MRH 73: 10 *Dhruv* MkI; 16 *Dhruv* MkIII; 24 SA316B *Alouette* III (*Chetak*); 23 SA319 *Alouette* III
  AEW ε12 Ka-31 *Helix* B
  TPT • Medium 5 *Sea King* Mk42C
UNINHABITED AERIAL VEHICLES
  CISR • Heavy 2 MQ-9A *Reaper* (leased)
  ISR 9: **Heavy** 4 *Heron*; **Medium** 5 *Searcher* Mk II
AIR-LAUNCHED MISSILES
  AAM • IR R-550 *Magic*/*Magic* 2; R-73 (RS-AA-11A *Archer*); **IR/SARH** R-27 (RS-AA-10 *Alamo*); **ARH**: R-77 (RS-AA-12A *Adder*)
  ASM *Rampage*
  AShM AGM-84 *Harpoon*; Kh-35 (RS-AS-20 *Kayak*)
  BOMBS • TV-guided KAB-500KR/OD

Marines ε1,200 (Additional 1,000 for SPB duties)

After the Mumbai attacks, the Sagar Prahari Bal (SPB), with 80 PBF, was established to protect critical maritime infrastructure

FORCES BY ROLE
SPECIAL FORCES
1 (marine) cdo force
MANOEUVRE
Amphibious
1 amph bde

Air Force 149,900

5 regional air comds: Western (New Delhi), Southwestern (Gandhinagar), Eastern (Shillong), Central (Allahabad), Southern (Trivandrum). 2 support comds: Maintenance (Nagpur) and Training (Bangalore)

FORCES BY ROLE
FIGHTER
3 sqn with MiG-29UPG *Fulcrum*; MiG-29UB *Fulcrum*
FIGHTER/GROUND ATTACK
5 sqn with *Jaguar* IB/IS
1 sqn with *Jaguar* IB/IM/IS
2 sqn with MiG-21 *Bison*
3 sqn with *Mirage* 2000E/ED/I/IT (2000H/TH) (secondary ECM role)
2 sqn with *Rafale* DH/EH
13 sqn with Su-30MKI *Flanker*
2 sqn with *Tejas*
ISR
1 unit with Global 5000 ISR
AIRBORNE EARLY WARNING & CONTROL
1 sqn with EMB-145AEW *Netra*
1 sqn with Il-76TD *Phalcon*
TANKER
1 sqn with Il-78 *Midas*
TRANSPORT
6 sqn with An-32/An-32RE *Cline*
2 sqn with C-130J-30 *Hercules*
1 sqn with C-17A *Globemaster* III
1 sqn with C295MW; HS-748
3 sqn with Do-228; HS-748
1 sqn with Il-76MD *Candid*
1 VIP sqn with B-737; B-737BBJ; B-777-300ER; EMB-135BJ
TRAINING
1 OCU sqn with Su-30MKI *Flanker*
1 unit with An-32; Do-228; *Hawk* Mk132; HJT *Kiran* MkI/II; *Jaguar* IS/IM; PC-7 MkII *Turbo Trainer*; 331613 *Alouette* III
1 sqdn with *Tejas* (forming)
ATTACK HELICOPTER
1 sqn with AH-64E *Apache Guardian*
1 sqn with LCH *Prachand*
2 sqn with Mi-25 *Hind*; Mi-35 *Hind*
TRANSPORT HELICOPTER
5 sqn with *Dhruv*
7 sqn with Mi-17/Mi-17-1V *Hip* H
12 sqn with Mi-17V-5 *Hip* H
2 sqn with SA316B *Alouette* III (*Chetak*)
1 flt with CH-47F *Chinook*; Mi-26 *Halo*
2 flt with SA315B *Lama* (*Cheetah*)
2 flt with SA316B *Alouette* III (*Chetak*)
ISR UAV
5 sqn with *Heron*; *Searcher* MkII
SURFACE-TO-SURFACE MISSILE
2 GLCM sqn with PJ-10 *Brahmos*
AIR DEFENCE
6 sqn with 9K33M3 *Osa-AKM* (RS-SA-8B *Gecko*)

8 sqn with *Akash*
2 sqn with *Barak*-8 MR-SAM
25 sqn with S-125M *Pechora*-M (RS-SA-3B *Goa*)
3 sqn with S-400 (RS-SA-21 *Growler*)
10 flt with 9K38 *Igla*-1 (RS-SA-18 *Grouse*)

EQUIPMENT BY TYPE

AIRCRAFT 721 combat capable
  FTR 58: 51 MiG-29UPG *Fulcrum*; 7 MiG-29UB *Fulcrum* B
  FGA 455: ε40 MiG-21 *Bison*; 37 MiG-21U/UM *Mongol*; 35 *Mirage* 2000E/I (2000H); 9 *Mirage* 2000ED/IT (2000TH); 8 *Rafale* DH; 28 *Rafale* EH; 261 Su-30MKI *Flanker* H; 37 *Tejas*
  ATK 110: ε23 *Jaguar* IB; ε77 *Jaguar* IS; ε10 *Jaguar* IM
  ISR 2 Global 5000 ISR
  AEW&C 5: 2 EMB-145AEW *Netra* (1 more in test); 3 Il-76TD *Phalcon*
  TKR 6 Il-78 *Midas*†
  TPT 279: **Heavy** 28: 11 C-17A *Globemaster* III; 17 Il-76MD *Candid*; **Medium** 12 C-130J-30 *Hercules*; **Light** 174: 23 An-32; 76 An-32RE *Cline*; 3 C295W; 40 Do-228-101; 28 Do-228-202; 4 EMB-135BJ; **PAX** 65: 1 A321; 1 B-707; 3 B-737; 3 B-737BBJ; 2 B-777-300ER; 55 HS-748
  TRG 370: 98 *Hawk* Mk132*; 86 HJT-16 *Kiran* MkI/IA; 41 HJT-16 *Kiran* MkII; 74 PC-7 *Turbo Trainer* MkII; 71 *Virus* SW-80

HELICOPTERS
  ATK 44: 22 AH-64E *Apache Guardian*; 5 LCH *Prachand*; 17 Mi-25/Mi-35 *Hind*
  MRH 401: 59 *Dhruv*; 35 Mi-17 *Hip* H; 45 Mi-17-1V *Hip* H; 148 Mi-17V-5 *Hip* H; 59 SA315B *Lama* (*Cheetah*); 39 SA316B *Alouette* III (*Chetak*); 16 *Rudra*
  TPT • **Heavy** 15 CH-47F *Chinook*; (3 Mi-26 *Halo* in store)

UNINHABITED AERIAL VEHICLES
  ISR • **Heavy** 8 *Heron*; **Medium** some *Searcher* MkII
  OWA *Harop*

AIR DEFENCE • **SAM**
  Long-range 24 S-400 (RS-SA-21 *Growler*)
  Medium-range 72: ε64 *Akash*; 8 *Barak*-8 (MRSAM)
  Short-range S-125M *Pechora*-M (RS-SA-3B *Goa*); *Spyder*-SR
  Point-defence 9K33M3 *Osa-AKM* (RS-SA-8 *Gecko*); 9K38 *Igla* (RS-SA-18 *Grouse*)

AIR-LAUNCHED MISSILES
  AAM • **IR** R-60 (RS-AA-8 *Aphid*); R-73 (RS-AA-11A *Archer*) R-550 *Magic*; **IIR** Mica IR; **IR/SARH** R-27 (RS-AA-10 *Alamo*); **SARH** Super 530D; **ARH** R-77 (RS-AA-12A *Adder*); *Meteor*; Mica RF
  AShM AGM-84 *Harpoon*; AM39 *Exocet*; Kh-31A (RS-AS-17B *Krypton*)
  ASM AASM; AS-30L; AGM-114L/R *Hellfire*; Kh-29 (RS-AS-14 *Kedge*); Kh-59 (RS-AS-13 *Kingbolt*); Kh-59M (RS-AS-18 *Kazoo*); *Popeye* II (*Crystal Maze*); *Rampage*
  ARM Kh-25MP (RS-AS-12A *Kegler*); Kh-31P (RS-AS-17A *Krypton*)
  LACM • **Conventional** *Brahmos*; SCALP-EG

BOMBS
  INS/SAT guided *Spice*; *Spice* 2000
  Laser-guided *Griffin*; KAB-500L; *Paveway* II
  TV-guided KAB-500KR

SURFACE-TO-SURFACE MISSILE LAUNCHERS
  GLCM • **Conventional** PJ-10 *Brahmos*

Coast Guard 13,350

EQUIPMENT BY TYPE

PATROL AND COASTAL COMBATANTS 138
  PSOH 25: 2 *Sankalp* (capacity 1 *Chetak/Dhruv* hel); 2 *Samar* with 1 76mm gun (capacity 1 *Chetak/Dhruv* hel); 11 *Samarth* (capacity 1 *Chetak/Dhruv* hel); 7 *Vikram* (capacity 1 *Dhruv* hel); 3 *Vishwast* (capacity 1 *Chetak/Dhruv* hel)
  PSO 3 *Samudra Prahari* with 1 hel landing platform
  PCC 43: 20 *Aadesh*; 8 *Rajshree* (Flight I); 5 *Rajshree* (Flight II) 5 *Rani Abbakka*; 5 *Sarojini Naidu*
  PBF 67: 6 C-154; 11 C-143; 50 C-401

AMPHIBIOUS • **UCAC** 14: 2 H-181 (*Griffon* 8000TD); 12 H-187 (*Griffon* 8000TD)

AIRCRAFT • **MP** 38 Do-228-101

HELICOPTERS • **MRH** 39: 4 *Dhruv* MkI; 16 *Dhruv* MkIII; 19 SA316B *Alouette* III (*Chetak*)

Gendarmerie & Paramilitary 1,616,050

Rashtriya Rifles 65,000

Ministry of Defence. 15 sector HQ

FORCES BY ROLE
MANOEUVRE
  Other
    65 paramilitary bn

Assam Rifles 65,150

Ministry of Home Affairs. Security within northeastern states, mainly army-officered; better trained than BSF

FORCES BY ROLE
Equipped to roughly same standard as an army inf bn
COMMAND
  7 HQ
MANOEUVRE
  Other
    47 paramilitary bn

EQUIPMENT BY TYPE
ARTILLERY • **MOR** 81mm 252

Border Security Force 263,900

Ministry of Home Affairs
FORCES BY ROLE
MANOEUVRE
  Other
    193 paramilitary bn
EQUIPMENT BY TYPE
Small arms, lt arty, some anti-tank weapons

ARTILLERY • MOR 81mm 942+
AIRCRAFT • TPT • Light 1 ERJ-135BJ
HELICOPTERS • MRH 21: 6 *Dhruv*; 6 Mi-17-1V *Hip*; 8 Mi-17V-5 *Hip*; 1 SA315B *Lama* (*Cheetah*)

Central Industrial Security Force 144,400 (lightly armed security guards)

Ministry of Home Affairs. Guards public-sector locations

Central Reserve Police Force 324,600

Ministry of Home Affairs. Internal-security duties, only lightly armed, deployable throughout the country

FORCES BY ROLE
MANOEUVRE
  Other
  208 paramilitary bn
  15 (rapid action force) paramilitary bn
  10 (CoBRA) paramilitary bn
  6 (Mahila) paramilitary bn (female)
  2 sy gp
COMBAT SUPPORT
  5 sigs bn

Defence Security Corps 31,000

Provides security at Defence Ministry sites

Indo-Tibetan Border Police 89,400

Ministry of Home Affairs. Tibetan border security SF/guerrilla-warfare and high-altitude-warfare specialists

FORCES BY ROLE
MANOEUVRE
  Other
  56 paramilitary bn

National Security Guards 12,000

Anti-terrorism contingency deployment force, comprising elements of the armed forces, CRPF and Border Security Force

Railway Protection Forces 70,000

Sashastra Seema Bal 87,600

Guards the borders with Nepal and Bhutan

FORCES BY ROLE
MANOEUVRE
  Other
  73 paramilitary bn

Special Frontier Force 10,000

Mainly ethnic Tibetans

Special Protection Group 3,000

Protection of ministers and senior officials

State Armed Police 450,000

For duty primarily in home state only, but can be moved to other states. Some bn with GPMG and army-standard infantry weapons and equipment

FORCES BY ROLE
MANOEUVRE
  Other
  144 (India Reserve Police) paramilitary bn

Reserve Organisations

Civil Defence 500,000 reservists

Operate in 225 categorised towns in 32 states. Some units for NBC defence

Home Guard 441,000 reservists (547,000 authorised str)

In all states except Arunachal Pradesh and Kerala; men on reserve lists, no trg. Not armed in peacetime. Used for civil defence, rescue and firefighting provision in wartime; 6 bn (created to protect tea plantations in Assam)

DEPLOYMENT

CENTRAL AFRICAN REPUBLIC: UN • MINUSCA 3

CYPRUS: UN • UNFICYP 1

DEMOCRATIC REPUBLIC OF THE CONGO: UN • MONUSCO 1,115; 1 inf bn; 1 med coy

LEBANON: UN • UNIFIL 897; 1 mech inf bn; 1 log coy; 1 med coy

MIDDLE EAST: UN • UNTSO 3

SOMALIA: UN • UNSOM 1

SOUTH SUDAN: UN • UNMISS 2,404; 2 inf bn; 1 engr coy; 1 sigs coy; 2 fd hospital

SUDAN: UN • UNISFA 593; 1 mech inf bn(-)

SYRIA/ISRAEL: UN • UNDOF 201; 1 inf pl, 1 MP pl, 1 log coy

WESTERN SAHARA: UN • MINURSO 3

FOREIGN FORCES

Total numbers for UNMOGIP mission in India and Pakistan
Argentina 3
Croatia 8
Czech Republic 1
Italy 2
Korea, Republic of 6
Mexico 3
Nigeria 1
Philippines 6
Romania 2
Sweden 2
Switzerland 3
Thailand 5
Uruguay 2

Indonesia IDN

Indonesian Rupiah IDR		2023	2024	2025
GDP	IDR	20.9qrn	22.5qrn	24.2qrn
	USD	1.37trn	1.40trn	1.49trn
Real GDP growth	%	5.0	5.0	5.1
Def bdgt	IDR	145trn	175trn	165trn
	USD	9.50bn	10.9bn	10.2bn
FMA (US)	USD	14m	14m	14m

Real-terms defence budget trend (USDbn, constant 2015)

Population	281,562,465				
Age	0–14	15–19	20–24	25–29	30–64	65 plus
Male	12.2%	4.3%	4.1%	3.9%	21.9%	3.7%
Female	11.6%	4.1%	3.9%	3.8%	22.3%	4.3%

Capabilities

The Indonesian National Armed Forces are the largest in Southeast Asia and are traditionally concerned with internal security, counter-insurgency and counter-terrorism. The army, deployed on counter-insurgency operations in West Papua and counter-terrorist operations in central Sulawesi, remains the dominant service. Joint service integration remains limited. However, the creation of three new tri-service theatre commands and a new tri-service counter-terrorism command in 2019 reflects greater emphasis on integration, while the creation of new two-star commands in 2018, one for every service, reflects focus on the military presence in the East. Indonesia also set up a part-time reserve component in 2021. Plans were unveiled in 2024 for a cyber branch and new Army Military Regional Commands. Tensions in the South China Sea have prompted plans for a greater military and coastguard presence in the area. Indonesia is drafting a new 25-year modernisation plan to replace the Minimum Essential Force plan, which expired in 2024 without being completed. The country has an interest in acquiring a suite of new capabilities, including satellites, UAVs, combat aircraft, submarines, frigates, and ballistic missile and air defence systems. Indonesia's defence industry has jointly produced fixed-wing and rotary-wing aircraft, landing platform docks and frigates. Indonesia has no formal defence alliances but has a number of defence cooperation agreements with regional and extra-regional partners. The country hosts multilateral military exercises and frequently participates in UN peacekeeping.

ACTIVE 404,500 (Army 300,400 Navy 74,000 Air 30,100) **Gendarmerie & Paramilitary 290,250**

Conscription liability 24 months selective conscription authorised (not required by law)

RESERVE 400,000

Army cadre units; numerical str n.k., obligation to age 45 for officers

ORGANISATIONS BY SERVICE

Army ε300,400

Mil Area Commands (KODAM)
15 comd (I, II, III, IV, V, VI, IX, XII, XIII, XIV, XVI, XVII, XVIII, Jaya & Iskandar Muda)

FORCES BY ROLE
MANOEUVRE
  Mechanised
  3 armd cav bn
  8 cav bn
  1 mech inf bde (1 cav bn, 3 mech inf bn)
  1 mech inf bde (3 mech inf bn)
  3 indep mech inf bn
  Light
  1 inf bde (3 cdo bn)
  1 inf bde (2 cdo bn, 1 inf bn)
  1 inf bde (1 cdo bn, 2 inf bn)
  2 inf bde (3 inf bn)
  3 inf bde (1 cdo bn, 1 inf bn)
  3 inf bde (2 inf bn)
  29 indep inf bn
  20 indep cdo bn
COMBAT SUPPORT
  1 SP arty bn
  11 fd arty bn
  11 cbt engr bn
COMBAT SERVICE SUPPORT
  4 construction bn
TRANSPORT
  1 tpt sqn
TRAINING
  1 hel trg unit
ATTACK HELICOPTER
  3 atk hel sqn
HELICOPTER
  1 hel sqn
AIR DEFENCE
  1 AD regt (2 ADA bn, 1 SAM unit)
  9 ADA bn
  3 SAM unit

Special Forces Command (KOPASSUS)
FORCES BY ROLE
SPECIAL FORCES
  3 SF gp (total: 2 cdo/para unit, 1 CT unit, 1 int unit)

Strategic Reserve Command (KOSTRAD)
FORCES BY ROLE
COMMAND
  3 div HQ
MANOEUVRE
  Armoured
  2 tk bn
  Mechanised
  1 mech inf bde (3 mech inf bn)
  Light

2 inf bde (3 cdo bn)
1 inf bde (2 inf bn)
Air Manoeuvre
3 AB bde (3 AB bn)
COMBAT SUPPORT
2 arty regt (1 SP arty bn; 1 MRL bn; 1 fd arty bn)
1 fd arty bn
2 cbt engr bn
AIR DEFENCE
3 AD bn

EQUIPMENT BY TYPE
ARMOURED FIGHTING VEHICLES
  MBT 103: 42 *Leopard* 2A4; 61 *Leopard* 2RI
  LT TK 353: 275 AMX-13 (partially upgraded); 18 *Harimau*; 60 FV101 *Scorpion*-90
  ASLT 32: 10 *Badak*; 22 *Black Fox*
  RECCE 142: 55 *Ferret* (13 upgraded); 69 *Saladin* (16 upgraded); 18 VBL
  IFV 75: 42 *Marder* 1A3; 33 *Pandur* II
  APC 872+
    APC (T) 267: 75 AMX-VCI; 34 BTR-50PK; 15 FV4333 *Stormer*; 143 M113A1-B
    APC (W) 614+: 397 *Anoa*; some *Barracuda*; 40 BTR-40; 45 FV603 *Saracen* (14 upgraded); 100 LAV-150 *Commando*; 32 VAB-VTT
    PPV some *Casspir*
  AUV 127: 14 APR-1; 18 *Bushmaster*; 22 *Commando Ranger*; 73+ *Komodo* 4×4
ENGINEERING & MAINTENANCE VEHICLES
  AEV 4: 3 PiPz-2RI *Dachs*; 1 M113A1-B-GN
  ARV 15+: 2 AMX-13; 6 AMX-VCI; 3 BREM-2; 4 BPz-3 *Buffel*; *Stormer*; T-54/T-55
  VLB 19: 10 AMX-13; 3 BPR *Biber*-1; 4 M3; 2 *Stormer*
ANTI-TANK/ANTI-INFRASTRUCTURE
  MSL • MANPATS FGM-148 *Javelin*; SS.11; *Milan*; 9K11 *Malyutka* (RS-AT-3 *Sagger*)
  RCL 90mm M67; **106mm** M40A1
  RL 89mm LRAC
ARTILLERY 1,243+
  SP 92: **105mm** 20 AMX Mk61; **155mm** 72: 54 CAESAR; 18 M109A4
  TOWED 133+: **105mm** 110+: some KH-178; 60 M101; 50 M-56; **155mm** 23: 5 FH-88; 18 KH-179
  MRL 127mm 63 ASTROS II Mk6
  MOR 955: **81mm** 800; **120mm** 155: 75 Brandt; 80 UBM 52
PATROL AND COASTAL COMBATANTS 4
  PBF 4 Combat Boat 18M (used as fast transports)
AMPHIBIOUS
  LANDING SHIPS • LST 2 ADRI LI with 1 hel landing platform (capacity 8 MBT; 500 troops)
  LANDING CRAFT 19
    LCU 17: 1 ADRI XXXII; 4 ADRI XXXIII; 1 ADRI XXXIX; 1 ADRI XL; 3 ADRI XLI; 2 ADRI XLIV; 2 ADRI XLVI; 2 ADRI XLVIII; 1 ADRI L

LCAC 2
AIRCRAFT
  TPT 7: **Light** 6 C-212 *Aviocar* (NC-212); **PAX** 1 Beech 390 *Premier* 1
HELICOPTERS
  ATK 14: 8 AH-64E *Apache Guardian*; 6 Mi-35P *Hind*
  MRH 65: 5 H125M (AS550C3) *Fennec* (armed); 6 H125M (AS555AP) *Fennec* (armed); 6 Bell 412 *Twin Huey* (NB-412); 24 Bell 412EPI *Twin Huey*; 9 Bell 412EPI *Twin Huey*; 15 Mi-17V-5 *Hip* H
  TPT • Light 22: 7 Bell 205A; ε12 Bo-105 (NBo-105) (armed); 2 H120 *Colibri*; 1 H125 (AS350B3) *Ecureuil*
  TRG ε12 Hughes 300C
UNINHABITED AERIAL VEHICLES
  CISR • Light *Blowfish* A3; *Elang Laut* 25 (reported); *Rajawali* 330 (reported)
AIR DEFENCE
  SAM • Point-defence 54+: *Kobra*; *Starstreak*; TD-2000B (*Giant Bow* II); 42 RBS-70; QW-3; 12 ZUR-23-2KG
  GUNS • TOWED 411: **20mm** 121 Rh 202; **23mm** *Giant Bow*; **40mm** 90 L/70; **57mm** 200 S-60
AIR-LAUNCHED MISSILES • ASM 9M120 *Ataka* (AT-9 *Spiral* 2) (reported); AGM-114R *Hellfire* II

Navy ε74,000 (including Marines and Aviation)

Three fleets: East (Sorong), Central (Surabaya) and West (Tanjung Uban)

EQUIPMENT BY TYPE
SUBMARINES • SSK 4:
  1 *Cakra* (GER Type-209/1300) with 8 single 533mm TT with SUT HWT
  3 *Nagapasa* (GER Type-209/1400) with 8 single 533mm TT with *Black Shark* HWT
PRINCIPAL SURFACE COMBATANTS 7
  FRIGATES 7:
    FFGHM 5:
      1 *Ahmad Yani* (ex-NLD *Van Speijk*) with 1 2-cell VLS with 3M55E *Yakhont* (RS-SS-N-26 *Strobile*) AShM; 2 twin *Simbad* lnchr (manual) with *Mistral* SAM, 2 triple 324mm SVTT Mk 32 ASTT with Mk 46 LWT, 1 76mm gun (capacity 1 Bo-105 (NBo-105) hel)
      2 *Ahmad Yani* (ex-NLD *Van Speijk*) with 2 twin lnchr with C-802 (CH-SS-N-6) AShM, 2 twin *Simbad* lnchr (manual) with *Mistral* SAM, 2 triple 324mm SVTT Mk 32 ASTT with Mk 46 LWT, 1 76mm gun (capacity 1 Bo-105 (NBo-105) hel)
      2 *R.E. Martadinata* (SIGMA 10514) with 2 quad lnchr with MM40 *Exocet* Block 3 AShM, 2 6-cell CLA VLS with VL MICA SAM, 2 triple 324mm ILAS-3 (B-515) ASTT with A244/S LWT, 1 *Millennium* CIWS, 1 76mm gun (capacity 1 med hel)
    FFHM 2 *Ahmad Yani* (ex-NLD *Van Speijk*) with 2 twin *Simbad* lnchr (manual) with *Mistral* SAM, 2 triple 324mm ASTT with Mk 46 LWT, 1 76mm gun (capacity 1 Bo-105 (NBo-105) hel)

PATROL AND COASTAL COMBATANTS 205
  CORVETTES 24
    FSGM 7:
      3 *Bung Tomo* with 2 quad lnchr with MM40 *Exocet* Block 2 AShM, 1 16-cell VLS with *Sea Wolf* SAM, 2 triple 324mm ASTT, 1 76mm gun (capacity: 1 Bo-105 hel)
      4 *Diponegoro* (SIGMA 9113) with 2 twin lnchr with MM40 *Exocet* Block 2 AShM, 2 quad *Tetral* lnchr with *Mistral* SAM, 2 triple 324mm ILAS-3 (B-515) ASTT with MU90 LWT, 1 76mm gun, 1 hel landing platform
    FSGH 1 *Nala* with 2 twin lnchr with MM38 *Exocet* AShM, 1 twin Bofors ASW Rocket Launcher System 375mm A/S mor, 1 120mm gun (capacity 1 lt hel)
    FS 16:
      2 *Fatahillah* with 2 triple 324mm SVTT Mk 32 ASTT with Mk 46 LWT, 1 twin 375mm A/S mor, 1 120mm gun
      14 *Kapitan Pattimura* (ex-GDR *Parchim* I) with 4 single 400mm ASTT, 2 RBU 6000 *Smerch* 2 A/S mor, 1 AK230 CIWS, 1 twin 57mm gun
  PCFG 3 *Mandau* with 4 single lnchr with MM38 *Exocet* AShM, 1 57mm gun
  PCG 4:
    2 *Sampari* (KCR-60M) with 2 twin lnchr for C-705 AShM, 1 57mm gun
    2 *Todak* with 2 single lnchr with C-802 (CH-SS-N-6), 1 57mm gun
  PCT 2 *Andau* with 2 single 533mm TT with SUT, 1 57mm gun
  PCO 1 *Bung Karno* (capacity 1 AS565MBe *Panther* hel)
  PCC 37: 4 *Dorang*; 4 *Kakap* with 1 hel landing platform; 2 *Pandrong*; 4 *Pari*; 2 *Pulau Rote*; 4 *Sampari* (KCR-60M) with 1 NG-18 CIWS, 1 57 mm gun; 15 *Tatihu* (PC-40); 2 *Todak* with 1 57mm gun
  PBG 8: 2 *Clurit* with 2 single lnchr with C-705 AShM, 1 AK630 CIWS; 6 *Clurit* with 2 single lnchr with C-705 AShM
  PBF 25+ Combat Boat 18M
  PB 101: 2 *Badau* (ex-BRN *Waspada*); 1 *Bawean*; 1 *Cucut* (ex-SGP *Jupiter*); 1 *Klewang*; 13 *Kobra*; 1 *Krait*; 1 *Kudungga*; 1 *Mumuja*; 8 *Sibarau*; ε39 *Sinabang* (KAL-28); 8 *Viper*; 25 other
MINE WARFARE • MINE COUNTERMEASURES 8
  MCO 4: 2 *Pulau Fani* (GER *Frankenthal* (Type-332)); 2 *Pulau Rengat*
  MSC 4 *Pulau Rote* (ex-GDR *Kondor* (Project 89))
AMPHIBIOUS
  PRINCIPAL AMPHIBIOUS VESSELS • LPD 4:
    4 *Makassar* (capacity 2 LCU or 4 LCVP; 13 tanks; 500 troops); 2 AS332L *Super Puma*)
  LANDING SHIPS • LST 23
    1 *Teluk Amboina* (capacity 16 tanks; 800 troops)
    4 *Teluk Bintuni* (capacity 4 LCVP; 470 troops; 15 APC or 10 MBT)
    2 *Teluk Cirebon* (ex-GDR *Frosch* II) (capacity 11 APC; 80 troops)
    9 *Teluk Gilimanuk* (ex-GDR *Frosch*) (capacity 11 APC; 80 troops)
    5 *Teluk Lada* with 1 hel landing platform (capacity 4 LCVP; 470 troops; 15 APC; 10 MBT)
    2 *Teluk Semangka* (capacity 17 tanks; 200 troops)
  LANDING CRAFT 52
    LCM 20
    LCU 2
    LCVP 30
LOGISTICS AND SUPPORT 26
  AGF 1 *Multatuli* with 1 hel landing platform
  AGOR 3: 1 *Pollux*; 2 *Rigel* (FRA Ocea OSV 190)
  AGSH 1 *Dewa Kembar* (ex-UK *Hecla*) with 1 hel landing platform
  AGS 1 *Leuser* (IDN *Soputan* mod)
  AH 4:
    1 *Dr Soeharso* (ex-*Tanjung Dalpele*) (capacity 2 LCU/LCVP; 500 troops; 2 AS332L *Super Puma*)
    2 *Dr Sudirohusodo* (*Semarang* mod) (capacity 2 med hel)
    1 *Semarang* (IDN *Makassar* mod) (capacity 2 LCM; 3 hels; 28 vehs; 650 troops)
  AK 1 *Mentawai* (HUN *Telaud*)
  AOR 4: 1 *Arun* (ex-UK *Rover*); 2 *Bontang* with 1 hel landing platform; 1 *Tarakan* with 1 hel landing platform
  AP 2: 1 *Tanjung Kambani* with 1 hel landing platform; 1 *Karang Pilang*
  ATF 1 *Soputan*
  AXL up to 5 *Kadet*
  AXS 3: 1 *Arung Samudera*; 1 *Bima Suci*; 1 *Dewaruci*
UNINHABITED MARITIME SYSTEMS • UUV
  MW PAP
  UTL *Hugin* 1000

Naval Aviation ε1,000
FORCES BY ROLE
ANTI-SUBMARINE WARFARE
  1 sqn with AS565MBe *Panther*
MARITIME PATROL
  1 sqn with Beech 350i *King Air* (VIP); C212-200 MPA
  1 sqn with C212-200 MPA; CN235-220 MPA
TRAINING
  1 sqn with Beech G36 *Bonanza*; Beech G38 *Baron*; Bell 505 *Jet Ranger* X; H120 *Colibri*; PA-28 *Archer* III; TB-9 *Tampico*; TB-10 *Tobago*
TRANSPORT HELICOPTER
  1 sqn with Bell 412 (NB-412) *Twin Huey*; Bell 412EP *Twin Huey*; Bo-105 (NBo-105)
EQUIPMENT BY TYPE
AIRCRAFT
  MP 9: 3 C212-200 MPA; 6 CN235-220 MPA
  TPT • Light 30: 1 Beech 350i *King Air* (VIP); 7 Beech G36 *Bonanza*; 2 Beech G38 *Baron*; 9 C-212-200 *Aviocar*; 7 PA-28 *Archer* III (trg); 2 TB-9 *Tampico*; 2 TB-10 *Tobago*
HELICOPTERS
  ASW 11 AS565MBe *Panther*

MRH 7: 4 Bell 412 (NB-412) *Twin Huey*; 3 Bell 412EP *Twin Huey*
CSAR 4 H225M *Caracal*
TPT • Light 11: 2 Bell 505 *Jet Ranger* X; ε6 Bo-105 (NBo-105); 3 H120 *Colibri*
UNINHABITED AERIAL VEHICLES
ISR • Light 1: H-6 *Poseidon*; 1 S-100 *Camcopter*; *ScanEagle* 2; STERNA IT180-120

Marines ε20,000
FORCES BY ROLE
SPECIAL FORCES
1 SF bn
MANOEUVRE
Amphibious
2 mne gp (1 cav regt, 3 mne bn, 1 arty regt, 1 cbt spt regt, 1 CSS regt)
1 mne gp (forming)
1 mne bde (3 mne bn)
EQUIPMENT BY TYPE
ARMOURED FIGHTING VEHICLES
LT TK 10: 10 AMX-10 PAC 90
RECCE 21 BRDM-2
IFV 114: 24 AMX-10P; 22 BMP-2; 54 BMP-3F; 2 BTR-4; 12 BTR-80A
APC 103: **APC (T)** 100 BTR-50P; **APC (W)** 3 BTR-4M
AAV 15: 10 LVTP-7A1; 5 M113 *Arisgator*
ARTILLERY 71+
TOWED 50: **105mm** 22 LG1 MK II; **122mm** 28 M-38
MRL 122mm 21: 4 PHL-90B; 9 RM-70; 8 RM-70 *Vampir*
MOR 81mm some
AIR DEFENCE • GUNS • 40mm 5 L/60/L/70; **57mm** S-60

Air Force 30,100
3 operational comd (East, Central and West) plus trg comd
FORCES BY ROLE
FIGHTER/GROUND ATTACK
1 sqn with F-16A/AM/B/BM *Fighting Falcon*
2 sqn with F-16C/D Block 25/32+ *Fighting Falcon*
1 sqn with Su-27SK/SKM *Flanker*; Su-30MK2 *Flanker*
2 sqn with Hawk Mk109*/Mk209*
1 sqn with T-50i *Golden Eagle**
GROUND ATTACK
1 sqn with EMB-314 (A-29) *Super Tucano**
MARITIME PATROL
1 sqn with B-737-200
1 sqn with CN235M-220 MPA; CN235M-110
TANKER/TRANSPORT
1 sqn with C-130B/KC-130B *Hercules*
TRANSPORT
1 sqn with C-130B/H *Hercules*; KC-130B *Hercules*; L-100-30
1 sqn with C-130H-30/J-30 *Hercules*; L-100-30
1 sqn with C-130H *Hercules*
1 sqn with C-212 *Aviocar* (NC-212/NC-212i)
1 sqn with C295M
1 VIP sqn with B-737-200/400/500; B-737-800; BAe 146-RJ85; *Falcon* 7X/8X
TRAINING
1 sqn with G 120TP
1 sqn with KT-1B
1 UAV flt with LH-D (forming)
TRANSPORT HELICOPTER
2 sqn with AS332L *Super Puma* (NAS332L); H225M; NAS332 C1+ *Super Puma*
1 sqn with H225M (forming)
1 sqn with H120 *Colibri*
1 VIP sqn with AS332L *Super Puma* (NAS332L)
COMBAT/ISR UAV
1 sqn with CH-4B
ISR UAV
1 sqn with *Aerostar*
AIR DEFENCE
1 SAM unit with NASAMS II
EQUIPMENT BY TYPE
AIRCRAFT 104 combat capable
FTR 4: 1 F-16A *Fighting Falcon*; 1 F-16B *Fighting Falcon*; 2 Su-27SK *Flanker*
FGA 45: 6 F-16AM *Fighting Falcon*; 2 F-16BM *Fighting Falcon*; 18 F-16C Block 25/32+ *Fighting Falcon*; 5 F-16D Block 25/32+ *Fighting Falcon*; 3 Su-27SKM *Flanker*; 11 Su-30MK2 *Flanker* G
MP 7: 3 B-737-200; 2 B-737-800; 2 CN235M-220 MPA
ISR 1 C295M
TKR/TPT 1 KC-130B *Hercules*
TPT 66: **Medium** 30: 4 C-130B *Hercules*; 11 C-130H *Hercules*; 6 C-130H-30 *Hercules*; 5 C-130J-30 *Hercules*; 4 L-100-30; **Light** 26: 9 C295; 7 C-212 *Aviocar* (NC-212); 5 C-212 *Aviocar* (NC-212i); 5 CN235M-110; **PAX** 10: 1 B-737-200; 3 B-737-400; 1 B-737-500; 1 B-737-800 BJ (VIP); 1 BAe 146-RJ85 (VIP); 1 *Falcon* 7X, 2 *Falcon* 8X
TRG 101: 13 EMB-314 (A-29) *Super Tucano**; 30 G 120TP; 7 *Hawk* Mk109*; 22 *Hawk* Mk209*; 16 KT-1B; 13 T-50i *Golden Eagle**
HELICOPTERS
TPT 36: **Heavy** 14 H225M (some CSAR); **Medium** 10: 9 AS332 *Super Puma* (NAS332L) (VIP/CSAR); 1 NAS332 C1+ *Super Puma*; **Light** 12 H120 *Colibri*
UNINHABITED AERIAL VEHICLES
CISR • Heavy 3+ CH-4B
ISR • Medium *Aerostar*; ε2 LH-D; **Light** *Wulung* (reported)
AIR-LAUNCHED MISSILES
AAM • IR AIM-9P *Sidewinder*; R-73 (RS-AA-11A *Archer*); **IIR** AIM-9X *Sidewinder* II; **IR/SARH** R-27 (RS-AA-10 *Alamo*)
ARH AIM-120C-7 AMRAAM; R-77 (RS-AA-12A *Adder*)

ASM AGM-65G *Maverick*; AR-1; AR-2; Kh-59M (RS-AS-18 *Kazoo*); Kh-59T (RS-AS-14B *Kedge*)
ARM Kh-31P (RS-AS-17A *Krypton*)
BOMBS
  INS/SAT-guided GBU-38 JDAM
  Laser & INS/SAT-guided GBU-54 Laser JDAM
AIR DEFENCE
  SAM • Medium-range NASAMS II

Special Forces (KOPASGAT)
FORCES BY ROLE
SPECIAL FORCES
  3 (KOPASGAT) SF wg (total: 6 spec ops sqn)
  4 indep SF coy
EQUIPMENT BY TYPE
AIR DEFENCE
  SAM • Point-defence *Chiron*; QW-3
  GUNS • TOWED 35mm 6 Oerlikon *Skyshield*

Gendarmerie & Paramilitary 281,250+

Police ε280,000 (including 14,000 police 'mobile bde' (BRIMOB) org in 56 coy, incl CT unit (Gegana))
EQUIPMENT BY TYPE
ARMOURED FIGHTING VEHICLES
  APC (W) 34 *Tactica*
AIRCRAFT • TPT 10: **Light** 7: 2 Beech 18; 1 Beech 1900D; 2 C-212 *Aviocar* (NC-212); 1 C295; 1 *Turbo Commander* 680; **PAX** 3: 1 B-737-800; 1 Hawker 400XP; 1 F-50
HELICOPTERS
  MRH 5: 3 AS365N3 *Dauphin*; 2 AW189
  TPT • Light 34: 9 AW169; 3 Bell 206 *Jet Ranger*; 3 Bell 429; 19 Bo-105 (NBo-105)

KPLP (Sea and Coast Guard Unit) ε9,000
Responsible to Military Sea Communications Agency
EQUIPMENT BY TYPE
PATROL AND COASTAL COMBATANTS 76
  PCO 7: 1 *Arda Dedali*; 3 *Chundamani*; 1 *Kalimasada*; 2 *Trisula*
  PB 69: 4 *Golok* (SAR); 5 *Kujang*; 6 *Rantos*; 54 (various)
LOGISTICS AND SUPPORT • ABU 7

Bakamla (Maritime Security Agency) 1,250
EQUIPMENT BY TYPE
PATROL AND COASTAL COMBATANTS 10
  PSO 4: 3 *Pulau Nipaa* with 1 hel landing platform; 1 *Tanjung Datu* with 1 hel landing platform
  PB 6 *Bintang Laut* (KCR-40 mod)

Reserve Organisations

Kamra People's Security ε40,000
Report for 3 weeks' basic training each year; part-time police auxiliary

DEPLOYMENT

CENTRAL AFRICAN REPUBLIC: UN • MINUSCA 255; 1 engr coy
DEMOCRATIC REPUBLIC OF THE CONGO: UN • MONUSCO 1,037; 1 inf bn; 1 engr coy
LEBANON: UN • UNIFIL 1,231; 1 mech inf bn; 1 log coy; 1 FSGM
SOUTH SUDAN: UN • UNMISS 4
SUDAN: UN • UNISFA 4
WESTERN SAHARA: UN • MINURSO 3

Japan JPN

Japanese Yen JPY		2023	2024	2025
GDP	JPY	593trn	610trn	630trn
	USD	4.22trn	4.07trn	4.39trn
Real GDP growth	%	1.7	0.3	1.1
Def bdgt	JPY	6.82trn	7.95trn	8.54trn
	USD	48.6bn	53.0bn	59.5bn

Real-terms defence budget trend (USDbn, constant 2015)

Population	123,201,945					
Age	0–14	15–19	20–24	25–29	30–64	65 plus
Male	6.3%	2.4%	2.4%	2.7%	21.9%	13.0%
Female	5.9%	2.2%	2.3%	2.3%	22.2%	16.5%

Capabilities

Tokyo's principal security challenges are a more assertive China and North Korean and Russian military activities. These challenges are reflected in the 2024 defence white paper, which builds on a series of national security policy documents published in December 2022. Japan is increasing its defence spending and has also pursued policy and legislative reforms to strengthen the Japan Self-Defense Forces (JSDF). These include a Permanent Joint Headquarters to unify the JSDF's command structure and greater coordination with civilian agencies. Legislative reforms will also enable a more active role for the JSDF in international security. The navy has strengths in anti-submarine warfare and air-defence, while the country's Amphibious Rapid Deployment Brigade focuses on the defence of remote islands. The country is also looking to improve equipment capabilities, including stand-off missile systems and air and missile defence. Japan is also developing capabilities in space, cyberspace and the electromagnetic spectrum through plans for 'multi-domain defence force'. The country faces challenges in attracting and retaining personnel, which are compounded by Japan's falling birthrate, private sector competition and poor perceptions of military life. Japan's alliance with the US is central to its defence policy, reflected by continued US basing, the widespread use of US equipment across all three services and regular joint training. However, Japan has also expanded its traditional defence and security ties through a series of defence cooperation agreements. It signed Reciprocal Access Agreements with Australia in 2022 and with the UK in 2023, and signed an Acquisition and

Cross-Servicing Agreement with Germany in 2024. Cooperation has also expanded into Japan's defence-industrial base which, despite being technologically advanced, has traditionally seen limited international cooperation. In 2022, Japan, Italy and the UK announced the joint development of new combat aircraft, the Global Combat Air Programme, due to enter service by 2035. Japan has long had highly restrictive arms export policies, though has reformed these to sell abroad. In March 2024, Japan revised its guidelines on exporting defence equipment, including domestically produced missiles and artillery.

ACTIVE 247,150 (Ground Self-Defense Force 150,250 Maritime Self-Defense Force 45,400 Air Self-Defense Force 47,000 Central Staff 4,500) Gendarmerie & Paramilitary 14,800

RESERVE 55,900 (General Reserve Army (GSDF) 46,000 Ready Reserve Army (GSDF) 8,000 Navy 1,100 Air 800)

ORGANISATIONS BY SERVICE

Space
EQUIPMENT BY TYPE
SATELLITES 11
  COMMUNICATIONS 2: 1 *Kirameki*-1; 1 *Kirameki*-2
  ISR 9 IGS

Ground Self-Defense Force 150,250
FORCES BY ROLE
COMMAND
  5 army HQ (regional comd)
SPECIAL FORCES
  1 spec ops unit (bn)
MANOEUVRE
  Armoured
  1 (7th) armd div (1 armd recce sqn, 3 tk regt, 1 armd inf regt, 1 hel sqn, 1 SP arty regt, 1 AD regt, 1 cbt engr bn, 1 sigs bn, 1 NBC bn, 1 log regt)
  1 indep tk bn
  Mechanised
  1 (2nd) inf div (1 armd recce sqn, 1 tk regt, 1 mech inf regt, 2 inf regt, 1 hel sqn, 1 SP arty regt, 1 AT coy, 1 ADA bn, 1 cbt engr bn, 1 sigs bn, 1 NBC bn, 1 log regt)
  1 (4th) inf div (1 armd recce bn, 3 inf regt, 1 inf coy, 1 hel sqn, 1 AT coy, 1 SAM bn, 1 cbt engr bn, 1 sigs bn, 1 NBC bn, 1 log regt)
  1 (6th) inf div (1 recce sqn, 1 mech inf regt; 3 inf regt, 1 hel sqn, 1 SAM bn, 1 cbt engr bn, 1 sigs bn, 1 NBC bn, 1 log regt)
  1 (9th) inf div (1 armd recce bn, 3 inf regt, 1 hel sqn, 1 SAM bn, 1 cbt engr bn, 1 sigs bn, 1 NBC bn, 1 log regt)
  1 (5th) inf bde (1 armd recce sqn, 1 tk bn, 1 mech inf regt, 2 inf regt, 1 hel sqn, 1 SP arty bn, 1 SAM coy, 1 cbt engr coy, 1 sigs coy, 1 NBC coy, 1 log bn)
  1 (11th) inf bde (1 armd recce sqn, 1 tk sqn, 3 inf regt, 1 hel sqn, 1 SP arty bn, 1 SAM coy, 1 cbt engr coy, 1 sigs coy, 1 NBC coy, 1 log bn)

  Light
  3 (1st, 3rd & 10th) inf div (1 armd recce bn, 3 inf regt, 1 hel sqn, 1 SAM bn, 1 cbt engr bn, 1 sigs bn, 1 NBC bn, 1 log regt)
  1 (8th) inf div (1 recce sqn, 3 inf regt, 1 hel sqn, 1 SAM bn, 1 cbt engr bn, 1 sigs bn, 1 NBC bn, 1 log regt)
  1 (13th) inf bde (1 armd recce bn, 3 inf regt, 1 hel sqn, 1 SAM coy, 1 cbt engr coy, 1 NBC coy, 1 sigs coy, 1 log bn)
  1 (14th) inf bde (1 recce sqn, 2 inf regt, 1 hel sqn, 1 SAM coy, 1 cbt engr coy, 1 NBC coy, 1 sigs coy, 1 log bn)
  1 (15th) inf bde (1 recce sqn, 1 inf regt, 1 avn sqn, 1 AD regt, 1 cbt engr coy, 1 NBC coy, 1 sigs coy, 1 log bn)
  Air Manoeuvre
  1 (1st) AB bde (3 AB bn, 1 fd arty bn, 1 cbt engr coy, 1 sigs coy, 1 log bn)
  1 (12th) air mob inf bde (1 armd recce bn, 3 inf regt, 1 avn sqn, 1 SAM coy, 1 cbt engr coy, 1 NBC coy, 1 sigs coy, 1 log bn)
  Amphibious
  1 amph bde (1 recce coy, 3 amph regt, 1 amph aslt bn, 1 mor bn, 1 log bn)
COMBAT SUPPORT
  1 (1st) arty bde (1 MRL regt (2 MRL bn); 3 AShM regt)
  1 (2nd) arty bde (1 fd arty regt (1 SP arty bn; 3 fd arty bn); 1 MRL coy; 2 AShM regt)
  2 fd arty regt (4 fd arty bn)
  1 fd arty regt (2 fd arty bn)
  4 engr bde
  1 engr unit
  1 EW bn
  5 int bn
  1 MP bde
  1 sigs bde
COMBAT SERVICE SUPPORT
  5 log unit (bde)
  5 trg bde
COASTAL DEFENCE
  1 AShM regt
TILTROTOR
  2 sqn with MV-22B *Osprey* (forming)
HELICOPTER
  1 hel bde (1 tpt sqn; 6 tpt hel sqn; 1 VIP tpt hel bn)
  5 hel gp (1 atk hel bn, 1 hel bn)
AIR DEFENCE
  2 SAM bde (2 SAM gp)
  3 SAM gp
EQUIPMENT BY TYPE
ARMOURED FIGHTING VEHICLES
  MBT 349: 111 Type-10; 238 Type-90
  ASLT 177 Type-16 MCV
  RECCE 110 Type-87
  IFV 68 Type-89
  APC 786
    APC (T) 226 Type-73

APC (W) 560: 179 Type-82 (CP); 381 Type-96
AAV 52 AAV-7
AUV 8 *Bushmaster*
ENGINEERING & MAINTENANCE VEHICLES
ARV 54: 5 Type-11; 19 Type-78; 30 Type-90
VLB 22 Type-91
NBC VEHICLES 55: 34 Chemical Reconnaissance Vehicle; 21 NBC Reconnaissance Vehicle
ANTI-TANK/ANTI-INFRASTRUCTURE
MSL
  SP 37 Type-96 MPMS
  MANPATS Type-79 *Jyu*-MAT; Type-87 *Chu*-MAT; Type-01 LMAT
RCL • 84mm *Carl Gustaf*
ARTILLERY 1,429
SP 155mm 150: 14 Type-19; 136 Type-99
TOWED 155mm 196 FH-70
MRL 227mm 21 M270 MLRS
MOR 1,062: **81mm** 656 L16 **120mm** 382 RT-61; **SP 120mm** 24 Type-96
COASTAL DEFENCE • AShM 100: 38 Type-12; 62 Type-88
AIRCRAFT • TPT • Light 8 Beech 350 *King Air* (LR-2)
TILTROTOR • TPT 14 MV-22B *Osprey*
HELICOPTERS
ATK 84: 39 AH-1S *Cobra*; 12 AH-64D *Apache*; 33 OH-1S
MRH 8 Bell 412EPX (UH-2)
TPT 218: **Heavy** 44: 3 CH-47D *Chinook* (CH-47J); 41 CH-47JA *Chinook*; **Medium** 42: 3 H225 *Super Puma* MkII+ (VIP); 39 UH-60L *Black Hawk* (UH-60JA); **Light** 132: 102 Bell 205 (UH-1J); 30 Enstrom 480B (TH-480B)
AIR DEFENCE
SAM 319+
  Medium-range 123: 45 Type-03 *Chu*-SAM; 12 Type-03 *Chu*-SAM Kai; 66 MIM-23B I-*Hawk*
  Short-range 22 Type-11 *Tan*-SAM
  Point-defence 174+: 84 Type-81 *Tan*-SAM; 90 Type-93 *Kin*-SAM; Type-91 *Kei*-SAM
GUNS • SP 35mm 52 Type-87
AIR-LAUNCHED MISSILES
AAM • IR Type-91
ASM AGM-114M *Hellfire* II; BGM-71 TOW

Maritime Self-Defense Force 45,400
EQUIPMENT BY TYPE
SUBMARINES • SSK 25:
  10 *Oyashio* (of which 2 in trg role) with 6 single 533mm TT with UGM-84C *Harpoon* Block 1B AShM/Type-89 HWT
  12 *Soryu* (of which 10 fitted with AIP and 2 fitted with lithium-ion fuel battery) with 6 single 533mm TT with UGM-84C *Harpoon* Block 1B AShM/Type-89 HWT
  3 *Taigei* (of which 1 in trg role) (fitted with lithium-ion fuel battery) with 6 single 533mm TT with UGM-84C *Harpoon* Block 1B AShM/Type-89 HWT/Type-18 HWT

PRINCIPAL SURFACE COMBATANTS 54
AIRCRAFT CARRIERS • CVH 4:
  2 *Hyuga* with 2 8-cell Mk 41 VLS with ASROC/RIM-162B ESSM SAM, 2 triple 324mm HOS-303 ASTT with Mk 46/Type-97 LWT, 2 Mk 15 *Phalanx* Block 1B CIWS (normal ac capacity 3 SH-60 *Seahawk* ASW hel; plus additional ac embarkation up to 7 SH-60 *Seahawk* or 7 MCH-101)
  2 *Izumo* (being converted to CVS) with 2 11-cell Mk 15 SeaRAM lnchr with RIM-116 SAM, 2 Mk 15 *Phalanx* Block 1B CIWS (normal ac capacity 7 SH-60 *Seahawk* ASW hel; plus additional ac embarkation up to 5 SH-60 *Seahawk*/MCH-101 hel)
CRUISERS • CGHM 4:
  2 *Atago* with *Aegis* Baseline 9 C2, 2 quad lnchr with SSM-1B (Type-90) AShM, 12 8-cell Mk 41 VLS (8 fore, 4 aft) with SM-2 Block IIIA/B SAM/SM-3 Block IA/IB/IIA SAM/ASROC A/S msl, 2 triple 324mm HOS-302 ASTT with Mk 46 LWT, 2 Mk 15 *Phalanx* Block 1B CIWS, 1 127mm gun (capacity 1 SH-60 *Seahawk* ASW hel)
  2 *Maya* (*Atago* mod) with *Aegis* Baseline 9 C2, w quad lnchr with SSM-1B (Type-90) AShM/SSM-2 (Type-17) AShM, 12 8-cell Mk 41 VLS (8 fore, 4 aft) with SM-2 Block IIIA/B SAM/SM-3 Block IA/IB/IIA SAM/Type-07 A/S msl, 2 triple 324mm HOS-303 ASTT with Mk 46 LWT, 2 Mk 15 *Phalanx* Block 1B CIWS, 1 127mm gun (capacity 1 SH-60 *Seahawk* ASW hel)
DESTROYERS 34
DDGHM 28:
  8 *Asagiri* with 2 quad lnchr with RGM-84C *Harpoon* Block 1B AShM, 1 octuple Mk 29 lnchr with RIM-7M *Sea Sparrow* SAM, 2 triple 324mm HOS-302 ASTT with Mk 46 LWT, 1 octuple Mk 112 lnchr with ASROC, 2 Mk 15 *Phalanx* CIWS, 1 76mm gun (capacity 1 SH-60 *Seahawk* ASW hel)
  4 *Akizuki* with 2 quad lnchr with SSM-1B (Type-90) AShM, 4 8-cell Mk 41 VLS with ASROC/RIM-162B ESSM SAM, 2 triple 324mm HOS-303 ASTT with Type-97 LWT, 2 Mk 15 *Phalanx* Block 1B CIWS, 1 127mm gun (capacity 1 SH-60 *Seahawk* ASW hel)
  2 *Asahi* (*Akizuki* mod) with 2 quad lnchr with SSM-1B (Type-90) AShM, 4 8-cell Mk 41 VLS with RIM-162B ESSM SAM/Type-07 A/S msl, 2 triple 324mm HOS-303 ASTT with Type-12 LWT, 2 Mk 15 *Phalanx* Block 1B CIWS, 1 127mm gun (capacity 1 SH-60 *Seahawk* ASW hel)
  9 *Murasame* with 2 quad lnchr with SSM-1B (Type-90) AShM, 1 16-cell Mk 48 mod 0 VLS with RIM-162C ESSM SAM, 2 triple 324mm HOS-302 ASTT with Mk 46 LWT, 2 8-cell Mk 41 VLS with ASROC, 2 Mk 15 *Phalanx* CIWS, 2 76mm gun (capacity 1 SH-60 *Seahawk* ASW hel)
  5 *Takanami* (improved *Murasame*) with 2 quad lnchr with SSM-1B (Type-90) AShM, 4 8-cell Mk 41 VLS with RIM-162B ESSM SAM/ASROC A/S msl, 2 triple 324mm HOS-302 ASTT with Mk 46 LWT, 2 Mk 15 *Phalanx* Block 1B CIWS, 1 127mm gun (capacity 1 SH-60 *Seahawk* ASW hel)

DDGM 6:
  2 *Hatakaze* (trg role) with 2 quad lnchr with RGM-84C *Harpoon* Block 1B AShM, 1 Mk 13 GMLS with SM-1MR Block VI SAM, 2 triple 324mm HOS-301 ASTT with Mk 46 LWT, 1 octuple Mk 112 lnchr with ASROC, 2 Mk 15 *Phalanx* CIWS, 2 127mm gun, 1 hel landing platform
  4 *Kongou* with *Aegis* Baseline 5 C2, 2 quad lnchr with RGM-84C *Harpoon* Block 1B AShM, 12 8-cell Mk 41 VLS (of which 2 only 5-cell and fitted with reload crane) with SM-2 Block IIIA/B SAM/SM-3 Block IA SAM/ASROC A/S msl, 2 triple 324mm HOS-302 ASTT with Mk 46 LWT, 2 Mk 15 *Phalanx* Block 1B CIWS, 1 127mm gun

FRIGATES 12
  FFGHM 6 *Mogami* with 2 quad lnchr with SSM-2 (Type-17) AShM, 1 11-cell Mk 15 SeaRAM GMLS with RIM-116 RAM SAM, 2 triple 324mm HOS-303 ASTT with Mk 46 LWT, 1 127mm gun (capacity 1 SH-60 *Seahawk* hel) (to be fitted with Mk 41 VLS)
  FFG 6 *Abukuma* with 2 quad lnchr with RGM-84C *Harpoon* Block 1B AShM, 2 triple 324mm HOS-301 ASTT with Mk 46 LWT, 1 octuple Mk 112 lnchr with ASROC A/S msl, 1 Mk 15 *Phalanx* CIWS, 1 76mm gun

PATROL AND COASTAL COMBATANTS 6
  PBFG 6 *Hayabusa* with 4 SSM-1B (Type-90) AShM, 1 76mm gun

MINE WARFARE • MINE COUNTERMEASURES 19
  MCCS 2:
    1 *Uraga* with 1 76mm gun, 1 hel landing platform (for MCH-101 hel)
    1 *Uraga* with 1 hel landing platform (for MCH-101 hel)
  MSC 14: 3 *Hiroshima*; 8 *Sugashima* (1 more non-operational); 3 *Enoshima*
  MSO 3 *Awaji*

AMPHIBIOUS
  PRINCIPAL AMPHIBIOUS SHIPS • LHD 3 *Osumi* with 2 Mk 15 *Phalanx* CIWS (capacity for 2 CH-47 hel) (capacity 10 Type-90 MBT; 2 LCAC(L) ACV; 330 troops)
  LANDING CRAFT 7
    LCM 1 LCU-2001
    LCAC 6 LCAC(L) (capacity either 1 MBT or 60 troops)

LOGISTICS AND SUPPORT 26
  AGBH 1 *Shirase* (capacity 2 AW101 *Merlin* hel)
  AGEH 1 *Asuka* (wpn trials) with 1 8-cell Mk 41 VLS (capacity 1 SH-60 *Seahawk* hel)
  AGOS 3 *Hibiki* with 1 hel landing platform
  AGS 3: 1 *Futami*; 1 *Nichinan*; 1 *Shonan*
  AOEH 2 *Mashu* (capacity 1 med hel)
  AOE 3 *Towada* with 1 hel landing platform
  AO 2 YOT-01
  ARC 1 *Muroto*
  ASR 2: 1 *Chihaya* with 1 hel landing platform; 1 *Chiyoda* with 1 hel landing platform
  ATF 5 *Hiuchi*

  AX 3:
    1 *Kashima* with 2 triple 324mm HOS-301 ASTT, 1 76mm gun, 1 hel landing platform
    1 *Kurobe* with 1 76mm gun (trg spt ship)
    1 *Tenryu* (trg spt ship); with 1 76mm gun (capacity: 1 med hel)

UNINHABITED MARITIME PLATFORMS • USV
  MW • Medium *Mogami* USV

UNINHABITED MARITIME SYSTEMS • UUV
  DATA REMUS 100
  MW OZZ-5; *SeaFox*

Naval Aviation ε9,800
7 Air Groups
FORCES BY ROLE
ANTI SUBMARINE/SURFACE WARFARE
  2 sqn with SH-60B (SH-60J)/SH-60K *Seahawk*
  3 sqn with SH-60K *Seahawk*
MARITIME PATROL
  2 sqn with P-1
  2 sqn with P-3C *Orion*
ELECTRONIC WARFARE
  1 sqn with EP-3C *Orion*; Learjet 36A
MINE COUNTERMEASURES
  1 sqn with MCH-101
SEARCH & RESCUE
  1 sqn with *Shin Meiwa* US-2
TRANSPORT
  1 sqn with Beech 90 *King Air* (LC-90); KC-130R *Hercules*
TRAINING
  1 sqn with Beech 90 *King Air* (TC-90)
  1 sqn with P-3C *Orion*
  1 sqn with T-5J
  1 hel sqn with H135 (TH-135); SH-60K *Seahawk*

EQUIPMENT BY TYPE
AIRCRAFT 66 combat capable
  ASW 66: 34 P-1; 32 P-3C *Orion*
  ELINT 5 EP-3C *Orion*
  ISR 2 Learjet 36A
  SAR 7 *Shin Meiwa* US-2
  TPT 24: **Medium** 6 C-130R *Hercules*; **Light** 18: 5 Beech 90 *King* Air (LC-90); 13 Beech 90 *King Air* (TC-90) (trg)
  TRG 30 T-5J
HELICOPTERS
  ASW 81: 7 SH-60B *Seahawk* (SH-60J); 72 SH-60K *Seahawk*; 2 SH-60L *Seahawk* (in test)
  MCM 10 MCH-101
  TPT 18: **Medium** 3 AW101 *Merlin* (CH-101); **Light** 15 H135 (TH-135) (trg)
AIR-LAUNCHED MISSILES
  ASM AGM-65 *Maverick*
  AShM AGM-84 *Harpoon*; ASM-1C (Type-90)

Air Self-Defense Force 47,000

7 cbt wg

FORCES BY ROLE
FIGHTER
 7 sqn with F-15J *Eagle*
 3 sqn with F-2A/B
 2 sqn with F-35A *Lightning* II
ELECTRONIC WARFARE
 1 sqn with EC-1; YS-11EA
ELINT
 1 sqn with RC-2; YS-11EB
AIRBORNE EARLY WARNING & CONTROL
 2 sqn with E-2C/D *Hawkeye*
 1 sqn with E-767
SEARCH & RESCUE
 1 wg with U-125A *Peace Krypton*; UH-60J *Black Hawk*
TANKER
 1 sqn with KC-46A *Pegasus* (forming)
 1 sqn with KC-767J
TRANSPORT
 1 sqn with C-1; C-2; Gulfstream IV (U-4)
 1 sqn with C-2
 1 sqn with C-130H *Hercules*; KC-130H *Hercules*
 1 VIP sqn with B-777-300ER
 Some (liaison) sqn with Gulfstream IV (U-4); T-4*
TRAINING
 1 (aggressor) sqn with F-15J *Eagle*
TEST
 1 wg with F-15J *Eagle*; T-4*
TRANSPORT HELICOPTER
 4 flt with CH-47J *Chinook*
ISR UAV
 1 sqn with RQ-4B *Global Hawk* (forming)

EQUIPMENT BY TYPE
AIRCRAFT 527 combat capable
 FTR 200: 156 F-15J *Eagle*; 44 F-15DJ *Eagle*
 FGA 130: 64 F-2A; 27 F-2B; 39 F-35A *Lightning* II
 EW 3: 1 Kawasaki EC-1; 2 YS-11EA
 SIGINT 4: 1 RC-2; 3 YS-11EB
 AEW&C 22: 10 E-2C *Hawkeye*; 8 E-2D *Hawkeye*; 4 E-767
 SAR 26 U-125A *Peace Krypton*
 TKR/TPT 11: 4 KC-46A *Pegasus*; 3 KC-130H *Hercules*; 4 KC-767J
 TPT 53: **Medium** 33: 13 C-130H *Hercules*; 4 C-1; 16 C-2; **PAX** 20: 2 B-777-300ER (VIP); 13 Beech T-400; 5 Gulfstream IV (U-4)
 TRG 246: 197 T-4*; 49 T-7
HELICOPTERS
 SAR 38 UH-60J *Black Hawk*
 TPT • Heavy 15 CH-47J *Chinook*
UNINHABITED AERIAL VEHICLES 3
 ISR • Heavy 3 RQ-4B *Global Hawk*

AIR-LAUNCHED MISSILES
 AAM • IR AAM-3 (Type-90); **IIR** AAM-5 (Type-04); **SARH** AIM-7 *Sparrow*; **ARH** AAM-4 (Type-99); AIM-120C5/C7 AMRAAM
 AShM ASM-1 (Type-80); ASM-2 (Type-93)
BOMBS
 Laser & INS/SAT-guided GBU-54 Laser JDAM
 INS/SAT-guided GBU-38 JDAM
 IIR-guided GCS-1

Air Defence

Ac control and warning. 4 wg; 28 radar sites

FORCES BY ROLE
AIR DEFENCE
 4 SAM gp (total: 24 SAM bty with M902 *Patriot* PAC-3)
 1 AD gp with Type-81 *Tan-SAM*

EQUIPMENT BY TYPE
AIR DEFENCE
 SAM 146+
  Long-range 120 M902 *Patriot* PAC-3
  Short-range ε26 Air Base Defense SAM
  Point-defence Type-81 *Tan-SAM*

Gendarmerie & Paramilitary 14,800

Coast Guard 14,800

Ministry of Land, Transport, Infrastructure and Tourism (no cbt role)

EQUIPMENT BY TYPE
PATROL AND COASTAL COMBATANTS 380
 PSOH 19: 1 *Mizuho* (capacity 2 hels); 1 *Mizuho* II (capacity 2 hels); 4 *Shikishima* (capacity 2 hels); 3 *Shunko* (capacity 2 hels); 1 *Soya* (capacity 1 hel) (icebreaking capability); 9 *Tsugaru* (*Soya* mod) (capacity 1 hel)
 PSO 52: 9 *Hateruma* with 1 hel landing platform; 3 *Hida* with 1 hel landing platform; 6 *Iwami*; 1 *Izu* with 1 hel landing platform; 1 *Itsukushima* (trg role); 1 *Kojima* (trg role) with 1 hel landing platform; 1 *Miura* (trg role) with 1 hel landing platform; 3 *Miyako* with 1 hel landing platform; 5 *Ojika* with 1 hel landing platform; 22 *Taketomi* with 1 hel landing platform
 PCO 13: 3 *Aso*; 9 *Katori*; 1 *Teshio* (icebreaker)
 PCC 22: 2 *Amami*; 20 *Tokara*
 PBF 50: 26 *Hayagumo*; 17 *Raizan*; 1 *Takatsuki*; 6 *Tsuruugi*
 PB 55: 4 *Asogiri*; 4 *Hamagumo*; 10 *Hayanami*; 15 *Katonami*; 1 *Matsunami*; 11 *Shimoji*; 10 *Yodo*
 PBI 169: 2 *Hakubai*; 3 *Hayagiku*; 4 *Hayakaze*; 160 *Himegiku*
LOGISTICS AND SUPPORT 24
 ABU 3 *Teshio*
 AGS 15: 6 *Hamashio*; 1 *Hamashio* II (*Katonami* mod); 1 *Jinbei*; 2 *Meiyo*; 2 *Peiyo*; 1 *Shoyo*; 1 *Takuyo*; 1 *Tenyo*
 AG 3: 1 *Aki Hikari*; 2 *Hakuun*
 AXL 3: 1 *Aoba*; 2 other

UNINHABITED MARITIME SYSTEMS • UUV
  DATA *Naminow*
AIRCRAFT
  MP 6 *Falcon 2000MSA*
  SAR 4 Saab 340B
  TPT 24: **Light** 22: 4 Cessna 172; 10 Beech 350 *King Air* (LR-2); 8 DHC-8-300 (MP); **PAX** 2 Gulfstream V (MP)
HELICOPTERS
  MRH 3 Bell 412 *Twin Huey*
  SAR 15 S-76D
  TPT 44: **Medium** 17: 2 AS332 *Super Puma*; 15 H225 *Super Puma*; **Light** 27: 21 AW139; 4 Bell 505 *Jet Ranger X*; 2 S-76C
UNINHABITED AERIAL VEHICLES
  CISR • **Heavy** 3 MQ-9B *Sea Guardian* (unarmed) (leased)

DEPLOYMENT

ARABIAN SEA & GULF OF ADEN: 200; 1 DDGHM
DJIBOUTI: 180; 2 P-3C *Orion*
SOUTH SUDAN: UN • UNMISS 4

FOREIGN FORCES

United States
US Indo-Pacific Command: 55,750
  Army 2,450; 1 corps HQ (fwd); 1 SF gp; 1 avn bn; 1 SAM bn with M903 *Patriot* PAC MSE
  Navy 22,200; 1 CVN; 2 CGHM; 8 DDGHM; 3 DDGM; 1 LCC; 4 MCO; 1 LHA; 2 LPD; 1 LSD; 2 FGA sqn with 10 F/A-18E *Super Hornet*; 1 FGA sqn with 10 F/A-18F *Super Hornet*; 1 FGA sqn with 10 F-35C *Lightning* II; 2 ASW sqn with 5 P-8A *Poseidon*; 2 EW sqn with 5 EA-18G *Growler*; 1 AEW&C sqn with 5 E-2D *Hawkeye*; 2 ASW hel sqn with 12 MH-60R *Seahawk*; 1 tpt hel sqn with MH-60S *Knight Hawk*; 1 base at Sasebo; 1 base at Yokosuka
  USAF: 13,000; 1 HQ (5th Air Force) at Okinawa–Kadena AB; 1 ftr wg at Misawa AB (2 ftr sqn with 22 F-16C/D *Fighting Falcon*); 1 ftr wg at Okinawa–Kadena AB (2 ftr sqn with 5 F-15C/D *Eagle*; 1 ftr sqn with 12 F-22A *Raptor*; 1 FGA sqn with 12 F-16C/D *Fighting Falcon*; 1 tkr sqn with 15 KC-135R *Stratotanker*; 1 AEW sqn with 2 E-3G *Sentry*; 1 CSAR sqn with 10 HH-60G *Pave Hawk*; 1 CISR UAV sqn with 4 MQ-9A *Reaper*); 1 tpt wg at Yokota AB with 10 C-130J-30 *Hercules*; 3 Beech 1900C (C-12J); 1 spec ops gp at Okinawa–Kadena AB with (1 sqn with 5 MC-130J *Commando* II; 1 sqn with 5 CV-22B *Osprey*); 1 ISR sqn with RC-135 *Rivet Joint*; 1 ISR UAV flt with 5 RQ-4A *Global Hawk*
  US Space Force 100
  USMC 18,000; 1 mne div; 1 mne regt HQ; 1 arty regt HQ; 1 recce bn; 3 mne bn; 1 arty bn; 1 FGA sqn at Iwakuni with 12 F/A-18C/D *Hornet*; 2 FGA sqn at Iwakuni with 12 F-35B *Lightning* II; 1 tkr sqn at Iwakuni with 15 KC-130J *Hercules*; 2 tpt sqn at Futenma with 12 MV-22B *Osprey*
US Strategic Command: 1 AN/TPY-2 X-band radar at Shariki; 1 AN/TPY-2 X-band radar at Kyogamisaki

Korea, Democratic People's Republic of DPRK

Definitive macro- and defence-economic data not available

Population	26,298,666					
Age	0–14	15–19	20–24	25–29	30–64	65 plus
Male	10.2%	3.3%	3.5%	3.7%	23.8%	4.2%
Female	9.7%	3.2%	3.5%	3.7%	24.0%	7.1%

Capabilities

North Korea continues to signal improvements in its nuclear weapons capacity. The country showcased a new tactical warhead design in 2023 and has conducted several claimed simulated nuclear strike drills. There remains concern that the country may renew nuclear testing. North Korea's continued investment in asymmetric capabilities, particularly the development of nuclear weapons and ballistic-missile delivery systems, reflects an awareness of the qualitative inferiority of its conventional forces. It tested a second solid-propellant ICBM design in November 2024. Efforts to further diversify shorter-range delivery systems continue. North Korea is also exploring new, potentially less vulnerable basing options, such as a rail-based system and additional submarine-launched designs. North Korea remains diplomatically isolated. While foreign defence cooperation is restricted by international pressure and sanctions, Pyongyang has developed military ties, including with Moscow. Western states assert that North Korea has delivered large quantities of artillery rounds to aid Russia's war on Ukraine and also started transferring short-range ballistic missiles by the end of 2023. In June 2024, the two countries signed and later ratified a comprehensive strategic partnership treaty. During October 2024, around 10,000 North Korean soldiers were transported to Russia, with some believed to have deployed to the Kursk region. The forces regularly conduct exercises, but the staged nature of those publicised is not necessarily representative of wider operational capability. Increasingly obsolete Soviet-era and Chinese-origin equipment is supplemented by a growing number of indigenous designs and upgrades. The precise capability of the locally made equipment is unclear. Pyongyang has maintenance, repair and overhaul capacity and the ability to manufacture light arms, armoured vehicles, artillery and missile systems.

ACTIVE 1,280,000 (Army 1,100,000 Navy 60,000 Air 110,000 Strategic Forces 10,000) **Gendarmerie & Paramilitary 189,000**

Conscript liability Army 5–12 years, Navy 5–10 years, Air Force 3–4 years, followed by compulsory part-time service to age 40. Thereafter service in the Worker/Peasant Red Guard to age 60

RESERVE ε600,000 (Armed Forces ε600,000), **Gendarmerie & Paramilitary 5,700,000**

Reservists are assigned to units (see also Paramilitary)

ORGANISATIONS BY SERVICE

Strategic Forces ε10,000

North Korea describes its ballistic missile force as nuclear capable, although there is no conclusive evidence to verify the successful integration of a warhead with any of these systems

EQUIPMENT BY TYPE (ε)
SURFACE-TO-SURFACE MISSILE LAUNCHERS
ICBM 17+: 6+ *Hwasong*-14/-15/-15 mod 1/-18 (all in test); 11+ *Hwasong*-17 mod 1 (in test); *Hwasong*-19 (in test; (Earlier *Hwasong*-13/-13 mod designs untested and presumed cancelled)
IRBM 10+: 10+ *Hwasong*-12/-12 mod 1 (in test); some *Hwasong*-16 (in test); some *Hwasong*-16B
MRBM 17+: ε10 *Hwasong*-7 (*Nodong* mod 1/mod 2); 7+ *Pukgusong*-2 (in test); some *Scud*-ER
SBRM 319+: 30+ *Hwasong*-5/-6 (RS-SS-1C/D *Scud*-B/C); 1+ *Hwasong*-8/-8 mcd 1 (in test); 17+ *Hwasong*-11A (KN-23) (road & rail mobile variants); 9+ *Hwasong*-11B (KN-24) (in test); 6+ *Hwasong*-11C (KN-23 mod 1) (in test); 250 *Hwasong*-11D; some *Hwasong*-11S (KN-23 mod 2) (in test); 6+ *Scud* (mod) (status uncertain)
GLCM some *Hwasal*-1/-1D-3/-2 (in test)

Army ε1,100,000
FORCES BY ROLE
COMMAND
10 inf corps HQ
1 (Capital Defence) corps HQ
MANOEUVRE
Armoured
1 armd div
15 armd bde
Mechanised
6 mech div
Light
27 inf div
14 inf bde
COMBAT SUPPORT
1 arty div
21 arty bde
9 MRL bde
5–8 engr river crossing/amphibious regt
1 engr river crossing bde

Special Purpose Forces Command 88,000
FORCES BY ROLE
SPECIAL FORCES
8 (Reconnaissance General Bureau) SF bn
MANOEUVRE
Reconnaissance
17 recce bn
Light
9 lt inf bde
6 sniper bde
Air Manoeuvre
3 AB bde
1 AB bn
2 sniper bde
Amphibious
2 sniper bde

Reserves 600,000
FORCES BY ROLE
MANOEUVRE
Light
40 inf div
18 inf bde

EQUIPMENT BY TYPE (ε)
ARMOURED FIGHTING VEHICLES
MBT 3,500+ T-34/T-54/T-55/T-62/Type-59/*Chonma*/*Pokpoong*/*Songun*/M-2020
LT TK 560+: 560 PT-76; M-1985
IFV 32 BTR-80A
APC 2,500+
  APC (T) BTR-50; Type-531 (Type-63); VTT-323
  APC (W) 2,500 BTR-40/BTR-60/M-1992/1/BTR-152/M-2010 (6×6)/M-2010 (8×8)
ANTI-TANK/ANTI-INFRASTRUCTURE
MSL
  SP 9K11 *Malyutka* (RS-AT-3 *Sagger*); M-2010 ATGM
  MANPATS 2K15 *Shmel* (RS-AT-1 *Snapper*); 9K111 *Fagot* (RS-AT-4 *Spigot*); 9K111-1 *Konkurs* (RS-AT-5 *Spandrel*)
RCL 82mm 1,700 B-10
ARTILLERY 21,600+
  SP/TOWED 8,600:
  SP 122mm M-1977; M-1981; M-1985; M-1991; **130mm** M-1975; M-1981; M-1991; **152mm** M-1974; M-1977; M-2018; **170mm** M-1978; M-1989
  TOWED 122mm D-30; D-74; M-1931/37; **130mm** M-46; **152mm** M-1937; M-1938; M-1943
  GUN/MOR 120mm (reported)
  MRL 5,500: **107mm** Type-63; VTT-323 107mm; **122mm** BM-11; M-1977 (BM-21); M-1985; M-1992; M-1993; VTT-323 122mm; **200mm** BMD-20; **240mm** BM-24; M-1985; M-1989; M-1991; **300mm** some M-2015 (KN-SS-X-09) (in test)
  MOR 7,500: **82mm** M-37; **120mm** M-43; **160mm** M-43
SURFACE-TO-SURFACE MISSILE LAUNCHERS
  SBRM 24+: 24 FROG-3/-5/-7; some M-2019 (KN-25) (in test); some *Toksa* (RS-SS-21B *Scarab* mod)
AIR DEFENCE
SAM
  Point-defence 9K35 *Strela*-10 (RS-SA-13 *Gopher*); 9K310 *Igla*-1 (RS-SA-16 *Gimlet*); 9K32 *Strela*-2 (RS-SA-7 *Grail*)‡
GUNS 11,000+
  SP 14.5mm M-1984; **23mm** M-1992; **37mm** M-1992; **57mm** M-1985
  TOWED 11,000: **14.5mm** ZPU-1/ZPU-2/ZPU-4; **23mm** ZU-23; **37mm** M-1939; **57mm** S-60; **85mm** M-1939 *KS*-12; **100mm** KS-19

Navy ε60,000
EQUIPMENT BY TYPE
SUBMARINES 71

SSB 1 *8.24 Yongung* (*Gorae* (*Sinpo*-B)) (SLBM trials) with 1 *Pukguksong*-1 SLBM (status unclear)/*Hwasong*-11S (KN-23 mod 2) SLBM (in test)

SSK ε20 Type-033 (*Romeo*) with 8 single 533mm TT with SAET-60 HWT

SSC ε40 (some *Sang-O* some with 2 single 533mm TT with 53–65E HWT; some *Sang-O* II with 4 single 533mm TT with 53–65E HWT)

SSW ε10† (some *Yugo* some with 2 single 406mm TT; some *Yeono* some with 2 single 533mm TT)

PRINCIPAL SURFACE COMBATANTS 2
FRIGATES • FFG 2:
1 *Najin* with 2 single lnchr with P-20 (RS-SS-N-2A *Styx*) AShM, 2 RBU 1200 *Uragan* A/S mor, 2 100mm gun, 2 twin 57mm gun

1 *Najin* with 2 twin lnchr with *Kumsong*-3 (KN-SS-N-2 *Stormpetrel*) AShM, 2 RBU 1200 *Uragan* A/S mor, 2 100mm gun, 2 twin 57mm gun (operational status unclear)

PATROL AND COASTAL COMBATANTS 374+
CORVETTES 7
FSGM 2 *Amnok* with 2 quad lnchr with *Hwasal*-2 LACM (operational status unclear, armament may vary between vessels), 1 sextuple GMLS with 9K310 *Igla*-1 (RS-SA-16 *Gimlet*), 4 RBU 1200 A/S mor, 2 AK630 CIWS, 1 100mm gun

FS 5: 4 *Sariwon* with 2 twin 57mm gun; 1 *Tral* with 1 85mm gun

(Two *Tuman*-class corvettes constructed since early 2010s; operational status unknown)

PCG 10 *Soju* (FSU Project 205 mod (*Osa*)) with 4 single lnchr with P-20 (RS-SS-N-2A *Styx*) AShM

PCC 18:
6 Type-037 (*Hainan*) with 4 RBU 1200 A/S mor, 2 twin 57mm gun

7 *Taechong* I with 2 RBU 1200 *Uragan* A/S mor, 1 85mm gun, 1 twin 57mm gun

5 *Taechong* II with 2 RBU 1200 *Uragan* A/S mor, 1 100mm gun, 1 twin 57mm gun

PBFG 31+:
6 *Komar* with 2 single lnchr with P-20 (RS-SS-N-2A *Styx*) AShM

8 Project 205 (*Osa* I) with 4 single lnchr with P-20 (RS-SS-N-2A *Styx*) AShM, 2 twin AK230 CIWS

6 *Sohung* (*Komar* mod) with 2 single lnchr with P-20 (RS-SS-N-2A *Styx*) AShM

1+ *Nongo* with 2 single lnchr with P-15 *Termit* (RS-SS-N-2 *Styx*) AShM (operational status unknown)

6+ *Nongo* with 2 twin lnchr with *Kumsong*-3 (KN-SS-N-2 *Stormpetrel*) AShM (operational status unknown)

4 Type-021 (*Huangfeng*) with 4 single lnchr with P-15 *Termit* (RS-SS-N-2 *Styx*) AShM, 2 twin AK230 CIWS

PBF 222: approx. 50 *Chong-Jin* with 1 85mm gun; 142 *Ku Song/Sin Hung/Sin Hung* (mod); approx. 30 *Sinpo*

PB 86: approx. 50 *Chaho*; 6 *Chong-Ju* with 2 RBU 1200 *Uragan* A/S mor, 1 85mm gun; 12 Type-062 (*Shanghai* II); 18 SO-1 with 4 RBU 1200 *Uragan* A/S mor, 2 twin 57mm gun

MINE WARFARE • MINE COUNTERMEASURES 20
MSC 20: 15 *Yukto* I; 5 *Yukto* II

AMPHIBIOUS
LANDING SHIPS • LSM 10 *Hantae* (capacity 3 tanks; 350 troops)

LANDING CRAFT 255
LCM 25
LCPL approx. 95 *Nampo* (capacity 35 troops)
UCAC 135 *Kongbang* (capacity 50 troops)

LOGISTICS AND SUPPORT 23:
AGI 14 (converted fishing vessels)
AS 8 (converted cargo ships)
ASR 1 *Kowan*

UNINHABITED MARITIME PLATFORMS • UUV
ATK • Extra-Large *Haeil*; *Haeil*-1/-2

Coastal Defence
FORCES BY ROLE
COASTAL DEFENCE
2 AShM regt with HY-1/*Kumsong*-3 (6 sites, some mobile launchers)

EQUIPMENT BY TYPE
COASTAL DEFENCE
ARTY 130mm M-1992; SM-4-1
AShM HY-1; *Kumsong*-3
ARTILLERY • TOWED 122mm M-1931/37; **152mm** M-1937

Air Force 110,000
4 air divs. 1st, 2nd and 3rd Air Divs (cbt) responsible for N, E and S air-defence sectors respectively; 8th Air Div (trg) responsible for NE sector. The AF controls the national airline

FORCES BY ROLE
BOMBER
3 lt regt with H-5; Il-28 *Beagle*

FIGHTER
6 regt with J-5; MiG-17 *Fresco*
4 regt with J-6; MiG-19 *Farmer*
5 regt with J-7; MiG-21F-13/FFM *Fishbed*
1 regt with MiG-15 *Fagot*
1 regt with MiG-21bis *Fishbed*
1 regt with MiG-23ML/P *Flogger*
1 regt with MiG-29A/S/UB *Falcrum*

GROUND ATTACK
1 regt with Su-25K/UBK *Frogfoot*

TRANSPORT
Some regt with An-2 *Colt*/Y-5 (to infiltrate 2 air-force sniper brigades deep into ROK rear areas); Il-62M *Classic*

TRAINING
Some regt with CJ-6; FT-2; MiG-21U/UM

TRANSPORT HELICOPTER
Some regt with Hughes 500D/E; Mi-8 *Hip*; Mi-17 *Hip H*; Mil-26 *Halo*; PZL Mi-2 *Hoplite*; Mi-4 *Hound*; Z-5

AIR DEFENCE
19 bde with S-75 *Dvina* (RS-SA-2 *Guideline*); S-125M1 *Pechora*-M1 (RS-SA-3 *Goa*); S-200 *Angara* (RS-SA-5 *Gammon*); 9K32 *Strela*-2 (RS-SA-7 *Grail*)‡; 9K34 *Strela*-3 (RS-SA-14 *Gremlin*); 9K310 *Igla*-1 (RS-SA-16 *Gimlet*)

EQUIPMENT BY TYPE
AIRCRAFT 545 combat capable
BBR 80 Il-28 *Beagle*/H-5‡ (includes some Il-28 for ISR)
FTR 401+: MiG-15 *Fagot*‡; 107 MiG-17 *Fresco*/J-5‡; 100 MiG-19 *Farmer*/J-6 (incl JJ-6 trg ac); 120 MiG-21F-13 *Fishbed*/J-7; MiG-21PFM *Fishbed*; 46 MiG-23ML *Flogger*; 10 MiG-23P *Flogger*; 18+ MiG-29A/S/UB *Fulcrum*
FGA 30 MiG-21bis *Fishbed* (18 Su-7 *Fitter* in store)
ATK 34 Su-25K/UBK *Frogfoot*
TPT 205: **Heavy** 3 Il-76 (operated by state airline); **Light** ε200 An-2 *Colt*/Y-5; **PAX** 2 Il-62M *Classic* (VIP)
TRG 215+: 180 CJ-6; 35 FT-2; some MiG-21U/UM

HELICOPTERS
MRH 80 Hughes 500D/E (some armed)
TPT 206: **Heavy** 4 Mi-26 *Halo*; **Medium** 63: 15 Mi-8 *Hip*/Mi-17 *Hip H*; 48 Mi-4 *Hound*/Z-5; **Light** 139 PZL Mi-2 *Hoplite*

UNINHABITED AERIAL VEHICLES
ISR • Medium some (unidentified indigenous type); **Light** *Pchela*-1 (*Shmel*) (reported)

AIR DEFENCE • SAM 209+
Long-range 10 S-200 *Angara*†(RS-SA-5 *Gammon*)
Medium-range 179+: some *Pongae*-5 (KN-SA-X-01) (status unknown); 179+ S-75 *Dvina* (RS-SA-2 *Guideline*)
Short-range ε20 S-125M1 *Pechora*-M1† (RS-SA-3 *Goa*)
Point-defence 9K32 *Strela*-2 (RS-SA-7 *Grail*)‡; 9K34 *Strela*-3 (RS-SA-14 *Gremlin*); 9K310 *Igla*-1 (RS-SA-16 *Gimlet*)

AIR-LAUNCHED MISSILES
AAM • IR R-3 (RS-AA-2 *Atoll*)‡; R-60 (RS-AA-8 *Aphid*); R-73 (RS-AA-11A *Archer*); PL-5; PL-7; **SARH** R-23/24 (RS-AA-7 *Apex*); R-27R/ER (RS-AA-10 A/C *Alamo*)
ASM 9M14 *Malyutka* (AT-3 *Sagger*); Kh-23 (RS-AS-7 *Kerry*)‡; Kh-25 (RS-AS-10 *Karen*); Kh-29L (RS-AS-14A *Kedge*)

Gendarmerie & Paramilitary 189,000 active

Security Troops 189,000 (incl border guards, public-safety personnel)
Ministry of Public Security

Worker/Peasant Red Guard ε5,700,000 reservists
Org on a province/town/village basis; comd structure is bde–bn–coy–pl; small arms with some mor and AD guns (but many units unarmed)

DEPLOYMENT
RUSSIA: Army 11,000; 4 inf bde

Korea, Republic of ROK

South Korean Won KRW		2023	2024	2025
GDP	KRW	2.40qrn	2.53qrn	2.63qrn
	USD	1.84trn	1.87trn	1.95trn
Real GDP growth	%	1.4	2.5	2.2
Def bdgt	KRW	57.1trn	59.4trn	61.6trn
	USD	43.8bn	43.9bn	45.5bn

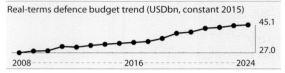
Real-terms defence budget trend (USDbn, constant 2015)

Population	52,081,799					
Age	0–14	15–19	20–24	25–29	30–64	65 plus
Male	5.8%	2.2%	2.8%	3.6%	27.2%	8.5%
Female	5.5%	2.1%	2.5%	3.2%	25.7%	10.8%

Capabilities

South Korea's forces are among the best equipped in the region. The country's defence policy is focused on the threat from North Korea, and Seoul continues to prioritise developing new capabilities to respond to Pyongyang's nuclear and conventional threat. The Defense Innovation 4.0 programme of March 2023 replaced the 2018 Defense Reform 2.0 project; that saw delays in the introduction of advanced weapon systems to offset reduced personnel numbers. As well as redesigning overall defence policy to focus on space, advanced technology and cyber security, South Korea pledges to develop a new integrated concept known as 'Kill Web' to deter DPRK threats, even at left-of-launch, to better support its three axis defence strategy comprising 'Kill Chain', 'Korea Air and Missile Defense' and 'Korea Massive Punishment and Retaliation' components. The alliance with the US is a central element of its defence strategy. The planned transfer of wartime operational control of forces to Seoul is now 'conditions based' with no firm date set. US military personnel and equipment are stationed in South Korea, along with THAAD missile-defence systems. South Korea inaugurated a space-operations centre in 2021 and launched two military surveillance satellites in the span of four months in 2023–24. South Korea has demonstrated the capacity to support small international deployments. The equipment inventory increasingly comprises modern systems. South Korea has developed a substantial domestic defence industry which supplies a large proportion of equipment requirements, although procures some equipment – notably the F-35A aircraft – from the US. Local defence companies are having growing international export success, though industry will have to carefully balance new export contracts against existing local orders.

ACTIVE 500,000 (Army 365,000 Navy 70,000 Air 65,000) **Gendarmerie & Paramilitary 13,500**

Conscript liability Army and Marines 18 months, Navy 20 months, Air Force 21 months

RESERVE 3,100,000

Reserve obligation of three days per year. First Combat Forces (Mobilisation Reserve Forces) or Regional Combat Forces (Homeland Defence Forces) to age 33

Reserve Paramilitary 3,000,000
Being reorganised

ORGANISATIONS BY SERVICE

Space
EQUIPMENT BY TYPE
SATELLITES 4
    COMMUNICATIONS 2 *Anasis*
    ISR 2 425 Project

Army 365,000
FORCES BY ROLE
COMMAND
  6 corps HQ
  1 (Capital Defence) comd HQ
SPECIAL FORCES
  1 (Special Warfare) SF comd (1 SF gp; 6 spec ops bde)
  5 cdo regt
  1 indep cdo bn
MANOEUVRE
  Armoured
  7 armd bde
  1 (Capital) armd inf div (1 armd cav bn, 2 armd bde, 1 armd inf bde, 1 SP arty bde, 1 engr bn)
  1 (8th) armd inf div (1 armd cav bn, 1 armd bde, 2 armd inf bde, 1 SP arty bde, 1 engr bn)
  1 (11th) armd inf div (1 armd cav bn, 3 armd inf bde, 1 SP arty bde, 1 engr bn)
  Light
  13 inf div (1 recce bn, 1 tk bn, 3 inf bde, 1 arty bde, 1 engr bn)
  2 indep inf bde
  1 mtn inf bde
  Air Manoeuvre
  1 air mob div (2 cdo bde)
  1 air aslt bde
  Other
  1 sy bde
  4 sy regt
  1 sy gp
SURFACE-TO-SURFACE MISSILE
  3 SSM bn
COMBAT SUPPORT
  6 arty bde
  1 MRL bde (3 MRL bn; 2 SSM bn)
  6 engr bde
  5 engr gp
  1 CBRN defence bde
  8 sigs bde

COMBAT SERVICE SUPPORT
  4 log spt comd
HELICOPTER
  1 (army avn) comd
AIR DEFENCE
  1 ADA bde
  5 ADA bn

Reserves
FORCES BY ROLE
COMMAND
  1 army HQ
MANOEUVRE
  Light
  24 inf div
EQUIPMENT BY TYPE
ARMOURED FIGHTING VEHICLES
  MBT 2,110: 1,000 K1/K1E1; 450 K1A1/K1A2; ε260 K2; ε400 M48A5
  IFV 540: ε500 K21; 40 BMP-3
  APC 2,800
    APC (T) 2,260: 1,700 KIFV; 420 M113; 140 M577 (CP)
    APC (W) 530; 20 BTR-80; ε60 K806; ε450 K808
  PPV 10 *MaxxPro*
ENGINEERING & MAINTENANCE VEHICLES
  AEV 207 M9; K600
  ARV 238+: 200 K1; K21 ARV; K288A1; M47; 38 M88A1
  VLB 56 K1; KM3
ANTI-TANK/ANTI-INFRASTRUCTURE
  MSL
    SP *Hyeongung*
    MANPATS 9K115 *Metis* (RS-AT-7 *Saxhorn*); *Hyeongung*; TOW-2A
  RCL 75mm; **90mm** M67; **106mm** M40A2
  GUNS 58
    SP 90mm 50 M36
    TOWED 76mm 8 M18 *Hellcat* (AT gun)
ARTILLERY 12,078+
  SP 2,480: **105mm** ε200 K105A1; **155mm** 2,280: ε1,240 K9/K9A1 *Thunder*; 1,040 M109A2 (K55/K55A1)
  TOWED 3,300+: **105mm** 1,500 M101/KH-178; **155mm** 1,800+ KH-179/M114
  MRL 298: **130mm** ε40 K136 *Kooryong*; **227mm** 58: 48 M270 MLRS; 10 M270A1 MLRS; **239mm** ε200 K239 *Chunmoo*
  MOR 6,000: **81mm** KM29 (M29); KM114; KM187 **107mm** M30; **120mm** Hanwha 120mm mortar
SURFACE-TO-SURFACE MISSILE LAUNCHERS
  SRBM • Conventional 30+: 30 *Hyunmoo* IIA/IIB; MGM-140A/B ATACMS (launched from M270/M270A1 MLRS)
  GLCM • Conventional *Hyunmoo* III
HELICOPTERS
  ATK 91: 55 AH-1F *Cobra*; 36 AH-64E *Apache*

MRH 175: 130 Hughes 500D; 45 MD-500
TPT 332: **Heavy** 33: 27 CH-47D *Chinook*; 6 MH-47E *Chinook*; **Medium** 287: ε200 KUH-1 *Surion*; 87 UH-60P *Black Hawk*; **Light** 12 Bo-105
UNINHABITED AERIAL VEHICLES
ISR • Medium 76: ε36 RQ-101 *Songolmae*; ε40 RQ-102K
AIR DEFENCE
SAM • Point-defence *Chiron*; *Chun Ma* (*Pegasus*); FIM-92 *Stinger*; *Javelin*; *Mistral*; 9K310 *Igla-1* (RS-SA-16 *Gimlet*)
GUNS 477+
  SP 317: **20mm** ε150 KIFV *Vulcan* SPAAG; **30mm** 167 K30 *Biho*; some K-808 *Cheonho* SPAAG
  TOWED 160: **20mm** 60 M167 *Vulcan*; **35mm** 20 GDF-003; **40mm** 80 L/60/L/70; M1
AIR-LAUNCHED MISSILES
  ASM AGM-114R1 *Hellfire* II

Navy 70,000 (incl marines)

Three separate fleet elements: 1st Fleet Donghae (East Sea/Sea of Japan); 2nd Fleet Pyeongtaek (West Sea/Yellow Sea); 3rd Fleet Busan (South Sea/Korea Strait); independent submarine command, three additional flotillas (incl SF, mine-warfare, amphibious and spt elements) and 1 Naval Air Wing (3 gp plus spt gp)

EQUIPMENT BY TYPE
SUBMARINES 21
  SSB 3 *Dosan An Chang-Ho* (KSS-III Batch I) (GER Type-214 mod) (fitted with AIP) with 6 SLBM (likely based on *Hyunmoo*-IIB), 8 single 533mm TT with K731 *White Shark*
  SSK 18:
    4 *Chang Bogo* (KSS-I) (GER Type-209/1200) with 8 single 533mm TT with SUT HWT/K731 *White Shark* HWT
    5 *Chang Bogo* (KSS-I) (GER Type-209/1200) with 8 single 533mm TT with UGM-84 *Harpoon* AShM/SUT HWT/K731 *White Shark* HWT
    9 *Son Won-Il* (KSS-II) (GER Type-214) (fitted with AIP) with 8 single 533mm TT with *Haeseong* III LACM/*Haeseong* I AShM/SUT HWT/K731 *White Shark* HWT
PRINCIPAL SURFACE COMBATANTS 26
  CRUISERS • CGHM 4:
    3 *Sejong* (KDD-III) with *Aegis* Baseline 7 C2, 6 8-cell K-VLS with *Haeseong* II LACM/*Red Shark* A/S msl, 4 quad lnchr with *Haeseong* I AShM, 10 8-cell Mk 41 VLS (6 fore, 4 aft) with SM-2 Block IIIA/B SAM, 1 21-cell Mk 49 GMLS with RIM-116 RAM SAM, 2 triple 324mm SVTT Mk 32 ASTT with K745 *Blue Shark* LWT, 1 *Goalkeeper* CIWS, 1 127mm gun (capacity 2 *Lynx* Mk99/AW159 *Wildcat* hels)
    1 *Jeongjo* (KDD-III Batch II) with *Aegis* Baseline KII, BMD capability, 5 8-cell K-VLS with *Haeseong* II LACM/*Red Shark* A/S msl, 4 quad lnchr with *Haeseong* I AShM, 6 8-cell Mk 41 VLS (2 fore, 4 aft) for SM-3/SM-6 SAM, 1 21-cell Mk 49 GMLS with RIM-116 RAM SAM, 2 triple 324mm SVTT Mk 32 ASTT with K745 *Blue Shark* LWT, 2 *Phalanx* CIWS, 1 127mm gun (capacity 1 MH-60R hel)
  DESTROYERS • DDGHM 6 *Chungmugong Yi Sun-Sin* (KDD-II) with 2 8-cell K-VLS with *Haeseong* II LACM/*Red Shark* A/S msl, 2 quad lnchr with RGM-84 *Harpoon* AShM/*Haeseong* I AShM, 4 8-cell Mk 41 VLS with SM-2 Block IIIA/B SAM, 1 21-cell Mk 49 GMLS with RIM-116 RAM SAM, 2 triple 324mm SVTT Mk 32 ASTT with Mk 46 LWT, 1 *Goalkeeper* CIWS, 1 127mm gun (capacity 1 *Lynx* Mk99/AW159 *Wildcat* hel)
  FRIGATES 16
    FFGHM 14:
      8 *Daegu* (*Incheon* Batch II) with 2 8-cell K-VLS with *Haeseong* II LACM/TSLM LACM/*Haegung* (K-SAAM) SAM/*Red Shark* A/S msl, 2 quad lnchr with TSLM LACM/*Haeseong* I AShM, 2 triple 324mm KMk. 32 ASTT with K745 *Blue Shark* LWT, 1 Mk 15 *Phalanx* Block 1B CIWS, 1 127mm gun (capacity 1 *Lynx* Mk99/AW159 *Wildcat* hel)
      3 *Gwanggaeto Daewang* (KDD-I) with 2 quad lnchr with RGM-84 *Harpoon* AShM, 2 8-cell Mk 48 mod 2 VLS with RIM-7P *Sea Sparrow* SAM, 2 triple 324mm KMk. 32 ASTT with K745 *Blue Shark* LWT, 2 *Goalkeeper* CIWS, 1 127mm gun (capacity 1 *Lynx* Mk99/AW159 *Wildcat* hel)
      6 *Incheon* with 2 quad lnchr with TSLM LACM/*Haeseong* I AShM, 1 21-cell Mk 49 lnchr with RIM-116 RAM SAM, 2 triple 324mm KMk. 32 ASTT with K745 *Blue Shark* LWT, 1 Mk 15 *Phalanx* Block 1B CIWS, 1 127 mm gun (capacity 1 *Lynx* Mk99/AW159 *Wildcat* hel)
    FFG 2 *Ulsan* with 2 quad lnchr with RGM-84 *Harpoon* AShM, 2 triple 324mm SVTT Mk 32 ASTT with Mk 46 LWT, 2 76mm gun
  PATROL AND COASTAL COMBATANTS 74
    CORVETTES • FSG 5:
      1 *Po Hang* (Flight IV) with 2 twin lnchr with RGM-84 *Harpoon* AShM, 2 triple 324mm ASTT with Mk 46 LWT, 2 76mm gun
      4 *Po Hang* (Flight V/VI) with 2 twin lnchr with *Haeseong* I AShM, 2 triple 324mm KMk. 32 ASTT with K745 *Blue Shark* LWT, 2 76mm gun
    PCFG 34: 18 *Gumdoksuri* with 2 twin lnchr with *Haeseong* I AShM, 1 76mm gun; 16 *Chamsuri* II with 1 12-cell 130mm MRL, 1 76mm gun
    PBF ε35 *Sea Dolphin*
  MINE WARFARE 12
    MINE COUNTERMEASURES 10
      MHO 6 *Kan Kyeong*
      MSO 4 *Yang Yang*
    MINELAYERS • ML 2:
      1 *Nampo* (MLS-II) with 1 4-cell K-VLS VLS with *Haegung* (K-SAAM) SAM, 2 triple KMk. 32 triple 324mm ASTT with K745 *Blue Shark* LWT, 1 76mm gun (capacity 1 med hel)
      1 *Won San* with 2 triple 324mm SVTT Mk 32 ASTT with Mk 46 LWT/K745 *Blue Shark* LWT, 1 76mm gun, 1 hel landing platform
  AMPHIBIOUS
  PRINCIPAL AMPHIBIOUS SHIPS 6

LHD 2:
  1 *Dokdo* with 1 Mk 49 GMLS with RIM-116 RAM SAM, 2 *Goalkeeper* CIWS (capacity 2 LCAC; 10 tanks; 700 troops; 10 UH-60 hel)
  1 *Marado* (*Dokdo* mod) with 1 4-cell K-VLS with *Haegung* (K-SAAM) SAM, 2 Mk 15 *Phalanx* Block 1B CIWS (capacity 2 LCAC; 6 MBT, 7 AAV-7A1, 720 troops; 7-12 hels)
LPD 4 *Cheonwangbong* (LST-II) (capacity 3 LCM; 2 MBT; 8 AFV; 300 troops; 2 med hel)
LANDING SHIPS • LST 4 *Go Jun Bong* with 1 hel landing platform (capacity 20 tanks; 300 troops)
LANDING CRAFT 29
  LCU 7+ *Mulgae* I
  LCT 3 *Mulgae* II
  LCM 10 LCM-8
  LCAC 9: 3 *Tsaplya* (capacity 1 MBT; 130 troops); 6 LSF-II (capacity 150 troops or 1 MBT & 24 troops)
LOGISTICS AND SUPPORT 11
  AG 1 *Sunjin* (trials spt)
  AOEH 1 *Soyangham* (AOE-II) with 1 Mk 15 *Phalanx* Block 1B CIWS (capacity 1 med hel)
  AORH 3 *Chun Jee*
  ARS 3: 1 *Cheong Hae Jin*; 2 *Tongyeong*
  AX 1 *Hansando* with 2 triple 324mm KMk. 32 ASTT with K745 *Blue Shark* LWT, 1 76mm gun (fitted for but not with K-VLS) (capacity 2 med hels; 300 students);
  AXL 2 MTB
UNINHABITED MARITIME PLATFORMS • UUV
  MARSEC • Extra-Large ASWUUV

Naval Aviation
FORCES BY ROLE
ANTI-SUBMARINE WARFARE
  1 sqn with Cessna F406 *Caravan* II; P-3C/K *Orion*; P-8A *Poseidon*
  2 sqn with P-3C/K *Orion*
  1 sqn with AW159 *Wildcat*; Lynx Mk99
  1 sqn with Lynx Mk99A
TRAINING
  1 sqn with Bell 205 (UH-1H *Iroquois*)
TRANSPORT HELICOPTER
  2 sqn with Bell 205 (UH-1H *Iroquois*); UH-60P *Black Hawk*
  1 VIP sqn with UH-60P *Black Hawk*
EQUIPMENT BY TYPE
AIRCRAFT 22 combat capable
  ASW 22: 8 P-3C *Orion*; 8 P-3CK *Orion*; 6 P-8A *Poseidon*
  TPT • Light 5 Cessna F406 *Caravan* II
HELICOPTERS
  ASW 31: 11 *Lynx* Mk99; 12 *Lynx* Mk99A; 8 AW159 *Wildcat*
  TPT 15: **Medium** 8 UH-60P *Black Hawk* **Light** 7 Bell 205 (UH-1H *Iroquois*)
UNINHABITED AERIAL VEHICLES
  ISR • Light 2+ S-100 *Camcopter*
AIR-LAUNCHED MISSILES • AShM AGM-84 *Harpoon*

Marines 29,000
FORCES BY ROLE
SPECIAL FORCES
  1 SF regt
MANOEUVRE
  Amphibious
  2 mne div (1 recce bn, 1 tk bn, 3 mne bde, 1 amph bn, 1 arty bde, 1 engr bn)
  1 mne bde (1 recce coy, 4 mne bn, 1 SP arty bn)
  1 mne bde (3 mne bn, 1 fd arty br)
  1 mne BG (1 mne bn, 1 SP arty bn)
HELICOPTER
  1 hel gp (1 atk hel sqn; 2 tpt hel sqn) (forming)
EQUIPMENT BY TYPE
ARMOURED FIGHTING VEHICLES
  MBT 100: 60 K1E1; 40 K1A2
  AAV 166 AAV-7A1
  APC • APC(W) ε20 K808
ANTI-TANK/ANTI-INFRASTUCTURE • MSL
  SP *Spike* NLOS
  MANPATS *Hyeongung*
ARTILLERY 238
  SP • 155mm 80: ε40 K9 *Thunder*; ε20 K9A1 *Thunder*; ε20 M109A2 (K55/K55A1)
  TOWED 140: **105mm** ε20 M101; **155mm** ε120 KH-179
  MRL • 239mm 18 K239 *Cheonmu*
  MOR 81mm KM29 (M29); KM114; K-M187
COASTAL DEFENCE • AShM RGM-84A *Harpoon* (truck mounted)
HELICOPTERS • TPT • Medium ε27 MUH-1 *Surion*
AIR DEFENCE
  GUNS • Towed • 20mm M167 *Vulcan* (direct fire role)

Naval Special Warfare Flotilla

Air Force 65,000
4 Comd (Ops, Southern Combat, Logs, Trg)
FORCES BY ROLE
FIGHTER/GROUND ATTACK
  5 sqn with F-5E/F *Tiger* II
  3 sqn with F-15K *Eagle*
  2 sqn with F-16C/D Block 32 MLU *Fighting Falcon*
  7 sqn with F-16C/D Block 52/Block 52 MLU *Fighting Falcon*
  2 sqn with F-35A *Lightning* II
  3 sqn with FA-50 *Fighting Eagle*
ISR
  1 wg with KA-1
  1 sqn with F-16C/D Block 52/Block 52 MLU *Fighting Falcon*
SIGINT
  1 sqn with *Falcon* 2000; Hawker 800RA/SIG
AIRBORNE EARLY WARNING & CONTROL
  1 sqn with B-737 AEW

SEARCH & RESCUE
1 sqn with AS332L *Super Puma*; Bell 412EP *Twin Huey*; Ka-32 *Helix* C
1 sqn with CH-47D *Chinook*; HH-47D *Chinook*
1 sqn with HH-60P *Black Hawk*

TANKER
1 sqn with A330 MRTT

TRANSPORT
2 sqn with C-130H/H-30/J-30 *Hercules*
2 sqn with CN235M-100/220
1 spec ops sqn with MC-130K *Hercules*
1 VIP sqn with B-737-300; B-747-8; CN235-220; S-92A *Superhawk*; VH-60P *Black Hawk*

TRAINING
1 sqn with F-5E/F *Tiger* II
1 sqn with F-16C/D *Fighting Falcon*
4 sqn with KT-1
1 sqn with KT-100
3 sqn with T-50/TA-50 *Golden Eagle**

ISR UAV
1 sqn with RQ-4B *Global Hawk* (forming)

SPECIAL FORCES
1 SF sqn

AIR DEFENCE
3 AD bde (total: 6 SAM bn with *Chunggung*; 2 SAM bn with M902 *Patriot* PAC-3 CRI)

EQUIPMENT BY TYPE
AIRCRAFT 508 combat capable
  FTR 103: ε75 F-5E *Tiger* II; ε28 F-5F *Tiger* II
  FGA 323: 59 F-15K *Eagle*; 27 F-16C Block 32 MLU *Fighting Falcon*; 89 F-16C Block 52/Block 52 MLU *Fighting Falcon* (some ISR); 7 F-16D Block 32 MLU *Fighting Falcon*; 42 F-16D Block 52/Block 52 MLU *Fighting Falcon* (some ISR); 39 F-35A *Lightning* II; 60 FA-50 *Fighting Eagle*
  AEW&C 4 B-737 AEW
  ISR 23: 4 Hawker 800RA; 19 KA-1
  SIGINT 6: 4 Hawker 800SIG; 2 *Falcon* 2000 (COMINT/SIGINT)
  TKR/TPT 4 A330 MRTT
  TPT 38: **Medium** 16: 4 C-130H *Hercules*; 4 C-130H-30 *Hercules*; 4 C-130J-30 *Hercules*; 4 MC-130K *Hercules*; **Light** 20: 12 CN235M-100; 8 CN235M-220 (incl 2 VIP); **PAX** 2: 1 B-737-300; 1 B-747-8 (leased)
  TRG 185: 83 KT-1; 49 T-50 *Golden Eagle**; 9 T-50B *Black Eagle** (aerobatics); 22 TA-50 *Golden Eagle**; 2 TA-50 *Golden Eagle* Block 2*; ε20 KT-100

HELICOPTERS
  SAR 16: 5 HH-47D *Chinook*; 11 HH-60P *Black Hawk*
  MRH 3 Bell 412EP
  TPT 27: **Heavy** 5 CH-47D *Chinook*; **Medium** 22: 2 AS332L *Super Puma*; 7 Ka-32 *Helix* C; 3 S-92A *Super Hawk*; 10 VH-60P *Black Hawk* (VIP)

UNINHABITED AERIAL VEHICLES
  ISR 7: **Heavy** 4 RQ-4B *Global Hawk*; **Medium** 3 *Searcher*
  OWA *Harpy*

AIR DEFENCE • SAM 120
  Long-range 48 M902 *Patriot* PAC-3 CRI
  Medium-range 76+:72 *Chunggung* (KM-SAM); 4+ *Chungung* II (KM-SAM II)
  GUNS • 30mm K30W *Cheonho*

AIR-LAUNCHED MISSILES
  AAM • IR AIM-9 *Sidewinder*; **IIR** AIM-9X *Sidewinder* II; **SARH** AIM-7 *Sparrow*; **ARH** AIM-120B/C-5/7 AMRAAM
  ASM AGM-65A *Maverick*; AGM-130
  AShM AGM-84L *Harpoon* Block II
  ARM AGM-88 HARM
  ALCM AGM-84H SLAM-ER; Taurus KEPD-350

BOMBS
  Laser-guided GBU-28; *Paveway* II
  INS/SAT-guided GBU-31/-32/-38 JDAM; GBU-39 SDB; KGGB; *Spice* 2000

Gendarmerie & Paramilitary 13,500 active

Civilian Defence Corps 3,000,000 reservists (to age 50)

Coast Guard 13,500
Part of the Ministry of Maritime Affairs and Fisheries. Five regional headquarters with 19 coastguard stations and one guard unit

EQUIPMENT BY TYPE
PATROL AND COASTAL COMBATANTS 111
  PSOH 16: 1 *Lee Cheong-ho* with 1 76mm gun; 1 *Sambongho*; 14 *Tae Pung Yang* with 1 med hel
  PSO 21: 3 *Han Kang* with 1 76mm gun, 1 hel landing platform; 5 *Han Kang* II with 1 76mm gun, 1 hel landing pllatform; 12 *Jaemin* with 1 hel landing platform; 1 *Sumjinkang*
  PCO 23 *Tae Geuk*
  PCC 21: 4 *Hae Uri*; 15 *Hae Uri* II; 2 *Hae Uri* III
  PB 30: 26 *Haenuri*; ε4 (various)

AMPHIBIOUS • LANDING CRAFT 8:
  UCAC 8: 1 BHT-150; 4 *Griffon* 470TD; 3 *Griffon* 8000TD

AIRCRAFT
  MP 5: 1 C-212-400 MP; 4 CN235-110 MPA
  TPT • PAX 1 CL-604

HELICOPTERS
  MRH 7: 5 AS565MB *Panther*; 2 AW139
  SAR 2 S-92
  TPT • Medium 10: 8 Ka-32 *Helix* C; 2 KUH-1 *Surion*

DEPLOYMENT

ARABIAN SEA & GULF OF ADEN: Combined Maritime Forces • CTF-151: 200; 1 DDGHM

INDIA/PAKISTAN: UN • UNMOGIP 6

LEBANON: UN • UNIFIL 252; 1 mech inf BG HQ; 1 mech inf coy; 1 inf coy; 1 log coy

MIDDLE EAST: UN • UNTSO 2

SOUTH SUDAN: UN • UNMISS 278; 1 engr coy

SYRIA/ISRAEL: UN • UNDOF 1

UNITED ARAB EMIRATES: 170 (trg activities at UAE Spec Ops School)

WESTERN SAHARA: UN • MINURSO 4

FOREIGN FORCES

Sweden NNSC: 5
Switzerland NNSC: 5
United States US Indo-Pacific Command: 28,500
Army 19,750; 1 HQ (8th Army) at Pyeongtaek; 1 div HQ at Pyeongtaek; 1 mech bde; 1 (cbt avn) hel bde with AH-64D/E *Apache*; CH-47F *Chinook*; UH-60L/M *Black Hawk*; 1 MRL bde with M270A1 MLRS; 1 AD bde with M902 *Patriot* PAC-3/FIM-92A *Avenger*; 1 SAM bty with THAAD; 1 (APS) armd bde eqpt set
Navy 350
USAF 8,150; 1 HQ (7th Air Force) at Osan AB; 1 ftr wg at Kunsan AB (2 ftr sqn with 20 F-16C/D *Fighting Falcon*); 1 ftr wg at Osan AB (1 ftr sqn with 20 F-16C/D *Fighting Falcon*, 1 atk sqn with 24 A-10C *Thunderbolt* II); 1 ISR sqn at Osan AB with U-2S
Space Force 100
USMC 150

Laos LAO

New Lao Kip LAK		2023	2024	2025
GDP	LAK	280trn	334trn	392trn
	USD	14.9bn	14.9bn	14.4bn
Real GDP growth	%	3.7	4.1	3.5
Def bdgt	LAK	n.k	n.k	n.k
	USD	n.k	n.k	n.k
Population	7,953,556			

Age	0–14	15–19	20–24	25–29	30–64	65 plus
Male	15.3%	4.8%	4.9%	4.4%	18.3%	2.2%
Female	14.9%	4.7%	4.8%	4.5%	18.6%	2.6%

Capabilities

The Lao People's Armed Forces (LPAF) form a vital pillar of Laos' state machinery alongside the ruling Communist Lao People's Revolutionary Party (LPRP) and the government apparatus. In addition to external security responsibilities, the LPAF is expected to protect the regime against internal threats. Laos has military-to-military contacts with the Cambodian, Chinese and Vietnamese armed forces. The country also has defence cooperation with Russia which, along with Vietnam, provides training support. The LPAF have participated in exercises, including some organised by the ADMM–Plus grouping involving ASEAN and some other states. Laos operates Soviet-era military equipment and relies on Russian supplies, as illustrated by deliveries of training aircraft, armoured reconnaissance vehicles and main battle tanks. The country has little defence-industrial capability and its maintenance capacity is limited.

ACTIVE 29,100 (Army 25,600 Air 3,500)
Gendarmerie & Paramilitary 100,000

Conscript liability 18 months minimum

ORGANISATIONS BY SERVICE

Space
EQUIPMENT BY TYPE
SATELLITES • **ISR** 1 *LaoSat*-1

Army 25,600
FORCES BY ROLE
4 mil regions
MANOEUVRE
 Armoured
  1 armd bn
 Light
  5 inf div
  7 indep inf regt
  65 indep inf coy
COMBAT SUPPORT
 5 arty bn
 1 engr regt
 2 (construction) engr regt
AIR DEFENCE
 9 ADA bn
EQUIPMENT BY TYPE
ARMOURED FIGHTING VEHICLES
 MBT 46: 15 T-54/T-55; 31+ T-72B1MS
 LT TK 10 PT-76
 RECCE BRDM-2M
 IFV 10+ BMP-1
 APC • **APC (W)** 50: 30 BTR-40/BTR-60; 20 BTR-152
 AUV Dongfeng Mengshi 4×4; ZYZ-8002 (CS/VN3)
ENGINEERING & MAINTENANCE VEHICLES
 ARV T-54/T-55
 VLB MTU
ANTI-TANK/ANTI-INFRASTRUCTURE • **RCL 57mm** M18/A1; **75mm** M20; **106mm** M40; **107mm** B-11
ARTILLERY 68+
 SP • **122mm** 6+ PCL-09
 MRL • **122mm** BM-21 *Grad*
 TOWED 62: **105mm** 20 M101; **122mm** 20 D-30/M-30 M-1938; **130mm** 10 M-46; **155mm** 12 M114
 MOR 81mm; **82mm**; **107mm** M-1938/M2A1; **120mm** M-43
AIR DEFENCE
 SAM
  Short-range 6 S-125M *Pechora*-M† (RS-SA-3 *Goa*)
  Point-defence 9K32M *Strela*-2M (RS-SA-7 *Grail*)‡;

9K35 *Strela*-10 (RS-SA-13 *Gopher*); 9K310 *Igla*-1 (RS-SA-16 *Gimlet*); some *Yitian* (CH-SA-13)

GUNS

SP 23mm ZSU-23-4

TOWED 14.5mm ZPU-1/ZPU-4; 23mm ZU-23; 37mm M-1939; 57mm S-60

Army Marine Section ε600

EQUIPMENT BY TYPE

PATROL AND COASTAL COMBATANTS • PBR some

AMPHIBIOUS • LCM some

Air Force 3,500

FORCES BY ROLE

GROUND ATTACK

1 regt with K-8W *Karakorum**; Yak-130 *Mitten**

TRANSPORT

1 regt with MA60; MA600

TRAINING

1 regt with LE500

TRANSPORT HELICOPTER

1 regt with Ka-32T *Helix* C; Mi-17 *Hip* H; Mi-17V-5 *Hip*; Z-9A

1 (VIP) flt with SA360 *Dauphin*

EQUIPMENT BY TYPE

AIRCRAFT 7 combat capable

TPT • Light 13: 1 An-26 *Curl* (reported); 8 LE500; 2 MA60; 2 MA600

TRG 7: ε4 K-8W *Karakorum**; 3 Yak-130 *Mitten**

HELICOPTERS

MRH 15: 6 Mi-17 *Hip* H; 5 Mi-17V-5 *Hip*; 4 Z-9A

TPT 4: Medium 1 Ka-32T *Helix* C; Light 3 SA360 *Dauphin*

Gendarmerie & Paramilitary

Militia Self-Defence Forces 100,000+

Village 'home guard' or local defence

Malaysia MYS

Malaysian Ringgit MYR		2023	2024	2025
GDP	MYR	1.82trn	2.00trn	2.15trn
	USD	400bn	440bn	488bn
Real GDP growth	%	3.6	4.8	4.4
Def bdgt	MYR	17.7bn	19.7bn	
	USD	3.89bn	4.34bn	

Real-terms defence budget trend (USDbn, constant 2015)

4.55 / 3.08
2008 — 2016 — 2024

Population		34,564,810				
Age	0–14	15–19	20–24	25–29	30–64	65 plus
Male	11.4%	3.8%	4.1%	4.6%	23.0%	4.1%
Female	10.8%	3.7%	4.0%	4.4%	21.7%	4.3%

Capabilities

The Royal Malaysian Armed Forces (RMAF) have a limited capacity for external defence. The army remains the dominant service, reflecting a longstanding focus on counter-insurgency. The 2019 defence white paper, Malaysia's first, and the 2021–25 Strategic Plan identified 'three pillars' of defence: 'concentric deterrence' (protection of national interests in 'core', 'extended' and 'forward' zones); 'comprehensive defence'; and 'credible partnerships.' These planning documents, as well as the 2022 Action Plan, identified new defence challenges, including tensions in the South China Sea, cyber threats and other 'mass non-kinetic crises'. They also outlined capability development priorities, including ISR, maritime-strike, air-defence, synthetic training, and the capacity to operate in multiple theatres. In 2023, the government announced plans for a new naval base and air base at Bintulu near the South China Sea as well as plans to relocate an army brigade to Bintulu. Procurement priorities inclue combat aircraft, maritime patrol aircraft, MALE UAVs, helicopters, surface ships, 155mm artillery, MRLs and long-range radars. However, budgetary constraints will likely limit defence resources, equipment modernisation and operational readiness. The RMAF regularly exercises with regional and international partners. In 2017, Malaysia began coordinated trilateral maritime and air patrols in the Sulu-Sulawesi Seas with Indonesia and the Philippines. The Sulu Sea remains an area of concern, given continued terrorist and pirate activity. Malaysia hosts Australian forces and the headquarters of the FPDA Integrated Area Defence System at RMAF Butterworth. Malaysia's defence industry focuses mainly on MRO, naval shipbuilding, and land-vehicle production via offset agreements.

ACTIVE 113,000 (Army 80,000 Navy 18,000 Air 15,000) Gendarmerie & Paramilitary 22,500

RESERVE 51,600 (Army 50,000, Navy 1,000 Air Force 600) Gendarmerie & Paramilitary 244,700

ORGANISATIONS BY SERVICE

Army 80,000

2 mil region

FORCES BY ROLE

COMMAND
  5 div HQ
SPECIAL FORCES
  1 spec ops bde (1 SF bn; 2 cdo bn)
MANOEUVRE
  Armoured
  1 tk regt
  Mechanised
  5 armd regt
  1 mech inf bde (4 mech bn, 1 cbt engr sqn)
  Light
  1 inf bde (5 inf bn)
  1 inf bde (4 inf bn, 1 fd arty bn)
  1 inf bde (4 inf bn)
  4 inf bde (3 inf bn, 1 fd arty bn)
  3 inf bde (3 inf bn)
  2 inf bde (2 inf bn, 1 fd arty bn)
  1 inf bde (2 inf bn)
  Air Manoeuvre
  1 (Rapid Deployment Force) AB bde (1 lt tk sqn, 4 AB bn, 1 fd arty bn, 1 engr sqn)
COMBAT SUPPORT
  3 fd arty bn
  1 MRL bde (2 MRL bn)
  1 STA bn
  1 cbt engr sqn
  3 fd engr regt (total: 7 cbt engr sqn, 3 engr spt sqn)
  1 construction regt
  1 int unit
  4 MP regt
  1 sigs regt
HELICOPTER
  3 hel sqn
AIR DEFENCE
  3 ADA regt
EQUIPMENT BY TYPE
ARMOURED FIGHTING VEHICLES
  MBT 48 PT-91M *Pendekar*
  RECCE 24 AV8 *Gempita*
  IFV 199: 31 ACV300 *Adnan* (25mm *Bushmaster*); 46 AV8 *Gempita* IFV25; 122 AV8 *Gempita* IFV30 (incl 54 with *Ingwe* ATGM)
  APC 352
    APC (T) 265: 149 ACV300 *Adnan* (incl 69 variants); 13 ACV300 *Adnan* AGL; 63 K200A; 40 K200A1
    APC (W) 35: 35 AV8 *Gempita* APC (incl 13 CP; 3 sigs; 9 amb)
    PPV 52: 20 Ejder *Yalcin*; 12 IAG *Guardian*; 20 *Lipanbara*
ENGINEERING & MAINTENANCE VEHICLES
  AEV 3 MID-M
  ARV 43: 15 ACV300; 4 K288A1; 6 WZT-4; 18 AV8 *Gempita* ARV
  VLB 5+: *Leguan*; 5 PMCz-90

NBC VEHICLES 4+: 4 AV8 *Gempita*; K216A1
ANTI-TANK/ANTI-INFRASTRUCTURE • MSL
  SP 8 ACV300 *Baktar Shikan*
  MANPATS 9K115 *Metis* (RS-AT-7 *Saxhorn*); 9K115-2 *Metis*-M1 (RS-AT-13); *Eryx*; *Baktar Shikan* (HJ-8); SS.11
  RCL 84mm *Carl Gustaf*
ARTILLERY 444
  TOWED 146: **105mm** 118: 18 LG1 MkIII; 100 Model 56 pack howitzer; **155mm** 28 G-5
  MRL 36 ASTROS II (equipped with 127mm SS-30)
  MOR 262: **81mm** 232; **SP 81mm** 14: 4 K281A1; 10 ACV300-S; **SP 120mm** 16: 8 ACV-S; 8 AV8 *Gempita*
HELICOPTERS
  MRH 6 MD-530G
  TPT • Light 10 AW109
AIR DEFENCE
  SAM • Point-defence 15+: 15 *Jernas* (*Rapier* 2000); *Anza*-II; HY-6 (FN-6) (CH-SA-10); 9K38 *Igla* (RS-SA-18 *Grouse*); *Starstreak*; VAMTAC with 9K38 *Igla* (RS-SA-18 *Grouse*); VAMTAC with *Starstreak*
  GUNS 52+
    SP 20mm K263
    TOWED 52: **35mm** 16 GDF-005; **40mm** 36 L40/70

Reserves

Territorial Army
Some paramilitary forces to be incorporated into a re-organised territorial organisation
FORCES BY ROLE
MANOEUVRE
  Mechanised
  4 armd sqn
  Light
  16 inf regt (3 inf bn)
  Other
  5 (highway) sy bn
COMBAT SUPPORT
  5 arty bty
  2 fd engr regt
  1 int unit
  3 sigs sqn
COMBAT SUPPORT
  4 med coy
  5 tpt coy

Navy 18,000

3 Regional Commands: MAWILLA 1 (Kuantan), MAWILLA 2 (Sabah) and MAWILLA 3 (Langkawi). A fourth is being formed (Bintulu).
EQUIPMENT BY TYPE
SUBMARINES 2
  SSK 2 *Tunku Abdul Rahman* (FRA *Scorpène*) with 6 single 533mm TT with SM39 *Exocet* AShM/*Black Shark* HWT

PRINCIPAL SURFACE COMBATANTS • FRIGATES 2
FFGHM 2 *Lekiu* (UK Yarrow F2000) with 2 quad lnchr with MM40 *Exocet* Block 2 AShM, 1 16-cell VLS with *Sea Wolf* SAM, 2 triple 324mm ILAS-3 (B-515) ASTT with A244/S LWT, 1 57mm gun (capacity 1 *Super Lynx* 300 hel)

PATROL AND COASTAL COMBATANTS 62
  CORVETTES 8
    FSG 2 *Kasturi* (GER HDW FS1500) with 2 quad lnchr with MM40 *Exocet* Block 2 AShM, 2 triple 324mm ILAS-3 (B-515) ASTT with A244/S LWT, 1 57mm gun, 1 hel landing platform
    FSH 6 *Kedah* (GER MEKO 100) with 1 76mm gun (fitted for but not with MM40 *Exocet* AShM & RAM SAM)
  PCFM 4 *Laksamana* with 1 *Albatros* quad lnchr with *Aspide* SAM, 1 76mm gun
  PCF 4 *Perdana* (FRA *Combattante* II) with 1 57mm gun
  PCC 4 *Keris* (Littoral Mission Ship) (PRC *Durjoy* mod)
  PBF 27: 10 Gading Marine FIC; 17 *Tempur* (SWE CB90)
  PB 15: 3 *Handalan* (SWE *Spica*-M) with 1 57mm gun (1 more non-op); 6 *Jerong* (GER Lurssen 45m) with 1 57mm gun; 2 *Pengawal*; 2 *Sri Perlis*; 2 *Sri Sabah* (UK Vosper 32m)

MINE WARFARE • MINE COUNTERMEASURES 4
  MCO 4 *Mahamiru* (ITA Lerici)

LOGISTICS AND SUPPORT 13
  AFS 2: 1 *Mahawangsa* with 2 57mm guns, 1 hel landing platform; 1 *Sri Indera Sakti* with 1 57mm gun, 1 hel landing platform
  AG 2: 1 *Bunga Mas Lima* with 1 hel landing platform; 1 *Tun Azizan*
  AGS 2: 1 *Dayang Sari*; 1 *Perantau*
  AP 2 *Sri Gaya*
  ASR 1 *Mega Bakti*
  ATF 1
  AXL 2 *Gagah Samudera* with 1 hel landing platform
  AXS 1 *Tunas Samudera*

Naval Aviation 160
FORCES BY ROLE
ANTI-SUBMARINE WARFARE
  1 sqn with *Super Lynx* 300
TRANSPORT HELICOPTER
  1 sqn with AS555 *Fennec*
  1 sqn with AW139
EQUIPMENT BY TYPE
HELICOPTERS
  ASW 4 *Super Lynx* 300
  MRH 7: 5 AS555 *Fennec*; 2 AW139
AIR-LAUNCHED MISSILES • AShM *Sea Skua*

Special Forces
FORCES BY ROLE
SPECIAL FORCES
  1 (mne cdo) SF unit

Air Force 15,000
1 air op HQ, 2 air div, 1 trg and log comd, 1 Intergrated Area Def Systems HQ
FORCES BY ROLE
FIGHTER/GROUND ATTACK
  1 sqn with F/A-18D *Hornet*
  1 sqn with Su-30MKM *Flanker*
  2 sqn with *Hawk* Mk108*/Mk208*
MARITIME PATROL
  1 sqn with Beech 200T
TANKER/TRANSPORT
  2 sqn with C-130H/H-30 *Hercules*; KC-130H *Hercules*
TRANSPORT
  1 sqn with A400M *Atlas*
  1 sqn with CN235M-220
  1 VIP sqn with A319CT; BD700 *Global Express*; CN235M-220; *Falcon* 900
TRAINING
  1 unit with Beech 350i *King Air* (leased)
  1 unit with PC-7 Mk II *Turbo Trainer*
TRANSPORT HELICOPTER
  4 (tpt/SAR) sqn with H225M *Super Cougar*; S-70A *Black Hawk*
  1 sqn with AW139
UNINHABITED AERIAL VEHICLE
  1 sqn (forming)
AIR DEFENCE
  1 sqn with *Starburst*
SPECIAL FORCES
  1 (Air Force Commando) unit (airfield defence/SAR)
EQUIPMENT BY TYPE
AIRCRAFT 42 combat capable
  FTR (8 MiG-29 *Fulcrum* (MiG-29N); 2 MiG-29UB *Fulcrum* B (MIG-29NUB) in store)
  FGA 26: 8 F/A-18D *Hornet* (some serviceability in doubt); 18 Su-30MKM (some serviceability in doubt)
  MP 3 CN235 MPA
  ISR 3 Beech 200T
  TKR/TPT 4 KC-130H *Hercules*
  TPT 23: **Heavy** 4 A400M *Atlas*; **Medium** 10: 2 C-130H *Hercules*; 8 C-130H-30 *Hercules*; **Light** 6: 2 Beech 350i *King Air* (leased); 4 CN235M-220 (incl 1 VIP); **PAX** 3: 1 A319CT (VIP); 1 BD700 *Global Express*; 1 *Falcon* 900
  TRG 33: 4 *Hawk* Mk108*; 12 *Hawk* Mk208*; 17 PC-7 Mk II *Turbo Trainer*; (7 MB-339C in store)
HELICOPTERS
  MRH 4 AW139 (leased)
  TPT 14: **Heavy** 12 H225M *Super Cougar*; **Medium** 2 S-70A *Black Hawk*
AIR DEFENCE • SAM • Point-defence *Starstreak*
AIR-LAUNCHED MISSILES
  AAM • IR AIM-9 *Sidewinder*; R-73 (RS-AA-11A *Archer*); **IIR** AIM-9X *Sidewinder* II; **IR/SARH** R-27 (RS-

AA-10 *Alamo*); **SARH** AIM-7 *Sparrow;* **ARH** AIM-120C AMRAAM; R-77 (RS-AA-12A *Aader*)
ASM AGM-65 *Maverick;* Kh-29T (RS-AS-14B *Kedge*); Kh-29L (RS-AS-14A *Kedge*); Kh-31P (RS-AS-17A *Krypton*); Kh-59M (RS-AS-18 *Kazoo*)
ARM Kh-31P (RS-AS-17A *Krypton*);
AShM AGM-84D *Harpoon;* Kh-31A (RS-AS-17B *Krypton*)
BOMBS
Electro-optical guided KAB-500KR; KAB-500OD
Laser-guided GBU-12 *Paveway* II

Gendarmerie & Paramilitary ε22,500

Police–General Ops Force 18,000
FORCES BY ROLE
COMMAND
5 bde HQ
SPECIAL FORCES
1 spec ops bn
MANOEUVRE
Other
19 paramilitary bn
2 (Aboriginal) paramilitary bn
4 indep paramilitary coy
EQUIPMENT BY TYPE
ARMOURED FIGHTING VEHICLES
APC • **APC (W)** AT105 *Saxon*
AUV ε30 SB-301

Malaysian Maritime Enforcement Agency (MMEA) ε4,500
Controls 5 Maritime Regions (Northern Peninsula; Southern Peninsula; Eastern Peninsula; Sarawak; Sabah), subdivided into a further 18 Maritime Districts. Supported by one provisional MMEA Air Unit
EQUIPMENT BY TYPE
PATROL AND COASTAL COMBATANTS 126
PSO 5: 1 *Arau* (ex-JPN *Nojima*) with 1 hel landing platform; 2 *Langkawi* with 1 57mm gun, 1 hel landing platform; 1 *Pekan* (ex-JPN *Ojika*) with 1 hel landing platform; 1 *Tun Fatimah* (Damen OPV 1800 mod) with 1 hel landing platform
PCC 6 *Bagan Datuk*
PBF 46: 12 *Penggalang* 16; 18 *Penggalang* 17 (TUR MRTP 16); 2 *Penggalang* 18; 14 *Tugau*
PB 69: 13 *Gagah*; 4 *Malawali*; 2 *Nusa* 22; 3 *Nusa* 28; 5 *Penyelamat* 20; 7 *Ramunia*; 1 *Rhu* (1 more non-op); 3 *Semilang*; 9 *Gemia* (*Sipadan Steel*); 20 *Pengawal*; 2 *Perwira*
LOGISTICS AND SUPPORT • **AXL** 1 *Marlin*
AIRCRAFT • **MP** 2 Bombardier 415MP
HELICOPTERS
SAR 2 AW139
MRH 3 AS365 *Dauphin*

Area Security Units 3,500 reservists
(Auxiliary General Ops Force)
FORCES BY ROLE
MANOEUVRE
Other
89 paramilitary unit

Border Scouts 1,200 reservists
in Sabah, Sarawak

People's Volunteer Corps (RELA) 240,000 reservists (some 17,500 armed)

DEPLOYMENT

DEMOCRATIC REPUBLIC OF THE CONGO: UN • MONUSCO 8
LEBANON: UN • UNIFIL 833; 1 mech inf bn(-); 1 engr coy; 1 sigs coy; 1 maint coy; 1 tpt coy
SUDAN: UN • UNISFA 2
WESTERN SAHARA: UN • MINURSO 9

FOREIGN FORCES
Australia 130; 1 inf coy (on 3-month rotational tours); 1 P-8A *Poseidon* (rotational)

Maldives MDV

Maldivian Rufiyaa MVR		2023	2024	2025
GDP	MVR	101bn	103bn	118bn
	USD	6.57bn	6.58bn	7.64bn
Real GDP growth	%	4.0	4.7	4.7
Def bdgt	MVR	1.69bn	1.69bn	
	USD	110m	110m	

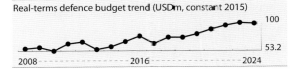

Population	388,858					
Age	0–14	15–19	20–24	25–29	30–64	65 plus
Male	11.4%	3.6%	4.0%	4.9%	24.2%	2.7%
Female	11.0%	3.3%	3.5%	4.3%	23.6%	3.5%

Capabilities

The Maldives National Defence Force (MNDF) is tasked with defence, security and civil-emergency response over the expansive and mostly oceanic territory of the archipelagic nation. The MNDF is maritime-centric, with a littoral coast guard, a marine corps and, as of March 2024, an air corps which replaced its air wing. The standing up of the new air corps featured the induction of uninhabited aerial vehicles from Türkiye. That same month, President Muizzu announced plans to mobilise resources to recondition neglected military resources as well as plans to double the capacity of the coast guard. The MNDF is focused on ISR, maritime security, counterterrorism and capability development. India had long been the MNDF's key defence partner, having supplied most of its major military platforms and offered training to MNDF personnel. However, the Maldives and China signed an agreement in March 2024 on Beijing's provision of military assistance. In 2020, Malé signed a defence agreement with the US and, in 2021, the MNDF started capacity building work with the US Army.

ACTIVE 4,000 (Maldives National Defence Force 4,000)

ORGANISATIONS BY SERVICE

Maldives National Defence Force 4,000

Special Forces
FORCES BY ROLE
SPECIAL FORCES
  1 SF sqn

Marine Corps
FORCES BY ROLE
SPECIAL FORCES
  1 spec ops unit
MANOEUVRE
  Mechanised
  1 mech sqn
  Amphibious
  7 mne coy
EQUIPMENT BY TYPE
ARMOURED FIGHTING VEHICLES
  IFV 2 BMP-2
  AUV 2 *Cobra*

Coast Guard
FORCES BY ROLE
SPECIAL FORCES
  1 spec ops unit
EQUIPMENT BY TYPE
PATROL AND COASTAL COMBATANTS 12
  PCF 1 *Huravee* (ex-IND *Tarmugli*)
  PCC 2: 1 *Ghazee* 1 *Shaheed Ali*
  PBF 8: 1 *Kaamiyaab*; 2 *Noordadheen*; 5 SM50 Interceptor
  PB 1 *Dhaharaat*
AMPHIBIOUS • LANDING CRAFT 4:
  LCU 1 L301
  LCP 3
LOGISTICS AND SUPPORT • AAR 2
AIRCRAFT
  MP 1 Do-228 (contractor operated)
HELICOPTERS
  MRH 2 *Dhruv* (contractor operated)

Air Corps
FORCES BY ROLE
EQUIPMENT BY TYPE
UNINHABITED AERIAL VEHICLES
  CISR • Medium 3 *Bayraktar* TB2
BOMBS
  Laser-guided MAM-L

Mongolia MNG

Mongolian Tugrik MNT		2023	2024	2025
GDP	MNT	70.4trn	81.7trn	95.2trn
	USD	20.3bn	23.7bn	27.2bn
Real GDP growth	%	7.4	5.5	7.0
Def bdgt	MNT	311bn	565bn	
	USD	89.6m	164m	
FMA (US)	USD	3m	3m	n.a

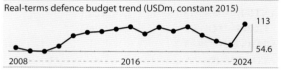
Real-terms defence budget trend (USDm, constant 2015)
113
54.6
2008 2016 2024

Population	3,281,676					
Age	0–14	15–19	20–24	25–29	30–64	65 plus
Male	13.1%	3.9%	3.4%	3.7%	22.0%	2.4%
Female	12.6%	3.8%	3.4%	3.8%	24.3%	3.6%

Capabilities

Mongolia's most recent defence policy document, from 2015, stresses the importance of peacekeeping and anti-terrorist capabilities. The country has no formal military alliances but pursues defence ties and bilateral training with regional states and others, including India, Turkiye and the US. The Mongolian prime minister made an inaugural visit to the Pentagon in 2023 for talks on military-to-military relations. Mongolia hosts the annual *Khaan Quest* multinational peacekeeping training exercise. The country's main exercise partners are India and Russia, though in 2024, China and Mongolia held a joint military exercise. There are longstanding ties with NATO, including cooperation in cyber security. Mongolia's most significant deployment is to the UN peacekeeping mission in South Sudan. The inventory generally comprises Soviet-era equipment, supplemented by deliveries of second-hand Russian weapons. In 2024, Mongolia has explored defence equipment cooperation with other countries, including Japan and the Czech Republic. Barring maintenance facilities, the country has no significant defence-industrial capabilities.

ACTIVE 9,700 (Army 8,900 Air 800) Gendarmerie & Paramilitary 7,500

Conscript liability 12 months for males aged 18–25

RESERVE 137,000 (Army 137,000)

ORGANISATIONS BY SERVICE

Army 5,600; 3,300 conscript (total 8,900)
FORCES BY ROLE
MANOEUVRE
  Mechanised
  1 MR bde

Light
1 (rapid deployment) lt inf bn
Air Manoeuvre
1 AB bn

COMBAT SUPPORT
1 arty regt

EQUIPMENT BY TYPE
ARMOURED FIGHTING VEHICLES
  MBT 420: 370 T-54/T-55; 50 T-72A
  RECCE 120 BRDM-2
  IFV 310 BMP-1
  APC • APC (W) 210: 150 BTR-60; 40 BTR-70M; 20 BTR-80
ENGINEERING & MAINTENANCE VEHICLES
  ARV T-54/T-55
ANTI-TANK/ANTI-INFRASTRUCTURE
  GUNS • TOWED • 100mm M-1944/MT-12
ARTILLERY 570
  TOWED ε300: **122mm** D-30/M-30 (M-1938); **130mm** M-46; **152mm** ML-20 (M-1937)
  MRL 122mm 130 BM-21
  MOR 140: **120mm**; **160mm**; **82mm**
AIR DEFENCE
  SAM Medium-range 2+ S-125-2M *Pechora*-2M (RS-SA-26)
  GUNS • TOWED 23mm ZU-23-2

Air Force 800

FORCES BY ROLE
FIGHTER
1 flt with MiG-29UB *Fulcrum* B
TRANSPORT
1 flt with An-24 *Coke*; An-26 *Curl*
ATTACK/TRANSPORT HELICOPTER
1 sqn with Mi-171; Mi-24 *Hind*; Mi-8 *Hip*
AIR DEFENCE
2 regt with S-60/ZPU-4/ZU-23

EQUIPMENT BY TYPE
AIRCRAFT 6 combat capable
  FTR 6 MiG-29UB *Fulcrum* B
  TPT • Light 3: 2 An-24 *Coke*; 1 An-26 *Curl*
HELICOPTERS
  ATK 2+ Mi-24 *Hind*
  TPT • Medium 12: 10 Mi-8 *Hip*; 2 Mi-171
AIR-LAUNCHED MISSILES
  IR R-73 (RS-AA-11A *Archer*)
AIR DEFENCE • GUNS • TOWED 150: **14.5mm** ZPU-4; **23mm** ZU-23; **57mm** S-60

Gendarmerie & Paramilitary 7,500 active

Border Guard 1,300; 4,700 conscript (total 6,000)

Internal Security Troops 400; 800 conscript (total 1,200)
FORCES BY ROLE
MANOEUVRE
  Other
    4 gd unit

Construction Troops 300

DEPLOYMENT

CENTRAL AFRICAN REPUBLIC: UN • MINUSCA 4
CYPRUS: UN • UNFICYP 3
DEMOCRATIC REPUBLIC OF THE CONGO: UN • MONUSCO 1
LEBANON: UN • UNIFIL 4
SOUTH SUDAN: UN • UNMISS 872; 1 inf bn
SUDAN: UN • UNISFA 3
WESTERN SAHARA: UN • MINURSO 4

Myanmar MMR

Myanmar Kyat MMK		2023	2024	2025
GDP	MMK	139trn	156trn	168trn
	USD	64.5bn	64.3bn	65.0bn
Real GDP growth	%	2.5	1.0	1.1
Def bdgt	MMK	5.64trn	6.40trn	
	USD	2.61bn	2.63bn	

Real-terms defence budget trend (USDbn, constant 2015)

Population	57,527,139					
Age	0–14	15–19	20–24	25–29	30–64	65 plus
Male	12.5%	4.1%	4.0%	4.1%	21.5%	3.1%
Female	11.9%	4.0%	4.0%	4.1%	22.7%	4.0%

Capabilities

Myanmar's Tatmadaw (armed forces) seized power in 2021 from the democratically elected National League for Democracy (NLD). Since the coup, there has been widespread civil unrest and clashes with ethnic armed organisations as well as People's Defence Force (PDF) groups subsequently formed by protestors. These tensions sharpened the Tatmadaw's focus on internal security and counter-insurgency. The Tatmadaw has been accused of widespread human rights abuses against non-combatants during such counter-insurgency operations. Human rights concerns gained international attention after the widely condemned actions targeting the Rohingya ethnic minority began in 2017. Ethnic armed organisations have fought the central government along Myanmar's border areas for decades. However, the current conflict has spread across the country to areas relatively untouched by violence in previous years. Escalating opposition from various non-state armed groups since 2023 has undermined the junta's hold on key strategic border areas in the country. Conscription laws have since been re-introduced to offset battlefield losses. The country has a limited small-arms industry organised through the Directorate of Defence Industries. While the country's defence-industrial capacity remains limited, naval-shipbuilding capabilities have developed in recent years, including at the Naval Dockyard in Thanlyinm while the Aircraft Production and Maintenance Base in Meiktila performs final assembly and maintenance, repair and overhaul services on trainer/light-attack aircraft and military helicopters. China and Russia are key defence cooperation partners.

ACTIVE 134,000 (Army 100,000 Navy 19,000 Air 15,000) **Gendarmerie & Paramilitary 70,000**

Conscript liability 24–36 months

ORGANISATIONS BY SERVICE

Army ε100,000

14 military regions, 7 regional op comd. Following the 2021 coup, and reports of desertions, combat losses and recruitment problems, personnel figures should be treated with caution

FORCES BY ROLE
COMMAND
  20 div HQ (military op comd)
  10 inf div HQ
  34+ bde HQ (tactical op comd)
MANOEUVRE
  Armoured
  10 armd bn
  Light
  100 inf bn (coy)
  337 inf bn (coy) (regional comd)
COMBAT SUPPORT
  7 arty bn
  37 indep arty coy
  6 cbt engr bn
  54 fd engr bn
  40 int coy
  45 sigs bn
AIR DEFENCE
  7 AD bn
EQUIPMENT BY TYPE
ARMOURED FIGHTING VEHICLES
  MBT 195+: 10 T-55; 50 T-72S; 25+ Type-59D; 100 Type-69-II; 10+ Type-90-II (MBT-2000)
  LT TK 108+: 3+ MMT-40; 105 Type-63 (ε60 serviceable)
  ASLT 21 PTL-02 mod
  RECCE 95+: ε50 AML-90; 33 BRDM-2MS (incl CP); 12+ EE-9 *Cascavel*; MAV-1
  IFV 36+: 10+ BTR-3U; 26+ MT-LBMSh
  APC 345+
    APC (T) 305: 250 ZSD-85; 55 ZSD-90
    APC (W) 30+ ZSL-92
    PPV 10+: BAAC-87; Gaia *Thunder*; 10 MPV

  AUV MAV-2; MAV-3
ENGINEERING & MAINTENANCE VEHICLES
  ARV Type-72
  VLB MT-55A
ANTI-TANK/ANTI-INFRASTRUCTURE
  RCL 84mm *Carl Gustaf*; **106mm** M40A1
ARTILLERY 443+
  SP 155mm 42: 30 NORA B-52; 12 SH-1
  TOWED 282+: **105mm** 150: 54 M-56; 96 M101; **122mm** 100 D-30; **130mm** 16 M-46; **155mm** 16 Soltam M-845P
  MRL 39+: **107mm** 30 Type-63; **122mm** BM-21 *Grad* (reported); Type-81; **240mm** 6+ M-1985 mod; **302mm** 3+ MAM-03
  MOR 80+: **82mm** Type-53 (M-37); **120mm** 80+: 80 Soltam; Type-53 (M-1943)
SURFACE-TO-SURFACE MISSILE LAUNCHERS
  SRBM • Conventional some *Hwasong*-6 (reported)
AIR DEFENCE
  SAM 12+
    Medium-range 12+: 12+ KS-1A (CH-SA-12); S-125-2M *Pechora*-2M (RS-SA-26); 2K12 *Kvadrat*-M (RS-SA-6 *Gainful*)
    Point-defence HN-5 (CH-SA-3) (reported); 9K310 *Igla*-1 (RS-SA-16 *Gimlet*)
  SPAAGM 30mm Some 2K22 *Tunguska* (RS-SA-19 *Grison*)
  GUNS 46
    SP 57mm 12 Type-80
    TOWED 34: **37mm** 24 Type-74; **40mm** 10 M1

Navy ε19,000
EQUIPMENT BY TYPE
SUBMARINES • SSK 2
  1 *Min Kyaw Htin* (ex-PRC Type-035B (*Ming*)) with 8 single 533mm TT with Yu-3/Yu-4 HWT
  1 *Min Ye Thein Kha Thu* (ex-IND *Sindhughosh* (Project 877EKM (*Kilo*))) with 6 single 533mm TT
PRINCIPAL SURFACE COMBATANTS • FRIGATES 5
  FFGHM 2 *Kyansitthar* with 2 twin lnchr with C-802 (CH-SS-N-6) AShM, 1 sextuple lnchr with MANPAD SAM, 2 RDC-32 A/S mor, 3 AK630 CIWS, 1 76mm gun (capacity 1 med hel)
  FFGM 1 *Aung Zeya* with 2 quad lnchr with DPRK AShM (possibly 3M24 derivative), 1 sextuple GMLS with MANPAD SAM; 4 AK630 CIWS, 2 RDC-32 A/S mor, 1 76mm gun, 1 hel landing platform
  FFG 2 *Mahar Bandoola* (ex-PRC Type-053H1 (*Jianghu* I)) with 2 quad lnchr with C-802 (CH-SS-N-6) AShM, 2 RBU 1200 *Uragan* A/S mor, 2 twin 100mm guns

PATROL AND COASTAL COMBATANTS 86
  CORVETTES 3
    FSGHM 1 *Tabinshwethi* (*Anawrahta* mod) with 2 twin lnchr with C-802 (CH-SS-N-6), 1 sectuple lnchr with unknown MANPADs, 2 RBU 1200 *Uragan* A/S mor, 2 NG-18 CIWS, 1 76mm gun (capacity 1 med hel)
    FSG 2 *Anawrahta* with 2 twin lnchr with C-802 (CH-SS-N-6) AShM, 2 RDC-32 A/S mor, 1 76mm gun, 1 hel landing platform
  PSOH 2 *Inlay* with 1 twin 57mm gun
  PCG 8: 6 *Maga* (PRC Type-037-IG (*Houxin*)) with 2 twin lnchr with C-801 (CH-SS-N-4) AShM; 2 FAC(M) mod with 2 twin lnchr with C-802 (CH-SS-N-6) AShM, 1 NG-18 CIWS
  PCT 2 *Yan Nyein Aung* (Project PGG 063) with 2 FQF 1200 A/S mor, 2 triple 324mm TLS with *Shyena* LWT, 1 twin 57mm gun
  PCO 2 *Indaw*
  PCC 7 *Yan Min Aung* (Ex-PRC Type-037 (*Hainan*)) with 4 RBU 1200 *Uragan* A/S mor, 2 twin 57mm guns
  PBFT 1 Type-201
  PBG 5 *Myanmar* with 2 single lnchr with C-801 (CH-SS-N-4) AShM, 1 NG-18 CIWS
  PBF 8 *Super Dvora* Mk III (ISR)
  PB 32: 3 PB-90; 6 PGM 401; 3 PGM 412; 15 *Myanmar*; 3 *Swift*; 2 other
  PBR 16: 4 *Sagu*; 9 Y-301†; 1 Y-301 (Imp); 2 other
AMPHIBIOUS
  PRINCIPAL AMPHIBIOUS VESSELS • LPD 1:
    1 *Moattama* (ROK *Makassar*) (capacity 2 LCVP; 2 hels; 13 tanks; 500 troops)
  LANDING CRAFT 40: **LCU** 9; **LCM** 31
LOGISTICS AND SUPPORT 14
  ABU 1
  AGS 3: 1 *Innya*; 2 other
  AH 1 *Thanlwin*
  AKL 7: 1 *Myitkyina*; 6 other
  AP 1 *Chindwin*
  AWT 1

Naval Infantry 800
FORCES BY ROLE
MANOEUVRE
  Light
  1 inf bn

Air Force ε15,000
FORCES BY ROLE
FIGHTER
  4 sqn with F-7 *Airguard*; FT-7; FTC-2000G; JF-17/JF-17B *Thunder*; MiG-29 *Fulcrum*; MiG-29SE/SM/UB *Fulcrum*; Su-30SM *Flanker* H
GROUND ATTACK
  2 sqn with A-5C *Fantan*
TRANSPORT
  1 sqn with ATR-72-600; F-27 *Friendship*; PC-6AB *Turbo Porter*; Y-12 (IV)
TRAINING
  2 sqn with G-4 *Super Galeb**; PC-7 *Turbo Trainer**; PC-9*
  1 sqn with K-8 *Karakorun* *
ATTACK/TRANSPORT HELICOPTER
  4 sqn with Bell 205; Bell 206 *Jet Ranger*; Ka-28 *Helix* A; Mi-17 *Hip* H; Mi-35P *Hind*; PZL Mi-2 *Hoplite*; PZL W-3 *Sokol*

EQUIPMENT BY TYPE
AIRCRAFT 168 combat capable
  FTR 63: 21 F-7 *Airguard*; 11 FT-7; 10 MiG-29 *Fulcrum*; 6 MiG-29SE *Fulcrum*; 10 MiG-29SM *Fulcrum*; 5 MiG-29UB *Fulcrum*
  FGA 16: 6 FTC-2000G; 4 JF-17 *Thunder* (FC-1 Block II); 2 JF-17B *Thunder* (FC-1 Block II); 4 Su-30SM *Flanker* H
  ATK 21 A-5C *Fantan*
  MP 2 ATR-42
  TPT 30: **Medium** 5: 4 Y-8D; 1 Y-8F-200W **Light** 23: 1 ATR-42; 1 ATR-72-600; 5 Beech 1900D; 2 C295 (reported); 3 F-27 *Friendship*; 5 PC-6A/B *Turbo Porter*; 6+ Y-12 (IV); **PAX** 2 F-70
  TRG 88: ε5 G-4 *Super Galeb**; 20 G 120; ε4 K-8 *Karakorum**; 12 PC-7 *Turbo Trainer**; 9 PC-9*; 18 Yak-130 *Mitten**
HELICOPTERS
  ATK 11 Mi-35P *Hind*
  ASW 2 Ka-28 *Helix* A
  MRH 9: 1 AS365; ε8 Mi-17 *Hip* H
  TPT 48: **Medium** 10 PZL W-3 *Sokol*; **Light** 38: 12 Bell 205; 6 Bell 206 *Jet Ranger*; 3 H120 *Colibri*; 17 PZL Mi-2 *Hoplite*
UNINHABITED AERIAL VEHICLES
  CISR • Heavy 4 CH-3
  ISR • Light S-100 *Camcopter*
AIR-LAUNCHED MISSILES
  AAM • IR PL-5; R-73 (RS-AA-11a *Archer*); PL-5E-II; **IR/SARH** R-27 (RS-AA-10 *Alamo*); **ARH** PL-12 (CH-AA-7a *Adze*); R-77 (RS-AA-12a *Adder*)
  AShM C-802A

Gendarmerie & Paramilitary 70,000

Coast Guard
EQUIPMENT BY TYPE
PATROL AND COASTAL COMBATANTS 10
  PB 10: 3 PGM 412; 7 other

People's Police Force 45,000

People's Militia 25,000

Nepal NPL

Nepalese Rupee NPR		2023	2024	2025
GDP	NPR	5.35trn	5.79trn	6.39trn
	USD	40.9bn	43.7bn	47.8bn
Real GDP growth	%	2.0	3.1	4.9
	NPR	55.0bn	58.8bn	59.9bn
	USD	421m	444m	448m

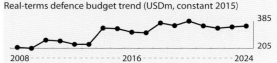

Real-terms defence budget trend (USDm, constant 2015)

Population	31,122,387					
Age	0–14	15–19	20–24	25–29	30–64	65 plus
Male	13.3%	4.8%	4.9%	5.0%	17.9%	3.1%
Female	12.6%	4.5%	4.8%	5.0%	20.9%	3.3%

Capabilities

Nepal has a history of deploying troops as UN peacekeepers, but also employs the armed forces to support internal security and humanitarian relief efforts. The all-volunteer force receives training support from countries such as China, India and the US. Following a 2006 peace accord with the Maoist People's Liberation Army, Maoist personnel underwent a process of demobilisation or integration into the armed forces. Gurkhas continue to be recruited by the British and Indian armed forces and the Singaporean police. A number of Nepali men reportedly joined the Russian armed forces to fight in its war against Ukraine. The small air wing provides limited transport and support capacity, but mobility remains a challenge, in part because of the country's topography. Nepal's logistics capability appears sufficient for internal-security operations; however, its UN peacekeepers are largely dependent on contracted logistics support. Modernisation efforts in recent years have included small enhancements to its air arm. The country has some maintenance capacities, but otherwise lacks a defence industry and is dependent on foreign suppliers for modern equipment.

ACTIVE 96,600 (Army 96,600) Gendarmerie & Paramilitary 15,000

ORGANISATIONS BY SERVICE

Army 96,600
FORCES BY ROLE
COMMAND
 2 inf div HQ
 1 (valley) comd
SPECIAL FORCES
 1 bde (1 SF bn, 1 AB bn, 1 cdo bn, 1 ranger bn, 1 mech inf bn)
MANOEUVRE
 Light
 18 inf bde (total: 62 inf bn; 32 indep inf coy)

COMBAT SUPPORT
 1 arty bde
 4 arty regt
 5 engr bn
 1 sigs bde
AIR DEFENCE
 2 AD regt
 4 indep AD coy
EQUIPMENT BY TYPE
ARMOURED FIGHTING VEHICLES
 RECCE 40 *Ferret*
 APC 253
  APC (W) 13: 8 OT-64C; 5 WZ-551
  PPV 240: 90 *Casspir*; 150 MPV
  AUV Dongfeng *Mengshi*; CS/VN3C mod 2
ARTILLERY 92+
 TOWED 105mm 22: 8 L118 Light Gun; 14 pack howitzer (6 non-operational)
 MOR 70+: 81mm; 120mm 70 M-43 (est 12 op)
AIR DEFENCE • GUNS • TOWED 32+: **14.5mm** 30 Type-56 (ZPU-4); **37mm** (PRC); **40mm** 2 L/60

Air Wing 320
EQUIPMENT BY TYPE†
AIRCRAFT • TPT • Light 6: 1 CN235M-220; 3 M-28 *Skytruck*; 2 PA-28 *Cherokee* (trg)
HELICOPTERS
 MRH 8: 2 AW139; 1 Bell 407GXP (VIP); 1 *Dhruv* MkIII; 1 Mi-17-1V *Hip* H; 3 Mi-17V-5 *Hip*
 TPT • Light 4: 2 AS350B2 *Ecureuil*; 2 Bell 206

Paramilitary 15,000

Armed Police Force 15,000
Ministry of Home Affairs

DEPLOYMENT

CENTRAL AFRICAN REPUBLIC: UN • MINUSCA 1,224; 2 inf bn; 1 MP pl
DEMOCRATIC REPUBLIC OF THE CONGO: UN • MONUSCO 1,149; 1 inf bn; 1 engr coy
IRAQ: UN • UNAMI 88; 1 sy unit
LEBANON: UN • UNIFIL 876; 1 mech inf bn; 1 log coy
LIBYA: UN • UNISMIL 231; 2 sy coy
MIDDLE EAST: UN • UNTSO 3
SOUTH SUDAN: UN • UNMISS 1,754; 2 inf bn
SUDAN: UN • UNISFA 107; 1 log coy
SYRIA/ISRAEL: UN • UNDOF 451; 1 mech inf coy; 1 inf coy; 1 engr pl
WESTERN SAHARA: UN • MINURSO 5

FOREIGN FORCES

United Kingdom 60 (Gurkha trg org)

New Zealand NZL

New Zealand Dollar NZD		2023	2024	2025
GDP	NZD	405bn	415bn	434bn
	USD	249bn	252bn	263bn
Real GDP growth	%	0.6	0.0	1.9
Def bdgt	NZD	4.94bn	5.19bn	5.45bn
	USD	3.03bn	3.15bn	3.30bn

Population	5,161,211				
Age	0–14	15–19	20–24	25–29	30–64	65 plus
Male	9.7%	3.3%	3.2%	3.4%	22.5%	7.9%
Female	9.2%	3.2%	3.0%	3.3%	22.3%	9.0%

Capabilities

The government issued its inaugural National Security Strategy in 2023 to address changes in Wellington's security environment, including rising tension in the South and East China seas and the consequences of Russia's 2022 invasion of Ukraine. The document called for a strategy of 'acting early and working together'. It was accompanied by a Defence Policy and Strategy Statement intended to guide defence planning and investment in an increasingly challenging and complex environment, and Future Force Design Principles which outline force development requirements over the next 15 years. New Zealand's closest defence partners are Australia and the United States, and Wellington considers defence relationships with Pacific Island states key to its and the region's security. The NZDF is looking to expand the army by 2035 but is facing recruitment challenges. In April 2023, the Australian and New Zealand armies agreed, under Plan ANZAC, to cooperate in areas such as training and readiness. The army is revamping its protected mobility capabilities with new systems and is experimenting with UAVs to inform future military requirements. New Zealand has a small defence industry consisting of private companies and subsidiaries of larger North American and European firms. These companies provide some maintenance, repair and overhaul capability, but significant work is contracted overseas.

ACTIVE 8,700 (Army 4,250 Navy 2,050 Air 2,400)

RESERVE 3,270 (Army 2,050 Navy 800 Air Force 420)

ORGANISATIONS BY SERVICE

Army 4,250
FORCES BY ROLE
SPECIAL FORCES
  1 SF regt
MANOEUVRE
  Light
  1 inf bde (1 armd recce regt, 2 lt inf bn, 1 arty regt (2 arty bty), 1 engr regt(-), 1 MP coy, 1 sigs regt, 2 log bn)

EQUIPMENT BY TYPE
ARMOURED FIGHTING VEHICLES
  IFV 74 NZLAV-25
  AUV 43 *Bushmaster*
ENGINEERING & MAINTENANCE VEHICLES
  AEV 7 NZLAV
  ARV 3 LAV-R
ANTI-TANK/ANTI-INFRASTRUCTURE
  MSL • MANPATS FGM-148 *Javelin*
ARTILLERY 56
  TOWED 105mm 24 L119 Light Gun
  MOR 81mm 32

Reserves

Territorial Force 1,850 reservists
Responsible for providing trained individuals for augmenting deployed forces
FORCES BY ROLE
COMBAT SERVICE SUPPORT
  3 (Territorial Force Regional) trg regt

Navy 2,050

Fleet based in Auckland. Fleet HQ at Wellington
EQUIPMENT BY TYPE
PRINCIPAL SURFACE COMBATANTS • FRIGATES 2
  FFHM 2 *Anzac* (GER MEKO 200) with 1 20-cell VLS with *Sea Ceptor* SAM, 2 triple SVTT Mk 32 324mm ASTT with Mk 46 mod 5 LWT, 1 Mk 15 *Phalanx* Block 1B CIWS, 1 127mm gun (capacity 1 SH-2G(I) *Super Seasprite* ASW hel)
PATROL AND COASTAL COMBATANTS 4
  PSOH (2 *Otago* (capacity 1 SH-2G(I) *Super Seasprite* ASW hel) (ice-strengthened hull) in reserve)
  PCC 1 *Lake* (1 more in reserve)
  PBF 3 *Littoral Manoeuvre Craft* (*Sentinel 1250*)
AMPHIBIOUS • LANDING CRAFT 2
  LCM 2 (operated off HMNZS *Canterbury*)
LOGISTICS AND SUPPORT • 2
  AKRH 1 *Canterbury* (capacity 4 NH90 tpt hel; 1 SH-2G(I) *Super Seasprite* ASW hel; 2 LCM; 16 NZLAV; 20 trucks; 250 troops)
  AORH 1 *Aotearoa* (capacity 1 NH90/SH-2G(I) hel)
UNINHABITED MARITIME SYSTEMS • UUV
  DATA REMUS 100/300
  UTL *Cougar* XT

Air Force 2,400
FORCES BY ROLE
MARITIME PATROL
  1 sqn with P-8A *Poseidon*
TRANSPORT
  1 sqn with B-757-200 (upgraded); C-130H *Hercules* (upgraded); C-130J-30 *Hercules*

ANTI-SUBMARINE/SURFACE WARFARE
1 (RNZAF/RNZN) sqn with SH-2G(I) *Super Seasprite*

TRAINING
1 sqn with T-6C *Texan* II
1 sqn with Beech 350 *King Air* (leased)

TRANSPORT HELICOPTER
1 sqn with AW109LUH; NH90

EQUIPMENT BY TYPE
AIRCRAFT 4 combat capable
  ASW 4 P-8A *Poseidon*
  TPT 10: **Medium** 4: 3 C-130H *Hercules* (upgraded); 1 C-130J-30 *Hercules*; **Light** 4 Beech 350 *King Air* (leased); **PAX** 2 B-757-200 (upgraded)
  TRG 11 T-6C *Texan* II
HELICOPTERS
  ASW 5 SH-2G(I) *Super Seasprite*
  TPT 13: **Medium** 8 NH90; **Light** 5 AW109LUH
AIR-LAUNCHED MISSILES
  AShM AGM-119 *Penguin* Mk2 mod 7

DEPLOYMENT
EGYPT: MFO 28; 1 trg unit; 1 tpt unit
MIDDLE EAST: UN • UNTSO 8
SOUTH SUDAN: UN • UNMISS 3
UNITED KINGDOM: Operation Tieke (*Interflex*) 71

Pakistan PAK

Pakistani Rupee PKR		2023	2024	2025
GDP	PKR	83.9trn	106trn	122trn
	USD	337bn	375bn	435bn
Real GDP growth	%	-0.2	2.4	3.2
Def bdgt [a]	PKR	1.97trn	2.38trn	2.80trn
	USD	7.91bn	8.40bn	10.0bn

[a] Includes defence allocations to the Public Sector Development Programme (PSDP), including funding to the Defence Division and the Defence Production Division.

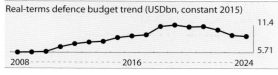
Real-terms defence budget trend (USDbn, constant 2015)

Population	252,363,571					
Age	0–14	15–19	20–24	25–29	30–64	65 plus
Male	17.6%	5.2%	4.7%	4.2%	17.0%	2.3%
Female	16.9%	4.9%	4.5%	4.0%	16.3%	2.6%

Capabilities

Pakistan's nuclear and conventional forces have traditionally been oriented and structured against a prospective threat from India. Recruitment and retention within the armed forces is high, though there are concerns about politicisation, radicalisation and pay, given Pakistan's growing political, security and fiscal crises. The army and air force have considerable operational experience from a decade of counter-insurgency operations in Pakistan's tribal areas. Since 2008, counter-insurgency and counter-terrorism have been the forces' main effort. Although an army-led counter-terrorism operation has improved domestic security, terrorist attacks continue. Pakistan's UAVs have targeted militants in Afghanistan. A 2021 mutual reaffirmation of the 2003 ceasefire agreement between India and Pakistan has reduced conflict across the Line of Control in the disputed region of Jammu and Kashmir. Overseas, they contribute a considerable number of personnel to UN peacekeeping missions, principally in Africa. China is Pakistan's main defence partner, with all three services employing a large amount of Chinese equipment. Although funds have been directed towards improving security and fencing on the border with Afghanistan, the Taliban regime provides little support to those efforts. Investments in military nuclear programmes continue despite budget pressures, including the testing of a nuclear-capable sea-launched cruise missile. Ending a lull in missile testing since April 2022, Pakistan in October 2023 tested the *Ababeel* ballistic missile, confirming its ambition to develop MIRVs. The navy and air force are modernising across a range of activities. The indigenous defence industry has well-developed maintenance facilities for combat aircraft and exports platforms, weapons and ammunition. Pakistan has close defence-industrial ties with China.

ACTIVE 660,000 (Army 560,000 Navy 30,000 Air 70,000) **Gendarmerie & Paramilitary 291,000**

ORGANISATIONS BY SERVICE

Strategic Forces

Operational control rests with the National Command Authority. The Strategic Plans Directorate (SPD) manages and commands all of Pakistan's military nuclear capability. The SPD also commands a reportedly 25,000-strong military security force responsible for guarding the country's nuclear infrastructure

Army Strategic Forces Command 12,000–15,000

Commands all land-based strategic nuclear forces

EQUIPMENT BY TYPE
SURFACE-TO-SURFACE MISSILE LAUNCHERS 60+
  MRBM • **Nuclear** 30+: ε30 *Ghauri*/*Ghauri* II (*Hatf*-V)/*Shaheen*-II (*Hatf*-VI); *Shaheen*-III (in test)
  SRBM • **Nuclear** 30+: ε30 *Ghaznavi* (*Hatf*-III – PRC M-11)/*Shaheen*-I (*Hatf*-IV); some *Abdali* (*Hatf*-II); some *Nasr* (*Hatf*-IX)
  GLCM • **Nuclear** *Babur*-I/IA (*Hatf*-VII); *Ra'ad* (*Hatf*-VIII – in test)

Air Force
1–2 sqn of F-16A/B or *Mirage* 5 may be assigned a nuclear-strike role

Army 560,000
FORCES BY ROLE
COMMAND
  9 corps HQ
  1 (Northern) comd

SPECIAL FORCES
2 SF gp (total: 4 SF bn)

MANOEUVRE
Armoured
2 armd div
7 indep armd bde
Mechanised
2 mech inf div
1 indep mech bde
Light
18 inf div
5 indep inf bde
4 (Northern Command) inf bde
Other
2 sy div

COMBAT SUPPORT
1 arty div
14 arty bde
7 engr bde

AVIATION
7 avn sqn

ISR
1 sqn

HELICOPTER
3 atk hel sqn
1 SAR hel sqn
4 tpt hel sqn
1 spec ops hel sqn
5 hel sqn

AIR DEFENCE
1 AD comd (3 AD gp (total: 8 AD bn))

EQUIPMENT BY TYPE
ARMOURED FIGHTING VEHICLES
MBT 2,537: 300 Al-Khalid (MBT 2000); ε110 Al-Khalid I; 315 T-80UD; ε500 Al-Zarrar; 400 Type-69; 268 Type-85-IIAP; 44 VT-4; ε600 ZTZ-59
APC 3,545
  APC (T) 3,200: 2,300 M113A1/A2/P; ε200 Talha; 600 VCC-1/VCC-2; ε100 ZSD-63
  APC (W) 120 BTR-70/BTR-80
  PPV 225 Maxxpro
AUV 10 Dingo 2

ENGINEERING & MAINTENANCE VEHICLES
ARV 262+: 175 Type-70/Type-84 (W653/W653A); Al-Hadeed; 52 M88A1; 35 Maxxpro ARV; T-54/T-55
VLB M47M; M48/60
MW Aardvark Mk II

ANTI-TANK/ANTI-INFRASTRUCTURE
MSL
  SP M901 TOW; ε30 Maaz (HJ-8 on Talha chassis)
  MANPATS HJ-8; TOW
RCL 75mm Type-52; 106mm M40A1 RL 89mm M20

GUNS 85mm 200 Type-56 (D-44)

ARTILLERY 4,619+
SP 552: 155mm 492: 200 M109A2; ε115 M109A5; 123 M109L; ε54 SH-15; 203mm 60 M110/M110A2
TOWED 1,629: 105mm 329: 216 M101; 113 M-56; 122mm 570: 80 D-30 (PRC); 490 Type-54 (M-1938); 130mm 410 Type-59-I; 155mm 292: 144 M114; 148 M198; 203mm 28 M115
MRL 88+: 107mm Type-81; 122mm 52+: 52 Azar (Type-83); some KRL-122; 300mm 36 A100
MOR 2,350+: 81mm; 120mm AM-50

SURFACE-TO-SURFACE MISSILE LAUNCHERS
MRBM • Nuclear 30+: ε30 Ghauri/Ghauri II (Hatf-V)/Shaheen-II (Hatf-VI); some Shaheen-III (in test)
SRBM 135+: Nuclear 30+: ε30 Ghaznavi (Hatf-III – PRC M-11)/Shaheen-I (Haif-IV); some Abdali (Haif-II); some Nasr (Hatf-IX); Conventional 105 Hatf-I
GLCM • Nuclear some Babur-I/IA (Hatf-VII)

AIRCRAFT
TPT • Light 30: 5 Beech 350 King Air; 3+ Beech 350i King Air; 2 Cessna T206H; 13 Cessna 208B; 1 Cessna 550 Citation; 1 Cessna 560 Citation; 1 Cessna 680 Sovereign; 4 Y-12(II)
TRG 87 MFI-17B Mushshak

HELICOPTERS
ATK 42: 38 AH-1F/S Cobra; 4 Mi-35M Hind
MRH 132+: 10 H125M Fennec; 12 AW139; 38 Bell 412EP Twin Huey; 38+ Mi-17 Hip H; 2 Mi-171E Hip; 12 SA315B Lama; 20 SA319 Alouette III
TPT 79: Medium 36: 31 SA330 Puma; 4 Mi-171: 1 Mi-172; Light 43: 16 H125 Ecureuil (SAR); 5 Bell 205 (UH-1H Iroquois); 5 Bell 205A-1 (AB-205A-1); 13 Bell 206B Jet Ranger II; 4+ F-280FX
TRG 10 Hughes 300C

UNINHABITED AERIAL VEHICLES
CISR • Heavy 5 CH-4
ISR • Light Bravo; Jasoos; Vector

AIR DEFENCE
SAM 27+
  Long-range some HQ-9/P
  Medium-range 27 LY-80 (CH-SA-16)
  Short-range FM-90 (CH-SA-4)
  Point-defence M113 with RBS-70; Anza-II; FN-6 (CH-SA-10); Mistral; QW-18 (CH-SA-11); RBS-70
GUNS • TOWED 1,933: 14.5mm 981; 35mm 248 GDF-002/GDF-005 (with 134 Skyguard radar units); 37mm 310 Type-55 (M-1939)/Type-65; 40mm 50 L/60; 57mm 144 Type-59 (S-60); 85mm 200 Type-72 (M-1939) KS-12

Navy 30,000 (incl ε3,200 Marines)

EQUIPMENT BY TYPE
SUBMARINES 8
SSK 5:
  2 Hashmat (FRA Agosta 70) with 4 single 533mm ASTT

with UGM-84 *Harpoon* AShM/F-17P HWT
3 *Khalid* (FRA *Agosta* 90B) (of which 2 fitted with AIP) with 4 single 533mm ASTT with SM39 *Exocet* AShM/*SeaHake* mod 4 (DM2A4) HWT

SSW 3 MG110 (SF delivery) each with 2 single 533mm TT with F-17P HWT

PRINCIPAL SURFACE COMBATANTS • FRIGATES 11
FFGHM 9:
1 *Babur* (TUR MILGEM mod) with 2 triple lnchr with AShM, 2 6-cell VLS with *Albatross*-NG (CAMM-ER) SAM, 2 triple 324mm ASTT with LWT, 1 *Gokdeniz* CIWS, 1 76mm gun (capacity 1 med hel)
4 *Sword* (F-22P) with 2 quad lnchr with C-802A AShM, 1 octuple lnchr with FM-90N (CH-SA-N-4) SAM, 2 triple 324mm ASTT with ET-52C (A244/S) LWT, 2 RDC-32 A/S mor, 1 Type 730B (H/PJ-12) CIWS, 1 76mm gun (capacity 1 Z-9C *Haitun* hel)
4 *Tughril* (PRC Type-054AP) with 2 twin lnchr with CM-302 (YJ-12A) AShM, 4 8-cell H/AJK-16 VLS with LY-80N (HHQ-16 CH-SA-N-16)) SAM, 2 triple 324mm ASTT with Yu-7 LWT, 2 H/PJ-11 CIWS, 1 76mm gun (capacity 1 Z-9C *Haitun* ASW hel)

FFGH 1 *Alamgir* (ex-US *Oliver Hazard Perry*) with 2 quad lnchr with RGM-84 *Harpoon* AShM, 2 triple 324mm ASTT with Mk 46 LWT, 1 Mk 15 *Phalanx* CIWS, 1 76mm gun

FFH 1 *Hunain* (Damen OPV 2600)

PATROL AND COASTAL COMBATANTS 21
CORVETTES • FSH 2 *Yarmook* (Damen OPV 1900) (fitted for but not with 2 quad lnchr for AShM) with 1 Mk 15 *Phalanx* CIWS (capacity 1 hel)
PCG 4: 2 *Azmat* (FAC(M)) with 2 quad lnchr with C-802A AShM, 1 AK630 CIWS; 2 *Azmat* (FAC(M)) with 2 triple lnchr with C-602 AShM, 1 AK630 CIWS
PBG 4: 2 *Jalalat* with 2 twin lnchr with C-802 (CH-SS-N-6) AShM; 2 *Jurrat* with 2 twin lnchr with C-802 (CH-SS-N-6) AShM
PBF 4: 2 *Kaan* 15 (TUR MRTP 15); 2 *Zarrar* (TUR MRTP 34)
PB 5: 1 *Larkana*; 4 M16 Fast Assault Boat
PBR 2 12T *Marine Assault Boat*

MINE WARFARE • MINE COUNTERMEASURES 5
MCC 5 *Munsif* (ex-FRA *Eridan*) (1 more in store)

AMPHIBIOUS • LANDING CRAFT 8
LCM 2
LCAC 2 *Griffon* 8100TD
UCAC 4 *Griffon* 2000TD

LOGISTICS AND SUPPORT 11
AGI 1 *Rizwan*
AGS 2: 1 *Behr Masa*; 1 *Behr Paima*
AOL 4: 2 *Gwadar*; 2 *Madadgar*
AORH 2: 1 *Moawin* with 2 Mk 15 *Phalanx* CIWS, 1 hel landing platform; 1 *Nasr* (PRC *Fuqing*) with 1 Mk 15 *Phalanx* CIWS (capacity 1 SA319 *Alouette* III hel)
AP 1 *Balochistan*
AXS 1

Marines ε3,200
FORCES BY ROLE
SPECIAL FORCES
1 cdo gp
MANOEUVRE
Amphibious
3 mne bn
AIR DEFENCE
1 AD bn

Naval Aviation
FORCES BY ROLE
ANTI-SUBMARINE WARFARE
1 sqn with P-3C *Orion*
1 sqn with *Sea King* Mk45
1 sqn with SA319B *Alouette* III
1 sqn with Z-9C *Haitun*
MARITIME PATROL
1 sqn with ATR-72-500; Hawker 850XP
EQUIPMENT BY TYPE
AIRCRAFT 10 combat capable
ASW 10: 7 P-3C *Orion*; 3 ATR-72-500
TPT 5: **Light** 4: 2 ATR-72-500; 2 Lineage 1000 (converting to MP); **PAX** 1 Hawker 850XP
HELICOPTERS
ASW 12: 7 *Sea King* Mk45; 5+ Z-9C *Haitun*
MRH 6 SA319B *Alouette* III
SAR 1 *Sea King* (ex-HAR3A)
TPT • Medium 5: 1 *Commando* Mk2A; 3 *Commando* Mk3; 1 *Sea King* (ex-HC4)
UNINHABITED AERIAL VEHICLES
ISR • Light 2 *Luna* NG
AIR-LAUNCHED MISSILES • AShM AGM-84L *Harpoon*; AM39 *Exocet*

Coastal Defence
FORCES BY ROLE
COASTAL Defence
1 AShM regt with *Zarb* (YJ-62)
EQUIPMENT BY TYPE
COASTAL DEFENCE • AShM *Zarb* (YJ-62)

Air Force 70,000
3 regional comds: Northern (Peshawar), Central (Sargodha), Southern (Masroor). The Composite Air Tpt Wg, Combat Cadres School and PAF Academy are Direct Reporting Units

FORCES BY ROLE
FIGHTER
3 sqn with F-7PG/FT-7PG *Airguard*
1 sqn with F-16A/B ADF *Fighting Falcon*
1 sqn with *Mirage* IIID/E (IIIOD/EP)
FIGHTER/GROUND ATTACK
1 sqn with F-16A/B MLU *Fighting Falcon*

1 sqn with F-16C/D Block 52 *Fighting Falcon*
1 sqn with J-10CE *Firebird*
1 sqn with JF-17 *Thunder* (FC-1 Block I)
1 sqn with JF-17 *Thunder* (FC-1 Block II)
2 sqn with JF-17 *Thunder* (FC-1 Block I/II)
1 sqn with JF-17 *Thunder* (FC-1 Block I/II/III); JF-17B *Thunder* (FC-1 Block II)
1 sqn with JF-17 *Thunder* (FC-1 Block III) (forming)
3 sqn with *Mirage* 5

ELECTRONIC WARFARE/ELINT
1 sqn with *Falcon* 20F

AIRBORNE EARLY WARNING & CONTROL
2 sqn with Saab 2000; Saab 2000 *Erieye*
1 sqn with ZDK-03

SEARCH & RESCUE
2 sqn with AW139
1 sqn with AW139 (liaison/SAR); Mi-171Sh
5 sqn with SA316 *Alouette* III

TANKER
1 sqn with Il-78 *Midas*

TRANSPORT
1 sqn with C-130B/E/H *Hercules*; L-100-20
1 sqn with C-130E *Hercules*; Saab 2000
1 sqn with CN235M-220
1 VIP sqn with A319; Beech 350i *King Air*; Cessna 560XL *Citation Excel*; CN235M-220; *Falcon* 20E; Global 6000; Gulfstream IVSP
1 (comms) sqn with EMB-500 *Phenom* 100; PA-46 Mk600; Y-12 (II)

TRAINING
1 OCU sqn with F-7P/FT-7P *Skybolt*; JF-17 *Thunder* (FC-1 Block II); JF-17B *Thunder* (FC-1 Block II)
1 OCU sqn with *Mirage* III/*Mirage* 5
1 OCU sqn with F-16A/B MLU *Fighting Falcon*
2 sqn with K-8 *Karakorum**
2 sqn with MFI-17
2 sqn with T-37C *Tweet*

AIR DEFENCE
1 bty with HQ-2 (CH-SA-1); 9K310 *Igla*-1 (RS-SA-16 *Gimlet*)
6 bty with *Crotale*
10 bty with SPADA 2000

EQUIPMENT BY TYPE
AIRCRAFT 465 combat capable
  FTR 107: 46 F-7PG *Airguard*; 20 F-7P *Skybolt*; 9 F-16A ADF *Fighting Falcon*; 4 F-16B ADF *Fighting Falcon*; 21 FT-7; 5 FT-7PG; 2 *Mirage* IIIB
  FGA 310: 23 F-16A MLU *Fighting Falcon*; 21 F-16B MLU *Fighting Falcon*; 12 F-16C Block 52 *Fighting Falcon*; 6 F-16D Block 52 *Fighting Falcon*; 20+ J-10CE *Firebird*; 49 JF-17 *Thunder* (FC-1 Block I); 57 JF-17 *Thunder* (FC-1 Block II); 23+ JF-17 *Thunder* (FC-1 Block III); 25 JF-17B *Thunder* (FC-1 Block II); 7 *Mirage* IIID (*Mirage* IIIOD); 30 *Mirage* IIIE (IIIEP); 25 *Mirage* 5 (5PA)/5PA2; 2 *Mirage* 5D (5DPA)/5DPA2; 10 *Mirage* 5PA3 (AS_W)
  ISR 10 *Mirage* IIIR* (*Mirage* IIIRP)
  ELINT 2 *Falcon* 20F
  AEW&C 12: 8 Saab 2000 *Erieye*; 4 ZDK-03
  TKR 4 Il-78 *Midas*
  TPT 51: **Medium** 19: 5 C-130B *Hercules*; 3 C-130E *Hercules*; 4 C-130H *Hercules*; 1 L-100-20; **Light** 20: 2 Beech 350i *King Air*; 2 Cessna 208B; 1 Cessna 560XL *Citation Excel*; 4 CN235M-220; 6 EMB-500 *Pherom* 100; 2 PA-46 M600; 3 Y-12 (II); **PAX** 12: 1 A319; 1 *Falcon* 20E; 2 Global 6000; 2 Gulfstream IV-SP; 6 Saab 2000
  TRG 140: 38 K-8 *Karakorum**; 79 MFI-17B *Mushshak*; 23 T-37C *Tweet*
HELICOPTERS
  MRH 29: 15 SA316 *Alouette* III; 14 AW139
  TPT • **Medium** 6 Mi-171Sh
UNINHABITED AERIAL VEHICLES
  CISR 18+: **Heavy** 13+: 1 *Bayraktar Akinci*; 5+ CH-3 (*Burraq*); CH-4 (reported); 2+ *Wing Loong* I; 1+ *Wing Loong* II; **Medium** 5: 3+ *Bayraktar* TB2; 2+ *Shahphar* II
  ISR • **Medium** *Falco*
AIR DEFENCE • **SAM** 190+
  Medium-range 6 HQ-2 (CH-SA-1)
  Short-range 184: 144 *Crotale*; ε40 SPADA 2000
  Point-defence 9K310 *Igla*-1 (RS-SA-16 *Gimlet*)
AIR-LAUNCHED MISSILES
  AAM • **IR** AIM-9L/P *Sidewinder*, *U-Darter*; PL-5E-II; **IIR** PL-10 (CH-AA-9); **SARH** Super 530; **ARH** AIM-120C AMRAAM; PL-12 (CH-AA-7A *Adze*); PL-15 (CH-AA-10 *Abaddon*)
  ASM AGM-65 *Maverick*; CM-400AKG; *Raptor* II
  AShM AM39 *Exocet*; C-802
  ARM MAR-1
  LACM • **Nuclear** *Ra'ad*
BOMBS
  INS/SAT-guided LS-6; *Takbir*
  Laser-guided Al-Battar 500; Al-Battar 2000; *Paveway* II

Gendarmerie & Paramilitary 291,000 active

Airport Security Force 9,000
Government Aviation Division

Pakistan Coast Guards
Ministry of Interior
EQUIPMENT BY TYPE
PATROL AND COASTAL COMBATANTS 5:
  PBF 4
  PB 1

Frontier Corps 70,000
Ministry of Interior
FORCES BY ROLE
MANOEUVRE

Reconnaissance
1 armd recce sqn

Other
11 paramilitary regt (total: 40 paramilitary bn)

EQUIPMENT BY TYPE
ARMOURED FIGHTING VEHICLES
APC (W) 45 UR-416

Maritime Security Agency ε2,000
FORCES BY ROLE
MARITIME PATROL
1 sqn with BN-2T *Defender*
EQUIPMENT BY TYPE
PATROL AND COASTAL COMBATANTS 23
PSO 2 *Kashmir* with 1 hel landing platform
PCC 10: 4 *Barkat*; 4 *Hingol*; 2 *Sabqat* (ex-US *Island*)
PBF 11 Response Boat-Medium (RB-M) (ex-US)
AIRCRAFT • TPT • Light 3 BN-2T *Defender*

National Guard 185,000
Incl Janbaz Force; Mujahid Force; Women Guards

Pakistan Rangers 25,000
Ministry of Interior

DEPLOYMENT

ARABIAN SEA & GULF OF ADEN: Combined Maritime Forces • CTF-151: 1 FFGHM

CENTRAL AFRICAN REPUBLIC: UN • MINUSCA 1,314; 1 inf bn; 2 engr coy; 1 hel sqn

CYPRUS: UN • UNFICYP 43

DEMOCRATIC REPUBLIC OF THE CONGO: UN • MONUSCO 383; 1 arty bty; 1 hel sqn with SA300 *Puma*

SOMALIA: UN • UNSOS 1

SOUTH SUDAN: UN • UNMISS 292; 1 engr coy

SUDAN: UN • UNISFA 593; 1 inf bn(-)

WESTERN SAHARA: UN • MINURSO 12

FOREIGN FORCES
Figures represent total numbers for UNMOGIP mission in India and Pakistan
Argentina 3
Croatia 8
Italy 2
Korea, Republic of 5
Mexico 3
Nigeria 1
Philippines 6
Romania 2
Sweden 2
Switzerland 3
Thailand 5
Uruguay 2

Papua New Guinea PNG

Papua New Guinea Kina PGK		2023	2024	2025
GDP	PGK	111bn	123bn	134bn
	USD	30.9bn	31.9bn	32.6bn
Real GDP growth	%	2.9	4.6	3.7
Def bdgt	PGK	348m	353m	
	USD	96.8m	91.3m	

Real-terms defence budget trend (USDm, constant 2015)
95.4
41.9
2008 -- 2016 -- 2024

Population 10,046,233

Age	0–14	15–19	20–24	25–29	30–64	65 plus
Male	18.9%	5.0%	4.5%	4.1%	16.3%	2.0%
Female	18.2%	4.8%	4.3%	3.9%	16.1%	2.0%

Capabilities

The Papua New Guinea Defence Force (PNGDF) has suffered from underfunding and lack of capacity. A 2013 defence white paper identified core roles, including defending the state and civil-emergency assistance and called for strengthening defence capability, with long-term plans calling for a 'division-sized force' of 10,000 personnel by 2030. The PNGDF have since announced the Force 2030 and Defence 50 strategies to build defence capability. The PNGDF has received substantial external military assistance from China, and there were discussions with China regarding a security and policing deal. The US and Papua New Guinea (PNG) signed a defence cooperation agreement in May 2023 that updated and expanded a status of forces agreement. PNG also signed a bilateral security deal with Australia in December 2023 alongside investment from Canberra to support PNG's defence and security priorities. In February 2024, PNG ratified a PNG-Indonesia Defence Cooperation Agreement. The PNGDF is not able to deploy outside the country without assistance and there have only been small PNGDF deployments as part of UN peacekeeping missions. The forces have a limited air arm. PNG has no significant defence industry, though there is some local maintenance capacity.

ACTIVE 4,000 (Army 3,700 Maritime Element 200 Air 100)

ORGANISATIONS BY SERVICE

Army ε3,700
FORCES BY ROLE
SPECIAL FORCES
1 spec ops unit
MANOEUVRE
Light
2 inf bn
COMBAT SUPPORT
1 engr bn
1 EOD unit

COMBAT SERVICE SUPPORT

1 spt bn (1 sigs sqn; 1 supply coy)

EQUIPMENT BY TYPE

ARMOURED FIGHTING VEHICLES

APC • APC (W) 4 WZ-551†

ARTILLERY • MOR 3+: 81mm Some; 120mm 3

Maritime Element ε200

HQ located at Port Moresby

EQUIPMENT BY TYPE

PATROL AND COASTAL COMBATANTS • PCO 4

Guardian (AUS *Bay* mod)

AMPHIBIOUS • **LANDING CRAFT** 2

LCT 1 *Buna* (ex-AUS *Balikpapan*) (trg role)

LCM 1 *Cape Gloucester*

Air Force ε100

FORCES BY ROLE

TRANSPORT

1 flt with CN235M-100; PAC-750XSTOL

TRANSPORT HELICOPTER

1 flt with Bell 212

EQUIPMENT BY TYPE

AIRCRAFT • **TPT** • **Light** 4: 1 CN235M-100 (1 more in store); 3 PAC-750XSTOL

HELICOPTERS • **TPT** • **Light** 2 Bell 212 (leased)

DEPLOYMENT

SOUTH SUDAN: UN • UNMISS 2

Philippines PHL

Philippine Peso PHP		2023	2024	2025
GDP	PHP	24.3trn	26.5trn	28.8trn
	USD	437bn	470bn	508bn
Real GDP growth	%	5.5	5.8	6.1
Def bdgt [a]	PHP	344bn	379bn	408bn
	USD	6.19bn	6.73bn	7.19bn
FMA (US)	USD	40.0m	40.0m	42.3m

[a] Excludes military pensions

Real-terms defence budget trend (USDbn, constant 2015)

Population	118,277,063				
Age	0–14	15–19	20–24	25–29	30–64	65 plus
Male	15.4%	4.9%	4.6%	4.2%	18.7%	2.2%
Female	14.8%	4.7%	4.4%	4.1%	18.6%	3.4%

Capabilities

Despite modest increases in defence funding in the decade up to 2023, the capabilities and procurement plans of the Armed Forces of the Philippines (AFP) remain limited. However, the country's strategic context has shifted significantly in recent years. The stand-off in the South China Sea between Chinese and Philippine vessels, originally centred around the BRP Sierra Madre in the Second Thomas Shoal, has expanded to Sabina Shoal and Scarborough Shoal. The 2018–22 National Defense Strategy and the 2022 Strategic Defense Review highlighted strategic priorities including ensuring sovereignty and territorial integrity, promoting internal stability, HADR preparedness and strengthening maritime and air defence. The 2023–28 National Security Policy signalled a reorientation from internal security towards territorial and external defence. This is central to the 2024 Comprehensive Archipelagic Defense Concept which also emphasises joint service integration and inter-agency cooperation. The US is an ally of the Philippines and supports the AFP's external security role and its counter-terrorism operations. In 2023, Manila granted the US rotational access to additional bases and published bilateral defence guidelines, reaffirming the 1951 Mutual Defence Treaty. Japan and the Philippines finalised a Reciprocal Access Agreement in 2024. The AFP continues to host the long-running Balikatan exercise series with US forces and participates in ADMM exercises. Priorities under the Horizon modernisation programme, currently in its third and final phase (2023–28), include combat aircraft, transport aircraft, ASW/MP aircraft, UAVs, submarines, frigates, and air- and coastal-defence systems. In 2024, the Philippines began receiving its first *BrahMos* coastal-defence systems. Concerns remain about some procurement ambitions due to budget concerns. The Philippine Aerospace Development Corporation has assembled a variety of small helicopters and aircraft and provides MRO services for military aircraft.

ACTIVE 146,250 (Army 103,200 Navy 25,450 Air 17,600) Gendarmerie & Paramilitary 30,700

RESERVE 131,000 (Army 100,000 Navy 15,000 Air 16,000) Gendarmerie & Paramilitary 50,000 (to age 49)

ORGANISATIONS BY SERVICE

Army 103,200

5 Area Unified Comd (joint service), 1 National Capital Region Comd

FORCES BY ROLE

SPECIAL FORCES

1 spec ops comd (1 ranger regt, 1 SF regt, 1 CT regt)

MANOEUVRE

Mechanised

1 armd div (2 mech bde (total: 3 lt armd bn, 7 armd cav coy, 6 mech inf bn), 1 cbt engr coy, 1 sigs coy, 1 avn regt)

Light

1 div (4 inf bde, 1 fd arty bn, 1 int bn, 1 sigs bn)

7 div (3 inf bde, 1 fd arty bn, 1 int bn, 1 sigs bn)

3 div (3 inf bde, 1 int bn, 1 sigs bn)

Other

1 (Presidential) gd gp

COMBAT SUPPORT
 1 SP arty bn
 2 MRL bty (forming)
 5 engr bde

SURFACE-TO-SURFACE MISSILE
 1 SSM bty (forming)

AIR DEFENCE
 1 AD bty

EQUIPMENT BY TYPE

ARMOURED FIGHTING VEHICLES
 LT TK 26: 7 FV101 *Scorpion*; 19+ *Sabrah* ASCOD
 IFV 54: 2 YPR-765; 34 M113A1 FSV; 18 M113A2 FSV
 APC 395
  APC (T) 168: 6 ACV300; 42 M113A1; 120 M113A2 (some with *Dragon* RWS)
  APC (W) 224: 73 LAV-150 *Commando*; 146 *Simba*; 5 VBTP-MR *Guarani*
  PPV 3 CS/VP-3

ENGINEERING & MAINTENANCE VEHICLES
 ARV 5+: ACV-300; M578; 4 M113 ARV; *Samson*; 1 *Sabrah* ASCOD ARV
 VLB 2+: some GQL-111; 2 *Merkava* MkIV AVLB

ANTI-TANK-ANTI-INFRASTRUCTURE •
 RCL 75mm M20; 90mm M67; 106mm M40A1
 MSL • MANPATS TOW-2

ARTILLERY 287+
 SP 155mm 12 ATMOS 2000
 TOWED 220: 105mm 204 M101/M102/Model 56 pack howitzer; 155mm 16: 10 M114/M-68; 6 Soltam M-71
 MOR 55+: 81mm M29; 107mm 40 M30; SP 120mm 15 M113 with *Cardom*

AIRCRAFT
 TPT • Light 6: 1 Cessna 170; 2 Cessna 172; 1 Cessna P206A; 1 Cessna 421; 1 Short 330UTT
 HELICOPTERS • TPT • Light 5: 3 Bo-105 (medevac); 2 R-44 *Raven* II

UNINHABITED AERIAL VEHICLES
 ISR • Medium *Blue Horizon*; Light *Skylark* 3

Navy 25,450
EQUIPMENT BY TYPE

PRINCIPAL SURFACE COMBATANTS • FRIGATES 2
 FFGHM 2 *Jose Rizal* (ROK HDF-3000) with 2 quad lnchr with *Haeseong* I AShM, 2 twin *Simbad*-RC lnchr with *Mistral* SAM, 2 triple 324mm SEA TLS ASTT with K745 *Blue Shark* LWT, 1 76mm gun (fitted for but not with 1 8-cell VLS) (capacity 1 AW159 *Wildcat*)

PATROL AND COASTAL COMBATANTS 54
 CORVETTES • FS 1 *Conrado Yap* (ex-ROK *Po Hang* (Flight III)) with 2 triple 324mm SVTT Mk 32 ASTT with Mk 46 LWT, 2 76mm guns
 PSOH 3 *Del Pilar* (ex-US *Hamilton*) with 1 76mm gun (capacity 1 Bo 105)
 PCF 3 *General Mariano Alvares* (ex-US *Cyclone*)
 PCO 3 *Emilio Jacinto* (ex-UK *Peacock*) with 1 76mm gun
 PBFG 8: 6 MPAC Mk3 with 1 *Typhoon* MLS-ER quad lnchr with *Spike*-ER SSM; 2 *Nestor Acero* (ISR *Shaldag* V) with 1 8-cell lnchr with *Spike*-NLOS SSM
 PBF 10: 6 MPAC Mk1/2; 4 *Nestor Acero* (ISR *Shaldag* V mod)
 PB 26: 2 *Alberto Navarette* (ex-US *Point*); 22 *Jose Andrada*; 2 *Kagitingan*

AMPHIBIOUS
 PRINCIPAL AMPHIBIOUS SHIPS • LPD 2:
  2 *Tarlac* (IDN *Makassar*) (capacity 2 LCVP; 3 hels; 13 tanks; 500 troops)
 LANDING SHIPS • LST 4:
  2 *Bacolod City* (US *Besson*) with 1 hel landing platform (capacity 32 tanks; 150 troops)
  2 LST-1/542 (ex-US) (capacity 16 tanks; 200 troops) (1 other permanently grounded as marine outpost)
 LANDING CRAFT 15
  LCM 2: 1 *Manobo*; 1 *Tagbanua* (capacity 100 tons; 200 troops)
  LCT 5 *Ivatan* (ex-AUS *Balikpapan*)
  LCU 4: 3 LCU Mk 6 (ex-US); 1 *Mamanwa* (ex-ROK *Mulgae* I)
  LCVP 4

LOGISTICS AND SUPPORT 5
 AGOR 1 *Gregorio Velasquez* (ex-US *Melville*)
 AGS 1 *Fort San Antonio Abad*
 AO 1 *Lake Danao*
 AP 1 *Ang Pangulo*
 AWT 1 *Lake Buluan*

UNINHABITED MARITIME SYSTEMS • USV
 UTL *Mantas* T12

Naval Aviation
EQUIPMENT BY TYPE

AIRCRAFT • TPT • Light 14: 5 Beech 90 *King Air* (TC-90); 3 BN-2A *Defender*; 4 Cessna 172; 2 Cessna 177 *Cardinal*

HELICOPTERS
 ASW 2 AW159 *Wildcat*
 TPT 10: Medium 4 Mi-171Sh; Light 6: 4 AW109E (2 armed); 2 R-22 *Raven*

UNINHABITED AERIAL VEHICLES
 ISR • Light *ScanEagle* 2

Marines 8,300
FORCES BY ROLE

SPECIAL FORCES
 1 (force recon) spec ops bn

MANOEUVRE
 Amphibious
 4 mne bde (total: 12 mne bn)

COMBAT SERVICE SUPPORT
 1 CSS bde (6 CSS bn)

COASTAL DEFENCE
1 coastal def bde (1 AShM bn (forming); 1 SAM bn (forming))

EQUIPMENT BY TYPE
ARMOURED FIGHTING VEHICLES
APC • **APC (W)** 42: 19 LAV-150 *Commando*; 23 LAV-300
AAV 67: 8 AAV-7A1; 4 LVTH-6†; 55 LVTP-7
ARTILLERY 37+
TOWED 37: **105mm** 31: 23 M101; 8 M-26; **155mm** 6 Soltam M-71
MOR 107mm M30

Naval Special Operations Group
FORCES BY ROLE
SPECIAL FORCES
1 SEAL unit
1 diving unit
10 naval spec ops unit
1 special boat unit
COMBAT SUPPORT
1 EOD unit

Air Force 17,600
FORCES BY ROLE
FIGHTER
1 sqn with FA-50PH *Fighting Eagle**
GROUND ATTACK
1 sqn with EMB-314 *Super Tucano**
1 sqn with OV-10A/C *Bronco**; SF-260F/TP*
ISR
1 sqn with Cessna 208B *Grand Caravan* EX mod
SEARCH & RESCUE
4 (SAR/Comms) sqn with Bell 205 (UH-1M *Iroquois*); AUH-76; W-3A *Sokol*
TRANSPORT
1 sqn with C-130B/H/T *Hercules*
1 sqn with C295M/W; F-27-200 MPA; F-27-500 *Friendship*
1 sqn with N-22B *Nomad*; C-212 *Aviocar* (NC-212i)
1 VIP sqn with C295M; F-28 *Fellowship*; Gulfstream G280; Hawker 800
TRAINING
1 sqn with S-211*
1 sqn with SF-260FH
1 sqn with T-41B/D/K *Mescalero*
1 hel sqn with Bell 205 (UH-1H *Iroquois*)
ATTACK HELICOPTER
1 sqn with AH-1S *Cobra*; MD-520MG
1 sqn with AW109E; T-129B
TRANSPORT HELICOPTER
1 sqn with Bell 205 (UH-1H *Iroquois*)
1 sqn with Bell 412EP *Twin Huey*
1 sqn with S-70i *Black Hawk*
1 VIP sqn with Bell 412EP *Twin Huey*; S-70A/i *Black Hawk*
ISR UAV
1 sqn with *Hermes* 450/900
AIR DEFENCE
2 bty with *Spyder*-MR
EQUIPMENT BY TYPE
AIRCRAFT 28 combat capable
FGA 12 FA-50PH *Fighting Eagle*
ISR 6: 3 Cessna 208B *Grand Caravan* EX mod; 1 OV-10A *Bronco**; 2 OV-10C *Bronco**
TPT 22: **Medium** 5: 1 C-130B *Hercules*; 2 C-130H *Hercules*; 2 C-130T *Hercules* (secondary MP role); **Light** 14: 2 C-212 *Aviocar* (NC-212i); 4 C295M; 3 C295W; 1 Cessna T210 *Centurion*; 1 F-27-200 *Friendship*; 1 F-27-500 *Friendship*; 2+ N-22B *Nomad*; **PAX** 3: 1 F-28 *Fellowship* (VIP); 1 Gulfstream G280 (VIP); 1 Hawker 800 (VIP)
TRG 38: 6 EMB-314 *Super Tucano**; 3+ S-211*; 10 SF-260FH; 4 SF-260TP*; 15 T-41B/D/K *Mescalero*
HELICOPTERS
ATK 8: 2 AH-1S *Cobra*; 6 T129B
MRH 38: 2 AUH-76; 8 AW109E (armed); 8 Bell 412EP *Twin Huey*; 2 Bell 412HP *Twin Huey*; 11 MD-520MG; 7 W-3A *Sokol*
TPT 24: **Medium** 21: 1 S-70A *Black Hawk* (SAR); 20 S-70i *Black Hawk*; **Light** 3+ Bell 205 (UH-1H *Iroquois*) (SAR) (10 more non-operational)
UNINHABITED AERIAL VEHICLES
ISR • **Medium** 15: 2 *Blue Horizon* II; 4 *Hermes* 450; 9 *Hermes* 900; **Light** *ScanEagle* 2
AIR-LAUNCHED MISSILES
AAM • **IR** AIM-9L *Sidewinder*
ASM AGM-65D *Maverick*; AGM-65G2 *Maverick*; AGR-20A APKWS; *Cirit*; GATR
BOMBS
INS/GPS-guided: GBU-49 *Enhanced Paveway* II
AIR DEFENCE • **SAM**
Medium-range 6 *Spyder*-MR

Gendarmerie & Paramilitary 30,700

Coast Guard 30,700
EQUIPMENT BY TYPE
PATROL AND COASTAL COMBATANTS 49
PSOH 3: 1 *Gabriela Silang* (OCEA OPV 270); 2 *Teresa Magbanua* (JPN *Kunigami* mod)
PCO 4 *San Juan* with 1 hel landing platform
PCC 10 *Parola* (MRRV)
PB 32: 4 *Boracay* (FPB 72 Mk II); 4 *Ilocos Norte*; 10 PCF 46; 12 PCF 50 (US *Swift* Mk1/2); 2 PCF 65 (US *Swift* Mk3)
LOGISTICS AND SUPPORT • **ABU** 1 *Corregidor*
AIRCRAFT • **TPT** • **Light** 3: 2 BN-2 *Islander*; 1 Cessna 208B *Grand Caravan* EX
HELICOPTERS • **TPT** • **Light** 2 H145

Citizen Armed Force Geographical Units
50,000 reservists

FORCES BY ROLE

MANOEUVRE

Other

56 militia bn (part-time units which can be called up for extended periods)

DEPLOYMENT

CENTRAL AFRICAN REPUBLIC: UN • MINUSCA 3
INDIA/PAKISTAN: UN • UNMOGIP 6
SOUTH SUDAN: UN • UNMISS 2

FOREIGN FORCES

Australia *Operation Augury* 100
United States US Indo-Pacific Command: 200

Singapore SGP

Singapore Dollar SGD		2023	2024	2025
GDP	SGD	673bn	708bn	742bn
	USD	501bn	531bn	562bn
Real GDP growth	%	1.1	2.6	2.5
Def bdgt	SGD	18.0bn	20.2bn	
	USD	13.4bn	15.2bn	

Real-terms defence budget trend (USDbn, constant 2015)

Population	6,028,459				
Age	0–14	15–19	20–24	25–29	30–64	65 plus
Male	7.6%	3.0%	3.7%	4.1%	25.0%	6.6%
Female	7.0%	2.7%	3.3%	3.7%	25.6%	7.7%

Capabilities

The Singapore Armed Forces (SAF) are the best equipped in Southeast Asia. The air force and navy are staffed mainly by professional personnel while, apart from a small core of regulars, the much larger army is based on conscripts and reservists. Although there are no publicly available defence-policy documents, it is widely presumed that the SAF's primary role is to deter attacks on the city-state or interference with its vital interests – particularly its sea lines of communication and its critical infrastructure. The SAF also is focused on counter-terror operations. To address significant personnel challenges from an ageing population, the defence ministry has introduced lean staffing measures and increased the use of technology. The SAF routinely trains abroad and has training units based long-term overseas, with plans also to expand overseas training and improve domestic facilities by making greater use of synthetic training. The SAF also engages extensively in bilateral and multilateral exercises, including with ASEAN member states and Five Power Defence Arrangements signatories, and has spearheaded many regional maritime-security initiatives. Singaporean forces have gradually become more involved in multinational operations, albeit on a small scale. While deployments have provided some operational experience, and training standards and operational readiness are high, the army's reliance on conscripts and reservists limits its capacity for sustained operations abroad. The SAF 2040 vision, launched in March 2022, underpins a new round of modernisation. The armed forces are modernising across domains to preserve Singapore's military edge over other Southeast Asian countries. The country has a small but sophisticated defence industry.

ACTIVE 51,000 (Army 40,000 Navy 4,000 Air 6,000 Digitial & Intelligence 1,000) **Gendarmerie & Paramilitary 7,400**

Conscription liability 22–24 months

RESERVE 252,500 (Army 240,000 Navy 5,000 Air 7,500)

Annual trg to age 40 for army other ranks, 50 for officers

ORGANISATIONS BY SERVICE

Space

EQUIPMENT BY TYPE

SATELLITES

ISR 4: 1 DS-EO; 1 DS-SAR; 1 NeuSAR; 1 TeLEOS-2

Army 40,000 (including 26,000 conscripts)

FORCES BY ROLE

COMMAND

4 (combined arms) div HQ
1 (rapid reaction) div HQ
4 armd bde HQ
9 inf bde HQ
1 air mob bde HQ
1 amph bde HQ

SPECIAL FORCES

1 cdo bn
1 (ADF) cdo bn

MANOEUVRE

Armoured
1 tk bn
3 armd inf bn

Mechanised
6 mech inf bn

Light
2 (gds) inf bn

Other
2 sy bn

COMBAT SUPPORT

2 arty bn
1 STA bn
2 engr bn
1 EOD bn
1 ptn br bn
1 int bn

2 ISR bn
1 CBRN bn
3 sigs bn
COMBAT SERVICE SUPPORT
3 med bn
2 tpt bn
3 spt bn

Reserves
Activated units form part of divisions and brigades listed above; People's Defence Force Comd (homeland defence) with 12 inf bn

FORCES BY ROLE
SPECIAL FORCES
1 cdo bn
MANOEUVRE
Armoured
6 armd inf bn
Mechanised
6 mech inf bn
Light
ε56 inf bn
COMBAT SUPPORT
ε12 arty bn
ε8 engr bn

EQUIPMENT BY TYPE
ARMOURED FIGHTING VEHICLES
MBT 96+ *Leopard* 2SG
LT TK (22 AMX-10 PAC 90; ε350 AMX-13 SM1 in store)
IFV 420+: 250 *Bionix* 25/*Bionix* II; ε120 *Hunter* AFV; 50+ M113A2 *Ultra*; (22 AMX-10P in store)
APC 1,635+
  APC (T) 1,350+: 250 *Bionix* 40/50; 700+ M113A1/A2; 400+ ATTC *Bronco*
  APC (W) 135 *Terrex* ICV; (250 LAV-150/V-200 *Commando*; 30 V-100 *Commando* in store)
  PPV 150: 84 *Belrex* (incl variants); 15 *MaxxPro Dash*; 51 *Peacekeeper*
ENGINEERING & MAINTENANCE VEHICLES
AEV 94: 18 CET; 54 FV180; 14 *Kodiak*; 8 M728
ARV *Bionix*; *Büffel*; *Hunter* AVLB; LAV-150; LAV-300
VLB 72+: *Bionix*; LAB 30; *Leguan*; M2; 60 M3; 12 M60
MW 910-MCV-2; *Trailblazer*
ANTI-TANK/ANTI-INFRASTRUCTURE
MSL • MANPATS *Milan*; *Spike*-SR; *Spike*-MR
RCL 90+: **84mm** *Carl Gustaf*; **106mm** M40A1
ARTILLERY 798+
SP 155mm 54 SSPH-1 *Primus*
TOWED 88: **105mm** (37 LG1 in store); **155mm** 88: 18 FH-2000; ε18 *Pegasus*; 52 FH-88
MRL 227mm 18 M142 HIMARS
MOR 638+
  SP 90+: **81mm**; **120mm** 90: 40 on *Bronco*; 50 on M113; some *Belrex Mortar*
TOWED 548: **81mm** 500; **120mm** 36 M-65; **160mm** 12 M-58 Tampella

Navy 4,000 (incl 1,000 conscripts)
EQUIPMENT BY TYPE
SUBMARINES • SSK 4:
  2 *Archer* (ex-SWE *Västergötland*) (fitted with AIP) with 3 single 400mm TT with Torped 431, 6 single 533mm TT with *Black Shark* HWT
  2 *Invincible* (GER Type-218SG) (fitted with AIP) with 8 single 533mm TT with *Black Shark* HWT
PRINCIPAL SURFACE COMBATANTS • FRIGATES 6
FFGHM 6 *Formidable* with 2 quad lnchr with RGM-84 *Harpoon* AShM, 4 8-cell *Sylver* A43 VLS with *Aster* 15 SAM, 2 triple 324mm ILAS-3 (B-515) ASTT with A244/S LWT, 1 76mm gun (capacity 1 S-70B *Sea Hawk* hel)
PATROL AND COASTAL COMBATANTS 27
  CORVETTES • FSM 8 *Independence* (Littoral Mission Vessel) with 1 12-cell CLA VLS with VL MICA, 1 76mm gun, 1 hel landing platform
  PCGM 6 *Victory* with 2 quad lnchr with RGM-84C *Harpoon* Block 1B AShM, 2 8-cell VLS with *Barak*-1 SAM, 1 76mm gun
  PCO 4 *Sentinel* (*Fearless* mod) with 1 76mm gun
  PBF 9: 1 Combat Craft Large; 2 SMC Type 1; 6 SMC Type 2
MINE WARFARE • MINE COUNTERMEASURES 4
  MCC 4 *Bedok*
AMPHIBIOUS
  PRINCIPAL AMPHIBIOUS SHIPS • LPD 4 *Endurance* with 2 twin *Simbad* lnchr with *Mistral* SAM, 1 76mm gun (capacity 2 hel; 4 LCVP; 18 MBT; 350 troops)
  LANDING CRAFT • LCVP 23; ε17 FCEP; 6 FCU
LOGISTICS AND SUPPORT 5
  ASR 1 *Swift Rescue*
  ATF 2
  AKR 1 *Mentor* (trg role)
  AXL 1 *Stet Polaris*
UNINHABITED MARITIME PLATFORMS • USV 4+
  MARSEC 2+: **Medium** 2 MARSEC USV; **Small** *Protector*
  UTL 2+: **Medium** 2 *Venus* 16; **Small** *Venus* 9; *Venus* 11
UNINHABITED MARITIME SYSTEMS • UUV
  DATA REMUS 100
  MW K-Ster C/I; MCM AUV

Naval Diving Unit
FORCES BY ROLE
SPECIAL FORCES
1 SF gp
1 (diving) SF gp
COMBAT SUPPORT
1 EOD gp

Air Force 6,000 (incl 3,000 conscripts)

5 comds

FORCES BY ROLE

FIGHTER/GROUND ATTACK
 2 sqn with F-15SG *Eagle*
 1 sqn with F-16C Block 52/Block 52 MLU *Fighting Falcon*; F-16D Block 52 SG/Block 52 SG MLU *Fighting Falcon*; (some ISR)
 1 sqn with F-16D Block 52 SG/Block 52 SG MLU *Fighting Falcon*; F-16D Block 52+/Block 52+ MLU *Fighting Falcon* (some ISR)

ANTI-SUBMARINE WARFARE
 1 sqn with S-70B *Seahawk*

MARITIME PATROL/TRANSPORT
 1 sqn with F-50; F-50 *Maritime Enforcer*

AIRBORNE EARLY WARNING & CONTROL
 1 sqn with G550-AEW

TANKER
 1 sqn with A330 MRTT

TANKER/TRANSPORT
 1 sqn with KC-130B/H *Hercules*; C-130H *Hercules*

TRAINING
 1 (aggressor) sqn with F-15SG *Eagle*; F-16C Block 52/Block 52 MLU *Fighting Falcon*; F-16D Block 52 SG/Block 52 SG MLU *Fighting Falcon*
 1 (FRA-based) sqn with M-346 *Master*
 3 (USA-based) units with AH-64D *Apache*; F-15SG; F-16C/D *Fighting Falcon*
 1 (AUS-based) sqn with PC-21
 1 hel sqn with H120 *Colibri*

ATTACK HELICOPTER
 1 sqn with AH-64D *Apache*

TRANSPORT HELICOPTER
 1 sqn with CH-47F *Chinook*; CH-47SD *Super D Chinook*
 2 sqn with AS532UL *Cougar*; H225M

ISR UAV
 1 sqn with *Hermes* 450
 2 sqn with *Heron* 1

AIR DEFENCE
 1 AD bn with *Mistral* (opcon Army)
 3 AD bn with RBS-70; 9K38 *Igla* (RS-SA-18 *Grouse*); Mechanised *Igla* (opcon Army)
 1 ADA sqn with Oerlikon
 1 AD sqn with SAMP/T
 1 AD sqn with *Spyder*-SR
 1 radar sqn with radar (mobile)
 1 radar sqn with LORADS

MANOEUVRE
 Other
 4 (field def) sy sqn

EQUIPMENT BY TYPE

AIRCRAFT 104 combat capable

FGA 99: 40 F-15SG *Eagle*; 19 F-16C Block 52/Block 52 MLU *Fighting Falcon* (some ISR); 20 F-16D Block 52 SG/Block 52 SG MLU *Fighting Falcon* (some ISR); 20 F-16D Block 52+/Block 52+ MLU *Fighting Falcon* (some ISR)
MP 5 F-50 *Maritime Enforcer**
AEW&C 4 G550-AEW
TKR/TPT 11: 6 A330 MRTT; 4 KC-130B *Hercules*; 1 KC-130H *Hercules*
TPT 9: **Medium** 5 C-130H *Hercules* (incl 2 ELINT); **PAX** 4 F-50 (secondary MP role)
TRG 31: 12 M-346 *Master*; 19 PC-21

HELICOPTERS
 ATK 19 AH-64D *Apache*
 ASW 8 S-70B *Seahawk*
 TPT 59: **Heavy** 42: 16 CH-47F *Chinook*; 10 CH-47SD *Super D Chinook*; 16 H225M (some SAR); **Medium** 12 AS532UL *Cougar*; (18 AS332M *Super Puma* in store); **Light** 5 H120 *Colibri* (leased)

UNINHABITED AERIAL VEHICLES
 ISR 17+: **Heavy** 8+ *Heron* 1; **Medium** 9+ *Hermes* 450; **Light** some *Orbiter*-4

AIR DEFENCE
 SAM 4+
  Long-range 4+ SAMP/T
  Short-range *Spyder*-SR
  Point-defence 9K38 *Igla* (RS-SA-18 *Grouse*); Mechanised *Igla*; *Mistral*; RBS-70
 GUNS 34
  SP 20mm GAI-C01
  TOWED 34+: **20mm** GAI-C01; **35mm** 34 GDF (with 25 *Super-Fledermaus* fire-control radar)

AIR-LAUNCHED MISSILES
 AAM • IR AIM-9P/S *Sidewinder*; *Python* 4; **IIR** AIM-9X *Sidewinder* II; *Python* 5; **SARH** AIM-7P *Sparrow*; **ARH** (AIM-120C5/7 AMRAAM in store in US)
 ASM: AGM-65B/G *Maverick*; AGM-114K *Hellfire* II; AGM-114L *Longbow Hellfire*; AGM-154A/C JSOW
 AShM AGM-84 *Harpoon*; AM39 *Exocet*

BOMBS
 Laser-guided GBU-10/12 *Paveway* II
 Laser & INS/GPS-guided GBU-49 Enhanced *Paveway* II; GBU-54 Laser JDAM
 INS/GPS-guided GBU-31 JDAM

Digital & Intelligence Service 1,000

Formed 2022 as fourth service of the Singapore Armed Forces, consolidating existing intelligence and cyber capabilities

Gendarmerie & Paramilitary 7,400 active

Civil Defence Force 5,600 (incl conscripts); 500 auxiliaries (total 6,100)

Singapore Gurkha Contingent 1,800

Under the Police
FORCES BY ROLE
MANOEUVRE
Other
6 paramilitary coy

DEPLOYMENT

AUSTRALIA: 2 trg schools – 1 with 12 AS332M1 *Super Puma*/AS532UL *Cougar* (flying trg) located at Oakey; 1 with PC-21 (flying trg) located at Pearce. Army: prepositioned AFVs and heavy equipment at Shoalwater Bay training area

BRUNEI: 1 trg camp with inf units on rotation; 1 hel det with AS332M1 *Super Puma*

FRANCE: 200: 1 trg sqn with 12 M-346 *Master*

TAIWAN: 3 trg camp (incl inf and arty)

THAILAND: 1 trg camp (arty, cbt engr)

UNITED STATES: Trg units with F-16C/D; 12 F-15SG; AH-64D *Apache*; 6+ CH-47D *Chinook*

FOREIGN FORCES

United States US Indo-Pacific Command: 200; 1 naval spt facility at Changi naval base; 1 USAF log spt sqn at Paya Lebar air base

Sri Lanka LKA

Sri Lankan Rupee LKR		2023	2024	2025
GDP [a]	LKR			
	USD			
Real GDP growth	%			
Def bdgt	LKR	410bn	424bn	
	USD	1.25bn	1.39bn	

[a] No IMF economic data available

Real-terms defence budget trend (USDbn, constant 2015)

Population	21,982,608					
Age	0–14	15–19	20–24	25–29	30–64	65 plus
Male	11.5%	4.2%	3.9%	3.3%	20.3%	5.2%
Female	11.0%	4.0%	3.8%	3.4%	22.1%	7.2%

Capabilities

Since the defeat of the Tamil Tigers, the armed forces have focused on peacetime internal-security. China has supported Sri Lanka's armed forces, an indication of growing military-to-military ties. India remained Sri Lanka's key maritime partner, including by providing maritime patrol aircraft. The US has eased its long-standing military trade restrictions on the country and Japan said it would increase maritime cooperation. Sri Lanka has little capacity for force projection but has contributed small troop numbers to UN missions. The navy has enhanced its capability, based on fast-attack and patrol boats, through the acquisition of offshore-patrol vessels. The US has gifted a former coast guard cutter and China a frigate. The army is reducing in size and spending on new equipment has been sparse since the end of the civil war. Sri Lanka is looking to launch procurements to fill capability gaps, but its ambitions are limited by budget constraints. The longer-term effects of the 2022 political and economic crisis on Sri Lanka's defence policy, the size of its armed forces and procurement are unclear. Beyond maintenance facilities and limited fabrication, such as at Sri Lanka's shipyards, there is no defence-industrial base.

ACTIVE 262,500 (Army 177,000 Navy 57,500 Air 28,000) Gendarmerie & Paramilitary 63,650

RESERVE 5,500 (Army 1,100 Navy 2,400 Air Force 2,000) Gendarmerie & Paramilitary 30,400

ORGANISATIONS BY SERVICE

Army 113,000; 64,000 active reservists (recalled) (total 177,000)

Regt are bn sized
FORCES BY ROLE
COMMAND
 7 region HQ
 21 div HQ
SPECIAL FORCES
 1 indep SF bde
MANOEUVRE
 Reconnaissance
 3 armd recce regt
 Armoured
 1 armd bde(-)
 Mechanised
 1 mech inf bde
 Light
 60 inf bde
 1 cdo bde
 Air Manoeuvre
 1 air mob bde
COMBAT SUPPORT
 7 arty regt
 1 MRL regt
 8 engr regt
 6 sigs regt
EQUIPMENT BY TYPE
ARMOURED FIGHTING VEHICLES
 MBT 62 T-55A/T-55AM2
 RECCE 15 *Saladin*
 IFV 62+: 13 BMP-1; 49 BMP-2; WZ-551 20mm
 APC 211+
  APC (T) 30+: some Type-63; 30 Type-85; some Type-89
  APC (W) 181: 25 BTR-80/BTR-80A; 31 *Buffel*; 20 WZ-551; 105 *Unicorn*
ENGINEERING & MAINTENANCE VEHICLES
 ARV 16 VT-55

VLB 2 MT-55

ANTI-TANK/ANTI-INFRASTRUCTURE
 MANPATS HJ-8
 RCL 40: 105mm ε10 M-65; 106mm ε30 M40
 GUNS 85mm 8 Type-56 (D-44)

ARTILLERY 908
 TOWED 96: 122mm 20; 130mm 30 Type-59-I; 152mm 46 Type-66 (D-20)
 MRL 122mm 28: 6 KRL-122; 22 RM-70
 MOR 784: 81mm 520; 82mm 209; 120mm 55 M-43

UNINHABITED AERIAL VEHICLES
 ISR • Medium 1 Seeker

Navy 44,500; ε13,000 active reserves (total 57,500)

Seven naval areas

EQUIPMENT BY TYPE
PATROL AND COASTAL COMBATANTS 178
 PSOH 6: 2 Gajabahu (ex-US Hamilton) with 1 76mm gun (capacity 1 med hel); 1 Parakramabahu (ex-PRC Type-053H2G (Jiangwei I)) with 1 twin 100mm gun (capacity 1 med hel); 1 Sayura (ex-IND Sukanya) (capacity 1 med hel); 2 Sayurala (IND Samarth) (capacity 1 med hel)
 PCO 2: 1 Samudura (ex-US Reliance) with 1 hel landing platform; 1 Sagara (IND Vikram) with 1 hel landing platform
 PCC 2 Nandimithra (ex-ISR Sa'ar 4) with 1 76mm gun
 PBF 81: 26 Colombo; 6 Shaldag; 4 Super Dvora Mk II; 6 Super Dvora Mk III; 5 Trinity Marine 25m; 34 Wave Rider
 PB 11: 2 Mihikatha (ex-AUS Bay); 2 Prathapa (PRC Haizhui mod); 3 Ranajaya (PRC Haizhui); 1 Ranarisi (ex-PRC Shanghai III); 3 Weeraya (ex-PRC Shanghai II)
 PBR 76

AMPHIBIOUS
 LANDING SHIPS • LSM 1 Shakthi (PRC Yuhai) (capacity 2 tanks; 250 troops)
 LANDING CRAFT 7
  LCM 2 Ranavijaya
  LCU 4: 2 Yunnan; 2 other
 UCAC 1 M 10† (capacity 56 troops)

LOGISTICS AND SUPPORT 4: 3 AP; 1 AX

Marines ε500

FORCES BY ROLE
MANOEUVRE
 Amphibious
 1 mne bn

Special Boat Service ε100

Reserve Organisations

Sri Lanka Volunteer Naval Force (SLVNF) 13,000 active reservists

Air Force 28,000 (incl SLAF Regt)

FORCES BY ROLE
FIGHTER
 1 sqn with F-7BS/G; FT-7
FIGHTER/GROUND ATTACK
 1 sqn with Kfir C-2/C-7/TC-2
 1 sqn with K-8 Karakorum*
MARITIME PATROL
 1 sqn with Beech 350/360ER/B200T King Air; Do-228-101; Y-12 (II)/(IV)
TRANSPORT
 1 sqn with An-32B Cline; C-130K Hercules; Cessna 421C Golden Eagle
 1 sqn Beech B200 King Air; MA60; Y-12 (II)/(IV)
TRAINING
 1 wg with PT-6, Cessna 150L
TRANSPORT HELICOPTER
 2 sqn with Mi-17 Hip H; Mi-171E/Sh
 1 sqn with Bell 206A/B (incl basic trg); Bell 212
 1 VIP sqn with Bell 212; Bell 412 Twin Huey; Bell 412EP Twin Huey; Mi-171E/Sh
ISR UAV
 1 sqn with Blue Horizon II
MANOEUVRE
 Other
 1 (SLAF) sy regt

EQUIPMENT BY TYPE
AIRCRAFT 12 combat capable
 FTR 4: 3 F-7GS; 1 FT-7 (3 F-7BS; 1 F-7GS non-operational)
 FGA 1 Kfir C-2 (2 Kfir C-2; 1 Kfir C-7; 2 Kfir TC-2 non-operational)
 MP 3: 2 Beech 350/360ER King Air; 1 Do-228-101
 ISR 1 Beech 200T King Air
 TPT 23: Medium (2 C-130K Hercules non-operational); Light 23: 3 An-32B Cline; 1 Beech B200 King Air; 6 Cessna 150L; 1 Cessna 421C Golden Eagle; 2 MA60; 6 Y-12 (II); 4 Y-12 (IV)
 TRG 12: 7 K-8 Karakorum*; 5 PT-6

HELICOPTERS
 ATK (6 Mi-24P Hind; 3 Mi-24V Hind E; 2 Mi-35V Hind all non-operational)
 MRH 10: 6 Bell 412 Twin Huey (VIP); 2 Bell 412EP (VIP); 2+ Mi-17 Hip H
 TPT 25: Medium 14: ε10 Mi-171E; 4 Mi-171Sh; Light 11: 1 Bell 206A Jet Ranger; 2 Bell 206B Jet Ranger; 8 Bell 212

UNINHABITED AERIAL VEHICLES
 ISR • Medium some Blue Horizon II; (some Searcher II non-operational)

AIR DEFENCE
 SAM • Point Defence 9K38 Igla (RS-SA-18 Grouse)
 GUNS • TOWED 27: 40mm 24 L/40; 94mm 3 (3.7in)

AIR-LAUNCHED MISSILES
 AAM • IR PL-5E

Gendarmerie & Paramilitary ε63,550

Home Guard 13,000

National Guard ε15,000

Police Force 30,200; 1,000 (women) (total 31,200) 30,400 reservists

Ministry of Defence Special Task Force 3,000
Anti-guerrilla unit

Coast Guard 1,350
Ministry of Defence
EQUIPMENT BY TYPE
PATROL AND COASTAL COMBATANTS 26
  PCO 1 *Suraksha* (ex-IND *Vikram*) with 1 hel landing platform
  PCC 1 *Jayasagara*
  PBF 18: 1 *Dvora*; 4 *Super Dvora* Mk I; 3 *Killer* (ROK); 10 *Wave Rider*
  PB 6: 2 Simonneau Type-508; 2 *Samudra Raksha*; 2 Type 501 (JPN)

DEPLOYMENT

CENTRAL AFRICAN REPUBLIC: UN • MINUSCA 114; 1 hel sqn

LEBANON: UN • UNIFIL 126; 1 inf coy

SOUTH SUDAN: UN • UNMISS 66; 1 fd hospital

WESTERN SAHARA: UN • MINURSO 2

Taiwan (Republic of China) ROC

New Taiwan Dollar TWD		2023	2024	2025
GDP	TWD	23.5trn	24.9trn	26.0trn
	USD	756bn	775bn	814bn
Real GDP growth	%	1.3	3.7	2.7
Def bdgt	TWD	580bn	607bn	
	USD	18.6bn	18.9bn	
FMA (US)	USD	n.a	n.a	100m

Real-terms defence budget trend (USDbn, constant 2015)
17.3
9.80
2008 2016 2024

Population	23,595,274					
Age	0–14	15–19	20–24	25–29	30–64	65 plus
Male	6.2%	2.2%	2.8%	3.4%	26.1%	8.5%
Female	5.9%	2.1%	2.7%	3.2%	26.6%	10.4%

Capabilities

Taiwan's security policy is dominated by its relationship with China and its attempts to sustain a credible military capability. Taiwan is looking to boost air defence in coastal areas. The 2021 Quadrennial Defense Review (QDR), for the first time, mentioned the need to counter the PLA's 'grey zone' threat. The armed forces exercise regularly, and in 2024, Taiwan's *Han Kuang* military exercises included unscripted combat scenarios that sought to test decentralised command, updated rules of engagement and nighttime operations. Demographic pressure has influenced plans for force reductions and a shift towards an all-volunteer force, which the 2021 QDR credited for helping the armed forces reach its staffing goals. Nonetheless, issues with recruitment and retention have reportedly created personnel challenges for combat units. In 2024, Taiwan initiated its one-year programme of conscripted service. Taiwan is also focused on expanding the reserve force, improving reservist training and civil defence, although these efforts are at an early stage of development. Taiwan's main security partnership is with the US, which under the 1979 Taiwan Relations Act pledges to 'provide Taiwan with arms of a defensive character'. In 2019, the US approved the sale of 66 F-16 Block 70 combat aircraft to Taiwan, though deliveries are delayed. In 2024, the defence minister announced four main areas for training and acquisition from the US, including asymmetric warfare capabilities, enhancing combat resilience, improving reserve forces and countering grey-zone tactics. Taiwan's own defence-industrial base has strengths in aerospace, shipbuilding and missiles. In 2023, Taiwan unveiled its first domestically built diesel-powered submarine, which is expected to be delivered in 2025.

ACTIVE 169,000 (Army 94,000 Navy 40,000 Air 35,000) **Gendarmerie & Paramilitary** 17,800

Conscript liability (19–40 years) 12 months for those born before 1993; four months for those born after 1994 (alternative service available)

RESERVE 1,657,000 (Army 1,500,000 Navy 67,000 Air Force 90,000)

Some obligation to age 30

ORGANISATIONS BY SERVICE

Space
EQUIPMENT BY TYPE
SATELLITES • **ISR** 1 *Formosat-5*

Army 94,000 (incl ε5,000 MP)
FORCES BY ROLE
COMMAND
  3 corps HQ
  5 defence comd HQ
SPECIAL FORCES/HELICOPTER
  1 SF/hel comd (5 spec ops bn, 2 hel bde)
MANOEUVRE
  Armoured
  4 armd bde
  Mechanised
  3 mech inf bde
COMBAT SUPPORT
  3 arty gp
  3 engr gp
  3 CBRN gp
  3 sigs gp

COASTAL DEFENCE
1 AShM bn

Reserves
FORCES BY ROLE
MANOEUVRE
 Light
  27 inf bde
EQUIPMENT BY TYPE
ARMOURED FIGHTING VEHICLES
 MBT 650: 200 M60A3; 450 CM-11 *Brave Tiger* (M48H); (100 CM-12 in store)
 LT TK ε100 M41A3/D
 IFV 305 CM-34 *Yunpao*
 APC 1,543
  APC (T) 875: 225 CM-21A1; 650 M113A1/A2
  APC (W) 668: 368 CM-32 *Yunpao*; 300 LAV-150 *Commando*
ENGINEERING & MAINTENANCE VEHICLES
 AEV 18 M9
 ARV 37+: CM-27A1; 37 M88A1
 VLB 22 M3; M48A5
NBC VEHICLES 48+: BIDS; 48 K216A1; KM453
ANTI-TANK/ANTI-INFRASTRUCTURE
 MSL
  SP M113A1 with TOW; M1045A2 HMMWV with TOW
  MANPATS FGM-148 *Javelin*; TOW
 RCL 500+: **90mm** M67; **106mm** 500+: 500 M40A1; Type-51
ARTILLERY 2,104
 SP 488: **105mm** 100 M108; **155mm** 318: 225 M109A2/A5; 48 M44T; 45 T-69; **203mm** 70 M110
 TOWED 1,060+: **105mm** 650 T-64 (M101); **155mm** 340+: 90 M59; 250 T-65 (M114); M44; XT-69; **203mm** 70 M115
 MRL 234: **117mm** 120 *Kung Feng* VI; **126mm** 103: 60 *Kung Feng* III/*Kung Feng* IV; 43 RT 2000 *Thunder*; **227mm** 11 M142 HIMARS
 MOR 322+
  SP 162+: **81mm** 72+: M29; 72 M125; **107mm** 90 M106A2
  TOWED 81mm 160+: 160 M29; T-75; **107mm** M30; **120mm** K5; XT-86
SURFACE-TO-SURFACE MISSILE LAUNCHERS
 SRBM • Conventional MGM-168 ATACMS (launched from M142 HIMARS)
COASTAL DEFENCE
 ARTY 54: **127mm** ε50 US Mk32 (reported); **240mm** 4 M1
 AShM *Ching Feng*
HELICOPTERS
 ATK 90: 61 AH-1W *Cobra*; 29 AH-64E *Apache*
 MRH 37 OH-58D *Kiowa Warrior*
 TPT 38: **Heavy** 8 CH-47SD *Super D Chinook*; **Medium** 30 UH-60M *Black Hawk*

 TRG 29 TH-67 *Creek*
UNINHABITED AERIAL VEHICLES
 ISR • Light *Mastiff* III
AIR LAUNCHED MISSILES
 AAM • IR AIM-9L *Sidewinder*
 ASM AGM-114L *Longbow Hellfire*
AIR DEFENCE
 SAM • Point-defence 76+: 74 M1097 *Avenger*; 2 M48 *Chaparral*; FIM-92 *Stinger*
 GUNS
  SP 40mm M42
  TOWED 40mm L/70

Navy 40,000
EQUIPMENT BY TYPE
SUBMARINES • SSK 4:
 2 *Hai Lung* with 6 single 533mm TT with UGM-84L *Harpoon* Block II AShM/SUT HWT
 2 *Hai Shih*† (ex-US *Guppy* II (used in trg role)) with 10 single 533mm TT (6 fwd, 4 aft) with SUT HWT
PRINCIPAL SURFACE COMBATANTS 26
 DESTROYERS • DDGHM 4 *Keelung* (ex-US *Kidd*) with 2 quad lnchr with RGM-84L *Harpoon* Block II AShM, 2 twin Mk 26 GMLS with SM-2 Block IIIA SAM, 2 triple 324mm SVTT Mk 32 ASTT with Mk 46 LWT, 2 Mk 15 *Phalanx* Block 1B CIWS, 2 127mm gun (capacity 1 S-70 ASW hel)
 FRIGATES 22
  FFGHM 21:
   8 *Cheng Kung* (US *Oliver Hazard Perry* mod) with 2 quad lnchr with *Hsiung Feng* II/III AShM, 1 Mk 13 GMLS with SM-1MR Block VI SAM, 2 triple 324mm SVTT Mk 32 ASTT with Mk 46 LWT, 1 Mk 15 *Phalanx* Block 1B CIWS, 1 76mm gun (capacity 2 S-70C ASW hel)
   2 *Meng Chuan* (ex-US *Oliver Hazard Perry*) with 1 Mk13 GMLS with RGM-84 *Harpoon* AShM/SM-1MR Block VI SAM, 2 triple 324mm SVTT Mk 32 ASTT with Mk 46 LWT, 1 Mk 15 *Phalanx* Block 1B CIWS, 1 76mm gun (capacity 2 S-70C ASW hel)
   5 *Chin Yang* (ex-US *Knox*) with 1 octuple Mk 16 lnchr with RGM-84C *Harpoon* Block 1B AShM/ASROC A/S msl, 2 triple lnchr with SM-1MR Block VI SAM, 2 twin lnchr with SM-1MR Block VI SAM, 2 twin 324mm SVTT Mk 32 ASTT with Mk 46 LWT, 1 Mk 15 *Phalanx* Block 1B CIWS, 1 127mm gun (capacity 1 MD-500 hel)
   6 *Kang Ding* with 2 quad lnchr with *Hsiung Feng* II AShM, 1 quad lnchr with *Sea Chaparral* SAM, 2 triple 324mm SVTT Mk 32 ASTT with Mk 46 LWT, 1 Mk 15 *Phalanx* Block 1B CIWS, 1 76mm gun (capacity 1 S-70C ASW hel)
  FFGH 1 *Chin Yang* (ex-US *Knox*) with 1 octuple Mk 112 lnchr with RGM-84C *Harpoon* Block 1B AShM, 2 twin 324mm SVTT Mk 32 ASTT with Mk 46 LWT, 1 Mk 15 *Phalanx* Block 1B CIWS, 1 127mm gun (capacity 1 MD-500 hel)

PATROL AND COASTAL COMBATANTS 46
  CORVETTES • FSGM 6 *Ta Jiang* (*Tuo Jiang* mod) with 4 twin lnchr with *Hsiung Feng* II AShM, 2 twin lnchr with *Hsiung Feng* III AShM, 2 octuple lnchr with *Tien Chien* 2N (*Sea Sword* II) SAM, 1 Mk 15 Phalanx CIWS, 1 76mm gun, 1 hel landing platform
  PCFG 1 *Tuo Jiang* (*Hsun Hai*) with 4 twin lnchr with *Hsiung Feng* II AShM, 4 twin lnchr with *Hsiung Feng* III AShM, 2 triple 324mm SVTT Mk 32 ASTT, 1 Mk 15 *Phalanx* Block 1B CIWS, 1 76mm gun
  PCG 7:
    2 *Jin Chiang* with 2 twin lnchr with *Hsiung Feng* II AShM, 1 76mm gun
    5 *Jin Chiang* with 1 twin lnchr with *Hsiung Feng* III AShM, 1 76mm gun
  PCC 1 *Jin Chiang* (test platform)
  PBG 31 *Kwang Hua* with 2 twin lnchr with *Hsiung Feng* II AShM
MINE WARFARE 11
  MINE COUNTERMEASURES 7
    MHC 6: 4 *Yung Feng*; 2 *Yung Jin* (ex-US *Osprey*)
    MSO 1 *Yung Yang* (ex-US *Aggressive*)
  MINELAYERS • ML 4 FMLB
COMMAND SHIPS • LCC 1 *Kao Hsiung*
AMPHIBIOUS
  PRINCIPAL AMPHIBIOUS SHIPS 2
    LPD 1 *Yu Shan* with 4 octuple lnchr with *Tien Chien* 2N (*Sea Sword* II) SAM, 2 Mk 15 *Phalanx* CIWS, 1 76mm gun (capacity 2 med hel; 4 LCM; 9 AAV-7A1; approx 500 troops)
    LSD 1 *Shiu Hai* (ex-US *Anchorage*) with 2 Mk 15 *Phalanx* CIWS, 1 hel landing platform (capacity either 2 LCU or 18 LCM; 360 troops)
  LANDING SHIPS 6
    LST 6:
      4 *Chung Hai* (ex-US LST-524) (capacity 16 tanks; 200 troops)
      2 *Chung Ho* (ex-US *Newport*) with 1 Mk 15 *Phalanx* CIWS, 1 hel landing platform (capacity 3 LCVP, 23 AFVs, 400 troops)
  LANDING CRAFT 44
    LCM ε32 (various)
    LCU 12 LCU 1610 (capacity 2 M60A3 or 400 troops) (minelaying capability)
  LOGISTICS AND SUPPORT 10
    AGF 1 *Kao Hsiung* (ex-US LST 542)
    AGOR 1 *Ta Kuan*
    AOEH 1 *Panshih* with 1 quad lnchr with *Sea Chaparral* SAM, 2 Mk 15 *Phalanx* CIWS (capacity 3 med hel)
    AOR 1 *Wu Yi* with 1 quad lnchr with *Sea Chaparral* SAM, 1 hel landing platform
    ARS 2: 1 *Da Hu* (ex-US *Diver*); 1 *Da Juen* (ex-US *Bolster*)
    ATF 4 *Ta Tung* (ex-US *Cherokee*)

Marines 10,000

FORCES BY ROLE
MANOEUVRE
  Amphibious
  2 mne bde
  Other
  1 (airfield def) sy gp
COMBAT SUPPORT
  Some cbt spt unit
EQUIPMENT BY TYPE
ARMOURED FIGHTING VEHICLES
  MBT 100 M60A3 TTS
  AAV 202: 52 AAV-7A1; 150 LVTP-5A1
ENGINEERING & MAINTENANCE VEHICLES
  ARV 2 AAVR-7
ANTI-TANK/ANTI-INFRASTRUCTURE
  SP ε25 CM-25
  RCL 106mm
ARTILLERY • TOWED 105mm; 155mm

Naval Aviation

FORCES BY ROLE
ANTI SUBMARINE WARFARE
  2 sqn with S-70C *Seahawk* (S-70C *Defender*)
  1 sqn with MD-500 *Defender*; S-70C *Seahawk* (S-70C *Defender*)
ISR UAV
  1 bn with *Albatross*
EQUIPMENT BY TYPE
HELICOPTERS
  ASW 28: 9 MD-500; 19 S-70C *Seahawk* (S-70C *Defender*)
  MRH 1 MD-500 *Defender*
UNINHABITED AERIAL VEHICLES
  ISR • Medium 25+ *Albatross*

Air Force 35,000

FORCES BY ROLE
FIGHTER
  3 sqn with *Mirage* 2000-5E/D (2000-5EI/DI)
FIGHTER/GROUND ATTACK
  6 sqn with F-16V(A/B) *Fighting Falcon*
  5 sqn with F-CK-1A/B/C/D *Ching Kuo*
ANTI-SUBMARINE WARFARE
  1 sqn with P-3C *Orion*
ELECTRONIC WARFARE
  1 sqn with C-130HE *Tien Gian*
ISR
  1 sqn with F-16V(A/B) *Fighting Falcon*; F-5E *Tigereye*
AIRBORNE EARLY WARNING & CONTROL
  1 sqn with E-2T *Hawkeye*
SEARCH & RESCUE
  1 sqn with H225; UH-60M *Black Hawk*
TRANSPORT
  2 sqn with C-130H *Hercules*

1 VIP sqn with B-727-100; B-737-800; Beech 1900; F-50

TRAINING

1 sqn with AT-3A/B *Tzu-Chung**

1 sqn with Beech 1900

3 sqn with T-5 *Yung Ying*

1 (basic) sqn with T-34C *Turbo Mentor*

EQUIPMENT BY TYPE

AIRCRAFT 386 combat capable

FTR 53: 9 *Mirage 2000-5D* (2000-5DI); 44 *Mirage* 2000-5E (2000-5EI)

FGA 269: ε103 F-CK-1C *Ching Kuo*; ε26 F-CK-1D *Ching Kuo*; 110 F-16V(A) *Fighting Falcon*; 30 F-16V(B) *Fighting Falcon*

ASW 12 P-3C *Orion*

EW 1 C-130HE *Tien Gian*

ISR 5 RF-5E *Tigereye**

AEW&C 5 E-2T *Hawkeye*

TPT 34: **Medium** 19 C-130H *Hercules*; **Light** 11 Beech 1900; **PAX** 4: 1 B-737-800; 3 F-50

TRG 111: 47 AT-3A/B *Tzu-Chung**; 34 T-34C *Turbo Mentor*; 30 T-5 *Yung Ying*

HELICOPTERS

TPT • Medium 17: 3 H225; 14 UH-60M *Black Hawk*

UNINHABITED AERIAL VEHICLES

OWA *Chien Hsiang*

AIR-LAUNCHED MISSILES

AAM • IR AIM-9J/M/P *Sidewinder*; R-550 *Magic* 2; *Shafrir*; *Sky Sword* I; **IIR** AIM-9X *Sidewinder* II; *Mica* IR; **ARH** *Mica* RF; **ARH** AIM-120C-7 AMRAAM; *Sky Sword* II

ASM AGM-65A *Maverick*

AShM AGM-84 *Harpoon*

ARM AGM-88B HARM; *Sky Sword* IIA

LACM • Conventional *Wan Chien*

BOMBS • Laser-guided GBU-12 *Paveway* II

Air Defence and Missile Command

FORCES BY ROLE

SURFACE-TO-SURFACE MISSILE

1 GLCM bde (3 GLCM bn with *Hsiung Feng* IIE)

AIR DEFENCE

1 (792) SAM bde (1 SAM bn with *Tien Kung* III; 2 ADA bn)

1 (793) SAM bde (1 SAM bn with Tien Kung II; 1 SAM bn with *Tien Kung* III; 1 SAM bn with M902 *Patriot* PAC-3)

1 (794) SAM bde (1 SAM bn with Tien Kung II; 1 SAM bn with M902 *Patriot* PAC-3)

1 (795) SAM bde (1 SAM bn with M902 *Patriot* PAC-3; 2 ADA bn)

EQUIPMENT BY TYPE

SURFACE-TO-SURFACE MISSILE LAUNCHERS

GLCM • Conventional ε12 *Hsiung Feng* IIE

AIR DEFENCE

SAM 202+

Long-range 122+: 72+ M902 *Patriot* PAC-3; ε50 *Tien Kung* II

Short-range 30 RIM-7M *Sparrow* with *Skyguard*

Point-defence *Antelope*

GUNS • 20mm some T-82; **35mm** 20+ GDF-006 with *Skyguard*

MISSILE DEFENCE *Tien Kung* III

Gendarmerie & Paramilitary 11,800

Coast Guard 11,800

EQUIPMENT BY TYPE

PATROL AND COASTAL COMBATANTS 170

PSOH 6: 2 *Chiayi*; 2 *Tainan*; 2 *Yilan*

PSO 5: 4 *Miaoli* with 1 hel landing platform; 1 *Ho Hsing*

PCF 6 *Anping* (*Tuo Jiang* mod)

PCO 13: 2 *Kinmen*; 1 *Mou Hsing*; 1 *Shun Hu* 1; 3 *Shun Hu* 7; 4 *Taichung*; 2 *Taipei*

PBF ε58 (various)

PB 82: 1 *Shun Hu* 6; ε81 (various)

FOREIGN FORCES

Singapore 3 trg camp (incl inf and arty)

Thailand THA

Thai Baht THB		2023	2024	2025
GDP	THB	17.9trn	18.3trn	19.1trn
	USD	515bn	529bn	545bn
Real GDP growth	%	1.9	2.8	3.0
Def bdgt	THB	195bn	198bn	199bn
	USD	5.60bn	5.73bn	5.67bn
FMA (US)	USD	10.0m	10.0m	3.25m

Real-terms defence budget trend (USDbn, constant 2015)

6.19
4.76
2008 — 2016 — 2024

Population	69,920,998				
Age	0–14	15–19	20–24	25–29	30–64	65 plus
Male	8.1%	3.0%	3.0%	3.4%	24.4%	6.7%
Female	7.7%	2.8%	2.9%	3.4%	26.0%	8.4%

Capabilities

Thailand has a large, well-funded military and its air force is one of the best equipped and trained in Southeast Asia. Facing an increasingly unstable regional security environment, the Royal Thai Armed Forces are emphasising deterrence. They also have a longstanding internal security role, particularly in the country's far south, where a Malay-nationalist insurgency continues, albeit at low levels. The US classes Thailand as a major non-NATO ally, although Bangkok has also developed closer defence ties with China since 2014. The armed forces regularly take part in international military exercises, notably the multinational annual *Cobra*

Gold series with the US and some of its allies and partners. The Vision 2026 defence modernisation plan, approved by the Defence Council in October 2017, outlined the armed forces' planned capability improvements through the mid-2020s. In February 2024, the Royal Thai air force issued a white paper which detailed acquisition and upgrade requirements, including combat aircraft, air defence, uninhabited capabilities and missiles. The paper emphasised the use of defence offsets during the procurement of major programmes to assist defence industrial development. The Royal Thai army published a white paper in July 2024 that detailed modernisation plans to 2037 and aimed to bolster R&D and production capacity. More broadly, the government has sought to reform defence procurement and offsets by expanding the role of the state-owned Defence Technology Institute.

ACTIVE 360,850 (Army 245,000 Navy 69,850 Air 46,000) Gendarmerie & Paramilitary 93,700

Conscription liability 24 months

RESERVE 200,000 Gendarmerie & Paramilitary 45,000

ORGANISATIONS BY SERVICE

Space
EQUIPMENT BY TYPE
SATELLITES • ISR 2 *Napa*

Army 130,000; ε115,000 conscript (total 245,000)

Cav, lt armd, recce and tk sqn are bn sized

FORCES BY ROLE
COMMAND
  4 (regional) army HQ
  3 corps HQ
SPECIAL FORCES
  1 SF div
  1 SF regt
MANOEUVRE
  Armoured
  1 (3rd) mech cav div (2 tk regt (2 tk sqn); 1 sigs bn; 1 maint bn; 1 hel sqn)
  Mechanised
  1 (1st) mech cav div (1 armd recce sqn; 2 mech cav regt (3 mech cav sqn); 1 indep mech cav sqn; 1 sigs bn; 1 maint bn; 1 hel sqn)
  1 (2nd) mech cav div (1 armd recce sqn; 2 (1st & 5th) mech cav regt (1 tk sqn, 2 mech cav sqn); 1 (4th) mech cav regt (3 mech cav sqn); 1 sigs bn; 1 maint bn; 1 hel sqn)
  1 (2nd) mech inf div (1 armd recce sqn; 1 tk bn; 3 mech inf regt (3 mech inf bn); 1 arty regt (4 arty bn); 1 engr bn; 1 sigs bn)
  1 (11th) mech inf div (2 mech inf regt (3 mech inf bn); 1 engr bn; 1 sigs bn)
  Light
  1 (1st) inf div (1 lt armd sqn; 1 ranger regt (3 ranger bn); 1 arty regt (4 arty bn); 1 engr bn; 1 sigs bn)
  1 (3rd) inf div (3 inf regt (3 inf bn); 1 arty regt (3 arty bn); 1 engr bn; 1 sigs bn)
  1 (4th) inf div (1 lt armd sqn; 2 inf regt (3 inf bn); 1 arty regt (3 arty bn); 1 engr bn; 1 sigs bn)
  1 (5th) inf div (1 lt armd sqn; 3 inf regt (3 inf bn); 1 arty regt (4 arty bn); 1 engr bn; 1 sigs bn)
  1 (6th) inf div (2 inf regt (3 inf bn); 1 arty regt (4 arty bn); 1 engr bn; 1 sigs bn)
  1 (7th) inf div (2 inf regt (3 inf bn); 1 arty regt (2 arty bn); 1 engr bn; 1 sigs bn)
  1 (9th) inf div (1 mech cav sqn; 3 inf regt (3 inf bn); 1 arty regt (3 arty bn); 1 engr bn; 1 sigs bn)
  1 (15th) inf div (1 mech cav sqn; 3 inf regt (3 inf bn); 1 engr bn; 1 sigs bn)
COMBAT SUPPORT
  1 arty div (1 arty regt (1 SP arty bn; 2 fd arty bn); 1 arty regt (1 MRL bn; 2 fd arty bn))
  1 engr div
COMBAT SERVICE SUPPORT
  4 economic development div
HELICOPTER
  1 bn with AW139; AW149; H125M (AS550) *Fennec*
  1 bn with AH-1F *Cobra*; Bell 212 (AB-212); Mi-17V-5 *Hip H*; UH-60L *Black Hawk*; UH-72A *Lakota*
  1 bn with AH-1F *Cobra*; Bell 212 (AB-212)
  1 bn with UH-60A/M *Black Hawk*
  1 bn with Mi-17V-5 *Hip H*; *Hermes* 450
ISR UAV
  1 UAV bn with *Hermes* 450; *Searcher* II
AIR DEFENCE
  1 ADA div (6 bn)

EQUIPMENT BY TYPE
ARMOURED FIGHTING VEHICLES
  MBT 394: 53 M60A1; 125 M60A3; 105 M48A5; 49 T-84 *Oplot*; 62 VT-4; (50 Type-69 in store)
  LT TK 194: 24 M41; 104 *Scorpion* (50 in store); 66 *Stingray*
  RECCE 42: 10 M1127 *Stryker* RV; 32 S52 *Shorland*
  IFV 220: 168 BTR-3E1; 52 VN-1 (incl variants)
  APC 1,265
    APC (T) 880: *Bronco*; 430 M113A1/A3; 450 Type-85
    APC (W) 285: 9 BTR-3K (CP); 6 BTR-3C (amb); 18 *Condor*; 142 LAV-150 *Commando*; 110 M1126 *Stryker* ICV
    PPV 100 REVA
ENGINEERING & MAINTENANCE VEHICLES
  ARV 69+: 2 BREM-84 *Atlet*; 13 BTR-3ERc; 22 M88A1; 6 M88A2; 10 M113; 5 Type-653; 11 VS-27; WZT-4
  VLB Type-84
  MW *Bozena*; *Giant Viper*
ANTI-TANK/ANTI-INFRASTRUCTURE
  MSL
    SP 30+: 18+ M901; 12 BTR-3RK
    MANPATS FGM-148 *Javelin*
  RCL 180: **75mm** 30 M20; **106mm** 150 M40
ARTILLERY 2,642
  SP 155mm 56: 30 ATMOS 2000; 6 CAESAR; 20 M109A5

TOWED 555: **105mm** 326: 24 LG1 MkII; 30 LG1 MkIII; 12 M-56; 200 M101A1; 60 L119 Light Gun; (12 M102; 32 M618A2 in store); **155mm** 229: 90 GHN-45 A1; 118 M198; 21 M-71 (48 M114 in store)

MRL 69: **122mm** 4 SR-4; **130mm** 60 PHZ-85; **302mm** 4: 1 DTI-1 (WS-1B); 3 DTI-1G (WS-32); **306mm** 1 PULS

MOR 1,962+: **81mm/107mm/120mm** 1,867; **SP 81mm** 39: 18 BTR-3M1; 21 M125A3; **SP 107mm** M106A3; **SP 120mm** 56: 8 BTR-3M2; 24 Elbit *Spear*; 12 M1064A3; 12 SM-4A

AIRCRAFT
TPT • Light 26: 2 Beech 200 *King Air*; 2 Beech 1900C; 2 C-212 *Aviocar*; 3 C295W; 3 Cessna 182T *Skylane*; 9 Cessna A185E (U-17B); 2 ERJ-135LR; 2 *Jetstream* 41; 1 PC-12NGX

TRG 33: 11 MX-7-235 *Star Rocket*; 22 T-41B *Mescalero*

HELICOPTERS
ATK 7 AH-1F *Cobra*

MRH 33: 8 H125M (AS550C) *Fennec* (armed); 10 AW139; ε5 AW149; 10 Mi-17V-5 *Hip* H

TPT 129: **Medium** 18: 3 UH-60A *Black Hawk*; 8 UH-60L *Black Hawk*; 7 UH-60M *Black Hawk*; **Light** 111: 27 Bell 206 *Jet Ranger*; 52 Bell 212 (AB-212); 21 Enstrom 480B; 6 H145M (VIP); 5 UH-72A *Lakota*

TRG 53 Hughes 300C

UNINHABITED AERIAL VEHICLES
ISR • Medium 4+: 4 *Hermes* 450; *Searcher*; *Searcher* II

AIR DEFENCE
SAM 10+
  Short-range *Aspide*; 2 VL MICA
  Point-defence 8+: 8 *Starstreak*; 9K338 *Igla*-S (RS-SA-24 *Grinch*)

GUNS 192
  SP 54: **20mm** 24 M163 *Vulcan*; **40mm** 30 M1/M42 SP
  TOWED 138: **20mm** 24 M167 *Vulcan*; **35mm** 8 GDF-007 with *Skyguard*; **37mm** 52 Type-74; **40mm** 48 L/70; **57mm** ε6 Type-59 (S-60) (18+ more non-operational)

AIR-LAUNCHED MISSILES • ASM BGM-71 TOW

Navy 44,000 (incl Naval Aviation, Marines, Coastal Defence); 25,850 conscript (total 69,850)

EQUIPMENT BY TYPE
PRINCIPAL SURFACE COMBATANTS 8
  AIRCRAFT CARRIERS • CVH 1 *Chakri Naruebet* with 3 sextuple *Sadral* lnchr with *Mistral* SAM (capacity 6 S-70B *Seahawk* ASW hel)

FRIGATES 7
  FFGHM 3:
    2 *Naresuan* with 2 quad lnchr with RGM-84 *Harpoon* AShM, 1 8 cell Mk 41 VLS with RIM-162B ESSM SAM, 2 triple SVTT Mk 32 324mm TT with Mk 46 LWT, 1 127mm gun (capacity 1 *Super Lynx* 300 hel)
    1 *Bhumibol Adulyadej* (DW3000F) with 2 quad lnchr with RGM-84L *Harpoon* Block II AShM, 1 8-cell Mk 41 VLS with RIM-162B ESSM SAM, 2 triple 324mm SEA TLS ASTT with Mk 54 LWT, 1 Mk 15 *Phalanx* Block 1B CIWS, 1 76mm gun (capacity 1 med hel)
  FFG 4:
    2 *Chao Phraya* (trg role) with 4 twin lnchr with C-802A AShM, 2 RBU 1200 *Uragan* A/S mor, 2 twin 100mm guns
    2 *Chao Phraya* with 4 twin lnchr with C-802A AShM, 2 RBU 1200 *Uragan* A/S mor, 1 twin 100mm gun, 1 hel landing platform

PATROL AND COASTAL COMBATANTS 68
  CORVETTES 5:
    FSGM 1 *Rattanakosin* with 2 twin lnchr with RGM-84 *Harpoon* AShM, 1 octuple *Albatros* lnchr with *Aspide* SAM, 2 triple 324mm SVTT Mk 32 ASTT with *Stingray* LWT, 1 76mm gun
    FSG 1 *Krabi* (UK *River* mod) with 2 twin lnchr with RGM-84L *Harpoon* Block II AShM, 1 76mm gun
    FS 3:
      1 *Makut Rajakumarn* with 2 triple 324mm ASTT, 2 114mm gun
      1 *Pin Klao* (ex-US *Cannon*) (trg role) with 2 triple 324mm SVTT Mk 32 ASTT, 3 76mm guns
      1 *Tapi* with 2 triple 324mm SVTT Mk 32 ASTT with Mk 46 LWT, 1 76mm gun
  PSO 1 *Krabi* (UK *River* mod) with 1 76mm gun
  PCT 3 *Khamronsin* with 2 triple 324mm ASTT with *Stingray* LWT, 1 76mm gun
  PCOH 2 *Pattani* (1 in trg role) with 1 76mm gun
  PCO 4: 3 *Hua Hin* with 1 76mm gun; 1 M58 Patrol Gun Boat with 1 76mm gun
  PCC 9: 3 *Chon Buri* with 2 76mm gun; 6 *Sattahip* with 1 76mm gun
  PBF 4 M18 Fast Assault Craft (capacity 18 troops)
  PB 40: 3 T-81; 5 M36 Patrol Boat; 1 T-227; 2 T-997; 23 M21 Patrol Boat; 3 T-991; 3 T-994

MINE WARFARE • MINE COUNTERMEASURES 17
  MCCS 1 *Thalang*
  MCO 2 *Lat Ya*
  MCC 2 *Bang Rachan*
  MSR 12: 7 T1; 5 T6

AMPHIBIOUS
  PRINCIPAL AMPHIBIOUS SHIPS • LPD 2:
    1 *Angthong* (SGP *Endurance*) with 1 76mm gun (capacity 2 hel; 19 MBT; 500 troops);
    1 Type-071E (PRC *Yuzhao*) (capacity 4 LCAC plus supporting vehicles; 800 troops; 60 armoured vehicles; 4 hel)

LANDING SHIPS 2
  LST 2 *Sichang* with 2 hel landing platform (capacity 14 MBT; 300 troops)

LANDING CRAFT 14
  LCU 9: 3 *Man Nok*; 2 *Mataphun* (capacity either 3–4 MBT or 250 troops); 4 *Thong Kaeo*
  LCM 2
  UCAC 3 *Griffon* 1000TD

LOGISTICS AND SUPPORT 13
  ABU 1 *Suriya*
  AGOR 1 *Sok*
  AGS 2: 1 *Chanthara*; 1 *Paruehatsabodi*
  AOL 5: 1 *Matra* with 1 hel landing platform; 2 *Proet*; 1 *Prong*; 1 *Samui*
  AORL 1 *Chula*
  AORH 1 *Similan* (capacity 1 hel)
  AWT 2
UNINHABITED MARITIME SYSTEMS
  UUV • MW *SeaFox* C

Naval Aviation 1,200
FORCES BY ROLE
ISR
  1 sqn with *Sentry* O-2-337
MARITIME PATROL
  1 sqn with Do-228-212; F-27-200 MPA*
TRANSPORT
  1 sqn with ERJ-135LR; 2 F-27-400M *Troopship*
HELICOPTER
  1 sqn with Bell 212 (AB-212); H145M
  1 sqn with *Super Lynx* 300; S-76B
  1 sqn with S-70B *Seahawk*; MH-60S *Knight Hawk*
ISR UAV
  1 sqn with S-100 *Camcopter*
EQUIPMENT BY TYPE
AIRCRAFT 2 combat capable
  ISR 9 *Sentry* O-2-337
  MP 4: 2 Do-228-212; 2 F-27-200 MPA*
  TPT • Light 9: 5 Do-228-212 (to be upgraded to MP); 2 ERJ-135LR; 2 F-27-400M *Troopship*
HELICOPTERS
  ASW 8: 6 S-70B *Seahawk*; 2 *Super Lynx* 300
  MRH 2 MH-60S *Knight Hawk*
  TPT • Light 16: 6 Bell 212 (AB-212); 5 H145M; 5 S-76B
UNINHABITED AERIAL VEHICLES • ISR • Light 5: *Orbiter* 3B; 1 RQ-21A *Blackjack*; ε4 S-100 *Camcopter*
AIR-LAUNCHED MISSILES • AShM AGM-84 *Harpoon*

Marines 23,000
FORCES BY ROLE
COMMAND
  1 mne div HQ
MANOEUVRE
  Reconnaissance
  1 recce bn
  Light
  3 inf regt (total: 6 bn)
  Amphibious
  1 amph aslt bn
COMBAT SUPPORT
  1 arty regt (3 fd arty bn, 1 ADA bn)

EQUIPMENT BY TYPE
ARMOURED FIGHTING VEHICLES
  LT TK 3 VN-16
  IFV 14 BTR-3E1
  APC • APC (W) 24 LAV-150 *Commando*
  AAV 33 LVTP-7
ENGINEERING & MAINTENANCE VEHICLES
  ARV 1 AAVR-7
ANTI-TANK/ANTI-INFRASTRUCTURE
  MSL
    SP 10 M1045A2 HMMWV with TOW
    MANPATS M47 *Dragon*; TOW
  RCL • SP 106mm M40A1
ARTILLERY 54
  SP 155mm 6 ATMOS-2000
  TOWED 48: **105mm** 36 M101A1; **155mm** 12 GC-45
AIR DEFENCE
  SAM • Point-defence QW-18

Air and Coastal Defence Command ε8,000
FORCES BY ROLE
COASTAL DEFENCE
  1 coastal arty regt (3 coastal arty bn)
AIR DEFENCE
  2 AD regt (3 AD bn)
EQUIPMENT BY TYPE
AIR DEFENCE • SAM
  Long-range FK-3 (HQ-22)
  Point-defence 9K338 *Igla*-S (RS-SA-24 *Grinch*)

Naval Special Warfare Command

Air Force ε46,000
4 air divs, one flying trg school
FORCES BY ROLE
FIGHTER
  1 sqn with F-16A/B *Fighting Falcon*; F-16A/B ADF *Fighting Falcon*
FIGHTER/GROUND ATTACK
  1 sqn with F-5TH(E/F) *Tiger* II
  1 sqn with F-16A/B MLU *Fighting Falcon*
  1 sqn with *Gripen* C/D
GROUND ATTACK
  1 sqn with *Alpha Jet**
  1 sqn with AU-23A *Peacemaker*
  1 sqn with T-50TH *Golden Eagle**
ELINT/ISR
  1 sqn with DA42 MPP *Guardian*
AIRBORNE EARLY WARNING & CONTROL
  1 sqn with Saab 340B; Saab 340 *Erieye*
TRANSPORT
  1 sqn with ATR-72-500/-600
  1 sqn with BT-67

1 sqn with C-130H/H-30 *Hercules*
1 (Royal Flight) VIP sqn with A319CJ; A320CJ; A340-500; B-737-800; SSJ-100-95LR

TRAINING
1 sqn with CT-4B/E *Airtrainer*; DA42M
1 sqn with DA40NG; DA42
1 sqn with T-6C *Texan* II
1 hel sqn with Bell 412EP *Twin Huey*; H135

TRANSPORT HELICOPTER
1 (CSAR) sqn with H225M *Super Cougar*
1 sqn with S-70i *Black Hawk*; S-92A

ISR UAV
1 sqn with *Aerostar*; *Dominator* XP
1 sqn with U-1

EQUIPMENT BY TYPE
AIRCRAFT 112 combat capable
FTR 28: 12 F-16A *Fighting Falcon*; 10 F-16A ADF *Fighting Falcon*; 5 F-16B *Fighting Falcon*; 1 F-16B ADF *Fighting Falcon*
FGA 42: 11 F-5TH(E) *Tiger* II; 2 F-5TH(F) *Tiger* II; 12 F-16A MLU *Fighting Falcon*; 6 F-16B ADF *Fighting Falcon*; 7 *Gripen* C; 4 *Gripen* D
ATK 12 AU-23A *Peacemaker* (CISR)
ISR 14 DA42 MPP *Guardian*
AEW&C 2 Saab 340 *Erieye*
ELINT 2 Saab 340 *Erieye* (COMINT/ELINT)
TPT 59: **Medium** 15: 6 C-130H *Hercules*; 6 C-130H-30 *Hercules*; 3 Saab 340B; **Light** 36: 3 ATR-72-500; 3 ATR-72-600; 3 Beech 200 *King Air*; 8 BT-67; 8 DA40NG; 10 DA42/42M; 1 P.180 *Avanti*; **PAX** 8: 1 A319CJ; 2 A320CJ; 1 A340-500; 1 B-737-800; 3 SSJ-100-95LR (1 A310-324 in store)
TRG 70: 16 *Alpha Jet**; 6 CT-4B *Airtrainer*; 19 CT-4E *Airtrainer*; 3 RTAF-6 (in test); 12 T-6C *Texan* II; 14 T-50TH *Golden Eagle**

HELICOPTERS
MRH 6 Bell 412EP *Twin Huey*
CSAR 12 H225M *Super Cougar*
TPT 14: **Medium** 8: 3 S-92A *Super Hawk*; 5 S-70i *Black Hawk*; **Light** 6 H135

UNINHABITED AERIAL VEHICLES • ISR 20: **Heavy** 3 *Dominator* XP; **Medium** *Aerostar*; **Light** ε17 U-1

AIR DEFENCE
SAM **Medium-range** 3+ KS-1C (CH-SA-12)

AIR-LAUNCHED MISSILES
AAM • IR AIM-9P/S *Sidewinder*; *Python* 3; IIR IRIS-T; *Python* 5 (reported); ARH AIM-120 AMRAAM; *Derby* (reported)
ASM AGM-65 *Maverick*
AShM RBS15F

BOMBS
Laser-guided GBU-10/-12 *Paveway* II; *Lizard*
INS/GPS-guided GBU-31/-38 JDAM; KGGB

Royal Security Command

FORCES BY ROLE
MANOEUVRE
Light
2 inf regt (3 inf bn)

Gendarmerie & Paramilitary ε93,700

Border Patrol Police 20,000

Marine Police 2,200
EQUIPMENT BY TYPE
PATROL AND COASTAL COMBATANTS 56
PCO 1 *Srinakrin*
PCC 2 *Hameln*
PB 53: 1 *Chai Jinda* (Incat Crowther 42m); 1 *Chasanyabadee*; 3 *Cutlass*; 2 M25; 2 *Ratayapibanbancha* (*Reef Ranger*); 1 *Sriyanont*; 2 *Wasuthep*; 41 (various)

Volunteer Defense Corps 45,000 – Reserves

Police Aviation 500
EQUIPMENT BY TYPE
AIRCRAFT 6 combat capable
ATK 6 AU-23A *Peacemaker*
TPT 17: **Light** 15: 2 Beech 350i *King Air*; 2 CN235; 3 DHC-6-400; 8 PC-6 *Turbo-Porter*; **PAX** 2: 1 F-50; 1 Falcon 2000
HELICOPTERS
MRH 32: 2 AS365N3 *Dauphin*; 4 AW189; 7 Bell 412EP *Twin Huey*; 8 Bell 412EPI *Twin Huey*; 2 Bell 412HP *Twin Huey*; 9 Bell 429
TPT 22: **Medium** 2 H175; **Light** 20: some Bell 205A; 2 Bell 206L *Long Ranger*; 13 Bell 212 (AB-212); 5 H155

Provincial Police 50,000 (incl ε500 Special Action Force)

Rangers (Thahan Phran) 21,000
Volunteer irregular force
FORCES BY ROLE
MANOEUVRE
Other
22 paramilitary regt (total: 275 paramilitary coy)

DEPLOYMENT

INDIA/PAKISTAN: UN • UNMOGIP 5
SOUTH SUDAN: UN • UNMISS 283; 1 engr coy
SUDAN: UN • UNISFA 2

FOREIGN FORCES

United States US Indo-Pacific Command: 100

Timor-Leste TLS

US Dollar USD		2023	2024	2025
GDP	USD	2.38bn	1.99bn	2.13bn
Real GDP growth	%	2.3	3.0	3.1
Def bdgt	USD	55.1m	46.4m	

Real-terms defence budget trend (USDm, constant 2015)

Population	1,506,909					
Age	0–14	15–19	20–24	25–29	30–64	65 plus
Male	19.9%	5.2%	4.9%	3.9%	13.8%	2.1%
Female	18.8%	5.0%	4.9%	4.0%	15.2%	2.3%

Capabilities

The small Timor-Leste Defence Force (F-FDTL) has been affected by funding, personnel and morale challenges since its establishment in 2001. The F-FDTL was reconstituted in the wake of fighting between regional factions in the security forces in 2006 but is still a long way from meeting the ambitious force-structure goals set out in the Force 2020 plan published in 2007. The government published a Strategic Defence and Security Concept (SDSC) in 2016, which outlined the roles of the F-FDTL, which include protecting the country from external threats and combating violent crime. However, this internal-security role has sometimes brought it into conflict with the national police force. The SDSC also stated that the F-FDTL needs to improve its naval capabilities, owing to the size of Timor-Leste's exclusive economic zone. The origins of the F-FDTL in the Falintil national resistance force and continuing training and doctrinal emphasis on low-intensity infantry tactics means that the force provides a deterrent to invasion. The F-FDTL has received training from Australian and US personnel. Timor-Leste signed a reciprocal Defence Cooperation Agreement with Australia in September 2022. Australia was due to provide two patrol boats in 2024 under its Pacific Maritime Security Program. Maintenance capacity is limited, and the country has no defence industry.

ACTIVE 2,250 (Army 2,250)

ORGANISATIONS BY SERVICE

Army 2,250

Training began in January 2001 with the aim of deploying 1,500 full-time personnel and 1,500 reservists. Authorities are engaged in developing security structures with international assistance

FORCES BY ROLE
MANOEUVRE
  Light
    2 inf bn
COMBAT SUPPORT
  1 MP pl
COMBAT SERVICE SUPPORT
  1 log spt coy

Naval Element 250
EQUIPMENT BY TYPE
PATROL AND COASTAL COMBATANTS 2
  PB 2 *Shanghai* II

Air Component
EQUIPMENT BY TYPE
AIRCRAFT
  ISR 1 Cessna T206H mod
  TPT • Light 1 Cessna 172

DEPLOYMENT

SOUTH SUDAN: UN • UNMISS 2

Tonga TON

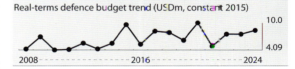

Tongan Pa'anga TOP		2023	2024	2025
GDP	TOP	1.22bn	1.30bn	1.37bn
	USD	520m	545m	571m
Real GDP growth	%	2.0	1.8	2.4
Def bdgt	TOP	20.4m	23.6m	
	USD	8.68m	9.92m	

Real-terms defence budget trend (USDm, constant 2015)

Population	104,889					
Age	0–14	15–19	20–24	25–29	30–64	65 plus
Male	14.9%	5.1%	4.7%	4.1%	18.0%	3.4%
Female	14.4%	4.8%	4.5%	4.1%	17.9%	4.1%

Capabilities

His Majesty's Armed Forces (HMAF) is a battalion-sized military based around the light infantry of the Tonga Royal Guards and the Royal Tongan Marines, and a small naval patrol squadron. The primary defence concerns include maritime security, counternarcotics and HADR. However, between 2002 and 2014, HMAF also contributed platoon-sized forces to multinational peacekeeping efforts in the Solomon Islands, and then international coalition operations in Iraq and Afghanistan. Australia, New Zealand and the US are Tonga's key external defence partners, but the armed forces also undertake defence-cooperation activities with China, India and the UK.

ACTIVE 600 (Royal Guards & Land Force 140 Navy 130 Other 330)

ORGANISATIONS BY SERVICE

Royal Guard & Land Force 140

FORCES BY ROLE
MANOEUVRE
  Light

1 inf coy(-)
Other
1 sy coy(-)

Navy 130
EQUIPMENT BY TYPE
PATROL AND COASTAL COMBATANTS 2
  PCO 2 *Guardian* (AUS *Bay* mod)
AMPHIBIOUS • LANDING CRAFT 1
  LCVP 1 *Late* (AUS)

Vietnam VNM

Vietnamese Dong VND		2023	2024	2025
GDP	VND	10.2qrn	11.3qrn	12.4qrn
	USD	434bn	468bn	506bn
Real GDP growth	%	5.0	6.1	6.1
Def bdgt	VND	ε176trn	ε189trn	
	USD	ε7.48bn	ε7.83bn	
FMA (US)	USD	12.0m	12.0m	13.5m

Real-terms defence budget trend (USDbn, constant 2015)

Population	105,758,975				
Age	0–14	15–19	20–24	25–29	30–64	65 plus
Male	12.2%	3.9%	3.6%	3.7%	23.4%	3.4%
Female	10.9%	3.5%	3.4%	3.6%	23.4%	4.9%

Capabilities

Vietnam has a strong military tradition, and the country's defence efforts benefit from broad popular support, particularly in the context of tensions with China over conflicting claims in the South China Sea. In 2018, Vietnam adopted a Law on National Defence that referred several times to Vietnam's differences with China and the need for both sides to 'put more effort into maintaining stability'. Hanoi has been strengthening naval and air capabilities with a clear focus on protecting its interests in the South China Sea. Those efforts include the development of an advanced submarine capability and the procurement of ISR, air-defence and anti-ship systems. In 2022, Vietnam and India signed a joint vision statement on defence cooperation and a logistics support agreement. Vietnam also has a defence cooperation agreement with Cuba. Although Russia has been Vietnam's dominant defence supplier, Hanoi is seeking to diversify its supplier base and is being courted by international suppliers; the US lifted its arms embargo on Vietnam in 2016, while the Czech Republic, India, Japan and South Korea are among those seeking to make inroads into Vietnam's defence market. The need for diversification became more acute as Russia's war in Ukraine caused Moscow to prioritise arms deliveries to its own forces. Vietnam is developing its defence-industrial capacities and has launched a defence-focused subsidiary of the state-owned Viettel Military Industry and Telecoms Group, called Viettel High Technology Industries Corporation, which focuses on defence electronics and communications. A 2019 white paper promoted investment in Vietnam's defence industry with the aim to become internationally competitive and join the 'global value chain' by 2030.

ACTIVE 450,000 (Army 380,000 Navy 40,000 Air 30,000) Gendarmerie & Paramilitary 40,000

Conscript liability 2 years army and air defence, 3 years air force and navy, specialists 3 years, some ethnic minorities 2 years

RESERVES Gendarmerie & Paramilitary 5,000,000

ORGANISATIONS BY SERVICE

Space
EQUIPMENT BY TYPE
SATELLITES • ISR 1 VNREDSat

Army ε380,000
8 Mil Regions (incl capital)
FORCES BY ROLE
COMMAND
  2 corps HQ
SPECIAL FORCES
  2 SF bde
MANOEUVRE
  Reconnaissance
  1 recce bde
  Armoured
  10 tk bde
  Mechanised
  2 mech inf div
  Light
  23 inf div
SURFACE-TO-SURFACE MISSILE
  1 SRBM bde
COMBAT SUPPORT
  13 arty bde
  1 arty regt
  11 engr bde
  1 engr regt
  1 EW unit
  3 sigs bde
  2 sigs regt
COMBAT SERVICE SUPPORT
  9 economic construction div
  1 log regt
  1 med unit
  1 trg regt
AIR DEFENCE
  11 AD bde

Reserve
FORCES BY ROLE

MANOEUVRE
Light
9 inf div
EQUIPMENT BY TYPE
ARMOURED FIGHTING VEHICLES
MBT 1,379: 45 T-34; 750 T-54/T-55; 100 T-54B mod; 70 T-62; 64 T-90S; 350 ZTZ-59;
LT TK 620: 300 PT-76; 320 ZTQ-62/ZTS-63
RECCE 100 BRDM-1/BRDM-2
IFV 300 BMP-1/BMP-2
APC 1,380+
APC (T) 280+: Some BTR-50; 200 M113 (to be upgraded); MT-LB; 80 ZSD-63
APC (W) 1,100 BTR-40/BTR-60/BTR-152
ENGINEERING & MAINTENANCE VEHICLES
AEV IMR-2
ARV BREM-1M
VLB TMM-3
ANTI-TANK/ANTI-INFRASTRUCTURE
MSL • MANPATS 9K11 *Malyutka* (RS-AT-3 *Sagger*); 9K111 *Fagot* (AT-4 *Spigot*); 9K113-1 *Konkurs* (AT-5 *Spandrel*); 9M14 mod
RCL 75mm PF-56; **82mm** PF-65 (B-10); **87mm** PF-51
GUNS
SP 100mm SU-100
TOWED 100mm T-12 (arty); M-1944
ARTILLERY 3,040+
SP 30+: **122mm** 2S1 *Gvozdika*; **152mm** 30 2S3 *Akatsiya*; **175mm** M107
TOWED 2,300: **105mm** M101/M102; **122mm** D-30/PL-54 (M-1938)/PL-60 (D-74); **130mm** M-46; **152mm** D-20; **155mm** M114
MRL 710+: **107mm** 360 Type-63; **122mm** 350 BM-21 *Grad*; **140mm** BM-14
MOR 82mm; **120mm** M-1943; **160mm** M-1943
SURFACE-TO-SURFACE MISSILE LAUNCHERS
SRBM • Coventional 9K72/9K77 (RS-SS-1C/D *Scud* B/C)
AIR DEFENCE
SAM • Point-defence 9K32 *Strela*-2 (RS-SA-7 *Grail*)‡; 9K310 *Igla*-1 (RS-SA-16 *Gimlet*); 9K38 *Igla* (RS-SA-18 *Grouse*)
SPAAGM 23mm ZSU-23-4M
GUNS 12,000
SP 23mm ZSU-23-4
TOWED 30mm/37mm/57mm/85mm/100mm

Navy ε40,000 (incl ε27,000 Naval Infantry)
EQUIPMENT BY TYPE
SUBMARINES 8
SSK 6 *Hanoi* (RUS Project 636.1 (Improved *Kilo*)) with 6 533mm TT with 3M14E *Klub*-S (RS-SS-N-30B) LACM/3M54E1/E *Klub*-S (RS-SS-N-27A/B) AShM (*Klub*-S AShM variant unclear)/53-65KE HWT/TEST-71ME HWT
SSW 2 *Yugo* (DPRK)
PATROL AND COASTAL COMBATANTS 70
CORVETTES 13:
FSGM 6:
1 BPS-500 with 2 quad lnchr with 3M24E *Uran*-E (RS-SS-N-25 *Switchblade*) AShM, 1 9K32 *Strela*-2M (RS-SA-N-5 *Grail*) SAM (manually operated), 2 twin 533mm TT, 1 RBU 1600 A/S mor, 1 AK630 CIWS, 1 76mm gun
2 *Dinh Tien Hoang* (RUS *Gepard* 3.9 (Project 11661E)) with 2 quad lnchr with 3M24E *Uran*-E (RS-SS-N-25 *Switchblade*) AShM, 1 3M89E *Palma* (*Palash*) CIWS with *Sosna*-R SAM (RS-CADS-N-2), 2 AK630M CIWS, 1 76mm gun, 1 hel landing platform
2 *Tran Hung Dao* (RUS *Gepard* 3.9 (Project 11661E)) with 2 quad lnchr with 3M24E *Uran*-E (RS-SS-N-25 *Switchblade*), 1 3M89E *Palma* (*Palash*) CIWS with *Sosna*-R SAM (RS-CADS-N-2), 2 twin 533mm TT with SET-53M HWT, 2 AK630M CIWS, 1 76mm gun, 1 hel landing platform
1 *Khukri* (ex-IND) with 2 twin lnchr with P-27 *Termit*-R (RS-SS-N-2D *Styx* AShM, 2 twin lnchr (manual aiming) with 9K32M *Strela*-2M (RS-SA-N-5 *Grail*) SAM, 2 AK630M CIWS, 1 76mm gun, 1 hel landing platform
FSG 1 *Po Hang* (Flight III) (ex-ROK) with 2 quad lnchr with 3M24E *Uran*-E (RS-SS-N-25 *Switchblade*) AShM, 2 76mm guns
FS 6:
3 Project 159A (ex-FSU *Petya* II) with 1 quintuple 406mm ASTT, 4 RBU 6000 *Smerch* 2 A/S mor, 2 twin 76mm gun
2 Project 159AE (ex-FSU *Petya* III) with 1 triple 533mm ASTT with SET-53ME HWT, 4 RBU 2500 *Smerch* 1 A/S mor, 2 twin 76mm guns
1 *Po Hang* (Flight III) (ex-ROK) with 2 76mm guns
PCFGM 12:
4 Project 1241RE (*Tarantul* I) with 2 twin lnchr with P-15 *Termit*-R (RS-SS-N-2D *Styx*) AShM, 1 quad lnchr with 9K32 *Strela*-2M (RS-SA-N-5 *Grail*) SAM (manually operated), 2 AK630M CIWS, 1 76mm gun
8 Project 12418 (*Tarantul* V) with 4 quad lnchr with 3M24E *Uran*-E (RS-SS-N-25 *Switchblade*) AShM, 1 quad lnchr with 9K32 *Strela*-2M (RS-SA-N-5 *Grail*) SAM (manually operated), 2 AK630M CIWS, 1 76mm gun
PCO 7: 1 Project FC264; 6 TT-400TP with 2 AK630M CIWS, 1 76mm gun
PCC 6 *Svetlyak* (Project 1041.2) with 1 AK630M CIWS, 1 76mm gun
PBFG 8 Project 205 (*Osa* II) with 4 single lnchr with P-20U (RS-SS-N-2B *Styx*) AShM
PBFT 1+ *Shershen*† (FSU) with 4 single 533mm TT
PBF 12
PBR 4 Stolkraft
PB 2 TP-01

PH 2 *Shtorm* (ex-FSU Project 206M (*Turya*))† with 1 twin 57mm gun
PHT 3 *Shtorm* (ex-FSU Project 206M (*Turya*))† with 4 single 533mm TT with 53-65KE HWT, 1 twin 57mm gun

MINE WARFARE • MINE COUNTERMEASURES 8
MSO 2 *Akvamaren* (Project 266 (*Yurka*))
MSC 4 *Sonya* (Project 1265 (*Yakhont*))
MHI 2 *Korund* (Project 1258 (*Yevgenya*))

AMPHIBIOUS
LANDING SHIPS 7
LST 2 *Tran Khanh Du* (ex-US LST 542) with 1 hel landing platform (capacity 16 Lt Tk/APC; 140 troops)
LSM 5:
1 *Polnochny* A (capacity 6 Lt Tk/APC; 200 troops)
2 *Polnochny* B (capacity 6 Lt Tk/APC; 200 troops)
2 *Nau Dinh*
LANDING CRAFT • LCM 13
8 LCM 6 (capacity 1 Lt Tk or 80 troops)
4 LCM 8 (capacity 1 MBT or 200 troops)
1 VDN-150

LOGISTICS AND SUPPORT 22
AGS 1 *Tran Dai Nia* (Damen Research Vessel 6613)
AH 1 *Khanh Hoa* (*Truong Sa* mod)
AKR 4 Damen Stan Lander 5612
AKL 10+
AP 1 *Truong Sa*
ASR 1 *Yết Kiêu* (Damen Rescue Gear Ship 9316)
ATF 2
AWT 1
AXS 1 *Le Quy Don*

Naval Infantry ε27,000
FORCES BY ROLE
SPECIAL FORCES
1 cdo bde
MANOEUVRE
Amphibious
2 mne bde
EQUIPMENT BY TYPE
ARMOURED FIGHTING VEHICLES
LT TK PT-76; ZTS-63
APC • APC (W) BTR-60

Coastal Defence
FORCES BY ROLE
COASTAL DEFENCE
4 AShM bde
1 coastal arty bde
EQUIPMENT BY TYPE
COASTAL DEFENCE • AShM 4K44 *Redut* (RS-SSC-1B *Sepal*); 4K51 *Rubezh* (RS-SSC-3 *Styx*); K-300P *Bastion*-P (RS-SSC-5 *Stooge*)
ARTILLERY • MRL 160mm AccuLAR-160; **306mm** EXTRA

Navy Air Wing
FORCES BY ROLE
ASW/SAR
1 regt with DHC-6-400 *Twin Otter*; H225; Ka-28 (Ka-27PL) *Helix* A; Ka-32 *Helix* C
EQUIPMENT BY TYPE
AIRCRAFT • TPT • Light 6 DHC-6-400 *Twin Otter*
HELICOPTERS
ASW 10 Ka-28 *Helix* A
TPT • Medium 4: 2 H225; 2 Ka-32 *Helix* C

Air Force 30,000
3 air div, 1 tpt bde
FORCES BY ROLE
FIGHTER/GROUND ATTACK
3 regt with Su-22M4/UM-3K *Fitter* (some ISR)
1 regt with Su-27SK/UBK *Flanker*
3 regt with Su-30MK2 *Flanker*
TRANSPORT
1 regt with An-2 *Colt*; Mi-8 *Hip*; Mi-17 *Hip H*
1 regt with An-2 *Colt*; C295M; Mi-8 *Hip*; Mi-17 *Hip H*
TRAINING
1 OCU regt with Yak-130 *Mitten**
1 regt with L-39 *Albatros*; L-39NG
1 regt with Yak-52
TRANSPORT HELICOPTER
2 regt with Mi-8 *Hip*; Mi-17 *Hip H*; Mi-171
AIR DEFENCE
6 AD div HQ
2 SAM regt with S-300PMU1 (RS-SA-20 *Gargoyle*)
3 SAM regt with *Spyder*-MR
3 SAM regt with S-75 *Dvina* (RS-SA-2 *Guideline*)
4 SAM regt with S-125-2TM *Pechora*-2TM
2 SAM regt with S-125M *Pechora*-M
4 ADA regt
EQUIPMENT BY TYPE
AIRCRAFT 82 combat capable
FGA 70: 16 Su-22M4 *Fitter* K (some ISR); 9 Su-22UM-3K *Fitter* G; 5 Su-27SK *Flanker*; 5 Su-27UBK *Flanker* B; 35 Su-30MK2 *Flanker* G
TPT • Light 12: 6 An-2 *Colt*; 3 C295M; 3 C-212 *Aviocar* (NC-212i)
TRG 72: 17 L-39 *Albatros*; ε8 L-39NG; 5 T-6C *Texan* II; 12 Yak-130 *Mitten**; 30 Yak-52
HELICOPTERS
MRH 6 Mi-17 *Hip H*
TPT • Medium 24: 16 Mi-8 *Hip*; 8 Mi-171 (incl 4 SAR)
AIR DEFENCE
SAM 98+:
Long-range 12 S-300PMU1 (RS-SA-20 *Gargoyle*)
Medium-range 65: ε25 S-75 *Dvina* (RS-SA-2 *Guideline*); ε30 S-125-2TM *Pechora*-2TM; ε10 *Spyder*-MR
Short-range 21+: 2K12 *Kub* (RS-SA-6 *Gainful*); 21

S-125M *Pechora*-M (RS-SA-3 *Goa*)
Point-defence 9K32 *Strela*-2 (RS-SA-7 *Grail*)‡; 9K310 *Igla*-1 (RS-SA-16 *Gimlet*)
GUNS 37mm; 57mm; 85mm; 100mm; 130mm
AIR-LAUNCHED MISSILES
AAM • IR R-60 (RS-AA-8 *Aphid*); R-73 (RS-AA-11A *Archer*); **IR/SARH** R-27 (RS-AA-10 *Alamo*); **ARH** R-77 (RS-AA-12A *Adder*)
ASM Kh-29L/T (RS-AS-14 *Kedge*); Kh-59M (RS-AS-18 *Kazoo*)
AShM Kh-31A (RS-AS-17B *Krypton*)
ARM Kh-28 (RS-AS-9 *Kyle*); Kh-31P (RS-AS-17A *Krypton*)

Gendarmerie & Paramilitary 40,000+ active

Border Defence Corps ε40,000

Coast Guard
EQUIPMENT BY TYPE
PATROL AND COASTAL COMBATANTS 77+
 PSOH 2 *Hamilton* (ex-US) with 1 76mm gun (capacity 1 med hel)
 PSO 4 DN2000 (Damen 9314)
 PCO 13+: 1 *Mazinger* (ex-ROK); 9 TT-400; 3+ other
 PCC 2 *Hae Uri* (ex-ROK)
 PBF 28: 26 MS-50S; 2 *Shershen*
 PB 28: 1 MS-50; ε12 TT-200; 14 TT-120; 1 other
LOGISTICS AND SUPPORT 5
 AFS 1
 ATF 4 Damen Salvage Tug
AIRCRAFT • MP 2 C-212-400 MPA

Local Forces ε5,000,000 reservists
Incl People's Self-Defence Force (urban units) and People's Militia (rural units); comprises static and mobile cbt units, log spt and village protection pl; some arty, mor and AD guns; acts as reserve

DEPLOYMENT

CENTRAL AFRICAN REPUBLIC: EU • EUTM RCA 2; **UN •** MINUSCA 8
SOUTH SUDAN: UN • UNMISS 38; 1 fd hospital
SUDAN: UN • UNISFA 192; 1 engr coy

Chapter Six
Middle East and North Africa

- Israel demonstrated its ability to maintain offensive operations in Gaza and degraded the capabilities of Hizbullah, while also mounting long-range strikes against Iranian targets. Air defence capabilities largely defeated complex Iranian missile and uninhabited aerial vehicle (UAV) attacks but Western air-defence support was required.
- Iran's April and October 2024 attacks on Israel revealed limitations in the ability of both its missiles and UAVs to penetrate advanced missile defences.
- Western navies have used a considerable amount of high-end ordnance amid efforts to protect international shipping from Ansarullah's (the Houthis') missile and UAV attacks. Magazine-depth and munition stockpile issues have prompted the US to re-examine at-sea reloads of vertical launch systems and explore the development of more cost-effective options to tackle threats such as UAVs.
- UAVs produced by Turkish firms are seen increasingly widely in regional inventories, driven by factors including US restrictions on armed UAV exports, the ability of Turkish companies to deliver quickly, and Turkiye and other countries' combat experience with these systems.
- Since 2022, defence spending growth across the Middle East and North Africa region has been very strong, averaging around 8% in real terms annually. In 2024, growth was particularly strong, driven by a 72.9% real-terms surge in Israeli spending but also by growth in markets like Algeria. The war in Gaza and wider regional instability have driven an increase in defence spending as a percentage of GDP, with the regional average rising to 4.3% in 2024, up from 4% in 2023.

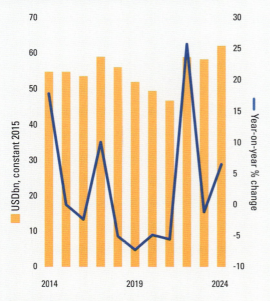

Saudi Arabia, real-terms defence budget trend, 2014–24 (USDbn, constant 2015)

Note: Defence budget only – excludes security expenditure.

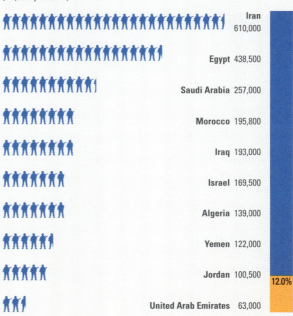

Active military personnel – top 10
(25,000 per unit)

Iran	610,000	
Egypt	438,500	
Saudi Arabia	257,000	
Morocco	195,800	
Iraq	193,000	
Israel	169,500	
Algeria	139,000	
Yemen	122,000	
Jordan	100,500	
United Arab Emirates	63,000	

Global total 20,629,000

Regional total 2,485,000 (12.0%)

Regional defence policy and economics 314
Arms procurement and defence-industrial trends 325
Armed forces data section 328

Middle East and North Africa: tactical combat aircraft, 2024

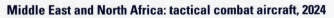

Note: Tactical combat aircraft includes fighter, fighter/ground-attack, and ground-attack aircraft.

Middle East and North Africa: attack-submarine inventories, 2024

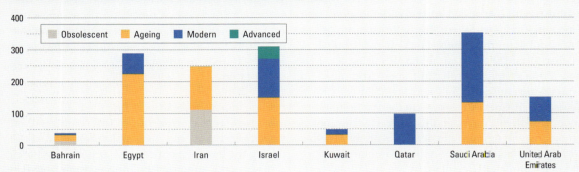

Middle East and North Africa: selected Iranian-designed ballistic missile families

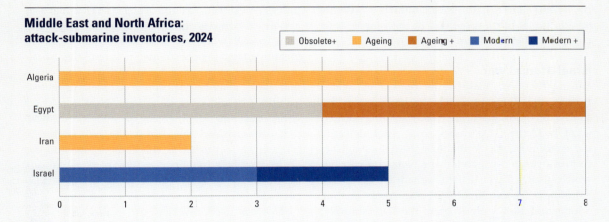

Middle East and North Africa

The 7 October 2023 attack by Hamas, and the Israel Defense Forces' (IDF) combined-arms response, largely shaped the Middle East in 2024. The conflict subsequently expanded to the wider region, with members of the so-called 'Axis of Resistance' such as Ansarullah (or the Houthis) in Yemen, Hizbullah in Lebanon and the Hashd al-Shaabi raising tensions on various fronts. Arab Gulf states continued to pursue detente with Iran and maintain calls for a ceasefire in Gaza. Russia strengthened its military cooperation with Iran, and the United States took a more forceful approach to dealing with the Houthis while also bolstering its regional military posture to deter Iran and Hizbullah. By the end of the year, however, Hizbullah in Lebanon had been weakened by Israeli attacks, with Iran's influence suffering an additional blow at the end of the year with the collapse of the Assad family's rule in Syria.

Israel–Hamas war

During the first phase of its operations against Hamas, the IDF launched a ground assault and conducted thousands of airstrikes, isolating northern Gaza in October–December 2023. After defeating the standing Hamas formations, the IDF established control over and expanded the Netzarim corridor, which bisects Gaza. It then turned to Hamas and Palestinian Islamic Jihad (PIJ) formations in Khan Younis and Rafah. By August, the IDF controlled the border between Gaza and Egypt along the Philadelphi corridor, cutting Hamas off from the tunnels to Egypt that are its main smuggling route. While through the year Hamas and PIJ retained the ability to reconstitute fighting formations to control the Gazan population, when they did so they faced IDF raids, but reports in late year pointing to attempts by Hamas to tackle criminality and looting may be indicative of an overall decline in the group's security control of Gaza following Israel's attacks, as well as its intent to restore its position.

In early November 2024, the Israeli government acknowledged that more than 5,000 IDF personnel had been wounded and over 700 killed on all fronts since 7 October, of which about 360 died during ground operations in Gaza. While these losses are significant, the IDF's standing personnel and reserve force was not materially affected. Throughout the year the IDF partially activated reserve brigades, with some mobilised several times and decommissioned in a matter of weeks. July saw the first time that conscription notices were issued to members of Israel's Haredi community, who were previously exempt from serving with the IDF.

The IDF's ground operations have included the fielding of new systems including the *Eitan* wheeled armoured vehicle (reportedly first employed on 7 October 2023), and the application of robotics during the employment of some armoured vehicles – M113s and armoured bulldozers were noted in some reports. Active protection systems have been utilised, designed to improve the survivability of armoured vehicles and their crew. At the same time, the IDF will likely be looking to learn lessons, including from the constrained nature of the urban-warfare environment in Gaza and the operations that have taken place under as well as above ground. Ground operations have been combined with a sustained deployment of modern airpower that demonstrated the devastating effects that it can deliver. Nevertheless, this combination and the destruction it wrought also prompted significant international concern and censure from certain circles and put pressure on Israel's leadership.

The war also revealed that Israel still relies heavily on the US, especially for precision-guided munitions and components for its *Iron Dome* system's *Tamir* interceptor missiles. At the same time, the IDF leadership showed great reluctance to occupy Gaza in any post-war scenario, when some Israeli political parties discussed that option. Israel's political leaders, meanwhile, faced the challenges of fulfilling their overall war aims of the destruction of Hamas and the return of hostages held in Gaza. Hamas frustrated attempts to strengthen local institutions in Gaza, fearing these could be the basis for a future administration free of their involvement.

The Gaza campaign marked a departure from the IDF's war-fighting doctrine, which aims for short wars and decisive battles. There had been doubts as to whether Israel could sustain a long campaign and

Table 7 Israel: selected air-force procurements since 2010

The Israeli Air Force (IAF) has significantly modernised its air domain capabilities since 2010. The principal focus has been on recapitalising its combat-aviation fleet through procuring the F-35I *Adir* multi-role combat aircraft from the United States. Israel sees this acquisition, primarily funded through the US Foreign Military Financing programme, as a key part of maintaining its qualitative military edge. In 2024, contracts were signed for a third squadron of F-35Is as well as a new squadron of 25 F-15IA multi-role combat aircraft, with an option for 25 more. In addition to new combat aircraft, the IAF has also sought to sustain its fleet of airborne enablers. Recent operations have highlighted the continuing importance of air-to-air refueling for the service, and it has ordered four KC-46A *Pegasus* tankers to replace the ageing fleet of KC-707 *Re'em* aircraft. Programme delays mean that the *Pegasus* deliveries are now expected to occur between 2025 and 2027. In March 2024, the IAF declared its *Oron* wide-area intelligence, surveillance and reconnaissance (ISR) aircraft operational. This aircraft joins the IAF's existing fleet of Gulfstream G550-based special-mission aircraft, such as the *Shavit* electronic-intelligence aircraft and the *Eitam* airborne early-warning and control aircraft, in addition to the service's inventory of uninhabited aerial vehicles.

Date	Equipment	Type	Quantity	Value (USD)	Prime contractor	Deliveries
Mar 2010	C-130J-30 *Hercules*	Medium transport aircraft	7	500 million	Lockheed Martin	2013–18
Sep 2010	F-35I *Adir*	Fighter/ground-attack (FGA) aircraft	19	2.62 billion	Lockheed Martin	2016–19
Jul 2012	M-346 *Master* (*Lavi*)	Training aircraft	30	1bn	Leonardo	2014–16
Feb 2015	F-35I *Adir*	FGA aircraft	14	2.38bn	Lockheed Martin	2019–22
2015	F-15D *Eagle* (*Baz*)	FGA aircraft	9	n.k.	US government surplus	2016–17
Aug 2017	F-35I *Adir*	FGA aircraft	17	2.8bn	Lockheed Martin	2022–26
2017	Gulfstream G550 *Oron*	ISR aircraft	1	n.k.	IAI	2021
Dec 2019	AW119Kx (*Ofer*)	Light transport helicopter	7	38.43m	Leonardo	2022
Feb 2022	CH-53K *King Stallion*	Heavy transport helicopter	12	2bn	Sikorsky	2025–27
Apr 2022	AW119Kx (*Ofer*)	Light transport helicopter	5	29.24m	Leonardo	2024
Aug 2022	KC-46A *Pegasus*	Tanker/transport aircraft	4	927m	Boeing	2025–27
Jun 2024	F-35I *Adir*	FGA aircraft	25	3bn	Lockheed Martin	From 2028
Nov 2024	F-15IA	FGA aircraft	25	5.2bn	Boeing	From 2031

Source: IISS, Military Balance+, milbalplus.iiss.org

---

stress has built up within Israeli society, with protests over the fate of the hostages, discontent with the leadership of Prime Minister Benjamin Netanyahu, and general concern about the disruption and negative impact that the war effort was having on the economy. Nonetheless, while the IDF may have caused severe attrition to Hamas, claiming to have killed upwards of 20,000 Hamas fighters (possibly including fighters from other militant organisations), in the process tens of thousands of Palestinian civilians have also been reported as killed and wounded.

Iran and the 'Axis of Resistance'

Iran and a network of militant groups that it supports joined the war against Israel, albeit to differing effect. Israel inflicted significant losses on Hizbullah after 7 October, killing more than 2,000 combatants by October 2024, including senior military commanders. Perhaps Israel's most high-profile operation came in September 2024, when it initiated explosive charges implanted in thousands of communications devices used by Hizbullah members, disrupting the group's ability to communicate. The IDF then ramped up its airstrikes, killing Hizbullah's leader Hasan Nasrallah, and launched a ground invasion of southern Lebanon in October. These setbacks revealed Hizbullah's deep operational security flaws and exposure to Israel's superior intelligence capabilities. Israel also struck Hizbullah's weapons-storage and logistics facilities in Lebanon and Syria, with US and Israeli officials claiming Israel had destroyed half of Hizbullah's stockpile of missiles and rockets.

Hizbullah struggled to calibrate its response, with Iran reluctant to risk an all-out war and the Lebanese population weary of another large-scale conflict. The US also positioned assets to deter Hizbullah, and Israel retained air and intelligence superiority. As such, Hizbullah remained keen to avoid radical transgressions of the rules of engagement, appearing to adhere to proportionality during most of its attacks. While not completely rejecting US diplomatic efforts, Hizbullah's leadership repeatedly insisted that only a ceasefire in Gaza would lead to one in Lebanon. Nevertheless, with Hizbullah under pressure from mounting losses, and Israel seeking some tangible security dividend for its northern population, in late November Washington was able to broker a fragile truce.

To the east, militias launched at least 190 attacks on US forces in Syria and Iraq, most of which took place between October 2023 and January 2024. In response to an attack that killed three US soldiers near Al-Tanf in Syria in late January, the US conducted retaliatory strikes. After that, militias refocused their efforts on striking Israel, with attacks against US forces decreasing significantly. In response, the IDF struck targets in the Syrian border town of Al-Bukamal, a centre of Islamic Revolutionary Guard Corps (IRGC) affiliates and a weapons transit point from Iraq. From mid-year the security situation in Syria remained unstable due to Israeli airstrikes, the resurgence of the Islamic State and renewed conflict between Hayat Tahrir al-Sham (HTS) and regime forces in the northwest. The rapid move south by HTS in November, and the sequential fall of major towns and cities, culminated in the collapse of Assad rule in early December. Other militias moved against regime forces from the south, while ISIS looked for an opportunity to expand its influence, prompting significant US airstrikes in the days around the government collapse. At time of writing, the Syrian armed forces, which had numbered nearly 170,000, had collapsed. Israel rapidly attacked military equipment and facilities, with apparent focus on combat aircraft and missile systems, but precise losses were unclear.

Iran's involvement in the Israel–Gaza conflict for the first six months was limited to moral and logistical support to militant groups. But on 13 April, Iran launched a major attack against Israeli targets in response to an IDF airstrike on an Iranian consulate in Damascus that killed a high-ranking IRGC officer. Iran's attack involved more than 100 ballistic missiles, several dozen cruise missiles and over 100 one-way-attack uninhabited aerial vehicles (OWA-UAVs). Israel, along with the US, United Kingdom, France and Jordan, reportedly intercepted most of the OWA-UAVs and cruise missiles outside of Israeli airspace using crewed fighter aircraft, with some endo- and exo-atmospheric interceptions of ballistic missiles achieved with Israeli *Arrow* 2 and *Arrow* 3 interceptors plus US SM-3 missiles – their first operational use. Although a few ballistic missiles reached Nevatim Air Base, their low accuracy resulted in only minor damage to the facility. While the attack demonstrated Iran's resolve and ability to conduct large and complex operations, it was unable to overcome Israeli and Western defences and inflict meaningful damage to military infrastructure. Further south, the Houthis launched several rounds of ballistic missiles, cruise missiles and OWA-UAVs against targets in southern Israel, though Israel's air and missile defences meant that these attacks caused little damage.

In many ways, the blunting of the Iranian assault compounded Tehran's strategic difficulties, even if the attack showed Israel's reliance on others to help in its defence. On 1 October 2024, Iran launched a second wave of around 180 ballistic missiles against Israel without warning and this time without the slow-flying OWA-UAVs. More than 30 missiles penetrated Israel's air defences and struck Nevatim Air Base, although damage appeared to have been limited. The strikes Israel mounted in response, moreover, appeared to underscore its military superiority and exposed weaknesses in Iran's capabilities, adding to the strategic dilemmas that Iran's leadership faces, which includes the degrading of its supposed trump card, its influence network. Reports also suggested that Israel had targeted not only air-defence sites, but also locations involved in the production of missile components and the related supply chain.

Red Sea crisis

Perhaps the most significant contrast to this picture has been the Houthis' campaign against merchant shipping in the Red Sea and the Gulf of Aden. While their missile and OWA-UAV hit rates were low, the level of risk created was sufficient for many shipping companies to divert their operations from these areas. Additionally, the Houthis began to increasingly use explosive uninhabited surface vessels, which pose a larger threat to shipping due to their greater payload. All this appeared to raise the Houthis' status as a significant regional actor, albeit again perhaps not an entirely welcome outcome from Tehran's perspective. In the Gulf of Oman and the Arabian Sea, the IRGC has been suspected of seizing and attacking several merchant vessels since October 2023.

Most regional countries did not publicly support the naval coalitions set up in response to the Houthi attacks, except for Bahrain. Internationally, efforts were fragmented between the US-led maritime-protection effort *Operation Prosperity Guardian*; the US- and UK-led *Operation Poseidon Archer*, which focused on offensive action against Houthi targets; the European Union's *Operation Aspides*; and the presence of a number of other discrete national deployments. There was limited tactical cooperation between these efforts, however, and the German and Dutch navies were among several European fleets for which the attacks exposed shortcomings in their systems integration.

US and UK strikes against Houthi targets did not deter the Houthis nor degrade their capabilities sufficiently to halt their anti-shipping campaign. Rather, they likely reduced their overall effectiveness, notwithstanding sporadic Houthi successes.

Navies operating in the area learned significant tactical lessons, employing a combination of area air defence and close protection systems. However, maintaining a long-term commitment will be a challenge, and the counter-Houthi campaign has highlighted trade-offs around the use of expensive air-defence missiles against high numbers of OWA-UAVs. Ultimately, this may be less about money and more about strategic stockpiles, magazine depths and reviving the ability to rearm at sea – something the US Navy is now urgently investigating. Red Sea operations will likely lead to increased focus on cost-effective air-defence and counter-UAV solutions in the future, including directed-energy weapons.

A purely military solution to the Red Sea situation seemed unlikely, since it would need to be on a scale involving troops on the ground that Western countries would not contemplate. Equally, a strategic approach involving diplomacy and a more robust approach to enforcing arms sanctions against the Houthis also looked challenging.

The Gulf

The April 2024 attack by Tehran and its non-state allies against Israel added new urgency to the long-standing goal of improving air and missile defence among Washington's Gulf Cooperation Council (GCC) partners. More than two decades after missile defence was first raised as a security priority, the issue has featured repeatedly on the US–GCC agenda. Delivering on the ambition, however, has until now proved beyond the collective will of the region. This time, a GCC meeting took place in Saudi Arabia a month after the attack, which included a US–GCC integrated air- and missile-defence working group that agreed to establish a GCC Early Warning Study.

In late 2023, the United Arab Emirates (UAE) became the first GCC country to publicly unveil a national-defence strategy, which was released alongside a Climate Change Strategy for the UAE Armed Forces announced on the sidelines of the COP28 meeting in Dubai. Although the national-defence strategy is a high-level document lacking explicit detail, it represents a small step towards some transparency and could be a useful strategic-communications tool. Its focus on advanced technology, the national defence industry and human capital as key drivers of future growth also help it to project the image of a future-focused force.

Extra-regional actors

Russia and Iran deepened their cooperation with the construction of a factory for manufacturing Iranian UAVs inside Russia, and Iran supplied ballistic missiles to Russian forces. Consequently, Russia-Israel ties have deteriorated markedly since the beginning of the Israel-Hamas war due to Russia's perceived pro-Hamas position. Even though the Assad regime had collapsed, at time of writing, Russia still maintained a presence in the Syrian port of Tartus and at the Khmeimim air base. Despite the wars in Ukraine and Gaza, Russia maintained positive relationships with most regional actors, including Iran and its allies, the GCC members, Jordan and Egypt, and it has clearly sought to exploit the regional crisis to promote an anti-Western narrative chiefly aimed at the Global South. However, the rapid progress of HTS militias in Syria from late November highlighted not only the incapacity of the Syrian army and the limitations apparent in Hizbullah's forces in Syria, but also the effect that Russia's heavy military commitment to the invasion of Ukraine had made to the degree to which it could militarily support the Syrian army. At time of writing, after the regime collapse in Syria, there were reports that Russia was contacting militias, likely in a bid to retain some foothold in the country.

Figure 27 Ansarullah (Houthis): selected missile forces

After seizing control of northern Yemen in 2014–15, the Houthis swiftly operationalised an array of short-range ballistic missile systems inherited from the pre-war Yemeni armed forces. This modest initial arsenal was soon bolstered by Iranian deliveries of various types of land-attack ballistic and cruise missiles, allowing the Houthis to stage ever-longer-range attacks against Saudi Arabia, the United Arab Emirates and, later, Israel. Tehran has provided some of its most advanced long-range missiles, such as the precision-guided, 1,300 kilometre-range *Kheibar Shekan*, indicating reduced concern over both the escalatory

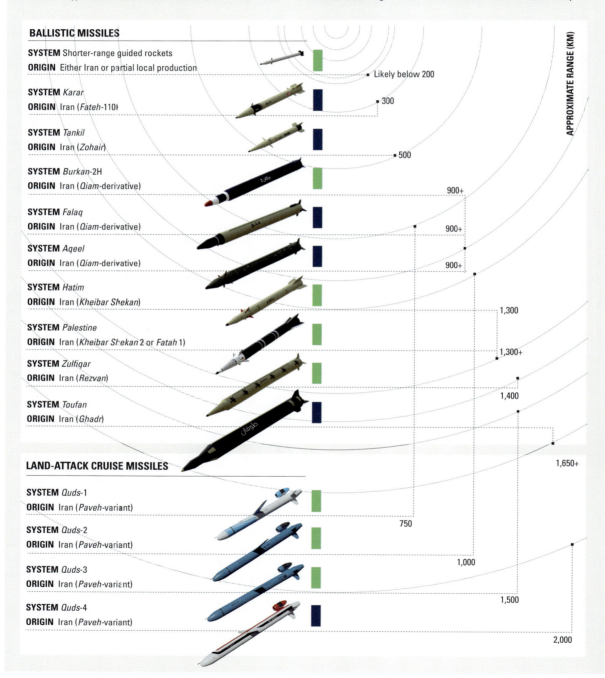

*The Soviet Union delivered the SAMs and Iran supplied the guidance kit.

potential of such transfers and the risk of foreign powers exploiting its technology. Beyond supplying advanced missiles, Iran also appears to have facilitated the Houthis' domestic production of shorter-range missiles, reflecting a strategy similar to its support for Hizbullah in Lebanon and Hamas and Palestinian Islamic Jihad in Gaza. Iran likely views Yemen as a testing ground for both missile technology and associated tactics, techniques and procedures. Houthi missiles have served as an effective tool of asymmetric warfare, allowing the group to exact a cost on adversaries and translate its willingness to escalate into political leverage.

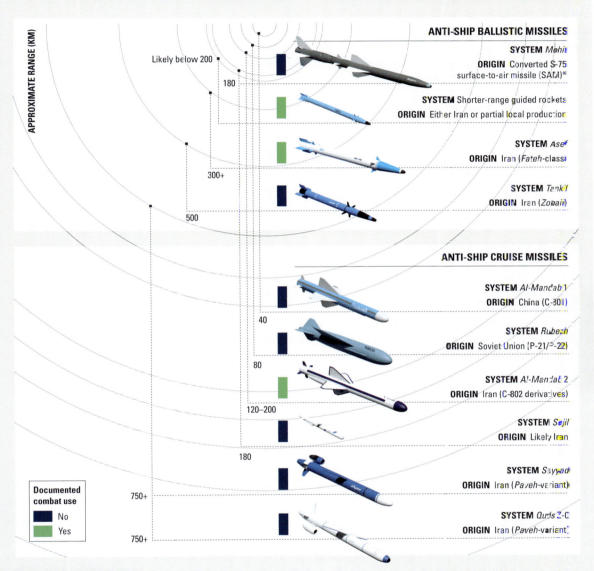

Anti-shipping capabilities

In addition to land-attack systems, Iran has also provided the Houthis with a diverse arsenal of anti-ship ballistic and cruise missiles. The use of anti-ship ballistic missiles, alongside uninhabited aerial vehicles (UAVs), has played a key role in the Houthis' campaign against merchant shipping in the Red Sea and the Gulf of Aden. The combat effectiveness of Houthi missiles, however, has been mixed. Their ballistic missiles have shown a relatively low success rate and Western ship-based ballistic missile defence systems have frequently intercepted them. Despite repeated attempts, the Houthis have yet to strike a Western warship. Nonetheless, their missile and UAV campaigns have still managed to disrupt global shipping and have proved resilient against Western military intervention.

Source: IISS

DEFENCE ECONOMICS

Defence spending across the Middle East and North Africa rose by 14.5% in 2024, to reach USD209.1 billion, or USD214.3bn including Foreign Military Financing (FMF) from the United States. Saudi Arabia remained the region's largest spender although Algeria, Iraq and Israel recorded the highest rates of growth. Increases here, and across the region, took place amid a worsening security situation, with the 7 October 2023 attacks against Israel precipitating an increasingly internationalised conflict. Defence spending as a percentage of GDP has increased, with the regional average rising to 4.3% in 2024, up from 4.0% in 2023, and significant uplifts evident in Algeria and Israel. In parallel, efforts at domestic industrial development continued apace, particularly in Israel and the Arab Gulf states, as countries seek to secure their own sovereign supply chains, as well as develop new technology to enable military capability development. Exports remained a clear, but largely elusive, goal for many regional manufacturers.

Defence budgets

Regional defence spending remains dominated by **Saudi Arabia**, although the country's share of regional spending has fallen in recent years, down to 34.3% in 2024 from a high of 38.8% in 2022. The 2022 spike was due to a 25.8% real-terms uplift made that year as Riyadh bolstered defence funding, after five years of stagnation in the wake of the 2016 collapse in oil prices. Saudi Arabia's regional share has fallen away since 2022 as growth has moderated and other countries, such as Algeria and Israel, have dramatically increased their defence budgets. Nonetheless, Riyadh's 2024 allocation of SAR269bn (USD71.7bn) still represents a real-terms increase of 6.6% on the previous year and raises funding to 6.5% of GDP, which is one of the highest levels globally. In addition to its ongoing modernisation efforts, the increased funding will help Riyadh restock, if not expand, its munitions holdings – an effort that will be aided by the lifting of the US ban on offensive-weapons sales to Saudi Arabia. For example, on 11 October 2024, the US Defense Security Cooperation Agency (DSCA) announced that the potential sale of up to 220 AIM-9X Block II *Sidewinder* air-to-air missiles had been approved. After including related equipment, spares and other support, the package was valued at USD251.8 million. On the same day, the DSCA approved the sale of up to 2,503 Lockheed Martin AGM-114R3 *Hellfire* II air-to-surface missiles in a total package valued at USD655m. At time of writing, these still required approval in Congress. In addition to offensive capabilities, Saudi Arabia is investing in new missile defence and, in July 2024, South Korea's Hanwha Systems announced that it will supply an upgraded multi-function radar for the Kingdom's forthcoming *Cheongung* II (KM-SAM II) medium-range surface-to-air missile system, ordered in 2019 (contracted in November 2023).

In 2024, **Israel's** military spending increased significantly, with the ongoing war requiring increased mobilisation, procurement and training. In local terms, the Ministry of Defense's (MoD) domestic budget jumped by almost 79%, reaching ILS125bn (USD33.7bn), up from ILS70.1bn (USD19.1bn) the year before. This pushed spending to 6.4% of GDP, a level not seen since the first Gaza war in 2008–09. In addition to domestic defence spending, Israel receives USD3.3bn in annual FMF allocations from the US, the majority of which is used to fund the acquisition of US materiel.

As the conflict has endured and escalated, it has also become increasingly internationalised. This includes **Iran**, which conducted its first-ever missile attack on Israel in April 2024, in retaliation for an Israeli airstrike in Damascus that killed several senior military commanders. A further Iranian missile attack was launched in October 2024; however, Tehran can ill afford a full-scale conflict. Domestically, unemployment remains high, while recent protests have been fuelled, in part, by the country's ongoing economic crisis. Indeed, inflation averaged near 30% across the past decade, with food inflation standing at over 24% by September 2024. Nonetheless, in 2024, Iran allocated IRR3.67 quadrillion to fund the army, the Ministry of Defence and the Islamic Revolutionary Guard Corps (IRGC) (The IISS does not include Law Enforcement Force (NAJA) funding in the defence budget as this is defined as security expenditure). This total for defence in 2024 equates to USD8.04bn, if using the country's official NIMA exchange rate, and rises substantially to USD87.3bn if using market rates. The full extent of Iranian military spending is likely to be considerably higher, as some reports suggest that the armed forces and IRGC receive further funding from oil revenues and from the National Development Fund. Regardless of the measure used, spending is likely to rise, if only to replenish stocks

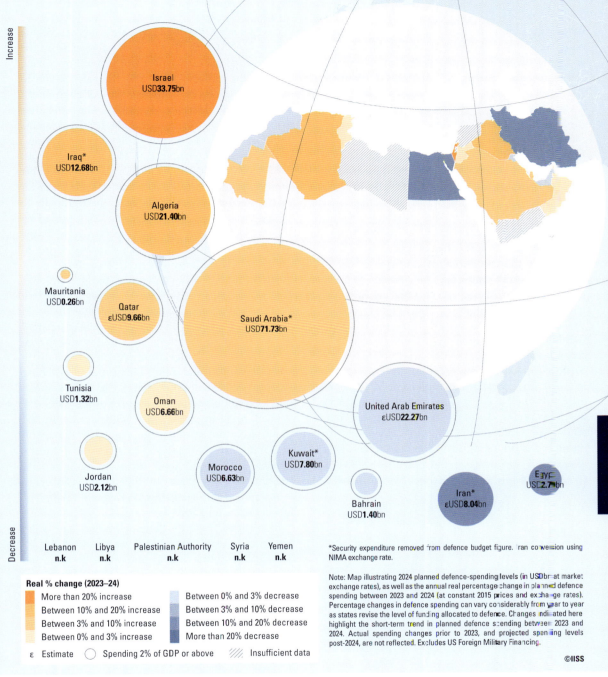

▲ Map 4 **Middle East and North Africa: regional defence spending** (USDbn, %ch yoy)

of cruise and ballistic missiles used in its campaigns and rebuild related facilities damaged or destroyed in Israeli missile strikes. Indeed, according to state-media reports in October 2024, Iran is considering increasing the defence budget by 200%, although it is not clear which budget figure is being referred to.

The war also encroached into **Lebanon**. Israeli forces exchanged fire with Hizbullah forces along the Israel–Lebanon border and Golan Heights in October 2023, though after a series of escalations, Israeli troops entered Lebanon in October 2024. The Lebanese Armed Forces (LAF) have long been hamstrung by Hizbullah's position in Lebanese national politics, while the country's prolonged economic depression and an ongoing governance crisis have further hampered capability development. As a result, securing sufficient resources for the LAF has remained challenging. In local terms, funding for defence has seen extensive increases in recent years, from LBP6.6bn (USD239m) in 2022 to LBP48.5bn (USD540m) in 2024, with a further jump to LBP71.3bn (USD793m) in 2025. However, the slump in the value of the Lebanese pound against the dollar and surges in the inflation rate (which exceeded 200% in 2023) erodes the effective value of these increases. Lebanon does receive FMF from the US, which came to USD150m in 2024.

Against this backdrop of decreasing stability, the **United Arab Emirates'** (UAE) defence budget reached an estimated AED81.8bn (USD22.3bn), making it the region's third-highest defence spender. The UAE has steadily increased its military capabilities, and in June 2024, its navy received its second of two *Bani Yas*-class (FRA *Gowind*-class) corvettes from France's Naval Group. Ordered in 2019, the corvettes complement a May 2021 order of four *Falaj* 3-class patrol vessels based on Singapore's *Fearless*-class oceangoing patrol craft. Like Saudi Arabia, the UAE also boosted its munitions stocks and, in October 2024, the DSCA announced approval for the potential sale of 259 Guided Multiple Launch Rocket System (GMLRS) M31A1 Unitary Pods and 203 Army Tactical Missile Systems (ATACMS) M57 Unitary Missiles from the US, in a total package worth USD1.2bn. Previously, in May, the US also approved the sale of kits to modify the UAE's existing inventory of High Speed Anti-Radiation Missiles (HARMs). The UAE has also increased its air- and missile-defence systems through the acquisition of US-made *Patriot* and South Korean *Cheongung* II (KM-SAM II) systems, purchased in 2022. The region has seen considerable interest in the KM-SAM, with **Iraq** placing an order for the system in September 2024, the third sale to the region in recent years. The sale is supported by Baghdad's increasing defence spending, with the country's budget rising by 15.3% in real terms in 2024, reaching IQD16.5 trillion (USD12.7bn).

Algeria doubled its defence budget in 2023 to DZD2.5trn (USD18.3bn) from DZD1.3trn (USD9.2bn) in 2022. Such growth comes amid strained relations with Morocco and persistent instability in Libya and the Sahel but is also driven by ongoing recapitalisation efforts. Growth in 2024 was more moderate, with funding reaching DZD2.9trn (USD21.4bn), but such uplifts mean that Algeria's budget as a proportion of GDP reached 8.2% in 2024 – the highest rate in the region. In addition to foreign acquisitions, Algeria is looking to continue developing its domestic defence capabilities, with forthcoming orders of Rheinmetall *Fuchs* 2 armoured personnel carriers to be assembled locally. Kit deliveries will take place between 2024 and 2028.

In contrast, **Egypt's** defence budget has fallen dramatically over the last two years, decreasing by 13.9% in real terms in 2023 and 17.0% in 2024. The budget is now estimated to be just USD3.8bn, down from USD5.4bn in 2022, with further reductions expected in 2025, though defence budgets will continue to be supplemented by the USD1.3bn in FMF from Washington. The cuts are likely due to the fiscal impact of the Israel–Hamas war. The 7 October 2023 attacks on Israel and the corresponding escalation of tensions in the Red Sea and Gulf affected Suez Canal transit receipts and – to a lesser extent – tourism, both of which are a significant source of revenue for the Egyptian government. Financial support from countries such as the UAE, and institutions like the IMF, World Bank and European Union, has provided some breathing space for Cairo as the macroeconomic challenges facing the economy have intensified in recent years.

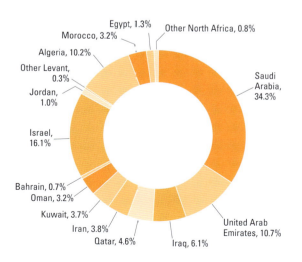

▲ Figure 28 **Middle East and North Africa: defence spending by country and sub-region, 2024**

▼ Figure 29 **Middle East and North Africa: defence spending** as % of GDP (average)

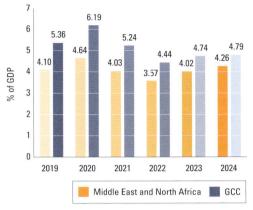

Note: Analysis excludes Lebanon, Libya, Palestinian Authority, Syria and Yemen.
Source: IISS analysis based on GDP data from IMF World Economic Outlook, October 2024 ©IISS

Defence industry

As tensions deepened, regional countries maintained focus on developing their defence industries, in efforts to decrease reliance on foreign suppliers while also increasing revenues and influence through arms exports. These dynamics were seen across the region, including Israel, which scaled up its defence industry to protect against potential embargoes and supply-chain disruptions. The war has pushed areas of Israel's defence-industrial base to capacity – notably ammunition production. For example, in May, Elbit Systems received contracts worth a total of USD760m to supply the Israeli MoD with munitions over a two-year period. However, as military operations continued, a further contract was awarded on 1 August 2024. Valued at USD340m, this covers a ten-year delivery period, including the construction of a new production line to support increased activity.

Research and development, particularly in counter-uninhabited aerial vehicle (UAV) technology, has been accelerated to meet the operational requirements of the Israel Defense Forces, in addition to the potential export market. Yet, despite the new operational demands, Israel's defence industry continued to bring in export revenues. According to the Israeli MoD, defence-export revenues reached just over USD13bn in 2023. This was an increase of USD500m on 2022 levels, and a new national record. Additionally, the MoD noted that 40% of sales were valued at more than USD100m, demonstrating that larger, high-value contracts were making up a significant portion of exports. Missiles, rockets and air-defence systems accounted for 36% of sales, including the sale of the *Arrow* 3 air-defence system to Germany and the *David's Sling* system to Finland. Radars and anti-aircraft systems comprised 11% of sales, as did weapons stations and launching systems.

In parallel, changes in US funding are also driving the co-location of production in the US. For example, the Off-Shore Procurement programme – under which up to a quarter of Israel's FMF grant can be used to buy Israeli-made equipment – began its planned phase-out in 2024. This followed gradual reductions in 2022 and 2023, from USD785m to USD775m respectively. Cuts will continue until the programme is phased out in 2028. Key programmes, including the *Roem* 155mm self-propelled artillery system, have begun moving to the US to ensure compliance with new funding processes.

Major developments also took place in Saudi Arabia and the UAE though their emphasis differed, with Saudi looking to localise defence capabilities, while the UAE looked abroad for growth. In line with the country's Vision 2030 strategy, in October 2023, Saudi's General Authority for Defence Development invested SAR664m (USD177m) through Saudi Arabian Military Industries (SAMI) – the national defence conglomerate – to develop Software Defined Radio systems and intelligence, surveillance and reconnaissance capabilities for counter-UAV systems. Similarly, in February 2024, Saudi authorities concluded an ammunition-manufacturing localisation agreement with India's Munitions India Limited, with a second contract with South Korea's LIG Nex1 for ground-based air-defence systems, also including localisation requirements. These deals expand on SAMI's success in localising maintenance, repair and overhaul capabilities, as do a raft of other February 2024 agreements that support the creation of the SAMI Industrial Complex for Land Systems Based in Al Kharj, the complex will assist manufacturing and future equipment integration. Also in February, the Kingdom's final *Hawk* advanced training aircraft, fitted with local components, rolled off the assembly line in Dhahran.

Such successes have contributed towards the Kingdom's goal of reaching 50% localisation of defence spending on equipment and services by 2030, though there are different estimates on the progress reached so far against this target. The Vision 2030 Annual Report for 2030, released in early 2024, stated that the level had reached 10.4% in 2023, while the then-SAMI CEO, Walid Abukhaled, said in November 2023 that the country had reached a localisation rate of approximately 15%. However, in November 2024, the governor of the General Authority for Military Industries, Ahmad Al-Ohali, said that the localisation rate at the end of 2023 was 19.35%.

As Saudi's defence-industrial base expanded, the UAE's consolidated, as key players sought to streamline operations, boost profitability and seek further internationalisation. National defence conglomerate EDGE Group remains the country's leading defence company, consolidating its position by absorbing the Strategic Development Fund – a venture-investment organisation – into its wider corporate structure in November 2023, as well as adding the International Golden Group (IGG) portfolio to its books in January 2024. Prior to its incorporation into EDGE, the IGG was the UAE's leading agent for high-end defence supplies, with the move allowing EDGE to offer more complete end-to-end services. In 2023, EDGE achieved a total order intake of over USD5bn which included orders for three corvettes for the Angolan Navy, and for MANSUP and MANSUP-ER anti-ship missiles for the Brazilian Navy. Contracts were also signed to supply an ammunition-production line to Indonesia's Pindad; an agreement to produce and integrate smart weapons with Azerbaijan; and one to develop aerospace and guided-weapons systems with Turkish industry. EDGE also ventured into space technologies, in September 2024, through a new firm called FADA. The company will be involved in developing and manufacturing satellite platforms and payloads and inherits the UAE Space Agency's *Sirb* (Flock) programme to implement a constellation of three fully IP-owned synthetic aperture radar satellites.

Egypt's efforts at revitalising its moribund defence-industrial base began to show signs of progress throughout 2024, as major procurement programmes began to move into the delivery phase. Key to these are naval and artillery projects. Alexandria Shipyard launched the first locally built ThyssenKrupp Marine Systems (TKMS) MEKO A200 frigate in December 2023. Named ENS *Al-Jabbar*, it is the fourth vessel acquired by the Egyptian Navy under a 2018 deal with TKMS. The first three vessels were built in Germany, with the fourth being built under licence over a two-year period. Egypt's acquisition of Hanwha K9A1 *Thunder* 155mm self-propelled artillery pieces from South Korea also includes localisation objectives.

Meanwhile, in Morocco the government continued to allocate defence funds specifically to help create a defence industry. Morocco's selection of the Tata Advanced Systems 8x8 Wheeled Armoured Platform (WhAP) further cemented defence-equipment ties with India, following on from the 2023 delivery of 92 LPTA 6x6 military trucks from the manufacturer. As part of the WhAP acquisition, a localised-production agreement was signed in September 2024, which will involve the manufacture of vehicles at a new site to be constructed in Casablanca. Potential exports to other markets from the Casablanca facility are also being considered. Other industrial developments have supported recent acquisitions and capability upgrades. Israel's BlueBird Aero Systems has reportedly opened a UAV-manufacturing facility in the country, and Morocco's acquisition of *Ofek* 13 surveillance satellites from Israel Aerospace Industries, as reported in the specialist press, would help to develop Morocco's space-based sensing and research capabilities, within the context of agreements signed in 2022.

Figure 30 **Middle East and North Africa: arms procurement and defence-industrial trends, 2024**

SURGE IN GULF STATES' UNINHABITED AERIAL VEHICLE (UAV) PROCUREMENT

Gulf states have sought to acquire armed UAVs since the United States demonstrated their effectiveness in the early 2000s. However, US reluctance to sell these UAVs allowed China to fill that vacuum. Beijing sold the *Wing Loong* I to the UAE around 2010 and then to Saudi Arabia a few years later. China built on that success with further UAV sales to the two countries, as well as to Oman. More recently, Turkiye has become the Gulf states' new preferred supplier, driven by frustration with some of the Chinese equipment. Turkish UAVs also gained traction because they have been extensively used in combat, including in Libya, Azerbaijan's conflict with Armenia, and Syria. Turkiye has also capitalised on its ability to deliver equipment quickly. Until around 2017, only the UAE and Saudi Arabia in the Arabian Peninsula had bought UAVs, but since then, Kuwait, Oman and Qatar have also ordered Turkish or Chinese UAVs, albeit in lower numbers. Meanwhile, Saudi Arabia awarded Turkiye's Baykar an approximately USD3 billion contract for UAVs in 2023, Ankara's largest-ever export deal. The UAE alone has placed orders for around 500 UAVs in recent years. Those include deals with Baykar for 60 *Bayraktar TB2* medium and 60 *Bayraktar Akinci* heavy UAVs, and with Swiss-headquartered Anavia to supply 200 rotary-wing UAVs. International Golden Group and ADASI, subsidiaries of Emirati defence conglomerate EDGE Group, are also on contract for uninhabited systems. Washington approved the possible sale of MQ-9B UAVs to the UAE in 2020 along with related weapons, although the status of this USD2.97bn deal is unclear.

UAE DIVERSIFICATION IN WEAPONS SUPPLIERS

Traditionally, the UAE has relied on US and European suppliers for its defence equipment needs. But during the past few years, the UAE has aggressively diversified its network of suppliers to include countries predominantly in Asia. In 2021, it purchased around 12 K239 *Chunmoo* self-propelled multiple rocket launchers from South Korea, followed in 2022 by the USD3.2bn acquisition of the *Cheongung* Block-2 surface-to-air missile system. From Indonesia, it purchased a USD408 million landing platform dock able to carry 500 troops, tanks, helicopters and small boats. At the Dubai Airshow 2023, the UAE's defence ministry confirmed it had closed a contract with China's CATIC to purchase 12 L-15 advanced trainers, with an option for an additional 36. Turkish UAV manufacturer Baykar reportedly inked deals with the UAE to sell it 60 *Bayraktar* TB2 and 60 *Bayraktar Akinci* UAVs sometime in 2022–23. Satellite imagery revealed that the UAE had deployed the *Barak* LRAD air-defence system in 2022. Reuters reported in September 2022 that Israel had agreed to sell the Rafael *Spyder* air-defence system. Other European countries also supply the UAE. Sweden sold it two Saab *GlobalEye* airborne early-warning and control aircraft, and Spain over 500 remotely operated weapon stations in 2023 to upgrade armoured vehicles in service with the UAE armed forces. Diversifying suppliers, along with developing a local defence industry, will help the UAE reduce end-user constraints and over-dependency on a single point of failure, all crucial in achieving greater strategic autonomy.

INTERNAL CONSOLIDATION OF AND ACQUISITIONS BY GULF DEFENCE CONGLOMERATES

National defence champions in the Gulf have conducted a wave of acquisitions and investments in recent years, both domestically and abroad. In 2019, Saudi Arabian Military Industries (SAMI) acquired a major stake in Aircraft Accessories and Components Company, a Saudi entity focusing on aircraft maintenance, repair and overhaul. A year later, SAMI announced it had formally acquired the Saudi-based Advanced Electronics Company. In 2022, the General Authority for Competition approved SAMI's acquisition of 51% of Saudi Rotorcraft Support Company. At the 2024 World Defense Show, former SAMI CEO Walid Abukhaled said that SAMI intended to acquire 100% of Alsalam Aerospace Industries and that the contract was almost completed. Qatar's Barzan Holdings has invested in US-based Electra.aero and SpinLaunch, as well as UK-based Aeralis. Electra.aero is developing electric, short take-off and landing aircraft, whereas SpinLaunch aims to launch satellites into space without rockets. As for Aeralis, it is developing a modular military training jet. Barzan also owns 49% of Turkish armoured-vehicle manufacturer BMC and has joint ventures with international partners like Rheinmetall. EDGE Group has been the most active, having conducted at least 13 acquisitions since it was established in 2019. Domestically, the conglomerate absorbed all other major state-owned defence companies, including Etimad Holding, Trust International Group, and International Golden Group. It also assumed full ownership of OryxLabs and the Strategic Development Fund, an investment firm focused on strategic technologies. Internationally, it has invested in or acquired Swiss VTOL-manufacturer Anavia, Estonian UGV company Milrem Robotics, Brazilian Condor Non-Lethal Technologies, Israeli air-traffic-management company Highlander, Polish light-jet developer Flaris, Brazilian smart-weapons and high-tech-systems specialist SIATT, and Jordanian UAV developer MARS Robotics. These countries are bringing disparate defence companies under one roof to integrate and streamline business processes. In addition to consolidating capabilities, it makes it easier to direct efforts and be strategic in developing the local defence industry. Given their bigger size, these conglomerates can also relate to major foreign defence companies on a more equal footing.

Figure 31 Saudi Arabia: defence industry

In 1953, Saudi Arabia established the Military Industries Corporation as a state-owned enterprise dedicated to producing ammunition, firearms and armoured vehicles. The late 1980s saw the creation of several other defence companies, including Advanced Electronics Co. (AEC), Aircraft Accessories and Components Co. (AACC) and Alsalam, often in partnership with foreign defence firms as part of major procurement offset agreements. With the launch of Vision 2030 in 2016, the Kingdom decided to channel its efforts into developing a strong and sustainable domestic defence industry, aiming to localise 50% of defence expenditure by 2030. To achieve this, it established Saudi Arabian Military Industries (SAMI) in 2017, a defence company owned by the Public Investment Fund and tasked with the development of the Saudi defence industry. Since 2017, SAMI has formed as many as ten joint ventures (JVs) with original equipment manufacturers to facilitate technology transfers, has absorbed several existing Saudi defence companies and is in the process of building production facilities for ammunition and armoured vehicles. Despite receiving significant financial backing, SAMI has struggled to export its products and to develop an attractive portfolio of locally produced defence systems. In addition to SAMI, several other organisations shape the defence landscape. The General Authority for Military Industries (GAMI) plays a key role as a regulator of the defence industry, while the General Authority for Defense Development (GADD) drives R&D efforts. At sea, a new entity called SOFON is poised to become the Kingdom's champion for the navy and marine industry, with large shipbuilding facilities in Ras Al-Khair. Furthermore, uninhabited aerial vehicle (UAV) manufacturing is rapidly expanding through both domestic initiatives and partnerships with foreign companies such as Türkiye's Baykar.

Timeline of defence localisation programmes in Saudi Arabia

Feb 2015	Saudi Arabia orders a second batch of 22 BAE Systems *Hawk* Mk165 training aircraft, with final assembly to be completed locally.
Apr 2018	Zamil Offshore Services concludes a deal with France's Constructions Mécaniques de Normandie (CMN) for the supply of 39 HSI 32 *Interceptor*s to Saudi Arabia, with CMN constructing 21 vessels and Zamil Offshore Services assembling the remainder in Saudi Arabia. The contract is subsequently extended to 58 vessels, with CMN building 31 and Zamil 27.
Feb 2021	Emirati company Nimr signs an agreement with SAMI to explore opportunities to manufacture the *Jais* 4×4 vehicle in Saudi Arabia. In March 2022, Nimr signs a manufacturing licence agreement with SAMI to transfer technology and enable the production of the *Jais* 4×4 in Saudi Arabia.
Mar 2021	Italian company Elsel signs an agreement with Saudi company Wahaj to jointly develop Elsel's *Livet* remote-controlled weapons station.
Mar 2022	China Electronics Technology Group Corporation signs an agreement with Saudi company ACES for knowledge transfer to locally manufacture UAV payload systems.
Mar 2022	Switzerland's Rheinmetall Air Defence and Saudi Arabia's MAZ Group form Radarabia, a joint venture that aims to manufacture and maintain air-defence systems in Saudi Arabia.
Feb 2024	Lockheed Martin awards a contract to Arabian International Company for Steel Structures to localise the manufacturing of THAAD missile round pallets in Saudi Arabia and to Middle East Propulsion Company to localise the production of THAAD interceptor canisters.
2024	UK-based New Technologies Global Systems signs an agreement with Saudi company Eraf to localise the manufacturing of the *Alakran* mobile mortar system in Saudi Arabia.
2024	TRD Singapore signs an agreement with Saudi company Rakaa Holding to create a JV called TRD Middle East Industry Co. The JV will develop the *Orion*-H9 soft-kill counter-UAV system in Saudi Arabia. TRD Singapore has also said it is looking to localise its other man-portable systems, such as the *Orion*-D C-UAS jammer and the mobile *Orion* C2 system.
2024	Munitions India signs an agreement with Nadrah Trading Company valued at over SAR1 billion (USD266.67 million) to set up a nanotechnology factory and localise ammunition production in Saudi Arabia.
2024	South Africa's Milkor says it received approval to fully assemble and manufacture the *Milkor* 380 armed UAV in Saudi Arabia if an acquisition goes ahead.
Mar	South Korea's Kia Corporation signs an MoU with SAMI Land Systems to build light tactical vehicles through collaboration, research and development.

Source: IISS

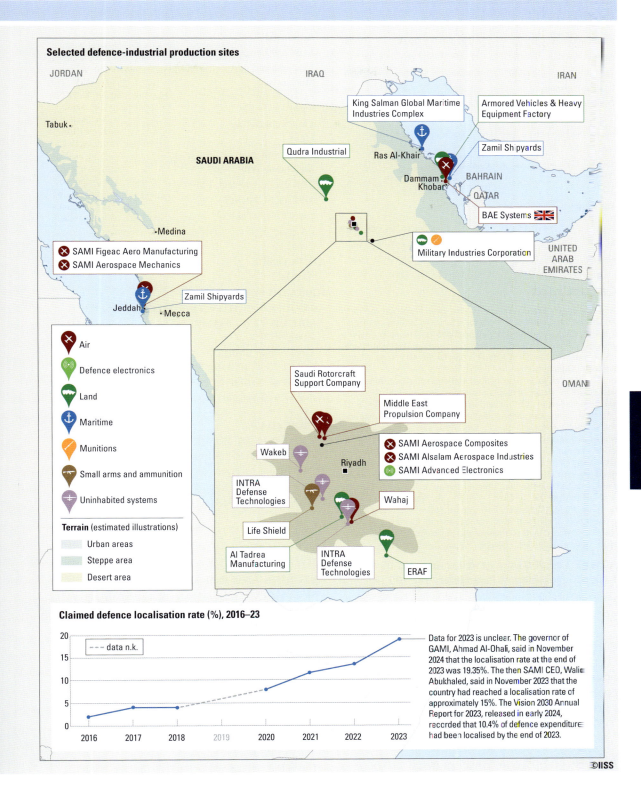

Algeria ALG

Algerian Dinar DZD		2023	2024	2025
GDP	DZD	32.6trn	35.6trn	38.3trn
	USD	240bn	260bn	264bn
Real GDP growth	%	4.1	3.8	3.0
Def bdgt	DZD	2.49trn	2.93trn	
	USD	18.3bn	21.4bn	

Real-terms defence budget trend (USDbn, constant 2015)
17.6
4.09
2008 — 2016 — 2024

Population	47,022,473					
Age	0–14	15–19	20–24	25–29	30–64	65 plus
Male	15.8%	4.0%	3.2%	3.3%	21.1%	3.4%
Female	15.0%	3.8%	3.0%	3.2%	20.7%	3.5%

Capabilities

Algeria's armed forces are among the best equipped in North Africa. The armed forces' primary roles relate to securing territorial integrity, internal security and regional stability. The army retains a key political position following its role in ending Abdelaziz Bouteflika's presidency in 2019. Algeria is part of the AU's North African Regional Capability Standby Force, hosting the force's logistics base. A November 2020 constitutional change allows Algeria to participate in UN peacekeeping missions. Tensions with Morocco, which increased in 2021, have persisted into 2024. In 2024, a trilateral regional cooperation initiative was agreed with Tunisia and the Tripoli-based Libyan government. Army and air force inventories consist of a core of modern, primarily Russian-sourced equipment, though China also supplied equipment, including armed UAVs and self-propelled artillery. Security cooperation with China could deepen after an agreement in 2024. The extent to which the Russia-Ukraine war has affected the supply of spare parts is unclear, though the air force received new training aircraft and self-propelled SAM systems from Russia. Algiers has recapitalised around half of its fixed-wing combat-aircraft inventory and the navy has invested in its submarine and frigate fleet. Algeria is starting to develop a domestic defence industry.

ACTIVE 139,000 (Army 110,000 Navy 15,000 Air 14,000) **Gendarmerie & Paramilitary 187,200**

Conscript liability 12 months

RESERVE 150,000 (Army 150,000) to age 50

ORGANISATIONS BY SERVICE

Space
EQUIPMENT BY TYPE
SATELLITES 4
  COMMUNICATIONS 1 ALCOMSAT
  ISR 3 ALSAT

Army 35,000; 75,000 conscript (total 110,000)
FORCES BY ROLE
6 Mil Regions
MANOEUVRE
  Armoured
    2 (1st & 8th) armd div (3 tk regt, 1 mech regt, 1 arty gp)
    2 indep armd bde
  Mechanised
    2 (12th & 40th) mech div (1 tk regt, 3 mech regt, 1 arty gp)
    4 indep mech bde
  Light
    1 indep mot bde
  Air Manoeuvre
    1 AB div (4 para regt; 1 SF regt)
COMBAT SUPPORT
  2 arty bn
  1 AT regt
  4 engr bn
AIR DEFENCE
  7 AD bn

EQUIPMENT BY TYPE
ARMOURED FIGHTING VEHICLES
  MBT 1,485: 270 T-55AMV; 290 T-62; 325 T-72M1/M1M; ε600 T-90SA
  TSV 26+: 13+ BMPT; 13+ BMPT-62
  RECCE 70: 44 AML-60; 26 BRDM-2
  IFV 980: ε220 BMP-2; 760 BMP-2M with 9M133 *Kornet* (RS-AT-14 *Spriggan*)
  APC 1,305
    APC (T) VP-6
    APC (W) 1,305: 250 BTR-60; 150 BTR-80; 150 OT-64; 55 M3 Panhard; ε600 *Fuchs* 2; 100 *Fahd*
    PPV some *Maxxpro*
  AUV Nimr *Ajban*; Nimr *Ajban* LRSOV
ENGINEERING & MAINTENANCE VEHICLES
  AEV IMR-2
  ARV BREM-1
  VLB MTU-20
  MW M58 MICLIC
ANTI-TANK/ANTI-INFRASTRUCTURE
  SP 92: 64 9P133 with 9M113 *Konkurs* (RS-AT-5 *Spandrel*); 28 9P163-3 *Kornet*-EM (RS-AT-14 *Spriggan*); BTR-60 with 9M133 *Kornet* (RS-AT-14 *Spriggan*); BTR-80 with 9M133 *Kornet* (RS-AT-14 *Spriggan*)
  MSL • MANPATS 9K11 *Malyutka* (RS-AT-3 *Sagger*); 9K111 *Fagot* (RS-AT-4 *Spigot*); 9K111-1 *Konkurs* (RS-AT-5 *Spandrel*); 9K115-2 *Metis*-M1 (RS-AT-13); 9K135 *Kornet*-E (RS-AT-14 *Spriggan*); Luch *Skif*; Milan
  RCL 180: **82mm** 120 B-10; **107mm** 60 B-11
ARTILLERY 1,127
  SP 224: **122mm** 140 2S1 *Gvozdika*; **152mm** 30 2S3 *Akatsiya*; **155mm** ε54 PLZ-45
  TOWED 393: **122mm** 345: 160 D-30 (incl some truck mounted SP); 25 D-74; 100 M-1931/37; 60 M-30; **130mm**

10 M-46; **152mm** 20 M-1937 (ML-20); **155mm** 18 PLL-01
MRL 180: **122mm** 48 BM-21 *Grad*; **140mm** 48 BM-14; **220mm** 36: 18+ SR5; ε18 TOS-1A; **240mm** 30 BM-24; **300mm** 18 9A52 *Smerch*
MOR 330+: **82mm** 150 M-37; **120mm** 120 M-1943; W86; **SP 120mm** Nimr *Hafeet* with SM5; SM4; W86 (SP); **160mm** 60 M-1943

SURFACE-TO-SURFACE MISSILE LAUNCHERS
SRBM 12+ *Iskander*-E

AIR DEFENCE
SAM
Point-defence 68+: ε48 9K33M *Osa* (RS-SA-8B *Gecko*); ε20 9K31 *Strela*-1 (RS-SA-9 *Gaskin*); 9K32 *Strela*-2 (RS-SA-7A/B *Grail*)‡; QW-2 (CH-SA-8)
SPAAGM 30mm 38 96K6 *Pantsir*-S1 (RS-SA-22 *Greyhound*); *Pantsir*-SM
GUNS ε425
SP 23mm ε225 ZSU-23-4
TOWED 200: **14.5mm** 100: 60 ZPU-2; 40 ZPU-4; **23mm** 100 ZU-23-2

Navy ε15,000
EQUIPMENT BY TYPE
SUBMARINES • SSK 6:
2 *Paltus* (FSU Project 877 (*Kilo*)) with 6 single 533mm TT with TEST-71ME HWT
4 *Varshavyanka* (RUS Project 636.1 (Improved *Kilo*)) with 6 single 533mm TT with 3M14E *Klub*-S (RS-SS-N-30B) LACM/3M54E1/E *Klub*-S (RS-SS-N-27A/B) AShM (*Klub*-S AShM variant unclear)/TEST-71ME HWT

PRINCIPAL SURFACE COMBATANTS • FRIGATES 5
FFGHM 5:
3 *Adhafer* (C-28A) with 2 quad lnchr with C-802A AShM, 1 octuple lnchr with FM-90 (CH-SA-N-4) SAM, 2 triple 324mm ASTT, 2 Type-730B (H/PJ-12) CIWS, 1 76mm gun (capacity 1 hel)
2 *Erradii* (MEKO A200AN) with 2 octuple lnchrs with RBS15 Mk3 AShM, 4 8-cell VLS with *Umkhonto*-IR SAM, 2 twin 324mm TT with MU90 LWT, 1 127mm gun (capacity 1 *Super Lynx* 300)

PATROL AND COASTAL COMBATANTS 29
CORVETTES 4
FSGM 1 *Al-Moutassadi* (PRC Type-056 mod) with 2 twin lnchr with C-802 (CH-SS-N-6) AShM, 1 octuple GMLS with FL-3000N (HHQ-10 (CH-SA-N-17)) SAM, 2 A/S mor, 1 76mm gun, 1 hel landing platform
FS 3 *Mourad Rais* (FSU Project 1159 (*Koni*)) with 2 twin 533mm TT, 2 RBU 6000 *Smerch* 2 A/S mor, 2 twin 76mm gun
PCGM 3 *Rais Hamidou* (FSU Project 1234E (*Nanuchka* II)) with 4 quad lnchr with 3M24E *Uran*-E (RS-SS-N-25 *Switchblade*) AShM, 1 twin lnchr with 4K33 *Osa*-M (RS-SA-N-4 *Gecko*) SAM, 1 AK630 CIWS, 1 twin 57mm gun
PCG 4:
3 *Djebel Chenoua* with 2 twin lnchr with C-802 (CH-SS-N-6) AShM, 1 AK630 CIWS, 1 76mm gun;
1 *Rais Hassen Barbiar* (*Djebel Chenoua* mod) with 2 twin lnchr with C-802 (CH-SS-N-6) AShM, 1 Type-730 (H/PJ-12) CIWS, 1 76mm gun
PBFG 9 Project 205 (ex-FSU *Osa* II)† with 4 single lnchr with P-20U (RS-SS-N-2B *Styx*) AShM
PB 9 *Kebir* with 1 76mm gun

MINE WARFARE • MINE COUNTERMEASURES 3
MCC 3 *El-Kasseh* (ITA *Gaeta* mod)

AMPHIBIOUS
PRINCIPAL AMPHIBIOUS SHIPS 1
LHD 1 *Kalaat Beni Abbes* with 1 8-cell *Sylver* A50 VLS with *Aster* 15 SAM, 1 76mm gun (capacity 5 med hel; 3 LCVP; 15 MBT; 350 troops)
LANDING SHIPS • LST 2 *Kalaat beni Hammad* (capacity 7 MBT; 240 troops) with 1 med hel landing platform
LANDING CRAFT • LCVP 3

LOGISTICS AND SUPPORT 4
AGS 2: 1 *Al-Masseh* (FRA OSV 95); 1 *El Idrissi*
AX 1 *Daxin* with 2 AK230 CIWS, 1 76mm gun, 1 hel landing platform
AXS 1 *El Mellah*

Naval Infantry ε7,000
FORCES BY ROLE
SPECIAL FORCES
1 cdo bn
MANOEUVRE
Amphibious
8 naval inf bn
EQUIPMENT BY TYPE
ARMOURED FIGHTING VEHICLES
APC • APC(W) BTR-80

Naval Aviation
EQUIPMENT BY TYPE
HELICOPTERS
MRH 9: 3 AW139 (SAR); 6 *Super Lynx* 300
SAR 9: 5 AW101 SAR; 4 *Super Lynx* Mk130

Coastal Defence
FORCES BY ROLE
COASTAL DEFENCE
1 AShM regt with 4K51 *Rubezh* (RS-SSC-3 *Styx*); CM-302 (YJ-12E)
EQUIPMENT BY TYPE
COASTAL DEFENCE
AShM 4K51 *Rubezh* (RS-SSC-3 *Styx*); CM-302 (YJ-12E)

Coast Guard ε500
EQUIPMENT BY TYPE
PATROL AND COASTAL COMBATANTS 74
PBF 6 *Baglietto* 20
PB 68: 6 *Baglietto Mangusta*; 12 *Jebel Antar*; 40 *Dezer*; 4 *El Mounkid*; 6 *Kebir* with 1 76mm gun

LOGISTICS AND SUPPORT 9
  AR 1 El Mourafek
  ARS 3 El Moundjid
  AXL 5 El Mouderrib (PRC Chui-E) (2 more in reserve†)

Air Force 14,000
FORCES BY ROLE
FIGHTER
  4 sqn with MiG-29S/UB Fulcrum
FIGHTER/GROUND ATTACK
  3 sqn with Su-30MKA Flanker H
GROUND ATTACK
  2 sqn with Su-24M/MK Fencer D
ELINT
  1 sqn with Beech 1900D
MARITIME PATROL
  2 sqn with Beech 200T/300 King Air
ISR
  1 sqn with Su-24MR Fencer E*
TANKER
  1 sqn with Il-78 Midas
TRANSPORT
  1 sqn with C-130H/H-30 Hercules; L-100-30
  1 sqn with C295M
  1 sqn with Gulfstream IV-SP; Gulfstream V
  1 sqn with Il-76MD/TD Candid
TRAINING
  2 sqn with Z-142
  1 sqn with Yak-130 Mitten*
  2 sqn with L-39C Albatros; L-39ZA Albatros*
  1 hel sqn with PZL Mi-2 Hoplite
ATTACK HELICOPTER
  3 sqn with Mi-24 Hind (one re-equipping with Mi-28NE Havoc)
TRANSPORT HELICOPTER
  1 sqn with AS355 Ecureuil
  5 sqn with Mi-171Sh Hip; Mi-8 Hip
  1 sqn with Ka-27PS Helix D; Ka-32T Helix
COMBAT/ISR UAV
  1 sqn with ASN-209; CH-3; CH-4; Seeker II; Wing Loong II; WJ-700; Yabhon Flash-20; Yabhon United-40
AIR DEFENCE
  3 ADA bde
  3 SAM regt with S-125M/M1 Pechora-M/M1 (RS-SA-3 Goa); 2K12 Kub (RS-SA-6 Gainful); S-300PMU2 (RS-SA-20 Gargoyle)

EQUIPMENT BY TYPE
AIRCRAFT 185 combat capable
  FTR 22 MiG-29S/UB Fulcrum; (11 MiG-25 PDS/RU Foxbat in store)
  FGA 73: 14 MiG-29M/M2 Fulcrum; 59 Su-30MKA Flanker H
  ATK 33 Su-24M/MK Fencer D
  ISR 3 Su-24MR Fencer E*; (4 MiG-25 RBSh Foxbat D in store)
  TKR 6 Il-78 Midas
  TPT 67: **Heavy** 11: 3 Il-76MD Candid B; 8 Il-76TD Candid; **Medium** 18: 8 C-130H Hercules; 6 C-130H-30 Hercules; 2 C-130J Hercules; 2 L-100-30; **Light** 32: 3 Beech C90B King Air; 5 Beech 200T King Air; 6 Beech 300 King Air; 12 Beech 1900D (electronic surv); 5 C295M; 1 F-27 Friendship; **PAX** 6: 1 A340; 4 Gulfstream IV-SP; 1 Gulfstream V
  TRG 101: 36 L-39ZA Albatros*; 7 L-39C Albatros; 18 Yak-130 Mitten*; 40 Z-142
HELICOPTERS
  ATK 72: 30 Mi-24 Hind; 42+ Mi-28NE/UB Havoc
  SAR 3 Ka-27PS Helix D
  MRH 11: 8 AW139 (SAR); 3 Bell 412EP
  TPT 136: **Heavy** 14 Mi-26T2 Halo; **Medium** 78: 4 Ka-32T Helix; 39 Mi-171Sh Hip; 35 Mi-8 Hip; **Light** 44: 8 AW119KE Koala; 8 AS355 Ecureuil; 28 PZL Mi-2 Hoplite
UNINHABITED AERIAL VEHICLES
  CISR • Heavy CH-3; CH-4; Wing Loong II; WJ-700; Yabhon United-40
  ISR • Medium ASN-209; Seeker II; Yabhon Flash-20
AIR DEFENCE • SAM
  Long-range 32+ S-300PMU2 (RS-SA-20 Gargoyle)
  Medium-range 20+ 9K317 Buk-M2E (RS-SA-17 Grizzly)
  Short-range 36+: 2K12 Kvadrat (RS-SA-6 Gainful); 9K331MK Tor-M2K (RS-SA-15 Gauntlet); 12 S-125M; Pechora-M (RS-SA-3 Goa); 24 S-125M1 Pechora-M1 (RS-SA-3 Goa)
AIR-LAUNCHED MISSILES
  AAM • IR R-60 (RS-AA-8 Aphid); R-73 (RS-AA-11A Archer); **IR/SARH** R-40/46 (RS-AA-6 Acrid); R-23/24 (RS-AA-7 Apex); R-27 (RS-AA-10 Alamo); **ARH** R-77 (RS-AA-12A Adder)
  ASM Kh-25 (RS-AS-10 Karen); Kh-29 (RS-AS-14 Kedge); Kh-59ME (RS-AS-18 Kazoo); ZT-35 Ingwe; 9M120 Ataka (RS-AT-9)
  AShM Kh-31A (RS-AS-17B Krypton)
  ARM Kh-25MP (RS-AS-12A Kegler); Kh-31P (RS-AS-17A Krypton)
BOMBS • Electro-optical guided KAB-500KR/OD

Air Commando Fusiliers
FORCES BY ROLE
SPECIAL FORCES
  2 cdo bn
MANOEUVRE
  Other
  6 sy bn

Gendarmerie & Paramilitary ε187,200

Gendarmerie 20,000
Ministry of Defence control; 6 regions
EQUIPMENT BY TYPE

ARMOURED FIGHTING VEHICLES
  RECCE AML-60
  APC • **APC (W)** 210: 100 TH-390 *Fahd*; 110 Panhard M3
HELICOPTERS • **TPT** • **Light** 12+: 12 AW109; Some PZL Mi-2 *Hoplite*

National Security Forces 16,000
Directorate of National Security. Equipped with small arms

Republican Guard 1,200
EQUIPMENT BY TYPE
ARMOURED FIGHTING VEHICLES
  RECCE AML-60

Legitimate Defence Groups ε150,000
Self-defence militia, communal guards (60,000)

DEPLOYMENT
DEMOCRATIC REPUBLIC OF THE CONGO: UN • MONUSCO 1

Bahrain BHR

Bahraini Dinar BHD		2023	2024	2025
GDP	BHD	17.3bn	18.0bn	18.6bn
	USD	46.1bn	47.8bn	49.5bn
Real GDP growth	%	3.0	3.0	3.2
Def bdgt [a]	BHD	527m	527m	
	USD	1.40bn	1.40bn	
FMA (US)	USD	4.00m	3.25m	1.00m

[a] Excludes funds allocated to the Ministry of the Interior and the National Security Agency

Real-terms defence budget trend (USDbn, constant 2015)

Population	1,566,888				
Age	0–14	15–19	20–24	25–29	30–64	65 plus
Male	9.2%	3.4%	4.7%	6.3%	34.3%	2.2%
Female	8.9%	3.0%	3.3%	3.8%	18.9%	2.1%

Capabilities
Bahrain occupies a strategic position between regional rivals Iran and Saudi Arabia. The armed forces are responsible for territorial defence and internal-security support. Bahrain's most critical security relationship is with Saudi Arabia, but it also has strong defence ties with the UK and US. The country has been a major non-NATO US ally since 2002 and the US 5th Fleet is headquartered in Bahrain, as is the US-led Combined Maritime Forces (CMF) and the GCC Unified Maritime Operations Center, while the UK has a naval support facility. Bahrain has periodically commanded CMF task forces. The armed forces carried out a limited expeditionary deployment in support of the Saudi-led intervention in Yemen and have also deployed in Somalia. Bahrain signed a security cooperation agreement with Israel in 2022 and a Comprehensive Security Integration and Prosperity Agreement with the US in 2023. Bahrain is modernising critical capabilities, including with F-16 fighters and *Patriot* air- and missile-defences, the latter housed at a new base opened in 2024. The country is also enhancing its combat rotorcraft fleet, frigate capacity and potentially its tank fleet. The armed forces have organic maintenance support, but there is little in the way of a defence-industrial base beyond the limited maintenance support provided by the Arab Shipbuilding and Repair Yard.

ACTIVE 8,200 (Army 6,000 Navy 700 Air 1,500)
Gendarmerie & Paramilitary 11,260

ORGANISATIONS BY SERVICE

Army 6,000
FORCES BY ROLE
SPECIAL FORCES
  1 SF bn
MANOEUVRE
  Armoured
  1 armd bde(-) (1 recce bn, 1 armd bn)
  Mechanised
  1 inf bde (2 mech bn, 1 mot bn)
  Light
  1 (Amiri) gd bn
COMBAT SUPPORT
  1 arty bde (1 hy arty bty, 2 med arty bty, 1 lt arty bty, 1 MRL bty)
  1 engr coy
COMBAT SERVICE SUPPORT
  1 log coy
  1 tpt coy
  1 med coy
EQUIPMENT BY TYPE
ARMOURED FIGHTING VEHICLES
  MBT ε50 M60A3
  RECCE 22 AML-90
  IFV 67: 25 YPR-765 PRI; 42 AIFV-B-C25
  APC 303+
    APC (T) 303: 300 M113A2; 3 AIFV-B
    APC (W) *Arma* 6×6
  AUV M-ATV
ENGINEERING & MAINTENANCE VEHICLES
  ARV 53 *Fahd* 240
ANTI-TANK/ANTI-INFRASTRUCTURE
  MSL
    SP 5+: 5 AIFV-B-*Milan*; HMMWV with BGM-71A TOW; 9P163-3 *Kornet*-EM (RS-AT-14 *Spriggan*)
    MANPATS BGM-71A TOW; *Kornet*-EM (RS-AT-14 *Spriggan*)
  RCL 31: **106mm** 25 M40A1; **120mm** 6 MOBAT
ARTILLERY 119

SP 26: **155mm** 20 M109A5; **203mm** ε6 M110A2 (56 more in store)
TOWED 36: **105mm** 8 L118 Light Gun; **155mm** 28 M198
MRL 13: **220mm** 4 SR5; **227mm** 9 M270 MLRS
MOR 44: **81mm** 12 L16; **SP 81mm** 20 VAMTAC with EIMOS; **SP 120mm** 12 M113A2

SURFACE-TO-SURFACE MISSILE LAUNCHERS
SRBM • Conventional MGM-140A ATACMS (launched from M270 MLRS)

AIR DEFENCE
SAM
Point-defence 9K338 *Igla-S* (RS-SA-24 *Grinch*) (reported); FIM-92 *Stinger*; RBS-70

Navy 700
EQUIPMENT BY TYPE
PRINCIPAL SURFACE COMBATANTS • FRIGATES 1
FFGHM 1 *Sabha* (ex-US *Oliver Hazard Perry*) with 1 Mk 13 GMLS with RGM-84C *Harpoon* Block 1B AShM/SM-1MR Block VI SAM, 2 triple 324mm SVTT Mk 32 ASTT with Mk 46 LWT, 1 Mk 15 *Phalanx* Block 1B CIWS, 1 76mm gun (capacity 1 Bo-105 hel)

PATROL AND COASTAL COMBATANTS 25
PSO 1 *Al Zubara* (ex-UK *River* (OPV) Batch 1 (mod)) with 1 hel landing platform
PCFG 4 *Ahmed el Fateh* (GER Lurssen 45m) with 2 twin lnchr with MM40 *Exocet* AShM, 1 76mm gun
PCG 2 *Al Manama* (GER Lurssen 62m) with 2 twin lnchr with MM40 *Exocet* AShM, 2 76mm guns, 1 hel landing platform
PCF 5 *Al-Gurairiyah* (ex-US *Cyclone*)
PB 6: 2 *Al Jarim* (US *Swift* FPB-20); 2 *Al Riffa* (GER Lurssen 38m); 2 *Masnhoor* (US Swiftships 35m)
PBF 7 Mk V FPB

AMPHIBIOUS • LANDING CRAFT 9
LCM 7: 1 *Loadmaster*; 4 *Mashtan*; 2 *Dinar* (ADSB 42m)
LCVP 2 *Sea Keeper*

Naval Aviation
EQUIPMENT BY TYPE
HELICOPTERS • TPT • Light 2 Bo-105

Air Force 1,500
FORCES BY ROLE
FIGHTER
1 sqn with F-5E/F *Tiger* II
FIGHTER/GROUND ATTACK
2 sqn with F-16C/D Block 40/70 *Fighting Falcon*
TRANSPORT
1 (Royal) flt with B-737–800; B-767; B-747; BAe-146; Gulfstream II; Gulfstream IV; Gulfstream 450; Gulfstream 550; S-92A
TRAINING
1 sqn with *Hawk* Mk129*
1 sqn with T-67M *Firefly*

ATTACK HELICOPTER
2 sqn with AH-1E/F *Cobra*; AH-1Z *Viper*; TAH-1P *Cobra*
TRANSPORT HELICOPTER
1 sqn with Bell 212 (AB-212); Bell 412EP *Twin Huey*
1 sqn with UH-60M *Black Hawk*
1 (VIP) sqn with Bell 505 *Jet Ranger X*; Bo-105; S-70A *Black Hawk*; UH-60L *Black Hawk*
AIR DEFENCE
1 AD bn (1 ADA bty, 3 SAM bty)

EQUIPMENT BY TYPE
AIRCRAFT 44 combat capable
FTR 12: 8 F-5E *Tiger* II; 4 F-5F *Tiger* II
FGA 26: 16 F-16C Block 40 *Fighting Falcon*; 4 F-16D Block 40 *Fighting Falcon*; 4 F-16C Block 70 *Fighting Falcon*; 2 F-16D Block 70 *Fighting Falcon*
TPT 14: **Medium** 2 C-130J *Hercules*; **PAX** 12: 1 B-737-800 (VIP); 1 B-767 (VIP); 2 B-747 (VIP); 1 Gulfstream II (VIP); 1 Gulfstream IV (VIP); 1 Gulfstream 450 (VIP); 1 Gulfstream 550 (VIP); 2 BAe-146-RJ85 (VIP); 1 BAe-146-RJ100 (VIP); 1 BAe-146-RJ170 (VIP); (1 B-727 in store)
TRG 9: 6 *Hawk* Mk129*; 3 T-67M *Firefly*

HELICOPTERS
ATK 34: 10 AH-1E *Cobra*; 12 AH-1F *Cobra*; 12 AH-1Z *Viper*
MRH 2+ Bell 412EP *Twin Huey*
TPT 30: **Medium** 13: 3 S-70A *Black Hawk*; 1 S-92A (VIP); 1 UH-60L *Black Hawk*; 8 UH-60M *Black Hawk*; **Light** 17: 3 Bell 505 *Jet Ranger X*; 11 Bell 212 (AB-212); 3 Bo-105
TRG 6 TAH-1P *Cobra*

AIR DEFENCE
SAM 15+
Long-range 2 M903 *Patriot* PAC-3 MSE
Medium-range 6 MIM-23B I-*Hawk*
Short-range 7 *Crotale*
Point-defence 9K338 *Igla-S* (RS-SA-24 *Grinch*) (reported); FIM-92 *Stinger*; RBS-70
GUNS 24: **35mm** 12 GDF-003/-005; **40mm** 12 L/70

AIR-LAUNCHED MISSILES
AAM • IR AIM-9P *Sidewinder*; **SARH** AIM-7 *Sparrow*; **ARH** AIM-120B/C AMRAAM
ASM AGM-65D/G *Maverick*; *Cirit*; TOW
BOMBS • Laser-guided GBU-10/-12 *Paveway* II

Gendarmerie & Paramilitary ε11,260

Police 9,000
Ministry of Interior
EQUIPMENT BY TYPE
ARMOURED FIGHTING VEHICLES
APC • PPV Otokar ISV
AUV *Cobra*
HELICOPTERS
MRH 2 Bell 412 *Twin Huey*
ISR 2 Hughes 500
TPT • Light 1 Bo-105

National Guard ε2,000
FORCES BY ROLE
MANOEUVRE
Other
3 paramilitary bn
EQUIPMENT BY TYPE
ARMOURED FIGHTING VEHICLES
APC • APC (W) *Arma 6×6; Cobra*

Coast Guard ε260
Ministry of Interior
PATROL AND COASTAL COMBATANTS 60
PBF 26: 2 *Ares* 18; 3 *Response Boat-Medium* (RB-M); 4 *Jaris*; 6 *Saham*; 6 *Fajr*; 5 *Jarada*
PB 34: 6 *Haris*; 1 *Al Muharraq*; 10 *Deraa* (of which 4 *Halmatic* 20, 2 *Souter* 20, 4 *Rodman* 20); 10 *Saif* (of which 4 *Fairey Sword*, 6 *Halmatic* 160); ε7 *Hawar*
AMPHIBIOUS
LANDING CRAFT • LCU 1 *Loadmaster* II

FOREIGN FORCES
United Kingdom *Operation Kipion* 1,000; 1 FFGHM; 2 MCO; 2 MHO; 1 LSD; 1 naval facility
United States US Central Command: 4,500; 1 HQ (5th Fleet); 4 MCO; 1 ESB; 1 ASW sqn with 3 P-8A *Poseidon*; 2 SAM bty with M903 *Patriot* PAC-3 MSE

Egypt EGY

Egyptian Pound EGP		2023	2024	2025
GDP	EGP	10.2trn	13.8trn	17.5trn
	USD	394bn	380bn	346bn
Real GDP growth	%	3.8	2.7	4.1
Def bdgt	EGP	92.4bn	102bn	116bn
	USD	3.58bn	2.79bn	2.28bn
FMA (US)	USD	1.30bn	1.30bn	1.30bn

Real-terms defence budget trend (USDbn, constant 2015)

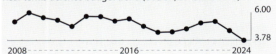

Population	111,247,248					
Age	0–14	15–19	20–24	25–29	30–64	65 plus
Male	17.4%	4.7%	4.2%	3.8%	18.5%	2.8%
Female	16.4%	4.4%	4.0%	3.6%	17.5%	2.8%

Capabilities

Egypt's armed forces are focused principally on maintaining territorial integrity and internal security, including tackling ISIS-affiliated groups in northern Sinai. The armed forces remain deeply involved in the civilian economy and retain a central role in internal politics. The US is a key partner and provides significant military assistance. Cairo has defence relations with Russia and other states, such as France and Italy, particularly regarding procurement. Relations are improving with Turkiye. Egypt hosts the annual multinational exercise *Bright Star*. The armed forces have a developing capacity to independently deploy abroad. It contributes to UN missions, has intervened militarily in Libya and supported the Saudi-led coalition in Yemen. In 2023, Egypt reportedly delivered military aid to the Sudanese government while engaging in Emirati-mediated negotiations with the Rapid Support Forces. There is tension with Ethiopia over the Grand Ethiopian Renaissance Dam, and Egypt signed a defence agreement with Somalia in 2024. Obsolete Soviet-era systems still dominate the armed forces' inventory. However, a recapitalisation programme has led to the addition of newer Western-origin and Russian equipment. Egypt will also acquire Turkish UAVs. The diversity of the inventory risks complicating military maintenance and sustainment. Egypt has an established defence industry, although it has heavily relied on license and co-production agreements with foreign companies.

ACTIVE 438,500 (Army 310,000 Navy 18,500 Air 30,000 Air Defence Command 80,000) Gendarmerie & Paramilitary 397,000

Conscription liability 12–36 months (followed by refresher training over a period of up to 9 years)

RESERVE 479,000 (Army 375,000 Navy 14,000 Air 20,000 Air Defence Command 70,000)

ORGANISATIONS BY SERVICE

Space
EQUIPMENT BY TYPE
SATELLITES 5
COMMUNICATIONS 1 TIBA-1
ISR 4: 1 *Egyptsat-A*; 2 *Horus* (reported); 1 *Mirsat-2*

Army ε310,000 (incl ε200,000 conscripts)
FORCES BY ROLE
SPECIAL FORCES
5 cdo gp
1 counter-terrorist unit
1 spec ops unit
MANOEUVRE
Armoured
4 armd div (2 armd bde, 1 mech bde, 1 arty bde)
4 indep armd bde
1 Republican Guard bde
Mechanised
8 mech div (1 armd bde, 2 mech bde, 1 arty bde)
4 indep mech bde
Light
2 indep inf bde
Air Manoeuvre
2 air mob bde
1 para bde
SURFACE-TO-SURFACE MISSILE
1 SRBM bde with FROG-7
1 SRBM bde with 9K72 *Elbrus* (RS-SS-1C *Scud-B*)

COMBAT SUPPORT
15 arty bde
6 engr bde (3 engr bn)
2 spec ops engr bn
6 salvage engr bn
24 MP bn
18 sigs bn

COMBAT SERVICE SUPPORT
36 log bn
27 med bn

EQUIPMENT BY TYPE
ARMOURED FIGHTING VEHICLES
MBT 2,480: 1,130 M1A1 *Abrams*; 300 M60A1; 850 M60A3; 200 T-62 (840 T-54/T-55; 300 T-62 all in store)
RECCE 412: 300 BRDM-2; 112 *Commando Scout*
IFV 690: 390 YPR-765 25mm; 300 BMP-1
APC 5,244+
  APC (T) 2,700: 2,000 M113A2/YPR-765 (incl variants); 500 BTR-50; 200 OT-62; SENA 200 (in test)
  APC (W) 1,560: 250 BMR-600P; 250 BTR-60; 410 *Fahd*-30/TH 390 *Fahd*; 650 *Walid*
  PPV 984+: 535 *Caiman*; some REVA III; some REVA V LWB; 360 RG-33L; 89 RG-33 HAGA (amb); ST-500; *Temsah* 2; *Temsah* 3
  AUV 173+: *Panthera* T6; 173 *Sherpa Light Scout*; ST-100

ENGINEERING & MAINTENANCE VEHICLES
ARV 367+: *Fahd* 240; BMR 3560.55; 12 *Maxxpro* ARV; 220 M88A1; 90 M88A2; M113 ARV; 45 M578; T-54/55 ARV
VLB KMM; MTU; MTU-20
MW *Aardvark* JFSU Mk4

ANTI-TANK/ANTI-INFRASTRUCTURE • MSL
SP 352+: 52 M901; 300 YPR-765 PRAT; HMMWV with TOW-2
MANPATS 9K11 *Malyutka* (RS-AT-3 *Sagger*) (incl BRDM-2); HJ-73; Luch *Corsar* (reported); *Milan*; *Stugna*-P (reported); TOW-2

ARTILLERY 4,468
SP 492+: **122mm** 124+ 124 SP 122; D-30 mod; **130mm** M-46 mod; **155mm** 368+: K9; 164 M109A2; 204 M109A5
TOWED 962: **122mm** 526: 190 D-30M; 36 M-1931/37; 300 M-30; **130mm** 420 M-46; **155mm** 16 GH-52
MRL 450: **122mm** 356 some ATS-59G; 96 BM-11; 60 BM-21; 50 *Sakr*-10; 50 *Sakr*-18; 100 *Sakr*-36; **130mm** 36 K136 *Kooryong*; **140mm** 32 BM-14; **227mm** 26 M270 MLRS; **240mm** (48 BM-24 in store)
MOR 2,564: **81mm** 50 M125A2; **82mm** 500; **SP 107mm** 100: 65 M106A1; 35 M106A2; **120mm** 1,848: 1,800 M-1943; 48 Brandt; **SP 120mm** 36 M1064A3; **160mm** 30 M-160

SURFACE-TO-SURFACE MISSILE LAUNCHERS
SRBM • Conventional 42+: 9 FROG-7; 24 *Sakr*-80; 9 9K72 *Elbrus* (RS-SS-1C *Scud*-B)

UNINHABITED AERIAL VEHICLES
ISR • Medium ASN-209; R4E-50 *Skyeye*

AIR DEFENCE
SAM 48+
  Medium-range 3+ IRIS-T SLM
  Point-defence *Ayn al-Saqr*; FIM-92 *Stinger*; 9K38 *Igla* (RS-SA-18 *Grouse*); 9K338 *Igla*-S (RS-SA-24 *Grinch*) (reported)
SPAAGM • 23mm 45 *Sinai*-23 with *Ayn al-Saqr*
GUNS 860
  SP 160: **23mm** 120 ZSU-23-4; **57mm** 40 ZSU-57-2
  TOWED 700: **14.5mm** 300 ZPU-4; **23mm** 200 ZU-23-2; **57mm** 200 S-60

Navy ε8,500 (incl 2,000 Coast Guard); 10,000 conscript (total 18,500)

EQUIPMENT BY TYPE
SUBMARINES • SSK 8
  4 Type-033 (PRC *Romeo*) with 8 single 533mm TT with UGM-84C *Harpoon* Block 1B AShM/Mk 37 HWT
  4 Type-209/1400 with 8 single 533mm TT with UGM-84L *Harpoon* Block II AShM/*SeaHake* mod 4 (DM2A4) HWT

PRINCIPAL SURFACE COMBATANTS • FRIGATES 16
FFGHM 12:
  3 *Al-Aziz* (GER MEKO A200) with 4 quad lnchr with MM40 *Exocet* Block 3 AShM, 4 8-cell CLA with VL MICA NG SAM, 2 twin 324mm ASTT with MU90 LWT, 1 127mm gun (capacity 1 med hel)
  4 *Alexandria* (ex-US *Oliver Hazard Perry*) with 1 Mk 13 GMLS with RGM-84C *Harpoon* Block 1B AShM/SM-1MR Block VI SAM, 2 triple 324mm ASTT with Mk 46 LWT, 1 Mk 15 *Phalanx* CIWS, 1 76mm gun (capacity 2 SH-2G *Super Seasprite* ASW hel)
  4 *Al-Fateh* (*Gowind* 2500) with 2 quad lnchrs with MM40 *Exocet* Block 3 AShM, 1 16-cell CLA VLS with VL MICA SAM, 2 triple 324mm ASTT with MU90 LWT, 1 76mm gun (capacity 1 med hel)
  1 *Tahya Misr* (FRA *Aquitaine* (FREMM)) with 2 quad lnchr with MM40 *Exocet* Block 3 AShM, 2 8-cell *Sylver* A43 VLS with *Aster* 15 SAM, 2 twin 324mm B-515 ASTT with MU90 LWT, 1 76mm gun (capacity 1 med hel)
FFGH 2 *Damyat* (ex-US *Knox*) with 1 octuple Mk 16 GMLS with RGM-84C *Harpoon* Block 1B AShM/ASROC, 2 twin 324mm SVTT Mk 32 TT with Mk 46 LWT, 1 Mk 15 *Phalanx* CIWS, 1 127mm gun (capacity 1 SH-2G *Super Seasprite* ASW hel)
FFHM 2 *Al-Galala* (ITA *Bergamini* (FREMM)) with 2 8-cell *Sylver* A50 VLS with *Aster* 15/30 SAM, 2 twin 324mm B-515 ASTT with MU90 LWT, 1 127mm gun, 1 76mm gun (fitted for but not with *Otomat* (*Teseo*) Mk2A AShM) (capacity 2 med hel)

PATROL AND COASTAL COMBATANTS 71
CORVETTES 3
  FSGM 2 *Abu Qir* (ESP *Descubierta*) (of which 1†) with 2 quad lnchr with RGM-84C *Harpoon* Block 1B AShM, 1 octuple *Albatros* lnchr with *Aspide* SAM, 2 triple 324mm SVTT Mk 32 ASTT with *Sting Ray* LWT, 1 twin

375mm Bofors ASW Rocket Launcher System A/S mor, 1 76mm gun

FS 1 *Shabab Misr* (ex-RoK *Po Hang*) with 2 76mm guns

PCFGM 4 *Ezzat* (US *Ambassador* Fast Missile Craft) with 2 quad lnchr with RGM-84L *Harpoon* Block II AShM, 1 21-cell Mk49 lnchr with RIM-116B RAM Block 1A SAM, 1 Mk15 mod 21 Block 1B *Phalanx* CIWS 1 76mm gun

PCFG 8:
  1 Project 12418 (RUS *Tarantul* IV) with 2 twin lnchr with 3M80E *Moskit* (RS-SS-N-22A *Sunburn*), 2 AK630 CIWS, 1 76mm gun
  6 *Ramadan* with 4 single lnchr with *Otomat* Mk2 AShM, 1 76mm gun
  1 *Tiger* with 2 twin lnchr with RGM-84 *Harpoon* AShM, 1 76mm gun

PCF 3 *Cyclone* (ex-US)

PCC 15: 5 *Al-Nour* (ex-PRC *Hainan*) (3 more in reserve†) with 2 triple 324mm TT, 4 RBU 1200 A/S mor, 2 twin 57mm guns; 1 Lurssen 41m; 9 *Omar Ibn El Khattab* (GER OPB 40)

PBFGM 8 Project 205 (ex-YUG *Osa* I) (of which 3†) with 4 single lnchr with P-20 (RS-SS-N-2A *Styx*) AShM, 1 9K32 *Strela*-2 (RS-SA-N-5 *Grail*) SAM (manual aiming)

PBFG 10:
  4 Type-024 (PRC *Hegu*) (2 additional vessels in reserve) with 2 single lnchr with SY-1 (CH-SS-N-1 *Scrubbrush*) AShM
  up to 6 *October* (FSU *Komar*)† with 2 single lnchr with *Otomat* Mk2 AShM (1 additional vessel in reserve)

PBFM 4 *Shershen* (FSU) with 1 9K32 *Strela*-2 (RS-SA-N-5 *Grail*) SAM (manual aiming), 1 12-tube BM-24 MRL

PBF 10: 6 *Kaan* 20 (TUR MRTP 20); 4 Project 205 (ex-FIN *Osa* II)

PB 6: up to 4 Type-062 (ex-PRC *Shanghai* II); 2 *Shershen* (FSU) (of which 1†) with 4 single 533mm TT, 1 8-tube BM-21 MRL

MINE WARFARE • MINE COUNTERMEASURES 14
  MHC 5: 2 *Al Siddiq* (ex-US *Osprey*); 3 *Dat Assawari* (US Swiftships)
  MSI 2 *Safaga* (US Swiftships)
  MSO 7: 3 *Assiout* (FSU T-43); 4 *Aswan* (FSU *Yurka*)

AMPHIBIOUS
  PRINCIPAL AMPHIBIOUS SHIPS • LHD 2 *Gamal Abdel Nasser* (FRA *Mistral*) (capacity 16 med hel; 2 LCT or 4 LCM; 13 MBTs; 50 AFVs; 450 troops)
  LANDING CRAFT 15:
    LCT 2 EDA-R
    LCM 13: 4 CTM NG; up to 9 *Vydra* (FSU) (capacity either 3 MBT or 200 troops)

LOGISTICS AND SUPPORT 23
  AE 1 *Halaib* (ex-GER *Westerwald*)
  AKR 3 *Al Hurreya*
  AOL 7 *Ayeda* (FSU *Toplivo*) (1 more in reserve)
  AR 1 *Shaledin* (ex-GER *Luneberg*)
  ARS 2 *Al Areesh*
  ATF 5 *Al Maks*† (FSU *Okhtensky*)

AX 2: 1 *El Horriya* (also used as the presidential yacht); 1 other

AXL 2: 1 *Al Kousser*; 1 *Iat shat*;

Special Forces

FORCES BY ROLE
SPECIAL FORCES
  1 SF bde
EQUIPMENT BY TYPE
ANTI-TANK/ANTI-INFRASTRUCTURE • MSL
  MANPATS *Akeron*

Coastal Defence

Army tps, Navy control
EQUIPMENT BY TYPE
COASTAL DEFENCE
  ARTY 100mm; 130mm SM-4-1; 152mm
  AShM 4K87 (RS-SSC-2B *Samlet*); *Otomat* MkII

Naval Aviation

All aircraft operated by Air Force
EQUIPMENT BY TYPE
AIRCRAFT • TPT • Light 4 Beech 1900C (maritime surveillance)
UNINHABITED AERIAL VEHICLES
  ISR • Light 2 S-100 *Camcopter*

Coast Guard 2,000

EQUIPMENT BY TYPE
PATROL AND COASTAL COMBATANTS 68
  PBF 14: 6 *Crestitalia*; 5 *Swift Protector*; 3 *Peterson*
  PB 54: 5 *Nisr*; 12 *Sea Spectre* MkIII; 25 *Swiftships*; some *Timsah*; 3 Type-83; 9 *Peterson*

Air Force 20,000; 10,000 conscript (total 30,000)

FORCES BY ROLE
FIGHTER
  1 sqn with F-16A/B *Fighting Falcon*
  8 sqn with F-16C/D *Fighting Falcon*
  1 sqn with *Mirage* 2000B/C
FIGHTER/GROUND ATTACK
  3 sqn with MiG-29M/M2 *Fulcrum*
  2 sqn with *Rafale* DM/EM
ANTI-SUBMARINE WARFARE
  1 sqn with SH-2G *Super Seasprite*
MARITIME PATROL
  1 sqn with Beech 1900C
ELECTRONIC WARFARE
  1 sqn with Beech 1900 (ELINT); *Commando* Mk2E (ECM)
ELECTRONIC WARFARE/TRANSPORT
  1 sqn with C-130H/VC-130H *Hercules*
AIRBORNE EARLY WARNING
  1 sqn with E-2C *Hawkeye*

SEARCH & RESCUE
  1 sqn with AW149
  1 unit with AW139
TRANSPORT
  1 sqn with An-74TK-200A
  1 sqn with C-130H/C-130H-30 *Hercules*
  1 sqn with C295M
  1 sqn with B-707-366C; B-737-100; Beech 200 *Super King Air*; *Falcon* 20; Gulfstream III; Gulfstream IV; Gulfstream IV-SP
TRAINING
  1 sqn with *Alpha Jet**
  3 sqn with EMB-312 *Tucano*
  1 sqn with Grob 115EG
  ε6 sqn with K-8 *Karakorum**
  1 sqn with L-39 *Albatros*; L-59E *Albatros**
ATTACK HELICOPTER
  1 sqn with Mi-24V
  2 sqn with AH-64D *Apache*
  1 sqn with Ka-52A *Hokum* B
  2 sqn with SA-342K *Gazelle*
TRANSPORT HELICOPTER
  1 sqn with AW149
  1 sqn with CH-47C/D *Chinook*
  1 sqn with Mi-8
  1 sqn with Mi-8/Mi-17-V1 *Hip*
  1 sqn with AW189; S-70 *Black Hawk*; UH-60A/L *Black Hawk*
UAV
  Some sqn with R4E-50 *Skyeye*; *Wing Loong* I
EQUIPMENT BY TYPE
AIRCRAFT 485 combat capable
  FTR 32: 26 F-16A *Fighting Falcon*; 6 F-16B *Fighting Falcon*
  FGA 257: 138 F-16C *Fighting Falcon*; 37 F-16D *Fighting Falcon*; 2 Mirage 2000B; 15 Mirage 2000C; 41 MiG-29M/M2 *Fulcrum*; 16 *Rafale* DM; 8 *Rafale* EM
  ELINT 2 VC-130H *Hercules*
  ISR ε6 AT-802 *Air Tractor**
  AEW&C 7 E-2C *Hawkeye*
  TPT 73: **Heavy** 2 Il-76MF *Candid*; **Medium** 24: 21 C-130H *Hercules*; 3 C-130H-30 *Hercules*; **Light** 36: 3 An-74TK-200A; 1 Beech 200 *King Air*; 4 Beech 1900 (ELINT); 4 Beech 1900C; 24 C295M; **PAX** 11: 1 B-707-366C; 3 *Falcon* 20; 2 Gulfstream III; 1 Gulfstream IV; 4 Gulfstream IV-SP
  TRG 328: 36 *Alpha Jet**; 54 EMB-312 *Tucano*; 74 Grob 115EG; 119 K-8 *Karakorum**; 10 L-39 *Albatros*; 35 L-59E*
HELICOPTERS
  ATK 104: 45 AH-64D *Apache*; ε46 Ka-52A *Hokum* B; ε13 Mi-24V *Hind* E
  ASW 10 SH-2G *Super Seasprite* (opcon Navy)
  ELINT 4 *Commando* Mk2E (ECM)
  MRH 104: 2 AW139 (SAR); 24 AW149 (incl 9 SAR); 8 AW189 (VIP); 65 SA342K *Gazelle* (some armed); 5 SA342L *Gazelle* (opcon Navy)
  TPT 96: **Heavy** 19: 3 CH-47C *Chinook*; 16 CH-47D *Chinook*; **Medium** 77: 2 AS-61; 24 *Commando* (incl 3 VIP); 40 Mi-8T *Hip*; 3 Mi-17-1V *Hip*; 4 S-70 *Black Hawk* (VIP); 4 UH-60L *Black Hawk* (VIP)
  TRG 17 UH-12E
UNINHABITED AERIAL VEHICLES
  CISR • Heavy 4+ *Wing Loong* I
  ISR • Medium R4E-50 *Skyeye*
AIR LAUNCHED MISSILES
  AAM • IR AIM-9M/P *Sidewinder*; R-73 (RS-AA-11A *Archer*); R-550 *Magic*; 9M39 *Igla*-V; **IIR** *Mica* IR; **ARH** *Mica* RF; R-77 (RS-AA-12 *Adder*); **SARH** AIM-7F/M *Sparrow*; R-530
  ASM 9M120 *Ataka* (RS-AT-9); AGM-65A/D/F/G *Maverick*; AGM-114F/K *Hellfire*; AS-30L; HOT; LJ-7 (AKD-10)
  LACM SCALP EG
  AShM AGM-84L *Harpoon* Block II; AM39 *Exocet*; Kh-35U (RS-AS-20 *Kayak*)
  ARM *Armat*; Kh-25MP (RS-AS-12A *Kegler*)
BOMBS
  Laser-guided GBU-10/12 *Paveway* II
  INS/SAT-guided AASM *Hammer* 250; *Al Tariq*

Air Defence Command 80,000 conscript; 70,000 reservists (total 150,000)

FORCES BY ROLE
AIR DEFENCE
  5 AD div HQ (geographically based)
  3 SAM bty with S-300V4 (RS-SA-23)
  4 SAM bty with 9K37M1-2/9K317 *Buk*-M1-2/M2E (RS-SA-11 *Gadfly*/RS-SA-17 *Grizzly*)
  11 SAM bty with MIM-23B *I-Hawk*
  38 SAM bty with S-75M *Volkhov* (RS-SA-2 *Guideline*)
  10 SAM bty with S-125-2M *Pechora*-2M (RS-SA-26)
  Some SAM bty with 2K12 *Kub* (RS-SA-6 *Gainful*)
  2 SAM bty with 9K331/9K331ME *Tor*-M1/M2E (RS-SA-15 *Gauntlet*)
  14 SAM bty with *Crotale*
  12 SAM bty with M48 *Chaparral*
  30 SAM bty with S-125M *Pechora*-M (RS-SA-3 *Goa*)
  18 AD bn with RIM-7M *Sea Sparrow* with *Skyguard*/GDF-003 with *Skyguard*
  12 ADA bde (total: 100 ADA bn)
EQUIPMENT BY TYPE
AIR DEFENCE
  SAM 777
    Long-range ε18 S-300V4 (RS-SA-23)
    Medium-range 323+: 40+ 9K37M1-2/9K317 *Buk*-M1-2/M2E (RS-SA-11 *Gadfly*/RS-SA-17 *Grizzly*); ε33 MIM-23B *I-Hawk*; ε210 S-75M *Volkhov* (RS-SA-2 *Guideline*); ε40 S-125-2M *Pechora*-2M (RS-SA-26)
    Short-range 300+: 56+ 2K12 *Kub* (RS-SA-6 *Gainful*); 10 9K331 *Tor*-M1 (RS-SA-15 *Gauntlet*); 10+ 9K331ME *Tor*-M2E (RS-SA-15 *Gauntlet*); 24+ *Crotale*; 80 RIM-7M *Sea Sparrow* with *Skyguard*; ε120 S-125M *Pechora*-M

(RS-SA-3 *Goa*)
Point-defence 136+: 50 M1097 *Avenger*; 50+ M48 *Chaparral*
GUNS 910
  SP • **23mm** 230 ZSU-23-4 *Shilka*
  TOWED 680: **35mm** 80 GDF-005 with *Skyguard*;
  57mm 600 S-60

Gendarmerie & Paramilitary ε397,000 active

Central Security Forces ε325,000
Ministry of Interior; includes conscripts
ARMOURED FIGHTING VEHICLES
  APC • **APC (W)** *Walid*
  AUV *Sherpa Light Scout*

National Guard ε60,000
Lt wpns only
FORCES BY ROLE
MANOEUVRE
  Other
    8 paramilitary bde (cadre) (3 paramilitary bn)
EQUIPMENT BY TYPE
ARMOURED FIGHTING VEHICLES
  APC • **APC (W)** 250 *Walid*

Border Guard Forces ε12,000
Ministry of Interior; lt wpns only
FORCES BY ROLE
MANOEUVRE
  Other
    18 Border Guard regt

DEPLOYMENT

CENTRAL AFRICAN REPUBLIC: UN • MINUSCA 1,023; 1 inf bn; 1 tpt coy

DEMOCRATIC REPUBLIC OF THE CONGO: UN • MONUSCO 6

SOUTH SUDAN: UN • UNMISS 7

SUDAN: UN • UNISFA 5

WESTERN SAHARA: UN • MINURSO 20

FOREIGN FORCES
Australia MFO (*Operation Mazurka*) 27
Canada MFO 55
Colombia MFO 275; 1 inf bn
Czech Republic MFO 18; 1 C295M
Fiji MFO 170; elm 1 inf bn
France MFO 1
Italy MFO 75; 3 PB
New Zealand MFO 26; 1 trg unit; 1 tpt unit
Norway MFO 3
United Kingdom MFO 2
United States MFO 465; elm 1 ARNG inf bn; 1 ARNG spt bn (1 EOD coy, 1 medical coy, 1 hel coy)
Uruguay MFO 41 1 engr/tpt unit

Iran IRN

Iranian Rial IRR		2023	2024	2025
GDP	IRR	143qrn	198qrn	262qrn
	USD	373bn	434bn	464bn
Real GDP growth	%	5.0	3.7	3.1
Def bdgt [a]	IRR	3.19qrn	3.67qrn	
	USD [b]	8.33bn	8.04bn	

[a] Excludes Law Enforcement Forces (NAJA)
[b] Conversions using NIMA exchange rate

Real-terms defence budget trend (USDbn, constant 2015)

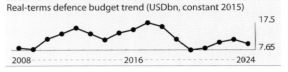

Population		88,386,937				
Age	0–14	15–19	20–24	25–29	30–64	65 plus
Male	11.9%	3.6%	3.3%	3.3%	25.4%	3.2%
Female	11.4%	3.5%	3.1%	3.1%	24.5%	3.7%

Capabilities

Iran's ambition is to become the dominant regional power and to check the power of Israel and the US. Iranian efforts to achieve this goal have centred on an asymmetric doctrine that combines territorial defence through national mobilisation, an inventory of one-way attack (OWA) UAVs, cruise and ballistic missiles, as well as an alliance of non-state actors equipped with long-range weaponry. These ambitions have been challenged following the Israel–Hamas war. An inventory of short- and medium-range ballistic missiles, land-attack cruise missiles and UAVs enables Iran to conduct long-range strikes in the absence of a capable air force. However, Iran's April and October 2024 attacks on Israel revealed limitations both in these systems' ability to penetrate advanced missile defences and to achieve the precision necessary to significantly damage military infrastructure. The rest of the conventional armed forces struggle with increasingly obsolescent equipment that ingenuity and asymmetric techniques can only partially offset. Ageing equipment is pronounced across the air force. Although Iran's naval force focuses on asymmetric approaches, such as the use of mines, anti-ship missiles, speedboats and small submarines, the service has shown interest in blue water operations and power projection. There are C2 problems between the regular forces and the IRGC. While unable to meet national needs for all major weapons, the domestic industry has achieved a high degree of proficiency in the production of certain types of advanced weapons. Iran also has developed expansive sanctions-evasion techniques to support its defence industry. Increased military cooperation with Moscow could offer Iran a conduit to more modern weaponry and technology.

ACTIVE 610,000 (Army 350,000 Islamic Revolutionary Guard Corps 190,000 Navy 18,000 Air 37,000 Air Defence 15,000) Gendarmerie & Paramilitary 40,000

Armed Forces General Staff coordinates two parallel organisations: the regular armed forces and the Islamic Revolutionary Guard Corps

Conscript liability 18–21 months (reported, with variations depending on location in which service is performed)

RESERVE 350,000 (Army 350,000, ex-service volunteers)

ORGANISATIONS BY SERVICE

Space
EQUIPMENT BY TYPE
SATELLITES • ISR 1 *Khayam* (reported)

Army 130,000; 220,000 conscript (total 350,000)
FORCES BY ROLE
5 corps-level regional HQ
COMMAND
  1 cdo div HQ
  4 armd div HQ
  2 mech div HQ
  4 inf div HQ
SPECIAL FORCES
  1 cdo div (3 cdo bde)
  6 cdo bde
  1 SF bde
MANOEUVRE
  Armoured
    8 armd bde
  Mechanised
    14 mech bde
  Light
    12 inf bde
  Air Manoeuvre
    1 AB bde
  Aviation
    Some avn gp
COMBAT SUPPORT
  5 arty gp
EQUIPMENT BY TYPE
Totals incl those held by IRGC Ground Forces. Some equipment serviceability in doubt
ARMOURED FIGHTING VEHICLES
  MBT 1,513+: 100 *Chieftain* Mk3/Mk5; 168 M47/M48; 150 M60A1; 540 *Safir*-74/T-54/T-55/ZTZ-59; 75+ T-62; 480 T-72S
  LT TK 80 *Scorpion*
  RECCE 35 EE-9 *Cascavel*
  IFV 610+: 210 BMP-1; 400 BMP-2 with 9K111 *Fagot* (RS-AT-4 *Spigot*); BMT-2 *Cobra*
  APC 640+
    APC (T) 340: 140 *Boregh* with 9K111 *Fagot* (RS-AT-4 *Spigot*); 200 M113
    APC (W) 300+: 300 BTR-50/BTR-60; *Rakhsh*
    PPV *Toofan*
ENGINEERING & MAINTENANCE VEHICLES
  ARV 20+: BREM-1 reported; 20 *Chieftain* ARV; M578; T-54/55 ARV reported
  VLB 15 *Chieftain* AVLB
  MW *Taftan* 1
ANTI-TANK/ANTI-INFRASTRUCTURE
  MSL • MANPATS 9K11 *Malyutka* (RS-AT-3 *Sagger*); 9K111 *Fagot* (RS-AT-4 *Spigot*); 9K111-1 *Konkurs* (RS-AT-5 *Spandrel/Towsan*-1); *Almaz*; *Dehlavieh* (*Kornet*); I-Raad; *Saeqhe* 1; *Saeqhe* 2; *Toophan*; *Toophan* 2
  RCL 200+: **75mm** M20; **82mm** B-10; **106mm** ε200 M40; **107mm** B-11
ARTILLERY 6,798+
  SP 292: **122mm** 60 2S1 *Gvozdika*; **155mm** 150 M109A1; **170mm** 30 M-1978; **175mm** 22 M107; **203mm** 30 M110
  TOWED 2,030+: **105mm** 150: 130 M101A1; 20 M-56; **122mm** 640: 540 D-30; 100 Type-54 (M-30); **130mm** 985 M-46; **152mm** 30 D-20; **155mm** 205: 120 GHN-45; 70 M114; 15 Type-88 WAC-21; **203mm** 20 M115
  MRL 1,476+: **107mm** 1,300: 700 Type-63; 600 HASEB *Fadjr* 1; **122mm** 157: 7 BM-11; 100 BM-21 *Grad*; 50 *Arash/Hadid/Noor*; **240mm** 19+: ε10 *Fadjr* 3; 9 M-1985; **330mm** *Fadjr* 5
  MOR 3,000: **81mm**; **82mm**; **107mm** M30; **120mm** HM-15; HM-16; M-65
SURFACE-TO-SURFACE MISSILE LAUNCHERS
  SRBM • Conventional ε30 CH-SS-8 (175 msl); *Fateh*-360; *Shahin*-1/*Shahin*-2; *Nazeat*; *Oghab*
AIRCRAFT • TPT 17 **Light** 16: 10 Cessna 185; 2 F-27 *Friendship*; 4 *Turbo Commander* 690; **PAX** 1 *Falcon* 20
HELICOPTERS
  ATK 50 AH-1J *Cobra*
  TPT 167: **Heavy** ε20 CH-47C *Chinook*; **Medium** 69: 49 Bell 214 (some armed); 20 Mi-171; **Light** 78: 68 Bell 205A (AB-205A); 10 Bell 206 *Jet Ranger* (AB-206)
UNINHABITED AERIAL VEHICLES
  CISR • Medium *Ababil* 3; *Ababil* 4; *Mohajer* 6
  ISR • Medium *Mohajer* 4; **Light** *Mohajer* 2; *Yasir*
  OWA *Ababil* T; *Akhgar*; *Arash*; *Omid*
AIR-LAUNCHED MISSILES
  ASM *Almas* (reported); *Heydar*-1; *Qaem* 114; *Shafaq* (mod)
BOMBS
  Laser-guided *Qaem*
  Electro-optical guided *Qaem* 5
AIR DEFENCE
  SAM
    Short-range FM-80 (CH-SA-4)
    Point-defence 9K36 *Strela*-3 (RS-SA-14 *Gremlin*); 9K32 *Strela*-2 (RS-SA-7 *Grail*)‡; *Misaq* 1 (QW-1); *Misaq* 2 (QW-18); 9K338 *Igla*-S (RS-SA-24 *Grinch*) (reported); HN-5A (CH-SA-3)
  GUNS 1,122
    SP 180: **23mm** 100 ZSU-23-4; **57mm** 80 ZSU-57-2
    TOWED 942+: **14.5mm** ZPU-2; ZPU-4; **23mm** 300 ZU-23-2; **35mm** 92 GDF-002; **37mm** M-1939; **40mm** 50 L/70; **57mm** 200 S-60; **85mm** 300 M-1939

Islamic Revolutionary Guard Corps 190,000

Islamic Revolutionary Guard Corps Ground Forces 150,000

Controls Basij paramilitary forces. Lightly staffed in peacetime. Primary role: internal security; secondary role: external defence, in conjunction with regular armed forces

FORCES BY ROLE
COMMAND
  31 provincial corps HQ (2 in Tehran)
SPECIAL FORCES
  3 spec ops div
  1 AB bde
MANOEUVRE
  Armoured
  2 armd div
  3 armd bde
  Light
  8+ inf div
  5+ inf bde

EQUIPMENT BY TYPE
SRBM • Conventional some *Fateh-360*
UNINHABITED AERIAL VEHICLES
  CISR • Medium *Mohajer 6*
  ISR • Light *Meraj 313*
  OWA *Meraj 532*
BOMBS
  Laser-guided *Qaem*
  Electro-optical guided *Qaem 5*

Islamic Revolutionary Guard Corps Naval Forces 20,000+ (incl 5,000 Marines)

FORCES BY ROLE
COMBAT SUPPORT
  Some arty bty
  Some AShM bty with HY-2 (CH-SSC-3 *Seersucker*)

EQUIPMENT BY TYPE
In addition to the vessels listed, the IRGC operates a substantial number of patrol boats with a full-load displacement below 10 tonnes, including *Boghammar*-class vessels and small *Bavar*-class wing-in-ground effect air vehicles

PATROL AND COASTAL COMBATANTS 131
  PCGM 3 *Shahid Soleimani* with 2 twin lnchr with *Ghader* AShM, 2 single lnchr with C-704 (*Nasr*) AShM, 2 3-cell VLS & 4 single cell VLS (likely fitted with SAM), 1 hel landing platform
  PBFG 56:
    5 C14 with 2 twin lnchr with C-701 (*Kosar*)/C-704 (*Nasr*) AShM
    10 Mk13 with 2 single lnchr with C-704 (*Nasr*) AShM, 2 single 324mm TT
    10 *Thondor* (PRC *Houdong*) with 2 twin lnchr with C-802A (*Ghader*) AShM, 2 AK230 CIWS
    25 *Peykaap* II (IPS-16 mod) with 2 single lnchr with C-701 (*Kosar*) AShM/C-704 (*Nasr*), 2 single 324mm TT
    6 *Zolfaghar* (*Peykaap* III/IPS-16 mod) with 2 single lnchr with C-701 (*Kosar*)/C-704 (*Nasr*) AShM
  PBG 1 *Shahid Rouhi* with 2 twin lnchr with C-704 (*Nasr*) AShM
  PBFT 15 *Peykaap* I (IPS -16) with 2 single 324mm TT
  PBF 35: 15 *Kashdom* II; 10 *Tir* (IPS-18); ε10 *Pashe* (MIG-G-1900)
  PB 21: ε20 *Ghaem*; 1 *Shahid Nazeri*

AMPHIBIOUS
  LANDING SHIPS • LST 3 *Hormuz* 24 (*Hejaz* design for commercial use)
  LANDING CRAFT • LCT 2 *Hormuz* 21 (minelaying capacity)

LOGISTICS AND SUPPORT 5
  AP 3 *Naser*
  ESB 2: 1 *Shahid Mahdavi* (multipurpose helicopter and UAV carrier) with 2 twin lnchr with C-802A (*Ghader*) AShM; 1 *Shahid Roudaki* with 4 twin lnchr with C-802A (*Ghader*) AShM

UNINHABITED MARITIME PLATFORMS
  UUV • ATK Some

COASTAL DEFENCE • AShM C-701 (*Kosar*); C-704 (*Nasr*); C-802 (*Noor*); HY-2 (CH-SSC-3 *Seersucker*)

HELICOPTERS
  MRH 5 Mi-171 *Hip*
  TPT • Light some Bell 206 (AB-206 *Jet Ranger*)

UNINHABITED AERIAL VEHICLES
  CISR • Medium *Ababil 3*; *Ababil 5*; *Mohajer 6*
  ISR • Medium *Mohajer 4*; **Light** *Yasir*
  OWA *Ababil T*; *Shahed 131*; *Shahed 136*

AIR-LAUNCHED MISSILES
  AShM CM-35A *Nasr* (C-704)

BOMBS
  Laser-guided *Qaem*
  Electro-optical guided *Qaem*

Islamic Revolutionary Guard Corps Marines 5,000+

FORCES BY ROLE
MANOEUVRE
  Amphibious
  1 mne bde

Islamic Revolutionary Guard Corps Aerospace Force 15,000

Controls Iran's strategic-missile force

FORCES BY ROLE
FIGHTER/GROUND ATTACK
  1 sqn with Su-22M4 *Fitter K*; Su-22UM-3K *Fitter* G
TRAINING
  1 sqn with EMB-312 *Tucano**

EQUIPMENT BY TYPE
SURFACE-TO-SURFACE MISSILE LAUNCHERS
  MRBM • Conventional 100+: *Dezful* (*Zolfaghar* mod);

Emad-1 (*Shahab*-3 mod); *Fattah*-1; *Ghadr*-1/-2 (*Shahab*-3 mod); *Kheibar Shekan*; *Khorramshahr*; *Rezvan* (*Qiam* mod); *Sajjil*-2;

SRBM • Conventional 100+: *Fateh*-110; *Fateh*-313; *Hormuz*-1/-2 (*Fateh*-110 mod); *Khalij Fars* (*Fateh*-110 mod ASBM); *Qiam*-1; *Zelzal*; *Zolfaghar* (IR-SS-1)

GLCM • Conventional *Paveh*; *Quds*-2; *Quds*-3

SATELLITES *See Space*

AIRCRAFT 22 combat capable

FGA 7: up to 6 Su-22M4 *Fitter* K; 1+ Su-22UM-3K *Fitter* G

TRG 15 EMB-312 *Tucano**

UNINHABITED AERIAL VEHICLES

CISR • Heavy *Shahed* 129; **Medium** *Ababil* 3; *Shahed* 133; *Shahed* 141; *Shahed* 181; *Shahed* 191

ISR • Medium *Shahed* 123

OWA *Shahed* 131; *Shahed* 136

AIR-LAUNCHED MISSILES

ASM *Almas* (reported); *Qaem* 114 (reported)

BOMBS

Laser-guided *Sadid*

Electro-optical guided *Sadid*

AIR DEFENCE

SAM

Medium-range *3rd Khordad*; *15th Khordad*; *Talash*
Point-defence *Misaq* 1 (QW-1); *Misaq* 2 (QW-18)

Islamic Revolutionary Quds Force 5,000

Navy 18,000

HQ at Bandar Abbas

EQUIPMENT BY TYPE

In addition to the vessels listed, the Iranian Navy operates a substantial number of patrol boats with a full-load displacement below 10 tonnes

SUBMARINES • TACTICAL 19

SSK 1 *Taregh* (RUS *Paltus* (Project 877EKM (*Kilo*))) (2 more non-operational) with 6 single 533mm TT

SSC 1 *Fateh* with 4 single 533mm TT with C-704 (*Nasr*-1) AShM/*Valfajr* HWT

SSW 17: 16+ *Ghadir* ((DPRK *Yeono* mod) with 2 single 533mm TT with *Jask*-2 (C-704 (*Nasr*)) AShM/*Valfajr* HWT (additional vessels in build); 1 *Nahang*

PATROL AND COASTAL COMBATANTS 69

CORVETTES 8

FSGM 3 *Jamaran* (UK Vosper Mk 5 derivative) with 2 twin lnchr with C-802 (*Noor*) (CH-SS-N-6) AShM, 2 single lnchr with SM-1 SAM, 2 triple 324mm SVTT Mk 32 ASTT, 1 76mm gun, 1 hel landing platform (1 more†)

FSG 5:
  2 *Alvand* (UK Vosper Mk 5) with 2 twin lnchr with C-802 (CH-SS-N-6) AShM, 2 triple 324mm SVTT Mk 32 ASTT, 1 114mm gun
  1 *Alvand* (UK Vosper Mk 5) with 2 twin lnchr with C-802 (CH-SS-N-6) AShM, 2 triple 324mm SVTT Mk 32 ASTT, 1 AK630M CIWS, 1 114mm gun
  1 *Bayandor* (US PF-103) (1 other non operational) with 2 twin lnchr with C-802 (CH-SS-N-6) AShM, 2 triple 324mm SVTT Mk 32 ASTT, 1 76mm gun
  1 *Hamzah* with 2 single lnchr with C-802 (*Noor*) (CH-SS-N-6) AShM

PCFG 15: up to 10 *Kaman* (FRA *Combattante* II) with 1 twin lnchr with C-802 (*Noor*) (CH-SS-N-6) AShM, 1 76mm gun; 5+ *Sina* with 1 twin lnchr with C-802 (*Noor*) (CH-SS-N-6) AShM, 1 76mm gun

PBG 9:
  3 *Hendijan* with 2 twin lnchr with C-802 (*Noor*) (CH-SS-N-6) AShM
  3 *Kayvan* with 2 single lnchr with C-704 (*Nasr*) AShM
  3 *Parvin* with 2 single lnchr with C-704 (*Nasr*) AShM

PBFT 3 *Kajami* (semi-submersible) with 2 324mm TT

PBF 1 MIL55

PB 33: 9 C14; 8 *Hendijan*; 6 MkII; 10 MkIII

MINE WARFARE • MINE COUNTERMEASURES 1

MCC 1 *Shahin*

AMPHIBIOUS

LANDING SHIPS 12

LST 3 *Hengam* with 1 hel landing platform (capacity 9 tanks; 225 troops)

LSM 3 *Farsi* (ROK) (capacity 9 tanks; 140 troops)

LSL 6 *Fouque*

LANDING CRAFT 11

LCT 2

LCU 1 *Liyan* 110

UCAC 8: 2 *Wellington* Mk 4; 4 *Wellington* Mk 5; 2 *Tondar* (UK *Winchester*)

LOGISTICS AND SUPPORT 15

AE 2 *Delvar*

AKL 3 *Delvar*

ESB 1 *Makran*

AO 2 *Bandar Abbas*

AWT 5: 4 *Kangan*; 1 *Delvar*

AXL 2 *Kialas*

COASTAL DEFENCE • AShM C-701 (*Kosar*); C-704 (*Nasr*); C-802 (*Noor*); C-802A (*Ghader*); *Ra'ad* (reported)

Marines 2,600

FORCES BY ROLE

MANOEUVRE

Amphibious

2 mne bde

Naval Aviation 2,600

EQUIPMENT BY TYPE

AIRCRAFT

TPT 16: **Light** 13: 5 Do-228; 4 F-27 *Friendship*; 4 Turbo Commander 680; **PAX** 3 *Falcon* 20 (ELINT)

HELICOPTERS

ASW ε10 SH-3D *Sea King*

MCM 3 RH-53D *Sea Stallion*

TPT • **Light** 17: 5 Bell 205A (AB-205A); 2 Bell 206 *Jet Ranger* (AB-206); 10 Bell 212 (AB-212)
UNINHABITED AERIAL VEHICLES
CISR • **Heavy** *Shahed* 129
BOMBS
Laser-guided *Sadid*
Electro-optical guided *Sadid*

Air Force 37,000
FORCES BY ROLE
Includes IRGC AF equipment
FIGHTER
1 sqn with F-7M *Airguard*; JJ-7*
2 sqn with F-14 *Tomcat*
2 sqn with MiG-29A/UB *Fulcrum*
FIGHTER/GROUND ATTACK
5 sqn with F-4D/E *Phantom* II
4 sqn with F-5E/F *Tiger* II
1 sqn with *Mirage* F-1B/E
GROUND ATTACK
1 sqn with Su-24MK *Fencer* D
MARITIME PATROL
1 sqn with P-3F *Orion*
ISR
1 (det) sqn with RF-4E *Phantom* II*
SEARCH & RESCUE
Some flt with Bell 214C (AB-214C)
TANKER/TRANSPORT
1 sqn with B-707; B-747; B-747F
TRANSPORT
1 sqn with B-707; *Falcon* 50; L-1329 *Jetstar*; Bell 412
2 sqn with C-130E/H *Hercules*
1 sqn with F-27 *Friendship*; *Falcon* 20
1 sqn with Il-76 *Candid*; An-140 (Iran-140 *Faraz*)
TRAINING
1 sqn with Beech F33A/C *Bonanza*
1 sqn with F-5B *Freedom Fighter*
1 sqn with PC-6
1 sqn with PC-7 *Turbo Trainer*
Some units with MFI-17 *Mushshak*; TB-21 *Trinidad*; TB-200 *Tobago*
TRANSPORT HELICOPTER
1 sqn with CH-47 *Chinook*
Some units with Bell 206A *Jet Ranger* (AB-206A); *Shabaviz* 2-75; *Shabaviz* 2061
EQUIPMENT BY TYPE
AIRCRAFT 265 combat capable
FTR 138: 15 F-5B *Freedom Fighter*; 54 F-5E/F *Tiger* II; 18 F-7M *Airguard*; ε10 F-14 *Tomcat*; 35 MiG-29A/UB *Fulcrum*; up to 6 *Azarakhsh* (reported)
FGA 73: 55 F-4D/E *Phantom* II; 2 *Mirage* F-1BQ; 10 *Mirage* F-1EQ; up to 6 *Saegheh* (reported)
ATK 29 Su-24MK *Fencer* D
ASW 3 P-3F *Orion*
ISR 6+ RF-4E *Phantom* II*
TKR/TPT 4: 2 B-707; ε2 B-747
TPT 116: **Heavy** 12 Il-76 *Candid*; **Medium** ε19 C-130E/H *Hercules*; **Light** 75: 11 An-74TK-200; 5 An-140 (Iran-140 *Faraz*); 10 F-27 *Friendship*; 1 L-1329 *Jetstar*; 10 PC-6B *Turbo Porter*; 8 TB-21 *Trinidad*; 4 TB-200 *Tobago*; 3 *Turbo Commander* 680; 14 Y-7; 9 Y-12; **PAX** 10: ε1 B-707; 1 B-747; 4 B-747F; 1 *Falcon* 20; 3 *Falcon* 50
TRG 128: 25 Beech F33A/C *Bonanza*; 14 JJ-7*; 25 MFI-17 *Mushshak*; 12 *Parastu*; 15 PC-6; 35 PC-7 *Turbo Trainer*; 2 Yak-130 *Mitten**
HELICOPTERS
MRH 2 Bell 412
TPT 38+: **Heavy** 2+ CH-47 *Chinook*; **Medium** 30 Bell 214C (AB-214C); **Light** 6+: 2 Bell 206A *Jet Ranger* (AB-206A); 4 Bell 212 (AB-212) (VIP); some *Shabaviz* 2-75; some *Shabaviz* 2061
UNINHABITED AERIAL VEHICLES
CISR • **Heavy** *Kaman* 22 (reported); **Medium** *Ababil* 4/5; *Kaman* 12; *Kaman* 22 (reported); *Mohajer* 6
AIR-LAUNCHED MISSILES
AAM • **IR** AIM-9J *Sidewinder*; PL-2A‡; PL-7; R-60 (RS-AA-8 *Aphid*); R-27T (RS-AA-10B *Alamo*) (reported); R-73 (RS-AA-11A *Archer*); **SARH** AIM-7E-2 *Sparrow*; R-27R (RS-AA-10A *Alamo*); **ARH** AIM-54 *Phoenix*†
ASM AGM-65A *Maverick*; Kh-25 (RS-AS-10 *Karen*); Kh-25ML (RS-AS-10 *Karen*); Kh-29L/T (RS-AS-14A/B *Kedge*)
AShM C-801K; CM-35A *Nasr* (C-704); CM-200A *Ghader* (C-802A)
ARM Kh-58 (RS-AS-11 *Kilter*)
LACM *Asef* (status uncertain)
BOMBS
Electro-optical guided GBU-87/B; *Qassed*

Air Defence Force 15,000
FORCES BY ROLE
AIR DEFENCE
16 bn with MIM-23B I-*Hawk*/*Shahin*
4 bn with S-300PMU2 (RS-SA-20 *Gargoyle*)
5 sqn with FM-80 (CH-SA-4); *Rapier*; HQ-2 (CH-SA-1); S-200 *Angara* (RS-SA-5 *Gammon*); 9K331 *Tor*-M1 (RS-SA-15 *Gauntlet*)
EQUIPMENT BY TYPE
AIR DEFENCE
SAM 410
Long-range 42+: 10 S-200 *Angara* (RS-SA-5 *Gammon*); 32 S-300PMU2 (RS-SA-20 *Gargoyle*); *Bavar*-373
Medium-range 59+: ε50 MIM-23B I-*Hawk*/*Shahin*; 9 HQ-2 (CH-SA-1); *Talash*/15th *Khordad*
Short-range 279: 250 FM-80 (CH-SA-4); 29 9K331 *Tor*-M1 (RS-SA-15 *Gauntlet*)
Point-defence 30+: 30 *Rapier*; *Misaq* 1 (QW-1); *Misaq* 2 (QW-18)
GUNS • **TOWED 23mm** ZU-23-2; **35mm** GDF-002

Gendarmerie & Paramilitary 40,000–60,000

Law-Enforcement Forces 40,000–60,000 (border and security troops); 450,000 on mobilisation (incl conscripts)

Part of armed forces in wartime

EQUIPMENT BY TYPE
PATROL AND COASTAL COMBATANTS • PB ε90
AIRCRAFT • TPT • Light 2+: 2 An-140; some Cessna 185/Cessna 310
HELICOPTERS • TPT • Light ε24 AB-205 (Bell 205)/AB-206 (Bell 206) *Jet Ranger*

Basij Resistance Force ε600,000 on mobilisation

Paramilitary militia with claimed membership of 12.6 million; ε600,000 combat capable

Iraq IRQ

Iraqi Dinar IQD		2023	2024	2025
GDP	IQD	332trn	343trn	352trn
	USD	252bn	264bn	271bn
Real GDP growth	%	-2.9	0.1	4.1
Def bdgt [a]	IQD	13.8trn	16.5trn	
	USD	10.5bn	12.7bn	
FMA (US)	USD	250m	75.5m	90.0m

[a] Excludes Ministry of the Interior and National Security Council budget

Population	42,083,436				
Age	0–14	15–19	20–24	25–29	30–64	65 plus
Male	17.7%	5.4%	4.8%	4.1%	16.7%	1.6%
Female	16.9%	5.2%	4.7%	4.0%	16.8%	2.0%

Capabilities

Iraq's armed forces have had success battling ISIS, though the threat has not been eliminated. US forces have remained in the country as advisors under Combined Joint Task Force – Operation Inherent Resolve (OIR) and the Pentagon conducts bilateral security cooperation activities, though an agreement in late 2024 heralded a reduction in US troop numbers. Iraq's budget foresees a sizeable expansion of the Popular Mobilization Forces (PMF), a grouping of 50-odd factions, some with links to Iran. Baghdad relies on the Counter-Terrorism Service (CTS) for offensive operations. The Iraqi Federal Police also operates as a military force. Turkiye targets the Kurdistan Workers Party in Northern Iraq and maintains bases there. The Kurdish region maintains two divisions under nominal control of the Ministry of Peshmerga Affairs, but the two main Kurdish factions maintain larger separate forces. Iraq has a mix of Soviet-era, Russian, European and US platforms, but has significant shortcomings in logistics support, joint fires and mission planning. Iraq is trying to modernise its armed forces and decrease dependence on the US, having ordered European helicopters, French radars and South Korean air defence systems. Iraq's defence industry is limited, focusing on light weapons and ammunition, and some maintenance.

ACTIVE 193,000 (Army 180,000 Navy 3,000 Air 5,000 Air Defence 5,000) **Gendarmerie & Paramilitary 266,000**

ORGANISATIONS BY SERVICE

Army ε180,000

Includes Counter-Terrorism Service

FORCES BY ROLE
SPECIAL FORCES
 3 SF bde
 1 ranger bde (3 ranger bn)
MANOEUVRE
 Armoured
 1 (9th) armd div (2 armd bde, 2 mech bde, 1 engr bn, 1 sigs regt, 1 log bde)
 Mechanised
 3 (5th, 8th & 10th) mech div (4 mech inf bde, 1 engr bn, 1 sigs regt, 1 log bde)
 1 (7th) mech div (2 mech inf bde, 1 inf bde, 1 engr bn, 1 sigs regt, 1 log bde)
 Light
 1 (6th) mot div (3 mot inf bde, 1 inf bde, 1 engr bn, 1 sigs regt, 1 log bde)
 1 (14th) mot div (2 mot inf bde, 3 inf bde, 1 engr bn, 1 sigs regt, 1 log bde)
 1 (1st) inf div (2 inf bde)
 1 (11th) inf div (3 lt inf bde, 1 engr bn, 1 sigs regt, 1 log bde)
 1 (15th) inf div (5 inf bde)
 1 (16th) inf div (2 inf bde)
 1 (17th Cdo) inf div (4 inf bde, 1 engr bn, 1 sigs regt, 1 log bde)
 1 inf bde
 Other
 1 (PM SF) sy div (3 inf bde)
HELICOPTER
 3 atk hel sqn with Bell T407; H135M
 1 atk hel sqn with Mi-28NE *Havoc*
 1 atk hel sqn with Mi-35M *Hind*
 1 ISR sqn with SA342M *Gazelle*
 1 sqn with Bell 205 (UH-1H *Huey* II)
 3 sqn with Mi-17 *Hip* H; Mi-171Sh
 2 trg sqn with Bell 206; OH-58C *Kiowa*
 1 trg sqn with Bell 205 (UH-1H *Huey* II)
 1 trg sqn with Mi-17 *Hip*
UNINHABITED AERIAL VEHICLE
 1 sqn with CH-4; CH-5
EQUIPMENT BY TYPE
ARMOURED FIGHTING VEHICLES
 MBT 401+: ε100 M1A1 *Abrams*; 178+ T-72M/M1; ε50

T-55; 73 T-90S

RECCE 53: 18 BRDM 2; 35 EE-9 *Cascavel*;

IFV 650: ε400 BMP-1; ε90 BMP-3M; ε60 BTR-4 (inc variants); 100 BTR-80A

APC 1,592+

    APC (T) 900: ε500 M113A2/*Talha*; ε400 MT-LB

    APC (W) VN22A (mod)

    PPV 692+: 12 *Barracuda*; 250 *Caiman*; *Gorets*-M; ε400 ILAV *Badger*; *Mamba*; 30 *Maxxpro*

    AUV 528+: *Abhar*; ε400 *Akrep*; 20 *Commando*; M-ATV; 108 T-Kat

ENGINEERING & MAINTENANCE VEHICLES

    ARV 222+: 180 BREM; 35+ M88A1/2; 7 *Maxxpro* ARV; T-54/55 ARV; Type-653; VT-55A

NBC VEHICLES 20 *Fuchs* NBC

ANTI-TANK/ANTI-INFRASTRUCTURE

    MSL • MANPATS 9K135 *Kornet* (RS-AT-14 *Spriggan*) (reported)

ARTILLERY 1,064+

    SP 48+: **152mm** 18+ Type-83; **155mm** 30: 6 M109A1; 24 M109A5

    TOWED 60+: **130mm** M-46/Type-59; **152mm** D-20; Type-83; **155mm** ε60 M198

    MRL 6+: **122mm** some BM-21 *Grad*; **220mm** 6+ TOS-1A

    MOR 950+: **81mm** ε500 M252; **120mm** ε450 M120;

HELICOPTERS

    ATK 6 Mi-35M *Hind*†; (11 Mi-28NE *Havoc*; 4 Mi-28UB *Havoc*; 15 Mi-35M *Hind* all non-operational)

    MRH 51+: 4+ SA342 *Gazelle*; 17 Bell IA407; 23 H135M; 7 Mi-17 *Hip* H/Mi-171Sh† (38 more non-operational)

    ISR 10 OH-58C *Kiowa*

    TPT • Light 51: 16 Bell 205 (UH-1H *Huey* II); 10 Bell 206B3 *Jet Ranger*; ε18 Bell T407; 7 Bell 505 *Jet Ranger* X

UNINHABITED AERIAL VEHICLES

    CISR • Heavy 12+: 12 CH-4; some CH-5

AIR-LAUNCHED MISSILES • ASM 9K114 *Shturm* (RS-AT-6 *Spiral*); AGR-20A APKWS; AR-1; *Ingwe*

BOMBS • INS/GPS-guided FT-9

Navy 3,000

EQUIPMENT BY TYPE

PATROL AND COASTAL COMBATANTS 32

    PCF (1 *Musa ibn Nusayr* (ITA *Assad*) with 1 76mm gun non-operational)

    PCO 2 *Al Basra* (US *River Hawk*)

    PCC 4 *Fateh* (ITA *Diciotti*)

    PB 20: 12 Swiftships 35; 5 *Predator* (PRC 27m); 3 *Al Faw*

    PBR 6: 2 Type-200; 4 Type-2010

Marines 1,000

FORCES BY ROLE

MANOEUVRE

    Amphibious

    2 mne bn

Air Force ε5,000

FORCES BY ROLE

FIGHTER/GROUND ATTACK

    2 sqn with F-16C/D *Fighting Falcon*

GROUND ATTACK

    1 sqn with Su-25/Su-25K/Su-25UBK *Frogfoot*

    1 sqn with L-159A; L-159T1

ISR

    1 sqn with CH-2000 *Sama*; SB7L-360 *Seeker*

    1 sqn with Cessna 208B *Grand Caravan*; Cessna AC-208B *Combat Caravan**

    1 sqn with Beech 350 *King Air*

TRANSPORT

    1 sqn with An-32B *Cline*

    1 sqn with C-130E/J-30 *Hercules*

TRAINING

    1 sqn with Cessna 172, Cessna 208B

    1 sqn with *Lasta*-95

    1 sqn with T-6A

    1 sqn with T-50IQ *Golden Eagle**

    1 sqn with *Super Mushshak* (forming)

EQUIPMENT BY TYPE

AIRCRAFT 88 combat capable

    FGA 32 F-16C/D *Fighting Falcon*

    ATK 30: 10 L-159A; 1 L-159T1; ε19 Su-25/Su-25K/Su-25UBK *Frogfoot*†

    ISR 10: 2 Cessna AC-208B *Combat Caravan**; 2 SB7L-360 *Seeker*; 6 Beech 350ER *King Air*

    TPT 27: **Medium** 12: 6 C-130J-30 *Hercules*; 6 An-32B *Cline* (2 combat capable); (3 C-130E *Hercules* in store); **Light** 15: 1 Beech 350 *King Air*; 5 Cessna 208B *Grand Caravan*; 9 Cessna 172

    TRG 64+: 8 CH-2000 *Sama*; 10+ *Lasta*-95; 8 *Super Mushshak*; 14 T-6A *Texan* II; 24 T-50IQ *Golden Eagle**

AIR-LAUNCHED MISSILES

    AAM • IR AIM-9L/M *Sidewinder*; **SARH** AIM-7M *Sparrow*

    ASM AGM-114 *Hellfire*

BOMBS

    Laser-guided GBU-10 *Paveway* II; GBU-12 *Paveway* II

Air Defence Command ε5,000

FORCES BY ROLE

AIR DEFENCE

    1 SAM bn with 96K6 *Pantsir*-S1 (RS-SA-22 *Greyhound*)

    1 SAM bn with M1097 *Avenger*

    1 SAM bn with 9K338 *Igla-S* (RS-SA-24 *Grinch*)

    1 ADA bn with ZU-23-2; S-60

EQUIPMENT BY TYPE

AIR DEFENCE

    SAM

        Point-defence M1097 *Avenger*; 9K338 *Igla-S* (RS-SA-24 *Grinch*)

    SPAAGM 30mm 24 96K6 *Pantsir*-S1 (RS-SA-22 *Greyhound*)

GUNS • TOWED 23mm ZU-23-2; 57mm S-60

Gendarmerie & Paramilitary ε266,000

Iraqi Federal Police ε36,000

Territorial Interdiction Force ε50,000

FORCES BY ROLE
MANOEUVRE
 Other
  4 sy bde
  11 sy bde (forming)

Popular Mobilisation Forces ε180,000

Includes Badr Organisation; Kataib Hizbullah; Kataib Imam Ali; Kataib Sayyid al-Shuhada

EQUIPMENT BY TYPE
ARMOURED FIGHTING VEHICLES
 MBT T-55; T-72B; T-72 Rakhsh
 IFV BMP-1 mod (23mm gun); BMP-2
 APC • PPV Toophan
ANTI-TANK/ANTI-INFRASTRUCTURE
 MANPATS Dehlavieh (Kornet); Toophan
ARTILLERY
 TOWED • 130mm M-46; 152mm D-20
 MRL • 122mm HM-20
UNINHABITED AERIAL VEHICLES
 CISR • Medium Mohajer 6
 OWA Ababil T; Shahed 101; Shahed 131
AIR DEFENCE
 SAM • Short-range Saqr-1 (358) (reported)
 GUNS • SP 23mm BMP-1 mod (ZU-23-2 on BMP-1 chassis)

FOREIGN FORCES

Australia Operation Inherent Resolve (Okra) 110 • NATO Mission Iraq 2
Bulgaria NATO Mission Iraq 2
Canada NATO Mission Iraq 14
Croatia Operation Inherent Resolve 3 • NATO Mission Iraq 7
Czech Republic Operation Inherent Resolve 60 • **NATO Mission Iraq** 5
Denmark NATO Mission Iraq 15
Estonia Operation Inherent Resolve 88 • NATO Mission Iraq 110; 1 inf coy
Fiji UNAMI 157; 2 sy unit
Finland Operation Inherent Resolve 70; 1 trg unit • NATO Mission Iraq 4
France Operation Inherent Resolve 6 • NATO Mission Iraq 4
Germany Operation Inherent Resolve 90 • NATO Mission Iraq 50
Greece NATO Mission Iraq 4
Hungary Operation Inherent Resolve 20 • NATO Mission Iraq 3
Italy Operation Inherent Resolve (Prima Parthica) 300; 1 trg unit; 1 hel sqn with 5 NH90 • NATO Mission Iraq 75
Latvia Operation Inherent Resolve 1 • NATO Mission Iraq 3
Lithuania NATO Mission Iraq 30
Macedonia, North NATO Mission Iraq 4
Montenegro NATO Mission Iraq 1
Nepal UNAMI 88; 1 sy unit
Netherlands Operation Inherent Resolve 7 • NATO Mission Iraq 280; 1 air mob coy; 1 hel flt
Norway Operation Inherent Resolve 30; 1 trg unit • NATO Mission Iraq 2
Poland Operation Inherent Resolve 208 • NATO Mission Iraq 51
Portugal NATO Mission Iraq 1
Romania Operation Inherent Resolve 30 • NATO Mission Iraq 2
Slovakia Operation Inherent Resolve 1 • NATO Mission Iraq 4
Slovenia Operation Inherent Resolve 3
Spain Operation Inherent Resolve 180; 1 trg units; 1 hel unit • NATO Mission Iraq 178
Sweden Operation Inherent Resolve 1 • NATO Mission Iraq 1
Turkiye Army 4,000 • NATO Mission Iraq 86
United Kingdom Operation Inherent Resolve (Shader) 70; 1 inf coy • NATO Mission Iraq 27
United States Operation Inherent Resolve 2,500; 1 inf bde(-); 2 atk hel bn with AH-64D Apache; MQ-1C Gray Eagle; 1 spec ops hel bn with MH-47G Chinook; MH-60M Black Hawk; 1 CISR UAV sqn with MQ-9A Reaper; 2 SAM bty with M903 Patriot PAC-3 MSE; • NATO Mission Iraq 16

Israel ISR

New Israeli Shekel ILS		2023	2024	2025
GDP	ILS	1.88trn	1.96trn	2.08trn
	USD	514bn	528bn	551bn
Real GDP growth	%	2.0	0.7	2.7
Def bdgt	ILS	70.1bn	125bn	
	USD	19.1bn	33.7bn	
FMA (US)	USD	3.30bn	3.30bn	3.30bn

Real-terms defence budget trend (USDbn, constant 2015)

Population	9,402,617					
Age	0–14	15–19	20–24	25–29	30–64	65 plus
Male	14.0%	4.1%	3.8%	3.5%	19.3%	5.6%
Female	13.4%	3.9%	3.7%	3.4%	18.6%	6.7%

Capabilities

The Israel Defense Forces (IDF) are highly trained and organised for territorial defence, short-term interventions in neighbouring states and limited regional power projection. The country is widely believed to possess nuclear weapons. In 2024, IDF forces continued to engage Hamas in Gaza and also Hizbullah in Lebanon. These operations have delayed the intended implementation of a new IDF multi-year defence programme, dubbed Ma'alot (Ascent). The US remains Israel's vital defence partner. Washington provides significant funding and is instrumental in several equipment programmes. The IDF has historically had high training levels despite its reliance on national service. Largely asymmetric threats in recent years have focused modernisation efforts on force-protection, missile defence and precision-strike capabilities, but have also raised questions about the forces' discipline and readiness for more conventional operations. Given its mission-set, the IDF's logistics capabilities are limited to sustaining operations within Israel itself or in immediately neighbouring territories, but the air force maintains a limited capability to conduct longer-range missions. Air defence capability was augmented by Western assistance in countering Iranian attacks, and in response Israel utilised capabilities including air-launched ballistic missiles. Israel maintains a broad defence-industrial base, with world-class capabilities in uninhabited systems, guided weapons, radars and sensors, and cyber security. Military aircraft and large naval vessels are imported and often modified with Israeli systems.

ACTIVE 169,500 (Army 126,000 Navy 9,500 Air 34,000) Gendarmerie & Paramilitary 8,000

Conscript liability Officers 48 months, other ranks 32 months, women 24 months (Jews and Druze only; Christians, Circassians and Muslims may volunteer)

RESERVE 465,000 (Army 400,000 Navy 10,000 Air 55,000)

Annual trg as cbt reservists to age 40 (some specialists to age 54) for male other ranks, 38 (or marriage/pregnancy) for women

ORGANISATIONS BY SERVICE

Strategic Forces

Israel is widely believed to have a nuclear capability – delivery means include F-15I and F-16I ac, *Jericho* 2 MRBM and, reportedly, *Dolphin/Tanin*-class SSKs with LACM

FORCES BY ROLE
SURFACE-TO-SURFACE MISSILE
 3 MRBM sqn with *Jericho* 2
EQUIPMENT BY TYPE
SURFACE-TO-SURFACE MISSILE LAUNCHERS
 MRBM • **Nuclear**: ε24 *Jericho* 2

Strategic Defences
FORCES BY ROLE
AIR DEFENCE
 3 bty with *Arrow* 2/3 ATBM with *Green Pine/Super Green Pine* radar and *Citrus Tree* command post
 10 bty with *Iron Dome* (incl reserve bty)
 2 bty with *David's Sling*

Space
EQUIPMENT BY TYPE
SATELLITES
 ISR 4: 2 *Ofeq*-5, 1 *Ofeq*-11; 1 *Ofeq*-13

Army 26,000; 100,000 conscript (total 126,000)

Organisation and structure of formations may vary according to op situations. Equipment includes that required for reserve forces on mobilisation

FORCES BY ROLE
COMMAND
 3 (regional comd) corps HQ
 2 armd div HQ
 1 (Multidimensional) div HQ
 5 (territorial) inf div HQ
 1 (home defence) comd HQ
SPECIAL FORCES
 1 SF bn
 1 spec ops bde (3 spec ops unit)
MANOEUVRE
 Armoured
 3 armd bde (1 recce coy, 3 armd bn, 1 AT coy, 1 cbt engr bn)
 1 (Multidimensional) armd inf/ISR bn
 Mechanised
 3 mech inf bde (3 mech inf bn, 1 cbt spt bn, 1 sigs coy)
 1 mech inf bde (1 recce bn, 4 mech inf bn, 1 cbt spt bn)
 1 indep mech inf bn
 Light
 2 indep inf bn
 Air Manoeuvre
 1 para bde (3 para bn, 1 cbt spt bn, 1 sigs coy)
 Other
 1 armd trg bde (3 armd bn)
 1 (Border Protection) sy bde (5 ISR bn; 5 sy bn)
COMBAT SUPPORT
 2 arty bde
 1 (special) arty bde
 1 engr bde (3 engr bn, 3 EOD coy)
 1 engr bn
 1 CBRN bn
 1 int bde (3 int bn)
 1 int unit
 1 SIGINT unit
 2 MP bn

Reserves 400,000+ on mobilisation
FORCES BY ROLE
COMMAND
 2 armd div HQ
 1 AB div HQ
SPECIAL FORCES
 1 spec ops bde
MANOEUVRE
 Armoured
 9 armd bde
 Mechanised
 8 mech inf bde
 Light
 16 (territorial/regional) inf bde
 Air Manoeuvre
 4 para bde
 Mountain
 1 mtn inf bde
 1 mtn inf bn

Other
1 sy bde (forming)
COMBAT SUPPORT
4 arty bde
COMBAT SERVICE SUPPORT
6 log unit
EQUIPMENT BY TYPE
ARMOURED FIGHTING VEHICLES
  MBT ε400 *Merkava* MkIV/Mk IV *Barak*; (ε700 *Merkava* MkIII; ε200 *Merkava* MkIV all in store)
  APC 390+
    APC (T) 320+: ε320 *Namer*; M113A2; *Nagmachon* (Centurion chassis); *Nakpadon* (5,100: ε100 *Achzarit* (modified T-55 chassis); 5,000 M113A1/A2 all in store)
    APC (W) ε70 *Eitan*
  PPV *Panter*
  AUV *Tigris*; *Sand Cat*; *Ze'ev*
ENGINEERING & MAINTENANCE VEHICLES
  AEV D9R; *Namera*; *Puma*
  ARV *Namer*; M88A1; M113 ARV
  VLB *Alligator* MAB; M48/60; MTU
NBC VEHICLES ε8 TPz-1 *Fuchs* NBC
ANTI-TANK/ANTI-INFRASTRUCTURE • MSL
  MANPATS IMI MAPATS; *Spike* SR/MR/LR/ER
ARTILLERY 530
  SP 250: **155mm** 250 M109A5; *Roem*; (**155mm** 30 M109A2; **175mm** 36 M107; **203mm** 36 M110 all in store)
  TOWED (**155mm** 171: 40 M-46 mod; 50 M-68/M-71; 81 M-839P/M-845P all in store)
  MRL 48: **227mm** 30 M270 MLRS; **306mm** ε18 *Lahav* (**160mm** 50 LAR-160; **227mm** 18 M270 MLRS; **290mm** 20 LAR-290 all in store)
  MOR 250: **81mm** 250 (**81mm** 1,100; **120mm** 650; **160mm** 18 Soltam M-66 all in store); **SP 120mm** *Khanit*
UNINHABITED AERIAL VEHICLES
  ISR • Light *Skylark* 3
AIR DEFENCE
  SAM • Point-defence *Machbet*; FIM-92 *Stinger*

Navy 7,000; 2,500 conscript (total 9,500)
EQUIPMENT BY TYPE
SUBMARINES 5
  SSK 5:
    3 *Dolphin* (GER HDW design) with 6 single 533mm TT with UGM-84C *Harpoon* Block 1B AShM/*SeaHake* (DM2A3) HWT/*SeaHake* mod 4 (DM2A4) HWT/*Kaved* HWT, 4 single 650mm TT with dual-capable LACM (reported)
    2 *Tanin* (GER HDW design) (fitted with AIP) with 6 single 533mm TT with UGM-84C *Harpoon* Block 1B AShM/*SeaHake* (DM2A3) HWT/*SeaHake* mod 4 (DM2A4) HWT/*Kaved* HWT, 4 single 650mm TT with dual-capable LACM (reported)
PATROL AND COASTAL COMBATANTS 51

CORVETTES • FSGHM 7:
  3 *Eilat* (*Sa'ar* 5) with 2 quad lnchr with RGM-84 *Harpoon* AShM/*Gabriel* V AShM, 4 8-cell VLS with *Barak*-8 SAM, 2 triple 324mm TT with Mk 46 LWT, 1 Mk 15 *Phalanx* CIWS (capacity 1 AS565SA *Panther* ASW hel)
  4 *Magen* (*Sa'ar* 6) with 2 quad lnchr with *Gabriel* V AShM, 2 20-cell VLS with *Tamir* (C-*Dome*) SAM, 4 8-cell VLS with *Barak* LRAD, 2 triple 324mm ASTT with Mk 54 LWT (capacity 1 AS565SA *Panther* ASW hel)
PCGM 8 *Hetz* (*Sa'ar* 4.5) with 2 quad lnchr with RGM-84 *Harpoon* AShM (can also be fitted with up to 6 single lnchr with *Gabriel* II AShM), 2 8-cell VLS with *Barak*-1 SAM, (can be fitted with 2 triple 324mm Mk32 TT with Mk46 LWT), 1 Mk 15 *Phalanx* CWIS, 1 76mm gun
PBF 34: 5 *Shaldag*; 2 *Shaldag* V; 3 *Stingray*; 9 *Super Dvora* Mk I (SSM & TT may be fitted); 2+ *Super Dvora* Mk II (SSM & TT may be fitted); 6 *Super Dvora* Mk II-I (SSM & TT may be fitted); 4 *Super Dvora* Mk III (SSM & TT may be fitted); 3 *Super Dvora* Mk III (SSM may be fitted)
AMPHIBIOUS
  LANDING SHIP • LSL 1 *Nahshon* (US *Frank Besson* mod) (capacity 24 MBT)
  LANDING CRAFT • LCVP 3 *Manta*
LOGISTICS AND SUPPORT
  AG 1 *Bat Yam* (ex-GER Type-745)
UNINHABITED MARITIME PLATFORMS
  USV • MARSEC • Small 10: 10 *Protector* (9m); *Seagull*; *Silver Marlin*
  UUV • MARSEC • Extra-large *Caesaron*

Naval Commandos ε300
FORCES BY ROLE
SPECIAL FORCES
  1 cdo unit

Air Force 34,000
Responsible for Air and Space Coordination
FORCES BY ROLE
FIGHTER & FIGHTER/GROUND ATTACK
  1 sqn with F-15A/B/D *Eagle* (*Baz*)
  1 sqn with F-15B/C/D *Eagle* (*Baz*)
  1 sqn with F-15I *Ra'am*
  5 sqn with F-16C/D *Fighting Falcon* (*Barak*)
  4 sqn with F-16I *Fighting Falcon* (*Sufa*)
  2 sqn with F-35I *Adir*
ANTI-SUBMARINE WARFARE
  1 sqn with AS565SA *Panther* (missions flown by IAF but with non-rated aircrew)
ELECTRONIC WARFARE
  1 sqn with Beech A36 *Bonanza* (*Hofit*); Beech 200/200T/200CT *King Air*
AIRBORNE EARLY WARNING & CONTROL
  1 sqn with Gulfstream G550 *Eitam*; Gulfstream G550 *Shavit*
TANKER/TRANSPORT
  1 sqn with C-130E/H *Hercules*; KC-130H *Hercules*

1 sqn with C-130J-30 *Hercules*
1 sqn with KC-707 (*Re'em*)
TRAINING
1 OPFOR sqn with F-16C/D *Fighting Falcon* (*Barak*)
1 sqn with F-35I *Adir*
1 sqn with M-346 *Master* (*Lavi*)
ATTACK HELICOPTER
1 sqn with AH-64A *Apache* (*Peten*)
1 sqn with AH-64D *Apache* (*Saraf*)
TRANSPORT HELICOPTER
2 sqn with CH-53D *Sea Stallion*
2 sqn with S-70A *Black Hawk*; UH-60A *Black Hawk*
1 medevac unit with CH-53D *Sea Stallion*
CISR UAV
2 sqn with *Hermes* 450 (*Zik*)
1 sqn with *Hermes* 900 (*Kochav*)
ISR UAV
1 sqn with *Heron* (*Shoval*); *Heron* TP (*Eitan*)
1 sqn with *Heron* (*Shoval*) (MP role)
1 sqn with *Orbiter* 4 (*Nitzoz*)
AIR DEFENCE
3 bty with *Arrow* 2/3
10 bty with *Iron Dome*
2 bty with *David's Sling*
SPECIAL FORCES
1 SF wg (2 SF unit, 1 CSAR unit, 1 int unit)
SURFACE-TO-SURFACE MISSILE
3 MRBM sqn with *Jericho* 2
EQUIPMENT BY TYPE
AIRCRAFT 340 combat capable
　FGA 310: 8 F-15A *Eagle* (*Baz*); 6 F-15B *Eagle* (*Baz*); 17 F-15C *Eagle* (*Baz*); 19 F-15D *Eagle* (*Baz*); 25 F-15I *Ra'am*; ε50 F-16C *Fighting Falcon* (*Barak*); 49 F-16D *Fighting Falcon* (*Barak*); 97 F-16I *Fighting Falcon* (*Sufa*); 39 F-35I *Adir*
　ISR 1 Gulfstream G550 *Oron*
　ELINT 3 Gulfstream G550 *Shavit*
　AEW 2 Gulfstream G550 *Eitam*
　TKR/TPT 10: 4 KC-130H *Hercules*; 6 KC-707 (*Re'em*)
　TPT 65: **Medium** 18: 5 C-130E *Hercules*; 6 C-130H *Hercules*; 7 C-130J-30 *Hercules*; **Light** 47: 3 AT-802 *Air Tractor*; 9 Beech 200 *King Air*; 8 Beech 200T *King Air*; 5 Beech 200CT *King Air*; 22 Beech A36 *Bonanza* (*Hofit*)
　TRG 66: 16 Grob G-120; 30 M-346 *Master* (*Lavi*)*; 20 T-6A
HELICOPTERS
　ATK 46: 26 AH-64A *Apache* (*Peten*); 20 AH-64D *Apache* (*Saraf*)
　ASW 7 AS565SA *Panther* (missions flown by IAF but with non-rated aircrew)
　ISR 12 OH-58B *Kiowa*
　TPT 80: **Heavy** 25 CH-53D *Sea Stallion*; **Medium** 49: 39 S-70A *Black Hawk*; 10 UH-60A *Black Hawk*; **Light** 6 Bell 206 *Jet Ranger*
UNINHABITED AERIAL VEHICLES
　CISR • **Medium** *Hermes* 450 (*Zik*); *Hermes* 900 (*Kochav*);
　ISR • **Heavy** *Heron* (*Shoval*); *Heron* TP (*Eitan*); RA-01 (reported); **Light** *Orbiter* 4 (*Nitzoz*)
　OWA *Harop*; *Harpy*
SURFACE-TO-SURFACE MISSILE LAUNCHERS
　MRBM • **Nuclear** ε24 *Jericho* 2
AIR DEFENCE
　SAM 40+:
　　Long-range (M901 *Patriot* PAC-2 in store)
　　Medium-range some *David's Sling*
　　Short-range up to 40 *Iron Dome*
　　Point-defence *Machbet*
　GUNS • **TOWED 20mm** M167 *Vulcan*
MISSILE DEFENCE • **SAM** 24 *Arrow* 2/*Arrow* 3
AIR-LAUNCHED MISSILES
　AAM • **IR** AIM-9 *Sidewinder*; *Python* 4; **IIR** AIM-9X *Sidewinder* II; *Python* 5; **ARH** AIM-120C AMRAAM
　ASM AGM-114 *Hellfire*; AGM-65 *Maverick*; *Delilah* AL; *Mikholit*; *Popeye* I/II; *Rampage*; *Spike* NLOS
　ALBM *Golden Horizon*; *Rocks*
BOMBS
　IIR guided *Opher*
　Laser-guided *Griffin*; *Lizard*; *Paveway* II
　INS/GPS-guided GBU-31 JDAM; GBU-39 Small Diameter Bomb (*Barad Had*); *Spice*; *Spice* 2000

Airfield Defence 3,000 active (15,000 reservists)

Gendarmerie & Paramilitary ε8,000

Border Police ε8,000

DEPLOYMENT

LEBANON: ε45,000; 4 div HQ; 1 spec ops bde; 4 armd bde; 4 mech bde; 2 inf bde; 2 AB bde; 1 mtn bde; 1 arty bde
PALESTINIAN TERRITORIES: ε25,000; 3 div HQ; 2 armd bde; 3 mech bde; 2 inf bde; 1 AB bde; 1 arty bde

FOREIGN FORCES

UNTSO unless specified. UNTSO figures represent total numbers for mission
Argentina 3 • UNDOF 1
Australia 12 • UNDOF 2
Austria 5
Belgium 1
Bhutan 4 • UNDOF 4
Canada 4
Chile 3
China 5
Czech Republic UNDOF 4
Denmark 10
Estonia 1
Fiji 2 • UNDOF 149; 1 inf coy
Finland 16

France 1
Ghana UNDOF 5
India 2 • UNDOF 201; 1 inf pl; 1 MP pl; 1 log coy
Ireland 12 • UNDOF 4
Kazakhstan UNDOF 140; 1 recce coy
Korea, Republic of 2 • UNDOF 1
Latvia 1
Nepal 3 • UNDOF 451; 1 mech inf coy; 1 inf coy; 1 engr pl
Netherlands 11
New Zealand 8
Norway 12
Poland 3
Russia 4
Serbia 1
Slovakia 3
Slovenia 2
Sweden 5
Switzerland 12
United States 2 • US Strategic Command; 200; 1 SAM bty with THAAD; 1 AN/TPY-2 X-band radar at Mount Keren
Uruguay UNDOF 211; 1 mech inf coy
Zambia 1 • UNDOF 3

Jordan JOR

Jordanian Dinar JOD		2023	2024	2025
GDP	JOD	36.1bn	37.8bn	39.8bn
	USD	50.9bn	53.3bn	56.1bn
Real GDP growth	%	2.6	2.4	2.9
Def bdgt [a]	JOD	1.45bn	1.50bn	
	USD	2.04bn	2.12bn	
FMA (US)	USD	425m	400m	400m

[a] Excludes expenditure on public order and safety

Real-terms defence budget trend (USDbn, constant 2015)

Population	11,174,024					
Age	0–14	15–19	20–24	25–29	30–64	65 plus
Male	15.9%	5.0%	4.8%	4.6%	20.0%	2.0%
Female	15.0%	4.8%	4.5%	4.1%	17.2%	2.2%

Capabilities

The Jordanian Armed Forces are structured to provide border security and an armoured response to conventional threats. They have recently focused on tackling narcotics- and weapons-smuggling from Syria. The government has issued no recent public statement on defence policy, but regional instability is a prime concern. Jordan is a major non-NATO ally of the US, with a close bilateral defence relationship, including a 2021 defence cooperation agreement. In 2024, NATO opened a liaison office in Jordan, building on an existing partnership between Amman and the alliance. The country has developed a special-forces training centre and has hosted training for numerous state and non-state military forces. Personnel are relatively well trained, particularly aircrew and special forces, who are highly regarded internationally.

Jordanian forces are able to independently deploy regionally and participated in ISAF operations in Afghanistan and in coalition air operations over Syria and Yemen. Jordan's inventory largely comprises older systems and procurements have typically been in small numbers, second-hand or donations. Although the state-owned Jordan Design and Development Bureau (JODDB) has demonstrated the capacity to upgrade vehicles, the army has largely recapitalised its armoured vehicle fleet with second-hand equipment from European countries. JODDB has produced some light-armoured vehicles for domestic use through agreements with foreign suppliers.

ACTIVE 100,500 (Army 86,000 Navy 500 Air 14,000) Gendarmerie & Paramilitary 15,000

RESERVE 65,000 (Army 60,000 Joint 5,000)

ORGANISATIONS BY SERVICE

Army 86,000
FORCES BY ROLE
SPECIAL FORCES
1 (Royal Guard) SF gp (1 SF regt, 1 SF bn, 1 CT bn)
1 spec ops bde (3 spec ops bn)
MANOEUVRE
Armoured
1 (40th) armd bde (2 tk bn, 1 armd inf bn)
1 (60th) armd bde (1 tk bn, 1 lt armd bn, 1 mech inf bn)
Mechanised
4 mech bde (1 tk bn, 2 mech inf bn)
4 mech bde (3 mech inf bn)
Light
1 (Border Gd) inf bde (6 inf bn)
1 (Border Gd) inf bde (4 inf bn)
1 (Border Gd) inf gp
Air Manoeuvre
1 AB bde (3 AB bn)
Other
1 (Royal Guard) gd bde
COMBAT SUPPORT
1 arty bde (5 SP arty bn)
1 arty bde (4 SP arty bn)
1 arty bde (2 SP arty bn)
1 MRL bde (1 fd arty bn, 2 MRL bn, 1 mor bn, 1 STA bn)
1 AD bde (3 AD bn)
3 AD bde (2 AD bn)
1 engr bn
COMBAT SERVICE SUPPORT
1 log bn
EQUIPMENT BY TYPE
ARMOURED FIGHTING VEHICLES
MBT 302: ε50 FV4034 *Challenger 1* (*Al Hussein*); 70 *Leclerc*; 182 M60A3
ASLT 80 B1 *Centauro* (61 more in store)
IFV 399: 13 AIFV-B-C25; 50 *Marder* 1A3; 336 YPR-765 PRI
APC 968+

APC (T) 729: 370 M113A1/A2 Mk1J; 269 M577A2 (CP); 87 YPR-765 PRCO (CP); 3 AIFV-B
PPV 239: some *Al-Wahsh*; 45 *Caiman*; 25 *Marauder*; 25 *Matador*; 100 *MaxxPro*; 44 *Nomad/Thunder*
AUV 35 *Cougar*

ENGINEERING & MAINTENANCE VEHICLES
ARV 85+: *Al Monjed*; 5 BPz-1; FV4204 *Chieftain* ARV; 32 M88A1; 30 M578; 18 YPR-806
MW 12 *Aardvark* Mk2

ANTI-TANK/ANTI-INFRASTRUCTURE • MSL
SP 115: 70 M901; 45 AIFV-B-*Milan*
MANPATS FGM-148 *Javelin*; TOW/TOW-2A; 9K135 *Kornet* (RS-AT-14 *Spriggan*); Luch *Corsar*; *Stugna*-P

ARTILLERY 1,285
SP 394: **155mm** 358 M109A1/A2; **203mm** 36 M110A2 (112 more in store)
TOWED 84: **105mm** 66: 54 M102; 12 M119A2; **155mm** 18 M114
MRL 32+: **220mm** 2+ SR5; **227mm** 12 M142 HIMARS; **273mm** 18 WM-80
MOR 777: **81mm** 359; **SP 81mm** 50; **107mm** 50 M30; **120mm** 300 Brandt; **SP 120mm** 18 *Agrab* Mk2

AIR DEFENCE
SAM • Point-defence 92+: 92 9K35 *Strela*-10 (RS-SA-13 *Gopher*); 9K36 *Strela*-3 (RS-SA-14 *Gremlin*); 9K310 *Igla*-1 (RS-SA-16 *Gimlet*); 9K38 *Igla* (RS-SA-18 *Grouse*); 9K338 *Igla*-S (RS-SA-24 *Grinch*)
GUNS • SP 108: **23mm** 48 ZSU-23-4 *Shilka*; **35mm** 60 *Gepard*

Navy ε500
EQUIPMENT BY TYPE
PATROL AND COASTAL COMBATANTS 9
PBF 2 Response Boat-Medium (RB-M)
PB 7: 4 *Abdullah* (US *Dauntless*); 3 *Al Hussein* (UK Vosper 30m)

Marines
FORCES BY ROLE
MANOEUVRE
Amphibious
1 mne unit

Air Force 14,000
FORCES BY ROLE
FIGHTER/GROUND ATTACK
2 sqn with F-16AM/BM *Fighting Falcon*
ISR
1 sqn with AT-802U *Air Tractor*
1 sqn with Cessna 208B
TRANSPORT
1 sqn with C-130E *Hercules*
TRAINING
1 OCU with F-16AM/BM *Fighting Falcon*

1 sqn with PC-21
1 sqn with Grob 120TP
1 hel sqn with Bell 505 *Jet Ranger* X; R-44 *Raven* II

ATTACK HELICOPTER
2 sqn with AH-1F *Cobra*

TRANSPORT HELICOPTER
1 sqn with AS332M *Super Puma*; UH-60A *Black Hawk*
1 sqn with EC635; UH-60A *Black Hawk*
1 sqn with UH-60M *Black Hawk*
1 sqn with Mi-26T2 *Halo*
1 (Royal) flt with VH-60M *Black Hawk*; AW 39

ISR UAV
1 sqn with S-100 *Camcopter*

AIR DEFENCE
2 bde with MIM-23B Phase III I-*Hawk*

EQUIPMENT BY TYPE
AIRCRAFT 57 combat capable
FGA 47: 33 F-16AM *Fighting Falcon*; 14 F-16BM *Fighting Falcon*
ATK (2 AC235 in store, offered for sale)
ISR 10: 6 AT-802 *Air Tractor**; 4 AT-802U *Air Tractor**
TPT 11: **Medium** 3 C-130E *Hercules* (1 C-130B *Hercules*, 4 C-130H *Hercules* in store); **Light** 7: 5 Cessna 208B; 2 M-28 *Skytruck*; **PAX** 1 CL-604 *Challenger*
TRG 25: 13 Grob 120TP; 12 PC-21; (12 Hawk Mk63* in store, offered for sale)

HELICOPTERS
ATK 12 AH-1F *Cobra* (17 more in store, offered for sale)
MRH 14: 3 AW139; 11 H135M (Tpt/SAR); (6 MD-530F in store, offered for sale)
TPT 71: **Heavy** 4 Mi-26T2 *Halo*; **Medium** 38: 10 AS332M *Super Puma*; 8 UH-60A *Black Hawk*; 5 UH-60L *Black Hawk*; 12 UH-60M *Black Hawk*; 3 VH-60M *Black Hawk*; **Light** 29: 10 Bell 505 *Jet Ranger* X; 7 EC635; 2 R-44 *Raven* II; (13 Bell 205 (UH-1H *Iroquois*) in store, offered for sale)

UNINHABITED AERIAL VEHICLES
CISR • Heavy (some CH-4B in store, offered for sale)
ISR • Light S-100 *Camcopter*

AIR DEFENCE
SAM • Medium-range 24 MIM-23B Phase III I-*Hawk*
GUNS • TOWED 40mm 22 L/70 (with *Flycatcher* radar)

AIR-LAUNCHED MISSILES
AAM • IR AIM-9J/N/P *Sidewinder*; **SARH** AIM-7 *Sparrow*; **ARH** AIM-120C AMRAAM
ASM AGM-65D/G *Maverick*; BGM-71 TOW

BOMBS
Laser-guided GBU-10/12 *Paveway* II

Gendarmerie & Paramilitary ε15,000 active

Gendarmerie ε15,000 active
3 regional comd
FORCES BY ROLE
SPECIAL FORCES
  2 SF unit
MANOEUVRE
  Other
  10 sy bn
EQUIPMENT BY TYPE
ARMOURED FIGHTING VEHICLES
  APC • APC (W) 25+: AT105 *Saxon* (reported); 25+ EE-11 *Urutu*
  AUV AB2 *Al-Jawad*

DEPLOYMENT

CENTRAL AFRICAN REPUBLIC: UN • MINUSCA 10
DEMOCRATIC REPUBLIC OF THE CONGO: UN • MONUSCO 9
SOUTH SUDAN: UN • UNMISS 5

FOREIGN FORCES

France *Operation Inherent Resolve* (*Chammal*) 300; 4 *Rafale* F3
Germany *Operation Inherent Resolve* 150; 1 A400M
United States US Central Command: *Operation Inherent Resolve* 3,000; 1 FGA sqn with 18 F-15E *Strike Eagle*; 1 CISR sqn with 12 MQ-9A *Reaper*; 2 SAM bty with M903 *Patriot* PAC-3 MSE

Kuwait KWT

Kuwaiti Dinar KWD		2023	2024	2025
GDP	KWD	50.3bn	49.7bn	49.8bn
	USD	164bn	162bn	162bn
Real GDP growth	%	-3.6	-2.7	3.3
Def bdgt [a]	KWD	2.38bn	2.40bn	
	USD	7.75bn	7.80bn	

[a] Includes National Guard

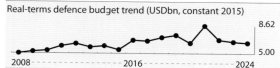

Population	3,138,355					
Age	0–14	15–19	20–24	25–29	30–64	65 plus
Male	12.0%	3.4%	4.8%	7.0%	28.9%	1.5%
Female	11.0%	3.1%	3.7%	4.3%	18.1%	2.0%

Capabilities

Kuwait's armed forces are postured to provide territorial defence through a strategy of holding out against a superior aggressor until allied forces can be mobilised to assist. Kuwait's key defence relationship is with the US. Washington designated Kuwait a major non-NATO ally in 2004, and a bilateral defence-cooperation agreement provides for a range of joint activities and mentoring, and the stationing and pre-positioning of US personnel and equipment. US force reductions from CENTCOM in 2021 mean that Kuwait's own capabilities are more critical to its security, as well as those of GCC partners. Kuwait has little expeditionary sustainment capacity, although it made a small air contribution to the Saudi-led coalition at the beginning of the Yemen conflict. Improvements in air and missile defence continue to be a priority, given the country's proximity to Iran. Kuwait is modernising its armoured force, and its combat air arm, although F/A-18 *Super Hornet* deliveries have been delayed. The country has also signed a contract with Turkiye to acquire UAVs. The navy is procuring undersea vehicles for mine-countermeasures missions. Kuwait has some local maintenance capacity bolstered by contractor support, but lacks a defence-industrial base. The country has offset requirements to help stimulate the wider industrial sector.

ACTIVE 17,500 (Army 11,500 Navy 2,000 Air 2,500 Emiri Guard 1,500) Gendarmerie & Paramilitary 7,100

Conscript liability 12 months, males 18–35 years

RESERVE 23,700 (Joint 23,700)

Reserve obligation to age 40; 1 month annual trg

ORGANISATIONS BY SERVICE

Army 11,500
FORCES BY ROLE
SPECIAL FORCES
  1 SF unit
  1 cdo bde
MANOEUVRE
  Armoured
  2 armd bde
  Mechanised
  3 mech inf bde
COMBAT SUPPORT
  1 arty bde
  1 engr bde
  1 MP bn
COMBAT SERVICE SUPPORT
  1 log gp
  1 fd hospital

Reserve
FORCES BY ROLE
MANOEUVRE
  Mechanised
  1 bde
EQUIPMENT BY TYPE
ARMOURED FIGHTING VEHICLES
  MBT 293: 218 M1A2K *Abrams* (being delivered); 75 M-84AB; (218 M1A2 *Abrams*; 75 M-84AB in store)
  IFV 537: 76 BMP-2; 122 BMP-3; 103 BMP-3M; 236 *Desert Warrior*† (incl variants)

APC 260
  APC (T) 260: 230 M113A2; 30 M577 (CP)
  APC (W) (40 TH 390 *Fahd* in store)
  AUV 300 *Sherpa Light Scout*
ENGINEERING & MAINTENANCE VEHICLES
  ARV 41+: 8 M88A1; 33 M88A2; Type-653A; *Warrior*
  MW *Aardvark* Mk2
NBC VEHICLES 12 *Fuchs*-2 NBC
ARTY 193
  SP 155mm 88: 37 M109A3; 51 PLZ-45
  MRL 300mm 27 9A52 *Smerch*
  MOR 78: **81mm** 60; **107mm** 6 M30; **120mm** ε12 RT-F1
ANTI-TANK/ANTI-INFRASTRUCTURE
  MSL
    SP 74: 66 HMMWV TOW; 8 M901
    MANPATS 9K135 *Kornet* (RS-AT-14 *Spriggan*); TOW-2
  RCL 84mm *Carl Gustaf*
AIR DEFENCE
  SAM • Point-defence *Starburst*; FIM-92 *Stinger*

Navy ε2,000 (incl 500 Coast Guard)
EQUIPMENT BY TYPE
PATROL AND COASTAL COMBATANTS 20
  PCFG 2:
    1 *Al Sanbouk* (GER Lurssen TNC 45m) with 2 twin lnchr with MM40 *Exocet* AShM, 1 76mm gun
    1 *Istiqlal* (GER Lurssen TNC 57m) with 2 twin lnchr with MM40 *Exocet* AShM, 1 76mm gun
  PBF 10 *Al Nokatha* (US Mk V PBF)
  PBG 8 *Um Almaradim* (FRA *Combattante* 1 derivative) with 2 twin lnchr with *Sea Skua* AShM
AMPHIBIOUS • LANDING CRAFT 8
  LCT 2 *Assafar* (ADSB 64m)
  LCM 1 *Abhan* (ADSB 42m)
  LCVP 5 ADSB 16m
LOGISTICS AND SUPPORT • AG 1 *Sawahil* with 1 hel landing platform

Marines 800

Air Force 2,500
FORCES BY ROLE
FIGHTER/GROUND ATTACK
  2 sqn with F/A-18C/D *Hornet*
SEARCH & RESCUE
  2 sqn with H225M (opcon Navy)
TRANSPORT
  1 sqn with C-17A *Globemaster* III; KC-130J *Hercules*; L-100-30
TRAINING
  1 OCU sqn with F/A-18C/D *Hornet*
  1 OCU sqn with Eurofighter *Typhoon*
  1 unit with EMB-312 *Tucano**; *Hawk* Mk64*
ATTACK HELICOPTER
  2 sqn with AH-64D *Apache*
  1 atk/trg sqn with SA342 *Gazelle* with HOT
TRANSPORT HELICOPTER
  1 sqn with AS532 *Cougar*; SA330 *Puma*
  1 (VIP) sqn with S-92A
EQUIPMENT BY TYPE
AIRCRAFT 63 combat capable
  FGA 49: 17 Eurofighter *Typhoon*; 25 F/A-18C *Hornet*; 7 F/A-18D *Hornet*
  TKR/TPT 3 KC-130J *Hercules*
  TPT 5: **Heavy** 2 C-17A *Globemaster* III; **Medium** 3 L-100-30
  TRG 14: 6 EMB-312 *Tucano**; 8 *Hawk* Mk64* (10 EMB-312 *Tucano** in store)
HELICOPTERS
  ATK 16 AH-64D *Apache*
  MRH 13 SA342 *Gazelle* with HOT
  TPT 37: **Heavy** 24 H225M; **Medium** 13: 3 AS532 *Cougar*; 7 SA330 *Puma*; 3 S-92A (SAR/VIP)
AIR-LAUNCHED MISSILES
  AAM • IR AIM-9L *Sidewinder*; R-550 *Magic*; **SARH** AIM-7F *Sparrow*; **ARH** AIM-120C7 AMRAAM
  ASM AGM-65G *Maverick*; AGM-114K *Hellfire*; HOT
  AShM AGM-84D *Harpoon* Block IC

Air Defence Command
FORCES BY ROLE
AIR DEFENCE
  1 SAM bde (7 SAM bty with M902 *Patriot* PAC-3)
  1 SAM bde (6 SAM bty with *Skyguard*/*Aspide*)
EQUIPMENT BY TYPE
AIR DEFENCE
  SAM 47
    Long-range 35 M902 *Patriot* PAC-3
    Short-range 12 *Aspide* with *Skyguard*
  GUNS • TOWED 35mm 12+ Oerlikon GDF

Emiri Guard 1,500
FORCES BY ROLE
MANOEUVRE
  Other
    1 (Emiri) gd bde

Gendarmerie & Paramilitary ε7,100 active

National Guard ε6,600 active
FORCES BY ROLE
SPECIAL FORCES
  1 SF bn
MANOEUVRE
  Reconnaissance
    1 armd car bn**Other**
    3 security bn

COMBAT SUPPORT
1 MP bn
EQUIPMENT BY TYPE
ARMOURED FIGHTING VEHICLES
RECCE 20 VBL
IFV ε150 Pandur (incl variants)
APC 67+
APC (W) 27+: 5+ Desert Chameleon; 22 S600 (incl variants)
PPV 40 Otokar ISV
AUV 120 Sherpa Light Scout
ENGINEERING & MAINTENANCE VEHICLES
ARV Pandur
HELICOPTERS
TPT • Heavy 6 E-225M

Coast Guard 500
EQUIPMENT BY TYPE
PATROL AND COASTAL COMBATANTS 32
PBF 12 Manta
PB 20: 3 Al Shaheed; 4 Inttisar (Austal 31.5m); 3 Kassir (Austal 22m); 10 Subahi
AMPHIBIOUS • LANDING CRAFT
LCU 4: 2 Al Tahaddy; 1 Saffar; 1 other
LOGISTICS AND SUPPORT • AG 1 Sawahil

FOREIGN FORCES

Canada Operation Inherent Resolve (Impact) 200
Italy Operation Inherent Resolve (Prima Parthica) 300; 4 Typhoon; 1 MQ-9A Reaper; 1 C-27J Spartan; 1 KC-767A; 1 SAM bty with SAMP/T
United Kingdom Operation Inherent Resolve (Shader) 50; 1 CISR UAV sqn with 8 MQ-9A Reaper
United States US Central Command: 10,000; 1 ARNG armd bn; 1 ARNG inf bn; 1 ARNG MRL bn; 1 (cbt avn) hel bde; 1 spt bde; 1 CISR UAV sqn with MQ-9A Reaper; 1 (APS) armd bde eqpt set; 1 (APS) inf bde eqpt set; 2 SAM bty with M903 Patriot PAC-3 MSE

Lebanon LBN

Lebanese Pound LBP		2023	2024	2025
GDP [a]	LBP			
	USD			
Real GDP growth	%			
Def bdgt	LBP	20.8trn	48.5trn	71.3trn
	USD	239m	540m	793m
FMA (US)	USD	100m	150m	150m

[a] No IMF economic data available for Lebanon

Real-terms defence budget trend (USDbn, constant 2015)

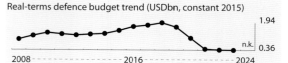

Population 5,364,482

Age	0–14	15–19	20–24	25–29	30–64	65 plus
Male	9.7%	3.7%	3.6%	3.6%	25.3%	4.1%
Female	9.2%	3.5%	3.5%	3.4%	25.1%	5.4%

Capabilities

The ability of the Lebanese Armed Forces (LAF) to fulfil its missions remains under strain from Hizbullah's position in national politics, the country's severe and prolonged economic depression and an ongoing governance crisis. This was further exacerbated by a significant escalation in fighting between Hizbullah and Israel in late 2024. The LAF is reliant on outside assistance to continue its operations, most notably from the US and Qatar. The economic crisis has left the government struggling to pay wages, while inflation has eroded the value of salaries. This has led to concern that troops are supplementing their wages with other employment or resigning. Training and operational assistance have traditionally been provided by the US, as well as France, Germany, Italy and the UK. The US is providing funding and expertise to help restore military facilities at the Beirut naval base damaged by a port explosion in 2020, as well as to upgrade Hamat Air Base. The LAF has no requirement and minimal capability for extra-territorial deployment. The military has been trying to secure the border against Syrian migrations. The LAF remains dependent on foreign support to replace and modernise its ageing equipment. Lebanon has no significant domestic defence industry.

ACTIVE 60,000 (Army 56,600 Navy 1,800 Air 1,600) Gendarmerie & Paramilitary 20,000

ORGANISATIONS BY SERVICE

Army 56,600
FORCES BY ROLE
5 regional comd (Beirut, Bekaa Valley, Mount Lebanon, North, South)
SPECIAL FORCES
1 cdo regt
MANOEUVRE
Armoured

1 armd regt
Mechanised
11 mech inf bde
Air Manoeuvre
1 AB regt
Amphibious
1 mne cdo regt
Other
1 Presidential Guard bde
6 intervention regt
4 border sy regt
COMBAT SUPPORT
2 arty regt
1 cbt spt bde (1 engr regt, 1 AT regt, 1 sigs regt; 1 log bn)
1 MP gp
COMBAT SERVICE SUPPORT
1 log bde
1 med gp
1 construction regt
EQUIPMENT BY TYPE
MBT 334: 92 M48A1/A5; 10 M60A2; 185 T-54; 47 T-55
RECCE 55 AML
IFV 56: 24 AIFV-B-C25; 32 M2A2 *Bradley*
APC 1,378
  APC (T) 1,274 M113A1/A2 (incl variants)
  APC (W) 96: 86 VAB VCT; 10 VBPT-MR *Guarani*
  PPV 8 *Maxxpro*
ENGINEERING & MAINTENANCE VEHICLES
  ARV 3+: 3 M88A1; M113 ARV; T-54/55 ARV (reported)
  VLB MTU-72 reported
  MW *Bozena*
ARTILLERY 718
  SP 155mm 36: 12 M109A2; 24 M109A5
  TOWED 281: **105mm** 13 M101A1; **122mm** 35: 9 D-30; 26 M-30; **130mm** 15 M-46; **155mm** 218 M198
  MRL 122mm 11 BM-21
  MOR 390: **81mm** 203; **82mm** 112; **120mm** 75: 29 Brandt; 46 M120
ANTI-TANK/ANTI-INFRASTRUCTURE
  MSL
    SP 35 VAB with HOT
    MANPATS *Milan*; TOW
  RCL 106mm 113 M40A1
AIR DEFENCE
  SAM • Point-defence 9K32 *Strela*-2M (RS-SA-7B *Grail*)‡
  GUNS • TOWED 77: **20mm** 20; **23mm** 57 ZU-23-2

Navy 1,800
EQUIPMENT BY TYPE
PATROL AND COASTAL COMBATANTS 16
  PCC 1 *Trablous*
  PBF 1

  PB 14: 1 *Aamchit* (ex-GER *Bremen*); 1 *Al Karamoun* (ex-FRA *Avel Gwarlarn*); 3 *Marine Protector*; 7 *Tripoli* (ex-UK *Attacker/Tracker* Mk 2); 1 *Naquora* (ex-GER *Bremen*); 1 *Tabarja* (ex-GER *Bergen*)
AMPHIBIOUS • LANDING CRAFT
  LCT 2 *Sour* (ex-FRA EDIC – capacity 8 APC; 96 troops)

Air Force 1,600
4 air bases
FORCES BY ROLE
GROUND ATTACK
  1 sqn with Cessna AC-208 *Combat Caravan*
  1 sqn with EMB-314 *Super Tucano**
ATTACK HELICOPTER
  1 sqn with SA342L *Gazelle*
TRANSPORT HELICOPTER
  4 sqn with Bell 205 (UH-1H *Iroquois*/*Huey* II)
  1 sqn with SA330/IAR330SM *Puma*
  1 trg sqn with R-44 *Raven* II
EQUIPMENT BY TYPE
AIRCRAFT 9 combat capable
  ISR 3 Cessna AC-208 *Combat Caravan**
  TRG 9: 3 *Bulldog*; 6 EMB-314 *Super Tucano**
HELICOPTERS
  MRH 14: 1 AW139; 5 MD530F+; 8 SA342L *Gazelle* (5 SA342L *Gazelle*; 5 SA316 *Alouette* III; 1 SA318 *Alouette* II all non-operational)
  TPT 41: **Medium** 13: 3 S-61N (fire-fighting); 10 SA330/IAR330 *Puma*; **Light** 28: 18 Bell 205 (UH-1H *Iroquois*); 6 Bell 205 (UH-1H *Huey* II); 4 R-44 *Raven* II (basic trg) (11 Bell 205; 7 Bell 212 all non-operational)
AIR LAUNCHED MISSILES
  ASM AGM-114 *Hellfire*; AGR-20A APKWS

Gendarmerie & Paramilitary ε20,000 active

Internal Security Force ε20,000
Ministry of Interior
FORCES BY ROLE
Other Combat Forces
  1 (police) judicial unit
  1 regional sy coy
  1 (Beirut Gendarmerie) sy coy
EQUIPMENT BY TYPE
ARMOURED FIGHTING VEHICLES
  APC • APC (W) 60 V-200 *Chaimite*

Customs
EQUIPMENT BY TYPE
PATROL AND COASTAL COMBATANTS 7
  PB 7: 5 *Aztec*; 2 *Tracker*

SOUTHERN LEBANON
Data here represents the de facto situation. This does not

imply international recognition. Hizbullah maintains a substantial inventory of rockets and missiles in Lebanon, reportedly bolstered by transfers from Syria and from the group's own facilities. Hizbullah's operations in Syria saw the organisation take on a more conventional military role and acquire heavy equipment from the Syrian Arab Army.

ACTIVE 40,000

ORGANISATIONS BY SERVICE

Hizbullah ε40,000 (incl mobilised reserves)
EQUIPMENT BY TYPE
ARMOURED FIGHTING VEHICLES
   MBT T-54/55; T-72 (all in Syria)
   APC • APC (T) M113; MT-LB (all in Syria)
ANTI-TANK/ANTI-INFRASTRUCTURE
   MSL • MANPATS *Almas*; *Dehlavieh* (*Kornet*); *Milan* 3; *Toophan*; 9K11 *Malyutka* (RS-AT-3 *Sagger*); 9K111 *Fagot* (RS-AT-4 *Spigot*); 9K115-2 *Metis*-M1 (RS-AT-13)
ARTILLERY
   SP 122mm 2S1 *Gvozdika* (in Syria)
   TOWED 122mm D-30; **130mm** M-46 (all in Syria)
   MRL 122mm BM-21 *Grad*; **220mm** *Fadi* 1; **240mm** *Fadjr* 3; **300mm** *Fadjr* 5; **302mm** *Fadi* 2
SURFACE-TO-SURFACE MISSILE LAUNCHERS
   SRBM • Conventional *Fateh*-110; M-600; SS-1D *Scud* C (reported); SS-1E *Scud* D (reported); *Qader* 1; *Qader* 2; *Zelzal* 2
COASTAL DEFENCE • AShM C-802 (*Noor*); C-704 (*Nasr*); *Yakhont* (reported)
UNIHABITED AERIAL VEHICLES
   CISR • Light *Mersad*
   ISR • Medium *Ababil* 2; *Sammad* 1; **Light** *Mohajer* 2
   OWA *Ababil* T (*Mersad* 1)
AIR DEFENCE
   SAM • Point-defence *Misaq*-2 (QW-18)
   GUN • SP 57mm ZSU-57-2; **85mm** KS-12 mod (on 2P25 chassis); **100mm** KS-19 mod (on 2P25 chassis) (all in Syria)

FOREIGN FORCES

Unless specified, figures refer to UNTSO and represent total numbers for the mission
Argentina 3 • UNIFIL 3
Armenia UNIFIL 1
Australia 12
Austria 5 • UNIFIL 161: 1 log coy
Bangladesh UNIFIL 120: 1 FSGM
Belgium 1
Bhutan 4
Brazil UNIFIL 11
Brunei UNIFIL 29
Cambodia UNIFIL 181: 1 EOD coy
Canada 4 (*Operation Jade*)
Chile 3
China, People's Republic of 5 • UNIFIL 418: 2 engr coy; 1 med coy
Colombia UNIFIL 1
Croatia UNIFIL 1
Cyprus UNIFIL 2
Denmark 10
El Salvador UNIFIL 52: 1 inf pl
Estonia 1 • UNIFIL 1
Fiji 2 • UNIFIL 1
Finland 16 • UNIFIL 163; 1 inf coy
France 1 • UNIFIL 578: 1 bn HQ; 1 recce coy; 1 log coy; 1 tpt coy; 1 maint coy; VBCI; VAB; VBL; *Mistral*
Germany UNIFIL 78: 1 FSGM
Ghana UNIFIL 873: 1 recce coy; 1 mech inf bn; 1 spt coy
Greece UNIFIL 131: 1 FFGHM
Guatemala UNIFIL 2
Hungary UNIFIL 15
India 2 • UNIFIL 897: 1 mech inf bn; 1 log coy; 1 med coy
Indonesia UNIFIL 1,231: 1 mech inf bn; 1 log coy; 1 FSGM
Ireland 12 • UNIFIL 355: 1 mech inf bn (-)
Israel Army: ε45,000; 4 div HQ; 1 spec ops bde; 4 armd bde; 4 mech bde; 2 inf bde; 1 AB bde; 1 mtn bde; 1 arty bde
Italy MIBIL 160 • UNIFIL 863: 1 bde HQ; 1 inf bn; 1 sigs coy; 1 tpt coy; 1 hel bn
Kazakhstan UNIFIL 7
Kenya UNIFIL 3
Korea, Republic of 2 • UNIFIL 252: 1 mech inf BG HQ; 1 mech inf coy; 1 inf coy; 1 log coy
Latvia 1
Macedonia, North UNIFIL 5
Malaysia UNIFIL 833: 1 mech inf bn(-); 1 engr coy; 1 sigs coy; 1 maint coy; 1 tpt coy
Malta UNIFIL 8
Moldova UNIFIL 32
Mongolia UNIFIL 4
Nepal 3 • UNIFIL 876: 1 mech inf bn; 1 log coy
Netherlands 11 • UNIFIL 1
New Zealand 8
Nigeria UNIFIL 1
Norway 12
Peru UNIFIL 1
Poland 3 • UNIFIL 195: 1 mech inf coy
Qatar UNIFIL 1
Russia 4
Serbia 1 • UNIFIL 182: 1 mech inf coy
Sierra Leone UNIFIL 3
Slovakia 3
Slovenia 2
Spain UNIFIL 677: 1 bde HQ; 1 mech inf bn(-); 1 engr coy; 1 sigs coy; 1 log coy
Sri Lanka UNIFIL 126: 1 inf coy
Sweden 5
Switzerland 12
Tanzania UNIFIL 125: 1 MP coy
Turkiye UNIFIL 92: 1 FSG
United Kingdom UNIFIL 1
United States 2
Uruguay UNIFIL 1
Zambia 1 • UNIFIL 2

Libya LBY

Libyan Dinar LYD		2023	2024	2025
GDP	LYD	212bn	218bn	233bn
	USD	44.0bn	44.8bn	48.0bn
Real GDP growth	%	10.2	2.4	13.7
Def bdgt	LYD	n.k.	n.k.	n.k.
	USD	n.k.	n.k.	n.k.

Population		7,361,263				
Age	0–14	15–19	20–24	25–29	30–64	65 plus
Male	16.5%	4.5%	3.7%	3.3%	20.9%	2.1%
Female	15.8%	4.3%	3.6%	3.2%	19.6%	2.5%

Capabilities

The formation of a Government of National Unity (GNU) in March 2021 failed to bring together the Tripoli-based Government of National Accord (GNA) and the Tobruk-based House of Representatives (HoR). National elections in 2021 were postponed and the two sides appointed rival ministers. The parties then agreed to form the 5+5 Joint Military Committee to unify the military forces of the GNU and the HOR-linked Libyan Arab Armed Forces (LAAF), controlled by General Khalifa Haftar. However, the unstable political and security situation worsened in 2024. The GNU has been weakened by internal divisions and both the GNU and the LAAF continue to receive foreign support. In 2024, a trilateral regional cooperation initiative was agreed with Algeria and Tunisia. Turkiye has delivered UAVs to the GNU, while Russia has increased its presence, establishing a training camp operated by a private military company and supplying equipment. The Tripoli-based GNU government has benefited from several military advisory and training programmes, such as the EUNAVFOR–MED maritime-security training for the navy and coast guard. EUNAVFOR Operation *Irini* continues to monitor the implementation of the UN arms embargo.

Forces loyal to the Government of National Unity (Tripoli-based)

ACTIVE n.k.

ORGANISATIONS BY SERVICE

Ground Forces n.k.
EQUIPMENT BY TYPE
ARMOURED FIGHTING VEHICLES
  MBT T-55; T-72
  IFV BMP-2
  APC
    APC (T) ACV-AAPC; Steyr 4K-7FA
    APC (W) Mbombe-6
    PPV Al-Wahsh; Kirpi-2; Vuran
  AUV Lenco Bearcat G3; Nimr Ajban; VPK Ural
ENGINEERING & MAINTENANCE VEHICLES
  ARV Centurion 105 AVRE
ANTI-TANK/ANTI-INFRASTRUCTURE • MSL
  SP 9P157-2 Khrizantema-S (RS-AT-15 Springer)
  MANPATS 9K115 Metis (RS-AT-7 Saxhorn)
ARTILLERY
  SP 155mm Palmaria
  TOWED 122mm D-30
UNINHABITED AERIAL VEHICLES
  CISR • Heavy Bayraktar Akinci (reported); **Medium** Bayraktar TB2 (reported)
AIR DEFENCE
  SAM • Point-defence QW-18 (CH-SA-11)
  GUNS • SP 14.5mm ZPU-2 (on tch); **23mm** ZU-23-2 (on tch)
BOMBS
  Laser-guided MAM-C (reported); MAM-L (reported)

Navy n.k.
A number of intact naval vessels remain in Tripoli, although serviceability is questionable
EQUIPMENT BY TYPE
PATROL AND COASTAL COMBATANTS 3+
  CORVETTES • FSGM (1 Al Hani (ex-FSU Project 1159 (Koni)) in Malta for refit since 2013 with 2 twin lnchr with P-22 (RS-SS-N-2C Styx) AShM, 1 twin lnchr with 4K33 Osa-M (RS-SA-N-4 Gecko) SAM, 2 twin 406mm ASTT, 1 RBU 6000 Smerch 2 A/S mor, 2 AK230 CIWS, 2 twin 76mm gun)
  PBFG 1 Sharaba (FRA Combattante II) with 4 single lnchr with Otomat Mk2 AShM, 1 76mm gun†
  PB 2+ PV30
AMPHIBIOUS
  LANDING SHIPS • LST 1 Ibn Harissa (capacity 1 hel; 11 MBT; 240 troops)
LOGISTICS AND SUPPORT 1
  ARS 1 Al Munjed (YUG Spasilac)†

Air Force n.k.
EQUIPMENT BY TYPE
AIRCRAFT 12 combat capable
  FGA 2 MiG-23BN
  ATK 1 J-21 Jastreb†
  TRG 9+: 3 G-2 Galeb*; ε5 L-39ZO*; 1+ SF-260ML*
HELICOPTERS
  ATK Mi-24 Hind
  TPT • Medium Mi-17 Hip
AIR-LAUNCHED MISSILES • AAM • IR R-3 (RS-AA-2 Atoll)‡; R-60 (RS-AA-8 Aphid); R-24 (RS-AA-7 Apex)

Paramilitary n.k.

Coast Guard n.k.
EQUIPMENT BY TYPE
PATROL AND COASTAL COMBATANTS 20
  PCC 1 Damen Stan 2909 with 1 sextuple 122mm MRL
  PBF 10: 4 Bigliani; 4 Fezzan (ex-ITA Corrubia); 2 Vittoria FPV350 (ITA)
  PB 9: 8 Burdi (Damen Stan 1605); 1 Ikrimah (FRA RPB 20)

FOREIGN FORCES

Bangladesh UNSMIL 1
Italy MIASIT 90
Nepal UNSMIL 231; 2 sy coy
Türkiye ε500; ACV-AAPC; *Kirpi*; 1 arty unit with T-155 *Firtina*; 1 AD unit with *Hisar*-O; *Korkut*; GDF-003; 1 CISR UAV unit with *Bayraktar* TB2
United States UNSMIL 1

EASTERN LIBYA

Data here represents the de facto situation. This does not imply international recognition

ACTIVE n.k.

ORGANISATIONS BY SERVICE

Libyan Arab Armed Forces n.k.

EQUIPMENT BY TYPE

ARMOURED FIGHTING VEHICLES
  MBT T-55; T-62; T-72
  RECCE BRDM-2; EE-9 *Cascavel*
  IFV BMP-1; *Ratel*-20
  APC
    APC (T) M113
    APC (W) *Al-Mared*; BTR-60PB; *Mbombe*-6; Nimr *Jais*; *Puma*
    PPV *Al-Wahsh*; *Caiman*; Streit *Spartan*; Streit *Typhoon*; *Vuran*; *Titan*-DS
  AUV *Panthera* T6; *Panthera* F9; *Terrier* LT-79

ANTI-TANK/ANTI-INFRASTRUCTURE
  MSL
    SP 9P157-2 *Khrizantema*-S (status unknown)
    MANPATS 9K11 *Malyutka* (RS-AT-3 *Sagger*); 9K111 *Fagot* (RS-AT-4 *Spigot*); 9K111-1 *Konkurs* (RS-AT-5 *Spandrel*); 9K135 *Kornet* (RS-AT-14 *Spriggan*); *Milan*
  RCL: 106mm M40A1; **84mm** *Carl Gustaf*

ARTILLERY
  SP 122mm 2S1 *Gvozdika*; **155mm** G5
  TOWED 122mm D-30
  MRL 107mm Type-63; **122mm** BM-21 *Grad*
  MOR M106

AIR DEFENCE
  SAM
    Short-range 2K12 *Kvadrat* (RS-SA-6 *Gainful*)
    Point-defence 9K338 *Igla*-S (RS-SA-24 *Grinch*)
  GUNS • SP 14.5mm ZPU-2 (on tch); **23mm** ZSU-23-4 *Shilka*; ZU-23-2 (on tch)

Navy n.k.

EQUIPMENT BY TYPE

PATROL AND COASTAL COMBATANTS 7+
  PB: 7+: 2 *Burdi* (Damen Stan 1605); 1 *Burdi* (Damen Stan 1605) with 1 73mm gun; 2 *Ikrimah* (FRA RPB20); 1 *Hamelin*; 1+ PV30

Air Force n.k.

EQUIPMENT BY TYPE

AIRCRAFT 33 combat capable
  FTR 2+: 2 MiG-23ML *Flogger* G; some MiG-29 *Fulcrum* (operator uncertain)
  FGA 13: ε10 MiG-21MF *Fishbed*; 1 *Mirage* F-1AD; 1 *Mirage* F-1ED; 1 Su-22UM3 *Fitter* G
  ATK some Su-24M *Fencer* D (operator uncertain)
  TRG 19: ε10 L-39ZO *Albatros**; 1+ MiG-21UM *Mongol* B; 8 SF-260ML*

HELICOPTERS
  ATK Mi-24/35 *Hind*
  MRH up to 3 SA341 *Gazelle*
  TPT • Medium 3: up to 3 H215 (AS332L) *Super Puma*; Mi-8/Mi-17 *Hip*

AIR-LAUNCHED MISSILES • AAM • IR R-3 (RS-AA-2 *Atoll*)‡; R-27T (RS-AA-10B *Alamo*); R-60 (RS-AA-8 *Aphid*); R-73 (RS-AA-11A *Archer*)

FOREIGN FORCES

Russia 3,500 (PMC)

Mauritania MRT

Mauritanian Ouguiya MRU		2023	2024	2025
GDP	MRU	389bn	423bn	440bn
	USD	10.6bn	10.8bn	11.1bn
Real GDP growth	%	6.5	4.4	4.2
Def bdgt	MRU	9.30bn	10.3bn	
	USD	255m	263m	

Real-terms defence budget trend (USDm, constant 2015)

Population	4,328,040					
Age	0–14	15–19	20–24	25–29	30–64	65 plus
Male	17.9%	5.1%	4.5%	3.9%	14.9%	1.9%
Female	17.8%	5.2%	4.7%	4.3%	17.3%	2.5%

Capabilities

The country's armed forces are tasked with maintaining territorial integrity, internal security and, in light of the regional threat from extremist Islamist groups, border security. In early 2021, the government approved a draft decree establishing a defence area along the northern border to prevent incursions by the Polisario Front. To help the army secure the country's borders, the latter approved the delivery of military aid through the European Peace Mechanism in December 2022. A new package focused on maritime surveillance was approved in July 2024. Deployment capabilities are limited, but the armed forces have demonstrated mobility and sustainment in desert regions. A Chinese firm built a new naval base in the south, possibly designed to enable improved protection of offshore gas fields. Mauritania has limited and ageing equipment. Naval equipment is geared toward coastal-surveillance missions and China's donation of a landing ship has helped establish a basic sealift capability. There is no domestic defence industry.

ACTIVE 15,850 (Army 15,000 Navy 600 Air 250)
Gendarmerie & Paramilitary 5,000
Conscript liability 24 months

ORGANISATIONS BY SERVICE

Army 15,000
FORCES BY ROLE
6 mil regions
MANOEUVRE
  Reconnaissance
  1 armd recce bn
  Armoured
  1 armd bn
  Light
  7 mot inf bn
  8 (garrison) inf bn
  Air Manoeuvre
  1 cdo/para bn
  Other
  2 (camel corps) bn
  1 gd bn
COMBAT SUPPORT
  3 arty bn
  4 ADA bty
  1 engr coy

EQUIPMENT BY TYPE
ARMOURED FIGHTING VEHICLES
  MBT 35 T-54/T-55
  ASLT 10 WMA-301
  RECCE 70: 20 AML-60; 40 AML-90; 10 *Saladin*
  APC • APC (W) 32: 5 FV603 *Saracen*; 7 *Bastion* APC; ε20 Panhard M3
  AUV 27: 12 *Cobra*; 15 MCAV-20
ENGINEERING & MAINTENANCE VEHICLES
  ARV T-54/55 ARV reported
ANTI-TANK/ANTI-INFRASTRUCTURE
  MSL
    SP 4+ VN-21 with HJ-9
    MANPATS *Milan*
  RCL • 106mm M40A1
ARTILLERY 180
  TOWED 80: **105mm** 36 HM-2/M101A1; **122mm** 44: 20 D-30; 24 D-74
  MRL 10: **107mm** 4 Type-63; **122mm** 6 Type-81
  MOR 90: **81mm** 60; **120mm** 30 Brandt
AIR DEFENCE
  SAM • Point-defence 8+: ε4 9K31 *Strela*-1 (RS-SA-9 *Gaskin*) (reported); 9K32 *Strela*-2 (RS-SA-7 *Grail*)‡; 4+ Yitian-L (CH-SA-13)

GUNS • TOWED 82: **14.5mm** 28: 16 ZPU-2; 12 ZPU-4; **23mm** 20 ZU-23-2; **37mm** 10 M-1939; **57mm** 12 S-60; **100mm** 12 KS-19

Navy ε600
EQUIPMENT BY TYPE
PATROL AND COASTAL COMBATANTS 12
  PCC 5: 1 *Aboubekr Ben Amer* (FRA OPV 54); 1 *Arguin*; 1 *Limam El Hidrami* (PRC); 2 *Timbedra* (PRC *Huangpu* mod)
  PB 7: 1 *El Nasr*† (FRA *Patra*); 4 *Mandovi*; 2 *Meçsem Bakker* (FRA RPB20 – for SAR duties)
AMPHIBIOUS • LANDING SHIPS 1
  LSM 1 *Nimlane* (PRC)

Fusiliers Marins
FORCES BY ROLE
MANOEUVRE
  Amphibious
  1 mne unit

Air Force 250
EQUIPMENT BY TYPE
AIRCRAFT 2 combat capable
  ISR 2 Cessna 208B *Grand Caravan*
  TPT 14: **Light** 13: 1 Beech 350 *King Air*; 2 BN-2 *Defender*; 1 C-212; 2 CN235; 3 G1; 2 PA-31T *Cheyenne* II; 2 Y-12(II);
  PAX 1 BT-67 (with sensor turret)
  TRG 8: 3 EMB-312 *Tucano*; 2 EMB-314 *Super Tucano**; 3 SF-260E
HELICOPTERS
  MRH 3: 1 SA313B *Alouette* II; 2 Z-9
  TPT • Light 2 AW109

Gendarmerie & Paramilitary ε5,000 active

Gendarmerie ε3,000
Ministry of Interior
FORCES BY ROLE
MANOEUVRE
  Other
  6 regional sy coy
EQUIPMENT BY TYPE
PATROL AND COASTAL COMBATANTS • PB 3: 1 *Awkar* (PRC 60); 2 Rodman 55

National Guard 2,000
Ministry of Interior

Customs
EQUIPMENT BY TYPE
PATROL AND COASTAL COMBATANTS • PB 4: 1 *Dah Ould Bah* (FRA *Amgram* 14); 2 *Saeta*-12; 1 *Yaboub Ould Rajel* (FRA RPB18)

DEPLOYMENT

CENTRAL AFRICAN REPUBLIC: UN • MINUSCA 467; 1 inf bn(-)
SOMALIA: UN • UNSOS 1
SUDAN: UN • UNISFA 3

Morocco MOR

Moroccan Dirham MAD		2023	2024	2025
GDP	MAD	1.46trn	1.56trn	1.65trn
	USD	144bn	157bn	169bn
Real GDP growth	%	3.4	2.8	3.6
Def bdgt [a]	MAD	63.5bn	65.8bn	70.2bn
	USD	6.27bn	6.63bn	7.15bn
FMA (US)	USD	10m	10m	10m

[a] Includes autonomous defence spending (SEGMA) and Treasury funding for "Acquisitions and Repair of Equipment for Royal Armed Forces"

Real-terms defence budget trend (USDbn, constant 2015)

Population	37,387,585				
Age	0–14	15–19	20–24	25–29	30–64	65 plus
Male	13.1%	4.2%	3.9%	3.6%	21.0%	4.1%
Female	12.6%	4.1%	3.9%	3.7%	21.5%	4.3%

Capabilities

The armed forces in early 2022 established an eastern military zone in addition to the northern and southern zones, in light of tensions with Algeria. A 30-year ceasefire between Morocco and the Polisario Front ended in late 2020 and the UN has reported that hostilities have resumed, albeit at a low level. Morocco has close defence ties with the US, receiving military training and equipment, and there is also cooperation with NATO. In 2016, Morocco was granted access to the Alliance's Interoperability Platform to strengthen the defence and security sectors. Defence relations with Israel have developed, having normalised relations in 2020. There is exercise cooperation with France and in October 2024, a French submarine joined a bilateral exercise with the Moroccan Navy for the first time. The armed forces have gained experience from UN peacekeeping deployments and multinational exercises. The country reintroduced conscription in early 2019. Morocco's military inventory comprises primarily of ageing French and US equipment, but the armed forces are procuring new air and maritime capabilities. The country relies on imports and donations for major defence equipment.

ACTIVE 195,800 (Army 175,000 Navy 7,800 Air 13,000) **Gendarmerie & Paramilitary 50,000**

Conscript liability 12 months for men aged 19–25

RESERVE 150,000 (Army 150,000)

Reserve obligation to age 50

ORGANISATIONS BY SERVICE

Space
EQUIPMENT BY TYPE
SATELLITES • ISR 2 *Mohammed* VI

Army 175,000
FORCES BY ROLE
2 comd (Northern Zone, Southern Zone)
MANOEUVRE
  Armoured
  1 armd bde
  11 armd bn
  Mechanised
  3 mech inf bde
  Mechanised/Light
  8 mech/mot inf regt (2–3 bn)
  Light
  1 lt sy bde
  3 (camel corps) mot inf bn
  35 lt inf bn
  4 cdo unit
  Air Manoeuvre
  2 para bde
  2 AB bn
  Mountain
  1 mtn inf bn
COMBAT SUPPORT
  11 arty bn
  7 engr bn
AIR DEFENCE
  2 AD gp

Royal Guard 1,500
FORCES BY ROLE
MANOEUVRE
  Other
  1 gd bn
  2 cav sqn
EQUIPMENT BY TYPE
ARMOURED FIGHTING VEHICLES
  MBT 703: 222 M1A1SA *Abrams*; 220 M60A1 *Patton*; 120 M60A3 *Patton*; 40 T-72B (being upgraded to T-72EA); 47 T-72EA; 54 Type-90-II (MBT-2000); (ε200 M48A5 *Patton* in store)
  LT TK (111 SK-105 *Kuerassier* in store)
  ASLT 80 AMX-10RC
  RECCE 284: 38 AML-60-7; 190 AML-90; 40 EBR-75; 16 *Eland*
  IFV 238: 10 AMX-10P; 30 *Ratel* Mk3-20; 30 *Ratel* Mk3-90; 45 VAB VCI; 123 YPR-765
  APC 1,225
    APC (T) 905: 400 M113A1/A2; 419 M113A3; 86

M577A2 (CP)
APC (W) 320 VAB VTT
AUV 36 *Sherpa Light Scout*

ENGINEERING & MAINTENANCE VEHICLES
ARV 85+: 10 *Greif*; 55 M88A1; M578; 20 VAB-ECH

ANTI-TANK/ANTI-INFRASTRUCTURE
MSL
SP 80 M901
MANPATS 9K11 *Malyutka* (RS-AT-3 *Sagger*); HJ-8L; M47 *Dragon*; *Milan*; TOW
RCL 106mm 350 M40A1
GUNS • **SP** 36: **90mm** 28 M56; **100mm** 8 SU-100

ARTILLERY 2,384
SP 354: **155mm** 326: 36 CAESAR; ε130 M109A1/A1B/A2/A3/A4; 70 M109A5; 90 Mk F3; **203mm** 60 M110
TOWED 118: **105mm** 50: 30 L118 Light Gun; 20 M101; **130mm** 18 M-46; **155mm** 50: 30 FH-70; 20 M114
MRL 83: **122mm** 35 BM-21 *Grad*; **300mm** 36 PHL-03; **306mm** 12 PULS
MOR 1,797: **81mm** 1,100 Expal model LN; **SP 107mm** 36 M106A2; **120mm** 550 Brandt; **SP 120mm** 110: 20 (VAB APC); 91 M1064A3

UNINHABITED AERIAL VEHICLES
ISR • **Medium** R4E-50 *Skyeye*

AIR DEFENCE
SAM 67+
Medium-range 24 *Tianlong*-50 (CH-SA-23)
Short-range 6+: *Barak* MX; DK-9 (CH-SA-5); ε6 VL-MICA (reported)
Point-defence 37+: 37 M48 *Chaparral*; 9K38 *Igla* (RS-SA-18 *Grouse*)
SPAAGM 30mm 12 2K22M *Tunguska*-M (RS-SA-19 *Grison*)
GUNS 390
SP 20mm 60 M163 *Vulcan*
TOWED 330: **14.5mm** 200: 150–180 ZPU-2; 20 ZPU-4; **20mm** 40 M167 *Vulcan*; **23mm** 75–90 ZU-23-2; **35mm** some PG-99

Navy 7,800 (incl 1,500 Marines)
EQUIPMENT BY TYPE
PRINCIPAL SURFACE COMBATANTS • FRIGATES 4
FFGHM 2:
1 *Mohammed VI* (FRA FREMM) with 2 quad lnchr with MM40 *Exocet* Block 3 AShM, 2 8-cell *Sylver* A43 VLS with *Aster* 15 SAM, 2 triple 324mm ILAS-3 (B-515) ASTT with MU90 LWT, 1 76mm gun (capacity 1 AS565MA *Panther*)
1 *Tarik ben Ziyad* (NLD SIGMA 10513) with 2 twin lnchr with MM40 *Exocet* Block 3 AShM, 1 12-cell CLA VLS with VL MICA SAM, 2 triple 324mm ILAS-3 (B-515) ASTT with MU90 LWT, 1 76mm gun (capacity 1 AS565MA *Panther*)
FFGH 2 *Mohammed V* (FRA *Floreal*) with 2 single lnchr with MM38 *Exocet* AShM, 1 76mm gun (fitted for but not with *Simbad* SAM) (capacity 1 AS565MA *Panther*)

PATROL AND COASTAL COMBATANTS 52
CORVETTES 3
FSGHM 2 *Sultan Moulay Ismail* (NLD SIGMA 9813) with 2 twin lnchr with MM40 *Exocet* Block 2/3 AShM, 1 12-cell CLA VLS with VL MICA SAM, 2 triple 324mm ILAS-3 (B-515) ASTT with MU90 LWT, 1 76mm gun (capacity 1 AS565MA *Panther*)
FSM 1 *Lt Col Errhamani* (ESP *Descubierta*) with 1 octuple *Albatros* lnchr with *Aspide* SAM, 2 triple 324mm ASTT with Mk46 LWT, 1 76mm gun
PSO 1 *Bin an Zaran* (OPV 70) with 1 76mm gun
PCG 4 *Cdt El Khattabi* (ESP *Lazaga* 58m) with 4 single lnchr with MM38 *Exocet* AShM, 1 76mm gun
PCO 5 *Rais Bargach* (under control of fisheries dept)
PCC 12:
4 *El Hahiq* (DNK *Osprey* 55, incl 2 with customs)
6 *LV Rabhi* (ESP 58m B-200D)
2 *Okba* (FRA PR-72) each with 1 76mm gun
PB 27: 6 *El Wacil* (FRA P-32), 10 VCSM (RPB 20); 10 Rodman 101; 1 other (UK *Bird*)

AMPHIBIOUS
LANDING SHIPS • **LST** 3 *Ben Aicha* (FRA *Champlain* BATRAL) with 1 hel landing platform (capacity 7 tanks; 140 troops)
LANDING CRAFT 2:
LCT 1 *Sidi Ifni*
LCM 1 CTM (FRA CTM-5)

LOGISTICS AND SUPPORT 7
AGOR 1 *Dar Al Beida* (FRA EHO2M)
AGS 1 Damen Stan Tender 1504
AK 2
AX 1 *Essaouira*
AXS 2

Marines 1,500
FORCES BY ROLE
MANOEUVRE
Amphibious
2 naval inf bn

Naval Aviation
FORCES BY ROLE
MARITIME PATROL
1 sqn Beech 350ER *King Air*
HELICOPTER
1 sqn with AS565MA *Panther*; Bell 412EPI
EQUIPMENT BY TYPE
AIRCRAFT • **MP** 2 Beech 350ER *King Air*
HELICOPTERS
ASW 2 Bell 412EPI
MRH 3 AS565MA *Panther*

Air Force 13,000
FORCES BY ROLE

FIGHTER/GROUND ATTACK
2 sqn with F-5E/F *Tiger* II
3 sqn with F-16C/D *Fighting Falcon*
1 sqn with *Mirage* F-1C (F-1CH)
1 sqn with *Mirage* F-1E (F-1EH)

ELECTRONIC WARFARE
1 sqn with EC-130H *Hercules*; *Falcon* 20 (ELINT)

MARITIME PATROL
1 flt with Do-28

TANKER/TRANSPORT
1 sqn with C-130H/KC-130H *Hercules*

TRANSPORT
1 sqn with CN235
1 VIP sqn with B-737BBJ; Beech 200/300 *King Air*; *Falcon* 50; Gulfstream II/III/V-SP/G550

TRAINING
1 sqn with *Alpha Jet**
1 sqn T-6C

ATTACK HELICOPTER
1 sqn with SA342L *Gazelle*

TRANSPORT HELICOPTER
1 sqn with Bell 205A (AB-205A); Bell 206 *Jet Ranger* (AB-206); Bell 212 (AB-212)
1 sqn with CH-47D *Chinook*
1 sqn with SA330 *Puma*

EQUIPMENT BY TYPE
AIRCRAFT 89 combat capable
FTR 22: 19 F-5E *Tiger* II; 3 F-5F *Tiger* II
FGA 48: 15 F-16C *Fighting Falcon*; 8 F-16D *Fighting Falcon*; 15 *Mirage* F-1C (F-1CH); 10 *Mirage* F-1E (F-1EH)
ELINT 1 EC-130H *Hercules*
TKR/TPT 2 KC-130H *Hercules*
TPT 47: **Medium** 17: 4 C-27J *Spartan*; 13 C-130H *Hercules*; **Light** 19: 4 Beech 100 *King Air*; 2 Beech 200 *King Air*; 1 Beech 200C *King Air*; 2 Beech 300 *King Air*; 3 Beech 350 *King Air*; 5 CN235; 2 Do-28; **PAX** 11: 1 B-737BBJ; 2 *Falcon* 20; 2 Falcon 20 (ELINT); 1 *Falcon* 50 (VIP); 1 Gulfstream II (VIP); 1 Gulfstream III; 1 Gulfstream V-SP; 2 Gulfstream G550
TRG 57: 12 AS-202 *Bravo*; 19 *Alpha Jet**; 2 CAP-10; 24 T-6C *Texan*; (9 T-34C *Turbo Mentor*; 14 T-37B *Tweet* all in store)
HELICOPTERS
MRH 25: 6 H135M; 19 SA342L *Gazelle* (armed)
TPT 70: **Heavy** 10 CH-47D *Chinook*; **Medium** 24 SA330 *Puma*; **Light** 36: 24 Bell 205A (AB-205A); 5+ Bell 206 *Jet Ranger* (AB-206); 3 Bell 212 (AB-212); 4 Bell 429

UNINHABITED AERIAL VEHICLES
CISR
Heavy *Wing Loong* II
Medium *Bayraktar* TB2
ISR
Heavy *Heron*
Medium 4 *Hermes* 900

AIR-LAUNCHED MISSILES
AAM • **IR** AIM-9J *Sidewinder*; R-550 *Magic*; *Mica* IR; **IIR** AIM-9X *Sidewinder* II; **ARH** AIM-120C7 AMRAAM; *Mica* RF
ASM AASM; AGM-65B/D/G *Maverick*; HOT
ARM AGM-88B HARM

BOMBS
Laser-guided *Paveway* II
Laser & INS/GPS-guided GBU-54 Laser JDAM
INS/GPS-guided GBU-31 JDAM

Gendarmerie & Paramilitary 50,000 active

Gendarmerie Royale 20,000
FORCES BY ROLE
MANOEUVRE
Air Manoeuvre
1 para sqn
Other
1 paramilitary bde
4 (mobile) paramilitary gp
1 coast guard unit
TRANSPORT HELICOPTER
1 sqn
EQUIPMENT BY TYPE
PATROL AND COASTAL COMBATANTS
PB 15 Arcor 53
AIRCRAFT
TPT • **Light** 12 BN-2T *Islander*
TRG 2 R-235 *Guerrier*
HELICOPTERS
MRH 14: 3 SA315B *Lama*; 2 SA316 *Alouette* III; 3 SA318 *Alouette* II; 6 SA342K *Gazelle*
TPT 25: **Medium** 11: 3 H225 *Super Puma*; 2 S-70A *Black Hawk* (VIP); 6 SA330 *Puma*; **Light** 14: 2 H125; 4 H135; 6 H145; 2 SA360 *Dauphin*

Force Auxiliaire 30,000 (incl 5,000 Mobile Intervention Corps)

Customs/Coast Guard
EQUIPMENT BY TYPE
PATROL AND COASTAL COMBATANTS
PB 36: 4 *Erraid*; 18 *Arcor* 46; 14 (other SAR craft)

DEPLOYMENT

CENTRAL AFRICAN REPUBLIC: UN • MINUSCA 772; 1 inf bn

DEMOCRATIC REPUBLIC OF THE CONGO: UN • MONUSCO 918; 1 inf bn; 2 fd hospital

SOUTH SUDAN: UN • UNMISS 3

SUDAN: UN • UNISFA 5

Oman OMN

Omani Rial OMR		2023	2024	2025
GDP	OMR	41.8bn	42.3bn	42.8bn
	USD	109bn	110bn	111bn
Real GDP growth	%	1.3	1.0	3.1
Def bdgt [a]	OMR	2.50bn	2.56bn	
	USD	6.51bn	6.66bn	

[a] Excludes security funding

Real-terms defence budget trend (USDbn, constant 2015)

Population		3,901,992				
Age	0–14	15–19	20–24	25–29	30–64	65 plus
Male	15.2%	3.9%	4.4%	5.4%	22.8%	1.9%
Female	14.5%	3.7%	3.8%	4.3%	17.8%	2.1%

Capabilities

The principal task for Oman's armed forces is ensuring territorial integrity, with a particular focus on maritime security. Oman maintains carefully calibrated relations with the US and is developing its defence agreements with the UK, a country with which Muscat has a long-standing defence and security relationship. Oman does not host a significant permanent presence of US or other foreign forces, but UK forces are frequently deployed to the country for training. In 2019, the UK and Oman signed a Joint Defence Agreement, followed by the establishment of a joint military training area. Both the UK and US make use of Omani air- and naval-logistics facilities, most notably the port at Duqm, where the UK has a Joint Logistics Support Base. Oman has also sought to strengthen ties with Asian states. Oman's navy has exercised with Western countries, India and China. Oman is a GCC member but did not participate in Saudi-led coalition operations in Yemen and has largely followed a semi-independent regional policy. Oman has recently recapitalised its core air- and naval-systems inventory, and is now looking to do the same in the land domain. Oman has very limited defence-industrial capacity, but it has begun local production of various types of ammunition and is looking to boost organic support capability, particularly in the air and land sectors.

ACTIVE 42,600 (Army 25,000 Navy 4,200 Air 5,000 Foreign Forces 2,000 Royal Household 6,400) Gendarmerie & Paramilitary 4,400

ORGANISATIONS BY SERVICE

Army 25,000
FORCES BY ROLE
(Regt are bn size)
MANOEUVRE
Armoured
1 armd bde (2 armd regt, 1 recce regt)
Light
1 inf bde (5 inf regt, 1 arty regt, 1 fd engr regt, 1 engr regt, 1 sigs regt)
1 inf bde (3 inf regt, 2 arty regt)
1 indep inf coy (Musandam Security Force)
Air Manoeuvre
1 AB regt
COMBAT SERVICE SUPPORT
1 tpt regt
AIR DEFENCE
1 ADA regt (2 ADA bty)
EQUIPMENT BY TYPE
ARMOURED FIGHTING VEHICLES
MBT 117: 38 *Challenger 2*; 6 M60A1 *Patton*; 73 M60A3 *Patton*
LT TK 37 FV101 *Scorpion*
RECCE 12 *Pars* III 6×6 (Recce)
IFV 72 *Pars* III 8×8 IFV
APC 262
    APC (T) 10 FV4333 *Stormer*
    APC (W) 252: 15 AT-105 *Saxon*; 15 *Pars* III 6×6 (incl 10 CP; 1 trg); 47 *Pars* III 8×8 (38 CP; 8 amb; 1 trg); 175 *Piranha* (incl variants);
AUV 143: 6 FV103 *Spartan*; 13 FV105 *Sultan* (CP); 124 VBL
ENGINEERING & MAINTENANCE VEHICLES
AEV 6 *Pars* III AEV
ARV 19: 4 *Challenger* ARV; 2 M88A1; 8 *Pars* III ARV; 2 *Piranha* ARV; 3 *Samson*
ANTI-TANK/ANTI-INFRASTRUCTURE • MSL
SP 8 VBL with TOW
MANPATS FGM-148 *Javelin*; *Milan*; BGM-71 TOW/TOW-2A
ARTILLERY 245
SP 155mm 24 G-6
TOWED 108: **105mm** 42 L118 Light Gun; **122mm** 30 D-30; **130mm** 24: 12 M-46; 12 Type-59-I; **155mm** 12 FH-70
MOR 113: **81mm** 69; **SP 81mm** VAMTAC with A3MS; **107mm** 20 M30; **120mm** 12 Brandt; **SP 120mm** 12 *Pars* III AMV
AIR DEFENCE
SAM • Point-defence *Mistral* 2; *Javelin*; 9K32 *Strela*-2 (RS-SA-7 *Grail*)‡
GUNS 26: **23mm** 4 ZU-23-2; **35mm** 10 GDF-005 (with *Skyguard*); **40mm** 12 L/60 (Towed)

Navy 4,200
EQUIPMENT BY TYPE
PRINCIPAL SURFACE COMBATANTS • FRIGATES 3
  FFGHM 3 *Al-Shamikh* with 2 twin lnchr with MM40 *Exocet* Block 3 AShM, 2 6-cell CLA VLS with VL MICA SAM, 1 76mm gun
PATROL AND COASTAL COMBATANTS 10
  CORVETTES • FSGM 2:
    2 *Qahir Al Amwaj* with 2 quad lnchr with MM40 *Exocet* AShM, 1 octuple lnchr with *Crotale* SAM, 1 76mm gun, 1 hel landing platform
  PCO 4 *Al Ofouq* with 1 76mm gun, 1 hel landing platform
  PCC 3 *Al Bushra* (FRA P-400) with 1 76mm gun
  PBF 1 1400 FIC
AMPHIBIOUS
  LANDING SHIPS • LST 1 *Nasr el Bahr†* with 1 hel landing platform (capacity 7 tanks; 240 troops)
  LANDING CRAFT 5: 1 LCU; 1 LCT; 3 **LCM**
LOGISTICS AND SUPPORT 7
  AGS 1 *Al Makhirah*
  AKL 1 *Al Sultana*
  AX 1 *Al-Mabrukah*
  AXS 1 *Shabab Oman* II
  EPF 3: 2 *Al Mubshir* (High Speed Support Vessel 72) (of which 1†) with 1 hel landing platform (capacity 260 troops); 1 *Shinas* (commercial tpt – auxiliary military role only) (capacity 56 veh; 200 tps)

Air Force 5,000
FORCES BY ROLE
FIGHTER/GROUND ATTACK
  1 sqn with Eurofighter *Typhoon*
  2 sqn with F-16C/D Block 50 *Fighting Falcon*
MARITIME PATROL
  1 sqn with C295MPA
TRANSPORT
  1 sqn with C-130H/J/J-30 *Hercules*
  1 sqn with C295M
  1 (VIP) flt with A320-300; Gulfstream IV
TRAINING
  1 sqn with *Hawk* Mk166
  1 sqn with Bell 206 (AB-206) *Jet Ranger*; MFI-17B *Mushshak*; PC-9*
TRANSPORT HELICOPTER
  4 (med) sqn; Bell 212 (AB-212); NH-90; *Super Lynx* Mk300 (maritime/SAR)
AIR DEFENCE
  2 sqn with NASAMS
EQUIPMENT BY TYPE
AIRCRAFT 47 combat capable
  FGA 35: 12 Eurofighter *Typhoon*; 17 F-16C Block 50 *Fighting Falcon*; 6 F-16D Block 50 *Fighting Falcon*;
  MP 4 C295MPA
  TPT 14: **Medium** 6: 3 C-130H *Hercules*; 2 C-130J *Hercules*; 1 C-130J-30 *Hercules* (VIP); **Light** 4 C295M; **PAX** 4: 2 A320-300; 2 Gulfstream IV
  TRG 27: 7 *Hawk* Mk166; 8 MFI-17B *Mushshak*; 12 PC-9*
HELICOPTERS
  MRH 15 *Super Lynx* Mk300 (maritime/SAR)
  TPT 26+ **Medium** 20 NH90 TTH; **Light** 6: 3 Bell 206 (AB-206) *Jet Ranger*; 3 Bell 212 (AB-212)
UNINHABITED AERIAL VEHICLES
  CISR • Heavy CH-4 (reported)
AIR DEFENCE • SAM
  Short-range NASAMS
AIR-LAUNCHED MISSILES
  AAM • IR AIM-9M/P *Sidewinder*; **IIR** AIM-9X *Sidewinder* II; **ARH** AIM-120C7 AMRAAM
  ASM AGM-65D/G *Maverick*
  AShM AGM-84D *Harpoon*
BOMBS
  Laser-guided EGBU-10 *Paveway* II; EGBU-12 *Paveway* II
  INS/GPS-guided GBU-31 JDAM

Royal Household 6,400
(incl HQ staff)
FORCES BY ROLE
SPECIAL FORCES
  2 SF regt

Royal Guard Brigade 5,000
FORCES BY ROLE
MANOEUVRE
Other
  1 gd bde (1 armd sqn, 2 gd regt, 1 cbt spt bn)
EQUIPMENT BY TYPE
ARMOURED FIGHTING VEHICLES
  ASLT 9 *Centauro* MGS (9 VBC-90 in store)
  IFV 14 VAB VCI
  APC • APC (W) ε50 Type-92
ANTI-TANK/ANTI-INFRASTRUCTURE
  MSL • MANPATS *Milan*
ARTILLERY • MRL 122mm 6 Type-90A
AIR DEFENCE
  SAM • Point-defence *Javelin*
  GUNS • SP 9: **20mm** 9 VAB VDAA

Royal Yacht Squadron 150
EQUIPMENT BY TYPE
LOGISTICS AND SUPPORT 3
  AP 1 *Fulk Al Salamah* (also veh tpt) with up to 2 AS332 *Super Puma* hel

Royal Flight 250
EQUIPMENT BY TYPE
AIRCRAFT • TPT • PAX 7: 1 A319; 1 A320; 1 B-747-

400; 1 B-747-8; 1 B-747SP; 2 Gulfstream IV
HELICOPTERS • TPT • Medium 6 EC225LP *Super Puma*

Gendarmerie & Paramilitary 4,400 active

Tribal Home Guard 4,000
org in teams of ε100

Police Coast Guard 400
EQUIPMENT BY TYPE
PATROL AND COASTAL COMBATANTS 73
  PCO 1 *Haras*
  PBF 17: 14 *Ares* 85; 3 *Haras* (US Mk V PBF)
  PB 55: 3 Rodman 101; 1 *Haras* (SWE CG27); 3 *Haras* (SWE CG29); 14 K13 Fast Intercept Craft; 14 Rodman 58; 1 D59116; 5 *Zahra*; up to 14 Other (Baltic Workboats)

Police Air Wing
EQUIPMENT BY TYPE
AIRCRAFT • TPT • Light 4: 1 BN-2T *Turbine Islander*; 2 CN235M; 1 Do-228
HELICOPTERS
  MRH 1 H145M
  TPT • Light 16: 3 AW109 (1 VIP); 11 AW139 (1 VIP); 2 Bell 205A

FOREIGN FORCES
United Kingdom 90

Palestinian Territories PT

Definitive macro- and defence-economic data not available

Population	5,385,012					
Age	0–14	15–19	20–24	25–29	30–64	65 plus
Male	19.3%	5.5%	4.9%	4.3%	15.1%	1.7%
Female	18.3%	5.3%	4.7%	4.2%	15.0%	1.8%

Capabilities

The Palestinian Territories remain effectively divided between Gaza and the West Bank. In Gaza, the Izz al-Din al-Qassam Brigades of Hamas have suffered significant losses in personnel and equipment in fighting with the Israel Defense Forces since October 2023, leading remaining forces to shift from territorial control to guerrilla operations. In the West Bank, the Fatah-dominated Palestinian Authority controls its own security forces, principally the National Security Forces (NSF), which have received support from the EU, Jordan and the US. Hamas have expanded their own operations in the West Bank since 2022.

ACTIVE 0 Gendarmerie & Paramilitary n.k.
Precise personnel-strength figures for the various Palestinian groups are not known

ORGANISATIONS BY SERVICE

There is little available data on the status of the organisations mentioned below. Following internal fighting in June 2007, Gaza has been under the de facto jurisdiction of Hamas, though security control is now tenuous in light of Israel's military action, while the West Bank is controlled by the Palestinian Authority.

Gendarmerie & Paramilitary

Palestinian Authority n.k.
Presidential Security ε3,000
Special Forces ε1,200
Police ε9,000
National Security Force ε10,000
FORCES BY ROLE
MANOEUVRE
  Other
  9 paramilitary bn
Preventative Security ε4,000
Civil Defence ε1,000
The al-Aqsa Brigades n.k.
Profess loyalty to the Fatah group that dominates the Palestinian Authority

Hamas ε15,000
Information as of October 2024
Izz al-Din al-Qassam Brigades ε15,000
Maritime Police n.k.

FOREIGN FORCES
Israel ε25,000; 3 div HQ; 2 armd bde; 3 mech bde; 2 inf bde; 1 AB bde; 1 arty bde

Qatar QTR

Qatari Riyal QAR		2023	2024	2025
GDP	QAR	775bn	806bn	823bn
	USD	213bn	221bn	226bn
Real GDP growth	%	1.2	1.5	1.9
Def bdgt [a]	QAR	ε32.8bn	ε35.2bn	
	USD	ε9.02bn	ε9.66bn	

[a] Defence budget figures derived from Defence and Security allocation in the 'Public Budget Statement'

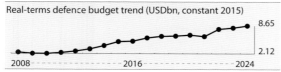

Real-terms defence budget trend (USDbn, constant 2015)

Population	2,552,088					
Age	0–14	15–19	20–24	25–29	30–64	65 plus
Male	6.6%	2.4%	5.5%	9.7%	51.7%	1.0%
Female	6.5%	1.8%	1.8%	2.5%	10.0%	0.5%

Capabilities

Qatar is attempting to transform its military capabilities and regional defence standing with significant equipment acquisitions. The size and capability of the country's air force and navy are increasing, reflecting the pace of spending and major construction of military infrastructure. The scale of the expansion has raised questions about the country's ability to develop and sustain the necessary personnel, infrastructure and maintenance capacity, given the small indigenous population. Qatar maintains close ties with Türkiye, which has a small military presence in the country. Tensions with some of Qatar's neighbours that culminated in the 2017 Gulf Crisis have subsided significantly. The US and other Western states base forces at Al-Udeid Air Base. In 2022, the US government designated Qatar a major non-NATO ally and the US has agreed a range of security cooperation agreements with Qatar, as has France. The air force has joint squadrons with the UK and Turkish air forces. Qatar is also improving training infrastructure for special operations forces. Qatari equipment modernisation efforts include new and upgraded naval and air capabilities, while coast guard equipment has improved with the acquisition of Turkish-made patrol craft. Qatar's limited indigenous defence industry includes small arms, small calibre munitions production and ship repair. Qatar is trying to upgrade its defence industrial capacity through Barzan Holdings, which has joint ventures with OEMs and several international investments.

ACTIVE 16,500 (Army 12,000 Navy 2,500 Air 2,000)
Gendarmerie & Paramilitary up to 5,000

Conscript liability 12 months, males 18–35 years. Voluntary national service for women

ORGANISATIONS BY SERVICE

Space
EQUIPMENT BY TYPE
SATELLITES • COMMUNICATIONS 2 Es'hail-2

Army 12,000 (including Emiri Guard)
FORCES BY ROLE
SPECIAL FORCES
  1 SF coy
MANOEUVRE
  Armoured
    1 armd bde (1 tk bn, 1 mech inf bn, 1 mor sqn, 1 AT bn)
  Mechanised
    3 mech inf bn
    1 (Emiri Guard) bde (3 mech regt)
COMBAT SUPPORT
  1 SP arty bn
  1 fd arty bn
EQUIPMENT BY TYPE
ARMOURED FIGHTING VEHICLES
  MBT 62 Leopard 2A7+
  ASLT 48: 12 AMX-10RC; 36 Piranha II 90mm
  RECCE 32 Fennek
  IFV 40 AMX-10P
  APC 418
    APC (T) 30 AMX-VCI
    APC (W) 168: 8 V-150 Chaimite; 160 VAB
    PPV 220+: 170+ Ejder Yalcin; 50 Kirpi-2; RG-31
  AUV 65+: 35 BMC Amazon; 14 Dingo 2; NMS; 16 VBL
ENGINEERING & MAINTENANCE VEHICLES
  AEV 6 Wisent 2
  ARV 3: 1 AMX-30D; 2 Piranha
ANTI-TANK/ANTI-INFRASTRUCTURE
  MSL
    SP 24 VAB VCAC HOT; Ejder Yalcin with Stugna-P; NMS with Stugna-P
    MANPATS FGM-148 Javelin; Milan; Kornet-EM
  RCL 84mm Carl Gustaf
ARTILLERY 89+
  SP 155mm 24 PzH 2000
  TOWED 155mm 12 G-5
  MRL 8+: 107mm PH-63; 122mm 2+ (30-tube); 127mm 6 ASTROS II Mk3
  MOR 45: 81mm 26 L16; SP 81mm 4 VAB VPM 81; 120mm 15 Brandt
SURFACE-TO-SURFACE MISSILE LAUNCHERS
  SRBM • Conventional 8+ BP-12A (CH-SS-14 mod 2)
AIR DEFENCE
  SAM • Point-defence NMS with Igla
  GUNS • SP 35mm 15 Gepard

Navy 2,500 (incl Coast Guard)
EQUIPMENT BY TYPE
PRINCIPAL SURFACE COMBATANTS • FRIGATES 4
  FFGHM 4 Al Zubarah with 2 quad lnchr with MM40 Exocet Block 3 AShM, 2 8-cell Sylver A50 VLS with Aster 30 SAM, 1 21-cell Mk 49 GMLS with RIM-116 RAM

SAM, 1 76mm gun (capacity 1 med hel)

PATROL AND COASTAL COMBATANTS 24

CORVETTES • FSGM 2 *Musherib* with 2 twin lnchr with MM40 *Exocet* Block 3 AShM, 1 8-cell CLA VLS with VL MICA SAM, 1 76mm gun

PCFGM 4 *Barzan* (UK *Vita*) with 2 quad lnchr with MM40 *Exocet* Block 3 AShM, 1 sextuple *Sadral* lnchr with *Mistral* SAM, 1 *Goalkeeper* CIWS, 1 76mm gun

PCFG 2 *Damsah* (FRA *Combattante* III) with 2 quad lnchr with MM40 *Exocet* AShM, 1 76mm gun

PBF 16: 3 MRTP 16; 6+ MRTP 20; 4 MRTP 24/U; 3 MRTP 34

AMPHIBIOUS 4

LCT 1 *Fuwairit* (TUR Anadolu Shipyard LCT)
LCM 2 *Broog* (TUR Anadolu Shipyard LCM)
LCVP 1 Anadolu 16m

LOGISTICS AND SUPPORT • AX 2 *Al Doha* with 1 hel landing platform

Coast Guard

EQUIPMENT BY TYPE

PATROL AND COASTAL COMBATANTS 28
PBF 11: 5 *Ares* 75; 2 *Ares* 150; 4 DV 15
PB 17: 10 *Ares* 110; 4 *Crestitalia* MV-45; 3 *Halmatic* M160

Coastal Defence

FORCES BY ROLE

COASTAL DEFENCE
1 bty with MM40 *Exocet* Block III
1 bty with *Marte* ER

EQUIPMENT BY TYPE

COASTAL DEFENCE • AShM 9: 3 MM40 *Exocet* Block III; 6 *Marte* ER

Air Force 2,000

FORCES BY ROLE

FIGHTER/GROUND ATTACK
1 sqn with Eurofighter *Typhoon*
1 sqn with Eurofighter *Typhoon* (personnel only) (joint QTR-UK unit)
3 sqn with F-15QA
3 sqn with *Rafale* DQ/EQ

ANTI-SUBMARINE WARFARE
1 sqn with NH90 NFH

TRANSPORT
1 sqn with C-17A *Globemaster* III; C-130J-30 *Hercules*
1 sqn with A340; B-707; B-727; *Falcon* 900

TRAINING
1 sqn with *Hawk* Mk167
1 sqn with M-346
1 sqn with PC-21; *Super Mushshak*

ATTACK HELICOPTER
1 sqn with SA341 *Gazelle*; SA342L *Gazelle* with HOT

TRANSPORT HELICOPTER
1 sqn with AW139
1 sqn with NH90 TTH

EQUIPMENT BY TYPE

AIRCRAFT 98 combat capable
FGA 98: 22 Eurofighter *Typhoon*; 40 F-15QA; 9 *Rafale* DQ; 27 *Rafale* EQ
TPT 18: **Heavy** 8 C-17A *Globemaster* III; **Medium** 4 C-130J-30 *Hercules*; **PAX** 6: 1 A340; 2 B-707; 1 B-727; 2 *Falcon* 900
TRG 41: 9 *Hawk* Mk167; 3 M-346; 21 PC-21; 8 *Super Mushshak*; (6 *Alpha Jet* in store)

HELICOPTERS
ATK 24 AH-64E *Apache*
ASW 9 NH90 NFH
MRH 34: 21 AW139 (incl 3 for medevac); 2 SA341 *Gazelle*; 11 SA342L *Gazelle*
TPT 10: **Medium** 9 NH90 TTH; **Light** 1 H125 *Ecureuil* (trg config)

UNINHABITED AERIAL VEHICLES
CISR • Medium 6 *Bayraktar* TB2

AIR DEFENCE
SAM
Long-range 34 M903 *Patriot* PAC-3 MSE
Medium-range NASAMS III
Point-defence FIM-92 *Stinger*; FN-6 (CH-SA-10); *Mistral*
GUNS • Towed 35mm 8 *Skynex*

RADAR 1 AN/FPS-132 Upgraded Early Warning Radar

AIR-LAUNCHED MISSILES
AAM • IR R-550 *Magic* 2; **IIR** AIM-9X *Sidewinder* II; ASRAAM; **ARH** AIM-120C-7 AMRAAM; *Meteor*; Mica RF
ASM *Apache*; AGM-114R *Hellfire*; AGR-20A APKWS; HOT
AShM AM39 *Exocet*; AGM-84L *Harpoon* Block II
ARM AGM-88B HARM
BOMBS • INS/GPS-guided AGM-154C JSOW

Gendarmerie & Paramilitary up to 5,000

Internal Security Force up to 5,000

DEPLOYMENT

LEBANON: UN • UNIFIL 1

FOREIGN FORCES

Turkiye 300 (trg team); 1 mech coy; 1 arty unit
United States US Central Command: 11,000; CAOC; 1 bbr flt with 4 B-52H *Stratofortress*; 1 ftr sqn with 12 F-22A *Raptor*; 1 atk sqn with 12 A-10C *Thunderbolt* II; 1 ISR sqn with 4 RC-135 *Rivet Joint*; 1 tkr sqn with 12 KC-46A *Pegasus*; 2 tkr sqn with 12 KC-135R/T *Stratotanker*; 1 tpt sqn with 4 C-17A *Globemaster*; 2 SAM bty with M903 *Patriot* PAC-3 MSE

Saudi Arabia SAU

Saudi Riyal SAR		2023	2024	2025
GDP	SAR	4.00trn	4.13trn	4.26trn
	USD	1.07trn	1.10trn	1.14trn
Real GDP growth	%	-0.8	1.5	4.6
Def bdgt [a]	SAR	248bn	269bn	
	USD	66.1bn	71.7bn	

[a] Military budget only - excludes security budget

Real-terms defence budget trend (USDbn, constant 2015)

Population		36,544 431				
Age	0–14	15–19	20–24	25–29	30–64	65 plus
Male	11.7%	4.0%	3.9%	4.2%	30.5%	2.3%
Female	11.2%	3.8%	3.6%	3.5%	19.2%	2.1%

Capabilities

Saudi Arabia has the largest and best-equipped armed forces in the GCC. Operations in Yemen allowed the Saudi armed forces to gain combat experience, but exposed areas of weakness and capability gaps, especially in the application of precision airpower, air-ground coordination and logistics. Meanwhile, cruise missile and UAV attacks on Saudi soil highlighted shortfalls in the Kingdom's air- and missile-defence capabilities, although the force has gained significant experience. In 2023, Riyadh agreed to re-establish diplomatic ties with Iran under a China-brokered deal. Saudi Arabia's most critical defence relationship is with the US and in August 2024, the US lifted a ban on sales of offensive weapons. Engagement has increased with Beijing. Over the years, Riyadh has sought to mitigate dependence on Washington by maintaining security relationships with France, the UK and others, and by diversifying procurement. Riyadh struck an agreement with Turkiye in 2023 to acquire UAVs. Equipment modernisation continues, including new naval vessels and there are reports that Riyadh is interested in joining the Global Combat Air Programme. Riyadh aims to spend 50% of its defence outlays locally as part of its Vision 2030. The government established the state-owned Saudi Arabian Military Industries to oversee the development of a defence industrial base and has been seeking other partnerships and technology transfers to boost its arms production capacity.

ACTIVE 257,000 (Army 75,000 Navy 13,500 Air 20,000 Air Defence 16,000 Strategic Missile Forces 2,500 National Guard 130,000) Gendarmerie & Paramilitary 24,500

ORGANISATIONS BY SERVICE

Army 75,000
FORCES BY ROLE
MANOEUVRE
  Armoured
  4 armd bde (1 recce coy, 3 tk bn, 1 mech bn, 1 fd arty bn, 1 AD bn, 1 AT bn, 1 engr coy, 1 log bn, 1 maint coy, 1 med coy)
  Mechanised
  5 mech bde (1 recce coy, 1 tk bn, 3 mech bn, 1 fd arty bn, 1 AD bn, 1 AT bn, 1 engr coy, 1 log bn, 1 maint coy, 1 med coy)
  Light
  2 lt inf bde
  Other
  1 (Al-Saif Al-Ajrab) gd bde
  1 (Royal Guard) gd regt (3 lt inf bn)
  Air Manoeuvre
  1 AB bde (2 AB bn, 3 SF coy)
  Aviation
  1 comd (3 hel gp)
COMBAT SUPPORT
  3 arty bde
EQUIPMENT BY TYPE
  MBT 1,085: 140 AMX-30; ε575 M1A2S *Abrams*; ε370 M60A3 *Patton*
  RECCE 300 AML-60/AML-90
  IFV 860: 380 AMX-10P; 380 M2A2 *Bradley*; 100 VAB Mk3
  APC 1,340
    APC (T) 1,190 M113A4 (incl variants)
    APC (W) 150 Panhard M3; (ε40 AF-40-8-1 *Al-Fahd* in store)
  AUV 1,200+: *Cobra* II; 100 *Didgori* (amb); 1,000+ M-ATV; *Al-Shibl* 2; 100 *Sherpa Light Scout*; Terradyne *Gurkha*
  ENGINEERING & MAINTENANCE VEHICLES
  AEV 15 M728
  ARV 275+: 8 ACV ARV; AMX-10EHC; 55 AMX-30D; *Leclerc* ARV; 122 M88A1; 90 M578
  VLB 10 AMX-30
  MW *Aardvark* Mk2
  NBC VEHICLES 10 TPz-1 *Fuchs* NBC
  ANTI-TANK/ANTI-INFRASTRUCTURE
  MSL
    SP 290+: 90+ AMX-10P (HOT); 200 VCC-1 ITOW; M-ATV with *Milan*
    MANPATS *Hyeongung*; Luch *Corsar* (reported); Luch *Skif* (reported); *Stugna*-P (reported); TOW-2A
  RCL 84mm *Carl Gustaf*; **90mm** M67; **106mm** M40A1
  ARTILLERY 880
  SP 155mm 224: 60 AU-F-1; 110 M109A1B/A2; 54 PLZ-45
  TOWED 201: **105mm** 91 LG1; (100 M101/M102 in store); **155mm** 110: 50 M114; 60 M198
  MRL 88: **127mm** 60 ASTROS II Mk3; **220mm** 10 TOS-1A; **239mm** ε18 K239 *Chunmoo*
  MOR 367: **SP 81mm** 70; **107mm** 150 M30; **120mm** 147: 110 Brandt; 37 M12-1535; **SP 120mm** M113A4 with 2R2M
  HELICOPTERS
  ATK 35: 11 AH-64D *Apache*; 24 AH-64E *Apache*
  MRH 21: 6 AS365N *Dauphin* 2 (medevac); 15 Bell 406CS *Combat Scout*
  TPT 90: **Heavy** 4+ CH-47F *Chinook*; **Medium** 67: 22 UH-60A *Black Hawk* (4 medevac); 36 UH-60L *Black Hawk*; 9 UH-60M *Black Hawk*; **Light** 19 Schweizer 333

AIR-LAUNCHED MISSILES
ASM AGM-114R *Hellfire* II
AIR DEFENCE • SAM
Short-range *Crotale*
Point-defence FIM-92 *Stinger*

Navy 13,500
Navy HQ at Riyadh; Eastern Fleet HQ at Jubail; Western Fleet HQ at Jeddah
EQUIPMENT BY TYPE
PRINCIPAL SURFACE COMBATANTS • FRIGATES 12
FFGHM 12:

5 *Al-Jubail* (ESP *Avante* 2200) with 2 quad lnchr with RGM-84L *Harpoon* Block II AShM, 2 8-cell Mk 41 VLS with RIM-162B ESSM SAM, 2 triple 324mm ASTT with Mk 46 LWT, 1 76mm gun (capacity 1 med hel)

3 *Al Riyadh* (FRA *La Fayette* mod) with 2 quad lnchr with MM40 *Exocet* Block 2 AShM, 2 8-cell *Sylver* A43 VLS with *Aster* 15 SAM, 4 single 533mm TT with F17P HWT, 1 76mm gun (capacity 1 AS365N *Dauphin* 2 hel)

4 *Madina* (FRA F-2000) with 2 quad lnchr with *Otomat* Mk2 AShM, 1 octuple lnchr with *Crotale* SAM, 4 single 533mm TT with F17P HWT, 1 100mm gun (capacity 1 AS365N *Dauphin* 2 hel)

PATROL AND COASTAL COMBATANTS 93
CORVETTES • FSG 4 *Badr* (US *Tacoma*) with 2 quad lnchr with RGM-84C *Harpoon* Block 1B AShM, 2 triple 324mm ASTT with Mk 46 LWT, 1 Mk 15 *Phalanx* CIWS, 1 76mm gun

PCFG 9 *Al Siddiq* (US 58m) with 2 twin lnchr with RGM-84C *Harpoon* Block 1B AShM, 1 Mk 15 *Phalanx* CIWS, 1 76mm gun

PBF 58 HSI 32

PB 22: 3 2200 FPB; 17 (US) *Halter Marine* 24m; 2 *Plascoa* 2200

MINE WARFARE • MINE COUNTERMEASURES 3
MHC 3 *Al Jawf* (UK *Sandown*)

AMPHIBIOUS • LANDING CRAFT 5
LCU ε2 *Al Qiaq* (US LCU 1610) (capacity 120 troops)
LCM 3 LCM 6 (capacity 80 troops)

LOGISTICS AND SUPPORT 1
AORH 1 *Boraida* (mod FRA *Durance*) (1 more non-operational and in drydock since 2017) (capacity either 2 AS365F *Dauphin* 2 hel or 1 AS332C *Super Puma*)

Naval Aviation
FORCES BY ROLE
ANTI-SUBMARINE WARFARE
1 sqn with MH-60R *Seahawk*
TRANSPORT HELICOPTER
1 sqn with AS365N *Dauphin* 2; AS565 *Panther*
1 sqn with AS332B/F *Super Puma*
EQUIPMENT BY TYPE
HELICOPTERS
ASW 10 MH-60R *Seahawk*

MRH 21: 6 AS365N *Dauphin* 2; 15 AS565 *Panther*
TPT • Medium 12 AS332E/F *Super Puma*
AIR-LAUNCHED MISSILES
AShM AM39 *Exocet*; AS-15TT

Marines 3,000
FORCES BY ROLE
SPECIAL FORCES
1 spec ops regt with (2 spec ops bn)
EQUIPMENT BY TYPE
ARMOURED FIGHTING VEHICLES
RECCE *Bastion Patsas*
APC • APC (W) 135 BMR-600P
AUV • *Jais* Mk 2

Air Force 20,000
FORCES BY ROLE
FIGHTER
4 sqn with F-15C/D *Eagle*
FIGHTER/GROUND ATTACK
3 sqn with Eurofighter *Typhoon*
4 sqn with F-15S/SA/SR *Eagle*
GROUND ATTACK
3 sqn with *Tornado* IDS; *Tornado* GR1A
AIRBORNE EARLY WARNING & CONTROL
1 sqn with E-3A *Sentry*
1 sqn with Saab 2000 *Erieye*
ELINT
1 sqn with RE-3A/B; Beech 350ER *King Air*
TANKER
1 sqn with KE-3A
TANKER/TRANSPORT
1 sqn with A330 MRTT
1 sqn with KC-130H/J *Hercules*
TRANSPORT
3 sqn with C-130H *Hercules*; C-130H-30 *Hercules*; CN-235; L-100-30HS (hospital ac)
2 sqn with Beech 350 *King Air* (forming)
TRAINING
1 OCU sqn with F-15SA *Eagle*
3 sqn with *Hawk* Mk65*; *Hawk* Mk65A*; *Hawk* Mk165*
1 sqn with *Jetstream* Mk31
1 sqn with MFI-17 *Mushshak*; SR22T
2 sqn with PC-9; PC-21
TRANSPORT HELICOPTER
4 sqn with AS532 *Cougar* (CSAR); Bell 212 (AB-212); Bell 412 (AB-412) *Twin Huey* (SAR)
COMBAT/ISR UAV
2 sqn with CH-4; *Wing Loong* I/II
EQUIPMENT BY TYPE
AIRCRAFT 449 combat capable
FTR 68 F-15C/D *Eagle*
FGA 220: 71 Eurofighter *Typhoon*; ε66 F-15S/SR *Eagle*; 83

F-15SA *Eagle*
ATK 65 *Tornado* IDS
ISR 14+: 12 *Tornado* GR1A*; 2+ Beech 350ER *King Air*
AEW&C 7: 5 E-3A *Sentry*; 2 Saab 2000 *Erieye*
ELINT 2: 1 RE-3A; 1 RE-3B
TKR/TPT 15: 6 A330 MRTT; 7 KC-130H *Hercules*; 2 KC-130J *Hercules*
TKR 7 KE-3A
TPT 47+: **Medium** 36: 30 C-130H *Hercules*; 3 C-130H-30 *Hercules*; 3 L-100-30; **Light** 11+: 10+ Beech 350 *King Air*; 1 *Jetstream* Mk31
TRG 203: 24 *Hawk* Mk65* (incl aerobatic team); 16 *Hawk* Mk65A*; 44 *Hawk* Mk165*; 20 MFI-17 *Mushshak*; 20 PC-9; 55 PC-21; 24 SR22T

HELICOPTERS
MRH 15 Bell 412 (AB-412) *Twin Huey* (SAR)
TPT 30: **Medium** 10 AS532 *Cougar* (CSAR); **Light** 20 Bell 212 (AB-212)

UNINHABITED AERIAL VEHICLES
CISR • Heavy some *Wing Loong* I (reported); some *Wing Loong* II (reported); some CH-4; **Medium** some *Haboob* (*Karayel*-SU) (reported)
ISR • Medium some *Falco*

AIR-LAUNCHED MISSILES
AAM • IR AIM-9P/L *Sidewinder*; **IIR** AIM-9X *Sidewinder* II; IRIS-T; **SARH** AIM-7 *Sparrow*; AIM-7M *Sparrow*; **ARH** AIM-120C AMRAAM
ASM AGM-65 *Maverick*; AR-1; *Brimstone*
AShM AGM-84L *Harpoon* Block II
ARM ALARM
ALCM *Storm Shadow*

BOMBS
Laser-guided GBU-10/12 *Paveway* II; *Paveway* IV; MAM-L (reported)
Laser & INS/GPS-guided GBU-54 Laser JDAM
INS/GPS-guided AGM-154C JSOW; FT-9; GBU-31 JDAM; GBU-39 Small Diameter Bomb (reported)

Royal Flight
EQUIPMENT BY TYPE
AIRCRAFT • TPT 24: **Medium** 8: 5 C-130H *Hercules*; 3 L-100-30; **Light** 3: 1 Cessna 310; 2 Learjet 35; **PAX** 13: 1 A340; 1 B-737-200; 2 B-737BBJ; 2 B-747SP; 4 BAe-125-800; 2 Gulfstream III; 1 Gulfstream IV
HELICOPTERS • TPT 3+: **Medium** 3: 2 AS-61; 1 S-70 *Black Hawk*; **Light** some Bell 212 (AB-212)

Air Defence Forces 16,000
FORCES BY ROLE
AIR DEFENCE
6 bn with M902 *Patriot* PAC-3
17 bty with *Shahine*/AMX-30SA
16 bty with MIM-23B I-*Hawk*

EQUIPMENT BY TYPE
AIR DEFENCE
SAM 817+
  Long-range 108 M902 *Patriot* PAC-3
  Medium-range 128 MIM-23B I-*Hawk*
  Short-range 181: 40 *Crotale*; 141 *Shahine*
  Point-defence 400+: LMM; 400 M1097 *Avenger*; Mistral
GUNS 218
  SP • 20mm 90 M163 *Vulcan*
  TOWED 128: **35mm** 128 GDF Oerlikon; **40mm** (150 L/70 in store)
DE • Laser Silent Hunter

Strategic Missile Forces 2,500
EQUIPMENT BY TYPE
MSL • TACTICAL
IRBM 10+ DF-3 (CH-SS-2) (service status unclear)
MRBM Some DF-21 (CH-SS-5 – variant unclear) (reported)

National Guard 130,000
FORCES BY ROLE
MANOEUVRE
Mechanised
5 mech bde (1 recce coy, 3 mech inf bn, 1 SP arty bn, 1 cbt engr coy, 1 sigs coy, 1 log bn)
Light
5 inf bde (3 combined arms bn, 1 arty bn, 1 log bn)
3 indep inf bn
Other
1 (Special Security) sy bde (3 sy bn)
1 (ceremonial) cav sqn
COMBAT SUPPORT
1 MP bn
HELICOPTER
3 hel bde
1 hel trg bde

EQUIPMENT BY TYPE
ARMOURED FIGHTING VEHICLES
ASLT 204: 204 LAV-AG (90mm); LAV 700 (105mm)
IFV 1,285: ε635 LAV-25; ε650 LAV 700 (incl variants)
APC 778
  APC (W) 514: 116 LAV-A (amb); 30 LAV-AC (ammo carrier); 296 LAV-CC (CP); 72 LAV-PC
  PPV 264 *Aravis*; some *Arive*
ENGINEERING & MAINTENANCE VEHICLES
AEV 58 LAV-E
ARV 111 LAV-R; V-150 ARV
MW MV5; MV10
ANTI-TANK/ANTI-INFRASTRUCTURE
MSL
  SP 182 LAV-AT
  MANPATS TOW-2A; M47 *Dragon*
RCL • 106mm M40A1

ARTILLERY 359+
  SP 155mm up to 132 CAESAR
  TOWED 108: **105mm** 50 M102; **155mm** 58 M198
  MOR 119+: **81mm** some; **SP 120mm** 119: 107 LAV-M; 12 LAV-M with NEMO
HELICOPTERS
  ATK 24 AH-64E *Apache*
  MRH 35: 23 AH-6i *Little Bird*; 12 MD530F (trg role)
  TPT • Medium ε50 UH-60M *Black Hawk*
AIR-LAUNCHED MISSILES
  ASM AGM-114R *Hellfire* II
AIR DEFENCE
  SAM 79
    Short-range 11 VL MICA
    Point-defence 68 MPCV
  GUNS • TOWED • 20mm 30 M167 *Vulcan*

Gendarmerie & Paramilitary 24,500+ active

Border Guard 15,000
FORCES BY ROLE
Subordinate to Ministry of Interior. HQ in Riyadh. 9 subordinate regional commands
MANOEUVRE
  Other
    Some mobile def (long-range patrol/spt) units
    2 border def (patrol) units
    12 infrastructure def units
    18 harbour def units
    Some coastal def units
COMBAT SUPPORT
  Some MP units
EQUIPMENT BY TYPE
ARMOURED FIGHTING VEHICLES
  APC • PPV *Caprivi* Mk1/Mk3
PATROL AND COASTAL COMBATANTS 108
  PCC 15 OPB 40
  PBF 85: 4 *Al Jouf*; 2 *Sea Guard*; 79 Plascoa FIC 1650
  PB 8: 6 Damen Stan Patrol 2606; 2 *Al Jubatel*
AMPHIBIOUS • LANDING CRAFT • UCAC 8: 5 *Griffon* 8000; 3 other
LOGISTICS AND SUPPORT 4: 1 **AXL**; 3 **AO**

Facilities Security Force 9,000+
Subordinate to Ministry of Interior

General Civil Defence Administration Units
EQUIPMENT BY TYPE
HELICOPTERS • TPT • Medium 10 Boeing *Vertol* 107

Special Security Force 500
EQUIPMENT BY TYPE
ARMOURED FIGHTING VEHICLES
  APC • APC (W) UR-416
  AUV 60+: *Gurkha* LAPV; 60 *Kozak*-5

DEPLOYMENT
YEMEN: 500

FOREIGN FORCES
France 50 (radar det)
Greece 100: 1 SAM bty with M901 *Patriot* PAC-2
United Kingdom 100; 1 SAM bty with FV4333 *Stormer* with *Starstreak*
United States US Central Command: 2,500; 2 FGA sqn with 12 F-16C *Fighting Falcon*; 1 tkr sqn with 12 KC-135R *Stratotanker*; 1 ISR flt with 4 E-11A; 1 AEW&C sqn with 4 E-3B/G *Sentry*; 1 SAM bty with M903 *Patriot* PAC-3 MSE; 1 SAM bty with THAAD • **US Strategic Command**: 1 AN/TPY-2 X-band radar

Syria SYR

Definitive macro- and defence-economic data not available

Population	23,865,423					
Age	0–14	15–19	20–24	25–29	30–64	65 plus
Male	16.9%	4.9%	4.6%	4.3%	17.5%	2.0%
Female	16.0%	4.6%	4.5%	4.5%	18.0%	2.2%

Capabilities

The Hayat Tahrir al-Sham (HTS)-initiated overthrow of the Assad regime in early December 2024 and the collapse of the Syrian armed forces have placed great uncertainty on the status of the former state's inventory and organisation. Subsequent Israeli air strikes against defence materiel seemed to target former armed forces' equipment that could be utilised for offensive purposes, including combat aircraft and missile systems. The protracted civil war depleted the combat capabilities of Syria's armed forces and transformed them into an irregularly structured militia-style organisation focused on internal security. Various nominally pro-government militias often formed around local or religious identity and were reportedly funded by local businessmen or foreign powers, raising questions over capacity, morale and loyalty. Russia had been the regime's principal partner and provided essential combat support and assistance, as well as replacement equipment. Russia was also involved in efforts to reconstitute the army's pre-war divisions, whilst Iran and Hizbullah trained militias and other ground forces. Washington has said that Russia and Iran showed signs of coordinating some of their efforts in Syria to confront US interests. Before the civil war, Syria did not have a major domestic defence industry, although it possessed facilities to overhaul and maintain its existing systems and some capacity in focused areas, such as ballistic missiles and chemical weapons.

ACTIVE n.k. (Army n.k. Navy n.k. Air n.k. Air Defence n.k.) Gendarmerie & Paramilitary n.k.

ORGANISATIONS BY SERVICE

Army n.k.
Status of former Syrian armed forces' units and assets uncertain after December 2024. Some equipment listed below will have been lost following HTS and militia

action, and Israeli air strikes, particularly focused on air defence and surface-to-surface missiles and other assets capable of unconventional weapons delivery. Data should be treated with caution.

EQUIPMENT BY TYPE

ARMOURED FIGHTING VEHICLES
  MBT T-55A; T-55AM; T-55AMV; T-62; T-62M; T-72; T-72AV; T-72B; T-72B3; T-72M1; T-90; T-90A
  RECCE BRDM-2
  IFV BMP-1; BMP-2; BTR-82A
  APC
    APC (T) BTR-50
    APC (W) BTR-152; BTR-60; BTR-70; BTR-80
    APC IVECO LMV

ENGINEERING & MAINTENANCE VEHICLES
  ARV BREM-1 reported; T-54/55
  VLB MTU; MTU-20
  MW UR-77

ANTI-TANK/ANTI-INFRASTRUCTURE • MSL
  SP 9P133 *Malyutka*-P (BRDM-2 with RS-AT-3C *Sagger*); 9P148 *Konkurs* (BRDM-2 with RS-AT-5 *Spandrel*)
  MANPATS 9K111 *Fagot* (RS-AT-4 *Spigot*); 9K111-1 *Konkurs* (RS-AT-5 *Spandrel*); 9K115 *Metis* (RS-AT-7 *Saxhorn*); 9K115-2 *Metis*-M (RS-AT-13); 9K135 *Kornet* (RS-AT-14 *Spriggan*); *Milan*

ARTILLERY
  SP 122mm 2S1 *Gvozdika*; 152mm 2S3 *Akatsiya*
  TOWED 122mm D-30; M-30 (M1938); 130mm M-46; 152mm D-20; ML-20 (M-1937); 180mm S-23
  GUN/MOR 120mm 2S9 NONA-S
  MRL 107mm Type-63; 122mm BM-21 *Grad*; 140mm BM-14; 220mm 9P140 *Uragan*; 300mm 9A52 *Smerch*; 330mm some (also improvised systems of various calibres)
  MOR 82mm some; 120mm M-1943; 160mm M-160; 240mm M-240

SURFACE-TO-SURFACE MISSILE LAUNCHERS
  SRBM • Conventional 8K14 (RS-SS-1C *Scud*-B); 9K72 *Elbrus* (RS-SS-1D *Scud* C) 9K72-1 (RS-SS-1E *Scud* D); *Scud* lookalike; 9K79 *Tochka* (RS-SS-21 *Scarab*); *Fateh*-110/M-600

UNINHABITED AERIAL VEHICLES
  ISR • Medium *Mohajer* 3/4; Light *Ababil*

AIR DEFENCE
  SAM
    Medium-range 9K37 *Buk* (RS-SA-11 *Gadfly*); 9K317 *Buk*-M2 (RS-SA-17 *Grizzly*)
    Point-defence 9K31 *Strela*-1 (RS-SA-9 *Gaskin*); 9K33 *Osa* (RS-SA-8 *Gecko*); 9K35 *Strela*-10 (RS-SA-13 *Gopher*); 9K32 *Strela*-2 (RS-SA-7 *Grail*)‡; 9K38 *Igla* (RS-SA-18 *Grouse*); 9K36 *Strela*-3 (RS-SA-14 *Gremlin*); 9K338 *Igla*-S (RS-SA-24 *Grinch*)
    SPAAGM 30mm 96K6 *Pantsir*-S1 (RS-SA-22 *Greyhound*)
  GUNS
    SP 23mm ZSU-23-4; 57mm ZSU-57-2
    TOWED 23mm ZU-23-2; 37mm M-1939; 57mm S-60; 100mm KS-19

Navy n.k.

Status of former Syrian armed forces' units and assets uncertain after December 2024. Some equipment listed below will have been lost following HTS and militia action, and Israeli air strikes, particularly focused on surface-to-surface missiles and other assets capable of unconventional weapons delivery. Data should be treated with caution.

EQUIPMENT BY TYPE

PATROL AND COASTAL COMBATANTS 15+:
  CORVETTES • FS 1 Project 159AE (*Petya* III)† with 1 triple 533mm ASTT with SAET-60 HWT, 4 RBU 2500 *Smerch* 1 A/S mor, 2 twin 76mm gun
  PBFG 6+:
    some Project 205 (*Osa* I/II)† with 4 single lnchr with P-22 (RS-SS-N-2C *Styx*) AShM
    6 *Tir* with 2 single lnchr with C-802 (CH-SS-N-6) AShM
  PB 8 *Zhuk*†

MINE WARFARE • MINE COUNTERMEASURES 7
  MHC 1 Project 1265 (*Sonya*) with 2 quad lnchr with 9K32 *Strela*-2 (RS-SA-N-5 *Grail*)‡ SAM, 2 AK630 CIWS
  MSO 1 *Akvamaren*-M (FSU Project 266M (*Natya*)) with 2 quad lnchr with 9K32 *Strela*-2 (RS-SA-N-5 *Grail*)‡ SAM
  MSI 5 *Korund* (Project 1258 (*Yevgenya*))

AMPHIBIOUS • LANDING SHIPS • LSM 3 *Polnochny* B (capacity 6 MBT; 180 troops)

LOGISTICS AND SUPPORT • AX 1 *Al Assad*

Coastal Defence

Status of former Syrian armed forces' units and assets uncertain. Some equipment will have been lost following HTS and militia action, and Israeli air strikes. Data should be treated with caution.

EQUIPMENT BY TYPE

COASTAL DEFENCE • AShM P-35 (RS-SSC-1B *Sepal*); P-15M *Termit*-R (RS-SSC-3 *Styx*); C-802; K-300P *Bastion* (RS-SSC-5 *Stooge*)

Naval Aviation

All possibly non-operational after vacating base for Russian deployment

EQUIPMENT BY TYPE

HELICOPTERS • ASW 9: 4 Ka-28 *Helix* A; 5 Mi-14 *Haze*

Air Force n.k.

Status of former Syrian armed forces' units and assets uncertain after December 2024. Some equipment listed below will have been lost following HTS and militia action, and Israeli air strikes, particularly focused on air defence and surface-to-surface missiles and other assets capable of unconventional weapons delivery. Data should be treated with caution.

EQUIPMENT BY TYPE
AIRCRAFT 184
FTR 55: ε25 MiG-23MF/ML/MLD/UM *Flogger*; ε30 MiG-29A/SM/UB *Fulcrum*
FGA 79: ε50 MiG-21MF/bis *Fishbed* J/L; 9 MiG-21U *Mongol* A; ε20 MiG-23BN/UB *Flogger*
ATK 30: 20 Su-22M3/M4 *Fitter* J/K; ε10 Su-24MK *Fencer* D
TPT 23: **Heavy** 3 Il-76 *Candid*; **Light** 13: 1 An-24 *Coke*; 6 An-26 *Curl*; 2 PA-31 *Navajo*; 4 Yak-40 *Codling*; **PAX** 7: 2 *Falcon* 20; 1 *Falcon* 900; 4 Tu-134B-3
TRG 20+: ε20 L-39ZA/ZO *Albatros**; some MBB-223 *Flamingo*†
HELICOPTERS
ATK 20+: ε20 Mi-24D *Hind* D; some Mi-24P *Hind* F
MRH 40: ε20 Mi-17 *Hip* H; ε20 SA342L *Gazelle*
TPT • **Medium** ε10 Mi-8 *Hip*
AIR-LAUNCHED MISSILES
AAM • **IR** R-60 (RS-AA-8 *Aphid*); R-73 (RS-AA-11 *Archer*); **IR/SARH**; R-23/24 (RS-AA-7 *Apex*); R-27 (RS-AA-10 *Alamo*); **ARH**; R-77 (RS-AA-12A *Adder*)
ASM Kh-25 (RS-AS-10 *Karen*); Kh-29T/L (RS-AS-14 *Kedge*); HOT
ARM Kh-31P (RS-AS-17A *Krypton*)

Air Defence n.k.

Status of former Syrian armed forces' units and assets uncertain after December 2024. Some equipment listed below will have been lost following HTS and militia action, and Israeli air strikes, particularly focused on air defence and surface-to-surface missiles and other assets capable of unconventional weapons delivery. Data should be treated with caution.

EQUIPMENT BY TYPE
AIR DEFENCE • **SAM**
Long-range S-200 *Angara* (RS-SA-5 *Gammon*)
Medium-range 36+: S-75 *Dvina* (RS-SA-2 *Guideline*); ε36 S-125-2M *Pechora*-2M (RS-SA-26)
Short-range 2K12 *Kub* (RS-SA-6 *Gainful*); S-125M/M1 *Pechora*-M/M1 (RS-SA-3 *Goa*)
Point-defence 9K32 *Strela*-2/2M (RS-SA-7A/B *Grail*)‡

Gendarmerie & Paramilitary n.k.

National Defence Force n.k.
This was an umbrella of disparate regime militias performing a variety of roles, including territorial control

Other Militias n.k.
Numerous military groups that fought for the Assad regime, including Afghan, Iraqi, Pakistani and sectarian organisations. Some received significant Iranian support

FOREIGN FORCES
Russia 4,000: 1 inf BG; 3 MP bn; 1 engr unit; ε10 T-72B3; ε20 BTR-82A; BPM-97; 12 2A65; 6 D-30; 4 9A52 *Smerch*; 10 Su-24M *Fencer*; 6 Su-34; 6 Su-35S; 1 Il-20M; 12 Mi-24P/Mi-35M *Hind*; 4 Mi-8AMTSh *Hip*; 1 UAV unit with *Forpost*-R; 1 AShM bty with 3K55 *Bastion* (RS-SSC-5 *Stooge*); 1 SAM bty with S-400 (RS-SA-21 *Growler*); 1 SAM bty with *Pantsir*-S1/S2; air base at Latakia; naval facility at Tartus

FORMER OPPOSITION GROUPS

Data here represents the de facto situation for selected former armed opposition groups and their observed equipment.

Syrian Democratic Forces n.k.

A coalition of predominantly Kurdish rebel groups in de facto control of much of northeastern Syria. Kurdish forces from the YPG/J (People's Protection Units/Women's Protection Units) provide military leadership and main combat power, supplemented by Arab militias and tribal groups.

EQUIPMENT BY TYPE
ARMOURED FIGHTING VEHICLES
MBT T-55; T-72 (reported)
IFV BMP-1
APC • **PPV** *Guardian*
AUV M-ATV
ANTI-TANK/ANTI-INFRASTRUCTURE
MSL • **MANPATS** 9K111-1 *Konkurs* (RS-SA-5 *Spandrel*)
RCL 73mm SPG-9; 90mm M-79 *Osa*
ARTILLERY
MRL 122mm BM-21 *Grad*; 9K132 *Grad*-P
MOR 82mm 82-BM-37; M-1938; **120mm** M-1943; improvised mortars of varying calibre
AIR DEFENCE • **GUNS**
SP 14.5mm ZPU-4 (tch); ZPU-2 (tch); ZPU-1 (tch); 1 ZPU-2 (tch/on T-55); **23mm** ZSU-23-4 *Shilka*; ZU-23-2 (tch); **57mm** S-60
TOWED 14.5mm ZPU-2; ZPU-1; **23mm** ZU-23-2

Syrian National Army & National Front for Liberation n.k.

In late 2019, the Syrian National Army (SNA) and the National Front for Liberation (NLF) began to merge under the SNA umbrella. The SNA formed in late 2017 from Syrian Arab and Turkmen rebel factions operating under Turkish command in the Aleppo governate and northwestern Syria, including Afrin province. The NLF is a coalition of surviving Islamist and nationalist rebel factions formed in 2018 operating in northwestern Syria, particularly in and around Idlib.

EQUIPMENT BY TYPE
ARMOURED FIGHTING VEHICLES
MBT T-54; T-55; T-62
IFV BMP-1
ANTI-TANK/ANTI-INFRASTRUCTURE
MSL • **MANPATS** 9K11 *Malyutka* (RS-AT-3 *Sagger*); 9K111 *Fagot* (RS-AT-4 *Spigot*); 9K113 *Konkurs* (RS-T-5 *Spandrel*); 9K115 *Metis* (RS-AT-7); 9K115-2 *Metis*-M (RS-

AT-13 *Saxhorn* 2); 9K135 *Kornet* (RS-AT-14 *Spriggan*); BGM-71 TOW; *Milan*
RCL **73mm** SPG-9; **82mm** B-10
ARTILLERY
TOWED **122mm** D-30
MRL **107mm** Type-63; **122mm** 9K132 *Grad*-P; BM-21 *Grad*; *Grad* (6-tube tech)
MOR **82mm** 2B9 *Vasilek*; improvised mortars of varying calibre
AIR DEFENCE
SAM • Point-defence MANPADS some
GUNS
SP **14.5mm** ZPU-4 (tch); ZPU-2 (tch); ZPU-1 (tch); **23mm** ZU-23-2 (tch); ZSU-23-4 *Shilka*; **57mm** AZP S-60
TOWED **14.5mm** ZPU-1; ZPU-2; ZPU-4; **23mm** ZU-23-2

Hayat Tahrir al-Sham (HTS) n.k.

HTS was formed by Jabhat Fateh al-Sham (formerly known as Jabhat al-Nusra) in January 2017 by absorbing other hardline groups. It is designated a terrorist organisation by the US government. This group's breakout from northern Syria was an important factor precipitating the fall of the Assad regime.

EQUIPMENT BY TYPE
ANTI-TANK/ANTI-INFRASTRUCTURE
MSL • MANPATS 9K11 *Malyutka* (RS-AT-3 *Sagger*); 9K113 *Konkurs* (RS-AT-5 *Spandrel*); 9K115-2 *Metis*-M (RS-AT-13); 9K135 *Kornet* (RS-AT-14 *Spriggan*)
RCL **73mm** SPG-9; **106mm** M-40
ARTILLERY
MRL **107mm** Type-63
MOR **120mm** some; improvised mortars of varying calibres
AIR DEFENCE
SAM
Point-defence 9K32M *Strela*-2M (RS-SA-7B *Grail*)‡
GUNS
SP **14.5mm** ZPU-1; ZPU-2; **23mm** ZU-23-2; **57mm** S-60

Guardians of Religion (Huras al-Din) n.k.

An al-Qaeda-affiliated group that operated in Idlib province. It is designated a terrorist organisation by the US government.

FOREIGN FORCES

Turkiye ε3,000; 3 armd BG; some cdo units; 1 gendarmerie unit
United States *Operation Inherent Resolve* 900; 1 spec ops bn(-); 1 armd inf coy; 1 fd arty bty with M777A2; 1 AD unit with M1097 *Avenger*; *Phalanx* (LPWS)

Tunisia TUN

Tunisian Dinar TND		2023	2024	2025
GDP	TND	151bn	163bn	176bn
	USD	48.5bn	52.6bn	54.7bn
Real GDP growth	%	0.0	1.6	1.6
Def bgt	TND	3.75bn	4.09bn	
	USD	1.21bn	1.32bn	
FMA (US)	USD	45m	45m	45m

Real-terms defence budget trend (USDm, constant 2015)

Population	12,048,847					
Age	0–14	15–19	20–24	25–29	30–64	65 plus
Male	12.6%	3.5%	3.0%	3.1%	22.4%	4.9%
Female	11.8%	3.4%	3.0%	3.2%	23.6%	5.5%

Capabilities

Tunisia's armed forces have limited capacities, but a modernisation process is underway. There is increased instability in western Libya, including near its borders. The US designated Tunisia a major non-NATO ally in 2015. A ten-year military-cooperation agreement signed with the US in 2020 provides training and after-sales support. Military education reform is supported by NATO's Defence Education Enhancement Programme. There is also defence and security cooperation with several European countries, primarily Italy. In 2024, a trilateral regional cooperation initiative was agreed with Algeria and the Tripoli-based Libyan government. After withdrawing from Mali at the end of the UN MINUSMA mission, Tunisia reinforced its contribution to the UN MINUSCA mission in the Central African Republic. The country hosted a component of the US AFRICOM-led multinational exercise *African Lion* 2024. The equipment inventory is ageing, although the country has been the recipient of surplus US systems. Developing relations with Turkiye were reflected in the delivery of Turkish UAVs. The country has limited defence industrial capability but manufactured patrol boats for the navy between 2015 and 2021.

ACTIVE 35,800 (Army 27,000 Navy 4,800 Air 4,000)
Gendarmerie & Paramilitary 12,000
Conscript liability 12 months selective

ORGANISATIONS BY SERVICE

Army 5,000; 22,000 conscript (total 27,000)
FORCES BY ROLE
SPECIAL FORCES
  1 SF bde
  1 (Sahara) SF bde
MANOEUVRE
  Reconnaissance
  1 recce regt
  Mechanised
  3 mech bde (1 armd regt, 2 mech inf regt, 1 arty regt, 1

AD regt, 1 engr regt, 1 sigs regt, 1 log gp)
COMBAT SUPPORT
1 engr regt
EQUIPMENT BY TYPE
ARMOURED FIGHTING VEHICLES
  MBT 84: 30 M60A1; 54 M60A3
  LT TK 48 SK-105 *Kuerassier*
  RECCE 60: 40 AML-90; 20 FV601 *Saladin*
  APC 480
    APC (T) 140 M113A1/A2
    APC (W) 110 Fiat 6614
    PPV 230: 4 *Bastion* APC: 71 *Ejder Yalcin*; 146 *Kirpi*; 9 *Vuran*
ENGINEERING & MAINTENANCE VEHICLES
  ARV 11: 5 *Greif*; 6 M88A1
ANTI-TANK/ANTI-INFRASTRUCTURE • MSL
  SP 35 M901 ITV TOW
  MANPATS *Milan*; TOW
ARTILLERY 276
  TOWED 115: **105mm** 48 M101A1/A2; **155mm** 67: 12 M114A1; 55 M198
  MOR 161: **81mm** 95; **SP 107mm** 48 M106; **120mm** 18 Brandt
AIR DEFENCE
  SAM • Point-defence 26+: 26 M48 *Chaparral*; RBS-70
  GUNS 100
    TOWED • 20mm 100 M-55

Navy ε4,800
EQUIPMENT BY TYPE
PATROL AND COASTAL COMBATANTS 45
  PSO 4 *Jugurtha* (Damen Stan MSOPV 1400) (of which 2 with 1 hel landing platform)
  PCFG 3 *La Galite* (FRA *Combattante* III) with 2 quad lnchr with MM40 *Exocet* AShM, 1 76mm gun
  PCC 3 *Bizerte* (FRA PR 48)
  PCFT 6 *Albatros* (GER Type-143B) with 2 single 533mm TT, 2 76mm guns
  PBF 9: 3 Safe 44; 4 Safe 65; 2 *Sentry* 44
  PB 20: 5 *Istiklal*; 3 *Utique* (ex-PRC Type-062 (*Haizhui* II) mod); 6 *Joumhouria*; 6 V Series
LOGISTICS AND SUPPORT 6:
  ABU 3: 2 *Tabarka* (ex-US *White Sumac*); 1 *Sidi Bou Said*
  AGS 1 *Khaireddine* (ex-US *Wilkes*)
  AWT 1 *Ain Zaghouan* (ex-ITA *Simeto*)
  AXL 1 *Salambo* (ex-US *Conrad*, survey)

Air Force 4,000
FORCES BY ROLE
FIGHTER/GROUND ATTACK
  1 sqn with F-5E/F *Tiger* II
TRANSPORT
  2 sqn with C-130B/H/J-30 *Hercules*
  1 sqn with G.222; L-410 *Turbolet*
  1 liaison unit with S-208A
TRAINING
  1 sqn with L-59 *Albatros**; T-6C *Texan* II
  1 sqn with SF-260
ATTACK HELICOPTER
  2 sqn with OH-58D *Kiowa Warrior*
TRANSPORT HELICOPTER
  2 sqn with AS350B *Ecureuil*; AS365 *Dauphin* 2; AB-205 (Bell 205); SA313; SA316 *Alouette* III; UH-1H *Iroquois*; UH-1N *Iroquois*
  1 sqn with HH-3E
COMBAT/ISR UAV
  1 sqn with Anka-S
EQUIPMENT BY TYPE
AIRCRAFT 20 combat capable
  FTR 11: 9 F-5E *Tiger* II; 2 F-5F *Tiger* II
  ISR 16: 4 Cessna 208B Grand Caravan EX mod; 12 *Maule* MX-7-180B
  TPT 19: **Medium** 14: 5 C-130B *Hercules*; 2 C-130H *Hercules*; 2 C-130J-30 *Hercules*; 5 G.222; **Light** 5: 3 L-410 *Turbolet*; 2 S-208A
  TRG 31: 9 L-59 *Albatros**; 14 SF-260; 8 T-6C *Texan* II
HELICOPTERS
  MRH 34: 1 AS365 *Dauphin* 2; 6 SA313; 3 SA316 *Alouette* III; 24 OH-58D *Kiowa Warrior*
  SAR 11 HH-3E
  TPT 39: **Medium** 8 UH-60M *Black Hawk*; **Light** 31: 6 AS350B *Ecureuil*; 15 Bell 205 (AB-205); 8 Bell 205 (UH-1H *Iroquois*); 2 Bell 212 (UH-1N *Iroquois*)
UNINHABITED AERIAL VEHICLES
  CISR • Heavy 5 *Anka-S*
AIR-LAUNCHED MISSILES
  AAM • IR AIM-9P *Sidewinder*
  ASM AGM-114R *Hellfire*

Gendarmerie & Paramilitary 12,000

National Guard 12,000
Ministry of Interior
EQUIPMENT BY TYPE
ARMOURED FIGHTING VEHICLES
  ASLT 2 EE-11 *Urutu* FSV
  APC 29+
    APC (W) 16 EE-11 *Urutu* (anti-riot); VAB Mk3
    PPV 13 Streit *Typhoon*
  AUV IVECO LMV
PATROL AND COASTAL COMBATANTS 27
  PCC 6 *Rais el Blais* (ex-GDR *Kondor* I)
  PBF 10: 4 *Gabes*; 6 *Patrouiller*
  PB 11: 5 *Breitla* (ex-GDR *Bremse*); 4 Rodman 38; 2 *Socomena*
HELICOPTERS
  MRH 8 SA318 *Alouette* II/SA319 *Alouette* III
  TPT • Light 3 Bell 429

DEPLOYMENT

CENTRAL AFRICAN REPUBLIC: UN • MINUSCA 838; 1 inf bn; 1 hel flt with 3 Bell 205
DEMOCRATIC REPUBLIC OF THE CONGO: UN • MONUSCO 10
SOUTH SUDAN: UN • UNMISS 2
SUDAN: UN • UNISFA 2

United Arab Emirates UAE

Emirati Dirham AED		2023	2024	2025
GDP	AED	1.89trn	2.00trn	2.09trn
	USD	514bn	545bn	569bn
Real GDP growth	%	3.6	4.0	5.1
Def bdgt [a]	AED	ε80.3bn	ε81.8bn	
	USD	ε21.9bn	ε22.3bn	

[a] Defence budget estimate derived from central MoD expenditure and a proportion of the Federal Services section of the Abu Dhabi budget.

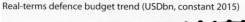
Real-terms defence budget trend (USDbn, constant 2015)

Population	10,032,213				
Age	0–14	15–19	20–24	25–29	30–64	65 plus
Male	8.4%	2.9%	3.0%	4.7%	47.3%	1.7%
Female	8.0%	2.5%	2.5%	3.2%	15.3%	0.5%

Capabilities

The UAE's armed forces are arguably the best trained and most capable of all GCC states. Iran remains a key defence concern, partly because of a continuing dispute over ownership of islands in the Strait of Hormuz. The UAE has shown a growing willingness to take part in operations and project power abroad, such as its involvement in the conflicts in Afghanistan and Libya. The UAE was also engaged in the Yemen conflict as part of the Saudi-led coalition but withdrew most of its forces in 2019. The country is becoming an increasingly active security partner in Africa. The UAE hosts a French naval base that was until 2024, home to the European Maritime Awareness in the Strait of Hormuz mission. Attempts to diversify security relationships, including with China, are complicating ties with the US, which remains the country's main extra-regional defence partner. The US Air Force continues to maintain a substantial force at the Al Dhafra airbase. The country's growing relationship with Israel has resulted in defence industrial ties and the purchase of Israeli air defence systems. The Emirati armed forces operate an advanced inventory of modern equipment across domains. The UAE has been trying to develop a domestic defence industry, through the state-owned EDGE Group. EDGE is now focusing on international exports and strengthening supply chain security.

ACTIVE 63,000 (Army 44,000 Navy 2,500 Air 4,500 Presidential Guard 12,000)

Conscript liability 11–36 months, males 18–30 years dependent on education level. Voluntary service enrolment for women

ORGANISATIONS BY SERVICE

Space
EQUIPMENT BY TYPE
SATELLITES 4
  COMMUNICATIONS 3 *Yahsat*
  ISR 1 *FalconEye*

Army 44,000
FORCES BY ROLE
MANOEUVRE
  Armoured
  2 armd bde
  Mechanised
  2 mech bde
  Light
  1 inf bde
COMBAT SUPPORT
  1 arty bde (3 SP arty regt)
  1 engr gp

EQUIPMENT BY TYPE
ARMOURED FIGHTING VEHICLES
  MBT 313: 45 AMX-30; 268 *Leclerc*
  LT TK 76 FV101 *Scorpion*
  RECCE 49 AML-90
  IFV 400 *Rabdan*
  APC 1,656
    APC (T) 136 AAPC (incl 53 engr plus other variants)
    APC (W) 185: 45 AMV 8×8 (one with BMP-3 turret); 120 EE-11 *Urutu*; 20 VAB
    PPV 1,335: ε460 *Caiman*; ε680 *Maxxpro* LWB; 150 Nimr *Hafeet* 630A (CP); 45 Nimr *Hafeet* (*Amb*)
    AUV 674+: MCAV-20; 650 M-ATV; Nimr *Ajban*; Nimr *Jais*; 24 VBL
ENGINEERING & MAINTENANCE VEHICLES
  AEV 53+: 53 ACV-AESV; *Wisent*-2
  ARV 158: 8 ACV-AESV Recovery; 4 AMX-30D; 85 BREM-L; 46 *Leclerc* ARV; 15 *Maxxpro* ARV
NBC VEHICLES 32: 8 Fuchs 2 BIO-RS; 16 *Fuchs* 2 NBC-RS; 8 Fuchs 2 NBC-CPS (CP)
ANTI-TANK/ANTI-INFRASTRUCTURE
  MSL
    SP 135: 20 HOT; 115 Nimr *Ajban* 440A with *Kornet*-E (RS-AT-14 *Spriggan*)
    MANPATS FGM-148 *Javelin*; Milan; TOW
  RCL 84mm *Carl Gustaf*
ARTILLERY 629
  SP 155mm 163: 78 G-6; 85 M109L47
  TOWED 99: **105mm** 73 L118 Light Gun; **130mm** 20 Type-59-I; **155mm** 6 AH-4
  MRL 140: **122mm** 74: ε24 *Firos*-25; ε18 *Jobaria*; **220mm** 24 SR5; **227mm** 32 M142 HIMARS; **239mm** ε12 K239 *Chunmoo*; **300mm** 6 9A52 *Smerch*

MOR 251: **81mm** 134: 20 Brandt; 114 L16; **120mm** 21 Brandt; **SP 120mm** 96 RG-31 MMP *Agrab* Mk2

SURFACE-TO-SURFACE MISSILE LAUNCHERS
SRBM • **Conventional** 6 *Hwasong*-5 (up to 20 msl); MGM-168 ATACMS (launched from M142 HIMARS)

UNINHABITED AERIAL VEHICLES
ISR • **Medium** *Seeker* II

AIR DEFENCE
SAM • **Point-defence** *Mistral*

Navy 2,500
EQUIPMENT BY TYPE
PRINCIPAL SURFACE COMBATANTS • FRIGATES 2
FFGHM 2 *Bani Yas* (FRA *Gowind*) with 2 quad lnchr with MM40 *Exocet* Block 3 AShM, 1 16-cell CLA VLS with VL MICA SAM, 1 21-cell Mk 49 GMLS with RIM-116C RAM Block 2 SAM, 2 triple 324mm ASTT with MU90 LWT, 1 76mm gun

PATROL AND COASTAL COMBATANTS 43
CORVETTES 7
FSGHM 6 *Baynunah* with 2 quad lnchr with MM40 *Exocet* Block 3 AShM, 1 8-cell Mk 56 VLS with RIM-162 ESSM SAM, 1 21-cell Mk 49 GMLS with RIM-116C RAM Block 2 SAM, 1 76mm gun
FSGM 1 *Abu Dhabi* with 2 twin lnchr with MM40 *Exocet* Block 3 AShM, 1 76mm gun
PCFGM 2 *Mubarraz* (GER Lurssen 45m) with 2 twin lnchr with MM40 *Exocet* AShM, 1 sextuple *Sadral* lnchr with *Mistral* SAM, 1 76mm gun
PCGM 4:
2 *Muray Jib* (GER Lurssen 62m) with 2 quad lnchr with MM40 *Exocet* Block 2 AShM, 1 octuple lnchr with *Crotale* SAM, 1 *Goalkeeper* CIWS, 1 76mm gun, 1 hel landing platform
2 *Ghantut* (*Falaj* 2) with 2 twin lnchr with MM40 *Exocet* Block 3 AShM, 2 3-cell VLS with VL-MICA SAM, 1 76mm gun, 1 hel landing platform
PCFG 6 *Ban Yas* (GER Lurssen TNC-45) with 2 twin lnchr with MM40 *Exocet* Block 3 AShM, 1 76mm gun
PBFG 12 *Butinah* (*Ghannatha* mod) with 4 single lnchr with *Marte* Mk2/N AShM
PBF 12: 6 *Ghannatha* with 1 120mm NEMO mor (capacity 42 troops); 6 *Ghannatha* (capacity 42 troops)

MINE WARFARE • MINE COUNTERMEASURES 1
MHO 1 *Al Murjan* (ex-GER *Frankenthal* Type-332)

AMPHIBIOUS
LANDING SHIPS • LST 3 *Alquwaisat* with 1 hel landing platform
LANDING CRAFT 19
LCM 5: 3 *Al Feyi* (capacity 56 troops); 2 ADSB 42m (capacity 40 troops and additional vehicles)
LCP 4 Fast Supply Vessel (multi-purpose)
LCT 10: 7 ADSB 64m; 2 *Al-Saadiyat* with 1 hel landing platform; 1 *Al Shareeah* (LSV 75m) with 1 hel landing platform

LOGISTICS AND SUPPORT 3:
AKL 2 *Rmah* with 4 single 533mm TT
AX 1 *Al Semeih* with 1 hel landing platform

Air Force 4,500
FORCES BY ROLE
FIGHTER/GROUND ATTACK
3 sqn with F-16E/F Block 60 *Fighting Falcon*
3 sqn with *Mirage* 2000-9DAD/EAD/RAD
AIRBORNE EARLY WARNING AND CONTROL
1 sqn with Global 6000; GlobalEye
SEARCH & RESCUE
2 flt with AW109K2; AW139
TANKER
1 flt with A330 MRTT
TRANSPORT
1 sqn with C-17A *Globemaster*
1 sqn with C-130H/H-30 *Hercules*; L-100-30
1 sqn with CN235M-100
TRAINING
1 sqn with Grob 115TA
1 sqn with *Hawk* Mk102*
1 sqn with PC-7 *Turbo Trainer*
1 sqn with PC-21
TRANSPORT HELICOPTER
1 sqn with Bell 412 *Twin Huey*

EQUIPMENT BY TYPE
AIRCRAFT 148 combat capable
FGA 128: 54 F-16E Block 60 *Fighting Falcon* (*Desert Eagle*); 24 F-16F Block 60 *Fighting Falcon*; 13 *Mirage* 2000-9DAD; 37 *Mirage* 2000-9EAD
MP 2 DHC-8 *Dash* 8 MPA
ISR 6 *Mirage* 2000 RAD*
SIGINT 2 Global 6000
AEW&C 5 GlobalEye
TPT/TKR 4 A330 MRTT
TPT 25: **Heavy** 8 C-17A *Globemaster* III; **Medium** 6: 3 C-130H *Hercules*; 1 C-130H-30 *Hercules*; 2 L-100-30; **Light** 11: 5 C295W; 4 CN235; 2 P.180 *Avanti* (MEDEVAC)
TRG 81: 12 Grob 115TA; 12 *Hawk* Mk102*; 2 L-15*; 30 PC-7 *Turbo Trainer*; 25 PC-21

HELICOPTERS
MRH 21: 12 AW139; 9 Bell 412 *Twin Huey*
TPT • **Light** 4: 3 AW109K2; 1 Bell 407

UNINHABITED AERIAL VEHICLES
CISR • **Heavy** *Wing Loong* I; *Wing Loong* II; **Medium** *Bayraktar* TB2
ISR • **Heavy** RQ-1E *Predator* XP

AIR-LAUNCHED MISSILES
AAM • **IR** AIM-9L *Sidewinder*; R-550 *Magic*; **IIR** AIM-9X *Sidewinder* II; **IIR/ARH** *Mica*; **ARH** AIM-120B/C AMRAAM
ASM AGM-65G *Maverick*; LJ-7; *Hakeem* 1/2/3 (A/B)

ARM AGM-88C HARM
LACM *Black Shaheen* (*Storm Shadow*/SCALP EG variant)
BOMBS
Laser-guided GBU-12/-58 *Paveway* II
Laser & INS/GPS-guided GBU-54 Laser JDAM
INS/SAT-guided *Al Tariq*

Air Defence
FORCES BY ROLE
AIR DEFENCE
2 AD bde (3 bn with *Barak* LRAD: M902 *Patriot* PAC-3)
3 (short range) AD bn with *Crotale*; *Mistral*; *Rapier*; RBS-70; *Javelin*; 9K38 *Igla* (RS-SA-18 *Grouse*); 96K6 *Pantsir*-S1 (RS-SA-22)
2 SAM bty with THAAD
EQUIPMENT BY TYPE
AIR DEFENCE
SAM 29+
Long-range 39+: 2+ *Barak* LRAD; 37 M902 *Patriot* PAC-3
Medium-range some *Cheongung* II (being delivered)
Short-range *Crotale*
Point-defence 9K38 *Igla* (RS-SA-18 *Grouse*); RBS-70; *Rapier*; *Mistral*
SPAAGM 30mm 42 96K6 *Pantsir*-S1 (RS-SA-22)
GUNS • Towed 35mm GDF-005
MISSILE DEFENCE 12 THAAD

Presidential Guard Command 12,000
FORCES BY ROLE
SPECIAL FORCES
1 SF bn
1 spec ops bn
MANOEUVRE
Reconaissance
1 recce sqn
Mechanised
1 mech bde (1 tk bn, 4 mech inf bn, 1 AT coy, 1 cbt engr coy, 1 CSS bn)
Amphibious
1 mne bn
EQUIPMENT BY TYPE
ARMOURED FIGHTING VEHICLES
MBT 50 *Leclerc*
IFV 340: 250 BMP-3; 90 BTR-3U *Guardian*
ANTI-TANK/ANTI-INFRASTRUCTURE
MSL • SP HMMWV with 9M133 *Kornet* (RS-AT-14 *Spriggan*)

Joint Aviation Command
FORCES BY ROLE
GROUND ATTACK
1 sqn with *Archangel*
ANTI-SURFACE/ANTI-SUBMARINE WARFARE
1 sqn with AS332F *Super Puma*; AS565 *Panther*

TRANSPORT
1 (Spec Ops) gp with AS365F *Dauphin* 2; AW139; Bell 407MRH; Cessna 208B *Grand Caravan*; CH-47C/F *Chinook*; DHC-6-300/400 *Twin Otter*; H125M *Fennec*; UH-60L/M *Black Hawk*
ATTACK HELICOPTER
1 gp with AH-64D *Apache*; AH-64E *Apache*
EQUIPMENT BY TYPE
AIRCRAFT 30 combat capable
ATK 23 *Archangel*
TPT • Light 14: 2 Beech 350 *King Air*; 7 Cessna 208B *Grand Caravan**; 1 DHC-6-300 *Twin Otter*; 4 DHC-6-400 *Twin Otter*
HELICOPTERS
ATK 29: 28 AH-64D *Apache*; 1 AH-64E *Apache*
ASW 7 AS332F *Super Puma* (5 ASuW)
MRH 53+: 4 AS365F *Dauphin* 2 (VIP); 9 H125M *Fennec*; 7 AS565 *Panther*; 3 AW139 (VIP); 20 Bell 407MRH; 4 SA316 *Alouette* III; 6+ UH-60M *Black Hawk* (ABH)
TPT 66: Heavy 22 CH-47F *Chinook*; Medium 44: 11 UH-60L *Black Hawk*; ε33 UH-60M *Black Hawk*
UNINHABITED AERIAL VEHICLES
ISR • Light S-100 *Camcopter*
AIR-LAUNCHED MISSILES
ASM AGM-114 *Hellfire*; *Cirit*; *Hydra*-70; HOT
AShM AM39 *Exocet*; AS-15TT

Gendarmerie & Paramilitary
National Guard
Ministry of Interior
EQUIPMENT BY TYPE
PATROL AND COASTAL COMBATANTS 78
PSO 2 *Al Wtaid*
PCM 2 *Arialah* (Damen Sea Axe 6711) with 1 11-cell Mk 15 SeaRAM GMLS with RIM-116C RAM Block 2 SAM, 1 57mm gun, 1 hel landing platform
PCC 3 *Shujaa* (Damen Stan Patrol 5009)
PBF 45: 11+ DV-15; 34 MRTP 16
PB 26: 2 *Protector*; 12 *Halmatic Work*; 12 *Al Saber*

DEPLOYMENT
SOMALIA: 180
YEMEN: 200

FOREIGN FORCES
Australia 400; 1 tpt det with 2 C-130J-30 *Hercules*
France 650: 1 armd BG (1 tk coy, 1 armd inf coy; 1 aty bty); *Leclerc*; VBCI; CAESAR; 7 *Rafale* F3
Korea, Republic of 170 (trg activities at UAE Spec Ops School)
United Kingdom 100
United States 5,000; 1 FGA sqn with 12 F-15E *Strike Eagle*; 1 ISR sqn with 4 U-2S; 1 ISR UAV sqn with RQ-4 *Global Hawk*; 1 ISR UAV flt with 2 MQ-4C *Triton*; 2 SAM bty with M903 *Patriot* PAC-3 MSE

Yemen, Republic of YEM

Yemeni Rial YER		2023	2024	2025
GDP	YER	25.5trn	29.4trn	36.0trn
	USD	18.8bn	16.2bn	16.2bn
Real GDP growth	%	-2.0	-1.0	1.5
Def bdgt	YER	n.k.	n.k.	n.k.
	USD	n.k.	n.k.	n.k.
Population	32,140,443			

Age	0–14	15–19	20–24	25–29	30–64	65 plus
Male	17.5%	5.7%	5.2%	4.5%	16.0%	1.5%
Female	16.9%	5.6%	5.1%	4.4%	15.6%	1.9%

Capabilities

Fighting between the Iran-backed Ansarullah (Houthi) group and forces aligned with the internationally recognised government has been largely contained after the UN negotiated an initially temporary round of ceasefires in 2022. However, occasional skirmishes continue. Tensions between the internationally recognised government and the Houthis have intensified, especially over economic control of key assets. The unity government exercises only limited control over the forces nominally allied against the Houthis. Irregular forces, such as Tareq Saleh's National Resistance, the Southern Giants Brigades and the Southern Transitional Council, are reportedly better paid and equipped than government forces. Many of these irregular forces also enjoy close political, financial and military support from regional actors. Saudi-Houthi talks have yet to produce a formal agreement, and Iran has not upheld its 2023 pledge to halt weapons shipments to the Houthis. Yemen's armed factions have been able to draw on large existing stockpiles of weapons and ammunition as well as external supplies, despite UN embargoes. Apart from the latent Houthi threat, government-controlled Yemen has also had to contend with a surge in attacks by Al-Qaeda in the Arabian Peninsula (AQAP) operatives. There is no domestic defence industry, barring some limited maintenance and workshop facilities.

ACTIVE 122,000 (Government forces 122,000)

ORGANISATIONS BY SERVICE

Government forces ε122,000 (incl militia)

Despite the establishment of the Presidential Leadership Council, central government control over the forces nominally allied together against the Houthis remains limited.

Hadrami Elite Forces ε7,000

Tribal forces trained by UAE for operations in Eastern Yemen.

Islah Affiliated Forces ε20,000

Militias and elements of the pre-war armed forces loyal to the Islah political party.

Joint Forces (West Coast) ε40,000

Includes the Guardians of the Republic, Southern Giants Brigades and Tihama Resistance forces.

Southern Transitional Council ε55,000

Southern Armed Forces and militias loyal to the STC.

EQUIPMENT BY TYPE
ARMOURED FIGHTING VEHICLES
  MBT Some M60A1; T-54/55; T-62; T-72
  RECCE some BRDM-2
  IFV BMP-2; BTR-80A; *Ratel*-20
  APC
    APC (W) BTR-60
    PPV Streit *Cougar*; Streit *Spartan*
  AUV M-ATV
ANTI-TANK/ANTI-INFRASTRUCTURE
  MSL • MANPATS 9K11 *Malyutka* (RS-AT-3 *Sagger*); M47 *Dragon*; TOW
  GUNS • SP 100mm SU-100†
ARTILLERY • SP 122mm 2S1 *Gvozdika*
AIRCRAFT • ISR 6 AT-802 *Air Tractor**
AIR DEFENCE • GUNS • TOWED 14.5mm ZPU-4; **23mm** ZU-23-2

FOREIGN FORCES

Saudi Arabia 500
United Arab Emirates 200

NORTHERN YEMEN

Insurgent forces ε185,000 (incl ε150,000 mobilised reservists)

The Ansarullah (Houthi) movement is the de facto administration of a large part of the country and has controlled northern Yemen since 2015. Iranian support has enabled the group to acquire significant military capabilities, including UAVs, loitering munitions and direct-attack munitions, long-range ballistic missiles and land-attack cruise missiles. In the maritime space, the Houthis have established capable asymmetric forces, operating anti-ship cruise- and ballistic-missiles, UAVs, USVs and speedboats. A 2022 ceasefire is largely holding between the Houthis and a Saudi-led coalition. In response to the Israel–Hamas war in Gaza, the Houthis used their missile and UAV capabilities to launch strikes against Israel as well as merchant shipping claimed to be connected to Israel and Western countries in the Red Sea and the Gulf of Aden. Western military action to safeguard freedom of navigation in the Red Sea and the Gulf of Aden had, by year-end, not succeeded in reducing the risk of Houthi attacks to a level acceptable for major shipping companies. Houthi attacks on Israel have largely been intercepted but still signal Houthi ambition to become a regional power within the so-called Axis of Resistance. With the help of Iran, the Houthis have established assembly and manufacturing facilities for various weapons systems inside Yemen, including UAVs, shorter-range missiles and naval mines. The Houthis have also expanded their air defence capabilities with Iranian assistance.

EQUIPMENT BY TYPE
ARMOURED FIGHTING VEHICLES
  MBT T-55; T-62; T-72
  IFV BMP-1; BMP-2; BTR-80A
  APC • **APC (W)** BTR-40; BTR-60
  AUV M-ATV
ARTILLERY
  MRL • **122mm** BM-21 *Grad*; **210mm** *Badr*
  MOR • **120mm**
ANTI-TANK1/ANTI-INFRASTRUCTURE
  MSL • **MANPATS** 9K111-1 *Konkurs* (RS-AT-5B *Spandrel*/*Towsan*-1); 9K115 *Metis* (RS-AT-7 *Saxhorn*); *Dehlavieh* (*Kornet*); *Toophan*
  RCL 82mm B-10; **73mm** SPG-9
SURFACE-TO-SURFACE MISSILE LAUNCHERS
  MRBM • **Conventional** *Aqeel*; *Borkan*-3 (*Qiam*-1 mod); *Hatim* (*Kheibar Shekan*); *Palestine* (*Kheibar Shekan* mod); *Toufan* (*Ghadr*)
  SRBM • **Conventional** *Borkan*-2H (*Qiam*-1); *Falaq*; *Fateh*-110; *Khalij Fars*
  GLCM • **Conventional** *Quds*-1; *Quds*-2; *Quds*-3; *Quds*-4

COASTAL DEFENCE • **AShM** C-801; C-802; *Sayyad*
AIRCRAFT 2 combat capable
  FTR 1 F-5E *Tiger* II
  FGA 1 Su-22M4 *Fitter* K
HELICOPTERS
  MRH 1 Mi-17 *Hip* H
  TPT • **Medium** 3 Mi-8 *Hip*
UNINHABITED AERIAL VEHICLES
  ISR • **Medium** *Sammad* 1; **Light** *Mersad* 1/2
  OWA *Qasef* 1 (*Ababil* T); *Qasef* 2K; *Sammad* 2; *Sammad* 3; *Shihab*; *Waed* 1 (*Shahed* 131); *Waed* 2 (*Shahed* 136); *Yafa* (*Sammad* 3 mod)
AIR DEFENCE
  SAM
    Short-range *Saqr*-1 (358)
    Point-defence 9K32 *Strela*-2 (RS-SA-7 *Grail*)‡; 9K34 *Strela*-3 (RS-SA-14 *Gremlin*); *Misaq*-1 (QW-1); *Misaq*-2 (QW-18)
  GUNS • **TOWED 20mm** M167 *Vulcan*; **23mm** ZU-23-2

THE ARMED CONFLICT SURVEY

THE WORLDWIDE REVIEW OF POLITICAL, MILITARY AND HUMANITARIAN TRENDS IN CURRENT CONFLICTS

2024

The Armed Conflict Survey 2024 provides an exhaustive review of the political, military and humanitarian dimensions of active armed conflicts globally in the period from 1 July 2023–30 June 2024.

The Armed Conflict Survey:
Paperback; 246mm x 189mm; 368pp;
ISBN 978-1-041-00457-8 Paperback
ISBN 978-1-003-60993-3 eBook

The Armed Conflict Survey 2024 includes maps, infographics, key statistics and the accompanying Chart of Armed Conflict.

The review is complemented by a strategic analysis of regional and global drivers and conflict outlooks, providing unique insights into the geopolitical and geo-economic threads linking conflicts regionally and globally, as well as into emerging flashpoints and political risks to monitor. This edition's regional-focused approach also includes Regional Spotlight chapters on selected key conflict trends of regional and global importance. Reflecting the growing significance of geopolitical factors in shaping current conflict trends across the world, *The Armed Conflict Survey 2024* features the fourth edition of the IISS Armed Conflict Global Relevance Indicator, which compares the global relevance of armed conflicts in terms of their geopolitical impact, as well as their human impact and intensity.

available at
amazon

OR

Routledge
Taylor & Francis Group

IISS

FURTHER DETAILS:
www.iiss.org/publications/armed-conflict-survey

Chapter Seven
Latin America and the Caribbean

- Brazil launched the third of four conventionally powered submarines built as part of the PROSUB deal with France, and continued work on developing infrastructure to support the nuclear-powered submarine also planned to be built as part of the project.
- Argentina has made progress in its effort to modernise its forces, signing an agreement with Demark to acquire 24 ex-Royal Danish Air Force F-16s. These are scheduled to arrive between 2025 and 2028.
- To recapitalise its combat-aircraft fleet, Brazil will soon start replacing its ageing fleet with 36 Saab *Gripen* E/Fs as part of a 2014 deal worth USD5.73 billion. Colombia, which is looking to replace its ageing aircraft, is reportedly considering the *Gripen* E, among other shortlisted candidates.
- The recent growth in Brazilian exports has been driven, in large part, by the success of Embraer's KC-390 *Millennium* medium-lift transport aircraft. The company has signed export contracts worth over USD4.75bn since 2019 as countries seek to replace legacy aircraft, such as older versions of the C-130 *Hercules*. Sweden has expressed its intent to acquire the KC-390, while other countries are also considering the platform.
- Ongoing economic difficulties and sanctions have limited Venezuela's ability to procure new defence technology, though its defence relationship with Iran has deepened under Nicolás Maduro, with the inventory now including *Mohajer* uninhabited aerial vehicles and *Peykaap* III-class fast patrol boats.
- Regional defence budgets grew for the second year since the COVID-19 pandemic. However, in real terms, budgets are yet to recover from pandemic-related cuts and remain below 2010 levels. Despite numerous countries seeking to modernise their forces, lingering financial pressures and low threat perceptions mean growth in defence spending remains subdued.

Latin America and the Caribbean defence spending, 2024 – top 5

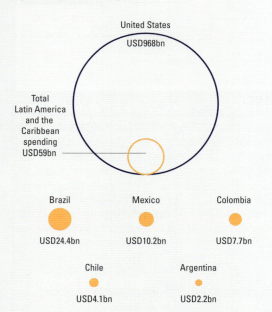

United States USD968bn
Total Latin America and the Caribbean spending USD59bn
Brazil USD24.4bn
Mexico USD10.2bn
Colombia USD7.7bn
Chile USD4.1bn
Argentina USD2.2bn

Active military personnel – top 10
(25,000 per unit)

Country	Personnel
Brazil	374,500
Mexico	287,000
Colombia	269,000
Venezuela	123,000
Peru	81,000
Argentina	72,100
Chile	68,500
Dominican Republic	56,800
Cuba	49,000
Ecuador	39,600

Global total 20,629,000
Regional total 1,581,000
7.7%

Regional defence policy and economics 382
Arms procurement and defence-industrial trends 392
Armed forces data section 393

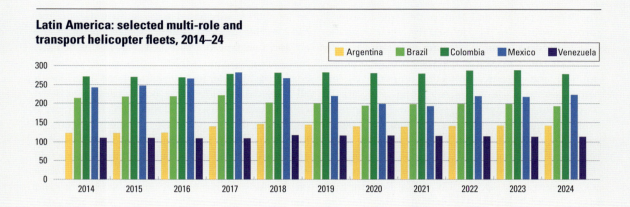

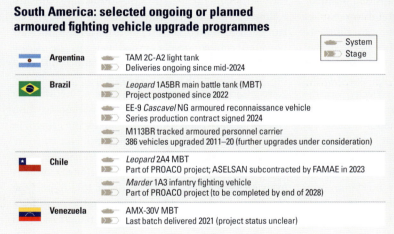

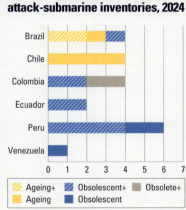

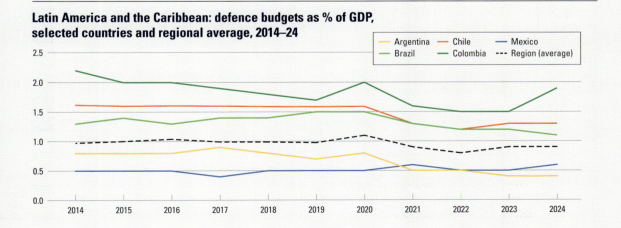

Latin America and the Caribbean

The defence policies and plans of the region's armed forces continue to be defined by their regional and geopolitical ambitions and domestic-security demands. At one end of the spectrum, economic, political and resource-protection imperatives led some countries, such as Argentina and Brazil, to continue to emphasise policy and equipment priorities including the development of power-projection capabilities. At the other end of the scale, other countries continue to struggle to tackle violent transnational crime and internal security issues, with governments such as Colombia, Ecuador and Mexico increasingly relying on their armed forces to deal with gangs, cartels and other criminal groups.

In **Brazil**, geopolitical ambitions and imperatives around resource protection continue to influence defence policy, with all three branches of the armed forces expanding their power-projection capabilities. Strategic continuity between the Lula government and previous administrations is reflected in the defence policy approved by the Brazilian Congress in May 2024, which emphasises international missions, including 'contributing to regional stability and international peace and security'. However, the armed forces are still carrying out internal security duties. *Operation Agata*, the long-standing border-security mission, continues, while the armed forces remain deployed to strengthen security in ports and airports as part of a campaign against criminal activity.

In 2018, the army initiated the Readiness Force project, Forças de Prontidão (FORPRON), in a bid to produce a high-readiness land capability that could form ad hoc task forces for interventions in internal crises, in response to international contingencies, or to deploy under United Nations command. FORPRON includes six 'strategic' brigades (Forças de Emprego Estratégico), several general-purpose brigades and independent special forces, psychological operations, artillery and cyber units. Certification activities for these units continued in 2024, utilising live and simulated environments. The army continues to test its initial batch of *Centauro* vehicles, and continues to moot upgrades to its *Leopard* 1 main battle tank capability (rather than a replacement), with its armour still mainly based in the south of the country. Most visible modernisation has taken place in the air and maritime domains. The navy launched the first *Tamandaré*-class (MEKO A100) frigate in August 2024, from an order for four ships placed in 2020 with all to be delivered by 2029. But Brazil's main naval effort remains focused on modernising its submarine fleet under the Submarine Development Programme (PROSUB). Brazil and France signed a partnership agreement in 2008 to collaborate on the construction of four conventionally powered submarines based on France's *Scorpène*-class attack submarine and one nuclear-powered submarine. The first two conventionally powered submarines are already commissioned and the third boat, *Tonelero* (S42), was launched in March 2024. Plans to launch a nuclear-powered conventionally armed variant, the *Álvaro Alberto*, remain under way, with launch planned for 2031. Infrastructure investments related to the conventional-submarine programme at the Madeira Island base and the Itaguaí naval-construction enterprise have been complemented by the growth in Brazil's capabilities in relation to reactor construction. In the air domain, Brazil's air force had received eight F-39E *Gripen* E fighter ground-attack aircraft by September 2024, out of an order for 36, and the air force was reported to be studying the possibility of reactivating the Pacau Squadron (1st/4th Aviation Group) for air-to-ground operations; the squadron currently operating the *Gripen* has an air-to-air role.

Brazil's interest in expeditionary missions, and internal mobility, is perhaps best demonstrated through its continued emphasis on expanding its airlift and air-to-air refuelling capabilities, not only by the acquisition of Embraer KC-390 medium transport aircraft, but also with the acquisition of two Airbus A330s in 2022 to be converted to tanker configuration by 2027. Despite these ambitions to develop capabilities that could be employed for power-projection tasks, challenges remain. Some analysts assess that internal coordination could be improved, along with the command structure. Individual services are responsible for most operational planning and conducting major exercises, despite the fact that these exercises may also

Figure 32 Latin America and the Caribbean: tactical-aviation fleets, 2014–24

Over the past two decades, Latin American tactical-aviation fleets have continued to shrink due to the retirement of ageing aircraft, financial limitations, and a focus on internal security. Countries are also not replacing their aircraft on a one-for-one basis.

Brazil is one of the few countries in the region beginning to recapitalise its combat-aircraft fleet. It will soon start to replace its ageing fleet of 40 Northrop F-5EM/FM *Tiger* II, seven AMX International AMX A-1M/BM, and 16 AMX A-1A/B aircraft with 36 Saab *Gripen* E/Fs as part of a 2014 deal worth USD5.73 billion. This includes establishing a joint Saab–Embraer *Gripen* production line in Brazil. As of the fourth quarter of 2024, assembly of the first aircraft on this line was nearly complete.

After years of uncertainty over any fighter acquisition, Argentina in 2024 finally appeared to have made progress. It has bought 24 ex-Danish Lockheed Martin F-16AM/BM *Fighting Falcon* aircraft for USD300 million, though as of October 2024, the first had yet to be delivered.

Colombia is looking to replace its 19 ageing Israel Aerospace Industries *Kfir* C-10/12 and *Kfir* TC-12 aircraft, which have suffered from maintenance issues. A *Kfir* replacement became even more urgent after Israel suspended the transfer of defence materiel to Colombia following the Colombian President's condemnation of the Israeli offensive in Gaza. Negotiations to acquire a new combat aircraft, however, had stalled as of November 2024. The Dassault *Rafale*, the Lockheed Martin F-16 *Fighting Falcon* and the Saab *Gripen* E are reportedly among the shortlisted candidates.

Issues with maintenance and spare parts have also affected parts of Venezuela's tactical aviation, while Western sanctions and arms embargoes have limited the operation of its F-16A/B *Fighting Falcon*s. The air force also operates Russian Sukhoi Su-30MKV *Flanker*s, which are reportedly being upgraded. Venezuela also purchased Chinese K-8W *Karakorum* trainers as a replacement for its retired VF-5D and NF-5B *Freedom Fighter*s and the North American Rockwell OV-10A *Bronco*s. It likely uses the K-8W *Karakorum* in a light attack role.

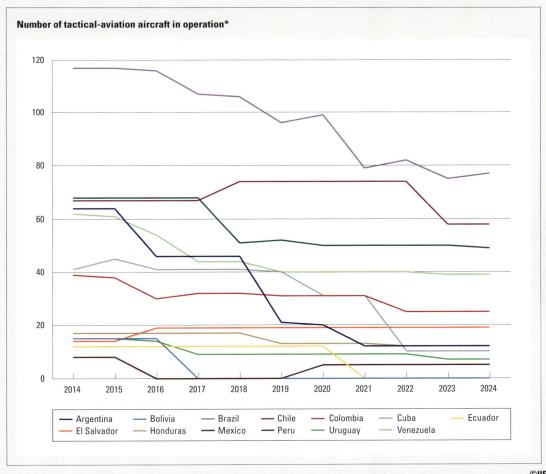

*Includes fighter, fighter/ground-attack, and ground-attack aircraft
Source: IISS, Military Balance+, https://milbalplus.iiss.org/

involve other military branches, as was the case with *Exercise Formosa* 2024, led by the navy and involving air and army units. The crisis triggered by Venezuela's threats to invade Guyana's Essequibo region and the building of military infrastructure by Venezuelan armed forces in the border region prompted Brazil's armed forces to increase their presence there, though this operation – involving a relatively small number of troops and 28 armoured vehicles – took 21 days to complete. Even taking distance and terrain into account, this highlighted continuing mobility challenges.

After four decades of underfunding, **Argentina** under President Javier Milei is continuing efforts to rebuild its defence capabilities. In April 2024 Argentina signed an agreement with Demark to acquire 24 ex-Royal Danish Air Force F-16s for USD300 million, which are scheduled to arrive between 2025 and 2028. This deal is significant because, in addition to being supported by the United States, it appeared to end Argentina's quest to acquire JF-17 *Thunder* fighter aircraft from China, an option explored by the previous government. Milei consolidated strategic ties with the US through plans that could lead to a US military presence in Ushuaia, in the southern province of Tierra del Fuego, again apparently undercutting reported discussions between the governor of Tierra del Fuego and Chinese representatives about the establishment of a Chinese logistical facility to support China's Antarctic operations. At the same time, Argentina's armed forces are expanding their involvement in internal security. They played a supporting role in the anti-criminal offensive launched by the government in the city of Rosario in March 2024, which saw the deployment of 120 troops, helicopters and patrol boats. This could herald broader participation in public-security missions if President Milei is successful in his attempt to change the current legal framework to expand the role of the armed forces in the fight against terrorism.

The armed forces in **Chile** have also increased their role in internal security. Since 2021, the Chilean armed forces have been deployed in the north of the country to prevent illegal immigration, drug trafficking and smuggling. In addition, 1,400 troops are assisting the police in fighting a low-level indigenous insurgency in Chile's southern regions. In March 2024, President Gabriel Boric said that he would not deploy the armed forces in the cities to respond to a rise in violent crime, arguing that they were not trained for those tasks. Public security has also become the dominant mission of **Ecuador's** armed forces, after President Daniel Noboa launched an anti-gang crackdown, declaring a state of war and deploying the military in the cities to try to stem an escalation in drug-fuelled violence. While these efforts have reduced crime, there is uncertainty as to their sustainability. The Ecuadorian army has been forced to drastically reduce its presence on the border with Colombia, the entry point for cocaine that fuels gang violence, in order to redeploy troops to conduct urban operations and take control over prisons.

The capabilities of the **Colombian** military are also under scrutiny. Budgetary limitations, in addition to political issues, have contributed to the cancellation of plans to replace ageing Israeli-made *Kfir* fighter ground-attack aircraft. The diplomatic rupture with Israel over its war in Gaza ended cooperation with a major supplier to the Colombian armed forces. At the same time, the peace talks and partial ceasefires negotiated by the government with various insurgent and criminal groups as part of the Total Peace project have restricted the freedom of action of the armed forces. The situation has become particularly serious along the border with Ecuador, where bilateral security cooperation has all but ceased, creating a vacuum exploited by criminal groups from both countries.

Under former president Andres Manuel López Obrador, the **Mexican** armed forces expanded their involvement in internal security matters and are likely to continue to do so under his successor, President Claudia Sheinbaum. A critical step in this process was the transfer of the national guard to the operational control of the secretary of defence, a move the recently elected president has promised to consolidate. The security plan presented in October 2024 by the new government also includes strengthening intelligence capabilities and improving coordination between the federal government and the state authorities. The expansion of the Mexican armed forces' role in fighting criminality has been accompanied by increased involvement in non-defence government affairs. For instance, the armed forces completed and became administrators of a railroad in southern Mexico in 2024. They also manage the operations of ports and airports throughout the country. The new president has announced she will continue relying on the military to build and manage strategic infrastructure. This involvement in civilian projects has given the military considerable economic and political influence, but has the potential to become a source of civil–military friction.

VENEZUELA

International sanctions, regional isolation and a long-standing economic crisis have restricted the capabilities of the Bolivarian Armed Forces (Fuerza Armada Nacional Bolivariana, FANB). Venezuela has tense relations with some of its neighbours. Guyana and Venezuela have a historical border dispute over the Essequibo region, which has heated up due to the discovery of offshore oil deposits in Guyana. In December 2023, Venezuela held a referendum over the Essequibo, and Caracas also deployed troops and equipment to the border, with this dispute prompting concerns in neighbouring countries including Brazil. Internally, the Venezuelan armed forces are tasked with combating transnational criminal organisations, particularly drug-trafficking entities, and tackling smuggling and environmental crimes such as illegal logging and illegal mining. However, the United States has accused (and charged) civilian authorities and military personnel of being engaged in criminal activities. The armed forces were internally deployed to suppress protests and protect critical infrastructure after the disputed elections in July 2024.

There is a heavy degree of politicisation, with promotions based on loyalty to the regime. In 2018, military officers were told to sign a 'loyalty act' to the Maduro government to procure promotions. After the elections in August 2024, the armed forces reiterated their 'absolute loyalty' to President Nicolás Maduro. Since the presidency of Hugo Chávez (1999–2013), the armed forces have grown in size, particularly at the senior levels. Around 230 generals, admirals and rear admirals, according to Caracas, were promoted in early July 2024. The regime's focus on self-preservation means that a high priority is given to identifying potential coup plotters among the FANB. In January 2024, Caracas announced the 'expulsion' of 33 officers, including one general and two colonels, it accused of plotting a military coup.

As well as the regular services, the Chávez government created the Bolivarian Militia (Milicia Nacional Bolivariana) in 2009. According to Caracas, the militia has around five million active personnel who mainly receive training in small arms and light weapons, though reportedly also including MANPADS. Although high oil prices during the Chávez years meant that the FANB acquired a range of military equipment from China and Russia – including T-72 main battle tanks, Su-30MKV *Flanker* fighter ground-attack aircraft and S-300VM long-range self-propelled surface-to-air missile systems – international sanctions and the ongoing economic crisis have significantly limited the country's ability to procure new technology from Beijing and Moscow. As a result, Caracas has turned to Tehran, another close partner, with this defence relationship deepening since Maduro came to power and the inventory now including *Mohajer* uninhabited aerial vehicles and *Peykaap* III-class fast patrol boats.

The Venezuelan armed forces have several agencies for maintenance and repair, including the DIANCA and UCOCAR shipyards. The army operates the CEMABLIN centre for armour maintenance, while the air force has the Aircraft Maintenance Service. Because of limited procurement capacity, much effort is given to repairs and upgrades to legacy systems, while the armed forces also repurpose legacy systems, such as one reported episode where at least two AMX-13 armoured vehicles were turned into mine-clearance vehicles.

The air force operates a mixed fleet of aircraft. In addition to Chinese and Russian systems, the service also flies F-16s, acquired before Chávez came to power. Given international sanctions, to keep at least some F-16s flying, the air force may be sourcing spares from other airframes, so reducing overall fleet readiness and availability. Similarly, the Venezuelan navy likely suffers from readiness issues. For instance, neither of its two submarines have been reported on deployment for a number of years, while the corvette *Warao*, which ran aground in 2012, has yet to be returned to service. While the Maduro regime and the armed forces regularly praise their capabilities, personnel losses against Colombian drug traffickers in 2021, the loss of the patrol vessel *Naiguatá* after a collision with a cruise ship in 2020, and apparent equipment issues – within the context of economic challenges and international sanctions – suggest problems with training and the overall operational status of maritime, land and aerial platforms. However, the re-election of President Maduro suggests that Venezuela's defence and security policies will remain unchanged.

DEFENCE ECONOMICS

In 2024, regional defence budgets in Latin America and the Caribbean reached USD59.5 billion, excluding Cuba, Suriname and Venezuela. This represented a nominal increase of 5.3%, with inflation reducing this to a 4.1% real-terms increase. Despite this uplift, regional budgets are yet to recover from COVID-19 pandemic-related cuts that, in real terms, pushed defence spending below 2008 levels. Even with two years of increases, lingering pandemic-related financial pressures and low threat perceptions have kept defence spending subdued.

Defence spending

Within the region, defence spending remains dominated by Argentina, Brazil, Chile, Colombia and Mexico.

These five countries make up more than 80% of the region's total, spending some USD48.7bn combined. **Brazil's** defence budget remains the largest, with its total 2024 allocation of BRL129.5bn (USD24.4bn) making up some 41.0% of the region's defence spending alone. This total amount includes a main budget of BRL126.5bn (USD23.8bn) and a smaller secondary budget of BRL3.0bn (USD565 million). The latter helps fund Brazil's EMGEPRON, a state-owned company linked to Brazil's Ministry of Defence, and NAV Brasil, which provides air-navigation services. Despite the country's total budget increasing by 2.7% in nominal terms, total spending in real terms decreased slightly because of inflation.

High and volatile inflation rates have long presented a challenge to Brazilian public finances, though rates have moderated in recent years. From the recent high of 9.3% in 2022, inflation fell to 4.3% in 2024, with projections seeing far lower rates to the end of the decade. However, even as this external pressure eases, Brazil's defence budget continues to face internal pressure from its high personnel burden. For example, in 2024 the country allocated 77.8% of its main budget to personnel and pension contributions, up from 67.5% in 2014. As a result, spending in other areas is being squeezed. Discretionary expenses have dropped by almost half since 2014, while investment spending forms just 6.8% of the 2024 main budget. This number includes funding provided under Brazil's 'new growth acceleration plan' (Novo PAC), which pledged to spend BRL27.8bn (USD5.2bn) by 2026. In contrast, NATO countries are supposed to spend at least 20% of their defence budgets on defence investments, and some countries have exceeded 30% in recent years.

Seeking to redress these issues, in 2023, members of Brazil's Congress proposed legal guarantees that the country would spend a minimum of 2% of GDP on defence annually, akin to NATO guidelines. Such constitutional amendments would effectively double Brazil's defence budget, which came to just 1.1% of GDP in 2024. Nonetheless, wider economic constraints mean such ambitions are unlikely, and in April 2024, Defence Minister José Múcio Monteiro expressed sympathy with the amendment's aims, though stopped short of endorsing it. Instead he emphasised the need for greater predictability in funding so the armed forces could honour their contracts and have clarity on future force planning.

Colombia, in 2024, allocated COP31.2 trillion (USD7.7bn) to defence, which was a nominal 29.3% increase in local currency terms and a real-terms uplift of 22.8% on the previous year. Like Brazil, Colombia is seeking to modernise its armed forces. However, after decades of fighting counter-insurgencies and drug traffickers, Colombia's modernisation primarily focuses on rebuilding its conventional capabilities and replacing old equipment. To this end, in February 2023, Colombia announced the completion of defence contracts worth USD1.1bn. This included major deals with Israel, including sales of Elbit Systems' ATMOS 2000 155mm self-propelled artillery and Israel Aerospace Industries' *Barak* MX medium-range surface-to-air missile system, with values of USD102.0m and USD131.2m, respectively.

However, uncertainty remains over the future of these sales. In May 2024, Bogota suspended diplomatic ties with Israel, in protest of Israel's conduct in Gaza. This represents a further decline

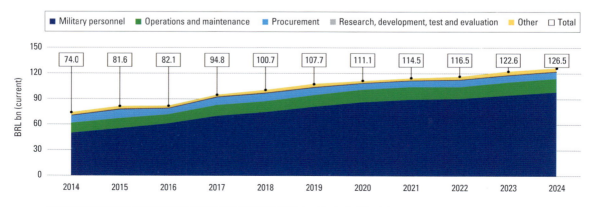

▲ Figure 33 **Brazil's annual core defence budget by function, 2014–24** (BRLbn, current)

from October 2023, when Bogota unilaterally suspended arms sales. This downturn in relations could have major repercussions as Israel supplies the country with equipment ranging from assault rifles to laser-guided bombs. Israel also provides extensive maintenance services for Colombia's fleet of *Kfir* fighter ground-attack aircraft, with a December 2022 maintenance contract expiring at the end of 2024. Any failure to renew the contract may accelerate plans to retire the *Kfir*, with local media reporting that the air force had already reduced its inventory due to the aircraft's age and difficulty in getting spare parts.

In 2024, **Chile** allocated CLP3.8trn (USD4.1bn) to defence, which was a 2.0% uplift in real terms compared to 2023 levels. The increase supports the country's modernisation plans, including the upgrade of its fleet of *Leopard* 2A4 tanks. After receiving an upgrade contract from the Chilean government in July 2023, Turkish defence company ASELSAN showcased planned upgrades at the FIDAE 2024 exhibition in Santiago, in April 2024, including ASELSAN's *Volkan* fire control system; other proposed enhancements include the integration of Identification Friend or Foe, active-protection, battle-management and enhanced-surveillance systems. Other high-profile programmes include Lockheed Martin's upgrade to the country's fleet of F-16s, the commissioning of the *Almirante Viel* icebreaker for Antarctic operations and the country's effort to acquire 40 infantry transport vehicles to replace its fleet of *Piranha* I wheeled armoured personnel carriers. The air force has already boosted its airborne early-warning capabilities, receiving retired E-3D *Sentry* airborne early-warning and control aircraft from the United Kingdom in 2022.

Argentina's defence budget declined again in real terms, with 2024 marking seven years of near-continuous real-terms cuts. To tackle persistently high inflation, President Javier Milei's incoming government saw ministerial budgets slashed across the board. Despite this, the Ministry of Defence's long-term decline in funding appears to have had some reprieve in the 2025 budget. Compared to an allocation of ARS2.3trn (USD2.2bn) in 2024, the 2025 budget allocated ARS4.4trn (USD2.4bn) to defence, which enabled the top line to stabilise, if not grow modestly. However, in terms of new investments, it is notable that in January 2024, the Milei government passed Administrative Decision 5/2024. This redefined the scope of the country's National Defence Fund (FONDEF), watering down its

▼ Figure 34 **Latin America and the Caribbean: defence spending by country and sub-region, 2024**

Note: Analysis excludes Cuba and Suriname. ©IISS

original role of procuring new defence equipment to now include more routine capital expenditures and supplier advances. Such moves may frustrate future procurement and upgrade programmes, although in September 2024, Argentina received the first of the four P-3C *Orion* aircraft acquired from Norway in October 2023. Additionally, in April 2024, Argentina signed a contract for the USD300m purchase of 24 second-hand F-16s from Denmark. This marks a significant shift from 2017, when Argentina scrapped plans to replace its grounded A-4 *Skyhawk* ground-attack aircraft due to the country's poor finances.

The sale of F-16s helps consolidate US defence ties in the region and has removed the need for Argentina to purchase JF-17 *Thunder* aircraft from China. The sale was also accompanied by USD40m in US Foreign Military Financing (FMF) to support the fighters and improve inter-operability with US forces, the first FMF support to Argentina since 2003. In addition, the country began receiving the first of its modernised TAM 2CA2 light tanks in July, and is considering new proposals for the army's wheeled armoured combat vehicle programme. In contrast, Argentina's navy continues to suffer from underinvestment. The navy now lacks any operational submarines while its principal surface combatants are listed as either obsolete or obsolescent, according to IISS judgements in the Military Balance+ database. However, plans to acquire new landing platform docks and landing ship tanks are being discussed, according to the Argentine navy's chief of the general staff, Rear Admiral Carlos María Allievi, speaking to local media in June 2024.

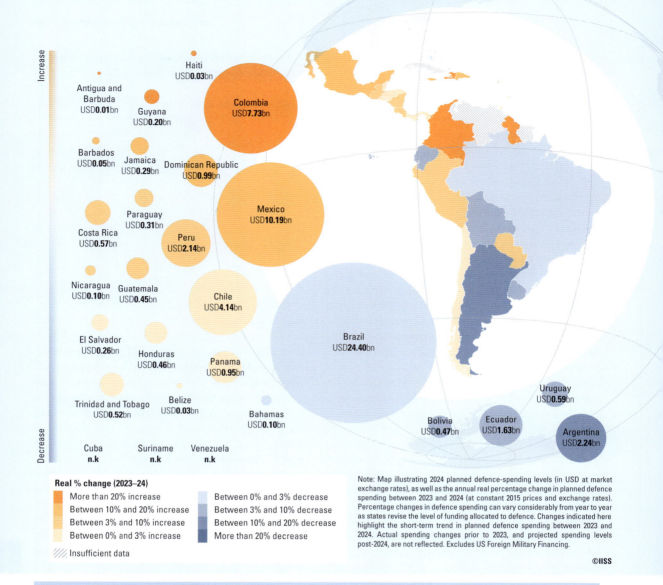

▲ Map 5 **Latin America and the Caribbean: regional defence spending** (USDbn, %ch yoy)

On face value, **Mexico's** defence budget more than doubled between 2023 and 2024, with the combined spending on the ministries of national and maritime defence jumping from MXN111bn (USD6.3bn) to MXN256bn (USD13.8bn). However, closer inspection shows that this includes major infrastructure projects, including airports and mass-transportation systems. After excluding spending on civilian infrastructure, Mexico's core defence budget was MXN189bn (USD10.2bn) for 2024, representing a real-terms increase of 16.2% over the previous year. In the long term, the air force has plans to acquire medium transport aircraft, while the navy has requested funds to build two multi-purpose logistics ships over the next two years.

Elsewhere in the region, tensions continued between Venezuela and Guyana, exacerbated by Caracas's military build-up along the border area and vote rigging in Venezuela's July 2024 election. Venezuela's territorial claims over its neighbour's oil-rich Essequibo region came amid protracted economic and social crises. Reflecting these difficulties, the country's defence budgets have declined considerably in recent years. For example, prior to the start of Venezuela's economic crisis in 2010, Caracas spent between USD3bn and USD4bn a year on defence, averaging 1.6% of GDP. In contrast, in 2024, Venezuela spent just VES30.3bn (in New Bolivars), equating to just USD649m and 0.61% of GDP. Nonetheless, Venezuela continues to invest in

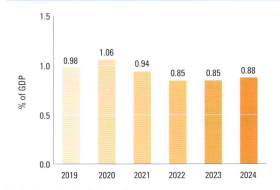

▼ Figure 35 **Latin America and the Caribbean: regional defence spending** as % of GDP (average)

Note: Analysis excludes Cuba, Suriname and Venezuela.
Source: IISS analysis based on GDP data from IMF World Economic Outlook, October 2024   ©IISS

new equipment, with procurements such as Iran's *Nasr* anti-ship missiles. In 2024, Guyana more than doubled its defence budget from GYD20.2bn (USD97.0m) to GYD42.2bn (USD203m).

Defence Industry

Brazil has Latin America's most developed defence industry, and in January 2024, the Brazilian government launched Nova Indústria Brasil – a new industrial policy that will guide the country's overall industrial development until 2033. The strategy seeks to re-capitalise Brazil's industrial base across the board, though Mission 6 of the plan notes the aspiration to produce half of the country's future 'critical defence technologies', across various priority areas. These areas include nuclear energy, communication and remote-sensing systems, propulsion systems and autonomously controlled vehicles. However, to meet such aspirations, the plan notes numerous challenges that Brazil will need to overcome, including the need to strengthen defence-related supply chains, the need to foster greater technological spillovers between the civil and military sectors, and the need to establish appropriate instruments to finance and promote the export of defence products. Indeed, uncertainty regarding funding can be seen by Banco do Brasil's January 2024 decision to stop funding defence-related activities. The decision brought the state-owned bank into line with private-banking practice, although the decision was later reversed, with Brazil's Ministry of Development, Industry, Commerce and Services announcing in February that the bank will maintain support for national defence exports.

The country already has the most advanced aviation industry in the region. In addition to national aviation champion Embraer, in May 2023, Saab inaugurated its aerostructures final-assembly line at Gavião Peixoto, Sao Paulo state. Following this, the company started the initial production of the first Brazilian *Gripen* E fighter ground-attack aircraft, with the first Brazilian-assembled single-seat aircraft expected to be delivered from 2025. Progress comes as Brazilian authorities continue to contemplate expanding *Gripen* orders.

At sea, in January 2024, Brazil commissioned the *Humaitá* (S41), the second out of four *Riachuelo*-class attack submarines based on French company Naval Group's *Scorpène* design, followed by the 27 March launch of the *Tonelero* (S42). In June, Brazil also laid the keel for the *Jerônimo de Albuquerque* (F201), the second out of four *Tamandaré*-class frigates, and in August the first frigate, the *Joaquim Marques Lisboa* (F200), was launched. The *Tamandaré* class, based on the MEKO A100 design, is being built by the Águas Azuis consortium, which includes Germany's ThyssenKrupp Marine Systems and Brazil's Embraer and Atech. Indeed, much of Brazil's modernisation relies on the strategic use of defence partnerships. High-profile partnerships include those with France, Germany and Sweden for the development of PROSUB, the *Tamandaré* and the *Gripen*, respectively.

Elsewhere in Latin America, industrial progress continued – mainly in shipbuilding, though with some progress in the aerospace sector. In Argentina, the engineering firm Redimec and national shipbuilder TANDANOR partnered to develop an uninhabited surface vessel to undertake routine patrol and survey tasks. In Peru, South Korea's HD Hyundai Heavy Industries began preparing technical files on shipbuilding projects with national shipbuilder SIMA Peru. Meanwhile, in Chile, national shipyard ASMAR progressed work to expand its shipbuilding and repair capabilities at its dry dock in Talcahuano, signing a development contract with Norwegian firm Syncrolift in June. In April 2024, Brazil's Embraer and the National Aeronautical Company of Chile announced two industrial and services cooperation agreements covering Embraer's EMB-314 *Super Tucano* training aircraft and the KC-390 *Millennium* medium transport aircraft. The deal deepens Embraer's supplier network across the region, with ENAER manufacturing components for Chile's fleet of 22 *Super Tucano*s and becoming a designated maintenance centre for the aircraft.

Figure 36 Brazil: defence industry

While the Brazilian defence industry has broad capabilities, it is in aerospace that it has had by far the most export success, principally through Embraer. The company has exported its *Super Tucano* turboprop aircraft widely to countries seeking a training aircraft or a low-cost ground-attack platform. More recently, the company's KC-390 *Millennium* medium transport aircraft has secured export contracts with six countries in as many years, of which four are NATO members, and is currently negotiating with India, Morocco and Sweden. This has eased production difficulties as Brazil's air force has sought to stagger deliveries due to budget pressures. Brazil now seeks to capitalise on this to achieve similar results in other sectors, such as land and space. Italian company Iveco Defence Vehicles' Brazilian business in Sete Lagoas has secured contracts, since 2014, with Ghana, Lebanon and the Philippines to supply 49 VBTP-MR *Guarani* 6×6 armoured vehicles worth over USD150 million.

The government has supported defence exports through financing derived in part from state-owned Banco do Brasil.

Major elements of Brazil's defence industry are entirely or partly owned by foreign primes. In 2023, 42.89% worth of Brazil's procurement spending, BRL8.87 billion (USD1.78bn), went to three companies: Embraer, Helicópteros do Brasil (Helibras) and Itaguaí Construções Navais (ICN). The share was 25.14% in 2022 and 29.06% in 2021. Of these, two companies, Helibras (Airbus subsidiary) and ICN (41% owned by Naval Group), have foreign owners. However, the COVID-19 pandemic and budgetary issues have caused difficulties for some companies in recent years. Guided-weapons firm Avibras Indústria Aeroespacial declared bankruptcy in 2022 due to a fall in exports, which had accounted for 80% of its revenue. Following ultimately unsuccessful Australian interest, the government is now evaluating other ownership options for the company.

M = Multinational.
Source: IISS, Military Balance+, milbalplus.iiss.org

Latin America and the Caribbean

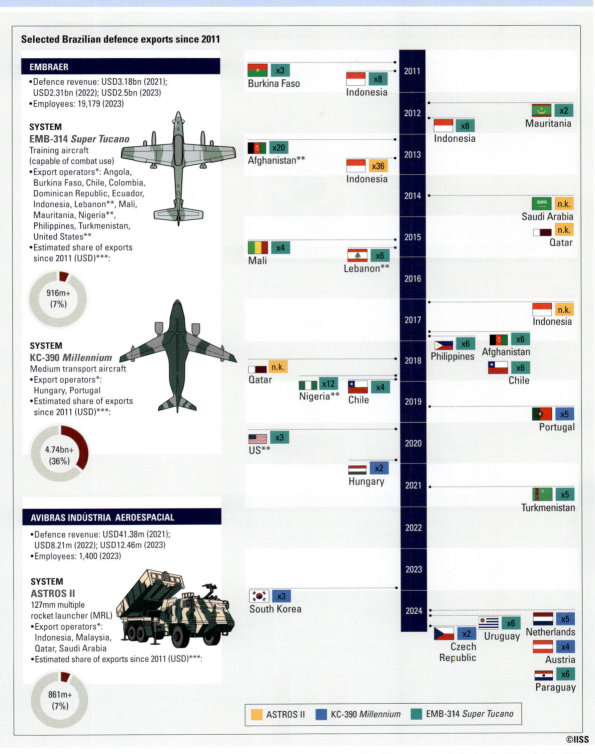

*Operators with in-service systems as of 2024. **Assembled/outfitted in the US. ***Total Brazilian defence export authorisations for 2011 to October 2024 are USD13.09bn. USD value is the sum of export contracts signed during this period and their corresponding percentage of the total export value.

Figure 37 **Latin America and the Caribbean: arms procurement and defence-industrial trends, 2024**

BRAZIL'S DEFENCE-INDUSTRIAL DEVELOPMENT FACES DIFFICULTIES

In July 2024, negotiations regarding the takeover of Brazilian guided-weapon company Avibras Indústria Aeroespacial by Australian company DefendTex fell through. This came 28 months after the COVID-19 pandemic caused Avibras to declare bankruptcy. Avibras relied heavily on exports, with 80% of the firm's revenue coming from sales abroad. The economic downturn led to a 75% decrease in revenue in 2022 to BRL42.42 million (USD8.21m). Before the pandemic, the company enjoyed healthier finances, with BRL950m (USD240.84m) of revenue in 2019. Following the end of talks with DefendTex, Brazil's National Congress initiated the nationalisation of Avibras. Over the last decade, Brazil has successfully lessened its dependence on imports whilst also growing its exports. This shift is in line with government plans laid out in successive national defence strategies since 2012, with the one released that year initiating a major reorganisation of the defence industry, benefitting local companies with a special tax system. Later, the 2016 strategy focused on promoting exports. Accordingly, Brazil's defence exports were 36.7% higher between 2019 and 2023 compared to the period from 2014 to 2018. Indeed, 2024 saw new heights, with exports for the year reaching USD1.65 billion by October 2024. Additionally, Brazil announced the *Nova Indústria Brasil* (New Industry Brazil) initiative in January 2024, in line with its May 2024 national defence strategy aiming to secure at least 50% of critical defence technologies like AI, propulsion and command-and-control systems from foreign industrial partners by 2033.

COLOMBIA CONTINUES MODERNISATION BUT NOW WITHOUT ISRAEL

The collapse of diplomatic ties between Colombia and Israel since 2023 due to Colombia accusing Israel of committing genocide in Gaza has negatively affected the Colombian armed forces' capability and modernisation plans. The heated disagreement has significantly impacted at least three publicly disclosed contracts signed in 2022, worth USD238.73m in total, placing them in limbo. This includes the acquisition of the *Barak* MX surface-to-air missile systems from Israel Aerospace Industries (IAI) to be delivered by 2026, 18 ATMOS 2000 155mm self-propelled howitzers from Elbit Systems to be delivered by 2032, and IAI's maintenance contract for the Colombian Air Force's *Kfir* multi-role fighter aircraft until December 2024. This puts pressure on other modernisation efforts. In the air domain, the *Kfir* replacement programme has stalled since a Colombian attempt attempt to acquire 16 Dassault *Rafale*s fell through in 2022. Colombia is now re-examining options to replace the *Kfir* aircraft. In the land domain, Colombia is still waiting to receive 55 of General Dynamics Land Systems-Canada's LAV III infantry fighting vehicles from the six-year-long contract it signed in 2023. In the maritime domain, the contract to licence-build up to five frigates based on Damen's SIGMA 10514 design at the state-owned COTECMAR shipyard in Cartagena was finally signed in August 2024, nine years after the *Plataforma Estratégica de Superficie* (Strategic Surface Platform) programme was launched. However, these are rare acquisitions of new-build equipment. Otherwise, Colombia relies on second-hand equipment donated by the US. This includes deliveries of 20 M1117 armoured utility vehicles, as well as five Bell 205 (UH-1H *Iroquois*), 60 Bell TH-67 *Creek* and 22 UH-60A *Black Hawk* helicopters, since 2016.

PERU'S DEFENCE-INDUSTRIAL AMBITIONS

Peru is looking to develop further its domestic defence industry, inaugurating the *Unidad Funcional de Industria para la Defensa* (Functional Unit for Defence Industry) in September 2024. The Functional Unit – temporarily affiliated directly to the *Dirección General de Recursos Materiales* (General Directorate of Material Resources) at Peru's Ministry of Defence – will formulate Peru's national defence-industrial policy regarding assembly, co-production and transfer of technology (ToT). The new institution will also closely collaborate with Peru's *Agencia de Compras de las Fuerzas Armadas* (ACFFAA, or Armed Forces Procurement Agency), established in 2012, which is responsible for procurement planning and contract execution on behalf of seven organisations, including the three armed services and the space agency. By forming the Functional Unit, Peru aims to better structure its defence-industrial policy amidst an effort to recapitalise its armed forces. Many of these contracts, totalling at least USD894m, have gone to South Korean companies since 2012. This includes 20 KT-1P training aircraft, five *Río Pativilca*-class coastal patrol craft, two *Pisco*-class landing platform docks and, in 2024, one 3,400-tonne frigate, one 2,200-tonne offshore patrol vessel, two 1,400-tonne amphibious vessels and 30 K808 armoured personnel carriers. All deals include local assembly, co-production and ToT with Peru's state-owned companies SIMA, SEMAN PERÚ and FAME. South Korea's donation of second-hand aircraft and corvettes to Peru was key to greater defence engagement and its penetration of the Peruvian market. In September 2024, Peru announced that it had approved a budget to acquire fighter aircraft (selection not yet decided) in 2025. This followed the signing of an agreement in July 2024 between Korea Aerospace Industries and SEMAN PERÚ for the latter to produce components of the FA-50 *Fighting Eagle* fighter ground-attack aircraft in Peru. The country's modernisation effort is funded, largely, through royalties from exploitation of the Camisea gas fields near Cusco.

Antigua and Barbuda ATG

East Caribbean Dollar XCD		2023	2024	2025
GDP	XCD	5.52bn	6.19bn	6.58bn
	USD	2.04bn	2.29bn	2.44bn
Real GDP growth	%	4.2	5.8	3.5
Def bdgt [a]	XCD	22.0m	29.5m	
	USD	8.13m	10.9m	

[a] Military spending, from within the Prime Minister's Office

Real-terms defence budget trend (USDm, constant 2015)

Population   102,634

Age	0–14	15–19	20–24	25–29	30–64	65 plus
Male	11.1%	3.5%	3.7%	3.9%	20.3%	4.5%
Female	10.8%	3.5%	3.8%	4.0%	24.7%	6.0%

Capabilities

The Antigua and Barbuda Defence Force (ABDF) focuses on internal security and disaster relief and contributes to regional counter-narcotics efforts. It comprises a light-infantry element, which carries out internal-security duties, and a coast guard, which is tasked with fishery protection and counter-narcotics. It has a limited air wing. Antigua and Barbuda has defence ties with the UK and US. The ABDF has participated in US SOUTHCOM's *Tradewinds* exercise, though it has no independent capacity to deploy other than in its immediate neighbourhood. There is no heavy land-forces equipment. The coast guard maintains ex-US patrol vessels and a number of smaller boats. Aside from limited maintenance facilities, the country has no defence industry.

ACTIVE 200 (Army 130 Coast Guard 50 Air Wing 20)

(all services form combined Antigua and Barbuda Defence Force)

RESERVE 80 (Joint 80)

ORGANISATIONS BY SERVICE

Army 130
FORCES BY ROLE
MANOEUVRE
  Light
  1 inf bn HQ
  1 inf coy
COMBAT SERVICE SUPPORT
  1 spt gp (1 engr unit, 1 med unit)

Coast Guard 50
EQUIPMENT BY TYPE
PATROL AND COASTAL COMBATANTS • PB 2: 1 *Dauntless*; 1 *Swift*

Air Wing 20
EQUIPMENT BY TYPE
AIRCRAFT • TPT • Light 2 BN-2A *Islander*

Argentina ARG

Argentine Peso ARS		2023	2024	2025
GDP	ARS	191trn	618trn	1.55qrn
	USD	646bn	604bn	574bn
Real GDP growth	%	-1.6	-3.5	5.0
Def bdgt	ARS	827bn	2.29trn	4.41trn
	USD	2.79bn	2.24bn	2.40bn
FMA (US)	USD	n.a	40m	n.a

Real-terms defence budget trend (USDbn, constant 2015)

Population   46,994,384

Age	0–14	15–19	20–24	25–29	30–64	65 plus
Male	12.0%	3.9%	3.8%	3.6%	20.8%	5.5%
Female	11.3%	3.7%	3.6%	3.5%	21.1%	7.4%

Capabilities

Argentina's armed forces have sufficient training and equipment to fulfil internal-security tasks, with power-projection limited by funding shortfalls. The armed forces principally focus on border security, surveillance and counter-narcotics operations, and they conduct some cooperation with their counterparts in Bolivia and Paraguay. Argentina's armed forces participate in multinational exercises and bilateral peacekeeping exercises with Chile. They also cooperate with the US. In 2024, talks took place on a potential partnership arrangement with NATO. Argentina's equipment inventory has faced increasing obsolescence, in part due to funding problems. However, the air force's air combat capability is set to receive a boost with the deal to buy surplus F-16 fighters from Denmark. Argentina has also received its first of four surplus Norwegian P-3 *Orion* maritime patrol aircraft. The navy's capability, however, has declined in areas such as anti-submarine warfare, mine warfare and airborne early warning, although it has received investment for offshore patrol vessels. Argentina possesses an indigenous defence-manufacturing and maintenance capacity covering land, sea, and air systems, although industry fortunes have dipped because of a lack of investment. Recent international procurement ambitions have been hampered by the UK's refusal to provide export licences for British defence-related components.

ACTIVE 72,100 (Army 42,800 Navy 16,400 Air 12,900) **Gendarmerie & Paramilitary 31,250**

ORGANISATIONS BY SERVICE

Army 42,800
Regt and gp are usually bn-sized
FORCES BY ROLE
MANOEUVRE

Mechanised

1 (1st) div (1 armd bde (1 armd recce regt, 3 tk regt, 1 mech inf regt, 1 SP arty gp, 1 cbt engr bn, 1 int coy, 1 sigs sqn, 1 log coy), 1 (3rd) jungle bde (2 jungle inf regt, 2 jungle inf coy, 1 arty gp, 1 engr coy, 1 int coy, 1 sigs coy, 1 log coy, 1 med coy); 1 (12th) jungle bde (2 jungle inf regt, 1 jungle inf coy, 1 arty gp, 1 engr bn, 1 int coy, 1 sigs coy, 1 log coy, 1 med coy), 2 engr bn, 1 int bn, 1 sigs bn, 1 log coy)

1 (3rd) div (1 armd bde (1 armd recce sqn, 3 tk regt, 1 mech inf regt, 1 SP arty gp, 1 cbt engr sqn, 1 int coy, 1 sigs sqn, 1 log coy); 1 mech bde (1 armd recce regt, 1 tk regt, 2 mech inf regt, 1 SP arty gp, 1 cbt engr bn, 1 int coy, 1 sigs coy, 1 log coy); 1 mech bde (1 armd recce regt, 1 tk regt, 2 mech inf regt, 1 SP arty gp, 1 cbt engr bn, 1 int coy, 1 sigs coy, 1 log coy); 1 int bn, 1 sigs bn, 1 log coy, 1 AD gp (2 AD bn))

1 (Rapid Deployment Force) div (1 SF gp; 1 mech bde (1 armd recce regt, 3 mech inf regt, 1 arty gp, 1 MRL gp, 1 cbt engr coy, 1 sigs coy,1 log coy); 1 AB bde (1 recce sqn, 2 para regt, 1 air aslt regt, 1 arty gp, 1 cbt engr coy, 1 sigs coy, 1 log coy))

Light

1 (2nd) mtn inf div (1 mtn inf bde (1 recce regt, 3 mtn inf regt, 1 mtn inf coy, 2 arty gp, 1 cbt engr bn, 1 sigs coy, 1 log coy); 1 mtn inf bde (1 recce regt, 3 mtn inf regt, 1 mtn inf coy, 1 arty gp, 1 cbt engr bn, 1 sigs coy, 1 log coy); 1 mtn inf bde (1 recce regt, 2 mtn inf regt, 2 arty gp, 1 cbt engr bn, 1 sigs coy, 1 construction coy, 1 log coy), 1 arty gp, 1 sigs bn)

1 mot cav regt (presidential escort)

COMBAT SUPPORT

1 engr bn

1 CBRN coy

1 sigs gp (1 EW bn, 1 sigs bn, 1 maint bn)

1 sigs bn

1 sigs coy

COMBAT SERVICE SUPPORT

3 maint bn

1 tpt bn

HELICOPTER

1 avn gp (bde) (1 avn bn, 1 tpt hel bn, 1 atk/ISR hel sqn)

EQUIPMENT BY TYPE

ARMOURED FIGHTING VEHICLES

MBT 231: 220 TAM, 6 TAM S21; 5 TAM 2C-A2

LT TK 117: 107 SK-105A1 *Kuerassier*; 6 SK-105A2 *Kuerassier*; 4 *Patagón*

RECCE 47 AML-90

IFV 232: 118 VCTP (incl variants); 114 M113A2 (20mm cannon)

APC 278

  APC (T) 274: 70 M113A1-ACAV; 204 M113A2

  APC (W) 4 WZ-551B1

ENGINEERING & MAINTENANCE VEHICLES

ARV *Greif*

ANTI-TANK/ANTI-INFRASTRUCTURE

MSL • SP 3 M1025 HMMWV with TOW-2A

RCL 105mm 150 M-1968

ARTILLERY 1,108

SP 155mm 42: 23 AMX F3; 19 VCA 155 *Palmaria*

TOWED 172: **105mm** 64 Model 56 pack howitzer; **155mm** 108: 28 CITEFA M-77/CITEFA M-81; 80 SOFMA L-33

MRL 8: **105mm** 4 SLAM *Pampero*; **127mm** 4 CP-30

MOR 886: **81mm** 492; **SP 107mm** 25 M106A2; **120mm** 330 Brandt; **SP 120mm** 39 TAM-VCTM

AIRCRAFT

ISR 1 DA62 MPP (survey)

TPT • Light 13: 1 Beech 80 *Queen Air*; 3 C-212-200 *Aviocar*; 4 Cessna 208EX *Grand Caravan*; 1 Cessna 500 *Citation* (survey); 1 Cessna 550 *Citation Bravo*; 2 DHC-6 *Twin Otter*; 1 Sabreliner 75A (*Gaviao* 75A)

TRG 5 T-41 *Mescalero*

HELICOPTERS

MRH 5: 4 SA315B *Lama*; 1 Z-11

TPT 62: **Medium** 3 AS332B *Super Puma*; **Light** 59: 15 AB206B1; 1 Bell 212; 25 Bell 205 (UH-1H *Iroquois* – 6 armed); 5 Bell 206B3; 13 UH-1H-II *Huey* II

AIR DEFENCE

SAM • Point-defence RBS-70

GUNS • TOWED 229: **20mm** 200 GAI-B01; **30mm** 21 HS L81; **35mm** 8 GDF-002 (*Skyguard* fire control)

Navy 16,400

Commands: Surface Fleet, Submarines, Naval Avn, Marines

FORCES BY ROLE

SPECIAL FORCES

1 (diver) SF gp

EQUIPMENT BY TYPE

SUBMARINES • SSK

1 *Santa Cruz* (GER TR-1700) (non-operational, undergoing MLU since 2015) with 6 single 533mm TT with SST-4 HWT

1 *Salta* (GER T-209/1100) (non-operational since 2013) with 8 single 533mm TT with Mk 37/SST-4 HWT)

PRINCIPAL SURFACE COMBATANTS 4

DESTROYERS • DDH 1 *Hercules* (UK Type-42) (utilised as a fast troop-transport ship), with 1 114mm gun (capacity 2 SH-3H *Sea King* hel)

FRIGATES • FFGHM 3 *Almirante Brown* (GER MEKO 360) with 2 quad lnchr with MM40 *Exocet* AShM, 1 octuple *Albatros* lnchr with *Aspide* SAM, 2 triple ILAS-3 (B-515) 324mm TT with A244/S LWT, 1 127mm gun (capacity 1 AS555 *Fennec* hel)

PATROL AND COASTAL COMBATANTS 24

CORVETTES 9:

FSGH 6 *Espora* (GER MEKO 140) with 2 twin lnchr with MM38 *Exocet* AShM, 2 triple 324mm ILAS-3 (B-515) ASTT with A244/S LWT, 1 76mm gun (capacity 1 AS555 *Fennec* hel)

FSG 3 *Drummond* (FRA A-69) (of which 2†) with 2 twin lnchr with MM38 *Exocet* AShM, 2 triple 324mm

ILAS-3 (B-515) ASTT with A244/S LWT, 1 100mm gun
PSOH 4 *Bouchard* (FRA OPV 87) (of which 1 ex-FRA *L'Adroit*) (capacity 1 hel)
PSO 1 *Teniente Olivieri* (ex-US oilfield tug)
PCFGT 1 *Intrepida* (GER Lurssen 45m) with 2 single lnchr with MM38 *Exocet* AShM, 2 single 533mm TT with SST-4 HWT, 1 76mm gun
PCF 1 *Intrepida* (GER Lurssen 45m) with 1 76mm gun
PCO 1 *Murature* (ex-US *King* – trg/river-patrol role) with 2 105mm gun
PB 7: 4 *Baradero* (ISR *Dabur*); 2 *Punta Mogotes* (ex-US *Point*); 1 *Zurubi*
AMPHIBIOUS 6 LCVP
LOGISTICS AND SUPPORT 18
ABU 3 *Red*
AFS 4 *Puerto Argentina* (ex-RUS *Neftegaz*)
AGB 1 *Almirante Irizar* (damaged by fire in 2007; returned to service in mid-2017)
AGS 2: 1 *Cormoran*; 1 *Puerto Deseado* (ice-breaking capability, used for polar research)
AGOR 2: 1 *Austral* (ex-GER *Sonne*); 1 *Commodoro Rivadavia*
AK 2 *Costa Sur* (capacity 4 LCVP)
AOR 1 *Patagonia* (ex-FRA *Durance*) with 1 hel platform
AX 2 *Ciudad de Ensenada*
AXS 1 *Libertad*

Naval Aviation 2,000
EQUIPMENT BY TYPE
AIRCRAFT 14 combat capable
  ASW 4: 2 S-2T *Tracker*; 1 P-3B *Orion*; 1 P-3C *Orion*
  TPT • Light 7 Beech 200F/M *King Air*
  TRG 10 T-34C *Turbo Mentor**
HELICOPTERS
  ASW 2 SH-3H (ASH-3H) *Sea King*
  MRH 1 AS555 *Fennec*
  TPT • Medium 6: 2 S-61T; 4 UH-3H *Sea King*
AIR-LAUNCHED MISSILES
  AAM • IR R-550 *Magic*
  AShM AM39 *Exocet*

Marines 2,500
FORCES BY ROLE
MANOEUVRE
  Amphibious
  1 (fleet) force (1 cdo gp, 1 (AAV) amph bn, 1 mne bn, 1 arty bn, 1 ADA bn)
  1 (fleet) force (2 mne bn, 2 navy det)
  1 force (1 mne bn)
EQUIPMENT BY TYPE
ARMOURED FIGHTING VEHICLES
  RECCE 12 ERC-90F *Sagaie*
  APC • APC (W) 31 VCR
  AAV 11 LVTP-7
ENGINEERING & MAINTENANCE VEHICLES
  ARV AAVR 7
ANTI-TANK/ANTI-INFRASTRUCTURE
  RCL 105mm 30 M-1974 FMK-1
ARTILLERY 89
  TOWED 19: **105mm** 13 Model 56 pack howitzer; **155mm** 6 M114
  MOR 70: **81mm** 58; **120mm** 12
AIR DEFENCE
  SAM • Point-defence RBS-70
  GUNS 40mm 4 Bofors 40L

Air Force 12,900
4 Major Comds – Air Operations, Personnel, Air Regions, Logistics, 8 air bde

Air Operations Command
FORCES BY ROLE
GROUND ATTACK
  2 sqn with A-4/OA-4 (A-4AR/OA-4AR) *Skyhawk*
  2 (tac air) sqn with EMB-312 *Tucano* (on loan for border surv/interdiction)
ISR
  1 sqn with Learjet 35A
SEARCH & RESCUE/TRANSPORT HELICOPTER
  2 sqn with Bell 212; Bell 407GXi; Bell 412; Mi-171, SA-315B *Lama*
TANKER/TRANSPORT
  1 sqn with C-130H *Hercules*; KC-130H *Hercules*; L-100-30
TRANSPORT
  1 sqn with Beech A200 *King Air* (UC-12B *Huron*); Cessna 182 *Skylane*
  1 sqn with DHC-6 *Twin Otter*; Saab 340
  1 sqn with F-28 *Friendship*
  1 sqn with Learjet 35A; Learjet 60
  1 (Pres) flt with B-737-700; B-757-23ER; S-70A *Black Hawk*, S-76B
TRAINING
  1 sqn with AT-63 *Pampa* II
  1 sqn with EMB-312 *Tucano*
  1 sqn with Grob 120TP
  1 sqn with IA-63 *Pampa* III*
  1 sqn with T-6C *Texan* II
  1 hel sqn with Hughes 369; SA-315B *Lama*
TRANSPORT HELICOPTER
  1 sqn with Hughes 369; MD-500; MD-500D
EQUIPMENT BY TYPE
AIRCRAFT 21 combat capable
  ATK 11: 9 A-4 (A-4AR) *Skyhawk* (of which 6†); 2 OA-4 (OA-4AR) *Skyhawk* (of which 1†)
  ELINT 1 Learjet 35A
  TKR/TPT 2 KC-130H *Hercules*
  TPT 28: **Medium** 5: 4 C-130H *Hercules* (incl 1 leased);

1 L-100-30; **Light** 19: 5 Beech A200 *King Air* (UC-12B *Huron*); 4 Cessna 182 *Skylane*; 2 DHC-6 *Twin Otter*; 3 Learjet 35A (of which 2 test and calibration and 1 medevac); 1 Learjet 60 (VIP); 1 PA-28-236 *Dakota*; 3 Saab 340 (jointly operated with LADE); **PAX** 4: 1 B-737; 1 B-737-700; 1 B-757-23ER; 1 F-28 *Fellowship*
TRG 47: 2 AT-63 *Pampa* II* (LIFT); 11 EMB-312 *Tucano*; 9 Grob 120TP; 9 IA-63 *Pampa* III*; 6 P2002JF *Sierra*; 10 T-6C *Texan* II (8 EMB-312 *Tucano* in store)

HELICOPTERS
MRH 29: 6 Bell 412EP; 11 Hughes 369; 3 MD-500; 4 MD-500D; 5 SA315B *Lama*
TPT 13: **Medium** 3: 2 Mi-171E; 1 S-70A *Black Hawk* (VIP); **Light** 10: 7 Bell 212; 1 Bell 407GXi; 2 S-76B (VIP)

AIR DEFENCE
GUNS 88: **20mm**: 86 Oerlikon/Rh-202 with 9 Elta EL/M-2106 radar; **35mm**: 2 GDF-001 with *Skyguard* radar

AIR-LAUNCHED MISSILES
AAM • IR AIM-9L *Sidewinder*; R-550 *Magic*; *Shafrir* 2‡

Gendarmerie & Paramilitary 31,250

Gendarmerie 18,000
Ministry of Security
FORCES BY ROLE
COMMAND
7 regional comd
SPECIAL FORCES
1 SF unit
MANOEUVRE
Other
17 paramilitary bn
Aviation
1 (mixed) avn bn
EQUIPMENT BY TYPE
ARMOURED FIGHTING VEHICLES
APC (W) 87: 47 *Grenadier*; 40 UR-416
ARTILLERY • MOR 81mm
AIRCRAFT
TPT 13: **Light** 12: 3 Cessna 152; 3 Cessna 206; 1 Cessna 336; 1 PA-28 *Cherokee*; 2 PC-6B *Turbo Porter*; 2 PC-12; **PAX** 1 Learjet 35
HELICOPTERS
MRH 2 MD-500C
TPT • Light 17: 3 AW119 *Koala*; 2 Bell 206 *Jet Ranger* (AB-206); 7 AS350 *Ecureuil*; 1 H135; 1 H155; 3 R-44 *Raven* II
TRG 1 S-300C

Prefectura Naval (Coast Guard) 13,250
Ministry of Security
EQUIPMENT BY TYPE
PATROL AND COASTAL COMBATANTS 71
PCO 7: 1 *Correa Falcon*; 1 *Delfin*; 5 *Mantilla* (F30 *Halcón* – undergoing modernisation)

PCC 1 *Mariano Moreno*
PB 58: 1 *Dorado*; 25 *Estrellemar*; 2 *Lynch* (US *Cape*); 18 *Mar del Plata* (Z-28); 1 *Surel*; 8 Damen Stan 2200; 3 Stan Tender 1750
PBF 4 *Shaldag* II
PBR 1 *Tonina*

LOGISTICS & SUPPORT 11
AAR 1 *Tango*
AG 3
ARS 1 *Prefecto Mansilla*
AX 3
AXL 2
AXS 1 *Dr Bernardo Houssay*

AIRCRAFT
MP 1 Beech 350ER *King Air*
TPT • Light 6: 5 C-212 *Aviocar*; 1 Beech 350ER *King Air*
TRG 2 Piper PA-28 *Archer* III

HELICOPTERS
SAR 3 AS565MA *Panther*
MRH 1 AS365 *Dauphin* 2
TPT 7: **Medium** 3: 1 H225 *Puma*; 2 SA330L (AS330L) *Puma*; **Light** 4: 2 AS355 *Ecureuil* II; 2 Bell 206 (AB-206) *Jet Ranger*
TRG 4 S-300C

DEPLOYMENT

CENTRAL AFRICAN REPUBLIC: UN • MINUSCA 2
CYPRUS: UN • UNFICYP 333; 2 inf coy; 1 hel flt with 2 Bell 212
INDIA/PAKISTAN: UN • UNMOGIP 3
LEBANON: UN • UNIFIL 3
MIDDLE EAST: UN • UNTSO 3
SYRIA/ISRAEL: UN • UNDOF 1
WESTERN SAHARA: UN • MINURSO 3

Bahamas BHS

Bahamian Dollar BSD		2023	2024	2025
GDP	BSD	14.3bn	14.8bn	15.3bn
	USD	14.3bn	14.8bn	15.3bn
Real GDP growth	%	2.6	1.9	1.7
Def bdgt	BSD	106m	105m	
	USD	106m	105m	

Real-terms defence budget trend (USDm, constant 2015)

Population	410,862					
Age	0–14	15–19	20–24	25–29	30–64	65 plus
Male	10.1%	3.8%	4.1%	4.5%	19.8%	3.8%
Female	11.3%	4.8%	5.1%	5.0%	22.8%	4.8%

Capabilities

The Royal Bahamas Defence Force (RBDF) is primarily a naval force tasked with disaster relief, maritime security and counter-narcotics duties. Its single commando squadron is responsible for base protection and internal security. The RBDF has training relationships with the UK and US. The RBDF has participated in US SOUTHCOM's *Tradewinds* exercise. There is little independent capacity to deploy abroad beyond recent regional disaster-relief efforts. The RBDF's Sandy Bottom Project, the largest-ever capital investment in the service, includes the acquisition of patrol craft and the development of bases and port facilities. Apart from limited maintenance facilities, the Bahamas has no indigenous defence industry.

ACTIVE 1,500

ORGANISATIONS BY SERVICE

Royal Bahamas Defence Force 1,500

FORCES BY ROLE

MANOEUVRE

  Amphibious

  1 mne coy (incl marines with internal- and base-security duties)

EQUIPMENT BY TYPE

PATROL AND COASTAL COMBATANTS 21

  PCC 2 *Bahamas*

  PB 19: 4 *Arthur Dion Hanna* (Damen Stan Patrol 4207); 2 *Dauntless*; 4 *Lignum Vitae* (Damen 3007); 1 Safe 33; 4 Safe 44; 2 Sea Ark 12m; 2 Sea Ark 15m

LOGISTICS & SUPPORT • **AKR** 1 *Lawrence Major* (Damen 5612)

AIRCRAFT • **TPT** • **Light** 3: 1 Beech A350 *King Air*; 1 Cessna 208 *Caravan*; 1 P-68 *Observer*

FOREIGN FORCES

Guyana Navy: Base located at New Providence Island

Barbados BRB

Barbados Dollar BBD		2023	2024	2025
GDP	BBD	13.4bn	14.4bn	15.3bn
	USD	6.72bn	7.20bn	7.65bn
Real GDP growth	%	4.1	3.9	3.0
Def bdgt [a]	BBD	87.1m	103m	
	USD	43.6m	51.6m	

[a] Defence & security expenditure

Real-terms defence budget trend (USDm, constant 2015)

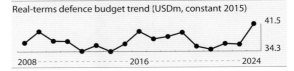

Population	304,139					
Age	0–14	15–19	20–24	25–29	30–64	65 plus
Male	8.3%	2.9%	3.0%	3.0%	24.1%	6.9%
Female	8.3%	3.0%	3.0%	3.0%	25.0%	9.4%

Capabilities

The main tasks of the Barbados Defence Force (BDF) are maritime security and resource protection, but it has a secondary public-safety role in support of the police force. The BDF has undertaken counternarcotics work, while troops have also been tasked with supporting law enforcement. There are plans to improve disaster-relief capabilities and to establish a medical Centre of Excellence. The Caribbean Regional Security System is headquartered in Barbados. The BDF has participated in US SOUTHCOM's *Tradewinds* exercise. There is limited capacity to deploy independently within the region, such as on hurricane-relief duties. The inventory consists principally of a small number of patrol vessels. Apart from limited maintenance facilities, Barbados has no indigenous defence industry.

ACTIVE 610 (Army 500 Coast Guard 110)

RESERVE 430 (Joint 430)

ORGANISATIONS BY SERVICE

Army 500

FORCES BY ROLE

MANOEUVRE

  Light

  1 inf bn (cadre)

Coast Guard 110

HQ located at HMBS Pelican, Spring Garden

EQUIPMENT BY TYPE

PATROL AND COASTAL COMBATANTS 6

  PB 6: 1 *Dauntless*; 2 *Enterprise* (Damen Stan 1204); 3 *Trident* (Damen Stan Patrol 4207)

Belize BLZ

Belize Dollar BZD		2023	2024	2025
GDP	BZD	6.14bn	6.68bn	6.98bn
	USD	3.07bn	3.34bn	3.49bn
Real GDP growth	%	1.1	5.4	2.5
Def bdgt [a]	BZD	56.4m	59.5m	
	USD	28.2m	29.7m	

[a] Excludes funds allocated to Coast Guard and Police Service

Real-terms defence budget trend (USDm, constant 2015)

Population	415,789					
Age	0–14	15–19	20–24	25–29	30–64	65 plus
Male	14.1%	4.8%	4.6%	4.3%	19.0%	2.8%
Female	13.7%	4.8%	4.8%	4.5%	20.0%	2.8%

Capabilities

The small Belize Defence Force (BDF) and a coastguard address national security tasks, particularly monitoring the borders with Guatemala and Mexico. In 2022, a new National Security Strategy underscored priorities including reducing transnational, cross-border and other violent crime; counter-terrorism; and reducing risk from natural human-caused hazards. The UK has a long-standing security relationship with Belize and maintains a small training unit there. The BDF also trains with US SOUTHCOM. The BDF does not, as a rule, deploy internationally and logistics support largely only for border-security missions. Nevertheless, Belize has taken tentative steps towards a limited deployment to Haiti as part of a UN security mission. Its conventional equipment inventory is limited but Belize has had a modest injection of US-donated trucks and a Cessna special-mission aircraft for surveillance. Apart from maintenance facilities there is no domestic defence industry.

ACTIVE 1,500 (Army 1,500) Gendarmerie & Paramilitary 550

RESERVE 700 (Joint 700)

ORGANISATIONS BY SERVICE

Army ε1,500
FORCES BY ROLE
SPECIAL FORCES
  1 SF unit
MANOEUVRE
  Light
    2 inf bn (3 inf coy)
COMBAT SERVICE SUPPORT
  1 spt gp
EQUIPMENT BY TYPE
ANTI-TANK/ANTI-INFRASTRUCTURE • RCL 84mm
  Carl Gustaf
ARTILLERY • MOR 81mm 6

Air Wing
EQUIPMENT BY TYPE
AIRCRAFT
  TPT • Light 3: 1 BN-2B *Defender†*; 1 Cessna 182 *Skylane†*; 1 Cessna 208B *Grand Caravan* EX
  TRG 1 T-67M-200 *Firefly*
HELICOPTERS
  TPT • Light 2: 1 Bell 205 (UH-1H *Iroquois*); 1 Bell 407

Reserve
FORCES BY ROLE
MANOEUVRE
  Light
    1 inf bn (3 inf coy)

Gendarmerie & Paramilitary 550

Coast Guard 550
EQUIPMENT BY TYPE
All operational patrol vessels under 10t FLD

FOREIGN FORCES
United Kingdom BATSUB 12

Bolivia BOL

Bolivian Boliviano BOB		2023	2024	2025
GDP	BOB	312bn	330bn	352bn
	USD	45.5bn	48.2bn	51.3bn
Real GDP growth	%	3.1	1.6	2.2
Def bdgt	BOB	3.24bn	3.26bn	
	USD	473m	475m	

Real-terms defence budget trend (USDm, constant 2015)

Population	12,311,974					
Age	0–14	15–19	20–24	25–29	30–64	65 plus
Male	14.6%	5.0%	4.6%	4.0%	18.9%	3.2%
Female	14.0%	4.8%	4.4%	4.0%	18.7%	3.8%

Capabilities

The armed forces are constitutionally tasked with maintaining sovereignty and territorial defence, though principal tasks are counter-narcotics and internal and border security. The government has formed and deployed joint task forces to border regions to combat smuggling and established several border posts. Airspace control is an emerging strategic priority. The armed forces have also been playing a greater role in disaster relief operations. The country has defence-technology ties with China and Russia. France is also a source of defence equipment. Regionally, Bolivia cooperates with Peru and Paraguay in providing disaster relief and countering illicit trafficking. In 2023, Bolivia signed an agreement with Iran to source UAVs for use in border surveillance. The armed forces have stressed the need to improve conditions for personnel amid greater internal deployments to border areas on counter-trafficking tasks. Cohesion challenges, and broader political tensions in the country, were highlighted by the attempted military coup in June 2024. The country has some maintenance, repair and overhaul capacity, and an aerospace R&D centre.

ACTIVE 34,100 (Army 22,800 Navy 4,800 Air 6,500)
Gendarmerie & Paramilitary 37,100

Conscript liability 12 months voluntary conscription for both males and females

ORGANISATIONS BY SERVICE

Army 9,800; 13,000 conscript (total 22,800)
FORCES BY ROLE
COMMAND
  6 mil region HQ
  10 div HQ
SPECIAL FORCES
  3 SF regt
MANOEUVRE
  Reconnaissance
  1 mot cav gp
  Armoured
  1 armd bn
  Mechanised
  1 mech cav regt
  2 mech inf regt
  Light
  1 (aslt) cav gp
  5 (horsed) cav gp
  3 mot inf regt
  21 inf regt
  Air Manoeuvre
  1 AB regt (bn)
  Other
  1 (Presidential Guard) inf regt
COMBAT SUPPORT
  6 arty regt (bn)
  6 engr bn
  1 int coy
  1 MP bn
  1 CBRN comd
  1 sigs bn
COMBAT SERVICE SUPPORT
  2 log bn
AVIATION
  2 avn coy
AIR DEFENCE
  1 ADA regt
EQUIPMENT BY TYPE
ARMOURED FIGHTING VEHICLES
  LT TK 54: 36 SK-105A1 *Kuerassier*; 18 SK-105A2 *Kuerassier*
  RECCE 24 EE-9 *Cascavel*
  APC 148+
    APC (T) 87+: 50+ M113, 37 M9 half-track
    APC (W) 61: 24 EE-11 *Urutu*; 22 MOWAG *Roland*; 15 V-100 *Commando*
  AUV 19 *Tiger* 4×4
ENGINEERING & MAINTENANCE VEHICLES
  ARV 4 *Greif*; M578 LARV
ANTI-TANK/ANTI-INFRASTRUCTURE
  MSL
    SP 2 *Koyak* with HJ-8
    MANPATS HJ-8
  RCL 90mm M67; 106mm M40A1
ARTILLERY 311+
  TOWED 61: 105mm 25 M101A1; 122mm 36 M-30 (M-1938)
  MOR 250+: 81mm 250 M29; Type-W87; 107mm M30; 120mm M120
AIRCRAFT
  TPT • Light 3: 1 Fokker F-27-200; 1 Beech 90 *King Air*; 1 C-212 *Aviocar*
HELICOPTERS • MRH 5 H425
AIR DEFENCE • GUNS • TOWED 37mm 18 Type-65

Navy 4,800
Organised into six naval districts with HQ located at Puerto Guayaramerín
EQUIPMENT BY TYPE
PATROL AND COASTAL COMBATANTS 7
  PBR 7: 1 *Santa Cruz*; 6 Type 928 YC
LOGISTICS AND SUPPORT 8
  AG 2: 1 LP-503; 1 *Mojo Huayna*
  AH 2
  AP 4

Marines 1,700 (incl 1,000 Naval Military Police)
FORCES BY ROLE
MANOEUVRE
  Mechanised
  1 lt mech inf bn
  Amphibious
  6 mne bn (1 in each Naval District)
COMBAT SUPPORT
  4 (naval) MP bn
EQUIPMENT BY TYPE
ARMOURED FIGHTING VEHICLES
  AUV 6: 6 *Tiger* 4×4

Air Force 6,500 (incl conscripts)
FORCES BY ROLE

GROUND ATTACK
1 sqn with K-8WB *Karakorum*

ISR
1 sqn with Cessna 206; Cessna 402; Learjet 25B/25D (secondary VIP role)

SEARCH & RESCUE
1 sqn with AS332B *Super Puma*; H125 *Ecureuil*; H145

TRANSPORT
1 (TAM) sqn with B-727; B-737; MA60
1 (TAB) sqn with C-130A *Hercules*; MD-10-30F
1 sqn with C-130B/H *Hercules*
1 sqn with F-27-400M *Troopship*
1 (VIP) sqn with Beech 90 *King Air*; Beech 200 *King Air*; Beech 1900; *Falcon* 50EX; *Falcon* 900EX; *Sabreliner* 60
6 sqn with Cessna 152/206; IAI-201 *Arava*; PA-32 *Saratoga*; PA-34 *Seneca*

TRAINING
1 sqn with DA40; T-25; Z-242L
1 sqn with Cessna 152/172
1 sqn with PC-7 *Turbo Trainer*
1 hel sqn with R-44 *Raven* II

TRANSPORT HELICOPTER
1 (anti-drug) sqn with Bell 205 (UH-1H *Iroquois*)

AIR DEFENCE
1 regt with Oerlikon; Type-65

EQUIPMENT BY TYPE

AIRCRAFT 6 combat capable
  TPT 77: **Heavy** 1 MD-10-30F; **Medium** 4: 1 C-130A *Hercules*; 2 C-130B *Hercules*; 1 C-130H *Hercules*; **Light** 64: 1 *Aero Commander* 690; 3 Beech 90 *King Air*; 2 Beech 200 *King Air*; 1 Beech 250 *King Air*; 1 Beech 350 *King Air*; 3 C-212-100; 6 Cessna 152; 2 Cessna 172; 18 Cessna 206; 3 Cessna 210 *Centurion*; 1 Cessna 402; 8 DA40; 1 F-27-400M *Troopship*; 4 IAI-201 *Arava*; 2 Learjet 25B/D; 2 MA60†; 1 PA-32 *Saratoga*; 4 PA-34 *Seneca*; 1 *Sabreliner* 60; **PAX** 8: 1 B-727; 3 B-737-200; 1 *Falcon* 50EX; 1 *Falcon* 900EX (VIP); 2 RJ70
  TRG 20: 4 K-8WB *Karakorum**; 6 T-25; 2 PC-7 *Turbo Trainer**; 8 Z-242L

HELICOPTERS
  MRH 1 SA316 *Alouette* III
  TPT 37: **Medium** 6 H215 *Super Puma*; **Light** 31: 2 H125 *Ecureuil*; 19 Bell 205 (UH-1H *Iroquois*); 4 H145; 6 R-44 *Raven* II

AIR DEFENCE • GUNS • TOWED 18+: **20mm** Oerlikon GAI; **37mm** 18 Type-65

Gendarmerie & Paramilitary 37,100+

National Police 31,100+
FORCES BY ROLE
MANOEUVRE
  Other
    27 frontier sy unit
    9 paramilitary bde
    2 (rapid action) paramilitary regt

Narcotics Police 6,000+
FOE (700) – Special Operations Forces

DEPLOYMENT

CENTRAL AFRICAN REPUBLIC: UN • MINUSCA 6
DEMOCRATIC REPUBLIC OF THE CONGO: UN • MONUSCO 2
SOUTH SUDAN: UN • UNMISS 3
SUDAN: UN • UNISFA 4

Brazil BRZ

Brazilian Real BRL		2023	2024	2025
GDP	BRL	10.9trn	11.6trn	12.3trn
	USD	2.17trn	2.19trn	2.31trn
Real GDP growth	%	2.9	3.0	2.2
Def bdgt [a]	BRL	126bn	129bn	136bn
	USD	25.2bn	24.4bn	25.6bn

[a] Recurring and investment defence budgets. Includes military pensions

Real-terms defence budget trend (USDbn, constant 2015)

Population	220,051,512				
Age	0–14	15–19	20–24	25–29	30–64	65 plus
Male	10.0%	3.7%	4.0%	3.9%	22.9%	4.7%
Female	9.6%	3.5%	3.9%	3.8%	23.8%	6.2%

Capabilities

The armed forces are among the most capable in Latin America. Brazil seeks to enhance its power-projection capabilities, boost surveillance of the Amazon region and coastal waters and further develop its defence industry. Security challenges from organised crime have seen the armed forces deploy on internal-security operations, while there is concern also about security on the northern border with Guyana and Venezuela. Brazil maintains military ties with most of its neighbours, including personnel exchanges and joint military training with Chile and Colombia. The country also has defence cooperation ties with France, Sweden and the US, centred on procurement, technical advice and personnel training. Brazil's air-transport fleet enables it to independently deploy forces and it contributes small contingents to several UN missions. The government has been pursuing a far-reaching investment plan to accelerate military modernisation. It is recapitalising equipment across domains. Brazil has a well-developed defence-industrial base, with the capability to design and manufacture land, air and naval equipment, including most recently submarines. Aerospace firms Avibras and Embraer also export. Local companies are involved in the SISFRON border-security programme. There are industrial partnerships, including technology transfers and research and development support.

ACTIVE 374,500 (Army 222,000 Navy 85,000 Air 67,500) **Gendarmerie & Paramilitary 395,000**

Conscript liability 12 months (can go to 18; often waived)

RESERVE 1,415,000

ORGANISATIONS BY SERVICE

Space
EQUIPMENT BY TYPE
SATELLITES 3
  COMMUNICATIONS 1 SGDC-1 (civil–military use)
  ISR 2 *Carcara*

Army 110,000; 112,000 conscript (total 222,000)
FORCES BY ROLE
COMMAND
  8 mil comd HQ
  12 mil region HQ
  7 div HQ (2 with regional HQ)
SPECIAL FORCES
  1 SF comd (1 SF bn, 1 cdo bn, 1 psyops bn, 1 spt bn)
  1 SF coy
MANOEUVRE
  Reconnaissance
  3 mech cav regt
  Armoured
  1 (5th) armd bde (1 mech cav sqn, 2 tk regt, 2 mech inf bn, 1 SP arty bn, 1 engr bn, 1 sigs coy, 1 log bn)
  1 (6th) armd bde (1 mech cav sqn, 2 tk regt, 2 mech inf bn, 1 SP arty bn, 1 AD bty, 1 engr bn, 1 sigs coy, 1 log bn)
  Mechanised
  2 (1st & 4th) mech cav bde (1 armd cav regt, 3 mech cav regt, 1 arty bn, 1 engr coy, 1 sigs coy, 1 log bn)
  2 (2nd & 3rd) mech cav bde (1 armd cav regt, 2 mech cav regt, 1 SP arty bn, 1 engr coy, 1 sigs coy, 1 log bn)
  1 (3rd) mech inf bde (1 mech cav sqn, 2 mech inf bn, 1 inf bn, 1 arty bn, 1 engr coy, 1 sigs coy, 1 log bn)
  1 (11th) mech inf bde (1 mech cav regt, 3 mech inf bn, 1 arty bn, 1 engr coy, 1 sigs coy, 1 MP coy, 1 log bn)
  1 (15th) mech inf bde (3 mech inf bn, 1 arty bn, 1 engr coy, 1 log bn)
  Light
  1 (4th) mot inf bde (1 mech cav sqn, 1 mot inf bn, 1 inf bn, 1 mtn inf bn, 1 arty bn, 1 sigs coy, 1 log bn)
  1 (7th) mot inf bde (3 mot inf bn, 1 arty bn)
  1 (8th) mot inf bde (1 mech cav sqn, 3 mot inf bn, 1 arty bn, 1 log bn)
  1 (10th) mot inf bde (1 mech cav sqn, 4 mot inf bn, 1 inf coy, 1 arty bn, 1 engr coy, 1 sigs coy)
  1 (13th) mot inf bde (1 mot inf bn, 2 inf bn, 1 inf coy, 1 arty bn)
  1 (14th) mot inf bde (1 mech cav sqn, 3 inf bn, 1 arty bn)
  8 inf bn
  1 (1st) jungle inf bde (1 armd recce bn, 2 jungle inf bn, 1 arty bn)
  4 (2nd, 16th, 17th & 22nd) jungle inf bde (3 jungle inf bn)
  1 (23rd) jungle inf bde (1 cav sqn, 4 jungle inf bn, 1 arty bn, 1 sigs coy, 1 log bn)
  Air Manoeuvre
  1 AB bde (1 cav sqn, 3 AB bn, 1 arty bn, 1 engr coy, 1 sigs coy, 1 log bn)
  1 (12th) air mob bde (1 cav sqn, 3 air mob bn, 1 arty bn, 1 engr coy, 1 sigs coy, 1 log bn)
  Other
  1 (9th) mot trg bde (1 mech cav regt, 3 mot inf bn, 1 arty bn, 1 sig bn, 1 log bn)
  1 (18th) sy bde (2 sy bn, 2 sy coy)
  1 sy bn
  7 sy coy
  3 gd cav regt
  1 gd inf bn
COMBAT SUPPORT
  2 SP arty bn
  6 fd arty bn
  2 MRL bn
  1 STA bty
  6 engr bn
  1 engr gp (1 engr bn, 4 construction bn)
  1 engr gp (4 construction bn, 1 construction coy)
  2 construction bn
  1 CBRN bn
  1 EW coy
  2 int bn
  3 int coy
  9 MP bn
  2 MP coy
  4 sigs bn
  2 sigs coy
COMBAT SERVICE SUPPORT
  5 spt bn
  5 log bn
  1 tpt bn
HELICOPTER
  1 avn bde (3 hel bn, 1 maint bn)
  1 hel bn
AIR DEFENCE
  1 ADA bde (5 ADA bn)
EQUIPMENT BY TYPE
ARMOURED FIGHTING VEHICLES
  MBT 292: 41 *Leopard* 1A1BE; 220 *Leopard* 1A5BR; 31 M60A3/TTS
  ASLT 2 *Centauro* 2
  RECCE 409 EE-9 *Cascavel*
  IFV 13 VBTP-MR *Guarani* 30mm
  APC 1,466
    APC (T) 660: 198 M113A1; 386 M113BR; 12 M113A2; 64 M577A2

APC (W) 806: 231 EE-11 *Urutu*; ε575 VBTP-MR *Guarani* 6×6
AUV 32 IVECO LMV (LMV-BR)
ENGINEERING & MAINTENANCE VEHICLES
  AEV 5 Pionierpanzer 2 *Dachs*
  ARV 35: 13 BPz-2; 8 M88A1; 14 M578 LARV
  VLB 5 Leopard 1 with *Biber*
ANTI-TANK/ANTI-INFRASTRUCTURE
  MSL • MANPATS *Eryx*; *Milan*; MSS-1.2 AC
  RCL • 84mm Carl Gustaf
ARTILLERY 2,263
  SP 109: **155mm** 109: 37 M109A3; 40 M109A5; 32 M109A5+
  TOWED 412: **105mm** 331: 231 M101/M102; 40 L118 Light Gun; 60 Model 56 pack howitzer; **155mm** 81 M114
  MRL • 127mm 38: 20 ASTROS II Mk3M; 18 ASTROS II Mk6
  MOR 1,704: **81mm** 1,436: 92 AGR Mrt Me Acg; 137 M1; 484 AGR M936; 651 Brandt; 72 L16; **120mm** 268 AGR M2
AIRCRAFT
  TPT • Light 4 Short 360 *Sherpa*
HELICOPTERS
  MRH 69: 3 AS565 *Panther* (HM-1); 30 AS565 K2 *Panther* (HM-1); 36 AS550A2 *Fennec* (HA-1) (armed)
  TPT 26: **Heavy** 14 H225M *Caracal* (HM-4); **Medium** 12: 8 AS532 *Cougar* (HM-3); 4 S-70A-36 *Black Hawk* (HM-2)
UNINHABITED AERIAL VEHICLES
  ISR • Medium 1 *Nauru* 1000C
AIR DEFENCE
  SAM • Point-defence RBS-70; 9K38 *Igla* (RS-SA-18 *Grouse*); 9K338 *Igla-S* (RS-SA-24 *Grinch*); RBS-70 NG
  GUNS • SP 35mm 34 *Gepard* 1A2

Navy 85,000

Organised into 9 districts with HQ I Rio de Janeiro, HQ II Salvador, HQ III Natal, HQ IV Belém, HQ V Rio Grande, HQ VI Ladario, HQ VII Brasilia, HQ VIII Sao Paulo, HQ IX Manaus

FORCES BY ROLE
SPECIAL FORCES
  1 (diver) SF gp
EQUIPMENT BY TYPE
SUBMARINES • SSK 4:
  2 *Riachuelo* (FRA *Scorpene*) with 6 533mm TT with SM39 *Exocet* AShM/F21 HWT
  1 *Tupi* (GER T-209/1400) with 8 single 533mm TT with Mk 48 HWT
  1 *Tikuna* (GER T-209/1450) with 8 single 533mm TT with Mk 24 *Tigerfish* HWT
PRINCIPAL SURFACE COMBATANTS 7
  FRIGATES 7
    FFGHM 6:
      1 *Greenhalgh* (ex-UK *Broadsword*) with 4 single lnchr with MM40 *Exocet* Block 2 AShM, 2 sextuple lnchr with *Sea Wolf* SAM, 2 triple 324mm STWS Mk.2 ASTT with Mk 46 LWT (capacity 2 *Super Lynx* Mk21A hel)
      5 *Niteroi* with 2 twin lnchr with MM40 *Exocet* Block 2 AShM, 1 octuple *Albatros* lnchr with *Aspide* SAM, 2 triple 324mm SVTT Mk 32 ASTT with Mk 46 LWT, 1 twin 375mm Bofors ASW Rocket Launcher System A/S mor, 1 115mm gun (capacity 1 *Super Lynx* Mk21A hel)
    FFGH 1 *Barroso* with 2 twin lnchr with MM40 *Exocet* Block 2 AShM, 2 triple 324mm SVTT Mk 32 ASTT with Mk 46 LWT, 1 115mm gun (capacity 1 *Super Lynx* Mk21A hel)
PATROL AND COASTAL COMBATANTS 45
  CORVETTES • FSGH 1 *Inhauma* with 2 twin lnchr with MM40 *Exocet* Block 2 AShM, 2 triple 324mm SVTT Mk 32 ASTT with Mk 46 LWT, 1 115mm gun (1 *Super Lynx* Mk21A hel)
  PSO 3 *Amazonas* with 1 hel landing platform
  PCO 6: 4 *Bracui* (ex-UK *River*); 1 *Imperial Marinheiro* with 1 76mm gun; 1 *Parnaiba* with 1 hel landing platform
  PCC 3 *Macaé* (FRA *Vigilante*)
  PCR 5: 2 *Pedro Teixeira* with 1 hel landing platform; 3 *Roraima*
  PB 23: 12 *Grajau*; 6 *Marlim* (ITA *Meatini* derivative); 5 *Piratini* (US PGM)
  PBR 4 LPR-40
MINE WARFARE • MINE COUNTERMEASURES 3
  MSC 3 *Aratu* (GER *Schutze*)
AMPHIBIOUS
  PRINCIPAL AMPHIBIOUS SHIPS 2
    LPH 1 *Atlantico* (ex-UK *Ocean*) (capacity 18 hels; 4 LCVP; 40 vehs; 800 troops)
    LPD 1 *Bahia* (ex-FRA *Foudre*) (capacity 4 hels; 8 LCM, 450 troops)
  LANDING SHIPS 1
    LSLH 1 *Almirante Saboia* (ex-UK *Sir Bedivere*) (capacity 1 med hel; 18 MBT; 340 troops)
  LANDING CRAFT 16:
    LCM 12: 10 EDVM-25; 2 *Icarai* (ex-FRA CTM)
    LCT 1 *Marambaia* (ex-FRA CDIC)
    LCU 3 *Guarapari* (LCU 1610)
LOGISTICS AND SUPPORT 42
  ABU 5: 4 *Comandante Varella*; 1 *Faroleiro Mario Seixas*
  ABUH 1 *Almirante Graça Aranha* (lighthouse tender)
  AGOR 4: 1 *Ary Rongel* with 1 hel landing platform; 1 *Almirante Maximiano* (capacity 2 AS350/AS355 *Ecureuil* hel); 1 *Cruzeiro do Sul*; 1 *Vital de Oliveira*
  AGS 11: 1 *Aspirante Moura*; 1 *Caravelas* (riverine); 1 *Antares*; 3 *Amorim do Valle* (ex-UK *River* (MCM)); 1 *Rio Branco*; 4 *Rio Tocantin*
  AH 5: 2 *Oswaldo Cruz* with 1 hel landing platform; 1 *Dr Montenegro*; 1 *Tenente Maximiano* with 1 hel landing platform; 1 *Soares de Meirelles*
  AOR 1 *Almirante Gastao Motta*

AP 3: 1 *Almirante Leverger*; 1 *Paraguassu*; 1 *Para* (all river transports)
ARS 3 *Mearim*
ASR 1 *Guillobel*
ATF 2 *Tritao*
AX 1 *Brasil* (*Niteroi* mod) with 1 hel landing platform
AXL 4: 3 *Nascimento*; 1 *Potengi*
AXS 1 *Cisne Branco*

Naval Aviation 2,100
FORCES BY ROLE
GROUND ATTACK
  1 sqn with A-4M (AF-1B) *Skyhawk*; TA-4M (AF-1C) *Skyhawk*
ANTI SURFACE WARFARE
  1 sqn with *Super Lynx* Mk21B
ANTI SUBMARINE WARFARE
  1 sqn with S-70B *Seahawk* (MH-16)
TRAINING
  1 sqn with Bell 206B3 *Jet Ranger* III
TRANSPORT HELICOPTER
  3 sqn with AS350 *Ecureuil* (armed)
  1 sqn with AS350 *Ecureuil* (armed); H135 (UH-17)
  1 sqn with H225M (AH-15B); H225M *Caracal* (UH-15/UH-15A)
  1 sqn with H225M *Caracal* (UH-15)
EQUIPMENT BY TYPE
AIRCRAFT 5 combat capable
  ATK 5: 4 A-4M (AF-1B) *Skyhawk*; 1 TA-4M (AF-1C) *Skyhawk*
HELICOPTERS
  ASW 11: 5 *Super Lynx* Mk21B (3 more being upgraded); 6 S-70B *Seahawk* (MH-16)
  MRH 3 H22M (AH-15B) (armed)
  CSAR 3 H225M *Caracal* (UH-15A)
  TPT 46: **Heavy** 7 H225M *Caracal* (UH-15); **Medium** 2 AS532 *Cougar* (UH-14); **Light** 37: 17 AS350 *Ecureuil* (armed); 8 AS355 *Ecureuil* II (armed); 10 Bell 206B3 *Jet Ranger* III (IH-6B); 2 H135 (UH-17)
AIR-LAUNCHED MISSILES • AShM: AM39 *Exocet*; AGM-119 *Penguin*

Marines 16,000
FORCES BY ROLE
SPECIAL FORCES
  1 SF bn
MANOEUVRE
  Amphibious
  1 amph div (1 lt armd bn, 3 mne bn, 1 amph aslt bn, 1 arty bn)
  6 (regional) mne gp
  3 rvn bn
COMBAT SUPPORT
  1 engr bn
COMBAT SERVICE SUPPORT
  1 log bn
EQUIPMENT BY TYPE
ARMOURED FIGHTING VEHICLES
  LT TK 10 SK-105 *Kuerassier*
  APC 60
    APC (T) 30 M113A1 (incl variants)
    APC (W) 18 *Piranha* IIIC
  AUV 12: 12 JLTV
  AAV 46: 22 AAV-7A1-P; 20 AAVP-7A1 RAM/RS; 2 AAVC-7A1 RAM/RS (CP); 2 AAV-7A1-C
ENGINEERING VEHICLES • ARV 3: 2 AAV-7A1-S; 1 AAVR-7A1 RAM/RS
ANTI-TANK/ANTI-INFRASTRUCTURE
  MSL• MANPATS RB-56 *Bill*; MSS-1.2 AC
ARTILLERY 65
  TOWED 34: **105mm** 26: 18 L118 Light Gun; 8 M101; **155mm** 8 M114
  MRL 127mm 6 ASTROS II Mk6
  MOR•TOWED 81mm 18 M29; **120mm** 6 K6A3
  AIR DEFENCE • GUNS 40mm 6 L/70 (with BOFI)

Air Force 67,500
4 air forces (I, II, III & V)
FORCES BY ROLE
SPECIAL FORCES
  1 sf gp
MANOEUVRE
  Other
  1 sy bde (28 sy gp)
FIGHTER
  2 sqn with F-5EM/FM *Tiger* II
FIGHTER/GROUND ATTACK
  2 sqn with AMX/AMX-T (A-1A/B); AMX A-1M/BM
  1 sqn with *Gripen* E (F-39E) (forming)
GROUND ATTACK/ISR
  4 sqn with EMB-314 *Super Tucano* (A-29A/B)*
MARITIME PATROL
  1 sqn with P-3AM *Orion*
  2 sqn with EMB-111 (P-95A/B/M)
ISR
  1 sqn with Learjet 35AM (R-35AM); EMB-110B (R-95)
AIRBORNE EARLY WARNING & CONTROL
  1 sqn with EMB-145RS (R-99); EMB-145SA (E-99M)
SEARCH & RESCUE
  1 sqn with C295M *Amazonas* (SC-105); UH-60L *Black Hawk* (H-60L)
TANKER/TRANSPORT
  1 sqn with KC-390 *Millennium*
TRANSPORT
  1 sqn with A330 (forming)
  2 sqn with C295M (C-105A)
  7 (regional) sqn with Cessna 208/208B (C-98/-98A); EMB-110 (C-95); EMB-120 (C-97)

1 sqn with EMB-121 (VU-9)
1 sqn with ERJ-145 (C-99A)
1 sqn with KC-390 Millennium
1 VIP sqn with A319 (VC-1A); EMB-190 (VC-2); AS355 Ecureuil II (VH-55)
1 VIP sqn with EMB-135BJ (VC-99B); ERJ-135LR (VC-99C); Learjet 35A (VU-35); Learjet 55C (VU-55C)

TRAINING
1 sqn with EMB-110 (C-95)
1 sqn with EMB-312 Tucano (T-27/T-27M)
1 sqn with T-25A/C

TRANSPORT HELICOPTER
1 VIP flt with H135M (VH-35); H225M Caracal (VH-36)
2 sqn with H225M Caracal (H-36)
1 sqn with AS350B Ecureuil (H-50); AS355 Ecureuil II (H-55)
2 sqn with UH-60L Black Hawk (H-60L)

ISR UAV
1 sqn with Hermes 900

AIR DEFENCE
3 AD gp

EQUIPMENT BY TYPE
AIR DEFENCE
SAM
Point-defence: 9K338 Igla-S (RS-SA-24 Grinch)
AIRCRAFT 173 combat capable
FTR 40: 36 F-5EM Tiger II; 4 F-5FM Tiger II
FGA 31: 16 AMX/AMX-T (A-1A/B); 6 AMX A-1M; 1 AMX A-1BM; 8 Gripen E (F-39E) (in test)
ASW 5 P-3AM Orion
MP 8 EMB-111 (P-95BM Bandeirulha)*
ISR 4 EMB-110B (R-95)
ELINT 6: 3 EMB-145RS (R-99); 3 Learjet 35AM (R-35AM)
AEW&C 5 EMB-145SA (E-99M)
SAR 7: 3 C295M Amazonas (SC-105); 4 EMB-110 (SC-95B)
TPT 152: **Medium** 7 KC-390 Millennium; **Light** 135: 11 C295M (C-105A); 6 Cessna 208 (C-98); 24 Cessna 208B (C-98A); 39 EMB-110 (C-95A/B/C/M); 17 EMB-120 (C-97); 5 EMB-121 (VU-9); 7 EMB-135BJ (VC-99B); 2 EMB-202A Ipanema (G-19A); 2 EMB-500 Phenom 100; 4 EMB-550 Legacy 500 (IU-50); 2 ERJ-135LR (VC-99C); 6 ERJ-145 (C-99A); 9 Learjet 35A (VU-35); 1 Learjet 55C (VU-55);
PAX 10: 1 A319 (VC-1A); 2 A330 (to be converted to A330 MRTT); 3 EMB-190 (VC-2); 4 Hawker 800XP (EU-93A – calibration)
TRG 173: 42 EMB-312 Tucano (T-27/-27M); 89 EMB-314 Super Tucano (A-29A/B)*; 42 T-25A/C

HELICOPTERS
MRH 2 H135M (VH-35)
TPT 55: **Heavy** 15 H225M Caracal (13 H-36 & 2 VH-36); **Medium** 16 UH-60L Black Hawk (H-60L); **Light** 24 AS350B Ecureuil (H-50)

UNINHABITED AERIAL VEHICLES
ISR 6: **Heavy** 2 Heron 1; **Medium** 4 Hermes 900

AIR-LAUNCHED MISSILES
AAM • IIR Iris-T; Python 4; ARH Derby; Meteor
AShM AGM-84L Harpoon

Gendarmerie & Paramilitary 395,000

Public Security Forces 395,000 opcon Army
State police organisation technically under army control. However, military control is reducing, with authority reverting to individual states

DEPLOYMENT

CENTRAL AFRICAN REPUBLIC: UN • MINUSCA 9
CYPRUS: UN • UNFICYP 2
DEMOCRATIC REPUBLIC OF THE CONGO: UN • MONUSCO 21
LEBANON: UN • UNIFIL 11
SOUTH SUDAN: UN • UNMISS 12
SUDAN: UN • UNISFA 5
WESTERN SAHARA: UN • MINURSO 10

Chile CHL

Chilean Peso CLP		2023	2024	2025
GDP	CLP	282trn	305trn	325trn
	USD	336bn	329bn	362bn
Real GDP growth	%	0.2	2.5	2.4
Def bdgt [a]	CLP	3.56trn	3.85trn	4.07trn
	USD	4.24bn	4.14bn	4.54bn

[a] Includes military pensions

Real-terms defence budget trend (USDbn, constant 2015)

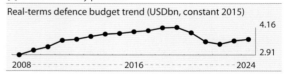

Population	18,664,652					
Age	0–14	15–19	20–24	25–29	30–64	65 plus
Male	9.8%	3.2%	3.3%	3.7%	23.4%	5.7%
Female	9.4%	3.1%	3.2%	3.6%	23.8%	7.8%

Capabilities

The core role of Chile's armed forces is to ensure sovereignty and territorial integrity, but there is growing emphasis on non-traditional military activities, such as disaster relief, countering human trafficking, as well as peacekeeping. The country maintains R&D cooperation ties and exchange programmes with Brazil and Colombia. Defence cooperation with the US is centred on procurement, technical advice and personnel training. The armed forces participate in international exercises. Chile has a limited capacity to deploy independently beyond its borders. The government is upgrading the country's F-16s to prolong their service life. Capability priorities reflect the focus on littoral and blue-water surveillance, and a satellite constellation is being developed. In 2024, the navy has commissioned a new icebreaker for Antarctic operations. Chile has a developed defence-industrial base.

ENAER conducts aircraft maintenance while shipyard ASMAR built the new icebreaker and is assembling new amphibious ships, and FAMAE works on land systems.

ACTIVE 68,500 (Army 37,650 Navy 19,800 Air 11,050) **Gendarmerie & Paramilitary 44,700**

Conscript liability Army 12 months; Navy 18 months; Air Force 12 months. Legally, conscription can last for 2 years

RESERVE 19,100 (Army 19,100)

ORGANISATIONS BY SERVICE

Space
EQUIPMENT BY TYPE
SATELLITES
  ISR 1 SSOT (Sistema Satelital de Observación de la Tierra)

Army 37,650
6 military administrative regions
FORCES BY ROLE
Currently being reorganised into 1 SF bde, 4 armd bde, 1 armd det, 4 mot bde, 2 mot det, 4 mtn det and 1 avn bde
COMMAND
  6 div HQ
SPECIAL FORCES
  1 SF bde (1 SF bn, 1 (mtn) SF gp, 1 para bn, 3 cdo coy, 1 log coy)
MANOEUVRE
  Reconnaissance
  4 cav sqn
  2 recce sqn
  2 recce pl
  Armoured
  1 (1st) armd bde (1 armd recce pl, 1 armd cav gp, 1 mech inf bn, 2 arty gp, 1 AT coy, 1 engr coy, 1 sigs coy)
  2 (2nd & 3rd) armd bde (1 armd recce pl, 1 armd cav gp, 1 mech inf bn, 1 arty gp, 1 AT coy, 1 engr coy, 1 sigs coy)
  1 (4th) armd bde (1 armd recce pl, 1 armd cav gp, 1 mech inf bn, 1 arty gp, 1 engr coy)
  1 (5th) armd det (1 armd cav gp, 1 mech inf coy, 1 arty gp)
  Mechanised
  1 (1st) mech inf regt
  Light
  1 (1st) mot inf bde (1 recce coy, 1 mot inf bn, 1 arty gp, 3 AT coy, 1 engr bn)
  1 (4th) mot inf bde (1 mot inf bn, 1 MRL gp, 2 AT coy, 1 engr bn)
  1 (24th) mot inf bde (1 mot inf bn, 1 arty gp, 1 AT coy)
  1 (Maipo) mot inf bde (3 mot inf regt, 1 arty regt)
  1 (6th) reinforced regt (1 mot inf bn, 1 arty gp, 1 sigs coy)
  1 (10th) reinforced regt (1 mot inf bn, 2 AT coy, 1 engr bn)
  1 (11th) mot inf det (1 inf bn, 1 arty gp)
  1 (14th) mot inf det (1 mot inf bn, 1 arty gp, 1 sigs coy, 1 AT coy)
  4 mot inf regt
  1 (3rd) mtn det (1 mtn inf bn, 1 arty gp, 1 engr coy)
  1 (9th) mtn det (1 mtn inf bn, 1 engr coy, 1 construction bn)
  2 (8th & 17th) mtn det (1 mtn inf bn, 1 arty coy)
COMBAT SUPPORT
  1 engr regt
  4 sigs bn
  1 sigs coy
  1 int bde (7 int gp)
  2 int regt
  1 MP regt
COMBAT SERVICE SUPPORT
  1 log div (2 log regt)
  4 log regt
  6 log coy
  1 maint div (1 maint regt)
AVIATION
  1 avn bde (1 tpt avn bn, 1 hel bn, 1 spt bn)
EQUIPMENT BY TYPE
ARMOURED FIGHTING VEHICLES
  MBT 170: 30 *Leopard* 1V; 140 *Leopard* 2A4
  IFV 191: 173 *Marder* 1A3; 18 YPR-765 PRI
  APC 445
    APC (T) 306 M113A1/A2
    APC (W) 139: 121 *Piranha* 6×6; 18 *Piranha* 8×8
ENGINEERING & MAINTENANCE VEHICLES
  AEV 6 Pionierpanzer 2 *Dachs*
  ARV 30 BPz-2
  VLB 13 *Biber*
  MW 8+: *Bozena* 5; 8 *Leopard* 1 MW
ANTI-TANK/ANTI-INFRASTRUCTURE
  MSL • MANPATS *Spike*-LR; *Spike*-ER
  RCL 84mm *Carl Gustaf*; **106mm** 213 M40A1
ARTILLERY 1,398
  SP 155mm 48: 24 M109A3; 24 M109A5+
  TOWED 239: **105mm** 191: 87 M101; 104 Model 56 pack howitzer; **155mm** 48 M-71
  MRL 160mm 12 LAR-160
  MOR 1,099: **81mm** 744: 295 ECIA L65/81; 192 FAMAE; 257 Soltam; **120mm** 284: 171 ECIA L65/120; 16 FAMAE; 97 M-65; **SP 120mm** 71: 35 FAMAE (on *Piranha* 6×6); 36 Soltam (on M113A2)
AIRCRAFT
  TPT • Light 10: 2 C-212-300 *Aviocar*; 2 Cessna 172; 3 Cessna 208 *Caravan*; 3 CN235
HELICOPTERS
  ISR 9 MD-530F *Lifter* (armed)
  TPT 17: **Medium** 12: 8 AS532AL *Cougar*; 2 AS532ALe *Cougar*; 2 SA330 *Puma*; **Light** 5: 4 H125 *Ecureuil*; 1 AS355F *Ecureuil* II
AIR DEFENCE
  SAM • Point-defence *Mistral*
  GUNS 41:
    SP 20mm 17 *Piranha*/TCM-20
    TOWED 20mm 24 TCM-20

Navy 19,800

5 Naval Zones; 1st Naval Zone and main HQ at Valparaiso; 2nd Naval Zone at Talcahuano; 3rd Naval Zone at Punta Arenas; 4th Naval Zone at Iquique; 5th Naval Zone at Puerto Montt

FORCES BY ROLE
SPECIAL FORCES
1 (diver) SF comd

EQUIPMENT BY TYPE
SUBMARINES • SSK 4:
2 *O'Higgins* (*Scorpene*) with 6 single 533mm TT with SM39 *Exocet* Block 2 AShM/*Black Shark* HWT
2 *Thomson* (GER Type-209/1400) (of which 1 in refit) with 8 single 533mm TT with SM39 *Exocet* Block 2 AShM/*Black Shark* HWT/SUT HWT

PRINCIPAL SURFACE COMBATANTS 8
FRIGATES • FFGHM 8:
3 *Almirante Cochrane* (ex-UK *Norfolk* Type-23) with 2 quad lnchr with RGM-84C *Harpoon* Block 1B AShM, 1 32-cell VLS with *Sea Ceptor* SAM, 2 twin 324mm ASTT with Mk 46 mod 2 LWT, 1 114mm gun (capacity 1 AS532SC *Cougar*)
2 *Almirante Latorre* (ex-AUS *Adelaide*) with 1 Mk 13 GMLS with RGM-84L *Harpoon* Block II AShM/SM-2 Block IIIA SAM, 1 8-cell Mk 41 VLS with RIM-162B ESSM SAM, 2 triple 324mm SVTT Mk 32 ASTT with MU90 LWT, 1 76mm gun (capacity 2 AS532SC *Cougars*)
2 *Almirante Riveros* (ex-NLD *Karel Doorman*) with 2 quad lnchr with MM40 *Exocet* Block 3 AShM, 1 8-cell Mk 48 VLS with RIM-7P *Sea Sparrow* SAM, 4 single 324mm SVTT Mk 32 mod 9 ASTT with Mk 46 mod 5 HWT, 1 76mm gun (capacity 1 AS532SC *Cougar*)
1 *Almirante Williams* (ex-UK *Broadsword* Type-22) with 2 quad lnchr with RGM-84 *Harpoon* AShM, 2 8-cell VLS with *Barak*-1 SAM; 2 triple 324mm ASTT with Mk 46 LWT, 1 76mm gun (capacity 1 AS532SC *Cougar*)

PATROL AND COASTAL COMBATANTS 12
PSOH 4: 2 *Piloto Pardo*; 2 *Piloto Pardo* with 1 76mm gun (ice-strengthened hull)
PCG 3:
2 *Casma* (ISR *Sa'ar* 4) with 6 single lnchr with *Gabriel* I AShM, 2 76mm guns
1 *Casma* (ISR *Sa'ar* 4) with 4 single lnchr with *Gabriel* I AShM, 2 twin lnchr with MM40 *Exocet* AShM, 2 76mm guns
PCO 5 *Micalvi* (1 used as med vessel)

AMPHIBIOUS
PRINCIPAL AMPHIBIOUS SHIPS • LPD 1 *Sargento Aldea* (ex-FRA *Foudre*) with 3 twin *Simbad* lnchr with *Mistral* SAM (capacity 4 med hel; 1 LCT; 2 LCM; 22 tanks; 470 troops)
LANDING SHIPS 3
LSM 1 *Elicura*
LST 2 *Maipo* (FRA *Batral*) with 1 hel landing platform (capacity 7 tanks; 140 troops)
LANDING CRAFT 3
LCT 1 CDIC (for use in *Sargento Aldea*)
LCM 2 (for use in *Sargento Aldea*)

LOGISTICS AND SUPPORT 11
ABU 1 *Ingeniero Slight* with 1 hel landing platform
AGBH 1 *Almirante Viel*
AGOR 1 *Cabo de Hornos*
AGS 1 *Micalvi*
AOR 2: 1 *Almirante Montt* (ex-US *Henry J. Kaiser*) with 1 hel landing platform; 1 *Araucano*
AP 1 *Aquiles* (1 hel landing platform)
ATF 3: 1 *Janequeo*; 1 *Lientur* (Ice capable); 1 *Veritas*
AXS 1 *Esmeralda*

Naval Aviation 600
EQUIPMENT BY TYPE
AIRCRAFT 14 combat capable
ASW 4: 2 C295ASW *Persuader*; 2 P-3ACH *Orion*
MP 4: 1 C295MPA *Persuader*; 3 EMB-111 *Bandeirante**
ISR 7 P-68
TRG 7 PC-7 *Turbo Trainer**
HELICOPTERS
ASW 5 AS532SC *Cougar*
MRH 8 AS365 *Dauphin*
TPT 11: **Medium** 2 H215 (AS332L1) *Super Puma*; **Light** 9: 4 Bo-105S; 5 H125
AIR-LAUNCHED MISSILES • AShM AM39 *Exocet*

Marines 3,600
FORCES BY ROLE
MANOEUVRE
Amphibious
1 amph bde (2 mne bn, 1 cbt spt bn, 1 log bn)
2 coastal def unit

EQUIPMENT BY TYPE
ARMOURED FIGHTING VEHICLES
LT TK (15 FV101 *Scorpion* in store)
IFV 22 NZLAV
APC • APC (W) 25 MOWAG *Roland*
ARTILLERY 39
TOWED 23: **105mm** 7 KH-178; **155mm** 16 M-71
MOR **81mm** 16
COASTAL DEFENCE • AShM MM38 *Exocet*
AIR DEFENCE • SAM • Point-defence 14: 4 M998 *Avenger*; 10 M1097 *Avenger*

Coast Guard
Integral part of the Navy
EQUIPMENT BY TYPE
PATROL AND COASTAL COMBATANTS 55
PBF 26 *Archangel*
PB 29: 18 *Alacalufe* (*Protector*); 4 *Grumete Diaz* (*Dabor*); 6 *Pelluhue*; 1 *Ona*

Air Force 11,050
FORCES BY ROLE

FIGHTER
1 sqn with F-5E/F *Tiger* III+
2 sqn with F-16AM/BM *Fighting Falcon*
FIGHTER/GROUND ATTACK
1 sqn with F-16C/D Block 50 *Fighting Falcon (Puma)*
ISR
1 (photo) flt with DHC-6-300 *Twin Otter*; Gulfstream IV
TANKER/TRANSPORT
1 sqn with B-737-300; C-130B/H *Hercules*; E-3D *Sentry*; KC-130R *Hercules*; KC-135 *Stratotanker*
TRANSPORT
3 sqn with Bell 205 (UH-1H *Iroquois*); C-212-200/300 *Aviocar*; Cessna O-2A; Cessna 525 *Citation* CJ1; DHC-6-100/300 *Twin Otter*; PA-28-236 *Dakota*; Bell 205 (UH-1H *Iroquois*)
1 VIP flt with B-767-300ER; B-737-500; Gulfstream IV
TRAINING
1 sqn with EMB-314 *Super Tucano**
1 sqn with Cirrus SR-22T; T-35A/B *Pillan*
TRANSPORT HELICOPTER
1 sqn with Bell 205 (UH-1H *Iroquois*); Bell 206B (trg); Bell 412 *Twin Huey*; S-70A *Black Hawk*
AIR DEFENCE
1 AD regt M163/M167 *Vulcan*
4 AD sqn with *Crotale*; NASAMS; *Mistral*; Oerlikon GDF-005
EQUIPMENT BY TYPE
AIRCRAFT 80 combat capable
 FTR 48: 10 F-5E *Tigre* III+; 2 F-5F *Tigre* III+; 29 F-16AM *Fighting Falcon*; 7 F-16BM *Fighting Falcon*
 FGA 10: 6 F-16C Block 50 *Fighting Falcon*; 4 F-16D Block 50 *Fighting Falcon*
 ISR 3 Cessna O-2A
 AEW&C 2 E-3D *Sentry*
 TKR 3 KC-135 *Stratotanker*
 TKR/TPT 2 KC-130R *Hercules*
 TPT 33: **Medium** 3: 1 C-130B *Hercules*; 2 C-130H *Hercules*; **Light** 24: 2 C-212-200 *Aviocar*; 1 C-212-300 *Aviocar*; 4 Cessna 525 *Citation* CJ1; 3 DHC-6-100 *Twin Otter*; 7 DHC-6-300 *Twin Otter*; 7 PA-28-236 *Dakota*; **PAX** 6: 1 B-737-300; 1 B-737-500 (VIP); 1 B-767-300ER (VIP); 3 Gulfstream IV (VIP/aerial photography)
 TRG 57: 8 Cirrus SR-22T; 22 EMB-314 *Super Tucano**; 27 T-35A/B *Pillan*
HELICOPTERS
 MRH 12 Bell 412EP *Twin Huey*
 TPT 25: **Medium** 7: 1 S-70A *Black Hawk*; 6 S-70i (MH-60M) *Black Hawk*; **Light** 18: 13 Bell 205 (UH-1H *Iroquois*); 5 Bell 206B (trg)
UNINHABITED AERIAL VEHICLES
 ISR • Medium up to 3 *Hermes* 900
AIR DEFENCE
 SAM
  Short-range 17: 5 *Crotale*; 12 NASAMS

  Point-defence *Mistral* (including some *Mygale/Aspic*)
 GUNS • TOWED 20mm M163/M167 *Vulcan*; **35mm** Oerlikon GDF-005
AIR-LAUNCHED MISSILES
 AAM • IR AIM-9J/M *Sidewinder*; *Python* 3; *Shafrir*‡; **IIR** *Python* 4; **ARH** AIM-120C AMRAAM; *Derby*
 ASM AGM-65G *Maverick*
BOMBS
 Laser-guided *Paveway* II
 INS/GPS guided JDAM

Gendarmerie & Paramilitary 44,700

Carabineros 44,700
Ministry of Interior; 15 zones, 36 districts, 179 *comisaria*
EQUIPMENT BY TYPE
ARMOURED FIGHTING VEHICLES
 APC • APC (W) 20 MOWAG *Roland*
ARTILLERY • MOR 81mm
AIRCRAFT
 TPT • Light 4: 1 Beech 200 *King Air*; 1 Cessna 208; 1 Cessna 550 *Citation* V; 1 PA-31T *Cheyenne* II
HELICOPTERS • TPT • Light 17: 5 AW109E *Power*; 1 AW139; 1 Bell 206 *Jet Ranger*; 2 BK-117; 5 Bo-105; 1 H125 *Ecureuil*; 2 H135

DEPLOYMENT

BOSNIA-HERZEGOVINA: EU • EUFOR (Operation Althea) 6
CYPRUS: UN • UNFICYP 6
MIDDLE EAST: UN • UNTSO 3

Colombia COL

Colombian Peso COP		2023	2024	2025
GDP	COP	1.57qrn	1.68qrn	1.79qrn
	USD	364bn	417bn	419bn
Real GDP growth	%	0.6	1.6	2.5
Def bdgt [a]	COP	24.1trn	31.2trn	34.6trn
	USD	5.57bn	7.73bn	8.09bn
FMA (US)	USD	38.5m	38.0m	38.5m

[a] Excludes security budget

Real-terms defence budget trend (USDbn, constant 2015)

Population	49,588,357				
Age	0–14	15–19	20–24	25–29	30–64	65 plus
Male	11.4%	3.9%	3.9%	4.0%	20.7%	4.9%
Female	10.9%	3.7%	3.8%	4.0%	22.5%	6.3%

Capabilities

Colombia's armed forces are largely focused on internal security, typically conducting counter-insurgency and counter-narcotics operations. The military has improved its training and overall capabilities in recent decades. In response to the humanitarian and security challenge from Venezuela, Colombia has strengthened cooperation with Brazil on border controls. The US is Colombia's closest international military partner, with cooperation in equipment procurement, and technical and personnel training. In 2017, Colombia became one of NATO's global partners. Although the equipment inventory mainly comprises legacy systems, Colombia has the capability to independently deploy force elements beyond national borders. The navy is acquiring new frigates based on a Dutch design, while the army is planning to modernise its armoured vehicles and the air force is still looking to replace its ageing *Kfir* aircraft. New medium transport aircraft will be equipped with ISR sensors to boost reconnaissance capabilities. Colombia's defence industry is active in all domains. CIAC is developing its first indigenous UAVs, while CODALTEC is developing an air-defence system for regional export. COTECMAR has supplied patrol boats and amphibious ships for national and export markets.

ACTIVE 269,000 (Army 195,400, Navy 58,000 Air 15,600) **Gendarmerie & Paramilitary 165,050**

Conscript liability 18 months' duration with upper age limit of 24, males only

RESERVE 34,950 (Army 25,050 Navy 6,500 Air 3,400)

ORGANISATIONS BY SERVICE

Army 195,400
FORCES BY ROLE

SPECIAL FORCES
1 SF div (1 (1st) SF regt (1 spec ops bn, 1 cdo bn); 1 (2nd) SF regt (3 SF bn); 1 (3rd) SF regt (1 spec ops bn, 2 sf bn))
1 (anti-terrorist) SF bn

MANOEUVRE
Mechanised
1 (1st) mech div (1 (2nd) mech bde (2 mech inf bn, 1 mtn inf bn, 1 engr bn, 1 MP bn, 1 spt bn, 2 Gaula anti-kidnap gp); 1 (10th) mech bde (1 armd recce bn, 1 mech cav bn, 1 mech inf bn, 1 mtn inf bn, 3 sy bn, 2 arty bn, 1 engr bn, 1 spt bn, 2 Gaula anti-kidnap gp, 1 ADA bn))

Light
1 (2nd) inf div (1 (1st) inf bde (1 mech cav bn, 2 inf bn, 1 mtn inf bn, 1 arty bn, 1 spt bn, 1 Gaula anti-kidnap gp); 1 (5th) inf bde (3 inf bn, 2 arty bn, 1 engr bn, 1 spt bn, 1 Gaula anti-kidnap gp, 1 ADA bn); 1 (30th) inf bde (1 mech cav bn, 2 inf bn, 1 arty bn, 1 engr bn, 1 spt bn, 1 Gaula anti-kidnap gp); 1 AD bn; 1 sy gp (1 (urban) spec ops bn, 4 COIN bn, 3 sy bn); 1 (rapid reaction) sy bde)
1 (3rd) inf div (1 (3rd) inf bde (2 inf bn, 2 mtn inf bn, 1 arty bn, 1 engr bn, 1 cbt spt bn, 1 MP bn, 1 log bn, 1 Gaula anti-kidnap gp); 1 (23rd) inf bde (1 lt inf bn, 2 sy bn, 1 engr bn, 1 spt bn, 1 log bn, 1 Gaula anti-kidnap gp); 1 (29th) mtn bde (1 mtn inf bn, 2 inf bn, 2 COIN bn, 1 spt bn, 1 log bn, 1 Gaula anti-kidnap gp); 1 mtn inf bn; 2 (rapid reaction) sy bde)
1 (4th) inf div (1 (7th) air mob bde (1 (urban) spec ops bn, 2 air mob inf bn, 1 lt inf bn, 1 sy bn, 1 COIN bn, 1 air mob engr bn, 1 EOD bn, 1 construction bn, 1 spt bn, 1 log bn, 2 Gaula anti-kidnap gp); 1 (22nd) jungle bde (1 air mob inf bn, 1 lt inf bn, 1 jungle inf bn, 1 spt bn, 1 log bn); 1 (31st) jungle bde (2 jungle inf bn))
1 (5th) inf div (1 (6th) lt inf bde (2 lt inf bn, 1 mtn inf bn, 1 spt bn, 1 Gaula anti-kidnap gp); 1 (8th) inf bde (1 inf bn, 1 mtn inf bn, 1 arty bn, 1 engr bn, 1 spt bn, 1 Gaula anti-kidnap gp); 1 (9th) inf bde (2 inf bn, 1 arty bn, 1 sy bn, 1 spt bn, 1 Gaula anti-kidnap gp); 1 (13th) inf bde (1 sf bn, 1 recce bn, 3 inf bn, 1 mtn inf bn, 1 air mob bn, 1 arty bn, 1 engr bn, 3 MP bn, 1 spt bn, 1 Gaula anti-kidnap gp))
1 (6th) inf div (1 (12th) inf bde (1 recce bn, 1 inf bn, 1 jungle inf bn, 1 mtn inf bn, 1 sy bn, 1 engr bn, 1 spt bn, 1 Gaula anti-kidnap gp); 1 (26th) jungle bde (1 jungle inf bn, 1 spt bn); 1 (27th) jungle inf bde (1 inf bn, 1 jungle inf bn, 1 sy bn, 1 arty bn, 1 engr bn, 1 spt bn); 1 (13th) mobile sy bde; 2 COIN bn)
1 (7th) inf div (1 (4th) inf bde (1 (urban) spec ops bn; 1 mech cav gp, 3 inf bn, 1 sy bn, 1 arty bn, 1 engr bn, 1 MP bn, 1 spt bn, 2 Gaula anti-kidnap gp); 1 (11th) inf bde (1 inf bn, 1 spt bn, 1 Gaula anti-kidnap gp); 1 (14th) inf bde (2 inf bn, 1 sy bn, 1 engr bn, 1 spt bn, 1 Gaula anti-kidnap gp); 1 (15th) jungle bde (2 mech bn, 1 inf bn, 1 jng inf, 1 engr bn, 1 spt bn); 1 (17th) inf bde (2 inf bn, 1 engr bn, 1 spt bn, 1 Gaula anti-kidnap gp))
1 (8th) inf div (1 (16th) lt inf bde (1 recce bn, 1 inf bn, 1 spt bn, 1 Gaula anti-kidnap gp); 1 (18th) inf bde (1 (urban) spec ops bn; 1 air mob gp, 5 sy bn, 1 arty bn, 1 engr bn, 1 spt bn); 1 (28th) jungle bde (1 sf bn, 1 mech inf bn, 1 jng inf bn, 1 COIN, 1, 1 cbt engr bn, spt bn); 1 (rapid reaction) sy bde, 4 COIN bn)
1 inf bn
3 COIN mobile bde (each: 4 COIN bn, 1 spt bn)
1 lt cav bde (4 lt cav gp)

COMBAT SUPPORT
1 cbt engr bde (1 SF engr bn, 1 (emergency response) engr bn, 1 EOD bn, 1 construction bn, 1 demining bn, 1 maint bn)
1 int bde (2 SIGINT bn, 1 log bn, 1 maint bn)

COMBAT SERVICE SUPPORT
2 spt/log bde (each: 1 spt bn, 1 maint bn, 1 supply bn, 1 tpt bn, 1 medical bn, 1 log bn)

AVIATION
1 air aslt div (1 counter-narcotics bde (4 counter-narcotics bn, 1 spt bn); 1 (25th) avn bde (4 hel bn; 5 avn bn; 1 avn log bn); 1 (32nd) avn bde (1 avn bn, 2 maint bn, 1 avn bn, 1 spt bn); 1 SF avn bn)

EQUIPMENT BY TYPE
ARMOURED FIGHTING VEHICLES
  RECCE 121 EE-9 *Cascavel*
  IFV 60: 28 *Commando Advanced*; 32 LAV III
  APC 112
    APC (T) 42: 28 M113A1 (TPM-113A1); 14 M113A2 (TPM-113A2)

APC (W) 56 EE-11 *Urutu*; BTR-80†
PPV 14+: some *Hunter* XL; 4 RG-31 *Nyala*; 1 *Titan-A*; 4 *Titan-B*; 5 *Titan-C*; *Meteoro*
AUV 189: 176 M1117 *Guardian*; 13 *Sand Cat*

ANTI-TANK/ANTI-INFRASTRUCTURE
MSL
  SP 77 *Nimrod*
  MANPATS TOW; *Spike*-ER
RCL 106mm 73 M40A1

ARTILLERY 1,808
TOWED 120: **105mm** 107: 22 LG1 MkIII; 85 M101; **155mm** 13 155/52 APU SBT-1
MOR 1,688: **81mm** 1,507; **SP 120mm**: 12 M113A2 with Brandt (with 105mm RCL); **120mm** 169

AIRCRAFT
ELINT 3: 2 Beech B200 *King Air*; 1 Beech 350 *King Air*
TPT • Light 21: 2 An-32B; 3 Beech 350 *King Air*; 1 Beech C90 *King Air*; 2 C-212 *Aviocar* (Medevac); 8 Cessna 208B *Grand Caravan*; 1 Cessna 208B-EX *Grand Caravan*; 4 *Turbo Commander* 695A

HELICOPTERS
MRH 19: 8 Mi-17-1V *Hip*; 6 Mi-17MD; 5 Mi-17V-5 *Hip*
TPT 89: **Medium** 53: 46 UH-60L *Black Hawk*; 7 S-70i *Black Hawk*; **Light** 36: 22 Bell 205 (UH-1H *Iroquois*); 14 Bell 212 (UH-1N *Twin Huey*)

AIR DEFENCE • GUNS • TOWED 40mm 4 M1A1

Navy 58,000 (incl 12,100 conscript)
HQ located at Bogota
EQUIPMENT BY TYPE
SUBMARINES 4
  SSK 2 *Pijao* (GER Type-209/1200) each with 8 single 533mm TT each with *SeaHake* (DM2A3) HWT
  SSC 2 *Intrépido* (ex-GER Type-206A) each with 8 single 533mm TT each with *SeaHake* (DM2A3) HWT

PATROL AND COASTAL COMBATANTS 58
  CORVETTES 6
    FSGHM 4 *Almirante Padilla* with 2 quad lnchr with *Haeseong* I AShM, 2 twin *Simbad* lnchr with *Mistral* SAM, 2 triple 324mm ILAS-3 (B-515) ASTT each with A244/S LWT, 1 76mm gun (capacity 1 Bo-105/AS555SN *Fennec* hel)
    FSG 1 *Almirante Tono* (Ex-ROK *Po Hang* (Flight IV)) 2 twin lnchr with *Haeseong* I AShM, 2 triple 324mm ASTT with Mk 46, 2 76mm guns
    FS 1 *Narino* (ex-ROK *Dong Hae*) with 2 triple 324mm SVTT Mk 32 ASTT with Mk 46 LWT
  PSOH 3: 2 *20 de Julio* (CHL *Piloto Pardo*); 1 *20 de Julio* (CHL *Piloto Pardo*) with 1 76mm gun
  PCR 10: 2 *Arauca* with 1 76mm guns; 8 *Nodriza* (PAF I-IV) with hel landing platform
  PBR 39: 5 *Diligente*; 16 LPR-40; 3 Swiftships; 9 *Tenerife* (US Bender Marine 12m); 2 PAF-L; 4 others

AMPHIBIOUS • LANDING CRAFT 16
  LCT 6 *Golfo de Tribuga*
  LCU 2 *Morrosquillo* (LCU 1466)
  UCAC 8 *Griffon* 2000TD

LOGISTICS AND SUPPORT 7
  ABU 1 *Quindio*
  AG 1 *Inirida*
  AGOR 2 *Providencia*
  AGS 2: 1 *Caribe*; 1 *Roncador*
  AXS 1 *Gloria*

Coast Guard
EQUIPMENT BY TYPE
PATROL AND COASTAL COMBATANTS 16
  PCO 2: 1 *San Andres* (ex-US *Balsam*); 1 *Valle del Cauca Durable* (ex-US *Reliance*) with 1 hel landing platform
  PCC 3 *Punta Espada* (CPV-46)
  PB 11: 1 *11 de Noviembre* (CPV-40) (GER Fassmer); 2 *Castillo y Rada* (Swiftships 105); 2 *Jaime Gomez* (ex-US Peterson Mk 3); 1 *Jorge Luis Marrugo Campo*; 1 *José Maria Palas* (Swiftships 110); 3 *Point*; 1 *Toledo* (US Bender Marine 35m)

LOGISTICS AND SUPPORT • ABU 1 *Isla Albuquerque*

Naval Aviation 150
EQUIPMENT BY TYPE
AIRCRAFT
  MP 3 CN235 MPA *Persuader*
  ISR 1 PA-31 *Navajo*
  TPT • Light 16: 1 ATR-42; 2 Beech 350 *King Air*; 1 Beech 360ER *King Air*; 2 Beech C90 *King Air*; 1 C-212 (Medevac); 4 Cessna 206; 3 Cessna 208 *Caravan*; 1 PA-31 *Navajo*; 1 PA-34 *Seneca*

HELICOPTERS
  SAR 2 AS365 *Dauphin*
  MRH 9: 1 AS555SN *Fennec*; 3 Bell 412 *Twin Huey*; 4 Bell 412EP *Twin Huey*; 1 Bell 412EPI *Twin Huey*
  TPT • Light 8: 1 Bell 212; 4 Bell 212 (UH-1N); 1 BK-117; 2 Bo-105

Marines 24,000
FORCES BY ROLE
SPECIAL FORCES
  1 SF bde (4 SF bn)
MANOEUVRE
  Amphibious
  1 mne bde (1 SF (Gaula) bn, 5 mne bn, 2 rvn bn, 1 spt bn)
  1 mne bde (1 SF bn, 2 mne bn, 2 rvn bn, 1 spt bn)
  1 rvn bde (1 SF bn, 1 mne bn, 2 rvn bn, 1 spt bn)
  1 rvn bde (4 rvn bn)
  1 rvn bde (3 rvn bn)
COMBAT SERVICE SUPPORT
  1 log bde (6 spt bn)
  1 trg bde (7 trg bn, 1 spt bn)
EQUIPMENT BY TYPE
ARMOURED FIGHTING VEHICLES
APC

PPV: *Meteoro*
ARTILLERY • MOR 82: 81mm 74; 120mm 8
AIR DEFENCE • SAM • Point-defence *Mistral*

Air Force 15,600

FORCES BY ROLE
FIGHTER/GROUND ATTACK
  1 sqn with *Kfir* C-10/C-12/TC-12
GROUND ATTACK/ISR
  1 sqn with AC-47T; ECN235; IAI *Arava*
  1 sqn with EMB-312 *Tucano**
  2 sqn with EMB-314 *Super Tucano** (A-29)
GROUND ATTACK
  1 sqn with AC-47T *Spooky* (*Fantasma*); Bell 205 (UH-1H *Huey* II); Cessna 208 *Grand Caravan*
  1 sqn with Cessna 208 *Grand Caravan*; C-212; UH-60L *Black Hawk*
EW/ELINT
  2 sqn with Beech 350 *King Air*; Cessna 208; SA 2-37; *Turbo Commander* 695
ELINT
  2 sqn with Cessna 560
TRANSPORT
  1 (Presidential) sqn with AW139; B-737BBJ; EMB-600 *Legacy*; Bell 412EP; F-28 *Fellowship*; UH-60L *Black Hawk*
  1 sqn with B-737-400; B-737-800; Beech C90GTx *King Air*; C-130H *Hercules*; C-212; C295M; CN235M; KC-767
  1 sqn with Beech 350C *King Air*; Bell 212; Cessna 208B; EMB-110P1 (C-95)
  1 sqn with Beech C90 *King Air*
TRAINING
  1 sqn with Cessna 172
  1 sqn with Lancair *Synergy* (T-90 *Calima*)
  1 sqn with T-6C *Texan* II
  1 hel sqn with Bell 206B3
  1 hel sqn with TH-67
HELICOPTER
  1 sqn with AH-60L *Arpia* III
  1 sqn with UH-60L *Black Hawk* (CSAR)
  1 sqn with Hughes 500M
  1 sqn with Bell 205 (UH-1H *Huey* II)
  1 sqn with Bell 206B3 *Jet Ranger* III
  1 sqn with Bell 212; Bell 205 (UH-1H *Huey* II)
ISR UAV
  1 sqn with *Hermes* 450; *Hermes* 900
EQUIPMENT BY TYPE
ARMOURED FIGHTING VEHICLES
APC
  PPV: *Meteoro*
AIRCRAFT 62 combat capable
  FGA 20: 8 *Kfir* C-10; 9 *Kfir* C-12; 3 *Kfir* TC-12
  ATK 6 AC-47T *Spooky* (*Fantasma*)
  ISR 11: 5 Cessna 560 *Citation* II; 6 SA 2-37
  ELINT 11: 3 Beech 350 *King Air*; 6 Cessna 208 *Grand Caravan*; 1 ECN235; 1 *Turbo Commander* 695
  TKR/TPT 1 KC-767
  TPT 71: **Medium** 7: 6 C-130H *Hercules*; 1 B-737F; **Light** 52: 7 ATR-42; 2 Beech 300 *King Air*; 2 Beech 350C *King Air* (medevac); 1 Beech 350i *King Air* (VIP); 2 Beech 350 *King Air* (medevac); 2 Beech C90 *King Air*; 3 Beech C90GTx *King Air*; 4 C-212; 6 C295M; 8 Cessna 172; 1 Cessna 182R; 12 Cessna 208B (medevac); 1 CN235M; 2 EMB-110P1 (C-95); **PAX** 12: 2 B-737-400; 2 B-737-800; 1 B-737BBJ (VIP); 2 ERJ-135BJ *Legacy* 600 (VIP); 2 ERJ-145; 1 F-28-1000 *Fellowship*; 1 F-28-3000 *Fellowship*; 1 Learjet 60
  TRG 65: 12 EMB-312 *Tucano**; 24 EMB-314 *Super Tucano* (A-29)*; 22 Lancair *Synergy* (T-90 *Calima*); 7 T-6C *Texan* II
HELICOPTERS
  MRH 18: 4 AH-60L *Arpia* III; 10 AH-60L *Arpia* IV; 1 AW139 (VIP); 1 Bell 412EP *Twin Huey* (VIP); 2 Hughes 500M
  TPT 48: **Medium** 16 UH-60L *Black Hawk* (incl 1 VIP hel); **Light** 32: 9 Bell 205 (UH-1H *Huey* II); 12 Bell 206B3 *Jet Ranger* III; 11 Bell 212
  TRG 60 TH-67
UNINHABITED AERIAL VEHICLES • ISR • Medium 8: 6 *Hermes* 450; 2 *Hermes* 900
AIR-LAUNCHED MISSILES
  AAM • IR *Python* 3; IIR *Python* 4; *Python* 5; ARH *Derby*; I-*Derby* ER (reported)
  ASM *Spike*-ER; *Spike*-NLOS
BOMBS
  Laser-guided *Paveway* II
  INS/GPS guided *Spice*

Gendarmerie & Paramilitary 165,050

National Police Force 165,050
EQUIPMENT BY TYPE
AIRCRAFT
  ELINT 5 C-26B *Metroliner*
  TPT • **Light** 41: 5 ATR-42; 3 Beech 200 *King Air*; 2 Beech 300 *King Air*; 2 Beech 1900; 3 BT-67; 3 C-26 *Metroliner*; 3 Cessna 152; 3 Cessna 172; 9 Cessna 206; 2 Cessna 208 *Caravan*; 2 DHC-6 *Twin Otter*; 1 DHC-8; 3 PA-31 *Navajo*
HELICOPTERS
  MRH 5: 2 Bell 407GXP; 1 Bell 412EP; 2 MD-500D
  TPT 83: **Medium** 25: 13 UH-60A *Black Hawk*; 9 UH-60L *Black Hawk*; 3 S-70i *Black Hawk*; **Light** 58: 34 Bell 205 (UH-1H-II *Huey* II); 6 Bell 206B; 5 Bell 206L/L3/L4 *Long Ranger*; 8 Bell 212; 5 Bell 407

DEPLOYMENT

CENTRAL AFRICAN REPUBLIC: UN • MINUSCA 2
EGYPT: MFO 275; 1 inf bn
LEBANON: UN • UNIFIL 1
WESTERN SAHARA: UN • MINURSO 2

FOREIGN FORCES
United States US Southern Command: 50

Costa Rica CRI

Costa Rican Colon CRC		2023	2024	2025
GDP	CRC	47.1trn	49.2trn	52.3trn
	USD	86.5bn	95.1bn	101bn
Real GDP growth	%	5.1	4.0	3.5
Sy Bdgt [a]	CRC	269bn	295bn	320bn
	USD	495m	570m	616m
FMA (US)	USD	7.5m	n.a.	n.a.

[a] Paramilitary budget

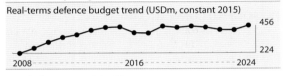
Real-terms defence budget trend (USDm, constant 2015)

Population	5,265,575					
Age	0–14	15–19	20–24	25–29	30–64	65 plus
Male	9.6%	3.6%	3.7%	4.0%	24.1%	5.1%
Female	9.2%	3.4%	3.6%	3.8%	24.0%	6.0%

Capabilities

Costa Rica relies on police and coastguard organisations for internal security, maritime and air domain awareness and counter-narcotics tasks. The armed forces were constitutionally abolished in 1949. Colombia and the US provide assistance and training to Costa Rica focused on policing and internal-security tasks. The Special Intervention Unit has received specialist training from non-regional states, including the US. The US and others have been assisting Costa Rica in building defences against cyber threats, after a 2022 cyber attack. Public force, coastguard and air surveillance units have little heavy equipment, and recent modernisation has depended on donations from countries such as China and the US. Apart from limited maintenance facilities, Costa Rica has no domestic defence industry.

Gendarmerie & Paramilitary 9,950

ORGANISATIONS BY SERVICE

Gendarmerie & Paramilitary 9,950

Special Intervention Unit
FORCES BY ROLE
SPECIAL FORCES
1 spec ops unit
EQUIPMENT BY TYPE
ARMOURED FIGHTING VEHICLES
APC • PPV Roshel *Senator*

Public Force 9,000
11 regional directorates

Coast Guard Unit 550
EQUIPMENT BY TYPE
PATROL AND COASTAL COMBATANTS 10
PB 10: 1 *Cabo Blanco* (US *Swift* 65); 1 Defiant 85; 1 *Isla del Coco* (US *Swift* 105); 3 *Libertador Juan Rafael Mora* (ex-US *Island*); 2 *Point*; 1 *Primera Dama* (US *Swift* 42); 1 *Puerto Quepos* (US *Swift* 36)

Air Surveillance Unit 400
EQUIPMENT BY TYPE
AIRCRAFT • TPT • **Light** 14: 2 Cessna T210 *Centurion*; 4 Cessna U206G *Stationair*; 2 PA-31 *Navajo*; 2 PA-34 *Seneca*; 1 Piper PA-23 *Aztec*; 1 Cessna 182RG; 2 Y-12E
HELICOPTERS
MRH 3: 1 MD-500E; 2 MD-600N
TPT • **Light** 4 Bell 212 (UH-1N)

Cuba CUB

Definitive macro- and defence-economic data not available

Population	10,966,038					
Age	0–14	15–19	20–24	25–29	30–64	65 plus
Male	8.4%	2.7%	3.0%	3.1%	24.7%	7.8%
Female	7.9%	2.5%	2.8%	2.8%	25.0%	9.4%

Capabilities

Cuba's armed forces are principally focused on protecting territorial integrity and rely on a mass mobilisation system. Military capability is limited by equipment obsolescence and the largely conscript-based force. Cuba maintains military ties with China and Russia, and the latter has supplied oil and fuel following Venezuela's economic collapse. Defence cooperation with Russia is largely centred around technical and maintenance support. Cooperation with China appears to be on a smaller scale and involves training agreements and personnel exchanges. In recent years, Cuba has sent medics and maintenance personnel to South Africa and has also trained some South African personnel in Cuba. The armed forces now have little logistical capability to support operational deployments abroad. The inventory is almost entirely composed of legacy Soviet-era systems with varying degrees of obsolescence. Serviceability appears problematic, with much equipment at a low level of availability and maintenance demands growing as fleets age. Much of the aviation fleet is reportedly in storage. It is unlikely that significant equipment recapitalisation can be financed in the near term. Cuba has little in the way of a domestic defence industry, apart from some upgrade and maintenance capacity.

ACTIVE 49,000 (Army 38,000 Navy 3,000 Air 8,000)
Gendarmerie & Paramilitary 26,500

Conscript liability 2 years

RESERVE 39,000 (Army 39,000) **Gendarmerie & Paramilitary 1,120,000**

Ready Reserves (serve 45 days per year) to fill out Active and Reserve units; see also Paramilitary

ORGANISATIONS BY SERVICE

Army ε38,000
FORCES BY ROLE
COMMAND
3 regional comd HQ
3 army comd HQ
SPECIAL FORCES
1 SF bde
3 SF regt
MANOEUVRE
Armoured
1 tk div (3 tk bde)
Mechanised
2 (mixed) mech bde
Light
2 (frontier) bde
AIR DEFENCE
1 ADA regt
1 SAM bde

Reserves 39,000
FORCES BY ROLE
MANOEUVRE
Light
14 inf bde
EQUIPMENT BY TYPE†
ARMOURED FIGHTING VEHICLES
MBT ε400 T-54/T-55/T-62
LT TK PT-76
ASLT BTR-60 100mm
RECCE BRDM-2;
IFV ε50 BMP-1/1P
APC ε500 BTR-152/BTR-50/BTR-60
ABCV BMD-1
ANTI-TANK/ANTI-INFRASTRUCTURE
MSL
SP 2K16 *Shmel* (RS-AT-1 *Snapper*)
MANPATS 9K11 *Malyutka* (RS-AT-3 *Sagger*)
GUNS 600+: **57mm** 600 ZIS-2 (M-1943); **85mm** D-44
ARTILLERY 1,715+
SP 40+: **100mm** AAPMP-100; CATAP-100; **122mm** 2S1 *Gvozdika*; AAP-T-122; AAP-BMP-122; *Jupiter* III; *Jupiter* IV; **130mm** AAP-T-130; *Jupiter* V; **152mm** 2S3 *Akatsiya*
TOWED 500: **122mm** D-30; M-30 (M-1938); **130mm** M-46; **152mm** D-1; M-1937 (ML-20)
MRL • SP 175: **122mm** BM-21 *Grad*; **140mm** BM-14
MOR 1,000: **82mm** M-41; **82mm** M-43; **120mm** M-43; M-38
AIR DEFENCE
SAM
Short-range 2K12 *Kub* (RS-SA-6 *Gainful*)

Pont-defence 200+: 200 9K35 *Strela*-10 (RS-SA-13 *Gopher*); 9K33 *Osa* (RS-SA-8 *Gecko*); 9K31 *Strela*-1 (RS-SA-9 *Gaskin*); 9K36 *Strela*-3 (RS-SA-14 *Gremlin*); 9K310 *Igla*-1 (SA-16 *Gimlet*); 9K32 *Strela*-2 (RS-SA-7 *Grail*)‡
GUNS 400
SP **23mm** ZSU-23-4; **30mm** BTR-60P SP; **57mm** ZSU-57-2
TOWED **100mm** KS-19/M-1939/**85mm** KS-12/**57mm** S-60/**37mm** M-1939/**30mm** M-53/**23mm** ZU-23

Navy ε3,000
Western Comd HQ at Cabanas; Eastern Comd HQ at Holquin
EQUIPMENT BY TYPE
SUBMARINES • SSW 1 *Delfin*
PATROL AND COASTAL COMBATANTS 9
PCG 2 *Rio Damuji* with two single P-22 (RS-SS-N-2C *Styx*) AShM, 2 57mm guns, 1 hel landing platform
PCM 1 Project 1241PE (FSU *Pauk* II) with 1 quad lnchr (manual aiming) with 9K32 *Strela*-2 (RS-SA-N-5 *Grail*) SAM, 2 RBU 1200 A/S mor, 1 76mm gun
PBF 6 Project 205 (FSU *Osa* II)† each with 4 single lnchr (for P-20U (RS-SS-N-2B *Styx*) AShM – missiles removed to coastal-defence units)
MINE WARFARE AND MINE COUNTERMEASURES 5
MHI 3 *Korund* (Project 1258 (*Yevgenya*))†
MSC 2 *Yakhont* (FSU Project 1265 (*Sonya*))†
LOGISTICS AND SUPPORT 2
ABU 1
AX 1

Coastal Defence
EQUIPMENT BY TYPE
ARTILLERY • TOWED 122mm M-1931/37; **130mm** M-46; **152mm** M-1937
COASTAL DEFENCE • AShM 4+: *Bandera* IV (reported); 4 4K51 *Rubezh* (RS-SSC-3 *Styx*)

Naval Infantry 550+
FORCES BY ROLE
MANOEUVRE
Amphibious
2 amph aslt bn

Anti-aircraft Defence and Revolutionary Air Force ε8,000 (incl conscripts)
Air assets divided between Western Air Zone and Eastern Air Zone
FORCES BY ROLE
FIGHTER/GROUND ATTACK
3 sqn with MiG-21bis/UM *Fishbed*; MiG-29/MiG-29UB *Fulcrum*
TRANSPORT
1 (VIP) tpt sqn with An-24 *Coke*; Mi-8P *Hip*
ATTACK HELICOPTER

2 sqn with Mi-17 *Hip* H; Mi-35 *Hind*

TRAINING
1 (tac trg) sqn with L-39C *Albatros* (basic); Z-142 (primary)

EQUIPMENT BY TYPE

AIRCRAFT 10 combat capable
FTR 5: 2 MiG-29 *Fulcrum*†; 3 MiG-29UB *Fulcrum*†
FGA 5: ε3 MiG-21bis *Fishbed*; ε2 MiG-21UM *Fishbed*
ISR 1 An-30 *Clank*†
TPT 23: **Heavy** 2 Il-76 *Candid*; **Light** 9: 1 An-24 *Coke* (Aerogaviota); 3 An-26 *Curl* (Aerogaviota); 5 ATR-42-500 (Cubana & Aergaviota); **PAX** 12: 6 An-158 (Cubana); 3 Il-96-300 (Cubana); 3 Tu-204E-100 (Cubana)
TRG 25+: ε25 L-39 *Albatros*; some Z-142C

HELICOPTERS
ATK 4 Mi-35 *Hind*† (8 more in store)
MRH 7 Mi-17 *Hip* H (12 more in store)
TPT • Medium 2 Mi-8P *Hip*

AIR DEFENCE • SAM
Medium-range S-75 *Dvina* (RS-SA-2 *Guideline*); S-75 *Dvina* mod (RS-SA-2 *Guideline* – on T-55 chassis)
Short-range S-125M/M1 *Pechora*-M/M1 (RS-SA-3 *Goa*); S-125M1 *Pechora*-M1 mod (RS-SA-3 *Goa* – on T-55 chassis)

AIR-LAUNCHED MISSILES
AAM • IR R-3‡ (RS-AA-2 *Atoll*); R-60 (RS-AA-8 *Aphid*); R-73 (RS-AA-11A *Archer*); **IR/SARH** R-23/24‡ (RS-AA-7 *Apex*); R-27 (RS-AA-10 *Alamo*)
ASM Kh-23‡ (RS-AS-7 *Kerry*)

Gendarmerie & Paramilitary 26,500 active

State Security 20,000
Ministry of Interior

Border Guards 6,500
Ministry of Interior
PATROL AND COASTAL COMBATANTS 20
  PCC 2 *Stenka*
  PB 18 *Zhuk*

Youth Labour Army 70,000 reservists

Civil Defence Force 50,000 reservists

Territorial Militia ε1,000,000 reservists

FOREIGN FORCES
United States US Southern Command: 550 (JTF-GTMO) at Guantanamo Bay

Dominican Republic DOM

Dominican Peso DOP		2023	2024	2025
GDP	DOP	6.82trn	7.45trn	8.15trn
	USD	122bn	126bn	136bn
Real GDP growth	%	2.4	5.1	5.0
Def bdgt	DOP	49.9bn	58.3bn	64.0bn
	USD	891m	988m	1.06bn

Real-terms defence budget trend (USDm, constant 2015)

Population	10,815,857					
Age	0–14	15–19	20–24	25–29	30–64	65 plus
Male	13.0%	4.4%	4.4%	4.2%	20.8%	3.7%
Female	12.6%	4.3%	4.3%	4.1%	20.3%	4.0%

Capabilities

The principal tasks for the Dominican armed forces include internal- and border-security missions as well as disaster relief. Training and operations increasingly focus on counter-narcotics and include collaboration with the police in an inter-agency task force. The US sends training teams to the country under the terms of a 2015 military-partnership agreement, and the navy has trained with French forces. The Dominican Republic has participated in US SOUTHCOM's *Tradewinds* exercise. In response to instability in Haiti, the government closed the border, the army has strengthened its presence along the frontier, establishing new surveillance posts, and the air force has carried out overflight operations. The country has little capacity to deploy and sustain forces abroad. The army's limited number of armoured vehicles are obsolete and likely difficult to maintain. The air force operates a modest number of light fixed-wing and rotary-wing assets, and the navy a small fleet of mainly ex-US patrol craft of varying sizes. The country has maintenance facilities, but no defence industry.

ACTIVE 56,800 (Army 29,500 Navy 11,200 Air 16,100) **Gendarmerie & Paramilitary 15,000**

ORGANISATIONS BY SERVICE

Army 29,500
5 Defence Zones
FORCES BY ROLE
SPECIAL FORCES
1 air cav bde (1 cdo bn, 1 (6th) mtn bn, 1 hel sqn with Bell 205 (op by Air Force); OH-58 *Kiowa*; R-22; R-44 *Raven* II)
3 SF bn
1 MP bn
MANOEUVRE
Light
3 (1st, 2nd & 3rd) inf bde (3 inf bn)
3 (4th, 5th & 6th) inf bde (2 inf bn)

1 (7th) inf bde (3 inf bn) (forming)
Other
1 (Presidential Guard) gd regt
1 (MoD) sy bn
COMBAT SUPPORT
1 cbt spt bde (1 lt armd bn, 1 arty bn)
COMBAT SERVICE SUPPORT
1 CSS bde (1 engr bn, 1 sig bn, 1 log bn)
EQUIPMENT BY TYPE
ARMOURED FIGHTING VEHICLES
LT TK 12 M41B (76mm)
APC • APC (W) 8 LAV-150 Commando
ANTI-TANK/ANTI-INFRASTRUCTURE
RCL 106mm 20 M40A1
GUNS 37mm 20 M3
ARTILLERY 104
TOWED 105mm 16: 4 M101; 12 Reinosa 105/26
MOR 88: 81mm 60 M1; 107mm 4 M30; 120mm 24 Expal Model L
HELICOPTERS
ISR 8: 4 OH-58A Kiowa; 4 OH-58C Kiowa
TPT • Light 6: 4 R-22; 2 R-44 Raven II
TRG 2 TH-67 Creek

Navy 11,200

HQ located at Santo Domingo
FORCES BY ROLE
SPECIAL FORCES
1 (SEAL) SF unit
MANOEUVRE
Amphibious
1 mne sy unit
EQUIPMENT BY TYPE
PATROL AND COASTAL COMBATANTS 17
PCO 1 Almirante Didiez Burgos (ex-US Balsam)
PCC 2 Tortuguero (ex-US White Sumac)
PB 14: 1 Altair (Swiftships 35m); 4 Bellatrix (US Sewart Seacraft); 1 Betelgeuse (Damen Stan Patrol 2606); 2 Canopus (Swiftships 110); 3 Hamal (Damen Stan Patrol 1505); 3 Point
AMPHIBIOUS • LANDING CRAFT
LCU 1 Neyba (ex-US LCU 1675)
LOGISTICS AND SUPPORT 1
AX 1 Almirante Juan Bautista Cambiaso

Air Force 16,100

FORCES BY ROLE
GROUND ATTACK
1 sqn with EMB-314 Super Tucano*
SEARCH & RESCUE
1 sqn with AW169; Bell 205 (UH-1H Huey II); Bell 205 (UH-1H Iroquois); Bell 430 (VIP); OH-58 Kiowa (CH-136); S-333
TRANSPORT
1 sqn with C-212-400 Aviocar; PA-31 Navajo
TRAINING
1 sqn with T-35B Pillan; TP75 Dulus
AIR DEFENCE
1 ADA bn with 20mm guns
EQUIPMENT BY TYPE
AIRCRAFT 8 combat capable
ISR 1 AMT-200 Super Ximango
TPT • Light 13: 3 C-212-400 Aviocar; 1 Cessna 172; 1 Cessna 182; 1 Cessna 206; 1 Cessna 207; 1 Commander 690; 3 EA-100; 1 PA-31 Navajo; 1 P2006T
TRG 21: 8 EMB-314 Super Tucano*; 11 T-35B Pillan; 2 TP75 Dulus
HELICOPTERS
ISR 9 OH-58 Kiowa (CH-136)
TPT • Light 24: 2 AW169; 14 Bell 205 (UH-1H Huey II); 5 Bell 205 (UH-1H Iroquois); 1 H155 (VIP); 2 S-333
AIR DEFENCE • GUNS 20mm 4

Gendarmerie & Paramilitary 15,000

National Police 15,000

Ecuador ECU

United States Dollar USD		2023	2024	2025
GDP	USD	119bn	121bn	126bn
Real GDP growth	%	2.4	0.3	1.2
Def bdgt	USD	1.67bn	1.63bn	
FMA (US)	USD	5m	5m	5m

Real-terms defence budget trend (USDbn, constant 2015)

Population 18,309,984

Age	0–14	15–19	20–24	25–29	30–64	65 plus
Male	13.7%	4.8%	4.5%	4.1%	18.2%	4.1%
Female	13.1%	4.6%	4.4%	4.1%	19.5%	5.0%

Capabilities

Ecuador's armed forces are focused on internal-security tasks. The political crisis in neighbouring Venezuela and resulting refugee flows have added to security challenges in the northern border area. These conditions led the armed forces to create a joint task force for counter-insurgency and counter-narcotics operations. The administration has proposed lifting the ban on foreign military bases. Defence cooperation with Peru includes demining efforts on the border. Quito signed a defence agreement with Colombia in 2022 to increase joint operations to counter drug trafficking and illicit smuggling. Military ties with Washington have been revived, leading to the re-establishment of bilateral training programmes and equipment donations. The armed forces have participated in multinational military exercises. The country has limited capability to deploy independently beyond national borders. The equipment inventory is increasingly obsolete, and low availability is a challenge. Modernisation plans are modest in scope and currently focused on armoured vehicles as well as maritime-patrol capabilities. Ecuador's defence industries are mostly state-owned, including shipyard ASTINAVE, which has some construction, maintenance and repair capabilities.

ACTIVE 39,600 (Army 24,000 Navy 9,400 Air 6,200)
Paramilitary 500

Conscript liability Voluntary conscription

RESERVE 118,000 (Joint 118,000)

Ages 18–55

ORGANISATIONS BY SERVICE

Army 24,000
FORCES BY ROLE
gp are bn sized
COMMAND
  4 div HQ
SPECIAL FORCES
  1 (9th) SF bde (3 SF gp, 1 SF sqn, 1 para bn, 1 sigs sqn, 1 log comd)
MANOEUVRE
  Mechanised
  1 (11th) armd cav bde (3 armd cav gp, 1 mech inf bn, 1 SP arty gp, 1 engr gp)
  1 (5th) inf bde (1 SF sqn, 2 mech cav gp, 2 inf bn, 1 cbt engr coy, 1 sigs coy, 1 log coy)
  1 (3rd) mech cav bde (2 mech cav gp, 1 hel gp) (forming)
  Light
  1 (1st) inf bde (1 SF sqn, 1 armd cav gp, 1 armd recce sqn, 3 inf bn, 1 med coy)
  1 (3rd) inf bde (1 SF gp, 1 mech cav gp, 1 inf bn, 1 arty gp, 1 hvy mor coy, 1 cbt engr coy, 1 sigs coy, 1 log coy)
  1 (7th) inf bde (1 SF sqn, 1 armd recce sqn, 1 mech cav gp, 3 inf bn, 1 jungle bn, 1 arty gp, 1 cbt engr coy, 1 sigs coy, 1 log coy, 1 med coy)
  1 (13th) inf bde (1 SF sqn, 1 armd recce sqn, 1 mot cav gp, 3 inf bn, 1 arty gp, 1 hvy mor coy, 1 cbt engr coy, 1sigs coy, 1 log coy)
  2 (17th & 21st) jungle bde (3 jungle bn, 1 cbt engr coy, 1 sigs coy, 1 log coy)
  1 (19th) jungle bde (3 jungle bn, 1 jungle trg bn, 1 cbt engr coy, 1 sigs coy, 1 log coy)
COMBAT SUPPORT
  1 (27th) arty bde (1 SP arty gp, 1 MRL gp, 1 ADA gp, 1 cbt engr coy, 1 sigs coy, 1 log coy)
  1 (23rd) engr bde (3 engr bn)
  2 indep MP coy
  1 indep sigs coy
COMBAT SERVICE SUPPORT
  1 (25th) log bde (1 log bn, 1 tpt bn, 1 maint bn, 1 med bn)
  9 indep med coy
AVIATION
  1 (15th) avn bde (2 tpt avn gp, 2 hel gp, 1 mixed avn gp)

AIR DEFENCE
  1 ADA gp
EQUIPMENT BY TYPE
ARMOURED FIGHTING VEHICLES
  LT TK 25 AMX-13
  RECCE 42: 10 EE-3 *Jararaca*; 32 EE-9 *Cascavel*
  APC 163
    APC (T) 102: 82 AMX-VCI; 20 M113
    APC (W) 49: 17 EE-11 *Urutu*; 32 UR-416
    PPV 12 *Mbombe* 6×6
  AUV 35: 20 *Cobra* II; 15 Otokar *Ural*
ARTILLERY 499
  SP 155mm 12 Mk F3
  TOWED 106: **105mm** 84: 36 M101; 24 M2A2; 24 Model 56 pack howitzer; **155mm** 22: 12 M114; 10 M198
  MRL 122mm 24: 18 BM-21 *Grad*; 6 RM-70
  MOR 81mm 357 M29
AIRCRAFT
  TPT • Light 10: 1 Beech 200 *King Air*; 2 C-212; 1 CN235; 2 Cessna 172; 1 Cessna 206; 1 Cessna 500 *Citation* I; 1 IAI-201 *Arava*; 1 M-28 *Skytruck*
  TRG 4: 2 MX-7-235 *Star Rocket*; 2 T-41D *Mescalero*
HELICOPTERS
  MRH 30: 7 H125M (AS550C3) *Fennec*; 3 Mi-17-1V *Hip*; 2 SA315B *Lama*; 18 SA342L *Gazelle* (13 with HOT for anti-armour role)
  TPT 12: **Medium** 8: 5 AS332B *Super Puma*; 1 Mi-171E; 2 SA330 *Puma*; **Light** 4: 2 H125 (AS350B2) *Ecureuil*; 2 H125 (AS350B3) *Ecureuil*
AIR DEFENCE
  SAM • Point-defence *Blowpipe*; 9K32 *Strela*-2 (RS-SA-7 *Grail*)‡; 9K38 *Igla* (RS-SA-18 *Grouse*)
  GUNS 240
    SP 20mm 44 M163 *Vulcan*
    TOWED 196: **14.5mm** 128 ZPU-1/-2; **20mm** 38: 28 M-1935, 10 M167 *Vulcan*; **40mm** 30 L/70/M1A1
AIR-LAUNCHED MISSILES • ASM HOT

Navy 9,400 (incl Naval Aviation, Marines and Coast Guard)
EQUIPMENT BY TYPE
SUBMARINES 2
  SSK 2 *Shyri* (GER T-209/1300) with 8 single 533mm TT each with A184 mod 3 HWT
PRINCIPAL SURFACE COMBATANTS • FRIGATES 2
  FFGH 2 *Moran Valverde* (ex-UK *Leander* batch II) with 1 quad lnchr with MM40 *Exocet* AShM, 2 triple 324mm ILAS-3 (B-515) ASTT with A244 LWT, 1 Mk 15 *Phalanx* CIWS, 1 twin 114mm gun (capacity 1 Bell 230 hel)
PATROL AND COASTAL COMBATANTS 9
  CORVETTES • FSGM 6
    5 *Esmeraldas* (ITA Tipo 550) with 2 triple lnchr with MM40 *Exocet* AShM, 1 quad *Albatros* lnchr with *Aspide* SAM, 2 triple 324mm ILAS-3 (B-515)

ASTT with A244 LWT, 1 76mm gun, 1 hel landing platform
1 *Esmeraldas* (ITA Tipo 550) with 2 triple lnchr with MM40 *Exocet* AShM, 1 quad *Albatros* lnchr with *Aspide* SAM, 1 76mm gun, 1 hel landing platform

PCFG 3 *Quito* (GER Lurssen TNC-45 45m) with 4 single lnchr with MM38 *Exocet* AShM, 1 76mm gun

LOGISTICS AND SUPPORT 8

AE 1 *Calicuchima*
AGOR 1 *Orion* with 1 hel landing platform
AGS 1 *Sirius*
AK 1 *Hualcopo* (ex-PRC *Fu Yuan Yu Leng* 999)
AKL 1 *Isla Bartolome* (operated by TRANSNAVE)
ATF 1 *Chimborazo*
AWT 1 *Atahualpa*
AXS 1 *Guayas*

Naval Aviation 380

EQUIPMENT BY TYPE
AIRCRAFT
   MP 2: 1 CN235-100; 1 CN235-300M
   ISR 3: 2 Beech 200T *King Air*; 1 Beech 300 *Catpass King Air*
   TPT • Light 2: 1 Beech 200 *King Air*; 1 Beech 300 *King Air*
   TRG 3 T-35B *Pillan*
HELICOPTERS
   TPT • Light 8: 3 Bell 206A; 3 Bell 206B; 1 Bell 230; 1 Bell 430
UNINHABITED AERIAL VEHICLES
   ISR 4: **Heavy** 2 *Heron*; **Medium** 2 *Searcher* Mk.II

Marines 1,950

FORCES BY ROLE
SPECIAL FORCES
   1 cdo bn
MANOEUVRE
   Amphibious
      5 mne bn
EQUIPMENT BY TYPE
ARTILLERY • MOR 32+ **81mm/120mm**
AIR DEFENCE • SAM • Point-defence 9K38 *Igla* (RS-SA-18 *Grouse*)

Air Force 6,200

Operational Command
FORCES BY ROLE
FIGHTER
   1 sqn with *Cheetah* C/D
GROUND ATTACK
   1 sqn with EMB-314 *Super Tucano**

Military Air Transport Group
FORCES BY ROLE
ISR
   1 sqn with Beech 350i *King Air*; Gulfstream G-1159; *Sabreliner* 40
SEARCH & RESCUE/TRANSPORT HELICOPTER
   1 sqn with AW119 *Koala*; Bell 206B *Jet Ranger* II; H145
   1 sqn with Cessna 206; PA-34 *Seneca*
TRANSPORT
   1 sqn with C295M
   1 sqn with DHC-6-300 *Twin Otter*
   1 sqn with B-727; B-737-200; C-130H *Hercules*; L-100-30
TRAINING
   1 sqn with DA20-C1
   1 sqn with G-120TP

EQUIPMENT BY TYPE
AIRCRAFT 17 combat capable
   TPT 20: **Medium** 2: 1 C-130H *Hercules*; 1 L-100-30; (2 C-130B *Hercules*; 1 C-130H *Hercules* in store); **Light** 11: 1 Beech E90 *King Air*; 1 Beech 350i *King Air*; 3 C295M; 1 Cessna 206; 3 DHC-6 *Twin Otter*; 1 PA-34 *Seneca*; 1 *Sabreliner* 40; **PAX** 7: 2 A320 (operated by TAME); 2 B-727; 1 B-737-200; 1 *Falcon* 7X; 1 Gulfstream G-1159
   TRG 36: 11 DA20-C1; 17 EMB-314 *Super Tucano**; 8 G-120TP
HELICOPTERS • TPT • Light 13: 4 AW119 *Koala*; 6 Bell 206B *Jet Ranger* II; 3 H145
AIR-LAUNCHED MISSILES • AAM • IR *Python* 3; R-550 *Magic*; **IIR** *Python* 4
AIR DEFENCE
   SAM • Point-defence 10+: 10 9K33 *Osa* (RS-SA-8 *Gecko*); 9K310 *Igla*-1 (RS-SA-16 *Gimlet*)
   GUNS • TOWED 52: **23mm** 34 ZU-23; **35mm** 18 GDF-002 (twin)

Paramilitary 500

Coast Guard 500
EQUIPMENT BY TYPE
PATROL AND COASTAL COMBATANTS 21
   PCC 7: 3 *Isla Fernandina* (*Vigilante*); 2 *Isla San Cristóbal* (Damen Stan Patrol 5009); 2 *Isla Floreana* (ex-ROK *Hae Uri*)
   PB 13: 2 *Espada*; 2 *Manta* (GER Lurssen 36m); 1 *Point*; 4 *Rio Coca*; 4 *Isla Santa Cruz* (Damen Stan 2606)
   PBR 1 *Rio Puyango*

DEPLOYMENT

CENTRAL AFRICAN REPUBLIC: UN • MINUSCA 2
SOUTH SUDAN: UN • UNMISS 3
SUDAN: UN • UNISFA 2
WESTERN SAHARA: UN • MINURSO 3

El Salvador SLV

United States Dollar USD		2023	2024	2025
GDP	USD	34.0bn	35.8bn	37.8bn
Real GDP growth	%	3.5	3.0	3.0
Def bdgt	USD	251m	261m	314m

Real-terms defence budget trend (USDm, constant 2015)

Population 6,628,702

Age	0–14	15–19	20–24	25–29	30–64	65 plus
Male	12.9%	3.8%	4.2%	4.6%	18.6%	3.6%
Female	12.3%	3.8%	4.2%	4.7%	22.3%	4.8%

Capabilities

The primary challenge for El Salvador's armed forces is tackling organised crime and aiding the National Civil Policy in combating narcotics trafficking. A spike in homicide rates in early 2020 led to emergency measures and widespread arrests. The government used large-scale personnel deployments, aimed at suppressing gang control in affected areas, with some of the measures winning domestic support but raising international human rights concerns. El Salvador participates in a tri-national border task force with Guatemala and Honduras. The armed forces have long-standing training ties with regional states and the US, focused on internal security, disaster relief and support to civilian authorities. El Salvador has deployed on UN peacekeeping missions up to company strength but lacks the logistical support to sustain independent international deployments. Most of its equipment is operational, indicating adequate support and maintenance. El Salvador lacks a substantive defence industry but has successfully produced light armoured vehicles based on commercial vehicles.

ACTIVE 26,000 (Army 22,000 Navy 2,000 Air 2,000)
Paramilitary 26,000

Conscript liability 12 months (selective); 11 months for officers and NCOs

RESERVE 9,900 (Joint 9,900)

ORGANISATIONS BY SERVICE

Army 22,000
FORCES BY ROLE
SPECIAL FORCES
  1 spec ops gp (1 SF coy, 1 para bn, 1 (naval inf) coy)
MANOEUVRE
  Reconnaissance
  1 armd cav regt (2 armd cav bn)
  Light
  6 inf bde (3 inf bn)
  Other
  1 (special) sy bde (2 border gd bn, 2 MP bn)
COMBAT SUPPORT
  1 arty bde (2 fd arty bn, 1 AD bn)
  1 engr comd (2 engr bn)
EQUIPMENT BY TYPE
ARMOURED FIGHTING VEHICLES
  RECCE 5 AML-90 (4 more in store)
  APC 46
    APC (W) 38: 30 VAL *Cashuat* (mod); 8 UR-416
    PPV 8 BMC *Vuran*
  AUV 5+ *SandCat*
ANTI-TANK/ANTI-INFRASTRUCTURE
  RCL 399: **106mm** 20 M40A1 (incl 16 SP); **90mm** 379 M67
ARTILLERY 233+
  TOWED 70+: **105mm** 58+: 36 M102; 18 M-56 (FRY); 4+ Oto Melara Mod 56; **155mm** 12 M198
  MOR 163: **81mm** 151 M29; **120mm** 12 UBM 52; (some M-74 in store)
AIR DEFENCE • GUNS 35: **20mm** 31 M-55; 4 TCM-20

Navy 2,000
EQUIPMENT BY TYPE
PATROL AND COASTAL COMBATANTS 12
  PB 12: 1 Bering 65; 3 Camcraft (30m); 1 Defiant 85; 1 Swiftships 77; 1 Swiftships 65; 4 Type-44 (ex-US); 1 YP 660
AMPHIBIOUS • LANDING CRAFT • LCM 4 LCM 8 (of which 3†)

Naval Inf (SF Commandos) 90
FORCES BY ROLE
SPECIAL FORCES
  1 SF coy

Air Force 2,000
FORCES BY ROLE
FIGHTER/GROUND ATTACK/ISR
  1 sqn with A-37B/OA-37B *Dragonfly*; O-2A/B *Skymaster**
TRANSPORT
  1 sqn with Cessna 208B *Grand Caravan* EX; Cessna 337G; IAI-202 *Arava*
TRAINING
  1 sqn with R-235GT *Guerrier*; SR22T; T-35 *Pillan*; T-41D *Mescalero*; TH-300; TH-300C
TRANSPORT HELICOPTER
  1 sqn with Bell 205 (UH-1H *Iroquois*); Bell 407; Bell 412EP *Twin Huey*; MD-530F; UH-1M *Iroquois*
EQUIPMENT BY TYPE
AIRCRAFT 25 combat capable
  ATK 14 A-37B *Dragonfly*
  ISR 11: 6 O-2A/B *Skymaster**; 5 OA-37B *Dragonfly**
  TPT • Light 5: 1 Cessna 208B *Grand Caravan* EX; 1 Cessna 337G *Skymaster*; 3 IAI-201 *Arava*
  TRG 11: 5 R-235GT *Guerrier*; 3 T-35 *Pillan*; 2 SR22T; 1 T-41D *Mescalero*
HELICOPTERS
  MRH 14: 4 Bell 412EP *Twin Huey* (of which 1 VIP); 8+

MD-530F; 2 UH-1M *Iroquois*
TPT • Light 8: 7 Bell 205 (UH-1H *Iroquois*); 1 Bell 407 (VIP tpt, govt owned)
TRG 4: 2 TH-300; 2 TH-300C; (4 more TH-300 in store)
AIR-LAUNCHED MISSILES • AAM • IR *Shafrir*‡

Gendarmerie & Paramilitary 26,000

National Civilian Police 26,000
Ministry of Public Security
EQUIPMENT BY TYPE
ARMOURED FIGHTING VEHICLES
    APC • PPV 8 BMC *Vuran*
AIRCRAFT
    ISR 1 O-2A *Skymaster*
    TPT • Light 1 Cessna 310
HELICOPTERS
    MRH 9: 2 MD-520N; 7 MD-500E
    TPT • Light 3: 1 Bell 205 (UH-1H *Iroquois*); 2 R-44 *Raven* II

DEPLOYMENT
LEBANON: UN • UNIFIL 52; 1 inf pl
SOUTH SUDAN: UN • UNMISS 2
SUDAN: UN • UNIFSA 1

FOREIGN FORCES
United States US Southern Command: 1 Cooperative Security Location at Comalapa Airport

Guatemala GUA

Guatemalan Quetzal GTQ		2023	2024	2025
GDP	GTQ	818bn	877bn	947bn
	USD	104bn	112bn	121bn
Real GDP growth	%	3.5	3.5	3.6
Def bdgt	GTQ	3.22bn	3.50bn	3.86bn
	USD	411m	449m	493m

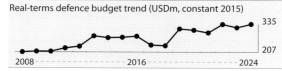
Real-terms defence budget trend (USDm, constant 2015)

Population		18,255,216			
Age	0–14	15–19	20–24	25–29	30–64	65 plus
Male	16.0%	4.9%	4.6%	4.5%	17.2%	2.4%
Female	15.4%	4.8%	4.6%	4.5%	18.1%	3.0%

Capabilities
The armed forces are refocusing on border security, having drawn down their decade-long direct support for the National Civil Police in 2018. Guatemala maintains an inter-agency task force with El Salvador and Honduras. The army has trained with US SOUTHCOM and regional partners such as Brazil and Colombia. Training for conventional military operations is limited by budget constraints and the long focus on internal security. Guatemala has participated in UN peacekeeping missions to company level and has pledged to send a larger contingent of military police to support the UN security mission in Haiti. The equipment inventory is small and ageing. The US has provided several soft-skinned vehicles to the army and helicopters to the air force. The air force's fixed-wing transport and surveillance fleet have seen modest recapitalisation. The country has no defence industry aside from limited maintenance facilities.

ACTIVE 18,050 (Army 15,550 Navy 1,500 Air 1,000)
Gendarmerie & Paramilitary 25,000

RESERVE 63,850 (Navy 650 Air 900 Armed Forces 62,300)

(National Armed Forces are combined; the army provides log spt for navy and air force)

ORGANISATIONS BY SERVICE

Army 15,550
15 Military Zones
FORCES BY ROLE
SPECIAL FORCES
    1 SF bde (1 SF bn, 1 trg bn)
    1 SF bde (1 SF coy, 1 ranger bn)
    1 SF mtn bde
MANOEUVRE
    Light
    1 (strategic reserve) mech bde (1 inf bn, 1 cav regt, 1 log coy)
    6 inf bde (1 inf bn)
    Air Manoeuvre
    1 AB bde with (2 AB bn)
    Amphibious
    1 mne bde
    Other
    1 (Presidential) gd bde (1 gd bn, 1 MP bn, 1 CSS coy)
COMBAT SUPPORT
    1 engr comd (1 engr bn, 1 construction bn)
    2 MP bde with (1 MP bn)

Reserves
FORCES BY ROLE
MANOEUVRE
    Light
    ε19 inf bn
EQUIPMENT BY TYPE
ARMOURED FIGHTING VEHICLES
    RECCE (7 M8 in store)
    APC 39
        APC (T) 10 M113 (5 more in store)
        APC (W) 29: 22 *Armadillo*; 7 V-100 *Commando*
        PPV 4: *Pit-Bull* VX
ANTI-TANK/ANTI-INFRASTRUCTURE

RCL 120+: **75mm** M20; **105mm** 64 M-1974 FMK-1 (ARG); **106mm** 56 M40A1

ARTILLERY 149
 TOWED 105mm 76: 12 M101; 8 M102; 56 M-56
 MOR 73: **81mm** 55 M1; **107mm** (12 M30 in store); **120mm** 18 ECIA
AIR DEFENCE • GUNS • TOWED 32: **20mm** 32: 16 GAI-D01; 16 M-55

Navy 1,500
EQUIPMENT BY TYPE
PATROL AND COASTAL COMBATANTS 11
 PB 11: 6 *Cutlass*; 1 *Dauntless*; 1 *Hunahpu* (US Metal Shark Defiant 85); 1 *Kukulkan* (US *Broadsword* 32m); 2 *Utatlan* (US *Sewart*)
AMPHIBIOUS • LANDING CRAFT 3
 LCT 1 *Quetzal* (COL *Golfo de Tribuga*)
 LCP 2 *Machete*
LOGISTICS AND SUPPORT • AXS 3

Marines 650 reservists
FORCES BY ROLE
MANOEUVRE
 Amphibious
 2 mne bn(-)

Air Force 1,000
2 air comd
FORCES BY ROLE
TRANSPORT
 1 sqn with Beech 90/200/300 *King Air*
 1 (tactical support) sqn with Cessna 206
TRAINING
 1 sqn with T-35B *Pillan*
TRANSPORT HELICOPTER
 1 sqn with Bell 212 (armed); Bell 407GX; Bell 412 *Twin Huey* (armed); Bell 429
EQUIPMENT BY TYPE
Serviceability of ac is less than 50%
AIRCRAFT
 TPT • **Light** 16: 1 Beech 90 *King Air*; 2 Beech 200 *King Air*; 2 Beech 300 *King Air* (VIP); 2 Cessna 206; 3 Cessna 208B *Grand Caravan*; 1 DHC-6 *Twin Otter*; 2 PA-28 *Archer III*; 1 PA-31 *Navajo*; 2 PA-34 *Seneca*; (5 Cessna R172K *Hawk* XP in store)
 TRG 1 SR22; (4 T-35B *Pillan* in store)
HELICOPTERS
 MRH 2 Bell 412 *Twin Huey* (armed)
 TPT • **Light** 7: 2 Bell 206B *Jet Ranger*; 2 Bell 212 (armed); 2 Bell 407GX; 1 Bell 429

Tactical Security Group
Air Military Police

Gendarmerie & Paramilitary 25,000
National Civil Police 25,000
FORCES BY ROLE
SPECIAL FORCES
 1 SF bn
MANOEUVRE
 Other
 1 (integrated task force) paramilitary unit (incl mil and treasury police)

DEPLOYMENT
CENTRAL AFRICAN REPUBLIC: UN • MINUSCA 4
DEMOCRATIC REPUBLIC OF THE CONGO: UN • MONUSCO 188; 1 spec ops coy
LEBANON: UN • UNIFIL 2
SOUTH SUDAN: UN • UNMISS 6
SUDAN: UN • UNISFA 3

Guyana GUY

Guyanese Dollar GYD		2023	2024	2025
GDP	GYD	3.55trn	4.80trn	5.10trn
	USD	17.1bn	23.0bn	24.5bn
Real GDP growth	%	33.0	43.8	14.4
Def bdgt	GYD	20.2bn	42.2bn	
	USD	97.0m	203m	

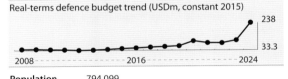
Real-terms defence budget trend (USDm, constant 2015)

Population	794,099				
Age	0–14	15–19	20–24	25–29	30–64	65 plus
Male	12.0%	4.5%	5.8%	4.8%	20.4%	3.6%
Female	11.5%	4.3%	5.5%	4.5%	18.7%	4.6%

Capabilities
The Guyana Defence Force (GDF) is focused on border control and support for law-enforcement operations. The government is planning to restructure the GDF to improve its flexibility. Guyana has close military ties with Brazil, with whom it cooperates on border security via annual regional military exchange meetings. The country also has bilateral agreements with France and the US. The GDF takes part in bilateral and multinational exercises. There has been some training cooperation with China. The military has no expeditionary or associated logistics capability. The air force has expanded its modest air-transport capabilities with some second-hand utility aircraft. The country is looking to recapitalise its land, maritime, air and cyber capabilities amid continued tension with Venezuela over the latter's claim to the Essequibo region. Apart from maintenance facilities, there is no defence-industrial sector.

ACTIVE 3,400 (Army 3,000 Navy 200 Air 200)

Active numbers combined Guyana Defence Force

RESERVE 670 (Army 500 Navy 170)

ORGANISATIONS BY SERVICE

Army 3,000
FORCES BY ROLE
SPECIAL FORCES
  1 SF sqn
MANOEUVRE
  Light
  3 inf bn
COMBAT SUPPORT
  1 arty coy
  1 (spt wpn) cbt spt coy
  1 engr bn
COMBAT SERVICE SUPPORT
  1 spt bn

Reserve
FORCES BY ROLE
MANOEUVRE
  Amphibious
  1 inf bn
EQUIPMENT BY TYPE
ARMOURED FIGHTING VEHICLES
  RECCE 6 EE-9 *Cascavel* (reported)
ARTILLERY 54
  TOWED 130mm 6 M-46†
  MOR 48: 81mm 12 L16A1; 82mm 18 M-43; 120mm 18 M-43

Navy 200
EQUIPMENT BY TYPE
PATROL AND COASTAL COMBATANTS 5
  PB 5: 4 *Barracuda* (ex-US Type-44); 1 Metal Shark Defiant 115

Air Force 200
FORCES BY ROLE
TRANSPORT
  1 unit with Bell 206; Do-228; Cessna 206; Y-12 (II)
EQUIPMENT BY TYPE
AIRCRAFT • TPT • Light 8: 2 BN-2 *Islander*; 1 Cessna 206; 2 Do-228; 2 SC.7 3M *Skyvan*; 1 Y-12 (II)
HELICOPTERS
  MRH 2: 1 Bell 412 *Twin Huey*†; 1 Bell 412EPI *Twin Huey*
  TPT • Light 2 Bell 206

Haiti HTI

Haitian Gourde HTG		2023	2024	2025
GDP	HTG	2.80trn	3.47trn	4.32trn
	USD	19.6bn	26.3bn	30.6bn
Real GDP growth	%	-1.9	-4.0	1.0
Def bdgt	HTG	2.26bn	3.66bn	7.91bn
	USD	15.8m	27.7m	56.1m
Population		11,753,943		

Age	0–14	15–19	20–24	25–29	30–64	65 plus
Male	15.2%	4.9%	4.8%	4.7%	17.8%	1.8%
Female	15.3%	5.0%	4.9%	4.7%	18.5%	2.4%

Capabilities

Haiti possesses almost no military capability. Violence and instability persists, and criminal groups are active in many areas. The UN Security Council in 2023 approved the deployment of an armed multinational force to Haiti. The limited armed forces also struggled to respond swiftly to the country's most recent earthquake. A small coast guard is tasked with maritime security and law enforcement and the country's army was still in the very early stages of development before unrest deepened in 2021. A road map for the re-establishment of the Haitian armed forces was distributed to ministers in early 2017, and in March 2018, an army high command was established. A 2018 agreement with Mexico saw small groups of Haitian troops travel to Mexico for training. Haiti has participated in US Southern Command's *Tradewinds* exercise. Haiti has neither heavy military equipment nor a defence industry.

ACTIVE 700 (Army 700) Gendarmerie & Paramilitary 50 Police ε9,000

ORGANISATIONS BY SERVICE

Army ε700
FORCES BY ROLE
MANOEUVRE
  1 inf bn (forming)

Gendarmerie & Paramilitary 50

Coast Guard ε50
EQUIPMENT BY TYPE
PATROL AND COASTAL COMBATANTS 5
  PB 5 *Dauntless*

National Police Force ε9,000
EQUIPMENT BY TYPE
ARMOURED FIGHTING VEHICLES
  AUV: 15 LT-79, 9 *Sentry/Geebor*

Honduras HND

Honduran Lempira HNL		2023	2024	2025
GDP	HNL	846bn	917bn	993bn
	USD	34.2bn	36.7bn	39.0bn
Real GDP growth	%	3.6	3.6	3.5
Def bdgt [a]	HNL	10.9bn	11.4bn	
	USD	440m	456m	

[a] Budget for Secretariat for Defence - security funding not included

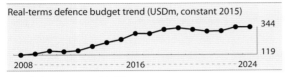
Real-terms defence budget trend (USDm, constant 2015)

Population			9,529,188			
Age	0–14	15–19	20–24	25–29	30–64	65 plus
Male	14.5%	4.9%	4.9%	4.4%	17.0%	2.4%
Female	14.2%	5.0%	5.1%	4.7%	19.6%	3.2%

Capabilities

The armed forces have been deployed in support of the police to combat organised crime and narcotics trafficking since 2011. The current government has pledged to focus on professionalisation, anti-corruption and human rights in the security forces. The US is its main security partner and provides assistance. Honduras hosts a US base at Soto Cano airfield and is part of a tri-national border-security task force with neighbouring El Salvador and Guatemala. Training for conventional military operations is limited and instead focused on internal- and border-security requirements. Honduras does not have the capability to maintain substantial foreign deployments. Most equipment is ageing with serviceability in doubt, but the air force is receiving new Airbus transport helicopters. Apart from limited maintenance facilities, the country has no defence industry.

ACTIVE 14,950 (Army 7,300 Navy 1,350 Air 2,300 Military Police 4,000) Gendarmerie & Paramilitary 8,000

RESERVE 60,000 (Joint 60,000; Ex-servicemen registered)

ORGANISATIONS BY SERVICE

Army 7,300
FORCES BY ROLE
SPECIAL FORCES
  1 (special tac) spec ops gp (2 spec ops bn, 1 inf bn; 1 AB bn; 1 arty bn)
MANOEUVRE
  Mechanised
  1 inf bde (1 mech cav regt, 1 inf bn, 1 arty bn)
  Light
  1 inf bde (3 inf bn, 1 arty bn)
  3 inf bde (2 inf bn)
  1 indep inf bn
  Other
  1 (Presidential) gd coy
COMBAT SUPPORT
  1 engr bn
  1 sigs bn
EQUIPMENT BY TYPE
ARMOURED FIGHTING VEHICLES
  LT TK 12 FV101 *Scorpion*
  RECCE 43: 3 FV107 *Scimitar*; 40 FV601 *Saladin*
  AUV 1 FV105 *Sultan* (CP)
ANTI-TANK/ANTI-INFRASTRUCTURE
  RCL 50+: **84mm** *Carl Gustaf*; **106mm** 50 M40A1
ARTILLERY 118+
  TOWED 28: **105mm**: 24 M102; **155mm**: 4 M198
  MOR 90+: **81mm**; **120mm** 60 FMK-2; **160mm** 30 M-66

Navy 1,350
EQUIPMENT BY TYPE
PATROL AND COASTAL COMBATANTS 15
  PCO 1 *General Cabanas* (ISR OPV 62 *Sa'ar*)
  PB 14: 2 *Lempira* (Damen Stan Patrol 4207 – leased); 1 *Chamelecon* (Swiftships 85); 1 *Tegucigalpa* (US *Guardian* 32m); 3 *Guaymuras* (Swiftships 105); 5 *Nacaome* (Swiftships 65); 1 *Rio Aguan* (Defiant 85); 1 *Rio Coco* (US PB Mk III)
AMPHIBIOUS • LANDING CRAFT 3
  LCT 1 *Gracias a Dios* (COL *Golfo de Tribuga*)
  LCM 3: 2 LCM 8; 1 *Punta Caxinas*
HELICOPTERS • TPT • Light 1 Bo-105S

Marines 1,000
FORCES BY ROLE
MANOEUVRE
  Amphibious
  2 mne bn

Air Force 2,300
FORCES BY ROLE
FIGHTER/GROUND ATTACK
  1 sqn with A-37B *Dragonfly*
  1 sqn with F-5E/F *Tiger* II
GROUND ATTACK/ISR/TRAINING
  1 unit with Cessna 182 *Skylane*; EMB-312 *Tucano*; MXT-7-180 *Star Rocket*
TRANSPORT
  1 sqn with Beech 200 *King Air*; C-130A *Hercules*; Cessna 185/210; IAI-201 *Arava*; PA-42 *Cheyenne*; Turbo Commander 690
  1 VIP flt with Bell 412EP/SP *Twin Huey*; PA-31 *Navajo*
TRANSPORT HELICOPTER
  1 sqn with Bell 205 (UH-1H *Iroquois*); Bell 412SP *Twin Huey*; Bo-105S

TRANSPORT HELICOPTER
  1 flt with *Skylark 3*
AIR DEFENCE
  1 ADA bn
EQUIPMENT BY TYPE
AIRCRAFT 12 combat capable
  FTR 6: 4 F-5E *Tiger II*†; 2 F-5F *Tiger II*†
  ATK 6 A-37B *Dragonfly*
  TPT 17: **Medium** 1 C-130A *Hercules*; **Light** 16: 1 Beech 200 *King Air*; 2 Cessna 172 *Skyhawk*; 2 Cessna 182 *Skylane*; 1 Cessna 185; 3 Cessna 208B *Grand Caravan*; 1 Cessna 210; 1 EMB-135 *Legacy* 600; 1 IAI-201 *Arava*; 1 L-410 (leased); 1 PA-31 *Navajo*; 1 PA-42 *Cheyenne*; 1 *Turbo Commander* 690
  TRG 15: 9 EMB-312 *Tucano*; 6 MXT-7-180 *Star Rocket*
HELICOPTERS
  MRH 7: 1 Bell 412EP *Twin Huey* (VIP); 4 Bell 412SP *Twin Huey*; 2 Hughes 500
  TPT • **Light** 7: 5 Bell 205 (UH-1H *Iroquois*); 1 H125 *Ecureuil*; 1 Bo-105S
UAV • ISR • **Light** 6 *Skylark* 3
AIR DEFENCE • GUNS 20mm 48: 24 M-55A2; 24 TCM-20
AIR-LAUNCHED MISSILES • AAM • IR *Shafrir*‡

Military Police 4,000
FORCES BY ROLE
MANOEUVRE
  Other
    8 sy bn

Gendarmerie & Paramilitary 8,000

Public Security Forces 8,000
  Ministry of Public Security and Defence; 11 regional comd

DEPLOYMENT
WESTERN SAHARA: UN • MINURSO 12

FOREIGN FORCES
United States US Southern Command: 400; 1 avn bn with 4 CH-47F *Chinook*; 12 UH-60L/HH-60L *Black Hawk*

Jamaica JAM

Jamaican Dollar JMD		2023	2024	2025
GDP	JMD	2.99trn	3.22trn	3.43trn
	USD	19.3bn	20.6bn	21.6bn
Real GDP growth	%	2.6	1.3	2.1
Def bdgt	JMD	38.3bn	45.2bn	
	USD	247m	289m	

Real-terms defence budget trend (USDm, constant 2015)

Population	2,823,713					
Age	0–14	15–19	20–24	25–29	30–64	65 plus
Male	12.1%	4.3%	4.3%	4.0%	19.8%	5.0%
Female	11.7%	4.1%	4.2%	4.0%	21.0%	5.5%

Capabilities

The Jamaica Defence Force (JDF) is focused principally on maritime and internal security, including support to police operations. Jamaica maintains military ties, including for training purposes, with Canada, the UK and the US. The JDF has participated in US SOUTHCOM's *Tradewinds* exercise. Jamaica is host to the Caribbean Special Tactics Centre, which trains special-forces units from Jamaica and other Caribbean nations. The JDF does not have any capacity to support independent deployment abroad. Funds have been allocated to procure new vehicles and helicopters, and new patrol craft are being procured. Jamaica has no defence industry except for limited maintenance facilities.

ACTIVE 5,950 (Army 5,400 Coast Guard 300 Air 250)
(combined Jamaican Defence Force)
RESERVE 2,580 (Army 2,500 Coast Guard 60 Air 20)

ORGANISATIONS BY SERVICE

Army 5,400
FORCES BY ROLE
MANOEUVRE
  Light
    4 inf bn
COMBAT SUPPORT
  1 engr regt (4 engr sqn)
  1 MP bn
  1 cbt spt bn (1 (PMV) lt mech inf coy)
COMBAT SERVICE SUPPORT
  1 spt bn (1 med coy, 1 log coy, 1 tpt coy)
EQUIPMENT BY TYPE
ARMOURED FIGHTING VEHICLES
  AUV 18 *Bushmaster*
ARTILLERY • MOR 81mm 12 L16A1

Reserves
FORCES BY ROLE
MANOEUVRE
   Light
      3 inf bn
COMBAT SERVICE SUPPORT
   1 spt bn

Coast Guard 300
EQUIPMENT BY TYPE
PATROL AND COASTAL COMBATANTS 9
   PCC 1 *Nanny of the Maroons* (Damen Fast Crew Supplier 5009)
   PB 8: 4 *Honour* (Damen Stan Patrol 4207); 4 *Dauntless*

Air Wing 250
Plus National Reserve
FORCES BY ROLE
MARITIME PATROL/TRANSPORT
   1 flt with Beech 350ER *King Air*; BN-2A *Defender*
SEARCH & RESCUE/TRANSPORT HELICOPTER
   1 flt with Bell 407
   1 flt with Bell 412EP
TRAINING
   1 unit with Bell 206B3 *Jet Ranger*; Bell 505; DA40-180FP *Diamond Star*
EQUIPMENT BY TYPE
AIRCRAFT
   MP 1 Beech 350ER *King Air*
   TPT • Light 2 DA40-180FP *Diamond Star* (1 BN-2A *Defender* in store)
HELICOPTERS
   MRH 1 Bell 412EP *Twin Huey* (1 more in store)
   TPT • Light 13: 1 Bell 206B3 *Jet Ranger*; 3 Bell 407; 3 Bell 429; 6 Bell 505

Mexico MEX

Mexican Peso MXN		2023	2024	2025
GDP	MXN	31.8trn	34.2trn	36.6trn
	USD	1.79trn	1.85trn	1.82trn
Real GDP growth	%	3.2	1.5	1.3
Def bdgt [a]	MXN	153bn	189bn	
	USD	8.61bn	10.2bn	

[a] Combined budgets for Ministries of national and maritime defence, excludes public infrastructure spending

Population	130,739,927					
Age	0–14	15–19	20–24	25–29	30–64	65 plus
Male	12.0%	4.6%	4.6%	4.2%	20.0%	3.5%
Female	11.3%	4.2%	3.9%	4.0%	23.1%	4.7%

Capabilities

Mexico's armed forces have been heavily involved in internal security support for nearly a decade. The National Plan for Peace and Security 2018–24 envisaged that the armed forces would hand over lead responsibility for tackling drug cartels and other organised crime to the National Guard. Mexico's Senate agreed in September 2024 to place the National Guard under military command. The US-Mexican security relationship is key to the country but has been under strain. The US has provided equipment and training to Mexican forces under the Mérida Initiative, as well as through bilateral programmes with the Pentagon. The armed forces have a moderate capability to deploy independently but do not do so in significant numbers. The country has plans to recapitalise its diverse and ageing conventional combat platforms across all three services. State-owned shipyards have produced patrol craft for the navy, which also has plans to modernise its frigate force. Army factories have produced light armoured utility vehicles for domestic use.

ACTIVE 287,000 (Army 186,000 Navy 71,000 Air 30,000) Gendarmerie & Paramilitary 136,900

Conscript liability 12 months (partial, selection by ballot) from age 18, serving on Saturdays; voluntary for women; conscripts allocated to reserves.

RESERVE 81,500 (National Military Service)

ORGANISATIONS BY SERVICE

Space
EQUIPMENT BY TYPE
SATELLITES 4
   COMMUNICATIONS 2 *Mexsat*
   ISR 2 *Painani*

Army 186,000
12 regions (total: 48 army zones)

FORCES BY ROLE
SPECIAL FORCES
1 (1st) SF bde (5 SF bn)
1 (2nd) SF bde (7 SF bn)
1 (3rd) SF bde (4 SF bn)
MANOEUVRE
  Reconnaissance
  3 (2nd, 3rd & 4th Armd) mech bde (2 armd recce bn, 2 lt mech bn, 1 arty bn, 1 (Canon) AT gp)
  28 mot recce regt
  Light
  1 (1st) inf corps (1 (1st Armd) mech bde (2 armd recce bn, 2 lt mech bn, 1 arty bn, 1 (Canon) AT gp), 3 (2nd, 3rd & 6th) inf bde (each: 3 inf bn, 1 arty regt, 1 (Canon) AT gp), 1 cbt engr bde (3 engr bn))
  3 (1st, 4th & 5th) indep lt inf bde (2 lt inf bn, 1 (Canon) AT gp)
  92 indep inf bn
  25 indep inf coy
  Air Manoeuvre
  1 para bde with (1 (GAFE) SF gp, 3 bn, 1 (Canon) AT gp)
COMBAT SUPPORT
  1 indep arty regt
EQUIPMENT BY TYPE
ARMOURED FIGHTING VEHICLES
  RECCE 223: 19 DN-5 *Toro*; 127 ERC-90F1 *Lynx* (7 trg); 40 M8; 37 MAC-1
  IFV 390 DNC-1 (mod AMX-VCI)
  APC 309
    APC (T) 73: 40 HWK-11; 33 M5A1 half-track
    APC (W) 236: 95 BDX; 16 DN-4; 2 DN-6; 28 LAV-100 (*Pantera*); 26 LAV-150 ST; 25 MOWAG *Roland*; 44 VCR (3 amb; 5 cmd post)
  AUV 379: 100 DN-XI; 247 *SandCat*; 32 VBL
ENGINEERING & MAINTENANCE VEHICLES
  ARV 7: 3 M32 *Recovery Sherman*; 4 VCR ARV
ANTI-TANK/ANTI-INFRASTRUCTURE
  MSL • SP 8 VBL with *Milan*
  RCL • 106mm 1,187+ M40A1 (incl some SP)
  GUNS 37mm 30 M3
ARTILLERY 1,390
  TOWED 123: **105mm** 123: 40 M101; 40 M-56; 16 M2A1; 14 M3; 13 NORINCO M90
  MOR 1,267: **81mm** 1,100: 400 M1; 400 Brandt; 300 SB **120mm** 167: 75 Brandt; 60 M-65; 32 RT-61
AIR DEFENCE • GUNS • TOWED 80: **12.7mm** 40 M55; **20mm** 40 GAI-B01

Navy 71,000
Two Fleet Commands: Gulf (6 zones), Pacific (11 zones)
EQUIPMENT BY TYPE
PRINCIPAL SURFACE COMBATANTS • FRIGATES 1
  FFGHM 1 *Benito Juárez* (Damen SIGMA 10514) with 2 quad lnchr with RGM-84L *Harpoon* Block II AShM, 1 8-cell Mk 56 VLS with RIM-162 ESSM SAM, 1 21-cell Mk 49 lnchr with RIM-116C RAM Block 2 SAM, 2 triple 324mm SVTT Mk 32 ASTT with Mk 54 LWT, 1 57mm gun (capacity 1 med hel) (fitted for but not with Mk 56 VLS with RIM-162 *Evolved SeaSparrow Missile*)
PATROL AND COASTAL COMBATANTS 124
  PSOH 8:
    4 *Oaxaca* with 1 76mm gun (capacity 1 AS565MB *Panther* hel)
    4 *Oaxaca* (mod) with 1 57mm gun (capacity 1 AS565MB *Panther* hel)
  PCOH 16:
    4 *Durango* with 1 57mm gun (capacity 1 Bo-105 hel)
    4 *Holzinger* (capacity 1 MD-902 *Explorer*)
    3 *Sierra* with 1 57mm gun (capacity 1 MD-902 *Explorer*)
    5 *Uribe* (ESP *Halcon*) (capacity 1 Bo-105 hel)
  PCO 9: 6 *Valle* (US *Auk* MSF) with 1 76mm gun; 3 *Valle* (US *Auk* MSF) with 1 76mm gun, 1 hel landing platform
  PCGH 1 *Huracan* (ex-ISR *Aliya*) with 4 single lnchr with *Gabriel* II AShM, 1 Mk 15 *Phalanx* CIWS
  PCC 2 *Democrata*
  PBF 72: 6 *Acuario*; 2 *Acuario B*; 48 *Polaris* (SWE CB90); 16 *Polaris* II (SWE IC 16M)
  PB 16: 3 *Azteca*; 3 *Cabo* (ex-US *Cape Higgon*); 10 *Tenochtitlan* (Damen Stan Patrol 4207)
AMPHIBIOUS • LANDING SHIPS
  LST 4: 2 *Monte Azules* with 1 hel landing platform; 1 *Papaloapan* (ex-US *Newport*) with 2 twin 76mm guns, 1 hel landing platform; 1 *Papaloapan* (ex-US *Newport*) with 1 hel landing platform
LOGISTICS AND SUPPORT 25
  AGOR 3: 2 *Altair* (ex-US *Robert D. Conrad*); 1 *Rio Tecolutla*
  AGS 8: 5 *Arrecife*; 1 *Onjuku*; 1 *Rio Hondo*; 1 *Rio Tuxpan*
  AK 1 *Rio Suchiate*
  AOL 2 *Aguascalientes*
  AP 1 *Isla Maria Madre* (Damen Fast Crew Supplier 5009)
  ARS 4 *Kukulkan*
  ATF 3 *Otomi* with 1 76mm gun
  AX 2 *Huasteco* (also serve as troop transport, supply and hospital ships)
  AXS 1 *Cuauhtemoc*

Naval Aviation 1,250
FORCES BY ROLE
MARITIME PATROL
  2 flt with CN235-300 MPA *Persuader*
ISR
  1 flt with Beech 350ER *King Air*
  1 flt with Z-143Lsi
TRANSPORT
  1 (VIP) sqn with AW109SP; Beech 350i *King Air*; CL-605 *Challenger*; DHC-8 *Dash 8*; Gulfstream 550; Learjet 31A/45/60

1 flt with C295M/W
TRAINING
1 sqn with Schweizer 300C; S-333; Z-242L
1 flt with MX-7-180 *Star Rocket*
3 flt with T-6C+ *Texan* II
SEARCH & RESCUE HELICOPTER
4 flt with AS565MB *Panther*; AS565MBe *Panther*
TRANSPORT HELICOPTER
6 flt with Mi-17-1V/V-5 *Hip*
2 flt with UH-60M *Black Hawk*
1 flt with H225M *Caracal*
EQUIPMENT BY TYPE
AIRCRAFT
MP 6 CN235-300 MPA *Persuader*
ISR 2 Z-143Lsi
TPT 20: **Light** 19: 5 Beech 350ER *King Air* (4 used for ISR); 3 Beech 350i *King Air*; 4 C295M; 2 C295W; 2 DHC-8 *Dash 8*; 2 Learjet 31A; 2 Learjet 45; 1 Learjet 60; **PAX** 2: 1 CL-605 *Challenger*; 1 Gulfstream 550
TRG 46: 7 MX-7-180 *Star Rocket*; 13 T-6C+ *Texan* II; 26 Z-242L
HELICOPTERS
MRH 19: 15 Mi-17-1V *Hip*; 4 Mi-17V-5 *Hip*
SAR 14: 4 AS565MB *Panther*; 10 AS565MBe *Panther*
TPT 22: **Heavy** 3 H225M *Caracal*; **Medium** 10: 2 H225 (SAR role); 8 UH-60M *Black Hawk*; **Light** 9: 1 AW109SP; 8 S-333
TRG 4 Schweizer 300C

Marines 21,500
FORCES BY ROLE
SPECIAL FORCES
3 SF unit
MANOEUVRE
Light
32 inf bn(-)
Air Manoeuvre
1 AB bn
Amphibious
1 amph bde (4 inf bn, 1 amph bn, 1 arty gp)
Other
1 (Presidential) gd bn (included in army above)
COMBAT SERVICE SUPPORT
2 spt bn
EQUIPMENT BY TYPE
ARMOURED FIGHTING VEHICLES
APC • APC (W) 29: 3 BTR-60 (APC-60); 26 BTR-70 (APC-70)
ANTI-TANK/ANTI-INFRASTRUCTURE
RCL **106mm** M40A1
ARTILLERY 22+
TOWED **105mm** 16 M-56
MRL **122mm** 6 *Firos*-25
MOR **81mm** some

AIR DEFENCE • SAM • **Point-defence** 9K38 *Igla* (RS-SA-18 *Grouse*)

Air Force 30,000
FORCES BY ROLE
FIGHTER
1 sqn with F-5E/F *Tiger* II
GROUND ATTACK/ISR
4 sqn with T-6C+ *Texan* II*
1 sqn with PC-7*
ISR/AEW
1 sqn with Beech 350ER *King Air*; EMB-145AEW *Erieye*; EMB-145RS
TRANSPORT
1 sqn with C295M; PC-6B
1 sqn with B-737
1 sqn with C-27J *Spartan*; C-130K-30 *Hercules*; L-100-30
5 (liaison) sqn with Cessna 182
1 (anti-narcotic spraying) sqn with Bell 206
1 (Presidential) gp with AW109SP; B-737; B-787; Gulfstream 450/550; H225; Learjet 35A; Learjet 36
1 (VIP) gp with B-737; Beech 350i *King Air*; CL-605 *Challenger*; Gulfstream 550; Learjet 35A; S-70A-24 *Black Hawk*
TRAINING
1 sqn with Cessna 182
1 sqn with PC-7; T-6C+ *Texan* II
1 sqn with Grob G120TP
TRANSPORT HELICOPTER
4 sqn with Bell 206B; Bell 407GX
1 (anti-narcotic spraying) sqn with Bell 206
1 sqn with MD-530MF/MG
1 sqn with Mi-17 *Hip*
1 sqn with H225M *Caracal*; Bell 412EP *Twin Huey*; S-70A-24 *Black Hawk*
1 sqn with UH-60M *Black Hawk*
ISR UAV
1 unit with *Hermes* 450; *Hermes* 900; S4 *Ehécatl*
EQUIPMENT BY TYPE
AIRCRAFT 80 combat capable
FTR 5: 4 F-5E *Tiger* II; 1 F-5F *Tiger* II
ISR 2 Cessna 501 *Citation*
ELINT 4: 2 Beech 350ER *King Air*; 2 EMB-145RS
AEW&C 1 EMB-145AEW *Erieye*
TPT 85: **Medium** 7: 4 C-27J *Spartan*; 2 C-130K-30 *Hercules*; 1 L-100-30; **Light** 72: 6 Beech 350i *King Air*; 6 C295M; 2 C295W; 52 Cessna 182; 2 Learjet 35A; 1 Learjet 36; 3 PC-6B; **PAX** 6: 2 B-737; 1 B-787; 1 CL-605 *Challenger*; 1 Gulfstream 450; 1 Gulfstream 550
TRG 100: 25 Grob G120TP; 20 PC-7* (30 more possibly in store); 55 T-6C+ *Texan* II*
HELICOPTERS
MRH 43: 17 Bell 407GX (incl 3 leased); 11 Bell 412EP *Twin Huey*; 15 Mi-17 *Hip* H
ISR 11: 3 MD-530MF; 8 MD-530MG

TPT 95: **Heavy** 12 H225M *Caracal*; **Medium** 24: 1 H225 (VIP); 6 S-70A-24 *Black Hawk*; 17 UH-60M *Black Hawk* **Light** 59: 5 AW109SP; 45 Bell 206; 1 Bell 206B *Jet Ranger II*; 8 Bell 206L

UNINHABITED AERIAL VEHICLES • ISR 9: **Medium** 4: 3 *Hermes* 450; 1 *Hermes* 900; **Light** 5 S4 *Ehécatl*

Gendarmerie & Paramilitary 136,900

Federal Ministerial Police 4,500

EQUIPMENT BY TYPE

HELICOPTERS

TPT • **Light** 25: 18 Bell 205 (UH-1H); 7 Bell 212

UNINHABITED AERIAL VEHICLES

ISR • **Heavy** 2 *Dominator* XP

National Guard 115,000

Public Security Secretariat. Gendarmerie created in 2019 from elements of the Army, Navy, Air Force and Federal Police.

FORCES BY ROLE

SPECIAL FORCES

1 sf unit

MANOEUVRE

Other

12 sy bde (3 sy bn)

EQUIPMENT BY TYPE

AIRCRAFT

ISR 1 DA42 MPP Guardian (shared with Federal Police)

TPT 5: **Light** 2: 1 CN235-100; 1 Do-328; **PAX** 3: 2 B-727; 1 Falcon 20

HELICOPTERS

MRH 5: 1+ Bell 407GX; 4 Mi-17 *Hip* H

TPT 18: **Medium** ε13 UH-60M *Black Hawk*; 5 H120 *Colibri*

Rural Defense Militia 17,400

FORCES BY ROLE

MANOEUVRE

Light

13 inf unit

13 (horsed) cav unit

DEPLOYMENT

CENTRAL AFRICAN REPUBLIC: UN • MINUSCA 2

INDIA/PAKISTAN: UN • UNMOGIP 3

WESTERN SAHARA: UN • MINURSO 5

Nicaragua NIC

Nicaraguan Gold Cordoba NIO		2023	2024	2025
GDP	NIO	650bn	710bn	767bn
	USD	17.8bn	19.4bn	21.0bn
Real GDP growth	%	4.6	4.0	3.8
Def bdgt	NIO	3.46bn	3.80bn	
	USD	94.9m	104m	

Real-terms defence budget trend (USDm, constant 2015)

Population	6,676,948					
Age	0–14	15–19	20–24	25–29	30–64	65 plus
Male	12.8%	4.5%	4.5%	4.6%	20.0%	2.7%
Female	12.3%	4.3%	4.4%	4.6%	22.0%	3.4%

Capabilities

Nicaragua's armed forces are tasked with border and internal security and supporting disaster relief efforts and ecological protection. Nicaragua has renewed its training relationship with Russia and has been expanding ties with China and Iran and, in 2024, the US tightened its restrictions on defence trade with the country. The mechanised brigade is reported to have received Russian training. The armed forces do not undertake significant deployments abroad and lack the logistical support for large-scale military operations, although the mechanised brigade can deploy internally. Equipment primarily consists of ageing Cold War-era platforms. Russia has helped re-equip the mechanised brigade and has supported the establishment of a repair workshop. The country has no defence industry.

ACTIVE 12,000 (Army 10,000 Navy 800 Air 1,200)

ORGANISATIONS BY SERVICE

Army ε10,000

FORCES BY ROLE

SPECIAL FORCES

1 SF bde (2 SF bn)

MANOEUVRE

Mechanised

1 mech inf bde (1 armd recce bn, 1 tk bn, 1 mech inf bn, 1 arty bn, 1 MRL bn, 1 AT coy)

Light

1 regional comd (3 lt inf bn)

1 regional comd (2 lt inf bn; 1 arty bn)

3 regional comd (2 lt inf bn)

2 indep lt inf bn

Other

1 comd regt (1 inf bn, 1 sy bn, 1 int unit, 1 sigs bn)

1 (ecological) sy bn

COMBAT SUPPORT

1 engr bn

COMBAT SERVICE SUPPORT
1 med bn
1 tpt regt
EQUIPMENT BY TYPE
ARMOURED FIGHTING VEHICLES
MBT: 20+ T-72B1MS; (127 T-55 in store)
LT TK (10 PT-76 in store)
RECCE 20 BRDM-2
IFV 17+ BMP-1
APC • APC (W) 126+: 41 BTR-152 (61 more in store); 45 BTR-60 (15 more in store); ε40 BTR-70M
ENGINEERING & MAINTENANCE VEHICLES
AEV IMR
VLB TMM-3
ANTI-TANK/ANTI-INFRASTRUCTURE
MSL
SP 12 9P133 *Malyutka* (RS-AT-3 *Sagger*)
MANPATS 9K11 *Malyutka* (RS-AT-3 *Sagger*)
RCL 82mm B-10
GUNS 281: **57mm** 174 ZIS-2; (90 more in store); **76mm** 83 ZIS-3; **100mm** 24 M-1944
ARTILLERY 766
TOWED 12: **122mm** 12 D-30; **152mm** some D-20; (30 D-20 in store)
MRL 151: **107mm** 33 Type-63; **122mm** 118: 18 BM-21 *Grad*; 100 *Grad* 1P (BM-21P) (single-tube rocket launcher, man portable)
MOR 603: **82mm** 579; **120mm** 24 M-43; (**160mm** 4 M-160 in store)
AIR DEFENCE • SAM • Point-defence 9K36 *Strela*-3 (RS-SA-14 *Gremlin*); 9K310 *Igla*-1 (RS-SA-16 *Gimlet*); 9K32 *Strela*-2 (RS-SA-7 *Grail*)‡
GUNS • TOWED: ZU-23-2

Navy ε800
EQUIPMENT BY TYPE
PATROL AND COASTAL COMBATANTS 13
PB 13: 3 *Dabur*; 2 *Farallones*; 4 Rodman 101; 2 *Soberania* (ex-JAM Damen Stan Patrol 4207); 2 (patrol/support)

Marines
FORCES BY ROLE
MANOEUVRE
Amphibious
1 mne bn

Air Force 1,200
FORCES BY ROLE
TRANSPORT
1 sqn with An-26 *Curl*; Beech 90 *King Air*; Cessna U206; Cessna 404 *Titan* (VIP)
TRAINING
1 unit with Cessna 172; PA-18 *Super Cub*; PA-28 *Cherokee*
TRANSPORT HELICOPTER
1 sqn with Mi-17 *Hip* H (armed)
AIR DEFENCE
1 gp with ZU-23
EQUIPMENT BY TYPE
AIRCRAFT
TPT • Light 9: 3 An-26 *Curl*; 1 Beech 90 *King Air*; 1 Cessna 172; 1 Cessna U206; 1 Cessna 404 *Titan* (VIP); 2 PA-28 *Cherokee*
TRG 2 PA-18 *Super Cub*
HELICOPTERS
MRH 7 Mi-17 *Hip* H (armed)†
TPT • Medium 2 Mi-171E
AIR DEFENCE • GUNS 23mm 18 ZU-23
AIR-LAUNCHED MISSILES • ASM 9M17 *Skorpion* (RS-AT-2 *Swatter*)

Panama PAN

Panamanian Balboa PAB		2023	2024	2025
GDP	PAB	83.4bn	87.3bn	91.7bn
	USD	83.4bn	87.3bn	91.7bn
Real GDP growth	%	7.3	2.5	3.0
Def bdgt [a]	PAB	903m	946m	
	USD	903m	946m	

[a] Public security expenditure

Real-terms defence budget trend (USDm, constant 2015)

Population		4,470,241				
Age	0–14	15–19	20–24	25–29	30–64	65 plus
Male	12.8%	3.9%	3.8%	3.9%	21.2%	4.7%
Female	12.2%	3.7%	3.7%	3.8%	20.8%	5.4%

Capabilities

Panama abolished its armed forces in 1990 but retains a border service, a police force and an air/maritime service for low-level security tasks. The country's primary security focus is on the southern border with Colombia, where the majority of the border service is deployed. Colombia and the US have provided training and support. Training is focused on internal and border security rather than conventional military operations and there is no capability to mount significant external deployments. None of Panama's security services maintain heavy military equipment, focusing instead on light-transport, patrol and surveillance capabilities. Aside from limited maintenance facilities, the country has no defence industry.

Gendarmerie & Paramilitary 27,700

ORGANISATIONS BY SERVICE

Gendarmerie & Paramilitary 27,700

National Border Service 4,000
FORCES BY ROLE
SPECIAL FORCES
1 SF gp
MANOEUVRE
Other
1 sy bde (5 sy bn(-))
1 indep sy bn

National Police Force 20,000
No hvy mil eqpt, small arms only
FORCES BY ROLE
SPECIAL FORCES
1 SF unit
MANOEUVRE
Other
1 (presidential) gd bn(-)

National Aeronaval Service 3,700
FORCES BY ROLE
TRANSPORT
1 sqn with Beech 250 *King Air*; C-212M *Aviocar*; Cessna 210; PA-31 *Navajo*; PA-34 *Seneca*
1 (Presidential) flt with ERJ-135BJ; S-76C
TRAINING
1 unit with Cessna 152; Cessna 172; T-35D *Pillan*
TRANSPORT HELICOPTER
1 sqn with AW139; Bell 205; Bell 205 (UH-1H *Iroquois*); Bell 212; Bell 407; Bell 412EP; H145; MD-500E
EQUIPMENT BY TYPE
PATROL AND COASTAL COMBATANTS 16
PCC 1 *Saettia*
PB 15: 5 *3 De Noviembre* (ex-US *Point*); 1 *Chiriqui* (ex-US PB MkIV); 1 *Cocle* (ex-US *Swift*); 1 *Omar Torrijos* (US Metal Shark Defiant 85); 2 *Panquiaco* (UK Vosper 31.5m); 1 *Taboga* (log/tpt role); 4 Type-200
AMPHIBIOUS • LANDING CRAFT 1
LCU 1 *General Estaban Huertas*
LOGISTICS AND SUPPORT 2
AG 1 *Lina María*
AKR 1 *Manuel Amador Guerror* (Damen Stan Lander 5612)
AIRCRAFT
TPT • Light 17: 1 Beech 100 *King Air*; 1 Beech 250 *King Air*; 1 Beech 350 *King Air*; 2 DHC-6-400 *Twin Otter*; 3 C-212M *Aviocar*; 1 Cessna 152, 1 Cessna 172; 2 Cessna 208B; 1 Cessna 210; 1 ERJ-135BJ; 1 PA-31 *Navajo*; 2 PA-34 *Seneca*
TRG (2 T-35D *Pillan* in store)
HELICOPTERS
MRH 10: 8 AW139; 1 Bell 412EP; 1 MD-500E
TPT • Light 13: 1 AW109; 8 Bell 205 (UH-1H *Iroquois*); 2 Bell 212; 2 Bell 407

Paraguay PRY

Paraguayan Guarani PYG		2023	2024	2025
GDP	PYG	313trn	334trn	359trn
	USD	43.0bn	44.9bn	46.8bn
Real GDP growth	%	4.7	3.8	3.8
Def bdgt	PYG	2.17trn	2.31trn	2.47trn
	USD	298m	310m	322m

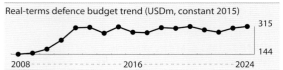
Real-terms defence budget trend (USDm, constant 2015)

Population		7,522,549				
Age	0–14	15–19	20–24	25–29	30–64	65 plus
Male	11.3%	3.8%	4.0%	4.5%	22.0%	4.5%
Female	10.9%	3.7%	4.0%	4.5%	21.9%	4.9%

Capabilities

The country's armed forces are small by regional standards, with largely obsolete equipment. Paraguay faces internal challenges from insurgency and transnational organised crime, chiefly drug trafficking. There is security cooperation with Argentina and Brazil in the Tri-Border Area. In 2017, Paraguay signed a defence cooperation agreement with Russia. The military ranks are increasingly top-heavy and conscript numbers have fallen in recent years. Key formations have long been under-strength. Paraguay has had a consistent, if limited, tradition of contributing to UN peacekeeping missions, and there is limited training with regional partners. It only has a limited ability to self-sustain forces abroad and no effective power-projection capacity. Recent acquisitions of heavy equipment have been confined to small quantities of engineering and transport capabilities. Paraguay plans to improve its air force capabilities with the acquisition, from 2025, of six *Super Tucano* aircraft from Brazil. The country has local maintenance capacity, but lacks defence industrial production facilities.

ACTIVE 13,950 (Army 7,400 Navy 3,800 Air 2,750)
Gendarmerie & Paramilitary 14,800

Conscript liability 12 months

RESERVE 164,500 (Joint 164,500)

ORGANISATIONS BY SERVICE

Army 7,400
Much of the Paraguayan army is maintained in a cadre state during peacetime; the nominal inf and cav divs are effectively only at coy strength. Active gp/regt are usually coy sized

FORCES BY ROLE
MANOEUVRE
Light
3 inf corps (total: 6 inf div(-), 3 cav div(-), 6 arty bty)
Other
1 (Presidential) gd regt (1 SF bn, 1 inf bn, 1 sy bn, 1 log gp)

COMBAT SUPPORT
1 arty bde with (2 arty gp, 1 ADA gp)
1 engr bde with (1 engr regt, 3 construction regt)
1 sigs bn

Reserves
FORCES BY ROLE
MANOEUVRE
  Light
  14 inf regt (cadre)
  4 cav regt (cadre)
EQUIPMENT BY TYPE
ARMOURED FIGHTING VEHICLES
  RECCE 28 EE-9 *Cascavel*
  APC 12+
    APC (W) 12 EE-11 *Urutu*
    PPV *Typhoon* 4×4
ARTILLERY 99
  TOWED 105mm 19 M101
  MOR 81mm 80
AIR DEFENCE • GUNS 22:
  SP 20mm 3 M9 half track
  TOWED 19: 40mm 6 L/60; 13 M1A1

Navy 3,800
EQUIPMENT BY TYPE
PATROL AND COASTAL COMBATANTS 18
  PCR 1 *Itaipu* (BRZ *Roraima*) with 1 hel landing platform
  PBR 17: 1 *Capitan Cabral*; 2 *Capitan Ortiz* (ROC *Hai Ou*); 2 *Novatec*; 4 Type-701 (US *Sewart*); 3 *Croq* 15 (AUS *Armacraft*); 5 others
AMPHIBIOUS • LANDING CRAFT • LCVP 3

Naval Aviation 100
FORCES BY ROLE
TRANSPORT
  1 (liaison) sqn with Cessna 150; Cessna 210 *Centurion*; Cessna 310
TRANSPORT HELICOPTER
  1 sqn with AS350 *Ecureuil* (HB350 *Esquilo*)
EQUIPMENT BY TYPE
AIRCRAFT • TPT • Light 5: 2 Cessna 150; 1 Cessna 210 *Centurion*; 2 Cessna 310
HELICOPTERS • TPT • Light 2 AS350 *Ecureuil* (HB350 *Esquilo*)

Marines 700; 200 conscript (total 900)
FORCES BY ROLE
MANOEUVRE
  Amphibious
  3 mne bn(-)
ARTILLERY • TOWED 105mm 2 M101

Air Force 2,750
FORCES BY ROLE
GROUND ATTACK/ISR
  1 sqn with EMB-312 *Tucano**
TRANSPORT
  1 gp with C-212-200/400 *Aviocar*; DHC-6 *Twin Otter*
  1 VIP gp with Beech 58 *Baron*; Bell 427; Cessna U206 *Stationair*; Cessna 208B *Grand Caravan*; Cessna 402B; PA-32R *Saratoga* (EMB-721C *Sertanejo*)
TRAINING
  1 sqn with T-25 *Universal*; T-35A/B *Pillan*
TRANSPORT HELICOPTER
  1 gp with AS350 *Ecureuil* (HB350 *Esquilo*); Bell 205 (UH-1H *Iroquois*)
MANOEUVRE
  Air Manoeuvre
  1 AB bde
EQUIPMENT BY TYPE
AIRCRAFT 6 combat capable
  TPT 18: **Light** 17: 1 Beech 58 *Baron*; 4 C-212-200 *Aviocar*; 1 C-212-400 *Aviocar*; 3 Cessna 208B *Grand Caravan*; 2 Cessna 208 *Grand Caravan* EX; 1 Cessna 310; 1 Cessna 402B; 2 Cessna U206 *Stationair*; 1 DHC-6 *Twin Otter*; 1 PA-32R *Saratoga* (EMB-721C *Sertanejo*); **PAX** 1 Cessna 680 *Sovereign*
  TRG 21: 6 EMB-312 *Tucano**; 6 T-25 *Universal*; ε4 T-35A *Pillan*; 5 T-35B *Pillan*
HELICOPTERS • TPT • Light 17: 3 AS350 *Ecureuil* (HB350 *Esquilo*); 12 Bell 205 (UH-1H *Iroquois*); 1 Bell 407; 1 Bell 427 (VIP)

Gendarmerie & Paramilitary 14,800

Special Police Service 10,800; 4,000 conscript (total 14,800)

DEPLOYMENT
CENTRAL AFRICAN REPUBLIC: UN • MINUSCA 4
DEMOCRATIC REPUBLIC OF THE CONGO: UN • MONUSCO 6
SOUTH SUDAN: UN • UNMISS 3

Peru PER

Peruvian Nuevo Sol PEN		2023	2024	2025
GDP	PEN	999bn	1.06trn	1.11trn
	USD	267bn	283bn	295bn
Real GDP growth	%	-0.6	3.0	2.6
Def bdgt	PEN	7.31bn	7.97bn	
	USD	1.95bn	2.14bn	

Population	32,600,249					
Age	0–14	15–19	20–24	25–29	30–64	65 plus
Male	13.2%	4.3%	3.9%	3.8%	20.4%	3.4%
Female	12.6%	4.1%	3.9%	3.9%	22.0%	4.6%

Capabilities

Peru's armed forces are primarily orientated towards preserving territorial integrity and security, counter-insurgency and counter-narcotics. The military is working on strengthening its disaster-relief capabilities. The armed forces are hampered by fiscal constraints and an increasingly ageing inventory. Peru maintains close ties with Colombia, including a cooperation agreement on air control, humanitarian assistance and counternarcotics. The armed forces are capable of independently deploying externally and contributing to UN missions abroad. Peru took part in the 2024 RIMPAC exercise. Peru has boosted its tanker/transport and anti-submarine warfare capabilities with the acquisition of second-hand equipment from Spain. The navy is looking to acquire new surface vessels, while its ageing fleet of submarines has yet to finish a modernisation process. Key players in Peru's defence industry include the state-owned shipyard SIMA, aviation firm SEMAN and munitions manufacturer FAME. Deepening ties with South Korea have improved defence industrial capability.

ACTIVE 81,000 (Army 47,500 Navy 24,000 Air 9,500)
Gendarmerie & Paramilitary 77,000

Conscript liability 12 months voluntary conscription for both males and females

RESERVE 188,000 (Army 188,000)

ORGANISATIONS BY SERVICE

Space
EQUIPMENT BY TYPE
SATELLITES • ISR PeruSAT-1

Army 47,500
4 mil region
FORCES BY ROLE
SPECIAL FORCES
1 (1st) SF bde (2 spec ops bn, 2 cdo bn, 1 cdo coy, 1 CT coy, 1 airmob arty gp, 1 MP coy, 1 cbt spt bn)
1 (3rd) SF bde (1 spec ops bn, 2 cdo bn, 1 airmob arty gp, 1 MP coy)
1 (6th) SF bde (2 spec ops bn, 2 cdo bn, 1 cdo coy, 1 MP coy)
MANOEUVRE
Armoured
1 (3rd) armd bde (2 tk bn, 1 mech inf bn, 1 arty gp, 1 AT coy, 1 cbt engr bn, 1 cbt spt bn, 1 AD gp)
1 (6th) armd bde (2 tk bn, 1 mech inf bn, 1 cbt engr bn, 1 log bn, 1 ADA gp)
1 (9th) armd bde (2 tk bn, 1 mech inf bn, 1 SP arty gp, 1 ADA gp)
Mechanised
1 (3rd) armd cav bde (3 mech cav bn, 1 mot inf bn, 1 arty gp, 1 AD gp, 1 engr bn, 1 cbt spt bn)
1 (1st) cav bde (4 mech cav bn, 1 MP coy, 1 cbt spt bn)
Light
2 (2nd & 31st) mot inf bde (4 mot inf bn, 1 arty gp, 1 MP coy, 1 log bn)
3 (1st, 7th & 32nd) inf bde (3 inf bn, 1 MP coy, 1 cbt spt bn)
1 (33rd) inf bde (4 inf bn)
1 (4th) mtn bde (1 armd regt, 3 mot inf bn, 1 arty gp, 1 MP coy, 1 cbt spt bn)
1 (5th) mtn bde (1 armd regt, 2 mot inf bn, 3 jungle coy, 1 arty gp, 1 MP coy, 1 cbt spt bn)
1 (6th) jungle inf bde (4 jungle bn, 1 engr bn, 1 MP coy, 1 cbt spt bn)
1 (35th) jungle inf bde (1 SF gp, 3 jungle bn, 3 jungle coy, 1 jungle arty gp, 1 AT coy, 1 AD gp, 1 jungle engr bn)
COMBAT SUPPORT
1 arty gp (bde) (4 arty gp, 2 AD gp, 1 sigs gp)
1 (3rd) arty bde (4 arty gp, 1 AD gp, 1 sigs gp)
1 (22nd) engr bde (3 engr bn, 1 demining coy)
COMBAT SERVICE SUPPORT
1 (1st Multipurpose) spt bde
AVIATION
1 (1st) avn bde (1 atk hel/recce hel bn, 1 avn bn, 2 aslt hel/tpt hel bn)
AIR DEFENCE
1 AD gp (regional troops)
EQUIPMENT BY TYPE
ARMOURED FIGHTING VEHICLES
MBT 165 T-55; (75† in store)
LT TK 96 AMX-13 (some with 9M133 *Kornet*-E)
RECCE 95: 30 BRDM-2; 15 Fiat 6616; 50 M9A1
APC 295
  APC (T) 120+: 120 M113A1; some BTR-50 (CP)†
  APC (W) 175: 150 UR-416; 25 Fiat 6614
ENGINEERING & MAINTENANCE VEHICLES
ARV M578
VLB GQL-111
ANTI-TANK-ANTI-INFRASTRUCTURE
MSL
  SP 22 M1165A2 HMMWV with 9K135 *Kornet* E (RS-AT-14 *Spriggan*)

MANPATS 9K11 *Malyutka* (RS-AT-3 *Sagger*); HJ-73C; 9K135 *Kornet* E (RS-AT-14 *Spriggan*); *Spike*-ER
RCL 106mm M40A1
ARTILLERY 1,025
SP 155mm 12 M109A2
TOWED 290: **105mm** 152: 44 M101; 24 M2A1; 60 M-56; 24 Model 56 pack howitzer; **122mm**; 36 D-30; **130mm** 36 M-46; **155mm** 66: 36 M114, 30 Model 50
MRL 122mm 49: 22 BM-21 *Grad*; 27 Type-90B
MOR 674+: **81mm/107mm** 350; **SP 107mm** 24 M106A1; **120mm** 300+ Brandt/Expal Model L
PATROL AND COASTAL COMBATANTS • PBR 1 *Vargas Guerra*
AIRCRAFT
TPT • Light 17: 2 An-28 *Cash*; 3 An-32B *Cline*; 1 Beech 350 *King Air*; 1 Beech 1900D; 4 Cessna 152; 1 Cessna 208 *Caravan*; 1 Cessna 560 *Citation*; 2 Cessna U206 *Stationair*; 1 PA-31T *Cheyenne* II; 1 PA-34 *Seneca*
TRG 4 IL-103
HELICOPTERS
MRH 7 Mi-17 *Hip* H
TPT 34: **Heavy** (3 Mi-26T *Halo* in store); **Medium** 21 Mi-171Sh; **Light** 13: 1 AW109K2; 2 F-280FX; 9 PZL Mi-2 *Hoplite*; 1 R-44
TRG 1 F-28F
AIR DEFENCE
SAM • Point-defence 9K36 *Strela*-3 (RS-SA-14 *Gremlin*); 9K310 *Igla*-1 (RS-SA-16 *Gimlet*); 9K32 *Strela*-2 (RS-SA-7 *Grail*)‡
GUNS 165
SP 23mm 35 ZSU-23-4
TOWED 23mm 130: 80 ZU-23-2; 50 ZU-23

Navy 24,000 (incl 1,000 Coast Guard)

Commands: Pacific, Lake Titicaca, Amazon River
EQUIPMENT BY TYPE
SUBMARINES • SSK 6:
  4 *Angamos* (GER Type-209/1200) with 8 single 533mm TT with SST-4 HWT (of which 1 in refit)
  2 *Islay* (GER Type-209/1100) with 8 single 533mm TT with SUT 264 HWT
PRINCIPAL SURFACE COMBATANTS • FRIGATES 6
FFGHM 6:
  2 *Aguirre* (ex-ITA *Lupo*) with 8 single lnchr with *Otomat* Mk2 AShM, 1 octuple Mk 29 lnchr with RIM-7P *Sea Sparrow* SAM, 2 triple 324mm ASTT with A244 LWT, 1 127mm gun (capacity 1 Bell 212 (AB-212)/SH-3D *Sea King*)
  2 *Aguirre* (ex-ITA *Lupo*) with 2 twin lnchr with MM40 *Exocet* Block 3 AShM, 1 octuple Mk 29 lnchr with RIM-7P *Sea Sparrow* SAM, 2 triple 324mm ASTT with A244 LWT, 1 127mm gun (capacity 1 Bell 212 (AB-212)/SH-3D *Sea King*)
  2 *Carvajal* (ITA *Lupo* mod) with 2 twin lnchr with MM40 *Exocet* Block 3 AShM, 1 octuple *Albatros* lnchr with *Aspide* SAM, 2 triple 324mm ASTT with A244 LWT, 1 127mm gun (capacity 1 Bell 212 (AB-212)/SH-3D *Sea King*)
PATROL AND COASTAL COMBATANTS 13
CORVETTES 7
  FSG 5 *Velarde* (FRA PR-72 64m) with 4 single lnchr with MM38 *Exocet* AShM, 1 76mm gun
  FS 2 *Ferré* (ex-ROK *Po Hang*) with 1 76mm gun
PCR 6: 2 *Amazonas* with 1 76mm gun; 2 *Manuel Clavero*; 2 *Marañon* with 2 76mm guns
AMPHIBIOUS
PRINCIPAL AMPHIBIOUS SHIPS • LPD 1 *Pisco* (IDN *Makassar*) (capacity 2 LCM; 3 hels; 24 IFV; 450 troops)
LANDING SHIPS • LST 1 *Paita* (capacity 395 troops) (ex-US *Terrebonne Parish*)
LANDING CRAFT • UCAC 7 *Griffon* 2000TD (capacity 22 troops)
LOGISTICS AND SUPPORT 24
AG 6 *Río Napo*
AGOR 1 *Humboldt* (operated by IMARPE)
AGORH 1 *Carrasco*
AGS 5: 1 *Zimic* (ex-NLD *Dokkum*); 2 *Van Straelen*; 1 *La Macha*, 1 *Stiglich* (river survey vessel for the upper Amazon)
AH 4 (river hospital craft)
AOL 2 *Noguera*
AORH 1 *Tacna* (ex-NLD *Amsterdam*)
ATF 1 *Morales*
AWT 1 *Caloyeras*
AXS 2: 1 *Marte*; 1 *Union*

Naval Aviation ε800
FORCES BY ROLE
ANTI-SUBMARINE WARFARE
  1 sqn with Bell 206B *Jet Ranger* II; Bell 212 ASW (AB-212 ASW); SH-2G *Super Seasprite*
  1 sqn with SH-3D *Sea King*; UH-3H *Sea King*
MARITIME PATROL
  1 sqn with Beech 200T; Fokker 50; Fokker 60
SEARCH & RESCUE
  1 flt with Bell 412SP
TRANSPORT
  1 flt with An-32B *Cline*; Mi-8T *Hip*
TRAINING
  1 sqn with T-34C/C-1 *Turbo Mentor*
  1 hel sqn with F-28F
EQUIPMENT BY TYPE
AIRCRAFT
  MP 6: 4 Beech 200T; 2 Fokker 60
  SIGINT 1 Fokker 50
  MP 1 Fokker 50
  TPT • Light 4: 2 An-32B *Cline*; 2 Fokker 60
  TRG 3: 2 T-34C *Turbo Mentor*; 1 T-34C-1 *Turbo Mentor*
HELICOPTERS
  ASW 16: 2 Bell 212 ASW (AB-212 ASW); 5 SH-2G

Super Seasprite; 9 SH-3D Sea King
MRH 3 Bell 412SP
TPT 10: **Medium** 7: 1 Mi-8T Hip; 6 UH-3H Sea King; **Light** 3 Bell 206B Jet Ranger II
TRG 5 F-28F
AIR-LAUNCHED MISSILES
ASM AGM-65D Maverick
AShM AM39 Exocet

Marines 4,000
FORCES BY ROLE
SPECIAL FORCES
3 cdo gp
MANOEUVRE
Light
2 inf bn
1 inf gp
Amphibious
1 mne bde (1 SF gp, 1 recce bn, 2 inf bn, 1 amph bn, 1 arty gp)
Jungle
1 jungle inf bn
EQUIPMENT BY TYPE
ARMOURED FIGHTING VEHICLES
APC • APC (W) 47+: 32 LAV II; V-100 Commando; 15 V-200 Chaimite
AUV 7 RAM Mk3
ANTI-TANK/ANTI-INFRASTRUCTURE
RCL 84mm Carl Gustaf; **106mm** M40A1
ARTILLERY 18+
TOWED 122mm D-30
MOR 18+: **81mm** some; **120mm** ε18
AIR DEFENCE • GUNS 20mm SP (twin)

Air Force 9,500
Divided into five regions – North, Lima, South, Central and Amazon
FORCES BY ROLE
FIGHTER
1 sqn with MiG-29S/SE Fulcrum C; MiG-29UBM Fulcrum B
FIGHTER/GROUND ATTACK
1 sqn with Mirage 2000E/ED (2000P/DP)
2 sqn with A-37B Dragonfly
1 sqn with Su-25A Frogfoot A; Su-25UBK Frogfoot B
ISR
1 (photo-survey) sqn with Learjet 36A; SA-227-BC Metro III (C-26B)
TRANSPORT
1 sqn with B-737; An-32 Cline
1 sqn with DHC-6 Twin Otter; DHC-6-400 Twin Otter; PC-6 Turbo Porter
1 sqn with L-100-20
TRAINING
2 (drug interdiction) sqn with EMB-312 Tucano

1 sqn with MB-339A*
1 (aerobatic) sqn with GB1 GameBird; Z-242
1 hel sqn with Enstrom 280FX; Schweizer 300C
ATTACK HELICOPTER
1 sqn with Mi-25†/Mi-35P Hind
TRANSPORT HELICOPTER
1 sqn with Mi-17-1V Hip
1 sqn with Bell 206 Jet Ranger; Bell 212 (AB-212); Bell 412 Twin Huey
1 sqn with Bo-105LS
AIR DEFENCE
6 bn with S-125 Pechora (RS-SA-3 Goa)
EQUIPMENT BY TYPE
AIRCRAFT 59 combat capable
FTR 19: 9 MiG-29S Fulcrum C; 3 MiG-29SE Fulcrum C; 5 MiG-29SMP Fulcrum; 2 MiG-29UBM Fulcrum B
FGA 11: 2 Mirage 2000ED (2000DP); 9 Mirage 2000E (2000P) (some†)
ATK 19: 15 A-37B Dragonfly; 2 Su-25A Frogfoot A; 2 Su-25UBK Frogfoot B; (8 Su-25A Frogfoot A; 6 Su-25UBK Frogfoot B in store)
ISR 5: 2 Learjet 36A; 3 SA-227-BC Metro III (C-26B)
TKR/TPT 2 KC-130H Hercules
TPT 38: **Medium** 6: 4 C-27J Spartan; 2 L-100-20; **Light** 29: 4 An-32 Cline; 1 Beech 360C King Air; 7 Cessna 172 Skyhawk; 3 DHC-6 Twin Otter; 12 DHC-6-400 Twin Otter; 1 PA-44; 1 PC-6 Turbo-Porter; **PAX** 3: 2 B-737; 1 Learjet 45 (VIP)
TRG 76: 8 CH-2000; 19 EMB-312 Tucano†; 1 GB1 GameBird; 20 KT-1P; 10 MB-339A*; 6 T-41A/D Mescalero; 12 Z-242
HELICOPTERS
ATK 18: 16 Mi-25 Hind D†; 2 Mi-35P Hind E
MRH 12: 2 Bell 412 Twin Huey; ε10 Mi-17-1V Hip
TPT 25: **Medium** 3 Mi-171Sh; **Light** 22: 8 Bell 206 Jet Ranger; 6 Bell 212 (AB-212); 6 Bo-105LS; 2 Enstrom 280FX
TRG 4 Schweizer 300C
AIR DEFENCE • SAM
Short-range S-125 Pechora (RS-SA-3 Goa)
Point-defence Javelin
AIR-LAUNCHED MISSILES
AAM • IR R-3 (RS-AA-2 Atoll)‡; R-60 (RS-AA-8 Aphid)‡; R-73 (RS-AA-11A Archer); R-550 Magic; **IR/SARH** R-27 (RS-AA-10 Alamo); **ARH** R-77 (RS-AA-12 Adder)
ASM AS-30; Kh-29L (RS-AS-14A Kedge)
ARM Kh-58 (RS-AS-11 Kilter)

Gendarmerie & Paramilitary 77,000

National Police 77,000 (100,000 reported)
EQUIPMENT BY TYPE
ARMOURED FIGHTING VEHICLES
APC (W) 120: 20 BMR-600; 100 MOWAG Roland

AIRCRAFT
TPT • Light 5: 1 An-32B *Cline*; 1 Beech 1900C; 3 Cessna 208B
HELICOPTERS
MRH 4 Mi-17 *Hip* H
TPT • Light 16: 5 H145; 2 Mi-171Sh; 9 UH-1H *Huey* II

General Police 43,000

Security Police 21,000

Technical Police 13,000

Coast Guard 1,000
Personnel included as part of Navy
EQUIPMENT BY TYPE
PATROL AND COASTAL COMBATANTS 44
  PCC 10: 6 *Rio Pativilca* (ROK *Tae Geuk*); 4 *Rio Nepena*
  PBF 1 *Rio Itaya* (SWE Combat Boat 90)
  PB 12: 6 *Chicama* (US *Dauntless*); 2 *Punta Sal* (Defiant 45); 1 *Rio Chira*; 3 *Rio Santa*
  PBR 21: 1 *Rio Viru*; 8 *Parachique*; 12 *Zorritos*
LOGISTICS AND SUPPORT • AH 1 *Puno*
AIRCRAFT
  TPT • Light 3: 1 DHC-6 *Twin Otter*; 2 F-27 *Friendship*

Rondas Campesinas
Peasant self-defence force. Perhaps 7,000 rondas 'gp', up to pl strength, some with small arms. Deployed mainly in emergency zone

DEPLOYMENT
CENTRAL AFRICAN REPUBLIC: UN • MINUSCA 234; 1 engr coy
DEMOCRATIC REPUBLIC OF THE CONGO: UN • MONUSCO 2
LEBANON: UN • UNIFIL 1
SOUTH SUDAN: UN • UNMISS 4
SUDAN: UN • UNISFA 3

Suriname SUR

Suriname Dollar SRD		2023	2024	2025
GDP	SRD	138bn	163bn	188bn
	USD	3.75bn	4.92bn	4.96bn
Real GDP growth	%	2.1	3.0	3.0
Def bdgt	SRD	n.k.	n.k.	n.k.
	USD	n.k.	n.k.	n.k.
Population		646,758		

Age	0–14	15–19	20–24	25–29	30–64	65 plus
Male	11.4%	4.0%	4.3%	4.2%	22.5%	3.1%
Female	11.1%	3.9%	4.1%	4.0%	23.0%	4.4%

Capabilities
The armed forces are principally tasked with preserving territorial integrity. They also assist the police in internal- and border-security missions, as well as tackling transnational criminal activity and drug trafficking, and have been involved in disaster relief and humanitarian assistance operations. Ties with Brazil, China, France, India and the US have been crucial for the supply of equipment, including a limited number of armoured vehicles and helicopters, as well as training activity. The armed forces participate in US SOUTHCOM's *Tradewinds* exercise. Resource challenges and limited equipment serviceability mean the armed forces are constrained in providing sufficient border and coastal control and surveillance. The country has no defence industrial production capacity and has looked abroad to improve training and maintenance capacity.

ACTIVE 1,840 (Army 1,400 Navy 240 Air 200)
(All services form part of the army)

ORGANISATIONS BY SERVICE

Army 1,400
FORCES BY ROLE
MANOEUVRE
  Mechanised
  1 mech cav sqn
  Light
  1 inf bn (4 coy)
COMBAT SUPPORT
  1 MP bn (coy)
EQUIPMENT BY TYPE
ARMOURED FIGHTING VEHICLES
  RECCE 6 EE-9 *Cascavel*
  APC • APC (W) 15 EE-11 *Urutu*
ANTI-TANK/ANTI-INFRASTRUCTURE
  RCL 106mm M40A1
ARTILLERY • MOR 81mm 6

Navy ε240
EQUIPMENT BY TYPE
PATROL AND COASTAL COMBATANTS 4

PB 3: 2 FPB 72 Mk II; 1 FPB 98 Mk I
PBR 1 Project 414

Air Force ε200
EQUIPMENT BY TYPE
HELICOPTERS • MRH 3 SA316B *Alouette* III (*Chetak*)

Trinidad and Tobago TTO

Trinidad and Tobago Dollar TTD		2023	2024	2025
GDP	TTD	189bn	190bn	197bn
	USD	28.0bn	28.1bn	29.2bn
Real GDP growth	%	1.1	1.6	2.4
Def bdgt	TTD	3.46bn	3.51bn	3.46bn
	USD	513m	519m	513m

Real-terms defence budget trend (USDm, constant 2015)

Population	1,408,966				
Age	0–14	15–19	20–24	25–29	30–64	65 plus
Male	9.5%	3.4%	3.2%	3.1%	24.5%	6.5%
Female	9.2%	3.3%	3.0%	2.9%	23.8%	7.5%

Capabilities

The Trinidad and Tobago Defence Force (TTDF) focuses on border protection and maritime security, as well as counter-narcotics tasks. Trinidad and Tobago is a member of the Caribbean Community and cooperates with other countries in the region in disaster-relief efforts. There are plans to establish a joint training academy in Trinidad and a proposal for a new coastguard base in Tobago. The TTDF has taken part in US SOUTHCOM's *Tradewinds* exercise and has sent personnel to the US and the UK for training. Trinidad and Tobago has no capacity to deploy and maintain troops abroad. Apart from maintenance facilities, there is no domestic defence industry.

ACTIVE 4,650 (Army 3,000 Coast Guard 1,600 Air Guard 50)
(All services form the Trinidad and Tobago Defence Force)
RESERVE 650

ORGANISATIONS BY SERVICE

Army ε3,000
FORCES BY ROLE
SPECIAL FORCES
  1 SF unit
MANOEUVRE
  Light
  2 inf bn

COMBAT SUPPORT
  1 engr bn
COMBAT SERVICE SUPPORT
  1 log bn
EQUIPMENT BY TYPE
ANTI-TANK/ANTI-INFRASTRUCTURE
  RCL 84mm *Carl Gustaf*
ARTILLERY • MOR 81mm 6 L16A1

Coast Guard 1,600
FORCES BY ROLE
COMMAND
  1 mne HQ
EQUIPMENT BY TYPE
PATROL AND COASTAL COMBATANTS 17
  PCO 3: 2 *Port of Spain* (AUS *Cape*); 1 *Nelson* II (ex-PRC *Shuke* III)
  PCC 6: 2 *Point Lisas* (Damen Fast Crew Supplier 5009); 4 *Speyside* (Damen Stan Patrol 5009)
  PB 8: 2 *Gaspar Grande*†; 6 *Scarlet Ibis* (Austal 30m)

Air Guard 50
EQUIPMENT BY TYPE
AIRCRAFT
  TPT • Light 2 SA-227 *Metro* III (C-26)
HELICOPTERS
  MRH 4 AW139
  TPT • Light 1 S-76

Uruguay URY

Uruguayan Peso UYU		2023	2024	2025
GDP	UYU	3.00trn	3.27trn	3.53trn
	USD	77.2bn	82.5bn	86.4bn
Real GDP growth	%	0.4	3.2	3.0
Def bdgt	UYU	23.2bn	23.4bn	
	USD	597m	592m	

Real-terms defence budget trend (USDm, constant 2015)

Population	3,425,330				
Age	0–14	15–19	20–24	25–29	30–64	65 plus
Male	9.6%	3.4%	3.7%	3.9%	21.5%	6.4%
Female	9.3%	3.3%	3.6%	3.8%	22.3%	9.3%

Capabilities

The armed forces are focused on assuring sovereignty, territorial integrity and the protection of strategic resources. Uruguay and China signed a defence-cooperation agreement in 2022, following a similar pact between Montevideo and Moscow in 2018 that provides for training exchanges. Uruguay and Argentina have a joint peacekeeping unit and exercise together. The country has long-established military ties with the US. The armed forces participate regularly in multinational exercises and deployments. The navy is being upgraded through the commissioning of ex-US Coast Guard patrol boats and the planned introduction of two new offshore patrol vessels to strengthen policing and coastguard capacities. The navy has created a tactical operations centre to oversee the deployment of surface and aerial assets to combat illegal maritime activities. The acquisition of air-defence radars may have improved the armed forces' ability to monitor domestic airspace, but the lack of sufficient interdiction capability will continue to limit the capacity to respond to contingencies. Much equipment is second-hand, and there is little capacity for independent power projection. Maintenance work is sometimes outsourced to foreign companies.

ACTIVE 21,100 (Army 13,500 Navy 5,000 Air 2,600) **Gendarmerie & Paramilitary 1,400**

ORGANISATIONS BY SERVICE

Army 13,500

Uruguayan units are substandard size, mostly around 30%. Div are at most bde size, while bn are of reinforced coy strength. Regts are also coy size, some bn size, with the largest formation being the 2nd armd cav regt

FORCES BY ROLE
COMMAND
  4 mil region/div HQ
MANOEUVRE
  Mechanised
  2 (1st & 2nd Cav) mech bde (1 armd cav regt, 2 mech cav regt)
  1 (3rd Cav) mech bde (2 mech cav regt, 1 mech inf bn)
  3 (2nd, 3rd & 4th Inf) mech bde (2 mech inf bn; 1 inf bn)
  1 (5th Inf) mech bde (1 armd cav regt; 1 armd inf bn; 1 mech inf bn)
  Light
  1 (1st Inf) inf bde (2 inf bn)
  Air Manoeuvre
  1 para bn
COMBAT SUPPORT
  1 (strategic reserve) arty regt
  5 fd arty gp
  1 (1st) engr bde (2 engr bn)
  4 cbt engr bn
  1 sigs bde (2 sigs bn)
AIR DEFENCE
  1 AD gp
EQUIPMENT BY TYPE
ARMOURED FIGHTING VEHICLES
  MBT 15 *Tiran-5*
  LT TK 47: 22 M41A1UR; 25 M41C
  RECCE 15 EE-9 *Cascavel*
  IFV 18 BMP-1
  APC 421
    APC (T) 27: 24 M113A1UR; 3 MT-LB
    APC (W) 360: 54 *Condor*; 11 EE-11 *Urutu*; 48 GAZ-39371 *Vodnik*; 53 OT-64; 47 OT-93; 147 *Piranha*
    PPV 34: 14 Mamba Mk7; 20 M-ATV
ENGINEERING & MAINTENANCE VEHICLES
  AEV MT-LB
ANTI-TANK/ANTI-INFRASTRUCTURE
  MSL • MANPATS *Milan*
  RCL 106mm 69 M40A1
ARTILLERY 195
  SP 16: **105mm** 10 M-108; **122mm** 6 2S1 *Gvozdika*
  TOWED 44: **105mm** 36: 28 M101A1; 8 M102; **155mm** 8 M114A1
  MRL • 122mm 4 RM-70
  MOR 135: **81mm** 91: 35 M1, 56 Expal Model LN; **120mm** 44 Model SL
UNINHABITED AERIAL VEHICLES • ISR • Light 1 *Charrua*
AIR DEFENCE • GUNS • TOWED 14: **20mm** 14: 6 M167 *Vulcan*; 8 TCM-20 (w/Elta M-2106 radar)

Navy 5,000

HQ at Montevideo
EQUIPMENT BY TYPE
PATROL AND COASTAL COMBATANTS 14
  PB 10: 1 *Colonia* (ex-US *Cape*); 9 Type-44
  PBF 1 *Huracan* (ex-ROK *Sea Dolphin*)
  PBI 3 *Rio Arapey* (ex-US *Marine Protector*)
MINE WARFARE • MINE COUNTERMEASURES 2
  MSO 2 *Temerario* (*Kondor* II)
AMPHIBIOUS 3: 2 LCVP; 1 LCM
LOGISTICS AND SUPPORT 8
  AAR 2 *Islas de Flores* (ex-GER *Hermann Helms*)
  ABU 1 *Sirius*
  AOR 1 *Artigas* (GER *Freiburg*, general spt ship with replenishment capabilities);
  ARS 1 *Vanguardia*
  ATF 1 *Maldonado* (also used as patrol craft)
  AXS 2: 1 *Capitan Miranda*; 1 *Bonanza*

Naval Aviation 210
FORCES BY ROLE
MARITIME PATROL
  1 flt with Beech 200T*; Cessna O-2A *Skymaster*
SEARCH & RESCUE/TRANSPORT HELICOPTER
  1 sqn with AS350B2 *Ecureuil* (*Esquilo*); Bell 412SP *Twin Huey*
TRANSPORT/TRAINING
  1 flt with T-34C *Turbo Mentor*
TRAINING
  1 hel sqn with Bell 412SP *Twin Huey*; OH-58 *Kiowa*
EQUIPMENT BY TYPE
AIRCRAFT 2 combat capable
  ISR 4: 2 Beech 200T*; 2 Cessna O-2A *Skymaster*
  TRG 2 T-34C *Turbo Mentor*
HELICOPTERS

ISR 1 OH-58 *Kiowa*

MRH 4: 2 Bell 412 (AB-412); 2 Bell 412SP *Twin Huey*

TPT • Light 1 AS350B2 *Ecureuil* (*Esquilo*)

Naval Infantry 700
FORCES BY ROLE
MANOEUVRE
Amphibious
1 mne bn(-)

Air Force 2,600
FORCES BY ROLE
FIGHTER/GROUND ATTACK
1 sqn with A-37B *Dragonfly*
ISR
1 flt with EMB-110 *Bandeirante*†
TRANSPORT
1 sqn with C-130B *Hercules*; C-212 *Aviocar*; EMB-120 *Brasilia*
1 (liaison) sqn with Cessna 206H; T-41D
1 (liaison) flt with Cessna 206H
TRAINING
1 sqn with PC-7U *Turbo Trainer*
1 sqn with Beech 58 *Baron* (UB-58); SF-260EU
TRANSPORT HELICOPTER
1 sqn with AS365 *Dauphin*; Bell 205 (UH-1H *Iroquois*); Bell 212

EQUIPMENT BY TYPE
AIRCRAFT 8 combat capable
ATK 7 A-37B *Dragonfly*
ISR 4: 1 EMB-110 *Bandeirante**†; 3 O-2A *Skymaster*
TKR/TPT 2 KC-130H *Hercules*
TPT 24: **Medium** 2 C-130B *Hercules*; **Light** 21: 1 BAe-125-700A; 2 Beech 58 *Baron* (UB-58); 6 C-212 *Aviocar*; 9 Cessna 206H; 1 Cessna 210; 2 EMB-120 *Brasilia*; **PAX** 1 C-29 Hawker
TRG 17: 5 PC-7U *Turbo Trainer*; 12 SF-260EU
HELICOPTERS
MRH 2 AS365N2 *Dauphin* II
TPT • Light 10: 5 Bell 205 (UH-1H *Iroquois*); 5 Bell 212

Gendarmerie & Paramilitary 1,400
Guardia Nacional Republicana 1,400

DEPLOYMENT
CENTRAL AFRICAN REPUBLIC: UN • MINUSCA 3
DEMOCRATIC REPUBLIC OF THE CONGO: UN • MONUSCO 742; 1 inf bn
EGYPT: MFO 41; 1 engr/tpt unit
INDIA/PAKISTAN: UN • UNMOGIP 2
LEBANON: UN • UNIFIL 1
SUDAN: UN • UNISFA 2
SYRIA/ISRAEL: UN • UNDOF 211; 1 mech inf coy

Venezuela VEN

Venezuelan Bolivar soberano VES		2023	2024	2025
GDP	VES	2.91trn	4.97trn	8.83trn
	USD	99.2bn	106bn	110bn
Real GDP growth	%	4.0	3.0	3.0
Def bdgt	VES	14.7bn	30.3bn	
	USD	502m	649m	
Population	31,250,306			

Age	0–14	15–19	20–24	25–29	30–64	65 plus
Male	12.8%	4.1%	3.9%	3.9%	21.0%	4.2%
Female	12.2%	4.0%	3.8%	3.8%	21.5%	5.0%

Capabilities

Venezuela's armed forces and national guard are tasked with protecting sovereignty, assuring territorial integrity and assisting with internal-security and counter-narcotics operations. Economic challenges have affected equipment availability, modernisation and training levels. Although Venezuela and Guyana agreed on a declaration in December 2023 to avoid a military clash, tensions persist along their border because of Venezuela's claim to Guyana's Essequibo region. Venezuela and Colombia recently re-established military relations that were strained by waves of migrants fleeing Venezuela because of the economic situation there, and the presence of armed groups in the border area that caused both countries to deploy troops. Caracas has close ties with China and Russia, relying on both to procure weapons and provide technical support. It also sources weapons from Iran. Venezuela has participated in exercises with China, Cuba, Iran and Russia. The military has little logistics capability to support deployments abroad. Venezuela's defence industry consists of small, state-owned companies, mainly focused on the production of small arms and munitions. Local platform production has been limited to small coastal-patrol boats and Empresa Aeronáutica Nacional (EANSA), a state-owned aerospace company established in 2020, produces an indigenous UAV based on Iran's *Mohajer*.

ACTIVE 123,000 (Army 63,000 Navy 25,500 Air 11,500 National Guard 23,000) Gendarmerie & Paramilitary 220,000

Conscript liability 30 months selective, varies by region for all services

RESERVE 8,000 (Army 8,000)

ORGANISATIONS BY SERVICE

Army ε63,000
FORCES BY ROLE
SPECIAL FORCES
1 (99th) spec ops bde (5 spec ops bn)
1 (94th) spec ops bde (3 spec ops bn)
MANOEUVRE
Reconnaissance
1 cav bde (3 recce bn, 1 mor bty, 1 cbt engr coy, 1 sigs coy, 1 maint coy)

Armoured
1 (11th) armd bde (1 recce sqn, 2 tk bn, 1 mech inf bn, 1 SP arty gp, 1 fd arty gp, 1 cbt engr coy, 1 sigs coy, 1 log coy, 1 maint coy)
1 (41st) armd bde (3 tk bn, 1 mech inf bn, 1 SP arty gp, 1 cbt engr coy, 1 sigs coy, 1 log coy)

Mechanised
1 (14th) mech inf bde (1 recce sqn, 1 tk bn, 2 mech inf bn, 1 fd arty gp, 1 cbt engr coy, 1 sigs coy, 1 log coy, 1 maint coy)
1 (25th) mech inf bde (1 recce sqn, 1 mech inf bn, 1 mot inf bn, 1 fd arty gp, 1 cbt engr coy, 1 sigs coy, 1 log coy, 1 maint coy)
1 (31st) mech inf bde (1 recce gp, 1 mech inf bn, 1 ranger bn, 1 fd arty gp, 1 cbt engr coy, 1 sigs coy, 1 log coy, 1 maint coy)

Light
1 (21st) mot inf bde (1 recce sqn, 3 mot inf bn, 2 fd arty gp, 1 cbt engr coy, 1 sigs coy, 1 log coy, 1 maint coy)
1 (13th) mot inf bde (1 recce gp, 3 mot inf bn, 1 fd arty gp, 1 cbt engr coy, 1 sigs coy, 1 log coy, 1 maint coy)
1 (22nd) mot inf bde (1 recce sqn, 2 mot inf bn, 1 fd arty gp, 1 cbt engr coy, 1 sigs coy, 1 log coy, 1 maint coy)
1 (92nd) ranger bde (1 recce sqn, 1 tk bn, 3 ranger bn, 1 fd arty gp, 1 cbt engr coy, 1 sigs coy, 1 log coy, 1 maint coy)
1 (12th) ranger bde (1 recce sqn, 1 mot inf bn, 3 ranger bn, 1 fd arty gp, 1 cbt engr coy, 1 sigs coy, 1 log coy, 1 maint coy)
1 (32nd) jungle inf bde (1 recce sqn, 3 jungle inf bn, 1 fd arty gp, 1 cbt engr coy, 1 sigs coy, 1 log coy, 1 maint coy)
1 (33rd) jungle inf bde (4 jungle inf bn)
2 (51st & 53rd) jungle inf bde (3 jungle inf bn, 1 fd arty gp, 1 cbt engr coy, 1 sigs coy, 1 log coy, 1 maint coy)
1 (52nd) jungle inf bde (1 recce sqn, 2 jungle inf bn, 1 fd arty gp, 1 cbt engr coy, 1 sigs coy, 1 log coy, 1 maint coy)

Airborne
1 AB bde (1 recce coy, 3 AB bn, 1 cbt engr coy, 1 sigs coy, 1 log coy)

Other
1 (93rd) sy bde (1 mot inf bn, 4 sy bn, 1 cbt engr coy, 1 sigs coy, 1 log coy, 1 maint coy)

COMBAT SUPPORT
1 arty bde (2 SP arty bn, 3 MRL bn)
1 engr bde (5 engr bn)
1 engr bde (2 cbt engr bn, 1 engr bn, 1 construction bn)
1 engr bde (1 cbt engr bn, 1 engr bn, 1 maint bn)
1 engr bde (3 railway bn)
1 MP bde (5 MP bn)
1 sigs bde

COMBAT SERVICE SUPPORT
1 (81st) log bde (4 log bn)
1 (82nd) log bde (5 log bn)
1 (83rd) log bde (3 log bn)

AVIATION
1 avn comd (1 tpt avn bn, 1 atk hel bn, 1 ISR avn bn)

Reserve Organisations 8,000

FORCES BY ROLE
MANOEUVRE
Armoured
1 armd bn
Light
4 inf bn
1 ranger bn
COMBAT SUPPORT
1 arty bn
2 engr regt

EQUIPMENT BY TYPE
ARMOURED FIGHTING VEHICLES
MBT 173: 81 AMX-30V; 92 T-72B1
LT TK 109: 31 AMX-13; 78 *Scorpion*-90
RECCE 121: 42 *Dragoon* 300 LFV2; 79 V-100/V-150
IFV 237: 123 BMP-3 (incl variants); 114 BTR-80A (incl variants)
APC • APC (W) 36 *Dragoon* 300

ENGINEERING & MAINTENANCE VEHICLES
ARV 5: BREM-L; 3 AMX-30D; BREM-1; 2 *Dragoon* 300RV; *Samson*
VLB *Leguan*
NBC VEHICLES 10 TPz-1 *Fuchs* NBC

ANTI-TANK/ANTI-INFRASTRUCTURE
MSL • MANPATS IMI MAPATS
RCL 106mm 175 M40A1
GUNS • SP 76mm 75 M18 *Hellcat*

ARTILLERY 515
SP 60: **152mm** 48 2S19 *Msta-S*; **155mm** 12 Mk F3
TOWED 92: **105mm** 80: 40 M101A1; 40 Model 56 pack howitzer; **155mm** 12 M114A1
MRL 56: **122mm** 24 BM-21 *Grad*; **160mm** 20 LAR SP (LAR-160); **300mm** 12 9A52 *Smerch*
GUN/MOR 120mm 13 2S23 NONA-SVK
MOR 270: **81mm** 165; **SP 81mm** 21 *Dragoon* 300PM; AMX-VTT; **120mm** 84: 60 Brandt; 24 2S12

AIRCRAFT
TPT • Light 28: 1 Beech 90 *King Air*; 1 Beech 200 *King Air*; 1 Beech 300 *King Air*; 1 Cessna 172; 6 Cessna 182 *Skylane*; 2 Cessna 206; 2 Cessna 207 *Stationair*; 1 IAI-201 *Arava*; 2 IAI-202 *Arava*; 11 M-28 *Skytruck*

HELICOPTERS
ATK 9 Mi-35M2 *Hind*
MRH 31: 10 Bell 412EP; 2 Bell 412SP; 19 Mi-17V-5 *Hip* H
TPT 9: **Heavy** 3 Mi-26T2 *Halo*; **Medium** 2 AS-61D; **Light** 4: 3 Bell 206B *Jet Ranger*, 1 Bell 206L3 *Long Ranger* II

Navy ε22,300; ε3,200 conscript (total ε25,500)
EQUIPMENT BY TYPE
SUBMARINES 1
SSK 1 *Sabalo* (in refit; 1 more non-operational) (GER T-209/1300) with 8 single 533mm TT with SST-4 HWT
PRINCIPAL SURFACE COMBATANTS • FRIGATES 2

FFGHM 2 *Mariscal Sucre* (ITA *Lupo* mod)† (1 more non-operational) with 8 single lnchr with *Otomat* Mk2 AShM, 1 octuple *Albatros* lnchr with *Aspide* SAM, 2 triple 324mm ASTT with A244 LWT, 1 127mm gun (capacity 1 Bell 212 (AB-212) hel)

PATROL AND COASTAL COMBATANTS 13
  CORVETTES • FSGH 2 *Guaiqueri* with 2 quadruple lnchr with C-802A AShM, 1 *Millenium* CIWS, 1 76mm gun
  PSOH 1 *Guaiqueri* with 1 *Millennium* CIWS, 1 76mm gun
  PBFG 2 *Peykaap* III(IPS-16 mod) with 2 single lnchr with C-701 (*Kosar*) AShM/C-704 (*Nasr*) AShM
  PBG 3 *Federacion* (UK Vosper 37m) with 2 single lnchr with *Otomat* Mk2 AShM
  PBF 2 *Peykaap* III (IPS-16 mod)
  PB 3 *Constitucion* (UK Vosper 37m) with 1 76mm gun
AMPHIBIOUS
  LANDING SHIPS • LST 3 *Capana* (ROK *Alligator*) capacity 12 tanks; 200 troops) (one more non-operational)
  LANDING CRAFT 3:
    LCU 2 *Margarita* (river comd)
    UCAC 1 *Griffon* 2000TD
LOGISTICS AND SUPPORT 10
  AGOR 1 *Punta Brava*
  AGS 2 *Gabriela*
  AKR 4 *Los Frailes*
  AORH 1 *Ciudad Bolivar*
  ATF 1 *Almirante Francisco de Miranda* (Damen Salvage Tug 6014)
  AXS 1 *Simón Bolívar*

Naval Aviation 500

FORCES BY ROLE
ANTI-SUBMARINE WARFARE
  1 sqn with Bell 212 ASW (AB-212 ASW)
MARITIME PATROL
  1 flt with C-212-200 MPA
TRANSPORT
  1 sqn with Beech 200 *King Air*; C-212 *Aviocar*; *Turbo Commander* 980C
TRAINING
  1 hel sqn with Bell 206B *Jet Ranger* II; TH-57A *Sea Ranger*
TRANSPORT HELICOPTER
  1 sqn with Bell 412EP *Twin Huey*; Mi-17V-5 *Hip* H
EQUIPMENT BY TYPE
AIRCRAFT 2 combat capable
  MP 2 C-212-200 MPA*
  TPT • Light 7: 1 Beech C90 *King Air*; 1 Beech 200 *King Air*; 4 C-212 *Aviocar*; 1 *Turbo Commander* 980C
HELICOPTERS
  ASW 4 Bell 212 ASW (AB-212 ASW)
  MRH 12: 6 Bell 412EP *Twin Huey*; 6 Mi-17V-5 *Hip* H
  TPT • Light 1 Bell 206B *Jet Ranger* II (trg)
  TRG 1 TH-57A *Sea Ranger*

Marines ε15,000
FORCES BY ROLE
COMMAND
  1 div HQ
SPECIAL FORCES
  1 spec ops bde
MANOEUVRE
  Amphibious
  1 amph aslt bde
  3 mne bde
  3 (rvn) mne bde
COMBAT SUPPORT
  1 cbt engr bn
  1 MP bde
  1 sigs bn
COMBAT SERVICE SUPPORT
  1 log bn
EQUIPMENT BY TYPE
ARMOURED FIGHTING VEHICLES
  LT TK 10 VN-16
  IFV 21: 11 VN-1; 10 VN-18
  APC • APC (W) 37 EE-11 *Urutu*
  AAV 11 LVTP-7
ENGINEERING & MAINTENANCE VEHICLES
  ARV 1 VS-25
  AEV 1 AAVR7
ANTI-TANK/ANTI-INFRASTRUCTURE
  RCL 84mm *Carl Gustaf*; **106mm** M40A1
ARTILLERY 30
  TOWED 105mm 18 M-56
  MRL 107mm ε10 *Fajr*-1
  MOR 120mm 12 Brandt
PATROL AND COASTAL COMBATANTS
  PBR 23: 18 *Constancia*; 2 *Manaure*; 3 *Terepaima* (*Cougar*)
AMPHIBIOUS • LANDING CRAFT • 1 LCU; 1 LCM; 12 LCVP

Coast Guard 1,000
EQUIPMENT BY TYPE
PATROL AND COASTAL COMBATANTS 25
  PSO 3 *Guaicamacuto* with 1 *Millennium* CIWS, 1 76mm gun (capacity 1 Bell 212 (AB-212) hel)
  PB 22: 1 *Fernando Gomez de Saa* (Damen Stan Patrol 4207); 12 *Gavion*; 3 *Pagalo* (Damen Stan Patrol 2606); 4 *Petrel* (US Point); 2 *Protector*
LOGISTICS AND SUPPORT 4
  AG 1 *Los Taques* (salvage ship)
  AKL 1
  AP 2

Air Force 11,500
FORCES BY ROLE
SPECIAL FORCES
  1 cdo unit

FIGHTER/GROUND ATTACK
1 sqn with F-5 *Freedom Fighter* (VF-5)
2 sqn with F-16A/B *Fighting Falcon*
4 sqn with Su-30MKV *Flanker*
2 sqn with K-8W *Karakorum**
GROUND ATTACK/ISR
1 sqn with EMB-312 *Tucano**
ELECTRONIC WARFARE
1 sqn with *Falcon* 20DC; SA-227 *Metro* III (C-26B)
TRANSPORT
1 sqn with A319CJ; B-737
1 sqn with C-130H *Hercules*; KC-137; Y-8
4 sqn with Cessna T206H; Cessna 750
1 sqn with Cessna 500/550/551; *Falcon* 20F; *Falcon* 900
1 sqn with G-222; Short 360 *Sherpa*
TRAINING
1 sqn with Cessna 182N; SF-260E
2 sqn with DA40NG; DA42VI
1 sqn with EMB-312 *Tucano**
TRANSPORT HELICOPTER
1 VIP sqn with AS532UL *Cougar*; Mi-172
3 sqn with AS332B *Super Puma*; AS532 *Cougar*
2 sqn with Mi-17 *Hip* H
ISR UAV
1 sqn with *Mohajer* 2
EQUIPMENT BY TYPE
AIRCRAFT 79 combat capable
  FTR 18: 15 F-16A *Fighting Falcon*†; 3 F-16B *Fighting Falcon*†
  FGA 21 Su-30MKV *Flanker*
  EW 4: 2 *Falcon* 20DC; 2 SA-227 *Metro* III (C-26B)
  TKR 1 KC-137
  TPT 75: **Medium** 14: 5 C-130H *Hercules* (some in store); 1 G-222; 8 Y-8; **Light** 56: 6 Beech 200 *King Air*; 2 Beech 350 *King Air*; 10 Cessna 182N *Skylane*; 12 Cessna 206 *Stationair*; 4 Cessna 208B *Caravan*; 1 Cessna 500 *Citation* I; 3 Cessna 550 *Citation* II; 1 Cessna 551; 1 Cessna 750 *Citation* X; 2 Do-228-212; 1 Do-228-212NG; 11 Quad City *Challenger* II; 2 Short 360 *Sherpa*; **PAX** 5: 1 A319CJ; 1 B-737; 1 *Falcon* 20F; 2 *Falcon* 900
  TRG 84: 24 DA40NG; 6 DA42VI; 19 EMB-312 *Tucano**; 23 K-8W *Karakorum**; 12 SF-260E
HELICOPTERS
  MRH 8 Mi-17 (Mi-17VS) *Hip* H
  TPT 21: **Medium** 14: 3 AS332B *Super Puma*; 7 AS532 *Cougar*; 2 AS532UL *Cougar*; 2 Mi-172 (VIP); **Light** 7+ Enstrom 480B
UNINHABITED AERIAL VEHICLES
  CISR • **Medium** *Mohajer* 6 (reported); **Light** ANSU-100 (in test)
  ISR • **Light** *Mohajer* 2
AIR-LAUNCHED MISSILES
  AAM • **IR** AIM-9L/P *Sidewinder*; PL-5E; R-73 (RS-AA-11A *Archer*); R-27T/ET (RS-AA-10B/D *Alamo*); **IR** *Python* 4; **SARH** R-27R/ER (RS-AA-10A/C *Alamo*); **ARH** R-77 (RS-AA-12 *Adder*)
  ASM Kh-29L/T (RS-AS-14A/B *Kedge*); Kh-59M (RS-AS-18 *Kazoo*)
  AShM Kh-31A (RS-AS-17B *Krypton*); AM39 *Exocet*
  ARM Kh-31P (RS-AS-17A *Krypton*)

Air Defence Command (CODAI)

Joint service command with personnel drawn from other services
FORCES BY ROLE
AIR DEFENCE
5 AD bde
COMBAT SERVICE SUPPORT
1 log bde (5 log gp)
EQUIPMENT BY TYPE
AIR DEFENCE
  SAM
    Long-range 12 S-300VM (RS-SA-23)
    Medium-range 53: 9 9K317M2 *Buk*-M2E (RS-SA-17 *Grizzly*); 44 S-125 *Pechora*-2M (RS-SA-26)
    Point-defence 9K338 *Igla*-S (RS-SA-24 *Grinch*); ADAMS; *Mistral*; RBS-70
  GUNS 440+
    SP 40mm 12+: 6+ AMX-13 *Rafaga*; 6 M42
    TOWED 428+: **20mm**: 114 TCM-20; **23mm** ε200 ZU-23-2; **35mm**; **40mm** 114+: 114+ L/70; Some M1

National Guard (Fuerzas Armadas de Cooperacion) 23,000

(Internal sy, customs) 9 regional comd
EQUIPMENT BY TYPE
ARMOURED FIGHTING VEHICLES
  APC 89:
    APC (T) 45: 25 AMX-VCI; 12 AMX-PC (CP); 8 AMX-VCTB (Amb)
    APC (W) 44: 24 Fiat 6614; 20 UR-416
  AUV 121 VN4
ARTILLERY • **MOR** 50 **81mm**
PATROL AND COASTAL COMBATANTS
  PB 34: 12 *Protector*; 12 *Punta*; 10 *Rio Orinoco* II
AIRCRAFT
  TPT • **Light** 34: 1 Beech 55 *Baron*; 1 Beech 80 *Queen Air*; 1 Beech 90 *King Air*; 1 Beech 200C *King Air*; 3 Cessna 152 *Aerobat*; 2 Cessna 172; 2 Cessna 402C; 4 Cessna U206 *Stationair*; 6 DA42 MPP; 1 IAI-201 *Arava*; 12 M-28 *Skytruck*
  TRG 3: 1 PZL 106 *Kruk*; 2 PLZ M2-6 *Isquierka*
HELICOPTERS
  MRH 13: 8 Bell 412EP; 5 Mi-17V-5 *Hip* H
  TPT • **Light** 18: 9 AS355F *Ecureuil* II; 4 AW109; 4 Bell 206B/L *Jet Ranger/Long Ranger*; 1 Bell 212 (AB 212);
  TRG 5 F-280C

Gendarmerie & Paramilitary ε220,000

Bolivarian National Militia ε220,000

Chapter Eight
Sub-Saharan Africa

- Following a series of coups earlier in the decade, France has reduced its military presence in the Sahel, drawing down its forces in Burkina Faso, Mali and Niger. In 2024, France announced that it will reduce its forces in Chad.
- Niger had been a key US regional hub for its counter-terror campaign, but following the July 2023 coup, many Western states withdrew their forces. France completed its withdrawal in December 2023, and US forces completed their withdrawal in September 2024.
- In February 2024, Somalia and Turkiye signed a defence agreement under which Turkiye will reconstruct, equip and train the Somali Navy.
- As regional states procure more uninhabited aerial vehicles, Turkiye has emerged as a leading supplier, counting Burkina Faso, Ethiopia and Mali among its recent customers.
- The UN's new Multidimensional Security Support Mission in Haiti is led by Kenya. Kenyan police landed in Haiti in July 2024, making this the first time that Kenya has led a multinational security mission outside of Africa.
- Defence spending declined across much of Sub-Saharan Africa, though rose substantially in the 'Alliance of Sahel States', which formed after military coups in Burkina Faso, Mali and Niger. In dollar terms, defence budgets increased across the three countries by over 20%, while spending by traditional security providers such as Nigeria fell. If sustained, such shifts will entrench changing security dynamics and consolidate long-term challenges of regional unity and stability.

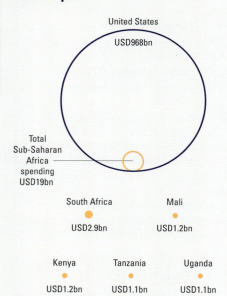

Sub-Saharan Africa defence spending, 2024 – top 5

- United States USD968bn
- Total Sub-Saharan Africa spending USD19bn
- South Africa USD2.9bn
- Mali USD1.2bn
- Kenya USD1.2bn
- Tanzania USD1.1bn
- Uganda USD1.1bn

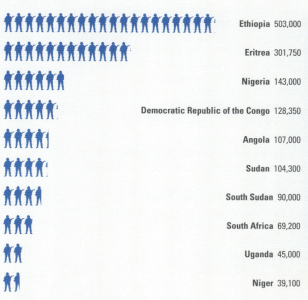

Active military personnel – top 10
(25,000 per unit)

- Ethiopia 503,000
- Eritrea 301,750
- Nigeria 143,000
- Democratic Republic of the Congo 128,350
- Angola 107,000
- Sudan 104,300
- South Sudan 90,000
- South Africa 69,200
- Uganda 45,000
- Niger 39,100

Global total 20,629,000
Regional total 2,038,000 — 9.9%

Regional defence policy and economics 442 ▶

Arms procurement and defence-industrial trends 451 ▶

Armed forces data section 453 ▶

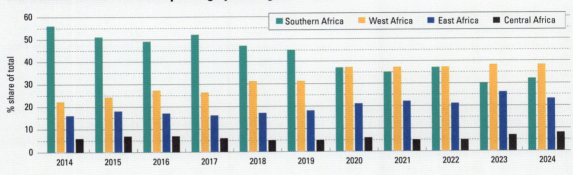

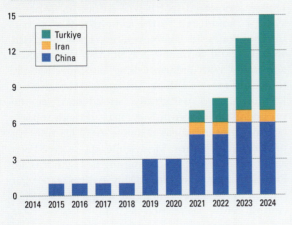

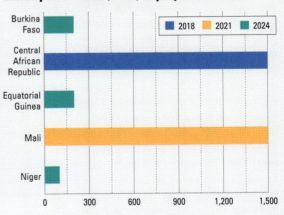

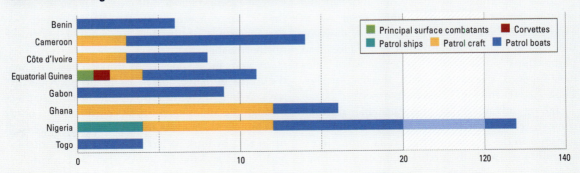

Sub-Saharan Africa

WEST AFRICA

For more than 15 years, armed groups across the Sahel region have challenged governments, and security has further deteriorated in recent years. A jihadist-based insurgency remains at the centre of the Sahel crisis, but chronic economic underdevelopment is also a factor. This instability and unrest has led to a succession of coups which has installed military rulers in the central Sahel states of Burkina Faso, Mali and Niger and is driving significant regional and international realignment.

The military juntas of these three countries set up the tripartite Alliance of Sahel States (Alliance des États du Sahel or AES) in September 2023, and announced in January 2024 they would leave the Economic Community of West African States (ECOWAS) after the mandatory one-year notice period. This decision was in large part due to the failures they perceived in ECOWAS, particularly in failing to stem regional security threats. The plan to leave ECOWAS is the latest step in what appears to be these states' shift away from traditional regional and Western allies. They have cut their long-established ties with France, many European Union countries and the United States. France completed its military withdrawal from Niger in December 2023 after its troops were asked to leave by the military government. US forces completed their withdrawal in September 2024. Previously, Niger had been the key US regional hub for its counter-terror campaign.

These departures are likely to undercut the counter-Islamist campaign, as they seem set to expose the limitations of the local forces. At the same time, a full-scale reconfiguration of alliances and partnerships is under way. The central Sahel states have opened discussions with Russia, Turkiye, India, Algeria and other possible partners.

Taking advantage of this unstable regional context, Russia has continued to expand its presence in the region, relying on its paramilitary capability – essentially a rebranding of the former Wagner Group – with now a more apparent line of control from Moscow. Russia has deployed trainers in the central Sahel states and delivered military equipment. However, personnel numbers may be limited, which may equally constrain the effect these forces can have, and there were reports that some Russian paramilitaries had been recalled to fight in Ukraine.

Further east, there is increased concern in the West over the strategic trajectory of Chad as it grapples with the potential spillover from threats on various fronts, including in the Sahel and Sudan and Libya to the north. In 2024, France retained a significant garrison of some 1,000 troops in the country, although its presence had become increasingly unpopular, and as part of its mid-2024 recalibration of its force presence in the Sahel, France announced that it will reduce its forces in Chad – though not to the same extent as it had in other states. In late November, however, Chad said it would terminate the military cooperation agreement with France, calling into question the future of France's military presence in the country. US forces had withdrawn in advance of the presidential election in May 2024, though reports late in the year indicated that a small US military presence may return. Meanwhile, there have been a number of reports of developing ties with Russia. President Mahamat Idriss Déby paid a state visit to Moscow at the beginning of 2024 and a Russian cultural centre has opened in Chad.

There are also growing fears of spillover effects for the states of the southern Sahel, notably Benin, Côte d'Ivoire, Ghana and Togo, where security forces are concerned by the threat posed by various armed groups heading southwards from northern Sahel.

In 2017, these states (plus Burkina Faso) set up the Accra Initiative, joined by Mali and Niger in 2019. While there has been information-sharing through the initiative, practical coordination is only developing. Meanwhile, the G5 Sahel joint force (set up in 2014 by Burkina Faso, Chad, Mali, Mauritania and Niger) and the ECOWAS Standby Force have only partially developed a coordinated regional response. Small-scale operations have taken place on a bilateral basis, but the withdrawal of the central Sahel states from these groupings will affect these efforts even more.

This growing instability, and the requirement for situational awareness that it generates, has seen some states, such as Benin, Côte d'Ivoire, Ghana and Togo, acquire uninhabited aerial vehicles. But it has also led to more internal deployments. Côte d'Ivoire deployed its security forces in its Northern Operational Zone in March 2021. New infrastructure is being established in Ghana's north to facilitate a more permanent security presence and, as elements of the armed forces move from a focus on peacekeeping operations to holding operations, interaction with local communities is seen as important to success. Togo has been raided by armed groups and the northern region remains under the threat posed by al-Qaeda in the Islamic Maghreb and associated groups. For its part, Benin is facing similar difficulties in the north and has deployed military units there under *Operation Mirador*, and its armed forces will receive military assistance financed by the European Peace Facility following a July 2024 EU decision.

EAST AFRICA

There has been much focus in the Horn of Africa and East Africa on the ripple effects of the anti-shipping campaign by the Ansarullah (Houthi) movement in Yemen centred on the southern Red Sea. But among the troubling new dynamics has been a memorandum of understanding (MoU) signed on 1 January 2024 between Ethiopia and Somaliland that would give Ethiopia access to land outside Berbera as a naval base in return for subsequent Ethiopian recognition of Somaliland as a sovereign state. Somalia responded sternly to the news, calling it 'an act of aggression'. Somalia considers Somaliland to be fully part of the Somali state and has strongly challenged the MoU in both the African Union and the United Nations, gathering international support against the agreement while also signing agreements, including on defence, with Kenya in May 2024.

In addition, in February 2024, Somalia and Turkiye signed a defence agreement under which Turkiye will reconstruct, equip and train the Somali Navy while receiving 30% of the revenue from Somalia's exclusive economic zone, including the Somaliland coast. In the same month, Turkiye and Djibouti agreed a military training cooperation agreement, a military financial cooperation agreement and a cash-aid implementation protocol, thus further establishing Turkiye's footprint in the area. At the same time, Turkiye hosted three rounds of talks between Somalia and Ethiopia in July, August and September 2024, and in late year Kenya and Uganda indicated that they would also mediate in the dispute. Meanwhile, Somalia and Egypt signed a military agreement protocol in August 2024, after Cairo had been vocal in its support for Mogadishu after the Ethiopia–Somaliland MoU. The August agreement was quickly followed by a deployment of Egyptian forces and military-equipment aid to Mogadishu. Altogether, these developments risked exacerbating already brittle relations between Egypt and Ethiopia.

Further complicating the issue is the December 2024 drawdown of the African Union Transition Mission in Somalia (ATMIS), to which Ethiopia is a key troop contributor, and its scheduled replacement by the African Union Support and Stabilization Mission in Somalia (AUSSOM) in January 2025. Somalia has refused to allow Ethiopia as a troop contributor to AUSSOM and Egypt has offered troops to the mission, replacing Ethiopia as a troop contributor. In the meantime, both the Somali federal member states of Jubaland and South West have said that Ethiopian troops present in their territories on a bilateral basis will remain. This leaves the possibility in 2025 of Ethiopian and Egyptian troops operating in the same areas in Somalia under different mandates and with their ability to coordinate and deconflict operations remaining uncertain.

Amid all these developments, the al-Shabaab threat has continued in Somalia, including an attack in February 2024 on a military training base in Mogadishu in which Emirati and Bahraini staff were killed.

Ethiopia's precarious security situation has driven a significant increase in defence spending. In addition, in March 2024 Ethiopia opened negotiations with India on an arms deal, representing a new foray into the African market for India while for Ethiopia, procuring from India would mark a move from predominantly Russian and Chinese equipment. Internal conflict continues, despite the Pretoria Peace Agreement signed with the Tigray People's Liberation Front. There is little sign of an end to conflict in Amhara between local Fano

Figure 38 — Sudan: confirmed aircraft losses in the Sudanese civil war since April 2023

More than a year after the Sudanese paramilitary Rapid Support Forces (RSF) began an offensive against the Sudanese Armed Forces (SAF) on 15 April 2023, the number of apparent SAF aircraft losses has slowed. The RSF destroyed numerous SAF attack and transport helicopters in its assault on Jebel Aulia air base on 15 April 2023. Its subsequent attack on Khartoum International Airport on 17 April 2023 damaged dozens of private transport aircraft and Sudanese air force transport aircraft, while its seizure of Merowe air base on the same day led to the destruction of several Egyptian MiG-29M/M2s, part of a Sudan–Egypt joint training contingent, as well as Sudanese FTC-2000Gs. The SAF eventually retook Merowe air base. In the RSF's attack on El Obeid air base, also on 17 April, it destroyed several Su-25Ks, while in its 27 July assault on Wadi Seidna air base it destroyed An-32s, MiG-29SE/UBs, Su-25K/UBKs and Su-24Ms. Between April and August 2023, the RSF also shot down some FTC-2000Gs, MiG-29SE/UBs, Su-25K/UBKs, and Mi-24/35s. Other unverified reports indicate that the RSF shot down Antonov transports, which the SAF have reportedly used to drop barrel bombs from their ramps. The most recent confirmed loss was the result of a first-person-view uninhabited aerial vehicle (UAV) colliding with a C-130H *Hercules* on 18 March 2024. Since then, the Sudanese air force has continued conducting airstrikes: predominantly in Khartoum and Darfur, parts of which are now RSF strongholds. Both the SAF and RSF have extensively employed UAVs.

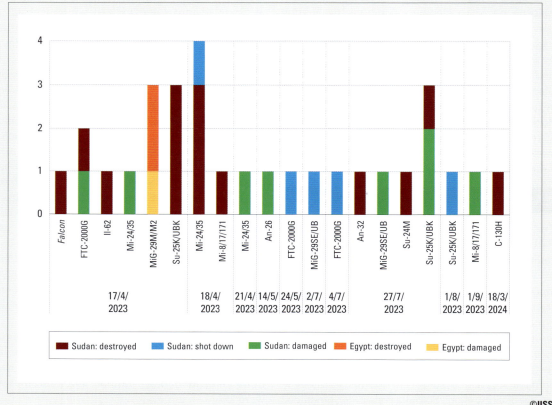

Note: Any aircraft not shot down was either destroyed or damaged (beyond repair) on the ground. Dates follow the DD/MM/YYYY format.
Source: IISS, Military Balance+, milbalplus.iiss.org

militias and the regional and federal governments, despite attempts to organise a peace process. Continuing conflict in Oromia between federal and regional forces and the Oromo Liberation Army means that overstretch continues to concern the Ethiopian National Defence Force and police. In this continuing conflict context, the delivery of the government's new transitional justice process, one of the deliverables of the Pretoria Agreement, risks being challenging and slow.

In Sudan, despite UN arms embargoes, both sides continue to receive weapons from outside the country. US-led Sudan peace talks in Geneva in August 2024 failed to bring the parties to agreement.

Progress is further hindered by international parties with differing agendas and lack of clarity on outcomes, including the US, Saudi Arabia and Switzerland; the African Union; the regional Intergovernmental Authority on Development (IGAD); and Egypt and Chad.

Russia, in its desire to establish a naval base on the Red Sea, also appears to be shifting its stance on Sudan's internal conflict. With the Sudanese Armed Forces and the ruling Transitional Sovereignty Council controlling Port Sudan, analysts consider that Moscow has been backing away from its alignment with the Rapid Support Forces. In South Sudan, political violence and instability persist between government forces and opposition factions. Security-sector reform and permanent constitution-making processes continue to be behind schedule.

Kenya took a significant step in its regional and international role during 2024. In October 2023, the UN Security Council authorised a new Multinational Security Support Mission for Haiti led by Kenya, for an initial period of 12 months. Following challenges in the Kenyan courts, the first Kenyan police landed in Haiti in July 2024. This is the first time Kenya has led a multinational security mission outside of Africa.

CENTRAL AND SOUTHERN AFRICA

The South Africa National Defence Force (SANDF) has been adversely affected by three decades of underfunding, aggravated by expanding missions. The operational status of most of its aircraft, ships and heavy army equipment is in doubt for lack of maintenance funding. The army is further hampered by large numbers of over-age personnel. These challenges were demonstrated by the SANDF's inability to provide air support and airlift for the South African Development Community (SADC) missions in Mozambique and the Democratic Republic of the Congo (DRC) and naval interdiction off Mozambique. Nonetheless, South Africa still provided the largest contingents for both missions, further overstretching an army that also has border-patrol and police-support tasks. Defence chiefs were thought to have advised against undertaking the DRC deployment, while all but one of the parties in parliament called for the mission to be terminated for lack of support to the deployed troops.

SADC has become more active in regional security matters, though the SADC Mission in Mozambique's northern Cabo Delgado province (SAMIM) was terminated in mid-2024, apparently due to lack of funding, just as the insurgency linked to the Islamic State (ISIS) regained momentum. Rwanda responded to the withdrawal by expanding its separate contingent, but it is focused around the Afungi Peninsula gas installations, while Tanzania extended its deployment to guard against spillover into its territory. That left the Mozambican security forces to cover the bulk of the province. They continued to face significant challenges despite an EU training mission there since 2021, and there is a possibility that the insurgency will be able to regain lost ground and spread. Indeed, should it establish itself along the coast south of the Rwandan deployment, this could also present maritime risk in the Mozambique Channel in particular, which has become of growing significance given the rerouting of global shipping because of the Houthi campaign in the southern Red Sea.

The SADC mission in the DRC began deploying in mid-2024, but this was hampered by a lack of airlift and initial elements were quickly probed by the M23 rebel movement, suffering casualties and losing vehicles in ambushes and attacks. The mission was further hampered again by a lack of air support and the means to counter M23's increasing use of relatively advanced weapons. It is unclear how the force is expected to achieve what the former UN mission, MONUSCO, could not, given the scale of the provinces affected by serious guerrilla activity. The number of groups with sometimes diverging agendas – M23, the ethnically Hutu Forces democratiques de liberation du Rwanda (FDLR), Islamist groups such as the Allied Democratic Forces and RED-Tabara, remnants of the Lord's Resistance Army, and some 120 assorted local militias – together with regionally deployed armed forces, makes any resolution yet more complex.

Angola is facing unrest in its east, particularly in the Lunda Sul, Lunda Norte and Moxico provinces, the former two being rich in diamonds but among the poorest parts of the country. The Lunda Tchokwe Protectorate Movement argues that the area was a protectorate and not part of the colony of Angola, and so should be independent. Angola also remains concerned regarding its exclave of Cabinda, the source of much of its oil income and which has been subject to claims by both the DRC and the Republic of Congo.

African Union

The African Union (AU) has sought to play a greater role in international affairs, especially in matters relating to global peace and security, in line with Article 3 of the AU Constitutive Act, which encourages the establishment of conditions for Africa to play a meaningful global role. In a demonstration of a new-found confidence and a departure from concentrating only on African peace and security issues, the AU has commented on conflicts in Ukraine and Gaza and sent a 'peace mission' to Ukraine and Russia.

The Ukraine conflict caused disruption of food and commodity imports across Africa, particularly wheat, fertilisers and steel. The conflict is also seen as a threat to multilateralism, potentially affecting the AU's, and therefore Africa's, position in global affairs. On Gaza, the AU has taken a clear and vocal stance. At the AU Assembly in February 2024, African leaders condemned Israel's military actions in Gaza, calling for an immediate cessation of hostilities.

Although unsuccessful, these developments illustrate the AU's new ambition for its Peace and Security Council (PSC) to more closely follow the model of the EU Peace and Security Council in considering conflict anywhere in the world that has continental implications. The United Nations has supported the strengthening of Africa's role in addressing global security and development challenges.

As a further sign of this evolution, the AU was granted full membership status in the G20 at the summit held in New Delhi in September 2023. This change is seen as giving Africa a more prominent voice in global economic discussions and decision-making. Rather than endorsing the AU's track record as such, this is a recognition of Africa's growing economic importance and potential and, with globalisation, the importance of Africa, given its young population and abundant natural resources, in the deliberations of the G20.

The UN and AU further cemented their partnership in addressing African peace and security when the UN adopted UN Security Council Resolution 2719 on 21 December 2023, approving a framework for the financing of AU Peace Support Operations (PSOs) from UN assessed contributions. The AU had argued for this since the adoption of the PSC Protocol in July 2002. It represents significant progress in the development of the UN–AU partnership in peace and security, allowing the UN to support the adequate, predictable and sustainable financing of AU-led PSOs. The first test case for this funding stream is the new African Union Support and Stabilization Mission in Somalia (AUSSOM), which replaced the African Union Transition Mission in Somalia (ATMIS) on 1 January 2025.

While the AU has demonstrated global ambitions, Africa remains challenged by many unresolved conflicts. The SADC Mission in Mozambique (SAMIM), deployed in July 2021, started to withdraw in April 2024 and withdrawal was completed in mid-July 2024 (though some logistics troops remained to repatriate equipment). Although it operated relatively successfully in northern Mozambique, the mission was unable to address the underlying causes of fragility and conflict in the region, and there is a risk that the insurgency might regain momentum.

The East African Community Regional Force (EACRF), stationed in the eastern DRC for a year as part of the Nairobi process, was not able to neutralise the M23 armed group, and the EACRF ceased operations when its mandate expired on 8 December 2023. The deployment of an SADC mission in the DRC, SAMIDRC, was scheduled to begin in December 2023 but by May 2024 only one-fifth had been deployed.

These regional approaches to peace and security, with the AU allowing regional primacy, illustrates a view that the regions know themselves best. This regional 'building block' approach to African peace and security brings its own challenges. In West Africa, relationships between the AU and the Economic Community of West African States (ECOWAS) have tended to be informal and cooperative. This loose arrangement has left ECOWAS hostage to the decisions of its member states. On 28 January 2024, the military leaders of Burkina Faso, Mali and Niger – who had recently formed the Alliance des États du Sahel (AES) – declared their withdrawal from ECOWAS, with immediate effect, though the rules of ECOWAS require a year's notice of withdrawal. Both ECOWAS and AES held summits in West Africa on 6 and 7 July 2024. The AES summit was held just one day before the ECOWAS summit as a challenge, testing ECOWAS's unity and stability. How this challenge will be resolved is not yet clear but ECOWAS, which used to be considered the most capable of the AU and African Standby Force Regional Economic Communities, has lost its position in African peace and security and analysts consider that a focused and inclusive approach will be required if ECOWAS is to retain its members and remain powerful in West Africa.

In Central Africa, political instability and armed conflicts in the DRC and the Central African Republic have led to similar challenges. The AU has supported the efforts of the Economic Community of Central African States to mediate and resolve conflicts but has struggled to assert a leading role. The AU's PSC has attempted to coordinate regional efforts, but its impact is often diluted by competing regional interests and limited resources. While the AU seeks greater global recognition and responsibility, it will also be mindful of the need to strive to keep the continent peaceful and secure if it is to play the effective global role to which it aspires, as set out in the AU's Constitutive Act and its ambitious Agenda 2063, which was first adopted in 2015.

DEFENCE ECONOMICS

High inflation rates and severe currency depreciations continue to affect defence spending in Sub-Saharan Africa. Despite some significant uplifts domestically, regional defence budgets fell by 3.7% in real terms in 2024 and also fell in dollar terms, with a collective spend of USD19.3 billion compared to USD20.5bn in 2023. Reductions in Angola, Ethiopia and Nigeria were mainly behind this fall, although budgets also fell or were largely flat in other key markets.

The countries that did implement increases, such as Burkina Faso, Mali and Niger, offset some of the decline but not enough to reverse the overall trend. These countries signed the Liptako-Gourma Charter in September 2023 to establish the Alliance of Sahel States (AES). The move followed military coups in each of the three countries and – in a rebuff to the Economic Community of West African States (ECOWAS) – the AES is seeking to redefine West African politics with a new economic, political and military alliance. To achieve this, defence budgets increased across the three by an average of 23.1% in dollar terms, consolidating the armed forces' hold over each country and entrenching the long-term challenges of regional unity and stability.

Defence spending

Despite the long-term stagnation in defence spending, **South Africa** remained Sub-Saharan Africa's top spender, with the country allocating ZAR52.7bn (USD2.9bn) to defence in 2024. The 2024 budget represents a nominal fall of 1.0% from the previous year, while the country has seen near-consistent annual real-terms declines for the past decade. Falls in defence spending come as the country seeks to balance high debt repayments with calls for free education and increased social protection. Yet this long-term decline is also materially affecting the country's defence capabilities. The defence budget has persistently remained below 1% of GDP since 2016 and, in 2024, represented just 0.7% of GDP. This is far below the regional average of 1.5% of GDP.

South Africa's defence budget now accounts for 14.8% of the region's total defence spending, down from a high of 28.6% in 2010. Nonetheless, operational requirements continue – particularly in the Democratic Republic of the Congo. Ambitions to remain a leading regional player will soon prompt difficult decisions, as ever-decreasing budgets raise questions about the affordability of future missions.

Angola's defence budget also continued to fall in real terms. The country's annual defence budget increased by a nominal 1.6% to AOA879.1bn (USD1.0bn) but fell in dollar terms and with inflation running at 28.4%, the budget actually fell by over 20% in real terms. The slowdown in Southern Africa's two largest defence spenders was somewhat offset by increases in neighbouring countries, which meant that spending remained flat across the sub-region, with total allocations of USD6.2bn matching 2023 levels.

In 2024, **Nigeria** allocated NGN1.6 trillion (USD1.0bn) to defence. Despite increasing by 14% in local naira, the budget translates into a decline of over 50% in dollar terms, and a real-terms decrease of 9.0%. This volatility reflects the country's ongoing struggle with high inflation and the naira's falling value after currency restrictions were relaxed in mid-2023. As a result, in 2024, Nigeria dropped from being the region's second-largest defence spender, to sixth position. The naira's declining value has the potential to affect the region's relative power balances and stability as Nigeria hosts one of Africa's strongest armed forces and is a cornerstone of regional peacekeeping. Yet this influence may be waning. In 2024, Nigeria formed just 14.3% of West Africa's spending, down from 27.9% in 2023, and 47.5% a decade before that.

The impact of Nigeria's declining budgets is made yet more acute as the fall coincides with large budget

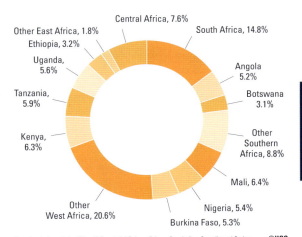

▲ Figure 39 **Sub-Saharan Africa: defence spending by country and sub-region, 2024**

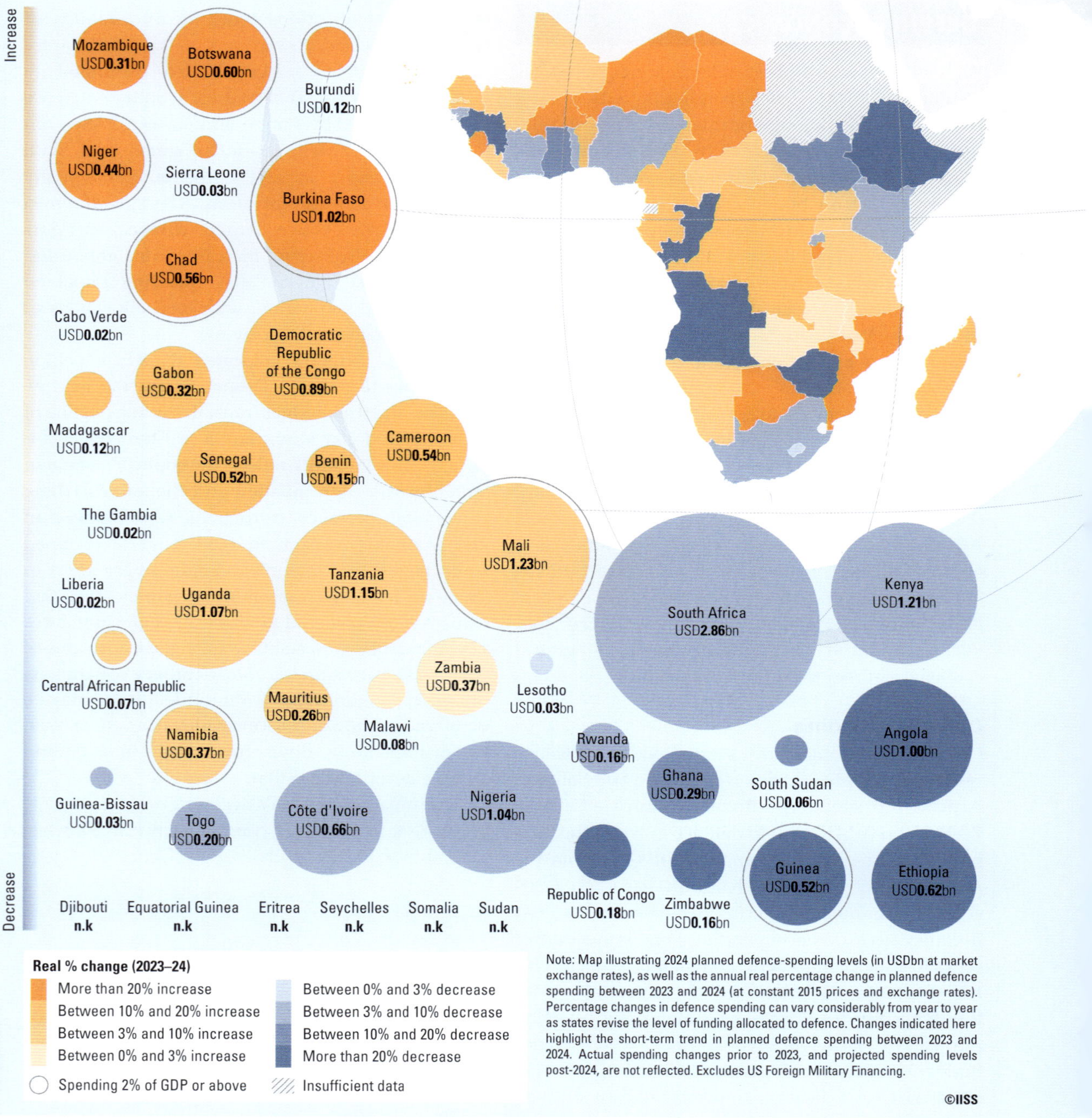

Map 6 Sub-Saharan Africa: regional defence spending (USDbn, %ch yoy)

Real % change (2023–24)
- More than 20% increase
- Between 10% and 20% increase
- Between 3% and 10% increase
- Between 0% and 3% increase
- Between 0% and 3% decrease
- Between 3% and 10% decrease
- Between 10% and 20% decrease
- More than 20% decrease
- ○ Spending 2% of GDP or above
- ▨ Insufficient data

Spending levels (USDbn):
- Mozambique USD 0.31bn
- Botswana USD 0.60bn
- Burundi USD 0.12bn
- Niger USD 0.44bn
- Sierra Leone USD 0.03bn
- Burkina Faso USD 1.02bn
- Chad USD 0.56bn
- Cabo Verde USD 0.02bn
- Gabon USD 0.32bn
- Democratic Republic of the Congo USD 0.89bn
- Madagascar USD 0.12bn
- Senegal USD 0.52bn
- Benin USD 0.15bn
- Cameroon USD 0.54bn
- The Gambia USD 0.02bn
- Mali USD 1.23bn
- Liberia USD 0.02bn
- Uganda USD 1.07bn
- Tanzania USD 1.15bn
- South Africa USD 2.86bn
- Kenya USD 1.21bn
- Central African Republic USD 0.07bn
- Mauritius USD 0.26bn
- Zambia USD 0.37bn
- Lesotho USD 0.03bn
- Angola USD 1.00bn
- Namibia USD 0.37bn
- Malawi USD 0.08bn
- Rwanda USD 0.16bn
- Ghana USD 0.29bn
- South Sudan USD 0.06bn
- Guinea-Bissau USD 0.03bn
- Togo USD 0.20bn
- Côte d'Ivoire USD 0.66bn
- Nigeria USD 1.04bn
- Guinea USD 0.52bn
- Ethiopia USD 0.62bn
- Republic of Congo USD 0.18bn
- Zimbabwe USD 0.16bn
- Djibouti n.k
- Equatorial Guinea n.k
- Eritrea n.k
- Seychelles n.k
- Somalia n.k
- Sudan n.k

Note: Map illustrating 2024 planned defence-spending levels (in USDbn at market exchange rates), as well as the annual real percentage change in planned defence spending between 2023 and 2024 (at constant 2015 prices and exchange rates). Percentage changes in defence spending can vary considerably from year to year as states revise the level of funding allocated to defence. Changes indicated here highlight the short-term trend in planned defence spending between 2023 and 2024. Actual spending changes prior to 2023, and projected spending levels post-2024, are not reflected. Excludes US Foreign Military Financing.

©IISS

---

increases in AES members. For example, within the alliance, each military government pushed through substantial defence allocations. In dollar terms, defence budgets for **Burkina Faso**, **Mali** and **Niger** increased by 23.6%, 13.4% and 32.3%, respectively. Indeed, Mali's allocation of XOF739bn (USD1.2bn) forms 16.9% of West Africa's defence spending, while Burkina Faso's XOF621bn (USD1.0bn) forms 14.1%. Niger's allocation of XOF264bn (USD439 million) adds a further 6.0% of the sub-region's total. These increases add to the already significant defence burden on some of the world's most impoverished countries, as illustrated by Burkina Faso's allocation of nearly a third of its state budget to defence and security in 2024. Moreover, elevated defence burdens are likely to continue. In Mali, a June 2023 referendum approved constitutional amendments that consolidated the military's domestic position, despite previous pledges to restore democratic rule by 2024. The amendments state that the armed forces shall participate in the economic, social and cultural development of the country and be provided with the necessary resources to fulfil their responsibilities – in terms of both personnel and equipment. In Burkina Faso, the military government delayed presidential elections by five years from July 2024, while in Niger, a month after the 2024 budget was published, new legislation exempted defence spending from future cuts and scrapped future reporting requirements. This consolidates the military's domestic position, obscures transparency and raises the risk of further corruption within the country. Increased defence funding across the three military governments also signals that they only conceive military solutions to their domestic armed conflicts, signalling the further entrenchment of long-term challenges such as low development amid regional instability.

In East Africa, **Kenya's** defence budget remained largely flat, in local currency terms, with 2024's approved defence budget of KES173.0bn (USD1.2bn) barely above the previous year's allocation. This meant a decline of 2.4%, in dollar terms, and 4.2% in real terms. This contrasts with the December 2023 proposed budget, where defence spending was planned to increase by 14% to KES198bn (USD1.4bn). The fall reflects Nairobi's wider financial difficulties, as seen in June 2024 when protests erupted throughout the country after controversial tax hikes were proposed. As a result, Kenya's President William Ruto scrapped proposed tax legislation and promised further reform through cuts to overall government spending and increased borrowing to alleviate widespread dissatisfaction. While Kenya struggled to balance its books, **Ethiopia's** defence budget saw a dramatic fall, declining by over 40% in local terms, from ETB84.0bn (USD1.5bn) in 2023 to ETB50.0bn (USD622.5m) in 2024. The fall – the largest in Sub-Saharan Africa – follows the success of the November 2022 ceasefire in the Tigray region, suggesting government confidence in the Cessation of Hostilities Agreement. As a result, trackable spending across East Africa declined to USD4.4bn in 2024, down from USD5.3bn the previous year.

Defence industry

South Africa's defence industry remains the region's most advanced producer, although the country's leading defence manufacturer, Denel, has struggled in recent years. The state-owned company ran at a loss between 2016 and 2020 and has failed to publish annual financial reports since then, which has raised concerns with South Africa's Standing Committee on Public Accounts. The company narrowly avoided liquidation in October 2021 following an out-of-court settlement with SAAB Grintek Defence. In the 2016–17 fiscal year, Denel employed nearly 5,000 employees but by 2024, staffing had reportedly fallen to just under 1,700. Looking to remedy the situation, in 2021 Denel began a process of restructuring, announcing in August that it was embarking upon a 'comprehensive five-year plan'. This included a reduction – from six to two – in operating divisions and a single subsidiary, corporate restructuring to realise cost efficiencies and the concentration of production at specific sites.

Further restructuring plans were announced in 2023, including the rationalisation of facilities and the sale of the company's property footprint. These measures, and government recapitalisation grants, have strengthened Denel's balance sheet and allowed some key programmes to continue. These include upgrades to South Africa's G-5 and G-6 155mm howitzers, and the *Badger* infantry fighting vehicle. A baseline product is now reportedly expected by the end of 2025. In addition, it was reported at September 2024's Africa Aerospace and Defence Exhibition (AAD) that delivery of Denel's A-*Darter*

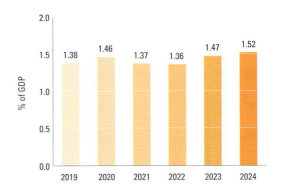

▲ Figure 40 **Sub-Saharan Africa: regional defence spending** as % of GDP (average)

air-to-air missile to the South African Air Force would begin in December 2024. Beyond Denel, South Africa's defence industry remains active in conceiving and developing defence products. Although innovation in ruggedised vehicles and turrets remains a mainstay of local development, South African companies, such as Paramount and Milkor, have also developed equipment in the uninhabited aerospace sector.

Nigeria's domestic production capabilities continue to slowly develop through partnerships with foreign producers. In April 2024, Nigeria awarded a contract to EPAIL Nigeria, a local defence firm, to supply an unspecified quantity of light tactical armoured vehicles (LTAVs) and heavy anti-mine armoured vehicles with ammunition for its armed forces. EPAIL Nigeria delivered the first 20 LTAVs to the Nigerian armed forces in May 2024, with the design of the vehicles reportedly based on China's Dongfeng *Mengshi* armoured utility vehicles, which the Nigerian Army has operated since at least 2021. The contract should help the company scale its production capabilities, and the first 20 locally produced vehicles were delivered to the Nigerian Army in May 2024. Nonetheless, Nigeria remains reliant on established producers for more sophisticated technology, for example, the supply of 12 Bell AH-1Z *Viper* attack helicopters which were granted as a Foreign Military Sale in March 2024. The contract, valued at USD455m, included associated engineering, programme management and logistics support.

As budgets in the region have remained small, Chinese and Russian companies that are able to offer equipment at lower prices than their Western competitors have dominated the market. However, as Russian industry prioritises its support of the Russian war effort in Ukraine, its ability to maintain exports globally, including to Sub-Saharan Africa, has reduced, creating opportunities that Chinese firms have typically benefited from. However, it has not ceased entirely, with Russia actively marketing at African defence shows such as AAD. Moreover, export of Russian equipment and services over the last three years has typically been to those countries where a *coup d'état* has led to the installation of an anti-Western, or specifically anti-French, government and to the deployment of Russian paramilitaries. For example, in September 2024, ministers from Burkina Faso, Mali and Niger announced a partnership with Russia's space company, Roscosmos, to establish telecommunications systems and satellite monitoring of their border areas. In addition to Russian and Chinese firms, Turkish and Emirati companies have also made inroads. For Turkiye, sales of armoured vehicles and combat ISR UAVs have been notable successes. These sales have often been either preceded or accompanied by the opening of a Turkish military mission or embassy in the country. Similarly, the United Arab Emirates has sought to deepen economic ties across Africa, with Angola being an important test case, with promises of significant investments across critical sectors such as energy, technology and maritime logistics.

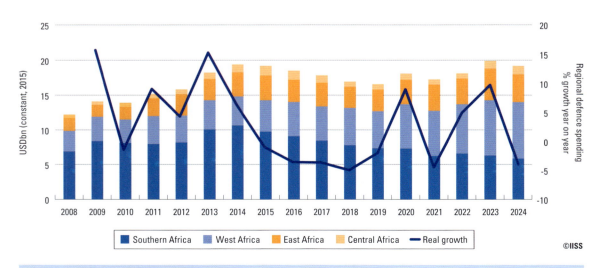

▲ Figure 41 **Sub-Saharan Africa: total defence spending by sub-region, 2008–24**

Figure 42 Sub-Saharan Africa: arms procurement and defence-industrial trends, 2024

GULF STATES' EQUIPMENT DELIVERIES TO SUB-SAHARAN AFRICA GROW

The transfer of defence equipment to African states by Gulf states, particularly the United Arab Emirates, is increasing. This trend started only a decade ago, with sporadic equipment deliveries from Qatar and Saudi Arabia. Deliveries from the UAE, primarily armoured vehicles, started at about the same time but have accelerated dramatically since then. By 2024, STREIT Group, a privately owned armoured-vehicle manufacturer with major production facilities in the UAE, had delivered vehicles to a multitude of clients, including the Democratic Republic of Congo (DRC), Mali, Nigeria, South Sudan and Sudan. Calidus, another Emirati armoured-vehicle manufacturer, has delivered its MCAV-20 to Chad, the DRC, Ethiopia, Mozambique, Rwanda and Sudan. Other UAE-based armoured-vehicle manufacturers such as Mezcal, Isotrex, MSPV and International Armored Group also appear to have supplied Sub-Saharan African countries. Beyond armoured vehicles, the UAE government transferred surplus AS550 *Fennec* helicopters to Kenya in 2018. More significantly, Emirati defence conglomerate EDGE Group signed a USD1.05 billion deal with Angola in 2023 for three corvettes, six rotary-wing uninhabited aerial vehicles (UAVs), and other smaller vessels. Qatar has also donated armoured vehicles to Burkina Faso, Mali and Somalia, while Saudi Arabia has transferred four helicopters to Djibouti and Riyadh-based ERAF recently sold at least 15 *Tares* armoured vehicles to Nigeria. With expected increases in the armoured-vehicle manufacturing capacity of Gulf states, as well as growing capabilities in other areas such as UAVs and munitions, these countries' defence industries could become a significant element of their growing influence across Sub-Saharan Africa.

ARMOURED-VEHICLE PRODUCTION SPREADS

For decades, Sub-Saharan Africa's armoured-vehicle production capabilities have been largely based in South Africa. Although this remains the case, other countries in the region are beginning to invest in their own companies, with some having recently secured their first export contracts. Nigeria's long-running counter-insurgency operations against Boko Haram have driven demand in the Nigerian armed forces and account for much of the growth. The army has ordered at least 80 *Ezugwu* 4×4s from the state-run Defence Industries Corporation of Nigeria. Local company Proforce has also supplied the army with a variety of vehicles and exported its *Ara*-2 to neighbouring Chad in 2019, Nigeria's first defence export. Similarly, Innoson Vehicle Manufacturing exported military trucks to Sierra Leone in 2022 and EPAIL Nigeria is now manufacturing Chinese Dongfeng *Mengshi* 4×4s. Elsewhere, Uganda's armed-forces-owned National Enterprise Corporation (NEC) opened a joint-venture facility with STREIT Group in 2022 to manufacture that company's designs. In 2018, Uganda had opened a similar facility in cooperation with South Africa's Twiga Services and Logistics. Sudan's Military Industries Corporation has supplied the armed forces of that country with a series of armoured vehicles, including the *Sarsar*-2, although the status of much of Sudanese industry today is unclear due to the civil war there. While countries in the region continue to import most of their defence equipment, growing defence budgets, particularly in West and East Africa, are creating opportunities for local companies, often in partnership with more established foreign firms.

RUSSIAN DEFENCE-INDUSTRY ACTIVITY IN AFRICAN STATES

Since 2017, Russian mercenary forces have deployed to at least four Sub-Saharan African states and established political and commercial links with many more. This increase in Russian influence in the region also has a defence-industrial angle, although equipment deliveries have declined since 2022 as Russian industry has focused on supporting the country's full-scale invasion of Ukraine. Exceptions to this include the delivery of armoured vehicles to Gabon and to the Rapid Support Forces in Sudan in 2024, and of surplus L-39 training aircraft to the Central African Republic in 2023. Elsewhere, Russia has concluded agreements to expand on military cooperation with Cameroon and the DRC, which include technical elements. The deployment of Russian mercenaries to Niger in 2024 will supposedly be followed by the delivery of an air-defence system. A USD100 million donation to the Ugandan armed forces in 2024 was accompanied by statements that both countries would work together to make Uganda a regional hub for maintenance and production of Russian-origin equipment, following the establishment of a facility to maintain Mi-17/24 helicopters in 2022. Russia has struggled since 2022 to supply some of its most important defence-industrial partners, such as India. As such, the extent to which its industry can support some of these ambitions in Sub-Saharan Africa is not clear. However, the lack of political stipulations that accompany cooperation with Russia, in contrast to assistance from the US and European states, still makes working with Russia attractive for those regional states which have either long been dictatorships or have recently become military-led.

Map 7 — Selected Turkish exports to Sub-Saharan Africa since 2018

Over the last six years, Turkish companies have enjoyed a surge in their exports to Sub-Saharan African countries, primarily through the sale of 4×4 armoured vehicles and armed uninhabited aerial vehicles (UAVs). This is due in large part to the much greater Turkish diplomatic engagement and presence in the continent over the last decade, including opening embassies (from 12 in 2002 to over 40 today), high-level visits, economic investment, military missions and, in the case of Somalia, a permanent military deployment. Turkish equipment is often of higher quality than Chinese rivals, cheaper than US and European alternatives and is sold liberally with few to no end-user restrictions, giving it a competitive advantage in many places. While these contracts are not as lucrative as the defence exports Turkiye has secured in the Middle East and South and Southeast Asia, they often act as a precursor to broader and much more significant commercial deals in areas such as energy, construction, mining and transportation.

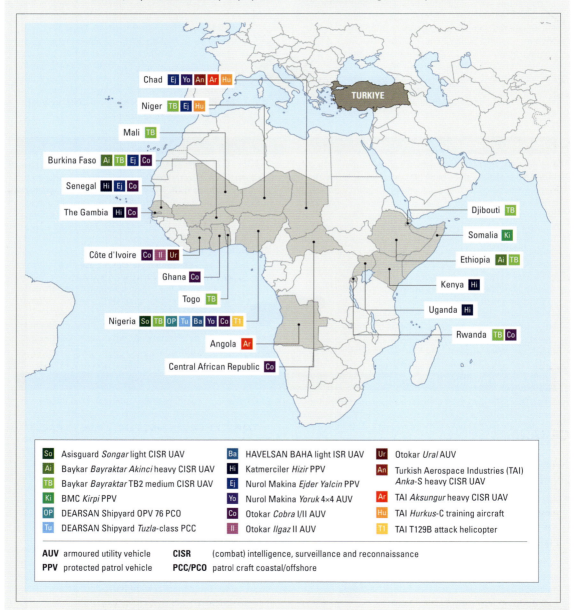

So	Asisguard *Songar* light CISR UAV
Ai	Baykar *Bayraktar Akinci* heavy CISR UAV
TB	Baykar *Bayraktar TB2* medium CISR UAV
Ki	BMC *Kirpi* PPV
OP	DEARSAN Shipyard OPV 76 PCO
Tu	DEARSAN Shipyard *Tuzla*-class PCC
Ba	HAVELSAN BAHA light ISR UAV
Hi	Katmerciler *Hizir* PPV
Ej	Nurol Makina *Ejder Yalcin* PPV
Yo	Nurol Makina *Yoruk* 4×4 AUV
Co	Otokar *Cobra* I/II AUV
Il	Otokar *Ilgaz* II AUV
Ur	Otokar *Ural* AUV
An	Turkish Aerospace Industries (TAI) *Anka*-S heavy CISR UAV
Ar	TAI *Aksungur* heavy CISR UAV
Hu	TAI *Hurkus*-C training aircraft
T1	TAI T129B attack helicopter

AUV armoured utility vehicle
PPV protected patrol vehicle
CISR (combat) intelligence, surveillance and reconnaissance
PCC/PCO patrol craft coastal/offshore

Source: IISS, Military Balance+, milbalplus.iiss.org

Angola ANG

New Angolan Kwanza AOA		2023	2024	2025
GDP	AOA	75.2trn	99.4trn	122trn
	USD	110bn	113bn	118bn
Real GDP growth	%	1.0	2.4	2.8
Def bdgt	AOA		865bn	879bn
	USD		1.26bn	1.00bn

Real-terms defence budget trend (USDbn, constant 2015)

Population	37,202,061				
Age	0–14	15–19	20–24	25–29	30–64	65 plus
Male	23.5%	5.4%	4.2%	3.3%	11.5%	1.0%
Female	23.4%	5.6%	4.4%	3.5%	12.8%	1.4%

Capabilities

Angola's armed forces are increasingly focused on the protection of offshore resources and maritime security cooperation with regional and external powers. Defence ties with Russia mainly involve equipment deliveries, though there have been plans to boost defence-industrial cooperation. Luanda is partnering with multiple countries in its pursuit of military modernisation, defence-industrial development and maritime security. Angola continues to deepen defence ties with the US, especially in capacity building and maritime security. Angola retains conscription but has volunteer components, such as the navy. The armed forces train regularly and have participated in multinational exercises. Angola is the only regional state with a strategic-airlift capacity. It has ordered three medium-lift aircraft for transport missions and maritime surveillance. The country curtailed equipment-purchasing plans in recent years due to defence budget challenges. The defence industry is limited to in-service maintenance facilities, but Angola aspires to develop greater capacity.

ACTIVE 107,000 (Army 100,000 Navy 1,000 Air 6,000) Gendarmerie & Paramilitary 10,000

Conscript liability 2 years

ORGANISATIONS BY SERVICE

Army 100,000
FORCES BY ROLE
MANOEUVRE
  Armoured
  1 tk bde
  Light
  1 SF bde
  1 (1st) div (1 mot inf bde, 2 inf bde)
  1 (2nd) div (3 mot inf bde, 3 inf bde, 1 arty regt)
  1 (3rd) div (2 mot inf bde, 3 inf bde)
  1 (4th) div (1 tk regt, 5 mot inf bde, 2 inf bde, 1 engr bde)
  1 (5th) div (2 inf bde)
  1 (6th) div (1 mot inf bde, 2 inf bde, 1 engr bde)
COMBAT SUPPORT
  Some engr units
COMBAT SERVICE SUPPORT
  Some log units
EQUIPMENT BY TYPE†
ARMOURED FIGHTING VEHICLES
  MBT 300: ε200 T-55AM2; 50 T-62; 50 T-72M1
  LT TK 10 PT-76
  ASLT 9+ WMA-301
  RECCE 603: 600 BRDM-2; 3+ *Cayman* BRDM
  IFV 250 BMP-1/BMP-2
  APC 276
    APC (T) 31 MT-LB
    APC (W) 200+: ε200 BTR-152/-60/-70/-80; WZ-551 (CP)
    PPV 45 *Casspir* NG2000
ENGINEERING & MAINTENANCE VEHICLES
  ARV 5+: 5 BTS-2; T-54/T-55
  MW *Bozena*
ARTILLERY 1,463
  SP 25+: **122mm** 9+ 2S1 *Gvozdika*; **152mm** 4 2S3 *Akatsiya*; **203mm** 12 2S7 *Pion*
  TOWED 575: **122mm** 523 D-30; **130mm** 48 M-46; **152mm** 4 D-20
  MRL 113+: **122mm** 110: 70 BM-21 *Grad*; 40 RM-70; **220mm**; 3+ 9P140MB *Uragan*-M; **240mm** BM-24
  MOR 750: **82mm** 250; **120mm** 500
ANTI-TANK/ANTI-INFRASTRUCTURE
  MSL • MANPATS 9K11 (RS-AT-3 *Sagger*)
  RCL 500: 400 **82mm** B-10/**107mm** B-11†; **106mm** 100 M40†
  GUNS • SP 100mm SU-100†
AIR DEFENCE
  SAM • Point-defence 9K32 *Strela*-2 (RS-SA-7 *Grail*)‡; 9K36 *Strela*-3 (RS-SA-14 *Gremlin*); 9K310 *Igla*-1 (RS-SA-16 *Gimlet*)
  GUNS
    SP 23mm ZSU-23-4
    TOWED 450+: **14.5mm** ZPU-4; **23mm** ZU-23-2; **37mm** M-1939; **57mm** S-60

Navy ε1,000
EQUIPMENT BY TYPE
PATROL AND COASTAL COMBATANTS 29
  PCO 2 *Ngola Kiluange* (NLD Damen 6210) with 1 hel landing platform (Ministry of Fisheries)
  PCC 5 *Rei Bula Matadi* (Ministry of Fisheries)
  PBF 12: 3 HSI 32; 5 PVC-170; 4 *Super Dvora* Mk III
  PB 10: 4 *Mandume*; 1 *Ocean Eagle 43*; 5 *Comandante Imperial Santana* (Ministry of Fisheries)
AMPHIBIOUS • LANDING CRAFT 1
  LCT 1 *RA 4 de Abril* (FRA CMN LCT 200-70) (capacity 3 MBT or 260 troops)

LOGISTICS AND SUPPORT 1

AGOR 1 *Baia Farta* (NLD Damen 7417) (Ministry of Fisheries)

Coastal Defence

EQUIPMENT BY TYPE

COASTAL DEFENCE • **AShM** 4K44 *Utyos* (RS-SSC-1B *Sepal* – at Luanda)

Marines ε500

FORCES BY ROLE

MANOEUVRE

Amphibious
1 mne bn

Air Force/Air Defence 6,000

FORCES BY ROLE

FIGHTER

1 sqn with Su-27/Su-27UB/Su-30K *Flanker*

GROUND ATTACK

1 sqn with EMB-314 *Super Tucano**

MARITIME PATROL

1 sqn with Cessna 500 *Citation* I; C-212 *Aviocar*; Kodiak 100 MP mod

TRANSPORT

3 sqn with An-12 *Cub*; An-26 *Curl*; An-32 *Cline*; An-72 *Coaler*; BN-2A *Islander*; C-212 *Aviocar*; C295M; EMB-135BJ *Legacy* 600 (VIP); Il-76TD *Candid*; Kodiak 100; MA60

TRAINING

1 sqn with Cessna 172R
1 sqn with EMB-312 *Tucano*
1 sqn with L-39 *Albatros*
1 sqn with PC-9*

ATTACK HELICOPTER

2 sqn with Mi-24/Mi-35 *Hind*; SA342M *Gazelle*

TRANSPORT HELICOPTER

1 sqn with AS565 *Panther*
1 sqn with Bell 212
1 sqn with Mi-8 *Hip*; Mi-17 *Hip* H
1 sqn with Mi-171Sh

AIR DEFENCE

5 bty with S-125M1 *Pechora*-M1 (RS-SA-3 *Goa*);
5 coy with 9K35 *Strela*-10 (RS-SA-13 *Gopher*)†; 2K12-ML *Kvadrat*-ML (RS-SA-6 *Gainful*); 9K33 *Osa* (RS-SA-8 *Gecko*); 9K31 *Strela*-1 (RS-SA-9 *Gaskin*)

EQUIPMENT BY TYPE†

AIRCRAFT 28 combat capable
FTR 18: 6 Su-27/Su-27UB *Flanker*; 12 Su-30K *Flanker*; (18 MiG-23ML *Flogger* in store)
FGA (8 MiG-23BN/UB *Flogger*; 13 Su-22 *Fitter* D all in store)
ATK (8 Su-25 *Frogfoot*; 2 Su-25UB *Frogfoot* in store)
MP 2: 1 Cessna 500 *Citation* I; 1 Kodiak 100 MP mod
TPT 53: **Heavy** 7 Il-76TD *Candid* (1 more in store); **Medium** 4 An-12 *Cub* (2 more in store); **Light** 42: 12 An-26 *Curl*; 2 An-32 *Cline*; 7 An-72 *Coaler* (1 more in store); 8 BN-2A *Islander*; 2 C-212 *Aviocar*; 1 C295M; 6 Cessna 172R; 1 EMB-135BJ *Legacy* 600 (VIP); 1 Kodiak 100; 2 MA60
TRG 37: 13 EMB-312 *Tucano*; 6 EMB-314 *Super Tucano**; 12 K-8W *Karakorum*; 2 L-39C *Albatros*; 4 PC-9*; (6 Z-142 in store)

HELICOPTERS
ATK 34 Mi-24/Mi-35 *Hind*
MRH 53: 8 AS565 *Panther*; 4 AW139; 8 SA342M *Gazelle*; 25 Mi-8 *Hip*/Mi-17 *Hip* H; 8 Mi-171Sh *Terminator*; (8 SA316 *Alouette* III (IAR-316) in store)
TPT • **Light** 10: 2+ AW109E; 8 Bell 212

AIR DEFENCE • **SAM** 73
Short-range 28: 16 2K12-ML *Kvadrat*-ML (RS-SA-6 *Gainful*); 12 S-125M1 *Pechora*-M1 (RS-SA-3 *Goa*)
Point-defence 45: 10 9K35 *Strela*-10 (RS-SA-13 *Gopher*)†; 15 9K33 *Osa* (RS-SA-8 *Gecko*); 20 9K31 *Strela*-1 (RS-SA-9 *Gaskin*)

AIR-LAUNCHED MISSILES
AAM
IR R-73 (RS-AA-11A *Archer*); **IR/SARH** R-23/24 (RS-AA-7 *Apex*)‡; R-27 (RS-AA-10 *Alamo*)
ASM 9M17M *Falanga*-M (RS-AT-2 *Swatter*); HOT
ARM Kh-28 (RS-AS-9 *Kyle*)

Gendarmerie & Paramilitary 10,000

Rapid-Reaction Police 10,000

Benin BEN

CFA Franc BCEAO XOF		2023	2024	2025
GDP	XOF	11.9trn	13.0trn	14.1trn
	USD	19.7bn	21.3bn	23.1bn
Real GDP growth	%	6.4	6.5	6.5
Def bdgt	XOF	77.5bn	93.5bn	
	USD	128m	154m	

Real-terms defence budget trend (USDm, constant 2015)

Population	14,697,052					
Age	0–14	15–19	20–24	25–29	30–64	65 plus
Male	22.9%	5.3%	4.7%	3.8%	11.6%	1.1%
Female	22.4%	5.2%	4.7%	4.0%	13.0%	1.3%

Capabilities

The armed forces focus on border- and internal-security issues but have been grappling with a deteriorating security situation in the northern part of the country. Border patrols and security have increased to address the regional threat from Islamist groups.

Maritime security remains a priority in light of continuing piracy in the Gulf of Guinea. The country reportedly is working to improve soldiers' living conditions. In July 2022, Benin struck a security cooperation agreement with Rwanda. The country also has a military cooperation agreement with France. French forces based in Senegal have provided training to boost Benin's border surveillance capacity. China has delivered armoured vehicles, while the US has helped train the army and national police and provided a patrol boat. Since July 2024, Benin also receives EU financial support for its armed forces as part of the European Peace Facility. Benin contributes personnel to the Multinational Joint Task Force fighting Islamist terrorist groups, though it has little capacity to deploy beyond neighbouring states without external support. It lacks a defence industry beyond maintenance capabilities.

ACTIVE 12,300 (Army 8,000 Navy 550 Air 250 National Guard 3,500) Gendarmerie & Paramilitary 4,800

Conscript liability 18 months (selective)

ORGANISATIONS BY SERVICE

Army ε8,000
FORCES BY ROLE
MANOEUVRE
  Armoured
    2 armd sqn
  Light
    1 (rapid reaction) mot inf bn
    8 inf bn
COMBAT SUPPORT
  2 arty bn
  1 engr bn
  1 sigs bn
COMBAT SERVICE SUPPORT
  1 log bn
  1 spt bn
EQUIPMENT BY TYPE
ARMOURED FIGHTING VEHICLES
  LT TK 18 PT-76†
  RECCE 24: 3 AML-90; 14 BRDM-2; 7 M8
  APC 65
    APC (T) 22 M113
    APC (W) 33: 2 *Bastion* APC; 31 VAB
    PPV 10 *Casspir* NG
  AUV 19: 9 Dongfeng *Mengshi*; 10 VBL
ARTILLERY 16+
  TOWED 105mm 16: 12 L118 Light Gun; 4 M101
  MOR 81mm PP-87; **120mm** W86

Navy ε550
EQUIPMENT BY TYPE
PATROL AND COASTAL COMBATANTS 6
  PB 6: 2 *Matelot Brice Kpomasse* (ex-PRC); 3 *Alibori* (FRA FPB 98); 1 *Couffo* (PRC 27m)

Air Force ε250
EQUIPMENT BY TYPE
AIRCRAFT
  TPT 4: **Light** 2: 1 DHC-6 *Twin Otter*†; 1 MA600; **PAX** 2: 1 B-727; 1 HS-748†
  TRG (1 LH-10 *Ellipse* non-operational)
HELICOPTERS
  MRH 2 H125M *Fennec*
  TPT 8: **Medium** 3 H215 (AS332M1) *Super Puma*; **Light** 5: 4 AW109BA; 1 AS350B *Ecureuil*†

National Guard ε3,500
FORCES BY ROLE
MANOEUVRE
  Air Manoeuvre
    1 AB bn

Gendarmerie & Paramilitary 4,800

Republican Police ε4,800
EQUIPMENT BY TYPE
ARMOURED FIGHTING VEHICLES
  APC • **PPV** *Casspir* NG

DEPLOYMENT

CENTRAL AFRICAN REPUBLIC: UN • MINUSCA 7
CHAD: Lake Chad Basin Commission • MNJTF 150
DEMOCRATIC REPUBLIC OF THE CONGO: UN • MONUSCO 8
SOUTH SUDAN: UN • UNMISS 8
SUDAN: UN • UNISFA 2

Botswana BWA

Botswana Pula BWP		2023	2024	2025
GDP	BWP	264bn	272bn	308bn
	USD	19.4bn	20.0bn	22.1bn
Real GDP growth	%	2.7	1.0	5.2
Def bdgt	BWP	6.54bn	8.13bn	
	USD		481m	597m

Population 2,450,668

Age	0–14	15–19	20–24	25–29	30–64	65 plus
Male	14.5%	4.5%	4.2%	4.1%	18.2%	2.4%
Female	14.2%	4.6%	4.4%	4.3%	20.9%	3.7%

Capabilities

The Botswana Defence Force's primary responsibility is to ensure territorial integrity. Its other tasks include tackling poaching. Botswana has a history of contributing to peacekeeping operations. The BDF has reportedly been working on a defence doctrine influenced by US concepts and practices. Botswana has a good relationship with the US, which provides regular training. The armed forces also train with several African states, including Namibia, with whom it holds biennial exercises. The operations centre for the Southern African Development Community (SADC) Standby Force is located in Gaborone. Recent personnel priorities include improving conditions of service and overhauling retirement ages. The air force has a modest airlift capacity. The country has shown interest in replacing its ageing combat aircraft, though financial pressures, have slowed progress. The country has a limited maintenance capacity but no defence-manufacturing sector.

ACTIVE 9,000 (Army 8,500 Air 500)

ORGANISATIONS BY SERVICE

Army 8,500
FORCES BY ROLE
MANOEUVRE
  Armoured
  1 armd bde(-)
  Light
  2 inf bde (1 armd recce regt, 4 inf bn, 1 cdo unit, 1 engr regt, 1 log bn, 2 ADA regt)
COMBAT SUPPORT
  1 arty bde
  1 engr coy
  1 sigs coy
COMBAT SERVICE SUPPORT
  1 log gp
AIR DEFENCE
  1 AD bde(-)

EQUIPMENT BY TYPE
ARMOURED FIGHTING VEHICLES
  LT TK 45: ε20 SK-105 *Kurassier*; 25 FV101 *Scorpion*
  IFV 35+ *Piranha* V UT-30
  APC 157:
    APC (W) 145: 50 BTR-60; 50 LAV-150 *Commando* (some with 90mm gun); 45 *Piranha* III
    PPV 12 *Casspir*
  AUV 70: 6 FV103 *Spartan*; 64 VBL
ENGINEERING & MAINTENANCE VEHICLES
  ARV *Greif*; M578
  MW *Aardvark* Mk2
ANTI-TANK/ANTI-INFRASTRUCTURE
  MSL
    SP V-150 TOW
    MANPATS TOW
  RCL 84mm *Carl Gustaf*
ARTILLERY 78
  TOWED 30: **105mm** 18: 12 L118 Light Gun; 6 Model 56 pack howitzer; **155mm** 12 Soltam M-68
  MRL 122mm 20 APRA-40
  MOR 28: **81mm** 22; **120mm** 6 M-43
AIR DEFENCE
  SAM
    Short-range 1 VL MICA
    Point-defence 9K32 *Strela*-2 (RS-SA-7 *Grail*)‡; 9K310 *Igla*-1 (RS-SA-16 *Gimlet*); *Javelin*; *Mistral*
  GUNS • TOWED 20mm 7 M167 *Vulcan*; **37mm** PG-65

Air Wing 500
FORCES BY ROLE
FIGHTER/GROUND ATTACK
  1 sqn with F-5A *Freedom Fighter*; F-5D *Tiger* II
TRANSPORT
  2 sqn with BD-700 *Global Express*; BN-2/-2B *Defender**; Beech 200 *King Air* (VIP); C-130B/H *Hercules*; C-212-300/400 *Aviocar*; CN-235M-100; Do-328-110 (VIP); PC-24
TRAINING
  1 sqn with PC-7 MkII *Turbo Trainer**
TRANSPORT HELICOPTER
  1 sqn with AS350B *Ecureuil*; Bell 412EP/SP *Twin Huey*; EC225LP *Super Puma*

EQUIPMENT BY TYPE
AIRCRAFT 28 combat capable
  FTR 13: 8 F-5A *Freedom Fighter*; 5 F-5D *Tiger* II
  TPT 23: **Medium** 4: 3 C-130B *Hercules*; 1 C-130H *Hercules*; **Light** 17: 4 BN-2 *Defender**; 6 BN-2B *Defender**; 1 Beech 200 *King Air* (VIP); 1 C-212-300 *Aviocar*; 2 C-212-400 *Aviocar*; 2 CN-235M-100; 1 Do-328-110 (VIP); **PAX** 2: 1 BD700 *Global Express*; 1 PC-24
  TRG 5 PC-7 MkII *Turbo Trainer**
HELICOPTERS
  MRH 7: 2 Bell 412EP *Twin Huey*; 5 Bell 412SP *Twin Huey*

TPT 9: **Medium** 1 EC225LP *Super Puma*; **Light** 8 AS350B *Ecureuil*

DEPLOYMENT

DEMOCRATIC REPUBLIC OF THE CONGO: UN • MONUSCO 3

Burkina Faso BFA

CFA Franc BCEAO XOF		2023	2024	2025
GDP	XOF	12.3trn	13.3trn	14.3trn
	USD	20.3bn	21.9bn	23.6bn
Real GDP growth	%	3.1	5.5	5.8
Def bdgt	XOF	502bn	621bn	
	USD	827m	1.02bn	

Population	23,042,199				
Age	0–14	15–19	20–24	25–29	30–64	65 plus
Male	21.1%	5.6%	5.0%	3.7%	12.2%	1.4%
Female	20.5%	5.5%	4.9%	4.0%	14.3%	1.9%

Capabilities

Burkina Faso suffered two coups in 2022 that brought a military regime to power. In September 2023, Burkina Faso became part of the Alliance of Sahel States with Mali and Niger, two other countries under military control after recent coups. French troops left in early 2023. Burkina Faso is increasing its cooperation and diplomatic ties with Russia and Iran. There are reports of Russian paramilitaries in the country. In recent years, the armed forces received a significant number of armoured vehicles and other equipment. Aviation capacity is slowly improving with the arrival of additional helicopters and acquisition of *Bayraktar* TB2 UAVs from Türkiye. Financial challenges and political instability might hinder broader capability developments. The military has a limited ability to deploy to neighbouring countries. Burkina Faso has some maintenance facilities but no defence-manufacturing sector.

ACTIVE 20,600 (Army 20,000 Air 600) Gendarmerie & Paramilitary 34,200

ORGANISATIONS BY SERVICE

Army 20,000

Six military regions.
FORCES BY ROLE
COMMAND
  1 inf bde HQ
  4 inf gp HQ
SPECIAL FORCES
  1 spec ops bn
  3 cdo unit
MANOEUVRE
  Mechanised
  1 mech bn
  Light
  11 inf bn
  25 inf bn (Rapid Intervention)
  Air Manoeuvre
  1 AB regt (incl 1 CT coy)
COMBAT SUPPORT
  1 arty bn (2 arty tp)
  1 engr bn
EQUIPMENT BY TYPE
ARMOURED FIGHTING VEHICLES
  ASLT 6 WMA-301
  RECCE 43: 19 AML-60/-90; 24 EE-9 *Cascavel*
  APC 231
    APC (W) 12: 11 *Bastion* APC; 1 WZ-551 (CP)
    PPV 219: 50 CS/VP14; 24 *Ejder Yalcin*; 6 *Gila*; 13+ *Phantom* II; 63 *Puma* M26-15; 21 Stark Motors *Storm*; 2 *Temsah*-2; 40 VP11
  AUV 46+: 8+ *Bastion Patsas*; 38 *Cobra*
ENGINEERING & MAINTENANCE VEHICLES
  MW 3 *Shrek*-M
ANTI-TANK/ANTI-INFRASTRUCTURE
  RCL 75mm Type-52 (M20); **84mm** *Carl Gustaf*
ARTILLERY 58+
  TOWED 14: **105mm** 8 M101; **122mm** 6
  MRL 9: **107mm** ε4 Type-63; **122mm** 5 APR-40
  MOR 35+: **81mm** Brandt; **82mm** 15; **SP 82mm** 8 CS/SS4; **120mm** 12
AIR DEFENCE
  SAM • Point-defence 9K32 *Strela*-2 (RS-SA-7 *Grail*)‡
  GUNS • TOWED 42: **14.5mm** 30 ZPU; **20mm** 12 TCM-20

Air Force 600

FORCES BY ROLE
GROUND ATTACK/TRAINING
  1 sqn with EMB-314 *Super Tucano**; SF-260WL *Warrior**
TRANSPORT
  1 sqn with AT-802 *Air Tractor*; B-727 (VIP); Beech 200 *King Air*; C295W; CN235-220; PA-34 *Seneca*; *Tetras*
ATTACK/TRANSPORT HELICOPTER
  1 sqn with AS350 *Ecureuil*; Mi-8 *Hip*; Mi-17 *Hip* H; Mi-17-1V *Hip*; Mi-26T *Halo*; Mi-35 *Hind*
EQUIPMENT BY TYPE
AIRCRAFT 5 combat capable
  ISR 1 DA42 MPP *Guardian*
  TPT 10: **Light** 9: 1 AT-802 *Air Tractor*; 2 Beech 200 *King Air*; 1 C295W; 1 CN235-220; 1 PA-34 *Seneca*; 3 *Tetras*; **PAX** 1 B-727 (VIP)
  TRG 5: 3 EMB-314 *Super Tucano**; 2 SF-260WL *Warrior**
HELICOPTERS

ATK 2 Mi-35 Hind
MRH 4: 1 AW139; 2 Mi-17 Hip H; 1 Mi-17-1V Hip
TPT 3: Heavy 1 Mi-26T Halo; Medium 1 Mi-8 Hip; Light 1 AS350 Ecureuil

UNINHABITED AERIAL VEHICLES
CISR 7: Heavy 2 Bayraktar Akinci; Medium 5+ Bayraktar TB2

BOMBS
INS/SAT HGK-82
Laser-guided MAM-L; MAM-T; Teber-82

Gendarmerie & Paramilitary 34,200

National Gendarmerie 4,200
Ministry of Defence and Veteran Affairs
FORCES BY ROLE
SPECIAL FORCES
1 spec ops gp (USIGN)
EQUIPMENT BY TYPE
ARMOURED FIGHTING VEHICLES
APC • APC (W) some Bastion APC

Homeland Defence Volunteeers 30,000

DEPLOYMENT
CENTRAL AFRICAN REPUBLIC: UN • MINUSCA 8
DEMOCRATIC REPUBLIC OF THE CONGO: UN • MONUSCO 5
SUDAN: UN • UNISFA 1

FOREIGN FORCES
Russia 200 (PMC)

Burundi BDI

Burundi Franc BIF		2023	2024	2025
GDP	BIF	10.9trn	13.0trn	16.3trn
	USD	4.24bn	4.29bn	2.15bn
Real GDP growth	%	2.7	2.2	3.5
Def bdgt	BIF	208bn	374bn	
	USD	80.9m	123m	

Real-terms defence budget trend (USDm, constant 2015)

Population 13,590,102

Age	0–14	15–19	20–24	25–29	30–64	65 plus
Male	21.3%	5.6%	4.6%	3.7%	13.0%	1.5%
Female	21.0%	5.6%	4.6%	3.8%	13.5%	1.9%

Capabilities
The country continues to face cross-border and internal security challenges. Security cooperation with external actors that was largely halted by the political crisis in 2015 and tested the cohesion of Burundi's armed forces has resumed in a limited fashion. Burundi signed a cooperation agreement with Russia in 2018 on counter-terrorism and joint training. The country also signed a security cooperation agreement with the DRC in 2023. Relations with Rwanda have again deteriorated. The armed forces have a limited capability to deploy externally and, in 2022, sent troops to the DRC to help stabilise the situation there. Burundi has long maintained a deployment in Somalia. The experience accumulated during UN operations has likely increased the skills of deployed troops. Peacekeeping missions help to fund the armed forces, though financial and equipment deficiencies restrict military effectiveness. The country has no defence industry apart from limited maintenance facilities.

ACTIVE 30,050 (Army 30,000 Navy 50) Gendarmerie & Paramilitary 1,000

ORGANISATIONS BY SERVICE

Army 30,000
FORCES BY ROLE
MANOEUVRE
  Mechanised
  2 lt armd bn (sqn)
  Light
  7 inf bn
  Some indep inf coy
COMBAT SUPPORT
  1 arty bn
  1 engr bn
AIR DEFENCE
  1 AD bn
EQUIPMENT BY TYPE
ARMOURED FIGHTING VEHICLES
  RECCE 48: 6 AML-60; 12 AML-90; 30 BRDM-2
  APC 114
    APC (W) 70: 20 BTR-40; 10 BTR-80; 10 Fahd-300; 9 Panhard M3; 15 Type-92; 6 Walid
    PPV 44: 12 Casspir; 12 RG-31 Nyala; 10 RG-33L; 10 Springbuck 4×4
  AUV 15 Cougar 4×4
ARTILLERY 120
  TOWED 122mm 18 D-30
  MRL 122mm 12 BM-21 Grad
  MOR 90: 82mm 15 M-43; 120mm ε75
ANTI-TANK/ANTI-INFRASTRUCTURE
  MSL • MANPATS Milan (reported)
  RCL 75mm Type-52 (M20)
AIR DEFENCE
  SAM • Point-defence 9K32 Strela-2 (RS-SA-7 Grail)‡
  GUNS • TOWED 150+: 14.5mm 15 ZPU-4; 135+ 23mm ZU-23/37mm Type-55 (M-1939)

Air Wing 200

EQUIPMENT BY TYPE

AIRCRAFT 1 combat capable

TPT • Light 2 Cessna 150L†

TRG 1 SF-260W *Warrior**

HELICOPTERS

ATK 2 Mi-24 *Hind*

MRH 2 SA342L *Gazelle*

TPT • Medium (2 Mi-8 *Hip* non-op)

Reserves

FORCES BY ROLE

MANOEUVRE

Light

10 inf bn (reported)

Navy 50

EQUIPMENT BY TYPE

PATROL AND COASTAL COMBATANTS • PB 4

AMPHIBIOUS • LCT 2

Gendarmerie & Paramilitary ε1,000

General Administration of State Security ε1,000

DEPLOYMENT

CENTRAL AFRICAN REPUBLIC: UN • MINUSCA 768; 1 inf bn

DEMOCRATIC REPUBLIC OF THE CONGO: Army: 1,000; 1 inf bn

SOMALIA: AU • ATMIS 2,300; 3 inf bn

SUDAN: UN • UNISFA 3

Cabo Verde CPV

Cape Verde Escudo CVE		2023	2024	2025
GDP	CVE	264bn	281bn	300bn
	USD	2.59bn	2.76bn	2.94bn
Real GDP growth	%	5.1	4.7	4.7
Def bdgt	CVE	1.51bn	1.76bn	1.74bn
	USD	14.8m	17.3m	17.0m

Population	611,014					
Age	0–14	15–19	20–24	25–29	30–64	65 plus
Male	13.3%	4.3%	4.2%	4.3%	20.0%	2.5%
Female	13.1%	4.3%	4.2%	4.4%	21.4%	3.9%

Capabilities

Cabo Verde's defence priorities include territorial defence, maritime security and protection of its EEZ and airspace. The country aspires to modernise the armed forces, including a revision of compulsory military service. It has developed a new Strategic Concept of National Defence aimed at upgrading the armed forces. Cabo Verde is trying to improve airspace monitoring and pursue related procurements, including new aircraft and helicopters. Portugal acts as the main security partner. The government is interested in greater regional and international defence engagement and, in 2022, signed agreements with Portugal and the US. International partners provide maritime security training support and both China and the US have strengthened the country's coast guard with patrol boat deliveries. The armed forces take part in multinational regional exercises and cooperative activities. Equipment capabilities remain limited and there is no defence industry, beyond maintenance facilities.

ACTIVE 1,200 (National Guard 1,000 Coast Guard 100 Air 100)

Conscript liability Selective conscription (14 months)

ORGANISATIONS BY SERVICE

National Guard 1,000

FORCES BY ROLE

SPECIAL FORCES

1 spec ops unit

MANOEUVRE

Light

2 inf bn (gp)

Amphibious

1 mne unit

COMBAT SUPPORT

1 mor bty

1 engr bn

1 MP unit

EQUIPMENT BY TYPE

ARMOURED FIGHTING VEHICLES

RECCE 10 BRDM-2

ARTILLERY • MOR 18: **82mm** 12; **120mm** 6 M-1943

AIR DEFENCE

SAM • Point-defence 9K32 *Strela* (RS-SA-7 *Grail*)‡

GUNS • TOWED 30: **14.5mm** 18 ZPU-1; **23mm** 12 ZU-23

Coast Guard ε100

EQUIPMENT BY TYPE

PATROL AND COASTAL COMBATANTS 7

PCC 2: 1 *Guardião* (NLD Damen Stan Patrol 5009); 1 *Vigilante* (ex-GDR *Kondor* I)

PB 4: 2 *Badejo*; 1 *Espadarte* (US Peterson Mk4); 1 *Tainha* (PRC 27m)

PBF 1 *Rei* (US *Archangel*)

LOGISTICS AND SUPPORT 2

AAR 2 *Ponta Nho Martinho* (ESP)

AIRCRAFT • TPT • Light 1 Do-228

Air Force up to 100

FORCES BY ROLE

MARITIME PATROL

1 sqn with An-26 *Curl*

EQUIPMENT BY TYPE

AIRCRAFT • TPT • Light 3 An-26 *Curl*†

Cameroon CMR

CFA Franc BEAC XAF		2023	2024	2025
GDP	XAF	29.9trn	32.1trn	34.5trn
	USD	49.3bn	53.4bn	57.7bn
Real GDP growth	%	3.2	3.9	4.2
Def bdgt	XAF	277bn	324bn	
	USD	457m	539m	

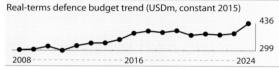

Real-terms defence budget trend (USDm, constant 2015)

Population	30,966,105				
Age	0–14	15–19	20–24	25–29	30–64	65 plus
Male	20.9%	5.4%	4.6%	3.9%	13.4%	1.5%
Female	20.6%	5.3%	4.6%	4.0%	13.9%	1.7%

Capabilities

Internal security is a key concern for Cameroon's armed forces, as is the cross-border challenge from Boko Haram in the Lake Chad region. The country is part of the Multinational Joint Task Force battling regional terrorist groups. Cameroon has a military-assistance agreement with China, which has assisted in the expansion of the deep-water port at Kribi. Cameroon also has long-standing military ties with France, including in relation to military training, receives US security assistance, renewed in 2023 its military cooperation agreement with Russia, and in early 2024 signed a framework agreement for naval cooperation with Spain. The AU maintains its continental logistics base at Douala. Although deployments continue to UN peacekeeping operations, the armed forces have limited organic power-projection capability without external support. The country is slowly updating its ageing equipment inventory, including armoured vehicles and ISR capabilities, while additional patrol vessels have in recent years improved Cameroon's maritime capability in the Gulf of Guinea. Cameroon has no defence industrial capacity bar maintenance facilities.

ACTIVE 38,000 (Army 35,500 Navy 1,500 Air 1,000)
Gendarmerie & Paramilitary 9,000

ORGANISATIONS BY SERVICE

Army 35,500

5 Mil Regions

FORCES BY ROLE

MANOEUVRE

Light

1 rapid reaction bde (1 armd recce bn, 1 AB bn, 1 amph bn)
1 mot inf bde (4 mot inf bn, 1 spt bn)
5 mot inf bde (3 mot inf bn, 1 spt bn)
6 rapid reaction bn
4 inf bn
1 rapid intervention bn

Air Manoeuvre

1 cdo/AB bn

Other

1 (Presidential Guard) gd bn

COMBAT SUPPORT

1 arty regt (5 arty bty)
5 engr regt

AIR DEFENCE

1 AD regt (6 AD bty)

EQUIPMENT BY TYPE

ARMOURED FIGHTING VEHICLES

ASLT 18: 6 AMX-10RC; ε12 WMA-301 (*Cara* 105)
RECCE 54: 31 AML-90; 15 *Ferret*; 8 M8
IFV 52: 8 LAV-150 *Commando* with 20mm gun; 14 LAV-150 *Commando* with 90mm gun; 22 *Ratel*-20 (Engr); ε8 Type-07P
APC 135
  APC (T) 12 M3 half-track
  APC (W) 66: 45 *Bastion* APC; 21 LAV-150 *Commando*
  PPV 57: 16 Gaia *Thunder*; 20 IAG *Rila*; 21 PKSV
AUV 19+: 6 *Cougar* 4×4; *Panthera* T6; 5 RAM Mk3; 3 *Tiger* 4×4; 5 VBL

ENGINEERING & MAINTENANCE VEHICLES

ARV WZ-551 ARV

ANTI-TANK/ANTI-INFRASTRUCTURE

MSL
  SP 24 TOW (on Jeeps)
  MANPATS *Milan*
RCL 53: **75mm** 13 Type-52 (M20); **106mm** 40 M40A2

ARTILLERY 114

SP 155mm 18 ATMOS 2000
TOWED 52: **105mm** 20 M101; **130mm** 24: 12 M-1982 (reported); 12 Type-59 (M-46); **155mm** 8 M-71
MRL 122mm 20 BM-21 *Grad*
MOR 24+: **81mm** (some SP); **120mm** 16 Brandt; **SP 120mm** 8 *Cardom*

AIR DEFENCE • GUNS

SP 20mm RBY-1 with TCM-20
TOWED 54: **14.5mm** 18 Type-58 (ZPU-2); **35mm** 18 GDF-002; **37mm** 18 Type-63

Navy ε1,500

HQ located at Douala

EQUIPMENT BY TYPE

PATROL AND COASTAL COMBATANTS 14

PCC 3: 1 *Dipikar* (ex-FRA *Flamant*); 2 *Le Ntem* (PRC Poly Technologies 60m)

PBF 1 *Night Hawk*
PB 10: 2 *Aresa 2400*; 2 *Aresa 3200*; 2 *Rodman 101*; 4 *Rodman 46*
PBR (2 *Swift-38* in reserve)
AMPHIBIOUS • LANDING CRAFT 5
LCU 2 Type-067 (ex-PRC *Yunnan*)
LCM 2: 1 Aresa 2300; 1 *Le Moungo* (ex-PRC *Yuchin*)
LCVP 1 Munson 44 (US)

Fusiliers Marin
FORCES BY ROLE
MANOEUVRE
Amphibious
3 mne bn

Air Force ε1,000
FORCES BY ROLE
FIGHTER/GROUND ATTACK
1 sqn with *Alpha Jet**†
TRANSPORT
1 sqn with PA-23 *Aztec*
1 VIP unit with AS332 *Super Puma*; AS365 *Dauphin* 2; Bell 206B *Jet Ranger*; Gulfstream III
TRAINING
1 unit with *Tetras*
ATTACK HELICOPTER
1 sqn with Mi-24 *Hind*
TRANSPORT HELICOPTER
1 sqn with Bell 206L-3; Bell 412; SA319 *Alouette* III
EQUIPMENT BY TYPE
AIRCRAFT 6 combat capable
ISR 2 Cessna 208B *Grand Caravan*
TPT 14: **Medium** (2 C-130H *Hercules*; 1 C-130H-30 *Hercules* non-operational); **Light** 13: 1 CN235; 2 J.300 *Joker*; 1 MA60; 2 PA-23 *Aztec*; 7 *Tetras*; (1 IAI-201 *Arava* in store); **PAX** 1 Gulfstream III
TRG 6 *Alpha Jet**†
HELICOPTERS
ATK 2 Mi-24 *Hind*
MRH 10: 1 AS365 *Dauphin* 2; 4 Bell 412 *Twin Huey*; 2 SA319 *Alouette* III; 3 Z-9; (5 Mi-17 *Hip* H non-operational)
TPT 5: **Medium** 3 AS332 *Super Puma*/SA330J *Puma*; **Light** 2: 1 Bell 206B *Jet Ranger*; 1 Bell 206L-3 *Long Ranger*
AIR-LAUNCHED MISSILES
ASM AKD-8

Fusiliers de l'Air
FORCES BY ROLE
MANOEUVRE
Other
1 sy bn

Gendarmerie & Paramilitary 9,000

Gendarmerie 9,000
FORCES BY ROLE
MANOEUVRE
Reconnaissance
3 (regional spt) paramilitary gp

DEPLOYMENT

CENTRAL AFRICAN REPUBLIC: UN • MINUSCA 759; 1 inf bn
DEMOCRATIC REPUBLIC OF THE CONGO: UN • MONUSCO 3

Central African Republic CAR

CFA Franc BEAC XAF		2023	2024	2025
GDP	XAF	1.60trn	1.71trn	1.84trn
	USD	2.63bn	2.82bn	3.03bn
Real GDP growth	%	0.7	1.4	2.9
Def bdgt	XAF	37.8bn	42.2bn	
	USD	62.4m	69.6m	

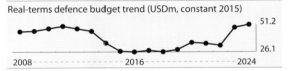
Real-terms defence budget trend (USDm, constant 2015)

Population	5,650,957					
Age	0–14	15–19	20–24	25–29	30–64	65 plus
Male	19.7%	5.6%	5.0%	4.3%	13.7%	1.5%
Female	18.8%	5.1%	4.6%	4.2%	15.5%	1.9%

Capabilities

Internal security challenges pose significant problems for the country's still-developing national defence and security institutions that suffer from the effects of violence in 2013 and ensuing political volatility. The UN's MINUSCA mission remains the principal security provider in the country but has been targeted by armed groups. In recent years, Russia has deepened its military ties in the CAR and has donated small arms, aircraft and armoured vehicles. Russian private military company personnel remain active in the country. The UN lifted an arms embargo on the country in 2024, though it said that members should avoid supplying arms to 'armed groups and associated individuals' in the CAR. The security forces continue to receive training from UN forces and an EU training mission. Poor infrastructure and logistics capacity limit the armed forces' ability to provide security across the country. There is no independent capability to deploy troops externally. The lack of financial resources and defence-industrial capacity makes equipment maintenance problematic.

ACTIVE 14,150 (Army 14,000 Air 150) **Gendarmerie & Paramilitary 1,000**

Conscript liability Selective conscription 2 years; reserve obligation thereafter, term n.k.

ORGANISATIONS BY SERVICE

Army ε14,000
FORCES BY ROLE
SPECIAL FORCES
  1 spec ops bn
  1 cdo bn
MANOEUVRE
  Light
   12 inf bn
  Amphibious
   1 amph bn
  Other
   1 gd bn
COMBAT SUPPORT
  1 engr bn
COMBAT SERVICE SUPPORT
  1 spt bn
EQUIPMENT BY TYPE
ARMOURED FIGHTING VEHICLES
  MBT 3 T-55†
  RECCE 28: 8 *Ferret*†; 20 BRDM-2
  IFV 18 *Ratel*
  APC • APC (W) 14+: 4 BTR-152†; 10+ VAB†
  AUV *Cobra* (reported); Dongfeng *Mengshi*
ARTILLERY • MOR 12+: **81mm**†; **120mm** 12 M-1943†
ANTI-TANK/ANTI-INFRASTRUCTURE
  RCL **106mm** 14 M40†
PATROL AND COASTAL COMBATANTS • PBR 9†

Air Force 150
EQUIPMENT BY TYPE
AIRCRAFT
  TPT 2: **Medium** (1 C-130A *Hercules* in store); **Light** 2 J.300 *Joker*; (1 Cessna 172RJ *Skyhawk* in store)
  TRG ε8 L-39 *Albatros*
HELICOPTERS
  ATK (1 Mi-24V *Hind* E in store)
  MRH some SA341B *Gazelle*
  TPT 1: **Medium** (1 Mi-8T *Hip* in store); **Light** 1 AS350 *Ecureuil*

FOREIGN FORCES
MINUSCA unless stated
Argentina 2
Bangladesh 1,421; 1 cdo coy; 1 inf bn; 1 med coy; 1 hel coy
Benin 7
Bhutan 187; 1 inf coy
Bolivia 6
Bosnia-Herzegovina EUTM RCA 3
Brazil 9
Burkina Faso 8
Burundi 768; 1 inf bn
Cambodia 345; 1 engr coy
Cameroon 759; 1 inf bn
Colombia 2
Congo 5
Côte d'Ivoire 185; 1 inf coy
Czech Republic 3
Ecuador 2
Egypt 1,023; 1 inf bn; 1 tpt coy
France 3
Gambia 9
Ghana 13
Guatemala 4
India 3
Indonesia 250; 1 engr coy
Jordan 7
Kazakhstan 1
Kenya 10
Lithuania EUTM RCA 1
Mauritania 458; 1 inf bn(-)
Mexico 1
Moldova 1
Mongolia 4
Morocco 767; 1 inf bn
Nepal 1,219; 2 inf bn; 1 MP pl
Niger 5
Nigeria 7
Pakistan 1,306; 1 inf bn; 2 engr coy; 1 hel sqn
Paraguay 2
Peru 229; 1 engr coy
Philippines 1
Poland EUTM RCA 2
Portugal 219; 1 AB coy • EUTM RCA 10
Romania EUTM RCA 60
Russia 10 • PMC 1,500
Rwanda 2,135; 3 inf bn; 1 fd hospital
Senegal 194; 1 inf coy
Serbia 70; 1 med coy • EUTM RCA 7
Sierra Leone 1
Spain EUTM RCA 2
Sri Lanka 114; 1 hel sqn
Tanzania 516; 1 inf bn(-)
Togo 7
Tunisia 835; 1 inf bn; 1 hel flt with 3 Bell 205
United States 10
Uruguay 3
Vietnam 7 • EUTM RCA 2
Zambia 927; 1 inf bn
Zimbabwe 2

Chad CHA

CFA Franc BEAC XAF		2023	2024	2025
GDP	XAF	10.7trn	11.3trn	12.0trn
	USD	17.6bn	18.7bn	19.6bn
Real GDP growth	%	4.9	3.2	3.8
Def bdgt	XAF	217bn	338bn	
	USD		358m	557m

Real-terms defence budget trend (USDm, constant 2015)

Population	19,093,595					
Age	0–14	15–19	20–24	25–29	30–64	65 plus
Male	23.2%	5.8%	4.6%	3.6%	11.4%	1.1%
Female	22.6%	5.7%	4.6%	3.6%	12.5%	1.4%

Capabilities

Chad's principal security concerns relate to instability in the Sahel and in the Lake Chad Basin area, where the armed forces conduct counter-insurgency operations against Boko Haram as part of the Multinational Joint Task Force. US special forces withdrew in May 2024 ahead of the presidential elections, but negotiations subsequently began on their return. There is uncertainty over the future of France's long-established military presence, while Hungary plans to deploy a small contingent. The UAE is showing increasing interest in Chadian security, donating military vehicles in 2023 and funding a field hospital in the north-east. There are also reports of growing ties with Russia. Deliveries of Turkish combat UAVs and guided munitions have strengthened the capabilities of the air force. Chadian military skills are widely recognised by partners, though training levels are not uniform across the force. Chad lacks the logistical capacity for routine rotations of deployed forces, relying on international partners for such operations. The US has donated military equipment to the country to bolster its ability to battle insurgents. Apart from maintenance facilities, there is no domestic defence-industrial capacity.

ACTIVE 33,250 (Army 27,500 Air 350 State Security Service 5,400) Gendarmerie & Paramilitary 11,900

Conscript liability Conscription authorised

ORGANISATIONS BY SERVICE

Army ε27,500

7 Mil Regions

FORCES BY ROLE
MANOEUVRE
  Armoured
    1 armd bn
  Light
    7 inf bn
COMBAT SUPPORT
  1 arty bn
  1 engr bn
  1 sigs bn
COMBAT SERVICE SUPPORT
  1 log gp

EQUIPMENT BY TYPE
Includes DGSSIE equipment
ARMOURED FIGHTING VEHICLES
  MBT 74: 60 T-55; ε14 ZTZ-59G
  ASLT ε14 WMA-301
  RECCE 265: 132 AML-60/-90; ε100 BRDM-2; 20 EE-9 *Cascavel*; 9 ERC-90CD *Sagaie*; 4 ERC-90F *Sagaie*
  IFV 131: 80 BMP-1; 42 BMP-1U; 9 LAV-150 *Commando* with 90mm gun
  APC 149
    APC (W) 103: 4+ *Bastion* APC; 24 BTR-80; 12 BTR-3E; ε20 BTR-60; ε10 *Black Scorpion*; 25 VAB-VTT; 8 WZ-523
    PPV 46: 20 *Ejder Yalcin*; 6+ KrAZ *Cougar*; 20 Proforce *Ara* 2
  AUV 110+: 22 *Bastion Patsas*; 7 MCAV-20; 31+ RAM Mk3; 30 *Terrier* LT-79; *Tiger* 4×4; ε20 *Yoruk* 4×4
ARTILLERY 34+
  SP 122mm 10 2S1 *Gvozdika*
  TOWED 13: **105mm** 5 M2; **122mm** 8+ D-74
  MRL 11+: **107mm** some PH-63; **122mm** 11: 6 BM-21 *Grad*; 5 PHL-81
  MOR 81mm some; **120mm** AM-50
ANTI-TANK/ANTI-INFRASTRUCTURE
  MSL • MANPATS *Eryx*; *Milan*
  RCL 106mm M40A1
AIR DEFENCE
  SAM 4+
    Short-range 4 2K12 *Kub* (RS-SA-6 *Gainful*)
    Point-defence 9K310 *Igla*-1 (RS-SA-16 *Gimlet*)
  GUNS
    SP 10: **23mm** 6 ZSU-23-4 *Shilka*; **37mm** 4+ M-1939 (tch)
    TOWED 14.5mm ZPU-1/-2/-4; **23mm** ZU-23-2

Air Force 350

FORCES BY ROLE
GROUND ATTACK
  1 unit with *Hurkus*-C*; Su-25 *Frogfoot*
TRANSPORT
  1 sqn with An-26 *Curl*; C-130H-30 *Hercules*; Mi-17 *Hip* H; Mi-171
  1 (Presidential) Flt with B-737BBJ; Beech 1900; DC-9-87; Gulfstream II
ATTACK HELICOPTER
  1 sqn with AS550C *Fennec*; Mi-24V *Hind*; SA316 *Alouette* III
MANOEUVRE
  Other
    1 sy bn

EQUIPMENT BY TYPE
AIRCRAFT 11 combat capable
  FTR (1 MiG-29S *Fulcrum* C in store)

ATK 7: 6 Su-25 *Frogfoot* (2 more in store); 1 Su-25UB *Frogfoot* B (1 more in store)
ISR 2 Cessna 208B *Grand Caravan*
TPT 10: **Medium** 3: 2 C-27J *Spartan*; 1 C-130H-30 *Hercules*; **Light** 4: 3 An-26 *Curl*; 1 Beech 1900; **PAX** 3: 1 B-737BBJ; 1 DC-9-87; 1 Gulfstream II
TRG 3 *Hurkus-C**; (2 PC-7; 1 PC-9 *Turbo Trainer*; 1 SF-260WL *Warrior* in store)
HELICOPTERS
ATK 5 Mi-24V *Hind*
MRH 8: 3 AS550C *Fennec*; 3 Mi-17 *Hip* H; 2 SA316
TPT • **Medium** 2 Mi-171
UNIHABITED AERIAL VEHICLES
CISR • **Heavy** 3: 1+ *Aksungur*; 2 *Anka*-S
AIR-LAUNCHED MISSILES • **ASM** *Cirit*
BOMBS • **Laser-guided** MAM-L

State Security Service General Direction (DGSSIE) 5,400

Gendarmerie & Paramiltary 11,900 active

Gendarmerie 4,500

National and Nomadic Guard (GNNT) 7,400

Police Mobile Intervention Group (GMIP)

DEPLOYMENT
WESTERN SAHARA: UN • MINURSO 4

FOREIGN FORCES
Benin MNJTF 150
France 1,000; 1 mech inf BG; 1 FGA flt with 3 *Mirage* 2000D; 1 tkr/tpt flt with 1 A330 MRTT; 1 C-130H; 2 CN235M

Congo, Republic of COG

CFA Franc BEAC XAF		2023	2024	2025
GDP	XAF	8.59trn	9.14trn	9.71trn
	USD	14.2bn	15.0bn	15.9bn
Real GDP growth	%	2.0	2.8	3.7
Def bdgt	XAF	173bn	110bn	132bn
	USD	285m	182m	216m

Population 6,097,665

Age	0–14	15–19	20–24	25–29	30–64	65 plus
Male	19.1%	5.4%	4.4%	3.8%	15.5%	1.9%
Female	18.8%	5.4%	4.4%	3.8%	15.3%	2.5%

Capabilities

Congo's armed forces have struggled to recover from the brief but devastating civil war in the late 1990s. They have low levels of training and limited overall capability and use ageing equipment. France provides advisory assistance and capacity-building support in military administration and military and police capability. Congo signed a military-cooperation agreement with Russia in 2019. The country has a limited ability to deploy to neighbouring countries without external support. The navy is largely a riverine force, despite maritime security requirements driven by the country's small coastline. Congo is modernising aspects of its armed forces, including acquiring armoured vehicles. Maintenance limitations have, in recent years, particularly affected the air force; there is no domestic defence-industrial capability.

ACTIVE 10,000 (Army 8,000 Navy 800 Air 1,200)
Gendarmerie & Paramilitary 3,500

ORGANISATIONS BY SERVICE

Army 8,000
FORCES BY ROLE
MANOEUVRE
Reconnaissance
1 recce gp
Mechanised
1 mech bn
1 mech inf bn
Light
1 inf bde (1 mech bn, 1 mot inf bn, 1 inf bn, 1 MRL gp, 1 ADA gp)
1 inf bde (1 mot inf bn, 2 inf bn)
1 mot inf bn
3 inf bn
Air Manoeuvre
1 AB bn
COMBAT SUPPORT
1 arty bn
1 engr bn
1 sigs bn
COMBAT SERVICE SUPPORT
1 maint bn
AIR DEFENCE
1 ADA bn
EQUIPMENT BY TYPE†
ARMOURED FIGHTING VEHICLES
MBT 40: 25 T-54/T-55; 15 ZTZ-59
LT TK 13: 3 PT-76; 10 ZTQ-62
RECCE 25 BRDM-1/BRDM-2
APC 142
APC (W) 78+: 28 AT-105 *Saxon*; 20 BTR-152; 30 BTR-60; Panhard M3
PPV 64: 18 *Mamba*; 37 *Marauder*; 9 Streit *Cobra*
AUV 7: 2 *Tigr*; 5 *Patrol*-A
ARTILLERY 56

SP 122mm 3 2S1 *Gvozdika*
TOWED 15+: 122mm 10 D-30; 130mm 5 M-46; 152mm D-20
MRL 10+: 122mm 10 BM-21 *Grad*; 140mm BM-14; 140mm BM-16
MOR 28+: 82mm; 120mm 28 M-43
ANTI-TANK/ANTI-INFRASTRUCTURE
RCL 57mm M18
GUNS 15: 57mm 5 ZIS-2 (M-1943); 100mm 10 M-1944
AIR DEFENCE • GUNS
SP 23mm ZSU-23-4 *Shilka*
TOWED 14.5mm ZPU-2/-4; 37mm 28 M-1939; 57mm S-60; 100mm KS-19

Navy ε800
EQUIPMENT BY TYPE
PATROL AND COASTAL COMBATANTS 8
PCC 4 *5 Fevrier 1979* (PRC Poly Technologies 47m)
PBR 4

Naval Infantry
FORCES BY ROLE
MANOEUVRE
Other
1 sy bn

Air Force 1,200
FORCES BY ROLE
FIGHTER/GROUND ATTACK
1 sqn with *Mirage* F-1AZ
TRANSPORT
1 sqn with An-24 *Coke*; CN235M-100; Il-76TD *Candid*
EQUIPMENT BY TYPE†
AIRCRAFT 3 combat capable
FGA ε3 *Mirage* F-1AZ
TPT 3: Heavy 1 Il-76TD *Candid*; Light 2: 1 An-24 *Coke*; 1 CN235M-100
HELICOPTERS
ATK (2 Mi-35P *Hind* in store)
TPT • Medium (3 Mi-8 *Hip* in store)
AIR-LAUNCHED MISSILES • AAM • IR R-3 (RS-AA-2 *Atoll*)‡

Gendarmerie & Paramilitary 3,500 active

Gendarmerie 2,000
FORCES BY ROLE
SPECIAL FORCES
1 CT unit
EQUIPMENT BY TYPE
ARMOURED FIGHTING VEHICLES
AUV 17: 10 *Tiger* 4×4; 2 *Tigr*; 5 *Patrol*-A

Republican Guard 1,500
FORCES BY ROLE
MANOEUVRE
Other
3 gd bn
EQUIPMENT BY TYPE
ARMOURED FIGHTING VEHICLES
APC • PPV 3 Streit *Cobra*
AUV 9: 6 MLS *Shield*; 3 *Tigr*

DEPLOYMENT
CENTRAL AFRICAN REPUBLIC: UN • MINUSCA 5

Côte d'Ivoire CIV

CFA Franc BCEAO XOF		2023	2024	2025
GDP	XOF	47.8trn	52.4trn	57.1trn
	USD	78.9bn	87.0bn	95.5bn
Real GDP growth	%	6.2	6.5	6.4
Def bdgt [a]	XOF	414bn	399bn	
	USD	682m	663m	

[a] Defence budget only - order and security expenses excluded

Real-terms defence budget trend (USDm, constant 2015)

Population	29,931,758					
Age	0–14	15–19	20–24	25–29	30–64	65 plus
Male	18.1%	5.7%	4.8%	4.1%	16.1%	1.3%
Female	18.0%	5.7%	4.8%	4.2%	15.6%	1.6%

Capabilities

The country is still regenerating its armed forces more than a decade after civil conflict in the country ebbed. The government has stepped up efforts to rebuild the military to address the deteriorating security in the north and the threat from Islamist insurgents. Security sector reforms have shown some progress. The 2021–25 National Development Plan indicated that efforts are being made to improve housing allowances for paramilitary personnel. The authorities have standardised promotion and salary structures to boost professionalisation and are looking to improve military infrastructure. The country has close defence ties with France and, while the French deployment is being reduced in size, a significant training mission remains. Security cooperation with the US includes IMET and GPOI assistance, and Côte d'Ivoire hosted AFRICOM's Exercise *Flintlock* 2024. The armed forces school at Zambakro runs courses for Ivorian as well as regional personnel. In 2021, with French assistance, Côte d'Ivoire opened the International Academy for the Fight Against Terrorism in Abidjan to help develop regional as well as Ivorian counterterrorist capability. Except for limited maintenance facilities, there is no domestic defence-industrial capability.

ACTIVE 27,400 (Army 23,000 Navy 1,000 Air 1,400 Special Forces 2,000) **Gendarmerie & Paramilitary** n.k.

ORGANISATIONS BY SERVICE

Army ε23,000
FORCES BY ROLE
MANOEUVRE
  Armoured
    1 armd bn
  Light
    7 inf bn
  Air Manoeuvre
    1 cdo/AB bn
COMBAT SUPPORT
  1 arty bn
  1 engr bn
COMBAT SERVICE SUPPORT
  1 log bn
AIR DEFENCE
  1 AD bn
EQUIPMENT BY TYPE
ARMOURED FIGHTING VEHICLES
  MBT 10 T-55†
  ASLT 9 VN22B
  RECCE 18: 13 BRDM-2; 5 *Cayman* BRDM
  IFV 10 BMP-1/BMP-2†
  APC 105
    APC (W) 56: 9 *Bastion* APC; 6 BTR-80; 12 Panhard M3; 13 VAB; 16 WZ-551
    PPV 49: 9 BATT UMG; 21 *Springbuck* HD; 1 *Snake*; 18 VP11
  AUV 20 *Cobra* II
ENGINEERING & MAINTENANCE VEHICLES
  VLB MTU
ANTI-TANK/ANTI-INFRASTRUCTURE
  MSL • MANPATS 9K111-1 *Konkurs* (RS-AT-5 *Spandrel*) (reported); 9K135 *Kornet* (RS-AT-14 *Spriggan*) (reported)
  RCL 106mm ε12 M40A1
ARTILLERY 40
  TOWED 4+: **105mm** 4 M-1950; **122mm** (reported)
  MRL 122mm 6 BM-21
  MOR 30+: **81mm**; **82mm** 10 M-37; **SP 82mm** 4 CS/SS4; **120mm** 16 AM-50
AIRCRAFT • TPT • Medium 1 An-12 *Cub*†
AIR DEFENCE
  SAM • Point-defence 9K32 *Strela*-2 (RS-SA-7 *Grail*)‡ (reported)
  GUNS 21+
    SP 20mm 6 M3 VDAA
    TOWED 15+: **20mm** 10; **23mm** ZU-23-2; **40mm** 5 L/60

Navy ε1,000
EQUIPMENT BY TYPE
PATROL AND COASTAL COMBATANTS 7
  PCO 2 *Esperance* (ISR OPV 45)
  PCC 1 *Contre-Amiral Fadika* (ex-FRA P400)
  PB 4: 3 *L'Emergence* (FRA Raidco RPB 33); 1 *Atchan* 2 (PRC 27m)
AMPHIBIOUS • LANDING CRAFT 1
  LCM 1 *Aby* (FRA CTM)

Air Force ε1,400
EQUIPMENT BY TYPE†
AIRCRAFT
  ISR 1 Beech C90 *King Air*
  TPT 6: **Light** 2: 1 An-26 *Curl*; 1 C295W; **PAX** 4: 1 A319CJ; 1 Gulfstream IV; 1 Gulfstream G450; 1 Gulfstream G550
HELICOPTERS
  ATK 3 Mi-24V *Hind* E
  MRH 3: 1 AW139; 2 Mi-8P *Hip*
  TPT • Medium 2 SA330L *Puma* (IAR-330L)

Special Forces ε2,000
FORCES BY ROLE
SPECIAL FORCES
  1 spec ops bde
EQUIPMENT BY TYPE
ARMOURED FIGHTING VEHICLES
  APC 16
    APC (W) 3 BTR-70MB
    PPV 13 BATT UMG

Gendarmerie & Paramilitary n.k.

Republican Guard n.k.

Gendarmerie n.k.
EQUIPMENT BY TYPE†
ARMOURED FIGHTING VEHICLES
  RECCE 3 *Cayman* BRDM
  IFV BMP-1
  APC
    APC (W) BTR-70MB; VAB
    PPV 11+: 5+ RG-31 *Nyala*; 6+ *Springbuck* HD; Streit *Spartan*
  AUV 26+: 10 *Cobra* II; 4 *Ilgaz*-II; LT-79 *Terrier*; 12 Otokar *Ural*
PATROL AND COASTAL COMBATANTS • PB 1 *Bian*

DEPLOYMENT

CENTRAL AFRICAN REPUBLIC: UN • MINUSCA 185; 1 inf coy
GUINEA-BISSAU: ECOWAS • ESSMGB 150
WESTERN SAHARA: UN • MINURSO 1

FOREIGN FORCES

France 600; 1 inf bn; 1 (army) hel unit with 2 SA330 *Puma*; 2 SA342 *Gazelle*; 1 (air force) hel unit with 1 AS555 *Fennec*

Democratic Republic of the Congo DRC

Congolese Franc CDF		2023	2024	2025
GDP	CDF	164trn	207trn	242trn
	USD	66.9bn	72.5bn	79.2bn
Real GDP growth	%	8.4	4.7	5.0
Def bdgt	CDF	1.82trn	2.54trn	3.37trn
	USD	744m	891m	1.10bn

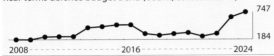

Population 115,403,027

Age	0–14	15–19	20–24	25–29	30–64	65 plus
Male	23.0%	5.3%	4.4%	3.8%	12.3%	1.1%
Female	22.7%	5.3%	4.4%	3.8%	12.4%	1.4%

Capabilities

The country's size and poor levels of military training, morale and equipment mean that the armed forces are unable to provide security throughout the country. Kinshasa has pursued several military-modernisation programmes, though efforts to reexamine doctrine and organisation have yielded few results. Violence has increased in the east since early 2024, with several non-state armed groups active in the area. The mandate of the UN's MONUSCO mission in the DRC currently runs to December 2024 and a phased withdrawal is being implemented. Since December 2023, the SADC's SAMIDRC mission has been deployed to support security in the east. The armed forces have incorporated several non-state armed groups. Training is provided through foreign assistance and capacity-building efforts. Deployment capability is limited, and the lack of logistics vehicles significantly reduces transport capacity while the lack of sufficient tactical airlift and helicopters is also a brake on military effectiveness. The country has acquired new equipment, but the absence of a defence sector apart from limited maintenance capability hinders military efficiency.

ACTIVE 128,350 (Army 103,000 Republican Guard 8,000 Navy 800 Air 2,550 Other 14,000)

ORGANISATIONS BY SERVICE

Army ε103,000

The DRC has 10 Military Regions divided between four Defence Zones. The actual combat effectiveness of many formations is doubtful.

FORCES BY ROLE
SPECIAL FORCES
  4 cdo bn
MANOEUVRE
  Light
  4 (Rapid Reaction) inf bde
  40+ inf regt
  3 jungle inf bn
COMBAT SUPPORT
  1 arty regt
  1 MP bn

EQUIPMENT BY TYPE†
(includes Republican Guard eqpt)
ARMOURED FIGHTING VEHICLES
  MBT 174: 32 T-55; 25 T-64BV-1; 100 T-72AV; 12–17 ZTZ-59
  LT TK 40: 10 PT-76; 30 ZTQ-62
  RECCE up to 50: up to 17 AML-60; 14 AML-90; 19 EE-9 *Cascavel*
  IFV 20 BMP-1
  APC 164:
    APC (T) 9: 3 BTR-50; 6 MT-LB
    APC (W) 155: 30–70 BTR-60PB; 20 *Mbombe*-4; 58 Panhard M3; 7 TH 390 *Fahd*
    PPV some *Hizir*
  AUV 30 MCAV-20
ANTI-TANK/ANTI-INFRASTRUCTURE
  RCL 57mm M18; 73mm SPG-9; 75mm M20; 106mm M40A1
  GUNS 85mm 10 Type-56 (D-44)
ARTILLERY 725
  SP 15: 122mm 5 2S1 *Gvozdika*; 152mm 10 2S3 *Akatsiya*
  TOWED 125: 122mm 77 M-30 (M-1938)/D-30/Type-60; 130mm 42 Type-59 (M-46)/Type-59-I; 152mm 6 D-20 (reported)
  MRL 57+: 107mm 12 Type-63; 122mm 24+: 24 BM-21 *Grad*; some RM-70; 128mm 6 M-51; 130mm 3 Type-82; 132mm 12
  MOR 528+: 81mm 100; 82mm 400; 107mm M30; 120mm 28: 10 Brandt; 18 other
AIR DEFENCE
  SAM • Point-defence 9K32 *Strela*-2 (RS-SA-7 *Grail*)‡
  GUNS • TOWED 64: 14.5mm 12 ZPU-4; 37mm 52 M-1939

Republican Guard 8,000

FORCES BY ROLE
MANOEUVRE
  Armoured
  1 armd regt
  Light
  3 gd bde
COMBAT SUPPORT
  1 arty regt

Navy 800

EQUIPMENT BY TYPE
PATROL AND COASTAL COMBATANTS 1
  PB 1 *Moliro* (Type-062 (PRC *Shanghai* II))†

Air Force 2,550
EQUIPMENT BY TYPE
AIRCRAFT 4 combat capable
  ATK ε4 Su-25 *Frogfoot*
  TPT 6: Heavy 2 Il-76MD *Candid*; **Medium** 1 C-130H *Hercules*; **Light** 1 An-26 *Curl*; **PAX** 2 B-727
HELICOPTERS
  ATK 5 Mi-24/Mi-24V *Hind*
  TPT 10: Medium 3: 1 AS332L *Super Puma*; 2 Mi-8 *Hip*; **Light** 7: 5 Bell 205 (UH-1H *Iroquois*); 2 Bell 206L *Long Ranger*
UNINHABITED AERIAL VEHICLES
  CISR • Heavy 3 CH-4B

Paramilitary

National Police Force
Incl Rapid Intervention Police (National and Provincial)

People's Defence Force

FOREIGN FORCES
All part of MONUSCO unless otherwise specified
Algeria 1
Bangladesh 1,774; 1 inf bn; 1 engr coy; 1 avn coy; 1 hel coy
Benin 8
Bhutan 1
Bolivia 2
Botswana 3
Brazil 21
Burkina Faso 5
Burundi Army: 1,000; 1 inf bn
Cambodia 1
Cameroon 3
Canada (*Operation Crocodile*) 7
Czech Republic 2
Egypt 6
France 2
Gambia 2
Ghana 15
Guatemala 188; 1 spec ops coy
India 1,115; 1 inf bn; 1 med coy
Indonesia 1,037; 1 inf bn; 1 engr coy
Jordan 9
Kazkahstan 2
Kenya 396; 1 inf coy(+)
Malawi 747; 1 inf bn
Malaysia 8
Malawi SAMIDRC 400
Mongolia 1
Morocco 918; 1 inf bn; 2 fd hospital
Nepal 1,149; 1 inf bn; 1 engr coy
Niger 4
Nigeria 69
Pakistan 383; 1 arty bty; 1 hel sqn with SA330 *Puma*
Paraguay 6
Peru 2
Poland 1
Romania 5
Russia 6
Rwanda Army: 3,000
Senegal 12
Sierra Leone 2
South Africa (*Operation Mistral*) 1,135; 1 inf bn; 1 hel sqn; SAMIDRC 600
Switzerland 1
Tanzania 859; 1 spec ops coy; 1 inf bn; SAMIDRC 300
Tunisia 10
Uganda Army: 3,000; 1 inf bde
United Kingdom 3
United States 3
Uruguay 742; 1 inf bn; 1 hel sqn
Zambia 6
Zimbabwe 3

Djibouti DJB

Djiboutian Franc DJF		2023	2024	2025
GDP	DJF	713bn	770bn	829bn
	USD	4.01bn	4.33bn	4.67bn
Real GDP growth	%	7.0	6.5	6.0
Def bdgt	DJF	n.k.	n.k.	n.k.
	USD	n.k.	n.k.	n.k.
FMA (US)	USD	6m	6m	6m
Population	994,974			

Age	0–14	15–19	20–24	25–29	30–64	65 plus
Male	14.3%	4.4%	4.6%	4.4%	15.8%	1.8%
Female	14.1%	4.6%	5.3%	5.6%	22.6%	2.4%

Capabilities
Djibouti's strategic location and relative stability have led a number of foreign states to station forces in the country. The main responsibility for its own armed forces is internal and border security, as well as counter-insurgency operations. A 2017 defence white paper highlighted a requirement to modernise key capabilities, though funding is limited. There is close defence cooperation with France, which has the largest foreign military base in the country. The US operates its Combined Joint Task Force–Horn of Africa from Djibouti. China, in 2017, opened its first overseas military base in the country, including dock facilities. Japan has based forces there for regional counter-piracy missions. Djibouti also hosts an Italian base that is focused on anti-piracy activities. France and the US provide training assistance. EU NAVFOR has delivered maritime security training and has based an MPA detachment in the country. Djibouti participates in several regional multinational exercises and contributes personnel to an international mission in Somalia but has limited capacity to independently deploy beyond its territory. Army equipment consists predominantly of older French and Soviet-era systems. Djibouti has maintenance facilities, but no defence manufacturing sector.

ACTIVE 8,450 (Army 8,000 Navy 200 Air 250)
Gendarmerie & Paramilitary 4,650

ORGANISATIONS BY SERVICE

Army ε8,000
FORCES BY ROLE
4 military districts (Tadjourah, Dikhil, Ali-Sabieh and Obock).
MANOEUVRE
  Mechanised
  1 armd regt (1 recce sqn, 3 armd sqn, 1 (anti-smuggling) sy coy)
  Light
  4 inf regt (3-4 inf coy, 1 spt coy)
  1 rapid reaction regt (4 inf coy, 1 spt coy)
  Other
  1 (Republican Guard) gd regt (1 sy sqn, 1 (close protection) sy sqn, 1 cbt spt sqn (1 recce pl, 1 armd pl, 1 arty pl), 1 spt sqn)
COMBAT SUPPORT
  1 arty regt
  1 demining coy
  1 sigs regt
  1 CIS sect
COMBAT SERVICE SUPPORT
  1 log regt
  1 maint coy
EQUIPMENT BY TYPE
ARMOURED FIGHTING VEHICLES
  ASLT 3+ WMA-301
  RECCE 23: 4 AML-60†; 17 AML-90; 2 BRDM-2
  IFV 28: 8 BTR-80A; 16-20 *Ratel*
  APC 67
    APC (W) 30+: 12 BTR-60†; 4+ AT-105 *Saxon*; 14 *Puma*
    PPV 37: 3 *Casspir*; some IAG *Guardian Xtreme*; 10 RG-33L; 24 *Puma* M36
    AUV 37: 10 *Cougar* 4×4 (one with 90mm gun); 2 CS/VN3B; 10 PKSV; 15 VBL
ANTI-TANK/ANTI-INFRASTRUCTURE
  RCL 106mm 16 M40A1
ARTILLERY 82
  SP 155mm 10 M109L
  TOWED 122mm 9 D-30
  MRL 12: **107mm** 2 PKSV AUV with PH-63; **122mm** 10: 6 (6-tube Toyota Land Cruiser 70 series); 2 (30-tube Iveco 110-16); 2 (30-tube)
  MOR 51: **81mm** 25; **120mm** 26: 20 Brandt; 6 RT-F1
AIR DEFENCE • GUNS 15+
  SP 20mm 5 M693
  TOWED 10: **23mm** 5 ZU-23-2; **40mm** 5 L/70

Navy ε200
EQUIPMENT BY TYPE
PATROL AND COASTAL COMBATANTS 14
  PCC 2 *Adj Ali M Houmed* (NLD Damen Stan Patrol 5009)
  PBF 3: 2 Battalion-17; 1 Safe 65
  PB 9: 1 PRC 27m; 2 Sea Ark 1739; 6 others
AMPHIBIOUS 2
  LANDING SHIPS • LSM 1 Type-074 (*Yuhai*) (capacity 6 light tanks)
  LANDING CRAFT • LCT 1 EDIC 700
LOGISTICS AND SUPPORT • AKR 1 *Col. Maj. Ali Gaad* (NLD Damen Stan Lander 5612)

Air Force 250
EQUIPMENT BY TYPE
AIRCRAFT
  TPT • Light 8: 1 Cessna U206G *Stationair*; 1 Cessna 208 *Caravan*; 1 L-410UVP *Turbolet*; 1 MA60; 2 Short 360 *Sherpa*; 2 Y-12E
HELICOPTERS
  ATK (2 Mi-35 *Hind* in store)
  MRH 6: 4 AS365 *Dauphin*; 1 Mi-17 *Hip* H; 1 Z-9WE
  TPT 3: **Medium** 1 Mi-8T *Hip*; **Light** 2 AS355F *Ecureuil* II
UNINHABITED AERIAL VEHICLES
  CISR • Medium 2+ *Bayraktar* TB2
BOMBS • Laser-guided MAM-L

Gendarmerie & Paramilitary ε4,650

Gendarmerie 2,000
Ministry of Defence
FORCES BY ROLE
MANOEUVRE
  Other
  1 paramilitary bn
EQUIPMENT BY TYPE
AFV • AUV 2 CS/VN3B

Coast Guard 150
EQUIPMENT BY TYPE
PATROL AND COASTAL COMBATANTS • PB 11: 2 *Khor Angar*; 9 other

National Police Force ε2,500
Ministry of Interior

DEPLOYMENT
SOMALIA: AU • ATMIS 450; 1 inf bn(-)

FOREIGN FORCES
China 400: 1 spec ops coy; 1 mne coy; 1 med unit; 2 ZTL-11; 8 ZBL-08
France 1,500: 1 SF unit; 1 combined arms regt (2 recce sqn, 2 inf coy, 1 arty bty, 1 engr coy); 1 hel det with 4 SA330 *Puma*; 3 SA342 *Gazelle*; 1 LCM; 1 FGA sqn with 4 *Mirage* 2000-5; 1 SAR/tpt sqn with 1 CN235M; 3 SA330 *Puma*
Italy BMIS 150
Japan 180; 2 P-3C *Orion*
Spain *Operation Atalanta* 60; 1 CN235 VIGMA

United States US Africa Command: 4,000; 1 tpt sqn with C-130H/J-30 *Hercules*; 1 tpt sqn with 12 MV-22B *Osprey*; 2 KC-130J *Hercules*; 1 spec ops sqn with MC-130J; PC-12 (U-28A); 1 CSAR sqn with HH-60G *Pave Hawk*; 1 CISR sqn with MQ-9A *Reaper*; 1 naval air base

Equatorial Guinea EQG

CFA Franc BEAC XAF		2023	2024	2025
GDP	XAF	7.26trn	7.83trn	7.88trn
	USD	12.0bn	12.9bn	12.9bn
Real GDP growth	%	-6.2	5.8	-4.8
Def bdgt	XAF	n.k.	n.k.	n.k.
	USD	n.k.	n.k.	n.k.
Population	1,795,834			

Age	0–14	15–19	20–24	25–29	30–64	65 plus
Male	18.4%	5.6%	5.0%	4.2%	17.8%	2.6%
Female	17.2%	4.7%	4.0%	3.4%	14.7%	2.4%

Capabilities

Internal security is the principal task for the armed forces. Equatorial Guinea has, for years, been trying to modernise its forces, which remain dominated by the army. French forces in Gabon have provided training. There are developing military ties with China, while there were reports in 2024 that Russia had sent military advisers. There is only limited capability for power projection. Recent naval investments include equipment and onshore-infrastructure improvements at Bata and Malabo, although naval capabilities remain limited. Maritime-security concerns in the Gulf of Guinea have resulted in a focus on boosting maritime-patrol capacity. There is limited maintenance capacity and no defence-industrial sector.

ACTIVE 1,750 (Army 1,100 Navy 550 Air 100)

ORGANISATIONS BY SERVICE

Army 1,100
FORCES BY ROLE
MANOEUVRE
  Mechanised
    1 mech inf bn
  Light
    3 inf bn(-)
EQUIPMENT BY TYPE
ARMOURED FIGHTING VEHICLES
  MBT 3 T-55
  ASLT 6 WMA-301
  RECCE 6 BRDM-2
  IFV 23: 20 BMP-1; 3 WZ-551 IFV
  APC 41
    APC (W) 16: 10 BTR-152; 6 WZ-551
    PPV 25 *Reva*
  AUV Dongfeng *Mengshi*

ANTI-TANK/ANTI-INFRASTRUCTURE
  MSL • MANPATS HJ-8
AIR DEFENCE
  SAM Point-defence QW-2 (CH-SA-8)
  GUNS • SP • 23mm ZU-23-2 (tch)

Navy ε550
EQUIPMENT BY TYPE
PRINCIPAL SURFACE COMBATANTS • FRIGATES 1
  FF 1 *Wele Nzas* with 2 MS-227 *Ogon'* 122mm MRL, 2 AK630 CIWS, 2 76mm guns, 1 hel landing platform
PATROL AND COASTAL COMBATANTS 10
  CORVETTES • FSG 1 *Bata* with 2 Katran-M RWS with *Barrier* SSM, 2 AK630 CIWS, 1 76mm gun
  PCC 2 OPV 62 (ISR *Sa'ar* 4.5 derivative)
  PBF 2 *Isla de Corisco* (ISR *Shaldag* II)
  PB 5: 1 *Daphne*†; 2 *Estuario de Muni*; 2 *Zhuk*
LOGISTICS AND SUPPORT
  AKRH 1 *Capitán David Eyama Angue Osa* with 1 76mm gun

Air Force 100
EQUIPMENT BY TYPE
AIRCRAFT 4 combat capable
  ATK 4: 2 Su-25 *Frogfoot*; 2 Su-25UB *Frogfoot B*
  TPT 4: **Light** 3: 1 An-32B *Cline*; 2 An-72 *Coaler*; **PAX** 1 *Falcon* 900 (VIP)
  TRG 2 L-39C *Albatros*
HELICOPTERS
  ATK 5 Mi-24P/V *Hind*
  MRH 3: 1 Mi-17 *Hip H*; 2 Z-9WE
  TPT 4: **Heavy** 1 Mi-26 *Halo*; **Medium** 1 Ka-29 *Helix*; **Light** 2 Enstrom 480

Gendarmerie & Paramilitary

Guardia Civil
FORCES BY ROLE
MANOEUVRE
  Other
    2 paramilitary coy

Coast Guard n.k.

FOREIGN FORCES
Russia 200 (PMC) (reported)

Eritrea ERI

Definitive macro- and defence-economic data not available

Population	6,343,956					
Age	0–14	15–19	20–24	25–29	30–64	65 plus
Male	17.9%	5.7%	4.8%	4.0%	15.2%	1.6%
Female	17.7%	5.7%	4.8%	4.2%	15.9%	2.4%

Capabilities

Eritrea maintains large armed forces mainly because of its historical conflict with Ethiopia. The easing of tensions following a 2018 peace agreement has afforded the armed forces the opportunity to consider restructuring and recapitalisation. Although Eritrea militarily supported the Ethiopian federal government in the conflict in the neighbouring Ethiopian province of Tigray, bilateral relations have since soured. Maritime insecurity, including piracy, remains a challenge. Eritrea has mandatory conscription and maintains a large army. For some, the term of service is reportedly indefinite, and significant numbers of conscripts have chosen to leave the country or otherwise evade service. These factors have likely affected overall military cohesion and effectiveness. Eritrea has demonstrated limited capacity to deploy beyond its immediate borders. The armed forces' inventory primarily comprises outdated Soviet-era systems and modernisation was restricted by the UN arms embargo until it was lifted in 2018. The arms embargo resulted in serviceability issues, notwithstanding allegations of external support. The navy remains capable of only limited coastal-patrol and interception operations. The country has limited maintenance capability but no defence manufacturing sector.

ACTIVE 301,750 (Army 300,000 Navy 1,400 Air 350)

Conscript liability 18 months (4 months mil trg) between ages 18 and 40

RESERVE n.k.

ORGANISATIONS BY SERVICE

Army ε300,000 (including mobilised reserves)

Div mostly bde sized

FORCES BY ROLE

COMMAND
  4 corps HQ

SPECIAL FORCES
  1 cdo div

MANOEUVRE
  Mechanised
  6 mech div
  Light
  ε50 inf div

EQUIPMENT BY TYPE

ARMOURED FIGHTING VEHICLES
  MBT 270 T-54/T-55
  RECCE 40 BRDM-1/BRDM-2
  IFV 15 BMP-1
  APC 35
    APC (T) 10 MT-LB†
    APC (W) 25 BTR-152/BTR-60

ENGINEERING & MAINTENANCE VEHICLES
  ARV T-54/T-55 reported
  VLB MTU reported

ANTI-TANK/ANTI-INFRASTRUCTURE
  MSL • MANPATS 9K11 *Malyutka* (RS-AT-3 *Sagger*); 9K111-1 *Konkurs* (RS-AT-5 *Spandrel*)
  GUNS 85mm D-44

ARTILLERY 258
  SP 45: **122mm** 32 2S1 *Gvozdika*; **152mm** 13 2S5 *Giatsint*-S
  TOWED 19+: **122mm** D-30; **130mm** 19 M-46
  MRL 44: **122mm** 35 BM-21 *Grad*; **220mm** 9 9P140 *Uragan*
  MOR 150+: **82mm** 50+; **120mm/160mm** 100+

AIR DEFENCE
  SAM • Point-defence 9K32 *Strela*-2 (RS-SA-7 *Grail*)‡
  GUNS 70+
    SP 23mm ZSU-23-4 *Shilka*
    TOWED 23mm ZU-23

Navy 1,400

EQUIPMENT BY TYPE

PATROL AND COASTAL COMBATANTS 25
  PBF 16: 6 Battalion-17; 4 Rodman 33; 6 other; (4 *Super Dvora* non-operational)
  PB 9 other (3 Swift 105 non-operational)

AMPHIBIOUS 4
  LANDING SHIP 2
    LST 2: 1 *Chamo*† (Ministry of Transport); 1 *Ashdod*†
  LANDING CRAFT 2
    LCU 2: 1 T-4† (in harbour service); 1 other

Air Force ε350

FORCES BY ROLE

FIGHTER/GROUND ATTACK
  1 sqn with MiG-29/MiG-29SE/MiG-29UB *Fulcrum*
  1 sqn with Su-27/Su-27UBK *Flanker*

TRANSPORT
  1 sqn with Y-12(II)

TRAINING
  1 sqn with MB-339CE*

TRANSPORT HELICOPTER
  1 sqn with Bell 412EP *Twin Huey*
  1 sqn with Mi-17 *Hip H*

EQUIPMENT BY TYPE

AIRCRAFT 14 combat capable
  FTR 8: 4 MiG-29 *Fulcrum*; 2 MiG-29UB *Fulcrum*; 1 Su-27 *Flanker*; 1 Su-27UBK *Flanker*
  FGA 2 MiG-29SE *Fulcrum*
  TPT • Light 5: 1 Beech 200 *King Air*; 4 Y-12(II)
  TRG 8: 4 MB-339CE*; 4+ Z-143/Z-242

HELICOPTERS

ATK 2 Mi-24 *Hind*
MRH 8: 4 Bell 412EP *Twin Huey* (AB-412EP); 4 Mi-17 *Hip* H
AIR-LAUNCHED MISSILES
AAM • IR R-60 (RS-AA-8 *Aphid*); R-73 (RS-AA-11A *Archer*); IR/SARH R-27 (RS-AA-10 *Alamo*)

DEPLOYMENT
Ethiopia: 40,000 (reported)

Ethiopia ETH

Ethiopian Birr ETB		2023	2024	2025
GDP	ETB	8.72trn	11.6trn	15.7trn
	USD	160bn	145bn	121bn
Real GDP growth	%	7.2	6.1	6.5
Def bdgt	ETB	84.0bn	50.0bn	65.7bn
	USD	1.54bn	623m	506m

Real-terms defence budget trend (USDm, constant 2015)

Population	118,550,298

Age	0–14	15–19	20–24	25–29	30–64	65 plus
Male	19.5%	5.3%	4.6%	3.9%	15.1%	1.5%
Female	19.2%	5.2%	4.6%	4.0%	15.3%	1.8%

Capabilities

Ethiopia's armed forces are among the region's largest. Prior to a November 2022 peace agreement with the Tigray People's Liberation Front (TPLF), Ethiopia's military was engaged in a two-year internal conflict in and around the Northern province of Tigray. Despite a November 2022 ceasefire, fighting continues between the ENDF and a number of rebel groups. In 2023, conflict broke out in the neighbouring Amhara region with the FANO militia group. Other tasks include countering al-Shabaab. They also support regional security initiatives, such as the AU presence in Somalia and the UN mission in South Sudan. Tensions have risen with Eritrea and Somalia because of ambitions to secure access to the Red Sea. Capability will have been degraded because of attrition during the War in Tigray, though the forces have looked to replace personnel losses. The inventory comprises mostly Soviet-era equipment, although surplus stocks have been acquired from China, Hungary, Ukraine and the US. Ethiopia purchased modern air-defence systems from Russia and, in response to the Tigray conflict, procured UAVs from Turkiye, China and reportedly also Iran. The country has a modest defence-industrial base, primarily centred on small arms, with some licensed production of light armoured vehicles. Ethiopia has adequate maintenance capability but only a limited ability to support advanced platforms.

ACTIVE 503,000 (Army 500,000 Air 3,000)

ORGANISATIONS BY SERVICE

Army ε500,000
Div mostly bde sized
FORCES BY ROLE
SPECIAL FORCES
1 cdo div
MANOEUVRE
Mechanised
5 mech inf div
Light
ε70 inf div
Other
1 (Republican Guard) gd div
EQUIPMENT BY TYPE
ARMOURED FIGHTING VEHICLES
   MBT 220: ε120 T-55/T-62; ε100 T-72B/UA1
   RECCE ε50 BRDM-1/BRDM-2
   IFV ε20 BMP-1
   APC 275+
      APC (T) ε200 ZSD-89
      APC (W) BTR-60; WZ-551
      PPV 75 Gaia *Thunder*
   AUV 35+: 35+ MCAV-20; some *Ze'ev*
ENGINEERING & MAINTENANCE VEHICLES
   ARV T-54/T-55 ARV reported; 3 BTS-5B
   VLB GQL-111; MTU reported
   MW *Bozena*
ANTI-TANK/ANTI-INFRASTRUCTURE
   MSL • MANPATS 9K11 *Malyutka* (RS-AT-3 *Sagger*); 9K111 *Fagot* (RS-AT-4 *Spigot*); 9K135 *Kornet*-E (RS-AT-14 *Spriggan*)
   RCL 82mm B-10; **107mm** B-11
   GUNS 85mm D-44
ARTILLERY 262+
   SP 42+: **122mm** 2S1 *Gvozdika*; WZ-551 with D-30; **152mm** 10 2S19 *Msta-S*; **155mm** 32 SH-15
   TOWED 200+: **122mm** ε200 D-30/M-30 (M-1938); **130mm** M-46; **155mm** AH2
   MRL 20+: **107mm** PH-63; **122mm** ε20 BM-21 *Grad*; **300mm** AR-2†
   MOR 81mm M1/M29; **82mm** M-1937; **120mm** M-1944
AIR DEFENCE
SAM 8
   Medium-range ε4 S-75M3 Volkhov (RS-SA-2 *Guideline*)
   Short-range ε4 S-125M1 *Pechora*-M1 (RS-SA-3 *Goa*)
   Point-defence 9K32 *Strela*-2 (RS-SA-7 *Grail*)‡; 9K310 *Igla*-1 (RS-SA-16 *Gimlet*)
SPAAGM 30mm ε6 96K6 *Pantsir*-S2 (RS-SA-22 *Greyhound*)
GUNS
   SP 23mm ZSU-23-4 *Shilka*
   TOWED 23mm ZU-23; **37mm** M-1939; **57mm** S-60

Air Force 3,000

FORCES BY ROLE

FIGHTER/GROUND ATTACK

1 sqn with Su-27/Su-27UB/Su-30K *Flanker*

1 sqn with MiG-23BN/UB *Flogger* H/C

GROUND ATTACK

1 flt with Su-25T/UBK *Frogfoot*

TRANSPORT

1 sqn with An-12 *Cub*; An-26 *Curl*; An-32 *Cline*; Beech 200GT *King Air*; C-130B *Hercules*; DHC-6 *Twin Otter*; L-100-30; Yak-40 *Codling* (VIP)

TRAINING

1 sqn with L-39 *Albatros*

1 sqn with G 120TP

1 sqn with Cessna 172

ATTACK/TRANSPORT HELICOPTER

2 sqn with Mi-24/Mi-35 *Hind*; Mi-8 *Hip*; Mi-17 *Hip* H; SA316 *Alouette* III

EQUIPMENT BY TYPE

AIRCRAFT 22 combat capable

FTR 13: 8 Su-27 *Flanker*; 3 Su-27UB *Flanker*; 2 Su-30K *Flanker*

FGA 6+ MiG-23BN/UB *Flogger* H/C

ATK 3: 1 Su-25T *Frogfoot*; 2 Su-25UB *Frogfoot*

TPT 19: **Medium** 8: 3 An-12 *Cub*; 2 C-130B *Hercules*; 2 C-130E *Hercules*; 1 L-100-30; **Light** 11: 1 An-26 *Curl*; 1 An-32 *Cline*; 1 Beech 200GT *King Air*; 4 Cessna 172; 3 DHC-6 *Twin Otter*; 1 Yak-40 *Codling* (VIP)

TRG 24: 12 G 120TP; 12 L-39 *Albatros*

HELICOPTERS

ATK 16: 15 Mi-24 *Hind*; 1 Mi-35 *Hind*

MRH 21: 3 AW139; 6 SA316 *Alouette* III; 12 Mi-8 *Hip*/Mi-17 *Hip* H

UNINHABITED AERIAL VEHICLES

CISR 4: **Heavy** 1+: 1 *Bayraktar Akinci*; some *Wing Loong* I; **Medium** 3+: some *Mohajer* 6 (reported); 3+ *Bayraktar* TB2

AIR-LAUNCHED MISSILES

AAM • IR R-3 (RS-AA-2 *Atoll*)‡; R-27ET (RS-AA-10D *Alamo*); R-60 (RS-AA-8 *Aphid*); R-73 (RS-AA-11A *Archer*); **SARH** R-27 (RS-AA-10 *Alamo*)

ASM Kh-25ML (RS-AS-12B *Kegler*); Kh-29T (RS-AS-14B *Kedge*); TL-2 (reported)

BOMBS

Laser-guided MAM-L

TV-guided KAB-500KR

DEPLOYMENT

SOMALIA: AU • ATMIS 2,400; 3 inf bn

SOUTH SUDAN: UN • UNMISS 1,524; 2 inf bn

FOREIGN FORCES

Eritrea Army: 40,000 (reported)

Gabon GAB

CFA Franc BEAC XAF		2023	2024	2025
GDP	XAF	12.2trn	12.6trn	12.5trn
	USD	20.1bn	20.9bn	21.0bn
Real GDP growth	%	2.4	3.1	2.6
Def bdgt [a]	XAF	161bn	194bn	
	USD	265m	321m	

[a] Includes funds allocated to Republican Guard

Real-terms defence budget trend (USDm, constant 2015)

Population	2,455,105				
Age	0–14	15–19	20–24	25–29	30–64	65 plus
Male	17.5%	5.7%	5.3%	5.0%	16.1%	2.2%
Female	17.2%	5.4%	4.9%	4.4%	14.2%	2.1%

Capabilities

Military officers seized power in August 2023. The country's oil revenues have allowed the government to support small but regionally capable armed forces. Gabon has benefited from a long-term presence of French troops acting as a security guarantor. French forces have provided training, including with regionally deployed naval units, to Gabon's armed forces, which also have worked with other international partners, including the US. Gabonese forces have taken part in the US Navy-led *Obangame Express* exercise series. Following the coup, the US suspended much assistance to the country, while France's military cooperation gradually resumed after a short cessation, in 2024, Paris announced that it would reduce its presence in the country. Gabon's armed forces have sufficient airlift to ensure mobility within the country, but limited capability to project power by sea and air. Apart from limited maintenance facilities, there is no defence industry.

ACTIVE 4,700 (Army 3,200 Navy 500 Air 1,000)
Gendarmerie & Paramilitary 2,000

ORGANISATIONS BY SERVICE

Army 3,200

Republican Guard under direct presidential control

FORCES BY ROLE

MANOEUVRE

Reconnaissance

1 armd recce bn

Light

1 (Republican Guard) gd gp (2 spec ops bn, 1 mech bn, 1 gd bn, 1 sy bn)

Air Manoeuvre

1 AB regt

COMBAT SUPPORT

1 cbt engr bn

COMBAT SERVICE SUPPORT

2 engr spt bn
1 log regt
EQUIPMENT BY TYPE
ARMOURED FIGHTING VEHICLES
  ASLT 10 WMA-301
  RECCE 60: 24 AML-60; 4 AML-90; 12 EE-3 *Jararaca*; 14 EE-9 *Cascavel*; 6 ERC-90F4 *Sagaie*
  IFV 22: 12 EE-11 *Urutu* (with 20mm gun); 10 VN-1
  APC 97
    APC (W) 35: 9 LAV-150 *Commando*; 5 *Bastion* APC; 3 WZ-523; 5 VAB; 12 VXB-170; 1 *Pandur*
    PPV 62: 8 *Aravis*; 34 *Matador*; 4 *Spartak*; 16 VP-11
  AUV 14 VBL
ANTI-TANK/ANTI-INFRASTRUCTURE
  MSL • MANPATS *Milan*
  RCL 106mm M40A1
ARTILLERY 67
  TOWED 105mm 4 M101
  MRL 24: **107mm** 16 PH-63; **140mm** 8 *Teruel*
  MOR 39: **81mm** 35; **120mm** 4 Brandt
AIR DEFENCE • GUNS 41
  SP 20mm 4 ERC-20
  TOWED 37+: **14.5mm** ZPU-4; **23mm** 24 ZU-23-2; **37mm** 10 M-1939; **40mm** 3 L/70

Navy ε500
HQ located at Port Gentil
EQUIPMENT BY TYPE
PATROL AND COASTAL COMBATANTS 9
  PB 9: 4 *Port Gentil* (FRA RPB 20); 4 *Awore* (ESP Rodman 66); 1 *Vice Amiral d'Escadre Jean Léonard Mbini* (PRC Poly Technologies 47m)
AMPHIBIOUS • LANDING CRAFT 1
  LCM 1 *Leconi II* (Ex-UK LCU Mk 9)

Air Force 1,000
FORCES BY ROLE
FIGHTER/GROUND ATTACK
  1 sqn with *Mirage* F-1AZ
TRANSPORT
  1 (Republican Guard) sqn with AS332 *Super Puma*; ATR-42F; *Falcon* 900; Gulfstream IV-SP/G650ER
  1 sqn with C-130H *Hercules*; C295W; CN-235M-100
ATTACK/TRANSPORT HELICOPTER
  1 sqn with Bell 412 *Twin Huey* (AB-412); SA330C/H *Puma*; SA342M *Gazelle*
EQUIPMENT BY TYPE
AIRCRAFT 8 combat capable
  FGA 6 *Mirage* F-1AZ
  MP (1 EMB-111* in store)
  TPT 7: **Medium** 1 C-130H *Hercules*; (1 L-100-30 in store); **Light** 3: 1 ATR-42F; 1 C295W; 1 CN-235M-100; **PAX** 3: 1 *Falcon* 900; 1 Gulfstream IV-SP; 1 Gulfstream G650ER
  TRG 2 MB-326 *Impala* I* (4 CM-170 *Magister* in store)

HELICOPTERS
  MRH 2: 1 Bell 412 *Twin Huey* (AB-412); 1 SA342M *Gazelle*; (2 SA342L *Gazelle* in store)
  TPT 7: **Medium** 4: 1 AS332 *Super Puma*; 3 SA330C/H *Puma*; **Light** 3: 2 H120 *Colibri*; 1 H135
AIR-LAUNCHED MISSILES • AAM • IR U-*Darter* (reported)

Gendarmerie & Paramilitary 2,000

Gendarmerie 2,000
FORCES BY ROLE
MANOEUVRE
  Other
  4 sy bn
  1 gd bn
COMBAT SUPPORT
  1 MP bn
COMBAT SERVICE SUPPORT
  1 spt bn
TRANSPORT HELICOPTER
  1 unit with AS350 *Ecureuil*; AS355 *Ecureuil* II
EQUIPMENT BY TYPE
HELICOPTERS • TPT • Light 4: 2 AS350 *Ecureuil*; 2 AS355 *Ecureuil* II

DEPLOYMENT
CENTRAL AFRICAN REPUBLIC: UN • MINUSCA 1

FOREIGN FORCES
France 350; 1 inf bn

Gambia GAM

Gambian Dalasi GMD		2023	2024	2025
GDP	GMD	148bn	174bn	198bn
	USD	2.36bn	2.69bn	3.01bn
Real GDP growth	%	5.3	5.8	5.8
Def bdgt	GMD	852m	993m	
	USD	13.6m	15.4m	

Real-terms defence budget trend (USDm, constant 2015)

Population	2,523,327					
Age	0–14	15–19	20–24	25–29	30–64	65 plus
Male	19.3%	5.7%	4.9%	4.2%	13.8%	1.6%
Female	18.9%	5.6%	4.9%	4.1%	14.8%	2.1%

Capabilities

Gambia has been reforming its security structure and the armed forces. A National Security Policy, updated in 2023, focused on cooperation with Senegal and the establishment of a governing Office of National Security. Gambia's small forces have traditionally focused on countering the trafficking of people and narcotics and on maritime security. Both have been strengthened, including through the establishment of a Committee for National Maritime Security in 2022 and an agreement with the EU's Seaport Cooperation Programme in 2023. Gambia also cooperates with neighbouring states and the African Union, which maintains a technical-support mission to assist in security sector reform. The Economic Community of West African States has deployed the ECOMIG mission to Gambia since 2017. The armed forces participate in some multinational exercises and have deployed in support of UN missions in Africa. The equipment inventory is limited, with donations a key source, and serviceability is in doubt for some types. The country has no significant defence industry and efforts to upgrade equipment remain limited.

ACTIVE 4,100 (Army 3,500 Navy 300 National Guard 300)

ORGANISATIONS BY SERVICE

Gambian National Army 3,500
FORCES BY ROLE
MANOEUVRE
Light
  4 inf bn
COMBAT SUPPORT
  1 engr sqn
EQUIPMENT BY TYPE
ARMOURED FIGHTING VEHICLES
  APC • **PPV** 4 *Hizir*
  AUV 2 *Cobra* II

Air Wing
EQUIPMENT BY TYPE
AIRCRAFT
  TPT 5: **Light** 2 AT-802A *Air Tractor*; **PAX** 3: 1 B-727; 1 CL-601; 1 Il-62M *Classic* (VIP)

Gambia Navy 300
EQUIPMENT BY TYPE
PATROL AND COASTAL COMBATANTS 9
  PBF 4: 2 Rodman 55; 2 *Fatimah* I
  PB 5: 1 *Bolong Kanta* (US Peterson Mk 4)†; 1 *Fankanta* (ex-ESP Rodman 101); 1 *Jambarr*; 2 *Taipei* (ROC *Hai Ou*) (2 more non-operational)

Republican National Guard 300
FORCES BY ROLE
MANOEUVRE
Other
  1 gd bn (forming)

DEPLOYMENT

CENTRAL AFRICAN REPUBLIC: UN • MINUSCA 9
DEMOCRATIC REPUBLIC OF THE CONGO: UN • MONUSCO 2
SOUTH SUDAN: UN • UNMISS 4
SUDAN: UN • UNISFA 1

FOREIGN FORCES

Ghana ECOMIG 50
Nigeria ECOMIG 200
Senegal ECOMIG 250

Ghana GHA

Ghanaian New Cedi GHS		2023	2024	2025
GDP	GHS	842bn	1.02trn	1.18trn
	USD	76.4bn	75.3bn	75.8bn
Real GDP growth	%	2.9	3.1	4.4
Def bdgt	GHS	3.74bn	3.89bn	
	USD	340m	287m	

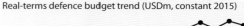

Real-terms defence budget trend (USDm, constant 2015)

Population	34,589,092					
Age	0–14	15–19	20–24	25–29	30–64	65 plus
Male	18.9%	5.0%	4.3%	3.7%	15.0%	2.0%
Female	18.5%	5.0%	4.3%	3.9%	17.0%	2.4%

Capabilities

Ghana's armed forces are among the region's most capable, with a long-term development plan. The ability to control its EEZ and maritime security are of increasing importance, which underpins the navy's expansion plans. Internal security is also a central military task, along with peacekeeping missions abroad. The EU, Germany, China, the UK and US provide training, support and equipment. The country has, in recent years, built up air force training, close-air support, rocket artillery and airlift capabilities. It also has strengthened naval capabilities through US donations and procurements from Singapore and China. The government is implementing plans to boost training and exercises and improve military infrastructure. Ghana opened a signals training school and a war college in 2023, and plans for a National Defence University. Ghanaian PME institutions act as a regional hub and regularly train personnel from neighbouring states. The development of forward-operating bases continues, with the principal objective of protecting energy resources in the Gulf of Guinea and the Volta estuary, as well as securing the northern border. The country has a limited defence-industrial base that delivers maintenance, ammunition manufacturing and, more recently, armoured-vehicle production.

ACTIVE 19,000 (Army 15,000 Navy 2,000 Air 2,000)

ORGANISATIONS BY SERVICE

Army 15,000
FORCES BY ROLE
COMMAND
  2 comd HQ
SPECIAL FORCES
  1 cdo bde (1 (rapid reaction) mot inf bn; 1 AB bn)
MANOEUVRE
  Reconnaissance
  1 armd recce bde (3 armd recce regt)
  Mechanised
  3 mech inf bn
  Light
  6 inf bn
COMBAT SUPPORT
  1 arty regt (1 arty bty, 2 mor bty)
  1 fd engr regt (bn)
  1 sigs bde (2 sigs regt)
  1 sigs regt
  1 sigs sqn
COMBAT SERVICE SUPPORT
  1 log gp
  1 tpt coy
  2 maint coy
  1 med coy
  1 trg bn
EQUIPMENT BY TYPE
ARMOURED FIGHTING VEHICLES
  RECCE 3 EE-9 *Cascavel*
  IFV 48: 24 *Ratel*-90; 15 *Ratel*-20; 4 *Piranha* 25mm; 5+ Type-05P 25mm
  APC 125
    APC (W) 75: 20 BTR-70; 46 *Piranha*; 9+ Type-05P
    PPV 50+: some *Maatla*; 50 Streit *Typhoon*
  AUV 73: 33 *Cobra*; 40 *Cobra* II
ARTILLERY 87
  TOWED 122mm 6 D-30
  MRL 3+: 107mm Type-63; 122mm 3 Type-81
  MOR 78: 81mm 50; 120mm 28 Tampella
ENGINEERING & MAINTENANCE VEHICLES
  AEV 1 Type-05P AEV
  ARV *Piranha* (reported)
ANTI-TANK/ANTI-INFRASTRUCTURE
  RCL 84mm *Carl Gustaf*
AIR DEFENCE
  SAM • Point-defence 9K32 *Strela*-2 (RS-SA-7 *Grail*)‡
  GUNS • TOWED 8+: 14.5mm 4+: 4 ZPU-2; ZPU-4; 23mm 4 ZU-23-2

Navy 2,000
Naval HQ located at Accra; Western HQ located at Sekondi; Eastern HQ located at Tema

EQUIPMENT BY TYPE
PATROL AND COASTAL COMBATANTS 16
  PCO 2 *Anzone* (ex-US *Balsam*)
  PCC 10: 4 *Snake* (PRC Poly Technologies 47m); ; 4 *Volta* (SGP *Penguin Flex Fighter*); 2 *Yaa Asantewa* (ex-GER *Albatros*)
  PBF 1 *Stephen Otu* (ex-ROK *Sea Dolphin*)
  PB 3: 2 *Aflao* (ex-US Marine Protector); 1 *David Hansen* (ex-US Peterson Mk3)
AMPHIBIOUS • LANDING CRAFT 1
  LCVP 1 Navdock

Special Boat Squadron
FORCES BY ROLE
SPECIAL FORCES
  1 SF unit

Air Force 2,000
FORCES BY ROLE
GROUND ATTACK
  1 sqn with K-8 *Karakorum**
ISR
  1 sqn with DA42; DA42 MPP; Z-9EH
TRANSPORT
  1 sqn with C295
TRAINING
  1 unit with Cessna 172
TRANSPORT HELICOPTER
  1 sqn with Mi-17V-5 *Hip* H; Mi-171Sh; Z-9EH
EQUIPMENT BY TYPE†
AIRCRAFT 4 combat capable
  ISR 2 DA42 MPP
  TPT 8: Light 7: 3 C295M; 3 Cessna 172; 1 DA42; PAX 1 Falcon 900EX (VIP); (1 F-28 *Fellowship* in store)
  TRG 4 K-8 *Karakorum**
HELICOPTERS
  MRH 7: 3 Mi-17V-5 *Hip* H; 4 Z-9EH
  TPT • Medium 3 Mi-171Sh

DEPLOYMENT
CENTRAL AFRICAN REPUBLIC: UN • MINUSCA 13
CYPRUS: UN • UNFICYP 1
DEMOCRATIC REPUBLIC OF THE CONGO: UN • MONUSCO 15
GAMBIA: ECOWAS • ECOMIG 50
GUINEA-BISSAU: ECOWAS • ESSMGB 150
LEBANON: UN • UNIFIL 873; 1 recce coy; 1 mech inf bn; 1 spt coy
SOMALIA: UN • UNSOM 1
SOUTH SUDAN: UN • UNMISS 737; 1 inf bn
SUDAN: UN • UNISFA 664; 1 inf bn; 1 fd hosptial
SYRIA/ISRAEL: UN • UNDOF 5
WESTERN SAHARA: UN • MINURSO 14

Guinea GUI

Guinean Franc GNF		2023	2024	2025
GDP	GNF	196trn	226trn	263trn
	USD	23.0bn	25.5bn	27.3bn
Real GDP growth	%	5.7	4.1	5.7
Def bdgt	GNF	5.27trn	4.62trn	
	USD		620m	521m

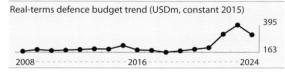

Real-terms defence budget trend (USDm, constant 2015)

Population	13,986,179					
Age	0–14	15–19	20–24	25–29	30–64	65 plus
Male	20.6%	5.2%	4.5%	3.8%	14.0%	1.8%
Female	20.3%	5.1%	4.5%	3.8%	14.2%	2.2%

Capabilities

Guinea's armed forces are limited in size and conventional capacity. Special forces troops initiated a coup in September 2021, with their leader sworn in as interim president a month later. ECOWAS sanctioned the coup leaders and called for elections within six months, though no election date has been set. Piracy in the Gulf of Guinea is a key concern, as is illegal trafficking and fishing. Guinea did not fully implement a military-programme law for 2015–20 due to funding issues. France and the US, prior to the coup, provided financial and training assistance, including for personnel earmarked for deployment to Mali. Much of the country's military equipment is ageing and of Soviet-era vintage; serviceability is questionable for some types. Guinea has limited organic airlift. France was supporting the development of a light aviation observation capability before the coup. Guinea is also attempting to improve its logistics and military-health capacities. There is no significant local defence industry.

ACTIVE 9,700 (Army 8,500 Navy 400 Air 800)
Gendarmerie & Paramilitary 2,600

Conscript liability 9–12 months (students, before graduation)

ORGANISATIONS BY SERVICE

Army 8,500
FORCES BY ROLE
MANOEUVRE
  Armoured
  1 armd bn
  Light
  1 SF bn
  5 inf bn
  1 ranger bn
  1 cdo bn
  Air Manoeuvre
  1 air mob bn
  Other
  1 (Presidential Guard) gd bn
COMBAT SUPPORT
  1 arty bn
  1 AD bn
  1 engr bn
  1 sigs coy
EQUIPMENT BY TYPE
ARMOURED FIGHTING VEHICLES
  MBT 8 T-54†
  LT TK 15 PT-76
  RECCE 27: 2 AML-90; 25 BRDM-1/BRDM-2
  IFV 2 BMP-1
  APC 205
    APC (T) 10 BTR-50
    APC (W) 30: 16 BTR-40; 8 BTR-60; 6 BTR-152
    PPV 165: ε100 *Cougar*; 10 *Mamba*†; some *Puma* M26-15; 9 *Puma* M36; 30 *Spartan*-MAV; 16+ Springbuck 4×4
  AUV Dongfeng *Mengshi*
ENGINEERING & MAINTENANCE VEHICLES
  ARV T-54/T-55 (reported)
ANTI-TANK/ANTI-INFRASTRUCTURE
  MSL • MANPATS 9K11 *Malyutka* (RS-AT-3 *Sagger*); 9K111-1 *Konkurs* (RS-AT-5 *Spandrel*)
  RCL 82mm B-10
  GUNS 6+: **57mm** ZIS-2 (M-1943); **85mm** 6 D-44
ARTILLERY 59+
  TOWED 24: **122mm** 12 M-1931/37; **130mm** 12 M-46
  MRL 15: **107mm** 8 PH-63; **122mm** 4 BM-21 *Grad*; **220mm** 3 9P140 *Uragan*
  MOR 20+: **82mm** M-43; **120mm** 20 M-1938/M-1943
AIR DEFENCE
  SAM • Point-defence 9K32 *Strela*-2 (RS-SA-7 *Grail*)‡
  GUNS • TOWED 24+: **30mm** M-53 (twin); **37mm** 8 M-1939; **57mm** 12 Type-59 (S-60); **100mm** 4 KS-19

Navy ε400
EQUIPMENT BY TYPE
PATROL AND COASTAL COMBATANTS 4
  PB 4: 1 Swiftships 77†; 3 *Zégbéla Togba Pivi* (FRA RPB 20)

Air Force 800
FORCES BY ROLE
ISR
  1 sqn with *Tetras* (observation)
EQUIPMENT BY TYPE†
AIRCRAFT
  FGA (2 MiG-21bis *Fishbed* L; 1 MiG-21UM *Mongol* B in store)
  TPT • Light 4 *Tetras* (observation)
HELICOPTERS
  ATK (4 Mi-24 *Hind* in store)
  MRH 3: 2 MD-500MD; 1 SA342K *Gazelle*; (2 Mi-17-1V

Hip H in store)

TPT 2: Medium 1 SA330 *Puma*; **Light** 1 AS350B *Ecureuil*

AIR-LAUNCHED MISSILES

AAM • IR R-3 (RS-AA-2 *Atoll*)‡

Gendarmerie & Paramilitary 2,600 active

Gendarmerie 1,000
Republican Guard 1,600
People's Militia 7,000 reservists

DEPLOYMENT

SOUTH SUDAN: UN • UNMISS 3
SUDAN: UN • UNISFA 1
WESTERN SAHARA: UN • MINURSO 5

Guinea-Bissau GNB

CFA Franc BCEAO XOF		2023	2024	2025
GDP	XOF	1.22trn	1.33trn	1.43trn
	USD	2.01bn	2.19bn	2.36bn
Real GDP growth	%	5.2	5.0	5.0
Def bdgt	XOF	15.3bn	ε15.4bn	
	USD	25.3m	ε25.4m	

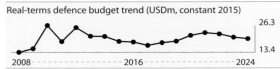

Population	2,132,325					
Age	0–14	15–19	20–24	25–29	30–64	65 plus
Male	21.3%	5.5%	4.6%	3.8%	12.4%	1.3%
Female	21.0%	5.6%	4.9%	4.1%	13.6%	1.8%

Capabilities

Guinea-Bissau's armed forces have limited capabilities and are undergoing various reform programmes. The UN has expressed concern about the armed forces' role in politics following political disputes linked to elections in 2019 and in 2024. Defence policy focuses mainly on tackling internal security challenges, particularly drug trafficking. An ECOWAS mission withdrew at the end of 2020, only to return in mid-2022 after an attempted coup that February. The armed forces suffer from limited training and recruitment and retention problems, while also needing to develop an adequate non-commissioned officer structure. Much of the country's military equipment is obsolescent and poor maintenance likely limits military effectiveness. There is no defence-manufacturing sector.

ACTIVE 4,450 (Army 4,000 Navy 350 Air 100)

Conscript liability Selective conscription

Personnel and eqpt totals should be treated with caution. A number of draft laws to restructure the armed services and police have been produced

ORGANISATIONS BY SERVICE

Army ε4,000

FORCES BY ROLE

MANOEUVRE

Reconnaissance

1 recce coy

Armoured

1 armd bn (sqn)

Light

5 inf bn

COMBAT SUPPORT

1 arty bn

1 engr coy

EQUIPMENT BY TYPE

ARMOURED FIGHTING VEHICLES

LT TK 15 PT-76

RECCE 10 BRDM-2

APC • APC (W) 55: 35 BTR-40/BTR-60; 20 Type-56 (BTR-152)

ANTI-TANK/ANTI-INFRASTRUCTURE

RCL 75mm Type-52 (M20); **82mm** B-10

GUNS 85mm 8 D-44

ARTILLERY 26+

TOWED 122mm 18 D-30/M-30 (M-1938)

MOR 8+: **82mm** M-43; **120mm** 8 M-1943

AIR DEFENCE

SAM • Point-defence 9K32 *Strela*-2 (RS-SA-7 *Grail*)‡

GUNS • TOWED 34: **23mm** 18 ZU-23; **37mm** 6 M-1939; **57mm** 10 S-60

Navy ε350

EQUIPMENT BY TYPE

PATROL AND COASTAL COMBATANTS 5

PB 5: 2 *Alfeite*†; 1 *N'Djamba Mane*; 2 Rodman 55

Air Force 100

EQUIPMENT BY TYPE

AIRCRAFT • TPT • Light 1 Cessna 208B

FOREIGN FORCES

Côte d'Ivoire ESSMGB 150
Ghana ESSMGB 150
Nigeria ESSMGB 86
Senegal ESSMGB 150

Kenya KEN

Kenyan Shilling KES		2023	2024	2025
GDP	KES	15.1trn	16.6trn	18.3trn
	USD	109bn	116bn	117bn
Real GDP growth	%	5.6	5.0	5.0
Def bdgt [a]	KES	172bn	173bn	
	USD	1.24bn	1.21bn	

[a] Includes national intelligence funding

Real-terms defence budget trend (USDm, constant 2015)

Population	58,246,378				
Age	0–14	15–19	20–24	25–29	30–64	65 plus
Male	18.0%	5.8%	5.0%	4.0%	15.7%	1.5%
Female	17.8%	5.8%	4.9%	4.0%	15.7%	1.8%

Capabilities

The armed forces are focused on threats to regional stability and tackling security challenges, including those emanating from neighbouring Somalia. Kenya has deployed forces to the DRC since late 2022 as part of an East African Community mission and from mid-2024 has led a UN policing mission in Haiti. Kenya signed a new five-year Defence Cooperation Agreement with the UK in 2021. It provides for a permanent UK training unit, support for maritime security and a counter-IED training centre. The country also has strong ties with the US. The Cooperative Security Location Manda Bay remains an operational base for US AFRICOM, and in September 2023, the two sides signed a five-year framework for defence cooperation and enhancing interoperability. Regular operational deployments have increased military experience and confidence, while demonstrating limited power projection capacity. Kenya has been a key contributor to AU peacekeeping operations in Somalia. The armed forces also contribute to UN missions and are a leading element of the East African Standby Force. Kenya's armed forces regularly participate in multinational exercises. Recent equipment investments have focused on improving counter-insurgency capabilities and transport capacity to support regional deployments. The country's limited defence industry is focused on equipment maintenance and the manufacture of small arms and ammunition.

ACTIVE 24,100 (Army 20,000 Navy 1,600 Air 2,500) **Gendarmerie & Paramilitary 5,000**

ORGANISATIONS BY SERVICE

Army 20,000
FORCES BY ROLE
SPECIAL FORCES
1 spec ops bn
1 ranger regt (1 ranger bn, 1 AB bn)
MANOEUVRE
Armoured
1 armd bde (2 armd recce bn, 2 armd bn)
Mechanised
1 mech inf bde (3 mech inf bn)
Light
3 inf bde (3 inf bn)
COMBAT SUPPORT
1 arty bde (3 arty bn, 1 ADA bn, 1 mor bty)
1 engr bde (2 engr bn)
HELICOPTER
1 air cav bn
EQUIPMENT BY TYPE
ARMOURED FIGHTING VEHICLES
MBT 78 Vickers Mk 3
RECCE 84: 72 AML-60/AML-90; 12 Ferret
APC 222
APC (W) 95: 52 UR-416; 31 WZ-551 (incl CP); 12 Bastion APC; (10 M3 Panhard in store)
PPV 127: 105 Puma M26-15; CS/VP14; 22 Mamba Mk7; Springbuck 4×4
AUV 2+ BOV M10 (CP)
ENGINEERING & MAINTENANCE VEHICLES
ARV 7 Vickers ARV
MW Bozena
ARTILLERY 112
SP 155mm 3+ NORA B-52
TOWED 105mm 47: 40 L118 Light Gun; 7 Model 56 pack howitzer
MOR 62: 81mm 50; 120mm 12 Brandt
ANTI-TANK/ANTI-INFRASTRUCTURE
MSL • MANPATS Milan
RCL 84mm Carl Gustaf
HELICOPTERS
MRH 42: 2 Hughes 500D†; 12 Hughes 500M†; 10 Hughes 500MD Scout Defender† (armed); 9 Hughes 500ME†; 6 MD-530F; 3 Z-9W
AIR DEFENCE • GUNS • TOWED 94: **20mm** 81: 11 Oerlikon; ε70 TCM-20; **40mm** 13 L/70
AIR-LAUNCHED MISSILES • ASM TOW

Navy 1,600 (incl 120 marines)
EQUIPMENT BY TYPE
PATROL AND COASTAL COMBATANTS 7
PCO 1 Jasiri with 1 AK630 CIWS, 1 57mm gun
PCF 2 Nyayo (UK Vosper 57m) with 1 76mm gun
PCC 3: 1 Harambee II (ex-FRA P400); 2 Shujaa with 1 76mm gun
PBF 1 Archangel
AMPHIBIOUS • LANDING CRAFT 2
LCM 2 Galana
LOGISTICS AND SUPPORT • AP 2

Air Force 2,500
FORCES BY ROLE
FIGHTER/GROUND ATTACK

2 sqn with F-5E/F *Tiger* II

TRANSPORT
1 sqn with DHC-8†; F-70† (VIP); C-27J *Spartan*; M-28 *Skytruck* (C-145A)

TRAINING
1 sqn with *Bulldog* 103/127†; EMB-312 *Tucano*†*; G 120TP

ATTACK HELICOPTER
1 sqn with AH-1F *Cobra*; H125M (AS550) *Fennec*

TRANSPORT HELICOPTER
1 sqn with AW139; Bell 205 (UH-1H *Huey* II); SA330 *Puma*†

EQUIPMENT BY TYPE†

AIRCRAFT 32 combat capable
  FTR 21: 17 F-5E *Tiger* II; 4 F-5F *Tiger* II
  TPT 10: **Medium** 3 C-27J *Spartan*; **Light** 6: 3 DHC-8†; 3 M-28 Skytruck (C-145A); (6 Do-28D-2 in store); **PAX** 1 F-70 (VIP)
  TRG 33: 8 *Bulldog* 103/127†; 11 EMB-312 *Tucano*†*; 5 G 120A; 9 G 120TP

HELICOPTERS
  ATK 3 AH-1F *Cobra*
  MRH 11: 3 AW139; 8 H125M (AS550) *Fennec*
  TPT 16: **Medium** 10 SA330 *Puma*†; **Light** 6 Bell 205 (UH-1H *Huey* II)

AIR-LAUNCHED MISSILES
  AAM • IR AIM-9 *Sidewinder*
  ASM AGM-65 *Maverick*

Gendarmerie & Paramilitary 5,000

Police General Service Unit 5,000
EQUIPMENT BY TYPE
ARMOURED FIGHTING VEHICLES
  APC • PPV 49: 25 CS/VP3; 24 *Maxxpro*
  AUV 30: some Streit *Cyclone*; 30 VN-4
PATROL AND COASTAL COMBATANTS 5
  PB 5 (2 on Lake Victoria)

Air Wing
EQUIPMENT BY TYPE
AIRCRAFT • TPT • Light 6: 2 Cessna 208B *Grand Caravan*; 3 Cessna 310; 1 Cessna 402
HELICOPTERS
  MRH 3 Mi-17 *Hip* H
  TPT 5: **Medium** 1 Mi-17V-5; **Light** 4: 2 AW139; 1 Bell 206L *Long Ranger*; 1 Bo-105
  TRG 1 Bell 47G

Coast Guard
Ministry of Interior
EQUIPMENT BY TYPE
PATROL AND COASTAL COMBATANTS 1
  PCC 1 *Doria* with 1 hel landing platform

DEPLOYMENT

CENTRAL AFRICAN REPUBLIC: UN • MINUSCA 17
DEMOCRATIC REPUBLIC OF THE CONGO: UN • MONUSCO 396; 1 inf coy(+)
LEBANON: UN • UNIFIL 3
SOMALIA: AU • ATMIS 2,400: 3 inf bn; **UN •** UNSOS 1
SOUTH SUDAN: UN • UNMISS 18
SUDAN: UN • UNISFA 3

FOREIGN FORCES
United Kingdom BATUK 350; 1 trg unit

Lesotho LSO

Lesotho Loti LSL		2023	2024	2025
GDP	LSL	41.5bn	45.1bn	48.8bn
	USD	2.21bn	2.30bn	2.42bn
Real GDP growth	%	2.2	2.8	2.3
Def bdgt	LSL	652m	680m	
	USD	34.8m	34.6m	

Real-terms defence budget trend (USDm, constant 2015)

Population	2,227,548					
Age	0–14	15–19	20–24	25–29	30–64	65 plus
Male	16.1%	5.3%	4.8%	4.2%	17.1%	2.0%
Female	15.9%	5.3%	4.7%	4.1%	17.2%	3.4%

Capabilities

The Lesotho Defence Force (LDF) has a small ground element and an air wing for light transport and liaison. The LDF is charged with protecting territorial integrity and sovereignty and ensuring internal security. Lesotho's government has expressed its desire to carry out defence reforms to de-politicise the security forces. India has provided training to the LDF since 2001 and, more recently, so has France. In April 2020, the army was briefly deployed internally by the prime minister. Lesotho has limited capacity to deploy and sustain missions beyond national borders, though the country sent personnel to Mozambique as part of the SADC mission there. Lesotho's limited inventory is obsolescent by modern standards and there is little possibility of significant recapitalisation, although there has been interest in acquiring light helicopters. Except for limited maintenance capacity, Lesotho lacks a defence-industrial base.

ACTIVE 2,000 (Army 2,000)

ORGANISATIONS BY SERVICE

Army ε2,000
FORCES BY ROLE

SPECIAL FORCES
  1 spec ops unit
MANOEUVRE
  Reconnaissance
  1 recce coy
  Light
  7 inf coy
  Aviation
  1 sqn
COMBAT SUPPORT
  1 arty bty(-)
  1 engr gp (incl 1 cbt engr unit)
  1 MP coy
  1 spt coy (with mor)
  1 sigs gp
EQUIPMENT BY TYPE
ARMOURED FIGHTING VEHICLES
  MBT 1 T-55
  RECCE 6: 4 AML-90; 2 BRDM-2†
  AUV 6 RAM Mk3
ANTI-TANK/ANTI-INFRASTRUCTURE
  RCL 106mm 6 M40
ARTILLERY 12
  TOWED 105mm 2
  MOR 81mm 10

Air Wing 110
AIRCRAFT
  TPT • Light 3: 2 C-212-300 *Aviocar*; 1 GA-8 *Airvan*
HELICOPTERS
  MRH 3: 1 Bell 412 *Twin Huey*; 2 Bell 412EP *Twin Huey*
  TPT • Light 4: 1 Bell 206 *Jet Ranger*; 3 H125 (AS350) *Ecureuil*

Liberia LBR

Liberian Dollar LRD		2023	2024	2025
GDP	LRD	4.39bn	4.76bn	5.05bn
	USD	4.39bn	4.76bn	5.05bn
Real GDP growth	%	4.6	5.1	5.8
Def bdgt	LRD	16.4m	17.5m	
	USD	16.4m	17.5m	

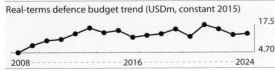
Real-terms defence budget trend (USDm, constant 2015)

Population	5,437,249					
Age	0–14	15–19	20–24	25–29	30–64	65 plus
Male	19.6%	5.6%	4.9%	4.3%	14.1%	1.5%
Female	19.4%	5.7%	5.1%	4.5%	13.8%	1.7%

Capabilities

Priorities in Liberia's 2022 National Strategic Defense Plan included contributing to peacekeeping operations and also improving capabilities including in engineering, military medicine and education, as well as infrastructure improvements. Authorities are examining training requirements for MoD civilians. Nigeria is supporting the development of an air wing. A National Maritime Strategy was issued in September 2023. US military assistance has in recent years focused on areas such as force health, including schemes to improve recruitment and retention, as well as maritime security, medical training and the provision of spare parts. The UK has delivered training including in C-IED and military medicine, and China has donated medical equipment. The armed forces are able to deploy and sustain small units, most recently to the former MINUSMA mission in Mali. Equipment recapitalisation will depend on finances and the development of a supporting force structure but will also be dictated by the armed forces' role in national development objectives. Apart from limited maintenance-support capacities, Liberia has no defence industry.

ACTIVE 2,010 (Army 1,950, Coast Guard 60)

ORGANISATIONS BY SERVICE

Army 1,950
FORCES BY ROLE
MANOEUVRE
  Light
  1 (23rd) inf bde with (2 inf bn, 1 engr coy, 1 MP coy)
COMBAT SERVICE SUPPORT
  1 trg unit (forming)
ARMOURED FIGHTING VEHICLES
  APC • PPV 53: 50 *Mamba* Mk7; 3+ Streit *Cougar*

Coast Guard 60
All operational patrol vessels under 10t FLD

DEPLOYMENT
SOUTH SUDAN: UN • UNMISS 2
SUDAN: UN • UNISFA 2

Madagascar MDG

Malagsy Ariary MGA		2023	2024	2025
GDP	MGA	69.9trn	77.8trn	87.1trn
	USD	15.8bn	17.2bn	18.1bn
Real GDP growth	%	3.8	4.5	4.6
Def bdgt	MGA		475bn	563bn
	USD		107m	125m

Real-terms defence budget trend (USDm, constant 2015): 106 / 53.2 (2008–2024)

Population	29,452,714					
Age	0–14	15–19	20–24	25–29	30–64	65 plus
Male	18.7%	5.3%	4.7%	4.2%	15.4%	1.8%
Female	18.3%	5.2%	4.6%	4.2%	15.4%	2.1%

Capabilities

Madagascar's principal defence priorities are ensuring sovereignty and territorial integrity. It also focuses on maritime security and the country is part of the EU funded Maritime Security Programme. The armed forces intervened in domestic politics in 2009. Madagascar is a member of SADC and its regional Standby Force. In 2018, the country signed an agreement with India to explore closer defence ties. Madagascar reportedly also signed an agreement with Russia on military cooperation that entered into force in 2022 and may have involved arms sales, development of military equipment and personnel training. China has also looked to foster closer ties with Madagascar. France provides some training. The armed forces have no independent capacity to deploy and support operations beyond national borders. The equipment inventory is obsolete, and, with economic development a key government target, equipment recapitalisation is unlikely to be a priority.

ACTIVE 13,500 (Army 12,500 Navy 500 Air 500)
Gendarmerie & Paramilitary 8,100

Conscript liability 18 months (voluntary) (incl for civil purposes)

ORGANISATIONS BY SERVICE

Army 12,500+
FORCES BY ROLE
MANOEUVRE
  Light
    2 (intervention) inf regt
    10 (regional) inf regt
COMBAT SUPPORT
  1 arty regt
  3 engr regt
  1 sigs regt
COMBAT SERVICE SUPPORT
  1 log regt

AIR DEFENCE
  1 ADA regt
EQUIPMENT BY TYPE
ARMOURED FIGHTING VEHICLES
  LT TK 12 PT-76
  RECCE 73: ε35 BRDM-2; 10 FV701 *Ferret*; ε20 M3A1; 8 M8
  APC • APC (T) ε30 M3A1 half-track
  AUV 6 *Panthera* T4
ANTI-TANK/ANTI-INFRASTRUCTURE
  RCL 106mm M40A1
ARTILLERY 25
  TOWED 17: 105mm 5 M101; 122mm 12 D-30
  MOR 8+: 82mm M-37; 120mm 8 M-43
AIR DEFENCE • GUNS
  TOWED 70: 14.5mm 50 ZPU-4; 37mm 20 PG-55 (M-1939)

Navy 500 (incl some 100 Marines)
EQUIPMENT BY TYPE
PATROL AND COASTAL COMBATANTS 10
  PCC 1 *Trozona*
  PB 9: 2 *Tselatra* (PRC 27m); 7 (ex-US CG MLB)

Air Force 500
FORCES BY ROLE
TRANSPORT
  1 sqn with Yak-40 *Codling*
  1 (liaison) sqn with Cessna 310; Cessna 337 *Skymaster*; PA-23 *Aztec*
TRAINING
  1 sqn with Cessna 172; J.300 *Joker*; *Tetras*
TRANSPORT HELICOPTER
  1 sqn with SA318C *Alouette* II
EQUIPMENT BY TYPE
AIRCRAFT • TPT 21: Light 19: 4 Cessna 172; 5 Cessna 206; 1 Cessna 310; 2 Cessna 337 *Skymaster*; 1 CN235M; 2 J.300 *Joker*; 1 PA-23 *Aztec*; 1 *Tetras*; 2 Yak-40 *Codling* (VIP); PAX 2 B-737
HELICOPTERS
  MRH 3 SA318C *Alouette* II
  TPT • Light 4: 3 AS350 *Ecureuil*; 1 BK117

Gendarmerie & Paramilitary 8,100

Gendarmerie 8,100

Malawi MWI

Malawian Kwacha MWK		2023	2024	2025
GDP	MWK	14.6trn	19.8trn	23.5trn
	USD	12.7bn	10.8bn	10.8bn
Real GDP growth	%	1.5	1.8	4.0
Def bdgt	MWK		112bn	153bn
	USD		97.5m	84.0m

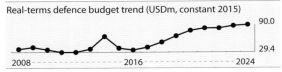

Real-terms defence budget trend (USDm, constant 2015)

Population	21,763,309					
Age	0–14	15–19	20–24	25–29	30–64	65 plus
Male	18.7%	5.7%	4.8%	4.1%	13.9%	1.7%
Female	19.0%	5.9%	5.0%	4.3%	14.7%	2.2%

Capabilities

The Malawi Defence Forces (MDF) are constitutionally tasked with ensuring the country's sovereignty and territorial integrity. Additional tasks include providing military assistance to civil authorities and supporting the police. In recent years, the army has been used to help with infrastructure development and controlling illegal deforestation. The MDF's small air force, previously an air wing, and its naval unit are used to counter human trafficking and poaching. The armed forces are trying to enhance combat readiness, military medicine and engineering. Malawi is a member of the SADC and its Standby Force. The armed forces have contributed to peacekeeping missions. The UK provided training and support for the deployment to the DRC and London also supports the MDF's counter-poaching operations. Discussions with US Africa Command to establish a training centre for non-commissioned officers are ongoing. In 2024, the North Carolina National Guard partnered with Malawi's defence forces. The armed forces have no independent capacity to deploy and support operations beyond national borders.

ACTIVE 10,700 (Army 10,500 Air Force 200)
Gendarmerie & Paramilitary 4,200

ORGANISATIONS BY SERVICE

Army 10,500
FORCES BY ROLE
MANOEUVRE
  Mechanised
  1 mech bn
  Light
  2 inf bde (2 inf bn)
  1 inf bde (1 inf bn)
  Air Manoeuvre
  1 para bn
COMBAT SUPPORT
  3 lt arty bty
  1 engr bn
COMBAT SERVICE SUPPORT
  12 log coy
EQUIPMENT BY TYPE
ARMOURED FIGHTING VEHICLES
  RECCE 58: 30 *Eland*-90; 8 FV701 *Ferret*; 20 FV721 *Fox*
  APC • PPV 31+: 14 *Casspir*; 9 *Marauder*; 8 *Puma* M26-15; some *Puma* M36
  AUV 8 RAM Mk3
ARTILLERY 107
  TOWED 105mm 9 L118 Light Gun
  MOR 81mm 98: 82 L16A1; 16 M3
AIR DEFENCE • GUNS
  TOWED 14.5mm 40 ZPU-4

Navy 220
EQUIPMENT BY TYPE
PATROL AND COASTAL COMBATANTS • PB 3: 1 *Kasungu* (ex-FRA *Antares*)†; 2 *Mutharika* (PRC)

Air Force 200
EQUIPMENT BY TYPE
AIRCRAFT • TPT • Light 2 MA600
HELICOPTERS • TPT 8: **Medium** 3: 1 AS532UL *Cougar*; 1 SA330H *Puma*; 1 H215 *Super Puma* **Light** 5: 1 AS350L *Ecureuil*; 4 SA341B *Gazelle*

Gendarmerie & Paramilitary 4,200

Police Mobile Service 4,200
EQUIPMENT BY TYPE
AIRCRAFT
  TPT • Light 4: 3 BN-2T *Defender* (border patrol); 1 SC.7 3M *Skyvan*
HELICOPTERS • MRH 2 AS365 *Dauphin 2*

DEPLOYMENT

DEMOCRATIC REPUBLIC OF THE CONGO: SADC • SAMIDRC 400; **UN** • MONUSCO 747; 1 inf bn
LEBANON: UN • UNIFIL 1
SOUTH SUDAN: UN • UNMISS 6
SUDAN: UN • UNISFA 7
WESTERN SAHARA: UN • MINURSO 4

Mali MLI

CFA Franc BCEAO XOF		2023	2024	2025
GDP	XOF	12.3trn	13.0trn	13.9trn
	USD	20.2bn	21.7bn	23.2bn
Real GDP growth	%	4.4	3.8	4.4
Def bdgt [a]	XOF	657bn	739bn	
	USD	1.08bn	1.23bn	

[a] Defence and security budget

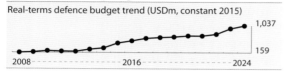
Real-terms defence budget trend (USDm, constant 2015)

Population 21,990,607

Age	0–14	15–19	20–24	25–29	30–64	65 plus
Male	23.5%	5.2%	4.0%	3.1%	11.3%	1.5%
Female	23.3%	5.5%	4.6%	3.8%	12.7%	1.6%

Capabilities

Mali's security situation has deteriorated because of military coups in August 2020 and May 2021 and policies implemented by the regime that strained security relationships with external partners. The regime has deepened its political and security partnership with Russia and hired Russia's Wagner Group to provide security to the regime and attempt to restore its control over the northern part of the country. Wagner forces deployed to the country in late 2021. The UN ended the MINUSMA mission to Mali in 2023, while the EU training mission ended in 2024. France suspended joint military operations in 2021 and officially ended its counter-insurgency mission, Operation Barkhane, in August 2022. Mali left the G5 Sahel security partnership in 2022 and is now part of the Alliance of Sahel States with the military-led regimes in Burkina Faso and Niger. The armed forces still suffer from operational deficiencies and broader institutional weakness. Despite vehicle deliveries by external partners and the acquisition of several aircraft from Russia, and UAVs from Turkiye, the armed forces remain under-equipped. Mali does not possess a defence-manufacturing industry and has limited equipment and maintenance capabilities.

ACTIVE 21,000 (Army 19,000 Air Force 2,000)
Gendarmerie & Paramilitary 20,000

ORGANISATIONS BY SERVICE

Army ε19,000
FORCES BY ROLE
MANOEUVRE
  Light
    9 mot inf bn
    1 inf coy (Special Joint Unit)
    5 inf coy (ULRI)
  Air Manoeuvre
    1 para regt
COMBAT SUPPORT
  1 arty regt
  1 engr bn
COMBAT SERVICE SUPPORT
  1 med unit
EQUIPMENT BY TYPE
ARMOURED FIGHTING VEHICLES
  LT TK 2+ PT-76
  RECCE 5+ BRDM-2
  IFV 6 VN2C
  APC 336:
    APC (W) 63: 27 Bastion APC; 10+ BTR-60PB; 11 BTR-70; 15+ WZ-551
    PPV 273: 50 Casspir; 16 IAG Guardian; 13 Marauder; 30 Puma M26-15/Puma M36; 23 Stark Motors Storm Light; 30 Streit Cougar; 4 Streit Gladiator; 5+ Streit Python; 29 Streit Typhoon†; 73+ VP-11
ARTILLERY 30+
  TOWED 122mm D-30
  MRL 122mm 30+: some Grad-P; 30+ BM-21 Grad

Air Force 2,000
FORCES BY ROLE
TRANSPORT
  1 sqn with BT-67; C295; Y-12E
TRAINING
  1 sqn with Tetras
TRANSPORT/ATTACK HELICOPTER
  1 sqn with H215; Mi-24D Hind; Mi-35M Hind
EQUIPMENT BY TYPE
AIRCRAFT 18 combat capable
  ISR 1 Cessna 208 Caravan
  TPT • Light 11: 2 C295; 7 Tetras; 2 Y-12E (1 An-24 Coke; 2 An-26 Curl; 2 BN-2 Islander; 1 BT-67 all in store)
  TRG 18: 3 A-29 Super Tucano*; ε15 L-39C Albratros*; (6 L-29 Delfin; 2 SF-260WL Warrior* all in store)
HELICOPTERS
  ATK 2 Mi-24D/Mi-24P/Mi-35M Hind
  TPT 7: Medium 7: 2 H215 (AS332L1) Super Puma; 5 Mi-8T /Mi-171Sh Hip; (3 Mi-8 Hip in store); Light (1 AS350 Ecureuil in store)
UNINHABITED AERIAL VEHICLES
  CISR • Medium ε16 Bayraktar TB2
BOMBS • Laser-guided MAM-L

Gendarmerie & Paramilitary 20,000 active

Gendarmerie 6,000
FORCES BY ROLE
MANOEUVRE
  Other
    8 paramilitary coy
    1 air tpt gp (2 sy coy; 1 tpt coy)
EQUIPMENT BY TYPE
ARMOURED FIGHTING VEHICLES
  APC • PPV 1+ RG-31 Nyala

National Guard 10,000

FORCES BY ROLE

MANOEUVRE

Reconnaissance

6 (camel) cav coy

Light

1 inf coy (Anti-terrorist special force)

EQUIPMENT BY TYPE

ARMOURED FIGHTING VEHICLES

APC • **PPV** 1+ RG-31 *Nyala*

National Police 1,000

Militia 3,000

FOREIGN FORCES

Russia 1,500 (PMC)

Mauritius MUS

Mauritian Rupee MUR		2023	2024	2025
GDP	MUR	659bn	730bn	785bn
	USD	14.6bn	15.9bn	16.5bn
Real GDP growth	%	7.0	6.1	4.0
Def bdgt [a]	MUR	10.9bn	11.8bn	12.6bn
	USD	241m	257m	265m

[a] Police service budget

Real-terms defence budget trend (USDm, constant 2015)

Population	1,310,504					
Age	0–14	15–19	20–24	25–29	30–64	65 plus
Male	7.7%	3.3%	3.6%	3.6%	24.8%	5.8%
Female	7.4%	3.1%	3.5%	3.6%	25.5%	8.2%

Capabilities

Responsibility for security lies with the Special Mobile Force (SMF), formed as a motorised infantry battalion. The SMF is tasked with ensuring internal and external territorial and maritime security. India provides support to the Mauritian Coast Guard. In 2024, the Indian-built airstrip and maritime jetty on Agaléga Island was inaugurated, in a bid by New Delhi to counter growing Chinese influence and maritime activities in the region. The SMF cannot deploy beyond national borders. Apart from very limited maintenance facilities, there is no defence industry. In 2024, the UK announced it would 'agree that Mauritius is sovereign over the Chagos Archipelago, including Diego Garcia', though it secured continued access to the UK and US base there for an initial period of 99 years.

ACTIVE NIL Gendarmerie & Paramilitary 2,550

ORGANISATIONS BY SERVICE

Gendarmerie & Paramilitary 2,550

Special Mobile Force ε1,750

FORCES BY ROLE

MANOEUVRE

Reconnaissance

2 recce coy

Light

5 (rifle) mot inf coy

COMBAT SUPPORT

1 engr sqn

COMBAT SERVICE SUPPORT

1 spt pl

EQUIPMENT BY TYPE

ARMOURED FIGHTING VEHICLES

IFV 2 VAB with 20mm gun

APC • **APC (W)** 12: 3 *Tactica*; 9 VAB

ARTILLERY • **MOR 81mm** 2

Coast Guard ε800

EQUIPMENT BY TYPE

PATROL AND COASTAL COMBATANTS 15

PCO 1 *Barracuda* (IND *Vikram* mod) with 1 hel landing platform

PCC 2 *Victory* (IND *Sarojini Naidu*)

PB 12: 10 Fast Interceptor Boat (IND); 1 P-2000 (UK *Archer* derivative); 1 *Guardian* (ex-IND SDB Mk 3)

AIRCRAFT • **TPT** • **Light** 4: 1 BN-2T *Defender*; 3 Do-228-101

Police Air Wing

EQUIPMENT BY TYPE

HELICOPTERS

MRH 10: 1 H125 (AS555) *Fennec*; 3 *Dhruv*; 1 SA315B *Lama* (*Cheetah*); 5 SA316 *Alouette* III (*Chetak*)

Mozambique MOZ

Mozambique New Metical MZN		2023	2024	2025
GDP	MZN	1.34trn	1.44trn	1.60trn
	USD	21.0bn	22.5bn	24.5bn
Real GDP growth	%	5.4	4.3	4.3
Def bdgt	MZN	13.3bn	20.1bn	
	USD	208m	314m	

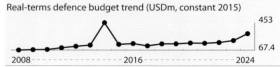

Population	33,350,954				
Age	0–14	15–19	20–24	25–29	30–64	65 plus
Male	22.6%	5.5%	4.6%	3.7%	11.4%	1.4%
Female	22.0%	5.4%	4.7%	3.9%	13.2%	1.5%

Capabilities

Mozambique faces a continued internal threat from Islamist groups in the northern provinces of Cabo Delgado and Nampula. The Mozambique government, in 2023, authorised the creation of local militias to help the armed forces fight insurgents. The SADC force withdrew in 2024 reportedly due to financial constraints. The country has received support from China, the EU, Portugal, Russia, Rwanda and the US, which has provided training in response to the Islamist threat. Several foreign countries help patrol the Mozambique Channel to thwart activities there, including illegal fishing and oil theft. Corruption in the armed forces is reportedly a concern. The armed forces have no capacity to deploy beyond Mozambique's borders without assistance. Soviet-era equipment makes up much of the inventory, making maintenance difficult, not least in the absence of a local defence industry. Recent economic performance limits the government's ability to recapitalise its inventory.

ACTIVE 12,050 (Army 10,000 Navy 1,050 Air 1,000)

Conscript liability 2 years

ORGANISATIONS BY SERVICE

Army ε9,000–10,000
FORCES BY ROLE
SPECIAL FORCES
  3 SF bn
MANOEUVRE
  Armoured
    1 tk bn
  Light
    7 inf bn
COMBAT SUPPORT
  2-3 arty bn
  2 engr bn
COMBAT SERVICE SUPPORT
  1 log bn

EQUIPMENT BY TYPE†
Equipment estimated at 10% or less serviceability
ARMOURED FIGHTING VEHICLES
  MBT 60+ T-54
  RECCE 30 BRDM-1/BRDM-2
  IFV 40 BMP-1
  APC 337
    APC (T) 30 FV430
    APC (W) 285: 160 BTR-60; 100 BTR-152; 25 AT-105 *Saxon*
    PPV 22+: 11 *Casspir*; 11 *Marauder*; some Tata Motors MRAP
  AUV 9+: Dongfeng *Mengshi*; MCAV-20; 9+ *Tiger* 4×4
ANTI-TANK/ANTI-INFRASTRUCTURE
  MSL • MANPATS 9K11 *Malyutka* (RS-AT-3 *Sagger*); 9K111 *Fagot* (RS-AT-4 *Spigot*)
  RCL 75mm; **82mm** B-10; **107mm** 24 B-12
  GUNS 85mm 18: 6 D-48; 12 PT-56 (D-44)
ARTILLERY 126
  TOWED 62: **100mm** 20 M-1944; **105mm** 12 M101; **122mm** 12 D-30; **130mm** 6 M-46; **152mm** 12 D-1
  MRL 122mm 12 BM-21 *Grad*
  MOR 52: **82mm** 40 M-43; **120mm** 12 M-43
AIR DEFENCE • GUNS 290+
  SP 57mm 20 ZSU-57-2
  TOWED 270+: **20mm** M-55; **23mm** 120 ZU-23-2; **37mm** 90 M-1939; (10 M-1939 in store); **57mm** 60 S-60; (30 S-60 in store)

Navy ε1,050
EQUIPMENT BY TYPE
PATROL AND COASTAL COMBATANTS 27
  PBF 23: 15 DV 15 (14 more in reserve); 2 HSI 32; 4 *Interceptor* (LKA Solas Marine); 2 *Namilti* (ex-IND C-401) (3 WP-18 non-operational)
  PB 4: 1 *Ocean Eagle* 43 (capacity 1 *Camcopter* S-100 UAV) (2 more in reserve); 1 *Pebane* (ex-ESP *Conejera*); 2 Other (fisheries patrol)
UNINHABITED AERIAL VEHICLES
  ISR • Light 1 S-100 *Camcopter*

Naval Infantry ε800
FORCES BY ROLE
MANOEUVRE
  Amphibious
  1 naval inf bn

Air Force 1,000
FORCES BY ROLE
FIGHTER/GROUND ATTACK
  1 sqn with MiG-21bis *Fishbed*; MiG-21UM *Mongol* B
ISR
  1 flt with *Mwari*

TRANSPORT
1 sqn with An-26 *Curl*; Cessna 150B; Cessna 172; CN235M; FTB-337G *Milirole*; L-410UVP-E; PA-34 *Seneca*

ATTACK/TRANSPORT HELICOPTER
1 sqn with Mi-24 *Hind*†

EQUIPMENT BY TYPE

AIRCRAFT 8 combat capable
FGA 8: 6 MiG-21bis *Fishbed*; 2 MiG-21UM *Mongol B*
ISR 5: 2 FTB-337G *Milirole*; ε3 *Mwari*
TPT 8: **Light** 7: 1 An-26 *Curl*; 2 Cessna 150B; 1 Cessna 172; 1 CN235M; 1 L-410UVP-E; 1 PA-34 *Seneca*; (4 PA-32 *Cherokee* non-op); **PAX** 1 Hawker 850XP
TRG 2 L-39 *Albatros*

HELICOPTERS
ATK 2 Mi-24V *Hind E*
MRH 2 SA314B *Gazelle*
TPT • **Medium** 2 Mi-8 *Hip*

FOREIGN FORCES

Austria EUMAM Mozambique 1
Belgium EUMAM Mozambique 2
Estonia EUMAM Mozambique 1
Finland EUMAM Mozambique 5
France EUMAM Mozambique 2
Greece EUMAM Mozambique 15
Italy EUMAM Mozambique 6
Lithuania EUMAM Mozambique 2
Portugal EUMAM Mozambqiue 50
Romania EUMAM Mozambique 6
Rwanda Army: 4,000
Spain EUMAM Mozambique 2
Tanzania Army: 290

Namibia NAM

Namibian Dollar NAD		2023	2024	2025
GDP	NAD	228bn	243bn	271bn
	USD	12.3bn	13.2bn	14.4bn
Real GDP growth	%	4.2	3.1	4.2
Def bdgt	NAD	6.29bn	6.74bn	
	USD	341m	366m	

Population	2,803,660					
Age	0–14	15–19	20–24	25–29	30–64	65 plus
Male	17.2%	5.2%	4.9%	4.3%	15.8%	1.7%
Female	16.9%	5.2%	4.8%	4.4%	17.4%	2.2%

Capabilities

The Namibian defence authorities aim to develop a small, well-trained, highly mobile and well-equipped professional force. The constitution assigns the Namibian Defence Force (NDF) territorial defence as the primary mission. Secondary roles include assisting civil authorities and supporting the AU, SADC and UN. The NDF's 4th National Defence Development Plan (2023–33) called for enhanced surveillance capabilities, developing quick reaction capabilities across all three domains and improving the local defence industry. The navy exercises as part of SADC's Standing Maritime Committee. It also has conducted multinational training missions organised by US forces. In 2021, Namibia and Botswana elevated annual meetings of a permanent commission on defence and security, chaired by the two countries' heads of state, to biannual status. The two countries also regularly conduct joint exercises. The NDF receives a comparatively large proportion of the state budget but has problems adequately funding training. There is limited capacity for independent power projection. The NDF is equipped, for the most part, with ageing or obsolescent systems, but economic difficulties make recapitalisation unlikely in the near term. The defence-manufacturing sector is limited, mainly focusing on armoured vehicles, tactical communications, and ammunition.

ACTIVE 11,600 (Army 9,000 Navy 1,600 Air Force 1,000) **Gendarmerie & Paramilitary 6,000**

ORGANISATIONS BY SERVICE

Army 9,000
FORCES BY ROLE
MANOEUVRE
  Reconnaissance
  1 recce regt
  Light
  3 inf bde (3 inf bn, 1 arty bn)
COMBAT SUPPORT
  1 arty bde (3 arty bn)
  1 AT regt
  1 engr regt
  1 sigs regt
COMBAT SERVICE SUPPORT
  1 log bn
AIR DEFENCE
  1 AD regt
EQUIPMENT BY TYPE
ARMOURED FIGHTING VEHICLES
  MBT T-54/T-55†
  RECCE 12 BRDM-2
  IFV 7: 5 Type-05P mod (with BMP-1 turret); 2 *Wolf Turbo 2* mod (with BMP-1 turret)
  APC 69
    APC (W) 13: 10 BTR-60; 3 Type-05P
    PPV 56: 20 *Casspir*; 8 RG-32M; 28 *Wolf Turbo 2*
ENGINEERING & MAINTENANCE VEHICLES
  ARV T-54/T-55 reported
ANTI-TANK/ANTI-INFRASTRUCTURE

RCL 82mm B-10
GUNS 12+: 57mm ZIS-2; 76mm 12 ZIS-3
ARTILLERY 72
    TOWED 140mm 24 G-2
    MRL 122mm 8: 5 BM-21 Grad; 3 PHL-81
    MOR 40: 81mm; 82mm
AIR DEFENCE
    SAM • Point-defence FN-6 (CH-SA-10)
    GUNS 65
        SP 23mm 15 Zumlac
        TOWED 50+: 14.5mm 50 ZPU-4; 57mm S-60

Navy ε1,600
EQUIPMENT BY TYPE
PATROL AND COASTAL COMBATANTS 7
    PSO 1 Elephant (PRC Zhonyang mod) with 1 hel landing platform
    PCC 3: 2 Daures (ex-PRC Type-037-IS (Haiqing)) with 2 FQF-3200 A/S mor; 1 Oryx
    PB 3: 1 Brendan Simbwaye (BRZ Grajaú); 2 Terrace Bay (BRZ Marlim)
AIRCRAFT • TPT • Light 1 F406 Caravan II
HELICOPTERS • TPT • Medium 1 S-61L

Marines ε700
FORCES BY ROLE
MANOEUVRE
    Amphibious
        1 mne bn

Air Force ε1,000
FORCES BY ROLE
FIGHTER/GROUND ATTACK
    1 sqn with F-7 (F-7NM); FT-7 (FT-7NG)
ISR
    1 sqn with O-2A Skymaster
TRANSPORT
    Some sqn with Falcon 900; Learjet 36; Y-12
TRAINING
    1 sqn with K-8 Karakorum*
ATTACK/TRANSPORT HELICOPTER
    1 sqn with H425; Mi-8 Hip; Mi-25 Hind D; SA315 Lama (Cheetah); SA316B Alouette III (Chetak)
EQUIPMENT BY TYPE
AIRCRAFT 10 combat capable
    FTR 7: 5 F-7 (F-7NM); 2 FT-7 (FT-7NG)
    ISR 5 Cessna O-2A Skymaster
    TPT 4: Light 3: 1 Learjet 36; 2 Y-12; (1 An-26 Curl in store); PAX 1 Falcon 900
    TRG 3+ K-8 Karakorum*
HELICOPTERS
    ATK 2 Mi-25 Hind D
    MRH 5: 1 H425; 1 SA315 Lama (Cheetah); 3 SA316B Alouette III (Chetak)
    TPT • Medium 1 Mi-8 Hip

Gendarmerie & Paramilitary 6,000
Police Force • Special Field Force 6,000 (incl Border Guard and Special Reserve Force)

DEPLOYMENT
SOUTH SUDAN: UN • UNMISS 5
SUDAN: UN • UNISFA 5

Niger NER

CFA Franc BCEAO XOF		2023	2024	2025
GDP	XOF	10.2trn	11.8trn	13.1trn
	USD	16.8bn	19.6bn	21.9bn
Real GDP growth	%	2.4	9.9	7.3
Def bdgt	XOF	201bn	264bn	
	USD	332m	439m	

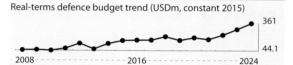
Real-terms defence budget trend (USDm, constant 2015)

Population	26,342,784				
Age	0–14	15–19	20–24	25–29	30–64	65 plus
Male	24.9%	5.7%	4.5%	3.4%	9.7%	1.3%
Female	24.5%	5.8%	4.7%	3.5%	10.5%	1.4%

Capabilities

Niger's armed forces took power in a bloodless coup in July 2023. In September that year, Niger formalised the Alliance of Sahel States with Mali and Burkina Faso, both also under military rule. Along with those countries, Niger withdrew from the G5 Sahel group and ECOWAS, announcing a joint anti-terrorism force in March 2024. After the French withdrawal in December 2023, the German, US and EU missions also ended in 2024, while the Italian mission resumed training activities. The new government has deepened ties with Russia. This included equipment deliveries and the deployment of mercenaries. Terrorist attacks have increased, inflicting loss of personnel and equipment. The armed forces are generally underequipped and under-resourced, although they have in recent years received a significant number of armoured vehicles. Equipment, including UAVs, has been procured from Turkiye since 2022. Apart from limited maintenance facilities, the country has no defence-industrial capability.

ACTIVE 39,100 (Army 39,000 Air 100) **Gendarmerie & Paramilitary 48,000**

Conscript liability Selective conscription, 2 years

ORGANISATIONS BY SERVICE

Army ε39,000
8 Mil Zones

FORCES BY ROLE
SPECIAL FORCES
  2 spec ops coy
  11 (intervention) cdo bn
MANOEUVRE
  Light
  26 (combined arms) inf bn
  Amphibious
  1 rvn coy
COMBAT SUPPORT
  1 arty bn
  1 engr coy
  1 int bn
COMBAT SERVICE SUPPORT
  1 log gp
AIR DEFENCE
  1 AD coy
EQUIPMENT BY TYPE
ARMOURED FIGHTING VEHICLES
  RECCE 155: 35 AML-20/AML-60; 90 AML-90; 30 BRDM-2
  APC 151
    APC (W) 53: 11 *Bastion* APC; 22 Panhard M3; 20 WZ-551
    PPV 98+: 15 IAG *Guardian Xtreme*; 57 *Mamba* Mk7; 21 *Puma* M26-15; 5+ *Puma* M36
    AUV 10+: 3+ *Tiger* 4×4; 7 VBL; *Bastion Patsas*
ANTI-TANK/ANTI-INFRASTRUCTURE
  RCL 14: **75mm** 6 M20; **106mm** 8 M40
ARTILLERY 52+
  TOWED 122mm 12 M-30
  MRL 107mm PH-63 (tch)
  MOR 40: **81mm** 19 Brandt; **82mm** 17; **120mm** 4 Brandt
AIR DEFENCE • GUNS 39
  SP 20mm 10 Panhard M3 VDAA
  TOWED 20mm 29

Air Force 100
EQUIPMENT BY TYPE
AIRCRAFT 5 combat capable
  ATK 2 Su-25 *Frogfoot*
  ISR 6: 4 Cessna 208 *Caravan*; 2 DA42 MPP *Twin Star*
  TPT 9: **Medium** 3 C-130H *Hercules*; **Light** 5: 1 An-26 *Curl*; 2 Cessna 208 *Caravan*; 1 Do-28 *Skyservant*; 1 Do-228-201; **PAX** 1 B-737-700 (VIP)
  TRG 3 *Hurkus*-C*
HELICOPTERS
  ATK 2 Mi-35P *Hind*
  MRH 8: 2 Bell 412HP *Twin Huey*; 1 Mi-17 *Hip*; 5 SA342 *Gazelle*
AIR-LAUNCHED MISSILES • ASM *Cirit*
BOMBS • Laser-guided *Bozok*

Gendarmerie & Paramilitary 48,000
  Gendarmerie 15,000
  National Guard 17,000
  National Police 16,000

DEPLOYMENT
CENTRAL AFRICAN REPUBLIC: UN • MINUSCA 5
DEMOCRATIC REPUBLIC OF THE CONGO: UN • MONUSCO 4

FOREIGN FORCES
Italy MISIN 250
Russia 100 (PMC)

Nigeria NGA

Nigerian Naira NGN		2023	2024	2025
GDP	NGN	234trn	302trn	352trn
	USD	364bn	200bn	195bn
Real GDP growth	%	2.9	2.9	3.2
Def bdgt	NGN	1.38trn	1.58trn	
	USD	2.15bn	1.04bn	

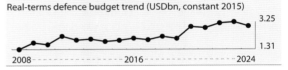

Real-terms defence budget trend (USDbn, constant 2015)

Population	236,747,130				
Age	0–14	15–19	20–24	25–29	30–64	65 plus
Male	20.6%	5.6%	4.9%	3.9%	13.9%	1.6%
Female	19.8%	5.4%	4.7%	3.8%	14.0%	1.8%

Capabilities

Nigeria is the region's principal military power. It faces numerous security challenges, including from Islamist groups and militants in the Niger Delta. The government is pursuing military reforms after counter-insurgency operations exposed operational weaknesses. Reforms target enhancing counter-insurgency tactics, forward-operating bases and quick-reaction groups. Nigeria is part of the Multinational Joint Task Force and is a key member of the ECOWAS Standby Force. Nigeria is strengthening its cooperation with Pakistan, while military and security assistance is either underway or being discussed with Germany, the UK and the US. The UK bases its British Defence Staff for West Africa in Nigeria. Contractors also provide training and maintenance. Nigeria can mount regional operations, though its deployment capacities remain limited. The government has been upgrading equipment across domains, including with the introduction of fighter ground-attack aircraft and combat-capable trainers, as well as new tanks and howitzers. Nigeria's navy is also being upgraded, in part to meet security requirements in the delta region and the Gulf of Guinea. Nigeria is developing its defence-industrial capacity, including local production facilities for small arms and protected patrol vehicles.

ACTIVE 143,000 (Army 100,000 Navy 25,000 Air 18,000) Gendarmerie & Paramilitary 80,000

Reserves planned

ORGANISATIONS BY SERVICE

Army 100,000
FORCES BY ROLE
SPECIAL FORCES
1 spec ops bn
3 spec ops bde
3 (mobile strike team) spec ops units
1 ranger bn
MANOEUVRE
Armoured
1 (3rd) armd div (1 armd bde, 1 inf bde, 1 arty bde, 1 engr bde (1 engr regt, 1 engr spt regt))
Mechanised
1 (1st) mech div (1 recce bn, 1 mech bde, 1 mot inf bde, 1 arty bde, 1 engr bde (1 engr regt))
1 (2nd) mech div (1 recce bn, 1 armd bde, 1 arty bde, 1 engr bde (1 engr regt, 1 engr spt regt))
1 (81st) composite div (2 recce bn, 1 mech bde, 1 arty bde, 1 engr bde (1 engr regt))
Light
1 (6th) inf div (1 amph bde, 2 inf bde)
1 (7th) inf div (1 spec ops bn, 1 armd bde, 7 (task force) inf bde, 1 arty bde, 1 engr bde (1 engr regt))
1 (8th Task Force) inf div (2 inf bde, 1 engr bde)
1 (82nd) composite div (1 recce bn, 3 mot inf bde, 1 arty bde, 1 engr bde (1 engr regt))
1 (Multi-National Joint Task Force) bde (2 inf bn(-))
Other
1 (Presidential Guard) gd bde (4 gd bn)
AIR DEFENCE
1 AD regt
EQUIPMENT BY TYPE
ARMOURED FIGHTING VEHICLES
MBT 319+: 100 T-55†; 10 T-72AV; 31 T-72M1; 172 Vickers Mk 3; 6+ VT-4
LT TK 154 FV101 *Scorpion*
ASLT 6+ ST-1
RECCE 312: 88 AML-60; 40 AML-90; 70 EE-9 *Cascavel*; 44 ERC-90F1 *Lynx*; 50 FV721 *Fox*; 20 FV601 *Saladin* Mk2
IFV 31: 9 BTR-4EN; 22 BVP-1
APC 956+
  APC (T) 373: 248 4K-7FA *Steyr*; 65 MT-LB; 60 ZSD-89
  APC (W) 172+: 10 FV603 *Saracen*; 110 AVGP *Grizzly* mod/*Piranha* I 6x6; 47 BTR-3UN; 5 BTR-80; some EE-11 *Urutu* (reported);
  PPV 411+: 14 *Caiman*; some *Conqueror*; 158 CS/VP3; 47 *Ezugwu*; up to 58 Isotrex *Legion*; up to 24 Isotrex *Phantom* II; some *Marauder*; 7+ *Maxxpro*; 8 Proforce *Ara-1*; 13 Proforce *Ara-2*; some Proforce *Viper*; 23 REVA III 4×4; 10 Streit *Spartan*; 9 Streit *Cougar* (*Igirigi*);
  25 Streit *Typhoon*; 15 *Tares*
AUV 302+: 106 *Cobra*; 120 Dongfeng *Mengshi*; FV103 *Spartan*; 4+ *Tiger* 4×4; 72 VBL
ENGINEERING & MAINTENANCE VEHICLES
ARV 17+: AVGP *Husky*; 2 *Greif*; 15 Vickers ARV
VLB MTU-20; VAB
ANTI-TANK/ANTI-INFRASTRUCTURE
MSL • MANPATS *Shershen*
RCL 84mm *Carl Gustaf*; 106mm M40A1
ARTILLERY 518+
SP 43+: 105mm 4+ SH-5; 122mm some SH-2; 155mm 39 *Palmaria*
TOWED 104: 105mm 49 M-56; 122mm 48 D-30/D-74; 130mm 7 M-46; (155mm 24 FH-77B in store)
MRL 122mm 41: 9 BM-21 *Grad*; 25 APR-21; 7 RM-70
MOR 330+: 81mm 200; 82mm 100; 120mm 30+
HELICOPTERS
TPT • Light 2 UH-1H *Iroquois*
UNINHABITED AERIAL VEHICLES
ISR • Light *Aerosonde*; *Blowfish* A2G
AIR DEFENCE
SAM • Point-defence 16+: 16 *Roland*; *Blowpipe*; 9K32 *Strela*-2 (RS-SA-7 *Grail*)‡
GUNS 89+
  SP 23mm 29 ZSU-23-4 *Shilka*
  TOWED 60+: 20mm 60+; 23mm ZU-23; 40mm L/70

Navy 25,000 (incl Coast Guard)
Western Comd HQ located at Apapa; Eastern Comd HQ located at Calabar; Central Comd HQ located at Brass
EQUIPMENT BY TYPE
PRINCIPAL SURFACE COMBATANTS • FRIGATES
FFGHM (1 *Aradu* (GER MEKO 360) (non-operational) with 8 single lnchr with *Otomat* Mk1 AShM, 1 octuple *Albatros* lnchr with *Aspide* SAM, 2 triple 324mm ASTT with A244/S LWT, 1 127mm gun (capacity 1 med hel))
PATROL AND COASTAL COMBATANTS 136
CORVETTES • FSM (1 *Erinomi* (UK Vosper Mk 9) (non-operational) with 1 triple lnchr with *Seacat*† SAM, 1 twin 375mm Bofors ASW Rocket Launcher System A/S mor, 1 76mm gun)
PSOH 4: 2 *Centenary* with 1 76mm gun (capacity 1 Z-9 hel); 2 *Thunder* (ex-US *Hamilton*) with 1 76mm gun
PCF 2 *Siri* (FRA *Combattante* IIIB) with 1 76mm gun
PCO 4 *Kyanwa* (ex-US CG *Balsam*)
PCC 2 *Kano* (Damen Fast Crew Supplier 4008)
PBF 33: 4 Aresa 1700; 4 C-Falcon; 4 *Manta* MkII (SGP Suncraft 17m); 12 *Manta* MkIII (SGP Suncraft 17m); 4 *Shaldag* II; 2 *Torie* (Nautic Sentinel 17m); 3 *Wave Rider*
PB 76: 1 *Andoni*; 3 *Dorina* (FRA FPB 98); 4 FPB 110 MkII; 8 *Okpoku* (FRA FPB 72); 6 *Irrua* (PRC Jianglong JL3880); 2 *Karaduwa*; 2 *Sagbama*; 2 *Sea Eagle* (SGP Suncraft 38m); up to 40 Suncraft 12m; 4 Swiftships; 2 *Town* (of which one laid up); 2 *Yola*†

PBR 15 *Stingray* (SGP Suncraft 16m)
MINE WARFARE • MINE COUNTERMEASURES 2
    MCC 2 *Ohue* (ITA *Lerici* mod)†
AMPHIBIOUS 5
    LANDING SHIPS • LST 1 *Kada* (NLD Damen LST 100) with 1 hel landing platform
    LANDING CRAFT • LCVP 4 *Stingray* 20
LOGISTICS AND SUPPORT 3
    AGOR 1 *Lana* (FRA Ocea OSV 190)
    AGS 1 *Zhizoko* (FRA Ocea OSV 115)
    AXL 1 *Prosperity* (ex-IRL *Emer*)
UNINHABITED MARITIME SYSTEMS
    USV • MARSEC *Sea Stalker*

Naval Aviation
EQUIPMENT BY TYPE
HELICOPTERS
    MRH 2 AW139 (AB-139)
    TPT • **Light** 8: 3 AW109E *Power*†; 5 AW109SP
UNINHABITED AERIAL VEHICLES
    ISR • **Light** AR3

Special Boat Service 200
EQUIPMENT BY TYPE
FORCES BY ROLE
SPECIAL FORCES
    1 SF unit

Air Force 18,000
FORCES BY ROLE
Very limited op capability
FIGHTER/GROUND ATTACK
    1 sqn with F-7 (F-7NI); FT-7 (FT-7NI); JF-17 *Thunder* (Block II)
GROUND ATTACK
    1 sqn with *Alpha Jet* A/E*
MARITIME PATROL
    1 sqn with ATR-42-500 MP; Do-128D-6 *Turbo SkyServant*; Do-228-100/200
ISR
    1 sqn with DA62 MPP
COMBAT SEARCH & RESCUE
    1 sqn with H215 (AS332) *Super Puma*
TRANSPORT
    1 sqn with C-130H *Hercules*; C-130H-30 *Hercules*; G-222
    1 sqn with ATR-42-500 MP; AW109LUH; Beech 350 *King Air*
    1 (Presidential) gp with AW189; A330; Beech 360ER *King Air*; Do-228-200; *Falcon* 7X; *Falcon* 900; Gulfstream IV/V
TRAINING
    1 unit with *Alpha Jet* A/E*; EMB-314 *Super Tucano* (A-29B)*
    1 unit with L-39ZA *Albatros*†*
    1 unit with *Air Beetle*†; *Super Mushshak*; DA40NG
    1 hel unit with AW109; AW109M; Mi-34 *Hermit*
ATTACK HELICOPTER
    1 sqn with Mi-24/Mi-35 *Hind*; H135; T129B
HELICOPTER
    1 (spec ops) flt with Bell 412EP
COMBAT/ISR UAV
    1 sqn with CH-3; *Wing Loong* II
EQUIPMENT BY TYPE
AIRCRAFT 61 combat capable
    FTR 11: 10 F-7 (F-7NI); 1 FT-7 (FT-7NI)
    FGA 3 JF-17 *Thunder* (Block II)
    ELINT 2 ATR-42-500 MP
    ISR 5: 1 Beech 350 *King Air*; 4 DA62 MPP
    MP (1 Cessna 525 *Citation* CJ3 non-operational)
    TPT 22: **Medium** 5: 1 C-130H *Hercules* (4 more in store†); 1 C-130H-30 *Hercules* (2 more in store); 3 G.222† (2 more in store†); **Light** 12: 1 Beech 350 *King Air*; 2 Beech 360ER *King Air* (VIP); 1 Cessna 550 *Citation*; 1 Do-228-100; 2 Do-228-101; 5 Do-228-200 (incl 2 VIP); **PAX** 5: 1 A330; 2 *Falcon* 7X; 1 *Falcon* 900 (1 more in store); 1 Gulfstream IV; 1 Gulfstream V
    TRG 115: 58 *Air Beetle*† (up to 20 awaiting repair); 1 *Alpha Jet* A*; 10 *Alpha Jet* E*; 2 DA40NG; 12 EMB-314 *Super Tucano* (A-29B)*; 23 L-39ZA *Albatros**†; 9 *Super Mushshak*
HELICOPTERS
    ATK 20: 2 Mi-24P *Hind*; 4 Mi-24V *Hind*; 3 Mi-35 *Hind*; 2 Mi-35P *Hind*; 5 Mi-35M *Hind*; 4 T129B
    MRH 13+: 6 AW109LUH; 2 AW189 (VIP); 2 Bell 412EP; 3+ SA341 *Gazelle*
    TPT 24: **Medium** 13: 2 AW101; 5 H215 (AS332) *Super Puma* (4 more in store); 3 AS365N *Dauphin*; 1 Mi-171Sh; 2 Mi-171E; **Light** 11: 4 H125 (AS350B) *Ecureuil*; 1 AW109; 2 AW109M; 1 Bell 205; 3 H135
UNINHABITED AERIAL VEHICLES 7
    CISR • **Heavy** 5: 1+ CH-3; 4+ *Wing Loong* II
    ISR 2: **Heavy** 1+ *Yabhon Flash*-20; **Medium** (9 *Aerostar* non-operational); **Light** 1+ *Tsaigami*
AIR-LAUNCHED MISSILES
    AAM • IR R-3 (RS-AA-2 *Atoll*)‡; PL-9C
    ASM AGR-20A APKWS; AR-1
    BOMBS • INS/GPS guided FT-9

Gendarmerie & Paramilitary ε80,000

Security and Civil Defence Corps 80,000
EQUIPMENT BY TYPE
ARMOURED FIGHTING VEHICLES
    APC 80+
        APC (W) 74+: 70+ AT105 *Saxon*†; 4 BTR-3U; UR-416
    PPV 6 *Springbuck* 4×4
    AIRCRAFT • TPT • Light 4: 1 Cessna 500 *Citation* I; 2 PA-31 *Navajo*; 1 PA-31-350 *Navajo Chieftain*

HELICOPTERS • TPT • Light 5: 2 Bell 212 (AB-212); 2 Bell 222 (AB-222); 1 Bell 429

DEPLOYMENT

CENTRAL AFRICAN REPUBLIC: UN • MINUSCA 7
DEMOCRATIC REPUBLIC OF THE CONGO: UN • MONUSCO 6
INDIA/PAKISTAN: UN • UNMOGIP 1
GAMBIA: ECOWAS • ECOMIG 200
GUINEA-BISSAU: ECOWAS • ESSMGB 86
LEBANON: UN • UNIFIL 1
SOUTH SUDAN: UN • UNMISS 14
SUDAN: UN • UNISFA 186; 1 inf coy
WESTERN SAHARA: UN • MINURSO 10

FOREIGN FORCES
United Kingdom 80 (trg teams)

Rwanda RWA

Rwandan Franc RWF		2023	2024	2025
GDP	RWF	16.4trn	18.3trn	20.5trn
	USD	14.1bn	13.7bn	14.0bn
Real GDP growth	%	8.2	7.0	6.5
Def bdgt	RWF	222bn	219bn	254bn
	USD	192m	164m	174m

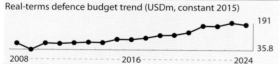

Population	13,623,302				
Age	0–14	15–19	20–24	25–29	30–64	65 plus
Male	18.8%	5.6%	4.8%	4.0%	14.6%	1.2%
Female	18.4%	5.6%	4.7%	4.1%	16.3%	1.8%

Capabilities

Rwanda is a principal security actor in East Africa, with disciplined and well-trained armed forces. Their key missions are to defend territorial integrity and national sovereignty. While the army is relatively large, units are lightly equipped with little mechanisation. Rwanda signed a Mutual Defence Treaty with Kenya and Uganda in 2014 and participates in East African Community military activities. It has deployed forces to Mozambique since 2021, including a small marine component. The country's professional military education establishments train regional as well as Rwandan personnel. In 2024, Rwanda hosted the East African Community FTX, having hosted the CPX in 2023. The lack of fixed-wing aircraft limits the armed forces' ability to independently deploy abroad beyond personnel, though they are capable of deploying and self-sustaining missions in the immediate region. There is limited maintenance capacity but no defence manufacturing sector.

ACTIVE 33,000 (Army 32,000 Air 1,000)
Gendarmerie & Paramilitary 2,000

ORGANISATIONS BY SERVICE

Army 32,000
FORCES BY ROLE
MANOEUVRE
Light
2 cdo bn
5 inf div (total of 13 inf bde)
COMBAT SUPPORT
1 arty bde
EQUIPMENT BY TYPE
ARMOURED FIGHTING VEHICLES
MBT 34: 24 T-54/T-55; 10 *Tiran*-5
RECCE ε90 AML-60/AML-90
IFV 38+: BMP; 13+ *Ratel*-23; 10 *Ratel*-60; 15 *Ratel*-90
APC 60+
    APC (W) 20+: BTR; *Buffalo* (Panhard M3); 20 WZ-551 (reported)
    PPV 40 RG-31 *Nyala*
AUV 92: 76 *Cobra/Cobra* II; 16 VBL
ENGINEERING & MAINTENANCE VEHICLES
ARV T-54/T-55 ARV reported
ANTI-TANK/ANTI-INFRASTRUCTURE
MSL • SP HJ-9A (on *Cobra*)
ARTILLERY 177
SP 17: **122mm** 12: 6 CS/SH-1; 6 SH-3; **155mm** 5 ATMOS 2000
TOWED 35+: **105mm** some; **122mm** 6 D-30; **152mm** 29 Type-54 (D-1)†
MRL 10: **107mm** PH-63; **122mm** 5 RM-70; **160mm** 5 LAR-160
MOR 115: **81mm**; **82mm**; **120mm**
AIR DEFENCE
SAM • Point-defence 9K32 *Strela*-2 (RS-SA-7 *Grail*)‡; some *Yitian* (CH-SA-13)
GUNS ε150: **14.5mm**; **23mm**; **37mm**

Air Force ε1,000
FORCES BY ROLE
TRANSPORT
1 flt with Cessna 208EX *Grand Caravan*
ATTACK/TRANSPORT HELICOPTER
1 sqn with Mi-17/Mi-17MD/Mi-17V-5/Mi-17-1V *Hip* H; Mi-24P/V *Hind*
EQUIPMENT BY TYPE
AIRCRAFT
TPT • Light 2 Cessna 208EX *Grand Caravan*
HELICOPTERS
ATK 5: 2 Mi-24V *Hind* E; 3 Mi-24P *Hind*
MRH 12: 1 AW139; 4 Mi-17 *Hip* H; 1 Mi-17MD *Hip* H; 1

Mi-17V-5 *Hip* H; 5 Mi-17-1V *Hip* H
TPT • **Light** 1 AW109S

Gendarmerie & Paramilitary

District Administration Security Support Organ ε2,000

DEPLOYMENT

CENTRAL AFRICAN REPUBLIC: UN • MINUSCA 2,144; 3 inf bn; 1 fd hospital
DEMOCRATIC REPUBLIC OF THE CONGO: Army 3,000
MOZAMBIQUE: Army 4,000
SOUTH SUDAN: UN • UNMISS 2,636; 3 inf bn; 1 hel sqn with 6 Mi-17
SUDAN: UN • UNISFA 4

Senegal SEN

CFA Franc BCEAO XOF		2023	2024	2025
GDP	XOF	18.8trn	20.3trn	22.6trn
	USD	30.9bn	33.7bn	37.8bn
Real GDP growth	%	4.6	6.0	9.3
Def bdgt	XOF	272bn	312bn	
	USD	449m	519m	

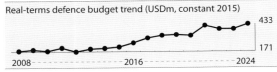

Population	18,847,519				
Age	0–14	15–19	20–24	25–29	30–64	65 plus
Male	20.7%	5.6%	4.6%	3.9%	13.0%	1.5%
Female	20.0%	5.4%	4.6%	3.9%	15.0%	1.9%

Capabilities

Senegal's armed forces are focused on internal and border security tasks, including counter-insurgency in the country's south and combating Islamist activity in neighbouring states. Senegal is improving PME, and newly established defence organisations include a naval academy and a higher war college. Modest upgrades have been made to the inventory in recent years. France remains Senegal's principal defence partner, though it plans to reduce its military presence in the country. Senegal also has defence cooperation ties with Spain, Russia and the UK, and it signed an agreement with Mauritania in 2021 regarding offshore energy-related maritime security. The US also provides security assistance, including to the national police and gendarmerie. The armed forces can deploy personnel using organic airlift, but short-notice movements of heavy equipment would be difficult without external assistance. Apart from maintenance facilities there is limited defence-industrial capability, though improving military technologies and defence industrial capacity is an ambition of the 2025–29 military planning law.

ACTIVE 14,150 (Army 11,900 Navy 1,500 Air 750)

Gendarmerie & Paramilitary 5,000

Conscript liability Selective conscription, 24 months

ORGANISATIONS BY SERVICE

Army 11,900 (incl conscripts)

7 Mil Zone HQ

FORCES BY ROLE
MANOEUVRE
  Reconnaissance
  5 armd recce bn
  Light
  1 cdo bn
  6 inf bn
  Air Manoeuvre
  1 AB bn
  Other
  1 (Presidential Guard) horse cav bn
COMBAT SUPPORT
  1 arty bn
  1 engr bn
  3 construction coy
  1 sigs bn
COMBAT SERVICE SUPPORT
  1 log bn
  1 med bn
  1 trg bn

EQUIPMENT BY TYPE
ARMOURED FIGHTING VEHICLES
  ASLT 27 WMA-301
  RECCE 67: 20 BRDM-2; 47 Eland-90
  IFV 26 *Ratel*-20
  APC 103
    APC (W) 28: 6+ *Bastion* APC; 2 *Oncilla*; 16 Panhard M3; 4 WZ-551 (CP)
    PPV 75: 8 *Casspir*; some *Hizir* II; 39 *Puma* M26-15; 28 *Puma* M36
  AUV 35: 27 RAM Mk3; ε8 CS/VN3
ENGINEERING & MAINTENANCE VEHICLES
  ARV 2 *Puma* M36 ARV
ANTI-TANK/ANTI-INFRASTRUCTURE
  MSL • **MANPATS** *Milan*
ARTILLERY 82
  TOWED 20: **105mm** 6 HM-2/M101; **155mm** 14: ε6 Model-50; 8 TR-F1
  MRL 122mm 6 BM-21 *Grad* (UKR *Bastion*-1 mod)
  MOR 56: **81mm** 24; **120mm** 32
AIR DEFENCE • **GUNS** • **TOWED** 39: **14.5mm** 6 ZPU-4 (tch); **20mm** 21 M693; **40mm** 12 L/60

Navy (incl Coast Guard) 1,500
FORCES BY ROLE

SPECIAL FORCES

1 cdo coy

EQUIPMENT BY TYPE

PATROL AND COASTAL COMBATANTS 14

PCGM 3 *Walo* (FRA OPV 58S) with 2 twin lnchr with *Marte* Mk2/N AShM, 1 twin *Simbad* lnchr with *Mistral* 3 SAM, 1 76mm gun

PCO 1 *Fouladou* (FRA OPV 190 Mk II)

PBF 6: 3 *Anambe* (ISR *Shaldag* II); 2 *Ferlo* (FRA RPB 33); 1 *Lac Retba* (ISR *Shaldag* V)

PB 4: 2 *Alphonse Faye* (FRA RPB 20); 1 *Conejera*; 1 *Kedougou* (FRA OPV 45)

AMPHIBIOUS • LANDING CRAFT 2

LCT 2 EDIC 700

LCVP 2 *Yoff* (ISR 24m)

LOGISTICS AND SUPPORT 3

ABU 1 *Samba Laobe Fall*

AGOR 1 *Itaf Deme*

AX 1 *Diender*

Air Force 750

FORCES BY ROLE

GROUND ATTACK

1 sqn with KA-1S*

MARITIME PATROL/SEARCH & RESCUE

1 sqn with CN235-220 MPA

TRANSPORT

1 sqn with ATR-42; Beech B200 *King Air*; C295W; F-27-400M *Troopship*

1 VIP flt with A320

TRAINING

1 sqn with TB-30 *Epsilon*

ATTACK/TRANSPORT HELICOPTER

1 sqn with Bell 206; Mi-24V/Mi-35P *Hind*; Mi-171Sh; Schweizer 300C

EQUIPMENT BY TYPE

AIRCRAFT 4 combat capable

MP 1 CN235-220 MPA

TPT 10: **Light** 8: 1 ATR-42; 2 C295W; 2 CN235; 2 Beech B200 *King Air*; 1 F-27-400M *Troopship* (2 more in store); **PAX** 2: 1 A320 (VIP); 1 B-727-200

TRG 10: 4 KA-1S*; 6 TB-30 *Epsilon*

HELICOPTERS

ATK 4: 2 Mi-24V *Hind* D; 2 Mi-35P *Hind*

MRH 1 AW139

TPT 4: **Medium** 2 Mi-171Sh; **Light** 2 Bell 206

TRG 1 Schweizer 300C

UNINHABITED AERIAL VEHICLES

ISR • Light *Black Eagle* 50H

Gendarmerie & Paramilitary 10,000

Gendarmerie 10,000

EQUIPMENT BY TYPE

ARMOURED FIGHTING VEHICLES

ASLT 4+ VN22B

APC 56

APC (W) 24: 7 *Bastion* APC; 5 EE-11 *Urutu*; 12 VXB-170†

PPV 32: 24 *Ejder Yalcin*; 8 *Gila*

AUV 36: 2 Bastion Patsas; 20 *Cobra* II; 11 RAM Mk3; ε6 CS/VN3C

DEPLOYMENT

CENTRAL AFRICAN REPUBLIC: UN • MINUSCA 194; 1 inf coy

DEMOCRATIC REPUBLIC OF THE CONGO: UN • MONUSCO 12

GAMBIA: ECOWAS • ECOMIG 250

GUINEA-BISSAU: ECOWAS • ESSMGB 150

FOREIGN FORCES

France 400; 1 *Falcon* 50MI

Spain 65; 2 C295M

Seychelles SYC

Seychelles Rupee SCR		2023	2024	2025
GDP	SCR	30.0bn	31.2bn	33.2bn
	USD	2.14bn	2.14bn	2.24bn
Real GDP growth	%	3.2	3.1	3.9
Def bdgt	SCR	n.k	n.k	n.k
	USD	n.k	n.k	n.k
Population	98,187			

Age	0–14	15–19	20–24	25–29	30–64	65 plus
Male	9.1%	3.0%	3.2%	3.5%	28.8%	4.3%
Female	8.6%	2.7%	2.8%	3.0%	25.3%	5.7%

Capabilities

The proximity of the Seychelles to key international shipping lanes increases its strategic significance. The Seychelles People's Defence Force (PDF) primarily focuses on maritime security and counter-piracy operations. The Seychelles has participated in Operation Prosperity Guardian with intelligence support capabilities. US forces conduct maritime patrols on a rotational basis. India maintains strong defence ties with the Seychelles, donating equipment, providing maintenance and supporting efforts to enhance its maritime-patrol and -surveillance capability. The government has plans to improve defence cooperation with China, which has already led to some equipment deliveries. Bahrain and the UAE have also donated equipment. The PDF does not deploy overseas and has a limited capacity to deploy and support troops. There are limited maintenance facilities but no domestic defence manufacturing sector.

ACTIVE 420 (Land Forces 200; Coast Guard 200; Air Force 20)

ORGANISATIONS BY SERVICE

People's Defence Force

Land Forces 200
FORCES BY ROLE
SPECIAL FORCES
  1 SF unit
MANOEUVRE
  Light
   1 inf coy
  Other
   1 sy unit
COMBAT SUPPORT
  1 MP unit
EQUIPMENT BY TYPE
ARMOURED FIGHTING VEHICLES
  RECCE 6 BRDM-2†
ARTILLERY • MOR 82mm 6 M-43†
AIR DEFENCE • GUNS • TOWED 14.5mm ZPU-2†; ZPU-4†; **37mm** M-1939†

Coast Guard 200 (incl 80 Marines)
EQUIPMENT BY TYPE
PATROL AND COASTAL COMBATANTS 11
  PCC 3: 2 *Topaz* (ex-IND *Trinkat*); 1 *Zoroaster* (IND *Car Nicobar* mod)
  PBF 4: 1 *Hermes* (ex-IND *Coastal Interceptor Craft*); 3 *Thorpe* (LKA *Wave Rider*)
  PB 4: 1 *Etoile* (PRC Poly Technologies 47m); 2 *Le Vigilant* (ex-UAE Rodman 101); 1 *Fortune* (ex-UK *Tyne*)
LOGISTICS AND SUPPORT • AKL 1 *Saya de Malha*

Air Force 20
EQUIPMENT BY TYPE
AIRCRAFT
  MP 2 Do-228 MP
  TPT • Light 3: 1 DHC-6-320 *Twin Otter*; 2 Y-12

Sierra Leone SLE

Sierra Leonean Leone SLL		2023	2024	2025
GDP	SLL	137trn	177trn	207trn
	USD	6.40bn	7.41bn	7.80bn
Real GDP growth	%	5.7	4.0	4.5
Def bdgt	SLL	441bn	818bn	
	USD	20.7m	34.3m	

Real-terms defence budget trend (USDm, constant 2015)

Population	9,121,049					
Age	0–14	15–19	20–24	25–29	30–64	65 plus
Male	20.2%	5.6%	4.8%	4.1%	13.6%	1.3%
Female	19.9%	5.5%	5.0%	4.6%	14.3%	1.3%

Capabilities

The primary task of the armed forces is to ensure internal, maritime and border security and provide forces for peacekeeping missions. Sierra Leone is building up its defence institutions, generating formal defence documentation and improving planning functions, mostly with international support. China, Nigeria, the UK and the US are among the countries supporting defence capacity-building. An ECOWAS stabilisation mission, scheduled for September 2024, has been delayed. Freetown's Horton Academy delivers professional military education training to national and regional personnel. The country launched its first National Security Policy and Strategy in August 2024. The armed forces' ability to deploy more than small units is constrained by force size and logistics-support capacity and the delivery of support vehicles is intended to start remedying deficiencies. The armed forces aim to develop an air-based surveillance capability. The country has limited maintenance capacity and no defence-manufacturing capability.

ACTIVE 8,500 (Joint 8,500)

ORGANISATIONS BY SERVICE

Armed Forces 8,500
FORCES BY ROLE
MANOEUVRE
  Reconnaissance
   1 recce unit
  Light
   4 inf bde (3 inf bn)
COMBAT SUPPORT
  1 engr regt
  1 int unit
  1 MP unit
  1 sigs unit
COMBAT SUPPORT
  1 log unit
  1 fd hospital

EQUIPMENT BY TYPE
ARMOURED FIGHTING VEHICLES
  APC • **PPV** 4: 3 *Casspir*; 1 *Mamba* Mk5
ANTI-TANK/ANTI-INFRASTRUCTURE
  RCL 84mm *Carl Gustaf*
ARTILLERY 37
  TOWED 122mm 6 PL-96 (D-30)
  MOR 31: **81mm** ε27; **82mm** 2; **120mm** 2
HELICOPTERS • **MRH** 2 Mi-17 *Hip* H/Mi-8 *Hip*†
AIR DEFENCE • **GUNS** • **TOWED 14.5mm** 3

Maritime Wing ε200
EQUIPMENT BY TYPE
PATROL AND COASTAL COMBATANTS 2
  PB 2: 1 *Mammy Yoko* (PRC 27m); 1 *Sir Milton* (ex-PRC Type-062/I (*Shanghai* III))†

DEPLOYMENT
CENTRAL AFRICAN REPUBLIC: UN • MINUSCA 7
DEMOCRATIC REPUBLIC OF THE CONGO: UN • MONUSCO 2
LEBANON: UN • UNIFIL 3
SOMALIA: UN • UNSOM 1
SOUTH SUDAN: UN • UNMISS 2
SUDAN: UN • UNISFA 4
WESTERN SAHARA: UN • MINURSO 1

Somalia SOM

Somali Shilling SOS		2023	2024	2025
GDP	USD	11.0bn	12.7bn	13.9bn
Real GDP growth	%	4.2	4.0	4.0
Def bdgt	USD	n.k	n.k	n.k
Population	13,017,273			

Age	0–14	15–19	20–24	25–29	30–64	65 plus
Male	20.7%	5.2%	4.6%	3.8%	14.7%	1.2%
Female	20.7%	5.3%	4.6%	3.7%	13.7%	1.6%

Capabilities

The Somali National Army (SNA) has limited in organisational and military capability. Internal stability remains fragile following decades of conflict and insurgency, with al-Shabaab and other extremist groups still retaining the ability to carry out attacks. Deployed international forces are trying to provide security, stabilisation and capacity-building assistance. Growing a domestic training capacity staff within the SNA to enable organic continuation training remains a challenge. This has required prolonged AU support, though ATMIS is due to hand over security responsibilities to the Somalia Security Forces, with a new AU Support and Stabilisation Mission in Somalia (AUSSOM) set to succeed ATMIS. US forces are also independently deployed to Somalia to tackle militant groups. The SNA remains reliant on external training programmes from several countries, organisations and private security companies to build capability. Turkiye has established a military training facility in Somalia. The military has no capacity to deploy beyond national borders and minimal national infrastructure to support domestic operations. Removal of the three decades-long UN arms embargo at the end of 2023 provides access to grow and modernise inventories. Somalia has no domestic defence-industrial capability.

ACTIVE 19,000 (Army 19,000) Gendarmerie & Paramilitary 700

ORGANISATIONS BY SERVICE

Army 19,000
FORCES BY ROLE
Almost all units are below establishment strength, and many are at half-strength or below.
SPECIAL FORCES
  3 cdo bde
MANOEUVRE
  Light
  1 (60th) inf div (4 inf bde)
  2 (21st & 27th) inf div (3 inf bde)
  2 (12th April & 43rd) inf div (2 inf bde)
  8 inf bde
  Other
  1 gd bde
  1 sy bde
COMBAT SUPPORT
  2 MP bde
EQUIPMENT BY TYPE
ARMOURED FIGHTING VEHICLES
  APC 73
    APC (W) 38+: 25+ AT-105 *Saxon*; 13 *Bastion* APC; Fiat 6614
    PPV 35+: *Casspir*; MAV-5; 20 *Kirpi*; 9+ *Mamba* Mk5; 6 *Puma* M36; RG-31 *Nyala*
  AUV 12 *Tiger* 4×4
HELICOPTERS • **MRH** 4+ Bell 412

Gendarmerie & Paramilitary 700

Coast Guard 700
EQUIPMENT BY TYPE
PATROL AND COASTAL COMBATANTS
All operational patrol vessels under 10t FLD

FOREIGN FORCES
Under UNSOM command unless stated
Burundi ATMIS 2,300; 3 inf bn
Djibouti ATMIS 450; 1 inf bn(-)
Ethiopia ATMIS 2,400; 3 inf bn
Finland EUTM Somalia 12
Ghana 1
India 1
Italy EUTM Somalia 150

Kenya ATMIS 2,400; 3 inf bn • UNSOS 1
Mauritania UNSOS 1
Pakistan UNSOS 1
Portugal EUTM Somalia 2
Romania EUTM Somalia 5
Serbia EUTM Somalia 6
Sierra Leone 1
Spain EUTM Somalia 21
Sweden EUTM Somalia 9
Turkiye 1 • Army: 200 (trg base)
Uganda 627; 1 sy bn • ATMIS 4,100; 3 inf bn • UNSOS 2
United Kingdom 2 • UNSOS 7 • Army: 65 (trg team)
United States US Africa Command: 100

PUNTLAND & SOMALILAND

Data presented here represents the de facto situation. This does not imply international recognition as sovereign states. Much of this equipment is in poor repair or inoperable

Puntland

Army ε3,000 (to be integrated into Somali National Army)

Maritime Police Force ε1,000
EQUIPMENT BY TYPE
PATROL AND COASTAL COMBATANTS
All operational patrol vessels under 10t FLD
AIRCRAFT • TPT 4: Light 3 Ayres S2R; PAX 1 DC-3
HELICOPTERS • MRH SA316 *Alouette* III

Somaliland

Army ε12,500
FORCES BY ROLE
MANOEUVRE
  Armoured
    2 armd bde
  Mechanised
    1 mech inf bde
  Light
    14 inf bde
COMBAT SUPPORT
  2 arty bde
COMBAT SERVICE SUPPORT
  1 spt bn
EQUIPMENT BY TYPE†
ARMOURED FIGHTING VEHICLES
  MBT T-54/55
  RECCE Fiat 6616
  APC • APC(W) Fiat 6614
ARTILLERY • MRL various incl BM-21 *Grad*
AIR DEFENCE • GUNS • 23mm ZU-23-2

Ministry of the Interior

Coast Guard 600

EQUIPMENT BY TYPE
PATROL AND COASTAL COMBATANTS • PB 2
Other operational patrol vessels under 10t FLD

FOREIGN FORCES

United Arab Emirates 180

South Africa RSA

South African Rand ZAR		2023	2024	2025
GDP	ZAR	7.02trn	7.42trn	7.87trn
	USD	381bn	403bn	418bn
Real GDP growth	%	0.7	1.1	1.5
Def bdgt	ZAR	53.3bn	52.7bn	
	USD	2.89bn	2.86bn	

Real-terms defence budget trend (USDbn, constant 2015)

Population	60,442,647					
Age	0–14	15–19	20–24	25–29	30–64	65 plus
Male	13.6%	3.9%	3.4%	3.5%	21.5%	3.2%
Female	13.6%	3.9%	3.6%	3.9%	21.6%	4.4%

Capabilities

South Africa's armed forces are the region's most capable on paper, but continuing economic and structural problems are eroding military capabilities. Its principal roles include maintaining territorial integrity and supporting the police service. A priority for the SANDF is to arrest the decline of critical military capabilities and equipment, but a lack of funds constrains its ability to renew equipment and meet performance targets. South Africa contributes personnel to UN operations, remains a key component of the Force Intervention Brigade in the DRC, and contributed forces to the SADC mission in Mozambique. Historically, the SANDF has also played a key role in training and supporting other regional forces. The SANDF can independently deploy its forces and it participates in national and multinational exercises as well as peacekeeping missions. However, reduced funding has undermined modernisation ambitions, resulting in delayed programmes and maintenance and availability challenges. Budget cuts are also likely to have afffected training. South Africa has the continent's most capable defence industry, including the state-owned Armaments Corporation of South Africa (ARMSCOR) and weapons manufacturer Denel, though both face financial difficulties.

ACTIVE 69,200 (Army 35,250 Navy 5,550 Air 8,900 South African Military Health Service 6,900 Other 12,600)

RESERVE 15,050 (Army 12,250 Navy 850 Air 850 South African Military Health Service Reserve 1,100)

ORGANISATIONS BY SERVICE

Army 35,250

FORCES BY ROLE
Regt are bn sized.
SPECIAL FORCES
2 SF regt(-)
MANOEUVRE
　Reconnaissance
　1 armd recce regt
　Armoured
　1 tk regt(-)
　Mechanised
　1 mech inf bde (2 mech inf bn, 1 mot inf bn)
　Light
　1 mot inf bde (2 mot inf bn)
　5 mot inf bn
　1 lt inf bde HQ
　1 lt inf bn
　Air Manoeuvre
　1 AB bde (1 AB bn, 1 air mob bn, 1 amph bn)
COMBAT SUPPORT
　1 arty regt
　1 engr regt
　1 construction regt
　4 sigs regt
COMBAT SERVICE SUPPORT
　1 engr spt regt
AIR DEFENCE
　1 ADA regt

Reserve 12,250 reservists (under-strength)
FORCES BY ROLE
MANOEUVRE
　Reconnaissance
　3 armd recce regt
　Armoured
　4 tk regt
　Mechanised
　6 mech inf bn
　Light
　1 mot inf bde HQ
　14 mot inf bn
　3 lt inf bn
　Air Manoeuvre
　1 AB bn
　2 air mob bn
　Amphibious
　1 amph bn
COMBAT SUPPORT
　2 SP arty regt
　2 fd arty regt
　1 MRL regt
　1 mor regt
　3 engr regt
　1 sigs regt

AIR DEFENCE
　5 AD regt
EQUIPMENT BY TYPE
ARMOURED FIGHTING VEHICLES
　MBT 24 *Olifant* 2 (133 *Olifant* 1B in store)
　ASLT 50 *Rooikat-76* (126 in store)
　IFV 534 *Ratel-20/Ratel-60/Ratel-90*
　APC • PPV 798: 358 *Casspir*; 60 *Mamba* (refurbished); 380 *Mamba*†
ENGINEERING & MAINTENANCE VEHICLES
　ARV *Gemsbok*
　VLB *Leguan*
　MW *Husky*
ANTI-TANK/ANTI-INFRASTRUCTURE
　MSL
　　SP ZT-3 *Swift*
　　MANPATS *Milan* ADT/ER
　RCL 106mm M40A1 (some SP)
ARTILLERY 1,240
　SP 155mm 2 G-6 (41 in store)
　TOWED 155mm 6 G-5 (66 in store)
　MRL 127mm 6 *Valkiri* Mk II MARS *Bataleur*; (26 *Valkiri* Mk I and 19 *Valkiri* Mk II in store)
　MOR 1,226: **81mm** 1,190 (incl some SP on *Casspir* & *Ratel*); **120mm** 36
UNINHABITED AERIAL VEHICLES
　ISR • Light ε4 *Vulture*
AIR DEFENCE
　SAM • Point-defence *Starstreak*
　GUNS 40
　　SP 23mm (36 *Zumlac* in store)
　　TOWED 35mm 40: 22 GDF-002; 18 GDF-005A/007

Navy 5,550
EQUIPMENT BY TYPE
SUBMARINES 2
　SSK 2 *Heroine* (GER Type-209/1400 mod) (1 additional boat in refit since 2014, awaiting funds to complete) with 8 533mm TT with SUT 264 HWT
PRINCIPAL SURFACE COMBATANTS • FRIGATES 4
　FFGHM 4 *Valour* (GER MEKO A200) with 2 quad lnchr with MM40 *Exocet* Block 2 AShM (upgrade to Block 3 planned); 2 16-cell VLS with *Umkhonto*-IR SAM, 1 Denel Dual Purpose Gun (DPG) CIWS, 1 76mm gun (capacity 1 *Super Lynx* 300 hel)
PATROL AND COASTAL COMBATANTS 4
　PCC 3: 1 *Warrior* (ISR *Reshef*) with 1 76mm gun; 2 *Warrior* II (NLD Damen Stan Patrol 6211)
　PB 1 *Tobie* (2 additional in reserve)
MINE WARFARE • MINE COUNTERMEASURES 2
　MHC 2 *River* (GER *Navors*) (limited operational roles; training and dive support) (2 more in reserve)
LOGISTICS AND SUPPORT 2

AGSH 1 *Protea* (UK *Hecla*) with 1 hel landing platform
AORH 1 *Drakensberg* (capacity 2 Oryx hels; 100 troops)

Maritime Reaction Squadron
FORCES BY ROLE
MANOEUVRE
  Amphibious
  1 mne patrol gp
  1 diving gp
  1 mne boarding gp
COMBAT SERVICE SUPPORT
  1 spt gp

Air Force 8,900
FORCES BY ROLE
FIGHTER/GROUND ATTACK
  1 sqn with *Gripen* C/D (JAS-39C/D)
GROUND ATTACK/TRAINING
1 sqn with *Hawk* Mk120*
TRANSPORT
  1 sqn with Beech 200 *King Air*; PC-12
  1 sqn with C-130BZ *Hercules*
  1 sqn with C-212-200/-300 *Aviocar*
  1 (VIP) sqn with B-737 BBJ; Cessna 550 *Citation* II; *Falcon* 50; *Falcon* 900
TRAINING
  1 unit with PC-7 Mk II *Astra*
  1 hel trg unit with AW109; *Oryx*
ATTACK HELICOPTER
  1 (cbt spt) sqn with AH-2 *Rooivalk*
TRANSPORT HELICOPTER
  4 (mixed) sqn with AW109; *Oryx*
EQUIPMENT BY TYPE
AIRCRAFT 27 combat capable
  FGA 3: 1 *Gripen* C (JAS-39C); 2 *Gripen* D (JAS-39D) (14 *Gripen* C; 7 *Gripen* D all non-operational)
  TPT 13: **Medium** 1 C-130BZ *Hercules* (4 more non-operational); **Light** 7: 2 Beech 200C *King Air* 1 C-212-200 *Aviocar*†; 1 C-212-300 *Aviocar*; 2 Cessna 550 *Citation* II; 1 PC-12†; (1 Beech 200C *King Air*; 1 Beech 300 *King Air*; 3 C-47TP; 9 Cessna 208 *Caravan* all non-operational); **PAX** 4: 1 B-737BBJ; 2 *Falcon* 50; 1 *Falcon* 900
  TRG 30: 24 *Hawk* Mk120* (of which 18†); 6 PC-7 Mk II *Astra* (29 more non-operational)
HELICOPTERS
  ATK 3 AH-2 *Rooivalk*† (8 more non-operational)
  MRH 1 *Super Lynx* 300 (3 more non-operational)
  TPT 11: **Medium** 5 *Oryx* (34 more non-operational); **Light** 14: 6 AW109; 8 BK-117 (of which 6†) (18 AW109 non-operational)
UNINHABITED AERIAL VEHICLES
  ISR • **Medium** 3+ *Seeker* 400
AIR-LAUNCHED MISSILES • **AAM** • IIR IRIS-T
BOMBS • **Laser-guided** GBU-12 *Paveway* II

Ground Defence
FORCES BY ROLE
MANOEUVRE
  Other
  12 sy sqn (SAAF regt)

South African Military Health Service 6,900

DEPLOYMENT
DEMOCRATIC REPUBLIC OF THE CONGO: SADC • SAMIDRC 600; UN • MONUSCO • *Operation Mistral* 1,135; 1 inf bn; 1 hel sqn
MOZAMBIQUE CHANNEL: Navy • 1 FFGHM

South Sudan SSD

South Sudanese Pound SSP		2023	2024	2025
GDP	SSP	6.69trn	13.5trn	28.9trn
	JSD	7.18bn	5.27bn	5.31bn
Real GDP growth	%	2.5	-26.4	27.2
Def bdgt [a]	SSP	60.3bn	142bn	
	USD	64.7m	55.7m	

[a] Security and law enforcement spending

Real-terms defence budget trend (USDm, constant 2015)

Population	12,703,714				
Age	0–14	15–19	20–24	25–29	30–64	65 plus
Male	21.5%	5.4%	5.0%	4.1%	13.6%	1.4%
Female	20.6%	5.3%	5.0%	3.7%	13.3%	1.2%

Capabilities

South Sudan's civil war formally ended in 2020, and a fragile cease-fire has largely remained intact. Although there has been some progress towards creating a unified force under the banner of the South Sudan People's Defence Forces (SSPDF), progress has been hampered by a lack of disarmament, demobilisation and reintegration for former rebels ineligible for inclusion. South Sudan lacks an independent capacity to deploy and sustain military units beyond national borders. Kenya facilitated a 2023 SSPDF deployment under the East African Community Regional Force. Equipment is primarily of Soviet origin, with some light arms of Chinese origin. There have been efforts to expand the small air force. Sanctions remain in place, with both the EU and UN arms embargoes widened in 2018 to include all types of military equipment. South Sudan has no domestic defence industry but has reportedly sought to develop an ammunition-manufacturing capacity.

ACTIVE 90,000 (Army 90,000)

ORGANISATIONS BY SERVICE

Army ε90,000

FORCES BY ROLE

3 military comd

MANOEUVRE

　Mechanised

　　1 lt mech div

　Light

　　10 inf div

　Other

　　1 gd div

COMBAT SUPPORT

　1 engr corps

EQUIPMENT BY TYPE

ARMOURED FIGHTING VEHICLES

　MBT 80+: some T-55†; 80 T-72AV†

　APC • PPV 10+: 10 Inkas *Titan-S*; Streit *Typhoon*; Streit *Cougar*; *Mamba*

ANTI-TANK/ANTI-INFRASTRUCTURE

　MSL • MANPATS HJ-73; 9K115 *Metis* (RS-AT-7 *Saxhorn*)

　RCL 73mm SPG-9 (with SSLA)

ARTILLERY

　SP 122mm 2S1 *Gvozdika*; **152mm** 2S3 *Akatsiya*

　TOWED 130mm Some M-46

　MRL 122mm BM-21 *Grad*; **107mm** PH-63

　MOR 82mm; **120mm** Type-55 look-alike

AIR DEFENCE

　SAM

　　Short-range 16 S-125 *Pechora* (RS-SA-3 *Goa*)†

　　Point-defence 9K32 *Strela*-2 (RS-SA-7 *Grail*)‡; QW-2

　GUNS 14.5mm ZPU-4; **23mm** ZU-23-2; **37mm** Type-65/74

Air Force

EQUIPMENT BY TYPE

AIRCRAFT 2 combat capable

　TPT • Light 1 Beech 1900

　TRG ε2 L-39 *Albatros**

HELICOPTERS

　ATK 3 Mi-24V/Mi-24V-SMB *Hind*

　MRH 5 Mi-17 *Hip H*

　TPT 2: **Medium** 1 Mi-172 (VIP); **Light** 1 AW109 (civ livery)

FOREIGN FORCES

All UNMISS, unless otherwise indicated

Albania 3
Australia 14
Azerbaijan 2
Bangladesh 1,631; 1 inf coy; 2 rvn coy; 2 engr coy
Benin 8
Bhutan 4
Bolivia 3
Brazil 12
Cambodia 85; 1 MP unit
Canada 9
China, People's Republic of 1,051; 1 inf bn; 1 engr coy; 1 fd hospital
Ecuador 3
Egypt 7
El Salvador 2
Ethiopia 1,524; 2 inf bn
Fiji 2
Gambia 4
Germany 11
Ghana 737; 1 inf bn
Guatemala 6
Guinea 3
India 2,404; 2 inf bn; 1 engr coy; 1 sigs coy; 2 fd hospital
Indonesia 4
Japan 4
Jordan 5
Kenya 18
Korea, Republic of 278; 1 engr coy
Kyrgyzstan 2
Liberia 2
Malawi 6
Moldova 4
Mongolia 872; 1 inf bn
Morocco 3
Namibia 5
Nepal 1,754; 2 inf bn
New Zealand 3
Nigeria 14
Norway 14
Pakistan 292; 1 engr coy
Papua New Guinea 2
Paraguay 3
Peru 4
Philippines 2
Poland 1
Romania 5
Russia 4
Rwanda 2,636; 3 inf bn; 1 hel sqn with 6 Mi-17
Sierra Leone 2
Sri Lanka 66; 1 fd hospital; 1 hel sqn
Switzerland 1
Tanzania 9
Thailand 283; 1 engr coy
Timor-Leste 2
Togo 2
Tunisia 2
Uganda 1
United Kingdom 4
United States 7
Vietnam 68; 1 fd hospital
Zambia 11
Zimbabwe 11

Sudan SDN

Sudanese Pound SDG		2023	2024	2025
GDP	SDG	26.8trn	64.8trn	154trn
	USD	38.1bn	29.8bn	30.0bn
Real GDP growth	%	-18.3	-20.3	8.3
Def bdgt	SDG	n.k	n.k	n.k
	USD	n.k	n.k	n.k
Population	50,467,278			

Age	0–14	15–19	20–24	25–29	30–64	65 plus
Male	20.4%	5.8%	5.1%	3.9%	13.3%	1.7%
Female	19.7%	5.7%	5.0%	3.7%	14.1%	1.6%

Capabilities

In mid-April 2023, fighting broke out between Sudan's regular armed forces and the paramilitary Rapid Support Forces. This followed internal divisions within the military junta that seized power in October 2021. The conflict has displaced millions with allegations of war crimes against civilians and has continued into 2024. Sudan also has border disputes with neighbouring Ethiopia. Sudan was part of the initial Saudi-led coalition that intervened in Yemen. Sudan struck a defence agreement with Iran in 2008 that reportedly included assistance in developing its domestic arms industry. Despite the current conflict, the Sudanese authorities have maintained close ties with Egypt after joint exercises in 2020 and 2021. The two signed an agreement to strengthen military cooperation in 2021. A UN arms embargo remains in place, though this is limited to equipment in the Darfur region, and there have been sustained reports that the embargo is being violated. The state-run Defense Industries System, formerly known as Military Industry Corporation, manufactures a range of ammunition, small arms and armoured vehicles and is under sanctions including by the US and the EU. The majority of the corporation's products are based on older Chinese and Russian systems.

ACTIVE 104,300 (Army 100,000 Navy 1,300 Air 3,000) Gendarmerie & Paramilitary 60,000

Conscript liability 2 years for males aged 18–30

ORGANISATIONS BY SERVICE

Space
EQUIPMENT BY TYPE
SATELLITES • ISR 1 SRSS-1

Army 100,000+
FORCES BY ROLE
SPECIAL FORCES
  5 SF coy
MANOEUVRE
  Reconnaissance
  1 indep recce bde
  Armoured
  1 armd div
  Mechanised
  1 mech inf div
  1 indep mech inf bde
  Light
  15+ inf div
  6 indep inf bde
  Air Manoeuvre
  1 air aslt bde
  Amphibious
  1 mne div
  Other
  1 (Border Guard) sy bde
COMBAT SUPPORT
  3 indep arty bde
  1 engr div (9 engr bn)
EQUIPMENT BY TYPE†
ARMOURED FIGHTING VEHICLES
  MBT *Al-Bashier* (Type-85-IIM); T-55A/AMV; T-72AV/B; Type-59D
  LT TK ZTQ-62; ZTS-63
  RECCE BRDM-2; *Cayman* BRDM
  IFV BMP-1; BMP-2; BTR-3; BTR-80A; WZ-523 IFV
  APC
    APC (T) BTR-50; M113
    APC (W) BTR-70M *Kobra* 2; BTR-152; OT-62; OT-64; *Rakhsh*; V-150 *Commando*; *Walid*; WZ-551; WZ-523
    PPV *Al-Wahsh*; *Sarsar*-2; Streit *Spartan*
  AUV MCAV-20; Nimr *Ajban* 440A
ANTI-TANK/ANTI-INFRASTRUCTURE
  MSL • MANPATS 9K11 *Malyutka* (RS-AT-3 *Sagger*); HJ-8; 9K135 *Kornet* (RS-AT-14 *Spriggan*)
  RCL 106mm M40A1
  GUNS 76mm ZIS-3; 100mm M-1944; 85mm D-44
ARTILLERY
  SP 122mm 2S1 *Gvozdika*; 155mm Mk F3
  TOWED 105mm M101; 122mm D-30; D-74; M-30; 130mm M-46; PL-59-I; 155mm M114A1
  MRL 107mm PH-63; 122mm BM-21 *Grad*; *Saqr*; PHL-81; 302mm WS-1
  MOR 81mm; 82mm; 120mm AM-49; *Boragh*; M-43; W86
AIR DEFENCE
  SAM • Point-defence 9K32M *Strela*-2M (RS-SA-7B *Grail*)‡; 9K33 *Osa* (RS-SA-8 *Gecko*); FN-6 (CH-SA-10)
  GUNS
    SP 20mm M163 *Vulcan*; M3 VDAA
    TOWED 14.5mm ZPU-2; 14.5mm ZPU-4; 20mm M167 *Vulcan*; 23mm ZU-23-2; 37mm Type-63; M-1939; 57mm S-60; 85mm M-1944

Navy 1,300
EQUIPMENT BY TYPE
PATROL AND COASTAL COMBATANTS 11
  PB 8: 2 13.5m; 1 14m; 2 19m; 3 41m (PRC)
  PBR 3 *Kurmuk*

AMPHIBIOUS • LANDING CRAFT • LCVP 5†
LOGISTICS AND SUPPORT 4
    AG 3
    AXL 1 *Petrushka* (ex-RUS)

Air Force 3,000
FORCES BY ROLE
FIGHTER
    2 sqn with MiG-29SE/UB *Fulcrum*
FIGHTER/GROUND ATTACK
    1 sqn with FTC-2000G
GROUND ATTACK
    1 sqn with Su-24M/MR *Fencer*
    1 sqn with Su-25K/UB *Frogfoot*
TRANSPORT
    Some sqn with An-30 *Clank*; An-32 *Cline*; An-72 *Coaler*; An-74TK-200/-300; C-130H *Hercules*; Il-76 *Candid*; Y-8
    1 VIP unit with *Falcon* 50; *Falcon* 900
TRAINING
    1 sqn with K-8 *Karakorum**
ATTACK HELICOPTER
    2 sqn with Mi-24/Mi-24P/Mi-24V/Mi-35P *Hind*
TRANSPORT HELICOPTER
    2 sqn with Mi-8 *Hip*; Mi-17 *Hip H*; Mi-171
EQUIPMENT BY TYPE
AIRCRAFT 42 combat capable
    FTR ε20 MiG-29SE/UB *Fulcrum* C/B
    FGA 3 FTC-2000G
    ATK 11: ε5 Su-24M/MR *Fencer*; ε6 Su-25K/UB *Frogfoot*; (15 A-5 *Fantan* in store)
    ISR 2 An-30 *Clank*
    TPT 18: **Heavy** 1 Il-76 *Candid*; **Medium** 3: 1 C-130H *Hercules*; 2 Y-8; **Light** 12: ε3 An-26 *Curl*; 2 An-32 *Cline*; 1 An-72 *Coaler*; 4 An-74TK-200; 2 An-74TK-300; **PAX** 2: 1 *Falcon* 50 (VIP); 1 *Falcon* 900
    TRG 11+: ε8 K-8 *Karakorum**; some SAFAT-03; 3 Utva-75
HELICOPTERS
    ATK ε11 Mi-24/Mi-24P/Mi-24V/Mi-35P *Hind*
    MRH ε3 Mi-17 *Hip H*
    TPT 7: **Medium** ε4 Mi-8 *Hip*/Mi-171; **Light** 3: 1 Bell 205; 2 Bo-105
    TRG some SAFAT 02
UNINHABITED AERIAL VEHICLES
    CISR • Heavy CH-3; CH-4; **Medium** *Mohajer*-6 (reported)
    ISR • Medium *Ababil* 2; *Ababil* 3
AIR DEFENCE • SAM • Medium-range: (18 S-75M *Dvina* (RS-SA-2 *Guideline*)‡ (non-operational))
AIR-LAUNCHED MISSILES • AAM • IR R-3 (RS-AA-2 *Atoll*)‡; R-60 (RS-AA-8 *Aphid*); R-73 (RS-AA-11A *Archer*); **ARH** R-77 (RS-AA-12A *Adder*)

Gendarmerie & Paramilitary 60,000

Central Reserve Police 60,000

TERRITORY WHERE THE GOVERNMENT DOES NOT EXERCISE EFFECTIVE CONTROL

Data here represents the de facto situation. This does not imply international recognition. The Rapid Support Forces exercise de facto control over large parts of western and southwestern Sudan, as well as significant parts of Khartoum and the surrounding area.

Rapid Support Forces 100,000+
EQUIPMENT BY TYPE
ARMOURED FIGHTING VEHICLES
    MBT T-55
    IFV BTR-80A; WZ-523 IFV
    APC • APC (W) BTR-70M *Kobra* 2
ANTI-TANK/ANTI-INFRASTRUCTURE
    MSL • MANPATS HJ-8
ARTILLERY
    SP 122mm *Khalifa*-1 (reported)
    MRL 107mm PH-63
    MOR 120mm M-74
AIR DEFENCE
    SAM • Point-defence 9K32M *Strela*-2M (RS-SA-7 *Grail*)‡; 9K38 *Igla* (RS-SA-18 *Grouse*); 9K338 Igla-S (RS-SA-24 *Grinch*); FN-6 (CH-SA-10); HN-5 (CH-SA-3)
    GUNS • SP 14.5mm ZPU-2 (tch); **23mm** ZU-23-2 (tch)

FOREIGN FORCES
All UNISFA unless otherwise indicated
Albania 1
Bangladesh 711; 1 inf bn(-)
Benin 2
Bhutan 2
Bolivia 4
Brazil 5
Burkina Faso 1
Burundi 3
Cambodia 1
China, People's Republic of 284; 1 inf coy; 1 hel flt with 2 Mi-171
Ecuador 2
Egypt 5
El Salvador 1
Gambia 1
Ghana 664; 1 inf bn; 1 fd hospital
Guatemala 3
Guinea 1
India 593; 1 mech inf bn(-)
Indonesia 4
Kenya 3
Kyrgyzstan 2
Liberia 2
Malawi 7
Malaysia 2
Mauritania 3

Mongolia 3
Morocco 5
Namibia 5
Nepal 107; 1 log coy
Nigeria 186; 1 inf coy
Pakistan 593; 1 inf bn(-)
Peru 3
Rwanda 4
Sierra Leone 4
Tanzania 1
Thailand 2
Tunisia 2
Uganda 2
Uruguay 2
Vietnam 192; 1 engr coy
Zambia 4
Zimbabwe 8

Tanzania TZA

Tanzanian Shilling TZS		2023	2024	2025
GDP	TZS	189trn	208trn	230trn
	USD	79.1bn	79.9bn	85.5bn
Real GDP growth	%	5.1	5.4	6.0
Def bdgt	TZS	2.71trn	2.99trn	3.33trn
	USD	1.14bn	1.15bn	1.23bn

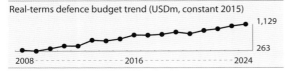

Population   67,462,121

Age	0–14	15–19	20–24	25–29	30–64	65 plus
Male	20.8%	5.4%	4.6%	3.9%	13.9%	1.4%
Female	20.4%	5.3%	4.5%	3.8%	14.1%	2.0%

Capabilities

Non-state actors pose the principal threat to Tanzania's security, with terrorism, poaching and piracy being of concern. In 2024, Tanzania hosted exercise Peace Unity 2024, which saw China dispatch troops and equipment to the country by air and sea. The armed forces take part in multinational exercises and have provided some training assistance to other African forces. Training relationships exist with other extra-regional armed forces, including the US. Tanzania's contribution to the UN's Force Intervention Brigade in the eastern DRC, notably its special forces, will have provided lessons for force development. However, there is only a limited capacity to project power independently beyond the country's borders. Budget constraints have limited recapitalisation, and heavy equipment is ageing. There are local ammunition facilities, but otherwise, Tanzania relies on imports for its military equipment.

ACTIVE 27,000 (Army 23,000 Navy 1,000 Air 3,000)
Gendarmerie & Paramilitary 1,400

Conscript liability Three months basic military training combined with social service, ages 18–23

RESERVE 80,000 (Joint 80,000)

ORGANISATIONS BY SERVICE

Army ε23,000
FORCES BY ROLE
SPECIAL FORCES
  1 SF unit
MANOEUVRE
  Armoured
  1 tk bde
  Light
  5 inf bde
COMBAT SUPPORT
  4 arty bn
  1 mor bn
  2 AT bn
  1 engr regt (bn)
COMBAT SERVICE SUPPORT
  1 log gp
AIR DEFENCE
  2 ADA bn
EQUIPMENT BY TYPE†
ARMOURED FIGHTING VEHICLES
  MBT 46: 30 T-54/T-55; 15 Type-59G; 1+ VT-2
  LT TK 57+: 30 FV101 *Scorpion*; 25 Type-62; 2+ Type-63A
  RECCE 10 BRDM-2
  APC • APC (W) 14: ε10 BTR-40/BTR-152; 4 Type-92
ANTI-TANK/ANTI-INFRASTRUCTURE
  RCL 75mm Type-52 (M20)
  GUNS 85mm 75 Type-56 (D-44)
ARTILLERY 344+
  TOWED 130: 122mm 100: 20 D-30; 80 Type-54-1 (M-30); 130mm 30 Type-59-I
  GUN/MOR 120mm 3+ Type-07PA
  MRL 61+: 122mm 58 BM-21 *Grad*; 300mm 3+ A100
  MOR 150: 82mm 100 M-43; 120mm 50 M-43

Navy ε1,000
EQUIPMENT BY TYPE
PATROL AND COASTAL COMBATANTS 14
  PCC 2 *Mwitongo* (ex-PRC *Haiqing*)
  PHT 2 Type-025 (ex-PRC *Huchuan*) each with 2 single 533mm ASTT
  PB 10: 2 *Ngunguri* (ex-UK *Protector*); 2 VT 23m; 4 *Mambwe* (Damen Fast Crew Supplier 3307); 2 41m
AMPHIBIOUS • LANDING CRAFT 3
  LCT 1 *Kasa*
  LCM 2 *Mbono* (ex-PRC *Yunnan*)

Air Defence Command ε3,000
FORCES BY ROLE
FIGHTER
  3 sqn with F-7/FT-7; FT-5; K-8 *Karakorum**

TRANSPORT
1 sqn with Cessna 404 *Titan*; DHC-5D *Buffalo*; F-28 *Fellowship*; F-50; Gulfstream G550; Y-12 (II)

TRANSPORT HELICOPTER
1 sqn with H215; H225

EQUIPMENT BY TYPE†

AIRCRAFT 16 combat capable
  FTR 11: 9 F-7 (F-7TN); 2 FT-7 (FT-7N)
  ISR 1 SB7L-360 *Seeker*
  TPT 12: **Medium** 2 Y-8; **Light** 7: 2 Cessna 404 *Titan*; 3 DHC-5D *Buffalo*; 2 Y-12(II); **PAX** 3: 1 F-28 *Fellowship*; 1 F-50; 1 Gulfstream G550
  TRG 8: 3 FT-5 (JJ-5); 5 K-8 *Karakorum**

HELICOPTERS
  TPT • Medium 4: 2 H215; 2 H225

AIR DEFENCE
  SAM
    Short-range 2K12 *Kub* (RS-SA-6 *Gainful*)†
    Point-defence 9K32 *Strela*-2 (RS-SA-7 *Grail*)‡
  GUNS 200
    TOWED 14.5mm 40 ZPU-2/ZPU-4†; **23mm** 40 ZU-23-2; **37mm** 120 M-1939

Gendarmerie & Paramilitary 1,400 active

Police Field Force 1,400
18 sub-units incl Police Marine Unit

Air Wing
EQUIPMENT BY TYPE
AIRCRAFT • TPT • Light 1 Cessna U206 *Stationair*
HELICOPTERS
  TPT • Light 4: 2 Bell 206A *Jet Ranger* (AB-206A); 2 Bell 206L *Long Ranger*
  TRG 2 Bell 47G (AB-47G)/Bell 47G2

Marine Unit 100
EQUIPMENT BY TYPE
PATROL AND COASTAL COMBATANTS
All operational patrol vessels under 10t FLD

DEPLOYMENT

CENTRAL AFRICAN REPUBLIC: UN • MINUSCA 516; 1 inf bn(-)

DEMOCRATIC REPUBLIC OF THE CONGO: SADC • SAMIDRC 300; **UN •** MONUSCO 859; 1 spec ops coy; 1 inf bn

LEBANON: UN • UNIFIL 125; 1 MP coy

MOZAMBIQUE: Army: 290

SOUTH SUDAN: UN • UNMISS 9

SUDAN: UN • UNISFA 1

Togo TGO

CFA Franc BCEAO XOF		2023	2024	2025
GDP	XOF	5.51trn	5.93trn	6.37trn
	USD	9.08bn	9.77bn	10.5bn
Real GDP growth	%	5.6	5.3	5.3
Def bdgt	XOF	120bn	118bn	
	USD	197m	195m	

Population 8,917,994

Age	0–14	15–19	20–24	25–29	30–64	65 plus
Male	19.6%	5.1%	4.2%	3.6%	14.9%	1.8%
Female	19.1%	5.0%	4.3%	3.7%	16.1%	2.5%

Capabilities

Security in the north has deteriorated in the face of jihadist activity, while piracy and illicit maritime activities in the Gulf of Guinea also cause concern. As a result, the government is pursuing stronger regional cooperation. In 2020, Togo adopted a new military-programming law, leading to the creation of a special forces group. Togo plans to bolster its forces and recently acquired modern APCs and armed UAVs. France continues to provide military training, including for Togolese peacekeeping contingents. The country also hosts a peacekeeping training centre in Lomé. The armed forces have taken part in multilateral exercises, including the US-led *Obangame Express*. Togo's deployment capabilities are limited without external support, while financial challenges limit capability development more broadly. Togo is home to limited maintenance facilities and lacks a defence-manufacturing sector.

ACTIVE 13,750 (Army 13,000 Navy 500 Air 250)
Gendarmerie & Paramilitary 5,000

Conscript liability Selective conscription, 2 years

ORGANISATIONS BY SERVICE

Army ε13,000
FORCES BY ROLE
MANOEUVRE
  Reconnaissance
  1 armd recce regt
  Mechanised
  1 armd bn
  Light
  2 cbd arms regt
  2 inf regt
  1 mot inf bn
  2 inf bn (rapid intervention)
  Air Manoeuvre
  1 cdo/para regt (3 cdo/para coy)

Other
1 (Presidential Guard) gd regt (1 gd bn, 1 cdo bn, 2 indep gd coy)
COMBAT SUPPORT
1 cbt spt regt (1 fd arty bty, 2 ADA bty, 1 engr/log/tpt bn)
EQUIPMENT BY TYPE
ARMOURED FIGHTING VEHICLES
MBT 2 T-54/T-55
LT TK 18 FV101 Scorpion
RECCE 55: 3 AML-60; 7 AML-90; 36 EE-9 Cascavel; 6 M8; 3 M20
IFV 20 BMP-2
APC 90
  APC (T) 4 M3A1 half-track
  APC (W) 36: 6 Mbombe 4; 30 UR-416
  PPV 50 Mamba Mk7
AUV 32: 29 Bastion Patsas; 1 FV103 Spartan; 2 VBL
ANTI-TANK/ANTI-INFRASTRUCTURE
RCL 75mm Type-52 (M20)/Type-56; 82mm Type-65 (B-10)
GUNS 57mm 5 ZIS-2
ARTILLERY 30+
SP 122mm 6
TOWED 105mm 4 HM-2
MRL 122mm PHL-81 mod (SC6 chassis)
MOR 82mm 20 M-43
AIR DEFENCE • GUNS • TOWED 43 14.5mm 38 ZPU-4; 37mm 5 M-1939

Navy ε500 (incl Marine Infantry unit)
EQUIPMENT BY TYPE
PATROL AND COASTAL COMBATANTS 4
  PBF 2 Agou (FRA Raidco RPB 33)
  PB 2: 1 Fazao (PRC 27m); 1 Kara (FRA Esterel)

Air Force 250
FORCES BY ROLE
TRANSPORT
1 sqn with Beech 200 King Air
1 VIP unit with DC-8; F-28-1000
TRAINING
1 sqn with TB-30 Epsilon*
TRANSPORT HELICOPTER
1 sqn with SA315 Lama; SA316 Alouette III; SA319 Alouette III; SA342L1 Gazelle
EQUIPMENT BY TYPE†
AIRCRAFT 3 combat capable
  TPT 5: Light 2 Beech 200 King Air; PAX 3: 1 DC-8; 2 F-28-1000 (VIP)
  TRG 3 TB-30 Epsilon* (3 Alpha Jet*; 4 EMB-326G* in store)
HELICOPTERS
  ATK 2 Mi-35M Hind
  MRH 8: 2 Mi-17 Hip H (reported); 2 SA315 Lama; 1 SA316 Alouette III; 1 SA319 Alouette III; 2 SA342L1 Gazelle
  TPT • Medium 2 Mi-8T Hip C
UNINHABITED AERIAL VEHICLES
  CISR • Medium Bayraktar TB2
BOMBS • Laser-guided MAM-L

Special Forces Group
FORCES BY ROLE
SPECIAL FORCES
1 SF unit

Gendarmerie & Paramilitary 5,000

Gendarmerie ε5,000
Ministry of Interior
FORCES BY ROLE
SPECIAL FORCES
  1 SF unit
MANOEUVRE
  Other
  1 (mobile) paramilitary sqn
ARMOURED FIGHTING VEHICLES • APC:
  APC (W) Bastion APC
  PPV Mamba Mk7

DEPLOYMENT
CENTRAL AFRICAN REPUBLIC: UN • MINUSCA 11
SOUTH SUDAN: UN • UNMISS 2
WESTERN SAHARA: UN • MINURSO 3

Uganda UGA

Ugandan Shilling UGX		2023	2024	2025
GDP	UGX	190trn	211trn	237trn
	USD	51.1bn	55.6bn	62.9bn
Real GDP growth	%	4.6	5.9	7.5
Def bdgt	UGX	3.77trn	4.08trn	4.75trn
	USD	1.01bn	1.07bn	1.26bn

Real-terms defence budget trend (USDm, constant 2015)

Population	49,283,041				
Age	0–14	15–19	20–24	25–29	30–64	65 plus
Male	23.8%	5.7%	4.5%	3.4%	10.4%	1.0%
Female	23.2%	5.7%	4.8%	3.9%	12.3%	1.4%

Capabilities
Uganda's armed forces are well-equipped and are important contributors to East African security. Operational experience and training have led to improvements in administration and planning, as

well as in military skills. Uganda is one of the largest contributors to the East Africa Standby Force and, in 2014, signed a Mutual Defence Treaty with Kenya and Rwanda. Forces train regularly with international partners, including at Ugandan facilities. Airlift is limited, though rotary-wing aviation has improved in recent years. Mechanised forces are relatively well equipped, though equipment is disparate and ageing. Uganda has limited defence-industrial capacity, with some manufacturing of light armoured vehicles, though, in late 2023, the UPDF announced plans to establish, with China's NORINCO, a UAV final assembly, testing and maintenance facility in the country.

ACTIVE 45,000 (Ugandan People's Defence Force 45,000) Gendarmerie & Paramilitary 1,400

RESERVE 10,000

ORGANISATIONS BY SERVICE

Ugandan People's Defence Force ε40,000–45,000

FORCES BY ROLE

MANOEUVRE

Armoured
1 armd bde

Light
1 cdo bn
5 inf div (3 inf bde)
1 mtn div (3 mtn inf bde)

Other
1 (Special Forces Command) mot bde

COMBAT SUPPORT
1 arty bde

AIR DEFENCE
2 AD bn

EQUIPMENT BY TYPE†

ARMOURED FIGHTING VEHICLES
 MBT 279+: 140 T-54/T-55; 45 T-55AM2; 40 T-72A; 10 T-72B1; 44 T-90S; some ZTZ-85-IIM
 LT TK ε20 PT-76
 RECCE 46: 40 Eland-20; 6 FV701 Ferret
 IFV 39: 37 BMP-2; 2+ VN2C
 APC 185
  APC (W) 58: 15 BTR-60; 20 Buffel; 4 OT-64; 19 Bastion APC
  PPV 127+: 42 Casspir; some Chui; 35 Hizir; 40 Mamba; 10 RG-33L
  AUV 15 Cougar

ENGINEERING & MAINTENANCE VEHICLES
 ARV 1 BTS-4; T-54/T-55 reported
 VLB MTU reported
 MW Husky

ARTILLERY 337+
 SP 155mm 6 ATMOS 2000
 TOWED 243+: 122mm M-30; 130mm 221; 155mm 22: 4 G-5; 18 M-839
 MRL 6+: 107mm (12-tube); 122mm 6+: BM-21 Grad; 6 RM-70
 MOR 82+: 81mm L16; 82mm M-43; 120mm 78 Soltam; SP 120mm 4+ SandCat with Spear

AIR DEFENCE
 SAM • Point-defence 9K32 Strela-2 (RS-SA-7 Grail)‡; 9K310 Igla-1 (RS-SA-16 Gimlet)
 GUNS • TOWED 20+: 14.5mm ZPU-1/ZPU-2/ZPU-4; 37mm 20 M-1939

Marines ε400

All operational patrol vessels under 10t FLD

FORCES BY ROLE

MANOEUVRE

Amphibious
1 mne bn

Air Wing

FORCES BY ROLE

FIGHTER/GROUND ATTACK
1 sqn with Su-30MK2 Flanker

TRANSPORT
1 unit with Cessna 208B; Y-12
1 VIP unit with Gulfstream 550

TRAINING
1 unit with Cessna 172; L-39ZA/ZO Albatros*

ATTACK/TRANSPORT HELICOPTER
1 sqn with Bell 205 (UH-1H Iroquois); Bell 412 Twin Huey; Mi-17/Mi-17A1/Mi-171E Hip; Mi-24V/P Hind E/F; Mi-28N/UB Havoc

EQUIPMENT BY TYPE

AIRCRAFT 13 combat capable
 FGA 6 Su-30MK2 Flanker (3+ MiG-21bis Fishbed; 1 MiG-21UM Mongol B non-operational)
 TPT 9: Light 8: 4 Cessna 172; 2 Cessna 208B; 2 Y-12; PAX 1 Gulfstream 550
 TRG 7 L-39ZA/ZO Albatros*

HELICOPTERS
 ATK 9: ε6 Mi-24V/P Hind E/F; 3+ Mi-28N/UB Havoc
 MRH 7: 2 Bell 412 Twin Huey; 5 Mi-17/Mi-171E Hip
 TPT 6: Medium 1 Mi-171A1 (VIP); Light 5 Bell 205 (UH-1H Iroquois)

AIR-LAUNCHED MISSILES
 AAM • IR R-73 (RS-AA-11A Archer); SARH R-27 (RS-AA-10 Alamo); ARH R-77 (RS-AA-12 Adder)
 ARM Kh-31P (RS-AS-17A Krypton) (reported)

Gendarmerie & Paramilitary ε600 active

Border Defence Unit ε600

Equipped with small arms only

DEPLOYMENT

DEMOCRATIC REPUBLIC OF THE CONGO: Army: 3,000; 1 inf bde

SOMALIA: AU • ATMIS 4,100; 3 inf bn; **UN** • UNSOM 627; 1 sy bn; **UN** • UNSOS 2
SOUTH SUDAN: UN • UNMISS 1
SUDAN: UN • UNISFA 2

Zambia ZMB

Zambian Kwacha ZMW		2023	2024	2025
GDP	ZMW	569bn	700bn	820bn
	USD	28.2bn	25.9bn	31.8bn
Real GDP growth	%	5.4	2.3	6.6
Def bdgt	ZMW	8.15bn	9.92bn	10.3bn
	USD	403m	367m	401m

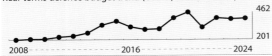
Real-terms defence budget trend (USDm, constant 2015)

Population 20,799,116

Age	0–14	15–19	20–24	25–29	30–64	65 plus
Male	21.2%	5.7%	4.7%	3.9%	13.3%	1.3%
Female	20.9%	5.7%	4.7%	3.9%	13.4%	1.5%

Capabilities

Zambia's armed forces are responsible for territorial integrity, border security, and participating in peacekeeping operations. However, their effectiveness is complicated by equipment obsolescence and a relatively small force. The country has emergent ties with China, including on military training and weapons sales. It has also acquired equipment from Israeli firms. The armed forces have participated in exercises with international and regional partners, including for the SADC Standby Force. Zambia's largest peacekeeping contribution is to the MINUSCA operation in the Central African Republic. In April 2017, Zambia signed a defence deal with Russia for spare-parts support. The US has provided funding and material support for army and air-force pre-deployment training as well as for general military training. The armed forces have limited capacity to independently deploy and sustain forces beyond national borders. The defence industry is limited to ammunition production.

ACTIVE 17,100 (Army 15,500 Air 1,600)
Gendarmerie & Paramilitary 1,400

RESERVE 3,000 (Army 3,000)

ORGANISATIONS BY SERVICE

Army 13,500
FORCES BY ROLE
COMMAND
  3 bde HQ
SPECIAL FORCES
  1 cdo bn
  1 cdo unit
MANOEUVRE
  Reconnaissance
  1 armd recce regt
  Armoured
  1 armd regt (1 tk bn)
  Mechanised
  1 mech inf bn
  Light
  5 inf bn
COMBAT SUPPORT
  1 arty regt (2 fd arty bn, 1 MRL bn)
  1 engr bn
  1 construction bde
  1 construction regt
AIR DEFENCE
  1 ADA regt
EQUIPMENT BY TYPE
Some equipment†
ARMOURED FIGHTING VEHICLES
  MBT 30: 10 T-55; 20 ZTZ-59
  LT TK 32 PT-76
  RECCE 35 BRDM-1/BRDM-2
  IFV 23 *Ratel*-20
  APC • APC (W) 47+: 13 BTR-60; 20 BTR-70; 10 BTR-80; 4+ WZ-551
  AUV 22 *Tigr*
ANTI-TANK/ANTI-INFRASTRUCTURE
  MSL • MANPATS 9K11 *Malyutka* (RS-AT-3 *Sagger*)
  RCL 12+: **57mm** 12 M18; **75mm** M20; **84mm** *Carl Gustaf*
ARTILLERY 172
  SP 6 ATMOS M-46
  TOWED 61: **105mm** 18 Model 56 pack howitzer; **122mm** 25 D-30; **130mm** 18 M-46
  MRL 122mm 18 BM-21 *Grad*
  MOR 97: **81mm** 55; **82mm** 24; **120mm** 12; **SP 120mm** 6+ Elbit *Spear* Mk2
AIR DEFENCE
  SAM • MANPAD 9K32 *Strela*-2 (RS-SA-7 *Grail*)‡
  GUNS
    SP 23mm 4 ZSU-23-4 *Shilka*
    TOWED 125: **14.5mm** ZPU-4; **20mm** 25 M-55 (triple); **23mm** ZU-23; **37mm** 47 M-1939; PG-65; **40mm** L/70; **57mm** 37 S-60; **85mm** 16 M-1939 (KS-12)

Reserve 3,000
FORCES BY ROLE
MANOEUVRE
  Light
  3 inf bn

Air Force 1,600
FORCES BY ROLE
FIGHTER/GROUND ATTACK

1 sqn with K-8 *Karakorum**
1 sqn with L-15*

TRANSPORT
1 sqn with MA60; Y-12(II); Y-12(IV)
1 (VIP) unit with AW139; HS-748
1 (liaison) sqn with Do-28

TRAINING
1 sqn with MFI-15 *Safari*

TRANSPORT HELICOPTER
1 sqn with Bell 412EP; Enstrom 480B; Mi-17 *Hip* H
1 (liaison) sqn with Bell 205 (UH-1H *Iroquois*/AB-205)

AIR DEFENCE
2 bty with S-125M *Pechora*-M (RS-SA-3 *Goa*)

EQUIPMENT BY TYPE†
Very low serviceability

AIRCRAFT 21 combat capable
TPT 19: Medium 2 C-27J *Spartan*; Light 15: 1 Cessna 208B *Grand Caravan*; 5 Do-28; 2 MA60; 3 Y-12(II); 4 Y-12(IV); PAX 2: 1 Gulfstream G650ER; 1 HS-748
TRG 40: 15 K-8 *Karakorum**; 6 L-15*; 8 MFI-15 *Safari*; 11 SF-260TW

HELICOPTERS
MRH 11: 1 AW139; 2 Bell 412EP; 4 Mi-17 *Hip* H; 4 Z-9
TPT • Light 14: 9 Bell 205 (UH-1H *Iroquois*/AB-205); 3 Bell 212 ; 2 Enstrom 480B

UNINHABITED AERIAL VEHICLES 3+
ISR • Medium 3+ *Hermes* 450

AIR DEFENCE
SAM • Short-range 6 S-125M *Pechora*-M (RS-SA-3 *Goa*)

AIR-LAUNCHED MISSILES
AAM • IR PL-5E-II
ASM 9K11 *Malyutka* (RS-AT-3 *Sagger*)

Gendarmerie & Paramilitary 1,400

Police Mobile Unit 700
FORCES BY ROLE
MANOEUVRE
  Other
    1 police bn (4 police coy)

Police Paramilitary Unit 700
FORCES BY ROLE
MANOEUVRE
  Other
    1 paramilitary bn (3 paramilitary coy)
EQUIPMENT BY TYPE
ARMOURED FIGHTING VEHICLES
  APC • PPV 9+: 3+ *Marauder*; 6 CS/VP3

DEPLOYMENT

CENTRAL AFRICAN REPUBLIC: UN • MINUSCA 934; 1 inf bn

DEMOCRATIC REPUBLIC OF THE CONGO: UN • MONUSCO 6
LEBANON: UN • UNIFIL 2
MIDDLE EAST: UN • UNTSO 1
SOUTH SUDAN: UN • UNMISS 11
SUDAN: UN • UNISFA 4
SYRIA/ISRAEL: UN UNDOF 3

Zimbabwe ZWE

Zimbabwe Dollar ZiG [1]		2023	2024	2025
GDP	ZiG	53.5bn	423bn	554bn
	USD	35.2bn	35.9bn	36.9bn
Real GDP growth	%	5.3	2.0	6.0
Def bdgt	ZiG	149m	1.89bn	
	USD	98.0m	161m	

[1] New currency issued in April 2024. Fluctuating valuations mean conversions to USD are indicative measures only

Real-terms defence budget trend (USDm, constant 2015)

Population	17,150,352					
Age	0–14	15–19	20–24	25–29	30–64	65 plus
Male	19.3%	4.7%	4.6%	4.0%	14.5%	1.6%
Female	19.0%	4.8%	4.7%	4.2%	16.3%	2.3%

Capabilities

Political instability and a weak economy remain key challenges for the government. Principal tasks for the Zimbabwe Defence Forces (ZDF) include ensuring territorial integrity, border security, and support to the police. The armed forces take an active political role. Zimbabwe is a member of the AU and the SADC and takes part in SADC Standby Force exercises. Zimbabwe sent troops as part of the SADC deployment to Mozambique. The country has defence ties with China and Russia, and links with India, Pakistan, Indonesia and Malaysia for military training. The government intends to improve defence infrastructure including housing and medical facilities, and ZDF leaders have identified training as a development priority. Equipment recapitalisation is a priority, including of armoured vehicles, though progress will depend on the country's economic health and, perhaps, the extent of Chinese and Russian support. A number of arms embargos remain in place. There are plans to revive state-owned small-arms and munitions manufacturer Zimbabwe Defence Industries, although these may be hindered by continuing Western sanctions.

ACTIVE 29,000 (Army 25,000 Air 4,000)
Gendarmerie & Paramilitary 21,800

ORGANISATIONS BY SERVICE

Army ε25,000
FORCES BY ROLE

SPECIAL FORCES
1 spec ops bde (1 spec ops regt; 1 cdo bn)

MANOEUVRE
Armoured
1 armd sqn
Mechanised
1 mech bde (2 mech inf bn)
Light
1 inf bde (3 inf bn)
2 inf bde (2 inf bn)
2 inf bde (1 inf bn)
6 inf bn
Air Manoeuvre
1 para bn
Other
3 gd bn
1 (Presidential Guard) gd gp

COMBAT SUPPORT
1 arty bde
1 fd arty regt
2 engr regt

AIR DEFENCE
1 AD regt

EQUIPMENT BY TYPE

ARMOURED FIGHTING VEHICLES
MBT 40: 30 ZTZ-59†; 10 ZTZ-69†
ASLT 8 WMA-301
RECCE 115: 20 Eland-60/-90; 15 FV701 Ferret†; 80 EE-9 Cascavel (90mm)
IFV 9: 7 WZ-551A; 2+ YW307
APC 45
  APC (T) 30: 8 ZSD-85 (incl CP); 22 VTT-323
  APC (W) 15 WZ-551B1

ENGINEERING & MAINTENANCE VEHICLES
ARV T-54/T-55 reported; ZJX-93 ARV
VLB MTU reported

ARTILLERY 254
SP 122mm 12 2S1 Gvozdika
TOWED 122mm 20: 4 D-30; 16 Type-60 (D-74)
MRL 76: **107mm** 16 Type-63; **122mm** 60 RM-70
MOR 146: **81mm/82mm** ε140; **120mm** 6 M-43

AIR DEFENCE
SAM • Point-defence 9K32 Strela-2 (RS-SA-7 Grail)‡
GUNS • TOWED 116: **14.5mm** 36 ZPU-1/ZPU-2/ZPU-4; **23mm** 45 ZU-23-2; **37mm** 35 M-1939

Air Force 4,000

FORCES BY ROLE

FIGHTER
1 sqn with F-7 II†; FT-7†

FIGHTER/GROUND ATTACK
1 sqn with K-8 Karakorum*

GROUND ATTACK/ISR
1 sqn with Cessna 337/O-2A Skymaster*

ISR/TRAINING
1 sqn with SF-260F/M; SF-260TP*; SF-260W Warrior*

TRANSPORT
1 sqn with BN-2 Islander; CASA 212-200 Aviocar (VIP)

ATTACK/TRANSPORT HELICOPTER
1 sqn with Mi-35 Hind; Mi-35P Hind; SA316 Alouette III; AS532UL Cougar (VIP); H215 (VIP)
1 trg sqn with Bell 412 Twin Huey, SA316 Alouette III

AIR DEFENCE
1 sqn

EQUIPMENT BY TYPE

AIRCRAFT 45 combat capable
FTR 9: 7 F-7 II†; 2 FT-7†
ISR 2 O-2A Skymaster
TPT • Light 20: 5 BN-2 Islander; 2 C-212-200 Aviocar; 13 Cessna 337 Skymaster*; (10 C-47 Skytrain in store)
TRG 33: 10 K-8 Karakorum*; 5 SF-260M; 8 SF-260TP*; 5 SF-260W Warrior*; 5 SF-260F

HELICOPTERS
ATK 5: 3 Mi-35 Hind; 2 Mi-35P Hind
MRH 8: 7 Bell 412 Twin Huey; 1 SA316 Alouette III
TPT • Medium 2: 1 AS532UL Cougar (VIP)†; 1 H215 (VIP) (reported)

AIR-LAUNCHED MISSILES • AAM • IR PL-2; PL-5 (reported)

AD • GUNS 100mm (not deployed); **37mm** (not deployed); **57mm** (not deployed)

Gendarmerie & Paramilitary 21,800

Zimbabwe Republic Police Force 19,500
incl air wg

Police Support Unit 2,300
EQUIPMENT BY TYPE
PATROL AND COASTAL COMBATANTS
All operational patrol vessels under 10t FLD

DEPLOYMENT

CENTRAL AFRICAN REPUBLIC: UN • MINUSCA 3

DEMOCRATIC REPUBLIC OF THE CONGO: UN • MONUSCO 3

SOUTH SUDAN: UN • UNMISS 11

SUDAN: UN • UNISFA 8

Reference

Explanatory notes

The Military Balance provides an assessment of the armed forces and defence economics of 174 countries and territories. Each edition provides a unique compilation of data and information, enabling the reader to discern trends by studying editions as far back as 1959. The data in the current edition is accurate according to IISS assessments as of November 2024, unless specified. Inclusion of a territory, country or state in *The Military Balance*, or terminology or boundaries used in graphics or mapping, does not imply legal recognition or indicate support for any government or administration.

General arrangement and contents

The Editor's Introduction is an assessment of key themes and content in the 2025 edition. An opening analytical essay examines developments in defence production. Regional chapters begin with analysis of the military and security issues that drive national defence policy developments, and key trends in regional defence economics. Detailed data on regional states' military forces and equipment, and defence economics, is presented in alphabetical order. The book closes with a reference section containing comparisons of defence economics and personnel statistics.

The Military Balance wall chart

The Military Balance 2025 wall chart is an overview of China's People's Liberation Army.

Using *The Military Balance*

The country entries assess personnel strengths, organisation and equipment holdings of the world's armed forces. Force-strength and equipment-inventory data is based on the most accurate data available, or on the best estimate that can be made. The data presented reflects judgements based on information available to the IISS at the time the book is compiled. Where information differs from previous editions, it is mainly because of changes in national forces or because the IISS has reassessed the evidence supporting past entries.

Country entries

Information on each country is shown in a standard format, although the differing availability of information and differences in nomenclature result in some variations. Country entries include economic, demographic and military data. Population figures are based on demographic statistics from the US Census Bureau. Military data includes personnel numbers, conscript liability where relevant, outline organisation, number of formations and units, and an inventory of the major equipment of each service. Details of national forces stationed abroad and of foreign forces stationed within the given country are also provided.

Arms procurements and deliveries

A series of thematic tables and graphics follows the regional text entries. These are designed to illustrate key trends, principal programmes and significant events in regional defence procurements. More detailed information on defence procurements, organised by country, equipment type and manufacturing company, can be found on the IISS Military Balance+ database (*https://www.iiss.org/the-military-balance-plus*). The information in this section meets the threshold for a *Military Balance* country entry and as such does not feature information on sales of small arms and light weapons.

Abbreviations and definitions[a]

'Up to'	Total is at most the number given, but could be lower
'Some'	Precise inventory is unavailable at time of press
'In store'	Equipment held away from front-line units; readiness and maintenance varies
Billion (bn)	1,000 million (m)
Trillion (trn)	1,000 billion
Quadrillion (qrn)	1,000 trillion
$	US dollars unless otherwise stated
ε	Estimated

*	Aircraft counted by the IISS as combat capable
(-)	Unit understrength or detached
+	Unit reinforced/total is no less than the number given
†	IISS assesses that the serviceability of equipment is in doubt[b]
‡	Missiles whose basic design is more than four decades old and which have not been significantly upgraded within the past decade[b]

[a] Selected
[b] Not to be taken to imply that such equipment cannot be used

Defence economics

Country entries include annual defence budgets (and expenditure where applicable), selected economic-performance indicators and demographic aggregates. All country entries are subject to revision each year as new information, particularly regarding actual defence expenditure, becomes available. On p. 520, there are also international comparisons of defence expenditure and military personnel, giving expenditure figures for the past three years in per capita terms and as a % of gross domestic product (GDP). The aim is to provide a measure of military expenditure and the allocation of economic resources to defence.

Individual country entries show economic performance and current demographic data. Where this data is unavailable, information from the last available year is provided. All financial data in the country entries is shown in both national currency and US dollars at current prices. US-dollar conversions are calculated from the exchange rates listed in the entry.

The use of market exchange rates has limitations, particularly because it does not consider the varying levels of development or the differing cost of inputs (principally personnel, equipment and investment) specific to each country's national context. An alternative approach is to make conversions using purchasing power parity (PPP) exchange rates, which at least partially takes these cost differentials into account.

However, the suitability of PPP conversions depends on the extent to which a country is self-sufficient in developing and producing the armaments required by its armed forces. For Russia and China they are appropriate, as imported systems play almost no role in Russia's case and only a small and decreasing one in that of China. However, PPP conversions are less suitable when assessing the spending of countries such as India and Saudi Arabia, which rely heavily on imports of military equipment from relatively high-cost producers. For those countries it would be necessary to adopt a hybrid approach to determine defence expenditure in dollars, with the market exchange rate used for converting defence procurement and the PPP conversion rate applied to all other defence expenditure (personnel, operations, etc.). As such, to produce standardised international comparisons, PPP conversions would have to be applied to all countries. In the absence of defence-based PPP rates, analysts would have to use the GDP-based PPP rates that are available for all countries. However, these are also statistical estimates and, as such, difficult to apply to military expenditure because they reflect the purchasing power of the wider economy, primarily civilian goods and services.

Definitions of terms

Despite efforts by NATO and the UN to develop a standardised definition of military expenditure, many countries prefer to use their own definitions (which are often not made public). In order to present a comprehensive picture, *The Military Balance* lists three different measures of military-related spending data.

- For most countries, an official defence-budget figure is provided.
- For those countries where other military-related outlays, over and above the defence budget, are known or can be reasonably estimated, an additional measurement referred to as defence expenditure is also provided. Defence-expenditure figures will naturally be higher than official budget figures, depending on the range of additional factors included.
- For NATO countries, a defence-budget figure, as well as defence expenditure reported by NATO in local-currency terms and converted using IMF exchange rates, is quoted.

NATO's military-expenditure definition (the most comprehensive) is cash outlays of central or federal governments to meet the costs of national armed forces. The term 'armed forces' includes strategic, land, naval, air, command, administration and support forces. It also includes other forces if they are trained, structured and equipped to support defence forces and are realistically deployable. Defence expenditures are reported in four categories: Operating Costs, Procurement and Construction, Research and Development (R&D) and Other Expenditure. Operating Costs include salaries and pensions for military and civilian personnel; the cost of maintaining and training units, service organisations, headquarters and support elements; and the cost of servicing and repairing military equipment and infrastructure. Procurement and Construction expenditure covers national equipment and infrastructure spending, as well as common infrastructure programmes. R&D is defence expenditure up to the point at which new equipment can be put in service, regardless of whether new equipment is actually procured. Foreign Military Assistance (FMA) contributions are also noted – primarily the IISS tracks Foreign Military Financing (FMF) allocations from the United States.

For many non-NATO countries the issue of transparency in reporting military budgets is fundamental. Not every UN member state reports defence-budget data (even fewer report real defence expenditures) to their electorates, the UN, the IMF or other multinational organisations. In the case of governments with a proven record of transparency, official figures generally conform to the standardised definition of defence budgeting, as adopted by the UN, and consistency problems are not usually a major issue. The IISS cites official defence budgets as reported by either national governments, the UN, OSCE or IMF.

For those countries where the official defence-budget figure is considered to be an incomplete measure of total military-related spending, and appropriate additional data is available, the IISS will use data from a variety of sources to arrive at a more accurate estimate of true defence expenditure. The most frequent instances of budgetary manipulation or falsification typically involve equipment procurement, R&D, defence-industrial investment, covert weapons programmes, pensions for retired military and civilian personnel, paramilitary forces and non-budgetary sources of revenue for the military arising from ownership of industrial, property and land assets. There will be several countries listed in *The Military Balance* for which only an official defence-budget figure is provided but where, in reality, true defence-related expenditure is almost certainly higher.

Percentage changes in defence spending are referred to in either nominal or real terms. Nominal terms relate to the percentage change in numerical spending figures, and do not account for the impact of price changes (i.e., inflation) on defence spending. By contrast, real terms account for inflationary effects, and may therefore be considered a more accurate representation of change over time.

The principal sources for national economic statistics cited in the country entries are the IMF, OECD, World Bank and three regional banks (the Inter-American, Asian and African Development banks). For some countries, basic economic data is difficult to obtain. GDP figures are nominal (current) values at market prices. GDP growth is real, not nominal growth, and inflation is the year-on-year change in consumer prices. When real-terms defence-spending figures are mentioned, these are measured in constant 2015 US dollars.

General defence data

Personnel

The 'Active' total comprises all service personnel on full-time duty (including conscripts and long-term assignments from the Reserves). When a gendarmerie or equivalent is under control of the defence ministry, they may be included in the active total. Only the length of conscript liability is shown; where service is voluntary there is no entry. 'Reserve' describes formations and units not fully manned or operational in peacetime, but which can be mobilised by recalling reservists in an emergency. Some countries have more than one category of reserves, often kept at varying degrees of readiness. Where possible, these differences are denoted using the national descriptive title, but always under the heading of 'Reserves' to distinguish them from full-time active forces. All personnel figures are rounded to the nearest 50, except for organisations with under 500 personnel, where figures are rounded to the nearest ten.

Units and formation strength

Company	100–200
Battalion	500–1,000
Brigade	3,000–5,000
Division	15,000–20,000
Corps or Army	50,000–100,000

Other forces

Many countries maintain forces whose training, organisation, equipment and control suggest that they may be used to support or replace regular military forces or be used more broadly by states to deliver militarily relevant effect. They include some forces that may have a constabulary role or are classed as gendarmerie forces, with more formal law-enforcement responsibilities. These are called 'Gendarmerie & Paramilitary' and are detailed after the military forces of each country. Their personnel numbers are not normally included in the totals at the start of each entry.

Forces by role and equipment by type

Quantities are shown by function (according to each nation's employment) and type, and represent what are believed to be total holdings, including active and reserve operational and training units. Inventory totals for missile systems relate to launchers and not to missiles. Equipment held 'in store' is not counted in the main inventory totals.

The IISS Military Balance+ database assesses the relative level of capability of certain equipment-platform types based on their technical characteristics. For land-domain equipment, these characteristics include the level of protection, main armament, and fire control and optics. For maritime-domain equipment, they include crew-to-displacement ratio, primary missile armament, sensor suites, signature reduction and propulsion. For air-domain equipment, they include avionics, weapons, signature management and upgrades.

Platform types assessed in this fashion are described as having either an 'obsolete', 'obsolescent', 'ageing', 'modern' or 'advanced' level of capability when compared with other designs within the same category of equipment. This should not be taken as an assessment of the physical age or remaining service life of a given platform or whether it can actually be employed offensively. Examples of these assessments appear in certain graphics within *The Military Balance*.

Deployments

The Military Balance mainly lists permanent bases and operational deployments abroad, including peacekeeping operations. Domestic deployments are not included, with the exception of overseas territories. Information in the country data sections details troop deployments and, where available, the role and equipment of deployed units. Personnel figures are not generally included for embassy staff or standing multinational headquarters.

Land forces

To make international comparison easier and more consistent, *The Military Balance* categorises forces by role and translates national military terminology for unit and formation sizes. Typical personnel strength, equipment holdings and organisation of formations such as brigades and divisions vary from country to country. In addition, some unit terms, such as 'regiment', 'squadron', 'battery' and 'troop', can refer to significantly different unit sizes in different countries. Unless otherwise stated, these terms should be assumed to reflect standard British usage where they occur.

Naval forces

Classifying naval vessels according to role is complex. A post-war consensus on primary surface combatants revolved around a distinction between independently operating cruisers, air-defence escorts (destroyers) and anti-submarine-warfare escorts (frigates). However, ships are increasingly performing a range of roles. Also, modern ship design has meant that the full-load displacement (FLD) of different warship types has evolved and in some cases overlaps. For these reasons, *The Military Balance* now classifies vessels by an assessed combination of role, equipment fit and displacement.

Air forces

Aircraft listed as combat capable are assessed as being equipped to deliver air-to-air or air-to-surface ordnance.

The definition includes aircraft designated by type as bomber, fighter, fighter/ground attack, ground attack and anti-submarine warfare. Other aircraft considered to be combat capable are marked with an asterisk (*). Operational groupings of air forces are shown where known. Typical squadron aircraft strengths can vary both between aircraft types and from country to country. When assessing missile ranges, *The Military Balance* uses the following range indicators:

- Short-range ballistic missile (SRBM): less than 1,000 kilometres;
- Medium-range ballistic missile (MRBM): 1,000–3,000 km;
- Intermediate-range ballistic missile (IRBM): 3,000–5,000 km;
- Intercontinental ballistic missile (ICBM): over 5,000 km.

Other IISS defence data

The Military Balance+ database is integrating information on military-owned cyber capacities. The research taxonomy focuses on enablers, including indicators of capability from the armed forces. The Military Balance+ also contains data on bilateral, multilateral and notable large or important military exercises held on a national basis. More broadly, the Military Balance+ enables subscribers to view multiple years of Military Balance data, and conduct searches for complex queries more rapidly than is possible by consulting the print book.

Attribution and acknowledgements

The International Institute for Strategic Studies owes no allegiance to any government, group of governments, or any political or other organisation. Its assessments are its own, based on the material available to it from a wide variety of sources. The cooperation of governments of all listed countries has been sought and, in many cases, received. However, some data in *The Military Balance* is estimated. Care is taken to ensure that data is as accurate and free from bias as possible. The Institute owes a considerable debt to a number of its own members, consultants and all those who help compile and check material. The Director-General and Chief Executive and staff of the Institute assume full responsibility for the data and judgements in this book. Comments and suggestions on the data and textual material contained within the book, as well as on the style and presentation of data, are welcomed and should be communicated to the Editor of *The Military Balance* at: The International Institute for Strategic Studies, Arundel House, 6 Temple Place, London, WC2R 2PG, UK, email: *milbal@iiss.org*. Copyright on all information in *The Military Balance* belongs strictly to the IISS. Application to reproduce limited amounts of data may be made to the publisher: Taylor & Francis, 4 Park Square, Milton Park, Abingdon, Oxon, OX14 4RN. Email: *society.permissions@tandf.co.uk*. Unauthorised use of data from *The Military Balance* will be subject to legal action.

Principal land definitions

Forces by role

Command:	free-standing, deployable formation headquarters (HQs).
Special Forces (SF):	elite units specially trained and equipped for unconventional warfare and operations in enemy-controlled territory. Many are employed in counter-terrorist roles.
Manoeuvre:	combat units and formations capable of manoeuvring. These are subdivided as follows:
Reconnaissance:	combat units and formations whose primary purpose is to gain information.
Armoured:	units and formations principally equipped with main battle tanks (MBTs) and infantry fighting vehicles (IFVs) to provide heavy mounted close-combat capability. Units and formations intended to provide mounted close-combat capability with lighter armoured vehicles, such as light tanks or wheeled assault guns, are classified as light armoured.
Mechanised:	units and formations primarily equipped with lighter armoured vehicles such as armoured personnel carriers (APCs). They have less mounted firepower and protection than their armoured equivalents, but can usually deploy more infantry.
Light:	units and formations whose principal combat capability is dismounted infantry, with few, if any, organic armoured vehicles. Some may be motorised and equipped with soft-skinned vehicles.
Air Manoeuvre:	units and formations trained and equipped for delivery by transport aircraft and/or helicopters.
Amphibious:	amphibious forces are trained and equipped to project force from the sea.
Other Forces:	includes security units such as Presidential Guards, paramilitary units such as border guards and combat formations permanently employed in training or demonstration tasks.
Combat Support:	combat support units and formations not integral to manoeuvre formations. Includes artillery, engineers, military intelligence, nuclear, biological and chemical defence, signals and information operations.
Combat Service Support (CSS):	includes logistics, maintenance, medical, supply and transport units and formations.

Equipment by type

Light Weapons:	small arms, machine guns, grenades and grenade launchers and unguided man-portable anti-armour and support weapons have proliferated so much and are sufficiently easy to manufacture or copy that listing them would be impractical.
Crew-Served Weapons:	crew-served recoilless rifles, man-portable ATGWs, MANPADs and mortars of greater than 80mm calibre are listed, but the high degree of proliferation and local manufacture of many of these weapons means that estimates of numbers held may not be reliable.
Armoured Fighting Vehicles (AFVs):	armoured combat vehicles with a combat weight of at least six metric tonnes, further subdivided as below:
Main Battle Tank (MBT):	armoured, tracked combat vehicles, armed with a turret-mounted gun of at least 100mm calibre and with a combat weight of between 35 and 75 metric tonnes.
Light Tank (LT TK):	armoured, tracked combat vehicles, armed with a turret-mounted gun of at least 75mm calibre and with a combat weight of between 15 and 40 metric tonnes.
Wheeled Assault Gun (ASLT):	armoured, wheeled combat vehicles, armed with a turret-mounted gun of at least 75mm calibre and with a combat weight of at least 15 metric tonnes.
Armoured Reconnaissance (RECCE):	armoured vehicles primarily designed for reconnaissance tasks with no significant transport capability and either a main gun of less than 75mm calibre or a combat weight of less than 15 metric tonnes, or both.
Infantry Fighting Vehicle (IFV):	armoured combat vehicles designed and equipped to transport an infantry squad and armed with a cannon of at least 20mm calibre.
Armoured Personnel Carrier (APC):	lightly armoured combat vehicles designed and equipped to transport an infantry squad but either unarmed or armed with a cannon of less than 20mm calibre.
Airborne Combat Vehicle (ABCV):	armoured vehicles designed to be deployable by parachute alongside airborne forces.
Amphibious Assault Vehicle (AAV):	armoured vehicles designed to have an amphibious ship-to-shore capability.
Armoured Utility Vehicle (AUV):	armoured vehicles not designed to transport an infantry squad, but capable of undertaking a variety of other utility battlefield tasks, including light reconnaissance and light transport.
Specialist Variants:	variants of armoured vehicles listed above that are designed to fill a specialised role, such as command posts (CP), artillery observation posts (OP), signals (sigs) and ambulances (amb), are categorised with their parent vehicles.

Engineering and Maintenance Vehicles:	includes armoured engineer vehicles (AEV), armoured repair and recovery vehicles (ARV), assault bridging (VLB) and mine-warfare vehicles (MW).
Nuclear, Biological and Chemical Defence Vehicles (NBC):	armoured vehicles principally designed to operate in potentially contaminated terrain.
Anti-Tank/Anti-Infrastructure (AT):	guns, guided weapons and recoilless rifles designed to engage armoured vehicles and battlefield hardened targets.
Surface-to-Surface Missile Launchers (SSM):	launch vehicles for transporting and firing surface-to-surface ballistic and cruise missiles.
Artillery:	weapons (including guns, howitzers, gun/howitzers, multiple-rocket launchers, mortars and gun/mortars) with a calibre greater than 100mm for artillery pieces and 80mm and above for mortars, capable of engaging ground targets with indirect fire.
Coastal Defence:	land-based coastal artillery pieces and anti-ship-missile launchers.
Air Defence (AD):	guns, directed-energy (DE) weapons and surface-to-air missile (SAM) launchers designed to engage fixed-wing, rotary-wing and uninhabited aircraft. Missiles are further classified by maximum notional engagement range: point-defence (up to 10 km); short-range (10–30 km); medium-range (30–75 km); and long-range (75 km+). Systems primarily intended to intercept missiles rather than aircraft are categorised separately as Missile Defence.

Principal naval definitions

To aid comparison between fleets, the following definitions, which do not always conform to national definitions, are used as guidance:

Submarines:	all vessels designed to operate primarily under water. Submarines with a dived displacement below 250 tonnes are classified as midget submarines (SSW); those below 500 tonnes are coastal submarines (SSC).
Principal Surface Combatants:	all surface ships designed for combat operations on the high seas, with an FLD above 2,200 tonnes. Aircraft carriers (CV), including smaller support carriers (CVS) embarking STOVL aircraft and helicopter carriers (CVH), are vessels with a flat deck primarily designed to carry fixed- and/or rotary-wing aircraft, without specialised amphibious capability. Other principal surface combatants include cruisers (C) (FLD above 9,750 tonnes), destroyers (DD) (FLD 4,500–9,749 tonnes with a primary area air-defence weapons fit and role) and frigates (FF) (FLD 2,200–9,000 tonnes and a primary anti-submarine/general-purpose weapons fit and role).
Patrol and Coastal Combatants:	surface vessels designed for coastal or inshore operations. These include corvettes (FS), which usually have an FLD between 500 and 2,199 tonnes and are distinguished from other patrol vessels by their heavier armaments. Also included in this category are offshore-patrol ships (PSO), with an FLD greater than 1,500 tonnes; patrol craft (PC), which have an FLD between 250 and 1,499 tonnes; and patrol boats (PB), with an FLD between ten and 250 tonnes. Vessels with a top speed greater than 35 knots are designated as 'fast'.
Mine Warfare Vessels:	all surface vessels configured primarily for mine laying (ML) or countermeasures. Countermeasures vessels are either: sweepers (MS), which are designed to locate and destroy mines in an area; hunters (MH), which are designed to locate and destroy individual mines; or countermeasures vessels (MC), which combine both roles.
Amphibious Vessels:	vessels designed to transport combat personnel and/or equipment onto shore. These include aviation-capable amphibious assault ships (LHA), which can embark rotary-wing or STOVL air assets and may have a well deck for landing craft air cushioned (LCAC) and landing craft; aviation-capable amphibious assault ships with a well dock for LCACs and landing craft (LHD), which can embark rotary-wing or STOVL assets; landing platform helicopters (LPH), which have a primary role of launch and recovery platform for rotary-wing or STOVL assets; landing platform docks (LPD), which do not have a through deck but do have a well dock and carry both combat personnel and equipment; and land ships docks (LSD) with a well dock but focused more on equipment transport. Landing ships (LS) are amphibious vessels capable of ocean passage and landing craft (LC) are smaller vessels designed to transport personnel and equipment from a larger vessel to land or across small stretches of water. Landing ships have a hold; landing craft are open vessels. LCAC are differentiated from utility craft air cushioned (UCAC) in that the former have a bow ramp for the disembarkation of vehicles and personnel.

Auxiliary Vessels:	vessels with an FLD above ten tonnes performing an auxiliary military role, supporting combat ships or operations. They generally fulfil six roles: logistics and replenishment (such as cargo ships (AK) and oilers (AO)), research and surveillance (such as intelligence collection vessels (AGI) and survey ships (AGS)), maintenance and rescue (such as repair ships (AR) and ocean-going tugs (ATF)), training (such as training craft (AX)), undersea support (such as auxiliary support submarines (SSA)) and special purpose (such as seagoing buoy tenders (ABU) and hospital ships (AH)).
Weapons Systems:	weapons are listed in the following order: land-attack cruise missiles (LACM), anti-ship missiles (AShM), surface-to-air missiles (SAM), heavy (HWT) and lightweight (LWT) torpedoes, anti-submarine weapons (A/S), CIWS, guns and aircraft. Missiles with a range less than 5 km and guns with a calibre less than 57mm are generally not included.
Organisations:	naval groupings such as fleets and squadrons frequently change and are shown only where doing so would aid qualitative judgements.
Uninhabited Maritime Platforms/Systems	maritime vehicles designed to operate wholly or partially without a crew, including both surface (USV) and underwater (UUV) vehicles. Platforms are larger, quantifiable vehicles that may complement larger naval vessels. Systems are typically networked with other systems and equipment to achieve an effect and may form part of an equipment fit for other vessels. Classified according to role: Attack (ATK) – vehicles with an integral warhead; Maritime Security (MARESEC) – vehicles designed for patrol or interceptor missions; Military Data Gathering (DATA) – vehicles whose primary purpose is to collect information on the maritime environment, including hydrographic survey; Mine Warfare (MW) – vehicles used for the identification or disposal of sea mines; Utility (UTL) – vehicles that do not fit into any of the above classifications or those that cover two or more of the above classifications. Platforms are further categorised according to physical size.
Legacy Platforms:	legacy-generation platforms, unless specifically modified for a new role, may be listed with their original designations although they may not conform fully with current guidance criteria.

Principal aviation definitions

Bomber (Bbr):	comparatively large platforms intended for the delivery of air-to-surface ordnance. Bbr units are units equipped with bomber aircraft for the air-to-surface role.
Fighter (Ftr):	aircraft designed primarily for air-to-air combat, which may also have a limited air-to-surface capability. Ftr units are equipped with aircraft intended to provide air superiority, which may have a secondary and limited air-to-surface capability.
Fighter/Ground Attack (FGA):	multi-role fighter-size platforms with significant air-to-surface capability, potentially including maritime attack, and at least some air-to-air capacity. FGA units are multi-role units equipped with aircraft capable of air-to-air and air-to-surface attack.
Ground Attack (Atk):	aircraft designed solely for the air-to-surface task, with limited or no air-to-air capability. Atk units are equipped with fixed-wing aircraft.
Attack Helicopter (Atk hel):	rotary-wing platforms designed for delivery of air-to-surface weapons, and fitted with an integrated fire-control system.
Anti-Submarine Warfare (ASW):	fixed- and rotary-wing platforms designed to locate and engage submarines, many with a secondary anti-surface-warfare capability. ASW units are equipped with fixed- or rotary-wing aircraft.
Anti-Surface Warfare (ASuW):	ASuW units are equipped with fixed- or rotary-wing aircraft intended for anti-surface-warfare missions.
Maritime Patrol (MP):	fixed-wing aircraft and uninhabited aerial vehicles (UAVs) intended for maritime surface surveillance, which may possess an anti-surface-warfare capability. MP units are equipped with fixed-wing aircraft or UAVs.
Electronic Warfare (EW):	fixed- and rotary-wing aircraft and UAVs intended for electronic warfare. EW units are equipped with fixed- or rotary-wing aircraft or UAVs.
Intelligence/Surveillance/Reconnaissance (ISR):	fixed- and rotary-wing aircraft and UAVs intended to provide radar, visible-light or infrared imagery, or a mix thereof. ISR units are equipped with fixed- or rotary-wing aircraft or UAVs.
Combat/Intelligence/Surveillance/Reconnaissance (CISR):	aircraft and UAVs that have the capability to deliver air-to-surface weapons, as well as undertake ISR tasks. CISR units are equipped with armed aircraft and/or UAVs for ISR and air-to-surface missions.

Explanatory Notes

COMINT/ELINT/SIGINT:	fixed- and rotary-wing platforms and UAVs capable of gathering electronic (ELINT), communications (COMINT) or signals intelligence (SIGINT). COMINT units are equipped with fixed- or rotary-wing aircraft or UAVs intended for the communications-intelligence task. ELINT units are equipped with fixed- or rotary-wing aircraft or UAVs used for gathering electronic intelligence. SIGINT units are equipped with fixed- or rotary-wing aircraft or UAVs used to collect signals intelligence.	**Transport (Tpt):**	fixed- and rotary-wing aircraft intended for military airlift. Light transport aircraft are categorised as having a maximum payload of up to 11,340 kilograms; medium up to 27,215 kg; and heavy above 27,215 kg. Light transport helicopters have an internal payload of up to 2,000 kg; medium transport helicopters up to 4,535 kg; heavy transport helicopters greater than 4,535 kg. Passenger (PAX) aircraft are platforms generally unsuited for transporting cargo on the main deck. Tpt units are equipped with fixed- or rotary-wing platforms to transport personnel or cargo.
Airborne Early Warning (& Control) (AEW (&C)):	fixed- and rotary-wing platforms capable of providing airborne early warning, with a varying degree of onboard command and control depending on the platform. AEW(&C) units are equipped with fixed- or rotary-wing aircraft.	**Trainer (Trg):**	fixed- and rotary-wing aircraft designed primarily for the training role; some also have the capacity to carry light to medium ordnance. Trg units are equipped with fixed- or rotary-wing training aircraft intended for pilot or other aircrew training.
Search and Rescue (SAR):	units are equipped with fixed- or rotary-wing aircraft used to recover military personnel or civilians.	**Multi-Role Helicopter (MRH):**	rotary-wing platforms designed to carry out a variety of military tasks including light transport, armed reconnaissance and battlefield support.
Combat Search and Rescue (CSAR):	units are equipped with armed fixed- or rotary-wing aircraft for recovery of personnel from hostile territory.	**Uninhabited Aerial Vehicles (UAVs):**	remotely piloted or controlled uninhabited fixed- or rotary-wing systems. Light UAVs are those weighing 20–150 kg; medium: 150–600 kg; and heavy: more than 600 kg. UAVs with an integral warhead that share some characteristics with both UAVs and cruise missiles are classified as one-way attack (OWA) UAVs.
Tanker (Tkr):	fixed- and rotary-wing aircraft designed for air-to-air refuelling. Tkr units are equipped with fixed- or rotary-wing aircraft used for air-to-air refuelling.		
Tanker Transport (Tkr/Tpt):	platforms capable of both air-to-air refuelling and military airlift.		

Reference

Table 8 List of abbreviations for data sections

AAM	air-to-air missile	aslt	assault	det	detachment
AAR	search-and-rescue vessel	ASM	air-to-surface missile	div	division
AAV	amphibious assault vehicle	ASR	submarine rescue craft	ECM	electronic countermeasures
AB	airborne	ASTT	anti-submarine torpedo tube	ELINT	electronic intelligence
ABCV	airborne combat vehicle	ASW	anti-submarine warfare	elm	element/s
ABM	anti-ballistic missile	ASuW	anti-surface warfare	engr	engineer
ABU/H	sea-going buoy tender/with hangar	AT	anti-tank	EOD	explosive ordnance disposal
ac	aircraft	ATF	ocean going tug	EPF	expeditionary fast transport vessel
AD	air defence	ATGW	anti-tank guided weapon	eqpt	equipment
ADA	air-defence artillery	Atk	attack/ground attack	ESB	expeditionary mobile base
adj	adjusted	AUV	armoured utility vehicle	ESD	expeditionary transport dock
AE	ammunition carrier	avn	aviation	EW	electronic warfare
AEM	missile support ship	AWT	water tanker	excl	excludes/excluding
AEV	armoured engineer vehicle	AX/L/S	training craft/light/sail	exp	expenditure/expeditionary
AEW(&C)	airborne early warning (and control)	BA	Budget Authority (US)	FAC	forward air control
AFD/L	floating dry dock/small	Bbr	bomber	fd	field
AFS/H	logistics ship/with hangar	BCT	brigade combat team	FF/G/H/M	frigate/with surface-to-surface missile/with hangar/with SAM
AFV	armoured fighting vehicle	bde	brigade	FGA	fighter/ground attack
AG	misc auxiliary	bdgt	budget	FLD	full-load displacement
AGB/H	icebreaker/with hangar	BG	battlegroup	flt	flight
AGF/H	command ship/with hangar	BMD	ballistic-missile defence	FMA	Foreign Military Assistance
AGE/H	experimental auxiliary ship/with hangar	bn	battalion/billion	FRS	fleet replacement squadron
AGI	intelligence collection vessel	bty	battery	FS/G/H/M	corvette/with surface-to-surface missile/with hangar/with SAM
AGM	missile range instrumentation vessel	C2	command and control	Ftr	fighter
		C4	command, control, communications, and computers	FTX	field training exercise
AGOR	oceanographic research vessel			FY	fiscal year
AGOS	oceanographic surveillance vessel	casevac	casualty evacuation	gd	guard
AGS/H	survey ship/with hangar	cav	cavalry	GDP	gross domestic product
AH	hospital ship	CBRN	chemical, biological, radiological, nuclear, explosive	GLCM	ground-launched cruise missile
AIP	air-independent propulsion	cbt	combat	GMLS	Guided Missile Launching System
AK/L	cargo ship/light	cdo	commando	gp	group
AKR/H	roll-on/roll-off cargo ship/with hangar	C/G/H/M/N	cruiser/with surface-to-surface missile/with hangar/with SAM/nuclear-powered	GPS	Global Positioning System
ALBM	air-launched ballistic missile			HA/DR	humanitarian assistance/disaster relief
ALCM	air-launched cruise missile	CIMIC	civil–military cooperation	hel	helicopter
amb	ambulance	CISR	combat ISR	HQ	headquarters
amph	amphibious/amphibian	CIWS	close-in weapons system	HUMINT	human intelligence
AO/L	oiler/light	COIN	counter-insurgency	HWT	heavyweight torpedo
AOE/H	fact combat support ship/with hangar	comd	command	hy	heavy
AOR/L/H	fleet replenishment oiler with RAS capability/light/with hangar	COMINT	communications intelligence	ICBM	intercontinental ballistic missile
		comms	communications	IFV	infantry fighting vehicle
AP	transport ship	coy	company	IIR	imaging infrared
APC	armoured personnel carrier	CP	command post	IMINT	imagery intelligence
AR/C	repair ship/cable	CS	combat support	imp	improved
ARG	amphibious ready group	CSAR	combat search and rescue	indep	independent
ARH	active radar homing	CSS	combat service support	inf	infantry
ARM	anti-radiation missile	CT	counter-terrorism	info ops	information operations
armd	armoured	CV/H/L/N/S	aircraft carrier/helicopter/light/nuclear powered/STOVL	INS	inertial navigation system
ARS/H	rescue and salvage ship/with hangar			int	intelligence
arty	artillery	CW	chemical warfare/weapons	IOC	Initial operating capability
ARV	armoured recovery vehicle	DD/G/H/M	destroyer/with surface-to-surface missile/with hangar/with SAM	IR	infrared
AS	anti-submarine/submarine tender			IRBM	intermediate-range ballistic missile
ASAT	anti-satellite	DDR	disarmament, demobilisation and reintegration	ISD	in-service date
ASBM	anti-ship ballistic missile			ISR	intelligence, surveillance and reconnaissance
ASCM	anti-ship cruise missile	DE	directed energy		
AShM	anti-ship missile	def	defence		

ISTAR	intelligence, surveillance, target acquisition and reconnaissance	NBC	nuclear, biological, chemical	SLBM	submarine-launched ballistic missile
		NCO	non-commissioned officer	SLCM	submarine-launched cruise missile
LACM	land-attack cruise missile	n.k.	not known	SLEP	service-life-extension programme
LC/A/AC/H/M/P/T/U/VP		O&M	operations and maintenance	SP	self-propelled
	landing craft/assault/air cushion/ heavy/medium/personnel/tank/ utility/vehicles and personnel	obs	observation/observer	SPAAGM	self-propelled anti-aircraft gun and missile system
		OCU	operational conversion unit		
		OP	observation post	Spec Ops	special operations
LCC	amphibious command ship	op/ops	operational/operations	spt	support
LGB	laser-guided bomb	OPFOR	opposition training force	sqn	squadron
LHA	aviation-capable amphibious assault ship	OPV	offshore patrol vessel	SRBM	short-range ballistic missile
		org	organised/organisation	SS	submarine
LHD	aviation-capable amphibious assault ship with well dock	OWA	one-way attack	SSA/N	auxiliary support submarine/ nuclear-powered
		para	paratroop/parachute		
LIFT	lead-in ftr trainer	PAX	passenger/passenger transport aircraft	SSB/N	ballistic missile submarine/ nuclear-powered
LKA	amphibious cargo ship				
lnchr	launcher	PB/F/G/I/M/R/T		SSC	coastal submarine
log	logistic		patrol boat/fast/with surface-to-surface missile/inshore/with SAM/ riverine/with torpedo	SSG	conventionally-powered attack submarine with dedicated launch tubes for guided missiles
LoI	letter of intent				
LP/D/H	landing platform/dock/helicopter				
LRIP	low-rate initial production	PC/C/F/G/H/I/M/O/R/T			
LS/D/L/H/M/T			patrol craft/coastal/fast/with surface-to-surface missile/with hangar/inshore/with CIWS missile or SAM/offshore/riverine/with torpedo	SSGN	nuclear-powered submarine with dedicated launch tubes for guided missiles
	landing ship/dock/logistic/with hangar/medium/tank				
lt	light			SSK	conventionally-powered attack submarine
LWT	lightweight torpedo	PGM	precision-guided munitions		
maint	maintenance	PH/G/M/T	patrol hydrofoil/with surface-to-surface missile/with SAM/with torpedo	SSM	surface-to-surface missile
MANPAD	man-portable air-defence system			SSN	nuclear-powered attack submarine
MANPATS	man-portable anti-tank system				
MARSEC	maritime security	PKO	peacekeeping operations	SSR	security-sector reform
MBT	main battle tank	pl	platoon	SSW	midget submarine
MC/C/CS/D/O		PNT	positioning, navigation, timing	strat	strategic
	mine countermeasure coastal/ command and support/diving support/ocean	PPP	purchasing-power parity	STOVL	short take-off and vertical landing
		PPV	protected patrol vehicle	surv	surveillance
		PRH	passive radar-homing	sy	security
MCM	mine countermeasures	PSO/H	peace support operations or offshore patrol ship/with hangar	t	tonnes
MCMV	mine countermeasures vessel			tac	tactical
mech	mechanised	psyops	psychological operations	tch	technical
med	medium/medical	ptn br	pontoon bridging	tk	tank
medevac	medical evacuation	qrn	quadrillion	tkr	tanker
MH/C/I/O	mine hunter/coastal/inshore/ ocean	quad	quadruple	torp	torpedo
		R&D	research and development	tpt	transport
mil	military	RAS	replenishment at sea	trg	training
MIRV	multiple independently targetable re-entry vehicle	RCL	recoilless launcher	trn	trillion
		RDT&E	research, development, test and evaluation	TSV	tank support vehicle
mk	mark (model number)			TT	torpedo tube
ML	minelayer	recce	reconnaissance	UAV	uninhabited aerial vehicle
MLU	mid-life update	regt	regiment	UCAC	utility craft air cushioned
mne	marine	RFI	request for information	UCAV	uninhabited combat air vehicle
mnv enh	manoeuvre enhancement	RFP	request for proposals	UGV	uninhabited ground vehicle
mod	modified/modification	RL	rocket launcher	UMV	uninhabited maritime vehicle
mor	mortar	ro-ro	roll-on, roll-off	USV	uninhabited surface vehicle
mot	motorised/motor	RPO	rendezvous and proximity operations	UTL	utility
MoU	memorandum of understanding			UUV	uninhabited underwater vehicle
MP	maritime patrol/military police	RV	re-entry vehicle	veh	vehicle
MR	motor rifle	rvn	riverine	VLB	vehicle launched bridge
MRBM	medium-range ballistic missile	SAM	surface-to-air missile	VLS	vertical launch system
MRH	multi-role helicopter	SAR	search and rescue/synthetic aperture radar	VSHORAD	very short-range air defence
MRL	multiple rocket launcher			WFU	withdrawn from use
MRO	maintenance, repair and overhaul	SARH	semi-active radar homing	wg	wing
MS/C/I/O/R		sat	satellite		
	mine sweeper/coastal/inshore/ ocean/river	SATCOM	satellite communications		
		SEAD	suppression of enemy air defence		
msl	missile	SF	special forces		
mtn	mountain	SHORAD	short-range air defence		
MW	mine warfare	SIGINT	signals intelligence		
n.a.	not applicable	sigs	signals		

Reference 519

Table 9 International comparisons of defence budgets and military personnel

	Defence Budget (current USDm) 2022	Defence Budget (current USDm) 2023	Defence Budget (current USDm) 2024	Defence Budget per capita (current USD) 2022	Defence Budget per capita (current USD) 2023	Defence Budget per capita (current USD) 2024	Defence Budget % of GDP 2022	Defence Budget % of GDP 2023	Defence Budget % of GDP 2024	Active Armed Forces (000) 2024	Estimated Reservists (000) 2024	Gendarmerie & Paramilitary (000) 2024
North America												
Canada	24,169	24,056	27,001	632	625	696	1.12	1.12	1.22	62	29	6
United States	838,814	919,765	967,962	2,487	2,708	2,831	3.23	3.32	3.32	1,316	797	0
Total	**862,983**	**943,821**	**994,963**	**1,559**	**1,666**	**1,763**	**2.17**	**2.22**	**2.27**	**1,378**	**826**	**6**
Europe												
Albania	288	397	489	93	128	157	1.51	1.74	1.87	8	0	0
Austria	3,633	4,415	5,297	408	494	591	0.77	0.85	0.99	23	107	0
Belgium	6,815	7,390	8,463	575	620	707	1.17	1.17	1.28	24	6	0
Bosnia-Herzegovina	165	217	218	43	57	57	0.67	0.80	0.77	11	6	0
Bulgaria	1,337	1,334	2,349	195	195	346	1.48	1.31	2.17	37	3	0
Croatia	1,303	1,119	1,250	311	268	301	1.81	1.35	1.39	17	21	0
Cyprus	533	567	603	411	434	456	1.82	1.76	1.73	12	50	0
Czech Republic	3,817	5,037	6,560	357	465	605	1.26	1.47	1.91	27	0	0
Denmark	5,044	5,346	5,484	852	899	918	1.25	1.31	1.33	13	44	0
Estonia	812	1,236	1,705	670	1,028	1,428	2.11	2.99	3.96	7	41	0
Finland	5,748	7,018	6,892	1,026	1,250	1,225	2.05	2.37	2.25	24	233	3
France	54,258	59,601	64,033	794	873	937	1.94	1.95	2.02	202	39	95
Germany*	54,902	67,058	85,975	651	796	1,022	1.32	1.48	1.83	180	34	0
Greece	7,846	7,309	7,765	745	696	742	3.60	3.07	3.07	132	289	7
Hungary	4,827	4,423	5,667	498	447	575	2.72	2.08	2.48	32	20	0
Iceland	41	40	49	115	112	134	0.14	0.13	0.15	0	0	0
Ireland	1,167	1,270	1,340	221	245	256	0.21	0.23	0.24	7	2	0
Italy	31,029	32,547	35,231	508	533	578	1.47	1.41	1.48	162	15	179
Kosovo	108	133	164	61	68	83	1.15	1.28	1.47	3	0	0
Latvia	857	1,046	1,436	465	574	797	2.12	2.40	3.15	7	16	0
Lithuania	1,580	2,025	2,498	589	762	950	2.22	2.60	3.02	16	13	18
Luxembourg	443	587	691	681	888	1,030	0.54	0.68	0.76	1	0	1
Macedonia, North	228	274	356	107	128	167	1.66	1.85	2.25	8	5	8
Malta	87	80	93	188	171	199	0.45	0.36	0.38	2	0	0
Montenegro	70	134	101	116	222	168	1.12	1.80	1.24	3	3	4
Netherlands	15,184	16,662	23,609	873	942	1,328	1.45	1.44	1.94	34	6	7
Norway	7,420	7,179	9,787	1,336	1,311	1,776	1.25	1.48	1.94	25	40	0
Poland	12,965	23,195	28,003	340	593	723	1.88	2.86	3.25	164	38	14
Portugal	2,584	2,796	3,106	252	273	304	1.01	0.97	1.02	22	24	23
Romania	5,640	8,475	9,204	305	462	507	1.88	2.41	2.42	70	55	57

	Defence Budget (current USDm) 2022	2023	2024	Defence Budget per capita (current USD) 2022	2023	2024	Defence Budget % of GDP 2022	2023	2024	Active Armed Forces (000) 2024	Estimated Reservists (000) 2024	Gendarmerie & Paramilitary (000) 2024
Serbia	1,218	1,484	1,464	181	222	220	1.92	1.97	1.77	28	50	4
Slovakia	2,002	2,657	2,848	369	477	512	1.73	2.00	2.00	13	0	0
Slovenia	880	1,016	1,160	419	484	553	1.47	1.47	1.58	6	1	0
Spain	14,966	19,291	19,435	317	409	411	1.03	1.19	1.12	122	14	81
Sweden	8,027	9,202	12,254	766	873	1,157	1.38	1.57	2.01	15	22	0
Switzerland	5,521	6,241	6,482	649	710	732	0.67	0.70	0.69	21	123	0
Türkiye	6,252	8,777	14,268	75	105	170	0.69	0.78	1.06	355	379	161
United Kingdom*	73,133	75,040	81,055	1,079	1,101	1,184	2.34	2.22	2.26	141	70	0
Total	**342,727**	**392,618**	**457,385**	**464**	**535**	**632**	**1.45**	**1.57**	**1.74**	**1,972**	**1,767**	**661**
Russia and Eurasia												
Armenia	781	1,277	1,366	260	427	459	4.00	5.30	5.41	43	210	4
Azerbaijan	2,641	3,129	3,777	255	295	355	3.35	4.32	4.99	68	300	15
Belarus	761	996	1,186	81	104	125	1.04	1.39	1.62	49	290	110
Georgia	315	479	506	64	97	103	1.26	1.57	1.53	21	0	5
Kazakhstan	1,867	2,508	2,622	96	125	129	0.83	0.95	0.90	39	0	32
Kyrgyzstan	n.k.	n.k.	n.k.	n.k.	n.k.	n.k.	n.k.	n.k.	n.k.	11	0	10
Moldova	48	94	108	14	26	30	0.33	0.57	0.60	5	58	1
Russia [a]	74,742	74,806	120,317	526	529	854	3.29	3.72	5.51	1,134	1,500	569
Tajikistan	108	141	176	12	14	17	1.03	1.19	1.35	9	20	8
Turkmenistan*	n.k.	n.k.	n.k.	n.k.	n.k.	n.k.	n.k.	n.k.	n.k.	37	0	20
Ukraine	4,099	23,403	28,414	94	672	797	2.55	13.17	15.43	730	0	260
Uzbekistan	n.k.	n.k.	n.k.	n.k.	n.k.	n.k.	n.k.	n.k.	n.k.	48	0	20
Total**	**85,362**	**106,834**	**158,473**	**156**	**254**	**319**	**1.96**	**3.57**	**4.15**	**2,193**	**2,378**	**1,053**
Asia												
Afghanistan	n.k.	n.k.	n.k.	n.k.	n.k.	n.k.	n.k.	n.k.	n.k.	172	0	0
Australia	33,197	34,374	36,404	1,270	1,299	1,360	1.93	1.97	2.02	58	22	0
Bangladesh	4,302	3,647	3,409	26	22	20	0.93	0.81	0.76	174	0	64
Brunei	433	462	597	907	952	1,213	2.60	3.05	3.80	7	1	1
Cambodia*	1,023	1,223	1,301	61	72	76	2.57	2.82	2.76	124	0	67
China	218,970	222,891	234,977	154	157	166	1.23	1.26	1.29	2,035	510	500
Fiji	43	48	69	45	51	72	0.86	0.89	1.19	4	6	0
India	72,768	75,358	74,363	52	54	53	2.17	2.11	1.91	1,476	1,155	1,616

	Defence Budget (current USDm) 2022	2023	2024	Defence Budget per capita (current USD) 2022	2023	2024	Defence Budget % of GDP 2022	2023	2024	Active Armed Forces (000) 2024	Estimated Reservists (000) 2024	Gendarmerie & Paramilitary (000) 2024
Indonesia	8,984	9,496	10,929	32	34	39	0.68	0.69	0.78	405	400	290
Japan	46,954	48,558	53,014	378	392	430	1.10	1.15	1.30	247	56	15
Korea, DPR of	n.k.	n.k.	n.k.	n.k.	n.k.	n.k.	n.k.	n.k.	n.k.	1,280	600	189
Korea, Republic of	42,287	43,754	43,876	816	842	842	2.35	2.38	2.35	500	3,100	14
Laos	n.k.	n.k.	n.k.	n.k.	n.k.	n.k.	n.k.	n.k.	n.k.	29	0	100
Malaysia	3,668	3,891	4,337	108	114	125	0.90	0.97	0.99	113	52	23
Maldives	102	110	110	262	282	283	1.66	1.67	1.57	4	0	0
Mongolia	91	90	164	28	28	50	0.53	0.44	0.69	10	137	8
Myanmar	1,987	2,606	2,631	35	46	46	3.22	4.04	4.09	134	0	70
Nepal	422	421	444	14	14	14	1.03	1.03	1.02	97	0	15
New Zealand	3,014	3,034	3,151	596	594	610	1.24	1.22	1.25	9	3	0
Pakistan	9,768	7,910	8,400	40	32	33	2.61	2.34	2.24	660	0	291
Papua New Guinea	98	97	91	10	10	9	0.31	0.31	0.29	4	0	0
Philippines	7,058	6,185	6,732	62	53	57	1.75	1.41	1.43	146	131	31
Singapore	12,346	13,388	15,174	2,085	2,240	2,517	2.48	2.67	2.86	51	253	7
Sri Lanka	1,156	1,251	1,388	50	57	63	1.55	n.k.	n.k.	263	6	64
Taiwan	17,298	18,625	18,861	734	790	799	2.27	2.46	2.43	169	1,657	12
Thailand	5,702	5,599	5,728	82	80	82	1.15	1.09	1.08	361	200	94
Timor-Leste	44	55	46	31	37	31	1.38	2.32	2.33	2	0	0
Tonga	8	9	10	77	83	95	1.70	1.67	1.82	1	0	0
Vietnam**	5,805	7,483	7,834	56	71	74	1.42	1.73	1.67	450	5,000	40
Total **	**497,530**	**510,564**	**534,037**	**308**	**323**	**352**	**1.60**	**1.70**	**1.76**	**8,983**	**13,287**	**3,508**
Middle East and North Africa												
Algeria	9,158	18,313	21,404	207	396	455	4.06	7.63	8.23	139	150	187
Bahrain	1,399	1,401	1,401	908	902	894	3.00	3.04	2.93	8	0	11
Egypt	5,211	3,582	2,793	48	33	25	1.10	0.91	0.73	439	479	397
Iran	8,021	8,326	8,042	92	95	91	2.13	2.23	1.85	610	350	40
Iraq	6,996	10,522	12,679	173	255	301	2.43	4.17	4.80	193	0	266
Israel	19,033	19,118	33,750	2,135	2,065	3,589	3.61	3.72	6.39	170	465	8
Jordan	1,933	2,039	2,120	176	184	190	3.97	4.01	3.98	101	65	15
Kuwait	7,812	7,750	7,798	2,546	2,497	2,485	4.25	4.73	4.82	18	24	7
Lebanon	248	239	540	47	45	101	1.01	1.00	n.k.	60	0	20
Libya	n.k.	n.k.	n.k.	n.k.	n.k.	n.k.	n.k.	n.k.	n.k.	n.k.	n.k.	n.k.
Mauritania	226	255	263	54	60	61	2.36	2.39	2.44	16	0	5
Morocco	6,071	6,270	6,625	165	169	177	4.64	4.34	4.22	196	150	50

Reference 523

	Defence Budget (current USDm) 2022	2023	2024	Defence Budget per capita (current USD) 2022	2023	2024	Defence Budget % of GDP 2022	2023	2024	Active Armed Forces (000) 2024	Estimated Reservists (000) 2024	Gendarmerie & Paramilitary (000) 2024
Oman	6,432	6,507	6,659	1,709	1,698	1,707	5.75	5.98	6.05	43	0	4
Palestinian Territories	n.k.	n.k.	n.k.	n.k.	n.k.	n.k.	n.k.	n.k.	n.k.	0	0	n.k.
Qatar	8,419	9,021	9,659	3,357	3,562	3,785	3.57	4.23	4.36	17	0	5
Saudi Arabia	65,333	66,133	71,733	1,848	1,840	1,963	5.89	6.19	6.52	257	0	25
Syria	n.k.	n.k.	n.k.	n.k.	n.k.	n.k.	n.k.	n.k.	n.k.	n.k.	n.k.	n.k.
Tunisia	1,146	1,207	1,319	96	101	109	2.57	2.49	2.51	36	0	12
United Arab Emirates	20,972	21,855	22,268	2,115	2,191	2,220	4.17	4.25	4.09	63	0	0
Yemen	n.k.	n.k.	n.k.	n.k.	n.k.	n.k.	n.k.	n.k.	n.k.	122	0	0
Total**	**168,411**	**182,538**	**209,052**	**980**	**1006**	**1135**	**3.57**	**4.02**	**4.26**	**2,485**	**1,683**	**1,052**
Latin America and the Caribbean												
Antigua and Barbuda	8	8	11	82	80	106	0.44	0.40	0.48	0	0	0
Argentina	3,352	2,788	2,236	72	60	48	0.53	0.43	0.37	72	0	31
Bahamas	94	106	105	266	262	256	0.72	0.74	0.71	2	0	0
Barbados	42	44	52	140	144	170	0.68	0.65	0.72	1	0	0
Belize	23	28	30	57	69	71	0.82	0.92	0.89	2	1	1
Bolivia	481	473	475	40	39	39	1.09	1.04	0.99	34	0	37
Brazil	22,966	25,233	24,396	106	115	111	1.18	1.16	1.11	375	1,415	395
Chile	3,672	4,244	4,139	199	229	222	1.22	1.26	1.26	69	19	45
Colombia	5,021	5,574	7,728	102	113	156	1.45	1.53	1.85	269	35	165
Costa Rica	418	495	570	80	95	108	0.60	0.57	0.60	0	0	10
Cuba	n.k.	n.k.	n.k.	n.k.	n.k.	n.k.	n.k.	n.k.	n.k.	40	30	27
Dominican Republic	761	891	988	71	83	91	0.67	0.73	0.78	57	0	15
Ecuador	1,581	1,666	1,633	91	92	89	1.36	1.40	1.34	40	118	1
El Salvador	257	251	261	39	38	39	0.80	0.74	0.73	26	10	26
Guatemala	408	411	449	23	23	25	0.43	0.39	0.40	18	64	25
Guyana	89	97	203	112	123	255	0.61	0.57	0.88	3	1	0
Haiti	13	16	28	1	1	2	0.07	0.08	0.11	1	0	9
Honduras	379	440	456	40	47	48	1.21	1.29	1.24	15	60	8
Jamaica	231	247	289	82	88	102	1.36	1.28	1.40	6	3	0
Mexico	7,027	8,613	10,191	54	66	78	0.48	0.48	0.55	287	82	137
Nicaragua	84	95	104	13	14	16	0.53	0.53	0.53	12	0	0
Panama	847	903	946	195	205	212	1.11	1.08	1.08	0	0	28

	Defence Budget (current USDm) 2022	2023	2024	Defence Budget per capita (current USD) 2022	2023	2024	Defence Budget % of GDP 2022	2023	2024	Active Armed Forces (000) 2024	Estimated Reservists (000) 2024	Gendarmerie & Paramilitary (000) 2024
Paraguay	279	298	310	38	40	41	0.67	0.69	0.69	14	165	15
Peru	1,821	1,953	2,138	56	60	66	0.75	0.73	0.75	81	188	77
Suriname	n.k.	n.k.	n.k.	n.k.	n.k.	n.k.	n.k.	n.k.	n.k.	2	0	0
Trinidad and Tobago	481	513	519	343	364	369	1.60	1.83	1.85	5	1	0
Uruguay	556	597	592	163	175	173	0.79	0.77	0.72	21	0	1
Venezuela	46	502	649	2	16	21	0.05	0.51	0.61	123	8	220
Total**	**50,938**	**56,488**	**59,495**	**95**	**102**	**112**	**0.85**	**0.85**	**0.88**	**1,581**	**2,207**	**1,272**
Sub-Saharan Africa												
Angola	1,837	1,263	1,002	53	35	27	1.29	1.15	0.88	107	0	10
Benin	97	128	154	7	9	10	0.56	0.65	0.72	12	0	5
Botswana	499	481	597	209	199	244	2.45	2.48	2.99	9	0	0
Burkina Faso	467	827	1,023	21	37	44	2.47	4.08	4.68	21	0	34
Burundi	67	81	123	5	6	9	1.70	1.91	2.87	30	0	1
Cabo Verde	11	15	17	19	25	28	0.50	0.57	0.63	1	0	0
Cameroon	417	457	539	14	15	17	0.94	0.93	1.01	38	0	9
Central African Rep	39	62	70	7	11	12	1.58	2.37	2.47	14	0	1
Chad	318	358	557	18	19	29	1.96	2.03	2.98	33	0	12
Congo	263	285	182	47	48	30	1.88	2.01	1.21	10	0	4
Côte d'Ivoire	608	682	663	6	23	22	0.87	0.86	0.76	27	0	n.k.
Dem Republic of the Congo	375	744	891	13	7	8	0.57	1.11	1.23	128	0	0
Djibouti	n.k.	n.k.	n.k.	n.k.	n.k.	n.k.	n.k.	n.k.	n.k.	8	0	5
Equatorial Guinea	n.k.	n.k.	n.k.	n.k.	n.k.	n.k.	n.k.	n.k.	n.k.	2	0	0
Eritrea	n.k.	n.k.	n.k.	n.k.	n.k.	n.k.	n.k.	n.k.	n.k.	302	n.k.	0
Ethiopia	425	1,538	623	4	13	5	0.36	0.96	0.43	503	0	0
Gabon	278	265	321	119	111	131	1.36	1.32	1.54	5	0	2
Gambia	14	14	15	6	6	6	0.63	0.58	0.57	4	0	0
Ghana	270	340	287	8	10	8	0.37	0.44	0.38	19	0	0
Guinea	447	620	521	34	46	37	2.28	2.69	2.04	10	0	3
Guinea-Bissau	25	25	25	12	12	12	1.43	1.26	1.16	4	0	0
Kenya	1,340	1,241	1,211	24	22	21	1.17	1.14	1.04	24	0	5
Lesotho	37	35	35	17	16	16	1.65	1.57	1.51	2	0	0
Liberia	19	16	18	3	3	3	0.47	0.37	0.37	2	0	0
Madagascar	103	107	125	4	4	4	0.68	0.68	0.72	14	0	8
Malawi	92	98	84	4	5	4	0.73	0.77	0.77	11	0	4
Mali	827	1,083	1,228	40	51	56	4.51	5.36	5.67	21	0	20

	Defence Budget (current USDm) 2022	2023	2024	Defence Budget per capita (current USD) 2022	2023	2024	Defence Budget % of GDP 2022	2023	2024	Active Armed Forces (000) 2024	Estimated Reservists (000) 2024	Gendarmerie & Paramilitary (000) 2024
Mauritius	235	241	257	180	184	196	1.82	1.65	1.62	0	0	3
Mozambique	170	208	314	5	6	9	0.90	0.99	1.39	12	0	0
Namibia	357	341	366	131	124	131	2.84	2.76	2.78	12	0	6
Niger	243	332	439	10	13	17	1.57	1.97	2.24	39	0	48
Nigeria	2,827	2,148	1,043	13	9	4	0.59	0.59	0.52	143	0	80
Rwanda	177	192	164	13	14	12	1.33	1.36	1.20	33	0	2
Senegal	422	449	519	24	24	28	1.52	1.45	1.54	14	0	5
Seychelles	n.k.	n.k.	n.k.	n.k.	n.k.	n.k.	n.k.	n.k.	n.k.	0	0	0
Sierra Leone	24	21	34	3	2	4	0.34	0.32	0.46	9	0	0
Somalia	n.k.	n.k.	n.k.	n.k.	n.k.	n.k.	n.k.	n.k.	n.k.	19	0	1
South Africa	3,195	2,889	2,860	56	48	47	0.79	0.76	0.71	69	0	15
South Sudan	61	65	56	5	5	4	0.76	0.90	1.06	90	0	0
Sudan	n.k.	n.k.	n.k.	n.k.	n.k.	n.k.	n.k.	n.k.	n.k.	104	0	60
Tanzania	1,024	1,139	1,146	16	17	17	1.38	1.44	1.43	27	80	1
Togo	170	197	195	20	23	22	2.08	2.17	2.00	14	0	5
Uganda	1,048	1,012	1,074	23	21	22	2.21	1.98	1.93	45	10	1
Zambia	450	403	367	23	20	18	1.55	1.43	1.42	17	3	1
Zimbabwe	349	98	161	23	6	9	1.07	0.28	0.45	29	0	22
Total**	**19,630**	**20,498**	**19,305**	**32**	**32**	**34**	**1.36**	**1.47**	**1.52**	**2,038**	**93**	**373**
Summary												
North America	862,983	943,821	994,963	1,559	1,666	1,763	2.17	2.22	2.27	1,378	826	6
Europe	342,727	392,618	457,385	464	535	632	1.45	1.57	1.74	1,972	1,767	661
Russia and Eurasia	85,362	106,834	158,473	156	254	319	1.96	3.57	4.15	2,193	2,378	1,053
Asia	497,530	510,564	534,037	308	323	352	1.60	1.70	1.76	8,983	13,287	3,508
Middle East and North Africa**	168,411	182,538	209,052	980	1,006	1,135	3.57	4.02	4.26	2,485	1,683	1,052
Latin America and the Caribbean	50,938	56,488	59,495	95	102	112	0.85	0.85	0.88	1,581	2,207	1,272
Sub-Saharan Africa	19,630	20,498	19,305	32	32	34	1.36	1.47	1.52	2,038	93	373
Global totals	**2,027,581**	**2,213,360**	**2,432,710**	**318**	**348**	**397**	**1.59**	**1.80**	**1.94**	**20,629**	**22,240**	**7,925**

* Estimates. **Totals exclude states where insufficient official information is available in order to enable approximate comparisons of regional defence-spending between years. Defence Budget per capita (current USD) and Defence Budget % of GDP totals are regional averages. [a] 'National Defence' budget chapter. Excludes other defence-related expenditures included under other budget lines (e.g. pensions) - see Table 5, p.161. All figures do not include US Foreign Military Financing allocations.

Table 10 Index of country/territory abbreviations

AFG	Afghanistan	
ALB	Albania	
ALG	Algeria	
ANG	Angola	
ARG	Argentina	
ARM	Armenia	
ATG	Antigua and Barbuda	
AUS	Australia	
AUT	Austria	
AZE	Azerbaijan	
BDI	Burundi	
BEL	Belgium	
BEN	Benin	
BFA	Burkina Faso	
BGD	Bangladesh	
BHR	Bahrain	
BHS	Bahamas	
BIH	Bosnia-Herzegovina	
BIOT	British Indian Ocean Territory	
BLG	Bulgaria	
BLR	Belarus	
BLZ	Belize	
BOL	Bolivia	
BRB	Barbados	
BRN	Brunei	
BRZ	Brazil	
BWA	Botswana	
CAM	Cambodia	
CAN	Canada	
CAR	Central African Republic	
CHA	Chad	
CHE	Switzerland	
CHL	Chile	
CIV	Côte d'Ivoire	
CMR	Cameroon	
COG	Republic of Congo	
COL	Colombia	
CPV	Cabo Verde	
CRI	Costa Rica	
CRO	Croatia	
CUB	Cuba	
CYP	Cyprus	
CZE	Czech Republic	
DJB	Djibouti	
DNK	Denmark	
DOM	Dominican Republic	
DPRK	Korea, Democratic People's Republic of	
DRC	Democratic Republic of the Congo	
ECU	Ecuador	
EGY	Egypt	
EQG	Equitorial Guinea	
ERI	Eritrea	
ESP	Spain	
EST	Estonia	
ETH	Ethiopia	
FIN	Finland	
FJI	Fiji	
FLK	Falkland Islands	
FRA	France	
GAB	Gabon	
GAM	Gambia	
GEO	Georgia	
GER	Germany	
GF	French Guiana	
GHA	Ghana	
GIB	Gibraltar	
GNB	Guinea-Bissau	
GRC	Greece	
GRL	Greenland	
GUA	Guatemala	
GUI	Guinea	
GUY	Guyana	
HND	Honduras	
HTI	Haiti	
HUN	Hungary	
IDN	Indonesia	
IND	India	
IRL	Ireland	
IRN	Iran	
IRQ	Iraq	
ISL	Iceland	
ISR	Israel	
ITA	Italy	
JAM	Jamaica	
JOR	Jordan	
JPN	Japan	
KAZ	Kazakhstan	
KEN	Kenya	
KGZ	Kyrgyzstan	
KWT	Kuwait	
LAO	Laos	
LBN	Lebanon	
LBR	Liberia	
LBY	Libya	
LKA	Sri Lanka	
LSO	Lesotho	
LTU	Lithuania	
LUX	Luxembourg	
LVA	Latvia	
MDA	Moldova	
MDG	Madagascar	
MDV	Maldives	
MEX	Mexico	
MHL	Marshall Islands	
MKD	Macedonia, North	
MLI	Mali	
MLT	Malta	
MMR	Myanmar	
MNE	Montenegro	
MNG	Mongolia	
MOR	Morocco	
MOZ	Mozambique	
MRT	Mauritania	
MUS	Mauritius	
MWI	Malawi	
MYS	Malaysia	
NAM	Namibia	
NCL	New Caledonia	
NER	Niger	
NGA	Nigeria	
NIC	Nicaragua	
NLD	Netherlands	
NOR	Norway	
NPL	Nepal	
NZL	New Zealand	
OMN	Oman	
PT	Palestinian Territories	
PAN	Panama	
PAK	Pakistan	
PER	Peru	
PHL	Philippines	
POL	Poland	
PNG	Papua New Guinea	
PRC	China, People's Republic of	
PRT	Portugal	
PRY	Paraguay	
PYF	French Polynesia	
QTR	Qatar	
ROC	Taiwan (Republic of China)	
ROK	Korea, Republic of	
ROM	Romania	
RSA	South Africa	
RUS	Russia	
RWA	Rwanda	
SAU	Saudi Arabia	
SDN	Sudan	
SEN	Senegal	
SER	Serbia	
SGP	Singapore	
SLB	Solomon Islands	
SLE	Sierra Leone	
SLV	El Salvador	
SOM	Somalia	
SSD	South Sudan	
STP	São Tomé and Príncipe	
SUR	Suriname	
SVK	Slovakia	
SVN	Slovenia	
SWE	Sweden	
SYC	Seychelles	
SYR	Syria	
TGO	Togo	
THA	Thailand	
TJK	Tajikistan	
TKM	Turkmenistan	
TLS	Timor-Leste	
TON	Tonga	
TTO	Trinidad and Tobago	
TUN	Tunisia	
TUR	Türkiye	
TZA	Tanzania	
UAE	United Arab Emirates	
UGA	Uganda	
UK	United Kingdom	
UKR	Ukraine	
URY	Uruguay	
US	United States	
UZB	Uzbekistan	
VEN	Venezuela	
VNM	Vietnam	
XKX	Kosovo	
YEM	Yemen, Republic of	
ZMB	Zambia	
ZWE	Zimbabwe	

Table 11 Index of countries and territories

Afghanistan AFG 231	Georgia GEO 174	Nicaragua NIC 426
Albania ALB 70	Germany GER 93	Nigeria NGA 489
Algeria ALG 328	Ghana GHA 475	Niger NER 488
Angola ANG 453	Greece GRC 97	Norway NOR 119
Antigua and Barbuda ATG 393	Guatemala GUA 418	Oman OMN 361
Argentina ARG 393	Guinea GUI 477	Pakistan PAK 286
Armenia ARM 168	Guinea-Bissau GNB 478	Palestinian Territories PT 363
Australia AUS 231	Guyana GUY 419	Panama PAN 427
Austria AUT 71	Haiti HTI 420	Papua New Guinea PNG 290
Azerbaijan AZE 169	Honduras HND 421	Paraguay PRY 428
Bahamas BHS 397	Hungary HUN 100	Peru PER 430
Bahrain BHR 331	Iceland ISL 102	Philippines PHL 291
Bangladesh BGD 234	India IND 251	Poland POL 121
Barbados BRB 397	Indonesia IDN 258	Portugal PRT 124
Belarus BLR 172	Iran IRN 337	Qatar QTR 349
Belgium BEL 72	Iraq IRQ 342	Romania ROM 127
Belize BLZ 398	Ireland IRL 102	Russia RUS 180
Benin BEN 454	Israel ISR 344	Rwanda RWA 492
Bolivia BOL 398	Italy ITA 103	Saudi Arabia SAU 366
Bosnia-Herzegovina BIH 74	Jamaica JAM 422	Senegal SEN 493
Botswana BWA 456	Japan JPN 262	Serbia SER 129
Brazil BRZ 400	Jordan JOR 348	Seychelles SYC 494
Brunei BRN 237	Kazakhstan KAZ 175	Sierra Leone SLE 495
Bulgaria BLG 75	Kenya KEN 479	Singapore SGP 294
Burkina Faso BFA 457	Korea, Democratic People's Republic of DPRK 267	Slovakia SVK 131
Burundi BDI 458	Korea, Republic of ROK 270	Slovenia SVN 133
Cabo Verde CPV 459	Kosovo XKX 108	Somalia SOM 496
Cambodia CAM 238	Kuwait KWT 350	South Africa RSA 497
Cameroon CMR 460	Kyrgyzstan KGZ 177	South Sudan SSD 499
Canada CAN 31	Laos LAO 275	Spain ESP 134
Central African Republic CAR 461	Latvia LVA 109	Sri Lanka LKA 297
Chad CHA 463	Lebanon LBN 352	Sudan SDN 501
Chile CHL 404	Lesotho LSO 480	Suriname SUR 433
China, People's Republic of PRC 239	Liberia LBR 481	Sweden SWE 138
Colombia COL 407	Libya LBY 355	Switzerland CHE 140
Congo, Republic of COG 464	Lithuania LTU 110	Syria SYR 369
Costa Rica CRI 411	Luxembourg LUX 112	Taiwan (Republic of China) ROC 299
Côte d'Ivoire CIV 465	Macedonia, North MKD 113	Tajikistan TJK 196
Croatia CRO 77	Madagascar MDG 482	Tanzania TZA 503
Cuba CUB 411	Malawi MWI 483	Thailand THA 302
Cyprus CYP 79	Malaysia MYS 276	Timor-Leste TLS 307
Czech Republic CZE 81	Maldives MDV 279	Togo TGO 504
Democratic Republic of the Congo DRC 467	Mali MLI 484	Tonga TON 307
Denmark DNK 82	Malta MLT 114	Trinidad and Tobago TTO 434
Djibouti DJB 468	Mauritania MRT 356	Tunisia TUN 372
Dominican Republic DOM 413	Mauritius MUS 485	Turkiye TUR 142
Ecuador ECU 414	Mexico MEX 423	Turkmenistan TKM 197
Egypt EGY 333	Moldova MDA 179	Uganda UGA 505
El Salvador SLV 417	Mongolia MNG 280	Ukraine UKR 199
Equatorial Guinea EQG 470	Montenegro MNE 115	United Arab Emirates UAE 374
Eritrea ERI 471	Morocco MOR 358	United Kingdom UK 146
Estonia EST 84	Mozambique MOZ 486	United States US 34
Ethiopia ETH 472	Multinational Organisations 116	Uruguay URY 434
Fiji FJI 250	Myanmar MMR 281	Uzbekistan UZB 204
Finland FIN 86	Namibia NAM 487	Venezuela VEN 436
France FRA 88	Nepal NPL 284	Vietnam VNM 308
Gabon GAB 473	Netherlands NLD 116	Yemen, Republic of YEM 377
Gambia GAM 474	New Zealand NZL 285	Zambia ZMB 507
		Zimbabwe ZWE 508

The Military Balance (Print ISSN 0459-7222, Online ISSN 1479-9022) is published annually for a total of one issue per year by Taylor & Francis Group, 4 Park Square, Milton Park, Abingdon, Oxon, OX14 4RN, UK.

Send address changes to Taylor & Francis Customer Services, Informa UK Ltd., Sheepen Place, Colchester, Essex CO3 3LP, UK.

Subscription records are maintained at Taylor & Francis Group, 4 Park Square, Milton Park, Abingdon, OX14 4RN, UK.

Subscription information: For more information and subscription rates, please see tandfonline.com/pricing/journal/tmib. Taylor & Francis journals are available in a range of different packages, designed to suit every library's needs and budget. This journal is available for institutional subscriptions with online only or print & online options. This journal may also be available as part of our libraries, subject collections, or archives. For more information on our sales packages, please visit: librarianresources.taylorandfrancis.com.

For support with any institutional subscription, please visit help.tandfonline.com or email our dedicated team at subscriptions@tandf.co.uk.

Subscriptions purchased at the personal rate are strictly for personal, non-commercial use only. The reselling of personal subscriptions is prohibited. Personal subscriptions must be purchased with a personal check, credit card, or BAC/wire transfer. Proof of personal status may be requested.

Back issues: Please visit https://taylorandfrancis.com/journals/customer-services/ for more information on how to purchase back issues.

Ordering information: To subscribe to the Journal, please contact: T&F Customer Services, Informa UK Ltd, Sheepen Place, Colchester, Essex, CO3 3LP, United Kingdom. Tel: +44 (0) 20 8052 2030; email: subscriptions@tandf.co.uk.

Taylor & Francis journals are priced in USD, GBP and EUR (as well as AUD and CAD for a limited number of journals). All subscriptions are charged depending on where the end customer is based. If you are unsure which rate applies to you, please contact Customer Services. All subscriptions are payable in advance and all rates include postage. We are required to charge applicable VAT/GST on all print and online combination subscriptions, in addition to our online only journals. Subscriptions are entered on an annual basis, i.e., January to December. Payment may be made by sterling cheque, dollar cheque, euro cheque, international money order, National Giro or credit card (Amex, Visa and Mastercard).

Permissions: See help.tandfonline.com/Librarian/s/article/Permissions

Disclaimer: The International Institute for Strategic Studies and our publisher Taylor & Francis make every effort to ensure the accuracy of all the information (the 'Content') contained in our publications. However, The International Institute for Strategic Studies and our publisher Taylor & Francis, our agents (including the editor, any member of the editorial team or editorial board, and any guest editors), and our licensors make no representations or warranties whatsoever as to the accuracy, completeness, or suitability for any purpose of the Content. Any opinions and views expressed in this publication are the opinions and views of the authors, and are not the views of or endorsed by The International Institute for Strategic Studies and our publisher Taylor & Francis. The accuracy of the Content should not be relied upon and should be independently verified with primary sources of information. The International Institute for Strategic Studies and our publisher Taylor & Francis shall not be liable for any losses, actions, claims, proceedings, demands, costs, expenses, damages, and other liabilities whatsoever or howsoever caused arising directly or indirectly in connection with, in relation to, or arising out of the use of the Content. Terms & Conditions of access and use can be found at http://www.tandfonline.com/page/terms-and-conditions.

All Taylor & Francis Group journals are printed on paper from renewable sources by accredited partners.